FROM TRAVELING SHOW
TO VAUDEVILLE

PUBLISHING FOR THE WORLD
125 Years

THE JOHNS HOPKINS UNIVERSITY PRESS

FROM
TRAVELING SHOW
TO
VAUDEVILLE

THEATRICAL SPECTACLE
IN AMERICA, 1830–1910

Edited by Robert M. Lewis

THE JOHNS HOPKINS UNIVERSITY PRESS
Baltimore and London

© 2003 The Johns Hopkins University Press
All rights reserved. Published 2003
Printed in the United States of America on acid-free paper
2 4 6 8 9 7 5 3 1

The Johns Hopkins University Press
2715 North Charles Street
Baltimore, Maryland 21218-4363
www.press.jhu.edu

Library of Congress Cataloging-in-Publication Data

From traveling show to vaudeville : theatrical spectacle in America, 1830–1910 /
edited by Robert M. Lewis.
p. cm.
Includes bibliographical references and index.
ISBN 0-8018-7087-9 (hardcover : alk. paper)
1. Performing arts—United States—History—19th century.
2. Performing arts—United States—History—20th century.
I. Lewis, Robert M., 1946–
PN2245 .E57 2003
791'.0973'09034—dc21
2002152161

A catalog record for this book is available from the British Library.

CONTENTS

PREFACE   *xi*

INTRODUCTION: *From Celebration to Show Business*   1

THE DIME MUSEUM   22

Early Museum Shows   24

Ethan Greenwood's account of his New England Museum, June 1824   *24* /
Nathaniel Hawthorne visits two sideshows in Salem, July 1838   *25* /
Abram Dayton's recollections of New York museums in the 1830s, 1882   *27*

Selling and Seeing Curiosities   29

Barnum's appeal to the family: *Sights and Wonders in New York* (1849)   *29* /
Barnum's advertising to visitors: Peleg Pettinghame to Timothy Touchmenot,
1861   *34* / Letters to a fellow showman: Barnum to Moses Kimball in Boston,
1843   *35* / Presenting Tom Thumb: *Sketch of Life . . . of Charles S. Stratton*
(1847)   *37* / Philip Hone and family visit Tom Thumb, 1843 and 1847   *40* /
Mark Twain's impressions of the "Wild Men of Borneo," 1853   *41* / Mark
Twain and the confidence-man's "Boney Part," 1852   *43* / *New York Tribune*
condemns "Disgusting Exhibitions," 1853   *46* / Fanny Fern meets the
Bearded Lady: *Fern Leaves*, 1854   *49* / *Autobiography of Petite Bunkum*'s
comic view of "The Whiskered Woman," 1855   *50* / Two upper-
class comments on Barnum's "What Is It?" in 1860 and 1861   *50* /
Sir Lyon Bouse's audience with a giantess, 1867   *53*

Commentary   57

The family show: *Gleason's* on the American Museum, 1853   *57* /
The Nation on "The Great Humbug," and Barnum's response, 1867   *58*

Contents

Dog Days of the Museum 61

Mark Twain sees a drab American Museum, 1867   61 / William Dean Howells goes slumming, 1902   62 / Journalist Rollin Lynde Hartt on the proletarian rabble, 1909   65

MINSTRELSY 66

Routines: Songs, Speeches, Dialogue, and Farce   71

Billy Whitlock's song of love and marriage: "Miss Lucy Long," 1842   71 / "Dandy Jim from Caroline" and bragging, 1843   72 / De Negro's Original Piano-Rama on gold fever, 1850   73 / End men chatter: Tambo and Bones on "Blackberrying," 1875   75 / Olio: Oh Hush! Or, the Virginny Cupids, 1853   76

Commentary: Rise and Fall of "Slave" Creativity   85

New York Knickerbocker praises the only true "American poets," 1845   85 / Putnam's Monthly regrets the bland "modern" songs, 1855   87 / The New York Tribune surveys "The Black Opera," 1855   89

Reminiscences   90

Ralph Keeler recalls his experiences as a teenage performer in the 1850s (1869)   90 / Mark Twain remembers the glories of the "real nigger show" in the 1840s (1906)   92 / Bayard Taylor observes minstrel songs among Sacramento miners, 1850   94

Musical Comedy: Harrigan's Mulligan Guard   95

Irish, Germans, and "Coloreds" at The Mulligan Guard Ball, 1879   95 / Edward Harrigan explains his interpretation of city realism, 1889   102 / William Dean Howells applauds Mulligan authenticity, 1886   104 /

Confessions of an African American Minstrel   105

Bert Williams on comedy and life, 1918   105

THE CIRCUS   108

The Circus Debated   110

The American Sunday-School Union warns the foolish young, 1840s   110 / Fanny Fern recommends a less-than-perfect circus to children, 1857   112 /

Contents

Performer Alfred Trumble justifies skills in the ring:
A *Spangled World* (1883)   *115*

The Early Circus   *116*

Nathaniel Hawthorne observes a circus performance and a traveling caravan,
1835, 1838   *116* / Henry David Thoreau visits a menagerie, 1851   *120* /
The circus comes to the village: The *Knickerbocker*, 1839   *121* /
Walt Whitman reviews Dan Rice's circus show in Brooklyn, 1856   *124* /
The New England itinerary of S. O. Wheeler's
Great International Circus, 1863   *126*

Big Business   *129*

Manager W. C. Coup reminisces in the 1890s: *Sawdust and Spangles*
(1902)   *129* / Barnum explains his operations to Mark Twain, 1875   *134* /
Barnum introduces children to the circus "curiosities," 1888   *135* /
Behind the scenes at Ringling Bothers, 1900   *137* / The itinerary of a
typical large circus, ca. 1900   *140*

The Audience   *147*

Hamlin Garland's memory of the circus parade in "Sun Prairie" in the late
1850s (1899)   *147* / William Dean Howells recalls the appeal to boys in an
Ohio small town, 1860s (1890)   *149* / Carl Sandburg remembers the sideshow
in Galesburg, Illinois, in the 1890s (1956)   *151* / A roustabout's story:
W. E. "Doc" Van Elstine, 1938   *153*

MELODRAMA   *155*

A Plea for an American Drama   *159*

James Kirke Paulding scorns a derivative postcolonial drama, 1827   *159*

Classic Melodrama   *162*

Charlotte Cushman's fictional tale of a professional actress, 1837   *162* /
Walt Whitman on the style of the sensation story-papers, 1858   *168* /
William B. English's novel, *Rosina Meadows, the Village Maid* (1843)   *169* /
Charles H. Saunders' stage adaptation of *Rosina Meadows*, 1855   *173* /
"Artemus Ward" and the abridged melodrama plot, 1865   *180*

Classic Melodrama's Audiences   *180*

Nathaniel Hawthorne at the National Theatre, Boston, 1850   *180* /
"Doesticks" slums with the Bowery B'hoys, 1855   *183*

Contents

The Ten-Twenty-Thirty Melodramas *185*

Porter Emerson Browne discovers the secrets of a good "mellodrammer,"
1909 *185* / Owen Davis explains the writer's formula, 1914 *187* / Rollin
Lynde Hartt among the "Neolithic" audience on the Lower East Side,
1909 *189* / Corse Payton's Friday matinée "pink tea" at the Academy
of Music, 1914 *193*

"LEG SHOW" BURLESQUE EXTRAVAGANZAS *195*

The Black Crook *198*

Joseph Whitton recalls the origins of a speculative venture, 1897 *198* /
Charles Barras's script of *The Black Crook*, 1866 *200* / *The Black Crook*'s most
popular song: "You Naughty, Naughty Men," 1866 *212*

A Burlesque of Burlesque *213*

Griffin and Christy's Minstrels' *The Black Crook Burlesque* (1866) *213*

Reactions to the Controversy *217*

Mabel Osgood Wright recalls the views of "Better New York," 1926 *217* /
George Templeton Strong on the "Feminine-Femoral School of Dramatic
Art," 1868 *218* / Mark Twain applauds the "beautiful clipper-built girls,"
1867 *219* / Charles Dickens sees "preposterous" leg shows in New York and
Boston, 1867–68 *222* / Louisa May Alcott is shocked at the "new world":
An Old-Fashioned Girl, 1870 *223* / Olive Logan spurns the "Leg Business"
as degrading, 1869 *225* / William Dean Howells is horrified by "The New
Taste in Theatricals," 1869 *229* / Richard Grant White salutes the
"Age of Burlesque," 1869 *231*

The Popular-Price Circuit *234*

Billy Watson and his Beef Trust Beauties in Brooklyn, 1911 *234*

THE WILD WEST SHOW *237*

Origins *241*

P. T. Barnum describes his "Indian Life on the Plains" show, 1875 *241* /
Buffalo Bill Cody explains the origins and aims of his Wild West, 1888 *242* /
McLoughlin Brothers tells young children of Buffalo Bill's "exhibition,"
1887 *243* / Manager Nate Salsbury reminisces, 1902 *245*

Contents

Extracts from Buffalo Bill's Wild West Programs   247

Cody and Carver's Rocky Mountain and Prairie Exhibition program, 1883   247 / "Buffalo Bill's 'Wild West,' Prairie Exhibition and Rocky Mountain Show," 1884   249 / America's National Entertainment on "Cody's Corral," 1885   256 / Buffalo Bill's Wild West and Congress of Rough Riders of the World program, 1893   258

Exhibiting Indians   264

Healy & Bigelow's Kickapoo medicine show program, 1890s   264 / *Harper's Weekly* journalists visit the Indian campgrounds, 1894 and 1898   265 / Luther Standing Bear remembers his years with Buffalo Bill, 1928   272 / The Commissioner of Indian Affairs and the dangers of the "show business," 1890   275 / Criticism by a "civilized" Indian: Chauncey Yellow Robe, 1914   277

SUMMER AMUSEMENT PARKS   279

Journalists and the "New" Coney   282

Julian Ralph compares the social freedom of the grand hotels and the Bowery, 1896   282 / Winthrop Alexander surveys the new fantasy "wonder-world" of Luna Park, 1903   285 / Architecture journalist Barr Ferree reviews Dreamland's buildings, 1904   290 / Trade journal *The Midway* on the significance of electricity, 1905   293

Showmen and the "Amusement Business"   294

Journalist Edwin Slosson celebrates the pleasures of peril, 1904   294 / Manager Frederic Thompson's theories of primitive childhood regained, 1907–10   295

Popular Responses   304

Two "undistinguished" immigrant women tell of Coney's escapism, 1902–3   304 / O. Henry's story of the search for the Greater Coney, 1906   305 / Josiah Allen's wife's experiences at Steeplechase, 1911   308

Two Critics of Coney's Banality   311

Maxim Gorky and the cowed masses, 1907   311 / Genteel critic James Huneker among the barbarians, 1915   312

Contents

VAUDEVILLE 315

Vaudeville Defined 319

The *Midway* surveys "the acme of variegated theatrical amusements,"
1905   319 / Edwin Milton Royle on the merits and convenience of "lunch-
counter" art, 1899   321 / "Something for everyone": Caroline Caffin on the
"democratic art," 1914   328

The Business 332

B. F. Keith explains the policy of the refined "continuous" show, 1898   332 /
Hartley Davis reports on the economy and efficiency of the "business," 1905,
1907   334 / Booking manager George Gottlieb explains how to organize a
program, 1915   335 / A master class on the "mechanics of emotion" in
vaudeville, 1913   338

Routines 340

Aaron Hoffman's sketch, "The Horse Doctor," 1911   340 / A hen-pecked
Jewish husband: "Abbie Cohen's Wedding Day," 1917   347

NOTES 351

BIBLIOGRAPHICAL ESSAY 363

INDEX 377

PREFACE

Compiling this anthology has been fun but also a protracted business. For many years I have taught courses on historical popular culture and, more recently, on show business. Finding movies and music for the modern period is a relatively simple task, but for the nineteenth century, I faced pedagogical difficulties not easily resolved. Many excellent monographs and periodical articles provide critical comment but the primary sources on which their arguments depend are seldom readily accessible even to scholars. There are many anthologies of the plays most frequently performed, but the minstrel monologues and comic dialogues issued by mass-market publishers like Denison or De Witt are now very scarce. Even the most comprehensive internet resources, including the Library of Congress's innovative and extensive American Memory website, give limited opportunities to read a showman's autobiography or to compare a typical theater program of the 1850s with a vaudeville bill of the 1890s. While researching in other fields in rare book collections, I began to collect documentary evidence of entertainments once popular so that students might understand how showmen fashioned their presentations and how spectators responded to shows.

This anthology has examples of major forms of commercial amusements in the nineteenth century. They may appear to be a miscellany without theme or focus, a jumble of songs and skits, of dances and dunces. But beneath the veneer of minstrel mask, theatrical grease-paint, or spangled costume, there were elements in common in the animal acts and acrobatic turns that appeared in circus rings, wild west arenas, vaudeville halls, or even in highbrow theaters. Performers were often versatile utility players who joined a repertory company for a season and were then able to adapt to the demands of the production of the moment. Impresarios had similarly broad experience of theatrical enterprises and were always sensitive to the wishes of a live audience and thus required to improvise. Throughout the century, most popular entertainments were variety shows with comedy and melodrama, and they were both resolutely commercial and decidedly American.

I hope that this anthology provokes wider research. Augustus Rapp seems to have been typical of the showmen who traveled by horse and buggy through

Preface

the Midwest and upper South at the turn of the century, but he was unusual in writing an autobiography. How small town audiences responded, and how Rapp managed to generate sufficient interest in a scattered community of a few thousand to sustain his week-long programs of magic, marionettes, music, and movies, is less clear. Local newspapers can tell us about the commercialization of entertainment, and research in the past generation on the minutiae of advertising and itineraries has transformed interpretations of the circus as a business. The distinctive ethnic and racial traditions of amusements, under-represented in this anthology, that made the multicultural nation quite different from its European counterparts, also require much closer attention. The diversity of popular entertainments, and the reflections and refractions of big-city shows in small towns and isolated farms, display the creative energy and entrepreneurial dynamism of a country determined to express its distinctive identity.

This project would not have been possible without assistance from the university libraries of Brown, California, Chicago, Cornell, Harvard, Princeton, Texas, and Yale, and from the collections of the Library Company of Philadelphia and the New-York Historical Society, and especially, of the British Library, the Library of Congress, and the New York Public Library. The interlibrary loans section of the University of Birmingham always made valiant efforts on my behalf, and the university made a research grant toward the cost of ordering documents. My students raised queries that prompted me to reconsider and review the project. John Walsh, the finest seminar teacher I have known, first stimulated my interest in American history. My friend and former colleague Brian Harding taught me most of the little I know about American literature. Forrest Robinson encouraged this anthology from the beginning, and Ron Walters was as generous as ever in recommending it. I have gained very much over the years from the scholarship and friendship of Lew Erenberg and Barney Mergen. Gwenda Morgan and Peter Rushton gave very constructive comments on the introduction. At the Johns Hopkins University Press, Robert J. Brugger and Melody Herr urged me to clarify my arguments, and Jack Kirshbaum was an efficient and gently critical copyeditor.

My foremost obligations are to two people who have not read one word of this. John Higham taught me that asking questions of significance was the most challenging and the most rewarding task for the historian. Half a lifetime later, I still marvel at the coherence of his argument, the elegance of his prose, and his ability to generalize and make connections. My wife, Jan, seldom complained when I missed family vacations, filled half the house with books and files, or used our bank account to fund research trips to New York or Washington or order more and more documents. She believed that this project would one day be completed, and certainly, without her patience, it would have remained unfinished.

FROM TRAVELING SHOW
TO VAUDEVILLE

INTRODUCTION
From Celebration to Show Business

Before Tin Pan Alley's phonograph and Hollywood's moving picture overshadowed the Broadway stage, live performance dominated American popular entertainment. In the early republic there were public spectacles open to all—communal celebrations, folk festivals, firework displays on the Fourth of July, processions of militia companies, and street parades that usually ran to the rowdy and raucous.[1] Later, traveling professionals offered escape for the price of admission. Even Americans who lived in remote villages—weary of toil in factory or on farm but lucky enough to have a dime or a quarter in their pockets—could enjoy the brief spectacles supplied by acrobats, animals exotic and extraordinary, "curiosities," conjurers, carousels, clowns, cowboys, dwarfs, dancers, dioramas, magicians, mechanical marvels, melodramas, menageries, and minstrels, often under the pretense of being educational. Whether organizers merely jumbled together these "clever turns" or expertly packaged them, whether they graced a tent, small-town "opera house," or urban "palace," the shows were almost always variety shows, and traveling was essential to any profitable amusement enterprise.

"The Decline of 'The Road,'" *Billboard* reported in late 1925, signaled the end of a century-long tradition of touring companies presenting live theater. According to a survey conducted by show business's trade paper, two-thirds of the halls that had welcomed itinerant performers fifteen years earlier now restricted their programs to moving pictures or vaudeville.[2] To many theater-owners, personal appearances seemed outdated: modern means of mechanical reproduction presented melodrama at lower cost and in novel form. The transition to machine-made culture had begun almost imperceptibly in the preceding generation, as showmen supplemented the standard routines of variety acts with the latest inventions, gimmicks, and gadgets. By 1925 small-town playhouses no longer needed one-night stands of repertory players "on the road": the photoplay and the picture show had supplanted them.

We might well wonder how this momentous change came about, and what it tells us of American society in the nineteenth century. The documents collected in this volume argue forcefully that the energy and enterprise of

1

showmen, along with the diffusion of new technologies, worked to transform the festivities of the early republic into the theatrical spectacles of the nineteenth and early twentieth century. But behind the showman's entrepreneurial zeal and fascinating techniques lay something else—a striking change in American attitudes to "diversions" and commercial entertainment itself.

Mr. Beecher and the Learned Pig

In the late 1860s actress and playwright Olive Logan poured scorn on the presumptions of self-styled "professionals" in the field of entertainment. In their view, she complained, "the Show Business" embraced any and every public performance given to a paying audience. Logan considered herself far more discriminating than the purveyors of cheap thrills. She valued good taste and genuine talent enriched by training, experience, and dedication to "art," whether in "the drama" or opera or ballet or in the lyceum lectures of Henry Ward Beecher. "I respect the actor who is an artist,—even the harmless clown of the pantomime, who makes us laugh without offending decency." Very different in character were the charlatans of the amusement world, the performers from dime museums, circus tents, and minstrel halls, who courted popularity by pandering to the prejudices and ignorance of the audience, and solely for monetary gain. The most despicable of all were the "clog-dancing creatures" of the "blonde burlesque," who merely exposed their bodies and uttered ribald remarks too coarse even for the lowly minstrel fool. In the past these disreputable players had been considered fit only for the low-class "concert-saloon" and "variety-show." Now they ventured into "the temples of the drama," and posing as actresses, sought equal status with the most esteemed in the legitimate theater. Their selfish and single-minded pursuit of profit excluded issues of taste, quality, and morality. This "leg business," Logan noted with disdain, was merely business, not art. According to these "professionals," all performers were in "the show business." "It must be a very wide world which should include Mr. Beecher with the learned pig," she commented sarcastically.[3]

The phrase "the show business"—what Olive Logan called a "curious" and "remarkably comprehensive term"—was of recent vintage. The first recorded use seems to have been in 1850. However, "show," or "shew," denoting a display or exhibition for the purpose of entertainment, had a much longer history. In the eighteenth and early nineteenth centuries, combinations derived from it further elaborated the original meaning of the word. The "show bill," "show board," and "show cloth" advertised the "show box," "show case," and "show piece" in the "show hall," "show place," "show room," and "show shop" operated by the "show folk," "show girl," and "show man." "Showmanship" appeared in 1859. "The show" also expanded as a concept. The "peepshow" had been typical of street entertainment that was "showy" or "showish" and primarily visual. However, Punch and Judy stands also had dialogue and music, and pantomime, traditionally mute, acquired words. Since Shakespeare's day, the "stage" had encompassed not only the raised platform for performances but the entertainers who appeared on it and the product of their endeavors. Commercial entertainment, Logan lamented, "embraces in its comprehensiveness all sorts of performances"—in the show or on the stage.[4]

The peepshow generally had a low reputation as a tawdry spectacle hawked on city streets or at seasonal fairs by dishonest tricksters.[5] Like Logan, entertainers who took pride in their artistic achievements wished to distinguish their wholesome diversions from vulgar "shows." Buffalo Bill's Wild West always insisted that its presentations were "exhibitions" or "expositions" of frontier skills. With pride, the 1893 program quoted journalist Brick Pomeroy's boast that the demonstrations of horsemanship were not theatrical pretense—"all this imaginary Romeo and Juliet business"—but reality. In 1898 it went further: "It is not a 'show' in any sense of the word, but it is a series of original, genuine and instructive object lessons."[6] Like the Wild West's publicity agents, impresario Dan Rice worried that the circus's tarnished reputation discouraged the respectable from attending. Rice's solution was to discard his clown's costume and rebrand his amusement package of spectacle and burlesque as Dan Rice's Great Show, "to make Equestrian exhibition worthy of the countenance of the intellectual and refined." "Dan has discarded the word 'Circus' as being unworthy of his exhibition," announced the *National Intelligencer* in 1860. For Rice, at least, his "Great Show" signified cultural uplift.[7]

Showmen remained sensitive to the public's perceptions, and so the language of show business, as Logan noted, was losing distinctive and pejorative meanings. Samuel Johnson in 1755 had defined "entertainment" in disparaging terms as "the lower comedy." "Recreation" and "amusement" had been nicely differentiated. "Whatever amuses serves to kill time, to lull the faculties, and banish reflection," George Crabbe wrote in *English Synonymes* in 1831. To "recreate," Webster's dictionary declared, was "to refresh after toil; to reanimate, as languid spirits or exhausted strength." By midcentury the liberal Frederic W. Sawyer dismissed such scruples as old-fashioned. "There is embraced under the head of amusements all those entertainments, diversions, sports, recreations, pastimes, games, and plays, that belong to the light, cheerful, and sportive employments of our powers of body and mind," he declared in *A Plea for Amusements*. In 1859, in the introduction to his pamphlet on leisure as a social problem, Presbyterian minister James L. Corning was equally dismissive of sophistry: "The words 'amusement' and 'recreation' are used interchangeably in the following chapters."[8] The old linguistic niceties seemed irrelevant in an era when commercial entertainment was expanding so rapidly throughout the country and gaining widespread acceptance.

Outdoor exhibitions and peep shows of traveling showmen were familiar sights in country and city. *Harper's Monthly Magazine* 9 (October 1854): 714.

Traveling Shows and Showmen

P. T. Barnum was the preeminent "showman" of Olive Logan's era. His bestselling autobiography recounted the exploits of a self-made entrepreneur in "the show line" who realized the commercial possibilities of all manner of "shows." He had managed a circus acrobat and juggler, arranged an exhibition of "wild sports of the Western Prairies" in Hoboken, supervised reenactments of city street cries in Vauxhall Garden, and organized concerts of the Swedish soprano Jenny Lind. In his American Museum on Broadway, he displayed human "curiosities" of all kinds, ranging from fat boys and thin men to waxworks and wild beasts. In the museum "Lecture Room," he presented melodrama and minstrelsy, acrobatic somersaults, and dancing "Rocky Mountain savages." Already by 1855, when he published his memoirs, Barnum's career illustrated the triumph of variety entertainment. His celebrity and his success in presenting babies and beauties to a receptive public gave credence to Olive Logan's warning that traditional distinctions between frivolous amusement and instructive recreation were being eroded.

The origins of variety entertainment lay in the traveling shows of the early nineteenth century. During the prosperous times before and especially after the Revolution, when New England and Mid-Atlantic farmers increased production of grain and dairy goods to purchase finished cotton cloth and tableware, itinerant peddlers carried imported English and American manufactures to the smallest town and farm. Along the rough tracks and river estuaries came the agents of what David Jaffee has called the "village enlightenment"— portrait painters, furniture makers, book dealers, school teachers, circuit preachers, patent-medicine vendors, tinsmiths, and artisans of all kinds, who wrought a cultural transformation of the northeast by the 1820s.[9] Showmen were less welcome, unless they exhibited mechanical marvels or beasts with unusual qualities that were deemed edifying and educational. The performances of itinerant actors, acrobats, and clowns were often considered among the vain amusements and frivolous diversions that threatened republican virtue. Connecticut's Act for the Suppressing of Mountebanks of 1773 prohibited "any games, tricks, plays, juggling or feats of uncommon dexterity and agility of body" that attracted "great numbers of people, to the corruption of manners, promoting of idleness, and the detriment of good order and religion."[10] In 1819 New York State made it unlawful to "exhibit or perform for gain and profit any puppet show, wire dance, or any other idle shows, acts or feats," but permitted "any museum or repository of natural curiosities, wax figures, useful works of art, or . . . the exhibition of any animal."[11]

Nevertheless, traveling showmen found ways to evade the punitive license fees and petty restrictions of local and state authorities. The canvas tent, first used by J. Purdy Brown as a pavilion in the 1820s, gave showmen greater flexibility; a fifty-foot round top could be quickly erected, provided seating for nearly a thousand in densely packed rows of backless seats, and was an effective substitute for the temporary wooden arenas that were too expensive and laborious to construct for anything other than an extended stay in the largest cities. Even in the 1820s, before canals, steamships, improved turnpike roads, and railroads made travel easier and quicker, there were a dozen circus troupes, each with some ten wagons and thirty employees, operating mainly along or near the northern seaboard, but venturing also into the Hudson River valley, into Ohio, and the southern seaboard states. A waxworks exhibition or some display of human skill was available to almost everyone. So familiar a figure was the wandering peddler of wonders with his portable cabinet of curiosities that the satirist Artemus Ward assumed the showman's persona for his stage "lectures" and his humorous essays on "the show bizness" in *Vanity Fair*. "I'm travelin with a tent, which is better nor [than] hirin hauls," Ward announced to his readers in 1859. "My show konsists of a serious of wax works, snakes, a paneramy kalled a Grand Movin Diarea of the War in the Crymear, komic songs and the Cangeroo." His catalogue of oddities was not mere whimsy. While on summer vacation in 1838, Nathaniel Hawthorne encountered entertainers on the road. One hawker had walked many miles over the thinly populated Berkshire hills to bring his hand organ and ingenious moving peepshow to the tavern in North Adams. A German carried his threadbare diorama in his wagon. For a few cents he offered "the very worst scratchings and daubings that can be imagined" of European cities ancient and modern, updated with scenes from the Napoleonic wars. The local farmers enjoyed both.[12]

In rural areas like western Massachusetts, where there were few large towns to support commercial entertainment, traveling shows needed very broad appeal to be successful. Performers had to be versatile. John Durang, one of the stars of the early circus, was a dancer, actor, clown, singer, tightrope walker, puppeteer, scene painter, and equestrian performer. He recalled that during a tour of Lower Canada with John Bill Ricketts in 1797, besides participating in stunts of all kinds on horseback: "I dancet on the stage, I was the Harlequin in the pantomimes, occasionally I sung a comic song. I tumbled on the slack rope and performed on the slack wire. I introduced mechanical exhibitions in machinery and transparencies. I produced exhibitions of fireworks. In short, I was performer, machinist, painter, designer, music compiler, the bill maker, and treasurer."[13]

Six years later Durang led his own small company by wagon through the towns of southern Pennsylvania and Maryland. Only in the largest cities of Philadelphia and Baltimore, with 41,000 and 26,000 inhabitants, did he stay for an extended period. Even then, he changed his program of song and dance, drama and opera, pantomime and farce, every day to encourage repeated visits.

Durang's versatility was typical of traveling showmen in rural America during the nineteenth century. For a generation, Hugh Lindsay combined managing a tavern and working irregularly as a clown with small circuses throughout southern Pennsylvania and adjoining states. When he joined John Miller's small "big show" and menagerie in 1823, the "business," he wrote in his memoirs, "was acting clown, singing comic songs, help to raise the canvas, [and] drive the camels after midnight from one stand to another, which averaged from 6 to 12 miles every night." Long distances between small settlements made touring unrewarding. In antebellum Missouri only bustling St. Louis had permanent professional theater; when Lexington, Boonville, and Hannibal were the only other cities with white populations greater than two thousand in 1850, troupes of players moving by boat or wagon struggled to finance their journey between the larger river towns, and avoided entirely the thinly populated central counties. To tempt adults to part with fifty cents—children and slave attendants, half price—the shows generally combined circus riding, minstrel song and humor, and a display of wild animals.[14]

Managers too gained broad experience from the traveling show, experience that shaped their plans for city playhouses. P. T. Barnum, who had been a storekeeper in Bethel, Connecticut, and in Brooklyn, was well-grounded in general salesmanship but a novice in entertainment matters. In 1835–36 he began his show business career in towns throughout the northern states by supervising appearances of the old and garrulous Joice Heth, supposedly the slave nurse of the infant George Washington, and of an acrobat-juggler, "Signor Vivalla." It was only when Barnum joined Aaron Turner's Old Columbian Circus in April 1836 that he learned more about general theatrical management. "To me," he admitted nearly twenty years later, "this travelling and performing in canvas tents was altogether new." After six months with the troupe of thirty-five, he led his own circus—"Barnum's Grand Scientific and Musical Theatre"—with the same acrobat-juggler, a clown, a minstrel, and musicians, on a tour through the South. He profited from that experience. In May 1840, in New York's Vauxhall Garden, he put on what he described as "a variety of performances, including singing, dancing, Yankee stories, etc." In January 1842, when he opened Barnum's American Museum in New York, among its miscellaneous amusements in the Lecture Room were the staples of the traveling show: "Industrious fleas, educated dogs, jugglers, automatons, ventriloquists, living statuary, tableaux, gipsies, albinoes, fat boys, giants, dwarfs, rope-dancers, caricatures of phrenology, and 'live Yankees,' pantomime, incidental music, singing and dancing in great variety (including Ethiopians,) etc. Dioramas, panoramas, models of Dublin, Paris, Niagara, Jerusalem, etc., mechanical figures, fancy glass-blowing, knitting machines and other triumphs in the mechanical arts, dissolving views, American Indians, including their warlike and religious ceremonies enacted on the stage, etc., etc."[15]

The most successful amusement entrepreneurs after Barnum had similarly broad experience. Dan Rice began his career in 1841 by exhibiting C. S. Kise's trained "pig of knowledge," made blackface "nigero dancing and singing" his specialty, became a circus strongman ("The Yankee Samson") and a comedian renowned for his burlesqued Shakespearean repertoire ("The Yankee Jester"). In the 1850s Rice performed in more than a dozen different circus combinations, and from 1852 to 1854 he owned a dime museum, supposedly containing a hundred thousand "curiosities," in New Orleans.[16] In 1846, at fourteen, Tony Pastor was a burnt-cork minstrel singer and comic in Barnum's Museum, and brought the skills he acquired in tumbling, riding, and mimicry to several traveling circuses in the 1850s. In the 1860s he became the leading pioneer of vaudeville in New York City, and in a career as performer-manager which spanned forty years, mixed circus comic burlesques and blackface "Negro extravaganzas" with pantomime, ballet, and opera in his three-hour bill. B. F. Keith was a businessman rather than a showman in vaudeville but was well prepared for variety theater. He performed in Bunnell's and Barnum's museums in the 1860s, in circuses in the 1870s, and in 1883 opened a dime museum in Boston with the usual miscellaneous exhibits—a chicken with a human face, "Baby Alice the Midget Wonder," a mermaid, and what he claimed was "the biggest hog in America"

—and much-abridged versions of Gilbert and Sullivan operettas. Buffalo Bill Cody's career in western melodrama began in city theaters in 1872, blossomed in a decade of winter touring, flourished in outdoor arenas in the 1880s, and ended in motion pictures. Informed by experience and by personal connections with successful impresarios, showmen mixed different strands of entertainment into a variety package.

Variety Entertainment

From financial necessity, city playhouses like Barnum's offered general entertainment for all tastes. "At the beginning of the nineteenth century," Lawrence Levine has pointed out, "the theater was a microcosm; it housed both the entire spectrum of the population and the complete range of entertainment, from tragedy to farce, juggling to ballet, opera to minstrelsy."[17] Managers still faced deep-seated antitheatrical sentiment from the Protestant churches. In the 1760s there had been only one small permanent playhouse in America, and Lewis Hallam's troupe of traveling players, excluded from New England, had depended on the upper classes of the middle and southern colonies and the Caribbean for patronage. After the Revolution the new states permitted public dramatic performances, and theaters were founded in the 1790s on the Atlantic seaboard, in Baltimore, Boston, New York, Philadelphia, Providence, Richmond, and Charleston, and a generation later, in the western river ports of Pittsburgh, Cleveland, Detroit, Louisville, Nashville, New Orleans, and St. Louis. Theaters constructed on the English model had three distinct spatial zones for the audience, often with separate entrances and differential prices of admission. The program had to appeal to the privileged in the boxes, to the clerks, mechanics, bootblacks, and newsboys in the pit close to the stage, and to the poorest groups in the upper balconies of the gallery. Managers and actors also depended directly on the audience for "benefit" performances, where named individuals received a share of the evening's box office receipts, to augment low salaries.

Even in metropolitan centers, theaters struggled to remain solvent and had to encourage regular attendance. In Boston, America's fourth biggest city, with a population of 136,000 in 1850, Moses Kimball, the manager of the Boston Museum, needed to fill two and a half thousand seats. Because of the competition from rival, low-cost places of amusement in the city, Kimball had to offer a different program almost every evening (except Saturdays and Sundays, when, determined to maintain a high moral tone, he respected Boston's sabbatarian customs and closed the theater). From 1843 to 1863, in every season of forty weeks, the museum staged a hundred and thirty dramatic pieces, half revivals of earlier successes and the rest entirely new. In the next twenty years, the number of productions was halved, and in the 1880s dropped to only fifteen a season. The stock company of the typical theater was small—from twelve to eighteen men, and fewer than half that number of women—but had to master tragedy, comedy, and light entertainment, often in the same evening. "There was rarely a program of a serious character that was not preceded by a farce," Boston Museum actress Kate Ryan remembered of the 1870s. The veteran comedian William Warren played nearly six hundred different roles in forty-two years at the museum, two hundred and six of them in the four seasons of 1847–51. William B. Wood listed nearly three hundred and fifty dramatic parts he played in fifty years on the Baltimore and Philadelphia stage, as well as hundreds of lesser roles, and hundreds more in melodrama, opera, farce, and pantomime.[18]

For most of the century every program in the theater was a variety show. Even the grand theaters of eighteenth-century London had surrounded solemn dramas with satirical comedy and the acrobatic turns and light musical offerings of city fairs. That legacy endured on both sides of the Atlantic. A typical evening's bill consisted of a play, usually abridged, and a comic afterpiece, with orchestral music. The play might be a Shakespearean tragedy or a contemporary melodrama, an eighteenth-century comedy or a new fairy-tale extravaganza, an opera or ballet. The melodramas that were a third of all plays performed at midcentury contained the most diverse elements. They were often vehicles for startling special effects, when stage managers conjured up sensational fires, waterfalls, volcanoes, or shipwrecks, or introduced horses, dogs, even an elephant. Entr'acte entertainment before and after the play included ventriloquists, magicians, jugglers, acrobats, dancers, minstrels, comedians, and singers of every description.[19]

George L. Fox's pantomime *Humpty Dumpty*, one of the century's most successful productions and one of the first to occupy a full evening's bill, was a variety show in miniature. As well as slapstick scenes of flying brickbats, rough-and-tumble fights, and acrobatics, it had a donkey cart and live pigs on stage, an improvised steamship, topical allusions to financial and political corruption, traditional dance that parodied the can-can, orchestral music that mixed opera and popular tunes, spectacular ballet sequences, and a concluding transformation scene of sensational visual splendor. It was, complained one critic, a "farrago of nonsense," "a medley of concert-saloon, minstrel-hall, and country circus attraction."[20] For the enthusiastic audience who flocked to more than a thousand performances of *Humpty Dumpty*, Fox's variety was a virtue rather than a vice. And mixed programs continued even in the most fashionable theater. In New York's Wallace's Theatre on Broadway and Thirteenth Street, the main attractions on May 31, 1880, were the third act of *Othello* and the second half of Dion Boucicault's comedy *London Assurance*, introduced, concluded, and linked by three brief farces.[21]

An evening bill in the Bowery Theatre in December 1832 illustrates the odd juxtaposition of high drama and low comedy. It was, a reporter noted, an unusual and "indescribably ludicrous" scene. Junius Brutus Booth, the fiery English actor, played Richard III, but the good-natured crowd became so excited that it filled the orchestra pit and most of the stage and wings. The effect was not quite what Shakespeare intended:

> It was every thing, or any thing, but a tragedy. In the scene with Lady Anne . . . the gallery spectators amused themselves by throwing pennies and silver on the stage, which occasioned an immense scrambling among the boys, and they frequently ran between King Richard and Lady Anne to snatch a stray copper. . . . The battle of Bosworth-field capped the climax—the audience mingled with the soldiers and raced across the stage, to the shouts of the people, the roll of the drums, and the bellowing of the trumpets; and when the fight between Richard and Richmond came on, they made a ring round the combatants to see fair play, and kept them at it for nearly a quarter of an hour.

When Thomas D. Rice, the best-known minstrel of the day, appeared on the bill later that evening, the spectators were so delighted with his grotesquely comic dance that they made him repeat his "Jim Crow" song twenty times.[22]

Americans had a penchant for burlesque productions that bridged highbrow and lowbrow tastes and transformed tragedy into comedy. If William Mitchell introduced the parodies popular on the London stage to the Bowery's Olympic Theatre in the 1830s, minstrel troupes added some of the nonsensical carnival spirit that pervaded the rowdy street parades. Comical minstrel burlesques of political oratory and erudite lectures mocked genteel pretension. Travesties of Italian opera were especially in vogue. Most assumed close knowledge of the music and plot of the originals. In the wake of Bellini's *La Sonnambula*, the ever-astute P. T. Barnum commissioned *The Sleep Walker*, described by one critic as "a dark version, . . . with a choice selection of music from that and other popular operas, and the favorite Ethiopian melodies."[23] There were humorous allusions to the American scene, sometimes adaptations of Shakespeare, sometimes skits on national peculiarities. *Po-ca-hon-tas, or, The Gentle Savage* (1855) by John Brougham, the master of dramatic burlesque, poked fun at the solemn verse of Longfellow; as Powhatan's associates, it had Kros-as-kan-be, Oso-char-ming, Lum-Pa-Shuga, and as medicine men, Kal-o-mel and Kod-liv-Royl. By the late 1860s the elaborate and ludicrous burlesques of Lydia Thompson's troupe filled most of the New York and Boston theaters. "Respecting nothing—neither taste, propriety, virtue, nor manners," *Appleton's Journal* complained, the British Blondes and their American imitators were determined "to throw ridicule on gods and men—to satirize everybody and everything."[24] Nothing escaped satire.

The hybrid combinations of comedy and drama, and song and dance were popular because they were miscellaneous. With burnt-cork make-up as the sole unifying link, the minstrel show grouped together short comic sketches, sentimental songs, instrumental solos, and speeches that mocked genteel oratory. "Leg-show" "burlesques" of fairy tales had even less coherence. Few observers were able to detect any narrative thread in *The Black Crook*, first produced in 1866 and renowned for its gorgeous array of girls in golden shells, and dressed (or undressed) as demons and Amazons. Some later "chorus-girl" spectacles, like *Robin Hood; or, The Maid That Was Arch and The Youth That Was Archer*, were so disjointed as to be almost beyond comprehension.[25] The circus was an incongruous mix of "wild" jungle animals with acrobats, equestrians, and clowns, and added midways of sideshow "curiosities" in the 1880s. The wild west show's program of Indians on horseback and "cow-boy fun"— riding, roping, shooting, and simulated displays of hunting the buffalo—gave way in the 1890s to "rough riders" from across the globe who had no connection with "exhibitions" of the American Far West.

As big-city amusements thrived, so did rural traveling shows. After the Civil War itinerant "combination" companies brought current New York productions and sensational melodramas like *Uncle Tom's Cabin* and *The Drunkard* that became perennial favorites in the small-town "opera" halls. Tent shows with improvised stages reached more dispersed settlements.[26] In the 1880s and 1890s showmen selling patent medicine also brought variety. Their greatest attraction was offering abridged versions of all or most of the popular styles. "Nevada Ned" Oliver, one of the stars of the Kickapoo Indian Medicine Company, recalled that he offered "drama, vaudeville, musical comedy, Wild West shows, minstrels, magic, burlesque, dog and pony circuses, not to mention Punch and Judy, pantomimes, movies, menageries." One branch of the Kickapoo Indians spent nine weeks at the Albany circus grounds in the summer of 1883. Every week, for ten cents' admission, the troupe of a dozen performers gave eight two-hour performances of rifle shooting, acrobatics, comedy, ventriloquism, a dog circus, and a comic afterpiece, interspersed with song and dance from the dozen Indians or lectures from Texas Charlie on the life-enhancing blessings of Indian Sagwa.[27]

However disparate variety entertainment seemed, there was cross-fertilization and fusion. The elaborate new amusement parks at New York's Coney Island, built between 1895 and 1904, exemplified that mixture. To an unsympathetic critic like James Huneker, Coney's Luna Park represented "topsyturvydom," with "the dwarfs and the dogs, the horses and the miniature railway" scrambled together in a bedlam of noisy funfair rides and lurid electric lights. Luna Park's designer Frederic Thompson had one original thought, journalist Dana Gatlin observed: he "conceived the idea of lumping together all the little, cheap concessions . . . and enclosing them, with one admission en-

11

A commercial stereograph of the E. and H. T. Anthony company recorded showbills near New York's City Hall Park in the 1860s, with bootblacks and newsboys in the foreground. Private collection. *American Photography in the Nineteenth Century*, ed. Martha Sandweiss (Fort Worth, Tex.: Amon Carter Museum, 1991), 6.

trance," and adding "novelties" and spectacles.[28] There were familiar dime-museum sideshows of fat ladies, minstrel and vaudeville acts, moving pictures, and exotic female dancers in the Streets of Cairo. There was a three-ring circus suspended over Luna's central lagoon, elephants in the Durbar of India, and Buckskin Bill's Wild West, which offered a faint glimmer of Cody's show. However, Luna Park was also unique, with distinctive features shared by no other entertainment form. It had space—portable tents and small city theaters could not offer hundreds of thousands of electric lights, exotic sham-fairylands, vast simulated disaster epics, and the lagoon of Shoot-the-Chutes. It encouraged participation—where rival amusements generally had only passive interaction between performers and spectators, here were thrilling, vertigo-inducing rides in a walled city of fun. Thompson was convinced that patrons of amusement rides did not appreciate lessons in intellectual or moral improvement. They left their dismal tenements not for enlightenment but for "bright days," for pleasant oblivion from daily cares. "Elaborated child's play" thrilled them. In carnival surroundings more surreal than any set designed for the conventional stage, the amusement park offered, he announced with pride, "a condensed Broadway"—"life, action, motion, sensation, surprise, shock, swiftness or else comedy."[29]

Popular Theater: English Heritage, American Enterprise

Throughout much of the nineteenth century, one significant difference between English and American variety entertainment was the predominance in England of the big-city amusement business. The English had advantages of every kind—a well-developed theatrical tradition, less intense criticism from the Protestant churches, a better-integrated system of transportation—but a more closely settled population was perhaps the most significant of all. There were traveling shows and portable theaters that generally followed circuits defined by seasonal hiring fairs and customary feast days, but Britain's large factory towns of the north and midlands also provided stable audiences for music hall and melodrama.[30] The contrast with the United States was marked. In 1800 less than 4 percent of America's population was living in centers of population greater than ten thousand. Fifty years later, when that figure had risen to 12 percent, it was still lower than the 20 percent of the population of England and Wales living in cities of that size in 1800. And by 1850, 40 percent of the population of England and Wales was congregated in the larger cities.[31] As New York became the nation's leading seaport, supplied by the Hudson River, Erie Canal, and coastal and transatlantic shipping, it also blossomed as the nation's theater capital. In 1860 its metropolitan population was only half that of London's but a million inhabitants supported twelve theaters, six lecture rooms, and several dozen exhibition halls. As the nation's urban population increased from nearly ten million in 1870 to almost forty-two million in 1910, commercial amusements also flourished, especially in the great cities.[32]

There were distinct class accents that modified the general picture of the theater as a gathering place for all classes. New York's Bowery district was the significant exception. In 1855 the humorist "Doesticks" dubbed it "the twenty-five cent area of town," "home of the unadulterated, undiluted sanguinary drama."[33] The Bowery was a thriving commercial area, processing food and producing garments, and profiting from the dockside warehouses of the nation's leading import-export emporium. By 1840 it was beginning to lose the checkerboard residential distribution of rich and poor characteristic of the early modern city; the wealthy had begun to move uptown, away from recent Irish and German immigrants. Boardinghouses provided cheap ac-

13

commodation for artisans, with bars and billiard rooms for male sociability. The Bowery Theatre had been built in grand style in 1826 to rival the elite Park Theatre, but within a few years, under manager Thomas S. Hamblin, it became notorious for low-priced, sensational entertainment and novelty acts. Hamblin took circus spectacles and comedy from the Bowery Amphitheatre, including Rice's minstrel song-and-dance act, and also adapted street performances from the Fulton Market nearby. William Mitchell's Olympic Theatre specialized in topical burlesques and blood-and-thunder melodramas, and he staged the early plays featuring the actor F. S. Chanfrau as Mose, the Bowery B'hoy, butcher and brawler.[34] The two outstanding early blackface troupes, the Virginia Minstrels and Christy Minstrels, gave their first performances in Bowery halls, and the Melodeon became the first specialized "Ethiopian opera house" in 1846. The theaters on Bowery and Chatham streets were never entirely working-class preserves—Aiken's *Uncle Tom's Cabin* in Purdy's National Theatre and George L. Fox's pantomimes in the Bowery attracted middle-class patronage in the 1850s. They demonstrated a successful formula for playhouses offering variety entertainment tailored to the needs of the locality.

The remarks of Frances Trollope and other English visitors critical of the manners of "mobocracy" at play give a misleading impression of unusually uncouth Americans. The audiences of London's cheap East End theaters, penny gaffs, and free-and-easy saloons were as boisterous and vociferous as the haunts of the Bowery b'hoys, but, like New York's popular theaters, also included the middle classes. Most Bowery melodramas were adaptations, improvisations, or imitations of popular English plays and copied their sensational style of presentation.[35] Hamblin and Mitchell, who joined the large cohort of English actors in the United States in the early 1830s, were the most successful managers of Bowery theaters. Mitchell brought the spirit and the tone of Madame Vestris's London Olympic to the Bowery's Olympic, but, like Hamblin, respected American patriotic feeling, and in his light musicals, travesties, and melodramas, he included themes familiar to the b'hoys in the pit. Mose's distinctive dress of red shirt, tall hat, high boots, his greased hair and long sideburns, and his colloquial expressions established him as the local champion who rescued damsels and dispatched villains. Mose, complained critic William K. Northall, was not merely on stage but "in the pit, the boxes and the gallery," as the respectable who once occupied the best seats shunned such "an unmitigated conglomeration of vulgarity and illiteracy."[36] Burlesques like those Mitchell staged and comedy portraying uniquely American characters helped integrate diverse themes in variety entertainment. Mose joined the pantheon of the phlegmatic Jonathan, created by George "Yankee" Hill, Nimrod Wildfire, the no-nonsense frontiersman in *The Lion of the West*, Adam Trueman, the plain-speaking yeoman in Anna Cora Mowatt's

Fashion, and the minstrel endmen who pricked the pomposity of the inter-locutor. Nuances of dress and dialogue, topical references, and specific details of locations were sufficient to transform the English heritage and to identify an American hero, comical and practical, who scorned pretension and in-justice.

By the early twentieth century, American inventiveness in variety enter-tainment began to prevail, even in England. American circuses, the minstrel show, Buffalo Bill's Wild West, and the large amusement park were exports as significant as American cotton or corn. In 1858 the British *Chambers's Journal* decried the "the age of shows," which it defined with the same broad brush as Olive Logan, as anything ranging from the Great Exhibition to "high-class" theater to "curiosities" at penny fairs, and it acknowledged Barnum as the model and master of the art of showmanship. Others denied obvious Ameri-can influences. "There is nothing that American showmen have ever done that Englishmen have not done first and better," 'Lord' George Sanger boasted. He confessed, however, that when Cushing's American circus came to Liverpool in 1856, it "was to eclipse all English circuses." In response, the English circus owner created his own band of "Indians." Sensing a money-making opportunity, Sanger also put on his own "Scenes from Buffalo Bill," with a few buffalo and more fake Indians, the year before the real Cody exhibition came to England in 1887.[37] American originality was most evident in vaudeville. Although it resembled English music hall in its program of short, miscellaneous acts, it also reflected the country's unique multiethnic and racial heritage and was distinguished by its efficient management: there was no English equivalent of Keith and Albee's vaudeville empire. On both sides of the Atlantic, successful showmen based their programs on their under-standing of popular taste, generally agreeing with Coney's Frederic Thomp-son that "child's play" and "happy days" were the essential elements.

Spectacles, Episodes, and Glad Mush

Other commentators agreed that popular entertainment lacked intellectual content. The modern theater audience, Joseph Jefferson noted with dismay in 1890, "has been accustomed to a supply of entertainments for the eye rather than for the ear." Gaudy scenery and special effects—"sugar-plums"—smoth-ered the "daintier morsels" of dialogue well written and well delivered. For almost forty years Jefferson had given countless performances in Dion Bouci-cault's *Rip Van Winkle*. The nation's most respected actor had built his reputa-tion on his convincing portrayal of the carefree young boy gradually trans-formed by life's experiences into the chastened and ineffectual old Rip. His delicately nuanced blend of comedy and sentiment was acclaimed as a master-piece of subtle characterization. "There is a depth of pathos, tenderness, and

15

beauty that charms like music and attunes the heart to the finest sense of pity," proclaimed a typical review in 1867. Jefferson resisted all suggestions to embellish the play with "realism"—with a retinue of pipe-smoking Knickerbockers, a Dutch windmill, real cows and a dog, and the Continental army patriotic with fife and drums. As the son and grandson of actors, he was proud to be an old-style professional who had never forgotten his early tours by road and riverboat to improvised stages in an age when audiences warmed to bravura oratory and gesture and when stagecraft was rudimentary. Those days, he declared, were now past.[38]

There was general consensus among early-twentieth-century critics that variety entertainment, regardless of the specific form, was trivial nonsense. Clayton Hamilton agreed with Jefferson that the modern drama "makes its appeal mainly to the eye." Why was the low-priced theater so popular? dramatist Harry James Smith wondered in 1907. Why did New York "shop girls" and their "steadies" spend ten, twenty, or thirty cents of their money, earned by long hours of labor in the garment factory or behind the department store counter, in watching poor quality melodrama in the Bowery's Thalia Theater? Why did they hiss villainous rogues intent on tricking childlike innocents into white slavery, or cheer street-smart bootblacks who mocked the silver-tongued seducers? What was so fascinating about *The Way of the Transgressor*, where at the climactic moment, one trained hound untied the helpless Gracie bound to the rails while the other climbed the ladder and pulled the rope over the signal's pulley to stop the advancing locomotive in the tunnel? There was no plot, no characterization, no coherent narrative.[39]

The audience, Smith concluded, "wanted to have their emotions stirred, their blood quickened," to escape the dull drudgery of drab, ill-paid work with three hours of forgetfulness in this "house of a thousand wonders." They wanted everyday life dramatized, so that "it becomes necessary to color it up, to provide it with glamour, with mystery, with terror, and with comicality. Realism and wild romance are curiously wedded in the result." The theater gave companionship; the visitors interacted with the performers and with each other—they whispered, whistled, commented, heckled, gripped the seat in front at times of tension, and applauded what they liked. They welcomed any and all expressions of emotion that transcended the ordinary so long as the "episodes" were brief: every isolated dramatic "situation" "must come to its culmination rapidly, directly, and by means which require no thought."[40]

There were, Smith noted, only two other forms of theatrical amusements favored by the Bowery poor—"the penny-in-the-slot Arcades" and vaudeville. Of vaudeville, he wrote, "could anything be more disjointed and scattering in its make-up?" And the "automatic" slot-machine kinetoscopes, mutoscopes, vitascopes, or phonographs, popular since the 1890s, offered merely brief, frenetic peepshows without sound or snatches of song without vision. Other commentators believed that modern amusement lacked narrative continuity. For Edwin Milton Royle vaudeville was "lunch-counter art" and, like the department store, comprised diverse elements assembled in one convenient package for city dwellers with limited time. "Vaudeville," Channing Pollock agreed in 1911, "addresses itself to amusement seekers incapable of giving, or unwilling to give, concentrated and continuous attention." Florence Sinow attributed its success to variety, editing, and fast pace, and reminisced: "the evening shifted from excitement to excitement, but—on different levels—high comedy, sophistication, slapstick, dancing, singing—sentimental—jazz—acrobats—animals—a panorama that was gorgeous, funny, tearful, each in turn—a kind of entertainment audiences could lose themselves in, individually and collectively."[41]

Modern variety amusements, the critic George Jean Nathan observed condescendingly, were merely "glad mush." Audiences did not wish to see social problems enacted on stage; they sought "life, colour, movement and gaiety"—"horse-play, belly laughter, pretty girls, ingenious scenery," "insane melodrama, lovely limbs, lively tunes, gaudy colours, loud humours, farce, flippancy, fol-de-rol." In 1913 Nathan had joined forces with George M. Cohan, the leading producer of musicals, and compiled a long list of the stage effects calculated to elicit appropriate emotional responses from those watching. For devising a successful show was an entirely predictable process, a matter of "mechanics," of applying the right formula of convention and invention. Some variant of the Cinderella story with a happy ending, he noted cynically, satisfied the great majority of theater-goers.[42]

Nathan and Cohan discussed the general techniques of theatrical production rather than its specific applications. By 1913 the legitimate theater and live drama with which they were familiar had a serious rival in moving pictures. A decade earlier, the journalist and critic Norman Hapgood dared to hope that the new "biograph" might be the salvation for the theater degraded by popular taste. If only the "spectacle-loving" masses could be diverted into "separate houses" managed by profit-hungry entrepreneurs and watch meretricious nonsense on the flickering screen, then the intellectual classes might be left alone to sponsor an "elevated" drama as culturally rich as Europe's.[43]

Illustrated Songs, Vaudeville, and the Moving-Picture Revolution

The "moving-picture revolution," popular writer Glenmore Davis declared triumphantly in 1910, "has put the biggest dent into theatricals that the amusement industry has ever received." In just two years, the movies, "an absolutely new form of popular amusement," had forced out of business cheap city melodrama houses and low-price vaudeville halls that had been the mainstay of popular drama for more than a generation. Small-time venture capitalists had grasped the rewards of lower costs of exhibition in storefront nickelodeons and outwitted the "Broadwayites" and the syndicates that traditionally controlled theatrical entertainments. By making live performances redundant, the "man at the crank" had thrown commercial theater into crisis. It was, Davis rejoiced, "a sudden and extraordinary change."[44] A few months earlier fellow journalist William Allen Johnston reflected on the implications of moving pictures as machine-made art. "All is mechanical, abbreviated, compressed, silent," he noted. In the "new style of theater," the "new form of drama" was "inanimate, compact, machine-like." "Gone are the glamour of the footlights and the interesting little world back of the curtain, which many found more luring than the play itself."[45]

The early kinetoscopes and vitagraphs had been little more than intriguing technological novelties, but Edison projectors made moving-picture entertainment social, even sociable, when groups gathered in a darkened room. There had been significant technological innovations during the nineteenth century that enhanced theatrical performances. In private homes, gifted amateurs with the energy and resources to amuse themselves made use of the new melodeon, piano, or of magic lantern, or sheet music or one of Dick and Fitzgerald's many guidebooks on parlor games and tableaux vivants that the rotary printing press produced inexpensively by the 1850s. For stagecraft in public arenas, gas and electric lighting allowed more subtle shading in painted scenery, more varied colors in costumes, and less garish make-up for actors, as producer David Belasco made famous in his "Drama of Illusion" at the turn of the century. Drop curtains, pulleys, water tanks, reflecting plate glass, and revolving stages encouraged extravagant stage effects. City audiences expected to see volcanoes erupting, houses burning, waterfalls gushing, lightning striking, ships sailing, or horses galloping. Nevertheless, these technological novelties did not fundamentally change the face-to-face encounter between performers and spectators that was the customary means of transmitting words and images.

In his survey of the amusement business published in 1910, Robert Grau concluded that the crucial stage in the triumph of the "cinematograph" was the introduction of the illustrated song in vaudeville. Using a projector and a set of colored slides keyed to the lyrics of well-known songs, the vocalist-exhibitor encouraged his listeners to join in the chorus and to be more than mere spectators. The show became a communal process, an improvised neighborhood gathering that domesticated the new technological form of machine-produced images .[46] Siegmund Lubin was a pioneer. A manufacturer of optical instruments, Lubin saw the potential, first of photographic song slides, and soon, of projectors and moving pictures. By March 1897 he displayed his short "Cineograph" films in C. A. Bridenbaugh's Dime Mu-

18

seum in Philadelphia, and in 1899 he opened his special-purpose Cineograph nickelodeon.[47]

Lubin had rivals. In 1898 the Sears, Roebuck mail-order catalogue offered a complete, ready-made, commercial entertainment "outfit" for traveling showmen. It supplied phonographs, moving-picture projectors with film footage, and magic-lantern slide projectors, sets of slides, and accompanying scripts, with rolls of tickets and blank posters to announce exhibitions. Budding entrepreneurs added the talent for performing, willingness to improvise from the set programs, and flair for business. A typical concern was the Cook and Harris High Class Moving Picture Company that toured upstate New York and northern New England from 1904 to 1911. The team of four comprised Bert Cook as singer and compère; his wife, Fannie Harris, as pianist; an advance man posting bills and seeking sponsorship from local organizations; and one special-effects assistant. The troupe presented a two-hour variety show, usually for one evening only, in very small towns with a population seldom larger than two thousand. The staple program included brief vaudeville sketches mixing comedy, melodrama, and music that were supplemented by brief sequences from current films of all kinds. In his advertising, Cook emphasized the mixture of sound and vision, with piano and sound effects to complement the silent films. The films were the main attraction but the slides and songs were the connecting thread—or as their program announced, "The Monotony of a Whole Evening of Moving Pictures is Relieved by the Introduction Now and Then of Some Beautiful Illustrated Song." Contact with local residents began with negotiations between the troupe's agent and charitable concerns, continued with advertising images that featured the audience as much as the film, and culminated in joint participation in illustrated songs.[48]

In Lexington, Kentucky, a medium-sized market town of 26,000 in 1900, illustrated songs and moving pictures also augmented the standard programs of traveling showmen. At the Lexington Opera House on 15 December 1896, the visiting Holmes and Wolford Company announced a "special attraction," "The Cinematograph": "The most marvelous invention of the nineteenth century will be on exhibition showing moving pictures life-size and very natural." In between acts of *The Smugglers*, a full-length "Sensational Melodrama," the repertory company screened a dozen, very brief, flickering scenes of Paris streetcars, waves breaking on a seaside beach, and comical "pickaninnies" bathing. The movies often came again to Lexington in the two decades after 1896, as a modern feature squeezed into the programs of traveling tent shows—Chautauqua, minstrels, circus, repertory theater. Lexington was unusual because it had no successful vaudeville hall until 1907, but it had a galaxy of other commercial amusements that provided variety entertainment, including movies and illustrated songs.[49]

19

By 1912 Cook and Harris had abandoned traveling and turned to managing a nickelodeon in a fixed location; Lexington now had two permanent motion-picture theaters. Only a few traveling shows like Lyman Howe's survived, as ten thousand special-purpose nickelodeons appeared across the nation between 1905 and 1910.[50] In 1907, Barton W. Currie, one of the first to acknowledge the "nickel madness," saw the advantages of these "tawdry little show-places": "Melodrama is served hot and at a pace the Bowery theatres can never follow." The content was much the same as the ten-twenty-thirty "mellowdrammer" theaters, but further edited and abridged to "episodes," presented within fifteen minutes, and without the expense of live performers. And, since film was silent, the descendants of the Bowery b'hoys could enjoy "French buffoonery," courtesy of Meliès and Pathé.[51] Motion-picture distributors made strenuous efforts to encourage family attendance in special-purpose, well-designed theaters.[52]

Glenmore Davis and William Allen Johnston believed that the coming of the movies marked the end of nineteenth-century tradition in live theatrical entertainments. However, they exaggerated the immediate effect of the "moving-picture revolution." The number of traditional theaters outside the major metropolitan centers that regularly hosted productions of visiting companies dropped steadily rather than suddenly. Julius Cahn's *Official Theatrical Guide* listed 1,746 "first-class houses" in 1905. In 1910 there were 1,549, but only 674 in 1925. In the 1920s Broadway productions still flourished, but elsewhere many of the old-style theaters that survived adjusted to new circumstances by replacing serious drama with lighthearted musicals and farces, and even then often had to screen movies on Saturday evenings to boost box office receipts. Even more striking was the loss of large "combination" companies touring the country with Broadway shows—339 in 1900, 236 in 1910, 95 in 1915, but only 39 in 1920.[53] The "tommers"—the troupes that visited the most remote areas with countless versions of the perennnial favorite *Uncle Tom's Cabin*—dropped from some 500 in the 1890s to 12 in 1927.[54] By 1920 the large circuses and wild west shows were also going out of business. Between 1910 and 1930 there was a decisive shift to mechanical reproduction of sound and vision that became characteristic of twentieth-century mass culture.

One form of live entertainment thrived a while longer. In underpopulated rural areas of the South and West, where permanent movie theaters were not viable, small troupes—perhaps 400 in 1927—brought "repertoire" drama and vaudeville in tent shows in spring and summer.[55] It was traditional variety in style and content. The J. Doug Morgan show that toured the Midwest and claimed to be the "World's Greatest Tented Amusement Enterprise" saw its role as presenting "A Grand Triple Alliance of Musical Comedy, Drama, and Vaudeville."[56] In the late 1920s the tent shows faced severe competition from "canned drama," especially talking pictures, and most failed in the Depression.[57]

Show Biz Old and New

After a long and successful career in Broadway musical theater, Jack Burton looked back nostalgically on the entertainments of his youth. Born in 1885, he recalled the excitement of the numerous touring companies that came to Aurora, Illinois, en route from Chicago to St. Louis. In the 1890s, at the Coulter Opera House and its successor, the Grand Opera House, he saw a regular succession of visiting attractions—minstrels, old-fashioned melodrama, the Holden Comedy Company, even the inspirational lectures of Theodore Roosevelt—and as a college student in Chicago, vaudeville, circus, and wild west shows too. The movies that replaced Aurora's live shows in 1913 lacked color: there was no dialogue, no comic punchline, no background music, no spontaneous song. What mechanical reproduction lacked most was a true sense of drama. The movies could not recapture a small boy's thrill of watching the bill poster announce the coming attraction, the anticipation of the grand street pageant, the unexpected improvisation on familiar themes. Recorded sound and vision lacked immediacy, intimacy, and spontaneity. In the opera house "homemade music" had blended with professional and amateur plays, church festivals, club pageants, and high school graduations graced the stage in the intervening weeks. Compared with the "road shows," the early movies were modern versions of peepshows—silent, remote, lacking the human warmth of direct engagement and empathy—and they were in black and white.[58]

THE DIME MUSEUM

Of the many "museums" on New York's Broadway and the Bowery, with ill-sorted collections of "curiosities," none was more renowned than Barnum's. From 1842 to 1868 Phineas Taylor Barnum's American Museum was the best-known "Congress of Wonders," an eclectic mix of enlightenment and entertainment to please both the many and the few. It was a minstrel hall and an art gallery, a repository of natural history and a theater for melodrama, a waxworks house of horrors and a collection of technological marvels. Barnum's pioneered the amusement business: it presented moral uplift with melodramatic publicity and wrapped sensational plays in sentimental rhetoric and polite decorum. There, the scientific and the sham enticed those enthralled by the diversity of the modern city, by its contrapuntal rhythms and contrasting experiences. Like other city dime museums, Barnum's offered teasing spectacles and fascinating puzzles served up with modern panache.

It was the display of "living curiosities"—the fat and the thin, giant and dwarf, real or fake—that distinguished Barnum's Museum from the other palaces of pleasure in the city. The novelist Henry James remembered its advertising "spurious relics and monsters in effigy, to say nothing of the promise within of the still more monstrous and abnormal living."[1] Some, like university professor Henry P. Tappan, scorned it as "a mere place of popular amusement." In 1852 he wrote that in America a museum was "a place for some stuffed birds and animals, for the exhibition of monsters, and for vulgar dramatic performances." In London, by contrast, the British Museum was an outstanding repository of art and science. Intellectuals often admired the dime museum's "scientific" menagerie of exotic animals, and sometimes acknowledged the worth of cases of geological specimens or flora and fauna gathered from afar; they usually disparaged the abnormal animal and human "curiosities" as crowd-pleasing and money-making distractions. However, Tappan's transatlantic comparison was overdrawn. London, with a larger population and a longer tradition, did have more specific sites for different forms of entertainment—for waxworks, for panoramas, for mechanical marvels. However, miscellaneous amusements gathered in one building were very common, even in England. In May 1846 the Egyptian Hall, London's premier venue, displayed at the very same time, Barnum's Tom Thumb, George Catlin's Indian Gallery, and the mawkish paintings of Benjamin Haydon. "Museums" in all cities in all nations in the early nineteenth century contained, as English visitor Isabella Bird observed of Barnum's in New York, both scientific objects of "real interest" and "spurious and contemptible" "monstrosities" fit only for the "vulgar gaze."[2]

"Living curiosities" were, Barnum proclaimed, "representatives of the wonderful."[3] In a Protestant country that cast doubt on the theater as an institution fit only for slothful men and filled with sinful women, the museum, Barnum insisted, exhibited God's mysterious creation for all to ponder —and enjoy. His most celebrated human "curiosities" were not mute waxworks but extraordinary living "wonders" who communicated with visitors and transformed passive viewing into an interactive experience. "Curiosities" made Barnum's reputation (or notoriety) as a loveable rogue and hoaxer. In 1835–36 he toured with the crippled Joice Heth, supposedly the ancient slave nurse of George Washington. In late 1842 he discovered the two exhibits that transformed his career. The Fejee Mermaid might be inanimate but Barnum's extensive publicity made the exotic half-monkey, half-fish another "missing link" demanding close scrutiny. Tom Thumb became not merely another midget exhibited but an entertainer whose burlesqued roles and repartee made him a charming companion as well as liminal "man-child" testing the borderlines between childhood innocence and adult knowingness. "Col. Frémont's Nondescript or Woolly Horse," supposedly found in 1849 during the explorer's expeditions in the Rocky Mountains, was typical of Barnum's stunts. Culture-seekers hoped it was a New World creature unknown to science; sensation-seekers enjoyed the jape with the beast with curly hair; all paid their twenty-five cents for admission. That was Barnum's genius.

During the Mexican War, Herman Melville wrote a series of short essays mocking the heroics of General Zachary Taylor. In the new humorous magazine *Yankee Doodle*, he mused how an astute showman might thrill the public eager for any contact with the all-conquering American warrior, by exhibiting curios which had "almost" been touched by the humble victor. Eventually, after touting for suitable relics, the impresario offers General Taylor a personal appearance alongside "General" Tom Thumb, "where you will be associated with all that is curious in nature and art, you will enjoy the society of a General almost as famous as yourself."[4] Who else would Melville choose as the people's showman-champion but Barnum?

Early Museum Shows

Ethan Greenwood was a typical showman-entrepreneur of the early nineteenth century. In 1818 he abandoned a career in portrait painting. For the next twenty years, he owned and managed the New England Museum and Gallery of Fine Arts in Boston and two other museums in Portland and Providence. Much of his time was spent in purchasing items for the collections, arranging for taxidermists to mount fish and animals, advertising in the local press, and traveling from Boston to Maine and Rhode Island. The staples of all his museums were the wonders of nature, preserved or sometimes live, waxworks, and fine art, supplemented by occasional special attractions like the "Wonderful dwarf," hired for a few weeks. Ethan Greenwood's journal for June 1824 outlined his activities.

Georgia Brady Barnhill, " 'Extracts from the Journals of Ethan A. Greenwood': Portrait Painter and Museum Proprietor," *Proceedings of the American Antiquarian Society* 103 (1993): 166–67.

June 1st., 1824. A Mermaid arrived here last week & I agreed to exhibit it. Busy setting up Shark.

2nd. Purchased some Indian Curiosities.

3rd. Bought four figures of an Italian $4.00.

5th. Bought four Busts of Voltaire, filling up jars of reptiles. . . .

7th. Artillery Election good run of business & in the eve a 'Glorious House' $342.75. Best day since the Museum began.

10th. Bought a young Shark.

12th. Preparing articles for Portland, closed exhibition of the Vampyre [of the Ocean (bought three weeks earlier for $150 in cash)].

14th. Dexter with his hand cart moved the Linnean Coll. After the Museum we rallied 15 men and removed the Vampyre into the lower hall of the Museum, this was a heavy job & took nearly 2 hours.

18th. Got ready to go to Portland. . . .

19th. Went on board at daylight & arrived in Portland on the 20th . . . . Last Friday I bought the Egyptian Mummy together with the cases & c for $350.00.

23d. Got out bills for the Mummy exhibit. . . .

26th. Went on a boat to Peake Island, & got 2 jaw bones of a Whale 14 feet long, out in a violent storm, got wet, & at one time in great danger. Put one bone in Museum here, & the other on board for Boston.

27th. On board Sloop for Boston.

Salem was one of the major seaports of the early republic; shipping generally, and especially the import-export trade with China and the East Indies, made it one of the wealthiest small cities in the country. On the Fourth of July

Early Museum Shows

1838, Nathaniel Hawthorne recorded his impressions of his visit to temporary sideshows on Salem common.

Nathaniel Hawthorne, *Hawthorne's Lost Notebook, 1835–1841*, ed. Barbara S. Mouffe (University Park: Pennsylvania State University Press, 1978), 66–69.

A very hot, bright sunny day; town much thronged. Booths on the common, selling gingerbread &c. sugar-plums and confectionery, spruce-beer, lemonade. Spirits forbidden, but probably sold stealthily. On the top of one of the booths a monkey, with a tail two or three feet long. He is fastened by a cord, which, getting tangled with the flag over the booth, he takes hold and tries to free it. The object of much attention from the crowd, and played with by the boys, who toss up ginger bread to him which he nibbles and throws down again. He reciprocates notice of some kind or other, with all who notice him. A sort of gravity about him. A boy pulls his long tail, whereat he gives a slight squeak, and for the future elevates it as much as possible. Looking at the same booth by and bye, find that the poor monkey has been obliged to betake him self to the top of one of the wooden joists that stick up high above.—Boys going about with molasses candy, almost melted down in the sun.—Shows, a mammoth rat; a collection of pirates, murderers &c. in wax. Smell of cigars, from Spanish down to immense long nines, smoking among the crowd. Constables in considerable number, parading about with their staves, sometimes communing with each other, producing an effect by their presence without having to interfere actively. One or two old salts or others rather the worse for liquor; in general people very temperate. At evening the aspect of things rather more picturesque; some of the booth keepers knocking down the temporary structures, and putting the materials in wagons to carry away; other booths lighted up; and the lights gleaming through rents in the sail-cloth top. Customers rather riotous, yet funny, calling loudly and whimsically for what they want,— young sailors &c; a young fellow and a girl coming arm in arm; perhaps two girls approaching the booth, and getting into conversation with the he-folks thereabout, while old knowing codgers wink to one another thereby indicating their opinion that these ladies are of easy virtue.—Perchance a knock-down between two half-stewed fellows in the crowd—a knock-down without a heavy blow, the receiver being scarcely able to keep his footing at any rate. Shoutings and hallooings, laughter,—oaths— generally a good-natured tumult; and the constables use no severity, but interfere, if at all, in a friendly sort of way. Talk with one about how the day has past, and bears testimony to the orderliness of the crowd, suspects one booth of selling liquor, relates one scuffle &c.—Perhaps a talkative and witty seller of gingerbread &c, holding forth to the people from his cart, making himself quite a noted character by his readiness of remark and humor; and selling off all his wares.—Late in the evening, during the fire works, people consulting how they are to get home, many having long miles to walk; a father with wife and children, saying it will be 12 °clock before they reach home, the children being already tired to death;—girls going home with their beaus; may they not linger by the wayside. The moon beautifully dark bright, not giving so white a light as

25

sometimes. The girls all look beautiful and fairy like in it, not exactly distinct, nor yet dim. The different character of female countenances as observed during the day—mirthful and mischievous, slyly humorous, stupid &c.; looking genteel generally, but when they speak, often betraying plebeianism by the tones of their voices—Two girls on the common very tired—one a pale, thin, languid looking creature; the other plump, rosy, rather over-burdened with her own little body. Conversation of the various groups.

Gingerbread figures in the shape of Jim Crow, and other popularities.

A little more than a week later, on July 13, 1838, Nathaniel Hawthorne visited a small waxworks sideshow in Salem. This was a house of horrors. Lurid narratives of execution sermons had been popular in eighteenth-century New England, and cheap bestsellers like *The Female Marine* (1815) added pirates to the constellation of evil-doers. The showmen kept representations up to date, with Chang and Eng, the Siamese Twins, first exhibited in the country in 1829. The most glamorous attraction was the wax figure of Helen Jewett, a young prostitute of respectable background murdered in New York on April 9, 1836. The subsequent trial and acquittal of Richard Robinson had kept the penny press enthralled for several months, largely because of revelations about the dark secrets of fashionable society and rumors of a cover-up. The wax museum in Salem, admission twenty-five cents, was a sideshow attached to the "National Menagerie" of June, Titus and Company, which toured New England in the early 1830s.

Nathaniel Hawthorne, *Hawthorne's Lost Notebook, 1835–1841*, ed. Barbara S. Mouffe (University Park: Pennsylvania State University Press, 1978), 75–77.

A show of wax figures, consisting almost wholly of murderers and their victims;— Gibbs and Wansley the Pirates; and the Dutch girl whom Gibbs kept and finally murdered. Gibbs and Wansl[e]y were admirably done, as natural as life; and many people, who had known Gibbs, would not, according to the showman, be convinced that this wax figure was not his skin stuffed. The two pirates were represented with halters round their necks, just ready to be turned off; and the sheriff behind them with his watch, waiting for the moment. The clothes, halters, and Gibbs' hair, were authentic. E. K. Avery and Cornell, the former a figure in black, leaning on the back of a chair, in the attitude of a clergyman about to pray;—an ugly devil, said to be a good likeness. Ellen Jewett and R. P. Robinson;—she dressed richly in extreme fashion, and very pretty; he awkward and stiff, it being difficult to stuff a figure to look like a gentleman. The showman seemed very proud of Ellen Jewett, and spoke of her somewhat as if this wax figure was a real creature. Strang and Mrs. Whipple, who together murdered the husband of the latter. Lastly the Siamese Twins. The showman is careful to call his exhibition the *"Statuary"*; he walks to and fro before the figures, talking of the history of the persons, the moral lessons to be drawn therefrom, and especially the excellence of the wax-work.

He has printed histories of the personages for sale. He is a friendly, easy-mannered sort of a half-genteel character, whose talk has been moulded by the persons who most frequent such a show—an air of superiority of information, a moral instructor, mingled with a good deal of real knowledge of the world. Inviting his departing guests to call again and bring their friends. Desiring to know whether they are pleased. Telling that he had a thousand people the 4th of July, and that they were all perfectly satisfied. Talking with the female visitors, and remarking on Ellen Jewett's person and dress to them—he having "spared no expense in dressing her," and all the ladies say that a dress never sat better; and he thinks he never knew a "handsomer female." He goes to and fro, snuffing the candles, and now and then holding one close to the face of a favorite figure; ever and anon, hearing steps upon the staircase, he goes to admit a new visitor. The visitors, a half bumpkin, half country-squire like man, who has something of a knowing air, and yet look and listens with a good deal of simplicity and faith, smiling between whiles;—a mechanic of the town;—several decent-looking girls and women, who eye Ellen Jewett with more interest than the other figures, all women having much curiosity about such ladies;—a gentlemanly sort of person, who looks somewhat ashamed of himself for being there, and glances at me knowingly, as if to intimate that he was conscious of being out of place; a boy or two; and myself, who examine wax faces and flesh ones with equal interest. A political or other satire might be made, by describing a show of wax figures of the prominent public men; and by the remarks of the showman and the spectators, their characters and public standing might be expressed.

In the early nineteenth century, the general-purpose exhibition hall reigned supreme. In Philadelphia, Charles Willson Peale lobbied in vain for government subsidy from Congress for his collections of original art and natural history. When attendance fees from middle-class visitors failed to meet expenses, he tried more sensational exhibits and more aggressive publicity, but with limited success. Rubens Peale modified his father's formula of "rational amusement." He diluted the informative, scientific content by adding more musicians, magicians, and performing animals—and in his New York museum in the late 1820s, a calf with two heads, six legs, and two tails as well as Indians and two fat girls. Even so, even in the 1840s, when sensational novelties and nonsensical minstrel songs were more of a draw than Egyptian mummies and prehistoric mastadons, the museum-going public still expected a modicum of genuine knowledge on display, and all proprietors displayed fossils as well as fat boys.

In 1871 Abram C. Dayton wrote a nostalgic memoir about the "Knicker-bocker" New York of his youth. It was a romantic tale of village-like intimacy ruined by class-embittered migrants and immigrants who had made the city ungovernable. Barnum was a symbol of this declension to a mercenary age. In the early nineteenth century, two cultural institutions had been outstanding: the old American Museum operated by the taxidermist John Scudder until his death in 1821 and by then by trustees, and Peale's New York Museum. When Barnum acquired them by devious means in 1841 and 1843, he sensed a market for "pious dollars," and lured the middle-class public with "high moral dramas" in the "Lecture Room." Barnum's hype and humbug, sharp practices, and sensational monsters, replaced genuine, old-fashioned, scientific emporia.

Abram C. Dayton, *Last Days of Knickerbocker Life in New York* (New York: George W. Harlan, 1882), pp. 142–45.

Both of these establishments were real museums, . . . clean, silent, systematic places for serious contemplation, and the study of the wonders and eccentricities of nature. Children on crossing the thresholds of these temples dedicated to science were awe-stricken by the sight presented, and clung tremblingly to their grandmothers for protection while gazing upon the trophies which had been culled from every nook of the civilized and barbarian world. These museums would have been pronounced duplicates by a casual observer. Each had on exhibition the wax presentment of Daddy [Daniel] Lambert, and this historic fat man was caged by well authenticated representations of heroes, criminals and murderers, whose romantic or villainous deeds had long been immortalized in nursery rhyme; so this wax department, when each figure had been pointed out and duly described by grandmother, was a grand attraction to youthful pilgrims in search of knowledge. Next in order of interest came the horrible boa constrictors, who were cruelly fed before our eyes with innocent live chickens and rabbits. During the process of his snakeship's meal the ears of the terrified young ones were wide open to listen, as the bland keeper gave an accurate statement as to what these monstrous reptiles would do if they had the chance, and we timidly calculated in primary rules of arithmetic what power of resistance the slim wire bars could offer should the boa resolve to change his steady diet and try a taste of baby by way of variety. So we slunk away from possible danger to feast our eyes upon the benign countenance of the Father of his Country, satisfied from early education that even his features on canvass were a sure protection against all assailants.

The portrait of Washington was surrounded by a bevy of notables: Napoleon, Franklin, Penn, Christopher Columbus, Jefferson, Madison, Sir Walter Raleigh, Queen Elizabeth, &c., backed up by way of nationality by the imaginary heads of Indian chiefs, who massacred and scalped our forefathers and *fore*mothers with their innocent babes, who had never done them any harm except to give them *fire water* and glass beads for their lands and rich furs. Next came a wonderful mummy, with the precise date of its sepulture marked on a piece of parchment, yellow with time or by reason of some chemical appliance. Indian war clubs, bows and arrows of curious workmanship, canoes of bark and hide, scalps of unfortunate pilgrims, dried bones of all sizes and shapes, ostrich eggs suspended from the ceiling, old pennies arranged in glass cases, a piece of the frigate Constitution, the signature of John Hancock, some specimens of Continental money, but any quantity of large and small stones duly labeled and designated in a body as *the Cabinet of Minerals,* over which our elders lingered long, and expatiated in grateful terms on the enterprise of the proprietor who gave them such a rare scientific treat at so little cost, *i.e.,* twenty-five cents, children half price. . . .

Each of these museums prided itself upon the attractions offered by its Lecture Room, where at a stated hour in the afternoon and evening an enthusiastic professor of something would learnedly hold forth on a subject about which he knew but little, but well aware of the fact that his slim audience knew less if possible. . . . But neither Scudder nor Peale confined themselves to dark-lantern *isms;* they did not pay in those hard-working practical days, when people gave a wide berth to everything which did not commend itself to sound common sense, so they were compelled to cater to that large class, who while they enjoyed occasional amusement, had been educated to the belief that the *theater* was "the gate of hell."

Selling and Seeing Curiosities

Barnum's American Museum faced strong competition from rivals in New York. By 1850 there were six theaters, four summer pleasure gardens, and more than sixty other amusement halls serving a population of nearly half a million. Part of Barnum's strategy was to offer more of everything, instructive and amusing. In the 1840s he greatly enlarged Scudder's rather shabby collection of curiosities of nature, added waxworks and copies of European art, purchased more space for a large menagerie and an aquarium, and increased the capacity of the Lecture Room to three thousand. With the pious rhetoric that so offended Abram Dayton, he touted his theatrical melodramas as "family" shows, morally elevating, for "all those who disapprove of the dissipations, debaucheries, profanity, vulgarity, and other abominations, which characterize our modern theatres."[5] The museum soon became a vast treasure-house of miscellaneous items, a department store of entertainment to rival A. T. Stewart's nearby marble-palace emporium of dry goods. The impact was often of a bewildering jumble. The satirist Mortimer Thomson described the collection "all mingled, mixed, and conglomerated, like a Connecticut chowder," with "bears, reptiles, reprobates, bugs, bulls, bells, bats, birds, petrifactions, putrefactions."[6]

However, the American Museum differed from its predecessors more in presentation than contents. In 1849 Barnum sponsored a twenty-four page illustrated pamphlet, costing twelve and a half cents, to promote the American Museum to family visitors. In it, Uncle Timothy Find-Out gives his two

BARNUM'S AMERICAN MUSEUM.

Of this magnificent establishment, embracing among its

SIX HUNDRED THOUSAND CURIOSITIES,

all that is rare and wonderful in the world of nature, or unique and striking in the world of art, it may be said in the words of Campbell;

"For *this* has science sought on weary wing,
By shore and sea each mute and living thing."

The Agents of the manager in all parts of the world, have instructions to spare neither labor nor expense, in adding *new wonders* to the exhibition, constituting as it does the

FOCAL POINT OF ATTRACTION,

TO THE LOVERS OF

RATIONAL AMUSEMENT,

FROM EVERY SECTION OF THE UNION.

Here, moulded in

LIFE-LIKE WAX,

the expressive facsimile of humanity—the HORRORS AND PENALTIES OF INTEMPERANCE are illustrated;

Celebrated Characters of the Old World and the New,

identical with the originals, in form, feature, attitude, and dress, seem in the act of introducing themselves to the spectator; while

The Solemn History of Christ,

from his birth to his betrayal and condemnation, is imbodied with extraordinary fidelity, in over one hundred life-size specimens of

SCRIPTURE STATUARY.

The walls of the immense pictorial saloon are surrounded with an

INTELLECTUAL CONGRESS OF AMERICAN SAGES,

PHILOSOPHERS, PATRIOTS, AND HEROES,

painted by the first Artists. The *Cosmoramas and Dissolving Views*, present a grand *coup d'œil* of the great Cities, and remarkable Scenery of both hemispheres; brilliant Experiments in Natural Philosophy delight the eyes and inform the minds of the curious; and the VAGARIES of NATURE in the human family are displayed in the towering proportions of GIANTS AND GIANTESSES, the minute forms of almost MICROSCOPIC DWARFS, the huge bulk of MAMMOTH BOYS, and in that extraordinary specimen of *magnified humanity*, the MAMMOTH LADY.

The inside cover of *Sights and Wonders in New York; including a description of the mysteries, miracles, phenomena, curiosities, and nondescripts, contained in that congress of wonders, Barnum's Museum* (1849) listed the major attractions. The Library Company of Philadelphia.

young nephews a guided tour, describing the main exhibits. He outlines Barnum's motto—"LOVE GOD AND BE MERRY"—ending with a homily: "Prosecute faithfully, as Mr. Barnum has done, the duties that fall to your lot; be vigilant, active, and industrious, as he has been; and, with the smiles of Fortune, you will find your highest hopes crowned with success." The pamphlet outlined the charms of the Museum.

Sights and Wonders in New York: including a description of the mysteries, miracles, marvels, phenomena, curiosities, and nondescripts, contained in that great congress of wonders, Barnum's Museum . . . (New York: J. S. Redfield, 1849), inside back cover, and pp. 1–2.

> Creation's wonders sought from pole to pole,
> Mingle and meet at this their common goal,
> Here, twice the measure of a five-foot staff,
> Towers that FOUR-FOOTED GIANT, the GIRAFFE
> There fiercely glare within their windowed dens,
> Life-like, though dead, the forests' denizens.
> The quaker pair, of giant bulk and stature,
> Formed (as the poet says), "to meet 'by Nature,'"
> Move through the spacious halls with stately mien,
> Beside the FAIRIES' LILLIPUTIAN QUEEN.
> A contrast this that all strange contrasts clinches,
> Full twice EIGHT FEET, to barely twice TWELVE INCHS
> Falstaff, that "tun of man," of size uncommon,
> Is here outweighed by HALF A TON OF WOMAN;
> And those BIG BUOYS, placed where our channel's bad,
> Are far out-girded by each MAMMOTH LAD.
> FIGURES OF WAX with more expression rife,
> Than that Prometheus kindled into life,
> With startling truth embody to the eye,
> The solemn scenes of SCRIPTURE HISTORY,
> Or the MAD DRUNKARD'S DOWNWARD PROGRESS show,
> A life of riot, and a death of wo.
> Those MOVING FIGURES on a smaller plan,
> And the MECHANIC COUNTERFEITS OF MAN.
> They write, dance, vault—they *all but* speak and sing,
> By the omnipotence of wheel and spring,
> And with the MONKEYS—almost human wise,
> Divide the applause, the laughter, the surprise,
> Now from the LECTURE-ROOM'S AMUSEMENT CALL,
> Summons the votaries to her LIGHTED HALL;
> HUMOR aloft on the proscenium springs,
> And waves his sceptre as each favorite sings;

THE DIME MUSEUM

While LAUGHTER holds his shaking sides in pain,
At WESTERN jokes in Gen'*wine* EASTERN strain.
Room for a *troupe* whose equal seldom met is,
Room for those prodigees the Marinettis!
Backward from stilts they bound, you scarce see where,
They vault, they lean, they whirl round in the air;
On bottles piled in pyramids they climb,
Or charm all eyes with matchless pantomime.
These, with more marvels than there's space to name,
From each spectator admiration claim,
This you'll acknowledge when you call to see 'em,
At Barnum's great American Museum.

Open every day in the year, except the Sabbath, from 7 o'clock, A.M. till 10 P.M. Such regulations are established and enforced, as render it perfectly safe and pleasant for LADIES and CHILDREN to visit the Museum in the daytime though unaccompanied by gentlemen. Exhibitions and Performances in the Lecture Room TWICE *every Day*, and oftener on Holydays.

The Price of Admission to the whole Museum, including the Entertainments, in the Lecture Room and all, is only TWENTY-FIVE *Cents.*

Children under 10 years of age Half Price.

The doggerel verse lauded the marvels of the natural world found inside:

Reader, pray lend me your attention,
While with much brevity I mention
Some of the wonders of creation,
Scattered throughout every clime and nation.
Of every other quadruped
The elephant stands at the head;
All other beasts that roam the field,
To him in bulk and strength must yield.
Then comes the huge rhinoceros,
With elk, and gnu or hornéd horse;
The tall giraffe and buffalo,
And camels which o'er deserts go;
The llama, zebra, deer, and goat,
And swiftly-bounding antelope;
And monkeys so much like a man,
Especially the orang-outang!
Lions, tigers, leopards rare,
The grizzly and the polar bear;

Selling and Seeing Curiosities

Panthers, hyenas, wolves, and foxes,
Such as are kept in cage or boxes;
Sable, ermine, marten, lynx,
Beaver, otter, muskrats, minks.
And birds that are in every land,
From Alpine rocks to desert sand:
The ostrich, eagle, vulture, hawk,
And crane with legs too long to walk;
Likewise swans, both black and white,
And paroquets with plumage bright;
And every kind of singing-bird
That eye hath seen or ear hath heard:
All fish that in the ocean swim,
From monstrous shark to herring trim;
Whale, walrus, porpoises, and seals,
And spurious ones, like snakes and eels!
The ichneume and crocodile,
Found near the banks of Egypt's Nile;
Serpents and reptiles, insects, all,
That walk or swim, or fly or crawl;
Choice specimens of antique art
From Pompeii's long-buried mart;
Or mummy, long in darkness hid
In catacomb or pyramid;
Or works of yet more modern dates,
From foreign climes or our own states—
As marble statue, plaster bust,
Armor of steel unsoiled by rust;
Portraits of great and noble men—
Columbus, Franklin, Howard, Penn,
Or of the great illustrious one,
Our own belovéd Washington
All these, and hundreds yet untold,
Which scarcely could be bought for gold.
Are near at hand, and, would you see 'em,
Go to the "American Museum."
There P. T. BARNUM's generosity
To satisfy your curiosity,
Has gathered all—and any day,
If but two shillings you will pay,
You're freely welcome to walk in,
And each strange creature to examine.

THE DIME MUSEUM

Barnum invested heavily in advertising in the cheap daily newspapers that blossomed in antebellum cities. An 1861 notice listed the charms of the Museum to visitors from the rural outskirts.

Advertisement, *New York Tribune*, March 1, 1861.

Barnum's American Museum.
Advice Given Gratis.
Peleg Pettinghame, in Town, to Timothy Touchmenot, in the Country.

When you to New-York City come, for pleasure or for pelf,
Just visit Barnum's Museum before you homeward turn.
"To see is to believe," you know; if witnessing yourself
The wonders of this unique show, the knowledge you thus learn
Will serve you in the days to come for story or for song,
When, gathered in your happy home, Time gently glides along.

For in this famous Museum are wondrous things untold,
Here, in the grand Aquaria, are fishes from all seas—
The angel fish, so beautiful in colors blue and gold;
The sticklebacks, the six-pound trout, gold-fish, or what you please;
You'll find them sportive and at play, as if in native sea
They took at ease their random way, conscious they were free.

A Black Sea Lion here is found; a Seal from Fundy's Bay;
A living Alligator, and a group of Crocodiles,
The famous Happy Family, with cats and mice at play,
While Monkeys, Owls, and Guinea Pigs, provoke a thousand smiles.
Here instinct seems herself at fault—opposing natures blend;
An enemy without the cage, within it is a friend.
Not these alone attention draw; Figures in Wax are found;
Classic and modern; Christian Sage and Heathen of renown;
All characters whose very names have a familiar sound.
A Mummy here, a Judas there—a "Tommy" done up brown;
A John Brown or an Albert Hinks—a Lambert and his wife,
The Siamese Twins and Albert Guelph—all true to life.

Not these alone attract the eye. The living wonders cause
Astonishment to all who see. The "What Is It?" is here;
Part monkey and part man it seems, defying Nature's laws;
And the Albino Family, from the Southern Hemisphere,
With pure white skin, and with pink eyes and soft white silken hair,
Are here on exhibition, under Barnum's watchful care.

34

The Aztec Children you can see—strangest of all strange sights—
Like, yet unlike, the Saxon, remnants of a now lost race;
And then, (Oh! Timothy!) the Bears; each with antic that delights,
With Herr Driesbach to exhibit them; 'tis here I fail of space
To talk of all the attractions of this famed Menagerie
Of Cougars and of Bears in all their wild variety.

Then to these add the Lecture room, where Drama proudly reigns,
("The Woman in White" is now the play. Read and resolve to come.)
Where the whole corps of Artists that Barnum here retains,
Unite to entertain the crowds that fill the Museum.
And all for five-and-twenty cents; a single quarter down,
Oh, Tim! is Open Sesame to the greatest place in town.

THE DRAMA OF THE WOMAN IN WHITE
is performed THIS AFTERNOON and EVENING, at 2 and 7½ o'clock, and all the living
wonders . . . are to be seen at all hours.

In late 1842 Barnum discovered in Bridgeport, Connecticut, the "Miniature Man" who made his fortune. Charles S. Stratton was four years old but only two feet in height and fifteen pounds in weight. He renamed him "General" Tom Thumb, after the legendary Tom Thumbe, a midget Knight of the Round Table in the court of King Arthur, whose exploits were part of children's storybook tradition. He added seven years to his age, billed him as English, schooled him in stagecraft and dialogue, and launched his act in December. The midget was precisely the premium he needed to enliven his staple collections of art and science, and induce patrons to make repeated visits. Barnum rotated star attractions between his museums in New York and Baltimore and, later, Philadelphia, and exchanged them with the Boston Museum, managed by his friend and associate, Moses Kimball. Barnum corresponded with Kimball about their collaboration generally and the "General" in particular.

Selected Letters of P. T. Barnum, ed. A. H. Saxon (New York: Columbia University Press, 1983), 13–14, 15, 16, 17.

American Museum [New York], 30 January 1843
Dear Moses,
. . . I send the General to Philadelphia on *Sunday next.* I shall run on & make arrangements next Thursday. He will probably be ready for you about lst to 10th of March. In a few days I will send you some fine *lithographs* of him so that you can be giving him *notoriety.* . . .
I *must* have the fat boy or some other monster [or] something new *in the course of this week* so as t[o be] *sure* to put them in the General's place *next Monday, [?so] don't*

fail! . . . Now more about the *General*. I pay him and his father $7 per week and board & travelling expenses for all three—father, mother, & son—and I have engaged my good frie[nd] Parson [Fordyce] Hitchcock at $12 per week, board & travelling expen[ses, to go w]ith him and shew him off. . . . He will do the same at Philadelphia & Baltimore. When the Genl. goes to Boston the Parson may continue with him, or he way remain here and attend to Peale's Museum while the boy & parents go to Boston, and you pick up some genteel person in Boston to do it. Just as you please. I dare not trust my singer with him, lest he may tamper with the parents and try to hire them away. Indeed, I fear the same from any person you might employ. Hitchcock's wages may seem high, but he is genteel, industrious, and knowing the ways of the boy well; I think he will well earn all I pay him, and of course before returning from Phil. & Baltimore he will be *thoroughly rehearsed*. So do as you please about Hitchcock; only if *he* don't go to Boston, you must employ some person who won't *tamper* with his parents. . . .

Don't fail to send me *some attraction* in time for next week.

Yours forever & a day,
Barnum

New York, 5 February 1843
My dear Moses,

. . . Tom Thumb left for Philadelphia today; yesterday was his (adver[tised)] *farewell* benefit. I took *$280*! Did you ever hear the like? [The] day previous took $90 odd. . . .

By the way, [Rubens] Peale wrote me the other day to ask If I c[ould] not send him a Tom Thumb or a two-headed man or [something] to create an *excitement*. . . . I replied that I could furnish [him with a] "beast with 7 heads & 10 horns" at short notice, or any other [?item] that he ordered; that Tom Thumb was made to my order six [?weeks] ago, and being now *nearly new* & without a rival, he was [very] *valuable*, that I thought he could take $1200 per week in Balti[more] Museum; and that he might engage him if he gave me [?half.] I shall let him chew upon that a few days. He certainly nev[er shall] have him for less than *half*.

. . . I have sent to London for a [pony] there for sale, 30 inches high. Do you know of one not over 3 feet? [I] want it for Tom Thumb, to ride about the room on.

As ever [thine,]
Barnum

A month later, Barnum wrote to Kimball, soothing his hurt feelings and empty pockets because the attractions Barnum sent to Boston proved disappointing.

American Museum, 8 March 1843
Oh Temperance! *Oh Moses*!!!

. . . In keeping *Thumb* longer south than I expected, I keep him out of my own museum as well as yours, and if he lives you shall have him, and at a time when you can make more money than he now could for you, and as for making *hay, excitement,* &c., it will be found an *easy* matter for you to raise an excitement on *Tommy* anytime, especially the *first* time. It hardly seems *sensible* to [go] to the expense of bringing him from the South where [he] is doing well, and then have to take him back there, perhaps in summer, when in fact *now* is the best season of the year to have him there. [?As to] the Big Boy, you may hold on to him as colla[teral] security for Tommy—or you may send him on whenever you please.

Do you want a pretty good-sized *bald eagle* skin? I bought two yesterday—shot on Long Island. . . .

As ever thine,

Barnum

After exhibiting Tom Thumb for little more than a year, Barnum took him to Europe from January 1844 to February 1847. On his return, he made the celebrity that the "General" gained in London and Paris the centerpiece of his publicity. A small, twenty-five cent souvenir booklet reintroduced Tom to the American public and lauded his unique virtues. People of abnormal appearance had for centuries attracted attention as smart court favorites or squalid fairground exhibits in Europe, but his theatrical talents and handsome features gave him advantages over midgets in rival exhibition halls. Barnum's skills of showmanship made Tom Thumb more famous than any of his peers or predecessors. "A thousand men might have taken hold of Tom Thumb and failed, but Barnum is a consummate manager in all such things," theatrical impresario William Northall wrote in 1851. "The public is lazy and will not take the trouble to seek after the curious; it must be brought right under its nose."[7] Unlike the barkers outside shabby Bowery dime museums or grubby traveling carnivals, Barnum did not summon the prurient merely to gawp at grotesque "monsters." His "human curiosities" appeared consenting and compliant, and they seemed companionable, even intimate, acquaintances. Tom Thumb could act out roles, sing, dance, appear in many guises, a man-child burlesquing conventional symbols of authority.

Sketch of the Life, Personal Appearance, Character and Manners of Charles S. Stratton, the man in miniature, known as General Tom Thumb, twenty-eight inches high, and weighing only fifteen pounds. With some account of remarkable dwarfs, giants, and other human phenomenon, of ancient and modern times. Also, General Tom Thumb's songs (New York: Van Norden and Amerman, 1847), 4–5, 7, 8–9, 11.

Many of . . . these tiny gentlemen have been much or partially deformed, and so pain has been felt whilst looking at them. But in the case of the hero of our narrative no such drawback exists, even as to the approach of a defect. All former dwarfs were, in shape as in size, far his inferiors. We now proceed to give some account of this most extraordinary human being.

THE DIME MUSEUM

GENERAL TOM THUMB

as he is best known, but whose real name is CHARLES S. STRATTON, first saw the light in the town of Bridgeport, Connecticut, U.S.A. His parents are persons about whom there exists no peculiarity, either in their mental or physical organization. At his birth, the General (for so he has been styled by the united voices of his thousands of friends and admirers) weighed nine pounds, and a half—which is far above the usual weight of children at birth, so that he bid fair to become—indeed *was* a bouncing boy. He grew, as other children do, day after day, until he attained to the age of seven months when nature put a *veto* on his further upward progress, and ordered him forever afterwards to remain in *status quo*. People, when he was twelve months' old, fancied he had never grown an inch for some time; measures (tape ones) were resorted to for the purpose of ascertaining his stationary condition; but although in *every other* respect he grew day by day, with great rapidity, never a hair's breadth more was added to his length. No longer—no shorter—no heavier—but much hand-somer—a great deal sharper, and considerable stronger; this was how matters stood. His appetite increased, although his stomach refused to grow larger; he never com-plained of sickness, partook freely of the dishes found upon the tables of the labouring classes, enjoyed refreshing sleep, *and has always exhibited the most perfect health,* with the exception of those slight colds to which the most robust are liable. His parents have two other children, who are well-grown, interesting girls of nine and eleven years of age. In fact, there is nothing in his history or appearance, or in that of his family, which furnishes the slightest clue to the astonishing phenomena which are presented by his miniature features and frame.

That trite but expressive saying, "He must be seen to be believed in," holds good in General Tom Thumb's case, for it is extremely difficult to form a proper idea of the personal appearance of this extraordinary being from descriptions, or even from draw-ings; all representations of him have an exaggerated appearance. The imagination cannot conceive of such extreme littleness, and we find it difficult, with the best artistic aids, to picture on the mental retina a perfect MINIATURE MAN, only TWENTY-EIGHT INCHES HIGH, perfect and elegant in his proportions, and weighing only FIFTEEN POUNDS!

When standing on the floor, or parading the room, which he does, dressed in a style of Bond-street elegance, and with all the grace, dignity and ease of a finished gentleman, his head scarcely reaches to the knees of a person of ordinary stature, and is about on a level with the seats of the chairs, sofas and ottomans of the drawing-room.

Unlike many other dwarfs, the General is exquisitely proportioned, his head being not large, but of the proper symmetry, and beautifully developed, and his hands and feet are the prettiest ever seen. His boots are perfect Wellingtons, made of the softest kid, by the most fashionable artists; his clothes are the production of the most distinguished tailors, and his gloves are of necessity furnished to order, for nothing so small and fairylike were ever before manufactured. . . . The General has a fair complexion, light hair, rosy cheeks, large beautiful dark eyes, a fine forehead, a handsome mouth, and great vivacity of expression and hilarity of manner. . . .

It could not be expected that his voice would be of the full depth of manhood, this *probably never can be*, from the size of the organ; and those who have seen Major Stevens will remember that, although he is forty years old, and much larger than the General, his voice is still pitched in "childish treble."

In strength, activity, and vivacity, the General is remarkable. He often amuses himself by taking hold of a cane with one or both hands, and being carried about the room, which a man can easily do with one hand. He is constantly engaged in walking about, talking, and in various pastimes and employments, from early in the morning till late at night, without showing any signs of fatigue, and seems the happiest little fellow in the world.

His personations of what are conventionally termed the "Grecian Statues," are among the most beautiful and wonderful portions of his performances. His "tableau" of Cupid, with his wings and quiver, is inimitable—his size and form being so perfect for that representation, that he looks as if he had just been removed from an Italian image-board. His "Samson carrying off the gates of Gaza" is a most extraordinary representation. His attitude is perfect, and the spectator for a moment loses his idea of the diminutive size of the representation of the *strong* man, so perfect is the representation. His personations of the "Fighting Gladiator," "The Slave whetting his knife," "Ajax," "Discobulus," "Cincinnatus," "Hercules with the Nemaean Lion" &c., exhibit a correctness of attitude, and develope in his motions a firmness and strength, combined with a spirit and intelligence, which prove his age beyond all question to be as represented. At times the General dresses as a sailor, and dances a horn-pipe to perfection. Again, we find him dressed as an English Fox Hunter, with his red coat, drab breeches, and top boots, the feet of which are three inches long, and one and a quarter inches wide!!!

His personations of NAPOLEON BONAPARTE and of FREDERICK THE GREAT, are perfection itself. His Court Costumes are elegant, but dressed as a HIGHLAND CHIEFTAIN, he carries his visiters by storm. Nothing can be conceived more perfect or more lovely.

Never was a human being, of any size, ever blessed with a kinder heart, or a more excellent disposition. He never forgets an acquaintance, and cherishes his friends with the greatest affection. There is something extremely winning in his manners, and this, with his strange beauty, has made many persons, and especially ladies, so strongly attached to him as to become his almost daily visiters. Children are always delighted with him, and little girls are his especial favourites. He receives all his visiters with a cordial and courtly grace; shaking hands and kissing the ladies, which it is difficult to prevent his doing, and which he appears to enjoy, especially when done roguishly, or by stealth, with extreme gusto. . . .

It is natural to suppose that the smallness of the brain should limit the development of his intellectual faculties; such, however, is not the case; but, from obvious circumstances, the General's education has, until recently, been neglected. There is no lack of intelligence or aptitude to learn, and the General is now advancing in reading, writing, music, &c., with every prospect of rapid proficiency.

It is gratifying to add, that the utmost care is devoted to his moral and religious education, and that his ideas regarding the Deity, and the essential requisites of the Gospel, are as lucid and correct as those of many of mature age. The General was never known to utter a falsehood, and his language is always unexceptionable. . . .

While at this popular Establishment, his levees, at all hours, were crowded with the wealth, fashion, and intelligence of the metropolis, and by thousands of strangers arriving and departing. These he welcomed in the great reception hall of the Museum, and after showing them the splendid Fountain and many thousand curiosities with which it was crowded, he appeared again on a raised platform in the Great Hall, on the third floor, where his Miniature Palace Furniture, and Equipage, caused almost as great a sensation as the General himself, and where, amid the millions of extraordinary productions of nature and art, he was still the greatest wonder.

At each performance in the splendid Exhibition Saloon, he walked upon the stage, gracefully saluting the crowded audiences, and mounted upon a chair by an assistant, sang, in a sweet voice, and with inimitable effect, a patriotic song, after which he retired, acknowledging, by frequent bows, the rapturous plaudits he never failed of receiving. A visit to the roof of the Museum, to view the city by gas or moonlight, and witness the ascension of the illuminated balloons, would close the pleasures and fatigues of one day of this strange existence. . . .

[W]e unhesitatingly declare him to be the greatest wonder of this wonderful age. Graceful, elegant, fascinating and clever. "We shall never look upon his like again." Should he live, and there is every prospect of it, he will doubtless become accomplished and brilliant, and surpass what he at present is in attainments, as much as he now does all other dwarfs who have ever lived before him. In conclusion, we know of no description so applicable to our little friend as a single line of Goldsmith's—he is, indeed,

"AN ABRIDGEMENT OF ALL THAT IS PLEASANT IN MAN."

Philip Hone, the wealthy former mayor of New York, recorded in his diary his responses to seeing Tom Thumb in the 1840s. He seems to have accepted uncritically all the claims made for the "boy wonder." Such was the midget's acclaim that Ralph Waldo Emerson went to view what he described as the "dwarf of dwarfs" in Boston in 1848. Tom Thumb was a particular favorite of the American Museum's "family" audience, a third of whom were children. On June 18, 1847, twelve-year-old Elizabeth Rogers Cabot Mason accompanied her wealthy parents to Kimball's Boston Museum and found the nine-year-old Tom Thumb (advertised as fifteen) and his tiny possessions, "certainly very remarkable," and was astonished at his doll-like size.[8] Both of Hone's visits were family outings with his wife or daughter.

Diary of Philip Hone, 1828–1850, ed. Allan Nevins, 2 vols. (New York: Dodd, Mead, 1927,), 2:664, 795–96.

June 12, 1843 . . . I went last evening with my daughter Margaret to the American Museum to see the greatest *little* mortal who has ever been exhibited; a handsome well-formed boy, eleven years of age, who is twenty-five inches in height and weighs fifteen pounds. I have a repugnance to see human monsters, abortions, and distortions . . . but in this instance I experienced none of this feeling. General Tom Thumb (as they call him) is a handsome, well-formed, and well-proportioned little gentleman, lively, agreeable, sprightly, and talkative, with no deficiency of intellect, as a phrenologist would certainly infer from his perfectly shaped head. At his birth he was of a proper size, but stopped growing when five months old, and is now about as large as infants usually are at that age. His hand is about the size of half a dollar and his foot three inches in length, and in walking alongside of him, the top of his head did not reach above my knee. When I entered the room he came up to me, offered his hand, and said "How d'ye do, Mr. Hone?"—his keeper having apprised him who I was. . . .

March 12, 1847 . . . My wife and I went this morning to see the celebrated Tom Thumb at the American Museum. He appears to have increased in *littleness* during his European visit. He is said to have realized by showing himself £150,000 sterling, and been kissed by a million pairs of the sweetest lips in Europe, from Queen Victoria down; and now he is making here a thousand dollars a day. He performs four or five times each day to a thousand or twelve hundred persons; dances, sings, appears in a variety of characters with appropriate costumes, is cheerful, gay, and lively, and does not appear to be fatigued or displeased by his incessant labors. He kisses the good-looking women, a favor which he does not grant indiscriminately, and in one way or another sends his audience away well satisfied, with their outlay of a quarter of a dollar each.

Few sights in New York City made a greater impression on the seventeen-year-old Mark Twain than the exhibition of the "Wild Men of Borneo." There was nothing in the small-town South quite like these "things." Brothers Hiram and Barney Davis were born in Weston, Massachusetts, in 1825 and 1827, blue-eyed and fair-skinned, the children of English immigrants, but as adults, were only three-and-a-half feet tall and mentally retarded. From 1852 showman Lyman Warner paraded them in rented halls as the missing links between men and beasts and having almost superhuman strength. Billed as Waino and Plutano, mysterious beings from the distant South Seas, and dressed in one-piece body-suits and shorts and with waist-length hair, they were exotic attractions, and in the 1860s joined Barnum.

The "Wild Men of Borneo," Hiram and Barney Davis, billed as
Waino and Plutano, were first exhibited by showman Lyman Warner
in 1852. Harry Ransom Humanities Research Center, University of
Texas at Austin.

Selling and Seeing Curiosities

In a letter to his mother, published a fortnight later in his local newspaper in Hannibal, Missouri, Twain described his prolonged scrutiny of the "animals."

Samuel Clemens [Mark Twain] to Jane Lampton Clemens, August 24, 1853, *Mark Twain's Letters*, vol. 1, *1853–1866*, ed. Edgar Marquess Branch, Michael B. Frank, and Kenneth M. Sanderson (Berkeley: University of California Press, 1988), 4.

I saw a curiosity to-day, but I don't know what to call it. Two beings, about like common people, with the exception of their faces, which are more like the "phiz" [physiognomy, face] of an orang-outang, than human. They are white, though, like other people. Imagine a person about the size of Harvel Jordan's oldest boy, with small lips and full breast, with a constant uneasy, fidgety motion, bright, intelligent eyes, that seems as if they would look through you, and you have these *things*. They were found in the island of Borneo (the only ones of the species ever discovered,) about twenty years ago. One of them is twenty three, and the other twenty five years of age. They possess amazing strength; the smallest one would shoulder three hundred pounds as easily as I would a plug of tobacco; they are supposed to be a cross between man and orang-outang; one is the best natured being in the world, while the other would tear a stranger to pieces, if he did but touch him; they wear their hair "Samson" fashion, down to their waists. They have no apple in their throats, whatever, and can therefore scarcely make a sound; no memory either; what transpires today, they have forgotten before to-morrow; they look like one mass of muscle, and can walk either on all fours or upright; when let alone, they will walk to and fro across the room, thirteen hours out of the twenty-four; not a day passes but they walk twenty-five or thirty miles, without resting thirty minutes; I watched them about an hour and they were "tramping" the whole time. The little one bent his arm with the elbow in front, and the hand pointing upward, and no two strapping six footers in the room could pull it out straight. Their faces and eyes are those of the beast, and when they fix their glittering orbs on you with a steady, unflinching gaze, you instinctively draw back a step, and a very unpleasant sensation steals through your veins. They are both males and brothers, and very small, though I do not know their exact hight. I have given you a very lengthy description of the animals, but I have nothing else to write about, and nothing from here would be interesting anyhow.

Nearly a year earlier, Sam Clemens had written a short story about a showman's duping naïve small-town hayseeds. With preacher-like dignity, the trickster tempts the unwary with the hope of seeing something suggestive—the "bony part" crossing the "rind," a euphemism for sexual intercourse. The bystanders greet the hoax with good humor, but Jim, the only one to complain, now becomes the "curiosity," and singled out for pious rebuke. Perhaps Barnum's well-known "humbugs" of Joice Heth or the Fejee Mermaid inspired this fiction. Many years later, in *Huckleberry Finn*, Twain depicted the

Duke and the King's deceiving the Arkansas hicks with "The King's Cameleopard or the Royal Nonesuch."

"Historical Exhibition—A No. 1 Ruse," *Hannibal Journal*, September 16, 1852, in *The Works of Mark Twain. Early Tales and Sketches*, vol. 1, *1851–1864*, ed. Edgar Marquess Branch and Robert H. Hirst (Berkeley: University of California Press, 1979), 79–82.

A young friend gives me the following yarn as fact, and if it should turn out to be a double joke, (that is, that he imagined the story to fool me with,) on his own head be the blame:

It seems that the news had been pretty extensively circulated, that Mr. Curts, of the enterprising firm of Curts & Lockwood, was exhibiting at their store, for the benefit of the natives, a show of some kind, bearing the attractive title of "Bonaparte crossing the Rhine," upon which he was to deliver a lecture, explaining its points, and giving the history of the piece, the price being "one dime per head, children half price." Well, the other day about dusk, a young man went in, paid his dime, "saw the elephant," and departed, apparently "with a flea in his ear," but the uninitiated could get nothing out of him on the subject; he was mum—had seen the varmint, and that was the full extent of the information which could be pumped out of him by his enquiring friends.

Well, everybody who saw the sight seemed seized with a sudden fit of melancholy immediately afterwards, and dimes began to grow scarce. But pretty soon Jim C—, with a crowd of eager boys at his heels, was seen coming down the street like half a dozen telegraphs. They arrived at the store, gasping and out of breadth, and Jim broke out with:

"Mr. Curts—want—to see—that—show! What's—price!"

"Oh, we let boys see it at half price—hand out your five cents."

Jim had got done blowing by this time, and threw down his money in as great a hurry as if life and death depended upon the speed of his movements, saying:

"Quick! Mr. Curts, I want to see it the worst kind."

"Yes, Oh yes; you want to see 'Bonaparte crossing the Rhine,' do you," said Abram, very deliberately.

"Yes, that's it—that's what I want to see," said Jim, who was so anxious to see the show that he could scarcely stand still.

"Well, you shall see it," said the worthy exhibitor, with a wise look, at the same time dropping the five cents into the money drawer, "and I hope by this show to impress upon your young minds, this valuable piece of history, and illustrate the same in so plain a manner that the silliest lad among you will readily comprehend it."

The juvenile audience was now breathless with expectation, and crowded around with eager looks, and not the slightest movement on the part of the learned lecturer was overlooked by them, as he drew from a drawer a piece of bone about three inches long, and holding it up before the wondering boys, he slowly and deliberately commenced his lecture, or explanation:

Selling and Seeing Curiosities

"My young friends, you now perceive—"

"Yes sir," interrupted Jim with mouth, eyes and ears wide open.

"As I was saying," continued Mr. Curts, "you now see before you the 'Bonaparte' —the'*Bony-part*,' you understand, the'*bony part*' of a hog's leg (house shakes with laughter from the crowd which had now assembled, but Jim did not join in the general merriment, but looked very sober, seeming to think there was very little about it to laugh at, at least on his side) yes, boys," said Abram, as grave and solemn as a judge about to pass sentence, "this is the bony-part of a hog's leg."

"Is—is—a—a—that all!" gasped Jim, beginning to look blue about the gills.

"Oh no," said the lecturer, "this is merely part of the exhibition," and he took from a shelf a piece of meat skin about as large as a piece of paper i.e. the size of a dollar bill, and presenting it to view he proceeded with the lecture.

"Now, my young hearers, this you see is the 'Rhine'—yes," he continued, as solemnly as before, "this is the 'Rhine,'—properly speaking, the hog's rind—a piece of hog's rind."

When the laugh had subsided, Mr. C. again went on with the explanation:

"Now, young gentlemen, draw near and give me your attention a moment, for this is the most interesting part of the exhibition," and old Abram looked and spoke, if possible, still more wise and solemn than before; then slowly passing the piece of bone back and forth across the skin, he said, "you see, boys this is the'bony part crossing the rind,' very lucidly explained—yes, (drawing his bone across again with the most imperturbable gravity imaginable, amid the roars of laughter) this sir, is, I may be allowed to say, a *very* apt illustration of that noted event in history, 'Napoleon crossing the Rhine.' You have now learned a valuable lesson—"

"Yes!" broke in Jim "I have that, but it's the last one you'll ever learn me—(laughter) you're nothing but an old swindler, anyhow—(renewed laughter, which somewhat riled our hero) yes, this is a swindling shop and a swindling show, and you don't do nothing but swindle people."

The laugh now became so universal, that poor Jim had to force a laugh and a "don't care" look, as he continued:

"I don't care, laugh, jest as much as you please—I ain't particular about the money, nohow: I know'd it was a swindle, 'fore I come down (a piece of knowledge which Jim, in the excitement had before unfortunately forgotten that he ever possessed,) yes I knowed it, and I jest come down for devilment—but I don't care, you can keep the money, I ain't particular about it (Jim seemed particularly anxious to impress this important fact upon the mind of the lecturer)—cause I know you need it worse'n I do, when you can swindle a feller out of it that way."

The crowd now laughed till they were completely exhausted, and Jim's face slowly relaxed from the ludicrous expression it had worn for a time. He now looked as if he had been suddenly bereft of every relation he had in the world—his face became lengthened to an alarming extent, and upon the said countenance the most woe-begone look settled, mingled with a most "sheep-stealing" expression; he was now

45

in a profound reverie, seemingly entirely unconscious of the jeers cast at him by the company. But Abram now broke in upon his meditations, and although he too had been enjoying his joke with a hearty laugh, he immediately assumed his former solemn look and grave tone, and thus addressed the cheap-looking "seeker after knowledge under difficulties."

"Young man, you have now learned an important historical lesson, and you are no doubt well pleased with it. I am anxious, however—ahem!—I am anxious, as I before remarked, that you should be entirely satisfied with the exhibition—if you did not understand it in its minutest details—if the illustration was not sufficiently lucid, and everything has not been exhibited to your entire satisfaction, I beg of you, my friend, to make it known; and if it has met with favor in your eyes, I shall hold myself under the greatest of obligations, (with a profound bow,) if you will use your influence in forwarding the cause of learning and knowledge, (another bow,) by inviting your friends to step in when they pass this way. What, may I ask, is your opinion of the exhibition?"

Poor Jim! He seemed not to have heard a word that had been spoken; but, with his eyes bent steadfastly upon some object that wasn't there, he moved not a muscle for the space of a minute, when, opening his lips, he slowly ejaculated the few, but significant words "Sold!—cheap - - - as - - - dirt!"

And striding out of the house he marched down the street in a profound fit of mental abstraction.

Since the above occurrence, if any one speaks to Jim, or asks him a question, he merely mutters "Bonaparte crossing—sold!"

Mr. Curts told one of Jim's companions to say to him, that his exhibition was merely an agency—that a noted wholesale firm of this city were the proprietors of the concern, that the apparatus belonged to them, that if Jim did not think his money well spent, they would in all probability refund it—but that being himself merely an agent, he did not feel authorized to do so.

W. EPAMINONDAS ADRASTUS BLAB.

Not everyone enjoyed what the English satirical magazine *Punch* derided in the 1840s as "Deformito-mania" promoted by the "monster-mongers." Horace Greeley liked and respected Barnum, but so many of the cheap dime museums in the Bowery and on Broadway fell short of his high-minded reform principles. In his newspaper editorial he scoffed at the fashion for storefront coffin displays and the singularly unpleasant and unedifying exhibitions of the "monstrous" that he believed so characteristic of New York City.

"Disgusting Exhibitions," *New York Tribune*, September 22, 1853, 4.

It would really seem that a portion of the community are only fully satisfied with the monstrous. In the matter of good exhibitions it is not sufficient that they bristle in the City, the spoils of Europe, artistically speaking, being laid at our feet . . . ; it is not sufficient that name what science or art we may, it has an exponent in some shape or other easily open to investigation; it is not sufficient that if the denizen of the City be weary of brick-walls, the dashing speed of our present mode of travel will place him in a few minutes in the country. All these sights and sounds are insufficient to please respectively the eye and ear and nurture the taste. The normal and beautiful are inadequate; the natural and hideous must be called into view.

Hence it is that Broadway is never without one or more damnable monsters on exhibition. Several now are prominently paraded there. The first that meets the eye on going up is a Fat Woman, weighing upwards, say the bills, of seven hundred pounds. A flying flag has a portrait of this oleagenous Venus, who appears rocking in a sea of what the doctors call adipose deposit and the butchers, suet. Is it really such an agreeable sight to behold a woman full five times heavier than she ought to be, according to the measurements of the classic girdle? Is beauty, that thing of joy forever, so palling to the sight that we must resort to the contemplation of a pyramid of panting tallow—a mountain of perspiring grease—to find out how far the age of undiseased mankind may be perverted by aberrations from nature, and huge and melancholy monstrosity take its place? Why should the misfortune of that woman be paraded in public? Why should her colossal folds of obesity be brazenly thrust in view, and even exaggerated and caricatured in the doubly disgusting flag which invites spectators to her apartments? It is enough that she is physically enormous, without being made personally public.

So too, the exhibition of the sleeping man. Here is a poor wretch, who . . . has less vitality than an oyster, placed before the general gaze. He has been asleep five years, except that, about every two or four months, he revives for a few minutes. He is wofully emaciated. He is inhumanly ugly. He is more horrible than a death-bed—more elegaic than a corpse. He is a living libel on human existence—a fierce degradation of manhood—not living, not dying, not dead—a shocking denial of precedents, facts and possibilities—a thing that should be kept out of sight and notice, and yet he is pushed into the van of publicities, and all the world called in to behold the sorry, wretched dreg of humanity.

Then comes—proh pudor—A Bearded Lady! Antique goddess of beauty what a descent is here! Mother of the graces—inspirer of kisses—alma mater—a woman with a beard! . . .

Then next on exhibition comes an hideous little dwarf; the King of Lilliputians, so called, a pale and trembling little whiffet—a living abortion—an idiot old at twenty months—a caricature at once of age and babyhood—the crib and the coffin cheek by jowl. Why should the existence of this poor little wretch be made the object of vicious curiosity, and hungry speculation? . . .

Out upon these hideous spectacles of abnormal nature and abused ingenuity! Let the appeals to the eye and the understanding be pure and real, and the vitiated taste which would hurl abominable sights into the face of the world be corrected, and a sound sentiment take its place.

Madame Josephine Boisdechene Clofullia was famous in London and Paris as the "Bearded Lady of Geneva" before Barnum brought her to New York. Thomas Easterly photographed the twenty-two-year-old during her visit to St. Louis in 1853. Missouri Historical Society.

Selling and Seeing Curiosities

Barnum's Museum on the corner of Ann and Broadway was at the hub of New York commerce, and close to both fashionable shopping and the Bowery workshops and tenements. One of Barnum's ploys was brash, garish advertising, with a spectacular fountain and reflecting light on the roof to attract passers-by. One hundred and four, large, oval, color transparencies decorated the facade of the five-story building. In March 1853 banners and posters celebrated the latest attraction, the Swiss Bearded Lady. The museum's official guide book later described her as a "genteel and accomplished lady—yet possessing as fine and *heavy Beard and Whiskers* as ever graced the face of a man, a freak of nature which the science of man has never been able to account for."[9]

Barnum was an obvious subject for one of the short, witty essays of "Fanny Fern," Sara Payson Willis Parton, who commented on issues in vogue for her female magazine readers. The tour of the Swedish opera-singer Jenny Lind Barnum that had arranged in 1850 had made him the talk of the nation. The abolitionist lectures of the Grimké sisters to "promiscuous" audiences, the Seneca Falls convention of 1848, and criticism of marriage, unequal property laws, and restricting dress had made women's rights a key issue. Naturally, Fanny Fern made Madame Clofullia's femininity the topic of discussion.

Fanny Fern, *Fern Leaves From Fanny's Port-Folio. Second Series* (Auburn, N.Y.: Ofton and Mulligan, 1854), 373–76.

It is possible that every stranger may suppose, as I did, on first approaching Barnum's Museum, that the greater part of its curiosities are on the outside, and have some fears that its internal will not equal its external appearance. But, after crossing the threshold, he will soon discover his mistake. The first idea suggested will perhaps be that the view, from the windows, of the motley, moving throng in Broadway—the rattling, thundering carts, carriages and omnibuses—the confluence of the vehicular and human tides which, from so many quarters, come pouring past the museum—is, (to adopt the language of advertisements,) "worth double the price of admission."

The visitor's attention will unquestionably be next arrested by the "Bearded Lady of Switzerland"—one of the most curious curiosities ever presented. A card, in pleasant juxtaposition to the "lady," conveys the gratifying intelligence that, "Visitors are allowed to touch the beard." Not a man in the throng lifts an investigating finger! Your penetration, Madame Clofullia, does you infinite credit. You knew well enough that your permission would be as good as a handcuff to every pair of masculine wrists in the company. For my own part, I should no more meddle with your beard, than with Mons. Clofullia's. I see no femininity in it. Its shoe-brush aspect puts me on my decorum. I am glad you raised it, however, just to show Barnum there is something "new under the sun," and to convince men in general that a woman can accomplish about anything she undertakes.

I have not come to New York to stifle my inquisitiveness. How did you raise that beard? Who shaves first in the morning? you, or your husband? Do you use a Woman's Rights razor? Which of you does the *strap*-ping? How does your baby know you from its father? What do you think of us, smooth-faced sisters? Do you (between you and me) prefer to patronize dress-makers, or tailors? Do you sing tenor, or alto? Are you master, or mistress of your husband's affections?

In the 1840s and 1850s Barnum's "living curiosities" were a favorite subject for humorists. As soon as *The Life of P. T. Barnum, Written by Himself* appeared in 1855, a parody appeared, based probably on prepublication connivance with Barnum. "Petite Bunkum, Esquire, late merchant, and now a hunter after curiosities and wonders," burlesqued the showman's frank exposition of his methods. Like Fanny Fern's, faux-Barnum's comments on the bearded lady centered on gender roles, with a particular focus on woman as the main wage earner.

The Autobiography of Petite Bunkum, the Showman: Showing his Birth, Education, and Bringing Up; His Astonishing Adventures by Sea and Land; His Connection with Tom Thumb, Judy Heath, the Woolly Horse, the Fudge Mermaid, and the Swedish Nightingale . . . Written by Himself (New York: P. F. Harris, 1855), 49–51.

THE WHISKERED WOMAN

This remarkable lady I imported from France, although she is a native of Switzerland. Her husband and father accompanied her, and showed themselves in connection with her. She was also attended by a red-headed interpreter; and, being blessed with two children, it will be acknowledged that she had a very pretty little family to support by the display of her beard.

For three strapping men to live upon the earnings of a woman's whiskers, is a novelty not often seen at the present day.

The lady was indeed blessed with a luxuriant jet-black beard that excited the wonder, admiration, and envy of all the bloods about town. She freely allowed everyone who wished, to stroke her whiskers, so that the public might be convinced of their being genuine, and no sham. Her neck, shoulders, and as much of her back as she saw proper to display, were thickly sprinkled with hairs. Her bust was feminine, and remarkably full. Several certificates, which had been written and signed by physicians who were present at her accouchement, were hung up in the hall of exhibition. These were to convince the spectators that Madame was indeed a woman, and no man, as many foolish persons might have been inclined to suppose. One blockhead summoned both me and the Whiskered Woman before the Police Court, swearing that she was a man, and that I had swindled him out of a quarter! The matter was soon settled in my favor—in what manner, I do not choose to explain.

George Templeton Strong, a wealthy lawyer by profession but an aesthete and dilettante by inclination, thought Barnum's "an eyesore." The brass band was raucous and irritating, the gaudy illustrations on the building's façade unattractive. Nevertheless, Strong always enjoyed the extensive natural history collections, and especially the menagerie. On March 2, 1860, he noted in his diary his reaction to Barnum's latest novelty. There had been "man-monkeys" before. In 1799 Charles Willson Peale had displayed a stuffed orangutan in his Philadelphia museum as the "Wild Man of the Woods," and asked his audience, "How like an old Negro?" Darwin's *Origin of Species* (1859) reopened the old controversy. Barnum's new exhibit was almost certainly "Zip," William Henry Johnson, clad in an ape-suit and with hair shaven to emphasize his cone-shaped head, and, like Peale's orangutan, holding a staff.

The "Man-Monkey," like the Swiss Bearded Lady, and many of the American Museum's prize exhibits defied conventional classification. The "nondescripts" seemed on the margins of two separate identities: the Fejee Mermaid, part woman, part fish; albino "White Negroes;" the "Leopard Child" with strangely pigmented black-and-tan skin; Miss Dora Dawson, dressed half as a woman and half as a man and singing both soprano and tenor; Jo-Jo, the "Dog-Faced Boy." For Strong, the intellectual puzzle justified close scrutiny of this curious, liminal figure.

The Diary of George Templeton Strong, 4 vols., ed. Allan Nevins and Milton Halsey Thomas (New York: Macmillan, 1952): March 2–3, 1860 [3:12–13]; June 6, 1860 [31]; September 3, 1863 [355]; November 27, 1863 [374]; July 13 1865 [4:17–18].

Stopped at Barnum's on my way downtown to see the much-advertised nondescript, the "What-is-it." Some say it's an advanced chimpanzee, others that it's a cross between nigger and baboon. But it seems to me clearly an idiotic negro dwarf, raised, perhaps, in Alabama or Virginia. The showman's story of its capture (with three other specimens that died) by a party in pursuit of the gorilla on the western coast of Africa is probably bosh. The creature's look and action when playing with his keeper are those of a nigger boy. But the anatomical details are fearfully simian, and he's a great fact for Darwin.

Strong went back the next day for a closer look, and decided the "What-is-it?" was "palpably a little nigger and not a good-looking one." Some months later, on June 6, he visited Barnum's on his way home from the office.

That specimen of showmen has resumed his functions, and his ancient and seedy museum is instinct with new life. The old wax figures are propped and brushed up and some of the more conspicuously mangy of the stuffed monkeys and toucans have disappeared. There is a colossal fat boy on exhibition (a real prodigy of hideousness), in addition to the miraculous calculator and the "What-is-it?" I went to see the aquaria. Sundry splendid tropical things from the Gulf of Mexico have been introduced there.

WHAT IS IT?—OR "MAN MONKEY".
ON EXHIBITION AT BARNUM'S MUSEUM, NEW YORK.
This is a most singular animal, with many of the features and other characteristics of both the HUMAN and BRUTE species. It was found in Africa, in a perfectly nude state, and with two others captured.—The others died on their passage to this country. At first it ran on all fours, and was with difficulty learned to stand as nearly erect as here represented. It is the opinion of most scientific men that he is a connecting link between the WILD NATIVE AFRICAN, AND THE ORANG OUTANG.
He is playful as a Kitten and every way pleasing interesting and amusing.
TO BE SEEN AT ALL HOURS.

Currier and Ives issued several lithographs of the "What Is It?" exhibit at Barnum's Museum. This one, from the early 1860s, emphasized the close association between the genteel family visitors and the "curiosity." Shelburne Museum, Shelburne, Vermont.

Sidney George Fisher retired early from business and devoted himself to scholarship and culture, and to his extensive social contacts among Philadelphia's elite. Like Strong, he did not share Barnum's populist view of the museum's function and admired only high-culture institutions. Nevertheless, on March 13, 1861, he attended Peale's former Philadelphia Museum, which Barnum had acquired in 1849 and "improved," and recorded his impressions. The "Aztec Children," Maximo and Bartola, reputed to be from an unknown race of gnomes from Yucatan, were favorite exhibits. In 1851 Nathaniel Parker Willis spent half an hour with the mentally retarded "little wonders" and held the hand of Bartola while Maximo sat on Willis's friend's lap. "With little intelligence, and skulls of such shape that no hope can be entertained of their being ever self-relying or responsible, they still inspire an indefinable feeling of interest" and affection, he concluded.[10] Fisher was more fastidious and reserved.

A *Philadelphia Perspective: The Diary of Sidney George Fisher Covering the Years 1834–1871*, ed. Nicholas B. Wainwright (Philadelphia: Historical Society of Pennsylvania, 1967), 382.

Went to see Barnum's exhibition of human curiosities, albinoes from Madagascar, a bushman from South Africa and two specimens, male and female, of what is said to be remnants of the Aztec race in Central America. The albinoes have white hair and pink eyes, but their faces are so intelligent and European that I doubt their being African. The bushman looks like a mulatto dwarf. She is about 4 feet 3 inches high, stout and 24 years old. The Aztecs were extraordinary creatures, heads very small, forehead and chin receding, idiotic expression, inarticulate cries, animated movements, brutified humanity, painful to look at. These, then, are lower states of what I am. Man in a state of arrested development.

For visitors to the museums, the great attraction of the human exhibits was their animated responses, even if only grunts and gestures. Part of the fascination was identifying—and even identifying with—these perplexing, bewildering, mysterious creations of God's universe. Barnum encouraged communication between viewer and viewed. Indeed, he disrupted the smooth, department-store order of scientific classification with "living curiosities" placed unexpectedly in dark corners among the display cases to startle the unwary. His giants and midgets were not like mute taxidermists' trophies seen from afar; they interacted with visitors in genteel surroundings, answered questions, sold pamphlets detailing their life histories, and, by the 1860s, signed photographic souvenirs of themselves.

Richard Grant White took the encounter between spectacle and spectator a step further. He imagined an English aristocrat's having to endure the niceties of polite conversation with one of the "curiosities" of a democratic, egalitarian nation. Perhaps the pseudonym and the familiar format of an English traveler's tale allowed the Anglophile White greater freedom of expression to comment on national peculiarities and on the American Museum as the "representative institootion of this country." As a noted theater critic, he mixed in New York society and intellectual circles and had almost certainly met Barnum. If the fictional account is based on fact, the giantess might have been Sylvia Hardy from Maine, or more likely, Anna Swan from Pictou, Nova Scotia—White's Miss Condor (the largest bird in the American hemisphere) being a play on her surname—billed by Barnum as "an extraordinary specimen of magnified humanity." White elaborated the dialogue between patron and patronized into a scenario of embarrassing social equality and unwelcome intimacy.

[Richard Grant White,] *The Adventures of Sir Lyon Bouse, Bart. in America, During the Civil War* (New York: American News, 1867), 32, 33–38.

I visited Barnum's Museum myself, but did not remain there long. A giant and giantess were on exhibition, and . . . as I had heard that the giantess, who is said to be taller then the giant, was an American, in fact a "Down-East" Yankee, and as I doubted very much the ability of New England to produce anything gigantic, except brag and swindles, I was anxious to see her. But, when I inquired for her, I was told that she was not then to be seen, as she had retired for a short time to rest. Here was another swindle, to begin with. This man Barnum advertised his giantess to be seen; I paid my money, and, when I asked to see her, she was *not* to be seen. I began to say very plainly what I thought of such an imposition; but the people around me, to my surprise, although they gathered near and listened, did not back me, or show much sympathy.

Presently a portly, curly-haired man in black approached, and I heard some one say, "There comes Mr. Barnum himself." He came up and asked what was the matter; adding, in the smoothest manner, that he hoped nothing had happened to dissatisfy the patrons of this establishment. I told him I wanted to see the giantess I had paid to see, and that she was not there. "Well," he said, "I'm sorry that she isn't here. But she's ben here all the morning; and we hev to be a little careful and easy with our giants. Giants ain't up to so much exhibition work, standin' round an' like, as people that isn't giants. An' so we spell 'em, particularly the lady giants. [What could he mean of spelling giants?] Our Belgian friend here'll have to go and take a rest pretty soon, and then the lady'll come out." The reader may be sure that I was not to be put off with any such chaff as this; and I told the man in pretty plain terms what I thought of his scoundrelly behavior, which, I added, was just what might be expected from a clock-making Yankee. To my surprise, he offered no apology, nor did he get angry but said to my very face, that, although he did not undertake to enforce good manners in his establishment, he always expected them, and from Yankees he always had them, whether they made clocks or not. Then, taking out a quarter of a dollar, he had the impudence to offer it to me, and to say, that, as I was dissatisfied, he would be pleased if I would take my money and go. But I was determined not to be put off in this manner; and so I told him that I didn't want my money back, and wouldn't take it. I wanted to see the giantess, and that I should be satisfied with nothing less. He looked at me a moment with a queer expression in his eyes, which I remember having seen in the eyes of many of his countrymen afterward, and said, "So you must see the giantess, must you?"—"Yes, of course I must."—"Well, then," taking me aside a little, "I think I shall hev to give you a private interview, if that'll suit." I was pleased to find that a little becoming self-assertion, and taking a decided stand, had produced a proper effect: a private exhibition was, of course, most acceptable to me.

Mr. Barnum disappeared for a few minutes, and, when he returned, he slipped his arm very coolly into mine, and he led me off to side room. As we entered, he asked me my name, and, on learning it, said, "Oh! I know you very well, sir, by reputation, although I have never had the pleasure of meeting you before." This was also gratifying. . . . Mr. Barnum led me up to a sofa where the giantess was sitting. I saw a huge, moony face, above a pair of monstrous shoulders, and a mass of female drapery. The face was on a level with my own, although I was standing. "Miss Condor," said Mr. B., with the formality of a master of ceremonies, "allow me to introduce Sir Lyon Bouse, of England; Sir Lyon Bouse, Miss Condor." I was very much taken aback. To have a private view of a curiosity is one thing, and is an attention quite suitable to one's reasonable expectations; but to be introduced to a giantess!—that's quite another. But the giantess herself was not at all discomposed, either by the introduction or by my rank; and, when I bowed, said, in a voice just like a woman's, "Good morning, sir; I'm very happy to have the pleasure of making your acquaintance." Mr. Barnum pointed to the sofa by the side of the monster in petticoats, and said: "Do sit down, Sir Lyon;" then, turning to her, "Sir Lyon is a devoted admirer of the ladies." This was more than I had bargained for; but I took the seat, as the best thing to be done under the circumstances.

Miss Condor received Mr. Barnum's remark in regard to my tastes with an enormous simper, and, giantess although she was, turned upon me that indescribable look a woman wears when she is expecting a compliment. I did not know exactly how to pay her one, the circumstances were so very extraordinary, and, I may even say, so embarrassing. So I sat still, and she and Mr. Barnum looked at me, until it seemed as if I was the show, instead of the giantess. It was beginning to be somewhat oppressive, this interview; yet neither of the other parties seemed to find it so, but looked at me with the utmost serenity, and at each other with no less complaisance.

At last Mr. Barnum said, "Miss Condor, will you be kind enough to rise? Sir Lyon is a great admirer of the human figure." All this formality with a giantess that I had expected to see stirred up like a she bear, considerately, of course, however! She rose in a dignified and almost solemn manner; and, as her face ascended, followed by her shoulders, and by her gradually unfolding drapery, I thought the process of her elongation would never be accomplished. When she stood I rose also, it would be hard for me to tell why[.] . . . Under the circumstances, I thought it would be well to pay Miss

Condor the compliment which it would appear that the singular customs of the country led giantesses to expect. But while I was thinking over my subject, and choosing my phrase, Mr. Barnum suddenly said, "Well, Sir Lyon, I hev business that calls me away; but don't let that disturb you. You can remain with Miss Condor until she is ready to resoome her dooties;" and then (I assure my readers that I am telling them the truth) "perhaps you will give her your arm out." Saying this, he departed.

I must confess that, admitting Mr. Barnum's civility in giving me a private view of one of his curiosities, in the shape the affair was taking, it did not seem to me at all like the delicate attention on his part that I had been led to expect. Determining, however, to put the best face upon the matter, I began a pretty speech; although I must admit that the combination of vastness and serenity on my companion's countenance—now my only companion—was not favorable to the formation of the dainty and well-turned phrases with which one likes to placate a lady of imposing presence. I said, however, that "I was delighted, in fact, quite charmed, to have the pleasure":—I don't think I got further, or much further than that, when the lady sidled toward me with a movement so tremendous, and beamed upon me with a smile so expansive, that I must confess I was somewhat disconcerted, and could not continue my speech with quite all the coherence and dignity which it is agreeable for a man to manifest in presence of one of the other sex, whatever her condition in life. The consequence was, that I found myself looking up speechless at this monstrous young woman, who continued to sidle and simper in her gigantic fashion. Now, to any one who happens to read these pages, this may appear a very trifling matter; but that can only be the opinion of men who have never been placed in my position. To have a lady pleased with one's company and with what one says is certainly very gratifying, especially if the lady herself is an attractive person; but, even in the intercourse of life under ordinary circumstances, the blandishments which are so charming in some women are not at all alluring in others.

I could name many women at home, and have even seen some in this country, whose gracious reception of my advances would excite in me only the liveliest emotions of pleasure; but I must own that the prospect of becoming the object of Miss Condor's colossal coquetry produced in me the most disagreeable sensation of the kind I can remember. There I was, quite at her mercy, as one may say. I candidly confess that nothing could have been more proper than her conduct; but I could not reflect, that, if she were a designing giantess, my reputation, and even my purse, was in her power. The situation was even more perilous than that of travelling at home in a railway carriage with an unprotected female. What if she should offer to kiss me? I should, of course, refuse; but would she ravish the salute? I was but imperfectly acquainted with the customs here; and above all, I was ignorant of the manners of giantesses in this strange country. My thoughts began to come with more rapidity than coherence, and I decided that the best thing I could do was to retire. So, after assuring the lady that I was delighted to make her acquaintance, and bowing to her as politely as possible, I went quickly out of the room and of the Museum, determined never again to be left alone with such a large female of my own species.

Commentary

Gleason's was one of the large-format, illustrated popular magazines. Its praise for the American Museum in 1853 showed how successful had been Barnum's strategy of cultivating the middlebrow public. Jenny Lind and temperance drama in the Lecture Room helped his campaign. Fine-art transparencies of European cities, statues, and the innumerable cases of natural history framed the main attractions, the spectacles of the living performers, animal and human. By 1863 the museum claimed 833 separate attractions and 850,000 items in the seven "saloons" on the five floors.

"American Museum, New York," *Gleason's Pictorial Drawing-Room Companion* 4 (January 29, 1853): 72, 73.

Located at the confluence of the two great thoroughfares of the city, it is an object of great attraction, from the flags, transparencies and paintings with which its exterior is decorated. On gala days, or other occasions of public interest, it bears off the palm by the number and beauty of its decorations; its location affording the finest possible opportunity for display. . . . We know that the name of Barnum and humbug are synonymous, but dropping the Fejee mermaid, Joyce Heth, and others of that elk, we cannot but give him the credit of offering the most pleasant and attractive place of amusement on this continent. Indeed, on a visit recently, we spent between three and four hours in viewing the attractions in two rooms only of this immense establishment, and left with the most pleasing impressions. . . . The "Happy Family," too, with which Barnum's name has become inseparably connected, is another of the manifold curiosities of this wonder-awakening establishment. Here are seen animals of the most incongruous natures eating out of the same dish, resting upon the same perch, and making their beds together. Owls and doves, eagles and rabbits, cats and rats, hawks and small birds, monkeys, guinea-pigs, mice, squirrels, and a host of others, "too numerous to mention," forming altogether one of the most incongruous collections ever put together. . . . [T]he Lecture Room . . . is one of the most elegant and recherche halls of its class to be found anywhere. It is fitted up in the most gorgeous style, yet so arranged as not to offend the eye with a multiplicity of ornament. All is harmonious, and there is nothing to detract from the general beauty of the whole. Of the performances in this room it is scarcely necessary for us to speak. The truth is, the public had long felt the want of a place of public entertainment in which a proper respect for the decencies and decorum of life were judiciously mingled with the broadest elements of mirth, and the refined vagaries of the most exuberant fancy. We have furnished in this lecture-room just such a place.—Every species of amusement, "from grave to gay, from lively to severe," is furnished—but so judiciously purged of every semblance of immorality, that the most fastidious may listen with satisfaction, and the most sensitive witness without fear.

In some measure the same influence is exercised by the American Museum, in

New York, as is the case with the Boston Museum. Thousands, who from motives of delicacy, cannot bring themselves to attend theatrical representations in a *theatre*, find it easy enough to reconcile a *museum*, and its vaudevilles and plays to their consciences. We confess that it is very difficult for us to make a distinction between the two, when the same plays are performed, the same actors employed, and the same effect given. If well conducted, we can realize no harm from either; but, on the contrary, consider that agreeable and often instructive amusement is thus afforded to the million, at a cheap rate. There are many sound moral principles that cannot be so thoroughly impressed in any other way as by theatrical representations; the more *lifelike* the example, the more impressive the contrast between good and evil—and a good play always holds up vice to disgrace, and elevates virtue and the love of right. Many of the plays of modern times are as good practical sermons as were ever preached from the pulpit, and, beyond a doubt, exert quite as exalted and purifying an influence. The play of "The Drunkard," as performed at the Boston Museum, not long since, doubtless exerted a strong and lasting influence in behalf of the cause of temperance, more potent than fifty lectures delivered before the same number of people upon this subject.

Barnum attracted much adverse comment when the local Republican convention nominated him as its candidate for Connecticut's Fourth Congressional District in 1867. The *Nation*, the influential reforming periodical edited by E. L. Godkin, commented that his skills of trickery epitomized the domination of market forces in the corrupt days of Reconstruction. The pretentious respectability with which he foisted fakes on the gullible public was a travesty of the true gentility expected of a representative. Nearly two years earlier, it had criticized the cultural pretensions of Barnum's "Congress of Wonders": the "heterogeneous heap" in such "so-called museums" merely "pandered to the most foolish curiosity and to the most morbid appetite for the marvellous." And more than a decade before, the *Christian Parlor Magazine* had protested that "latterly our museums have been transformed into petty theatres with the lowest order of farce, not to study the wonders of nature or the beauties of art."[11]

"'The Two Hundred Thousand and First Curiosity' in Congress," *Nation* 4 (March 7, 1867): 191–92.

He is the personification—and, so far from concealing or denying it, boasts of it—of a certain low kind of humbug; humbug so petty, and producing so little apparent mischief, that people are rather disposed to be utilitarian in their way of judging it, and smile at it. It is a kind of humbug, too, into which the Yankee "smartness," in its last and worst stages, appears to run naturally; but which, funny as it often appears, eats out the heart of religion and morality even more effectually than the display of great crimes or great vices, and which, if it were to spread, might easily end in presenting us with a community regular in its praying and singing and decent in external crust, but in which all below was rottenness and uncleanness, in which the men were without truth and the women without virtue. He has passed his life in ransacking the world for curiosities to exhibit—or, in other words, as a "showman." We do not concur in the low estimate in which a showman's calling is popularly held. If it be honorable or instructive to go to see strange or queer things, it is honorable to collect and exhibit them; and if Barnum had confined himself to this . . . we should not accuse him, as we now do, of having been for twenty or thirty years a depraving and demoralizing influence. His success in money-getting, so far from atoning for his offences, . . . only aggravates them; because it makes his example the more corrupting to the thousands of young men who leave home each year in New England with money-getting set before them as their mission in life. We laugh over the woolly horse, the mermaids, the Circassian girl, and the dozen other devices to which he every year resorts to extract quarters from the country people who visit New York; and there has been so much laughing about it, and he himself joins in the laughing so readily, that we forget that it is simply swindling on a small scale, and that the spirit which prompts it and sustains it is the very same spirit which fills the jails with forgers and embezzlers and "sneak-thieves." What makes all it all the more revolting, too, is his own efforts to deceive himself and his victims into the belief that he makes his trade moral by keeping up an appearance of respectability in his museum, and excluding all "indecent allusions or gestures," as he piously announces in his play-bills, from the stage of what, with all a humbug's deference for the prejudices of the religious world, he calls his "lecture room." We say nothing here of the intense and concentrated vulgarity— we do not use the word as the antithesis of "gentility"—of the atmosphere which surrounds him. . . . Nor would we dwell even on the knavishness of his career for the mere purpose of injuring his business, or trying to cure the depraved or debasing taste for monstrosities to which he so laboriously panders, knowing, as we do, how delighted he is with anything which increases his notoriety. . . . Anyone who wants a good illustration of Mr. Barnum's career and calling can hardly do better than to visit his "lecture room," and witness the great "moral drama" of the "Christian Martyrs," which is now presented there to "delighted thousands." It is an affecting portrayal of Christian sufferings and constancy in the worst days of the pagan empire; the dresses are gorgeous, the pious rant is unexceptionable, and the scenery imposing; the martyrs are delivered in the arena to Van Amburgh's lions, brought up from the lower floor of the museum for their bloody work—and all for thirty cents a head. In the final tableau, Constantine's cross appears in the sky, and the Roman empire is converted amidst bursts of applause, whereupon the curtain falls and is seen to be covered thickly with puffs of "Horse Linament," "Yahoo Bitters," "Ready Reliefs" and "Pain Extractors," and other quack medicines.

Barnum was so angered by the *Nation*'s attack on his reputation that he wrote a letter to the editor. He admitted the American Museum was less scientific and less academically respectable than the great institutions of Europe. He proposed a free national museum in New York, perhaps in Central Park, funded by Congress, which might display surplus treasures from the Smithsonian Institution and government departments, and banish the calumny that profit-making destroyed art and culture. The old American Museum might have given too little enlightenment, but it was never, he protested, guilty of promoting debased standards of morality.

"Mr. Barnum on Museums," *Nation* 4 (August 10, 1867): 171.

I am not so thin skinned, and I know my Museum was not so refined or classic or scientifically arranged as the foreign government institutions, for mine had to support my family, while those require annually from the government thousands of pounds. "That class for which it would seem to have been originally intended" would *not support* a proper museum pecuniarily. More's the pity—but such is the stern fact. Hence, to make it self-supporting, I was obliged to popularize it, and while I still held on to the "million of curiosities," millions of persons were only induced to see them because, at the same time, they could see whales, giants, dwarfs, Albinoes, dog shows, et cetera. But it is a great error to state that I ever permitted "vulgar sensation dramas." No vulgar word or gesture, and not a profane expression, was ever allowed on my stage! Even in Shakespeare's plays, I unflinchingly and invariably cut out vulgarity and profanity. It is equally incorrect that "respectable citizens did not take their wives and daughters" "to see a play on that stage." Your writer doubtless supposed he was stating facts, but let him enquire, and he will find that nothing could be further from the truth. I am sensitive on these points, because I was always extremely squeamish in my determination to allow nothing objectionable on my stage.

I permitted no intoxicating liquors in the Museum. I would not even allow my visitors to "go out to drink" and return again without paying a second time, and this reconciled them to the "ice-water" which was always profuse and free on each floor of the Museum. I could not personally or by proxy examine into the character of every visitor, but I continually had half a score of detectives dressed in plain clothes, who incontinently turned into the street every person of either sex whose actions indicated loose habits. My interest even depended upon my keeping a good reputation for my Museum, and I did it to a greater degree than one out of ten could attain who had charge of a free museum, or even a free picture gallery. Now, I beg of you to submit the above to the writer of the article in question, and ask him, as an act of justice, to set me right before the public. Humbug with me has had its day, and, although I always gave the money's worth of that which was not demoralizing, I often grieved that the taste of the million was not elevated.

Dog Days of the Museum

"The Happy Family" menagerie, one of its best-loved attractions, exemplified this appeal. Within the one large cage, predator and prey coexisted harmoniously, "contentedly playing and frolicking together, without injury or discord."[12] Puzzled visitors marveled that human agency could create the peaceable kingdom foretold in the Bible where natural enemies might lie side by side. Mark Twain was less than impressed by the condition of Barnum's Museum in 1867. The old museum had burned to the ground in July 1865 and Barnum had opened a new premises with an entirely new collection farther up Broadway, between Spring and Prince Streets. But it was smaller, dingy, and for all Barnum's resilence and waning enthusiasm, less interesting.

Mark Twain's Travels with Mr. Brown, being heretofore uncollected sketches written by Mark Twain for the San Francisco Alta California in 1866 & 1867, describing the adventures of the author and his irrepressible companion in Nicaragua, Hannibal, New York, and other spots on their way to Europe, ed. Franklin Walker and G. Ezra Dane (New York: Knopf, 1940), 116–19.

. . . I went to his museum yesterday, along with the other children. There is little or nothing in the place worth seeing, and yet how it draws! It was crammed with both sexes and all ages. One could keep on going up stairs from floor to floor, and still find scarcely room to turn. There are numerous trifling attractions there, but if there was one grand, absorbing feature I failed to find it. There is a prodigious woman, eight feet high, and well proportioned, but there was no one to stir her up and make her show her points, so she sat down all the time. And there is a giant, also, just her size; but he appears to be sick with love for her, and so he sat morosely on his platform, in his astonishing military uniform, and wrought no wonders. If I was impressario of that menagerie, I would make that couple prance around some, or I would dock their rations. Two dwarfs, unknown to fame, and a speckled negro, complete the list of human curiosities. They profess to have a Circassian girl there, but I could not find her. I think they moved her out, to make way for another peanut stand. In fact, Barnum's Museum is one vast peanut stand now, with a few cases of dried frogs and other wonders scattered here and there, to give variety to the thing. You can't go anywhere without finding a peanut stand, and an impudent negro sweeping up hulls. When peanuts and candy are slow, they sell newspapers and photographs of the dwarfs and giants.

There are some cages of ferocious lions, and other wild beasts, but they sleep all the time. And also an automaton card writer; but something about it is broken, and it don't go now. Also a good many bugs, with pins stuck through them; but the people do not seem to enjoy bugs any more. There is a photograph gallery in one room and an oyster saloon in another, and some news depots and soda fountains, a pistol gallery, and a raffling department for cheap jewelry, but not any barber shop. A plaster of Paris statue of Venus, with little stacks of dust on her nose and her eyebrows, stands

61

neglected in a corner, and in some large glass cases are some atrocious waxen images, done in the very worst style of the art. Queen Victoria is dressed in faded red velvet and glass jewelry, and has a bloated countenance and a drunken leer in her eye, that remind one of convivial Mary Holt, when she used to come in from a spree to get her ticket for the County Jail. And that cursed eye-sore to me, Tom Thumb's wedding party, which airs its smirking imbecility in every photograph album in America, is not only set forth here in ghastly wax, but repeated! Why does not some philanthropist burn the Museum again?

The Happy Family remains, but robbed of its ancient glory. A poor, spiritless old bear—sixteen monkeys—half a dozen sorrowful raccoons—two mangy puppies—two unhappy rabbits—and two meek Tom cats, that have had half the hair snatched out of them by the monkeys, compose the Happy Family—and certainly it was the most subjugated-looking party I ever saw. The entire Happy Family is bossed and bullied by a monkey that any one of the victims could whip, only that they lack the courage to try it. He grabs a Tom cat by the nape of the neck and bounces him on the ground, he cuffs the rabbits and the coons, and snatches his own tribe from end to end of the cage by the tail. When the dinner-tub is brought in, he gets boldly into it, and the other members of the family sit patiently around till his hunger is satisfied or steal a morsel and get bored heels over head for it. The world is full of families as happy as that. The boss monkey has even proceeded so far as to nip the tail short off one of his brethren, and now half the pleasures of the poor devil's life are denied him, because he hain't got anything to hang by. It almost moves one to tears to see that bob-tailed monkey work his stump and try to grab a beam with it that is a yard away. And when his stump naturally misses fire and he falls, none but the heartless can laugh. Why cannot he become a philosopher? Why cannot he console himself with the reflection that tails are but a delusion and a vanity at best.

Barnum puts a play on his stage called the "Christian Martyr," and in the third act all the mules and the lions, and sheep, and tigers, and pet bulls, and other ferocious wild animals, are marched about the stage in grand procession preparatory to going through the Christian. In the final act they throw the Christian into a cage with a couple of lions, but they were asleep, and all the punching the Martyr could do, and all the cursing he could get off under his breath failed to wake them; but the ignorant Roman populace on the stage took their indifference for Providential interference, and so they let the doomed Christian slide. Barnum's lions prefer fresh beef to martyrs. I suspect they are of the same breed as those we read of that were too stuck up to eat good old Daniel.

A generation later, William Dean Howells, noted novelist and dramatist, turned his journalist's eye on the dime museum. He had criticized the legitimate theatre for being too elitist, with high prices and unrealistic plots. Through the words of a fictitious "friend," Howells commented on popular taste and on the varied entertainments of a cheap but respectable Bowery museum that lacked Barnum's resources.

Dog Days of the Museum

William Dean Howells, "At a Dime Museum," in *Literature and Life: Studies* (New York: Harper and Brothers, 1902), 194–98.

I don't contend that it is intellectual, but I say that it is often clever and charming at the ten-cent shows. . . . I think the average of propriety is rather higher than it is at the two-dollar theatres; and it is much more instructive at the ten-cent shows, if you come to that. The other day . . . I went to a dime museum for an hour that I had between two appointments, and I must say that I never passed an hour's time more agreeably. In the curio hall, as one of the lecturers on the curios called it, they had several lecturers in white wigs and scholars' caps and gowns—there was not a great deal to see, I confess; but everything was very high-class. There was the inventor of a perpetual motion, who lectured upon it and explained it from a diagram. There was a fortune-teller in a three-foot tent whom I did not interview; there were five macaws in one cage, and two gloomy apes in another. On a platform at the end of the hall was an Australian [aborigine] family a good deal gloomier than the apes, who sat in the costume of our latitude, staring down the room with varying expressions all verging upon melancholy madness, and gave me such a pang of compassion as I have seldom got from the tragedy of the two-dollar theatres. They allowed me to come quite close up to them, and to feed my pity upon their wild dejection in exile without stint. I couldn't enter into conversation with them, and express my regret at finding them so far from their native boomerangs and kangaroos and pine-tree grubs, but I know they felt my sympathy, it was so evident. I didn't see their performance, and I don't know that they had any. They may simply have been there ethnologically, but this was a good object, and the sight of their spiritual misery was alone worth the price of admission.

After the inventor of the perpetual motion had brought his harangue to a close, we all went round to the dais where a lady in blue spectacles lectured us upon a fire-escape which she had invented, and operated a small model of it. None of the events were so exciting that we could regret it when the chief lecturer announced that this was the end of the entertainment in the curio hall, and that now the performance in the theatre was about to begin. He invited us to buy tickets at an additional charge of five, ten, or fifteen cents for the gallery, orchestra circle, or orchestra.

I thought I could afford an orchestra stall, for once. We were three in the orchestra, another man and a young mother, not counting the little boy she had with her; there were two people in the gallery, and a dozen at least in the orchestra circle. An attendant shouted, "Hats off!" and the other man and I uncovered, and a lady came up from under the stage and began to play the piano in front of it. The curtain rose, and the entertainment began at once. It was a passage apparently from real life, and it involved a dissatisfied boarder and the daughter of the landlady. There was not much coherence in it, but there was a good deal of conscience on the part of the actors, who toiled through it with unflagging energy. The young woman was equipped for the dance she brought into it at one point rather than for the part she had to sustain in the drama. It was a very blameless dance, and she gave it as if she was tired of it, but was

63

not going to falter. She delivered her lines with a hard, Southwestern accent, and I liked fancying her having come up in a simpler-hearted section of the country than ours, encouraged by a strong local belief that she was destined to do Juliet and Lady Macbeth, or Peg Woffington at the least; but very likely she had not.

Her performance was followed by an event involving a single character. The actor, naturally, was blackened as to his skin, and at first glance I could see that he had temperament. I suspect that he thought I had, too, for he began to address his entire drama to me. This was not surprising, for it would not have been the thing to single out the young mother; and the other man in the orchestra stalls seemed a vague and inexperienced youth, whom he would hardly have given the preference over me. I felt the compliment, but upon the whole it embarrassed me; it was too intimate, and it gave me a publicity I would willingly have foregone. I did what I could to reject it, by feigning an indifference to his jokes; I even frowned a measure of disapproval; but this merely stimulated his ambition. He was really a merry creature, and when he had got off a number of very good things which were received in perfect silence, and looked over his audience with a woebegone eye, and said, with an effect of delicate apology, "I hope I'm not disturbing you any," I broke down and laughed, and that delivered me into his hand. He immediately said to me that now he would tell me about a friend of his, who had a pretty large family, eight of them living, in Philadelphia; and then for no reason he seemed to change his mind, and said he would sing me a song written expressly for him—by an express-man; and he went on from one wild gayety to another, until he had worked his audience up to quite a frenzy of enthusiasm, and almost had a recall when he went off.

I was rather glad to be rid of him, and I was glad that the next performers, who were a lady and a gentleman contortionist of Spanish-American extraction, behaved more impartially. They were really remarkable artists in their way, and though it's a painful way, I couldn't help admiring their gift in bow-knots and other difficult poses. The gentleman got abundant applause, but the lady at first got none. I think perhaps it was because, with the correct feeling that prevailed among us, we could not see a lady contort herself with so much approval as a gentleman, and there was a wound to our sense of propriety in witnessing her skill. But I could see that the poor girl was hurt in her artist pride by our severity, and at the next thing she did I led off the applause with my umbrella. She instantly lighted up with a joyful smile, and the young mother in the orchestra leaned forward to nod her sympathy to me when she clapped. We were fast becoming a domestic circle, and it was very pleasant, but I thought that upon the whole I had better go. . . .

It was all very pathetic, in a way. Three out of those five people were really clever, and certainly artists. That colored brother was almost a genius, a very common variety of genius, but still a genius, with a gift for his calling that couldn't be disputed. He was a genuine humorist, and I sorrowed over him—after I got safely away from his intimacy—as I should over some author who was struggling along without winning his public.

Dog Days of the Museum

The journalist Rollin Lynde Hartt visited a small city dime museum early in the twentieth century. The old-style shows lacked the glamor of the better-financed vaudeville theatres, and even the "dim, flickering, bespeckled" films Hartt saw there were now offered at the local nickelodeons. This "temple of inanity," he decided, was unpretentious—"art plays second-fiddle to freaks"— and gave the human detritus of the city who were unable or unwilling to think, precisely what they wanted: "a vast and beneficent foolishness."

Rollin Lynde Hartt, *The People at Play* (Boston: Houghton, Mifflin, 1909), 87–88, 89–90, 92, 110–12.

The lowly, argue those who know not, repair thither to gloat over the affliction of their over-sized, under-sized, and otherwise peculiar fellow mortals. Then how comes it that they scan the exhibits with awe-struck reverence? that they keep a straight face while the lecturer heaps grandiloquent adulation upon his freaks? that every curio esteems himself a special pet of Providence, as who should say, "Behold the marvels that God hath wrought in my person!" . . .

Who are we that we should scoff when the ignorant—those who now stand marveling before the pictures and presently slouch toward the ticket-window—worship the rare accidents and misdemeanors of variation, forgetting that by virtue of their consistent normality it is they themselves who will constitute the only really marvelous exhibits in Curio Hall?

I counsel you to follow them in. They represent the substratum of society. Upon their foolishness rests the perpetuity of our institutions. . . .

Whereas you treasure monstrosities in marble, in bronze, and in deckle-edged editions, the humble do but treasure the only monstrosities that fall within their ken. . . . You press forward, and come to a tall room with square posts to prop its ceiling, walls freely kalsomined [color-washed] in red and yellow, and along the walls the cages, booths, thrones, and stages of greatness. This is Curio Hall. No seats; everybody is standing, gazing open-mouthed upon a freak, and listening with rapt deference while the "professor" declaims his "lecture." You get an impression of weather-worn Derby hats, with here and there a tawdry bonnet, . . . showing them to be inferior, in stature, in development, in endurance, and in comeliness, to the well-to-do. . . .

But it is the social philosopher, methinks, who should be most grateful to Curio Hall. Its existence spells safety for the existing social order. Think you it is the progress of enlightenment that sanctions and perpetuates our scheme of human relationships? Far otherwise. Rather is it the survival of benightedness. So long as endures the gallery of "exclusive living oddities," with pitiful blockheads to gape at them, so long will there abound those scullions, scavengers, stokers, flunkies, and wretched wage-minions upon whose docility we depend for our maintenance. Given intelligence to perceive the joke implied in their adoration of abnormalities, they might detect the huge, historic, practical joke played upon them by destiny.

MINSTRELSY

Londoners at the Adelphi Theatre in June and July 1843 were entertained by another American novelty. The city had already seen Barnum's Tom Thumb and George Catlin's Indian Gallery. Now the *Times* drew attention to the new "Ethiopian concert, by four Virginian minstrels, in which some of the original airs of the interior of Africa, modernized if not humanized in the slave states of the Union, and adapted to ears polite, have been introduced by the musical conductor of the theatre." This "negro concert" featured a band in blackface make-up playing banjo, violin, "bone castanetts," and tambourine, with impersonations of black speech and dance. Only five months before, the performers—Dan Emmett, Frank Brower, Billy Whitlock and Dick Pelham—had introduced to New York what became known as the minstrel show in its classic form.[1]

Minstrelsy developed further the long tradition in the English theater of characterizations of "Negroes," usually not depicted with the aid of black make-up. In the late eighteenth century, sentimental songs and speeches had depicted the sufferings of Africans far from home. More common were portrayals of comic servants in the West Indies who spoke a strange Africanized English and had wild, uncontrolled movements. In 1824 the actor Charles Mathews created a sensation in London with his caricatures of Agamemnon, the fat runaway slave fiddler, and his parody of the pretentious black Hamlet in the "Niggers Theatre," both based, he claimed, on close observation of the originals during the eighteen months he spent in America.

Significant as these rather mannered characterizations were, the main impulse behind minstrelsy was American and popular. Early blackface entertainers drew on sources of protest both traditional and modern. Anglo-Americans had long used masquerade, in which morris dancers and mummers adopted blackface disguise, and in carnival mood and loud noise had protested against social forces and figures undermining community solidarity. In the late 1820s and 1830s the main support for blackface comic acts in the theater came from urban manual laborers. W. T. Lhamon Jr. has argued that the carters, sailors, riggers, and longshoresmen who lived and worked along the wharves of canals and seaports had a class loyalty, a "mudsill mutuality," which transcended many, but not all, of the barriers of race and ethnicity. They were accustomed to ethnic mingling and made black style and gesture their vehicle for expressing dissent. When relations between apprentices and masters became more distant and city sweatshops more common, the rough and raucous humor of blackface conveyed this heightened sense of class conflict.[2] One of the first entertainers to modify the English genteel model of blackface entertainment was George Washington Dixon. Dixon, who called himself "a buffo singer and comedian," was born of poor parents in Richmond and traveled with circuses along the Atlantic seaboard. In 1827 or 1828 he first performed "Coal Black Rose," a "buffo" (burlesque) of the conventional courtship song. Dixon's appearances at New York's Bowery and Chatham Theatres in 1829 brought him in contact with the rowdy, boisterous, working-class audiences of the Five Points district. It was no coincidence that this was the crucible of minstrelsy. Living close to the docks and warehouses near Catherine Market were New York's poorest. Those who lacked artisan skills struggled for a living in the new metropolis and resented the new code of gentility and reform. Here, too, was easy access to black folk style. Almost a tenth of New York's population was black. They were not segregated in large ghettoes, as they would be later in the century, but clustered in small "tender-loins" or "little Africas" throughout the city. In an age when one-fifth of all American sailors was black, the nation's busiest seaport was also host to many sailors. That presence was all the more striking in the 1820s before large-scale Irish and German immigration.

The most inventive and original early minstrel performer was Thomas Dartmouth Rice. Rice was born in the Bowery's Catherine Street, apprenticed as a ship's carver, and then became an itinerant actor and circus comic in the river towns of the Ohio Valley and the Upper South. Probably in 1830 he first performed "Jim Crow," the song which made his fortune. In 1832 he appeared in the major Mid-Atlantic cities and toured throughout the northeast for the next four years before his triumphant success in London. Rice's act was the product of a medley of influences. His songs had some of the irreverent humor of the Crockett Almanacs, but his ridicule of gentility was less impolite, less scurrilous. "Coal Black Rose" always remained part of his repertoire, so it is clear that Dixon was one model. More influential were the streets of the Bowery. Growing up one block away from Catherine Market, Rice had seen blacks "dancing for eels." The dancer raised his hands over his head, wheeled about, and jumped vigorously to the percussive beat of a drum and clapping. This was the model for the ragged Jim Crow and his erratic, anarchic jig.

Race mattered in the 1830s. New York state had finally ended the long process of gradual emancipation in 1827, but "amalgamation" remained an emotive issue. Dixon's parody of "Zip Coon," the overdressed and ambitious black dandy, owed much to comic prints like the unflattering illustrations of Edward Clay and David Claypoole Johnson. The male audiences in the Bowery and Chatham Theatres who responded so enthusiastically to Dixon and Rice were familiar with the complex cultural references involving blackface. They applauded when the lowly clown mocked the powerful and pretentious, and enjoyed the robust, uninhibited humor, the exuberant, expressive physicality, and the new songs with lyrics of contemporary relevance set to familiar Irish melodies and interpreted with mimic-black body language.

Much of this noisy, carnival spirit was tamed in the 1840s, as more women attended. The first two minstrel troupes of 1842–43—Emmett's Virginia Minstrels and Christy's Virginia Minstrels in Buffalo—set a precedent for larger bands of four or six entertainers. The program gradually became more standardized, with acts more closely themed and coordinated. By the 1850s, the largest troupes, like the Christy Minstrels, structured the show loosely into three parts. The first element introduced the whole company in music and comedy and closed with a rousing song from all. What distinguished the variety of acts was the interchange between the flamboyant bones and tambourine players seated at the ends of a semicircle who mocked the dignified interlocutor acting as master of ceremonies. After the intermission, the olio, the second part, featured the specialized variety routines of individuals in short, virtuoso turns, impersonating "wenches," performing dances, delivering stump speeches, or pleasing the crowd with the sentimental songs of Stephen Foster. The concluding section was the most coherently organized with some semblance of a plot. The one-act farce, sometimes a parody of serious drama, more often a sketch set in plantation or city, blended music and dance with slapstick comedy, and a "walkaround" finale by the entire troupe. Charley White specialized in arranging and adapting these "Darkey Plays."

The essence of minstrelsy was burlesque. Audiences delighted in parodies of European high culture. The southern "common nigga" joined the western backwoodsman and the northern Yankee in a panoply of regional American folk heroes who ridiculed pretention. There were burlesque speeches, burlesque operas, burlesque ballets. The humorous lecture at a militia muster or the church sermon, given in broad dialect and with nonsensical words, mocked the learned orations and mastery of language so admired by the genteel. The "Ethiopian *Pas de Deux*" showed the grotesque antics of a crossdressed "nigger wench." And, most prominently, there were comic versions of the latest European successes. Opera had wide appeal. Traveling opera companies brought the ballads of Bellini, Balfe, and Verdi to the larger towns of the northeast. Blackface musicians soon transformed familiar scenes and songs: Donizetti's *Lucia di Lammermoor* became *Lucy-do-lam-her-more* or *Lucy-Did-Sham-Amour*. Minstrels who elevated the simple protagonists of Charley White's burlesque operas to equality with the Italian pantheon, William J. Mahar argues, "inverted that social order" of upper-class exclusiveness in opera houses "by exalting the American vernacular both in language and music" and asserting the common man's culture.[3]

Genteel magazines generally welcomed minstrelsy in its early years. It was vibrant and vigorous, if rather coarse and unrefined. A little reluctantly, Henry James the elder admitted a "fondness" for the "negro" song "that goes directly to the heart, and makes Italian trills seem tame." Some cultural nationalists saw in it those signs of originality which proved the blessings of republican liberty extended, if not to all the fine arts, then at least to the people's music. The *Knickerbocker* rejoiced that the "American national opera" was derived from the songs of slaves, the group "most secluded from foreign influences," and had "electrified the world." Praise from Charles Dickens seemed confirmation of coming glory.[4]

By the 1850s minstrelsy had lost much of its critical, questioning spirit and its distinctive identity. Few followed Margaret Fuller or Walt Whitman in heralding it as a praiseworthy achievement of the democratic culture; it was vulgar, if not debased. After the Civil War, blackface troupes boasted of their large companies, with Leavitt's Gigantean Ministrels challenging Cleveland's Colossals. Burlesque of polite culture remained central, but as mainstream entertainment blackface offered little more than a themed version of the general variety show. Often, after the war, even the plantation was missing from the program of miscellaneous sentimental songs, skits about women's rights, readings from Shakespeare, and longer sketches of life among the lowly. By the 1870s genuine blacks in blackface were a significant force in minstrelsy, and by the 1890s they had begun to dominate virtuoso dancing. Even in decline, for two generations after the Civil War burnt cork performers remained speciality acts in vaudeville, beyond Al Jolson's famous roles, with the young Judy Garland one of the last stars to don blackface.

Minstrel depictions of "Negro eccentricities" were much more than an expression of fellow feeling with black partners in a class crusade against middle-class convention. If there was admiration, jealousy, and envy for the actions of the black fools, there was also an unmistakable tone of racial denigration. As Eric Lott has shown, there was an undercurrent of sexual longing in the content and imagery of blackface performances. Blackface was a convenient disguise for cathartic release of repressed emotions and views on taboo subjects. Derogatory comments about "niggers" were common even among the educated, and there was generally little sensitivity to appropriate language in references to race and ethnicity. The humorist Mortimer Thomson described all "darkies" as having "foot of suitable dimensions for a railroad bridge,

Dan Bryant, pictured in blackface make-up, "fright" wig, and tambourine led one of the most successful New York minstrel troupes of the 1850s and 1860s. © Bettmann/CORBIS.

and mouth big enough for the depot." If minstrelsy appropriated black culture, and both rejoiced in it and maligned it, under the simple mask of "Ethiopian delineation," it also lampooned many elite and European cultural forms. It was complex and ambiguous—"collage entertainment where moods and meanings tumbled after one another with incredible quickness," manifesting both "respect and fear, affection and hate, need and scorn, caring and exploitation."[5]

Routines: Songs, Speeches, Dialogue, and Farce

Billy Whitlock, one of the original Virginia Minstrels, composed the most popular minstrel song of the 1840s. Its combination of sentimentality, comic nonsense, and a simple, repetitive tune made it a success with amateur and professional performers. It was topical, with mention of the Cachucha, a fast-paced Spanish dance popularized by the European ballerina Fanny Ellsler during her American tour of 1840–42. The role of Miss Lucy may have been the first for a cross-dressed "wench." The song celebrates male freedom; rebuffed in marriage, the would-be husband boasts of casting her off if she proves difficult.

S. Damon Foster, *Series of Old American Songs* (Providence, R.I.: Brown University Library, 1936).

Miss Lucy Long (1842)

I've come to see you again,
I'll sing another song,
Jist listen to my story,
It isn't very long.

Chorus: Oh, take your time Miss Lucy,
Take your time Miss Lucy Long,
Oh, take your time Miss Lucy,
Take your time Miss Lucy Long.

Miss Lucy, she is handsome,
And Miss Lucy, she is tall;
To see her dance Cachucha,
Is death to niggers all.

Oh! Miss Lucy's teeth is grinning,
Just like an ear ob corn,
And her eyes dey look so winning,
Oh! I would I'd ne'er been born.

I axed her for to marry
Myself de toder day,
She said she'd rather tarry,
So I let her hab her way.

If she makes a scolding wife,
As sure as she was born,

71

I'll tote her down to Georgia,
And trade her off for corn.

My Mamma's got de tisic,
And my daddy's got de gout:
Good morning, Mister Physick!
Does your mother know you're out.

Dan Emmett claimed to have written "Dandy Jim." Like the "Long-Tail'd Blue," made famous by George Washington Dixon, it was another song satirizing the gaudy male peacock and charlatan, the confidence-man. It proved more enduringly popular in minstrel programs than "Zip Coon" (1833), perhaps because Zip the "larned scholar" commented extensively, but narrowly, on Jacksonian politics. "Dandy Jim" had broad reference beyond the slave South to the city streets where boastful "swells," like Mose, the "Bowery B'hoy," with his greased ringlocks and flashy red shirt, promenaded and displayed themselves. There are least ten different versions of "Dandy Jim."

S. Damon Foster, *Series of Old American Songs* (Providence, R.I.: Brown University Library, 1936).

Dandy Jim from Caroline (1843)

I've often heard it said ob late,
Dat Souf Carolina was de state,
Whar a handsome nigga's bound to shine,
Like Dandy Jim from Caroline.

Chorus: For my ole missus tole me so,
I was de best looking nigga in de country, O,
I look in de glass and found 'twas so,
Just what massa tole me, O.

I drest myself from top to toe,
And down to Dinah I did go,
Wid pentaloons strapped down behind,
Like Dandy Jim from Caroline.

De bull dog cleared me out ob de yard,
I tought I'd better leabe my card,
I tied it fast to a piece ob twine,
Signed "Dandy Jim from Caroline."

She got my card and wrote me a letter,
And ebery word she spelt de better,

72

Routines: Songs, Speeches, Dialogue, and Farce

For ebery word an ebery line,
Was Dandy Jim from Caroline.

Oh, beauty is but skin deep,
But wid Miss Dinah none compete,
She changed her name from lubly Dine,
To Mrs. Dandy Jim from Caroline.

And ebery little nig she had,
Was the berry image ob de dad,
Dar heels stick out three feet behind,
Like Dandy Jim from Caroline.

I took dem all to church one day,
An hab dem christened widout delay,
De preacher christened eight or nine,
Young Dandy Jims from Caroline.

When Emerson and other prominent ministers and moralists became popular lecturers on the lyceum circuit, minstrels mocked the wise. Emotional sermons and pompous Fourth of July orations were favorite subjects for burlesque, with inappropriate nonsense words ridiculing pretentious sentiments. Any newsworthy subject, from the revolutions of 1848 to Manifest Destiny to the California Gold Rush, became suitable material.

De Negro's Original Piano-Rama, of Southern, Northern and Western Songs, to airs of all quarters, embracing de operatic de serenade and de soul combustion ballad, all sighentifically surplayed by three colored muses ob de plantation, de parlour an de kitchen (Philadelphia: Fisher and Brother, 1850), 67–69.

Grand Original, Local, Locomotive, Dog-matical, Grog-matical, Gold Fever-ical, An Prophetical
LECTURE!
For De Twenty-One Million

"Ah can ye not discover, by de signs ob de times."
Brodern an Sistern, Fellow Citizens, and animal exotics, an native indigeniouses:
De rounaboutationary resolution ob dis yar sub-lunar caustic globe, am fast comproximatin toward de WHOLE HALF ob de nineteenth century, an as it turns, 'cordin to de laws ob Sir Humphrey Gravy, a little bit more faster on its axes, its rebolution am symphietic, an de people feelin de strong percussion, am forcibly chucked into a state ob rebolution-eye-zation, an pitched clar up against de big wall of monarchy, custock-crazy, hygo-crazy, and all de oder-crazys, till dey get demo-crazy demselves.
Darfore, hence aroses de great parpetual comotion an spawn-taneous combus-

73

tion in de pole-cat-a-call, physicall at-most-fear, an de airth, like a great aeolian appa-rat-us, has warmed up her eggs, an hatched forth

"New signs ob de times."

Dar in France, she hatched out some republican game chickens, an de king-cock had to cut without a comb to his head, an take a roost on de horns ob de British Bull; some said a cow, bekase it looked cow-ardly, but while de French quarrelled how to feed de publican chickens, a sly hawk walked in an picked 'em so bare dat all we can see am de bony-part. De Dutch king cock got shook from his roost, but he squeezed enough ob royal sour-crout out ob de nation's cellar to crawl back agin, an now he picks at de rebel chickens, wrings de necks ob de game rooster, an he Kuss-eth dar heads for rebel tators.

But my bruddern an feller sisterns, let him look out for de "Signs ob de times," an beware ob de terrible tater peelin to come, for de 19th century can no more, an will no more warm up royal roosten eggs, dan a tumbler bug can hatch eagles.

Now, we'll succeed to de Delighted States ob de Americum Unicorn, whose territory extends from de extreme point ob day break, to de todder side ob sun navigation, an it is bounded by de roley boley-alls on de Norf, de ant-ark-tick pole on de Souf, de risin sun on de East, an on de West de day ob judgment. It possesses Noah's flood, divides into lakes an rivers, de entire garden ob Eden, wid all de creepen' an flyin' critters; de whole ob de milky way for nourishment, an de whole ob de tunder an lightin an shootin stars for a standin' army. De rainbow for a coat ob arms, de planets for a library, an de entire part ob immensity for mine diggins. Now den, let us look at her signs ob de times. Dar dey am, written in red hot letters ob Calaforny gold, to wit:

"Go ahead, in all things, wid a season ticket, all de way, clar through to Eternity."

Dar's de boys, dat go ahead so fast in larnin dat instruction gits out ob water, an lights up a piece ob nothin to keep de grintellects in fuel, an de women know so much dat dey have to go wid dar arms an necks bare to let off de surplus rebenue ob knowledge, an thar obliged to nail de scalp ober de skull wid silver combs to keep de high pressure ob knowledge, from mount vesuviation, an dar so far advanced in modesty, dat dey won't receive a fortune dat's left 'em, 'kase it's a leg-i-see.

An, dar so religious dat dey eat pies at tea, so dat dey may hab pie-ous deams. An as for de men, dey go into reform by machinery, an some ob de reformers can shove any part ob de sinful world into dar lecture mill, and it comes out millenium. Some am so perfect dat dey reject all sincerity bekase it begins wid sin.

What am de fashion signs? Why, de ladies am so fond ob payin visits dat dey war 'em on dar backs, an dey am so economical dat dey carry five yard purses, so dat dey can't get down to de money to spend it.

But gold am de fashionable fever; de epidemical confluensa; everybody splits his calabash for California's goold diggins; de miners dig de earth's pockets, and speck-letator's dig de miner's pockets. Now I'll splain to you how all dis discovery come for to be uncovered:—You'se all heard ob dem spots in de sun what ain't sunny spots. Well, de kase ob dat was, dat de sun one day in 'Octember, looked eleventeen hours in a mortified tater field, an cotch de tater rot in his face, an bein somewhat short ob sunshine, he throwed a sun-set, turned himself behind his back, an dis brought his gold side to de airth, an de fect ob dat was, dat it gold-vanized de bowels ob de airth an distracted all de goold from de centre toward de surface darof, an jis stumped his toe again a lump ob de dust, an it turned yaller, an fell agin a white man, dat white man fell agin anudder, an everybody become goold struck, and 'come 'fected wid goold yaller ganders, an eber since arter dat, de whole at-most-fear 'come pregnated wid gold. De sun am gold mounted, de gals wear gold in dar gums, de gemmen tie demselves fast to dar watches by gold ropes, an de wedder rooster ob dar minds all point toward California, an de great metal physical question dat seems to us, is am wedder de gold bug or de hum-bug will soonest make de human bug come out a big bug.

Publishers Dick and Fitzgerald advertised *Tambo's End Men's Ministrel Gags* as "a complete Hand-Book of Burnt Cork Drollery, which will be found alike useful to the professional and amateur. Everything new and rich," for thirty cents in paper covers or fifty cents cloth. The exchange between Brudder Tambo and Brudder Bones, the two "musicians" at the ends of the semicircular "line," was typical minstrel humor.

Minstrel Gags and End Men's Hand-Book. Being a collection of Ethiopian Dialogues, Plantation Scenes, Eccentric Scenes, Humorous Lectures, Laughable Interludes, End Men's Jokes, Burlesque Speeches, Witticisms, Conundrums, Yarns, Plantation Songs and Dances, etc. (New York: Dick and Fitzgerald, 1875), 60–62.

Blackberrying

"Ah! Tambo, she's gone dead."

"Is she dead, Bones?"

"Yes, Tambo. She sent for me three days after she died."

"Oh, no, Bones, you mean three days previous to her decease."

"No; she had no niece; she was an orphan."

"I mean three days before she departed this earthly tenement."

"Sir?"

"That is three days before she died."

"Oh, yes! Well, I went down to see her; went up to de bedside wid de bed in my eyes."

"You mean with the tears in your eyes?"

"Yes, wid de pillows in my eyes. Sez she, 'Bones, I'm goin' to leave this world of care'."

"What did you reply?"

"I sed I didn't care much. Den she axed me if I would go down to the 'pothecary shop for some medicine. I sed yes; so I went down to Dr. Night Bell—"

"No, not to Dr. Night Bell; that's the name of the bell on the door—the night bell."

"Well, I called him 'Dr. Night Bell,' anyhow."

"I presume he was a pretty good physician?"

"No, he wasn't fishin', he was home."

"Oh, no, I mean he was a physician of some note."

"Yes, he was counting out his notes when I went in."

"No, Bones, you do not understand. I mean he was a doctor of some standing."

"No, he wasn't standin', he was sittin' on a three-legged stool."

"Well, what did the doctor give you?"

"He gabe me a piece of paper."

"A prescription?"

"No, it was paper."

"Of course, it was on paper, but nevertheless a prescription. What did it say on the paper?"

"It was full of chalk-marks made wid a pencil. He sed I must get two dozen fish-hooks, No. 7, and put them in a quart ob molasses an boil it down, den gib her de broth, so I went up to de bar—"

"No, you mean the counter."

"He didn't count dem; he weighed 'em out."

"Well, was there any efficacy in the dose?"

"No: noffin' in it but fish-hooks!"

"I mean was the medicine any way efficacious?"

"Now, look here, Tambo, be so kind as to 'dress me in de English language."

"Well, then, Bones, I mean did the medicine do her any good?"

"It wouldn't have cured her, but the poor gal in an absence of mind, instead of takin' the broth, took de fish-hooks, and dey killed her."

"Then that must have been her funeral I saw last Wednesday?"

"No, it wasn't. De doctor says I can't bury her until next summer."

"Why not, Bones?"

"Kase dat's de best time to go out *Blackberryin'*."

The farce, *Oh, Hush! or, the Virginny Cupids*, went through several stages of evolution. George Washington Dixon expanded his "Coal Black Rose" (1827) into a skit, *Love in a Cloud* (1829), and then a longer farce, *The Duel; or, Coal Black Rose*. Thomas D. Rice performed it as *Long-Island Juba; or, Love in a Bushel* in 1833, and it remained popular from the late 1840s to the 1870s. Christy and Wood's Minstrels, the most successful troupe of their time, gave it as *The Virginia Cupids; or, The Rival Darkies* in 1853. Charles White was a minstrel impresario of note, and published dozens of his arrangements of old farces, probably little changed from earlier acting versions.

Charles White, *Oh! Hush! Or, The Virginny Cupids: an operatic olio in one act and three scenes arranged by Charles White* (New York: Happy Hours, 1873).

Illustrations of African Americans in minstrel songsheets like George Washington Dixon's "Coal Black Rose" in the 1830s were unflatteringly grotesque. The Free Library of Philadelphia.

OH, HUSH!
OR,
THE VIRGINNY CUPIDS.
an operatic olio,
in one act, and three scenes,
arranged by CHARLES WHITE.

CAST OF CHARACTERS
SAMBO JOHNSON (a retired bootblack)
CUFF (a boss bootblack)
PETE WILLIAMS (Cuff's foreman)
COLONEL BEN (an old polisher)
MISS DINAH ROSE (a fascinating wench)
KNIGHTS OF THE BRUSH

SCENE 1
Street. THE CHARACTERS *discovered blacking boots, some sitting down.* SAM JOHNSON *sits on a chair, R, his feet resting on a barrel. He is reading a newspaper which he holds upside down.* ALL *laugh and begin to get up as the curtain rises.*

CUFF. Pete, I hab been round to all the hotels to-day, an' I got so many boots to black by four o'clock dat I don't tink I can do it. Now, den, boys, if you polish dem by dat time, I'll gib you all a holiday dis ebenin'.

PETE. Ah! dat's right, Cuff, we'll gib'em de shine ob de best Day and Martin—but, Cuff, gib us a song.

CUFF (*sings*).
Come all you Virginny gals, and listen to my noise,
Neber do you wed wid de Carolina boys;
For if dat you do, your portion will be,
Cowheel and sugar cane, wid shangolango tea.

FULL CHORUS.
Mamzel ze marrel-ze bunkum sa?
Mamzel ze marrel-ze bunkum sa?

When you go a courting, de pretty gals to see,
You kiss 'em and you hug 'em like de double rule oh free.
De fust ting dey ax you when you are sitting down,
is, "Fetch along de Johnny cake—it's gitting radder brown."
CHORUS—Mamzel ze marrel, etc.

Before you are married, potatoes dey am cheap,
But money am so plenty dat you find it in the street.
But arter you git married, I tell you how it is—
Potatoes dey am berry high, and sassengers is riz.

CHORUS—Mamzel ze marrel, etc.

CUFF (*turning round after the song, discovers JOHNSON*). I say, Pete, who is dat consumquencial darkey ober dar, dat is puttin' on so many airs?

PETE. I don't know, Cuff. He stopped here a few minutes arter you went away, an' he'been reading dar eber since. Speak to him.

CUFF (*approaching JOHNSON, scrutinizes his person*). Why, it am Sam Johnson!
ALL. Sam Johnson!
CUFF. Yes, to be sure it am.

JOHNSON (*looking through his eyeglass*). Gemblem, is you distressing your conversation to me?

CUFF. Yes, sar, I is distressing my observation to you inderwidually, collectively, skientifically and alone. (*Seats himself on the barrel.*)

JOHNSON (*rising*). Well, sar, den I would hab you to know dat my name, sar, is Mr. Samuel Johnson, Exquire, an' I don't wish to be addressed by such—(*pointing to *crowd*) low, common, vulgar trash! You had better mind your business and brack your filthy boots. (*He sits down again.*)

CUFF (*gets off the barrel*). I say, Pete, I'll tell you whar I seed dat darkey. He used to work in de same shop wid me for old Jake Simmons, but he drawed a high prize in de lottery, and retired from de 'spectable perfession of bracking boots. De last time I seed him he was down in old Virginny on a coon hunt. I'll tell you suffin' 'bout it. (*He sings.*)

'Way down in old Virginny, 'twas in de arternoon,
    Oh! Roley, boley!
Wid de gun dat massa gib me, I went to shoot the coon.

    CHORUS.
Wid my hiddy-co-dink-er—mi! who dar?
    Good-mornin', ladies fair.
Wid my hiddy-co-dink-er—mi! who call?
    Good-mornin', ladies all.

He sat on a pine branch, whistlin' a tune,
    Oh! Roley, boley!
I up wid my gun, and brought down Mr. Coon.

    CHORUS.—Wid my hiddy-co-dink-er, etc.

PETE. I tell you what, Cuff; speak to him in a more eliphant manner.

CUFF. Yes, I will. (*goes over to* JOHNSON *in his best style*) Johnson! (*no answer*) Mr. Johnson! (*no answer*) I'll fetch him dis time, Pete. Mr. Samuel Johnson, Exquire!

JOHNSON (*rises and bows politely*). Sar, I am at your sarbice.

CUFF. Excuse my interrupting you, for I see you am busy readin' de paper. Would you be so kind as to enlighten us upon de principal topicks ob de day?

JOHNSON. Well, Mr. Cuff, I hab no objection, 'kase I see dat you common unsophisticated gemmen hab not got edgemcation yourself, and you am 'bliged to come to me who has. So spread around, you unintellumgent bracks, hear de news ob de day discoursed in de most fluid manner. (*He reads out some local items.*) Dar has been a great storm at sea and de ships hab been turned upside down. CUFF (*looks at the paper*). Why, Mr. Johnson, you've got the paper upside down. (ALL *laugh heartily.*)

JOHNSON. Well, yes, so I is. Golly! I didn't take notice ob dat. (*He starts with amazement.*) Oh, what do I see? Has de perfession come to dis degraded persition?

ALL (*shout*). What is it?

JOHNSON. Does my eyes deceibe me! Bracking boots on de Canal street plan for free cents a pair!

ALL (*grab at the paper, which is torn in pieces, and cry*). Whar? Wharabouts?

79

CUFF. I say, Pete, I can't see nuffin' like dat here. (*to* JOHNSON*)* Mr. Johnson, show me dat? (*holds the torn piece to him*)

JOHNSON. Oh, I can't show you now—it's torn out.

CUFF. It won't do, Mr. Johnson. Say, darkeys, don't you tink dat nigger am in lub?

ALL. Yes, yes! (JOHNSON *paces the stage in anger*.) CUFF *sings*.

Sam Johnson, why so solitacious?
    Hah, hah, hah, hah, hah?
'Tis lub dat makes you so vexatious,
    Sam Johnson, ho!

Does your lub lib in Philumdelphy?
    Hah, hah, hah, hah, hah?
Oh! is she poor, or am she wealthy?
    Sam Johnson, ho!

Now, gib him boots and make him travel,
    Hah, hah, hah, hah, hah!
Oh, chuck dem at him widout cavil,
    Sam Johnson, ho!

(JOHNSON *exits.* ALL *throw a perfect shower of boots at* JOHNSON *as soon as he leaves, and begin laughing*.)

CUFF. Dar he goes, Pete. I radder guess Mr. Samuel Johnson, Exquire, won't trouble dis crowd any more wid his presence. (*He sings*.)

De greatest man dat eber libed was Day and Martin,
    Johnny, my lango la!
For he was de fust ob de boot black startin'.
    CHORUS—Johnny, my lango la!

Did you eber see a ginsling made out of brandy?
    Johnny, my lango la!
Did you eber see a pretty gal lickin' lasses candy?
    CHORUS—Johnny, my lango la!

    FULL CHORUS.
Ah, oh—ah! ah, oh-ah! oh—oo-o-o-o!
Ah, oh—ah! ah, oh-ah! oh—oo-o-o-o!

WATCHMAN (*crosses in front, or he may sing outside*).
Past twelve o'clock and a cloudy mornin',
    Johnny, my lango la!
Past twelve o'clock and de daylight dawning,
    Johnny, my lango la!

CUFF (*resumes singing*).
Dat's de old watchman, we're going to fool him,
     Johnny, my lango la!
If he stays outside, de weder will cool him.
     CHORUS—Johnny, my lango la!

Now, cut your sticks, niggers, de daylight's dawning,
     Johnny, my lango la!
We'll meet right here quite early in de mornin'.
     CHORUS—Johnny, my lango la!
(ALL *exit R and L, singing very piano*.)

SCENE II

Exterior of Rose's house. Dark stage. Staccato music. JOHNSON enters with banjo or guitar to serenade.

JOHNSON. Tank heaben! I hab got clar ob dem ruffian darkeys at last. I neber was so grossly insulted in all my life. Dey nearly spiled my best clothes, and—but let's see, I promised to gib my lubly Rosa a serenade dis ebenin', and if I can only find de house. (*goes up to house*) Yes, here is de house—I know it from a tack in de door. (*sings*)
     SONG—"LUBLY ROSA."
Oh! lubly Rosa, Sambo has cum
To salute his lub wid his tum, tum, tum.
So open de door, Rose, and luff me in,
For de way I lub you am a sin.

ROSE (*appears at window and sings*).
Ah, who's dat knocking at my door,
Making such a noise wid his saucy jaw?
I'se looking down upon de stoop,
Like a henhawk on a chicken-coop.
     So clar de kitchen.
JOHNSON.
'Tis Sambo Johnson, dearest dove,
Come like Bacchus, God of Love;
To tell his lubly Rosa how
He's quit his old perfesion now.
     So clar de kitchen.
ROSE.
Oh, hold yer hat and cotch de key,
Come into de little back room wid me;
Sit by de fire and warm your shin,

81

And on de shelf you'll find some gin.
  So clar de kitchen.

(*She drops the key.* JOHNSON *catches it in his hat and exits in house.*)

SCENE III
Interior of Rose's house. Table set—cups and saucers for two—two chairs.

CUFF (*enters R, and sings*).
  SONG—"COAL BLACK ROSE!"
I wonder whar de debil my lubly Rosa's gone,
She's luff me half an hour sittin' all alone.
If she don't come back an' tell me why she didn't stay wid me,
I'll drink all de sassengers and eat up all de tea.

  CHORUS.
Oh, Rose! you coal-black Rose!
I neber lub a gal like I lub dat Rose.

ROSE (*enters R, and sings*).
Now, get up you Cuffy, and gib up dat chair,
Mr. Johnson'll pay de dickens if he cotch you sitting dar.
CUFF.
I doesn't fear de devil, Rose, luff alone dat Sam.
If dat nigger fool his time wid me, I'll hit him
  I'll be—(*breaks a plate*)

  CHORUS—Oh, Rose, etc.

ROSE. Now, get you in de cupboard, Cuff, a little while to stay,
I'll give you plenty applejack when Sambo's gone away.
CUFF. I'll keep my eye upon him—if he 'tempts to kiss or hug,
I'll be down upon him like a duck upon a bug.

(ROSE *conducts* CUFF *to the closet, puts him in, and closes the door.*)

JOHNSON (*heard singing without*)—
Oh, make haste, Rose, for sure as I am born,
I'm trembling like a sweep-oh on a frosty morn.
ROSE. Walk in, Sambo, and don't stand dar a-shakin',
De fire am a-burnin' and de hoe-cake am a-bakin'.

82

Routines: Songs, Speeches, Dialogue, and Farce

JOHNSON (*enters left, looks around the room, and converses ad libitum; he then discovers the table, starts with surprise and sings*).

From de chairs around de table and de two cups of tea,
I see you been to supper and had some company.
ROSE. 'Twas de missionary preacher, dey call him Dr. Birch,
He come to raise a 'scription to build hisself a church.
Come sit you down, Sambo, an' tell me how you've bin.
(JOHNSON *laughs*.)
Why, la bress you, honey, what does make you grin?
JOHNSON. I'd laugh to tink if you was mine, my dear, my lub, my Rose,
I'd gib you eberyting dat's nice, de Lord above knows,
Dar's possum fat an' hominy, and sometimes—
CUFF (*sings out from closet*).   Rice!
JOHNSON. Cowheel an' sugar cane, an' eberyting dat's—
CUFF (*sings out from the closet*).   Nice!
JOHNSON (*gets up, comes front and sings*).
I thought I heard a noise, Rose, it come from ober dar,
ROSE. It was de plaster fallin' down upon de chair.
JOHNSON. But it hollered out rice! as sure as I'm Sambo.
ROSE. It was dat nigger Cuffy upstairs, dat jumps Jim Crow.
JOHNSON. I wish I was a glove, Rose, upon dat lubly hand,
I'd be de happiest nigger ob all in dis land.
My bosom am so full ob lub—'twould soon find some relief,
When you took de glove to wipe your nose instead ob a handkerchief.
        CHORUS—Oh, Rose, etc.
ROSE. My love is strong, and of it's strength dar's none but you can tell.
CUFF. Half past twelve o'clock and all's not well.
JOHNSON. Dat's de old watchman took me up de udder night.
CUFF. Half past twelve o'clock, dar's going to be a fight.
        CHORUS—Oh, Rose, etc.
ROSE. Johnson, now you'd better go, for you see it's getting late,
An' missus will be coming home from de freminate.
JOHNSON. Well, gib me one kiss, Rose—(*tries to kiss her*).
ROSE. Why, Sam, what is you at?
JOHNSON. Why, I'll hug you like a grizzly—what de debil noise am dat?
(CUFF *is trying to get down the gun from shelf, falls down and spills the flour over him.* JOHNSON *gets up stage, brings* CUFF *down front and sings*.)
Who is you, and from whar did you cum?
ROSE. Oh, it am dat nigger Cuff—foreber I'm undone.
CUFF. I'se been out whitewashin' an' feelin' a little tire,
I merely cum to ax Miss Rose for a shobelful ob fire.

JOHNSON. Tell me, you saucy nigger, how you do on dat shelf?

CUFF. I was pretty well, I thank you, pray, how do you find yourself?

JOHNSON. Come, no prevarication or I'll smash dat calabash.

ROSE. Oh, Johnson, be advised by me—he's noffin's else but trash.

JOHNSON. Is dis your constancy, Miss Rose, you tell me ob all day!

CUFF. Why, de wench she am dumbfounded, and don't know what to say.

ROSE. I neber saw his face before—his berry sight I hates

I believe he am a runaway from de nullifying States.

CUFF. Say, tell me, Mr. Johnson, what dat nigger jaculates?

JOHNSON. Why, she says you am a runaway from de nullifyin' States.

CUFF. Dat's enuff to make a jaybird split his shin in two,

For here's my free papers dat I carry in my shoe.

(*shows his papers*)

    CHORUS—Oh, Rose, etc.

By dat darkey's peroration and his sarcarmastus grin,

1'll bet he gets a lickin' afore he does begin.

JOHNSON. Be off, you common nigger!

CUFF. Not until we hab a fight.

And, Rose, don't you interfere, I'll show dis moke a sight.

(*clinches* JOHNSON, *and they fight*)

    ROSE (*screams, seizes frying pan, and strikes* CUFF *over his head, breaking the* bottom).

Fire! help! murder, suicide, all sorts ob death!

JOHNSON. Stand off, you common nigger, gib me time to draw a breff.

(PETE *and* OTHERS *enter.*)

PETE. What's de matter, Rose, dat you gib dat Injun yelp?

ROSE. Why, it's Cuffy killin' Sambo, and I was cryin' out for help.

PETE (*raises and supports* CUFF, *while someone does the same to* JOHNSON).

Cuffy, is you much hurt?

CUFF. Oh, no, I'm only drawing my last breff. You'd better take me to the hoss-pistol.

PETE. Why, Cuff!

CUFF. Oh, I don't know; but I hardly tink I shall live more dan twenty-five years longer. (CUFF *and* JOHNSON *have now regained their feet.*)

JOHNSON (*starts*). Why, Cuff!

CUFF. Why Johnson!

JOHNSON. Rose, my love, pray tell me how this cum so?

ROSE. Well, dear, I will, since you really want to know:

You see, he sweeps de street, and blacks de gemmen's shoes,

But when he gets de liquor in, he don't know what he does.

CUFF (*sings to* ROSE).

If I'd married you, Miss Rose, I'd surely had a curse,

I offered for to take you for better or for worse;
But I was blind wid lub, your faults I couldn't see.
You is a deal sight worser dan I took you for to be.
    CHORUS—Oh, Rose, etc.

JOHNSON (*crosses over to* CUFF). Mr. Cuff, I ax your pardon.
CUFF. Mr. Johnson, dar's my hand. An Rose, I'm glad to find my head was harder dan your pan. But dar's no use to keep up grievances, since love am all by chance. So jest hand down de fiddle, Pete, and let us hab a dance. Come, darks, take your places and I'll saw the catgut.

(*They form and go through a reel.* CUFF *gets excited while* ROSE *and* JOHNSON *are dancing, and, jumping up, he breaks the fiddle over* JOHNSON*'s head.* ROSE *faints and is caught by* SOME ONE. JOHNSON *falls at her feet.* CUFF *stands with uplifted hands.*)
    ALL FORM PICTURE

Commentary: Rise and Fall of "Slave" Creativity

The New York *Knickerbocker* interpreted the popularity of minstrels in England as recognition of the New World's potential for genuinely original cultural achievements. The best of America's writers had composed in the English idiom, and distinguished as many were, their poetry was not "*peculiarly of America.*" Now, at last, here was an answer to the Rev. Sydney Smith's jibe. Most of the minstrel songs were copied from the slaves who, because of their isolation and ignorance, had little contact with European literature. These were most certainly "strongly of the locality" and uniquely American.

[J. K.], "Who Are Our National Poets?" *Knickerbocker* 26 (October 1845): 331–32, 335–36, 341.

Foreigners read BRYANT, and HALLECK, and LONGFELLOW, and hearing these called our best poets, and perceiving nothing in their poems which might not just as well have been written in England, or by Englishmen, they infer that as the productions of those who stand highest among our poets have nothing about them which savors *peculiarly* of America, therefore America has no national poetry; a broad conclusion from narrow premises. . . .

Applying this rule to America, in which class of our population must we look for our truly original and American poets? What class is most secluded from foreign influences, receives the narrowest education, travels the shortest distance from home, has the least amount of spare cash, and mixes least with any class above itself? Our negro slaves, to be sure! *That* is the class in which we must expect to find our original poets, and there we do find them. From that class come the Jim Crows, the Zip

Coons, and the Dandy Jims, who have electrified the world. From them proceed our only truly national poets.

When Burns was *discovered*, he was immediately taken away from the plough, carried to Edinburgh, and feted and lionized to the "fulness of satiety." James Crow and Scipio Coon never were discovered, personally; and if they had been, their owners would not have spared them from work. Alas! that poets should be ranked with horses, and provided with owners accordingly! In this, however, our negro poets are not peculiarly unfortunate. . . .

Who is the man of genius? He who utters clearly that which is dimly felt by all. He who most vividly represents the sentiment, intellect and taste of the public to which he addresses himself. He to whom all hearts and heads respond. Take our "national poets," for example, who being unknown individually, we may personify collectively as the American SAMBO. Is not Sambo a genius? All tastes are delighted, all intellects are astonished, all hearts respond to his utterances; at any rate, all pianofortes do, and a hundred thousand of the sweetest voices in christendom. What more convincing proof of genius was ever presented to the world? Is not Sambo the incarnation of the taste, intellect and heart of America, the ladies being the judges? Do not shrink from the answer, most beautiful, accomplished, delicate and refined lady-reader! You cannot hold yourself above him, for you imitate him; you spend days and weeks in learning his tunes; you trill his melodies with your rich voice; you are delighted with his humor, his pathos, his irresistible fun. Say truly, incomparable damsel! is not Sambo the realization of your poetic ideal?

But our national melodists have many imitators. Half of the songs published as theirs are, as far as the words are concerned, the productions of "mean whites"; but base counterfeits as they are, they pass current with most people as genuine negro songs. Thus is it ever with true excellence! . . . Every imitator acknowledges the superior excellence of his model. The greater the number of imitators, the stronger is the evidence of that superiority; the warmer their reception by the public, the more firmly becomes established the genius of the original.

But the music and the dancing are all Sambo's own. No one attempts to introduce any thing new *there*. In truth they, with the chorus, constitute all that is essentially permanent in the negro song. The blacks themselves leave out old stanzas, and introduce new ones at pleasure. Travelling through the South, you may, in passing from Virginia to Louisiana, hear the same tune a hundred times, but seldom the same words accompanying it. This necessarily results from the fact that the songs are unwritten, and also from the habit of extemporizing, in which the performers indulge on festive occasions. Let us picture one of these scenes, which often occur on the estates of kind masters, seldom on those of the cruel. So true is this, that the frequent sound of the violin, banjo, or jaw-bone lute, is as sure an indication of the former, as its general absence is of the latter. . . .

Give heed to foreign reviewers; doubt no longer that nationality is the highest merit that poetry can possess; uneducate yourselves; consult the taste of your fair

Commentary: Rise and Fall of "Slave" Creativity

countrywomen; write no more English poems; write negro songs, and Yankee songs in negro style; take lessons in dancing of the celebrated Thomas Rice; appear upon the stage and perform your own operas; do this, and not only will fortune and fame be yours, but you will thus vindicate yourselves and your country from the foul imputation under which both now rest! With *your* names on the list with Crow and Coon, who *then* will dare to say that America has no national poets?

Ten years later, a writer in *Putnam's Monthly* also believed that the original, "ancient" minstrel songs of the 1820s and 1830s had authentic folk roots in the plantation songs of southern black slaves. However, Y. S. Nathanson believed a far greater proportion of the songs of the 1840s had been "peculiar, genuine and unadulterated," and was dismayed that current offerings were so inferior to the "ancient" minstrel compositions.

[Y. S. Nathanson], "Negro Minstrelsy—Ancient and Modern," *Putnam's Monthly* 5 (January 1855): 72–74, 75–76, 79.

It is now some eighteen or twenty years since an enterprising Yankee . . . produced upon the boards of one of our metropolitan theatres, a musical sketch entitled "Jim Crow." . . . To those (if there can be any such) who are unacquainted with its character and general scope, it may be proper to remark that "Jim Crow" is what may be called a dramatic song, depending for its success, perhaps more than any play ever written for the stage, upon the action and mimetic powers of the performer. Its success was immediate and marked. It touched a chord in the American heart which had never before vibrated, but which now responded to the skilful fingers of its first expounder. . . . Popularity like this laughs at anathemas from the pulpit, or sneers from the press. The song which is sung in the parlor, hummed in the kitchen, and whistled in the stable, may defy oblivion. But such signal and triumphant success can produce but one result. Close upon the heels of Jim Crow, came treading, one after the other, "Zip Coon," "Long-Tailed Blue," "Ole Virginny neber tire," "Settin' on a Rail," and a host of others, all of superior merit, though unequaled alike in their intrinsic value, and in their participation in public approval. The golden age of negro literature had commenced. Thenceforward for several years the appearance of a new melody was an event whose importance can hardly be appreciated by the coming generation. It flew from mouth to mouth, and from hamlet to hamlet, with a rapidity which seemed miraculous. . . .

The prevailing characteristics of the melodies which this period produced are their perfect and continual lightness, spirit, and good humor; but the true secret of their favor with the world is to be found in the fact that they are genuine and real. They are no useless and ridiculous imitations forged in the dull brain of some northern self-styled minstrel, but the veritable tunes and words which have lightened the labor of some weary negro in the cotton fields, amused his midnight hours as he fished, or waked the spirits of the woods as he followed in the track of the wary racoon. It is . . . impossible to counterfeit, or successfully imitate, one of these songs. . . .

MINSTRELSY

In the terseness and fitness of the language, the oft-repeated idiomatic expressions, the occasional looseness and negligence in respect to rhyme, the carelessness and license in the metre, and above all, in the incoherence of the constantly recurring refrain, the lover of negro minstrelsy is constantly reminded of the old, plain songs which Shakespeare loved. . . .

The lightness and prevailing good humor of the negro songs, have been before remarked upon. A true southern melody is seldom sentimental, and never melancholy. And this results directly from the character and habits of the colored race. No hardships or troubles can destroy, or even check their happiness and levity. . . .

In or about the year 1841, a descriptive ballad, entitled "Ole Dan Tucker," first made its appearance, and speedily acquired a renown and popularity hardly excelled, even by that of "Jim Crow." This may be partly attributable to the fact that less histrionic talent is required to give it a fitting interpretation, and partly to its intrinsic worth. In some respects Ole Dan Tucker may be regarded as the best of what I have denominated the ancient negro ballads. The melody was far superior to anything that had preceded it. In its vivacity and liveliness, the music occasionally reminds us of some of Donizetti's happiest efforts, while its simplicity and quaintness at times breathe of Auber. The words, too, came more dearly home to the heart of the American people, than those of its predecessors. The song, it is needless to say, consists of a series of vivid pictures, disconnected in themselves, varying as rapidly as the changes in a kaleidoscope, and yet presenting to us the character of the hero, as a most artistic whole. The most searching test of popularity can be applied to "Ole Dan Tucker" with perfect confidence. It has been sung, perhaps, oftener than any melody ever written.

I have said that this was in some aspects the best of these songs. It was the last. With that ballad African minstrelsy may be said to have culminated. From that period its decline and fall was rapid and saddening. Hardly a song has been produced since that time which does not present the most glaring marks of barefaced and impudent imposition. . . . Vile parodies, sentimental love songs, dirges for dead wenches who are generally sleeping under the willow, on the bank of some stream, and melancholy reminiscences of negroic children fill the places once allotted to the grand old ballads of former days. . . . They have lost their country grace without acquiring a city polish. This inundation of trash has swept away in its might all the ancient landmarks of song. . . .

Instead of the lyrics which once stirred the heart of the nation, our wives and children . . . are fortunate if they get to bed without being wearied and disgusted with some crude burlesque on a popular opera, served up with vulgar caricatures of the style and manner of well-known artists. . . . It is from the purpose of negroic minstrelsy, whose end at the first was, and now ought to be, to present to the lovers of original poetry and music, a class of songs, peculiar, genuine, and unadulterated. A thoughtful, reflective man, can hardly leave one of the temples devoted to such barbaric sacrifices, without reasonable and just despondency and alarm. . . .

Commentary: Rise and Fall of "Slave" Creativity

It is earnestly to be desired that collections of genuine plantation songs may be made. The grateful incense of posterity would embalm the memory of him who should hand down to them authentic ballads, which another generation may sweep from the face of the earth forever.

The liberal *New York Tribune* considered "the black opera" the equal to Italian opera in the enjoyment it gave its audience. Unfortunately, conditions for the southern slaves who inspired such music had declined in twenty years and their more serious songs were reflected in the loss of inspiration and originality in the large minstrel troupes. At its best, the music of the "Ethiopian" banjo had been as expressive as the "lyre of the ancients" and appealed to the young.

"The Black Opera," *New York Tribune*, June 30, 1855.

Absurd as may seem negro minstrelsy to the refined musician, it is nevertheless beyond doubt that it expresses the peculiar characteristics of the negro as truly as the great masters of Italy represent their more spiritual and profound nationality. And although the melody of "Long-tailed Blue" may not possess the intellectual properties of an aria by Bellini, yet it will contain as much truth to the humanity of which it assumes to be the exponent, and quite as much enthusiasm will be manifested by its listeners. . . .

Mr. T. D. Rice made his debut in a dramatic sketch entitled "Jim Crow," and from that moment everybody was "doing just so," and continued "doing just so" for months, and even years afterward. Never was there such an excitement in the musical or dramatic world; nothing was talked of, nothing written of, and nothing dreamed of but "Jim Crow." The most sober citizens began to "wheel about, and turn about, and Jump Jim Crow." It seemed as though the entire population had been bitten by the tarantula; in the parlor, in the kitchen, in the shop and in the street, Jim Crow monopolised public attention. It must have been a species of insanity, though of a gentle and pleasing kind, for it made hearts lighter, and merrier, and happier; it smoothed away frowns and wrinkles, and replaced them with smiles. Its effects were visible alike on youth and age.

The success of Mr. Rice called out numerous imitators. . . . The homeliness, the truthfulness of these compilations, established their popularity. There was nothing factitious in them; they filled a void in public amusement, which was beginning to be sensibly experienced, and from their very naturalness, appealed to the sympathy of the multitude. Particularly was this the case with the younger portion of our population, most of whom have grown up to be men and women since then. For if the songs were of a humorous character, it was humor of a gushing, positive kind—boisterous fun, just suited to the exuberant nature of youth, and not without its effect upon the risibilities of the oldest; or if the air was a saddened one, there was a pathos in its mournful simplicity, quite as impressive as any waves of melody which ever gushed from the soul of a composer. Who has not often observed the tear of sensibility moistening the cheek of youth, while listening to the primitive strains of "Uncle Ned"—that poor old colored gentleman, who has gone "where the good darkies go"? Ah, these tears constituted one of the blessings of that youth, which has now departed. Sorrow and disappointment have doubtless weighed heavily upon many a heart since that spring of life passed away, with its smiles and tears. We can no longer smile at "Lucy Neal," nor weep at the pathetic story of "Uncle Edward." And in the meantime, has there been no change in the feelings of the true originators of this music—the negroes themselves? Are the great mass of those held to labor on Southern plantations the same careless, brutalized race they were twenty years ago? We believe not. Let the Southern traveler of to-day compare notes with one who went over the ground even ten years ago, and he will find a striking change in the mental characteristics of this unhappy people. The gay laugh and cheerful song are not heard with former frequency; there is loss of that noisy exuberance which not long since was regarded as a trait in the African disposition. The old, unmeaning compositions of the plantation have fallen into disuse, and if they sing now there is memory in their songs. Plaintive and slow, the sad soul of the slave throws into his music all that gushing anguish of spirit which he dare not otherwise express. And yet the careless reviewer of events, observing not the causes or consequences, mourns what he terms the decadence of national negro minstrelsy! . . .

There is some truth in the assertion that the music has deteriorated. We find that Miss Nancyism of vulgarity assuming a place in the concert room among the votaries of burnt cork, bones, and banjo. The sickly sentimentality which has of late characterized the productions of the majority of these companies, so well as the wholesale plagiarism of music now sysytematically pursued, has had the impact of injuring the claims of minstrelsy to originality. Let us hope that this will not be longer tolerated by the directors of the colored orchestra.

Reminiscences

Ralph Keeler was only twelve years old, orphaned and living with a relative in Detroit, when he witnessed minstrel song and dance. Constant practice and a natural talent for dance allowed him to escape being a newspaper seller and to enjoy a brief show business career with a series of small minstrel companies traveling on railroads and riverboats throughout the South and West in the early 1850s.

Ralph Keeler, "Three Years as a Negro Minstrel," *Atlantic Monthly* 24 (July 1869): 71, 73–74, 75, 77.

Negro minstrels were, I think, more highly esteemed at the time of which I am about to write than they are now; at least, I thought more of them then, both as individuals and as ministers to public amusement, than I have ever since. The first troupe of the kind I saw was the old "Kunkels," and I can convey no idea of the pleasurable thrill I felt at the banjo solo and the plantation jig. I resolved on the spot to be a negro minstrel. . . . Meanwhile I bought a banjo, and had pennies screwed on the heels of my boots, and practised "Jordan" on the former, and the "Juba" dance with the latter, till my boarding-house keeper gave me a warning. . . . It may be owned that I had no natural aptness for the banjo, and was always an indifferent player; but for dancing I had, I am confident, such a remarkable gift as few have ever had. Up to this day, I do not think I ever have seen a step done by man or woman that I could not do as soon as I saw it,—not saying, of course, how gracefully. . . .

I was still so small of stature, and yet capable of producing so much noise with the coppers on my heels, that, by the wholesale clerks and young bloods about town, I was considered in the light of a prodigy, and made to shuffle my feet at almost all hours and in almost all localities. It was by this means, at some place of convivial resort, that I attracted the notice and admiration of a conductor on the Michigan Southern and Northern Indiana Railroad. He determined to have so much talent with him all the time, and prevailed upon me to be his train-boy [selling books and papers]. . . .

[In a Toledo bar, he met Johnny Booker and joined his minstrel troupe for five dollars and expenses a week.] It is impossible to convey an idea of the gratified ambition with which I prepared for my first appearance on the stage. The great Napoleon, in the coronation robes which can be seen any day in the Tuileries, was not prouder than I made my initial bow before the foot-nights, in my small Canton flannel knee-pants, cheap lace, gold tinsel, corked face, and woolly wig. I do not remember any embarrassment, for I was only doing in public what I had already done for the majority of the audience in private. . . .

We now started on our travels, staying from one night to a week in a city, according to its size, stopping always at the best hotels, and leading the merriest of lives generally. . . . It was deemed a good advertisement, as well as in some metaphysical way conducive to the morale of the company, to dress as nearly alike as we could, when off the stage. This had the effect, as will be readily understood, of pointing me out more prominently than ever as the juvenile prodigy, whose portrait and assumed name were plastered about over the towns and cities through which we took our triumphal march. The first part of our performances we gave with white faces, and I had so improved my opportunities that I was now able to appear as the Scotch girl in plaid petticoats, who executes the inevitable Highland fling in such exhibitions. By practising in my room through many tedious days, I learned to knock and spin and toss about the tambourine on the end of my forefinger; and having rehearsed a budget of stale jokes, I was promoted to be one of the "end-men" in the first part of the negro performances. . . . In addition to my jig, I now appeared in all sorts of *pas de deux*, took the principal part in negro ballets, and danced "Lucy Long." I am told that I looked the wench admirably.

MINSTRELSY

In late 1906 Mark Twain dictated memories of his youth. In these auto-biographical fragments, published posthumously, he remembered fondly the first minstrels he had seen as a small boy in Hannibal, Missouri, in the early 1840s. Twain's mother, however, respected the sentiments of the fundamentalist denominations and regarded both the circus and the minstrel show as hostile to religion and morality.

Mark Twain in Eruption: Hitherto Unpublished Pages about Men and Events, ed. Bernard de Voto (New York: Harper and Row, 1940), 110–18.

[T]he real nigger show—the genuine nigger show, the extravagant show, the extravagant nigger show—the show . . . to me had no peer and whose peer has not yet arrived, in my experience. We have the grand opera; and I have witnessed and greatly enjoyed the first act of everything which Wagner created, but the effect on me has always been so powerful that one act was quite sufficient; whenever I have witnessed two acts I have gone away physically exhausted; and whenever I have ventured an entire opera the result has been the next thing to suicide. But if I could have the nigger show back again in its pristine purity and perfection, I should have but little further use for opera. It seems to me that to the elevated mind and the sensitive spirit, the hand organ and the nigger show are a standard and a summit to whose rarefied altitude the other forms of musical art may not hope to reach.

I remember the first negro musical show I ever saw. It must have been in the early forties. It was a new institution. In our village of Hannibal we had not heard of it before, and it burst upon us as a glad and stunning surprise.

The show remained a week and gave a performance every night. Church members did not attend these performances, but all the worldlings flocked to them and were enchanted. Church members did not attend shows out there in those days. The minstrels appeared with coal-black hands and faces and their clothing was a loud and extravagant burlesque of the clothing worn by the plantation slave of the time; not that the rags of the poor slave were burlesqued, for that would not have been possible; burlesque could have added nothing in the way of extravagance to the sorrowful accumulation of rags and patches which constituted his costume; it was the form and color of his dress that was burlesqued. Standing collars were in fashion in that day, and the minstrel appeared in a collar which engulfed and hid the half of his head and projected so far forward that he could hardly see sideways over its points. His coat was sometimes made of curtain calico with a swallowtail that hung nearly to his heels and had buttons as big as a blacking box. His shoes were rusty and clumsy and cumbersome, and five or six sizes too large for him. There were many variations upon this costume and they were all extravagant, and were by many believed to be funny.

The minstrel used a very broad negro dialect; he used it competently and with easy facility, and it was funny—delightfully and satisfyingly funny. However, there was one member of the minstrel troupe of those early days who was not extravagantly dressed and did not use the negro dialect. He was clothed in the faultless evening costume of the white society gentleman and used a stilted, courtly, artificial, and painfully grammatical form of speech, which the innocent villagers took for the real thing as exhibited in high and citified society, and they vastly admired it and envied the man who could frame it on the spot without reflection and deliver it in this easy and fluent and artistic fashion. "Bones" sat at one end of the row of minstrels, "Banjo" sat at the other end, and the dainty gentleman just described sat in the middle. This middleman was the spokesman of the show. The neatness and elegance of his dress, the studied courtliness of his manners and speech, and the shapeliness of his undoctored features made him a contrast to the rest of the troupe and particularly to "Bones" and "Banjo." "Bones" and "Banjo" were the prime jokers and whatever funniness was to be gotten out of paint and exaggerated clothing they utilized to the limit. Their lips were thickened and lengthened with bright red paint to such a degree that their mouths resembled slices cut in a ripe watermelon.

The original ground plan of the minstrel show was maintained without change for a good many years. There was no curtain to the stage in the beginning; while the audience waited they had nothing to look at except the row of empty chairs back of the footlights; presently the minstrels filed in and were received with a wholehearted welcome; they took their seats, each with his musical instrument in his hand; then the aristocrat in the middle began with a remark like this:

"I hope, gentlemen, I have the pleasure of seeing you in your accustomed excellent health, and that everything has proceeded prosperously with you since last we had the good fortune to meet."

"Bones" would reply for himself and go on and tell about something in the nature of peculiarly good fortune that had lately fallen to his share; but in the midst of it he would be interrupted by "Banjo," who would throw doubt upon his statement of the matter; then a delightful jangle of assertion and contradiction would break out between the two; the quarrel would gather emphasis, the voices would grow louder and louder and more and more energetic and vindictive, and the two would rise and approach each other, shaking fists and instruments and threatening bloodshed, the courtly middleman meantime imploring them to preserve the peace and observe the proprieties—but all in vain, of course. Sometimes the quarrel would last five minutes, the two contestants shouting deadly threats in each other's faces with their noses not six inches apart, the house shrieking with laughter all the while at this happy and accurate imitation of the usual and familiar negro quarrel, then finally the pair of malignants would gradually back away from each other, each making impressive threats as to what was going to happen the "next time" each should have the misfortune to cross the other's path; then they would sink into their chairs and growl back and forth at each other across the front of the line until the house had had time to recover from its convulsions and hysterics and quiet down.

The aristocrat in the middle of the row would now make a remark which was surreptitiously intended to remind one of the end men of an experience of his of a humorous nature and fetch it out of him—which it always did. It was usually an experience of a stale and moldy sort and as old as America. One of these things, which always delighted the audience of those days until the minstrels wore it thread-bare, was "Bones's" account of the perils which he had once endured during a storm at sea. The storm lasted so long that in the course of time all the provisions were consumed. Then the middleman would inquire anxiously how the people managed to survive.

"Bones" would reply, "We lived on eggs." "You lived on eggs! Where did you get eggs?"

"Every day, when the storm was so bad, the Captain laid to."

During the first five years that joke convulsed the house, but after that the popula-tion of the United States had heard it so many times that they respected it no longer and always received it in a deep and reproachful and indignant silence, along with others of its caliber which had achieved disfavor by long service.

The minstrel troupes had good voices and both their solos and their choruses were a delight to me as long as the negro show continued in existence. In the begin-ning the songs were rudely comic, such as "Buffalo Gals," "Camptown Races," "Old Dan Tucker," and so on; but a little later sentimental songs were introduced, such as "The Blue Juniata," "Sweet Ellen Bayne," "Nelly Bly," "A Life on the Ocean Wave," "The Larboard Watch," etc.

The minstrel show was born in the early forties and it had a prosperous career for about thirty-five years; then it degenerated into a variety show and was nearly all variety show with a negro act or two thrown in incidentally. The real negro show has been stone dead for thirty years. To my mind it was a thoroughly delightful thing, and a most competent laughter-compeller and I am sorry it is gone.

Bayard Taylor was the most renowned American travel writer of his day. During a trip to Gold Rush California, he visited the only theater in the territory in Sacramento. Miners were attracted to the nightlife shows by the drinking and gambling and by the minstrelsy, including Stephen Foster's song "Oh! Susanna" of 1847, which was one of the earliest imports from the East.

Bayard Taylor, *Eldorado, or, Adventures in the Path of Empire, comprising a voyage to California, via Panama; life in San Francisco and Monterey; pictures of the gold region; and experiences of Mexican travel* (1850; New York: G. P. Putnam's Sons, 1882), 275.

Some of the establishments have small companies of Ethiopian melodists, who nightly call upon "Susanna!" and entreat to be carried back to Old Virginny. These songs are universally popular, and the crowd of listeners is often so great as to embar-rass the player at the monte tables and injure the business of the gamblers. I confess to a strong liking for the Ethiopian airs, and used to spend half an hour every night in listening to them and watching the curious expressions of satisfaction and delight in the faces of the overland emigrants, who always attended in a body. The spirit of the music is always encouraging; even its most doleful passages had a grotesque touch of cheerfulness—a mingling of sincere pathos and whimsical consolation, which some-how took hold of all moods in which it might be heard, raising them to the same notch of careless good-humor. The Ethiopian melodies well deserve to be called, as they are in fact, the national airs of America. Their quaint, mock-sentimental cadences, so well suited to the broad absurdity of the words—their reckless gaiety and irreverent famil-iarity with serious subjects—and their spirit of antagonism and perseverance—are true expressions of the more popular sides of the national character. They follow the American race in all its emigrations, colonizations and conquests, as certainly as the Fourth of July and Thanksgiving Day. The penniless and half despairing emigrant is stimulated to try again by the sound of "It'll never do to give it up so!" and feels a pang of home-sickness at the burthen of the "Old Virginia Shore."

Musical Comedy: Harrigan's Mulligan Guard

Edward Harrigan was of distant Irish descent but grew up in New York's Lower East Side in a proud, working-class, Irish American culture. His specialty in the theater was an Irish comic and blackface minstrel. In 1871 he teamed up with Tony Hart (Anthony J. Cannon) in a highly successful partnership which lasted thirteen years. Their main repertoire was comic sketches of urban life interspersed with songs to music composed by David Braham. A ten-minute act that Harrigan wrote in 1873 was expanded into *The Mulligan Guard Ball* in 1879. Six more plays continuing the saga of the Mulligan family followed in the next two years, and two more in 1883–84. The narrative thread was the social activities surrounding the Irish-American target company led by Daniel Mulligan, and its interaction with local residents, primarily Germans and blacks. Other immigrant groups—Italians and Chinese, and, occasionally, Jews—were added to the Mulligan series in the 1880s.

Harrington's productions were formulaic. They played on what contem-poraries saw as affectionate ethnic stereotypes, on garish, ill-fitting uniforms, on elements of farce—slapstick fights and explosions—and the obligatory three or four jaunty songs. *The Mulligan Guard Ball* was first performed at Broadway's Theatre Comique from January 13 to May 19, 1879, and revived twice in the 1880s. Tommy, son of Dan Mulligan, and Katy, daughter of the local German butcher, Gustavus Lochmuller, are secretly in love. The rivalry of their fathers, and the pretensions of the "colored" barber Simpson Primrose and preacher Palestine Puter, provide most of the comic interest and oppor-tunities for song. Inadvertently, both the Irish Mulligan Guard and the black Skidmore Guard hold their annual dances in different rooms in the Harp and Shamrock hall. There are uniformed crowd roles for ill-assorted Guards and their gaudy ladies, for six "Dutch" butchers, and two blackface "wenches."

Edward Harrigan, *The Mulligan Guard Ball* (1879), in *Dramas from the American Theatre, 1762–1909*, ed. Richard Moody (Boston: Houghton Mifflin, 1966), 555–58, 559.

MINSTRELSY

Act I Scene 3

A barber shop with two chairs R.H. and a hair dresser's L.H. A division piece with practical door from barber shop to hair dresser's. Set door L.H. of hair dresser's. Table and wig block with wig on in hair dresser's—and table with papers R.H. of barber shop. Hooks for coats. Barber utensils. At opening, MAGGIE KIERNEY discovered in hair dresser's combing a wig. SIM PRIMROSE brushing Skidmore uniform at table, R.H. of barber shop.

SIM: I'd give a hundred dollars to know de man dat dropped dat kerosene on dat coat. I only wore it once in parade—last 'Mancipation Day. Dar'll be some hot coons at de Skids tonight, and I wouldn't have anybody smell kerosene on me for a million dollars.

Enter Dan Mulligan and Lochmuller D. in F. [Down in Front.] Dan takes off coat, hanging it up, and Lochmuller in evening dress. Both hang clothes up without observing each other and get in chairs.

SIM: Next—[*With razor and paper, going to Lochmuller*]

DAN: Look here, sir—I'm next.

SIM: [*Going to Dan*] 'Scuse me, sir—I didn't observe—

LOCHMULLER: Here, look here once—Mr. Primrose, I'm next.

DAN: Yis, that's right, he's next after me.

LOCHMULLER: [*In chair*] No, I am next before you.

SIM: My apprentice will be here in a minute.

LOCHMULLER: No—I wont be shaved by de printer, I have got my cup and razor here—

DAN: Go on, Primrose, shave me first. If you don't, the Divel a one of the Mulligans 'ill never lather here again.

SIM: Gemmen, I'm sorry. If I was a Simese twin I could shave both.

LOCHMULLER: Shave me first. I have as much pull in de Mulligan Guard as any man in de city, and Dan Mulligan is my friend.

DAN: [*Getting up on stage from chair*] That's my name, sir—and no man is my friend.

[*Lochmuller who has got on stage*] Oh—[*Aside*] If it wasn't for the 35 dollars.

LOCHMULLER: Mister Mulligan excuse me—I thought you vas somebody vat I didn't know—

DAN: Oh, that's all right.

SIM: [*With lather and brush*] When you settle de little difference, I'm ready, gemmen—

LOCHMULLER: Oh, dat's all right. I would fight for Dan Mulligan to-morrow—or de Mulligan Guards neither.

DAN: Oh, I know that. [*Aside*] Oh, if the ball was over—

LOCHMULLER: My wife und my little boy und Katy is all dressed for de ball, und so im I, und my wife is waiting for me on de corner. So uf you will let me shave first—why—

DAN: My wife is waiting for me—and I'm not dressed yet—so I must shave first.

SIM: I'll tell you, gemmen—I'll settle it. I want no quarrelling in de shop. I'll shave one half of you, and den I'll shave half of you—den you'll both get shaved at de same time.

DAN: That's all right. Free trade and sailor's rights is all I ax for—[*Getting into chair*]

LOCHMULLER: I don't want any domestic trouble. [*Getting into chair*] I'm satisfied.

SIM: Gemmen, dar's nuffing like a mutual friend—I'll begin on Germany, if Ireland will allow me—[*Going to Lochmuller and lathering one side of his face*]

DAN: Have you the *Clipper*?

SIM: Yes [*Getting paper from table R.H.*] Dar it is, de latest. [*Gives paper to Dan. Sim begins to shave Lochmuller*]

DAN: I see here where Buck McCarthy licked the Dutch Butcher in two rounds—

LOCHMULLER: [*Sitting up*] Yes, I know, but what kind of fair play vas dat—when all de goes out men jumped in and cut de rope?

DAN: I have here the referee's decision. Money and belt given to McCarthy.

SIM: Orlando Whippletree, de colored teacher in de gymasim—I see in de *Christian Observer* has challenged McCarthy and de Butcher together.

DAN: Oh, he's a walk away for Duck.

LOCHMULLER: Do you suppose a German would fight mit a nigger?

SIM: Say, look here—do you see dis razor—I'm Sim Primrose, Captain of de Skidmore Guard. Every man of them is N. G., a nice gemman. Now I want you to apologize or I'll draw dis across your jugular.

DAN: A man has no right to insult a colored man to his face.

SIM: Take it back.

LOCHMULLER: I mean dat a colored man could whip any German in de world.

SIM: Well dat settles it. [*Getting lather and brush and going to Dan*] Now I'll take de grass off of Ireland—[*Lathers one side of Dan's face*]

LOCHMULLER: Jiminy Christmas, I can't say nutting. I must get my other side shaved—Have you got de German paper here—[*Going to table*] Yes, here is de German *Puck*—I read it. [*Sits in chair and reads. Enter Tommy Mulligan and Katrine Lochmuller in hairdresser apartment L.H.*]

KATY: Oh, Maggie—[*Kissing her*]

MAGGIE: Oh, Katy—All ready for the ball, eh—

KATY: No, not quite, just fix my hair a little.

MAGGIE: How do you do, Tommy. Sit down. [*Puts chair for Tommy near door in division piece*] Now, Katy. [*Sits Katy in chair which Maggie has vacated and fixes her hair*]

KATY: He—he—he [*Laughing*]

LOCHMULLER: I hear dat laugh before—dat's funny. [*Reads*]

MAGGIE: What's the matter, Katy?

KATY: Tell her, Tommy.

TOMMY: Maggie, Katy ain't got spunk enough to tell you—I've got to go to the Mulligan Ball with the Guards, and Katy is going with her father and mother—Well, I never put up a job like this. [*Looking at hair modestly*]

SIM: I tell you we're going to have a hot ball tonight.

DAN: [*In agony*] Yes—but look!

SIM: All de first class colored families on Sixth Avenue 'ill be dar.

DAN: [*In agony*] Hay—

TOMMY: What's that next door, Maggie?

MAGGIE: A barber shop—no body but Skidmores shave there.

TOMMY: Oh—

SIM: Dares no military organization in de world like de Skidmore Guard. [*Going to shelf*]

DAN: Oh, I thought you were talking about the Mulligans.

SIM: I never mix wid dem kind of people. 'Scuse me, gemmen, I'm out of bay rum—I'll be back in a minute. [*Exit door in flat*]

TOMMY: Well, Maggie, what I was going to say was—[*Bashfully*]

DAN: That sounds like Tommy's voice. I'll see—[*Looks through keyhole*] There's nothing there—[*Going to chair*]

TOMMY: That my old man don't want me to marry Katy, and her old man don't like me, nor my old man either—and [*Bashfully*]

DAN: [*With paper*] There is more Irish in our district than there is German, Lochmuller.

LOCHMULLER: Yes, but dare is more German babies in Avenue A, dan dare is tombstones in Greenwood Cemetery.

DAN: Well, I'll not argue—

TOMMY: And we want to know if you will come to the ball and when we run away at intermission, will you stand up for Katy—when we get married?

MAGGIE: [*Aloud*] Will I, Tommy, certainly, and I know two people who will go crazy—

KATY: Who, Maggie?

MAGGIE: Mister Mulligan and Mister Lochmuller. [*Katy and Maggie and Tommy laugh heartily. Lochmuller and Mulligan get out of chairs*]

DAN: I'll go crazy.

LOCHMULLER: Lochmuller go crazy. [*Both go to door and pull one another away twice when Dan gets a peep*]

DAN: [*Aside*] Be the mortal Harry, it's my boy Tommy with the Dutchman's daughter.

LOCHMULLER: [*Looks in keyhole. Aside*] It's my Katrine, mit Tommy Mulligan.

TOMMY: I'll give the old man the laugh—eh. Maggie? [*Laughing*]

DAN: He'll give me the laugh—Oh, if it wasn't for the thirty-five dollars.

KATY: Won't the Swiss warbler kick when he finds out I'm married, eh, Tommy?

LOCHMULLER: [*Aside*] She laugh at Mr. Krime, de baritone singer—Oh, Katrine—[*Looking at Mulligan*] Off it vas not dat I lose his custom—

TOMMY: Come, Katy, hurry—don't give it away, Maggie—Remember intermission time.

KATY: Good-bye, Maggie—[*Exit Tommy and Katy door in F. at back of hair dresser's*]

DAN: [*To Lochmuller*] I owe you thirty-five dollars, let it go—I want to ax you father to father—What do you want to let your girl come around my boy for? Let the thirty-five dollars go.

LOCHMULLER: Yes let de thirty-five dollars go—I want to know why Katrine is dare mit Tommy Mulligan.

DAN: I don't want to quarrel when I'm going out for pleasure. My wife is waiting for me.

LOCHMULLER: Und my wife is waiting for me—Und before I see my Katrine make love mit Tommy Mulligan, I kill myself mit a cleaver.

DAN: And if I find Tommy Mulligan making love to a Dutch girl, I'll lick every German from Hamburg to Gowanus.

LOCHMULLER: Maybe—maybe—

MAGGIE: [*Who has put on hat and shawl during dialogue between Mulligan and Lochmuller, enters door into barber shop*] I'll get Primrose to have an eye on the store.

Mulligan and Lochmuller seize her and bring her front

LOCHMULLER: My good woman, tell me if Katrine Lochmuller is dare—

DAN: Was it Tommy Mulligan's voice I heard in there—answer me, I'm his father—

MAGGIE: Why you must be crazy.

LOCHMULLER: Yes, she said I was crazy—But on my knees—[*Getting on knees*] Please tell me if my child Katrine was dare.

Enter Bridget Lochmuller and Gustavus Lochrnuller Jr., dressed neatly for the ball. Bridget sees Lochmuller and seizes him throwing him around. Maggie exits into hair dresser's and then exits door in back flat. Dan going up and down stage in agony. Bridget shaking Lochmuller

BRIDGET: An' is this what I married you for—A dacent Irish girl—that had her twelve dollars a week in a feather factory, and to marry you, a bologna pudding butcher—and raise a family—to find you making love on your knees to a woman here in a barber shop—Oh, Lochmuller, Lochmuller—[*Weeping*]

LOCHMULLER: Bridget my darling—hear me once—

BRIDGET: An' me all dressed for the Mulligan Ball—and little Gustavus to see his father on his knees—[*Crying*] Oh, why did I marry among the Dutch.

DAN: [*To Bridget*] Are you that man's wife?

BRIDGET: Yis—But I'll lave him.

DAN: You have a daughter Katy?

BRIDGET: I have—Oh, Katy darling, when you hear of your father—

DAN: [*On knees*] Oh, my good woman hear me. Save a father's feelings. Keep her away from Tommy Mulligan. You're a County Cork woman—don't let your daughter run away with my boy—

Lochmuller going up and down stage. Enter Mrs. Mulligan, door in flat. Mrs.

Mulligan seizes Dan Mulligan, throwing him around.

MRS. MULLIGAN: And is this what you came to get shaved for—On your knees making love to another woman in a public bath house—Oh, you wretch! [*Going to Bridget*] And you—Who are you that dares to make trouble in my family?

BRIDGET: I am Bridget Lochmuller. I'm a lady—and raise your hand to me if you dare.

MRS. MULLIGAN: I'd tear the hair out of your head.

BRIDGET: Tear it—tear it—there's me hair tear it—[*Holding her head down*]

MRS. MULLIGAN: I will—[*Pulls Bridget's hair which falls loose*]

BRIDGET: Oh, let me at her—

LOCHMULLER: [*Getting in front of her and holding her*] Bridget, my darling, I am here your husband—Gustavus Lochmuller—Don't be mad, I'm a slaughter house butcher.

DAN: [*Holding Mrs. Mulligan*] Cordelia—Cordelia, what do you mean?

MRS. MULLIGAN: Let me at her—

BRIDIGET: Let her come.

LOCHMULLER: Take your wife away, Mulligan.

DAN: If you interfere, I'll pulverize you.

Enter August Sneider, in night shirt and nightcap. Bridget and Mrs. Mulligan run off and Gustavus, Jr., door in F.

SNEIDER: What's de matter here? I can't sleep in my tailor shop.

LOCHMULLER: My wife, Bridget darling—[*Exit door in flat*]

DAN: Cordelia—Cordelia—[*Exit after Lochmuller, door in flat*]

SNEIDER: Wake me out of my sleep, Mister Primrose. I get satisfaction—[*Breaks a shaving cup. Enter Primrose, seizes him. Bus. for finish.*]

There are short comic interludes as the Mulligans and Lochmullers, man and wife, quarrel about Tommy and Katy. The entrance of the Skidmores is an excuse for a song before separate scenes of dancing at the two balls, more fighting, ending with "General melee and curtain."

Scene 4

Local street. Enter Skidmore Guard Left. Sim Primrose as Captain and Puter as Chaplain

SIM: Halt. [*Business*] Members, I ordered you to carry arms to-night at de Skidmore Fancy Ball, kase we was forced to give up Lyric Hall, and take de Harp and Shamrock. Dar's no telling how many Irish will be in hambush dare. So, going in de hall, you can put your muskets in de hat rack, and every man have his razor sharpened. No one must interfere wid our pleasure.

PUTER: I'm agin de shedding of blood, but when it comes to dem people, why, you all know me.

COMPANY: Um—Um—

CAPTAIN SIM:

Song

"Skidmore's Fancy Ball"

Here we go, so nobly, oh,
   De colored Belvideres,
A number one, we carry a gun,
   We beat de Fusiliers.
Talk about your dances
   When we hear de cornet call,
We'll wing and wing, the dust we'll sling,
   At the Skidmore Fancy Ball.

   CHORUS
Hallelulah, glory, oh,
   Balance down de middle,
I tell you what, um um it's hot,
   Like gravy in a griddle.
Forward four, hold on de floor,
   Spread out through de hall,
Every coon's as warm as June,
   At the Skidmore Fancy Ball.

Supper served at one G.M.
   By Brown, the caterer.
Turk and goose, oh, cut me loose,
   Just lem me in de door.
Chairs reserved for ladies,
   Umbrellas in de hall,
Dar's etiquette in every set,
   At the Skidmore Fancy Ball.
   Hands around
   Keep off the ground,
We'll dance the plaster from de wall,
   Get in and sail, hold your trail,
At the Skidmore Fancy Ball.
   CHORUS

Every hat—when dey get at
   Dis colored coterie,
Will cost a half, you needn't laugh,

Help de colored mil it ia.
We're gwine down to Newport,
    Just next summer in de fall,
So follow suit and contribute
    To the Skidmore Fancy Ball.
Waltz away—mazourka,
    Dance de plaster from de wall,
Caledone—have a tone
    At de Skidmore Fancy Ball.
    CHORUS

In 1889 *Harper's Weekly* arranged a forum on the state of the theatrical arts and published the views of a few prominent American dramatists, a director, and a critic. Edward Harrigan reflected on his method and purpose in the *Mulligan* series.

"American Playwrights on the American Drama," *Harper's Weekly* [supplement] 33 (February 2, 1889): 97–98.

Perhaps the only general rule of valuing a dramatic composition is by applying the question, "Does it contain enough powerful, interesting, humorous, or beautiful features to attract and hold public attention?" This touchstone does away with all the stand-points referred to [financial and moral], and enables us to form a fair opinion of modern dramatic values.

At the outset of my career I found that whenever I tried to portray a type, I was warmly applauded by the audience, and praised by the press the next day. This, in all probability, is what gave me a decided bent, and has confined all my work to certain fields. It began with the New York "boy," the Irish-American, and our African brother. As these grew in popularity I added the other prominent types which go to make up life in the metropolis, and in every other large city of the Union and Canada. These are the Irishman, Englishman, German, Low German, Chinese, Italian, Russian, and Southern darky. I suppose ere long I shall add the Bohemian, Hungarian, Roumanian, Polak, and Scandanavian. As yet, however, their turn has not come. This system has given my pieces their peculiar polyglot character.

Though I use types and never individuals, I try to be as realistic as possible. Not only must the costuming and accessories be correct, but the speech or dialect, the personal "make-up," the vices and virtues, the habits and customs, must be equally accurate in their similarity to the facts. Each drama is a series of photographs of life to-day in the Empire City. As examples, the bar-room in one of the Mulligan series was copied from a saloon in Roosevelt Street, the opium den in *Investigation* [1884] from a "joint" in Pell Street, and the "dive" in *Waddy Googan* [1888] from an establishment in the neighborhood of the Bowery.

If I have given undue prominence to the Irish and negro, it is because they form about the most salient features of Gotham humanity, and also because they are the two races who care the most for song and dance. They are at least three hundred organizations in New York like the Mulligan Guards, and probably fifty like The Full Moons.

In constructing a plot, I use one that is simple and natural—just like what happens around us every day. Sometimes I'll start with only a germ, and let it develop of its own accord as I write. While I do my best to obtain realism in the plot, I try to avoid that whose sole value is local or temporary, and construct something that will interest and amuse ten or even twenty years hence. With the plot fixed or started, and with the types and places in my mind, it is easy to construct the characters and write the piece. When my work is done, my work, unlike that of most playwrights, is just begun. The next stage is "smoothing and brightening the raw material." Here I elaborate what situations I have sketched out and create new ones, arrange antitheses between the characters and between the different scenes, increase the wit and humor of the dialogue and the fun or nonsense of the climaxes. The third stage sees it cast and rehearsed. I can now see what effect it is going to have upon an audience, and can practically realize the good points and bad. The first stage is the shortest, and the third the longest of the three.

It is seldom I use any material but what I described. Polite society, wealth, and culture possess little or no color and picturesqueness. The chief use I make of them is as a foil to the poor, the workers, and the great middle class. The average gentleman is so stereotyped that he has no value except in those plays where he is a pawn on the chess-board of melodramatic vice or tragic sin.. . . .

It may be that I have struck a new idea in confining my work to the daily life of the common people. Why some other playwright does not try the same experiment, I cannot say. Their trials and troubles, hopes and fears, joys and sorrows, are more varied and more numerous than those of the Upper Ten. Whoever puts them on the stage appeals to an audience of a million. . . . And human nature is very much the same the world over. It thins out and loses all strength and flavor under the pressure of riches and luxury. It is most virile and aggressive among those who know only poverty and ignorance. It is also then the most humorous and odd. . . .

In the realism which I endeavor to employ I believe in being truthful to the laws which govern society as well as to the types of which it is composed. A playwright drops to a low level when he tries being a moralist, but to a much lower level when he gilds vice and sin and glorifies immorality. All of these are parts of life, and as such are entitled to be represented in the drama. The true realist will depict them as they are. Though he make the drunkard a source of infinite merriment to the multitude, he will not conceal the rags, misery, and disease which follow in his footsteps; though he discover virtue in criminals and tramps, he will not be blind to the qualities which outweigh and crush it down; and above all he will portray the fact that right-doing, kindness, and good-nature are in the majority, and "control the machine."

Though there are shams everywhere to be picked and ridiculed, and humbugs to be exposed and laughed out of existence, these are only incidents which, though they appear and disappear incessantly, are not parts of the real humanity beneath. The adage "To hold the mirror up to nature" is as applicable to the swarming myriads of New York as to the Greek warriors before Priam's city, or the lords and nobles who surrounded the TUDORS.

William Dean Howells was editor of the middlebrow *Harper's Monthly* and one of the most influential critics. In 1886 he saluted Edward Harrigan as the last best hope of the American theater. As a practical dramatist who wrote, acted, and managed, Harrigan, Howells concluded, cared little for "the highly decorated husk and gilded shell," and was willing to sacrifice literary artifice for dramatic effect. His peculiar genius was capturing the spirit of New York in a setting "singularly perfect and entirely sufficient."

[William Dean Howells], "Editor's Study," *Harper's New Monthly Magazine* 73 (July 1886): 315–16.

Mr. Harrigan accurately realizes in his scenes what he realizes in his persons; that is, the actual life of this city. He cannot give it all; and he has preferred to give its Irish-American phases in their rich and amusing variety, and some of its Teutonic and African phases. It is what we call low life, though whether it is essentially lower than fashionable life is another question. But what it is, it is; and it remains for others, if they can, to present other sides of our manifold life with equal perfection; Mr. Harrigan leaves a vast part of the vast field open. In his own province we think he cannot be surpassed. The art that sets before us all sorts and conditions of New York Irishmen, from the laborers in the street to the most powerful of the ward politicians and the genteelest of the ladies of that interesting race, is . . . the joyous yet conscientious art of the true dramatist in all times who loves the life he observes. . . . Mr. Harrigan shows us the street-cleaners and contractors, the grocery-men, the shysters, the politicians, the washer-women, the servant-girls, the truckmen, the policemen, the risen Irishman and Irish woman, of contemporary New York. . . . In fact, nothing could be better than the neatness, the fineness, with which the shades of character are given in Mr. Mulligan's Irish people; and this literary consciousness is supplemented by acting which is worthy of it. Mr. Harrigan is himself a player of the utmost natural-ness, delicate, restrained, infallibly sympathetic; and we have seen no one on his stage who did not seem to have been trained to his part through entire sympathy and intelligence. In certain moments of *Dan's Tribulations* the illusion is so perfect that you lose the sense of being in the theatre; you are out of that world of conventions and traditions, and in the presence of the facts.

All the Irish aspects of life are treated affectionately by this artist, as we might expect from one of his name; but the colored aspects do not fare so well under his touch. Not all the Irish are good Irish, but all the colored are bad colored people. They are of the gloomy, razor-bearing variety; full of short-sighted lies and prompt dishonesties, amusing always, but truculent and tricky; and the sunny sweetness which we all know in negro character is not there. . . .

In spite of such lapses, however, we recognize in Mr. Harrigan's work the spring of a true American comedy, the beginning of things which may be great things. We have more than intimated its limitations; let us say that whatever its limitations, it is never, so far as we have seen it, indecent. . . .

At any rate, loving reality as we do, we cannot do less than cordially welcome reality as we find it in Mr. Harrigan's comedies. Consciously or unconsciously, he is part of the great tendency toward the faithful representation of life which is now animating fiction.

Confessions of an African American Minstrel

By the 1880s, African American performers were becoming prominent as singers, dancers and comedians in minstrelsy. In 1896, Bert Williams and George Walker blacked up as "The Two Real Coons." Williams's success in all-black musicals, notably *In Dahomey* (1903), and his song "Nobody" (1906), established his reputation and made him a well-paid star of the prestigious Ziegfeld Follies after 1910. Williams was always conscious of his mixed-race, British-Caribbean origins and sensitive to prejudice. But as a thoughtful and consummate artiste, he explained to a prominent monthly magazine that the segregation that separated the races gave him the opportunity to articulate the views of the forgotten man, unknown to most Americans, through the medium of the minstrel fool.

Bert Williams, "The Comic Side of Trouble," *American Magazine* 85 (January 1918):, 33–34, 58–60.

One of the funniest sights in the world is a man whose hat has been knocked in or ruined by being blown off—provided, of course, it is the other fellow's hat! All the jokes in the world are based on a few elemental ideas, and this is one of them. The sight of other people in trouble is nearly always funny. This is human nature. . . . The man with the real sense of humor is the man who can put himself in the spectator's place and laugh at his own misfortunes.

That is what I am called upon to do every day. Nearly all of my comic songs have been based on the idea that I am getting the worst of it. I am the "Jonah Man," the man who, even if it rained soup, would be found with a fork in his hand and no spoon in sight, the man whose fighting relatives come to visit him and whose head is always dented by the furniture they throw at each other. There are endless variations of this idea, fortunately; but if you sift them, you will find the principle of human nature at the bottom of them all. . . .

It was not until I was able to see myself as another person that my sense of humor developed. For I do not believe there is any such thing as innate humor. It has to be developed by hard work and study, just as every other human quality. I have studied it all my life, unconsciously during my floundering years, and consciously as soon as I began to get next to myself. It is a study that I shall never get to the end of, and a work that never stops, except when I am asleep. There are no union hours to it and no let-up. It is only by being constantly on the lookout for fresh material, funny incidents, funny speeches, funny traits in human nature that a comedian can hope to keep step with his public.

I find material by knocking around in out of the way places and just listening. For among the American colored men and negroes there is the greatest source of simple amusement you can find anywhere in the world. . . . But Americans for the most part know little about the unconscious humor of the colored people and negroes, because they do not come in contact with them. . . .

Many of the best lines I have used came to me by that sort of eavesdropping. For, as I have pointed out, eavesdropping on human nature is one of the most important parts of a comedian's work. . . .

People ask me if I would not give anything to be white. I answer, in the words of the song, most emphatically, "No." How do I know what I might be if I were a white man? . . . In truth, I have never been able to discover that there was anything disgraceful in being a colored man. But I have found it inconvenient—in America. . . .

It was [in California] that I first ran up against the humiliations and persecutions that have to be faced by every person of colored blood, no matter what his brains, education or the integrity of his conduct. How many times have hotel keepers said to me, "I know you, Williams, and I like you, and I would like nothing better than to have you stay here, but you will see we have Southern gentlemen in the house and they would object."

Frankly, I can't understand what it is all about. I breathe like other people, eat like them—if you put me at a dinner table you can be reasonably sure that I won't use the ice cream fork for my salad; I think like other people. I guess the whole trouble must be that I don't look like them. They say it is a matter of race prejudice. But if it were prejudice a baby would have it, and you will never find it in a baby. It has to be inculcated on people. For one thing, I have noticed that this "race prejudice" is not to be found in people who are sure enough of their position to be able to defy it. . . .

Then, one day at Moore's Wonderland in Detroit, just for a lark I blacked my face and tried the song, "Oh, I don't know, you're not so warm." Nobody was more surprised than I when it went like a house on fire. Then I began to find myself. By that time I had met George Walker, and we used to travel around the country together. I took to studying the dialect of the American negro, which to me was just as much a foreign dialect as that of the Italian. . . .

After [success at Koster & Bial's in New York] I went to Europe frequently, not only because I found kinder treatment there but in order to learn my trade. I used to go over every summer for a while and study pantomime from Pietro, the great pantomimist. He is the one artist from whom I can truthfully say that I have learned. He taught me gesture, facial expression—without which I would ever have been able to do the poker game stunt that was so popular. And above all he taught me the value of poise, repose and pauses. He taught me that the pause after a gesture or a movement is frequently more important than the gesture itself, because it emphasizes the gesture. . . It was Pietro who taught me that the entire aim and object of art is to achieve naturalness. The more simple and real the manner of your walking or talking the more effective, and that is the purpose of art.

THE CIRCUS

"Friday I tasted life. It was a vast morsel," Emily Dickinson wrote to her sister. "A circus passed the house—I still feel the red in my mind though the drums are out."[1] In early May 1866 a caravan traveled through Amherst, Massachusetts, and on to towns along the Connecticut Valley. For Dickinson the show of the show—not the performance, but the parade and the brass band—was a rare treat. To Dickinson in the quiet college town, the circus brought excitement to a humdrum existence of seriousness, duty, and toil. Most of all, it conveyed a sense of movement and dynamism. Small caravans slowly wending their way across the country reached towns too small to support other professional companies. In the early nineteenth century the circus was the most complete amusement package available. In the one spectacle was mastery of the human body exhibited in daring feats and supremacy over the rarest of animals. Those who flocked to the circus thrilled to see man's control over wildness and anarchy as well as displays of the human body disciplined and brute creation tamed.

The modern circus emerged in the 1830s. Its roots lay in combining the exhibition of exotic beasts with displays of horsemanship and gymnastics. In the eighteenth century traveling menageries were judged to be educational and edifying, rather than merely frivolous dissipation. The respectable were drawn to the unusual of God's creation: caged wild cats, polar bears and porcupines, camels and zebras, buffalo and bears, or as much of a Noah's Ark as the noble educator could assemble. The great attraction of the "natural curiosities" was that they were living, not stuffed as in a dime museum. The first elephant appeared in 1796, the rhinoceros in 1826, the giraffe or "cameleopard" in 1837, and the hippopotamus or "blood-sweating behemoth" in the 1850s. However, showmen blurred the boundaries between enlightenment and entertainment. They soon added amusing acts demonstrating man's control over the animal kingdom. In 1798 William Pinchbeck announced to the people of Newburyport, Massachusetts, the astounding sight of a "Pig of Knowledge" who "reads print or writing, spells, tells the time of day, both the hours and minutes, by any persons watch in the company, the date of the year, the day of the month."[2] The "Philosophical Fish," "Sapient Dog," and "Learned Goat" soon followed.

Hippodrama introduced from England staged astonishing acrobatic feats on horseback. Philip Astley, a former cavalry officer, pioneered the modern circus in suburban London in 1768. One of his rivals, John Bill Ricketts, brought exhibitions of trick riding to Philadelphia in 1793 and toured seaboard cities, performing in specially built wooden arenas or in the open air. Opposition to itinerant players remained strong in New England and the northern states. Equestrian performers were often grouped with "mountebanks," defined by Connecticut state legislature in 1798 as those who "exhibit tricks of tumbling, ropewalking or dancing, puppet shows or any uncommon feats of agility of the body for money." Saratoga Springs allowed a playhouse in the 1820s, but a law of 1836 gave power to the city trustees to restrict "caravans of living animals, or other natural or artificial curiosities, or shows, or exhibitions for money."[3] Elsewhere, particularly in New York State, the circus began to thrive. After an equestrian circus joined forces with a menagerie with a zebra, camels, and a pony-riding monkey in 1828, the arrangement soon became standard practice. In the 1830s the novel use of tents made traveling shows independent of rented barns for arenas. By 1835 the first small tent of 1826 had ballooned to a hundred and twenty thousand square feet, sufficient for five thousand spectators.

The parade to the campground provided a free show and the greatest advertisement. With the strident sound of the large brass band came the procession—fifty carriages and a hundred and fifty horses in Van Amburgh's on Broadway in 1846. By the 1860s horse-drawn vehicles encrusted with carved dragons, eagles, and rococo decorations and painted in gaudy colors were standard. The Great Egyptian Dragon Chariot of Crane and Company's Great Oriental Circus was drawn by ten camels in 1849, and Howes and Cushing's huge parade organ needed forty horses in 1857. The Buffalo *Courier* described the impact of the Great European Circus's "pageant" through the city's streets in 1868. "First came the immense band chariot . . . suggestive of wealth and splendor, bearing the golden statue of Alexander's famous horse Bucephalus, containing the silver cornet band, and drawn by a team of gaily-decked dromedaries from the desert of Saharah." Many other monstrous wagons followed, some in fantastic shapes, like the "fairy chariot" drawn by twelve small ponies and escorted by knights and their ladies. The "grand feature" of the long procession was the "colossal leonine car, bearing beautiful women, in the centre of which was a large living lion, uncaged and un-chained, reposed in all his native majesty near his keeper."[4]

Within the next decade, the circus was transformed, particularly by improved management. Faster railroad travel eliminated loss-making stops; doubling the performance rings expanded the program. Barnum's alliance with the master-organizer James A. Bailey in the late 1880s produced one of the famous combinations in a highly competitive business. Small family tented shows survived, especially in the rural south and west, but twenty large, highly capitalized enterprises traversing almost half the country dominated. By 1895 Ephraim, Lewis, and Peter Sells of Columbus, Ohio, a typically large circus, employed almost five hundred and traveled nearly fourteen thousand miles in thirty-two weeks. There were still a hundred circuses in 1903, but only a few of the "mammoth," "colossal" combinations aspired to continental coverage. The *Barnum and Bailey Greatest Show on Earth*, billed in the 1890s as "The World's Largest, Grandest, Best Amusement Institution," failed, was purchased by Ringling Brothers in 1907, and the shows merged in 1918. By then, the grand parade had proved too costly to organize for one-day visits and almost disappeared.

The Circus Debated

Throughout the century, evangelical Christians condemned the circus as an insidious and pernicious amusement that sapped the virtue of the republic's citizens. Insidious, because what appeared to be merely a novel display of skill enticed, excited, and deluded the innocent; pernicious, because it ensnared the young, the most vulnerable, into a thoughtless love of pleasure that led to vice. In response, the interdenominational agencies that flourished in the generation after the Revolution launched a campaign, indeed, a crusade, to inform children, with cautionary tales written in the colloquial language of mass-market fiction. Some narratives, like the American Sunday-School Union's *Slim Jack: or, The History of a Circus-Boy* (1847), depicted in mawkish detail the sad fate of a foolish acrobat betrayed and abandoned by a callous entrepreneur. Most, however, were simple dialogues between the innocent and the wise. In a Sunday-School Union pamphlet, the worthy Mr. Brown explained to his young sons why circus exhibitions were morally unsound.

The Circus (Philadelphia: American Sunday-School Union, n.d. [1840s]).

Alfred and Silas Brown were brothers, and went to the same school. When they were coming home one day, they saw a man with a large parcel of papers under his arm, and in his hand he carried a pot of paste and a brush. The man stopped by a high fence, and put down the pot of paste and spread out his papers, just as the boys came near him. They stopped to look at these papers, and saw that there were a great many as large as a newspaper; but they were covered by bright red pictures, and all these pictures were men and horses. Some of the horses were running. Some seemed as if they were almost flying, for none of their feet were made to look as if they touched the ground; and the men were not riding as we are used to see them, but were standing on the horses. Some were standing on one foot, and some were driving two horses and had one foot on each of them.

Alfred and Silas did not know what to make of these fine looking pictures. So Alfred, who was the oldest, said to the man, "Will you please to tell me, sir, what this picture is about?"

By this time the man had put some paste on one of the sheets of paper, and was pasting it to the high fence where he had stopped.

"O yes, my little man," said he, "to be sure I will tell you. We are going to have a fine show here in a few days. We shall have a great many horses, that will do almost anything they are told to do, and fine music, and many other pretty sights. Here," said he, "take one of these papers and show it to all your school-mates, and tell them to save their money and come to the show. I cannot stop to talk to you about it now, but I belong to the circus, (for that is the name of the show,) and when you come there, I will tell you all you want to know about it."

"O thank you, sir," said Alfred, taking the paper, "I will ask my father to let me come;" and, taking Silas by the hand, he started to go home.

"Stop, my little lad," said the man. "If you think your father will not let you come, you had better not say anything to him about it; but you and little bub," (for so he called his brother Silas,) "can come after school, and be sure to bring your money, and I will show you something worth seeing. And see that you show the paper to your school-mates."

This was a wicked man. It is as wicked to persuade others to do wrong as to do it ourselves.

Off ran the little boys, and Alfred ran so fast he almost pulled Silas down, for his little legs were so short, he could scarcely keep up with him; so when they got home they were almost out of breath.

"O mother," said Alfred, "such a kind man! and he says that if I will come there, he will show me all the fine things."

"Not so fast, my son," said his mother. "Stop and rest, and then begin slowly, and I shall know what you are talking about."

"Where is the picture, Silas? Then look here, mother, see these fine horses."

"I should think that man would fall down and hurt himself," said little Silas, pointing to a man in the picture, who was standing with only one foot on a horse who was running very fast.

Just at this time the door opened, and Mr. Brown came in. Both the boys ran to him.

"May we go, father, to the show?" said Alfred. "Come look at all the horses; they know how to do every thing."

When Mr. Brown saw the picture, and heard his little boys talk about going to see the show, at first he felt sorry that he had heard anything about it; but afterwards he thought this was a good time to tell them what he thought of the circus. He knew that, as they should grow older, they would hear more about it; and if they did not know what kind of places they are, where such amusements are found, they might desire to go and see for themselves. So their father spread the picture on a table, and told the little boys to bring chairs and sit down by him, and he would tell them something about the circus.

He said, "I know little boys are very fond of horses, and it is very wonderful to see how much they can be taught. But whenever I think about it, I feel very sorry for the poor animals; for they have to be whipped very hard and treated very cruelly, before they can be taught all these things. This is not the only reason, however, why I am unwilling that you should go to the circus. The men who belong to it are generally idle and worthless people, who go about from place to place, and get their living by taking money of many persons who cannot afford to spend it so foolishly. Then there is a great deal of drinking and gambling about a circus; and I always think it a very sad thing for a village when the circus comes into it.

"Besides all this, it makes all the boys, who see it, want to do just as the men do; and some of them get so fond of seeing such shows, that as soon as they get a chance, they join themselves to a circus, and then there is no hope of their making useful men.

"When I was a little boy, there was such a show came to the place where I lived. My father talked to me as I have talked to you, and of course I did not go; but many of my school-mates went. After the circus had left, the boys tried to do as the circus men did, and one little boy tried to ride a horse while standing on his back. The old horse, who would have carried the little boy very safely if he had rode him in the usual way, did not know what to make of this new fashion of riding; for he had been brought up to good habits, and had never been in a circus. Soon he began to trot, and moved about so much, that the little boy, who did not know how to keep steady, fell off and broke his arm. He suffered a great deal of pain, and never tried to ride like the circus men again.

"So, my little boys," said Mr. Brown, "I shall not take you to the circus, but in a short time there is to be a show of wild beasts; and then I will take you to see it, if we live."

"Thank you, thank you, father," said Alfred, "that will do a great deal better. Come, Silas, let us go and play."

Mr. Brown's "show of wild beasts" had almost universal approval; *The Menagerie: A Reward for Good Children* (1835) explained the moral distinction between the "rational" display of wild animals and the "foolish" show of dancing puppets which merely frittered away God's time. A few children's authors, like "Fanny Fern," the pioneering journalist and feminist Sara Payson Willis Parton, openly defended the circus, while acknowledging its failings. More daringly, Parton hoped that commercial reality might transcend racial prejudice. As in all public entertainment before the Civil War, segregation was the norm. Some claimed that the circus transcended the usual social barriers. "Everybody went—all classes, ages, colors and conditions," the New England humorist Hiram Fuller wrote in 1858 of the circus's visit to Newport, Rhode Island. "There were as many as five thousand people there, all mixed up with the most democratic indiscrimination—Fifth Avenue belles sitting on narrow boards with their dresses under their arms, alongside of Irish chambermaids and colored persons of all sizes and sexes."[5] However, it is more likely, as Fanny Fern suggests, that African Americans like "black Nanny" were allowed to sit in the sections reserved for whites only because they sat with their employers. In the 1830s the New York Zoological Institute had a prominent sign outside its amphitheater at 37 Bowery: "The proprietors wish it to be understood, that PEOPLE OF COLOR are *not permitted to enter*, EXCEPT WHEN IN ATTENDANCE ON CHILDREN AND FAMILIES."[6]

Fanny Fern [Sara Payson Willis Parton], *The Play-Day Book; or, New Stories for Little Folks* (New York: Mason Brothers, 1857), 45–49.

What a mob of boys! There's Bill Saunders, and Ned Hoyt, and Tom Fagin, and Lewis Coates, and John Harris; and, sure as the world, there's that little tomtit, Harry Horn, without a sign of a cap on, jumping up and down as if there were pins in his trowsers. What can be the matter, I wonder? Now they shout, "Hurra—hurra!"—but then boys are always screaming hurra. I have done breaking my neck leaning out of the window to see what is the matter. I won't look at the little monkeys. There it goes again—"Hurra! hurra!" One would think General Washington, Lafayette, or same other great person, was coming down street. Now they move to one side—ah, now I see what all the fuss is about! A great flaming red and yellow hand-bill is posted on the fence; and on it is written, "Pat Smith's Circus! next Wednesday afternoon and evening." Circus! no wonder little Harry Horn forgot to put his hat on, and jumped up and down as if he were trying to jump out of his trowsers.

If there is anything that drives boys crazy, it is a circus. I should like to know why; I have a great mind to go to Pat Smith's Circus myself; just to find out; for I never was in a circus in my life. Yes, I will go, and I will take Nelly; she never was in a circus either. No, I won't; I will leave her at home with black Nanny. No, I won't; I will take black Nanny too; but then I am not sure Pat Smith allows colored people in his circus. Well, if he is such a senseless Pat as that, he may go without three twenty-five cent pieces, that's all, for Nanny likes a little fun as well as if her skin were whiter; and if Nanny can't come in, Nelly and I won't. But Nanny can; Pat is not such a fool. So, come along, Nanny; come along, Nelly; it don't matter what you wear. Walk a little faster, both of you; we must get a good seat, or we shall lose half the fun. Short people are apt to fare badly in a crowd. Here we are! This a circus! this round tent? How funny! Music inside; that's nice; I like music; so do Nelly and Nanny.

Here's your money, Mr. Pat Smith. Goodness! you don't mean that we have got to clamber up in those high, rickety-looking seats, without any backs? Suppose we should fall through on the ground below? Suppose the seats should crack, and let all these people down? I think we'll climb up to the highest seat, for in case they do break, I had rather be on the top of the pile than underneath it. That's it; here's a place for you, Nanny. Bless me, what a "many people," as little Harry Horn says. Little babies, too, as I live;—well, I suppose their poor tired mothers wanted a little fun too; but the babies are better off than we, because they can have a drink of milk whenever they are thirsty. Ah, I was a little too fast there, for Pat Smith has provided lemonade, and here comes a man with a pailful. Circus lemonade!—no, I thank you; it may be very good, but I prefer taking your word for it.

How the people flock in! What's that coming in at yonder door? Nanny! Nelly!—look! Is it a small house painted slate-color? No—it is an elephant—a live elephant. What a monster! what great flapping ears! what huge paws! and what a rat-ty looking tail! I don't like his tail; but his trunk is superb. I am afraid he has had a deal of whipping to make him behave so well. How he could make us all fly, if he chose; what mince-meat he could make of those little fat babies yonder. I am glad he don't want to; they are too pretty to eat. What are they going to do with him, I wonder? It can't be that they mean to make him walk up that steep pair of stairs. Yes—see him! Would you believe such a great monster could do it so gracefully? He lifts his paws as gently as a kitten. Now that's worth seeing; but how in the world are they going to get him down, now that he has reached the top? See—he is going to back down; not one false step does he make; now he has reached the bottom. Clever old monster! It seems a shame to make such a great, grand-looking, kingly creature, perform such dancing-master tricks. Now his master lies flat on his back on the ground, and the old elephant is going to walk over him. Suppose he should set that great paw of his on his master's stomach, and crush him as flat as a pancake? No; see how carefully he steps over him with those big legs; never so much as touching his gay scarlet-and-white tunic. Splendid old fellow, to have so much strength, and yet never use it to the harm of those who torment him with all this nonsense. How I should like to see you in your native jungles, old elephant, with all your baby elephants; your little big babies, old fellow. There he goes. I am glad they have done with him. It makes me sad to see him. Good-bye, old Samson.

What now? a lady on horseback, Mr. Pat Smith's wife; she sets her horse very well, but that's nothing remarkable; I can set a horse as well as that myself; but I couldn't make a leap on her back over that five-barred gate—mercy, no—he will break her neck, I know he will; I am afraid Mr. Pat Smith wants a second wife. Oh, see, the horse has come down safe with her on the other side of the gate. Now she is going to try it again; what a woman that is! I hope Mr. Pat Smith gives her half the money that he takes this hot night, for I am sure she has earned it; but wives don't always get what they earn, and I dare say Mrs. Pat Smith don't.

Now here comes a parcel of fellows in white tights, tight as their skin, tumbling head over heels, up side down, standing on each others' heads, and cutting up untold and untellable capers. I must say their strong limbs are quite beautiful, just as God intended limbs should grow, just as I hope yours will grow, one of these days, though I think it may be done without your being a circus tumbler. See how nimble they are, and how like eels they twist and squirm about, leaping on each others' shoulders like squirrels, leaping down again, running up tall poles and sitting on the top, and playing there with half a dozen balls at once, which are tossed up at them from below. It is really quite wonderful, and yet I can't help thinking had they taken as much pains to learn something really useful, as they have to learn to be funny, how much good they might do; for after all, a monkey, or a squirrel, or all ourang-outang could do all that quite as well as a man, who is so much superior to them, quite as gracefully, and without any teaching, too. But, bless me, a circus is no place to think, and yet I wish those men's heads were as well trained as their heels; if you listen you will find out they are not; just hear those stupid jokes they are making, how badly they pronounce, how ungrammatically they express themselves, and hear—oh, no—*don't* hear that! what a pity they should say anything *indelicate* before ladies and pure little children. *Now* I know why fathers and mothers do not like their little boys and girls to go to the circus. Mr. Pat Smith, Mr. Pat Smith, you must leave off those stupid bad jokes, if you want to draw ladies and little children.

I wish somebody would get up a *good* circus without these faults. I cannot think so badly of the people as to believe that they would like it less if it were purified. I think it might be made a very pleasant and harmless amusement for little children, who seem to want to go so much, and who have often felt so badly because their parents were not willing. Perhaps there are such good circuses, that I may not have heard of. I like good schools, I like study, but I should like to write over every schoolroom door— "All work and no play makes Jack a dull boy!"

A generation later, the circus had acquired more respectability. In 1883, Richard Kyle Fox, publisher of the sensationalist *National Police Gazette*, issued a small booklet by the acrobat Alfred Trumble. Trumble described the lives of the circus performers with their "spangled" or glittering, sequined costumes, but Fox embellished the plain narrative with characteristically lurid *Gazette* engravings of "show girls" in skimpy dresses—"Favorites of the Footlights"—and advertisements for such Fox publications as *Folly's Queens; or, Women whose Loves have ruled the World*, and *The Female Sharpers of New York*, all "handsomely illustrated." Indeed, semipornographic views of "leg-show" performers on horseback or trapeze in short skirt and tights undermined Trumble's justifications.

[Alfred T. Trumble,] *A Spangled World; or, Life with the Circus* (New York: Richard Fox, proprietor *Police Gazette*, 1883), 8, 21, 83.

I always pity the people who have so much to say against the circus. What poor creatures they are to look at, with their skinny, solemn faces and their rusty black suits! I believe the cause of their hatred of the circus may be found in their envy of the clown. He never looks dismal, he don't dress in rusty black, and who ever yet saw a clown who was not fat enough to kill?

The beauty of the circus is that everyone can understand it, a deaf and dumb boy can enjoy it, and a blind man could revel in the music and laugh at the clown's jokes. Youth, and age, irrespective of nationality, can feast upon the splendors of the saw-dust circles and understand it all. If you go to the play and don't understand what the actors are saying you have but a poor time of it. But what does it matter what they say at the circus, as long as they do only half the things they promise on the bills. . . .

Now let us look at the people who constitute the circus.

The chief of these, as the reader will admit, are the riders. Who has not felt his heart stop beating as these gorgeous apparitions burst upon him from the mysterious recesses of the dressing-room? What a dream they were! Velvets, tinsel, tarletan skirts, pink tights, gold braid, feathers and spangles, flying through the air like gigantic birds of paradise. . . .

The circus is a great humanizer. Its popularity is due chiefly to the fact that every-one can understand it, and it rouses in every one a sympathy of sentiments which levels the barriers fortune and station set up. The millionaire gets no more for his money than the man who sweeps the crossing for him, at the circus. He can only see, hear and enjoy, and those prerogatives nature and not fortune confers on man.

Look at the motley throng which makes up the audience of a circus. At the theatre you see not only silks and laces and diamonds, but here flannel shirt jostles broadcloth coat, and calico wrapper brushes sealskin; here diamonds gleam beside brass, and os-trich plumes quiver next to Bowery ribbons at five cents a yard. Artisan and banker, scul-lion and mistress, make up the swarm who turn out when the circus comes to town.

All this, as much as the performances themselves, lend interest to the show. If the act in the ring is dull, one can study one's neighbors, and be interesting in spite of the clown's antediluvian jokes and the ringmaster's familiar replies and apostrophes. This was never better shown than in the success the circus meets with in foreign coun-tries. Even a Frenchman will laugh at the, to him, incomprehensible witticisms of an American clown. He knows it is the clown's business to be funny and takes it for granted that he is so. It is well for the clown, sometimes, that he does take it for granted, perhaps.

The Early Circus

On May 28, 1835, Nathaniel Hawthorne noted his impressions of the circus performance he had seen in Salem and used it as the basis for his brief essay in the *American Magazine of Useful and Entertaining Knowledge* in April 1836. Perhaps the accent on tradition gave the skills greater legitimacy.

Nathaniel Hawthorne, *Hawthorne's Lost Notebook, 1835–1841*, ed. Barbara S. Mouffe (University Park: Pennsylvania State University Press, 1978), 3.

The Early Circus

The Circus—A dancing horse, keeping excellent time to the music, with all four feet. Mr Dakin says, that two horses, who had learned to dance, dropt down dead during their performance. The physical exertion seems very moderate; it must be the mental labor that kills them—The Clown in his dress of motley, making fun of everything—Mr. Merryman—the most antique character, I suppose, now existing; just the same, probably, that he used to be five hundred years ago; and perhaps playing-off many of the identical jokes that all those successive generations have roared at.—A fellow who kept up several balls in the air at once; and also several knives;—this, too, is a feat of great antiquity, practised by the Saxon gleemen.—Excellent horsemanship,—one rider with a boy on his shoulders; another man got into a sack, and after riding a few minutes, behold a woman emerged from the sack—Feats of strength, by a young fellow of no great bulk, but very solid muscle; lifting a table and a boy on it, with his teeth; sustaining an anvil on his breast, whereon another man smote with a sledge-hammer; laying out horizontally, with his feet against a stout pole, high up in the air, and letting a boy walk out on his back. The fellow seemed awkward in deportment, and made a very quick and bashful bob of his head, by way of bow to the spectators—A small white dog, of divers accomplishments—Vaulting and tumbling— one fellow threw fourteen somersets in succession.

In the summer of 1838 Hawthorne took a two-month vacation in the Berkshire hills in western Massachusetts. During his extended stay in North Adams, he relaxed with his new-found friend, Orrin Smith, a local widower. There he met an agent making advance preparations for a menagerie. The Zoological Institute had pooled the resources of thirteen itinerant companies in 1835, but the cartel soon failed in the depression of 1837. June, Titus, Angevine and Company, one of the institute's former subdivisions, arrived in Worcester on August 17 and spent a few days in Springfield and Chicopee. It had a choice of directions to North Adams: to go north along the Connecticut Valley toward Deerfield and Greenfield and then west along the Mohawk Trail via Charlemont, or to cross the Berkshires to Pittsfield and travel through Cheshire. This was good territory for traveling shows. It was in West Springfield in 1836 that Barnum began his six-month tour with his juggler Signor Vivalla as part of Aaron Turner's equestrian Old Columbian Circus. Hawthorne was intrigued by the agent's rude energy, and, as was his custom, made quick notes on August 18, 1838.

Nathaniel Hawthorne, *The American Notebooks*, ed. Claude M. Simpson (Columbus: Ohio State University Press, 1972), 117–18.

One of the proprietors or superintendents of a Caravan of Animals:—a large, portly-paunched, dark-complexioned, brandy burnt, heavy-faced man of about fifty; with a diminutive nose in proportion to the size of his face—thick, heavy lips;—nevertheless the air of a man who has seen much, and derived such experience as was for his purpose. Also, the air of a man not in subordinate station, though vulgar and coarse. He arrived in a wagon with a handsome span of grey horses; and ordered dinner. He had left his Caravan at Worcester, and came from thence, and over the mountain hither, to settle stopping-places for the caravan. His nearest to this, I believe, was at Charlemont, —the penultimate at Greenfield. In stopping at such a village as this, they do not expect much profit, if any; but would be content to pay their travelling expenses, and gather gain at larger places. In this village, it seems, the selectmen had resolved not to license any public exhibition of the kind; and it was interesting to attend to the consultations whether it were feasible to overcome their objections, and what might be the best means. Orrin and the chance passers-by took part in the discussion:—the scruple is, that the factory girls &c having ready money by them, spend it for these nonsenses, quitting their work;—whereas, were it a mere farming town, the Caravan would take little in proportion to their spendings. The opinion was generally, that the license could not be obtained;—and the portly man's face grew darker and downcast at the prospect; and he took out a travelling map, and looked it carefully over to discover some other station. This is somewhat like the planning of the route of an army. It was finally resolved to enlist the influence of a brother-in-law of the head selectman, and to try to gain his consent;—whereupon the caravan-man and the brother-in-law (who, being a tavern-keeper, was to divide the custom of the caravan-people with our house) went to make the attempt;—the caravan man stalking along with stiff awkward bulk and stature, yet preserving a respectability withal, though with somewhat of the blackguard. Before he went he offered a wager of "a drink of rum to a chaw of tobacco" that he did not get in. When he came back, there was a flush on his face and a sparkle in his eye that did not look like failure; but I know not what was the result. He took a glass of wine with the brother-in-law—a grave, thin, frosty-haired, shrewd-looking, yeoman in his shirt-sleeves—then ordered his horses, paid his bill, and rode off, accompanied still by the said yeoman, perhaps to get the permission of the other two selectmen. If he does not get a license here, he will try at Cheshire.

Two weeks later, on September 4, 1838, Hawthorne wrote about the show day in North Adams. The star attraction of June, Titus, Angevine, and Company was the elephant Siam. The menagerie added human intervention to enliven the traditional caged displays in the tent. Isaac Van Amburgh first entered the lions' cage in 1834 and astounded spectators by putting his head in the beast's open mouth. The novelty rapidly became established tradition and a bridge to other feats of human daring; thereafter, if posters displayed wild cats, almost always it was with the brave keeper in the cage.

Nathaniel Hawthorne, *The American Notebooks*, ed. Claude M. Simpson (Columbus: Ohio State University Press, 1972), 140–41.

This day, an exhibition of animals in the vicinity of the village—under a pavillion of sailcloth, the floor being the natural grass, with here and there a rock partially protrud-

The Early Circus

ing. A pleasant, mild shade; a strip of sunshine, or a spot of glimmering brightness in some parts. Crowded—row above row of women, on an amphitheater of seats, on one side. In an inner pavilion, an exhibition of anacondas, four, which the showman took one by one from a large box, under some blankets, and hung round his shoulders. They seemed almost torpid when first taken out; but gradually began to assume life, to extend, to contract; to twine and writhe about his neck and person, thrusting out their tongues, and erecting their heads. Their weights were as much as he could well bear; and they hung down almost to the ground, when not contorted; big round as a mans thigh—almost. Spotted and richly variegated. Then he thrust them into the box again, their heads emerging, and writhing forth—which he thrust back again. He gave a descriptive and historical account of them, and some fanciful and jocose &c. A man put his arm and head into the lion's mouth,—all the spectators looking on, so attentively that a breath could not be heard. That was impressive—its effect on a thousand people, more than the thing itself.

In the evening, the caravan people at our house, talking of their troubles in coming over the mountain, the overturn of a cage containing two leopards and a hyena. They are a rough, ignorant set of men, apparently incapable of taking any particular enjoyment from the life of variety and adventure which they lead. There, was the man who put his head in the lion's mouth, and, I suppose, the man whom the anaconda's twined about, talking about their suppers, and blustering for hot meat, and calling for something to drink, without anything of the wild dignity of men familiar with the *nobility of nature*.

A character of a desperate young man, who employs high courage and strong faculties in these sort of dangers, and wastes his talents in wild riot, addressing the audience as a snake man—keeping the ring while the monkey rides the poney—singing negro and other songs.

The country boors were continually getting within the barriers and venturing too near the cages. The great lion lay with his four paws extended, and a calm, majestic, but awful countenance. He looked on the people as if he had seen many such concourses. The hyaena was the most ugly and dangerous looking beast, full of spite, and on ill terms with all nature—looking a good deal like a hog with the devil in him. The ridge of hair along his back bristling. He was in the cage with a leopard and a panther; and the latter seemed continually on the point of laying his claw upon the hyaena, who snarled, and showed his teeth. It is strange to see, though, how these wild beasts acknowledge and practise a degree of mutual forbearance, and of obedience to man—with their wild nature yet in them. The great white bear seemed in distress from the heat, moving his head and body in a strange fantastic way—and eagerly swilling water when given it. He was thin and lank.

The caravan men were so sleepy, Orrin says, that he could hardly wake them in the morning. They turned over on their faces to shun him.

Coming out of the caravan, there were the mountains, in the quiet sunset; and many men drunk, swearing and fighting. Shanties with liquor for sale.

The elephant lodged in our barn.

The combined circus-menagerie of J. J. Nathans and Richard Sands and partners publicized its five clowns in a large lithographed poster, eleven feet by nine, in 1856. Prints and Photographs Division, Library of Congress.

Henry David Thoreau thrilled at the wildness of the animals exhibited in menageries. He gave a lyrical description of the canvas "pagoda in perfection," with its lingering smell of trampled grass and cigar smoke, that seemed mysterious, graceful, exotic, Oriental.[7] On August 1, 1851, he described his second visit in two months to the traveling show. His chief complaint was its overtly commercial intent.

Henry David Thoreau, *Journal*, vol. 2., *The Writings of Henry David Thoreau*, ed. Bradford Torrey (1906; New York: AMS Press, 1968), 367–68, 369.

I went to a menagerie the other day, advertised by a flaming show-bill as big as a barn-door. The proprietors had taken wonderful pains to collect rare and interesting animals from all parts of the world, and then placed by them a few stupid and ignorant fellows, coachmen or stablers, who knew little or nothing about the animals and were unwilling even to communicate the little they knew. You catch a rare creature, interesting to all mankind, and then place the first biped that comes along, with but a grain more reason in him, to exhibit and describe the former. . . . Not a cage was labelled. There was nobody to tell us how or where the animals were caught, or what they were. . . . I go not there to see a man hug a lion or fondle a tiger, but to learn how he is related to the wild beast. . . . Let it be a travelling zoölogical garden, with a travelling professor to accompany it. At present, foolishly, the professor goes alone with his poor painted illustrations of animals, while the menagerie takes another road, without its professor,—only its keepers, stupid coachmen. . . The present institution is imperfect precisely because its object is to enrich Van Amburgh & Co., and their low aim unfits them for rendering any more valuable service.

The *Knickerbocker*, the prestigious New York literary magazine, published the first American essay on the circus in 1839. It depicted a village accustomed to itinerants, but so excited by the circus's annual visit that the minister's warnings are ignored. The acts described—the youth's transformation into the lady rider, and the comic Tailor's Ride to Brentford—were standard English tradition. Unusually, the writer draws attention to the African Americans segregated among the spectators. The usual custom in the North was to put blacks in a separate "enclosure"; in the South they were often excluded entirely.

"The Circus," *Knickerbocker* 13 (January 1839): 68–69, 70, 72, 74–76.

A travelling caravan is an integral portion of the great institute in the metropolis. When the summer comes, it is broken up into parts, which are dispersed in every section of the country, that the imprisoned beasts may have the benefit of pure air. These consist, for the most part, of a lion, a tiger, a black bear, a camel, a wild cat, a hyena, some torpid snakes, coiled up in a box, and in a separate apartment a pan-

For patrons of Clyde Wixom's circus in the 1890s, one of the chief attractions was the display of caged exotic animals in the sideshow. Collections of the Henry Ford Museum and Greenfield Village.

orama, and a man who "sings Jim Crow." This latter is the most noxious beast of the whole clan. Besides these, a great number of monkeys, apes, and ring-tailed baboons are shut up in a community. These be capital fellows, full of spirits, which go the whole length of their ropes, and are better worth seeing, the spectators themselves being judges, than all the tigers, zebras, and hump-back camels, put together. Among themselves, they are "hale fellows," chattering and grinning, jibing, and cracking their jokes, as if in some forest of Africa, save when a bystander rolls in an "apple of discord," or a cake, and then the big ones flog the small ones unmercifully; and herein consists the kernel of the joke. A Shetland pony goes round and round in a circle, surmounted by a jocko in scarlet uniform, who proves himself an indomitable horseman. He leaps on and off, handles the reins with address, and cracks his whip like a Jehu. Sometimes a small African elephant is made to kneel down, and receive a tower on his shoulders. Those of the company who desire to ride, are requested to step forward, "ladies first, gentlemen after-*wards*." After a deal of hesitation, a servant-maid gathers courage, and simpering and dimpling, ambles into the arena. Her the showman politely assists to ascend. Another follows, and another, until all the seats are taken up. Then the beast moves once around, with his slow and heavy tramp, the *ladies* descend from their airy height, and are able to go home and say that they have "ridden on the elephant." Last of all, a negro is encouraged to mount the animal's bare back, and broadly grinning, is looking down upon the crowd below, when the latter, being privy to a joke, gives a violent shrug, and hurls him, as from a terrific precipice, to the ground. . . .

The menagerie is a very popular entertainment, unexceptionable on the score of morals, and visited by the "most straitest sects" of the people. . . .

It is a season of still deeper excitement, in such a retired country village, when once a year, after several days' heralding, a train of great red wagons is seen approaching, marked in large letters, CIRCUS, 1, 2, 3, 4, and so on. . . . A discussion waxes warm among the graver part of the community, about the lawfulness of these amusements. Some of the young are troubled with doubts. The old people hesitate, demur, and at last give their consent. They have been young once themselves—such opportunities do not occur everyday. Indeed, it would be very difficult for anyone to demur, after reading the "bill of fare," a great blanket sheet, full of wood cuts and pictures; horses on the full run, and men bent into all possible shapes and contortions. "Unrivalled Attraction! Grand entrée. Four-and-twenty Arabian horses. Celebrated equestrian Mr. Burke. Feats in the ring. Grand leap. Cups and ball. The entertainments to conclude with the laughable farce of Billy Button, or the Hunted Tailor." . . .

The sun is just resting on the borders of the horizon, and making the summer evening lovely, when the whole equestrian *corps*, a signal being given, sally forth and wind through the grass-skirted lanes of the village. A band of music goes before, drawn in a chariot by four dappled horses. The notes of the bugle floating exquisitely on the tranquil air, fill the rustic bosom with enthusiasm. The equestrians follow in gorgeous, spangled dresses, the clown standing up on one leg, with a straw in his mouth, and giving a foretaste of those facetious inanities which he will exhibit at even. Just at dusk, they return to the pavilion. A motley crowd rushes hurriedly through the streets. The minister of the parish looks out from his window, and weeps. He is a good man, and God will shelter his little flock from harm. The scrupulous and the wavering are now decided. Those who but yesterday said, crabbedly, that they had "no time, nor money nother, for such wild doings," bustle off, "just to see what's going on." Many persons of approved gravity attend, who "suld have known better." To the negro population, the occasion is a heyday and holiday. The Pompeys are there, and the Catos are there, and the noble lineage of the Caesars. Thus all the population are collected beneath the great tent. . . .

The area of the enclosure is divided into the ring, pit, and boxes. A circular wooden frame-work depends [hangs down] in the centre, containing a great many tarnished lamps, and magniloquently called a chandelier. . . .

Are there any in the whole area who will experience more genuine satisfaction, than the descendants of Ham? They are huddled together in one corner, dark, cloud-like, a distinct people. How will smiles and pleasantry be diffused over their features, like light bursting from the darkness! How will the whites of those eyes be uprolled in extacy, those even teeth glisten like ivory, and laughter break forth from the bottom of their souls, every laugh being worth a dollar! . . . It is high time that the performances commenced. "Music! music!" shout the crowd; and the orchestra without more ado plays a national air. Another piece is performed, and the tramping of horses is heard without. . . .

Tramp, tramp, tramp! There they come. Observe the grand entrée, by four-and-twenty Arabian horses, while the rustic mother claps her infant to her breast, scared by these terrible sports. At the first irruption of the cavalcade, the audience are be-wildered with the general splendor of the scene. The horses, beautifully marked and caparisoned, are obedient to the slightest will of the rider, and yet by their proud looks and haughty bearing, seem conscious of their lineage; while the equestrians vie with each other in rich costume, and their plumes dropping softly over their painted faces, make them as bright as Lucifer, in the eyes of the crowd. They ride gracefully, display-ing to advantage their elastic forms, swollen into full proportion by exercise and train-ing. As soon as the audience is sufficiently recovered to particularize the different members of the troop, they are attracted by the grotesque behaviour of the clown, who has got upon his horse the wrong way, and sits preposterously facing the tail. In this manner he slips on and off, encouraged with immense laughter. Next the remarks go round, and everyone praises to his neighbor the remarkable lightness and agility of a juvenile equestrian. He has not yet completed his eleventh summer, and not a horseman in the troop can vie with him in daring. The ladies who adorn the dress circle, regard him with smiles and approbation. *O! pulchrum puerum!* What a fair boy! How his ringlets flutter over his brow, in beautiful dishevelment, fanned by the wan-ton breeze. They could almost pluck him from his flying steed, and arrest his course with kisses. So light and agile is he, that he appears not human, but, as he flies round the ring with a daring rapidity, and his snow-white trowsers and gemmed vest mingle their colors, and become indistinct, he seems like an apple-blossom floating on the air. But look! look! What the devil is that fellow at, disrobing himself? He has kicked himself out of his pantaloons, and thrown away his coat, his horse flying all the while. "Angels and ministers of grace defend us!" he is plucking off his very—shirt! Nay, nay, do not be so alarmed, nor turn away your heads, ye fair ones, timidly blushing. Look again, and behold a metamorphosis more wonderful than any in Ovid; for lo! he pursues his swift career in the flowing robes of a woman! And now the pony is to perform a no less wonderful exploit, and leap through a balloon on fire. . . .

The second part of the diversions is a fescennine [scurrilous] dialogue, made up of alternate strokes of rude raillery, interspersed with songs and merriment, affording as keen a relish as the best Attic salt. . . .

Last of all, comes BILLY BUTTON, OR THE HUNTED TAILOR. I forget the plot of this piece, exactly, which is yearly enacted with much acceptation in every considerable village in the country. There are some very good points about it, that never come amiss to a rural audience, as when the perverse pony shakes off the cabbaging [thieving] tailor from his back, not allowing him to mount, or, dangerously acting on the offensive, chases him around the ring. And now the entertainments are about to conclude, let us indulge a wish that the ladies who have been seated near the crevices in the awning, may not catch their death a-cold, and that no evil whatever may result from the occasion. The clown bounces into the arena with a bow; doffs his harlequin aspect, and assumes the serious air of an every-day man. "Ladies and gentlemen, the entertainments of the evening are concluded. We thank you for your polite atten-dance." In a twinkling the canvass is rent down over your heads, the lights are ex-tinguished, and while the equestrians are already preparing to depart to the next village, the motley assemblage moves homeward through the dark night, yelping like savages.

Dan Rice, the most famous clown at midcentury, came annually to Brook-lyn's Fulton Street campground. An anonymous reporter, most probably Walt Whitman, a prolific writer of brief essays about city life, saw his show of riders, acrobats, and comics in 1856 on either August 20 or 21. For the essayist, the circus typified the nation's youthful and physical vitality.

[Walt Whitman], "The Circus," *Life Illustrated* (August 30, 1856), in *New York Dis-sected: A Sheaf of Recently Discovered Newspaper Articles by the Author of Leaves of Grass*, ed. Emory Holloway and Ralph Adimari (New York: R. R. Wilson, 1936), 193–96.

To witness the feats of the Ring is, to a very large proportion of our people, the only public amusement which breaks the monotony of the year. The Circus is a na-tional institution. Though originating elsewhere, and in ages long previous to the beginning of History, it has here reached a perfection attained nowhere else. . . . Doubtless, some of the funny things we saw Mr. Dan Rice doing in his tent in Brooklyn last week, have amused young humanity for a hundred years. Nothing is so tenacious of life as a joke.

Yes—we spent an evening perched on one of the excruciatingly narrow boards of Mr. Dan Rice's big tent, and we must avow that we were entertained exceedingly, and that we saw nothing and heard nothing calculated to do harm to any human being. Once or twice there was perhaps an approach to a double entendre on the part of the clown, which should have been avoided. It may have been unintentional, however. The manager of such an establishment, which amuses a million persons a year, should regard himself somewhat in the light of a public instructor. He should consider that seven-tenths of his audience are *boys*, upon all of whom his performances produce a thrilling effect, and who will be likely to catch a moral tone, as well as the ingenious tricks, of the Ring. As a general rule, the clown's jokes and the master's grandiloquent speeches are extremely virtuous and intensely patriotic—which makes it all the more desirable that the faintest appearance of indecency should be absolutely forbidden. The presence of ladies (in thousands) has tended no doubt to the purification of the circus. If clergymen—in country places—would make a point of attending the performances occasionally, it would have an excellent effect upon the performers, upon the audiences, and upon themselves. . . .

There is no use in decrying the circus. Even if it were the bad thing which some narrow good people think it is, it could not be put down. It is exactly suited to the place it fills. Residing in Brooklyn near where Dan Rice pitched his mighty tent, we had an opportunity of observing the intense interest which is awakened, and the intense delight which the performances gave. A week before its arrival, the fences broke out with bills announcing the coming of the "Great Show." From that day young Brooklyn was agog. On the evening when we formed one of a compressed mass of human beings melting under the tent, there was not a foot of space vacant. Seven thousand persons were present. They were seated in great, ascending circles around the ring— a stilled whirlpool of human faces. The mere seating of this great concourse was a moral lesson. The quiet, easy way in which the regulations were enforced, the ready acquiescence of nearly every one in those regulations, the summary but passionless ejectment of any boy or youth who refused to observe them, the care taken of the ladies, the perfect order that prevailed everywhere, the universal *right feeling* of the audience, the manly civility of the attendants, were all admirable to witness. No policemen were necessary, though a few were present. All were effected by the three or four employees of the circus.

The performers, we have said above, were unexceptionable. But they were more than that—they were of remarkable excellence. Dan Rice, as a clown, is not equal to his reputation; his jokes were not of extra quality, and he pronounces the English language in a "stewen-jew-ous" manner. But the sight of such beautiful and sagacious horses as he has, is worth the time it costs. His riders, too, and strong men, and dancers, are all perfect in their several ways, and afford a lively evidence of what *practice* will enable men to do. It can do no harm to boys to see a set of limbs displaying all their agility. It is pity, we admit, that the education of any man should be confined to his brain. But if we do not scruple to let children see men, and go to school to men who have no other than a brain development, let us not refuse occasionally to let them attend the evening school of these wonderfully leg-developed individuals. A circus performer is the other half of a college-professor. The perfect man has more than the professor's brains and a good deal of the performer's legs.

If, therefore, this circus of Mr. Dan Rice is a fair specimen of the circuses going about the country, we conclude that the circus is, to say the least, not a bad thing. It might be better. It ought to be scrupulously decent. The slightest looking down toward impropriety should be promptly hissed down. But on the whole we are glad we went, glad to see a circus in Brooklyn to go to, and glad that the circus is an established institution of the country. Something very good may come of it, by-and-by.

Silas Wheeler managed a medium-sized circus based in Boston in the 1860s. It probably carried a standard hundred-foot-diameter tent capable of seating a thousand and had a dozen canvasmen to erect it promptly. One of its key attractions was the Great Polka Horse Keil. There were probably five riders, notably Mme. Louise Tournaire and her daughter Josephine, the "fairy star." Other performers were four acrobats, including Mlle. Jeanette Ellsler on the tightrope and the Brothers Snow, Nat Austin and another clown, and perhaps three musicians in Prof. Silloway's Cornet Band. Wheeler charged a fee of two hundred dollars for candy stand concessions, and four hundred for sideshows whose chief exhibits in 1863 were Hiram and Barney Davis, the Wild Men of Borneo. The main expenses were wages, hotels and stables, printing and bill-posting. Perhaps because it had no menagerie that year, it traveled quite rapidly—about twenty miles a day, usually overnight—during the six-month tour of northern New England and the Maritimes. Some details of the Wheeler circus's itinerary are missing.

Copeland MacAllister, *Uncle Gus and the Circus: The Circus Activities of Augustine Constant from 1850 to 1871* (Framingham, Mass.: n.p., 1984), 12.

ITINERARY OF S.O. WHEELER'S GREAT INTERNATIONAL CIRCUS 1863

Date		Town	Miles
April	20	Cambridgeport, Mass.	
	21	Waltham	14
	22	Roxbury	15
	23	South Boston	4
	24	East Boston	5
	25	Chelsea	2
Sunday			
	27	Weymouth Landing	15

	28	East Abington	9
	29	North Bridgewater	5
	30	South Bridgewater	9
May	1	Taunton	9
	2	New Bedford	20
Sunday			
	4	Newport, R.I.	25
	5	Fall River, Mass.	18
	6	Pawtucket, R.I.	20
	7	Providence	5
	8	Providence	
	9	Phenix	10
Sunday			
	11	Woonsocket	24
	12	Milford, Mass.	12
	13	Worcester	19
	14	Natick	25
	15	Charlestown	19
	16	Lynn	8
Sunday			
	18	Salem	4
	19	Lawrence	19
	20	Lowell	10
	21	Lowell	
	22	Nashua, N.H.	12
	23	Manchester	15
Sunday			
	25	Haverhill, Mass.	25

* *

	28	Portsmouth, N.H.	
	29	Exeter	11
	30	Dover	18
Sunday			
June	1	Saco, Me.	35
	2	Portland	16
	3	Portland	
	4	Gray Corners	15
	5	Lewiston Falls	15
	6	Augusta	30
Sunday			
	8	Gardiner	8

* *

	17	Bangor	
	18	Bangor	
	* *		
	24	Eastport	
	25	Calais	25
	26	Journey to Canada: in St.John's, New Brunswick on July 14	
August	26	Gorham, N.H.	
	27	Lancaster	27
	28	Littleton	20
	* *		
Sept.	1	Plymouth	
	2	Laconia	24
	3	Franklin	12
	4	Concord	18
	5	Hillsborough	21
Sunday			
	7	Newport	28
	8	Lebanon	24
	9	Cornish Bridge	15
	10	Claremont	10
	11	Walpole	22
	12	Keene	15
Sunday			
	14	Brattleboro, Vt.	16
	15	Greenfield, Mass.	20
	16	Northampton	19
	17	Holyoake	10
	19	Springfield	
Sunday			
	* *		
	25	Athol	
	26	Winchendon	14
Sunday			
	30	Fitchburg	
	* *		
Oct.	13	South Danvers	
	14	Gloucester	15
	15	Marblehead	20
	16	Lynn	7
	17	East Boston	9

Sunday		
19	Charlestown	2
20–24	Boston Fairgrounds	2
	end of season	

Big Business

William Cameron Coup was the managerial genius of the modern circus. After joining the circus in Indiana as a teenager, he supervised sideshows in the south and midwest for more than twenty years before joining Barnum and Dan Castello. "P. T. Barnum's Museum, Menagerie and Circus, International Zoological Garden, Polytechnic Institute and Hippodrome" was organized in 1871. His greatest achievement, possibly suggested by Barnum, was converting the traditional horse-drawn wagon show to railroad cars in 1872. He exploited the new network of railroads and planned schedules across half the continent, bypassing towns now too small to cover the costs of performing. A moving army of thirty wagons mounted on railroad flatcars, supported by an advertising party of advance men and bill posters scouting ahead, traveled a hundred miles a day, and gave three three-hour performances a day in one huge tent with two show rings, and subsidiary sideshow tents. The Barnum circus partners introduced the second ring, and later the third ring, and made the show much more of an elaborate spectacle. Electric arc lights illuminated nighttime performances. The circus under the Barnum partners became synonymous with aggressive advertising: the half-page woodcut in newspapers in the 1830s, revolutionary at the time, was dwarfed by vast color posters—an 1882 hundred-sheet bill, twelve feet by ninety-six feet, was the biggest single picture ever printed.

After Coup's death in 1895, his recollections, recorded in the early 1890s, were rewritten by Forrest Crissey as anecdotal reminiscences depicting the golden age of the modern circus.

W. C. Coup, *Sawdust and Spangles: Stories and Secrets of the Circus* (Chicago: H. S. Stone, 1901), 59–60, 61, 64, 68–69, 63, 104, 105, 106–7, 107–8, 110, 124, 129, 130, 132, 133–34, 135, 136–38.

It requires several months of hard labor to prepare any show for the road, even those already organized, for, as a rule, all shows, "lay off" during the winter. . . . The manager then decides on his route for the coming season. This, in itself, is an arduous labor, for the cost of transportation becomes, necessarily, a most important consideration in his calculations.

The manager of a large show, however, can do this with comparative ease, since he does not fear opposition so much as does the manager of the small show and consequently, may choose his own territory, while his small opponent must skirmish around to get out of the way of the larger show. . . .

Therefore, the route of the big show is completed on paper not later than the first of February, and the first agent, usually the railroad contractor, begins his duties. . . .

Previous to 1872 the "railroad circus" was an unknown quantity. Like all other circuses of the day, the big show of which I was the manager traveled by wagon. During our first season our receipts amounted in round numbers to $400,000, exclusive of side shows, concerts and candy stands. Of course, we showed in towns of all sizes and our daily receipts ranged from $1,000 to $7,000. Finding that the receipts in the larger towns were frequently twice and three times as much as in the smaller ones, I became convinced that we could at least double our receipts if we could ignore the small places and travel only from one big town to another, thereby drawing the cream of the trade from the adjacent small towns instead of trying to give a separate exhibition in each. This was my reason for determining to move the show by rail the following season. . . .

Small shows had, prior to this time, traveled to a limited extent by rail; but not with accommodations like ours. Such shows consisted of seven or eight cars, whereas ours numbered sixty-one. . . .

Now we had Pullman cars for the artists, sleeping cars for the laborers, box cars for the extra stuff, palace cars for the horses and other large animals, such as were required for teaming, parades, etc., and platform cars for wagons, chariots, cages and carriages. Thus the Herculean task of putting the first railroad show of any magnitude on its own cars was successfully accomplished. . . .

Finally, however, system and good order came out of chaos. Once properly launched on our season, we were able to give three performances daily, and quite often made jumps of one hundred miles in one night. The scheme, as I had predicted, completely revolutionized the show business. . . . It also greatly advertised us, vast crowds assembling at the depots to see us load and unload. . . .

Our experience with the vast crowds of the season before had given us the idea of building two rings and giving a double performance. This, of course, doubled our company, but it kept the audience in their seats, since they were precisely as well off in one part of the canvas as in another, whereas in the old one-ring show we found it impossible to prevent the people who were farthest from the ring from standing up. They would rush to the front and thus interfere with many other people. This two-ring arrangement seemed to obviate this difficulty, and, as it at once hit the popular fancy, it proved a great drawing-card for us and others, for within a few months smaller showmen all over the country began to give two-ring performances. . . .

It may not be generally known to the public, but it is a fact, that nearly one-half of the entire expenditure of a circus is incurred in the work of the advance brigades. The advertising material, its distribution, express, freight and cartage, together with the salaries, transportation and living expenses of seventy-five to one hundred men, amount to vast sums of money. . . .

Big Business

Though, of course, there is a limit to possible receipts, there is no doubt that the business secured is in proportion to the sum used in advertising, and it is almost impossible to draw the line at which judicious advertising should stop. . . .

In 1880, in order to boom the "Newly United Monster Shows," I arranged some very peculiar and novel advertising features in the way of three cars especially fitted out for the use of my advance agents. The first brigade was accompanied by an enormous organ, for which a car was built, the latter being drawn through the streets by an elephant. . . . This, of course, attracted the people, and the brigade would then advertise the show by a lavish distribution of handbills. . . .

My second advertising car was fitted up with another enormous organ of far-reaching power, and attracted much attention, while my third and last advertising brigade rejoiced in the possession of an engine to which was attached a steam whistle of such power and discordant tone that it could be heard for miles. . . .

As that car with its whistle would steam into a town, its inhabitants would flock as one man to see what it was that had so disturbed their peace, and thus it was that we were enabled to advertise more thoroughly than any show before or since. . . .

Between these three advertising brigades I had smaller companies, accompanied by a colored brass band, which discoursed pleasant music while my bill posters decorated the dead walls and boards. The band also gave concerts at night upon the public square and, between pieces, a good speaker would draw attention to the excellences of the coming show.

A uniformed brigade of trumpeters was also sent through the country on horseback, and a band of Jubilee [gospel] singers marched through the streets singing the praises of the "Newly United Shows." Added to these attractions were two stereopticons that pictured, from some house-top or window, the main features of the show. This, together with perhaps the most liberal newspaper advertising that ever had been done, made the whole advance work as near absolute perfection in show business as possible. . . .

The printing bills of a first-class show are enormous. My lithograph bill alone, the last successful season of my show, amounted to $40,000, and this was before the days of extensive lithographing. . . .

Shows thrive best on bluster and buncombe [bunkum]. Years of experience have taught me that the traveling show business handled by capitalists who have never been trained in other lines of enterprise can never succeed. I have often been reproved by business men who were astounded at the lavish and apparently wasteful expenditures of the circus for "show and blow," and who have insisted that these expenses should be cut in half. It is true that such reckless expenditures in any ordinary commercial undertaking would be disastrous, but it is the life of the big show. When it is possible thoroughly to arouse the curiosity of the public, expense should be a secondary consideration. . . .

I have often been asked what it costs to start a circus and menagerie. This is a most difficult question to answer, since it depends entirely on the size and pretensions of the enterprise in question. Shows vary in size from cheap affairs, capable of being carried in three railroad cars, to the elaborate institutions which require two long special trains for their transportation. The expense of running a large show is enormous, although in advertising this expense is usually exaggerated. . . .

In the eye of the law a circus must have feats of horsemanship in its program, and such shows have to pay a "circus" license, which in some states and cities is very high. If, however, the shows do not give any riding, their performance simply consisting of leaping, tumbling, and athletic feats, then a license may be taken out at a greatly reduced price; and this accounts for the almost numberless small shows which annually tour the country. Of the circus and menagerie show proper I do not think there are more than twenty in America; but of tented exhibitions, billed as "railroad shows," there are several hundred. The tented exhibitions employ from fifty to six hundred men each, and the capital invested in them runs from $5,000 to $250,000. . . .

The flat and stock cars used by circuses are much more substantially constructed than the ordinary ones used in the railroad freight business, and are considerably larger, most of them being sixty feet in length and fitted with springs similar to those of passenger trains. Cars of this description cost from $500 to $800 each. . . .

The small circuses that hover around Chicago and the larger cities of the West in summer usually use a tent about eighty feet across, with two thirty-foot middle pieces. This, equipped with poles, seats and lights, costs about $800. These tents are made of light material. The larger canvases have to be made of stouter stuff, and a tent suitable for hippodrome or spectacular shows, which must be about 225 feet in width and 425 or 450 feet in length, would cost about $7,000. . . .

The draught horses . . . bought by me averaged $200 each; the usual circus horse, however, costs much less, and so long as it does its work all right [in parades and general haulage] the main purpose is answered. . . . Ring horses, whether for a "pad" or a "bare-back" act, must have a regular gait, as without it the rider is liable to be thrown. They are frequently and generally owned by the performers themselves, and I have known a crack rider to pay as high as $2,000 for one whose gait exactly suited him. . . .

Though it would be comparatively easy to start a circus and menagerie equipped almost entirely with second-hand paraphernalia, the reader will see from the following figures that the cost of starting a new first-class circus and menagerie is another proposition. Here are a few official figures on the cost of a first-class circus and menagerie which have never before been made public. They are taken from my private record, or invoice book:

20 cages at $350,	$7,000.00
2 Band wagons at $1,500 each,	3,000.00
3 Chariots at $3,000 each,	9,000.00
1 Wardrobe wagon,	800.00
1 Ticket wagon,	400.00

The above for the parade.
Animals to fill these cages will average about:

2 Lions,	2,000.00
2 Royal Tigers,	2,000.00
2 Leopards,	400.00
1 Yak,	150.00
1 Horned Horse,	500.00
2 Camels,	300.00
2 Elephants,	3,000.00

(As small elephants have been delivered here for
$1,000 each, this is probably a fair average.)

1 Hippopotamus,	5,000.00
1 Rhinoceros,	5,000.00
2 Cages of monkeys,	1,000.00
1 Kangaroo,	200.00
1 Cassowary,	200.00
1 Ostrich,	500.00
1 Giraffe,	1,500.00

Other small animals including hyenas, bears,
ichneumon [mongoose],

birds, etc.,	2,000.00
12 Baggage wagons at $200,	2,400.00
4 Roman chariots,	1,000.00
125 Horses at $125 each,	15,625 .00

This price is above the average.

125 Harnesses at $15,	1,875.00
2 Advertising cars,	5,000.00
Wardrobe,	3,000.00
2 Sleepers,	5,000.00
10 Flat cars at $400,	4,000.00
6 Horse cars at $400,	2,400.00
Elephant car,	500.00
Tents,	4,000.00
	$88,750.00

This could be reduced by eliminating the rhinoceros, hippopotamus, giraffe, and other very expensive animals, but to this must be added considerable money for stakes, shovels, picks, stake pullers, extra ropes, tickets, blank contracts and all necessary printing, which would bring the cost of the usual "million dollar" circus and menagerie up to about $86,000.

On all this property there is not one dollar of insurance. Once, when on the road, a live stock insurance company came to me to insure our horses, but at the rate at which they wanted to insure them I soon convinced them that we could not make any money.

I might add that a circus and menagerie at the figures I have given would be far better and larger than the average "million dollar show" now on the road, there being certainly not more than three aggregations that cost more than the amount I have given. No man should attempt the show business who has not a fortune, and also plenty of that other kind of capital quite as essential to his success—long experience on the road.

Apart from a brief tour of the South in 1836 and organizing the Asiatic Caravan in the early 1850s, P. T. Barnum had comparatively little direct experience of circuses. His partnership with Coup and Castello in the 1870s involved him in publicity and finance rather than daily management, but, as he informed his friend Mark Twain, he took an interest in all details.

Selected Letters of P. T. Barnum, ed. A. H. Saxon (New York: Columbia University Press, 1983), 189–90.

Bridgeport, 19 January 1875
My dear Clemens,
. . . My *daily* expenses in New York are nearly $5000. They will be more than that while travelling. Last August I had an immense tent made, over 800 feet long by 400 broad, and transported it to Boston, where I built seats to accommodate 11,000 persons, & I transported my entire hippodrome to Boston. There were over 1200 men, women, & children engaged by me; 750 horses, including 300 blooded race horses & ponies; camels, elephants, buffaloes, English stag and stag hounds, ostriches, &c. &c. (Don't mention menagerie of lions, tigers, & other wild beasts, for I don't take them *travelling* with hippodrome.)

Now the cost of tent, seats, and transporting the entire hippodrome & paraphernalia to Boston by rail was over $50,000. And yet though I was in Boston but 3 weeks, I was fully reimbursed and had a handsome surplus. We accommodated over 20,000 persons to our two performances each day and frequently turned away visitors for want of room. Cheap excursion trains ran daily on all the roads leading into Boston, and thousands daily came in them.

Now by having *two* of these 800 feet tents, so as to keep one continually a day ahead, I shall next summer take the entire hippodrome on 125 railroad cars of my own to all the *larger* towns in New England and the middle & western states, frequently stopping but one day in a town. I can easily lose half a million of dollars next summer *unless* I can in advance so awaken and electrify the country as to have *everybody* join in getting up excursion trains so as to hit me where I open the hippodrome. If I *can* do this, I can *make* half a million, so it is a pretty big stake to play for—hence my anxiety. I take along *sleeping* cars wherein nearly all my 1200 employees lodge every night (I put up berths in ordinary passenger cars), and I take along cooks and cooking tents where all except 150 of my 1200 employees get every meal they eat during the travelling season. Horse tents also accommodate my horses, elephants, camels, &c. I carry blacksmiths & blacksmith tents to do all my horse-shoeing, repairing of chariots, wagons, &c. I also carry harness makers. I carry carpenters and builders who precede the show ten days to build the seats. I carry wardrobe men and women to repair and care for the wardrobe, which has cost me over $70,000 and which I use in processions and all the various plays, scenes, and the great street procession which occurs every morning. I take two immense bands of music, first-class.

My hippodromic exhibitions include the Roman chariot races and many other acts that were shown in the Roman Colosseum 1600 years ago, and on a scale that has not been witnessed in this world during the last thousand years. My Roman chariots are driven by Amazons instead of men.

But I show besides scores of thrillingly interesting scenes which Rome never saw. . . .

The great English stag hunt wherein 150 ladies and gentlemen appear on horseback all dressed in appropriate hunting costumes, with the English stags and a large pack of real English stag hounds, depicts a scene worth going a hundred miles to see.

Then of course we have hurdle races by ladies; Roman standing races (the riders standing on bareback horses); flat races by English, American, and French jockeys, with the best blooded race horses to be found in Europe; races by camels ridden by Arabs; elephant races; liberty races by 40 wild horses turned loose; ostrich races, monkey races, and the most remarka[ble] performances by elephants and other animals. Taken altogether, this is a colossal travelling exhibition *never* before equalled and what no other man in this generation will ever dare to wish. It involves a capital of nearly a million of dollars. My expectation is to take it all to Europe next autumn, for it will prove even a greater wonder there than here.

Truly yours,
P. T. Barnum

In 1884 the Barnum circus upgraded its dime museum "Congress of Nations" to the "Ethnological Congress of Savage Peoples," and billed as central attractions, "Bestial Australian Cannibals; Mysterious Aztecs; Embruited Big-Lipped Botocudoes; Wild Moslem Nubians; Ferocious Zulus; Buddhist Monks; Invincible Afghans; Pagan Burmese Priests; Ishmaelitish Todars; Dusky Idolatrous Hindus; Sinuous Nautch Girls; Annamite Dwarfs; Haughty Syrians; Oriental Giants; Herculean Japanese; Kaffres; Arabs; Persians; Kurds; Ethiopians; Cicassians; Polynesians; Tasmanians; Tartars; Partans; Etc."[8]

In the 1888 illustrated guidebook for junior readers, Barnum leads his New York "child-friends," Tom and his younger sisters, through his circus. After they meet the performers, and before they see the animals, they go "Among The Curiosities."

THE CIRCUS

P. T. Barnum and Sarah J. Burke, *P. T. Barnum's Circus and Menagerie: Text and Illustrations Arranged for Little People* (New York: White and Allen, 1888).

"Look at the dhirty nagurs, Bridget!"

This is what Tom heard an Irishman say, and he turned his head to see a band of Nubians, black as crows, but not at all dirty.

"I don't like them," said Gay; so Mr. Barnum took them to look at the Chinese baby, sitting in its mama's lap. It clutched its little hand tight in Gay's lace cap, but she only laughed. Tom soon left the "dhirty nagurs" for the Afghan chiefs, one of whom let Tom handle his sword. Oh, how he longed to keep it! He thought—he was only nine, you know—how it would make the fellows on his block stare! But just then he happened to spy the Zulu warriors, and they were so much more horrible than the Afghans, that Tom returned the sword with thanks.

"Do Zulu *women* fight?" asked Trixie, seeing a fierce-looking woman in the group.

"You bet!" said the shortest of the Zulu men, in very good English, while he rolled his eyes toward the ceiling, with a sigh.

"I say, Trix," said Tom, wandering back to examine some old English coats of mail which had escaped his attention before, "wouldn't you like to see a tournament?"

Mama had read to him one of Sir Walter Scott's stories, with its magnificent description of the tournaments of early days in Merry England. Many a night as he lay in bed, he had tried to picture to himself the scenes that the great story-teller had described, and had fallen asleep to dream of Good Queen Bess and her gallant knights and lovely ladies.

"What is a tournament?" asked Trixie.

"Why, don't you know? A tournament is—a tournament was"—

"Was a sham fight between knights on horseback," said Mr. Barnum, coming to his assistance. "It was one of the ways in which the kings and queens of Europe entertained their royal guests, hundreds of years ago."

"Well, I should rather see a tournament than a bull fight," said Trixie.

Bull-fights and tournaments! Such difficult subjects for a baby to understand! But Gay could appreciate what she called the "Skye-dog people."

"She means Skye terrier—she is so little!" said Trixie, sweetly.

Oh, how the children laughed at the dog-faced family! "Sure enough, they are like terriers in petticoats," said Trixie, "and they look as though their bangs had slipped down on their cheeks!" She almost expected ro hear them cry, "Yap! Yap!" but they didn't.

"I wonder how he does it!" said Tom to himself, looking at the tattooed man. "I'm going to ask him! I'd like to try it on some little out-of-the-way place on myself." But, when questioned, the curious fellow said that it could only be done with a dry black feather, plucked from the wing of a hokey-pokey—"and," he added, "hokey-pokeys are very scarce in America." So Tom gave up the idea.

"What a grumpy old lot!" he complained later, refering to the Indian family. He had been teasing them, and Mr. Barnum knew it. "Ugh! Ugh!" they had sighed, in turn and in chorus.

"Tom," said Mr. Barnum frowning, "I'm ashamed of you!" and I am glad to say that Tom felt ashamed of himself.

The fattest old chief then turned to the fattest old squaw, and said something which I am sure meant, in English, "That boy ought to be scalped, and I'd like to be the one to do it!"

Quite as unsociable as the Indians were the wild Australians. They were throwing boomerangs, or curved sticks of wood, which, if they struck nothing, returned to the hand of the thrower. "It would save a deal of scamper and looking if a fellow's ball would do that," said Tom.

In 1884 the five Ringling brothers from Baraboo, Wisconsin, introduced the grandly named Yankee Robinson's Great Show, Ringling Brothers' Carnival of Novelties, and DeNar's Museum of Living Wonders. They were successful from the start and began to eliminate their competitors, and in 1907 they purchased the major rival, Barnum and Bailey's Greatest Show on Earth. In 1910 Alfred Ringling gave magazine readers a "behind-the-scenes" insight into the operations of the show.

Alfred T. Ringling, "What the Public Does Not See at a Circus," *National Magazine* 12 (1900): 189–92.

The wonders of a big modern circus are not so much in the show the audience sees, strange though this may be, as in the working details that lie hidden just beyond the public's view. On the other side of the tri-colored curtains that separate the dressing-rooms from the spectators, is found the real life of the actor-folk; the rings and stages are merely the screens upon which such parts of the view judged to be most pleasing to the circus-goers are shown.

As a characteristic of American life, "circus day," no matter on what day it occurs, is a semi-public holiday. We have other holidays, but there is only one circus day.

In the rush and activity of city life, the coming and passing of the circus, though no less interesting, is not so emphasized by its surroundings as in a country town. Here one may see to-day a meadow where only the peaceful grazing of the cows gives life to the scene, and to-morrow, Aladdin-like, a great city of white tents has arisen, its many flags and acres of canvas undulating in the morning breeze, its inhabitants, numbering many hundreds, moving about with the nonchalance of old settlers, yet there only for the day.

Enchantment played no part in the erection of the tents. Hard work and quick, intelligent action, dominated by system, comprised the magic that reared this city of an hour, which has its blacksmith shop with ringing anvil, barber shop, hotel, wagon shop, post office and paint shop. In fact, all it needs to be a town in itself is a state charter and a village council: for it has its doctor, its 1awyer, its veterinary surgeon, its mail carrier and its detective.

To transport the Ringling Brothers' circus and menagerie, sixty-five cars, averaging sixty feet in length, are required. Every cage, chariot, horse, elephant or other animal has an individual spot on one of the cars for it. Everything is loaded at night with special reference to the order in which it will be required on the morrow, and the several trains follow each other in regular order, as well.

The first train of cars carries the superintendents and working people, the draught horses, tent and pole wagons and canvas. As soon as this train reaches the next town, the superintendent of tents, with his assistants, starts for the show grounds to "lay out" the lot. With tape lines the location of each tent is soon measured out and a perfect plan of the grounds made. In a few minutes more, hundreds of small steel pins mark the places where the stakes which hold the tent ropes are to be driven.

The canvasmen are detailed in squads of six and eight pounding at one stake, their rapid strokes following each each other like the regular swing of a pendulum. It takes ten minutes to lay out the lot and about a half hour to drive the stakes, and then the welcome sound of the breakfast horn is heard.

While the chef and his assistants are cooking the breakfast, the waiters, dishwashers and other cook-tent employees erect the dining tents, place the tables in position and get them ready for an army of employees. Forty minutes to build a hotel, and on its completion to have a meal ready for hundreds of hungry men! It is quick time, but it is part of the system, and a very necessary part, for it has a great deal to do with the driving of the tent stakes. It accelerates the speed of the sledge gangs, who know that they will not be ready for breakfast any sooner than breakfast will be ready for them.

All of the working people of the circus eat on the show grounds. The performers, musicians and principals have meals served to them in specially constructed Pullman dining cars.

While the canvasmen are eating breakfast, tentage in immense bales, ropes and long poles accumulate on the lot until a sight is presented which to the novice seems chaotic, but the speed with which the long poles are raised skyward, the tents unrolled and laced together and ropes fastened to hold everything in place, shows that every bit of circus paraphernalia is unloaded by the teamsters just where needed.

The first show for the public is the parade. In one-day stands, except in the event of some unusual delay, it leaves the show grounds at ten o'clock. In this long cavalcade of hundreds of horses, uniformed people and gaily trapped animals everything has its place.

On the return of the parade to the show grounds the cages and dens are wheeled into the menagerie tent. The cages must be placed snugly together. Horses cannot do this, so two men take a short tongue and thus guide each vehicle into place while an elephant pushes it. The intelligence displayed by these big beasts in performing this work is truly remarkable and as interesting as any of their feats in the rings.

I remember once seeing one of our elephants called "Babe" pushing with all her might to move the hippopotamus den into place. The ground was muddy, and the big pachyderm's efforts merely tended to sink the big van deeper into the yielding sod. After several attempts to move the den, Babe stepped back a few feet, stood as if reflecting a moment and then deliberately wound her trunk around the axle and raised the wagon out of the mud, at the same time pushing it forward while the men in front "poled" it into position.

In teaching an elephant to perform in the ring the trainer depends upon the animal's intelligence and memory, while the horse learns to do things from habit. It would seem from this that a greater degree of patience is necessary in training a horse. This, however, is not the case, for the horse, after being induced to do a thing many times, will from force of habit repeat the thing, while the elephant has enough of the reasoning sense in him to question the utility of repeating his lessons at times.

In the winter quarters of our circus is a large brick building where the elephants are housed. In the center of the structure is a training ring of the regulation circus size. All winter the trainers are busy teaching the elephants new tricks and rehearsing them in the old ones. To teach an elephant to dance a hornpipe, to play a barrel-organ, to beat a drum and to play upon a brass trombone are achievements which require patient hours and many of them; and these are given ungrudgingly by the trainers during the long winter months while the circus is at rest—and what is called "rest" with a circus is really a continuation under different circumstances of the "strenuous life" of the showman.

The hardest task in teaching an elephant is to make him stand on his front feet, while his rear extremities point in the direction of ten o'clock. Only by years of patient work can this be done, and the elephant selected for the work must be a young animal so that the muscles needed to maintain a position so unnatural for such a heavy beast may be developed and strengthened for the feat. There is no particular rule for training an elephant to do thing of this kind. The trainer simply uses his resources to get the animal in the position desired as often as possible.

Madame Noble's horse, Jupiter, which walks across the ring in a vertical position, while the daring horsewoman maintains her position in the saddle, was taught the feat while a colt by being fed apples from a point high above his head, which he could reach only by raising himself to the position for which he has since become famous. The tender muscles of the colt were thus developed to sustain him in a position unnatural to the horse of everyday life; and the task of afterward making him perform this work in a place where apples could not be fed to him from a derrick, was solved by rewarding him immediately after he passed from the big tent into the passage-way to the stables.

Kindness, patience and perseverance are the key to the training of all animals. Of the sixty-one horses in the O'Brien act, which is such a leading feature of our ring performances, each animal had to be first trained individually; and only after many months of patient work could more than one horse be added at a time, the number training together being increased by twos and fours gradually, until the entire sixty-one were brought together.

Every animal has some inherent trait by which he is made to learn. All animals in varying degrees are reached by their sense of taste. A dominant and sensitive chord in the horse is pride, and the trainer must sound it at proper moments. He must be a diplomat in dispensing flattery to the proud animal. He needs all the finesse of a suitor wooing a high-strung belle of the season. While the animals of a circus are worked hard and long to perfect them in their feats, the people who perform in the rings, on the stages, hippodrome and races, each working from a personal motive and imbued with individual ambitions, submit themselves to a most rigid discipline of training.

Abstemiousness is a positive necessity to the performer who would have his nerves and muscles steady and strong for his "stunts." The regime of exercise to which he applies himself both winter and summer produces a physical type so sound that there is no thirst for stimulants. Fresh air, and lungs developed to receive it, shower baths and a good digestion make him a normal, physical type who, in consequence, enjoys moral health as well.

Probably the most mysterious part of the circus, and the one which is hidden the most securely from the public eye, is the dressing room which is divided into two compartments, one for the men and one for the women. Each one of these enclosures has a row of trunks laid around the sides, while the center is mapped out like the streets of a town. Each trunk is a dressing table, and it is not unusual to see 150 persons dressing in the aisles of either room.

Those who have seen the wonderful act of Millie Turnore, have, perhaps, never thought of her except as a young woman of nerve and courage.

As they watch her swinging in the dome of the tent on the slender rod of the trapeze, never once touching her hands, they are too lost in amazement to inquire into that part of her life which is beyond the tent. To the spectator she is a circus performer, but those acquainted with her domestic life know her as a loving mother. In a seminary in the east there are three girls, who twice each week write to this brave woman. One is just finishing her education and the other two are steadily advancing in their studies. The money that is providing these daughters with a college education is earned by the woman whose performance has thrilled thousands.

In the 1890s circuses published route books of the year's itinerary. At the turn of the century, in a year beginning on April 2 and ending on November 19, one unnamed circus [probably Barnum and Bailey's] traveled 11,569 miles, visiting 167 towns and cities in 26 states and provinces in the eastern United States and Canada. Sunday was the rest day for the performers human and animal, an arrangement that also recognized local sabbatarian wishes.

Big Business

W. C. Thompson, *On the Road with a Circus* (n.p.: Goldmann, 1903), 208–13.

DATE		TOWN	STATE	RAILROAD	MILES
APRIL	2–19	New York	N.Y.		
		Sunday			
	21–26	Philadelphia	Pa.	Penn R.R.	99
		Sunday			
	28–29	Baltimore	Md.		113
	30	Washington	D.C.		50
MAY	1	Washington			
	2	Hagerstown	Md.	B. & O. R.R.	77
	3	Cumberland	Md.		124
		Sunday			
	5	Clarksburg	W.Va.		124
	6	Fairmont	W.Va.		82
	7	Connellsville	Pa.		70
	8	Washington	Pa.		96
	9–10	Pittsburg	Pa.		42
		Sunday			

In 1906, Harry C. Rubincam, a member of Alfred Steiglitz's Photo-Secession group, captured a rare view of a circus equestrienne who has just leaped over the banner stretched across the ring. Hallmark Collection.

12	Johnstown	Pa.	Penn R.R.	79
13	Altoona	Pa.		39
14	Lewistown	Pa.		75
15	York			97
16	Reading	Pa.		89
17	Pottsville	Pa.		36
	Sunday			
19	Wilkesbarre	Pa.		118
20	Scranton	Pa.	C.R.R. of N.J.	18
21	Allentown	Pa.		103
22	Easton	Pa.		17
23	Elizabeth	N.J.		62
24	Jersey City	N.J.	Penn R.R.	14
	Sunday			
26–31	Brooklyn	N.Y.	Ferry	
JUNE 2	Paterson	N.J.	Erie R.R.	17
3	Newburg	N.Y.		47
4	Kingston	N.Y.	West Shore	32
5	Schenectady	N.Y.		70
6	Gloversville	N.Y.	W.S.F.J. & G.	37
7	Utica	N.Y.	N.Y.C. & H.R.	61
	Sunday			
9	Poughkeepsie	N.Y.	N.Y.C. & H.R.	165
10	Danbury	Conn.	N.Y.N.H.& H.	63
11	Ansonia	Conn.	N.Y.N.H.& H.	30
12	Meriden	Conn.	N.Y.N.H.& H.	31
13	Holyoke	Mass.	B. & M.	49
14	Greenfield	Mass.	B. & M.	38
	Sunday			
16	Gardner	Mass.	B. & M.	40
17	Lowell	Mass.	B. & M.	46
18	Lawrence	Mass.	B. & M.	13
19	Concord	Mass.	B. & M.	45
20	Manchester	N.H.	B. & M.	18
21	Haverhill	Mass.	B. & M.	33
	Sunday			
23	Portsmouth	N.H.	B. & M.	33
24	Biddeford	Me.	B. & M.	43
25	Portland	Me.	B. & M.	15
25	Lewiston	Me.	Grand Trunk	35
26	Berlin	N.H.	Grand Trunk	74
27	Sherbrooke	Quebec	Grand Trunk	99

		Sunday			
	30	Montreal	Quebec	C.P.	102
JULY	1	Montreal	Quebec	C.P.	
	2	Valleyfield	Quebec	C.P. & C.A.	51
	3	Ottawa	Ontario	C.A.	52
	4	Cornwall	Ontario	N.Y. & O.	85
	5	Kingston	Ontario	Grand Trunk	57
		Sunday			
	7	Belleville	Ontario	Grand Trunk	51
	8	Peterboro	Ontario	Grand Trunk	64
	9	Barrie	Ontario	Grand Trunk	88
	10	Toronto	Ontario	Grand Trunk	64
	11	Hamilton	Ontario	Grand Trunk	39
	12	Brantford	Ontario	Grand Trunk	27
		Sunday			
	14	Guelph	Ontario	Grand Trunk	36
	15	Stratford	Ontario	Grand Trunk	40
	16	Woodstock	Ontario	Grand Trunk	23
	17	London	Ontario	Grand Trunk	29
	18	St. Thomas	Ontario	L.E. & D.R.	15
	19	Chatham	Ontario	Grand Trunk	62
		Sunday			
	21	Buffalo	N.Y.	Grand Trunk	186
	22	Rochester	N.Y.	N.Y.C. & H.R.	69
	23	Geneva	N.Y.	N.Y.C. & H.R.	51
	24	Auburn	N.Y.	N.Y.C. & H.R.	26
	25	Cortland	N.Y.	Lehigh Valley	43
	26	Binghamton	N.Y.	D.L. & W.	43
		Sunday			
	28	Ithaca	N.Y.	D.L. & W.	55
	29	Elmira	N.Y.	D.L. & W.	70
	30	Williamsport	Pa.	Penn. Line	78
	31	Lock Haven	Pa.	Penn. Line	25
AUGUST	1	Dubois	Pa.	Penn. Line	101
	2	Butler	Pa.	Penn. Line	122
		Sunday			
	4	Wheeling	W.Va.	B. & O.	110
	5	Zanesville	Ohio	B. & O.	83
	6	Mansfield	Ohio	B. & O.	87
	7	Lima	Ohio	P. Ft. W. & C.	86
	8	Springfield	Ohio	D. S.	67
	9	Columbus	Ohio	Big Four	45

	Sunday				
11	Piqua	Ohio	P. C. C. & St. L.	73
12	Richmond	Ind.	P. C. C. & St. L.	47
13	Indianapolis	Ind.	P. C. C. & St. L.	68
14	Anderson	Ind.	Big Four	36
15	Marion	Ind.	Big Four	33
16	Logansport	Ind.	P. C. C. & St. L.	40
	Sunday				
18	Springfield	Ill.	Wabash	195
19	Jacksonville	Ill.	Wabash	34
20	Quincy	Ill.	Wabash	87
21	Keokuk	Iowa	Burlington	43
22	Burlington	Iowa	Burlington	43
23	Galesburg	Ill.	Burlington	40
	Sunday				
25	Kewanee	Ill.	Burlington	32
26	Sterling	Ill.	Burlington	92
27	Aurora	Ill.	C. & N.W.	70
28	Elgin	Ill.	C. & N.W.	27
29	Racine	Wis.	C. & N.W.	72
30	Waukesha	Wis.	C. & N.W.	42
	Sunday				
SEPT. 1	Marinette	Wis.	C. & N.W.	205
2	Green Bay	Wis.	C. & N.W.	52
3	Oshkosh	Wis.	C. & N.W.	48
4	Janesville	Wis.	C. & N.W.	103
5	Freeport	Wis.	C.M & St.P.	50
6	Rock Island	Ill.	C.M & St.P.	93
	Sunday				
8	Peoria	Ill.	C.R.I. & P.	100
9	Lincoln	Ill.	C. & A.	93
10	Pontiac	Ill.	C. & A.	64
11	Bloomington	Ill.	C. & A.	35
12	Danville	Ill.	Big Four	80
13	Lafayette	Ind.	Wabash	47
	Sunday				
15	Huntington	Ind.	Wabash	84
16	Defiance	Ohio	Wabash	84
17	Toledo	Ohio	Wabash	29
18	Findlay	Ohio	T. & O. C.	44
19	Bellefontaine	Ohio	Big Four	63
20	Dayton	Ohio	Big Four	58

Big Business

		Sunday			
	22	Chillicothe	Ohio	C.H. & D.	81
	23	Athens	Ohio	B. & O. S. W.	60
	24	Charleston	W. Va.	T. & O. C.	103
	25	Huntington	W. Va.	C. & O.	50
	26	Mt. Sterling	Ky.	C. & O.	107
	27	Lexington	Ky.	C. & O.	33
		Sunday			
	29	Chattanooga	Tenn.	I. & C.	254
	30	Tullahoma	Tenn.	N.C. & St.L.	82
OCT.	1	Nashville	Tenn.	N.C. & St.L.	69
	2	Paris	Tenn.	N.C. & St.L.	117
	3	Jackson	Tenn.	N.C. & St.L.	80
	4	Memphis	Tenn.	N.C. & St.L.	85
		Sunday			
	6	Tupelo	Miss.	K.C.S.F. & M.	105
	7	Birmingham	Ala.	K.C.S.F. & M.	146
	8	Anniston	Ala.	Southern	64
	9	Rome	Ga.	Southern	62
	10	Atlanta	Ga.	Southern	74
	11	Athens	Ga.	S.A.L.	73
		Sunday		S.A.L.	
	13	Augusta	Ga.	S.A.L.-C. & W. C.	119
	14	Anderson	S.C.	C. & W. C.	103
	15	Greenwood	S.C.	C. & W. C.-S. A. L.	63
	16	Greenville	S.C.	Southern	59
	17	Spartanburg	S.C.	Southern	32
	18	Charlotte	N.C.	Southern	70
		Sunday			
	20	Wilmington	N.C.	S.A.L.	187
	21	Florence	[S].C.	A.C.L.	110
	22	Columbia	[S].C.	A.C.L.	82
	23	Sumter	[S].C.	A.C.L.	43
	24	Charleston	[S].C.	A.C.L.	94
	25	Savannah	Ga.	A.C.L.	115
		Sunday			
	27	Jacksonville	Fla.	A.C.L.	172
	28	Waycross	Ga.	A.C.L.	75
	29	Valdosta	Ga.	A.C.L.	59
	30	Thomasville	Ga.	A.C.L.	45
	31	Albany	Ga.	A.C.L.	58
NOV.	1	Americus	Ga.	C. of G.	36

A SUPERB, GLORIOUS, ORIGINAL DEPARTURE!
⇒←⇒⇒ SOMETHING NEW ⇐⇐⇐→←

TREMENDOUS FREE SPECTACULAR STREET CARNIVAL

CAMPBELL BROTHERS GREAT CONSOLIDATED SHOWS

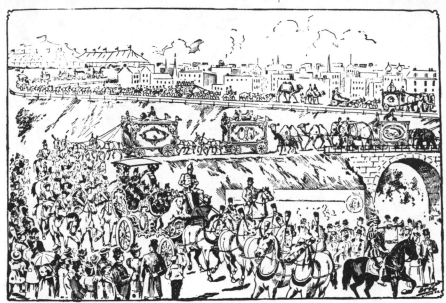

BIG NEW STREET PARADE
OLD IDEAS ABANDONED
A POSITIVE INNOVATION

MAGNIFICENT FLOATS, HUGE SIGHTS OF MILITARY GORGEOUSNESS. IMMENSE CHARIOTS, FIERCE
WILD BEASTS, MANY KINDS OF MUSIC, FINEST HORSES. A VISION OF BEAUTY AND
SPLENDOR NEVER SEEN BEFORE. A FORTUNE IN TRAPPINGS AND ACCESSORIES.

ALL NEW ORIGINAL AND UNIQUE
EACH SECTION A PARADE IN ITSELF FORMING A MOST STUPENDOUS

Free Public Pageant Every Morning at 10 A. M.

Campbell Brothers circus toured the Midwest, and its 1905 poster trumpeted the glories of the free street parade. Ed Brady, *The Story of the Campbell Brothers Circus: The Canvas That Covered the Plains* (Traverse City, Neb.: n.p., 1981).

	Sunday			
3	Macon	Ga.	C. of G.	70
4	Columbus	Ga.	C. of G.	100
5	Montgomery	Ala.	C. of G.	95
6	Selma	Ala.	W. of A.	50
7	Meridian	Miss.	M. & O.	73
8	West Point	Miss.	Ill.Ct.Y. & M.V.	9
	Sunday			
10	Kosciusko	Miss.	Y. & M.V.	70
11	Greenwood	Miss.	Y. & M.V.	73
12	Greenville	Miss.	Y. & M.V.	132
13	Vicksburg	Miss.	Y. & M.V	82
14	Fort Gibson	Miss.	Y. & M.V	30
15	Baton Rouge	La.	Y. & M.V	116
	Sunday			
17	New Orleans	La.	Y. & M.V	89
18	New Orleans	La.		
19	New Orleans	La.		

The Audience

Hamlin Garland grew up in many different communities in the Midwest. For those engaged in the hard, unrelenting toil and lonely misery of farm life, the traveling circus offered hope and escape. In late middle age Garland remembered the appeal of the annual visit of the horse-drawn caravans as the canvas "mushrooms" suddenly appeared in June in "Sun Prairie."

Hamlin Garland, *Boy Life on the Prairie* (New York: Macmillan, 1899), 231–32, 234–36, 237–38, 243–47.

There were always three great public holidays,—the Fourth of July, the circus, and the Fair, which was really an autumn festival. . . . Of all these, the circus was easily the first of importance; even the Fourth of July grew pale and of small account in the "glittering, gorgeous Panorama of Polychromatic Pictures," which once a year visited the country town, bringing the splendors of the great outside world in golden clouds, mystic as the sky at sunset. . . .

No one but a country boy can rightly measure the majesty and allurement of a circus. To go from the lonely prairie or the dusty corn-field and come face to face with the "amazing aggregation of world-wide wonders" was like enduring the visions of the Apocalypse. From the moment the advance man flung a handful of gorgeous bills over the corn-field fence, to the golden morning of the glorious day, the boys speculated and argued and dreamed of the glorious "pageant of knights and ladies, glittering chariots, stately elephants, and savage tigers," which wound its way down the yellow posters, a glittering river of Elysian splendors, emptying itself into the tent, which housed the "World's Congress of Wonders." . . .

Teams came streaming in over every road till the town was filled as if it were the Fourth of July. Accustomed to the silence of the fields, or the infrequent groups of families in the school-houses, the prairie boys bowed with awe before the coming together of two thousand people. . . . Neighbors greeted each other in the midst of the throng with such fervor as travellers show when they unexpectedly meet in far-off Asiatic cities.

Every child waited in nervous impatience for the parade, which was not a piece of shrewd advertising to them, but a solemn function. A circus without a parade was unthinkable. It began somewhere—the country boys scarcely knew where—far in the mystery of the East and passed before their faces,—the pageantry of "Ivanhoe" and the "Arabian Nights," and red Indians, and Mohammedanism and negro slavery,—in procession. It trailed a glorified dust, through which foolish and slobbering camels, and solemn and kingly lions, and mournful and sinister tigers, moved, preceded by the mountainous and slow-moving elephants, two and two, chained and sullen, while closely following, keeping step to the jar of great drums and the blaring voices of trumpets, ladies, beautiful and haughty of glance, with firmly-moulded busts, rode on parti-colored steeds with miraculous skill, their voices sounding small in the clangor of the streets. They were accompanied by knights corsletted in steel, with long plumes floating from their gleaming helmets. They, too, looked over the lowly people of the dusty plains with lofty and disdainful glance. . . .

The town boys, alert and self-sufficient, ran alongside the open chariot where the lion-tamer sat, surrounded by his savage pets, but the country boys could only stand and look, transfixed with pleasure and pain,—the pleasure of looking upon it, the pain of seeing it pass. They were wistful figures, standing there in dusty, ill-fitting garments, sensitive, subtle instruments on which the procession played, like a series of unrelated grandiose chords. As the lion passed, vague visions of vast deserts rose in their minds. Amid toppling towers these royal beasts prowled in the vivid moonlight. The camels came, reaching long necks athwart the shadows of distant, purple pyramids, and on hot stands at sunset, travellers, with garments outblown by the sirocco, passed near a crouching Arab. Mounted on elephants with uplifted trunks, tiger-hunters rode through long yellow grass. The feudal tournaments rolled back with the glittering knights. The wealth of the Indies shone in the golden chariots of the hippopotami. The jungles of Hindoostan were symbolized in the black and yellow bodies of the tigers, the heat of Africa shone from their terrible eyes. All that their readers, histories, and geographies had taught them seemed somehow illustrated, illuminated, irradiated, by this gorgeous pageantry. . . .

As they came out upon the green, the huge white tents, the fluttering flags, the crowds of people, the advertisements of the side-shows, the cries of the ticket-sellers and lemonade and candy men, appalled the country-boys. . . . The tumult was benumbing. On the left of the path was a long line of side-shows, with enormous

148

billowing canvas screens, on which were rudely painted the wonders within,—a pig playing a violin, an armless man sewing with his toes, a bearded lady, a fat boy, a man taking a silk hat from a bottle, while on a stool before each door stood alert and brazen-voiced young men, stern, contemptuous, and alien of face, declaring the virtues of each show, and inviting the people to enter. . . .

[T]he boys . . . moved slowly round the circle of the chariots, wherein the strange animals from the ends of the earth were on view. The squalling of parrakeets, the chatter and squawk of monkeys, the snorting of elephants, the deep, short, gusty elemental *ough* of the lions, the occasional snarl of the leopards, restlessly pacing, with yellow-green eyes glaring, the strange, odd, hot smells,—all these made the human fist very small and of no account. These beings whose footfalls were like velvet on velvet, whose bodies were swift as shadows and as terrible as catapults, whose eyes emitted the blaze of undying hate; these monstrous, watery, wide-mouthed, warty, uncouth creatures from rivers so remote that geographers had not reached them; these birds that outshone the prairie flowers in coloring; these serpents whose lazy, glittering coils concealed the strength of a hundred chains,—. . . and then, on top of it all, came the men and women of the circus proper. . . .

[T]he ring of the circus . . . crackled with the cries of alert men selling fans, ice-cream, sticks of candy, and bags of peanuts. It was already packed with an innumerable throng of people, whose faces were as vague to the boys as the fans they swung. Overhead the canvas lifted and billowed, and the poles creaked and groaned, and the rope snapped with the strain of the brisk outside wind. . . .

The band flared out into a strongly accentuated march, and forth from the mystic gateway came the knights and their ladies, riding two and two on splendid horses, and the boys thrilled with the joy of it. . . . The color, the glitter, the grace of gesture, the precision of movement, all so alien to the plains—so different from the slow movement of stiffened old farmers and faded and angular women, as well as from the shy and awkward manners of the beaux and belles of the country dances; the pliant joints and tireless limbs, the cool, calm judgment, the unerring eyes, the beautiful muscular bodies of the fearless women—a thousand impressions, new and deep-reaching, followed. . . .

Oh, to be one of those fine and splendid riders, with no more corn to plough, or hay to rake, or corn to husk. To go forth into the great, mysterious world, in the company of those grand men and lovely women; to be always admired by thousands, to bow and graciously receive thanks, . . . to be able to live under the shining canvas in the sound of music.

In William Dean Howells' nostalgic, semiautobiographical account of his youth in Hamilton, Ohio in the 1850s, the circus was uniquely exciting. The menagerie's parade was also colorful, but the performance of the exotic animals in the ring lacked action and drama. Most of all, it lacked the sense of moral danger that the spangled gods and goddesses of the circus ring had for small boys.

THE CIRCUS

William Dean Howells, *A Boy's Town* (New York: Harper and Brothers, 1890), 99–102.

The boys liked to be at the circus early so as to make sure of the grand entry of the performers into the ring, where they caracoled [wheeled] around on horseback, and gave a delicious foretaste of the wonders to come. The fellows were united in this, but upon other matters feeling varied—some liked tumbling best; some the slack-rope; some bare-back riding; some the feats of tossing knives and balls and catching them. There never was more than one ring in those days; and you were not tempted to break your neck and set your eyes forever askew, by trying to watch all the things that went on at once in two or three rings. The boys did not miss the smallest feats of any performance, and they enjoyed them every one, not equally, but fully. They had their preferences, of course, as I have hinted; and one of the most popular acts was that where a horse has been trained to misbehave, so that nobody can mount him; and after the actors have tried him, the ring-master turns to the audience, and asks if some gentleman among them wants to try it. Nobody stirs, till at last a tipsy country-jake is seen making his way down from one of the top-seats towards the ring. He can hardly walk, he is so drunk, and the clown has to help him across the ring-board, and even then he trips and rolls over on the sawdust, and has to be pulled to his feet. When they bring him up to the horse, he falls against it; and the little fellows think he will certainly get killed. But the big boys tell the little fellows to shut up and watch out. The ring-master and the clown manage to get the country-jake on to the broad plat-form on the horse's back, and then the ring-master cracks his whip, and the two supes who have been holding the horse's head let go, and the horse begins cantering round the ring. The little fellows are just sure the country-jake is going to fall off, he reels and totters so; but the big boys tell them to keep watching out; and pretty soon the country-jake begins to straigthen up. He begins to unbotton his long long gray over-coat, and then he takes it off and throws it into the ring, where one of the supes catches it. Then he sticks a short pipe into his mouth, and pulls on an old wool hat, and flourishes a stick that the supe throws to him, and you see that he is an Irishman just come across the sea; and then off goes another coat, and you see a British soldier in white duck trousers and red coat. That comes off, and he is an American sailor, with his hands on his hips dancing a hornpipe. Suddenly away flash wig and beard and false-face, the pantaloons are stripped off with the same movement, the actor stoops for the reins lying on the horse's neck, and James Rivers, the greatest three-horse rider in the world nimbly caters on the broad pad, and kisses his hand to the shouting and cheering spectators as he dashes from the ring past the braying and bellowing brass-band into the dressing-room!

The big boys have known all along that he was not a real country-jake; but when the trained mule begins, and shakes everybody off, just like the horse, and another country-jake gets up, and offers to bet that he can ride that mule, nobody can tell whether he is a real country-jake or not. This is always the last thing in the perfor-

150

mance, and the boys have seen with heavy hearts many signs openly betokening the end which they knew was at hand. The actors have come out of the dressing-room door, some in their everyday clothes, and some with just overcoats on over their circus-dresses, and they lounge about near the band-stand watching the performance in the ring. Some of the people are already getting up to go out, and stand for this last act, and will not mind the shouts of "Down in front! Down there!" which the boys eagerly join in, to eke out their bliss a little longer by keeping away even the appearance of anything transitory in it. The country-jake comes stumbling awkwardly into the ring, but he is perfectly sober, and he boldly leaps astride the mule, which tries all its arts to shake him off, plunging, kicking, rearing. He sticks on, and everybody cheers him, and the owner of the mule begins to get mad and to make it do more things to shake the country-jake off. At last, with one convulsive spring, it flings him from its back, and dashes into the dressing-room, while the country-jake picks himself up and vanishes among the crowd.

Carl Sandburg was born in Galesburg, Illinois, and lived on East Berrien Street near the Chicago, Burlington and Quincy Rail Road depot. In old age, the famous poet and writer reminisced about the parochialism of his youth surrounded by neighbors also of Scandinavian descent. In the 1890s the agricultural fair and the circus were rare events which shook the small town out of its torpor. For Sandburg, the sideshow had the greatest allure.

Carl Sandburg, *Always the Young Strangers* (New York: Harcourt Brace, 1956), 189–90, 191–92, 193.

When the circus came to town we managed to shake out of sleep at four o'clock in the morning, grab a slice of bread and butter, and make a fast walk to the Q. yards to watch the unloading in the early daylight. A grand clear voice the man had who rode his horse a half block ahead of the elephants in the parade and cried out as though there might be hell to pay, "The elephants are coming, watch your horses!" First to one side of the street and then to the other he cried it and those who had skittish horses watched them.

After the unloading we went home for a quick breakfast and a run to the circus grounds, a big pasture at Main and Farnham near the city limits. If we were lucky we got jobs at carrying water for the elephants or lugging to the big tent the boards for the audience to sit on. After three or four hours of this useful and necessary work we were presented with slips of paper that let us in to see the big show in the afternoon. . . .

I walked round to the Side Show. There out front as a free show I saw the man with the elastic skin. He would pull it out from his face and neck and it would snap back into place. There I saw the tattooed man with fish, birds, brunette girls, ships, and many other shapes inked deep into his skin—and there too the Oriental Dancing Girl wearing few clothes and smiling about it to some giggling farm hands. The spieler, a man with a thick upcurled mustache, leaned toward the farm hands and said in a voice as if for them only to hear, "Go inside, boys. You can't lose. She takes off everything, every last stitch, and her muscles shake like a bowl of jelly. She makes a sick man feel like a wild monkey. What did you come here for, boys? She's got it. You can't lose."

Then the spieler dropped his confidential way and turned to the main crowd and let go in a smooth, loud voice. You could tell he was used to what he was saying and had spoken the same words in the same way a thousand times. "La-deez and gen-tul-men, beneath yon canvas we have the curi-aw-si-ties and mon-straw-si-ties—the Wild Man of Borneo, the smallest dwarf ever seen of mankind and the tallest giant that ever came into existence, the most marvelous snake ever brought to your fair city, a man-eating python captured in the darkest jungles of Africa ever penetrated by man. And I would call your particular attention to Jo Jo the dog-faced boy, born forty miles from land and forty miles from sea." . . . And we learned too from the spieler, the barker, about the dime. "The price of admission, la-deez and gen-tul-men, is a dime, ten cents only, the tenth part of a dollar. Buy your tickets now before the big rush comes."

I had a dime and a nickel in my pocket. With the dime, the tenth part of a dollar, I bought a ticket. I went in and heard the ventriloquist and his dummy: "Will you spell a word for me, Danny?" "I'll try, what's the word?" "Constantinople." "Why do you tell me you can't stand on an apple?" I saw the Wild Man of Borneo and I could see he was a sad little shrimp and his whiskers messy. The Fat Woman, the Dwarf, the Giant, they seemed to me to be mistakes God had made, that God was absent-minded when he shaped them. I hung around the midget and his wife, watched them sign their names to photographs they sold at ten cents—and they were that pleasant and witty that I saw I had guessed wrong about them and they were having more fun out of life than some of the men in the Q. shops.

I stood a long time watching the Giant and noticed that he was quiet and satisfied about things and he didn't care one way or another whether people looked at him. He was so easy and calm about the way things were going that he reminded me of a big horse that didn't have to work and eats regular—and never buys patent medicines. If a smarty asked, "How's the weather up there?" he might lift one eye-brow and let it pass, for he had heard it often enough. Nor did I feel sorry for the python. He may have been a man-eater but he was sleeping as if he had forgotten whoever it was he had swallowed and digested. After a third and fourth time around, the only one I felt sorry for was the Wild Man of Borneo. He could have been the only lonely creature among all the freaks. The Oriental Dancing Girl certainly was no freak, an average good-looking showgirl, somewhat dark of skin and probably a gypsy. She twirled, she high-kicked, did a few mild wiggles, and when it was over I heard a farm hand saying, "It's a sell. I thought from the way he talked outside that we was going to see a belly dance." "Yeah," said another, "and she didn't take off a stitch. It's a sell."

Years later it came over me that at first sight of the freaks I was sad because I was

152

bashful. Except at home and among playmates, it didn't come easy for me to be looked at. . . . And there at the side show were these people, the freaks—and the business, the work, of each of them was to be looked at by thousands of people and they were paid to be looked at. . . .

Then I came to a man sitting on the ground, a deep-chested man with a face that had quiet on it and wouldn't bawl at you. I noticed he was barefoot. I looked up from his bare feet to see his arms gone, only stumps of arms at his shoulders. Between the first two toes of his right foot he held a card and lifted it toward me and said, "Take it and read it." I read a perfect handwriting, every letter shaped smooth and nice. It said, "I can write your name for you on a card for you to keep. The charge is only ten cents." I looked into his face. I said, "I would if I had the ten cents. All I've got is a nickel." I took out the nickel and turned my pockets inside out and showed him that besides the nickel there was only a knife, a piece of string, and a buckeye. He took the nickel in his left foot. He put a pen between the first two toes of his right foot and on the card wrote "Charles A. Sandburg," lifted the foot up toward me, and I took the card. I looked at it. It was the prettiest my name had ever been written. His face didn't change. All the time it kept that quiet look that didn't strictly belong with a circus. I was near crying. I said some kind of thanks and picked up my feet and ran.

As a teenager, W. E. "Doc" Van Elstine ran away from his middle-class New York family to join the Mighty Yankee Robinson Circus. His first escape was brief, but after studying medicine in dilatory fashion, he abandoned a conventional career and served as a roustabout in charge of seats and tents in various circuses from the 1870s until he retired in 1917. In July 1938, aged ninety-one, he was interviewed for the Federal Writers' Project on "Circus Days and Ways," and he explained the joys of the traveling life.

W. E. "Doc" Van Elstine, interviewed by A. C. Herbert in Portland, Oregon, and transcribed on January 13, 1939, for Oregon Folklore Studies, Federal Writers' Project, Works Progress Administration [American Memory: American Life Histories: Manuscripts From the Federal Writers' Project, 1936–1940, http://memory.loc.gov].

I been asked to draw a comparison between the circus of today and the circus of the past. Well, they just ain't no comparison. The circus in this day and age seems really to be the stupendous, gigantic, colossal exhibition the advance billing and the "barkers," "spielers," and "grinders," claim for it. The oldtime circus was a puny forerunner of the mammoth aggregations now on the road. The circus your grandfather went to see as a boy, was nothin' more than a variety, or vaudeville, show under canvas. Pretty near all the acts they done in the circus could of been put on in even the ordinary theaters of that time. Could you imagine the Ringling Brothers' B[arnum &] B[ailey] show of today tryin' to squeeze itself into any theater, auditorium, or indoor arena in any town, say, like Portland?

The people who works for circuses today is all trained specialists. Everybody has only one job, and he's supposed to do that one thing well. The oldtime trouper was a Jack-of-all-trades. He could shoe a horse, if he had to, he could clown, drive a ten-horse team, lay out canvas, and fill in at anything around the lot except perhaps aerial acrobatics, and believe it or not, many of the old-timers could even "double" in acrobatics.

The circus has always been one of the world's most progressive enterprises. New inventions, if they was something the circus could use, was grabbed up by the circus as soon as they come out. The circus was always away ahead of anybody else in lighting equipment. When stores and business places throughout the country was still using tallow dips for light, the circus was using calcium flares bright enough to almost blind you. The pressure gaslights used by circuses in the early part of this century was intensely brilliant by contrast with the dim, dinky lights of the average town the circus visited. Many small-town oldtimers will tell you they first saw Edison's marvelous incandescent lamps when some circus came to town.

Yes, the circus of today is bigger and better in every way than circuses was, even twenty-five years ago. But the kids of today ain't so wide-eyed and amazed at what they see at a circus as they was a quarter of a century ago. So many marvelous things goes on all the time in this day and age that kids probably expect more from a circus now than it's humanly possible to give.

In my more than a half century with circuses I worked on all the big shows one time or another. The circus has took me to the four corners of both hemispheres, and has give me many exciting experiences. I seen circuses miraculously missed by cyclones in the prairie states. When you're standin' in the middle of a couple million dollars' worth of circus equipment, it's always a thrill to see a blackish, greenish cloud with its trailing, death-dealing funnel, bearing down on your show. The 'stock' in the 'animal top' (menagerie tent) knows a storm is comin' same as you do. Makes you feel kind of funny in the pit of the stomach, to hear them snarl, howl, whine, bellow and roar as the storm gets nearer. They get nervous, testy, mean, and it all adds to the confusion on the lot.

MELODRAMA

In Stephen Crane's novel *Maggie* (1896), sensational drama offers life-enhancing make-believe as well as pleasing fantasy and forgetfulness. The evening's entertainment allows the poor seamstress to forget her drunken mother and the squalid tenement apartment in Rum Alley, and the day spent sewing cuffs and collars in the garment factory. Everyone in the cheap Bowery variety saloon responds enthusiastically to the dime-novel plot. Even the rogues watching "revolted from the pictured villainy," "hissed vice and applauded virtue" with "untiring zeal." More than a decade later the Progressive reformer Jane Addams labeled the neighborhood nickelodeon the "house of dreams" because it so captured the imagination of the young. In similar fashion, the cheap theater gave Maggie hope—"raised spirits" and "made her think"—that middle-class gentility might be within reach for a sweatshop machinist. This entertainment was not mere escapism: "To Maggie and the rest of the audience, this was transcendental realism."[1]

Melodrama was not the antithesis of realism; it included sufficient and sufficiently realistic details to make the narrative credible. According to the late-eighteenth-century formulation, it had originally been pantomime set to music. However, although music remained a signifier of emotional stress and dramatic tension in the nineteenth century, visual spectacle became the dominant strain. In the 1830s and 1840s, Thomas Hamblin, the English-born manager of the Bowery Theatre, introduced the popular songs, farces, and melodramatic plays of adventure that had proved so popular in London, but given contemporary relevance with flamboyant staging and lighting. Where novel blackface representations thrived, so did plays distantly European in origin but with an American accent. Authentic details of locale mattered.

What audiences expected was hyper-reality. "Common sense was not wanted in the highest level of melodrama," writes David Grimsted, "but rather something stylized, refined, elevated above the level of ordinary existence."[2] Melodrama suited an age of class conflict, of industrial capitalism, of sudden urbanization and the onset of a market economy, of evangelical religion and its armies of the damned and the almost-saved. Sin was generally depicted as the product of character rather than circumstance. When self-help literature told of ascent from log cabin to White House and from the factory floor to business magnate, it taught that determined individuals, and not grand impersonal forces, lay behind such transformations. In frothy dime-novel romances of mill girls and millionaires or tramps and tycoons, Michael Denning has shown, "the pressure of the real persisted."[3] The more successful melodramas transported fairy-tale characters to recognizable local scenes stocked with familiar social types in a dramatic form that melded folk tale and modern saga.

Within melodrama there were class accents. The mainly working-class audiences of New York's Bowery and Chatham Theatres enjoyed action-packed scenes of emotional and physical conflict. Bruce McConachie has described these melodramas as "apocalyptic." Amid scenes of general catas-trophe—fire, flood, shipwreck, massacre, all displayed graphically with every scenic effect in the producer's arsenal—the villain met divine retribution. Vengeance for past wrongs was inevitable. Heroes of sound republican virtue triumphed over villains and rescued helpless damsels in distress. John Au-gustus Stone's *Metamora, or The Last of the Wampanoags* (1828), where the doomed Indian chief bravely defended land, honor, and womanhood, was a platform for Edwin Forrest, the actor favored by the Bowery. Forrest moved, wrote a less-than-enthusiastic critic, with exaggerated physical vigor, with "a sudden entrance, impressive invocations to heaven, certain menacing falls of the brow, and numerous seizures of a sort of histrionic asthma or shortness of breath."[4]

The middle classes retreated to more salubrious dime museum lecture rooms. There were fewer thrilling chases in their favorite "sensation" plays of moral uplift, but vivid emotional turmoil. The temptation, ruin, and shame, and occasionally, reformation, of drunkards and slaveholders gave both diver-sion and reassurance. If virtuous individuals died, virtuous moral principle ascended triumphant. The best-known scene was the conclusion of George L. Aiken's dramatization of Harriet Beecher Stowe's *Uncle Tom's Cabin*, with appropriate symbolism in unmistakeably vast form: "Gorgeous clouds, tinted with sunlight. Eva, robed in white, is discovered on the back of a milk-white dove, with expanded wings, as if just soaring upwards. Her hands are extended in benediction over St. Clare and Uncle Tom, who are kneeling, and gazing up to her. Impressive music—Slow curtain."[5]

Melodrama was a study in contrasts. It depicted the extremes of emotion, rather than delicate shades and nuances. To many in the audience, awakened by revivals, Hell was a living reality, and sin, a vivid and ever-present tempta-tion. They appreciated the stark alternatives posed of damnation or redemp-tion. What mattered was action, energy, movement, plot, and not nice de-velopment of character. On stage, motivation was indicated by a code of

gestures that were part of the nineteenth-century actor's canon and understood by the audience. The villain was malevolent, often comic, sometimes
foreign, brutal, and overbearing, and as black-hearted as his dress, or a sweet-
talking seducer and roué disguised in the latest fashion. The heroine was a
passive innocent, naïvely trusting in the sincerity of others, and, if saved from
destruction, owed her salvation to the almost-divine intervention of those
more worldly-wise.

In the popular media of the 1840s the modern metropolis was depicted as
a site of moral conflict. Fact met fiction. In the largest Atlantic coast cities the
Irish and German foreign-born and their children were a majority or near
majority, and most native-born inhabitants were recent arrivals from the
country. There seemed few certain landmarks, physical or moral, and few
individuals experienced in city ways. Amid unprecedented change, the detective story, the new penny press, the pamphlets issued by the many reform
agencies, and most of all, the cheap, sensational novels, exposed the horrors of
crime and turpitude. English and American authors—G. M. W. Reynolds'
Mysteries of London (1849) or George Lippard's lurid tales of the "Quaker
City"—copied Eugène Sue's sensational style. George G. Foster's accounts of
"sunshine and shadow" among the "upper ten thousand" and "lower million"
of New York claimed to be based on direct observation of the dens and pits
where dissolute high society joined in an unholy alliance with the disreputable many.

Sensational plays made tangible the moral panic about vice. Rich and
debauched "sporting men," "swells," and "bloods" mingled with confidence
men and devised cunning ploys to seduce, rob, and murder the innocent.
Naïve greenhorns and country "rubes" and "jakes" were their natural prey.
Appearances were deceptive, when these wolves in sheep's clothing were adept
in disguising foul thoughts with fair words. Most at risk were young women who
trusted the words of the sly deceiver, and who either trusted innocently or were
tied by family obligations. Their natural protectors were the honest, low-
comedy men of the lower classes. Mose, the Bowery B'hoy, the butcher and
volunteer fireman, was the no-nonsense, street-wise, pugnacious defender of
honor in Benjamin Baker's *A Glance at New York in 1848* and a dozen more
plays. Also too shrewd to be hoodwinked by tricksters and charlatans were the
plainly dressed, plain-speaking, country yokels, such as Adam Trueman in
Anna Cora Mowatt's *Fashion* (1845), natural democrats, suspicious of privilege
and dishonesty. With such stock characters, easily recognizable to the Bowery
audiences, melodramas served as guidebooks through the bewildering chaos
of the city.

Appreciation was robust, genteel etiquette ignored. In industrial Pittsburgh, James Parton saw an all-male audience, scrubbed clean after duty in
the iron mills, ignoring the management's signs for politeness. During the

program of farces, comic songs, and chorus-line dancing, "the people would keep up such a roar of laughter, that for many seconds at a time not a word could be heard from the stage."[6] Nineteenth-century audiences went to the theater expecting to be moved physically as well as emotionally. Phrenology and psychology taught that there was an intimate connection between the outer body and the inner mind, between appearance and character, between action and intention. What was required was experience and knowledge in interpreting the signs. The task of the talented actor was to convey by appropriate gesture those signs of motivation to the audience, and in the popular theater at least, for appreciative response of jeers or tears. The interaction of the interpretative actor and sympathetic spectator was robust, open, and physically exuberant.

In Charles M. Sheldon's *In His Steps* (1896), wealthy Felicia is already troubled in conscience by Calvin Bruce's sermon, but an English melodrama about the London poor prompts her to deeper thought about Chicago. The scenery depicting the pauper's hovel was "almost too realistic" and she "found herself living those scenes over and over." Sister Rose was less convinced:

> "But the slum scene was horrible. I think they ought not to show such things in a play. They are too painful."
>
> "They must be painful in real life, too," replied Felicia.
>
> "Yes, but we don't have to look at the real thing. It's bad enough at the theater where we pay for it."[7]

Years before, Herman Melville explained why fantastic exaggerations of the everyday appealed. In an interlude in *The Confidence-Man* he anticipated criticisms that his central character, the mysterious and ambiguous cosmopolitan, was too unreal to be believed. More liberal readers of fiction, he explained, "with that unreserve permitted to the stage . . . look not only for more entertainment, but at bottom, even for more reality, than real life can show. . . . Thus, though they want novelty, they want nature too, but nature unfettered, exhilarated, in effect transformed." Like melodrama, fiction transcended reality: "it should present another world, and yet one to which we feel the tie."[8]

After the Civil War, confrontations on stage were less elaborate. Gone were galloping horses, pirate ships, fights with brigands and highwaymen—or at least on the same grand scale. The plays of Dion Boucicault and Augustin Daly in the 1870s and 1880s had thrilling adventures and near disasters, but the plots tended to be more credible and the narrative more fully developed. The last flowering of the melodrama came with the "ten-twenty-thirty" theaters in the two decades before World War One. As well as low prices and frequent change of program, impresarios like Corse Payton at Brooklyn's Lee Avenue offered inducements—receptions, souvenirs, and for the women of the neighborhood who were a third of the audience, an annual baby show and a nursery.

One of the innovations was the "tabloid drama," the one-act play popular as a vaudeville turn. What was remarkable, reported Hartley Davis, was that "realism is not successful. Audiences want something apart from the routine of their own lives." The plays involved commonplace characters in sensational exploits. Critic Harry James Smith found the Thalia's melodramas overwrought but lively, compared with Broadway's pale creations. What the "shop girls" and their "steadies" enjoyed, he noted, was the gamut of emotions, however implausible and bewildering the plot. "The melodrama," he concluded, "is full of comedy; it is sure to follow every scene of pathos or violence."[9] When theatrical syndicates were at their peak, the Stair-Havlin group had thirty-five houses across the country where touring "combination" companies presented a different melodrama weekly. Numerous repertory tent shows also visited small towns offering scaled-down versions of popular plays. The cheap-theater market proved intensely competitive. Always challenged by vaudeville and musical comedy, by 1910 the ten-twenty-thirty theaters faced the threat of the new nickelodeons recast as grand "palaces." When movie producers switched from documentary realism to dramatic fiction, the melodrama theaters were too expensive to operate. In 1924 the experienced journalist Marian Spitzer reported on the cheap theater's demise. The revival of the old favorite, Theodore Kremer's *Fatal Wedding, or, the Little Mother*, which had run for years in the Bowery, failed after only eight performances. Movie melodramas had triumphed over melodramatic theater.[10]

A Plea for an American Drama

The novelist James Kirke Paulding was one of the most passionate advocates for a drama celebrating American nationality. He was stung by the jibes of British commentators like the Rev. Sydney Smith that the new republic lacked cultural achievement of note, and wrote the satirical *Diverting History of John Bull and Brother Jonathan* (1812). Others looked to literature, but Paulding also had high hopes for the theater as a moral and intellectual force, and he spurned both spineless deference to English traditions and absurd, sensationalist, crowd-pleasing melodrama. Later, his comedy *The Lion of the West* (1830) cast as hero, good-natured frontiersman Nimrod Wildfire chiding English snobs and their servile American imitators.

[James Kirke Paulding,] "American Drama," *American Quarterly Review* 1 (June 1827): 332, 333–34, 336, 338, 356.

Of all popular amusements ever devised, dramatic exhibitions are, when properly conducted, the most elegant and instructive. They address themselves both to the understanding and the senses, and carry with them the force of precept and example. In witnessing them, we are excited by the passions of others instead of our own. . . .

It is by this mode of giving play and excitement to the mind, by mimic representations, that the force of the operations of the passions in real life, is unquestionably tempered and restrained; and hence it has always been held with justice, that the stage, in its legitimate and proper state, is a most powerful agent in humanizing and refining mankind. It operates also in other ways in bringing about this salutary result. It allures the people from an attendance upon barbarous and brutifying spectacles—from brawls, boxing-matches, and bull-baitings;—it accustoms them, in a certain degree, to intellectual enjoyments and rational recreations; and substitutes innocent amusement, if not actual instruction, in the place of those which afford neither one nor the other. A theatre, where the price of admittance is within the means of the ordinary classes of the people, is a substitute, and a most salutary one, for tavern brawls and low debauchery. Those whose faculties are too obtuse to relish or comprehend the intrinsic excellence of a plot, the lofty morality or classic ease of the dialogue, are still instructed and amused through the medium of their eyes, and actually see before them examples to imitate or avoid. If it be said, that these examples are too removed from the ordinary sphere of those who witness them, to be of any use, still it may be replied, that chastity, fortitude, patriotism, and magnanimity, are virtues of all classes of mankind, and that all can feel and comprehend them, though they may be exercised in circumstances and situations in which they never expected to be placed. . . .

It is generally, we believe, considered a sufficient apology in behalf of the persons who preside over this most delightful of all intellectual banquets, that the degradation of the stage originated in the necessity of administering to a taste already vitiated. The public must be pleased, that the manager may live. If the people require the attractions of a menagerie and a puppet-show combined, and will relish nothing living, but horses, dogs, dromedaries, and elephants, prancing in the midst of pasteboard pageantry, conflagrations, bombardments, springing of mines, blowing up of castles, and such like accumulations of awful nursery horrors, it is alleged that there is no help for it. The taste must be gratified, like the appetites of other animals that chance to prefer raw meat, and offals, to the highest delicacies of the table. This may be true to a certain extent; but we are, notwithstanding, satisfied in our own judgment, that it is very materially in the power of the managers of theatres, to give a better direction to the public taste; and that it would eventually lead to the most profitable results, were they to take equal pains and incur equal expense, to cater for a good taste, that they do to pamper a bad one.

We are quite sure, that a theatre, devoted to the exhibition of none but legitimate dramas, in the hands of competent actors, would prove permanently attractive; rally around it almost all the more enlightened portions of society, and, by a natural consequence, all the inferior classes; and finally prove far more profitable to the manager than one devoted to expensive spectacles, one of which costs more to get up than a dozen first-rate tragedies and comedies. If one-half of the sums laid out on pasteboard, tinsel, and trumpery, were offered as a premium for good actors, a first-rate company might be collected, permanently, and fully adequate to give effect to the finest efforts of the dramatist. There would then be no necessity to depend on perpetual novelty, which supplies the place of good acting; and perpetual shows substituted for the beautiful creations of genius. . . .

We are therefore of opinion, that no small portion of this bad taste which we deplore, in relation to the stage, may be fairly laid to the charge of managers, who, if we mistake not, have been at least accomplices in producing that very state of things which they now offer as an apology for persevering the same course by which it was brought about. . . .

The perpetual exhibition of shows, possessing no other merit but that of imitating or rather caricaturing nature most vilely, has by degrees rendered the more refined classes of society quite indifferent to the stage. . . .

Another reason, probably, why so few writers attempt the stage of late, is the utter hopelessness of seeing justice done to their productions by the actors. Large as are our modern theatres, they can accommodate but one good performer at a time. . . . Only one sun can blaze in the heavens; and but one *star*, of all the galaxy of stars, can display its nightly glories, and twinkle us blind, at the theatres. If it should, therefore, unfortunately happen, that the author has developed more than one character in his piece, which requires something beyond the ordinary talent of a candle-snuffer to personate, it will almost inevitably happen that the piece is condemned. The really good actors belonging to the company, are kept in reserve, while the *star* is exhibiting its splendours; or if brought forward at all, are condemned to toil through their parts neglected and unapplauded, while the course of the *star*, however wayward and eccentric, is hailed with shouts of admiration. . . .

By the prevalence of this absurd vanity on the part of actors, and the equally absurd credulity of the public, our theatres are deprived of any permanent attractions other than those of gorgeous spectacles, prodigious dancers, and prodigious wild beasts. . . .

The want of a National Drama is the first thing that strikes us in this inquiry. By a national drama, we mean, not merely a class of dramatic productions written by Americans, but one appealing directly to the national feelings; founded upon domestic incidents—illustrating or satirizing domestic manners—and, above all, displaying a generous chivalry in the maintenance and vindication of those great and illustrious peculiarities of situation and character, by which we are distinguished from all other nations. . . .

We have no peculiar language to create an identity of our own; and it must, in a great measure, be in its apt and peculiar application to ourselves, our situation, character, government and institutions, that our literature would seem destined to become national. . . .

This land is full of materials—such as novelty of incident, character, and situation. Like the forests of our country which have never been cut down, those materials remain unemployed and unexhausted—fresh and novel, with all the bold features of primeval strength and vigour. It only requires a brave, original intellect to convert them into the materials of excellence. It has been often imagined as one of the obstacles which stand in the way of a national drama, that we lack variety in our national character. No idea, we think, can possibly be more erroneous than this. There is, probably, no country in the world, which affords more numerous and distinct characters than the United States. Our cities are full of bipeds from every quarter of the old world, bringing with them all their peculiarities, to be exhibited in a new sphere. From the city on the sea-side, to the frontier settler—from him to the white hunter, more than half savage— to the savage himself—there are continual gradations in the characters and situation of mankind; and every state in the Union is a little world by itself, exhibiting almost the same degrees of difference that we observe in the English, the Scotch, and the Irish. Their manners, habits, occupations, prejudices, and opinions, are equally various and dissimilar. For these reasons, we believe that there is no want of sufficient varieties of character in the United States, to afford ample materials for a diversified drama. . . . But even conceding, for one moment only, that complaints of a want of variety of character are just; still no one will deny, that there is an abundant field for novelty of situation; and novelty of situation is the best possible substitute for novelty of character, if it does not in reality create it. . . .

The first requisite for producing a National Drama is national encouragement. We do not mean pensions and premiums—but liberal praise and rewards to success—and a liberal allowance for failures. The second, is a little more taste and liberality in the managers of our theatres; and the third, is the presence of competent performers, collected in companies of sufficient strength to give effectual support to a new piece, and sufficient talent to personate an original character, without resorting to some hacknied model, which has descended from generation to generation, and like all copies, lost something of the original in the hands of each succeeding imitator.

Classic Melodrama

Charlotte Cushman became the leading tragic actress of her day. As a beginning professional, she wrote a short story for fashionable *Godey's Lady's Book* magazine in 1837. In chapter 1, the innocent Leoline learns of her father's fate and her brother's unwillingness to assist mother and sister; as her mother tells her, this is "but one page in the volume of earthly selfishness, now spread open before you, and from which I fear you will have to learn much that will cast a blight upon your advancing years." The fiction was partly autobiographical. Charlotte, too, in an age when women in the theater had a low reputation, took to the stage to support her mother when her apparently wealthy father died suddenly and in debt. Charlotte, too, had an unhappy love match from which she never recovered emotionally. The style, the plot, and the sentiments of the story are archetypically melodramatic.

Classic Melodrama

Charlotte S. Cushman, "The Actress," *Godey's Lady's Book* 14 (February 1837): 70–73.

> "How little do they see what is, who frame
> Their hasty judgment upon that which seems."

The world teems with painted misery—the misery that banquets upon the heart yet is not written upon the brow, and which goes forth into society, robed in the drapery of joy, wearing a smile for the gay, and bland words of content and peace wherewith to mislead the curious.

Happy are they who can thus make the features the defensive barriers, behind which their griefs may be screened from vulgar observation; and by a system of excusable moral deception, ply jest and song, while over the bruised sensibilities of the soul, is pouring a lava-like flood of bitter anguish, scorching the affections of the heart, and making the brain whirl with the tortures of its pent up agony.

All may not thus play a part so foreign to their inward emotions, and gild the shattered column of hope with the mellow hues of peace; but there are some spirits so constituted, as to wreathe the lip with smiles, even when despair battens upon its fibres, and dissemble with well set phrase, when impertinence seeks to lift the Mokanna veil, and read the heart's language in its naked outpourings. There are some few who can school themselves thus, but however well the mummery prospers, yet, within, the strife is fiercer and more destructive than it would be, if the confined agonies could gain an outlet through the parched channels of the eye, or waste away in the cold calculating medium of words. To borrow the strong language of Bryon—

> Full many a stoic eye and aspect stern
> Mask hearts where grief hath little left to learn,
> And many a withering thought lies hid, not lost
> In smiles that least befit, who wears them most.

To such minds, so organized, and embodying all that may darken the horizon of life, and nothing to chase away for a moment its gloom, happiness ever wears a negative aspect, while sorrow looms frowningly over every hope, rendering the past a type of the future—the present rayless, and futurity ominous and to be feared.—With them the joy of to-day is rendered valueless by the uncertainty that enwraps the morrow, and they fear to quaff from the goblet of human affections lest the compounds of subsequent suffering are contained in its lees.—Dating the disease of the imagination from the experience which is gained in battling with early misfortune, the mind rarely, if ever, recovers from the shock it sustains, and intellect, hope, too often reason itself, fall into ruins, leaving the victim of a perverse destiny, the choice of incurring the world's scorn, by the open expression of misfortune, or of learning to govern the features and enacting a mask in the great revel of human folly.

But there are moments when the mask will drop off, and the too highly excited sensibilities refuse obedience to the artificial mechanism that directs them; then is the moment when speculation may resolve itself into certainty, and the gazer may read in fact, what has long been surmised, learning in an hour of agonized confidence, what will teach a more correct lesson than a century's examination of the drilled visage could impart. It is then that the sufferer renounces for a brief while the actor's part, and vents the surcharged feelings of the heart to any who may be disposed to become the recipient.

From such a source have I drawn the story of Leoline, and an apology would be offered for the seeming violation of confidence did not the mantle of the grave enshroud the breathless form of her, concerning whom my tale. . . .

CHAPTER II

'Tis not immortals to command success;
But we'll do more, Sempronius, we'll deserve it.

The performance was "King Lear," kindly chosen by the manager, as being calculated by the stirring character of its several heroines, to give encouragement to the new actress during this, her first appearance. She personated the youngest daughter of Lear.

_____ poured forth its hundreds to witness the *debut* of her, whose presence they had so often greeted under other and brighter auspices. The vast building was thronged with the young and beautiful, and faces well remembered met the agitated vision of Leoline, as from the "wings" she stole a furtive glance at the features of those, who but a few months since, had hailed her their associate, and welcomed her coming in their social circles. Her bosom throbbed painfully as she surveyed their countenances, where selfish curiosity shone conspicuous. But when her eye wandered to another part of the theatre, and she noticed her callous-hearted brother, and a group of equally unprincipled relatives, a change came over her spirit, nerving it to brave unflinchingly the ordeal through which she was about to pass.

"They shall not witness my failure," she murmured; "that were too much—no, here at least I will strive to curtail their selfish triumph." A smile flitted across the blanched cheek of the proud girl, and the bitterness that had, up to this hour, wrung her heart, passed away. At this moment a hurried step was heard, and her mother gazed enquiringly into her face.

"Fear not, mother," she said, "I am calm," and she joined the royal pageant as it moved across the stage, pacing some gay saloon, herself its mistress. Every eye was riveted upon her. She *felt* this, but wavered not; a hum of mingled voices struck upon her now acutely gifted ear; but she only nerved herself the more effectually to enunciate calmly, and with precision, her answer to the silly question of the dotard monarch, as he turned to her. As she progressed, a profound silence reigned over the spacious building, and when, ere learning the presence of her imperious sisters, she addressed to them the taunting language of the immortal bard; there was a withering sarcasm in her words, a dash of bitter, heart spoken feeling in her tones, that found a shaming echo in the breasts of her callous kindred. She felt that she had triumphed, and as she disappeared behind the scenes there arose a deafening shout of approbation, loud, fervent and long.

The Rubicon was passed, and the career of Leoline promised now to prove as unclouded and brilliant as its opening had seemed lowering. Gifted in the intellectual accomplishments of her sex, she found in the profession she had chosen many congenial spirits; and keenly relishing the society of the talented, the leisure moments she enjoyed were passed with the brilliant, though sometimes faulty members of the dramatic corps of the Theatre of _____, which, at that time, and in fact ever since, numbered among its components, some high-minded and intellectual spirits.

No sorrows of a pecuniary nature weighed upon her sensitive mind; her mother was in a state, if not affluent, at least beyond want—the public regarded her with warm feelings of esteem; she was respected by her fellow labourers in the dramatic vineyard. Even they, the haughty members of her own family, who had left her to struggle with misfortune alone and unfriended, were now disposed to extend the hand of social friendship, but indignant at the meanness of their present motives, and painfully alive to their past heartlessness, she passed over with contemptuousness their overtures for a reconciliation.

I say that the career of Leoline *promised* to be brilliant, but one false step—one fatal act of indiscretion again dashed from her lips the cup of happiness, and gave a colouring of woe to the years that remained to her on earth. Constituted as the mind of Leoline was, even the excitement of her present life left a void in her bosom which required filling up with something having more power to tranquilize than force the already strained energies of her character, and it was not to be wondered that some one, from the number who knelt in homage before the beautiful actress, should captivate a heart, eminently endowed with those imaginative fancies which give to love in the spring time of life a romantic and seemingly eternal youth. Experience had taught Leoline to despise those whose perfidy had been revealed by the agency of circumstances; but yet she had not learned the policy, so essential to the young, of weighing well the character of those around, before she reposed confidence in their lip eloquence. And when there came one, who, ardent and imaginative himself, spoke his admiration in terms sincere and respectful, she fondly [foolishly] listened and believed. She fondly hoped that now she should realize the fervent aspirations of her girlhood, and as imagination stretched its deluded eye over the broad, the boundless, and in appearance, unclouded future, a new divinity took possession of her heart, and all guileless and enthusiastic she responded to her lover with a tear in her eye which had in it nothing of sorrow—

And all the burning tongues the passions teach
Found *in that tear* the best interpreter!

She was won! Alas, poor Leoline!

MELODRAMA

CHAPTER III

Man's love is of man's life, a thing apart'
'Tis woman's whole existence

Almost with the transition of a drama did the history of Leoline please in incident. We have seen her supporting, with patient resignation, the defeat of all her hopes, when death snatched away her father, and the success that crowned her exertions upon the boards of _____ theatre, changed not her feelings. We now behold her at her bridal, giving her young and unsullied heart, with its priceless affections to one, who seemed too mercurial to estimate aright the responsibility he was assuming. But no doubts hung their gloomy drapery around her as she now plighted her faith and gave her hand to him who had won her heart. She trusted fully and implicitly, and the light of love and truth gleamed from her soft eye, extorting from all who gazed upon her the exclamations of "how beautiful."

* * * * *

Twelve months passed—in Love's Calendar scarce a day—yet the young wife thought she could see in the demeanour of her spouse some indications of indifference. Volatile and heedless, he disliked the quiet joys of home, and plunged recklessly into dissipation; yet his apologies for a time served to lull her fears. Any pretext, no matter how groundless, will serve the trusting heart for a place of safety, whereon to rest the ark of Hope, and Leoline gauging her husband's affections by her own, relied upon their unchangeableness with a tenacity which gives fresh energies to the shipwrecked seaman so long as he has a single plank between him, and the yawning wave. Well and truly has the wayward author of Don Juan written,

Alas! the love of woman! It is known
To be a lovely and a fearful thing.

Slight, however, was the thread upon which she suspended her hopes, and each progressive day gave her doubts wider range. She read that in her husband's glance that told volumes to her sorrowing heart, and as if to dash away the last, the only pillar of consolation, he, with the habits of a bacchanal, also associated the tone, and treated her with coarse and unfeeling rudeness. In vain her remonstrances—vainer still her tears. The brute passion of the wretched man were too strong to bow before the arguments she would advance, and even when she drove him to reflection by the magic which woman can so powerfully exert, when love prompts, and truth sanctifies the motive, he would resort again to the wine-cup, and drown his reason in the inebriating element.

The delusion was over, and all feebly did the heart of Leoline strive against the sweeping tide of misery that poured over her long cherished images of hope and joy.

It was a pleasant, but too brief dream, from which she was now fully awakened, and the bitterness of her present situation was only exceeded by the dark vista that lay spread out in the future. To live with the degraded wretch who had violated every

166

claim to her respect, was to subject herself to continual insult, without the remotest hope of ever reclaiming him from error, yet to forsake him would, she well knew, open the floodgate of calumny, and expose her to the censures of the unfeeling and misjudging. Long and doubtful was the conflict in the bosom of the sorrowing wife, but a fresh outrage from him, whose conduct gave rise to her sorrow, at length determined her as to the line of conduct she should pursue, and with a heavy heart, she, with her grief-worn parent, quitted the roof, under which she had spent so many checquered hours.

Fourteen months had passed since she quitted the stage, and again she was announced as about to appear.

CHAPTER IV

Dryden has truly observed—

The noisy praise
Of the giddy crowds is unchangeable as winds.

For so in most cases will be found the applause of those, who, governed partly by the impulse of the moment, praise in one breath, and condemn in the next.

Our heroine experienced this in its fullest and most withering sense; for although she had retired from the theatre of her dramatic glory, followed by the regrets of all, yet none of those marked ebullitions of popular esteem, which gratify the professional pride of the performer, greeted her return to the boards.

It was evident to all that the spirit which had characterized her formerly was gone; there seemed no desire to please, and when, in the course of her engagement, it was required that she should personate the gay Rosalind, in "As You Like It," there seemed something in her tones, strangely at variance with the jesting arrangement of the sentences, while her laughter contrasted singularly with the melancholy that hung upon her brow. A feeling of awe pervaded the spectators; no note of approbation came from their midst, and all who felt interested in her success, judged truly that the terrible struggle she made to appear composed were in themselves sufficient to defeat that object. The struggle proved too great for her agitated nerves, and when the curtain fell, she sank senseless upon the stage, and was thence borne delirious to her chamber.

Weeks elapsed before she again appeared, and all were surprised at the change that had been effected in her demeanour. Gay, almost to frivolity, she seemed the divinity of mirth, sporting in the enjoyment of hope and joy, without aught in the past to sadden her memory, nor a single cloud in the Heaven of the present. There was one, however, who read the heart of Leoline better than did they who gleaned their opinion from the external appearance of the gay and lively actress. That one was her mother, whose solicitude was fearfully excited by these strange symptoms in the condition of her child. And often in the silent watches of the night would she sit and tremble, as from the lips of Leoline, in her feverish slumbers, there would burst a torrent of anguished, frenzied expressions, telling too plainly the tortures her mind endured. The sleeper's fancy would roam away to the golden moments of the past, ransacking the caves of memory, bringing thence all that was bright and beautiful; and then, ere she had time to heap them together, would come a change over the character of her dream, and the laugh would die upon her lips, her brow would contract, as though the Sirocco's breath had passed over it, while from her wedged teeth, a stifled moan of sorrow would come forth, sounding upon the mother's ear like a dirge, and then she would start up, and collecting her faculties, chide her parent playfully for not taking some repose. In concert—coterie—or upon the stage, would she exert herself to please, with such winning grace, that loud bursts of applause would follow. And she could retire from the gay pageant, leaving the impression upon the minds of all, that she had outlived the remembrances of the dark incidents in her life's history. Little did they imagine, who thus surmised, that within her bosom despair had erected his throne, and reigned sole sovereign, that the joyous tones she uttered came not from the heart; and that even when she seemed the queen of mirth, woe was eating away the chords of life, and hurrying her passage to the sepulchre, for the quiet repose of which she panted, as does the weary pilgrim in the desert thirst after the cool spring and branching palm-tree. But this contest of the mind could not last. The mental energies were too strained, and the physical powers bent beneath the weight of the mind's cares.

Why lengthen out this true yet mournful story. She died ere twenty summers had kissed her brow, yet the chill of three-score winters could not have wrought a more withering lesson upon a form and features where beauty had stamped its choicest and loveliest proportions. She hailed the approach of the grim conqueror with joy, at a period in life when others first launch the bark of life upon the great ocean of circumstances; but misfortune had forced her out upon the waves, and the hopes of her girlish years—the love of her womanhood were all wrecked and sent back upon her heart stripped of their gay streamers. The grave was to her a resting place, and her last words to the heart broken parent, who watched her dying couch, testified that her only regret was in leaving that parent to the further endurance of a life of affliction.

Poor Leoline! The grass watered by the tears of the few who still cherish thy memory has scarcely grown upon thy humble grave, yet in the minds of the thousands who once knew thee as endowed with genius and worth, far superior to the general order, thou art forgotten, and thy name never mentioned by the kindred who forsook thee in life, and left thee to pass over the dark isthmus that divides Time from Eternity, without expressing a single regret at thy untimely demise!

For twenty years, Walt Whitman wrote brief wide-ranging essays on urban life for Brooklyn newspapers. Among his favorite subjects were the drama and popular literature, and in 1858 he commented on the melodramatic imagination that linked the two. The *New York Atlas* (for which Barnum wrote letters during his European tour in the 1840s) and Robert Bronner's best-selling *New York Ledger* weekly were the publications Whitman had in mind.

Classic Melodrama

Walt Whitman, Brooklyn *Daily Times*, December 13, 1858, in *The Uncollected Poetry and Prose of Walt Whitman*, , 2 vols., ed. Emory Holloway (New York: Doubleday, 1922), 2:19–20.

They are immense in blood and thunder romances with alliterative titles and plots of startling interest.—These stories are curious productions in their way, and the cultivated reader on the lookout for amusement may enjoy a hearty laugh at any time over such sanguinary tales as the "Bloody Burglar of Babylon"; the "Maniac Maiden's Fate"; or the "Red-Headed Ragamuffin's Revenge." All these unique publications have second and often third titles of the most mysterious, thrilling, harrowing and altogether insane description—calculated to impress the uninitiated reader with awe and to inflame his curiosity for the "coming events" that cast such portentous shadows before. These things are to literature what the Bowery melodramas are to the stage, and are read by the same class that would hang with rapture over the latter. When the pirate chief drinks the blood of his victims in the largest of gory goblets, and with a burst of savage laughter flings the cup at the head of his trembling prisoner, the appreciative newsboy who reads the eloquent account is impelled to shout "Hi! Hi!" in a transport of enthusiasm. When the virtuous young mechanic rescues the lovely but unhappy milliner's apprentice from the base violence of the fast young aristocrat, what delight thrills the reader's breast! When the heroine has been stolen in infancy from her Fifth Avenue father, who is possessed of princely wealth, and when in chapter the last, after years of unheard-of privations, she is at length restored to the paternal arms, what Sunday-paper lover of any sensibility but must feel a sympathetic throb when that venerable man falls upon her breast in a burst of confidence and a shower of tears, and ejaculates:—"Ke-ind Heaven, I thank thee!—it is—it is indeed my long-lost che-ild!"

To say the truth, these publications, which obtained the *acme* of their popularity in the *Ledger* are not the choicest in composition or conception of plot and character, but after all, we doubt very much whether the outcry raised against them in some quarters is sustained by common sense. It may be said with tolerable safety that a large proportion of the admirers of this kind of literature might do worse if debarred from the enjoyment of their favorite mental *pabulum*. . . . The public for whom these tales are written require strong contrasts, broad effects and the fiercest kind of "intense" writing generally.

William B. English specialized in writing inexpensive, paperbound, sensational novels for the Boston publishers Redding and Company. *Rosina Meadows* had themes similar to *Gertrude Howard, The Maid of Humble Life; or, Temptation Resisted* (1843), *Morton, or Smiles and Tears; a Story of the Past and Present* (1845), and *Hazards of the Heart; or, Woman's Wrongs, and Woman's Revenge* (1840s). The introduction summarized the plot.

William B. English, *Rosina Meadows, The Village Maid: or, Temptations Unveiled. A Story of City Scenes and Every Day Life* (Boston: Redding , 1843), [2], 3–4, 21–22, 32.

The frontispiece of William W. English's sensational novel, *Rosina Meadows, the Village Maid: or, Temptations Unveiled. A Story of City Scenes and Every Day Life* (1843), announced its theme: the danger of the wolf in sheep's clothing.

> "Vice is a monster of such hideous mien,
> That to be HATED, needs but to be SEEN."

The story of ROSINA MEADOWS is one of *real life,* and it has been the aim of the author to illustrate in her career the numerous *temptations, snares and trials* of the city, which beset the path of the young and unsophisticated maiden, on her first setting out upon the journey of life. In lifting the veil from the tempter, and his subtle and seductive arts, care has been taken to "hold the mirror up to nature," and to exhibit vice in its proper forms and colors, without introducing any thing exceptionable to the reader. The beginning shows *Virtue* in all her transcendent loveliness, and the end exhibits *Vice* in its most "hideous mien," thus showing how *to obtain the one* and *shun the other.*

The scenes and incidents portrayed in this volume are no ideal pictures, and the author has endeavored as far as possible, to divest them of the garb of fiction or other extraneous matter. It is believed that the utility of works of this character cannot be questioned by the most rigid moralist, when he reflects that the impressions formed in youth exercise a powerful influence over the character for life. The bloom and beauty of virtue lasts through all declining years; and if this volume be the means of

170

unveiling the temptations to those who would deviate from the path of duty and honor, and pointing out to them the way of virtue, "whose ways are pleasantness, and whose paths are peace," then will his labors be well repaid. . . .

The narrator finds the village maiden:

A short cut through a thicket, and two or three scrambles up hill and through dale, brought me to a stile in front of the cottage. And here, reader, let us pause for a few moments to view the scene before us. The sun is bathing the eastern horizon with a sea of gold and silver, and all Nature is awakening once more in her freshness and beauty; the air is balmy, fragrant with flowers, over which it steals so softly as scarcely to disturb the gathering dew. . . .

And the cottage how beautiful it looks; like a dimple set in the midst of Nature's loveliness. . . . A short distance from the cottage door was a bower, formed by the branches of a tree, neatly united by ribbands and trellised around by running vines. . . . The cows and sheep were browsing in the meadow and gamboling about as happily as Nature herself. As far off as the eye could reach, was the village church with its old, weather-beaten spire, rising almost as high as the trees that surrounded it, and in the lap of a valley, near it, was the school-house and play-ground which stood there as the proud temple of Minerva, and the landmark of the village. . . .

A thousand pleasant, happy thoughts took possession of my mind, while under the magic influence of the scene before me; and every thing I saw, showed that happiness and contentment crowned the little cottage and its domain with their smiles. I began involuntarily to hum "Home, sweet home," aloud. . . .

How shall I describe her—how picture to the mind that gentle-eyed, confiding creature that stood before me, . . . sent from the paradise of love? No painting could express her beauty—it dwelt not alone in her face,—in her ruby lips, her rosy cheeks, full of the flush and glow of health, in the magic glances of her bright eyes, or her glossy ringlets, that fell luxuriantly over her pure, transparent neck, wooing the gentle zephyrs as they passed. It was not alone in her graceful form and elastic step, but it enshrined her person with that inherent purity of mind and thought, formed by the honest impulses of nature. That fairy spot, far away from the turmoil of the world, and the sordid dominions and empty pageantry of fashion, had been her constant dwelling-place; and each of those familiar and delightful scenes had tranquillized her life, and imparted to her existence all its ripening charms.

Rosina seeks her fortune in Boston and is betrayed and abandoned by the wealthy libertine Harry Mendon. Falsely accused of prostitution, she is sentenced to the House of Correction. Afterward, her low reputation deprives her of honest work, and, pregnant, when she can find no assistance from Mendon's family, she turns to "that vice which had been her ruin."

MELODRAMA

No female ever plunged precipitately into the gulf of vice—she is led on step by step, lured progressively to the monster until her ruin is complete. . . . The libertine who invades the happy and peaceful fireside, and pollutes the fair shrine of female innocence with the impure emanations of his heart, who betrays a poor trusting and affectionate girl—robs the kind parent of their beloved daughter, in whom is concentrated the only cheering hope of their old age, and leaves them to weep over the ruin he has made, is again welcomed by the world—his dark and wicked deeds are attributed to youthful folly, and are soon forgotten. But how dreadful is the lot of the victim of his base designs—she is shunned, degraded and lost forever. The situation of a young and friendless girl, is indeed a sad one.—Her path in life is continually surrounded by the numerous temptations to sin which society is filled with—every step she takes is strewed with snares, each of which is filled with perils and ills, and if she errs it is human—it is often the error of circumstances, not the error of the heart. . . . Could those who witness with indifference the gradual downfall of a young and beautiful girl, once full of constancy and truth, once beloving and beloved, whose only fault is that she "loved not wisely but too well," and was wronged and betrayed in an unguarded hour, could they see her pining away in sorrow, the flower of her youth wasting under a cold world's scorn and contumely—avoided and despised by her own sex, a scoff and a by-word to the most depraved of man—treated by every one as though all sense and feeling were extinct in their breast—the cruel, bitter tongue of slander magnifying her errors in every breath, and her heart scorching and riven with every word of reproach, could they but witness her struggles in this dreadful sea of agony—see her grasping with a woman's earnest power at every new hope that breaks before her, that she might again regain her good name with the world; struggling every moment to protect those remaining barriers of her honor, until the heart grows sick—her spirits become wearied and exhausted, and the waters of affliction close over each hope forever, how different would be the course pursued. . . .

Harry wastes his fortune in drunken gambling and is imprisoned for life for armed robbery. After various escapes, Rosina commits suicide, and the city watchman discovers her.

Rosina opened her glassy eyes, but oh, how horrible and vacant was their glance. Her pale, thin lips, relaxed slightly, and bending his ear to them, he heard her say— "Mother, dear Mother,—I come—God forgive me—my child—dying—cold—dying— oh! oh! dy—." She could utter no more—the poison had stopped forever the river of life;—a slight tremor shook her thin worn body,—and her head fell back powerless. Her features were still calm as the unclouded sky of summer, but oh!, how white and wasted! Those once bright and laughing eyes, were now glazed and fixed in the seal of death; that form, which was once so full of grace and beauty, and cheered all hearts with its presence was now so worn, and stiffened, and cold,—those lips which had so often pressed a fond father's and mother's cheek, and gave utterance to the pure thought, that like a spirit of light dwelt within her heart—were now closed forever, and the poor, wronged, degraded, fallen, and crushed soul, that so lately dwelt upon them, had fled from its mortal clay, and gone before the God that gave it. . . .

Thus perished Rosina Meadows—her career on earth was short, as are the days of the wicked, and full of bitterness, and may her sad end prove a warning to her sex, in the hour of temptation.

Charles H. Saunders was a jobbing playwright and actor who compiled more than fifty melodramas. He adapted *Rosina Meadows* for the stage as soon as the novel was published. It proved exceptionally popular, and played for two months continuously at Frank Chanfrau's New National Theatre in 1849, in Barnum's American Museum in 1851, and in the National Theatre in Boston. In the preface to the play, published a dozen years after it was first performed, Saunders conceded that it was not a literary masterpiece, but an "effective acting piece," because "the incidents are local, the characters real, and not too highly colored." He retained much of English's dialogue, but greatly simplified the plot and added Jethro, the simple, good-natured, low-comedy Yankee who goes to Boston to sell his anti-appetite pills to the city slickers. The synopsis outlines the plot.

Rosina Meadows, the Village Maid; or, Temptations Unveiled. A Local Domestic Drama in three acts. As originally performed at the National Theatre, Boston, with extraordinary success. Adapted by Charles H. Saunders, from the popular novel of that name by Wm. B. English (New York: Samuel French, n.d. [1855–60]), [iii], 9, 11, 14–15, 17–18, 25–26, 40, 43–44, 45–46, 51–52.

ACT I

Opening chorus—"In merry, merry May." Preparations for the May-day festival. Arrival of Harry Mendon. The city spark and the Yankee girl. Chivalric spirit of Jethro. The unconscious father folds the serpent to his bosom. The village maid. The first encounter. Rustic meal; the father's warning; the libertine's resolve. The dance on the green, and crowning of Rosina as the "Queen of May." The last interview between the lover and his betrothed. Preparations for departure. Arrival of the coach. The farewell. The father's blessing. . . .

ACT II

The intelligence office. Rosina in search of employment. The design of Florence frustrated by the interference of Bartley. Rosina escapes from the snare. A view of Faneuil Hall and the adjacent buildings. Mendon's first encounter with Rosina in the city. False representations. Misplaced confidence of Rosina. The Restaurant. Another snare — Rosina in the house of Alice Warren. Ballad, Rosina, "Home, sweet Home." Alice a confederate of Mendon's. The unwilling consent. The ball and the fatal promise. . . .

ACT III

The father in search of his lost child. Jethro communicates intelligence of the mother's death. The resolve. Local scene, Court-street. "We won't go home till morning." The once happy Rosina a supplicant for charity. The fruits of error. Interview between the stranger lad and the father. The father's curse. Wharf. The robbery. Mendon a thief. Arrest and escape. Sal Pentland's house. Mendon seeks refuge from the officers. Encounter of the father and seducer. Death of Rosina and the father's terrible revenge.

The play opens with the inhabitants of the village assembled on the green in front of the Meadows' cottage, celebrating spring in song and dance:

> In merry, merry May, all nature is gay,
> In merry, merry May, all nature is gay;
> Cold winter is driven, is driven to his lair,
> Cold winter is driven, is driven to his lair.
> The goat and the wether browse together on the heather,
> And the trees, and the trees don their liveries rare;
> The goat and the wether browse together on the heather,
> And the trees, and the trees don their liveries rare.
> (*End of verse all dance.*)
>
> In peace and content, so bounteously sent,
> In peace and content, so bounteously sent;
> Shall lighten every toil, every toil each day,
> Shall lighten every toil, every toil each day.
> And when the shades of evening draw the curtains of heaven,
> On the green, on the green, we will dance blithe and gay;
> And when the shades of evening draw the curtains of heaven,
> On the green, on the green, we will dance blithe and gay.

Into this Eden comes Harry Mendon, the worldly stranger from Boston, who comments:

Here is a village apparently enjoying its primitive simplicity; but, I fear that the frequent and easy communication with the city by the railroad's iron arm may even now have tinctured it with its vices.

He meets the kindly Meadows, his wife, and beautiful daughter Rosina, and is invited to share their "frugal fare."

MENDON. O, sir! no city noble, sheltered in his proud mansion, ever feasted so joyously as I do now! Yours is the bread of industry sweetened with content, made doubly so by youth, beauty and innocence—nature's heaven-born handmaids!

174

OLD MEADOWS. The gentleman pleases to flatter you, Rose, as well as us, wife. Ah! it almost makes the tears come into my old eyes, when I think the dear girl leaves us to-day!

MENDON. Leaves you, for what?

OLD MEADOWS. Why, sir, she goes to Boston, to seek what the girls call her fortune. Pray Heaven it may be a good one!

MENDON. Does she go there for the first time?

OLD MEADOWS. Ay, she was cradled here in the woods! She has spent her childhood here, and has grown up a girl of seventeen, without being from the sight of this humble cottage. . . .

MENDON. So young and innocent a girl will find many snares and temptations in the city. I fear her course is over a wild and tumultuous sea, full of rocks and quick-sands.

OLD MEADOWS. But while virtue and modesty are her guides, she has nothing to fear from dangers such as those. She has learned both from the great book of Nature, written by the hand of God!

MENDON. His hand is indeed here, and every leaf and blossom invites us to his love. God made the country; man made the town. There vice is clothed in the tempta-tions that misguided our first parents, and brought sin and death into the world. Heaven forfend that so fair a blossom as Rosina Meadows should be untimely nipped!

OLD MEADOWS. Amen to that! I love my daughter,—words cannot express how much I love her; but I would rather see her a corse at my feet, and follow her to the cold grave, the headstone marking where sleeps the child of virtue, than harm should befall her!

George Milton, the local farmer's son, is betrothed to Rosina, and bids her farewell, but warns:

MILTON. I do not doubt you, Rosina; but I know the temptations that beset a young female's path in a great city! O, beware the garb of friendship! Villainy often lurks unseen—thousands pollute the air with their pestilential breath—they mount the flowery path where innocence presides, and even the domestic fireside is not safe from its evil eyes! You will ever, dear Rosa, bear in mind the advice I gave you last night! O, remember, dearest, there is a heart which will be true to you wherever you may go! Heaven preserve you from all harm!

ROSINA. I have engraved it on my heart with the pen of affection! Nay, I can remember the very words;—and I remember that, I am going to a gay and thoughtless city. Temptations will be thrown in my way—vice is there to deceive the young and innocent! The libertine is there—he pollutes the air with his pestilential breath, and, like the deadly upas [a poisonous influence], destroys all who come within its deadly circle! His presence darkens every avenue, and even the domestic fireside is not safe from his evil eyes! Be assured, dear George, I shall remember your counsel!

175

MELODRAMA

During her first week in the city, Rosina seeks work at the employment agency and escapes being sent to a brothel only by the intervention of a stranger. Then she meets again Harry Mendon who offers help, and marriage.

MENDON. I have been long acquainted with your father, Miss Rosina, and would be proud to render a service to his daughter. Permit me to interest myself for you. You would prefer some light work; a milliner's employment might suit your views. Rosina, do not think me rude—the time, the place is unseasonable for such a question, but forgive me—my heart will admit of no longer delay—are your affections engaged?

ROSINA. Sir, I fear you mock me, when the wealthy and beloved son of the Mendons declares his love for Rosina Meadows, an humble farmer's daughter! (*Turns from him.*)

MENDON. Do not turn from me, Rosina, but cheer me with those beauteous eyes, if words refuse to reply.

ROSINA. I have been taught to look with distrust upon every one—even upon you!

MENDON. Miss Meadows, you judge too harshly; there are those in this city to whom innocence and beauty such as thine are incentives to wicked and unholy thoughts. I look with shame and pity upon the thousands who sacrifice all the purest feelings of nature upon the altar of sensuality; far be it from me to indulge for one moment in such base motives. Your parents, before I left them, requested me to keep a watchful eye upon you, and I will fulfil the trust. I feel the prize I love never can be mine, and I will henceforth devote my energies to the advancement of your welfare. Let not your fears refuse me so trifling a boon as the favor of walking by your side. Could you read my heart, you would be assured that I am governed by the purest motives in tendering my, perhaps, unwelcome assistance!

ROSINA. I believe you, Mr. Mendon, and will rely on you.

MENDON. You may, Rosina; let me have your confidence, and you will attain all you desire. (*Aside.*) And so shall I.

In the following months, Rosina is led to believe that George Milton no longer loves her, and is deceived by Harry's smooth talk and betrayed by a fake marriage ceremony. Meanwhile, Rosina's father and George Milton travel to Boston to search for her, and learn that she has been deceived and then abandoned.

OLD MEADOWS. 'T is true, all true—every word of it—I feel it here. O, my child, why could you not see the snare that was weaving around you? Why did you not hear the loud laugh of the libertine as he exulted over his anticipated conquests? She was then the child of innocence. She dwelt around the paradise, created by her own holy thoughts, and saw not the serpent that lay beneath her feet!

MILTON. I hear the villain that has caused all this desolation has fallen from his high estate, and ranks among villains, gamblers, and other notorious characters that prowl about the city.

OLD MEADOWS. A terrible retribution upon the seducer of my child! O thou, who knowest all things; who saw the villain smile when dark, unholy thoughts were rife within his heart; who heard that solemn vow of marriage; O, place me face to face with the despoiler; let me meet his eye, and if my gaze does not strike death to his coward heart, then shall my hands tear from him the guilty life who lives on sufferance now!

Rosina has no means of support, and in desperation, disguises herself and seeks out Harry Mendon in his drinking den.

MENDON. For Heaven's sake, what do you want with me, woman! (*Draws aside her veil.*) Great God! is it you, Rosina, out so late at night, and in such a dress; what can you be in search of? Can this be Rosina whom I once loved so dearly?

ROSINA. Base man! that holy feeling never entered your heart! Look upon me—do you know me? 'T is true, I wear not now upon my cheek the ruddy glow of innocence—the pure air of my native village has not fanned my cheek for many a day. The dishonored blandishments of a false heart have driven me from the roof of virtue to the house of vice!

MENDON. I have not driven you there! What are your misfortunes to me? I know naught of them!

ROSINA. Ay, but you will—you will! The recording angel has it there! there in his eternal book! 'T is recorded with a diamond pen. He who stood before the altar, with the habiliments of the man of God, falsely pronounced us man and wife before Heaven's great tribunal! And he who sits in majesty upon the high throne of Heaven will give the sentence of the convicted destroyer of honor!

MENDON. Hush! Speak lower, Rosina, or they will hear you! I would not have my friends there think that the wretched object before me was the once—There, don't speak—I know all; but what want you of me?

ROSINA. Want! (*Kneels.*) Yes, I'm crushed and cannot sink any lower! I want money—I am famishing, houseless, and friendless—give me money! Shall I pray for you or fear you that a father's curse would cling to the prayer on its passage to the judgment-seat, or that a dead mother standing before the eternal throne will plead against the supplication?

MENDON. You are disgraced now; you are not what you once were; but why do you not leave me? I will give you anything, so you leave me. Do not notice me in the streets, or let me hear your voice. I will give you money, anything—here, take this, young woman, and see you use it properly!

STANLEY. Holloa, Harry! you are getting liberal, to waste a five-dollar-bill on a girl that walks the streets!

MENDON. This is a poor beggar, and has told me a piteous story of her wants!

ROSINA. O, may Heaven forgive you!

MENDON. Amen! but go—there's a good girl!

ROSINA. I will, and seek my father! The darkness of the night shall not prevent me. Heaven, thou art the last to deceive the wanderer—thou wilt guide my steps!

Still disguised, Rosina finds her father and listens in shame to his tale.

OLD MEADOWS. My daughter went there full of bright hopes; the rosy hue of health was on her cheek, and innocence in her dark eye; she promised to bring back both to her parents; we waited a long while, but she came not; and, at last, we heard—

ROSINA. I cannot support it. You had a daughter there?

OLD MEADOWS. Did you know her, sir?

ROSINA. Too well! Alas! too well!

OLD MEADOWS. If you thus feel for her, what must be the feelings of her poor heart-broken father! What are your sorrows compared to mine? Poverty I could have borne. With her I could buffet every stream of adversity which Providence might have cast upon me, and smile and feel happy amidst every calamity! O, God! what are all earthly woes, compared to the feelings of a disgraced, broken-hearted and doting father?

ROSINA. She lives, and may yet be saved!

OLD MEADOWS. Ay, she lives, but she has lost that which alone makes life valuable to woman—her honor! You may show me the casket, but the jewel is lost forever!

ROSINA. Is there no hope?

OLD MEADOWS. Ask the mariner who stands upon the wreck of his own proud vessel, as it breaks piece by piece beneath the angry billows, and while the thunders roll, and the lightnings flash, and display the death which awaits him, ask him to hope!

ROSINA. And may she not return to her home, and, falling on her knees as I do now, look up to you with clasped hands and contrite heart, and implore, in the face of God, your forgiveness?

OLD MEADOWS. Yes, let her come, if she can, and see this bleeding heart; let her look upon these bitter, scalding tears—this hollow cheek and death-struck form; let her look upon these white hairs, disgraced by her—the never-sleeping agony that rends this mind with its fearful delirium! Let her come and see the work she has wrought, and hear the curse, the terrible curse of a heart-broken father!

(ROSINA *throws off disguise and closely clings to* MEADOWS *as he goes up centre.*)

ROSINA. Father, in Heaven's name, do not curse me!—do not! I am your—O, God!—your child ! I am your once-beloved child!—your Rosina! Heaven look down, and have mercy on me!

(*Tableau.* ROSINA *falls at the feet of her father. Scene closes them in.*)

Harry Mendon gambles away his fortune, and is caught by city watchmen while attempting to rob one of the dockyard offices. Rosina hears of Harry's capture and rushes in.

ROSINA. Behold, Harry Mendon, this is thy work!

(ROSINA *falls,* R.C.)

OLD MEADOWS. (*Outside.*) Ah, that voice! that name! Where is he?

(*Rushes on with* GEORGE MILTON *through door in C.* GEORGE *goes to* ROSINA, *kneels and raises her head.* ROSINA *recognizes him.*)

OLD MEADOWS. Heaven, thou hast heard my prayer! Villain! thy race of wickedness is run! Thy time is come!—seducer! murderer of my child! look upon her father! Sweet, crushed flower, I forgive you! Bless you! bless you! . . .

ROSINA. (*On R..*) Then, I die happy!

(*Dies in the arms of* GEORGE MILTON.)

OLD MEADOWS. (C.) She's gone. Now, villain, prepare!—the fiat hath gone forth which said blood for blood!

MENDON. (L.C.) Officers, protect me from this madman!

OLD MEADOWS. Mad! 'T is false! I am not mad; for I look on a scene like this, and the tears course each other down my cheeks, and my heart will break with grief! Come, you are waited for! Why should you remain, while she is bounding towards the skies?

MENDON. Stand off, maniac!

OLD MEADOWS. No, my wife, my child, are torn from me—I have no one to clasp—you shall supply their places! Come, kneel with me at the altar of my child's lost honor! How?—will you not mind ?—Nay, then—

(*The officers, &c., have their backs to the audience, and do not observe the movement of* MEADOWS.)

MENDON. Mercy!

OLD MEADOWS. Thou didst have no mercy, and canst expect none! Nay, do not shriek—she cannot hear thee—her spirit is even now hovering over thee, impatient to denounce thee at the judgment-seat! 'T is time for the sacrifice! (*Seizes him.*) Villain! Seducer!—Murderer! Die! Die!

(*Music. He strangles him. The watchmen and citizens rush forward to rescue* MENDON *from the grasp of* MEADOWS—*as they take him from* MEADOWS, MENDON *falls dead. The watchmen stand at the side of* MEADOWS, *in C., who stands with one hand pointing to heaven, the other to* ROSINA, *on R.C.*).

TABLEAU.

Curtain falls to slow music.

MELODRAMA

Charles Farrar Browne, best known as Artemus Ward, was one of the most popular humorists on both sides of the Atlantic in the 1860s. His comic lectures and brief sketches burlesqued popular culture, including the melodrama.

Artemus Ward, "A Romance.—Only a Mechanic," in *Artemus Ward; His Travels* (New York: Carleton, 1865), 65–66.

In a sumptuously furnished parlor in Fifth Avenue, New York, sat a proud and haughty belle. Her name was Isabel Sawtelle. Her father was a millionaire, and his ships, richly laden, ploughed many a sea.

By the side of Isabel Sawtelle sat a young man with a clear, beautiful eye, and a massive brow.

"I must go," he said, "the foreman will wonder at my absence."

"The *foreman*?" asked Isabel in a tone of surprise.

"Yes, the foreman of the shop where I work."

"Foreman—shop—*work*! What! do *you* work?"

"Aye, Miss Sawtelle! I am a cooper!" and his eyes flashed with honest pride.

"What's that?" she asked; "it is something about barrels, isn't it!"

"It is!" he said, with a flashing nostril. "And hogsheads."

"Then go!" she said, in a tone of disdain—go *away*!"

"Ha!" he cried, "you spurn me, then, because I am a mechanic. Well, be it so! though the time has come, Isabel Sawtelle," he added, and nothing could *exceed* his looks at this moment—

"when you will bitterly remember the cooper you now so cruelly cast off! *Farewell*!"

Years rolled on. Isabel Sawtelle married a miserable aristocrat, who recently died of delirium tremens. Her father failed, and is now a raving maniac, and wants to bite little children. All her brothers (except one) were sent to the penitentiary for burglary, and her mother peddles clams that are stolen for her by little George, her only son that has his freedom. Isabel's sister Bianca rides an immoral spotted horse in the circus, *her* husband having long since been hanged for murdering his own uncle on his mother's side. Thus we see that it is always best to marry a mechanic.

Classic Melodrama's Audiences

During a fortnight in Boston in 1850, Nathaniel Hawthorne went to William Pelby's National Theatre on the evening of May 7. The National, situated in the working-class North End, offered the same kind of dramatic spectacles and melodrama as New York's Bowery theaters. As usual, Hawthorne made a detailed pen-portrait in his notebook.

Nathaniel Hawthorne, *The American Notebooks*, ed. Claude M. Simpson [*The Cente-*

Matthew Brady's daguerreotype of the early 1850s depicted the celebrated actress Charlotte Cushman as Meg Merrilies in *Guy Mannering* and illustrated her intensely melodramatic style. Prints and Photographs Division, Library of Congress.

nary Edition of the Works of Nathaniel Hawthorne, vol. 8] (Columbus: Ohio State University Press, 1972), 501–4.

I went, last night, to the National Theatre to see a pantomime; it was Jack the Giant Killer, and somewhat heavy and tedious. The audience was more noteworthy than the play. The theatre itself is for the middling and lower classes; and I had not taken my seat in the most aristocratic part of the house; so that I found myself surrounded chiefly by young sailors, Hanover-street shopmen, mechanics, and other people of that kidney. It is wonderful the difference that exists in the personal aspect and dress, and no less in the manners, of the people in this quarter of the city, compared with others. One would think that Oak Hall should give a common garb and air to the great mass of the Boston population; but it seems not to be so; and perhaps what is most singular is, that the natural make of the men has a conformity and suitableness to their dress. Glazed caps and Palo Alto hats were much worn. It is a pity that this picturesque and comparatively graceful hat should not have been generally adopted, instead of falling to the exclusive use of a rowdy class.

In the next box to me were two young women, with an infant of perhaps three or four months old (if so much) but to which of them appertaining, I could not at first discover. One was a large, plump girl, with a heavy face, a snub nose, coarse looking, but good-natured, and with no traits of evil; save, indeed, that she had on the vilest gown—of dirty white cotton, so pervadingly dingy that it was white no longer, as it seemed to me—the sleeves short, and ragged at the borders—and an old faded shawl, which she took off on account of the heat—the shabbiest of dress, in a word, that I ever saw a woman wear. Yet she was plump, as aforesaid, and looked comfortable in body and mind. I imagine that she must have had a better dress at home, but had come to the theatre extemporaneously, and not going to the dress-circle, considered her ordinary gown good enough for the occasion. The other girl seemed as young, or younger than herself; she was small, with a particularly intelligent and pleasant face, not handsome, perhaps, but as good or better than if it were. It was mobile with whatever sentiment chanced to be in her mind; as quick and vivacious in its movements as I have ever seen; cheerful, too, and indicative of a sunny, though I should think it might be a hasty temper. She was dressed in a dark gown, (chintz, I suppose the women call it,) a good homely dress, proper enough for the fireside, but a strange one to appear at a theatre in. Both these girls seemed to enjoy themselves very much; the large and heavy one, in her own duller mode; the smaller manifesting her interest by gestures, pointing at the stage, and so vivid a talk of countenance that I could sympathize as well as if she had spoken. She was not a brunette; and this made her vivacity of expression all the more agreeable. Her companion, on the other hand, was so dark that I rather suspected her to have a tinge of African blood.

There were two men who seemed to have some connection with these girls; one was an elderly, gray-headed personage, well stricken in liquor, talking loudly and foolishly, but good-humouredly; the other a young man, sober, and doing his best to keep his elder friend quiet. The girls seemed to give themselves no uneasiness about the matter. Both these men wore Palo Alto hats. I could not make out whether either of the men were the father of the child, or what was the nature of the union among them; though I was inclined to set it down as a family-party.

As the play went on, the house became crowded, and oppressively warm; and the poor little baby grew dark red, or purple almost, with the uncomfortable heat in its small body. It must have been accustomed to discomfort, and have concluded it to be the condition of mortal life; else it never would have remained so quiet. . . . Perhaps it had been quieted with a sleeping potion. The two young women were not negligent of it, but passed it to-and-fro between them, each willingly putting herself to inconvenience for the sake of tending it. But I really feared it might die in some kind of fit; so hot was the theatre; so purple with heat, yet so strangely quiet, was the child. I was glad to hear it cry, at last; but it did not cry with any great rage and vigor, as it should, but in a stupid kind of way. Hereupon, the smaller of the two girls, after a little efficacious dandling, at once settled the question of maternity, by uncovering her bosom, and presenting it to the child, with so little care of concealment that I saw, and anyone else might have seen, the whole breast, and the apex which the infant's little lips compressed. Yet there was nothing indecent in this; but a perfect naturalness. The child sucked a moment or two, and then became quiet, but still looked very purple. Children must be hard to kill, however injudicious the treatment. The two girls, and their cavaliers, remained till nearly the close of the play. I should like well to know who they are—of what condition in life—and whether reputable as members of the class to which they belong. My own judgement is, that they are so.

Throughout the evening, drunken young sailors kept stumbling into and out of the boxes, calling to one another from different parts of the house, shouting to the performers, and singing the burthens of songs. It was a scene of life in the rough.

Mortimer Q. Thomson ["Doesticks"] wrote humorous essays for publications like *The Spirit of the Times* in the 1850s. New to the big city, he delighted in city sights and scenes. He devoted one book to urban entertainments of all kinds—target-company excursions, Barnum's Museum, street sideshows, but especially the popular theater. Two debunking essays on the overwrought style of melodrama, another disparaging commentary on "colored theatricals" ["Shakspeare Darkeyized"] were paired with a scathing review of the newsboys' pulp drama at the Bowery Theatre.

Q. K. Philander Doesticks, P. B. [Mortimer Q. Thomson], *Doesticks: What He Thinks* (New York: Edward Livermore, 1855), 228–34.

I also desired to go over to the twenty-five cent side of the town, and behold the splendors of their dramatic world. Accordingly, I've been to the Bowery Theatre—the realm of orange-peel and peanuts—the legitimate home of the unadulterated, undiluted sanguinary drama—the school of juvenile Jack-Sheppardism, where adolescent "shoulder hitters" and politicians in future take their first lessons in rowdyism.

Where the seeds of evil are often first planted in the rough bosom of the uncared-for boy, and, developed by the atmosphere of this moral hot-house, soon blossom into crime.

Where, by perverted dramatic skill, wickedness is clothed in the robes of romance and pseudo-heroism so enticingly as to captivate the young imagination, and many a mis-taught youth goes hence into the world with the firm belief that to rival Dick Turpin or Sixteen-String Jack is the climax of earthly honor.

A place where they announce a grand "benefit" five nights in the week, for the purpose of cutting off the free-list, on which occasions the performance lasts till the afternoon of the next day.

Where the newsboys congregate to see the play, and stimulate, with their discriminating plaudits, the "star" of the evening.

For this is the spawning-ground of theatrical luminaries unheard-of in other spheres; men who having so far succeeded in extravagant buffoonery, or in that peculiar kind of serious playing which may be termed mad-dog tragedy, as to win the favor of this audience, forthwith claim celestial honors, and set up as "stars."

And a star benefit-night at this establishment is a treat; the beneficiary feasts the whole company after the performance, and they hurry up their work as fast as possible so as to begin their jollification at the nearest tavern; they have a preliminary good time behind the scenes with such viands and potables as admit of hurried consumption. . . .

But the Bowery audiences are, in their own fashion, critical, and will have everything, before the curtain, done to suit their taste.

An actor must do his utmost, and make things ring again; and wo be to him who dares, in a ferocious struggle, a bloody combat, or a violent death, to abate one single yell, to leave out one bitter curse, or omit the tithe of a customary contortion. He will surely rue his presumption, for many a combatant has been forced to renew an easily won broadsword combat, adding fiercer blows, and harder stamps—and many a performer who has died too comfortably, and too much at his ease to suit his exacting audience, has been obliged to do it all over again, with the addition of extra jerks, writhings, flounderings, and high-pressure spasms, until he has "died the death" set down for him.

An actress, to be popular at this theatre, must be willing to play any part, from Lady Macbeth to Betsey Baker—sing a song, dance a jig, swallow a sword, ride a barebacked horse, fight with guns, lances, pistols, broadswords, and single-sticks—walk the tight-rope, balance a ladder on her nose, stand on her head and even throw a back-summerset. She must upon occasion play male parts, wear pantaloons, smoke cigars, swear, swagger, and drink raw-whiskey without making faces.

The refined taste which approbates these qualifications is also displayed in the selection of dramas suitable for their display. Shakspeare, as a general thing, is too slow. Richard III might be endured, if they would bring him a horse when he calls for it, and let him fight Richmond and his army singlehanded, and finally shoot himself with a revolver, rather than give up beat.

Macbeth could only expect an enthusiastic welcome, if all the characters were omitted but the three witches and the ghost of Banquo; but usually nothing but the most slaughterous tragedies and melo-dramas of the most mysterious and sanguinary stamp, give satisfaction.

A tragedy hero is a milk-sop, unless he rescues some forlorn maiden from an impregnable castle, carries her down a forty-foot ladder in his arms, holds her with one hand, while with the other he annihilates a score or so of pursuers, by picking up one by the heels, and with him knocking out the brains of all the rest, then springs upon his horse, leaps him over a precipice, rushes him up a mountain, and finally makes his escape with his prize amid a tempest of bullets, Congreve rockets, Greek fire and bombshells.

Thus it may be supposed that no ordinary materials will furnish stock for a successful Bowery play. Probabilities, or even improbable possibilities, are too tame. Even a single ghost to enter in a glare of blue light, with his throat cut, and a bloody dagger in his breast, and clanking a dragging-chain, would be too commonplace.

When the boys are in the chivalric vein, and disposed to relish a hero, to content them he must be able, in defence of distressed maidens, (the Bowery boys are ragged knights-errant in their way, and greatly compassionate forlorn damsels,) to circumvent and destroy a small-sized army, and eat the captain for luncheon.

If they are in a murderous mood, nothing less than a full-grown battle, with a big list of killed and wounded, will satisfy their thirst for blood; and if they fancy a touch of the ghastly, nothing will do but new-made graves, coffins, corpses, gibbering ghosts, and grinning skeletons.

I went by the old, damaged "spout-shop" the other day—saw a big bill for the evening, and stopped to read—magnificent entertainment—to commence with a five-act tragedy, in which the hero is pursued to the top of a high mountain, and after slaying multitudes of enemies, he is swallowed up by an earthquake, mountain and all, just in time to save his life.

Professor Somebody was to go from the floor to the ceiling on a tight rope, having an anvil tied to each foot, and a barrel of salt in his teeth—then the interesting and bloody drama, "the Red Revenging Ruffian Robber, or Bold Blueblazo of the Bloody Bradawl"—after which, a solo on the violin, half a dozen comic songs, three fancy dances, and a recitation of the "Sailor Boy's Dream," with a real hammock to "spring from," three farces, and a comic opera—then Bullhead's Bugle Band would give a concert, assisted by the Ethiopian Minstrel Doves—then an amateur would dance the Shanghae Rigadoon on a barrel-head—after which Madame Jumpli Theo. Skratch would display her agility by leaping through a balloon over a pyramid, composed of a hose truck, two beer barrels, and a mountain of green fire.

Numberless other things were promised, in the shape of firemen's addresses, songs, legerdemain, acrobatic exercises, ventriloquism, &c., the whole to conclude with an original extravaganza, in which the whole company would appear.

The Ten-Twenty-Thirty Melodramas

The playwright Porter Emerson Browne's description of the "mellowdrammer" at a "humble abode of Thespis" was a mocking but affectionate portrait of the popular theater and its conventions.

MELODRAMA

Porter Emerson Browne, "The Mellowdrammer," *Everybody's Magazine* 21 (September 1909): 349, 354.

If you are at all familiar with the mellowdrammer as she is writ, you must know that the construction of one is a science as exact as is the making of a custard pie. They have rules for making them—just as they do for lobster à la Newburg, or deviled crabs, or stuffed tomatoes. It is a recipe that any one may obtain for the price of an admission ticket and a little observation.

Lest, however, you have not the money for the one nor the time for the other, I am glad herewith to give the recipe; and if you have the needed ingredients, I am sure that you'll have no difficulty in making as good a mellowdrammer as was ever cooked up by the best chefs in the business.

Here you are:

Take one good and beautiful heroine (peroxide, if possible), one poor but honest hero, one villain the size of an egg, a comedian (Irish, Dutch, Chinese or Rube), a soubrette with dropstitch stockings and a voice like a planing-mill, a villainess who has suspiciously buried three husbands, and half a dozen other assorted characters. Put the whole into a large stage and then beat the heroine for two hours. You may also beat the hero, as well, though care should be taken not to touch the villain and villainess. Sprinkle in the other characters from time to time. Season with large lumps of pathos, great gobs of heart interest, and cupfuls of unstrained humor. Flavor to taste with railroad trains, saw-mills, runaway horses, automobiles, steam-rollers, earthquakes, cyclones, forest fires, wild steers, and volcanoes.

When almost done, take out the hero and heroine and knead them carefully together. Throw the villain and villainess under the sink. You should be very careful to call the hero Harold Wintergreen, Reginald Worthington, or some such simple name. The villain should always wear riding breeches and papier maché puttees in the first act, a misfit business suit with high-water pants in the second, and a hired dress suit in the third and fourth. He should be called Sir Marmaduke Mungummery or Archibald Mainwaring or some similar name. You can always procure good names from Ouida or Laura Jean Libbey or any other old, established dealer.

Don't be afraid of seasoning too highly, nor of cooking too fiercely. You can't do it. . . .

Throughout the whole, harrowing story of the trials and tribulations of Lizzie, the Beautiful Saleslady, the audience swings from one emotion to another with all the easy facility with which monkeys in a cage gyrate from trapeze to trapeze. In the pathetic parts (or rather the bathetic parts), they shed salt tears into saturated handkerchiefs with the arrant prodigality of those obsessed by personal suffering—that is, the female element does; and the male element tries not to, and looks foolish. The laugh taps are turned on just as easily; and every time the hero and the heroine save each other's lives, the girl next to you almost swallows her gum, while the eyes of the man at your other side snap brightly and his hands clench.

The Ten-Twenty-Thirty Melodramas

The audience from gallery to orchestra joins in hungrily hissing the villain; they adore the leading man with devout eyes and long-drawn sighs; they love and pity the heroine and excoriate their hearts in tempestuous sympathy for her hard lot. And I, for one, think it is a mighty good thing that they don't see her after the performance eating fifteen cents' worth of chop-suey and rice, complaining the while because she gets only half salary in Holy Week and explaining how, if it weren't for managerial "fatheadedness," she'd be "headin' her own comp'ny on Broadway and givin' some o' them favored ham actorines a run for their money." It's just as well, too, that they don't see the leading man and the villain hobnobbing together over a glass of beer and making a free lunch counter look like a locust-ridden wheat-field in a dry season, as they tell each other what good actors they are and lie about their salaries.

In the vernacular, the melodramatic audience is a "warm" house to play to—it "eats" a "show."

And why not? It's real to them; as real as is life itself—and sometimes even more real than life itself. True, the audience has no taste, no discrimination, no sense of the ridiculous to obscure or destroy appreciation. It cannot tell pathos from bathos, and to it the exaggerated, affected acting and mannerisms and enunciation of the players; the dull, tawdry absurdity of the scenery; the glaring inconsistencies in both production and text; the utter lack of logic; the hopeless impossibility of situation, convey only the impression of actual things that actually exist, of events actually happening before its very eyes. Melodramatic audiences are the children of the theatre—the Peter Pans of stageland.

After our operas; after our skilfully woven, consistently created, glitteringly dialogued plays; after our gorgeous spectacular and musical productions; after our wonderfully written, wonderfully staged, wonderfully played pieces of all descriptions, we can loll back critically in our chairs, and cast amused and tolerant eyes upon these children of the theatre. But away down in our hearts, don't we, now, honestly wish that we could get out of a dramatic offering one thousandth part of the amusement and excitement and entertainment that these do. Don't we envy them, just a little, that infinite capacity for enjoyment that is theirs? I do.

In the first decade of the twentieth century, Owen Davis was the most successful playwright in melodrama, and, at his peak, wrote one play a month, which he also directed. Davis's *Nellie, the Beautiful Cloak Model* (1906) ran for five seasons on the Lower East Side. Each of the four acts had a moment of high tension when the villain threatened the life of the department-store heroine: she was pushed under a descending escalator, thrown off the Brooklyn Bridge, tied to the tracks of the elevated railroad, threatened by early-morning intrusion into her bedroom. "I have never taken my characters from real life," Davis explained. He preferred larger-than-life protagonists and based his plots on "a little more highly colored" events that spiced everyday reality and were reported in the press. When he decided to seek critical recognition in the legitimate theater, he explained the formula for success in the less demanding popular circuit.

Owen Davis, "Why I Quit Writing Melodrama," *American Magazine* 128 (September 1914): 29–30.

The plays that we produced were written largely by rule. In fact the actual writing of one of these sensational melodramas I had reduced to a formula, about as follows:

TITLE (at least fifty per cent of success)

PLOT: Brief story of the play.

CAST: *Leading Man*, very (even painfully) virtuous.

Leading Woman, in love with him.

Comedy Man, always faithful friend of Hero.

Soubrette, very worthy person (poor but honest) and always in love with *Comedian*.

Heavy Man, a villain, not for any special reason, but, like "Topsy," "born bad."

Heavy Woman,—here I had a wider choice, his lady, being allowed to fasten her affections upon either *Hero* or *Villain* (sometimes both) but never happily.

Father (or *Mother*), to provide sentiment.

Fill in as desired with character parts.

ACT I—Start the trouble.

ACT II—Here things look bad. The lady having left home, is quite at the mercy of *Villain*.

ACT III—The lady is saved by the help of the Stage Carpenter. (The big scenic and Mechanical effects were always in Act III.)

ACT IV—The lovers are united and the villains are punished.

I suppose that I have been responsible for as many executions as the Queen in "Alice in Wonderland." I am honest enough to admit my cold-blooded attitude; but apply this chart to many plays of authors who consider their work inspired, and see if it fits.

These plays depended very greatly upon scenic effect, sensational dramatic title, and enormously melodramatic pictorial display on the bill boards. I think we touched upon every theme known to man, and every location. We limited ourselves, however, to American subjects. We always had a clear and dominant love interest, which we crossed with an element of danger, usually furnished by a rather impossible villain or adventuress. The themes of some of these plays were absolutely legitimate and the stories in many cases, with different dressing, would have done for a Broadway theater of the present day. But we had to, or fancied we had to, have such an over-abundance of climactic material that our plays resulted in an undigested mass of unprepared situations. Where one carefully prepared and well-developed episode would really have been of far greater dramatic value, we made a rule of dividing our plays into no less than fifteen scenes, the end of each being a moment of perilous suspense or terrifying danger. This gave the playwright rather less than seven minutes to instruct his audience, to prepare his climaxes, to plant the seed for the next scene, and to *reach* his climaxes, which of course was absurdly impossible and resulted, I feel sure, in a form of entertainment which was only too ready to yield to the encroachment of the cheap vaudeville and moving pictures.

At the turn of the century, the journalist Rollin Lynde Hartt visited a cheap, inner-city, melodrama theater, probably the most famous, the Grand Opera House on New York's Bowery. His interest was primarily in the reaction of the lower-class audience, whom he labeled "Neolithic," to the staple blood-and-thunder fare of "Ten Commandments in red fire." He characterized the melodrama by citing the jingle of the lyricist Nathaniel P. Adams:

Rollin Lynde Hartt, *The People At Play* (Boston: Houghton, Mifflin, 1909), 158, 160, 161–67, 174–75, 182–83, 185–86, 188–90.

> If you want a receipt for a melodramatical,
> Thrillingly thundery popular show,
> Take an old father, unyielding, emphatical,
> Driving his daughter out into the snow;
> The love of a hero, courageous and Hacketty,
> Hate of a villain in evening clothes;
> Comic relief that is Irish and racketty;
> Schemes of a villainess muttering oaths;
> The bank and the safe and the will and the forgery—
> All of them built on traditional norms—
> Villainess dark and Lucrezia Borgery
> Helping the villain until she reforms;
> The old mill at midnight, a rapid delivery;
> Violin music, all scary and shivery;
> Plot that is devilish, awful, nefarious;
> Heroine frightened, her plight is precarious;
> Bingo!—the rescue!—the movement goes snappily—
> Exit the villain and all endeth happily!
> Take of these elements any you care about,
> Put 'em in Texas, the Bowery, or thereabout;
> Put in the powder and leave out the grammar,
> And the certain result is a swell melodrammer. . . .

Reduce the conventional theatre to a state of dog-eared shabbiness; write commercial advertisements on the curtain; borrow a whiff or so of the Dime Museum's aroma, and fill the house with office-boys, bell-boys, messengers, common laborers, factory-girls, shop-girls, waitresses, and "generals." There you have the Grand, wanting only the music, in which the drum predominates. To you, its incessant throbbing becomes oppressive. Not to those about you, though. One and all, they would endorse the sentiment if you quoted:—

Bang-whang-whang! goes the drum. Tootle-te-tootle, the fife!
No keeping one's haunches still; it's the greatest pleasure in life!

And now the curtain goes up. It little matters what scene it discloses. Be it Chinatown or the Riverside Drive, New Orleans or the Bad Lands, the same thrilling deeds of derring-do will be enacted by the same conventional machine-made characters as in the famous "Boulevard du Crime" two hundred years ago. Milieu may vary, types never.

Consider those types, those presumably immortal types, so dear to the popular heart. First the heroine:—She is "in-no-cent." With "quivering lips and moistened eye, her hands clasped meekly across her breast as though life was too heavy to bear," she tremulously reiterates the fact. Yet upon her, despite that aureole of angelic hair, those eyes so virtuously limpid, that rounded, maidenly figure, and the madonna-like sweetness of her ways, they have fastened accusations of arson, safe-cracking, forgery, and the murder of her husband. She is driven from home and kin. She is hounded by detectives. As the plot thickens, she grows eloquent. "Oh misery, misery!" she sobs. "I am alone forever! The thought will drive me frantic! I am wretched, mad! What is left to me now but the deepest, darkest despair? Oh, I cannot bear it! My heart will break! Why do I not die?—why do I not die?" She has life in her, though; lots of it. Wait till the villain sets about feeding her baby to the stone-crusher. It is with no little vigor, then, that she shrieks, "Me child! Me chi-i-i-ild!!!"

Or wait till he makes love to her. Zounds, what a counterblast! "Thou cur!" she snaps. "Unhand me, coward! The devilish cunning of your nature makes me shudder!" In moments like these she towers up in a physical grandeur well suiting her moral sublimity. And she needs a quite marvelous vitality, you discover, to go through the harrowing and terrific adventures this villain prepares her. He loves her furiously and it would be gentler if he understood. But villainy is not to be ranked among the learned professions. It is singularly without intellect. In "Nellie, the Beautiful Cloak-Model," the villain begins by causing the heroine to fall from the Brooklyn Bridge. Next, he pitches her overboard in mid-Atlantic. After that, he throws her under a freight elevator. Ultimately he says to her, "Why do you fear me, Nellie?"

What made him a villain, "no fellow can find out." He is a villain out of a clear sky, without motive or provocation, a "bold bad man" by nature, who has done all in his power to cultivate the gift. Hence a huge and horrid unpopularity, which he persistently augments till even the tiniest, tenderest gallery-god thirsts for his gore. The audience becomes so enraged that it hisses every time he comes on. Some cherish an abiding hatred; meeting him on the street next day, they openly insult him. In Texas, villains have been shot at. And as a final proof of villainy, the fiend glories in his shame, taking obloquy as a sort of laurel-crown, a tribute to his art.

Art it is, gadzooks! To be called "liar," "scoundrel," "puppy," "toad," yet never reply in more ferocious terms than "A time—will—come! Ha! Ha!"—this, methinks, argues that self-command which is the soul of virtuosity. Splendid, too, is the villain's talent for dropping flat when only half poked at by the hero; for never recognizing a detective disguised in a Piccadilly collar; for falling back foiled, although armed to the teeth, when the "comic relief" comes at him with bare knuckles, and for purloining wills and looting safes only at moments when witnesses swarm at his elbow. Moreover, if "genius is patience," this demon possesses a really dazzling brand of genius. "Foiled again"—and again and again—he pursues the evil tenor of his way.

And now the hero. Whereas the villain is completely and exhaustively villainous, the hero is completely and exhaustively heroic. You know it by his grand-opera stride, his righteously erect carriage, and the ring in his voice. Also by the creditable sentiments he exclaims while posing like any Olympian. "What! tell a falsehood? Let me die first! Fear a treacherous foe? Never, while a brave heart beats within me bosom!" "I swear that with the last drop of me blood I will defend yonder hunted but innocent girl!" To live up to this last proclamation requires a certain acrobatic nimbleness and a downright marvelous clairvoyance. Just when the heroine is about to be disintegrated by the sausage-machine, or reduced to longitudinal sections by the buzz-saw, or run over by the express-train as she lies bound across the rails, or blown to bits by the powder-barrel as the fuse sputters nearer and nearer, then—whoop-la!—in jumps the hero, who has foreseen all and turned up not a second too late. Down chimneys he comes, up woodchuck-holes, over yawning chasms, across tottering bridges, and along the ridgepoles of flaming buildings, to thwart the villain and succor beauty in distress. A demigod, that hero! . . .

And melodrama itself,—I find it perfect. Consider its problem. Wanted: By an incredibly dull audience, ten thousand thrills. To deliver those thrills takes something stronger, quicker, and simpler than the conventional play. Something stronger because the very dull require powerful stimulants to stave off torpor. These are they who love Salvationist rantings and whoopings, the yellow journal's tom-tom, and the dime novel's inspired hydrophobia; mild appeals leave them listless. Hence the merits of melodrama's wild and outrageous fury. . . .

Meanwhile, in the nine-and-twenty hair's-breadth-escape scenes of a melodrama, rapidity is everything. For three reasons. First, the audience knows what's coming; familiarity with "hurrah stuff" enables it to keep at least a minute ahead of the action. In the next place, it absolutely forgets itself. "Save her!" it shrieks. "Save her!" Or even, "Look out, Bill, he's under the sofa!" They tell how Salvini once choked his Desdemona in good faith; here it is the audience that is run away with by the convincing potency of art. And that mood won't last; one must strike while the iron is hot. Finally, melodrama is not got up for psychologists. Its devotees care nothing for the portrayal of the inner life, save in its crudest, most ferocious manifestations; a few wild cries suffice. They want "sump'n doin'." Strip the action, therefore, of all those interpretative, significant, philosophic touches that make it human. Give it go. Give it noise and bluster as it goes. Let it career madly, in a cloud of dust and with sparks flying.

And make it simple. The reason, really, why blood-and-thunder has for two centuries adhered to the rules set by the French *mélodrames*, is that their simplicity was absolute and final. They reduced character, incident, structure, and ideas to their lowest terms, enabling the Neolithic mind (and such is the Grand's) to comprehend. . . .

In the Grand's audience, pray notice, there are many who have had first-hand—or at least second-hand—acquaintance with the melodramatic. From among the Neolithic come firemen, policemen, seamen, and those who gain their bread in trades replete with danger and daring. Meanwhile the tenement street has its daily melodramas, such as these are,—melodramas of crime, drunkenness, and frightful vice, though generally lacking the completeness that would fit them for the stage. You know what happens when philanthropists transplant a family from the slum to the village. The family returns. It returns because its removal has involved an exchange of melodrama for "the legitimate." . . .

While the life of the people gives a tremendous reality to the melodramatic, their reading super-emphasizes that reality. In your evening newspaper, somewhere among the items under inconspicuous headlines, you are told that when Mrs. Ahearn, who dwells in a certain remote city, stood shrieking at the window of a blazing tenement, it was her own son, Terence (of Hook-and-Ladder Three), who carried her fainting to the ground. In the Neolithic newspaper, on the other hand, the story fills half a page, with colossal headlines and thrilling illustrations. A dozen despatches of international importance are "killed" to make room for it. So you need hardly marvel that, when the Grand presents incidents familiar through experience and reading, the people accept them. They are plausible, stirring, and readily comprehended. . . .

However wild and unrepresentative the incident, and however crude (even to grotesquerie) the depiction of character, the underlying notions must consist solely of platitudes,—or, to put it more genially, of fundamental verities. Mr. [G. K.] Chesterton remarks with absolute justice, "Melodrama is popular because it is profound truth; because it goes on repeating the things which humanity has found to be central facts. This endless repetition profoundly annoys the sensitive artist inside you and me. But it ought to profoundly please the realist. The melodrama is perpetually telling us that mothers are devoted to their children, because mothers are devoted to their children. Humanity may in time grow tired of hearing this truth; but humanity will never grow tired of fulfilling it. The melodramas say that men are chiefly sensitive upon honor and upon their personal claim to courage. Men are. It bores one to hear one's honor reiterated; but it would startle one to hear it denied. In so far as the melodrama is really bad, it is not bad because it expresses old ideas; it is bad because it so expresses them as to make them seem like dead ideas."

The Ten-Twenty-Thirty Melodramas

Dead ideas? So they may seem to Mr. Chesterton while "hurrah stuff" rages before his eyes and chills-and-fever music rings in his ears. So they most emphatically do not seem to the Neolithic.

Corse Payton was often proclaimed "King of the Ten-Twenty-Thirty." As actor-manager, with Etta Reed, his wife and leading lady, he brought repertory theater to the small-town circuit of "opera houses" and "academies of music" in the Midwest in the 1890s. He applied much the same practices of "popular-priced" melodrama and weekly change of program—mixed motion pictures and short drama—at a permanent location, his Lee Avenue theater in Brooklyn, in 1901. Soon, he operated a circuit of four theaters in Greater New York, in association with his sister, Mary Gibbs Spooner. At his Friday matinee teas, where he served the pink lemonade favored by "candy butchers" at circuses and carnivals, Payton encouraged the audience to meet his stock company. Journalist Arthur Ruhl observed the clublike interaction at Payton's Union Square theater in 1911.

Arthur Ruhl, "Ten-Twenty-Thirty," *Outlook* 98 (August 1911): 890–91.

Letting people choose their own plays is one of the specialities of the ten-twenty-thirty houses. At the Academy of Music, where a stock company has been playing steadily since last August, they send out some eight thousand circulars a week, merely to give their patrons a general notion of next week's play. Often the audience chooses the plays to be put on, and the subscribers have the same seats for one evening a week throughout the winter.

Mr. Girard [the company's "heavy"] told how the audiences in Brooklyn said how-de-you to each other as they took their seats, and how you soon got to remember the faces out in front. And you couldn't fool the audience about the people on the stage. Send on one of their favorites in a pitch-dark scene as a detective or a burglar, and they'd recognize him, no matter what his disguise, and give him a hand. . . .

Mr. Corse Payton has done more than any one else, probably, to make the ten-twenty-thirty cent theater a family institution. He has been at it ten years now, and has four companies and something like a hundred players working for him. A Friday matinée . . . is a veritable orgy of this sort of thing that such an audience genuinely likes. A pink tea is one of Mr. Payton's great ideas. A big sign in the lobby announces it as the crowd comes in. Corse himself issues another invitation from the stage just before the last act, and as soon as the curtain falls the crowd pile up on the stage by way of the left-hand boxes—fat ladies in limp shirt-waists, pounding the scenery to see how real it is; giggling young girls, half-awed, half-contemptuous, in this behind-the-scenes world. . . .

Then there is a very good orchestra, and between the acts moving pictures, if you are at the Academy; if at the Grand Opera House, a versatile young man, who shifts scenery or something at other times, comes out in front of the curtain and sings an illustrated song. There is a picture on the screen of a girl in a pink dress in a garden, and the athletic young tenor cries:

"Let's make love among the roses, dearie,
You and I,
Stealing little hugs, and tender kisses
On the sly."

After the chorus has been sung once or twice the words themselves are flashed on the curtain. The vague hum that has followed the song comes out more confidently on the spearmint-scented air—there is a sort of pathos in the sibilant s's in the twilight—and the following the one man's voice are many feminine voices, a little off the key, perhaps, faltering, yet evidently in deadly earnest groping for the tune. . . .

[Corse Payton] suddenly shoots out in front of the curtain just before the last act, with a "Hello, audience!" and, swinging his arms, walks rapidly up and down the footlights, talking as he goes. Now and then he stops, whacks his head, or, elaborately twisting one hand round with the other, slaps his wrist, and continues his promenade.

"Next week we'll revive that grand old melodrama, 'The Count of Monte Christo.' Splendid play—brings out the full strength of the company. After that, Mrs. Elinor Glyn's 'Three Weeks.' Beautiful scenic effects—good show—don't miss it. Prices same as usual—ten, twenty, and thirty cents. Dollar twenty a dozen. Ten cents admission—ten cents for 'Three Weeks.' Cheaper than room rent." The audience adore it. They wish he would go on forever. "If there's anything you'd like, let us know. Lists of plays out in the lobby—a hundred of 'em. Pick out the one you like and tell us about it. That's what we're here for. Pretty soon we're going to put on a revival of the greatest melodrama ever written, 'The Two Orphans.' Prices same as usual. Ten cents admission—five cents an orphan. (Slap). And if there's any thing you want, just vote for it. We'll play it. We play anything from 'Hamlet' to polo. Good-by, people"—and Corse goes slashing off, swinging his arms—"I'll come back."

Anything from Hamlet to polo—with moving pictures and pink lemonades and the glad news from the curtain advertisements, that somebody's gum aids digestion and that your credit is good at Spink's. Of course, the *ingénue* is rather too giggly, and the juvenile in wiping out the lines of care doth his face so brilliantly incarnadine [color pink] that his eyes are but two black spots like the lumps of coal in a snow-man. The comic aunt overdoes her make-up by hanging a green parrot on the very rim of her bonnet, so that it flops up and down absurdly every time she moves her head.

There are all sorts of exaggerations, over-accents, a continuous scaling-down. You see the author's work through a glass darkly, perhaps. But you do see. For thirty cents (fifty in the evening) you see plays of established merit, while Broadway is paying two dollars to see plays tried out.

"LEG SHOW" BURLESQUE
EXTRAVAGANZAS

"The Forty Flirts," or "40 la belle Par-
isiennes 40," were the highlight of the twice-daily "burlesque" show at the
Folly, a low-comedy Brooklyn theater that Rollin Lynde Hartt attended at the
turn of the century. For the price of twenty cents, in the company of men he
described as a "herd" of petty criminals, he watched the dancers, billed as "a
bevy of bouncing, bewitching, bewildering blondes" but sadly depleted in
number and long past their prime, appear as soldiers, sailors, gondoliers,
geishas, football players, college students, Moorish beauties. Ethnic comedy
filled the gap between the frequent changes of costume. Fifty years before,
Hartt noted, citing William Dean Howells as authority, burlesque had arrived
from Europe as "a sensational and spectacular travesty upon legend and
romance."[1] By contrast, this Folly show was a plotless, witless display of wom-
en's bodies, neither sensational nor spectacular, and if burlesque, had lost any
hint of credible travesty. Most critics believed that the decline had been
precipitated by the opening of *The Black Crook* in New York in September
1866. This musical extravaganza, part melodrama, part ballet, was, the de-
lightedly shocked *Clipper* reported at the time, an "undress piece" that made
women's "symmetrical legs and alabaster bosoms" a theatrical spectacle, and
had influenced the rise of the "chorus girl" as a theatrical phenomenon.[2]

Never had there been such an expensive and lavish production as *The
Black Crook*. A cast of several hundred appeared on stage, with three hundred
costumes, two hundred stagehands attending, and the most brilliant effects
yet seen. "The scenery is magnificent; the ballet is beautiful; the drama is—
rubbish," William Winter of the *Tribune* concluded, after attending the opening night. The other critics agreed. "The text of the play is little else than
stuffing to use up time while the great scenes are arranged," *Spirit of the Times*
reported.[3] Charles M. Barras's plot was childishly simple—the English version
some years later subtitled it *The Naughty Fairy*. How banal the saga of two
lovers in a medieval castle, a dungeon, a cruel stepmother and a wicked
count, a hunchbacked alchemist making a pact with the devil, demons and
monsters as cheerleaders, a fairy queen in a grotto. It was the work of "glean-
ers," as the *Tribune* put it: a pastiche of Goethe's *Faust* and Weber's opera *Der*

Freischutz, and the chorus of water nymphs from *The Naiad Queen* of 1861. It was a burlesque in the sense that the comic episodes mocked operatic conventions. The main characters, Amina and Rodolfo (Rodolphe), were taken from Vincenzo Bellini's *La Sonnambula*, the most popular opera in America since its first staging in 1835.

However, the production most resembled the genre of song-and-dance melodramas which the French called the *féerie* and the English and Americans, the "Fairy Burlesque Spectacular Extravaganza." Supernatural elements —sprites clad in gold and silver, allegorical monsters, the struggle between angels and devils—were combined with the march of the Amazons. Visual splendor gave some coherence to fantasy and nonsense. The outstanding feature was the transformation scenes. Gradually one scene faded into another —even prolonged to fifteen minutes—with the aid of all that nineteenth-century lighting, chemical fire, stage machinery, painted sets, and grandiose props could muster. Such transformations were common in London or Paris theaters but had been attempted only rarely in America. *Bluebeard, or Female Curiosity*, an "Eastern spectacle" and "grand dramatic romance," with song, dance, and thrills and horrors of the mysterious Turkish castle, was a favorite at the Boston Museum. In 1843 New York's Olympic Theatre staged *Diana's Revenge, or, the Fate of Aetaeon*, "an Extravaganzical Burletta," with music and dance. In New York, transformation scenes had been employed in *The Enchanted Temple, or, The Spectre of the Nile* in 1855, by George L. Fox in *Planche, or the Lively Fairies* for Christmas 1856, and by Laura Keene in her "Birth of Cupid in the Bower of Ferns" in her production of *The Three Sisters* in 1860. However, *The Black Crook* added dance formations of women in skimpy dresses.

Controversy over the theatrical display of "nude" female bodies had smouldered for two decades. Foreign showmen were blamed for introducing corruption into the New World Eden. On the English stage, managers had for comic and dramatic effect cast women dressed provocatively in abbreviated men's costume that accentuated their figures. In the 1820s Madame Vestris became famous for her "breeches" roles in London, and since then Vestris imitators, provocatively cross-dressed, had become a subgenre of actresses. Americans were more circumspect—or pretended to be. None of this mattered to the fashionable who filled most of the three thousand seats nightly for an unprecedented four hundred and seventy-five consecutive performances of *The Black Crook*. The success encouraged look-alike productions—*The White Fawn*, also by Jarrett and Palmer, *The Devil's Auction, or The Golden Branch* (1866), and *The Crimson Shield, or Nymphs of the Rainbow* (1868).

All criticism of *The Black Crook* paled in comparison with the wave of English pantomime-spectaculars which triumphed in New York and Boston in 1868–72. Gone were the ballet dances and the transformation scenes; in

196

their stead was an all-female cast of strange Minotaurs, half men, half women, in men's roles. Lydia Thompson's Blondes were the agents of this new style. When it opened in London in 1863, *Ixion; or, The Man at the Wheel* had been thought a trivial, silly, but rather shocking, exploitation of women's bodies. The English critic John Ruskin, who saw *Ali Baba* at Covent Garden in 1867, was bewildered by the sheer silliness of the show. "The Forty Thieves were girls," he wrote. "The Forty Thieves and their forty companions were in some way mixed up with almost forty hundred and forty fairies, who were girls. There was an Oxford and Cambridge boat-race, in which the Oxford and Cambridge men were girls."[4] But when *Ixion* crossed the Atlantic a few years later, in its wake also came in swift succession, *Ernani; or, The Horn of a Dilemma*, then *Field of the Cloth of Gold*, then *The Forty Thieves; or, Striking Oil in Family Jars*, then *Robinson Crusoe*, then *Sinbad the Sailor; or, The Ungenial Genii and the Cabin Boy*, then *Robin Hood; or, The Maid That Was Arch and The Youth That Was Archer*. The mocking tone and blatant sexuality of the English shows was more "dangerous," the *New York Times* claimed, than *The Black Crook*: "Its object is to upset decorum, to upset gravity, to disarm judgment, and to intoxicate the senses."[5] The Blondes not only exposed their legs but by burlesquing masculine behavior, exposed fragile male egos.

By the turn of the century, burlesque had a new and popular meaning, not as satire of well-known drama, but as a show of scantily dressed or undressed women. Late in life, Lydia Thompson complained of the vulgar tone she had found by the late 1880s. "When I first crossed the Atlantic for the six consecutive seasons I played here ladies and children were my greatest patrons," she explained to an American journalist. "But now when the word burlesque is put up men are the first patrons."[6]

The "leg show" had a divided legacy. If it generated the tawdry cheap "burlesque house" and the seedy Earl Carroll *Vanities* of the 1920s, it also inspired—with European sophistication added via Parisian revues—the glittering and costly Ziegfeld *Follies* fantasies of 1907–30. Perhaps the most unlikely offshoot was the Turkish harem floorshow for suburban shoppers. "Spectacular extravaganzas" were a feature of the elegant turn-of-the-century department stores. To promote retail sales, New York's Siegal-Cooper, like other large metropolitan stores, had become a general service center, offering club-room facilities, amenities, and entertainment, especially for women customers. In its elegant music auditorium on the fifth floor, it advertised and hosted free afternoon concerts twice a week in season. For 1903 its grand themed event was the "Carnival of Nations." During "Oriental Week," it presented *Phantasma, the Enchanted Bower*, with a "glimpse of the Orient—a Turkish harem, a parade of Turkish dancing girls, a 'genie of the lamp,' and 'Cleopatra of the Nile.'" The next year, Siegal-Cooper's held the *Amazma*

Show, with "weird transformations," "startling and beautiful electrical displays," and "incandescent illusions."[7] The shows might be only a fraction of the length of *The Black Crook*, but the setting of luxury and privilege—carpets, chandeliers, marbled interiors, liveried attendants—imitated the elegant fantasy of Niblo's Garden.

The Black Crook

The origins of *The Black Crook* lay in a speculative theatrical venture. Two New York entrepreneurs, Henry C. Jarrett, a young and ambitious producer, and his business partner Henry Palmer, believed that a big-budget musical show would be highly successful. They planned a visual feast of female dancers in a multi-media production with the most modern special effects. The gamble was no mere whim: European pantomime and opera had proved enduringly popular in the United States. In the 1850s the French troupe known as the Ravels and the Marinetti Family had combined acrobatic skills with pantomime, and they toured throughout the country with great success. However, few large ballet troupes had crossed the Atlantic. A grand spectacular with European cachet was still a novelty. Jarrett and Palmer toured London, Paris, Berlin, and Milan, offering high salaries to trained ballerinas. They purchased three hundred of the most expensive costumes from French designers and shipped one hundred and ten tons of the most elaborate scenery and the latest stage machinery from London technicians.

Now, all the producers needed was a production. They had vague plans to present one of the currently popular English or French spectacles at New York's prestigious Academy of Music. When that theater burned down, they formed a partnership with William Wheatley, the manager of Niblo's Garden. A profusion of trapdoors, a deep pit for a water tank, large plate-glass mirrors, a vast network of wires to support airborne fairies, and reconstruction of the entire backstage were needed to accommodate the special-effects machinery imported from London. Even with Niblo's huge stage, these necessary changes cost fifty thousand dollars.

Joseph Whitton claimed that his account, written thirty years after *The Black Crook* opened in New York, was the only true record. As the controller of finances at Niblo's Garden theater, and the aide closest to Wheatley, only he had had intimate knowledge of the production. The title of Whitton's pamphlet referred to a hostile sermon, "The Nuisances of New York, Particularly The Naked Truth," preached by the Rev. Charles B. Smyth on November 18, 1866, which, when reported by the hostile *Herald* newspaper, gave the show notoriety—and its most effective publicity.

Joseph Whitton, *"The Naked Truth:" An Inside History of the Black Crook* (Philadelphia: H. W. Shaw, 1897), [5]–6, 10, 32.

The Black Crook

Early in the summer of '66 Messrs. Jarrett & Palmer—the wide-famed theatrical managers and speculators of those days—returned from Europe, whose principal cities they had ransacked in search of some gigantic attraction with which to dazzle and monopolize the attention of American theatre-goers and draw enough dollars from their pockets to comfortably line their own.

After ripe deliberation they decided that a Grand Ballet would be the proper thing. Jarrett's reasons for this were cogent, and his argument—as coming events were to prove—thoroughly sound. "Legs are staple articles, and will never go out of fashion while the world lasts. They top the list of the 'Beauties of Nature,' and we will gather an array of them that will make even the surfeited New Yorker open his eyes and his pocket and hold his breath in astonishment."

Upon this line the cunning managers began their work. The most accomplished artistes and the prettiest women were picked from the leading theatres of London, Paris, Berlin, and Milan. No Ballet so complete in its *ensemble*, and with so ravishing a collection of the "Beauties of Nature," was ever before seen, or, if it were, certainly not by cisatlantic eyes.

The Ballet being completed, the next care of the managers was the costumes. These they had made in Paris, and with no regard to cost. The most expensive satins and silks were used, provided the needed effect and gorgeousness could not be obtained without them. No brummagem, no cheap sheen of paper-muslin, so long relied upon by the old-time economic manager to cheat the eyes of his patrons. All a true dream of splendor, a picture of glittering reality, to be hereafter displayed in a frame of bewildering enchantment.

Wheatley showed Whitton the manuscript of a minor dramatist, Charles M. Barras.

Patiently did I devote myself to the task, and soon saw, what Wheatley had already seen, that here was the very piece to fit the Ballet—a clothes-line, as it were, on which to hang the pretty dresses, besides affording abundant opportunities for scenic display. True, there was no originality in the plot—if it had a plot at all—[but] . . . originality was matter of little moment. It was just the wanted piece in every other respect, and if the plot had no originality, the title certainly had enough of it to insure, as I thought, the success of the play. . . .

I have said nothing of the literary merits of the *Crook*, for the best of reasons—it had none. This, however, is no serious fault. Elegant writing, with its daintily picked words and smooth-flowing sentences, is all well enough in its place; but that place is not in the drama of this prosy, money-grabbing age. The playgoer doesn't relish it. What he wants is something to please his eye and tickle his ear—something to strangle his cares and cut the throat of his troubles—something to make him laugh and forget he has a note to pay to-morrow, with no money to meet it. This is what he is after, and shrewd managers will show their shrewdness by accommodating him.

199

The sights and sounds and comedy of *The Black Crook* were its real glory. There were many subplots. Amina loves the impoverished artist Rodolphe but is matched by her stepmother Dame Barbara with the rich Count Wolfenstein. To restore his fading magical powers, the sorcerer Hertzog (known as the Black Crook because of his hunched or "crooked" back, and not for robbery and crime), makes a pact with the evil Zamiel to deliver a fresh soul to the devil every year. Rodolphe rescues Stalacta, the Fairy Queen, when she is trapped in the form of a dove, and is rewarded with precious jewels in the grotto. There are many comic characters, notably Carline, Barbara's impudent maid, and Greppo, first Hertzog's "drudge" and then Rodolphe's companion, and von Puffengruntz, Barbara's fat suitor. Comedy and fantastic scenes and "fairy" dances in the grotto predominate.

Act II, scene 4, introduces the fairies in the grotto, an excuse for songs and dances and a display of showy glitter. There were fishes swimming, a sea monster, a boat sinking, child-fairies asleep in shells, gems glittering on the foreshore. Theater-goers were astonished. The *Tribune* questioned its dramatic purpose but conceded that "Scenic Art has never, within our knowledge, been so amply and splendidly exemplified." *Spirit of the Times* praised as "absolutely miraculous" the "voluptuous moving forms, with the rocks and trees and babbling waters, the gorgeous caves and grottoes, the gems and gold of fairy land, the bewildering maze of all that is dazzlingly beautiful."[8]

Charles M. Barras, *The Black Crook, An Original, Magical and Spectacular Drama in Four Acts* (Chicago: Rounds and James, 1866), 28–30; *The Black Crook and Other Nineteenth-Century American Plays*, ed. Myron Matlaw (New York: Dutton, 1966), 349–63, 373–74.

The grotto of Golden Stalactites. A grand and comprehensive water-cavern of gold, deeply perspective, with stalactiform, arched roof. Vistas, running parallel and harmonizing with the main Grotto, the mouth of which discloses an open lake and distant shore at back. Transparent silver waters, in which are seen sporting fishes and nondescript amphibea. Diminutive fairies asleep on the waters of the Grotto in golden shells. Ground—or shore—piece, richly studded with gold and jewels. Masses of emerald and gold, upon and at the foot of which are reclining gnomes and amphibea.

Fairies asleep in poses. The moon, seen through the opening at back and over the distant shore of the lake, shows red upon its face at opening of scene.

Music.

DRAGONFIN, *who has been asleep on a jeweled mass on the shore, slowly awakens, rises and stretches himself. Upon turning, he sees the red upon the face of the moon.*

Music—chord.

DRAGONFIN. (*Uttering a cry of alarm.*) Awake. Awake.

(*Music—hurry. Gnomes and amphibea spring to their feet. Fairies and water nymphs enter hurriedly. Diminutive sprites in shells and fairies in poses, awaken.*)

Behold, there's blood upon the face of the moon—our Queen's in danger! To arms, to arms!

(*Music. The sprites in the shells disappear. The gnomes, amphibea and fairies rush off and immediately re-enter armed, the first-named with knotted clubs and tridents, the fairies with javelins. During the action the red disappears from the face of the moon, and it resumes its natural color.*)

(*Seeing the change.*) Stay—'tis past. Hark.

(*Queen STALACTA is heard singing beneath the waters. All bend forward and listen to her song.*)

(*After song.*) 'Tis she, our queen.

(*All kneel. Music. STALACTA rises from the waters and steps on shore, assisted by DRAGONFIN.*)

STALACTA. Arise, my loving subjects.

(*All rise.*)

DRAGONFIN. (*Pantomimes.*) Mistress, but now the light in yon great sapphire died out and stains of blood flushed in the face of the pale moon. You have 'scaped some deadly peril.

STALACTA. Thou art right. Listen, all. Tonight, while wandering in the fastnesses of the Hartz, without my protecting talisman, I heedlessly trod within one of the charmed circles of our enemy, the arch-fiend Zamiel.

ALL. Ha!

STALACTA. On the instant I was transformed into a white dove with shorn pinions. From beneath the rank leaves of an adder-plant glided a huge serpent. Its eyes were burning coals, its tongue a living flame. I was paralysed with fear and powerless to move. Nearer and nearer it came. I felt its stifling breath displace the purer air—I saw its venomed fangs glistening in the pale moonlight. Rising from out its deadly coil preparing itself to strike, when suddenly a youth, a mortal, strangely present in that wild, weird spot, seeing the danger of the trembling bird, seized a dead bough, which chance had fashioned like a Holy Cross, and smote the foul thing dead. Then he bore me safely from the charmed spot and gave me life and liberty.

DRAGONFIN. Revenge, revenge on the minions of Zamiel! (*Goes quietly off.*)

ALL. Revenge—revenge!

STALACTA. Nay, let no thought other than of joy mingle with this happy time. Remember, 'tis my natal hour, and I would have it, as in the past, a festal one. Let the invisible harmonies of this our realm breathe sweetest concord only.—And you, bright Crystaline, with your fair sisters, chase with flying feet the silver hours. (*Seats herself on bank.*)

(*Music. The Fairies form for dance. After the first pose, a loud, prolonged warning note, as if from a shell, is heard outside. All start in alarm, and hold the attitude of listening. The sound is repeated.*)

201

(*Music—hurry. The pose is broken and the fairies, gnomes and amphibea, the latter seizing their arms, form in alarm on either side. DRAGONFIN appears quickly.*)

STALACTA. (*who at the first sound has sprung to her feet.*) Speak, what danger threatens?

DRAGONFIN. The sentinel shells, played upon by the watchful winds, give alarm. Two daring mortals, armed with the enchanted magnet of the Black Crook, approach the secret entrance. Already they have passed the white whirlpool in safety. They come to despoil our realm of its glittering wealth.

STALACTA. Fear not, the talisman they bear is powerless against the spells that guard the portal.

ALL. Ho-ho-ho!

(*Echoes without and above. Music. Chorus—by gnomes, amphibea and fairies.*)

"Rejoice, rejoice, rejoice!

Sprites of the golden realm, rejoice.

Daring mortals mock our power

Flushed with the drink that the heart makes bold

They madly rush on the fatal hour.

Dark spells arise! Smite their longing eyes

That they never may gaze on the glittering prize!

Rejoice, rejoice, rejoice!

Sprites of the golden realm rejoice!

STALACTA. My faithful subjects—your Queen commends your zeal with which you would guard from mortal sight our beauteous realm. But ere these rash intruders perish, I would gratify a strange desire. Speed hence, good Dragonfin. Catch me their shadows from the bosom of the moon-lighted lake and cast them upon my faithful mirror. I would look upon them ere they fade forever.

(*Music. DRAGONFIN prostrates himself before STALACTA, springs into the water and disappears.*)

Begin the spell!

(*Music. This is either spoken by her or sung by fairy-chorus.*)

"Mortal shadows dimly cast

By the moonbeams' mystic ray

On the bosom of the lake

Hither, hither, fly away,

Flitting through the silver sheen

Come at summons of our Queen

Guardian spirits, let them pass,

Cast their shadows on the glass."

(*Music. DRAGONFIN springs from the water, and after prostrating himself before the Queen, rises and points to the water.*)

(*Music. Fairies wave their wands. A small arched-headed frame of gold and coral sta-lactites rises at the distant entrance of the Grotto, showing small figures of RODOLPHE*) and GREPPO *in boat, the former at the prow, gazing anxiously forward, the latter aft, in the attitude of paddling.*)

(STALACTA *who turns when the picture is fully shown. Chord of music.*)

(*Starting.*) Ha—'tis he! He must not perish. Invisible spirits, avert this peril.

"Shades of mortals hovering near

Join your masters—disappear."

(*Music—hurry. The mirror and figures quickly sink.*)

Dragonfin, come hither. Fly with swiftest speed to the rocks beneath the waters of the guarded entrance. When the frail bark which now approaches shall be rent asunder by the relentless spells that guard our realm, be it your task to snatch from death these daring mortals and bear them safely hither.

ALL. (*All start forward inquiringly, exclaiming.*) Mistress!

STALACTA. Nay, question me not, away, away,

Slaves of my power, obey, obey.

(*Music—hurry.* DRAGONFIN *bows low, springs into the water and disappears.*)

(*Music. A small boat, with two mechanical figures or small doubles of* RODOLPHE *and* GREPPO *as they appeared in the mirror, appears from the distant entrance of the cavern, and moves very slowly across. When it reaches the center it sinks at the sound of the gong and flash of lightning at back.*)

(*Music—hurry. All the gnomes, amphibea, etc., utter exclamations of delight and indulge in extravagant antics, until checked by a gesture from* STALACTA.)

(*Soft Music.* DRAGONFIN *rises slowly from the water, supporting on either side* RODOLPHE *and* GREPPO, *the latter gulping and grasping violently for breath as his head appears. They step on shore,* RODOLPHE *and* GREPPO *lost in bewilderment.* DRAGONFIN *bows low before* STALACTA. *The other amphibea and gnomes make a demonstration of attack.*)

(*Stepping between.*) Forbear! Who moves again 'till I alone command shall perish.

(*They retire.*)

RODOLPHE. (*Rubbing his eyes.*) Is this a phantasm—this glittering gold, yon flashing gems, these strange fantastic shapes? Have I then passed the portal of an unknown world, or am I dreaming?

STALACTA. Welcome, brave mortal, to our bright domain. And you, my subjects, know and greet your Queen's preserver.

(*Music. Gnomes and amphibea cluster around* RODOLPHE *and* GREPPO, *rolling at their feet and indulging in various grateful antics, after which the fairies surround them and evince their delight.*)

RODOLPHE. (*Still bewildered.*) If this indeed be not a dream, tell me, Bright Being, you whose simple motion seems to sway the moves and passions of this Elfin Band, who art thou, and where am I?

STALACTA. I am called Stalacta, Queen of this dazzling realm. The glittering wonders that assail thine eyes are not creations of phantastic dreams but nature's handiwork, wrought with the cunning fingers in a bounteous mood.

GREPPO. (*Who has picked up a large mass of gold at the back, comes forward.*) 'Tis true, 'tis true. Behold the shining nugget.

STALACTA. Who is thy droll companion?

RODOLPHE. My simple henchman, a faithful guide and servitor.

STALACTA. I bid him welcome, for his master's sake.

GREPPO. Thanks, thanks, your Resplendent Majesty, thanks, thanks.

RODOLPHE. You spoke of service done; have we then met before?

STALACTA. Yes, once.

RODOLPHE. Indeed? When?

STALACTA. This very night.

RODOLPHE. Tonight?

STALACTA. Tonight, in the glen of firs, but not as now—then, a poor, weak, fluttering, charm-encompassed bird, you snatched me trembling from the jaws of death, broke the dark spell of transformation, and gave to me the priceless boon of liberty.

RODOLPHE. I do remember—

GREPPO. And so do I. Phew, how the sparks flew when Master smashed the head of the scaly monster, and such a smell of brimstone, I do believe it was one of Beelzebub's own imps in disguise.

STALACTA. Again thou art welcome. This is my natal hour. Wilt view the sports of this, our carnival?

RODOLPHE. Most willingly.

STALACTA. And while the revels proceed, thou shalt tell me thy story.

(*Music—ballet. Seats are brought forward by amphibea.* STALACTA *and* RODOLPHE *sit.* GREPPO *amuses himself with* DRAGONFIN. *Gnomes and amphibea present him from time to time with nuggets of gold and jewels, which he thrusts into his pockets until they become greatly distended, during which action the diminutive sprites reappear in shells on the water, floating to and fro, fishing. The fairies form for dance. Grand ballet action by principals and full corps de ballet, during which the fishers in the shells are seen to catch small silver fish.*)

GREPPO. (*After the dance terminates.*) Ha, ha. Dancing. All very well in its way. But there's the sport for me, fishing! Look, Master, look. See the little rogues hook the silly shiners. Oh, if there is one thing in the world I love more than another, it is fishing—such fun to feel the greedy rascals snatch and see them wriggle. There's another—oh, I can't stand it any longer! Fishing is like the measles, it's catching. (*Turning to amphibea and gnomes.*) Would any of you handsome gentlemen oblige me with a spare hook and line.

(DRAGONFIN *nods assent and brings him rod and line.*)

Well, upon my word! I am very much obliged to your Scaly Magnificence. I'll do as much for you someday. By the way, is your Amphibious Majesty fond of fish? (DRAGONFIN *nods affirmatively.*)

What kind?

(DRAGONFIN, *business of indicating that he likes large ones.*)

Like large ones, eh? All right, I'll make you a present of the first ten-pounder that I catch.

(*Music. He fishes from the shore and catches two small fishes, the last quite diminutive. Amphibea, gnomes and fairies laugh boisterously as each fish is drawn forth.*)

(*Coming down, chapfallen.*) Pshaw—mere sprats and sardines—not my kind at all. This is too much like taking advantage of confiding innocence. (*To* DRAGONFIN.) Couldn't your Finny Excellency oblige me with a more tempting bait, something that would seduce some big, greedy, wiggly, waggly fellow, into taking a nibble? (DRAGONFIN *nods affirmatively. Music.* DRAGONFIN *goes to the margin of the water and draws forth a large crab, which he places on the hand of* GREPPO. *It seizes him by the fingers to the great delight of the amphibea, gnomes and fairies. He struggles frantically to extricate himself, and is finally released by* DRAGONFIN, *who baits the hook with the crab and gives him the rod and line.*)

(*Taking* DRAGONFIN *apart confidentially.*) I don't know about this. Excuse me for asking a question, but as an unprejudiced observer, don't you think this style of bait more likely to bite the fish than the fish to bite the bait?

(DRAGONFIN *shakes his head and indicates that a large fish will take it.*)

All right. Here goes then.

(*Music. He casts the line into the water. A moment after it is violently seized and a frantic struggle ensues, during which he is nearly drawn overboard two or three times. Suddenly an amphibious monster springs from the water and pursues* GREPPO *around, off and on the stage to the great delight of the amphibea, gnomes and fairies, who indulge in boisterous laughter.*)

(GREPPO, *in his terror, throws himself at the feet of* STALACTA *for protection. She rises and waves her hand. The monster retires and is pacified by* DRAGONFIN.)

GREPPO. (*Coming forward.*) Really, my fishy-fleshy friend, you must excuse me. I beg ten thousand pardons. I hadn't the remotest idea in the world that any of you bottle-green gentlemen were lying around loose on the bottom, watching for a supper of raw crabs. Indeed I hadn't. (*The monster growls and makes a start at him.*) (*Music.* DRAGONFIN *interposes and pacifies the monster. by patting him on the back. Then, taking its hand, passes it into that of* GREPPO.)

GREPPO. (*Shaking the monster's hand cordially.*) All right, I accept your apology. (*Then turning to* DRAGONFIN.) Now you're what I call a true friend—a friend in need, you stick by a fellow when he hasn't the courage to stick by himself. This is the second time you've done me a service. Once in saving me from too much water and now in saving me from too much luck, and I'll let you see that I can be grateful. You like fish?

(DRAGONFIN *nods affirmatively.*)

GREPPO (*passing the monster over to him.*) Consider him yours.

(*All the amphibea, gnomes and fairies laugh and go up.*)

STALACTA. (*Rising and leading* RODOLPHE *forward.*) Thy story claims for thee my pity and my aid.

RODOLPHE. And Hertzog the Black Crook—

STALACTA. Is a vile sorcerer whose dark, unhallowed spells were wrought for thy destruction.

RODOLPHE. How?

STALACTA. Beneath the entrance to this charmed spot, intertwined amid the branches of the coraline, are whole hecatombs of human bones, the whitened relics of adventurous mortals who like thyself have sought the realm. Until tonight no human eye has ever seen the dazzling splendor of this wondrous dome. No human footsteps save thine own and his who follows thee have ever pressed these sands of gold. Had not thy coming been to me foreshadowed and all my power been interposed to snatch thee from the impending doom, then thou too had'st joined the hapless throng that mouldering lies beneath yon depths.

RODOLPHE. Then is thy debt to me already paid.

STALACTA. Not so—I am still thy debtor and must ever be. Thou art environed by danger and need the power of my protection. Return unto the outer world again, thy happiness is there. She whom thou lovest is worthy of thy love, therefore return.

RODOLPHE. Amina, dear Amina.

STALACTA. In the secret cell of these caverns, whose walls are solid gold, lie countless hoards of richest treasure, gleaned for ages by the tireless gnomes. In the crystal depths of these waters sparkle gems richer by far than human eyes have ever gazed upon. Of these thou shalt bear with thee the choicest. Behold my gift.

(*Music. A jeweled stalactiform etagere with strong light from calcium falling upon it rises in front of ground-piece, bearing upon its different shelves rich vases filled with gold and various-colored jewels which* DRAGONFIN, *gnomes, and amphibea remove, performing a series of grotesque evolutions to marked music. Etagere sinks—after which music.* STALACTA *waves her wand; a golden boat studded with jewels glides on.*)

This bark, protected by a potent spell, shall bear thee safely to your neighboring shore. My faithful gnomes shall he thy treasure bearers. But ere we part, take thou this jeweled circlet. *(Gives him a ring from her finger.)* Should danger threaten—as perchance it will, for baffled malice has a thousand stings—press but thy lips upon the gem and thou wilt find me by thy side.

(*Music.* RODOLPHE *kneels and kisses her hand. She raises him.*)

Farewell.

(*Music. He slips into the boat.* GREPPO, *bearing a large mass of gold, affectionately embraces* DRAGONFIN, *shakes hands with the gnomes and amphibea, kisses the fairies, bows low to* STALACTA *and gets into the boat. A dolphin, glittering in green and gold, rises from waters with principal danseuse bearing a vase of treasure; other dolphins float with diminutive sprites bearing treasure. Copious shower of gold, the other sprites on the water catching the flakes in shells of silver. Poses by gnomes, amphibea and fairies. The whole scene brilliantly lighted. Slow curtain.*)

206

The Black Crook

ACT III Scene 1

A lapse of six months.

Illuminated gardens of Wolfenstein by moon-light, with terrace and illuminated castle at back. This scene, standing as it does the entire act, should be elaborate and beautiful.

Music.

Masqueraders in ball costumes discovered promenading. Grand Ballet divertissement, after which the masquers gradually disappear at different entrances.

Enter from the terrace DAME BARBARA, *masked, falutingly dressed and carrying a huge fan. She is followed by* CARLINE.

BARBARA. (*Unmasking and coming forward.*) Phew, what a relief. Thank the saints his Countship's birthday comes but once a year. Another such festival would be the death of me. Ah! I'm stewed, fried, broiled and roasted. (*Fans herself vigorously.*)

CARLINE. (*Aside.*) And still as tough as Dame Gretchen's gander, what was twenty-one last Easter. (*Aloud.*) Why, Madam Barbara, I thought you enjoyed it.

BARBARA. So I do, child, so I do; particularly the masquerading. One has so many pleasant things whispered in one's ear; but I can't say so much for the waltzing. It's such a terrible thing to take the starch out of one's linen.

CARLINE. La, Madam Barbara, what's a little starch? Nothing. If I waltzed as gracefully as you (BARBARA *makes a gesture of satisfaction.*) and had such an inviting waist—(BARBARA *pinches her waist.*)—I'd keep at it until I was as limp as a boiled cabbage leaf.

BARBARA. Then you—you think me graceful, eh?

CARLINE. (*Aside.*) As a hippopotamus. (*Aloud.*) As a sylph. You were the envy of all the ladies and the admiration of all the other sex. Did you notice that courtly gentleman in the blue mask?

BARBARA. And what of him?

CARLINE. Nothing, only he was frantic to get an introduction to you.

BARBARA. No! Was he?

CARLINE. Yes indeed, Madam. And when his Lordship, the Count, engaged the lady Amina for a moment, he turned to me and slipping a golden crown into my palm with one hand, pressing his heart with the other and pointing to you with the other, asked with a sweet, sighing, silvery voice, trembling with emotion: "Who is that lovely being?"

BARBARA. No—did he?

CARLINE. Yes indeed, Madam. (*Aside.*) The saints forgive me for lying. (*Aloud.*) And Mynheer von Puffengruntz, who overheard him, turned pea-green with jealousy.

BARBARA. (*Fanning herself and pressing her hand upon her heart.*) Be still, little trembler, be still. I declare, my silly heart is fluttering like a poor little starling in a gold cage.

CARLINE. (*Aside.*) More like a big buzzard in a steel trap.

BARBARA. Carline, take my fan, child. (*Gives it.*) The exertion will make my complexion too ruddy.

CARLINE. So it will, Madam, and ruddy complexions are not genteel—allow me. (*Fans her vigorously.*)

BARBARA. Not so violent, girl, you'll disarrange my hair. Gently, very gently, a sort of sportive zephyr.

CARLINE. I understand. Madam. You want a mild sort of tickling sensation. something like one feels on one's neck when a gentleman whispers in one's ear—

BARBARA. (*Languidly.*) Y-e-s. (*Sighs.*) And he called me a—a—what did he call me?

CARLINE. A swan-like creature. (*Aside.*) A goose.

BARBARA. (*Sighs.*) Who can he be, I wonder.

CARLINE. Nobody appears to know exactly. I heard his Lordship, the Count, whisper to the Baron von Stuffencram that he suspected the mysterious blue mask to be no other than the young prince Leopold.—Once, while dancing, his domino came open at the breast and I saw a collar of jewels fit for an emperor. However, as everybody is to unmask at the grand banquet, we will then know all about him.

BARBARA. Eh, what, the Prince Leopold?

CARLINE. So his Lordship, the Count, thinks.

BARBARA. Why, he is already affianced, as everybody knows, to the young Princess Frederica.

CARLINE. Dear me, so he is—how unfortunate.

BARBARA. Poor young man—how I pity him. What a terrible thing it is to be of royal blood and not have the liberty to choose for one's self. Heigh-ho! I know it is a sad, cruel, wicked thing to blight a young and budding affection, but as the right honorable foster-mother that-*is*-to-be of her right honorable Ladyship that-is-to-be, I mustn't encourage his highness in a hopeless passion. (*Displays herself.*)

(*Enter* VON PUFFENGRUNTZ.)

VON PUFFENGRUNTZ. (*At back, admiringly.*) There she is! What a grace, what a dignity, what a walk. (*Coming forward.*) Ah-a-a.

BARBARA. (*Sighing.*) There's another victim to love's cruel dart; my fan, child.

CARLINE. (*Giving it.*) Be careful, use it gently, Madam. Remember your complexion. (*Aside.*) What a lovely couple—powder and puff.

VON PUFFENGRUNTZ. (*Aside.*) What a golden opportunity. (*Aloud.*) Young woman, as I left the grand hall I heard your mistress asking for you.

CARLINE. (*Aside.*) Of course, I understand—cunning old walrus. (*Aloud.*) May I retire, Madam?

BARBARA. Yes. certainly, child, that is, if her Ladyship requires you. (*Coquettes with her dress, etc.*)

CARLINE. (*Aside.*) I thought so, willing old pelican. She's beginning to dress her feathers already. Never mind. I shall have another flirtation with the prince's equerry, the drollest and most agreeable fellow in the world, and *such* a rogue. (*Exits.*)

208

(VON PUFFENGRUNTZ *gazes admiringly at* BARBARA *and sighs.*)

BARBARA. (*Casting sidelong glances at him.*) Heigh-ho! There he is. My charms tonight have completed the conquest. He is fast-bound in the bonds of rosy cupid. I see a proposal in one eye and a marriage settlement in the other. But I mustn't draw him in too suddenly. These men are like trout; they must be played with a little.

VON PUFFENGRUNTZ. Full moon of the festival, why have you so cruelly robbed the grand hall of your light, and left us to grope about in the dull glimmer of the sickly stars?

BARBARA. Don't talk to me about moonshine and sickly stars, you heartless, gay deceiver.

VON PUFFENGRUNTZ. Deceiver?

BARBARA. Deceiver! Didn't I see you gallivanting with the Fraulein von Skragneek, the rich Burgomaster's daughter?

VON PUFFENGRUNTZ. Politeness, my dear Madam Barbara, merely politeness, on my honor. The fact is I—I had the misfortune to tread on the lady's favorite bunion, and what you mistook for tenderness was only an apology—an apology, believe me, my dear Madam Barbara, only an apology.

BARBARA. Oh, you men, you deceiving men! You are always ready with an excuse.

VON PUFFENGRUNTZ. On the honor of a von Puffengruntz, I swear I speak the truth. The Fraulein von Skragneek indeed! Haven't I got eyes? Ah, cruel fair one, compared with her and all others, you are as the stately sunflower in a meadow of dandelions. As—as the queenly holly-hock in a garden of chickweed.

(*Music—tremulo-piano.*)

(DRAGONFIN, *ascends quickly, steps forward and listens.*)

BARBARA. (*Aside.*) It's coming at last. I know it's coming. (*Pressing her heart.*) What a strange flutter. I hope I'm not going to faint. Dear me, what poor weak, silly creatures we are. I must nerve myself for the trying occasion. How fortunate it is that I happen to have my smelling-salts about me. (*Draws flask from her pocket, turns her back to* VON PUFFENGIRUNTZ, *and drinks.*)

VON PUFFENGRUNTZ. (*Aside.*) She's moved. She's overcome with emotion. She turns to hide her blushes. She yields, and now, like a conqueror, I'll gather in the fruits of victory.

(*He kneels with difficulty at the feet of* BARBARA. *His face is half-averted, and he is about to take her hand, when* DRAGONFIN *glides quietly back of and between them, extends his left hand to* VON PUFFENGRUNTZ *and takes* BARBARA's *in the other. They both sigh.* VON PUFFENGRUNTZ *squeezes the hand of* DRAGONFIN, *who shakes with* suppressed *laughter.*)

Poor, frightened thing, how she trembles.

BARBARA. (*Aside.*) Dear me, how strangely the tender passion affects him. He's shaking like an aspen and his hand is as cold as ice.

VON PUFFENGRUNTZ. Bewitching siren, listen to the voice of love.

BARBARA. Oh, Mynheer von Puffengruntz, how can you?

VON PUFFENGRUNTZ. Don't call me von Puffengruntz. Call me Maximilian, call me your Maximilian. (*Squeezes* DRAGONFIN's *hand.* DRAGONFIN *squeezes* BARBARA's *hand.*)

BARBARA. Oh, don't, you naughty man, you—you hurt my hand.

VON PUFFENGRUNTZ. No, did I? Queen of Love and Beauty, then let me heal the bruise.

(*Kisses the hand of* DRAGONFIN *rapturously, who, at the same time kisses* BARBARA's.)

And now that I've healed it, let me call it mine. (*Looks for the first time attentively at the hand; continues the inspection up the arm until he encounters the grinning face of* DRAGONFIN, *when in speechless terror he drops the hand, makes various floundering attempts to regain his feet and exits, hurriedly.*)

BARBARA. (*Aside.*) Shall I keep him a little longer with Cupid's dart sticking in his bosom, or shall I end his misery. (*Aloud.*) Ahem, you'll—you'll never be a naughty boy again?

(DRAGONFIN *squeezes her hand.*)

And you'll promise never to tread on the Fraulein von Skragneek's favorite bunion. (DRAGONFIN *squeezes her hand.*)

(*Aside.*) Poor fellow, joy has made him speechless, he can only answer with a squeeze of the hand. (*Aloud.*) Well then, Maximilian, I'm yours! (*Falls into* DRAGONFIN's *arms; looks up into his face.*)

(*Music. She utters a piercing scream and rushes off.*)

(DRAGONFIN *imitates and indulges in extravagant antics until music changes— when he starts, inclines his ear to the ground and listens—rises, moves cautiously, starts, points off, shakes his clenched hand threateningly, and quickly disappears.*)

HERTZOG. (*Entering hurriedly and disturbed.*) Foiled, tricked, crossed in the hour of my victory! A life desperately played for and fairly won, snatched from the jaws of death. He lives, my chosen victim lives, and flushed with triumph and vast hoards of gold, stalks boldly forth to mock me. Oh, curse the interposing power that stepped between us, a withering palsy light upon her arm and blight and pestilence infect the air she breathes! Oh, impotent, oh driveling fool! To work, to work. A soul once tampered with must be pursued, not cast aside to tempt another, so runs the bond which I've sealed. 'Tis well, 'tis well. I'll track him as the sleuth-hound tracks the stag. He must, he *shall* be mine.

(*Music. Exit hurriedly.*)

(*March of Amazons.*)

ACT IV Scene 6

Pandemonium. ZAMIEL *in council, seated on an illuminated throne of skulls and flame. Lesser thrones, one occupied by* REDGLARE, *with pen and open book, another* by a secretary, writing. At the foot of the central throne, two dwarf demon pages with wands, in attendance.

Music.

Fiends discovered in a chorus of demoniacal yells and fiendish laughter, dancing around a flaming chasm. After the action is continued a brief time, ZAMIEL waves his scepter.

Demons separate.

ZAMIEL. 'Tis well. Let silence reign awhile. How stands the record of the dying year? Has every seed brought sinful fruit? Is all the harvest gathered in—is every bond fulfilled?

REDGLARE. All—all save one.

ZAMIEL. Who plays the laggard.

REDGLARE. One who sought to rival thy great power—Hertzog, the Black Crook.

ALL THE FIENDS. Ho, ho, ho.

(*Echoed without and above, followed by a single wild blast of infernal music.*)

ZAMIEL. If when the brazen tongue of clamorous Time, now trembling on the midnight's verge, proclaims the appointed hour, the wail of no fresh soul by him betrayed breaks on the air of Hell, let him be summoned. (*Music.*)

(*The demons utter a wild wail of delight and resume the dance. The gong strikes twelve. At the first stroke, the demons cease dancing and hold separate pictures of exultation. At the termination of each stroke a single brazen blast of demoniacal music. At the twelfth stroke, loud and continued thunder. Demons utter a wild cry. ZAMIEL rises and waves his scepter.*)

(*If possible, the scene backs away and discloses vistas of Pandemonium teeming with infernal life and wreaths of flame, from which appear illuminated heads of demons, skeletons and nondescript monsters.*)

(*Gong sounds. HERTZOG is dragged on by Fiends, and is dashed into the flaming chasm. Demons howl and dance around.*)

Act IV Scene 7

Subterranean gallery of emerald and crystal stalactites.

Music.

Characteristic march. Grand procession of amphibea and gnomes bearing in their arms and upon their heads salvers, shells, and quaint vases filled with gold and jewels. They are followed by amazons in armor, led by STALACTA. They march, double the march, and vary the evolutions, till the transformation is ready, when they exit and the scene breaks away to

Act IV Scene 8

Music.

An elaborate mechanical and scenical construction of the Realms of STALACTA, occupying the entire stage. This scene must be of gradually-developing and culminating beauty, introducing during its various transformations STALACTA, *the entire host of fairies, sprites, water nymphs, amphibea, gnomes, etc., bearing treasure.* RODOLPHE, AMINA, GREPPO *and* CARLINE.

Calcium lights, brilliant fires, and slow curtain.

In act I, scene 4, of *The Black Crook*, Carline, the village girl who becomes Amina's maid and companion, sings "You Naughty, Naughty Men" in Count Wolfenstein's castle. The English singer Milly Cavendish played Carline. The cheeky song of the battle of the sexes, typical of the English music hall, suited such a free spirit who delights in tricking and teasing the vain Dame Barbara.

The Black Crook Songster: a collection of choice, jolly and happy songs, now published for the first time: including "You naughty men!" as sung at Niblo's with great applause by the late Millie Cavendish (New York: R. M. De Witt, 1867?), 2–3.

You Naughty, Naughty Men (1866)

I will never more deceive you, nor of happiness bereave you,
But I'll die a maid to grieve you, oh! you naughty, naughty men;
You may talk of love, and sighing, say for us you're nearly dying;
All the while you know you're trying to deceive, you naughty men;
You may talk of love, and sighing, say for us you're nearly dying;
All the while you know you're trying to deceive, you naughty, naughty men.

When you want a kiss or favour, you put on your best behaviour,
And your looks of kindness savour, oh, you naughty, naughty men;
Of love, you set us dreaming, and when with hope we're teeming;
We find you are but scheming, you naughty, naughty men,
Of love you set us dreaming; and when with hope we're teeming;
We find you are but scheming, you naughty, naughty, naughty men.

If a fortune we inherit, you see in us every merit,
And declare we're girls of spirit, oh! you naughty, naughty men,
But too often, matrimony, is a mere matter of money,
We get bitters 'stead of honey, from you naughty, naughty men,
But too often, matrimony, is a mere matter of money,
We get bitters 'stead of honey, from you naughty, naughty men.

And when married how you treat us, and of each fond wish defeat us,
And some will even beat us, oh! you naughty, naughty men,
You take us from our mothers, from our sisters, and our brothers,
When you get us, flirt with others, oh! you cruel wicked men,
You take us from our mothers, from our sisters, and our brothers,
When you get us, flirt with others, oh! you cruel wicked men,

But with all your faults, we clearly, love you wicked fellows dearly,

Yes, we dote upon you dearly, oh! you naughty, naughty men,

We've no wish to distress you, we'd sooner far caress you,

And when kind we'll say, oh, bless you, oh! you naughty, dear, delightful men,

We've no wish to distress you, we'd sooner far caress you,

And when kind we'll say, oh, bless you, oh! you naughty, dear, delightful men.

A Burlesque of Burlesque

The Black Crook's triumph invited copycat productions and parodies. In the winter season of 1866–67, George Fox enlivened the traditional English pantomime *Humpty Dumpty* by adding original and playful flourishes that pleased the eye, most notably a roller-skating ballet. There were also many one-act burlesques. *The Black Crook, Jr.* competed with *The Black Rook, The Black Rook with a Crook, The Red Crook*, and *The White Crook*. Most minstrel troupes included small-scale spectacles with transformation scenes, and by mocking the original's pretensions to art, added to its fame. In February 1867, just five months after *The Black Crook* opened, George Griffin and George Christy performed one of the earliest burlesques of the new sensation. Like the original, it was essentially visual, relying on scenery and dance, and on blackface conventions for comic effect, and with a topical reference to the conflict between the president and Congress about Reconstruction. George Griffin was the author of countless, ephemeral minstrel afterpieces and sketches, few of which were published.

The Black Crook burlesque, written and arranged by G. W. H. Griffin, and performed by Griffin & Christy's minstrels, for a succession of ninety nights, at the Fifth avenue opera house, 2 and 4 West Twenty-fourth street, N. Y. (New York: Samuel French, n.d. [1870s?]).

THE BLACK CROOK BURLESQUE
written and arranged by G. W. H. GRIFFIN and performed by
GRIFFIN & CHRISTY'S MINSTRELS
for a succession of ninety nights, at the Fifth Avenue Opera House.

CAST OF CHARACTERS
WOLFGANG HEDGEHOG (Black Crook)
LUCIFER
MOLLY BONFANTI
BETSY REGALIA
LUCALICO
DUCKLEGS
RITALANDA SOMECALLUS

MISERY
GOSSIPER

SCENE I.

A wood—den of the BLACK CROOK. At rise of curtain, wild music, allegro.

(Enter BLACK CROOK, Right. He is dressed in black tights, black blouse reaching to the knee, black belt, black shoes with buckles, black wig with hair standing in all directions. If done in blackface, the forehead should be washed clean with a sponge, leaving it perfectly white; rub a little of the black off from under the eyes, so as to give the face a wild expression. If done in white, the forehead must be painted green. He carries a cane to lean upon—it should be an old fashioned one with a cross piece for handle. He is nearly bent double as he enters leaning upon cane. He walks around two or three times, then stops in center of stage. Music stops.)

BLACK CROOK. Now to conjure up the spell

That shall do my bidding well!

More of riches I must have,

More of pleasure still I crave.

But should the spell impotent prove,

While the sprites of earth I move,

Then my power on earth is done!

Then I'll invoke the Evil One!

(Music repeats. BLACK CROOK takes cane and draws circle on stage, then uses cane in flourishes, as if invoking evil spirits. Music ceases. BLACK CROOK walks down left in despair, then putting his hand to his forehead, speaks:)

BLACK CROOK. Alas! I fear I have no power

To aid me in this trying hour.

What shall I do? My brain grows wild.

And through the air on fire I ride!

I'll call to aid the Evil One,

He's just come on from Washington.

He'll aid me in my dire distress,

Then send me on to con-ge-ress!

(Wild chord by the orchestra. LUCIFER appears, either through trap, or from right. Flash of lightning and sound of gong. He is dressed in red tights, with red hood on his head, and two horns. In his right hand he holds a scroll with which he points at BLACK CROOK, who shrinks from him in fear.)

LUCIFER. Well, here I am! all right, you see,

Now what is it you want of me?

BLACK CROOK. *(creeps up to him).*

I want a dozen magic lamps,

To aid through life in picking up stamps.

LUCIFER. Thou hast thy wish, fool, even now,

A Burlesque of Burlesque

The stamp of Cain is on thy brow.
Come, tell me what thou dost desire—
I'm getting cold without a fire.
BLACK CROOK. Well, then, I s'pose I must tell all,
The best of men will sometimes fall.
The people call me the "Black Crook,"
Because I read the "Magic Book."
They've robbed me of my magic spell,
And now myself to you I'll sell.
LUCIFER. Out with it, knave! name the condition
On which you'll join me in perdition.
You are the kind I wish to see,
For such as you resemble me.
BLACK CROOK. Then, first, I want the privilege
To be the first on "Broadway Bridge,"
Then I'd be pointed out to all,
As the young man, graceful and tall,
Who was the first to cross the street
Without wading through mud twelve inches deep.
LUCIFER. The first I grant! Now name the other,
Come, hurry up! I've no time to bother!
BLACK CROOK. Then first I'd know, as you're a resident,
About what time they'll impeach the President?
LUCIFER. Bosh!
BLACK CROOK. Another thing I wish you'd tell,
As you are bound to go to quell
Disturbance in this land of ours,
Who, at the next election, will hold the bowers?
LUCIFER. You shall know all, avaricious fool,
If you'll bring to me each year a soul;
Each year, when the clock strikes the hour of night,
A soul from you shall be my right.
BLACK CROOK. Enough! each year a "sole" I'll steal,
And with it bring you a toe and heel,
And, if your majesty it suits,
Next year I'll bring you a pair of "boots."
LUCIFER. 'Tis well, now I must be a going,
Methinks, I hear some "rooster" crowing;
Now don't forget, on land or sea,
That crooked trunk belongs to me.
(LUCIFER *vanishes Right through flame, of redfire.* BLACK CROOK *hobbles off Left.*)

215

SCENE II.

A garden.

"GRAND ENSEMBLE DE BALLET."

In this scene can be introduced as many Ballet Girls as you please; however, six or eight is the usual number. They are all dressed in burlesque style, excepting one, who is to be a good dancer in order to show a contrast between herself and the others. The ladies who compose the Grand Ballet are dressed in white gauze dresses, reaching nearly to the knee; without hoops. The waists are red or blue satin, abundantly stuffed to form immense bosom, large heavy shoes, white stockings stuffed, to form "big limbs" fashionable lady's wig, with tremendous waterfall, green wreaths upon the head.

At change of scene they come from all the entrances upon their toes, with hands elevated; moving to "slow music." Move around awkwardly for about thirty-two bars, then change to

SECOND MOVEMENT.—WALTZ BY BALLET.

THIRD MOVEMENT.

The leading dancer comes from Right, dressed in beautiful style, and executes LA ARIEL. Moving over to each corner alternately, and tending gracefully back, each Ballet Girl, as she approaches, strikes comical attitude. At end of dance she retires back.

FOURTH MOVEMENT.

LA SYLPHIDE is burlesqued by one of the comedians, after which someone from the gallery throws a large cabbage, with large envelope stuck in it. Dancer takes it, kisses envelope, looks up at gallery, and puts envelope in his bosom.

FIFTH MOVEMENT.—VILLAGE HORNPIPE—Burlesque.

SIXTH MOVEMENT.—LA BAYADEN—Burlesque.

SEVENTH MOVEMENT.—MAY POLE DANCE

MAN brings on May Pole and holds it on stage—it has six strings of different colored muslin hanging from the top. Each Ballet Girl takes one, and they all dance MAY POLE DANCE. They finally get entangled in the muslin, winding up the man's head, &c., and all run off with May pole. Then immediately re-enter and form for the last scene.

PALACE OF DEW DROPS.

With real water streaming from EMERALD FOUNTAINS. Members of the "Corps de Ballet" form on each side of the stage in comical attitudes. Fancy Dancer is placed upon a soap box, Center. Two little demons, dressed in red, rush out from either side with pans of red fire, and form each side of Fancy Dancer, forming Tableaux on their knees, in front of stage. At each corner is placed two Irish women upon boxes, pouring water from green wateringpots into a tub. A string of stuffed legs, boots, strings of onions, little dolls, cabbages, old clothes, bottles, &c. is let down from above by means of a rope held by some one, and kept moving slowly up and down. LUCIFER

and BLACK CROOK *swing off, holding onto ropes suspended from beams above. They swing back and forth. Music appropriate.*
THE END

Reactions to the Controversy

Writing sixty years later, Mabel Osgood Wright remembered fondly the elite circles in which her father Samuel Osgood moved as a prominent Unitarian minister to a wealthy congregation. "Better New York" remained loyal to opera and the theater throughout the Civil War, and the leading opera singers performed at private parties. "It was by way of the theatre, or the drama, as Father preferred to call it," she recalled, "that my longing for color, romance, and the beautiful things in life was first satisfied and unconsciously trained." The opening of *The Black Crook* at Niblo's posed a dilemma. The Osgoods were friends of the actor Edwin Booth, and Mabel's sister's fiancé was the nephew of Niblo's manager William Wheatley. Ministers, however, were overwhelmingly opposed to the scandalous European import.

Mabel Osgood Wright, *My New York* (New York: MacMillan, 1926), 124–26, 131–32.

The fuss was all about a new play that had been put on at Niblo's Garden that autumn, also as to whether [sisters] Bea and Gatha might go to see it, or if Father and Mother were reasonable to forbid them unless they first saw and judged the play for themselves and not by hearsay. The matter seemed very strange to me because our family always went to see plays when they had a chance. . . .

Hence the production of the daring *Black Crook* had more social ramifications than met the casual eye. Wives and mothers of sons frowned upon it, preachers railed against it. Conservative public opinion ran so high that for a time even Father was a bit shaken.

A lull followed the first discussion of our family's attendance, then came the crisis—a box at Niblo's Garden was sent Mother with Mr. Wheatley's compliments, at the same time that I, aged seven, was asked to go to a children's matinee party with Ross and Lawrence Miller. The box was declined for reasons of prudence, yet my sisters went with Brother George. It must have been a fairy spectacle and would have been taken only as such by a beauty-loving child, but as a line had to be drawn somewhere, it was drawn at me. However, I played *Black Crook* with Ross and Larrie Miller, for Mr. Wheatley sent them a miniature theatre with scenic backgrounds and all the characters of the play made of cardboard with colored costumes. As these figures were mounted on firm supports that did not wobble, we could make our own combinations and the amusement was endless. . . .

With the carefully preserved program of this play now before me, plus the mature vision that can look in many directions,—the social revolution that *The Black Crook* caused in New York is clearly cut, though scarcely to be understood by those of a later generation. Yet even today this spectacular bill of the play will rival the announcements of a Hollywood thriller. . . .

New York in the sixties, strong for "the legitimate drama," was very young, as was all America, along lines of artistic staging. It was but a little over a century before that there had been a law against all acting in New England, which was not set aside until the seventeen-nineties, when an English company dared to appear in Boston, to be followed the next year by the opening of the Federal Street Theatre.

There was dramatic blood in my mother's line, for English-born Aunt Susanna Rowson, sister of Great-grandfather Haswell, not only acted in the Chestnut Street Theatre, Philadelphia, and the Federal Street Theatre, but wrote a play that was put on there called *Americans in England*.

Minstrelsy long had held its place and many of our best "legitimates" started life as "nigger minstrels," even Booth and [Joseph] Jefferson having had their turn at it, Jefferson making the Jim Crow song famous. But *The Black Crook* was New York's first absolute "Leg Show";—beautiful, novel and very well presented. But the crux of the whole matter was, judged from afar, that a barrier was broken down, never to he replaced, for it was then discovered that some of the dancers as well as actresses could personally be really fine women, whom several of the "sparks" (ancient for "Johnnies") took honorably to wife. Thus a precedent was set for all time.

It was found that nimble feet and shapely bodies may be topped by intelligence, keen wit and real morality. This had been fully realized in England when the daughter of a Presbyterian minister, Ada[h] Isaacs Menken, the Mazeppa against whom sermons were preached and virtuous eyes veiled, was capable of holding the loyal and aboveboard friendship of men of the intelligence of Dickens, Swinburne and the elder Dumas.

A little space ago I heard two veteran playgoers speaking of *The Black Crook*. In discussing this spectacle in comparison with the dancing of later days, it was only a certain crudeness of setting, that obtained everywhere in the theatre, which came under their criticism, not in any way the moral side. But New York Society then felt that such things belonged only to debased overseas countries, and not to its severe Republican purist New World. It was mistaken. Americans paid out one hundred thousand dollars of their good money in a little less than a year and a half to see the play it had tried to frown down, at the rate of one dollar and a half for the best single seat and ten dollars for a stage box. Yet the coming of these dancers and the following development and change of public opinion in New York was a species of moral and social revolution; for *The Black Crook* and its train broke into many families beside ours, with a crack akin to the storming of the front windows by a mob.

On January 29 1868, George Templeton Strong went with two male companions to see Lydia Thompson's new sensation. More than two months earlier, his wife had seen *The Black Crook*, probably with women friends, and

218

Strong, as a worldly connoisseur of music and the theatre, had no moral objections to the show. The style of acting was simply inane.

The Diary of George Templeton Strong, 4 vols., ed. Allan Nevins and Milton Halsey Thomas (New York: Macmillan, 1952), 4:183.

I went through the weather to see *The White Fawn* at Niblo's—a grand new show piece, manifestly got up at very great cost, and said to surpass *The Black Crook* itself, which drew crowded houses for a year and a half. Ballet, spectacle, machinery, and pink legs are its chief constituents. The dialogue is senseless, the plot undiscoverable, and the music commonplace—plagiarism from the *Grande Duchesse* excepted. But the dresses, properties, decorations, and the like, are novel and lavish, except the costumes of the ballet girls, are the reverse of the lavish in quantity, though various and pretty in design and color. A grand procession of fishes, oysters and lobsters is very grotesque and carefully equipped. The final tableau or "transformation scene" is particularly elaborate and pretty. A scene shifter would call it gorgeous. In a meretricious sort of way it is quite artistic, with its slowly shifting masses of color, changing lights, and groups of good-looking young women (with very little on) nestling or hanging about everywhere. But the whole production depends for its success mainly on the well-formed lower extremities of female humanity. It is doubtless the most showy, and the least draped, specimen of what may be called the *Feminine-Femoral* School of Dramatic Art ever produced in New York. House packed—men mostly—and enthusiastic.

Curious "progress" has the drama made since the days of old Samuel Johnson, E. Burke, J. Reynolds, and Davy Garrick!

The British Blondes arrived at a time when traditional womanliness was attacked. With the lower classes frequenting German beer-halls and admiring skimpy costumes, and the new-wealthy fawning over French daring and English legs, the old moral standards seemed lost.

Many believed that the age of "shoddy"—wartime profiteering and corruption in business—had lowered the moral tone. The display of women's bodies as "Living Statues" clad in flesh-colored body-suits depicting "Venus Rising from the Sea" and other "classical" poses in Bowery concert saloons scandalized the New York press in the winter of 1847–48. In 1850, George Foster had reported in salacious detail, the tableaux "exhibitions" of the English Dr. Collyer with "lank-sided, flabby-breasted" "model artists" in baggy "fleshings."[9] The appearance in 1861 of the American Adah Issacs Menken in *Mazeppa*, strapped to a galloping horse and wearing the short tunic of a Tartar warrior (and little else), caused a sensation. When cheap concert saloons began to proliferate on the outer fringes of the Broadway theater district, the New York Sabbath Committee led the assault against "Continental" customs. In its pamphlet of 1866 on *Sunday Theatres, 'Sacred Concerts,' and Beer Gar-*

Inexpensive cartes de visite, like this 1866 photograph of the young ballet dancer Betty Rigl in her "Demon Dance" costume from *The Black Crook*, popularized an enticingly scandalous image of the burlesque actress. Harvard Theatre Collection.

dens, the Sabbath Committee condemned "pretty waiter-girls" in short skirts who danced lasciviously and welcomed male customers with more than drink.

Mark Twain saw *The Black Crook* in February 1867. Now the scantily dressed were in the heart of the fashionable Broadway theater district, and managers were recruiting even "padded, painted, slab-sided, lantern-jawed old hags" to meet public demand.

Reactions to the Controversy

Mark Twain's Travels with Mr. Brown, being heretofore uncollected sketches written by Mark Twain for the San Francisco Alta California in 1866 & 1867, describing the adventures of the author and his irrepressible companion in Nicaragua, Hannibal, New York, and other spots on their way to Europe, ed. Franklin Walker and G. Ezra Dane (New York: Knopf, 1940), 84–87 [originally published in the *San Francisco Alta California*, March 28, 1867].

When I was here in '53, a model artist show had an ephemeral existence in Chatham street, and then everybody growled about it, and the police broke it up. . . . But now, things are changed. The model artists play nightly to admiring multitudes at famous Niblo's Garden . . . [and] they call that sort of thing a "Grand Spectacular Drama," and everybody goes. It is all in a name. And it is about as spectacular as anything I ever saw without sinking right into the earth with outraged modesty. It is the wickedest show you can think of. You see there is small harm in exhibiting a pack of painted old harlots, swathed in gauze, like the original model artistes, for no man careth a cent for them but to laugh and jeer at them. Nakedness itself, in such a case, would be nothing worse than disgusting. But I warn you that when they put beautiful clipper-built girls on stage in this new fashion, with only just barely enough clothes on to be tantalizing, it is a shrewd invention of the devil. It lays a heavier siege to public morals than all the legitimate model artist shows you can bring into action.

The name of this new exhibition that so touches my missionary sensibilities is the "Black Crook." The scenic effects—the waterfalls, cascades, fountains, oceans, fairies, devils, hells, heavens, angels—are gorgeous beyond anything ever witnessed in America, perhaps, and these things attract the women and the girls. Then the endless ballets and splendid tableaux, with seventy beauties arrayed in dazzling half-costumes; and displaying all possible compromises between nakedness and decency, capture the men and boys—and so Niblo's has taken in twenty-four hundred dollars a night, (seven nights and a matinee a week,) for five months, and sometimes twenty-seven hundred dollars. It is claimed that a multitude equal to the entire population of the State of California, Chinamen included, have visited this play. The great *Herald* newspaper pitched into it, and a sensation parson preached a sermon against it; this was sufficient to advertise it all over the continent, and so the proprietor's fortune was made.

The scenery and the legs are everything; the actors who do the talking are the wretchedest sticks on the boards. But the fairy scenes—they fascinate the boys! Beautiful bare-legged girls hanging in flower-baskets; others stretched in groups on great sea shells; others clustered around fluted columns; others in all possible attitudes; girls—nothing but a wilderness of girls—stacked up, pile on pile, away aloft to the dome of the theatre, diminishing in size and clothing, till the last row, mere children, dangle high up from invisible ropes, arrayed only in a camisa [tunic]. The whole tableau resplendent with columns, scrolls, and a vast ornamental work, wrought in gold, silver and brilliant colors—all lit up with gorgeous theatrical fires, and witnessed through a great gauzy curtain that counterfeits a soft silver mist! It is the wonders of the Arabian Nights realized.

Those girls in ballet, dressed with a meagreness that would make a parasol blush. And they prance around and expose themselves in a way that is scandalous to me. Moreover, they come trooping on the stage in platoons and battalions, in the most princely attire I grant you, but always with more tights in view than anything else. They change their clothes every fifteen minutes for four hours, and their dresses become more beautiful and rascally all the time. . . .

Edwin Booth and the legitimate drama still draw immense houses, but the signs of the times convince me that he will have to make a little change by-and-by and peel some women. Nothing else can chain the popular taste, the way things are going now.

As a keen amateur actor, a playwright, and a close friend of acting professionals, Charles Dickens enjoyed all kinds of popular entertainments, from the circus to music-hall acts in London's working-class East End. He was familiar with Adah Menken's *Mazeppa* in London. On his second trip to the United States, in 1867–68, the few leisure moments that he had between giving public readings from his works he spent in visits to the theater. Even so, Dickens found his unusually wide experience did not prepare him for the display of female flesh. In letters to friends in England, he reported on the latest American fashion.

The Letters of Charles Dickens, vol. 11, *1865–1867*, ed. Graham Storey et al. (Oxford: Clarendon Press, 1999), 511–12. *The Letters of Charles Dickens*, vol. 12, *1868–1870*, ed. Graham Storey et al. (Oxford: Clarendon Press, 2002), 81.

To John Forster   New York, 15 December 1867

 . . . Niblo's great attraction, the *Black Crook*, has now been played every night for 16 months (!), and is the most preposterous peg to hang ballets on that was ever seen. The people who act in it have not the slightest idea of what it is about, and never had; but; after taxing my intellectual powers to the utmost, I fancy that I have discovered Black Crook to be a malignant hunchback leagued with the Powers of Darkness to separate two lovers; and that the Powers of Lightness coming (in no skirts whatever) to the rescue, he is defeated. I am quite serious in saying that I do not suppose there are two pages of *All The Year Round* in the whole piece (which acts all night); the whole of the rest of it being ballets of all sorts, perfectly unaccountable processions, and the Donkey out of last year's Covent Garden pantomime! At the other theatres, comic operas, melodramas, and domestic dramas prevail all over the city, and my stories play no inconsiderable part in them.

To W. C. Macready   Springfield, Mass. Saturday Twenty-First March

 . . . To pass from Boston personal, to New York Theatrical, I will mention here that one of the Proprietors of my New York hotel is one of the Proprietors of Niblo's and the most active. Consequently, I have seen *The Black Crook* and *The White Faun,* in majesty from an armchair in the first entrance P.S. [prompt side] more than once. Of these astonishing dramas, I beg to report (seriously) that I have found no human creature "behind," who has the slightest idea what they are about ('pon my honor, my Dearest Macready!) and that, having some amiable small talk with a neat little Spanish woman who is the premiere danseuse, I asked her, in joke, to let me measure her skirt with my dress glove. Holding the glove by the tip of the forefinger, I found the skirt to be just three gloves long—and its length was much in excess of the skirts of 200 other ladies whom the carpenters were, at that moment, getting into their places for a transformation scene—on revolving columns—on wire and travellers—on iron cradles —up in the flies—down in the cellars—on every impossible description of float that Wilmot gone distracted could imagine.

In *An Old-Fashioned Girl,* one of the series of novels that appeared soon after *Little Women,* Louisa May Alcott told of Polly Martin's shocked reaction to unfeminine women performing in the musical theater. Coming from the country, Polly felt like "a stranger in a strange land" in the city, and out of step with wealthy, teenage girls who thought only of the latest Grecian Bend dresses and reading sensational novels. Later, in *Work: A Story of Experience* (1873), Alcott showed Christie, cast as a song-and-dance Queen of the Amazons, disillusioned with the theater's "enchanted world": "Fairies, in rubberboots and woollen head-gear, disported themselves on flowery barks of canvas, or were suspended aloft with hooks in their backs. . . Demons, guiltless of hoof or horn, clutched their victims with the inevitable 'Ha! ha!' and vanished darkly, eating pea-nuts."[10]

Alcott may have seen one of the latest sensation shows when she lived in Boston and was editing *Merry's Museum*—Thompson burlesques played at five of the seven Boston theaters in the winter season of 1868–69, when she began the novel. For two decades she had acted in private theatricals and had written a dozen thrillers under a pseudonym, so she had no objections to professional drama. But like "old-fashioned" Polly, Alcott found the "new world" of two dozen female jockeys flirting with the audience too immodest and too "French."

Louisa May Alcott, *An Old-Fashioned Girl* (London: Sampson Low, Son, and Marston, 1870), 12–15.

[I]n came Fanny with the joyful news that Clara Bird had invited them both to go to the theatre with her that very evening, and would call for them at seven o'clock. Polly was so excited by this sudden plunge into the dissipations of city life, that she flew about like a distracted butterfly, and hardly knew what happened, till she found herself seated before the great green curtain in the brilliant theatre. Old Mr. Bird sat on one side, Fanny on the other, and both let her alone, for which she was very grateful, as her whole attention was so absorbed in the scene around her, that she couldn't talk.

Polly had never been much to the theatre, and the few plays she had seen were the good old fairy tales, dramatized to suit young beholders, lively, bright, and full of the harmless nonsense which brings the laugh without the blush. That night she saw one of the new spectacles which have lately become the rage, and run for hundreds of nights, dazzling, exciting, and demoralizing the spectator by every allurement French ingenuity can invent, and American prodigality execute. Never mind what its name was, it was very gorgeous, very vulgar, and very fashionable; so, of course, it was much admired, and every one went to see it. At first Polly thought she had got into fairy-land, and saw only the sparkling creatures who danced and sung in a world of light and beauty; but presently she began to listen to the songs and conversation, and then the illusion vanished; for the lovely phantoms sang negro melodies, talked slang, and were a disgrace to the good old-fashioned elves whom she knew and loved so well.

Our little girl was too innocent to understand half the jokes, and often wondered what people were laughing at; but as the first enchantment subsided, Polly began to feel uncomfortable, to be sure her mother wouldn't like to have her there, and to wish she hadn't come. Somehow, things seemed to get worse and worse as the play went on; for one small spectator was being rapidly enlightened by the gossip going on all about her, as well as by her own quick eyes and girlish instincts. When four-and-twenty girls, dressed as jockeys, came prancing onto the stage, cracking their whips, stamping the heels of their top-boots, and winking at the audience, Polly did not think it at all funny, but looked disgusted, and was glad when they were gone; but when another set appeared in a costume consisting of gauze wings, and a bit of gold fringe around the waist, poor unfashionable Polly didn't know what to do; for she felt both frightened and indignant, and sat with her eyes on her play-bill, and her cheeks getting hotter and hotter every minute.

"What are you blushing so for?" asked Fanny as the painted sylphs vanished.

"I'm so ashamed of those girls," whispered Polly, taking a long breath of relief.

"You little goose, it's just the way it was done in Paris, and the dancing is splendid. It seems queer at first, but you'll get used to it, as I did."

"I'll never come again," said Polly, decidedly; for her innocent nature rebelled against the spectacle, which, as yet, gave her more pain than pleasure. She did not know how easy it was to "get used to it," as Fanny did; and it was well for her that the temptation was not often offered. She could not explain the feeling, but she was glad when the play was done and they were safe at home, where kind Grandma was waiting to see them comfortably into bed.

"Did you have a good time, dear?" she asked, looking at Polly's feverish cheeks and excited eyes.

"I don't wish to be rude, but I didn't," answered Polly. "Some of it was splendid; but a good deal of it made me want to go under the seat. People seemed to like it, but *I* don't think it was proper."

As Polly freed her mind, and emphasized her opinion with a decided rap of the boot she had just taken off, Fanny laughed, and said, while she pirouetted about the room like Mademoiselle Therese, "Polly was shocked, Grandma. Her eyes were as big as saucers, her face as red as my sash, and once I thought she was going to cry. Some of it *was* rather queer; but of course it was proper or all our set wouldn't go. I heard Mrs. Smythe Perkins say, 'It was charming, so like dear Paris;' and she has lived abroad, so of course she knows what is what."

"I don't care if she has. I know it *wasn't* proper for little girls to see, or I shouldn't have been so ashamed!" cried sturdy Polly, perplexed, but not convinced, even by Mrs. Smythe Perkins.

"I think you are right, my dear; but you have lived in the country, and haven't yet learned that modesty has gone out of fashion." And with a good-night kiss, Grandma left Polly to dream dreadfully of dancing in jockey costume on a great stage, while Tom played a big drum in the orchestra, and the audience all wore the faces of her father and mother, looking sorrowfully at her, with eyes like saucers, and faces as red as Fanny's sash.

Olive Logan was the most vocal critic of the "Leg Business." Logan came from a well-known theatrical family, had been successful as both playwright and actress, but had retired from the stage in 1867. In May 1869, in a speech to the Equal Rights Association convention, she criticized the theater for its discrimination against women, and in a letter to the *New York Times* the same month, specified the unseemly physical requirements that managers made of "actresses." *The Black Crook* had at least some genuine ballerinas, but the "English burlesque blondes" merely exhibited their "nude" bodies. Logan defined nude by Samuel Johnson's definition, as "ill-supplied with garments." Her complaint was on economic as well as moral grounds: the unadorned display of women's bodies was not only degrading but restricted their freedom in the marketplace. Unfortunately, when the pressing issues of the Reconstruction suffrage amendments were being discussed, Logan's speech had little support from feminists.

Olive Logan, *Apropos of Women and Theatres. With a Paper or Two on Parisian Topics* (New York: Carleton, 1869), 128–30, 132–36, 137,142–43, 145–46, 152–53.

How, then, does it happen that in attacking these yellow-haired nudities, I am compelled to say that they disgrace the dramatic profession?

In this wise: These creatures occupy the temples of the drama; they perform in conjunction with actors and actresses, on the same stage, before the same audience, in the same hour. They are made legitimate members of our theatrical companies, and take part in those nondescript performances which are called burlesques, spectacles, what you will. They carry off the chief honors of the hour; their names occupy the chief places on the bills; and . . . they win the chief prizes in the theatrical world.

A woman who has not ability enough to rank as a passable "walking lady" in a good theatre, on a salary of twenty-five dollars a week, can strip herself almost naked, and be thus qualified to go upon the stage of two-thirds of our theatres at a salary of one hundred dollars and upwards.

Clothed in the dress of an honest woman, she is worth nothing to a manager. Stripped as naked as she dare—and it seems there is little left when so much is done— she becomes a prize to her manager, who knows that crowds will rush to see her, and pays her a salary accordingly. . . .

There are certain accomplishments which render the Nude Woman "more valuable to managers in the degree that she possesses them." I will tell you what these accomplishments are, and you shall judge how far they go toward making her, in any sense, an actress.

They are: 1. The ability to sing. 2. The ability to jig. 3. The ability to play on certain musical instruments. . . .

You, no doubt, will at once remark that these accomplishments have hitherto been peculiar to that branch of the show business occupied by the negro minstrel. But in the hands of the negro minstrel, these accomplishments amuse us without disgusting us. They are not wedded to bare legs, nor suggestive feminine leers and winks; nor is there a respectable minstrel band in the United States to-day which would tolerate in its members the *double entendres* which fly about the stages of some of the largest temples of the drama in this city. The minstrels would not dare utter them. Their halls would be vacated, and their business ruined. It requires that a half-naked woman should utter these ribaldous inuendoes, before our fastidious public will receive them unrebukingly.

To what branch of the show business, then, do these creatures belong?

I answer, to that branch which is known by the names of variety-show, concert-saloon, music-hall, and various other titles, which mean nothing to you unless you already know they mean.

No one in the show business needs to be told what a variety-show is. It is certainly not a theatre.

Until the reign of the nude woman set in, variety-halls were the resort of only the lowest and vilest, and women were not seen in the audience.

The nude woman was sometimes seen upon the stage, but she was only one of a large variety of attractions,—she was a tid-bit, hugely relished by the low and vile who went to see her; but only permitted to exhibit herself economically, for fear of cloying the public appetite.

Delicate caution! but how useless, her later career in our theatres has shown.

There, she is exhibited ceaselessly for three hours, in every variety which an indecent imagination can devise.

When the *Black Crook* first presented its nude woman to the gaze of a crowded auditory, she was met with a gasp of astonishment at the effrontery which dared show so much. Men actually grew pale at the boldness of the thing; a death-like silence fell over the house, broken only by a band of *claqueurs* around the outer aisles;

226

but it passed; and, in view of the fact that these women were French ballet-dancers after all, they were tolerated.

By slow and almost imperceptible degrees, this shame has grown, until to-day the indecency of that exhibition is far surpassed. Those women were ballet-dancers from France and Italy, and they represented in their nudity imps and demons. In silence they whirled about the stage; in silence trooped off. Some faint odor of ideality and poetry rested over them.

The nude woman of to-day represents nothing but herself. She runs upon the stage giggling; trots down to the foot-lights, winks at the audience, rattles off from her tongue some stupid attempts at wit, some twaddling allusions to Sorosis, or General Grant, or other subject prominent in the public eye, and is always and peculiarly herself,—the woman, that is, whose name is on the bills in large letters, and who considers herself an object of admiration to the spectators.

The sort of ballet-dancer who figured in the *Black Crook* is paralleled on the stage of every theatre in this city, except one, at this time.

She no longer excites attention.

To create a proper and profitable sensation in the breast of man, she no longer suffices. Something bolder must be devised,—something that shall utterly eclipse and outstrip her.

Hence, the nude woman of to-day,—who outstrips her in the broadest sense. And, as if it were not enough that she should be allowed to go unhissed and unrotten-egged, she must be baptized with the honors of a profession for which Shakespeare wrote!

Managers recognize her as an actress, and pay her sums ranging from fifty to a thousand dollars a week, according to her value in their eyes. Actresses, who love virtue better than money, are driven into the streets by her; and it becomes a grave and solemn question with hundreds of honorable women what they shall do to earn a livelihood.

I say that it is nothing less than an insult to the members of the dramatic profession, that these nude women should be classed among actresses and hold possession of the majority of our theatres. Their place is in the concert-saloons or the circus tents. Theatres are for artists. . . .

Women in society conceal all the lower part of their bodies with drapery,—and for good and sufficient reasons, which, no man, who has a wife or mother, should stop to question. . . .

I take up next an anonymous letter, dated at Boston, and signed, "A Sister Member of the Profession."

The writer says she is a respectable actress, and professes to be ignorant that gross evils prevail in the theatrical world.

She refers to my letter in the New York *Times*, and asks at what theatre such questions were ever put to an applicant for employment.

In my letter to the *Times*, I said,—

"I referred the other night to decent young women who are not celebrities,—merely honest, modest girls, whose parents have left them the not very desirable heritage of the stage, and who find it difficult to obtain any other employment, being uneducated for any other. When these girls go into a theatre to apply for a situation now, they find that the requirements of managers are expressed in the following questions,—

"1. Is your hair dyed yellow?

"2. Are your legs, arms, and bosom symmetrically formed, and are you willing to expose them?

"3. Can you sing brassy songs, and dance the can-can, and wink at men, and give utterance to disgusting half-words, which mean whole actions?

"4. Are you acquainted with any rich men who will throw you flowers, and send you presents, and keep afloat dubious rumors concerning your chastity?

"5. Are you willing to appear to-night and every night, amid the glare of gas-lights, and before the gaze of thousands of men, in this pair of satin breeches, ten inches long, without a vestige of drapery upon your person?

"If you can answer these questions affirmatively, we will give you a situation; if not, there's the door." . . .

It is not necessary, I suppose, to give with the accuracy of a criminal trial report the exact questions which pass between managers and actresses, who seek for employment. Their purport is unmistakable. . . .

I respect the theatre in its purity. I respect the actor who is an artist,—even the harmless clown of the pantomime, who makes us laugh without offending decency. That I love so many good and lovely women who are actresses, is my chief reason for deploring the reign of a class of women who are neither good nor lovely,—but coarse, indecent, painted, padded, and dyed.

If it were possible to treat the Nude Woman Question, and leave the nude woman herself out of it, I should be glad to do so. I am the last to wish to give pain to any person; but, in the path of clear duty, there is no choice. When it becomes a question between suffering, struggling virtue, and vice which rolls in luxury, and gathers unto itself wealth by the sheer practice of its wickedness, no woman who loves honor in her sex can hesitate as to the course to be taken. . . .

I see no other way to effect a cure of this nude woman evil but to make it odious. To that end, I shall do what in me lies. This article is but a beginning. I shall not cease to combat the encroachments of the nude woman upon the domain which should be occupied by true artists, and by virtuous men and women.

Firm in the belief that this indecent army *can* be routed, I call on all honorable souls, both in and out of the profession, to stand by my side and strike hard blows. We shall get hard blows in return, no doubt; but poor indeed must be the panoply of that warrior who can not hold his own against the cohorts of the nude woman. Whatever falls on my head in consequence of my words, I promise to give thrust for thrust. I do not fear the issue.

"Thrice is he armed that hath his quarrel JUST."

The British Blondes were not well liked by newspaper critics, apart from the *Clipper*. They were seen to be defying convention openly and outrageously. Their use of artifice, especially dyed hair, and notoriously, padding to display a more rounded profile of legs, hips and bust, was questioned at a time when the respectable still frowned on cosmetics. They also did not behave in a demure and ladylike manner. At a time when men played "nigger wenches" on stage, the Blondes performed minstrel clog dances and played trumpet and banjo. They jiggled and wiggled. They were loud, brash, and brazen. The most disturbing aspect was the cross-dressing that challenged notions of gender. Lydia Thompson favored classical or exotic dress, but her version of a man's Roman toga or Oriental robe revealed her bare legs and the corset exaggerated her female curves. Her "male" body language—smoking, staring boldly, and crossing her legs—rebuked modest femininity and notions of vulnerability.

William Dean Howells, beginning his career as a novelist and playwright and as drama critic for the prestigious *Atlantic Monthly*, was shocked by the "physical unreserve" of the new English burlesque actresses that he saw in Boston. Thompson, he wrote, "had a raucous voice, an insolent twist of the mouth, and a terrible trick of defying her enemies by standing erect, chin up, hand on hip, and right foot advanced, patting the floor."

William Dean Howells, "The New Taste in Theatricals," *Atlantic Monthly* 16 (May 1869): 640–44.

As for the burlesques themselves, they were nothing, the performers personally everything. . . . [T]here was commonly a flimsy ravelling of parodied myth, that held together the different dances and songs, though sometimes it was a novel or an opera burlesqued; but there was always a song and always a dance for each lady, song and dance being equally slangy, and depending for their effect mainly, upon the natural or simulated charms of the performer.

It was also an indispensable condition of the burlesque's success, that the characters should be reversed in their representation,—that the men's *rôles* should be played by women, and that at least one female part should be done by a man. It must be owned that the fun all came from this character, the ladies being too much occupied with the more serious business of bewitching us with their pretty figures to be very amusing; whereas this wholesome man and brother, with his blond wig, his *panier* [basket], his dainty feminine simperings and languishings, his falsetto tones, and his general air of extreme fashion, was always exceedingly droll. He was the saving grace of these stupid plays. . . . But otherwise, the burlesques were as little cheerful as profitable. The playwrights who had adapted them to the American stage —for they are all of English authorship—had been good enough to throw in some political allusions which were supposed to be effective with us, but which it was sad to see received with apathy. . . .

The burlesque chiefly betrayed its descent from the spectacular ballet in its undressing; but that ballet, while it demanded personal exposure, had something very observable in its scenic splendors, and all that marching and processioning in it was rather pretty; while in the burlesque there seemed nothing of innocent intent. No matter what the plot, it led always to a final great scene of breakdown,—which was doubtless most impressive in that particular burlesque where this scene represented the infernal world, and the ladies gave the dances of the country with a happy conception of the deportment of lost souls. There, after some vague and inconsequent dialogue, the wit springing from a perennial source of humor (not to specify the violation of the seventh commandment), the dancing commenced, each performer beginning with the Walk-round of the negro minstrels, rendering its grotesqueness with a wonderful frankness of movement, and then plunging into the mysteries of her dance with a kind of infuriate grace and a fierce delight very curious to look upon. It was perfect of its kind, that dancing, but some things one witnesses at the theatre nowadays had better be treated as a kind of confidence. . . . I dare not say how sketchily these ladies were dressed, or indeed, more than that they were dressed to resemble circus-riders of the other sex, but as to their own deceived nobody,—possibly did not intend deceit. . . .

Yet it was to be noted with regret that our innocence, our respectability, had no restraining influence upon the performance; and the fatuity of the hope cherished by some courageous people, that the presence of virtuous persons would reform the stage, was but too painfully evident. The doubt whether they were not nearer right who have denounced the theatre as essentially and incorrigibly bad would force itself upon the mind, though there was a little comfort in the thought that if virtue had been actually allowed to frown upon these burlesques, the burlesques might have been abashed into propriety. . . .

Commonly, however, the members of these burlesque troupes, though they were not like men, were in most things as unlike women, and seemed creatures of a kind of alien sex, parodying both. It was certainly a shocking thing to look at them with their horrible prettiness, their archness in which was no charm, their grace which put to shame. . . .

The new taste, as has been said before, is not our taste. It came to us like any other mode from abroad, but, unlike the fashions in dress, received no modification or impression from our life; so that, though curiosity led thousands, not in Boston alone, but in all our great cities, to look at these lewd travesties, it could not be said that we naturalized among us a form of entertainment involving fable that we could not generally understand, satire that we cared nothing about, lascivious dancing, singing that expressed only a depraved cockneyism. . . .

Reactions to the Controversy

But after we have praised these modern plays to their full desert, we must again recur to their foreign character. They have no relation to our life as a people; we can only appreciate them through our knowledge of English life derived from novel reading. Their interest all depends upon the conditions of English society; their characters are English; their scenes are English. . . .

It is very probable that we shall not see the burlesques again next winter, and that what has been here called the new taste in theatricals will then be an old-fashioned folly, generally ignored because it is old-fashioned, if not because it is folly. This belief is grounded, not so much upon faith in the power of the stage to reform itself, or the existence of a principle in the theatre-going public calculated to rebuke the stage's wantonness, as upon the fact that matters have already reached a point beyond which they cannot go. In the direction of burlesque, no novelty now remains which is not forbidden by statute.

Of all the theater critics, Richard Grant White was the most charitable to the "burlesque" actresses (and reputed to have had an affair with the Blondes star, Pauline Markham). In a telling allusion, he compared the cross-dressed women with a "set of chess-men which a mischievous boy had taken apart and screwed together with the black pieces on the white standards, and the white on the black, the bodies and heads of the pieces being misplaced in a like manner." Their dancing might be "vulgar and gross," but their articulation of language was excellent. If the extravaganzas were trivial, the spirit of the age that rejected expressions of emotion was to blame.

Richard Grant White, "The Age of Burlesque," *Galaxy* 8 (August 1869): 256–60, 266.

It means something, this outbreak of burlesque acting all over the world. No mere accident has made so monstrous a kind of entertainment equally acceptable to three publics so different as those of Paris, London, and New York. And by monstrous I do not mean wicked, disgusting, or hateful, but monstrously incongruous and unnatural. The peculiar trait of burlesque is its defiance both of the natural and the conventional. Rather, it forces the conventional and the natural together just at the points where they are most remote, and the result is absurdity, monstrosity. Its system is a defiance of system. It is out of *all* keeping. Its ideal figure, if it has an ideal, might be Julius Caesar in top boots and spectacles, carrying a baggy green cotton umbrella. Now the great dictator might have been the better for the services of all these articles. His moral majesty did not lift him above the every-day needs of men; but in our idea he is at least removed from them. The anachronism would not be all of the absurdity. We cannot think of him as blowing his nose on a red bandanna handkerchief more than we could so think of Jupiter. But burlesque casts down all the gods from their pedestals. . . . This trait of burlesque reached its fullest development in the mingling of the ancient and the modern, the heroic and the common-place, in "La Belle Helène," and in "The Forty Thieves," in which the forty robbers were represented by forty young

231

women, who, as a part of their daily drill, at the command of their captain, pulled out forty matches and lit forty cigarettes; in which a donkey danced a break-down, and Morgiana, pouring the poison into the jars in which the forty were concealed, exclaimed, "They do die beautiful."

Now, in such performances as this, there is plainly no dramatic interest. They have not even the coherence of farce, which is a dramatic caricature of nature. But a caricature must have a certain conformity to nature, or it cannot be caricature, which exaggerates or over-charges the characteristics of nature, whence it receives its name. In burlesque there is caricature; but it is without the relations of parts to a whole, without design, without coherence. It would seem as if a composition or performance of which these remarks are true could not be recognized in any sense as a work of art, as if in such work there could never be any scope for genius. . . . The motive of burlesque is always satire. If this did not pervade it there would not be life enough in it to keep it sweet and make it hold together. The pleasure, the instruction, and the comfort that we all derive from seeing the vices and the follies of others held up to ridicule are so great that we do not scrutinize too closely the manner in which they are conveyed. And in these days ridicule is, more than ever before, the sieve through which all men and things are sifted. There is a great deal of earnest thinking done; but even earnestness must not be too obtrusive, if it would escape ridicule, caricature, burlesque. Caricature has become a social and political power in all civilized communities. There is a disposition to criticise and to derogate from all high pretensions, not only pretensions to place, and power, and social distinction, but to virtue, to knowledge, to sentiment, and even to genuine feeling. At such pretensions we are inclined to scoff. . . .

Men used even to profess sentiment, and it was thought a fine thing to give way to emotion. Now we repress, as much as we are able, all such manifestations in ourselves, and we look with dislike, and even with suspicion, on them in others. We seem not to be equal to a grand scene; our nervous system will not bear the strain; we cower under a tempest of feeling; and seek refuge in scorn and ridicule. When we are threatened with a flood of feeling we take the tone and the language of the antediluvian, and declare that there is not going to be much of a shower. . . .

But the tragic, the emotional, even the tender, we can hardly bear to look upon. Our grandmothers vaunted their sensibility, and even our grandfathers prided themselves on their sentiment. But the very words sensibility and sentiment convey to us some sense of the ridiculous. . . .

This being the temper of the time, we cannot endure tragedy, or even the ideal presentation of life in high comedy, when tragedy and comedy assume a concrete form on the stage. . . . I do not believe that our repression of the manifestation of feeling has really deadened our sensibilities; for at no period of the world's history was there more active sympathy with real suffering, or so candid an appreciation of the claims of individual prejudice to consideration, or of the genuineness of a sentimental grievance. . . .

Reactions to the Controversy

Observation of men around us seems to support us in our assumption that sensitiveness of soul is in inverse proportion to manifestation of feeling. Certainly it is so in the relations of men to dramatic art. The same acting of grand tragedy or of sentimental comedy, which, in the last generation, would have pleased what was called genteel society, is now acceptable only to the coarsest and most sluggish natures—those who are immovable except by hard blows oft repeated. . . .

Of such a condition of the public mind in regard to the drama and dramatic part of life, burlesque is the legitimate and inevitable outcome. Join to this the craving for the enjoyment of material splendor and sensuous beauty, and the result is "The Black Crook," "La Grande Duchesse de Gerolstein," "La Belle Helène," "The Forty Thieves," and "Sinbad the Sailor."

The next step to the repression of manifestations of real feeling, is the caricature of such manifestations in art. And then, as mere caricature in acting is insufficient in its interest, the element of beauty is added, and in a monstrous form—that of women playing men's parts, and dressed for incongruity's sake, as well as for a display of their beauty, in the costumes of men centuries ago; while many of the personages are in the dress of the present day, and in some cases both costumes are mingled. Extravagance in all these respects could not go farther than it has gone in some of the burlesques recently produced in Europe and in this country. . . .

But going there [to Niblo's for *The Forty Thieves*] at a morning's performance, in search of a needed laugh, which I confess I do not get, I was surprised, not only with the merit of the lady herself, and of some of her companions, but with the character of the audience. The latter I expected to find made up of coarse and flashy people; but on the contrary, it was notable in the main, for simple and almost homely respectability. Comfortable, middle-aged women from the suburbs, and from the remoter country, their daughters, groups of children, a few professional men, bearing their quality in their faces, some sober, farmer-looking folk, a clergyman or two, apparently, the usual proportion of nondescripts, among whom were not very many young men, composed an audience less respectable than I had seen in Fourteenth street, but at least respectable. And the Lydia Thompson, in whom I had expected to find a coarse, Anglo-Saxon exaggeration of Mlle. Tostée, I found one of the most charming comic actresses it has been my good fortune to see. She played burlesque with a daintiness with which few actresses of note are able to flavor their acting, even in high comedy. She was doing hard work, no doubt, but her heart must have been in it, for she was the enbodiment of mirth, and moved others to hilarity by being moved herself. It was as if Venus, in her quality of the goddess of laughter, had come upon the stage. And if there was a likeness to Venus in the costume, as well as in manner, I must confess that I saw in it no chance of harm to myself or to any of my fellow spectators, old or young, male or female. Indeed, it seems rather to be desired that the points of a fine woman should be better known, and more thought of among us than they have been. They seem to me quite as important, and I think they are quite as interesting as those of a fine horse; and I should be sorry to believe that they are more harmful, either to taste or to morals.

Some of the outcry that we hear against the costume of which the burlesque actresses wear, in the way of their profession, has in it such a tone of personal injury,
that it might come from mammas and papas who, having a very poor article of young
woman lying heavy on their hands, are indignant that there should be so good and so
easy an opportunity of trying it by a very high standard. As to any impropriety in this
costume, in its place, that is, seriously speaking, a matter of individual opinion; but if
there is any, it is far less, both in degree and in kind, than that of the ordinary ballet
dancer, with her flying petticoat, alternately concealing and revealing the attractions of
her figure, which we have looked at ever since we were children, even in this dear old
Niblo's Garden, without a thought of shamefacedness, and very much less than that
of the tilting hoops, which lent such peculiar attractions to the "German" in fashionable society only two years ago. . . .

The drama, as an intellectual diversion of the mind from one channel of thought
into another, has passed away, I think, forever. The public, even the cultivated public,
in all countries, prefers that kind of theatrical entertainment at which it is not required
to think. It asks, not diversion, a *turning* of the mind from one object to another, but the
pleasure of the senses while the mind lies dormant. It seeks only to be amused. Of
this mood, burlesque or "spectacular extravaganza" is the natural and inevitable product. We, of Anglo-Saxon race at least, have probably seen the last of our legitimate
drama.

The Popular-Price Circuit

By the turn of the century the cheap variety halls had abandoned any pretence
at satire. In a Brooklyn theater the journalist Arthur Ruhl found a "rough-
house" musical comedy, a poor man's Harrigan and Hart, knock-about ethnic
caricature which featured the "Beef Trust Beauties," everyone weighing about
two hundred pounds. It was traditional: the Beauties' boxing ballad, "Throw
Him Down McClusky," had been made famous by Maggie Cline, the Irish
star, in the 1880s. The old-fashioned shows in Brooklyn or the Bowery were
quite unlike the genuinely creative travesties of Weber and Fields on Broadway, but, by holding amateur talent contests, had retained a direct personal
link between the regular stock company and the public, a link which had
been lost in the "cold business houses up-town."

Arthur Ruhl, *Second Nights: People and Ideas of the Theatre To-Day* (New York:
Scribner's, 1914).

It was a sign on a Ninth Avenue ash can,

    BILLY WATSON AND HIS BEEF TRUST BEAUTIES

which lured me to the outskirts of farthest Brooklyn for a somewhat closer study of
burlesque. It was one of those raining winter days when the sponge-like sky, not
content to squeeze itself over the town, seems to sag into the very streets and the

world is so muffled and opaque that one is almost surprised to find its ordinary wheels still turning.

Under the river and out again, through interminable streets, alike in dismalness and dismal still under the cold winter rain, and then, when it seemed as if one must have taken the wrong car, there was a big, warm, crowded theatre, full of band music and smoke and the smell of chocolate and spearmint, and men and women and children roaring at *Krausmeyer's Alley.*

Where they came from, how they could leave their homes or work—they and the thousands like them crowding similar houses in Eighth Avenue, the Bronx, Cincinnati, Minneapolis, goodness knows where, every afternoon in the week—that is one of the mysteries. Here they were, at any rate, there on the stage was Mr. Billy Watson— baggy comedian's clothes, toothpick in his mouth, red nose, cuffs tied in ribbons, hatchet in his pocket—a sort of mixed-up Cyrano striding, impudent and serene, through this slapstick epic of the "Irish an' the Dutch."

Mr. Watson, as one might gather from the name bestowed on his assistants—its enchanting connotation flashed across his mind at the time of the beef-trust investigation and he has used it ever since—belongs to the classic or Boeotian school of burlesque, uncontaminated, or nearly so, by the soft Ionian refinements of musical comedy. *Krausmeyer's Alley* goes back to the days when there were shanties and goats in New York where apartment-houses stand now. Krausmeyer's shanty and Grogan's are perched on adjoining rocks with a clothes-line between, or, in more spirited moments, a shower of cats. You will have seen this shower of cats on some back-street billboard, perhaps, and thought it but a fanciful decoration, a flower of the same order of lithography as that from which has sprung the comic valentine, but Krausmeyer and Grogan actually throw them in the play and have been throwing them these eighteen or twenty years.

The action throughout is set in this simple Elizabethan key. The slapstick has gone out even among such classicists as Mr. Watson, but a hatchet takes its place, and he would be lost without it as a Drury Lane villain without his gold cigarette case. How roguish its appearance as he asks, "Has anyone here seen Grogan?" and as he embraces the leading lady, how wittily—unseen by her—he taps her on the back with it, while the bass drum goes *"Pom!"* or the orchestra makes a sound like rapping a hollow cocoanut.

When Krausmeyer enters Grogan thinks he "smells a muskrat," and Grogan, planting his feet on the table, is requested to take them off and "give the limburger a chance." We are scarcely introduced to the alley before there is a general fight. And the first act ends—after the Beef Trust Beauties, appropriately dressed in red silk tights, red claw-hammer coats, and red top-hats to represent "Fifth Avenue swells," have danced and sung—in a "fight, battle scene, riot."

We go to Ireland in the next act, where a medley of Irish songs are sung by the company's handsome soloist and the Beef Trust Beauties appear as the "French girls invited from the Parisienne," and then Grogan and Krausmeyer fight again. Then the scene shifts to New York and the christening of little Philip Krausmeyer, with the Beef Trust Beauties metamorphosed into "grown-up kids from the alley." There is vivid repartee about little Philip's resemblance to Grogan, ending with what the programme describes as a "fight to the finish," and down goes the curtain on "Auld Lang Syne." Spirited, slap-bang stuff, it will be observed, fit for a generation which sang "Throw him down, McClusky!" from the heart and knew naught of tea dances or cabarets. . . .

Shows like *Krausmeyer's Alley* will doubtless soon be no more. Pale wraiths of musical comedy are continually crossing the once scornful frontiers and moving pictures flicker where once the slap-stick rang. The Bowery is not what it once used to be when it was full of shooting-galleries and sailors and strong-arm men and poor girls drank carbolic on the dance-floor at McGuirk's; nor is burlesque what it was when on a summer's evening, you could hear the chorus at Tony Pastor's through the open windows at Tammany Hall; when Annie Yeamans was singing "Maggie Murphy's Home," and Lillian Russell was a girl.

THE WILD WEST SHOW

Unlike other great powers in the nineteenth century, the United States had "free land" to acquire immediately adjacent to its settled border. England and France annexed huge areas overseas in Africa and Asia; America found its "empire" beyond the Atlantic's hinterland, and moved rapidly to the Mississippi, the Rocky Mountains, and the Pacific. Europeans brought home "tribesmen," "natives," and "jungle" animals as imperial trophies and exhibits for fairground sideshows; Americans had their "Indians," "cowboys," and captive buffalo. In the 1830s and 1840s, in New York, London, and Paris, George Catlin staged dances of a few "wild" midwestern Indians against a backdrop of their authentic artefacts and his paintings of their camps and customs. Dime showmen often included western "warriors" among their human oddities, but only in the 1880s did a fully fledged "Wild West" show emerge. Its personnel were billed as distinctively American, demonstrating New World skills of horsemanship with the guns of conquest. Where Catlin used drama to enliven his lectures and art, the new wild west shows relegated education to the program, not the platform. What interested audiences in the West performed was not homesteads and harvests, grain silos and gold mines, plows and Pullmans, but Fenimore Cooper's woodsmen modernized as American knights of the plains. No one was more instrumental in promoting this American historical drama than Buffalo Bill.

William Frederick Cody transformed history into myth. His real-life exploits in the 1860s and 1870s were the stuff of frontier romance. He was a Pony Express rider, a buffalo hunter for the Kansas Pacific railroad construction gangs, and a scout with the Fifth Cavalry in the Indian campaigns on the Great Plains. In November 1869 Ned Buntline published *Buffalo Bill, the King of the Border Men* in the *New York Weekly*. It became a Bowery Theatre play two years later, but was regarded as lighthearted fantasy; within a month it was burlesqued in Hooley's Opera House in Brooklyn as *Bill Buffalo, with His Great Buffalo Bull*. The larger-than-life adventures of "Buffalo Bill" Cody were promoted by the *Weekly* serial's editors as "The Greatest Romance of the Age." Dozens of dime novels followed. National fame launched Cody's second career as an entertainer and impresario of frontier skills. Gradually he learned the arts of showmanship. In 1872, with official permission from the U.S. Army, he organized a hunting expedition for the Grand Duke Alexis of Russia, in which he included a demonstration of a hundred Brulé Sioux, led by Spotted Tail, using bow and arrow to kill buffalo. In the fall and winter of 1872 he toured eastern theaters as a performance artist, and in 1873 he formed his own company, the Buffalo Bill Combination. For ten years Cody and other authentic westerners, dressed in elaborately fringed buckskin outfits, and occasionally genuine Indians, played themselves in action-melodramas contrived by Buntline. These were pure sensation-spectacles, dime novels animated, with little dialogue of consequence. *The Scouts of the Prairie; or Red Deviltry As It Is* was typical. The nonsensical plot involved fights with outlaws, horses on stage, shooting, a prairie fire, and a Scalp Dance; the love-interest was the exotic Dove Eye, a former ballerina from *The Black Crook*, described not unkindly by the Chicago *Tribune* critic as "a beautiful Indian maiden with an Italian accent and a weakness for scouts."[1]

Soon, life and art became indistinguishable. In 1876, while serving as an army scout, Cody killed the Cheyenne warrior, Yellow Hand. The gaudy vaquero costume of black velvet with silver buttons and lace trim which he had worn during that Nebraska campaign became a genuine prop for his theatrical performances. Within a few months, he was using it, and Yellow Hand's hair as trophy, in *The Red Right Hand: or, Buffalo Bill's First Scalp for Custer.* Cody moved on to grander performances. On July 4, 1882, he arranged the "Old Glory Blow-Out," an Independence Day celebration in his home town of North Platte, Nebraska. It incorporated the staples of his entertainment package for the next decade—genuine Indians, a buffalo chase, and "cow-boy" skills of roping, riding, and shooting. In May 1883 Cody joined Dr. William Frank Carver in Omaha in the Wild West, Rocky Mountain and Prairie Exhibition. The partnership foundered after a few months, and Cody teamed up with actor-manager Nate Salsbury to form Buffalo Bill's Wild West—America's National Entertainment. Tours of the East in 1885 and 1886, of England in 1887 and 1892, and France, Italy, and Germany in 1889–92 established the Wild West's reputation.

As the "Knight of the Plains," the "Last of the Plainsmen," or the "Last of the Great Scouts," Cody was a nostalgic symbol for the "disappearing" west of the buffalo, pioneer, hunter, and cattle trails in the new age of the railroad, the settler, and the mining company. Buffalo Bill's Wild West ignored the current western issues of exploiting the land, farmers' protests, railroad regulation, and free silver, and dwelt on dime-novel heroic dashes and clashes. Staged frontier melodramas had already shaded distinctions between hunting, scouting, and Indian fighting on the plains and ranching in the southwest. Prentiss Ingraham had scripted one of Cody's plays in 1879, and in February 1887 produced the first fictional cowboy hero in his Beadle half-dime novel, *Buck*

Taylor, King of the Cowboys; or, The Raiders and the Rangers, A Story of the Wild and Thrilling Life of William L. Taylor. The constellation of white western warriors was now complete.

Throughout the 1880s and early 1890s, Buffalo Bill's Wild West program remained substantially the same. Displays of horsemanship were key. The European hippodrama was recast with an explicitly American and western theme of "cow-boy fun" in roping and breaking-in mustangs and chasing Indians. Guns were the weapons of conquest. Shooting at all kinds of targets—glass balls, coins, cards—from every possible position (including a poodle's head) made up a quarter of the program. Markswomen like Annie Oakley demonstrated expertise with the rifle, but glamorous "Western girls" in lady-like divided skirts and buckskin fringes also rode and shot. Indians inside and outside the arena fascinated visitors. In his first large-scale "exhibition" in Nebraska in 1883, Cody advertised the Indian Camp as "a Living, Picturesque Reproduction of Savage Life." Easterners were even more curious: family groups at home, surrounded by "tribal" artefacts and adorned with animal skins and face paint, were always popular attractions and photographic souvenirs. Melodramatic action against the painted canvas backdrop in the large open-air arena was supposed to link the diverse western scenes of racing and chasing. But after a few years of experimentation, Cody and Salsbury became aware that hunting buffalo, trick-shooting, and rescuing white maidens from villains lacked thematic unity. In 1886 they enlisted the talents of the theater director Steele MacKaye, and for the winter season at New York's Madison Square Garden, MacKaye reorganized the program to illustrate "epochs" in the evolving "Drama of Civilization" of America's founding. MacKaye's vivid special effects of prairie fire and cyclonic winds proved too elaborate and impractical for itinerant performances across the nation, where tent shows lacked the necessary machinery, but his narrative gave the Wild West more dramatic coherence and the lessons were never entirely lost.

Buffalo Bill's Wild West always claimed authenticity. It was never advertised as a "show," which suggested Barnum's humbug, but as an "exhibition" or "exposition," "the real thing." John M. Burke, the general manager, publicized it as "in no wise partaking of the nature of a 'circus,'" but illustrating "life as it is witnessed on the plains," and "at once new, startling, and instructive."[2] During its heyday, the Wild West was an action-packed, patriotic pageant. Following after the bitter squabbles over Civil War and Reconstruction and the scandals of the Gilded Age, the spectacle of the frontier tamed gave reassurance of the triumph of civilization and national reconciliation.

During the 1890s the Old West theme began to be displaced by explicit comparisons between horsemen of the Old World and the New. After the 1892 London season the show added novelty acts and inflated its title to Buffalo Bill's Wild West and Congress of the Rough Riders of the World. Nate

Salsbury explained that for the grand international Columbian Exposition in Chicago in 1893 it had assembled "the most unique congregation of equestrians since the creation . . . for the *first time* in history—from far distant countries—differing in race, language, habits, customs, dress, as well as in skill, style and methods of horsemanship."[3] "Civilized" English Lancers, German Uhlans, French chasseurs, and U.S. cavalry competed for honors, and were matched against "primitive" horsemen—American Indians and Arabs, Argentinean gauchos and Russian cossacks.

When James A. Bailey of Barnum and Bailey's Circus became responsible for transportation, the Wild West developed a more efficient schedule. In the 1895 season it spent a hundred and ninety days in travel for a hundred and thirty-one one-day stands. By 1898 it was a huge company, requiring eight sleeping coaches for nearly seven hundred employees, fifteen cars for the eighteen buffalo and five hundred horses, sixteen flatcars for equipment (including electrical generators for lighting the night shows), and thirty-five wagons for general baggage. The show occupied almost eleven acres, and its arena, canvassed over on three sides and seating as many as fifteen thousand spectators, was a huge stage, fifty yards wide and more than a hundred yards long, and with seven panoramas, two hundred feet long and thirty feet high, as backdrops. Gradually, more traditional circus elements were added. As well as the customary white "squaw men," their Indian wives, and half-breed families, the sideshow exhibits in 1902 included a snake charmer, a fire eater, and a bearded lady. However, keeping the show on the road cost four thousand dollars a day, and as Cody's debts grew, he was compelled to merge Buffalo Bill's Wild West with Pawnee Bill's Historic Far West and Great Far East in 1908. Major Gordon W. Lillie ("Pawnee Bill") had had two failures in show business before succeeding with Pawnee Bill's Historical Wild West, Mexican Hippodrome, Indian Museum, and Grand Fireworks Exhibition in 1893. Lillie added pure circus spectacle to the program in 1909. The pageant, "The Far East, or A Dream of the Orient," brought together Rossi's Musical Elephants, a camel caravan, Bedouin and Japanese acrobats, Australian boomerang throwers, and dancers from Russia and Ceylon. "An Ethnological Congress of Strange Tribes, Clans, Races, and Nations of Peculiar Peoples"—Whirling Dervishes, Sudanese, Syrians, Moors, Persians, Dahomeans and South Sea Islanders—brought the sideshow center stage.

During its late, imperialist phase, the Wild West lost its distinctiveness. In the 1901–2 season the Indians doubled up as Chinese Boxers in the action-drama of "The Battle of Tien-Tsin" and fought under "The Royal Standard of Paganism" against the Allied "Banners of Civilization." New technology also made the touring shows obsolete, although Cody, ever hopeful for a new business opportunity, experimented with movie making, most notably in 1913. However, even before Cody's death in 1917, when scores of rivals toured the northeast and midwest, the Wild West show was in rapid decline. Motion-picture drama and outdoor locations were more profitable. For live performances the Old West had become little more than a cultural storehouse of nostalgic memory to spice circus acts and thrilling spectacles.

Origins

One possible influence on Cody's Wild West was the exhibition of Plains Indians which P. T. Barnum arranged for his "Congress of Nations" in his New York Roman Hippodrome arena in late 1874. Barnum had displayed several small groups of Indians in the museum Lecture Room as early as 1843, and published *Life and Adventures of the Indian Chiefs, Warriors and Squaws, of the Winnebago Tribe, now exhibiting at Barnum's American Museum, New York* in 1863, perhaps profiting from interest aroused by the Minnesota Sioux uprising of 1862. He had proposed a much more ambitious show in his 1869 autobiography. Such schemes were not uncommon—John P. Clum presented "Wild Apaches" in St. Louis in 1876. In his letter to Mark Twain, Barnum explained that the Indian-Mexican battle was sandwiched between Amazon chariot races and an English fox hunt. It is possible that Cody saw it during his stay in the city for his winter theater season or during the brief tour of the Congress of Nations through eastern cities before Barnum dissolved the company.

Selected Letters of P. T. Barnum, ed. A. H. Saxon (New York: Columbia University Press, 1983), 190.

Bridgeport, 19 January 1875
My dear Clemens,

. . . I give a scene called *Indian Life on the Plains* wherein scores of Indians of various tribes appear with their squaws, pappooses, ponies, and wigwams travelling as they do in the Indian territory. They encamp, erect their wigwams, engage in buffalo hunts with real buffaloes, give their Indian war dances, their Indian pony races, snowshoe races, foot races against horses, lasso horses and other animals, and both Indians and squaws give the most amazing specimens of riding at full speed. The Indian camp is surprised by Mexicans, and then ensues such a scene of savage strife and warfare as is never seen except upon our wild western borders.

The first "autobiography" of "Buffalo Bill," building on his dime-novel fame, appeared in 1879. A decade later, Cody's "camp-fire chats"—probably ghost-written by "Arizona" John Burke, the Wild West's publicist—was sold at the show's ticket booths. Before beginning a narrative of his life, Cody explained the grander meaning of frontier expansion.

Story of the Wild West and Camp-Fire Chats, by Buffalo Bill (Hon. W. F. Cody.) A full and complete history of the renowned pioneer quartette, Boone, Crockett, Carson and Buffalo Bill. Replete with graphic descriptions of wild life and thrilling adventures of famous heroes of the frontier . . . (Philadelphia: Historical Publishing, 1888), v–vi, 694–95.

I have sought to describe that great general movement westward—that irresistible wave of immigration which, arrested for a time by the Alleghenies, rose until at last it broke over and spread away across mountain, stream and plain, leaving States in its wake, until stopped by the shores of the Pacific.

The evolution of government and of civilization, the adaptation of one to the other, are interesting to the student of history; but particularly fascinating is the story of the reclamation of the Great West and the supplanting of the wild savages that from primeval days were lords of the country but are now become wards of the Government, whose guardianship they were forced to recognize. This story is one well calculated to inspire a feeling of pride even in the breasts of those whose sentimentality impels to commiserate the hard lot of the poor Indian; for, rising above the formerly neglected prairies of the West are innumerable monuments of thrift, industry, intelligence, and all the contributory comforts and luxuries of a peaceful and God-fearing civilization; those evidences that proclaim to a wondering world the march of the Anglo-Saxon race towards the attainment of perfect citizenship and liberal, free, stable government.

Cody described how the idea of the Wild West evolved, after his winter triumphs on the stage, and gave no credit to his one-time partner, William Frank "Doc" Carver. In May 1883 Cody joined Carver in Omaha in the Wild West, Rocky Mountain and Prairie Exhibition, billed as "REALITY ECLIPSING ROMANCE," with "Many Types of the Pioneers and Vanguard of Civilization," and "Representatives of THE RUGGED LIFE OF PRIMITIVE MAN."[4]

When the season of 1882–83 closed I found myself richer by several thousand dollars than I had ever been before, having done a splendid business at every place where my performance was given in that year. Immense success and comparative wealth, attained in the profession of a showman, stimulated me to greater exertion and largely increased my ambition for public favor. Accordingly, I conceived the idea of organizing a large company of Indians, cow-boys, Mexican vaqueros, famous riders and expert lasso throwers, with accessories of stage coach, emigrant wagons, bucking horses and a herd of buffaloes, with which to give a realistic entertainment of wild life on the plains. To accomplish this purpose, which in many respects was a herculean undertaking, I sent agents to various points in the far West to engage Indians from several tribes, and then set about the more difficult enterprise of capturing a herd of buffaloes. After several months of patient work, I secured the services of nearly fifty cow-boys and Mexicans skilled in lasso-throwing and famous as daring riders, but when these were engaged, and several buffaloes, elk and mountain sheep were obtained, I found all the difficulties had not yet been overcome, for such exhibitions as I had prepared to give could only be shown in large open-air enclosures, and these were not always to be rented, while those I found suitable were often inaccessible by such popular conveyances as street cars. The expenses of such a show as I had determined to give were so great that a very large crowd must be drawn to every exhibition or a financial failure would be certain; hence I soon found that my ambitious conception, instead of bringing me fortune, was more likely to end in disaster. But having gone so far in the matter I determined to see the end whatever it might be.

In the spring of 1883 (May 17th) I opened the Wild West Show at the fair grounds in Omaha, and played to very large crowds, the weather fortunately proving propitious. We played our next engagement in Springfield, Ill., and hence in all the large cities, to the seaboard. The enterprise was not a complete financial success during the first season, though everywhere our performances were attended by immense audiences.

Though I had made no money at the end of the first year, the profit came to me in the way of valuable experience and I was in no wise discouraged. Flattering offers were made me by circus organizations to go on the road as an adjunct to their exhibitions, but I refused them all, determined to win success with my prairie Wild West Show or go down in complete failure. The very large patronage I received during my first season convinced me that if I could form a partnership with some one capable of attending to the management and business details that the enterprise would prove a magnificent success, a belief that I am glad to say was speedily realized.

My career on the stage threw me in contact with a great many leading stars, and I came to have an acquaintanceship with nearly all my contemporary American actors. Among those with whom I became most intimate was Nate Salsbury, a comedian whose equal I do not believe graces the stage of either America or England today. Aside from his popularity and wealth, acquired in legitimate comedy, I knew him to be a reliable friend, and withal endowed with a rare business sagacity that gave him a reputation of being one of the very best, as well as successful, managers in the show business. Knowing his character as such, I approached him with a proposition to join me as an equal partner, in putting the Wild West entertainment again on the road. The result of my overtures was the formation of a partnership that still continues, and under the new management and partnership of Cody & Salsbury, the Wild West has won all its glory.

McLoughlin Brothers, the New York publisher and manufacturer of children's games and toys, issued a small, illustrated book of verse for the young in 1887, endorsing the Wild West. It celebrated the West as the land of the buffalo, settlers and Indians, and epic struggle between the wild and the civilizing. Buffalo Bill was central to the destiny of all three.

A Peep at Buffalo Bill's Wild West (New York: McLoughlin, 1887).

THE WILD WEST SHOW

The Indian village again set up,
    The squaws must remain at home
With the younger brood, to prepare the food,
    While the warriors further roam.

And girt with the weapons that they have won
    From enemies they have slain,
They watch and wait both early and late
    The approach of the settlers train.

And Buffalo Bill, who knows their ways,
    And the evil that they would do,
Puts foot to horse, and soon comes across
    The track of the sneaking Sioux.

And lucky for him if the band is small
    And the weapons they hold but few,
For he and his men may easily then
    Disperse the blood-thirsty crew.

. . . .

O Buffalo Bill like a spirit rides
    And dashes across the plain;
His wonderful steed to his voice gives heed
    And answers the touch of the rein.

And swiftly the light lasso is flung,
    And seldom is it at fault,
For it stops the speed of the flying steed
    That's brought to a sudden halt.

And to tame them and train them for further use
    Is a joy to Buffalo Bill,
And the cow-boys and he are as fond as can be
    Of the sport that demands such skills.

And almost human the beasts become,
    And though under the control of the reins
They are almost as free as they used to be
    When roaming wild o'er the plains.

. . . .

Some horses there are that a man can trust,
    But oh! it requires great pluck,
It does, indeed, to manage a steed
    That is always disposed to "buck."

Origins

Then there's a fight between horse and man,
 And the strength of the will is shown;
And sometimes, alas! it comes to pass
 That the rider is finally thrown.

And all these doings recorded here
 In the haunts of the Buffalo,
Where the cowboys dwell, and the Indians yell
 Are part of the WILD WEST SHOW.

In his manuscript "Reminiscences," written the year before his death in 1902, Nate Salsbury claimed to have originated the concept of the Wild West. As an actor-manager, he had taken his company, the Salsbury Troubadors, throughout the English-speaking world in the 1870s. The inspiration for a Wild West show had first come to him, he recalled, while arguing the merits of frontier American horsemen with fellow ship passengers while returning from Australia in 1877. He conceded that Cody also experimented with cowboy shows at the same time, but Buffalo Bill was an undisciplined drunkard and lacked business sense. Only Salsbury's managerial competence had transformed the Cody-Carver combination. By 1901 Salsbury's failing health and bitter quarrels had ended their partnership. His recollections were perhaps less than charitable about Cody's energy and charisma. Salsbury had had experience of professional stage management—in farce and melodrama—but for a realistic depiction of "cow-boy" life needed the expert knowledge of the frontier and the contacts with authentic performers which Cody had.

"Nate Salsbury Originated Wild West Show Idea," *Colorado Magazine* 32 (July 1955): 206–8. A slightly different text is published as "Reminiscences by Nate Salsbury," ed. Roger Hall, *Journal of American Drama and Theatre* 5 (winter 1993): 44–46, 47–48.

[In 1877] I ventured the opinion that our Cowboy and Mexican riders could beat the civilized, or uncivilized world in all that the term horsemanship implies. . . . [T]he subject stuck in my mind even after I had gone to bed that night, and the train of thought thus engendered grew upon me until it naturally turned into professional channels and I began to construct a show in my mind that would embody the whole subject of horsemanship and before I went to sleep I had mapped out in my mind a show that would be constituted of elements that had never been employed in concerted effort in the history of the show business. Of course I knew that various circus managers had tried to reproduce the riding of the plains, in made up professional riders, but I knew they had never had the real thing.

Some years passed but I had never lost sight of my plan to originate my show and put it on the road. Finally the thing took the form of resolve and I began to look up the elements of the show. I decided that such an entertainment must have a well known figure head to attract attention and thus help to quickly solve the problem of advertising a new idea. After a careful consideration of the plan and scope of the show I resolved to get W. F. Cody as my central figure. To this end I waited a favorable opportunity to confide the scheme to him and in 1882 while we were both playing an engagement in Brooklyn or perhaps he was in New York, I made an appointment with him to meet me. . . .

As he was about at the end of his profit string on the stage I dare say he was pleased at the chance to try something else, for he grew very enthusiastic over the plan as I unfolded it to him, and was sure that the thing would be a great success. It was arranged at that lunch that I would go to Europe the following summer and look the ground over with a view to taking the show to a country where all its elements would be absolutely novel. I was quite well aware that the Dime Novel had found its way to England especially and wherever the Dime Novel had gone Cody had gone along for Ned Buntline had so firmly written Cody into contemporary history of the Great Plains that he had made a hero on paper at first hand. While on this subject I want to note what I consider a most remarkable fact. The man who today is known in the uttermost parts of the earth as a showman, would never have been a showman at all if Ned Buntline had not made him notorious and he had dripped from the point of Buntline's pen as a hero. Buntline was looking for somebody to make a hero of and first tried to boost Major Frank North into that position but the Major being a real hero would not listen to that sort of thing but said, "If you want a man to fill that bill he is over there under that wagon." Buntline went over to the wagon and woke up the man he made famous as Buffalo Bill. Between story and the stage Cody became a very popular man with a certain class of the public and was notorious enough for my purpose.

As agreed upon I went to Europe the following summer and looked the ground over. I came to the conclusion that it would take a lot of money to do the thing right and told Cody that we must be well provided with money when we made the plunge and that so far as I was concerned I did not feel rich enough to undertake my share of the expense and that I would have to wait another year before I could go into the scheme in proper shape. To this Cody did not demur, but said that he was in about the same fix as myself. So far we had arrived at a perfect understanding that we were to share and share alike in the venture. So far so good.

But, Cody must have agreed to drop the matter for another year with a strong mental reservation for I was astonished in the spring of 1883 to get a telegram (which I now have in my possession) asking me if I wanted to go into the show for this country if DR. CARVER DID NOT OBJECT. Of course I was dumbfounded and replied that I did not want to have anything to do with Doctor Carver who was a fakir in the show business and as Cody once expressed it "Went West on a piano stool."

Events proved that Cody did not wait for our plan to go to Europe to ripen but no sooner had my ideas than he began to negotiate with Carver who had a reputation as a marksman to go in with him and was kind enough, when they had laid all their plans, to let me in as a partner. Of course I turned them down and they went on the road and made a ghastly failure. Their failure was so pronounced, that they separated at the end of the season, each blaming the other for the failure.

I was playing an engagement in Chicago, while they were there, and Cody came to see me and said that if I did not take hold of the show he was going to quit the whole thing. He said he was through with Carver and that he would not go through such another summer for a hundred thousand dollars. As I had seen their show and knew that they had not developed my ideas in putting it together at all I felt that there was still a lot of money in it if properly constructed. At the end of their term in Chicago they divided the assets of their firm and I took hold of the show under a partnership contract between Cody and myself which was drawn by John P. Altgeld who at that time was my legal adviser when I needed one.

What followed the signing of that contract is a history of the Wild West Show and is too long to recite here. I should never have put this relation of the origin of the Wild West Show on paper if there had not been in all the years that have passed a most determined effort on the part of John Burke and the other hero worshippers who have hung onto Cody's coattails for their sustenance to make Cody the originator of the show for in doing so they can edge in their own feeble claims to being an integral part of the success of the show. The men I speak of were all participants in the failure that followed the first venture by Cody and were retained by me in the management of the show by the request of Cody who lives in the worship of those who bleed him. . . .

Burke and [Jule] Keen [treasurer of the Wild West] and the rest of the Codyites who have followed the show from the day I took hold of it have never forgiven me for taking the reins of management out of their hands where they had been placed by Cody and Carver. They have always resented my presence with the show because it unseated their hero in the business saddle of the show which needed somebody that could ride it. . . .

I know that there will be a word of protest to these lines, but that the Wild West Show was an invention of my own entirely, is proven by the letters in Cody's own hand, which I have preserved, as indeed I have preserved every scrap of writing he has ever signed and addressed to me. It is lovely to be thus fortified against protestations and abuse that would surely follow if proof did not exist of what I have stated.

Extracts from Buffalo Bill's Wild West Programs

The first Wild West program of 1883 drew attention to the exhibitions of shooting and the variety of exotic equestrian acts assembled.

The Wild West, Cody and Carver's Rocky Mountain and Prairie Exhibition, with the famed Scout and Indian Fighter, Buffalo Bill (Hon. W. F. Cody) and Dr. W. F. Carver, King of riflemen, and acknowledged champion marksman of the world, will soon appear in this city. A Camp of Cheyenne, Arappahoe, Sioux and Pawnee Indians; A Group of Mexican

THE WILD WEST SHOW

Vaqueros: Round-up of Western Cow-boys; Company of Prairie Scouts; A Host of Western Celebrities; A Herd of Wild Buffaloes: A Corral of Indian Mexican Burros. Artistically Blending, Life-Like, and Thrilling Pictures of Western Life (Hartford, Conn.: Calhoun Printing, 1883).

Western Cyclone!

Grand Parade

Allegorical representation of the March: Progress of Civilization. National Parks the Playground! General Equestrianism and Feats of Horsemanship! Indian Foot Races! Feats of Archery! Broncho Lassoing! Riding of Pack Ponies! Chase! Lassoing! Tying Down the Texas Bovine! Bareback Races and Trials of Speed between the Anglo-Saxon, Castilian, and Indian! The Historic Relic of the Overland Route! Indian Attack on the Deadwood Stage Coach! Rescue by the Scouts! A mimic Border War!

Indian Buffalo Dance

BUFFALO BILL in a series of Feats of agility, Grace and Skill

Dr. W. F. CARVER, and CAPTAIN BOGARDUS,

Revelations in Clay Pigeon Contests.

Mexicans, Cow-Boys, Sioux and Pawnees Struggling for Prize and Honor in Familiar Sports.

The GREAT BOGARDUS at his Shot-Gun

JOHN NELSON, 'Cha-sha-na-po-ge-o,' Hunter, Trapper, Whip-Interpreter

Major FRANK NORTH, "White Chief of the Pawnees," the Pilot of the Prairies, Protector of the Border

BUCK TAYLOR, the Centaur Ranchman of Prairies

JIM LAYDON, the mad Matador—Emperor of the Rope

ELK RACES,

BUFFALO HUNT

MULES, MULETEERS,

MULE RACES, Etc, Etc.

GRAND SHOOTING FETE

On Foot and Horseback, Rifle and Shot-gun

Ne Plus Ultra in Sharp-Shooting. The Phenomenally Eagle-Eyed Dr. W. F. Carver, Famed Bogardus, Old Reliable Buffalo Bill. The Whirlwind Ride of the Montezumas, surpassing the stimulating delirium of Ancient Roman Races. Attack on the Wagon Train, Deadly Combat for Love and Life between the Red Warriors and White Pioneers. Vivid War and Scalp Dances, Night-Illuminating Bon-Fires, Lurid Flames of Vivid Light, revealing Scenes of Savage Weirdness. Grand Pyrotechnic Novelties! Dazzling Wonders, forming a Brilliant Finale, delighting Thousands.

Cody and Salsbury took care to have the program copyrighted as the only legal and authentic "Wild West," "the whole invented and arranged by W. F.

Cody," to distinguish it from four other rival shows. Mark Twain wrote to Cody (as the program duly reported) that the show "stirred me like a war song."

"Buffalo Bill's 'Wild West' Prairie Exhibition, and Rocky Mountain Show, A Dramatic-Equestrian Exposition of Life on the Plains, with accompanying monologue and incidental music. The whole invented and arranged by W. F. Cody. W. F. Cody and N. Salsbury, proprietors and managers who hereby claim as their special property the various effects introduced in the public performances of Buffalo Bill's 'Wild West'" (copyright deposit typescript in the Library of Congress, entered December 22, 1883, granted June 1, 1885). Reprinted in A *Treasury of American Folklore: Stories, Ballads and Traditions of the American People*, ed. B. A. Botkin (New York: Crown, 1945), 150–56.

BUFFALO BILL'S "WILD WEST"
PRAIRIE EXHIBITION, AND ROCKY MOUNTAIN SHOW,
A DRAMATIC-EQUESTRIAN EXPOSITION
OF
LIFE ON THE PLAINS,
WITH ACCOMPANYING MONOLOGUE AND INCIDENTAL MUSIC.
THE WHOLE INVENTED AND ARRANGED BY
W. F. CODY

W. F. CODY AND N. SALSBURY, PROPRIETORS AND MANAGERS
WHO HEREBY CLAIM AS THEIR SPECIAL
PROPERTY THE VARIOUS EF-
FECTS INTRODUCED IN
THE PUBLIC PER-
FORMANCES
OF
BUFFALO BILL'S "WILD WEST."

MONOLOGUE

Ladies and Gentlemen,

I desire to call your attention to an important fact. From time to time it will be my pleasure to announce to you the different features of the programme as they occur. In order that I may do so intelligently, I respectfully request your silence and attention while I am speaking. Our agents will pass among you with the biographical history of the life of Hon. William F. Cody ("Buffalo Bill,") and other celebrities, who will appear before you this afternoon. The management desires to vouch for the truth and accuracy of all the statements obtained in this book, and respectfully submitted to your attention, as helping you to understand and appreciate our entertainment. Before the entertainment begins, however, I wish to impress on your minds that what you are about to witness is not a performance in the common sense of that term, but an exhibition of skill, on the part of the men who have acquired that quality while gaining a livelihood. Many unthinking people suppose that the different features of our exhibition are the result of what is technically called "rehearsals." Such, however, is not the fact, and anyone who witnesses our performance the second time, will observe that men and animals alike are the creatures of circumstances, depending for their success upon their own skill, daring and capacity. In the East, the few who excel are known to all. In the Far West, the names we offer to you this afternoon are the synonyms of skill, courage and individual excellence. At the conclusion of the next overture our performance will commence with a grand processional parade of the "Wild West."

Overture, grand processional parade of cowboys,
Mexicans, and Indians, with incidental music.

I will introduce the different groups and individual celebrities as they pass before you in review.

Enter a group of Pawnee Indians. Incidental music. Enter
Chief. Music. Enter a group of Mexican vaqueros. Music.
Enter a group of Wichita Indians. Music. Enter Chief.
Music. Enter a group of American cowboys. Music. Enter
King of Cowboys. Music. Enter Cowboy Sheriff of the
Platte. Music. Enter a group of Sioux Indians. Music.
Enter Chief. Music.

I next have the honor of introducing to your attention a man whose record as a servant of the government, whose skill and daring as a frontiersman, whose place in history as the king of the scouts of the United States Army, under such generals as Sherman, Sheridan, Hancock, Terry, Miles, Hazen, Royal, Merrit, Crook, Carr and others, and whose name as one of the avengers of the lamented Custer, and whose adherence throughout an eventful life to his chosen principle of "true to friend and foe," have made him well and popularly known throughout the world. You know to whom I allude—the Honorable William F. Cody, "Buffalo Bill."

Enter Cody. Bugle Call. Cody speaks.

Ladies and gentlemen: allow me to introduce the equestrian portion of the Wild West Exhibition.

Turns to review.

Wild West, are you ready? Go!

Exeunt omnes.

First on our programme, a——mile race, between a cow boy, a Mexican, and an Indian, starting at——. You will notice that these horses carry the heaviest trapping, and that neither of the riders weigh less than 145 pounds.

———

Next on the programme, the Pony Express. The Pony Express was established long before the Union Pacific Rail Road was built across the continent, or even before the telegraph poles were set, and when Abraham Lincoln was elected president of the United States, it was important that the election returns from California should be brought across the mountains as quickly as possible. Mr. William Russell, the great government freighter, who at the time was in Washington, first proposed the Pony Express. He was told it would take too long—17 or 18 days. The result was a wager of $200,000 that the time could be made in less than ten days, and it was, the actual time being nine days, seventeen hours, leaving seven hours to spare, and winning the wager of two hundred thousand dollars. Mr. Billy Johnson will illustrate the mode of riding the Pony Express, mounting, dismounting and changing the mail to fresh horses.

Music. Enter Express rider, changing horse in front of the
grand stand, and exit.

Next on our programme, a one hundred yard race between an Indian on foot, and an Indian on an Indian pony, starting at a given point, running fifty yards, and returning to the starting point—virtually a race of a hundred yards.

Race as described above. Music.

Next on our programme, an historical representation between Buffalo Bill and Yellow Hand, fought during the Sitting Bull war, on the 17th. of July, 1876, at War Bonnet Creek, Dakota, shortly after the massacre of Custer. The fight was witnessed by General Carr's command and the Sioux army, and resulted in the death of Yellow Hand, and the first scalp taken in revenge of Custer's fate.

Duel as described above. Cody, supported by cow boys,
etc., Yellow Hand by Indians. Music.

I have the pleasure of introducing Mr. Seth Clover. Mr. Clover will give an exhibition of his skill, shooting with a Winchester repeating rifle, at composition balls thrown from the hand.

Clover shoots as above.

Shooting two balls thrown in the air at the same time. You will notice that Mr. Clov[er] is obliged to replace the discharged cartridge before he can shoot at the second ball.

Shoots as above.

Obscuring the sight by placing a card over the rifle.

Shoots as above.

If any gentleman has a half-dollar he would like to have mutilated and take home as a pocket piece, if he will throw it in upon the track, where we can get it, Mr. Clover will try and oblige him.

Shoots coin as above.

Shooting at a nickel.

Shoots as above.

Shooting at a marble. You will notice that the mark is hardly larger than the bullet shot at it.

Shoots as above.

Shooting a number of composition balls thrown in rapid succession.

Shoots as above. Exit.

———————

I have the pleasure of introducing Master Johnny Baker of North Platte, Neb., known as the Cow Boy Kid. Master Johnny is 16 years of age, and the holder of the boy's champion badge, for rifle and revolver shooting, and stands ready to meet any opponent of his age. Master Baker will give an exhibition of his skill, holding his rifle in various positions.

Holding the rifle sideways.

Holding the rifle to the left shoulder.

Holding the rifle upside down, on the top of his head.

Standing with his back to the target, bending forward, and shooting between his knees.

Leaning backward, over a support, and shooting over his head.

Standing with his back to the target, and taking aim by the aid of a small mirror.

Shooting composition balls thrown in air.

Shoots each shot as above. Exit.

———————

Miss Annie Oakley, the celebrated wing and rifle shot. Miss Oakley will give an exhibition of her skill, shooting with a shot gun at Ligowsky patent clay pigeons, holding the gun in various positions.

Shoots pigeons sprung from trap.

Shooting double, from two traps, sprung at the same time.

Shoots as above.

Picking the gun from the ground after the trap is sprung.

Shoots as above.

Shooting double in the same manner.

Shoots as above.

Shooting three composition balls, thrown in the air in rapid succession, the first with the rifle held upside down upon the head, the second and third with the shot gun.

Shoots as above. Exit.

———————

Next on our programme, the Cow Boy's Fun, or the riding of bucking ponies and mules, by Mr. ____, Mr. ____, and Mr. ____. There is an impression in the minds of many people that these horses are taught or trained to buck, or that they are compelled to do so by having foreign substances placed under their saddles. This, however, is not the fact. Bucking, the same as walking or running away is a natural trait of the animal, confirmed by habit.

Riders announced, and mount in succession.

Watch Mr. Taylor pick up his hat.

Taylor rides past at full sped, leans out of the saddle and

Extracts from Buffalo Bill's Wild West Programs

picks up hat from the ground.
Watch Mr. Taylor pick up handkerchief.
*Taylor rides past at full sped, leans out of the saddle and
picks up handkerchief.*

Hon. William F. Cody, Champion All-Round Shot of the World.
Enter Mr. Cody.
Mr. Cody will give an exhibition of his skill, shooting with shot gun rifle and revolver at clay pigeons and composition balls, shooting first with a shot gun at clay pigeons, pulling the traps himself, (*Shoots.*) shooting clay pigeons in the American style of holding the gun, the butt of the gun below his elbow. (*Shoots.*)

Shooting clay pigeons in the English style of holding the gun, the butt of the gun below the arm-pit. Please notice the change of position. (*Shoots.*)

Shooting clay pigeons standing with his back to the trap, turning and breaking the pigeon while it is in the air. (*Shoots.*)

Shooting with his back to the trap, gun over his shoulder, turning and pulling the traps himself. (*Shoots.*)

Holding the gun with one hand. (*Shoots.*)

Holding the gun with one hand, pulling the trap with the other. (*Shoots.*)

Shooting clay pigeons double from two traps, sprung at the same time. (*Shoots.*)

Shooting clay pigeons double, pulling the traps himself. (*Shoots.*)

Shooting twenty clay pigeons inside of one minute and thirty seconds. Any gentleman desiring to hold the time on this feat, will please take it, not from the pulling of the trap, but from the first crack of the gun. (*Shoots.*)

Mr. Cody will shoot next with a Winchester repeating rifle, at composition balls, thrown from the hand while he rides upon his horse. (*Shoots.*)

Missing with the first shot, hitting with the second. (*Shoots.*)

Missing twice, hitting the third time. (*Shoots.*)

Hitting three balls thrown in the air at the same time. (*Shoots.*)

Hitting a ball thrown from behind. (*Shoots.*)

Hitting a ball thrown to either side. (*Shoots.*)

Hitting a number of balls thrown in the air in rapid succession. (*Shoots.*)

Hitting a ball thrown in the air while he rides past it at full speed, a shot accomplished by no other marksman. (*Shoots.*)

Mr. Cody will next attempt the great double shot, hitting two balls thrown in the air at the same time, as he rides past at full speed. (*Shoots.*)

Hitting composition balls thrown in the air, while marksman and object thrower ride side by side at full speed, thus forming a picture of combined horsemanship and marksmanship never before presented to a public audience. (*Shoots.*)

Hitting composition balls thrown in the air with an ordinary Colt's army revolver. (*Shoots.*)

THE WILD WEST SHOW

Next on our programme, the Deadwood Stage coach, formerly the property of Gilmore, Salsbury, & Co., and plying between Deadwood and Cheyenne. The coach has an immortal place in American history, having been baptised many times by fire and blood. The gentleman holding the reins, is Mr. John Higby, an old stage driver, and formerly the companion of Hank Monk, of whom you have all probably read. Seated beside him is Mr. John Hancock, known in the West as the wizard hunter of the Platte Valley. Broncho Bill will act as out rider, a position he has occupied in earnest many times with credit. Upon the roof of the coach is seated Mr. Con Groner, the cow boy sheriff of the Platte, to whose intrepid administration of that office for several consecutive terms, covering a period of six years, Lincoln County, Neb., and its vicinity are indebted for the peace and quiet that now reigns. Mr. Groner's efforts having driven out the cattle thief and hoodlum element that formerly infested that section of the county, noticeably, the notorious Middleton gang. The coach will start upon its journey, be attacked from an ambush by a band of fierce and warlike Indians, who in their turn will be repulsed by a party of scouts and cow boys, under the command of Buffalo Bill. Will two or three ladies and gentlemen volunteer to ride as passengers.

After passengers are seated in coach.

It is customary to deliver parting instructions to the driver as he starts on his perilous journey, something in the following fashion: Mr. Higby, I have intrusted you with valuable lives and property. Should you meet with Indians, or other dangers, *en route,* put on the whip, and if possible, save the lives of your passengers. If you are ready, go!

Coach is driven down track, meets Indians, turns, followed by Indians. Battle back to stand. Cody and cow boys come to rescue. Battle past stand. Cody, coach and cow boys return to stand. Exit omnes.

———

Next on our programme, a one-quarter mile race between Sioux boys and on bare backed Indian ponies from the Honorable William F. Cody's ranch at North Platte, Neb., starting at———.

Race as above. Music.

———

I would next call to your attention to an exciting race between Mexican thoroughbreds. These animals are bred with great care and at considerable expense, their original cost being sixteen dollars per dozen. All up! No jockeying! Go!

Race as above. Music. "We Won't Come Home Til Morning."

———

A portion of the Pawnees and Wichita tribes will illustrate their native sports and pastimes, giving first the war dance.

War dance by Indians.

Next the grass dance.

Extracts from Buffalo Bill's Wild West Programs

Grass dance by Indians.
Next, the scalp dance, in which the women of the tribe are allowed to participate.
Scalp dance by Indians and squaws.

Keep your eye on the burros!
Burros return. Music. "Home Again!" or "We never
speak, as, etc."
I have the pleasure of introducing "Mustang Jack," or as the Indians call him, "Pet-ze-ka-we-cha-cha," the great high jumper. Jack is the champion jumper among the cow boys of the West, and stands ready to jump with anybody in any manner or style for any amount of money. He will give you an exhibition of his skill, jumping over various animals, beginning with the small burro.
Jack jumps over burro.
Jumping twenty-four feet in two jumps, and clearing the burro in the second jump.
Jack jumps as above.
Jumping the Indian pony, Cha-sha-sha-na-po-geo, a feat which gave him the name of
"Mustang Jack."
Jumps as above.
Next, jumping the tall white horse "Doc. Powell," sixteen and a half hands high. The best recorded standing high jump is one of five feet and three inches made by Mr. Johnson, of England. In order to clear this horse, Jack is obliged to make a jump of nearly six feet, thus beating the record daily.
Jumps as above.

Next on our programme the roping, tyeing and riding of wild Texan steers by cow boys and Mexicans.
Performance as above.

Next on our programme the riding of a wild elk, by Master Voter Hall, a Feejee Indian from Africa.
Saddled elk ridden as above.

Next on our programme the attack upon a settler's cabin by a band of marauding Indians, and their repulse, by a party of scouts and cow boys, under the command of Buffalo Bill. After our entertainment you are invited to visit the Wild West camp. We thank you for your polite attention, and bid you all good afternoon.
Battle as above. Review before the grand stand. Adieus
and dismissal by Mr. Cody.
FINIS.
Programme.
Subject to Changes and Additions

THE WILD WEST SHOW

1.—GRAND PROCESSIONAL REVIEW.

2.—ENTREE. Introduction of individual Celebrities, Groups, etc.

3.—RACE between Cow-boy, Mexican, and Indian on Ponies.

4.—PONY EXPRESS, ridden by Billy Johnson, Illustrating Mode of Conveying Mails on the Frontier.

5.—RIFLE SHOOTING by Johnnie Baker, the "Cow-boy Kid."

6.—DUEL between BUFFALO BILL and Chief Yellow Hand, and Indian Battle, "First Scalp for Custer."

7.—WING SHOOTING, by Miss Annie Oakley.

8.—THE COW-BOY'S FUN. Throwing the Lariat, Riding Bucking Ponies and Mules, by Buck Taylor, Bill Bullock, Tony Esquival, Jim Kidd, Dick Johnson, and Cow-boys.

9.—RIFLE SHOOTING, by Miss Lillian F. Smith, "The California Girl."

10.—RACE, ridden by Lady Riders.

11.—ATTACK UPON THE DEADWOOD STAGE COACH, by Indians. Repulsed by Cow-boys commanded by BUFFALO BILL.

12.—RACE between Sioux Boys on bareback Indian Ponies.

13.—RACE between Mexican Thoroughbreds.

14.—PHASES OF INDIAN LIFE. A nomadic tribe camps upon the prairie, the attack of the hostile tribe, followed by scalp, war, and other dances.

15.—MUSTANG JACK (Petz-ze-ka-we-cha-cha), the Wonderful Jumper.

16.—Hon. W. F. CODY, "BUFFALO BILL," America's Great Practical All-Around Shot.

17.—RIDING AND ROPING OF WILD TEXAS STEERS by Cow-boys and Mexicans.

18.—THE BUFFALO HUNT, BUFFALO BILL assisted by Sioux, Pawnee, Wichita, and Comanche Indians.

19.—THE ATTACK ON THE SETTLER'S CABIN by Marauding Indians; the Battle and Repulse by BUFFALO BILL Leading Cow-boys and Mexicans.

20.—SALUTE.

The Wild West began its third season on April 11, 1885, by moving from winter quarters in New Orleans to Mobile, Alabama. Before closing at St. Louis Fair on October 11, it visited more than forty of the larger cities in the eastern United States and Canada. Chief Sitting Bull of the Hunkpapa Sioux joined the Grand Processional at Buffalo in June for his one and only season. The program contained snippets of information on western topics, including a poem reprinted from *Beadle's Weekly*. The stilted, archaic language typified the dime novel.

Buffalo Bill's Wild West. America's National Entertainment led by the famed scout and guide Buffalo Bill (Hon. W. F. Cody) (Hartford, Conn.: Calhoun Printing, 1885).

Extracts from Buffalo Bill's Wild West Programs

Cody's Corral; or, the Scouts and the Sioux
By "Buckskin Sam."

A mount-inclosed valley, close sprinkled with fair flowers,
As if a shattered rainbow had fallen there in showers;
Bright-plumaged birds were warbling their songs among the trees,
Or fluttering their tiny wings in the cooling Western breeze.
The cottonwoods, by mountain's base, on every side high tower,
And the dreamy haze in silence marks the sleepy noontide hour.
East, south, and north, to meet the clouds the lofty mounts arise,
Guarding this little valley—a wild Western Paradise
Pure and untrampled as it looks, this lovely flower-strewn sod—
One scarce would think that e'er, by man, had such a sward been trod.
But yonder, see those wild mustangs by lariat held in check,
Tearing up the fairest flora, which fairies might bedeck;
And, near a camp fire's smoke, we see man standing all around—
'Tis strange, for from them has not come a single word or sound.
Standing by cottonwood, with arms folded on his breast,
Gazing with his eagle eyes up to the mountain's crest,
Tall and commanding is his form, and graceful is his mien;
As fair in face, as noble, has seldom here been seen,
A score or more of frontiersmen recline upon the ground,
But starting soon upon their feet, by sudden snort and bound!
A horse has sure been frightened by strange scent on the breeze,
And glances now by all are cast beneath the towering trees.
A quiet sign their leader gives, and mustangs now are brought;
And, by swift-circling lasso, a loose one fast is caught.
Then thundering round the mountain's dark adamantine side,
A hundred hideous, painted, and fierce Sioux warriors ride;
While, from their throats, the well-known and horrible death-knell,
The wild, blood-curdling war-whoop, and the fierce and fiendish yell
Strikes the ears of all, now ready to fight, and e'en to die,
In that mount-inclosed valley, beneath that blood-red sky!
Now rings throughout the open, on all sides clear and shrill,
The dreaded battle-cry of him whom men call Buffalo Bill!
On, like a whirlwind, then they dash—the brave scouts of the plains
Their rifles soft caressed by mustangs' flying manes!
On, like an avalanche, they sweep through the tall prairie grass;
Down, fast upon them, swooping, the dread and savage mass!
Wild yells of fierce bravado come, and taunts of deep despair;
While, through the battle-smoke, there flaunts each feathered tuft of hair.

And loudly rings the war-cry of fearless Buffalo Bill;
And loudly ring the savage yells, which make the blood ring chill!
The gurgling death-cry mingles with the mustang's shrillest scream,
And sound of dull and sodden falls, and bowie's brightest gleam.
At length there slowly rises the smoke from heaps of slain,
Whose wild war-cries will nevermore ring on the air again.
Then, panting and bespattered from the showers of foam and blood,
The scouts have once more halted 'neath the shady cottonwood.
In haste they are reloading, and preparing for a sally,
While the scattered foe, now desperate, are yelling in the valley.
Again are heard revolvers, with their rattling, sharp report;
Again the scouts are seen to charge down on that wild cohort.
Sioux fall around, like dead reeds when fiercest northers blow,
And rapid sink in death before their hated pale-face foe!
Sad, smothered now is the music from the mountain's rippling rill,
But wild hurrahs instead are heard from our brave Buffalo Bill,
Who, through the thickest carnage, charged ever in the van,
And cheered faint hearts around him, since first the fight began!
Deeply demoralized, the Sioux fly fast with bated breath,
And glances cast of terror along that vale of death;
While their victors quick dismounted, and looking all around,
On their dead and mangled enemies, whose corses strewed the ground.
"I had sworn I would avenge them"—were the words of Buffalo Bill—
"The mothers and their infants they slew at Medicine Hill.
Our work is done—done nobly—I looked for that from you;
Boys, when a cause is just, you need but to stand firm and true!"

In 1893 the Wild West had a large site between 62d and 63d Streets outside the World's Fair grounds in Chicago, and opposite the elevated railroad station and close to the Midway Plaisance funfair. With two shows a day, and a covered grandstand capable of holding eighteen thousand, Cody and Salsbury enjoyed their best season with the crowds who came to the Columbian Exposition and made perhaps a million dollars' profit in six months. After nearly a decade touring, experience had confirmed which elements were popular with the crowds, and the program had a more coherent narrative structure of struggle and contest. European horsemen added dashing uniforms and international rivalry.

Buffalo Bill's Wild West and Congress of Rough Riders of the World: Historical Sketches and Programme (Chicago: n.p., 1893), [1], 4, 9–10, 62, 23, 13.

BUFFALO BILL'S
WILD WEST

Extracts from Buffalo Bill's Wild West Programs

AND

CONGRESS OF ROUGH RIDERS OF THE WORLD

PROGRAMME

OVERTURE, "Star Spangled Banner" . . Cowboy Band, Wm. Sweeny, Leader

1—GRAND REVIEW introducing the Rough Riders of the World and Fully Equipped Regular Soldiers of the Armies of America, England, France, Germany, and Russia.

2—MISS ANNIE OAKLEY, Celebrated Shot, who will illustrate her dexterity in the use of Fire-arms.

3—HORSE RACE between a Cowboy, a Cossack, a Mexican, an Arab, and an Indian, on Spanish-Mexican, Broncho, Russian, Indian and Arabian Horses.

4—PONY EXPRESS. The Former Pony Post Rider will show how the Letters and Telegrams of the Republic were distributed across the immense Continent previous to the Railways and the Telegraph.

5—ILLUSTRATING A PRAIRIE EMIGRANT TRAIN CROSSING THE PLAINS. Attack by marauding Indians repulsed by "Buffalo Bill," with Scouts and Cowboys.

N.B.—The wagons are the same as used 35 years ago.

6—A GROUP OF SYRIAN AND ARABIAN HORSEMEN will illustrate their style of Horsemanship, with Native Sports and Pastimes.

7—COSSACKS, of the Caucasus of Russia, in Feats of Horsemanship, Native Dances, etc.

8—JOHNNY BAKER, Celebrated Young American Marksman.

9—A GROUP OF MEXICANS from Old Mexico, will illustrate the use of the Lasso, and perform various Feats of Horsemanship.

10—RACING BETWEEN PRAIRIE, SPANISH AND INDIAN GIRLS.

11—COWBOY FUN. Picking Objects from the Ground, Lassoing Wild Horses, Riding the Buckers.

12—MILITARY EVOLUTIONS by a Company of the Sixth Cavalry of the United States Army; a Company of the First Grand Uhlan Regiment of His Majesty King William II, German Emperor, popularly known as the "Potsdamer Reds"; a Company of French Chasseurs (Chasseurs a Cheval de la Garde Republique Francaise); and a Company of the 12th Lancers (Prince of Wales' Regiment) of the British Army.

13—CAPTURE OF THE DEADWOOD MAIL COACH BY THE INDIANS, which will be rescued by "Buffalo Bill" and his attendant Cowboys.

N.B.—This is the identical old Deadwood Coach, called the Mail Coach, which is famous on account of having carried the great number of people who lost their lives on the road between Deadwood and Cheyenne 18 years ago. Now the most famous vehicle extant.

14—RACING BETWEEN INDIAN BOYS ON BAREBACK HORSES.

15—LIFE CUSTOMS OF THE INDIANS. Indian settlement on the Field and "Path."

16—COL. W. F. CODY, ("Buffalo Bill"), in his Unique Feats of Sharpshooting.

17—BUFFALO HUNT, as it is in the Far West of North America—"Buffalo Bill" and Indians. The last of the only known Native Herd.

THE WILD WEST SHOW

18—THE BATTLE OF THE LITTLE BIG HORN, Showing with Historical Accuracy the scene of CUSTER'S LAST CHARGE.
19—SALUTE.
CONCLUSION.

The program's introduction drew attention to the epic struggle, with a hero to match. "Young, sturdy, a remarkable specimen of manly beauty, with the brain to conceive and the nerve to execute, Buffalo Bill *par excellence* is the exemplar of the strong and unique traits that characterize *a true American frontiersman.*"

SALUTATORY.

There is probably no field in modern American history more fascinating in the intensity of its interest than that which is presented in our rapidly-extending frontier. The pressure of the white man, the movement of the emigrant train, and the extension of our railways, together with the military power of the General Government, have, in a measure, broken down the barriers behind which the Indian fought and defied the advance of civilization; but the West, in many places, is still a scene of wildness, where the sternness of the law is upheld at the pistol point, and the white man and outlaw has become scarcely less dangerous than his red-skinned predecessor. (*This last, while perfectly true when written* (1883), *is at present* [ten years later] *inapplicable, so fast does law and order progress and pervade the Grand West*).

The story of our country, so far as it concerns lif e in the vast Rocky Mountain region and on the plains, has never been half told; and romance itself falls far short of the reality when it attempts to depict the career of the little vanguard of pioneers, trappers, and scouts, who, moving always in front, have paved the way—frequently with their own bodies—for the safe approach of the masses behind. The names of "OLD JIM BRIDGER," "KIT CARSON," "WHITE BEAVER," "WILD BILL," "CALIFORNIA JOE," "BUFFALO WHITE," "TEXAS JACK," "BUFFALO BILL," "MAJOR NORTH," and scores of others, have already become identified with what seem to be strange legends and traditions, and yet the lives and labors of these men form a part of the development of the great West. Most of them have died fighting bravely, and all of them, in their way, have been men around whose exploits contemporaneous writers in and out of the army have thrown the halo of heroism. Our most distinguished officers have repeatedly borne tribute to their usefulness and valor, and to-day the adventures of the Army Scout constitute a theme of never-ending interest. Keen of eye, sturdy in build, inured to hardship, experienced in the knowledge of Indian habits and language, familiar with the hunt, and trustworthy in the hour of extremest danger, they belong to a class that is rapidly disappearing from our country.

In the Eastern States, or even east of the Mississippi, the methods of these people are comparatively unknown, and it is for the purpose of introducing them to the public that this little pamphlet has been prepared. HON. WILLIAM F. CODY ("BUF-

260

Extracts from Buffalo Bill's Wild West Programs

FALO BILL"), in conjunction with MR. NATE SALSBURY, the eminent American actor (a ranch owner), has organized a large combination that, in its several aspects, will illustrate life as it is witnessed on the plains; the Indian encampment; the cowboys and vaqueros; the herds of buffalo and elk; the lassoing of animals; the manner of robbing mail coaches; feats of agility, marksmanship, archery, and the kindred scenes and events that are characteristic of the border. The most completely appointed delegation of frontiersmen and Indians that ever visited the East will take part in the entertainment, together with a large number of animals; and the performance, while in no wise partaking of the nature of a "circus," will be at once new, startling, and instructive.

JOHN M. BURKE,

North Platte, Neb., May 1, 1883.   *General Manager*

———

The exhibitions given by "BUFFALO BILL'S" Wild West have nothing in common with the usual professional exhibitions. Their merits are dependent on training of a natural kind.

Our aim is to make the public acquainted with the manners and customs of daily life of the dwellers in the far West of the United States, through the means of actual and realistic scenes from life. At each performance marked skill and daring are presented. Not only from the standpoint of the spectator, but also from a critical point of view, we assure the auditor that each scene presents a faithful picture of the habits of these folk, down to the smallest detail.

All the horses are descendants of those brought to America by the Spaniards, under Ferdinand Cortez. The whole material of harness, etc., is genuine, and has already been seasoned by many years' experienced use in their original wilds. We congratulate ourselves as being the first to successfully unite in an entertainment all their historic peculiarities.

After having earned the applause of the public and the flattering opinion of the press of the world, . . . we have the honor to place ourselves once more at the service of the American public, presenting in conjunction with the original Wild West features, a congress of the Rough Riders of the World. This assemblage of primitive horsemen meet for the *first time* in history—from far distant countries—differing in race, language, habits, customs, dress, as well as in skill, style and methods of horsemanship, forming the most unique congregation of equestrians since the creation.

NATE SALSBURY, *Vice-President and Manager*

. . . The nationally known Brick Pomeroy thus writes:—". . . The true Western man is free, fearless, generous and chivalrous. Of this class, Hon. Wm. F. Cody, 'Buffalo Bill,' is a bright representative. As a part of his rushing career he has brought together material for what he correctly terms a Wild West Exhibition. I should call it a Wild West Reality. The idea is not merely to take in money from those who witness a very lively exhibition, but to give people in the East a correct representation of life on the plains,

261

and the incidental life of the hardy, brave, intelligent pioneers, who are the first to blaze the way to the future homes and greatness of America. He knows the worth and sturdiness of true Western character, and as a lover of his country, wishes to present as many facts as possible to the public, so that those who will, can see actual pictures of life in the West, brought to the East for the inspection and education of the public.

" 'Buffalo Bill' has brought the Wild West to the doors of the East. There is more of real life, of genuine interest, of positive education in this startling exhibition, than I have ever before seen, and it is true to nature and life as it really is with those who are smoothing the way for millions to follow. All of this imaginary Romeo and Juliet business sinks to utter insignificance in comparison to the drama of existence as is here enacted, and all the operas in the world appear like pretty playthings for emasculated children by the side of the setting of reality, and the muse of the frontier as so faithfully and extensively presented, and so cleverly managed by this incomparable representative of Western pluck, coolness, bravery, independence, and generosity.
. . .

He deserves well for his efforts to please and to instruct in matters important to America, and incidents that are passing *never more to return.*" . . .

[I]t cannot be denied that an added chapter to Indian history, and the Wild West's peculiar province of truthfully exhibiting the same, is rendered more valuable to the student of primitive man, and to the ethnologists' acquaintance with the strange people whose grand and once happy empire (plethoric in all its inhabitants needed) has been (rightfully or wrongfully) brought thoroughly and efficiently under the control of our civilization, or (possibly more candidly confessed) under the Anglo-Saxon's commercial necessities. . . . [O]ur boasted civilization has a wonderful adaptability to the good soils, the productive portions and the rich mineral lands of the earth. . . .

A sentimental view is thus inspired, when long personal association has brought the better qualities of the Indian to one's notice, assisting somewhat to dispel the prejudices engendered by years of savage brutal wars (conducted with a ferocious vindictiveness foreign to our methods). The savageness of Indian warfare, born in the victim, and probably intensified by the instinctive knowledge of a despairing weakness that renders desperate the fiery spirit of expiring resistance, which latter (in another cause) might be held up for courage and tenacity. . . .

But then again the practical view of the non-industrious use of nature's cornucopia of world-needed resources and the inevitable law of *the survival of the fittest*, must "bring the flattering unction to the soul" of those—to whom the music of light, work, and progress, is the charm, the *gauge* of existence's worth, and to which the listless must hearken, the indolent attend, the weak imbibe strength from—whose ranks the red man must join, and advancing with whose steps march cheerily to the tune of honest toil, industrious peace, and placid fireside prosperity.

The program's sixty-four pages carried lengthy endorsements of the show's authenticity, biographies of its stars, and a narrative of its success in Europe.

Extracts from Buffalo Bill's Wild West Programs

Among the background stories of frontier "history almost passed away," were tributes to the weapons of struggle on the frontier with which savage met civilized.

The Rifle as an Aid to Civilization

There is a trite saying that "the pen is mightier than the sword." It is an equally true one that the bullet is the pioneer of civilization, for it has gone hand in hand with the axe that cleared the forest, and with the family bible and school book. Deadly as has been its mission in one sense, it has been merciful in another; for without the rifle ball we of America would not be to-day in the possession of a free and united country, and mighty in our strength.

And so has it been in the history of all people, from the time when David slew Goliath, down through the long line of ages, until, in modern times, science has substituted for the stone from David's sling the terrible missiles that now decide the fate of nations. It is not, therefore, so harsh an expression as it seems to be at first sight, that it is indeed the bullet which has been the forerunner of growth and development.

It is in the far West of America, however, and along our frontier, that the rifle has found its greatest use and become a part of the person and the household of the venturesome settler, the guide, the scout, and the soldier; for nowhere else in Christendom is it so much and so frequently a necessity for the preservation of life and the defence of home and property. It is here, too, among the hunters on the plains and in the Rocky Mountains, that one sees the perfection of that skill in marksmanship that has become the wonder of those who are not accustomed to the daily use of weapons. Yet if it were not possessed—if there were not the quick eye, the sure aim, coolness in the moment of extreme danger, whether threatened by man or beast—life in that section would be of little value, and a man's home anything but a safe abiding place.

There are exceptional cases of men like Buffalo Bill, Dr. Carver, and others, whose names are more or less familiar among the mighty hunters of the West, who excel in the use of rifle and pistol, and to which, time and time again, they and those around them have owed their lives. And they are the worthy successors of a long line of marksmen, whose names are also "familiar as household words." Who does not recall David Crockett and his death-dealing rifle in the Alamo? Daniel Boone, of Kentucky, and the heroic exploits that have been written concerning them in the early pages of our country's history?

It is to the end that the people of the East, or rather those who are not acquainted with the rough life of the border, and especially that portion of it in which the rifle plays so important a part, may personally witness some of the feats of Western men, that Messrs. Cody & Carver have determined to introduce in their "great realistic pictures of Western life" a series of shooting exhibitions, in which they will both have the assistance of the celebrated pigeon shot, Capt. Bogardus. The manner in which buffalo are hunted, the exciting chase at close quarters, the splendidly trained horses who participate in the chase, the hunt for elk, the stealthy devices of Indians in capturing the fleet-footed animals—all these will be illustrated in a manner that never have been witnessed east of the Mississippi River. . . .

The Bow and Arrow

The bow is the natural weapon of the wild tribes of the West. Previous to the introduction of firearms it was the weapon supreme of every savage's outfit—in fact his principal dependence, backed by personal skill in its use for sustenance for himself and his pappooses. It still retains its favor, as it is not always safe to rely on the white man's mechanism, as in case of lack of ammunition or deranged lock or trigger, time and location prevent its being "mended." As a weapon of economy it is also to be commended, as the hunting arrow is made so that the rear shoulders of the long tapering blade slope backward, thus facilitating its withdrawal from the wounded game. On the other hand, in the war arrow, the rear shoulders slope forward, forming barbs, as it is intended to remain and eventually kill. The possession, therefore, of firearms has not affected the Indian's love of this reliable weapon of the chase, which being his first childish plaything is still, no matter how well armed or rich he may be, an indispensable possession. At short distances it is a terribly effective arm, and the Indian expert can seize five to ten arrows in his left hand and dispatch them with such rapidity that the last will be on its flight before the first touches the ground. In close quarters they prefer to rely on it to depending on the rifle, as it can be of deadly force at thirty to forty yards, and creating a bad wound at much greater distance. In buffalo hunting, where the horseman can approach near, it is invaluable and economic, and is often buried to the feathers. "Two Lance," an Indian chief, during the Grand Duke's hunt, sent an arrow clear through a bison, Alexis retaining the light-winged messenger of death as a souvenir of his hunt on the American Plains.

Exhibiting Indians

Hundreds of medicine-show "Indians," accompanied by a few white "Indian fighters," visited small towns in the late nineteenth century, dispensing cure-alls flavored with free entertainment. The troupes most imitated were the "encampments" of the Kickapoo Indian Medicine Company, founded by John Healy and Charles Bigelow in 1881. In the open air, in tents, or in town halls, warriors from the Kickapoo wigwams danced with blood-curdling cries and then, guided by the lecturer, explained in broken English the life-enhancing qualities of their Sagwa, the restorative which gave the savages such remarkable health. In towns far too small ever to host the huge Buffalo Bill extravaganza, the tent shows mixed vaudeville sketches with romance. Many of the Indians were genuine, if never Kickapoo. The mock Wild West posters and program offered trick-shooting by the Cody-lookalikes, Nevada

Ned Oliver or Texas Charlie, and insight into Indian "ways, customs and habits" by a dozen exotic purveyors of patent medicine. Carl Sandburg recalled the summer visits to Galesburg, Illinois, of the Kickapoo "stomping and howling their lonesome war songs," and remembered the slick barkers touting the various concoctions which dressed piles or developed the squaw's chest. And all for free, or only fifty cents or a dollar for Sagwa or salve or worm killer.

Life and Scenes among the Kickapoo Indians; their manners, habits and customs. Containing a Graphic Description of Texas Charlie's adventures in the Wild West among the Indians, and the discovery of the wondrous Kickapoo Medicine Men, together with their remedies and the marvellous cures effected by them (New Haven: Healy and Bigelow, n.d. [1890s]), 94.

In order to Portray to the Civilized World Genuine scenes in Indian Life, Messrs. Healy & Bigelow, the Eastern Agents of the Kickapoo Indians, have, at an enormous outlay, perfected arrangements whereby they will be enabled to make
A GRAND TOUR OF THE UNITED STATES,
VISITING THE PRINCIPAL CITIES AND TOWNS,
Bringing with them their Squaws, Medicine Men
AND PAPPOOSES,
Encamping out in the Summer Time in their Wigwams and Tents,
As they do on the Plains,
And in the Winter time in Public Halls.
BY THIS UNIQUE PLAN
Genuine Indian Life and Scenes
WILL BE
BROUGHT TO YOUR OWN DOOR
By these Children of the Forest.
In order to more fully illustrate life on the Plains, they will give
FREE EXHIBITIONS
During their visit, introducing the
Scalp, Buffalo and War Dances,
Together with other wonderful and curious features of the aborigines of the Far West.

Buffalo Bill's Wild West spent the 1894 season in greater New York. For five cents, patrons could travel from Manhattan's Battery to the 39th Street ferry in South Brooklyn and pay fifty cents for general admission to the Ambrose Park grounds. However, in the summer, when the journalist Julian Ralph and the artist Frederick Remington visited the Indian encampment outside the show arena, times were difficult. The covered grandstand held 20,000, but was rarely full for the two performances a day at 3:00 and 8:15.

The 1894 Wild West poster gave precise directions to Ambrose Park in Brooklyn. Buffalo Bill Historical Center, Cody, Wyoming.

Even before Nate Salsbury fell ill, the show failed to meet its daily expenses of $4,000, and losses mounted. John Burke, the Wild West's shrewd publicist, played a key role in briefing journalists and encouraging favorable reports. Julian Ralph had spent two years traveling in the Far West reporting for *Harper's*, and in both books he published in 1893—*Our Great West* and *Chicago and the World's Fair*—he showed particular interest in the "primitive" family in its "native habitation."

Julian Ralph, "Behind The 'Wild West' Scenes," *Harper's Weekly* 38 (August 18, 1894): 775–76.

Buffalo Bill's camp in Brooklyn contains thirty acres fenced in. . . . [The interpreter] Changro took us to the tepees of the Indians, already colored richly at their tops like meerchaum pipes, as tepees do, and we saw the Indians at rest hours before the afternoon performance. They may not be Arapahoes and Crows and Shoshones and Blackfeet, and all the rest that the orator in the amphitheatre says they are. I suspect such a mixture would result in continuous bloodshed that would marvellously increase the death rate in Brooklyn. But if they are mainly Sioux, they have the conspicuous merit that belongs to all parts of this show—that of being genuine. They are genuine Indians, and some are so very genuine that the Indian agents were glad to get rid of them as being the malcontents of their bands. It is a queer reflection upon our management of the red men that for one simple reason "bad Injuns" should be willing to leave their homes—the last thing the natural Indian wants to do—and showmen should be glad to take them. That simple reason is that with three good meals a day a bad Indian becomes a good one.

We saw the Indians take one of their square meals. It was served in a building open at one side, like a carriage-shed, and set with long tables between benches. The bucks stalked in with lengthy, noiseless strides—the head men wearing a feather, or more elaborate hair-dresses, and the plain warriors showing only the wrinkled faces and black tresses that render them so like women that one must sometimes look at the foot-coverings to determine an Indian's sex. The fat squaws rolled along, and the pappooses came as children of any sort would, rolling their plump faces around, and even walking backward so as to see something in the background without losing a minute of dinner-time. I saw two of the pappooses—little boys—after dinner, squatted on their heels and smoking cigarettes, with their faces painted and streaked with the artistic taste of a Chinese devil. A boy in a Spanish suit of yellow silk and black velvet was talking to them, and they were grunting back to him just as a pig does when he is eye-deep in mud and you scratch his back to make him still more happy.

At dinner the Indians edged along on the benches and turned up their granite-ware cups to have them filled with coffee by a white youth who looked quite as tough as they did—precisely the sort of youth whom I heard say to an Englishman in a hotel in Calgary, Canada: "Yer don't like the coffee, eh? Well, that's what yer git, just the same." With that mixture of pride and dignity which is a rich portion of the plains Indian, the bucks at the end of the table crooked their elbows under their blankets and pushed them over the table so that I should not watch them as they ate. Then they looked like potato-sacks feeding themselves with spoons that went in and out of the pucker-holes at the top, and as that was not interesting, I withdrew. I saw them all, later on, assembled for a dance, and never, even in Indian camps out West, have I seen a more gaudy, brilliant, and bewildering spectacle than they then presented. For clothing they wore only breech-clouts and moccasins, but for ornaments they had full suits of yellow and blue and green paint, and many pounds of feathers, fur tails, elk teeth, pocket-mirrors, buckskin fringe, bone breastplates, beribboned lances, fringed and feathered *coup* sticks, bits of beadwork, bear claws, and all the rest that makes a soulless idiot liken the Indians to rag-bags, but which appeals to a sense of the romantic and the picturesque as no other costume in the world begins to do. We hired one of the shapeliest of the bucks to pose for Mr. Remington. We started to walk with him to the stables, but without effort he strode ahead, leaving us as if we were tied to the ground.

"He's walking like an Indian," said I.

"He walk lazy," said Changro.

The buck went to where the 450 ponies and horses are kept, and taking a halter with him, put it over the nose of a pony and led the beast into the open, where he mounted him. Leading the pony was like leading a fraction of an exploding boiler, and mounting him was like straddling a loose barrel on a ship's deck in a storm. The buck had on all his toggery, and after that was sketched he was bidden to undress and be pictured in his skin. This buck was as modest as all the plains Indians with whom I have dealt. He looked around for a place to undress in, apart from us, and found no other than a theatrical cabin made on the plan of a bird-cage. In a corner of this, in plain sight, he squatted to remove his upper coverings. Then he stood up to take off his "chaps" or trousers. When he came out he still kept his blanket around him. When told to take that off, he mounted his pony and coiled the blanket around his waist. At a second bidding he threw that off, and then he was seen to be all-sufficiently clothed— from the Indian stand-point—for he wore his breech-clout, and he was painted like a tropical bird. On the plains, or in the Brooklyn amphitheatre, along with his fellows, a public appearance in the light and airy attire of a "living picture" would seem perfectly proper. But to undress before two fully clothed white men in a retired corner hurt either the buck's pride or his modesty—call it which we will.

The inside of a tepee would interest the average visitor to the show, but visitors can with no more reason expect to see the quarters of the braves than they may ask to be shown the dressing-rooms of actors and actresses in a theatre. To see Colonel Cody's tent and then to visit a tepee twenty-five feet away is to be able to compare the quarters of a modern general with the refuge of a Celtic outlaw in the seventeenth century. By just so much have we advanced; by just so much has the Indian stood still. In Buffalo Bill's tent—the size of a small farm-house—we see the space divided into rooms. We see a telephone, curtains, bric-à-brac, carpets, pictures, desks, lounges, easy-chairs, an ornate buffet, a refridgerator, and all the furnishings of a cozy home. In the best tepee we see a circular board floor (it should be of dirt) within a ring of canvas. On a sheet of metal are the smouldering embers of the fire that makes a tepee at once a home and a chimney. Forever seated with their backs to the canvas and their feet to the fire are the Indians, the leader exactly opposite the door flap and the women close beside it, enjoying Indian "women's rights," which are the rights to do everything that a man refuses to do. Rolled up and stuffed around the edges of the tent, in bundles, are the belongings of the family. Like Caesar's ashes, they "serve to keep the wind away." A young brave is painting his bare legs bright yellow with factory-made water-color. A little boy is admiring his painted face in a broken bit of mirror. The adults are sitting, stolidly as if they were stunned, around the circle, and a tender baby propped up against the tent-side is looking even more grave than its parents, reflecting, per-haps, that it wants to cry, but that Indian babies commit the unpardonable sin when they do that, and that they get cuffed and grunted at, which is worse. If any of the Indian men understand any English it is very little, and it has got in their heads pre-cisely as water gets on a cat's feet—against their will. The squaws understand more— for a reason that is not creditable to them. Sometimes a squaw will be seen to grin behind her hand when a white man says something funny or flattering.

Out-of-doors at two or half past two o'clock, just before the first public perfor-mance, the space behind the amphitheatre is worth visiting. Scarcely could there have been such another human hodgepodge in an amphitheatre in ancient Rome. Standing about in groups, or playing for fun the very games and exercises they are hired to show in public, are many sorts of men who are all as nearly like centaurs as men can be. Some are soldiers of France and Russia, Africa and Germany, glittering, gaudy, trim, or, if from Africa, moving about with garments that blow out like balloons as they move in the wind. The Cossacks have the waists of fashionable women, and their long gabardines, each breasted with a row of tiny ivory powder-horns, reach to the middle of dainty, glossy boots. The gauchos of Argentina simply tie up their feet in rudely-dressed cow-skin that leaves their toes bare, and from their loins to their ankles are thin cloths wound about so as to make their very Oriental-looking trousers. The armorer of the show, an English boy who has been an American soldier, shoots eternally at whatever any one will throw up in the air before him. The gauchos just as eternally practise with the bola. Make a pawnbroker's three-ball emblem out of three stones and three lengths of limber rawhide, and you have a bola. All over the grounds they sling this queer implement at posts and poles, scurrying it over the dirt in the hope that it will tangle itself around what they aim at, as it is meant to tangle itself around a cow's legs.

The cowboys, first to mount their ponies, fall to roping one another, until the champion Mexican roper comes along to play with his lariat. Then they admit with unexpected frankness that what he does "can't be beat; it's out of sight." And truly it is. The Mexican—a handsome, finely built fellow, worth all the rest of his band in appearance—can make silent music, or poetry, with his rope. He sends its broad loop curving and circling and lilting round and round, above him, below him, under his feet, and out again over his head, with a motion that is graceful and easy and beautiful beyond the power of words to describe. And whenever he wants to do so, by a mere twist of his wrist he reverses its relation to his hand, and throws it unerringly over and around whatever he wishes to tether with it. When he plays, the cowboys—who are past masters of roping—simply line up their horses and look on, just as the public stares at the same thing a little later in the day. Sergeant Major-r-r Mur-r-r-dock, commanding the Irish Lancers, sits his horse and also looks on like a statue, until he speaks, when he becomes a hero right out of Kipling's army stories. "Me men all detest me," he says; "but, begorra, they fear me!" That is a little joke of his, indicative of his strict discipline, which is so terrible that he will not even allow himself a drink of rum until he gets back to Ireland.

When three o'clock draws near, the horse-mounting becomes general, and all over the space behind the scenes are spirited horses resisting the endeavors of Arabs, Indians, soldiers, gauchos, cowboys, and greasers who want to mount them. That is, indeed, a scene for a military painter. Suddenly the band plays in the amphitheatre, and Buffalo Bill takes his place behind a peep-hole in the back scene, mounted on a little covered platform. The dozen troops of rough riders form in parade or squadron formation, awaiting his orders. As the orator in the ring announces each band, Buffalo Bill gives the corresponding order, and each restless company springs as if from the ground into the air, and flies ahead of a cloud of dust into the view of the multitude on the benches.

The Indians attracted much more attention from the press than the cowboys. In 1898 a *Harper's* reporter made another visit to the Indian "encampment," this time to the quarters within New York's premier indoor arena.

Ernest L. Blumenschein, "Behind the Scenes at a 'Wild West' Show," *Harper's Weekly* 42 (April 22, 1898): 422.

Bedouins are whirling and "tumbling," through the sawdust and the sunshine; scene-painters retouching the marvellous blue mountains of the great long curtain; Indians trailing fractious ponies; and Mexicans, blanket on arm, Cossacks, Cubans, and cowboys lazily whiling away the early morning hours in the great arena at the Madison Square Garden. The employees take and scrape the dirt or scatter fresh sawdust, and a group of spectators watch the agile Arabs as they mass on one man's shoulders, or twirl their supple bodies through the air from one end of the ring to the other. Mounting the narrow stairway back of the old stage-coach brings one to quarters one would never imagine existed behind so elegant an exterior. Every square inch of space from floor to ceiling is filled with a chaos of costumes from all ends of the earth. In one corner, surrounded by elegant leather saddles, great heavy hats, velvet jackets trimmed with gold lace, tight-fitting breeches, spurs, harness, pistols, belts, etc., a few lazy Mexicans are visible.

Cowboys, soldiers, and employees are crowded in a large room, many asleep on their cots, and one English chap, propped up with saddles and blankets, trying to recover from a broken leg. Eight or ten Cossacks are partitioned off in a boxlike corner, where they pass most of the day singing their national hymns.

Indians performing dance at Ambrose Park, Brooklyn, 1894. Denver Public Library.

Exhibiting Indians

On the stairway, by the window, and occasionally gathering his thoughts by gazing abstractedly into the busy New York street, is a handsome young Indian writing a letter. Looking over his shoulder, I get a glimpse of interest—"New York, Madson Squir Gordin: Ui' nad' nishu' tawa bi' tan' wu—" (which means, "I am flying about the earth") etc.

In writing he uses the English characters. He has evidently finished, for, while chewing the point of his pencil, he gives his letter a final looking over, puts it into the addressed envelope, and turning to me, licks his finger and points to the corner. I have a stamp, which I donate, with an offer to mail the letter. He looks me over carefully, and gradually lets the letter slip from his hand into mine. A glance at the address explains the caution, for it is addressed to "Miss Alice Lone Bear, Pine Ridge Agency, Kyle P.O., So. Dakota."

Past the romantic red man, up another flight, and I enter a large room with low ceiling, in which one sees only the thousands of vari-colored feathers attached to war-bonnets, shields, belts, and dresses. An Indian jumps to his feet, and shouting out, causes about twenty strapping young fellows to leap from their blankets under the eaves of the roof and surround me, clamoring and jostling. It is rather a surprising greeting, and I feel my small stature as several ugly-looking bucks push me around. Knowing something of the Indian nature (which strongly resembles the schoolboy's), I shove a big fellow away and back into the rest.

"What's the matter with you, boys?" I ask.

"One dollar! One dollar!" is about the only English word in the answer, and repeated with vigor.

I laugh at them, take off my overcoat, open my sketch-book, and look around for a subject. I am soon at work on old Flat Iron, who, propped up in a chair, tries to keep his small eyes open. The young men leave me, to return to their card games, or doze away in their blankets on the floor. A few old men in the room are arranging feathers for a new bonnet, or stringing beads and lead for skirts; the fat and industrious squaws are beading moccasins, or braiding the little girls' hair (which is kept scrupulously clean and neat), while away in one corner an accomplished black-haired youth performs "Daisy Bell" on a mouth-organ. Occasionally the young fellows break into an Indian song . . . which is echoed from the floor below by a Russian hymn from the Cossacks. The Indians seem very contented; repartee passes from one side of the room to the other, and a point well made unfailingly brings a laugh.

The card game grows very exciting, attracting to the six squatting figures quite an audience of interested onlookers, who often add to the intenseness by throwing their recent pay into the circle to bet on a "draw." The Indian plays cards with great fervor, drawing the edge of the second card slowly over his first, to get the full benefit of the excitement should fortune fall his way and he have a "suit." If he has high cards, how he does bet! and the lookers on behind him bet. Then with quick breath he takes his next card. An ace of his "suit." Whoop! Hi-y!! those behind him joining in the yelling, to the discomfiture of the apparently stolid losers. And Black Heart goes to stock himself with tobacco for the week.

Twelve-thirty, and all start down for dinner. Old Flat Iron, whom I have been sketching, makes known to me in the sign language that I must bring him some tobacco for his trouble, fumbles around in his buckskin pouch for his dinner check, and dextrously sweeping his dirty blanket around half of him, ambles down the stairs to his place at the long table.

All connected with the show eat in the great room on the ground-floor. Here, in their working-clothes, or in the picturesque attire of their homes (for Cossack, Mexican, Bedouin, and Indian refuse civilized costume), they give the rather commonplace impression of a laboring-class satisfied to work hard for their daily bread.

Dinner over, preparation for the afternoon performance begins at once, and the scenes in the narrow dressing-rooms are animated. With pigments, a good Indian type is made hideous in a short interval, and but for the many deep furrows time has ploughed in the forehead of Flat Iron, one could never tell his yellow-streaked face from that of his son Leaping Antelope. Bodies and limbs are painted half white, half green, or with circles (representing the sun) and crescents and stars, and one Indian leaves the imprint of a vermilion-smeared hand on his cheek. The feathers come off the wall; the many sleigh-bells jingle and tinkle; the boys break into song; the squaws "ti-ti" in their high shrill voices; even the dignified old chiefs are gay, arrayed in all their glory. A blast from a bugle starts them off to saddle their ponies, on which they are soon mounted, ready for the grand entry. The cowboy band starts up "Hail, Columbia," the bugle sounds again, the great canvas curtain is drawn, and the howling warriors dash wildly into the public gaze.

The curtain is redrawn—the curtain with the distant blue mountains, the blue pine-trees, and the blue tepees. Before, it is the romance and pleasure; behind, the reality and labor. Both sides are interesting.

Luther Standing Bear acted as interpreter for seventy-five Sioux during the Wild West tour of England in 1898–99. At the age of eleven, he had been taken away from the tribe and boarded for four years at the Carlisle Indian School in Pennsylvania. After a short spell in Wanamaker's department store in Philadelphia, he returned as a school teacher and then operated a post office and general store on reservations in South Dakota for more than ten years during the Ghost Dance troubles. In 1898 he traveled to nearby Rushville, Nebraska, where William McCune hired Indians for the Buffalo Bill show. He sold them costumes suitable for the performance and signed on as interpreter. As an acculturated son of a chief, Standing Bear was presumed to have natural authority over the Sioux. He was responsible for enforcing the strict measures to guard against alcohol abuse; he operated a ticket-check system to limit their free movements outside the hotel or camp and withheld half their wages until the end of the tour. After a career as a stage Indian in the shows and early movies punctuated by more mundane storekeeping, he reflected in his autobiography on his first season with the Wild West in England, nearly thirty years before. Buffalo Bill had been less prejudiced than the cowboys, and very aware that in Europe, the Indians were key attraction on stage and off.

Luther Standing Bear, *My People, the Sioux*, ed. E. A. Brininstool (London: Williams and Norgate, 1928), 252, 254, 260–61, 263, 265–66.

[In London's Olympia Theatre arena] we found our horses—black, white, bay, and buckskin-colored animals . While all the Indians belonged to the Sioux tribe, we were supposed to represent four different tribes, each tribe to ride animals of one color. . . .

Buffalo Bill was well pleased to note how well the Indians minded me in all our work. I was wearing a very fine outfit, and the damp weather of London was not doing it any good. So after we had given a few shows, Johnny Baker came to me one day and said it would be a good plan if I did not wear my best clothes on the days when the attendance was not large, but that on such days I might take the part of a cowboy if I chose. This was a change for me and I enjoyed it very much. . . .

Breakfast would shortly be ready. Our appetites were sharpened by the work we had been doing. In the dining-room was one long table for the Indians, with other tables for the various other nationalities represented in the show. We always had plenty to eat, so there was no complaint in that direction.

One morning as I came into the dining-tent I noticed that everybody but the Indians had been served with hot cakes. This did not bother me very much, as Indians do not eat such food. At dinner-time that same day, when I sat down to our table, I saw to my surprise that there were pancakes before us. These were the "left-overs" from the morning, and now the cook wanted to feed them to us. Although I was very angry, I made no remark, but quietly left the table and went over where Buffalo Bill and the head officials of the show were eating dinner.

Colonel Cody asked, "What is it, Standing Bear?" "Colonel Cody," I replied, "this morning all the other races represented in the show were served with pancakes, but the Indians were not given any. We do not object to that, as we do not care for them; but now the cook has put his old cold pancakes on our table and expects us to eat what was left over from breakfast, and it isn't right." "Buffalo Bill's eyes snapped," as he arose from the table. "Come with me, Standing Bear," he exclaimed. We went direct to the manager of the dining-room, and Colonel Cody said to him, "Look here, sir, you are trying to feed my Indians the left-over pancakes from the morning meal. I want you to understand, sir, that I will not stand for such treatment. My Indians are the principal feature of this show, and they are the one people I will not allow to be misused or neglected. Hereafter see to it that they get just exactly what they want at meal-time. Do you understand me, sir?"

"Yes, sir, oh, yes, sir," exclaimed the embarrassed manager. After that we had no more trouble about our meals. . . .

There were a great many cowboys with the show. There was a chief of the cowboys who had general supervision over both horses and men. When an unbroken horse would be brought in, this cowboy chief would give it to an Indian to ride bareback. After the animal was well broken, it would be taken away from the Indian and given to a cowboy to ride. Then the Indian would be given another unbroken horse. For quite a while we said nothing about it, but finally it began to be just a little too much to stand. One day one of the Indians came to me just before it was time to enter the arena. His horse was saddled and bridled but he was leading the animal by the bridle. I asked him what was the matter, and he said it was a wild horse and he was not going to ride it into the arena.

I went to the chief cowboy and said, "I do not think you are doing right. You know our Indian boys have to ride bareback, but you always give them the wild horses to ride. Then, when they have the horse nicely broken, you give it to a cowboy. Why don't you give the wild horses to the cowboys to break in? They ride on saddles, and it would not be so hard for them."

But the chief cowboy said, "Well, I can't be bothered by a little thing like that. You will have to see Buffalo Bill about the horses."

But I retorted, "You know very well that Buffalo Bill does not know what you do with the horses. He does not know that you give the wild ones to the Indian boys to ride until they are broken in. Give that horse back to that Indian boy or he will not go into the arena today."

That was all—but the boy got his horse in time to enter the arena with the others. Just as I was ready to go back to the Indians, I looked at Buffalo Bill. and he had a twinkle in his eye. After that, we had no more trouble with the horses. Although Buffalo Bill never said anything to me, I knew he had fixed things to our satisfaction. . . .

While we were showing in Birmingham, a little daughter was born to us. The morning papers discussed the event in big headlines that the first full-blooded Indian baby had been born at the Buffalo Bill show grounds. Colonel Cody was to be its godfather and the baby was to be named after the reigning Queen of England. The child's full name was to be Alexandra Birmingham Cody Standing Bear.

The next morning Colonel Cody came to me and asked if baby could be placed in the side-show. He said the English people would like to see the face of a newly born Indian baby lying in an Indian cradle or "hoksicala postan." I gave my consent, and the afternoon papers stated that the baby and mother could be seen the following afternoon.

Long before it was time for the show to begin, people were lining up in the road. My wife sat on a raised platform, the little one in the cradle before her. The people filed past, many of them dropping money in a box for her. Nearly every one had some sort of little gift for her also. It was a great drawing card for the show; the work was very light for my wife, and as for the baby, before she was twenty-four hours old she was making more money than my wife and I together.

With the coming of the new baby came added cares, of course. Our little boy, who was named after me (Luther), had to be rigged up for the part he took in the show. He had a full costume of buckskin, very much like the one I wore, and every day his face must be painted and his hair braided for the two performances. The Indian boys seemed to think it was a pleasure to get the little chap ready for the exhibition. After he was "all fixed up," he would stand outside the tipi, and the English-speaking people would crowd around to shake his hand and give him money. This he would put in a little pocket in his buck-skin jacket, and when it was full he would refuse to accept any more, although the crowd would try to force it on him. Then he would leave, in apparent disgust, and come inside the tipi. He kept us all laughing.

As Commissioner of Indian Affairs, Thomas Jefferson Morgan objected strongly to the participation of Indians in Wild West shows. John H. Oberly, his predecessor, had also complained that traveling with the shows and immoral showmen "is not only most demoralizing to the present and future welfare of the Indian, but it creates a roaming and unsettled disposition." "The show business," the reformist Indian Rights Association stated in 1899, "teaches the Indian that what the white man really wants of him is amusement furnished by exhibitions of picturesque barbarism; not the acquisition of those sober, unpicturesque but absolutely necessary qualities which alone can make him equal to the battle of life."[5] Morgan's annual report to secretary of the Interior John W. Noble articulated his deep concerns. In practice, to prevent an Indian from exercising his right to leave the reservation if he chose was difficult to enforce, but the Bureau and reformers complained that the shows hampered the policy of individual landholding and assimilation that the Dawes Severalty Act of 1887 had begun.

Report of September 5, 1890, in *House Executive Document*, no.1, pt. 5, vol. 2, 51 Congress, 2d session, serial 2841, lvii–lix, in *Americanizing the American Indians: Writings by "Friends of the Indian," 1880–1900*, ed. Francis Paul Prucha (Cambridge: Harvard University Press, 1973), 309–12.

The practice which has prevailed for many years of occasionally permitting Indians to travel with "Wild West" and similar shows throughout the country and abroad, for the purpose of giving exhibitions of frontier life and savage customs, has been very harmful in its results. I have from the beginning steadily refused to sanction any permits, and I heartily welcome your letter dated August 4, 1890, directing that no more be granted.

In all cases where these engagements have been authorized their employers have been required to enter into written contracts with the Indians, obligating themselves to pay them fair, stipulated salaries for their services, to supply them with proper food and raiment, to meet their traveling and needful incidental expenses, including medical attendance, etc. to protect them from immoral influences and surroundings, and to employ a white man of good character to look after their welfare, etc. They have also been required to execute bonds with good and sufficient securities, payable to the Secretary of the Interior, conditioned upon the faithful fulfillment of their contracts.

While these contracts have been complied with in some instances, in others wellgrounded complaints have been made of the abandonment of the Indians and the failure of their employers to pay them their salaries. These complaints will be investigated and steps will be taken to recover the amounts due by instituting suit on the bonds given by the employers.

November 1, 1889, I addressed a circular letter to the agents of agencies from which the Indians have been taken for exhibition purposes, calling for the fullest information upon the subject, with a view to suggesting such modifications in the policy of the Department as the facts might warrant. The replies of the agents fully confirmed my previous impressions that the practice is a most pernicious one, fraught with dangerous results, economically, physically, and morally. It is not only injurious to the Indians who engage in the business, but also to those who remain at home, who, from their peculiar status and isolation, are influenced in a large degree by those who have been absent on such enterprises.

The policy of granting permission for Indians to engage in shows of this character has doubtless rested upon the idea that in addition to readily earning money, they would, by extensive travel through the States, and possibly in Europe, become familiar with the manners and customs of civilized life. But travel is not necessarily elevating or profitable. While they may earn a little money and see something of civilized life, their employment is, from the very nature of the case, temporary, and they are frequently brought into association with some of the worst elements of society. Their representations of feats of savage daring, showing border life as it formerly existed, vividly depicting scenes of rapine, murder, and robbery, for which they are enthusiastically applauded, is demoralizing in an extreme degree. They become self-important and strongly imbued with the idea that the deeds of blood, etc., which they portray in their most realistic aspects, are especially pleasing to the white people, whom they have been taught to regard as examples of civilization.

Their surroundings in these tours are generally of the worst, and they pick up most degrading vices. Instead of being favorably impressed with the religion of the white man, it is more than likely that they come to distrust it through what they unavoidably see, hear, and experience. Traveling about the country on these expeditions fosters the roving spirit already so common among them, encourages idleness and a distaste for steady occupation, and during their absence their families often suffer for want of their care and assistance. They frequently return home bankrupt in purse, wrecked morally and physically, and, in such cases, their influence and example among the other Indians is the worst possible.

The influence of these shows is antagonistic to that of the schools. The schools elevate, the shows degrade. The schools teach industry and thrift, the shows encourage idleness and waste. The schools inculcate morality, the shows lead almost inevitably to vice. The schools encourage Indians to abandon their paint, blankets, feathers, and savage customs, while the retention and exhibition of these is the chief attraction of the shows. Owing to the steady growth of public opinion with reference to the possibility of civilizing the Indians through the education of their children, Congress appropriated this year nearly $2,000,000 for Indian education. The popular impression of the Indians obtained from Wild West Show exhibits is that they are incapable of civilization, and this impression works directly and powerfully against the Government in its benevolent work.

I have endeavored through the various agents to impress upon the minds of the Indians the evil resulting from connecting themselves with such shows and the importance of their remaining at home and devoting their time and energies to building houses, establishing permanent homes, cultivating farms, and acquiring thrifty, industrious habits, thus placing themselves in fit position for absorption into our political and civil life.

Chauncey Yellow Robe, a Sioux Indian from Rapid City, South Dakota, spoke before the Fourth Annual Convention of the Society of American Indians in October 1914. The society was a pan-Indian association founded in 1911, and led by acculturated mixed-bloods, often Sioux. His main complaint was the "evil and degrading influence of commercializing the Indian," and the U.S. government's abdication of responsibility.

Chauncey Yellow Robe, "The Menace of the Wild West Show," *Quarterly Journal of the Society of American Indians* 2 (July–September 1914): 224–25.

It is now more than four centuries ago since Columbus came to our shores and claimed the country and gave us the name of Indians, and at the same time inaugurated the first Indian show by importing some of the Indians across the water for exhibition before the Spanish throne, and to-day the practice continues to exist in the wild-west shows.

Some time ago, Judge Sells, the United States Commissioner of Indian Affairs, said, "Let us save the American Indian from the curse of whiskey." I believe these words hold the key to the Indian problem to-day, but how can we save the American Indian if the Indian Bureau is permitting special privileges in favor of the wild-west shows, moving-picture concerns, and fair associations for commercializing the Indian? This is the greatest hindrance, injustice, and detriment to the present progress of the American Indians toward civilization. The Indian should be protected from the curse of the wild-west show schemes, wherein the Indians have been led to the white man's poison cup and have become drunkards.

In some of the celebrations, conventions, and county fairs in Rapid City and other reservation border towns, in order to make the attraction a success, they think they cannot do without wild-west shows, consequently certain citizens have the Indian show craze. In fact, South Dakota State Fairs have largely consisted of these shows. We can see from this state of affairs that the white man is persistently perpetuating the tribal habits and customs. We see that the showman is manufacturing the Indian plays intended to amuse and instruct young children, and is teaching them that the Indian is only a savage being. We hear now and then of a boy or girl who is hurt or killed by playing savage. These are the direct consequences of the wild-west Indian shows and moving pictures that depict lawlessness and hatred. . . .

I am not speaking here from selfish and sensitive motives, but from my own point of view, for cleaner civilization, education, and citizenship for my race. . . . "To the American Indian let there be given equal opportunities, equal responsibilities, equal education."

SUMMER AMUSEMENT PARKS

By the mid-nineteenth century, as metropolitan city populations doubled in a generation, the psychological, social, and physical costs of congestion became apparent. Greater New York was the extreme case; its population increased twofold between 1850 and 1870, and again by 1900, reaching a total of more than four and three-quarter million by 1910. Urbanism seemed a mixed blessing. The great city was progressive and civilized but seemed artificial and impersonal without familiar rural surroundings as a counterpoise. There were various opportunities for relaxation and relief. In the landscaped "rural oases" of Central Park and Prospect Park, created in the 1850s and 1860s, New York's and Brooklyn's weary found recuperation in informal walks close to "greensward" and on the promenades, where music from bandstands soothed shattered nerves. Suburban picnic sites near scenic falls or on the banks of gently flowing rivers were equally popular. Sea-bathing had few advocates but picturesque views from beaches on the Jersey shore and on the islands close to Manhattan gave solace from Bowery hustle. However, even in the 1830s these seaside havens were never simply "rural retreats" for the contemplation of pastoral scenery. At Hoboken, on the other side of the Hudson River, the attractions at the Elysian Fields belied its name. From April to October, steamships carried passengers on scheduled trips to Hoboken's games pitches and racetracks, and vendors tempted visitors with pleasures of every kind. The era of popular summer resorts had begun.

All major cities in the western world saw similar developments. Smart residential hotels in Brighton offered vacationing middle classes the sophisticated entertainments of London in the more relaxed setting of a seaside location. More disturbing to genteel observers were the numerous tawdry funfairs that mushroomed near the seashore. London's Margate or Manchester's Blackpool had iron "pleasure piers" where cheap attractions lured the poor on day-trips from the metropolis. Americans were as eager to develop low-cost, funfair amusements; by the 1890s the largest seaside resorts rivaled the English in size and scale and in the lavish use of electricity and iron. And none was more celebrated as the exemplar of unashamed, exuberant pleasure-seeking than Coney Island, a dozen miles from New York City.

In the 1850s Coney Island was merely one of many picnic and bathing areas on Long Island. Around its five-mile stretch of sandy beaches sprouted an unplanned constellation of small and often disreputable beer gardens, dance halls, eating places, and sports arenas. Far greater capital investment followed construction of the Brooklyn Bridge in 1882 and the opening of new steamship and railroad routes. In the late 1870s the Prospect Park and Coney Island Railroad offered speedy transportation from Brooklyn for thirty-five cents. The muddy creek was drained, allowing easy access from the mainland. Coney Island became a fashionable resort. Three grand racetracks were opened. At Brighton Beach and Manhattan Beach to the east, magnificent hotels were built for middle-class families on vacation and day-trippers from New York and Philadelphia. Speculative developers at West Brighton a few miles away began constructing the untidy complex of cheap amusement concessions that formed the nucleus of the enclosed parks in the early twentieth century.

By the 1890s Coney Island was thoroughly commercialized. Even more than Atlantic City, it had a reputation for flamboyant showmanship, for mechanical amusements, and for the use of artificial light. Fifty thousand visitors gathered there on a summer Saturday evening in the early 1880s. A guidebook on summer excursions close to Philadelphia depicted the glare of Coney Island hotels and beaches: "As night comes the bright suns of the electric light blaze out to illuminate the pier, and myriads of light are seen along the shore, while to the eastward fireworks go up."[1] An Island resort complex sponsored one of the first electric signs of the 1890s, fifteen hundred multicolored bulbs on a board fifty feet high and eighteen feet wide, in Times Square:

SWEPT BY OCEAN BREEZES
THE GREAT HOTELS
PAIN'S FIREWORKS
SOUSA'S BAND
SEIDL'S GREAT ORCHESTRA
THE RACES
NOW—MANHATTAN BEACH—NOW[2]

Between 1895 and 1904 entrepreneurs grouped together familiar attractions within several amusement park complexes along Surf Avenue. Enclosure was the most novel development. Earlier sporting entrepreneurs had set the precedent. Circuses had fenced temporary amphitheaters and charged admission; from the early 1860s baseball magnates had enclosed sports grounds and built stands for spectators to games of professional players from neighboring cities. In 1895 Captain Paul Boynton, a renowned diver and swimmer, opened Sea Lion Park, Coney's first walled mini-city of fun. Its centerpiece was a water slide, Shoot-the-Chutes, which sent its passengers hurtling into the lagoon where forty trained sea lions amused spectators. Two years later George Tilyou built Steeplechase Park and packed its fifteen acres with an astonishing variety of entertainments.

The inspiration for Sea Lion and Steeplechase Parks was the Midway Plaisance at the World's Columbian Exposition in Chicago in 1893. Like other world's fairs organized after London's Great Exhibition of 1851, Chicago's combined entertainment and education. Separated from the more austere classical buildings of the White City was the Midway strip, a mile long and two hundred yards wide. Ranged along the Midway were amusement concessions, most notably the giant ferris wheel, and a galaxy of villages of "native" people demonstrating the unique customs of Sudan or Samoa. Visitors rode on camels at the Streets of Cairo and watched exotic hootchy-cootchy dancers in the Persian Palace of Eros. The juxtaposition of anthropological oddities in architectural fantasylands, of technological thrills and traditional fairground attractions, became the characteristic feature of the larger suburban summer parks.

Frederic Thompson and Elmer Dundy raised the amusement park to new grandeur in 1903, when they opened Luna Park on the old Sea Lion site. In 1901 Tilyou had brought to Steeplechase the cosmorama-fantasy A Trip to the Moon, managed by Thompson and Dundy, that had proved so popular at the Pan-American Exposition at Buffalo the year before. At Luna Park, Thompson made good use of his brief draftsman's training and his experience of a dozen exposition midways to devise a bold architectural fancy. He retained Sea Lion's lagoon and the chutes, and around them constructed a dreamworld of a thousand lath-and-plaster minarets and towers. The fifteen-acre Dreamland park followed in 1904, more classical in form (and more expensive, with construction costs of three and a half million dollars), with even more spectacular lighting. Well over a million people, from a total population of four million in greater New York in 1905, flocked to the island on a summer weekend. "Coney is an empire among its kind," Reginald Wright Kauffman claimed, "a great American industry" for "a carnival all summer long."[3]

The Coney Island parks became models for similar enterprises throughout the United States and beyond. Luna Park attracted unprecedented publicity in newspapers and magazines, but intellectual property rights were impossible to protect. Scores of copies of the Luna name and design, and even the tell-tale crescent symbol, soon appeared in America's largest cities, and in London, Paris, Berlin, Moscow, and Melbourne. The most enterprising of the speculators, the Ingersoll Construction Company, built two of the most successful Luna Parks in Cleveland and Pittsburgh in 1905. The more austere and formal Dreamland spawned fewer White City clones. But everywhere, the old summer parks founded by street railway companies at lakeside picnic

281

grounds and trolley intersections in the last decades of the nineteenth century were modernized and upgraded in imitation of Coney. Landscaped grounds, croquet lawns, and sportsfields were sacrificed, and small fairground rides replaced by dance-halls, nickelodeons, roller coasters, freak-show "aborigines," and scaled-down disaster epics. The Coneyized trolley parks used superfluous electric light to broadcast their attractions to the city patrons of their streetcar lines.

Many middle-class commentators were shocked by the uninhibited pleasure-seeking in the old funfairs and in the "new" parks. On summer weekends visitors from the most densely inhabited city on earth paid twenty cents, a dime, or even a nickel for the journey of forty minutes or more from Manhattan. Then, as soon as they left the pier or rail station and entered the small enclosed parks—never more than five city blocks square—they were packed together in a swirling tide of humanity. In O. Henry's story, "Brickdust Row," the wealthy Blinker arrives at Coney by ship and is at first startled by being jostled and hustled along by the mob "shrieking, struggling, hurrying, panting, hurling itself in incontinent frenzy, with unabashed abandon, into the ridiculous sham palaces of trumpery and tinsel pleasures" in "Fairyland."[4] Carnival surroundings encouraged merry-making. Jollity became frivolity. The screams of delight of underdressed youth cavorting on shore and sea by day added to the general hubbub enveloping the joyrides on the Bowery and Surf Avenue by night.

In a 1911 pamphlet sponsored by the amusement park industry, Irvin S. Cobb attempted to define "The Spirit of Coney." New Yorkers, he explained, were accustomed to crowds, to banter and ballyhoo. On a Saturday evening the brief journey by boat or train released them from office and factory, kitchen and nursery. At dusk on Surf Avenue, the "vast geyser of sound" from the "painted city" and the brash ticket-sellers gave even the most miserable and lonely "the tincture of broad tolerance, of genial responsibility, of what-do-I-care-ativeness, that . . . glows and radiates . . . human fellowship and good nature." The journalist Rollin Lynde Hartt also believed that city-dwellers sought a "counter-irritant" as a cure for "Manhattanitis." Relief and restoration came not, as the genteel fondly hoped throughout the nineteenth century, in pastoral bliss and tranquil contemplation of the seashore. It was in sights and sounds of "wild hilarity" that the patrons of Thompson's and Tilyou's summer parks found brief respite. Night added disguise and the alluring glow of a million lights. To escape Babylon, the day-trippers added Babel.[5]

Journalists and the "New" Coney

Journalist Julian Ralph went to Coney Island during the heyday of the grand hotels: the Manhattan Beach, the Brighton Beach, and the Oriental. Coney was already, he announced in 1896, "the pioneer with modern improvements for giving the crowds a good time; it remains *sui generis*, enthroned, the king of all the popular resorts." What impressed him most were class differences within the "popular" market. There were essentially two very distinct Coney Islands at play. Affluent visitors near hotels to the east differed radically in their tastes from the less well-off day-trippers at the "hurly-burly" attractions clustered around the extravagantly exotic Elephant Hotel and the Bowery at West Brighton. For to the west was the dynamic commercial development: the three hundred-foot iron tower from the Philadelphia Centennial Exposition, LaMarcus Thompson's novel "Switchback Railway," and Charles Feltman's Ocean Pavilion, with room for three thousand dancers and a restaurant seating eight thousand. Real-estate speculators Peter and George Tilyou were developing the Bowery abutting Surf Avenue; soon it rivaled Manhattan's notorious district, with carnival sideshows, penny arcades, fortune tellers, variety music-halls, shooting galleries, boxing booths, and scores of taverns.

Ralph observed that although few swam in the sea, the beach provided the essential setting of social freedom.

Julian Ralph, "Coney Island," *Scribner's Magazine* 20 (July 1896): 14–20.

[W]hether it was that the water was chilly, or whether it was due to the unpleasantness of soaking one's apparel with brine and sand, it was a fact that few of us went into the billows for more than a ceremonious plunge. Instead, we lolled in the sun upon the hot, dry sand, and chatted with the girls and women and embanked their limbs in grave-like hillocks the while we anticipated in our chatter the delights of the music and the dinner that were to come. I noticed, too, a very strange fact strongly indicative of a popular sharing of my own pessimistic opinion of surf-bathing, and that was the general habit of smoking in bath uniform on the part of the men. Nearly all of them had brought cigars or cigarettes out of their dressing-rooms to enjoy as they lounged on the sand. . . . I came away with the new idea that what brought my neighbors into that bath enclosure was the barbarous but natural desire to free themselves from the fetters of prim modern dress and revel, loose and free, in the sunshine and the sand.

After the bath there was a choice of concerts. One was by Seidl's orchestra straining to be popular, and the other was by Sousa's band straining to be classical. . . . At night, the concerts compete with a grand fireworks exhibition—a London diversion, the like of which we never saw anywhere else but here, and still believe to be as splendid and dazzling a sight as the hand of man can create.

These were the novelties and triumphs for whose delights we owe gratitude to Coney Island. It will be noticed that they confine their territory to the newer or east end of the island, for it is a fact that the house in the shape of an elephant and, possibly, the iron steamboats and the old iron pier into the ocean were the only innovations that the older or western half of the resort brought forward. . . . For a transplanted Old World fair is what the older portion of Coney Island suggests—the amusement annex of such a fair at least; and on a scale so large as to make the hodge-podge seem a novelty. The principal avenue through it is a well called "the Bowery," a title which is at once amply and minutely descriptive to the born New Yorker, who has all his life called that which is cheap and yet pretentious, that which is loud, that which is beer-sodden, and that which is "faked" or made-up or make-believe—all by the comprehensive term "Bowery." There is not a thing (except the fireworks), on the higher-priced end of the island that cannot be obtained or witnessed at the cheaper end, but there are scores of attractions at the hurly-burly end that the more exclusive region does not hold forth. The peculiar theory of some religionists that we shall have differing heavens, to conform to our mundane ideas and tastes, gets some confirmation from the fact that ten go to the Bowery where one frequents the better beaches. Most excursionists who set apart a day for Coney Island put aside a generous sum to spend there—to "throw away" as we say. The resolution is eloquently expressed in the manners of the men, whether they are rotund old fellows in fine cloth ordering the "best" for their exquisite wives at Manhattan Beach, or wide-eyed mechanics clutching the arms of pallid sweethearts and pushing them through the perspiring mob around the elephant. And some, near the elephant, have set aside money sufficient for a day within sound of Seidl's orchestra, yet they prefer the oom-pah bands of rusted brass. They would rather have a luncheon of Frankfurters and lager and a dinner of roasted clams and melted butter, than the finicky food and precise surroundings away from the hurly-burly where nostalgia eats up appetite. And the queer thing is, that each sort of persons makes his cast-iron, habitual choice and calls it "seeing life;" whereas if the masses sent a deputation to Brighton and Manhattan and a few spent an occasional day in the Bowery, they would really see life and learn a great deal, and alas! be more or less unhappy. . . .

[W]estern Coney Island . . . is the most bewildering, noisy approach to bedlam that we know in America . . . [,] still the seat of a delirium of raw pleasure. Physically, the place is a sort of Chinatown of little frame buildings set about, helter-skelter, like a cityful of houses in a panic. Aurally, it is a riot of the noises of roller-coasters, from two to six stories high; of test-your-lungs and test-your-strength and test-your-grip machines; of shooting-galleries and "see-if-you-can-hit-the-nigger's head" contrivances; of those strange merry-go-rounds which seem to be manufactured exclusively in New Utrecht, L. I., of animals designed by a baker of ginger-bread; of razzle-dazzle rings that go all ways at once, like a ship's compass; of a band of howling Sioux; of the yells of the shouters in front of the freak museums; of rocking-boat devices that would make Neptune seasick if he rode in them; of the "ring-the-cane-and-get-a-cigar" layouts; of hand-organs, of yelling sea-bathers; in short, of pandemonium.

I like to go there, once in a while, to see the iron steamboats and the steam and trolley cars fling their loads of the poorer city folk upon the sands, complacent and at ease, beside the nervous, uncertain country people who come, a thousand at a time, upon the regular excursion boats. What Barney and Julia, from the tenements, go to "the Bowery" for I do not know, unless it is to enjoy the triumph of their own sagacity

284

in not ever, by any chance, being victimized by the fakirs who prey upon the unsophisticated. Barney looks on, from the outside, at all the clumsy traps for the unwary, and loves to guy the touts, who stand without, coaxing the people in.

"Say, cully," he says when he catches the eye of the roper-in, "is de fish bitin' good today?"

And Julia says of him proudly, to the other girls in the tenement at home: "Dere was a man tried to git Barney to take a chance on a watch, but Barney don't buy gold bricks an' he never blows out de gas."

What Barney and Julia like at Coney island is the bathing in the afternoon when Barney "berhaves terrible—" by endeavoring to duck his sweetheart; wherefore he chases her, screaming, all through the crowds—and the dancing. There are what are called dancing pavilions at the western end, where the music scarcely pauses between seven o'clock and that hour which is invariably called "de las' boat." . . . The city boys and girls described their own fashion of dancing when they gave the name of "pivoters" to the thousands of girls who are seized with such a madness for dancing that they spend every night in the dance halls and the picnic parks. Julia stands erect, with her body as rigid as a poker and with her left arm straight out from her shoulder like an upraised pump-handle. Barney slouches up to her, and bends his back so that he can put his chin on one of her shoulders and she can do the same by him. Then, instead of dancing with a free, lissome, graceful, gliding step, they pivot or spin, around and around, within the smallest circle that can be drawn around them. The expression on Barney's face is usually that of grim, determined effort, like that of one who is taking part in a trial of endurance; but Julia's eyes are uplifted, like those of a maid in her devotions, and a settled, almost sanctified calm is upon her features. On the last boat a great crowd of these honest young people is apt to gather on the upper deck, aft, where the young men practise that repartee which is quite as sharp and vastly more kindly than the wit of the London street folk. . . .

This glance at all parts of Coney Island shows us that while it has some of the main features of the great watering-places of Europe, it is yet different from all of them in being purely and wholly an excursion resort. . . . What is peculiar to Coney Island is that no one lives there. Other resorts offer change and rest, but Coney Island offers only change. A reporter having to announce the formal opening of one of the beaches there, put the case of Coney Island in a verbal nutshell in this brief sentence, one day: "Manhattan Beach has opened, and now New Yorkers have a place by the seaside where they may go for dinner, spend an evening enjoyably, and get home at a reasonable time." . . . How grand an acquisition it is for us to possess a beach to which we can go in an hour at the cost of a quarter of a dollar, to get a new environment and have old ocean's pure tonic breath blow the cobwebs out of our brain—and then, as the chronicler saith, "get home at a reasonable time."

In 1903 Frederic Thompson mounted a very successful advertising campaign to persuade press and public that his park-enclave was "new," a "renaissance," cleaner, brighter, and free from the crime and corruption that had tainted the island. It was, he proclaimed, the "electric city by the sea." "By day a paradise . . . At night, Arcadia!" "Harnessed Lightning in Flashing Fountains!"[6] A quarter of a million lights gave the free-form scramble of orange crescents, gold dragons, and oriental glitter some thematic unity. Entertainments were jumbled together: elephants and Eskimos, the Canals of Venice and the Japanese tea garden, the disaster epic "Fire and Flames" and the Durbar of India, a three-ring circus suspended over the lagoon, the old-fashioned Helter-Skelter, and the ultramodern Premature Baby Incubators.

Journalist Winthrop Alexander responded to the media event. What distinguished Luna Park, he thought, were the picturesque illusions. Such simulated "journeys" to exotic locations far in place, space, and time had been one of the most popular features of world's fair midways in the 1890s. Now, there were novel futuristic "voyages" for those who could not afford to travel abroad. Popular science-fiction novels like H. G. Wells's *The First Men in the Moon* (1901) or Jules Verne's fantasies seemed to be made real. It soon became legend. A few years later, in O. Henry's short-story "The Lickpenny Lover," Maisie, the beautiful but worldy-wise salesgirl, mistakes millionaire Irving Carter's genuine offer to show her the real gondolas of Venice for the usual ploy of a cheap daytrip to dreamland. For Alexander, this "wonder-world" was Coney's hallmark.

Winthrop Alexander, "Coney Island's New Wonder-World," *New Metropolitan Magazine* 18 (1903): 311–19.

Summer brings many hours of leisure to the millions of people dwelling in this big city of New York. It is the season when, as at no other time of the year, they seek to amuse themselves; or, to put it more correctly, when they seek to be amused; and they accomplish this by a variety of means which is truly multi-form. The avidity of their quest for opportunity to extract all the sunshine possible from the golden hours is such an incentive to invention and enterprise that every season is an occasion for new wonder at the ingenuity manifested and the amount of capital expended in adding to the attractiveness of popular resorts, and in the new ones which will appeal to the love of novelty.

Coney Island has been for years the great focussing point for New Yorkers, and for visitors to the metropolis, led thither by the desire and the intention to make the fullest and the lightest use of a summer day or evening. . . .

In the meantime, a practical work of reformation has been inaugurated by a class of men interested in amusement enterprises, who have discovered by their own successes that the competition of clean and well-ordered places of entertainment presenting meritorious and interesting attractions is overshadowing the business and undermining the influence of such cheap, meretricious and questionable shows as have prospered here in the past. One of the results of what these men, who are actually reformers without making any profession in that direction, is that Coney Island is developing a new and better character, attracts a growing proportion of the respectable elements in metropolitan life, and is freeing itself from the domination of the coarser elements in the creation of the local color and atmosphere. A fresh and impressive evidence of the solidity of this reformation has been presented in the inauguration this summer of a single amusement enterprise which represents an investment of something more than one million dollars, and which, strange as the fact may appear, derives none of its support from the sale of liquor nor from spectacles wherein the woman performer of the so-called soubrette type is a feature.

In various ways, Luna Park, the new attraction to which reference is here made, is entitled to more than ordinary notice, inasmuch as it represents upon an extensive scale the marked improvement in the estimate placed by promoters of amusement enterprises upon the tone and taste of the average pleasure-seeker. Occupying an area of twenty-two acres, it is a wonder of architectural splendor and artistic land-scape effects. There are touches of the incongruous and the grotesque, it must be admitted, but these are not obtrusive. The general effect is a realization of what imagination might paint as a fairy city, and the visitor is bewildered by the beautiful picture presented on every hand. It is as fascinating in its details as in its *ensemble*. Perhaps those features in the architectural and landscape effects which are most likely to excite and maintain interest are those representative of other lands than our own, and of wonderful regions in our own country with which the majority of people are acquainted only through what they have learned from story and picture. The visitor experiences no difficulty in recognizing the Venetian canal, with its little bridges and the ornate palace rising above foundations laved by the sluggish waters. In fact, the first impressions received of the place as a whole are suggestive of what one knows or has read of the "Queen of the Adriatic," although every path leading from the Court of Honor, with its picturesque lagoon and encircling sky-line of towers, domes and minarets takes the visitor into other portions of the world—here an old German village, with its Rath Haus, or convention hall; there a typical Irish village nestling under the walls of Blarney castle; in another place an Alpine mill and torrent; then a quaint Japanese village; elsewhere the early Californian mining camp, the Southern darkey in the field as he was before the war, the Filipinos in their home, and so on till one has passed from the artistic evidences of refined civilization to the rugged picturesque-ness of nature in such regions as the Grand Canyon of the Colorado, the Yosemite Falls and Yellowstone Park. There is life to add to the interest of every scene; and the large permanent population of this wonderful summer city, which represents so fully the whole world in miniature—the multitude whose homes and employment for the summer are here—is literally a congress of nations.

Even though seen only as a massing of spectacular effects, Luna Park is worth a visit; and much time can be spent in an agreeable manner without patronizing any of the several exhibitions which are to be seen in some of the larger buildings among the many on the grounds. Day and night the grounds alone present a mammoth display of

Luna Park at night, 1904. Prints and Photographs Division, Library of Congress.

ingenuity and art. Then there is an almost limitless possibility of amusement in seeing how others amuse themselves. Evening scenes are, of course, especially fascinating because of the liberal use made of electric-lighting effects, the brilliant display center- ing at the tower which rises from the lagoon, near its head or broadest part, to a height of about two hundred feet. There is a triteness in the expression about turning night into day which emphasizes itself in such a place as this, inasmuch as the gorgeous- ness of the scene at night, while it lacks the splendor of a perfect summer day has a glory of its own, pervaded by a glamor which is irresistible, and which only the night makes possible. Under its witchery the imaginative visitor might dream many a pretty romance. Perhaps there are actually romances developing in those boats shooting the White Horse Rapids, and in gondolas floating lazily over the surface of the lagoon or threading the grand canal. However that may be, it is certain that many people will

288

carry hence some mid-summer night's dream, which will float into memory now and then in later years as a pleasant reminiscence of idle hours, during which life seemed all sweetness and light. Over the portals of this fairy city there might be placed the antithesis of that dread inscription which Dante's muse found over the gates of the Inferno, the change of only one word making it new and seductive—"Abandon care all ye who enter here!" . . .

Amusement, pure and, simple, is aimed at in all the other exhibitions, although there is in some of them that which might add to the sum of the visitor's knowledge. There are two, characterized as illusions, which undoubtedly provoke a great deal of hard thinking in the minds of people who "Wonder how it is done." One of these is the famous "Trip to the Moon," which was one of the most startling and successful novelties at the Pan-American Exposition in Buffalo. As a Coney Island attraction it renewed its success last summer, and became the inspiration of the larger enterprise now under notice. It is in recognition of this success that the name, Luna Park, has been adopted for the new resort. In "A Trip to the Moon" the visitor leaves the earth, or experiences the sensation of leaving it, upon a large air-ship, which rises through space and alights upon the moon. Leaving the air-ship, the pilgrim under competent guidance, explores the weird valleys and caverns of our satellite, discovering for one thing that the "man in the moon" is not a solitary individual, but bobs up at every turn, extremely elfin in appearance, though of genuine flesh and blood, and evidently one of a numerous family. In fact, despite their elfishness, the people of the moon appear to be very distinctly related to our own terrestrial race, and the writer happened to hear one of them say to another, in a most mundane way, "Well, this is the day the ghost walks!"

The lunar journey culminates in the sacrifice of the adventurous traveler to a creature of terrific aspect, named the "moon-calf," which swallows him whole, but considerately deposits him on Coney Island again, unharmed, though considerably shaken up by an experience such as Jonah might have been able to describe. . . .

If, as may be, "A Trip to the Moon" suggests to the aerial voyagers a suspicion that they are in the power of a necromancer such a suspicion will be even stronger during the journey of "Twenty Thousand Leagues Under the Sea." This is an entirely new illusion, which affords a sensation quite opposite to that experienced in the older one. Like the "Trip to the Moon," it occupies a huge building especially planned and constructed for it, and the scenic and other effects have been secured by a combination of engineering and artistic skill incomprehensible except by the favored few who are admitted "behind the scenes." When those persons who are ambitious to emulate the hero of Jules Verne's story disappear through the man-hole of the big model of Holland's submarine boat, the people standing by see the man-hole securely closed and the boat sink beneath the water at their feet. The passengers in the strange craft hear the splash of the liquid element as they drop into its depths. They feel the vibration of machinery and experience the sensation of moving rapidly through the water, and by means of the conning ports in the side of the boat, which are glazed with heavy but clear plate glass, they behold all sorts of marine life and vegetation, as they pass from zone to zone. Tropic seas are traversed, and the frozen north is reached, when the boat grounds amid the ice, and the adventurers leave it for an arctic exploration under the guidance of genuine Eskimos with their dogs and sledges. Boreal blasts give chilly realism to the experience, which may be a trifle uncomfortable for those in summer attire, but they forget anything of this kind in witnessing the marvelous display of the Aurora Borealis, which greets them as the exploration nears its end. This is in itself a scenic triumph as startling as it is beautiful, an explanation of which, if it could be given without breach of confidence, would be more interesting than any description of the scene itself. When the wonders of the frozen north are exhausted the travelers re-embark on their submarine boat, and make a return trip under the seas which affords fresh views and new experiences. The voyage ends happily at the point of departure, where the boat rises to the surface in full view of the amazed spectators who generally extend a pleasant greeting to the returning adventurers as they emerge from the dripping man-hole.

These two features of Luna Park are selected for this extended mention because they are emphatically novel in character. All the other exhibitions on the grounds have been equipped upon a similarly large and costly plan. Luna Park, like all great shows, is advertised in that somewhat flamboyant style which is looked for, but is invariably discounted in the minds of those who have frequently perceived the lack of unity, which differentiates the work of the poster artist from that of the people who shaped the show. In this instance, however, no claims are set forth, and no expectations are raised which are not fully met. If the proprietors had set out to create an exposition which would eventually do its own advertising through the stories carried away by delighted visitors, certainly the idea will be crowned with success.

Dreamland hoped to emulate Luna Park's success when it opened in 1904. Indeed, with a construction budget four times as large and four times as many lights, the Beacon Tower nearly twice as tall, and two shoot-the-chutes, the venture capitalists headed by former state senator William H. Reynolds intended to eclipse it in grandeur. Classical-styled buildings, with a vast sculpture for the showpiece entrance, followed the more chaste and formal plan of the White City. The attractions were broadly similar—illusion rides, thrills and spills, disaster epics. Soon after the "Gibraltar of the Amusement World" opened in 1904, Barr Ferree reviewed its architecture for a trade journal. It had, he admitted, no stylistic unity. However, pleasure seekers expected variety, and as a commercial showplace, it succeeded brilliantly. He singled out for particular praise the all-white "palace" of twenty-five thousand square feet and ten thousand electric lights built on Dreamland pier built to serve the dance craze where romantically inclined youth swayed to music "over the waves."

Barr Ferree, "The New Popular Resort Architecture. Dreamland, Coney Island," *Architect's and Builder's Magazine* 5 (August 1904): 499–513.

Journalists and the "New" Coney

The value of architecture as an aid to civic betterment has seldom been more aptly illustrated than in the creation of the new popular resort at Coney Island known as "Dreamland." The purification and reformation of that well-known place has long baffled public authorities and thoughtful people. As a place of recreation in the honest, healthy sense of the word, it has long been not only a farce, but an impossibility. That it was popular was well attested by the enormous crowds of people who thronged its heated streets and alleys, surged into its ridiculous music halls and, in general, patronized the inane if not vulgar entertainments spread forth for the delectation of the multitude who wanted to be amused badly enough, and who only took the frivolities that were given it because there was nothing else.

Coney Island has been a favorite topic with reformers who said a great deal and, like many contemporary of that ilk, accomplished very little. Then a change came. The patent fact that decent amusements will pay finally penetrated the minds of some amusement caterers, and a new Coney Island was created in a new place that has since been known to fame as Luna Park. The astonishing idea that any part of Coney Island could be "good," shocked the island from end to end. And it never recovered from the blow. More than that, it has thoroughly awakened to the fact that not only can Coney Island be good, but that goodness pays, and pays handsomely. This, indeed, is the supreme test of Coney Island success; for it thrives on no philanthropic basis; it is money, money, money, all the time; money extracted from the visitor in the delusive amounts of five and ten cents—until, after a few inspections, the unwary one suddenly discovers that a trip that was estimated to cost a few cents, has mounted up into the dollars. As a "cheap" family resort, Coney Island has long since proved itself to be the most colossal fraud now on public view. . . .

But first of all, it is well to take to heart the caution that, even in Dreamland, one must not be too serious. It is a play place and a place for play. It has not been created as an exhibition of architecture, as an example of high art, as a realization of a long pondered dream. But it stands apart and alone among the seaside resorts around New York as an honest effort to employ intelligent architecture in an intelligent way as an aid to popular entertainment. In other words, the motto of its projectors may very well be supposed to have been "Let us not only have many pleasant forms of amusement, but let us have a pleasant place in which people may be amused." . . .

One is quite justified in going about with one's mouth open at what one sees. Verily this is Dreamland, and one rubs one's eyes and pinches one's arm to see if one be really awake. Such splendor was never before seen at Coney Island; and this is the first and overwhelming fact. But Dreamland is more than simply superior to anything Coney Island has had before; it stands on its own merits, and it stands on them solidly and firmly. Nevertheless, it is so wholly unlike what one has been accustomed to in Coney Island, that it is not until one has turned once more into Surf Avenue and seen the same old atrocities that have so long defaced that misnamed street, breathed once more the vitiated atmosphere of that horrible thoroughfare, been jostled in the crowds, been saluted, nasally, by its frying sausages and ancient fish, that one comes

291

down to mother earth and awakes to the painful thought that perhaps after all it was only a dream, and the visit to Dreamland was a mind's journey only. . . .

Dreamland is, therefore, a collection of buildings put to every imaginable entertaining use. One can do almost everything here, from sliding boisterously down a bumpy incline to sitting decorously and looking at the unnatural performances of wild beasts. It is impossible to be dignified in such a place, and if the facades of structures behind which such strange doings are carried on are of a commendable excellence, very much has been accomplished and a new note set in popular resort architecture.

For it is an important point to remember that the attractions of Dreamland, as is the case with all the attractions of Coney Island, are not in the buildings themselves, but in the things within them. . . .

Decoration in color is, in fact, the distinguishing merit of Dreamland. The American public has become thoroughly accustomed to the decoration of buildings by sculpture. . . . The dominant color note in Dreamland is white; this is the natural color of all the buildings. One or two of them are tinted, but the first impression, and perhaps the last one, is that we are here in a mimic White City. One speedily realizes, however, that other arts than architecture have contributed to the general effect. Sculpture has been but sparingly used . . . where it could be used naturally; but there is not that superabundance that has characterized some of our later World's Fairs.

The architects of Dreamland, however, have very wisely called in the aid of the painter, and used, for the first time in any considerable sense—considering the area at their disposal—painted decorations as an aid to architecture. [The paintings on the illusions of Venice, Pompeii and the Scenic Railway] all count in the color scheme, all relieve the buildings of the brilliancy of whiteness, all help in producing a new result, and perhaps most important of all, give a distinct individuality to the whole at a very much less cost than sculpture. . . .

Crossing the bridge one finds oneself immediately at the Bowery. Not the old horrible place that once desecrated the sands of old Coney Island, but a new Bowery than runs out into the ocean on the old iron pier. Here are gathered a multitude of minor matters of too small importance to need a separate structure, a somewhat dreary place and quite remote from the centre of interest. The outward form of the pier is the least satisfactory feature of Dreamland. It is not satisfactory at all; but a barn-like structure, redolent of the Coney Island of the past. One forgets its sordid exterior when one has mounted to the upper story and walked out an almost interminable distance to the ball room, which is truly sumptuous—a regal apartment of quite metropolitan significance. It is two stories in height, the roof supported with columns and arches, between which are balconies for the better observing of the dancing below. It is a brilliant room, superbly lighted at night; a room so fine and splendid in its proportions and its architecture—for it is quite undecorated—that one entirely fails to realize that the waters of the Atlantic are washing the props on which it is supported. . . .

But Dreamland must be seen at night to realize the fulness of its possibilties. If the

292

tower is beautiful by day, it is supreme by night when its every part is outlined with light, and it raises its proudly gemmed head far above the surrounding buildings. Every part of Dreamland glows with light at night; every building is lit, every post, it almost appears, is capped with its globe of fire, every point that can be illuminated, is illuminated. It is a wonderful night spectacle, brilliant in the fullest sense of the word, a vision of loveliness and wonder, a veritable Dreamland realized in actuality.

In an age when most homes still lacked electric light, and when the bright department store window was a source of wonder, funfair illumination was unsurpassed. Visitors to Coney were often overawed. One traveling at night by ship from Manhattan wrote of observing "far across the restless black expanse, a glow-worm shimmer on the Atlantic Coast" suddenly transformed, when "from its narrowing tail, from time to time, there rose a fountain of green and crimson and golden fire" from Surf Avenue.[7] A journalist attributed the "Renaissance of Coney" to the use of bright light, as well as to astute showmanship. "The age of electricity and science . . . which has destroyed our illusions has created in its place something which is as near Fairyland as we have ever dreamed of." Man-made "fire" was Coney's emblem and summons to play.[8]

The Midway: An Illustrated Magazine of Amusement Resorts and Attractions was a short-lived, monthly trade journal. For a dime a month or a dollar a year, would-be entrepreneurs read promotional articles on investment possibilities; for two dollars per column inch, manufacturers of equipment advertised the latest novelties. *Midway* claimed in 1905 that there were close to a thousand parks which did more business in the summer season than all the vaudeville houses. Electricity, it assured readers, was the key to the industry's future.

Charles Carter, "Electricity in Amusement Parks," *Midway* 1 (January 1905): 29–30.

It is safe to assume . . . that had the electric lighting and power system never been discovered, the summer park as we know it now would never have evolved. . . .

To begin with, to the various electric railroad companies was due the first real summer park. Usually this was situated at the end of a comparatively non-paying stretch of track. Some brainy man with keen observation saw a way to make that stretch of track pay dividends, and with that idea was born the American amusement park. Naturally, as soon as the property was obtained it became necessary to light it in order to make it available at night, when the crowds would naturally appear. Having lighted the park it became necessary to furnish an attraction, for nature unadorned, while undoubtless beautiful, is hardly the material out of which dividends are gathered.

Following the necessity for attractions came the electric scenic theatres, the electrically operated swings, scenic railways and such kindred devices. Gradually a form of design managed to evolve itself, and things moved along systematic lines. . . . The big electric towers, glittering with enormous numbers of lights, the light-fringed lagoons, the fire-rimmed buildings, all became necessities to attract the eye, and in addition to furnishing light to lend themselves to decorative effect.

There is nothing in this wide wide world so easily manipulated for decorative purposes as electricity. It is a willing servant ready to heat, light or drive railways or anything else that may be required. Few scenic effects or illusions could be accomplished without its aid, and in fact the summer park would be but a dreary wilderness without it.

The projector of the amusement park must remember one fact and work with that fact closely in mind. The park must be attractive at night. To make it attractive by night you must use electricity, and to use electricity to fill these requirements you must purchase the energies of the man or men who know what effect they wish to create, and have the ability to produce it. The electric tower at first glance may seem a useless luxury, yet it is doubtful if there is anything so brilliantly attractive as this feature. The case of Dreamland at Coney Island is an example. The big tower can be seen for miles at sea, looming up over the horizon like a living shaft of fire. What must be the thoughts of the immigrant approaching New York harbor by night in the summer time? Inland the tower can be seen from Brooklyn Bridge, from the heights of Manhattan, and it is like a beckoning finger to the multitude.

Showmen and the "Amusement Business"

Journalists from the popular monthly magazines of the Progressive era used the new language of sociology and psychology to explain the appeal of the "new" Coney Island. "It is blatant, it is cheap, it is the apotheosis of the ridiculous," wrote one.[9] It was successful, he noted, precisely because of its range of options—because it offered so many different opportunities for uninhibited interaction. As the "Tom-Tom of America," Coney Island satisfied a primitive impulse, explained Richard Le Gallienne: "orgiastic escape from respectability—that is, from the world of What-we-have-to-do into the world of What-we-would-like-to-do."[10] Separated from the rational city plan and the purposeful movement of business life by the journey to pier or station, fun-seekers looked forward to anarchic zigzag routes and dizzy spins.

What puzzled Edwin W. Slosson was that so many of the mechanical rides were merely variants of the transportation park patrons used every day in the city. The novelty of these "exaggerations of the ordinary," he believed, was that they gave a sudden feeling of vertigo, a stimulating jolt of danger, ephemeral but intoxicating for those eager to escape from the mundane and conventional.

Edwin E. Slosson, "The Amusement Business," *Independent* 57 (July 21, 1904): 137–39.

Not only do our modern entertainers cater to the ordinary senses by music, colored lights and food, but in many of the most popular amusements they provide titillation for a more obscure sense, only recently recognized by psychologists, the sense of equilibrium, the sense which is affected when the motion of the body is changed in direction or speed, a sense located in part in the semicircular canals of the ears. This sense, like all the others, is a source of acute misery, the fear of falling and the feeling of seasickness, when stimulated too suddenly or too long, but, when gently excited, gives a sensation of pleasure. The magnified merry-go-rounds, the mountainous railways, the big steel arms which lift and swing and whirl people high in the air, the chutes, the loop, all act chiefly on this sense.

With these must be classed as causing the same sensations the illusions of motion. The haunted swing, where the room turns round and the spectator feels himself to be standing on his head, and the airship in which one goes to the moon both give the false interpretations of the visual impressions the same feeling of delightful dizziness.

To the pleasure of rapid and unusual motion is added in many of the amusements the delight of danger. This is, of course, mostly an illusion, for accidents to the participants are rare, but the apparent risk gives one a sense of personal daring very gratifying to us all, and as each boat load plunges down the chutes into the lagoon this finds expression in a cry for protection from feminine and an answering shout of triumph from masculine throats.

The pleasures of peril are enjoyed vicariously by looking at women escape from the burning building by a leap into the fire net, the trapeze performers and wire walkers, the bicycle rider looping the gap, and the man who dares to be a Daniel and go into the lions' den. . . .

After all, the social feature is the important one in popular amusements. Does any one go to Coney Island alone? To get away for a holiday, to "go some place," is the common desire. Hospitality and visiting in the country sense being impossible in city flats people must meet in public, and little trips by sea or land afford this opportunity. The reference to "dear little Coney Isle" in the folk love songs show what a part it has played as a matchmaker. Many a young couple have been so well satisfied with each other in this short journey that they have decided to continue traveling together through life, and a sudden clutch of his arm when the boat goes through the mill-race has often brought a young man to realize how pleasant it would be to have the right to protect and cheer the maiden by his side.

Luna Park's Frederic Thompson emerged as the most articulate and publicity-conscious of the amusement park showmen, eager to enhance his reputation as the "Regenerator of Coney." In a half dozen essays and interviews to boost his personal and business ambitions, especially building the huge Hippodrome theater in New York in 1905, he explained successful management and crowd pschology. Ten years' experience of exposition midways had convinced him that pretensions to education and formal architectural grandeur were not commercially viable. Adults were "children of maturer years" who had never lost their primitive sense of terror. Surprise, even shock, made them forget workday normality and rationality. "Amusement, pure and simple"—thrills and spills, often in exotic fantasylands that stimulated their imagination and suspended their natural caution and reserve—promoted childlike escapism and blissful forgetfulness of life's cares.

Frederick [sic] A. Thompson, "The Summer Show," *Independent* 62 (June 20, 1907): 1460–63.

Fred Thompson, "Fooling the Public: The Growth of the Big Show, as Described by a Master Showman," *Delineator* 69 (February 1907): 264–66.

Frederic Thompson, "Amusing the Million," *Everybody's Magazine* 19 (September 1908): 378–87.

Frederic Thompson, "Amusing People," *Metropolitan Magazine* 32 (August 1910): 601–10.

When people come down to the seaside for an afternoon or evening of enjoyment they are not in a serious mood, and do not want to encounter seriousness. They have enough seriousness in their every-day lives, and the keynote of the thing they do demand is change. Everything must be different from their ordinary experience. What is presented to them must have life, action, motion, sensation, surprise, shock, swiftness or else comedy. . . .

When a stranger arrives in Coney Island, the great headquarters of summer shows, the first thing that impresses him is change—difference. His eyes tell him he is in a different world—a dream world, perhaps a nightmare world—where all is bizarre and fantastic—crazier than the craziest part of Paris—gayer and more different from the every-day world.

This spirit pervading the whole place, strangeness and irresponsible gaiety captures the visitor and leads him along, and he is prepared to accept all sorts of extravagances—things that everywhere would be impossible—in perfect good faith for the time being.

The summer outdoor public wants to be amused. At the Island we are not dealing with New Yorkers as they are in New York, but with big children who have come to fairyland and want the fairies to make them laugh and show them strange things.

Hence the trip to the moon and to Mars, the journey to the center of the earth, the descent into the coal mine, the floods and earthquakes and fires and battles are all real to the spectators while the experience lasts.

But in spite of this complaisant mood of the visitors, poor imitations of things represented will not do. To succeed, whatever is shown or given must be the product of the highest art of its kind. The day of roughness and crudity has gone by, and no expense or pains is spared in making the spectacles, the illusions, the performances as perfect as they can be made.

The showmen have educated Coney Island's visitors till they are very discriminating, and the visitors have also educated the showmen. They have taught for one thing

Showmen and the "Amusement Business"

that the fun must be innocent—that it must be such as women and children can enjoy. It must be respectable. Coney Island is frisky, but it knows where to draw the line, and this knowledge is largely the result of the lessons given by the crowds themselves. The clean show pays; the other goes to the wall. . . .

Sometimes I am asked whether Coney Island makes any contribution to morality, and I say decidedly it does. . . . Innocent play is a moral antiseptic, and innocent play has certainly won the victory at Coney Island. Whatever of the other there may still be there has had to take to the caves. . . .

Coney is frankly devoted to fun, the fantastic, the gay, the grotesque. . . .

The Island deserves well of the people. It gives them bright days.

Looking carefully, calmly, over my career in the "show" business, I have come to the conclusion that while some of the people want to be fooled some of the time, and while some of the people want to be fooled all the time, the showman who starts in on the theory that the public is aching to have his kind of fooling twelve months of the year is bound to come to calamity. . . .

Let me explain at the beginning, what I mean by "fooling the public." There isn't any other business that I know of where you are really expected to "fool" the people who come to you and where there is a just ground for complaint unless you do. In the higher forms of the drama the public goes to the theater for intellectual stimulus; it wants to be made to think, and it has the right to demand and to expect a certain amount of intellectual and moral sincerity. But in the lighter forms of amusement—your farces, your vaudeville, your circus, your "big show,"—the attitude of the public is entirely different. It is one that says: "We are young, and being young we want to be made to laugh, no matter how foolish is the method by which you do it; we are young and we believe everything, therefore do the most impossible things and we will pretend to believe them and applaud; we are poor,"—it says,—"make us forget that there are luxuries and perhaps, necessities beyond our means—stir us so that we will remember the hours that we are spending with you for months to come; we are tired and weary and overworked—don't add to our burdens, lighten them by your most fantastic and foolish endeavors." In other words, "fooling the public" for the show-man means amusing it. . . .

People will recall that there has never been anything like the Summer-show idea which has sprung up in every large city during the last ten years. These Summer shows are due, first, to the modern exposition idea, then, to an increasing demand on the part of the poorer people for healthy entertainment, then to shrewd business judgment on the part of men who own land near a city, or stock in a trolley company. . . .

I stood at the entrance of the Pan-American Exposition the morning after "Midway Day," and looking over its classical architecture I saw Luna Park complete, no definite style of architecture being in my mind, a number of palaces in free Renaissance, well proportioned and balanced, the skyline broken with countless towers and minarets,

297

the whole thing a rather Oriental dream; and in that architectural plan lies what I consider the better sort of "fooling the public."

The difference between the theatre and the big amusement park is the difference between the Sunday-school and the Sunday-school picnic. The people are the same; the spirit and the environment are wholly different. It is harder to make the picnic successful than successfully to conduct a session of the school; and it is harder to make a success of a big amusement park than of a theatre. There isn't any irreverence in this comparison with the Sunday-school, for if the amusement park doesn't attract people who are interested in the Sunday-school, it isn't going to succeed.

For I want to say at the beginning that ninety-five per cent of the American public is pure and good, and it is this public that it pays to serve. . . .

In the theatre and in the Sunday-school conventional standards of behavior are accepted as a matter of course. The picnic and the open-air park are designed to give the natural, bubbling animal spirits of the human being full play, to give people something fresh and new and unusual, to afford them respite from the dull routine of their daily lives.

The one thing that makes a picnic or an amusement park a success—it doesn't make any difference whether the picnic is made up of ten people or ten thousand, whether the park is a little one or a great international exposition—the one thing absolutely necessary is the carnival spirit. Without that no show in the open, nothing that has to do with people in the mass, can hope to succeed. Whenever any enterprise that is intended to appeal to the million fails, the failure can always be traced to the lack of carnival enthusiasm.

This spirit of gaiety, the carnival spirit, is not spontaneous, except on extraordinary occasions, and usually its cause can be easily traced. Almost always it is manufactured. . . . The first step, as far as the public is concerned, is to create an impression that there will be things doing, to get emotional excitement into the very air. . . .

In big amusement enterprises that appeal to the masses the spirit of gaiety is manufactured just as scenery, lights, buildings, and the shows generally are manufactured. That's the business of the showman—to create the spirit of gaiety, frolic, carnival; and the capacity to do this is the measure of his mastery of the craft. . . .

To create a carnival spirit a showman may use other means than ballyhoos—which means the sample shows on the outside, with the patter of the barkers—bands, freak shows, and free circuses. I use architecture. . . . The very architecture must be in keeping with the spirit of carnival. It must be active, mobile, free, graceful, and attractive. It must be arranged so that visitors will say, "What is this?" and "Why is that?"
. . . .

I stuck to no style. I adapted what I thought was best in Free Renaissance, but reserved the right to use all the license in the world and to inject into everything I did the graceful, romantic curves of the Oriental.

One result is Luna Park, the sky-line of which is utterly unlike anything of its kind in

298

the two Americas. The architecture of Luna Park helps rather than hinders the spirit of carnival. Luna Park has been, and is, tremendously successful. There are other amusement parks in the vicinity that are chastely beautiful from an artistic standpoint, but that so far as dollars and cents are concerned are utter failures. Visitors admire the buildings—and don't go near the shows. I have built their sort of buildings, too, but not for a Luna Park. They don't pay. An exposition is a form of festivity, and serious architecture should not enter into it if it will interfere with the carnival spirit.

In amusing the million there are other essential elements besides gaiety. One is decency—the absolutely necessary quality in every line of the world's business. There is nothing that pays so well. When Coney Island used to have a pretty bad reputation, there were good shows there, and clean shows, but the influence of evil dives was dominant. . . . It's different now. The clean, decent shows have driven the dives out of business. They can't pay the rents the good places easily afford. . . .

Courtesy on the part of the employee is as necessary as decency on the part of the visitor. If I hear of one of my employees resenting an insult offered by a visitor, I dismiss him. I tell him that so long as he wears my uniform he is representing me, and that I am the only person who can be insulted inside the gates.

An amusement park is a condensed Broadway, if that is understood to represent metropolitan theatreland. In a park the best things of a theatrical nature must be presented in capsule form. The shows must be diversified because the appeal must be universal. The whole gamut of the theatre must be run, and no show can last more than twenty minutes. If you have a two-hour show, it should be boiled down to a quarter of an hour. It is foolish to make people serious or to point a moral. . . .

People are just boys and girls grown tall. Elaborated child's play is what they want on a holiday. Sliding down cellar doors and the make-believes of youngsters are the most effective amusements for grown-ups. An appreciation of that fact made the "Trip to the Moon" possible, and "The Trip to the Moon" made for me and my partner, Dundy, half a million dollars. "The Tickler," "Bump the Bumps," and "The Virginia Reel" are nothing more than improved cellar doors. "The Trip to the Moon," "Night and Morning," "The Witching Waves," and "The Lost Girl" are only elaborations of the doll-house stunts of childhood, and they are successful largely for that reason. But they must be short and decisive. I would rather have a good show that lasts three minutes than a better one that runs an hour. And I prefer one that is over in a minute but enables the spectator to become a part of it to one that runs three minutes and never permits him to become more than an onlooker.

Speed is almost as important a factor in amusing the millions as is the carnival spirit, decency, or a correct reflection of school days. Speed has become an inborn American trait. We as a nation are always moving, we are always in a hurry, we are never without momentum. "Helter Skelters," "The Dragon's Gorge," and the thousand and one varieties of roller-coasters are popular for the same reason that we like best the fastest trains, the speediest horses, the highest powered motor-cars, and the swiftest sprinters.

SUMMER AMUSEMENT PARKS

Not only must some rides be speedy and all shows be short, but the employees must work fast visibly, thereby promoting by suggestion speed in the mind, heart, and steps of the most laggard visitors. . . .

To keep up the carnival spirit everybody and everything must be on the "go." There can be no carnival without speed. The moment a crowd of folk who are slowly meandering around catch this spirit they walk faster, they laugh, they spend money, they have a good time.

If I were asked (although, of course, nobody would ever think of asking me), what I considered to be the most typically American Institutions, I should very unhesitatingly say the Genius for Industrial Organization, the American Girl and Summer Amusement. And I should bracket the American Girl and Summer Amusement—they are so very inextricably interwoven.

When I say summer amusement, I mean, of course, what you mean: that thing which draws millions of people to hundreds of places, in scores of cities, over the very broad acres of our land. I mean those places which cause railroad terminals to be choked on hot evenings, and decent Saturdays and almost any sort of Sundays, and crowd and delay trolley-cars, and make much worry for the traffic authorities. If you really want to be more specific: Picture many white steeples, and numerous minarets, and innumerable highly-decorated buildings of every conceivable architecture, from the prototype of a Turkish mosque to the styles obtaining among the more imaginative of the Japanese, with a strain of the architectural fashions which are creditably supposed to obtain in fairyland; imagine swirling things, and tortuous things, and very quickly moving things, and gentlemen with rather bright clothes and (unfortunately) somewhat hoarse voices who make vigorous announcements of activities within; imagine countless crowds of women in white and quite as many men in many colors, strolling, waiting, peering, laughing; being borne off in curious contrivances that rush and dash; being carried again by other curious contrivances that jump and dance— imagine the sounds of distant bands and present chatter; above all, imagine movement, movement, movement everywhere—and you have a tolerable idea of summer amusement to-day, as people understand summer amusement. . . .

Think, then, of the cellar door—the cellar door of childhood. . . . Because that little door had within it the mystery, the thrill, the glamorous uncertainty which is the foundation of all success in the corridors of summer amusements.

You remember—they opened that little door and there was blackness there. They closed it on you and you trembled, trembled deliciously. You wondered what would happen if they forgot about you. You shivered for a little while there in the black and then you issued forth again with a strange exultancy. Your little nerves had cried to be thrilled—and they were thrilled. Henceforth, you regarded that little cellar door with a strange reverence, a joyous fear. And it was a versatile thing, too, because when the thrill of the dark wore off you could slide down its slippery surface and that was another thrill—a thrill that never ceases.

300

Showmen and the "Amusement Business"

It was not until you grew up and got beyond it that you craved the thrill of something else. And that craving to thrill, that undeniable, universal craving to thrill which possesses every man or woman, boy or girl—is the objective point at which all summer amusement providers aim. We develop many amplifications of the little door, all over the country. . . .

But the thrill is the thing. It has been so throughout the evolution of American summer amusement. When the fat ladies and the tall ladies and the bearded ladies and the thin ladies, and the abnormally strong men and the sword-swallowing persons appeared before you, it was with the simple idea that you should be thrilled. When the raucous-voiced "spielers" of the old fashion proclaimed the thrilling merits of the man from Borneo it was with the same virtuous intent. When they announced "the most stoopenjious creat-uuu-ure" who was "half a dorg and half a man," they aimed at precisely the same thing. And the moving terrors pictured on the old brown posters— those old brown, canvas, weather-beaten posters which we knew so well—had a similar moving aim. It was the little cellar door again—vulgarised—but that same little cellar door. . . .

And the first thing which the summer amusement provider has to recognize is that men and women are not really men and women at all, but only children grown up. He comes to recognize that the average mature human is not the complex thing which he had previously imagined. He comes to learn that all people are primitive in their tastes and pleasures. He comes more directly to his point, it is true, than the exponent of the high-brow drama; but the governing principles are essentially the same. Suspense, thrill and—grateful satisfaction—this is the body and the spirit of all amusement, high, low and middle-browed. Even in the most removed of dramas there must be a thrilling moment. The summer amusement provider learns that he must make his thrilling moments more frequent, more personal than any which have gone before. . . .

This child-nature is the first thing which you must sedulously follow, and study and refuse to be parted from it if you would be a successful promoter of summer amusement. You must learn, for instance, that no truly great success can be other than simply arrived at—provided, of course, that the necessary amount of thrill is there. You will find that the most popular appeals are those which are the most starkly primal— and blood-related to some children's game. Taking a ride, for instance. Only this must be a longer ride, a steeper ride, a more thrilling ride than that which the other children —the children not grown up—demand. The cellar door must be enlarged.

And now begin the problems to be solved when you cater to these children long since grown. Their nature, it is true, undergoes no change. But their tendencies do. . . . These grown-up children want new toys all the time and new dolls are headless ere they are well dressed up. You must make newer cellar doors, more elaborate ones all the time, to replace those old affairs which are flying from the hinge. . . . And as the days go on these characteristics come forth more boldly. Each season the grown children become more insatiable. They are thrill-hungry. They ask a new thought; they demand a new laugh; they clamor for a new sensation. The devices of yesterday have

301

become older than the pyramids. It is part of the psychology of summer amusements that you must unite to-day and to-morrow.

It is only necessary to look back a few years for illustrations. The humble old merry-go-round which fascinated our fathers and beguiled our mothers to joy—the old merry-go-round with its wooden horses, drawn through the country village by a horse —is gone into the limbo of things. New desires have created the devices which cause you to plunge down steel inclines into water, and turn somersaults in the air, and jump over abysses, and make lightning dashes through gorges and caverns and multifarious other things which must get quicker and steeper and more joyously terrifying all the time if they are to succeed. The cyclorama, not so very long ago too, was looked upon as a desirable and uplifting thing. Viewing the anxieties of others was found to be wholesome and gratifying. You used to watch a shipwreck and be perfectly satisfied. You viewed the fragments of the train wreck with active pleasure. The appeal to the eye then wholly satisfied. All that you desired in those early days was optical satisfaction. Now, however, you must hear the boat crash or the train fall apart; or you must have the sensation of going down some dizzy incline. You are the victim of the snowball of sensation which promoters must follow. It gets greater all the time. . . .

All the subjects may be incalculably varied, but deep-set, within the bosom of each, must be the same potentiality of exaggerated child's play blended with apparent physical hazard. These absolutely must be present or your device will be a failure. . . .

There is one necessary thing, however, which, in addition to thrill, every idea should have. Your idea must be simple in order to be successful. The child-man, or woman, may have more strenuous ideas of excitement than when they viewed the little cellar door, but the fascination of the barbarically simple never dies within the human breast. Your average person does not want a conception to be suggested to him. He wants a conception to dazzle, to stun him, to hit him on the head like the crack of doom.

Neither, in this relation, does the child-nature of men and women ever outgrow that other element which is so much a part of child-nature—vanity.

These, indeed, are the only two appeals which you can make to people in the matter of amusement—thrill and vanity. I have spoken of the average person's inborn hungering for terror, that most overpowering of all human delights. An understanding of the psychology of vanity is almost as important to the summer amusement provider. The promoter of summer devices for amusement comes to understand as no other man does, the overpowering ambition of those grown-up children called the human race to be seen "doing things." . . .

So an amusement promoter comes to learn that the average man wants to prove that he can do things better than anybody else. And the amusement promoter advances—as an amusement promoter—because he knows this, and gives that average man every opportunity in the world to do it. It is for this reason that most of the devices which you see and which can appeal to vanity are placed where every opportunity for observation exists. This, too, has a double effect. A certain opportunity to view things, or the portions of things, exercises an influence in inducing other people to "do" them too. You make provision in this way also to draw people who take pleasure in watching other people "do it." And it is really to general admission that I look for profit.

A promoter comes to learn, too, that it is futile to make any appeal to class in the matter of amusement. The human race is a great democracy in the matter of amusement. The summer promoter comes to know that all his attractions must appeal to primitive desires—because all people are primitive. . . .

Having got, then, your foundation of thrill and vanity, and your knowledge of the child-nature of man and woman, the aim is, as far as possible, to scientifically cover the whole broad ground of the human senses. . . . If you want to be shocked—electrically shocked—you can become shocked. The sensations of speed, or the rushing of cool air, of falling, of bumping, of twisting, of turning—all are provided in innumerable variety. But the psychology of entertainment demands that the eyes likewise shall be pleased by some little suggestion of mystery or wonderment, for which the human race is ever hungry. And here is explained the fantastic suggestiveness of the architecture. The aim is, as far as possible, to duplicate the cities of fairy stories, in the material—to appeal to the child-imagination in sight as well as feeling. So when you see the imitation mosques and the minarets next time, think of this and follow the mental process of its creation. Notice the classical form and the fantastic shape and know the reason for each of these things, which is an attempt to make the universal appeal to that which exists in varying proportions to varying people.

And in the matter of hearing—bands, bands, bands, for the reason that they exhilarate, and unconsciously excite and prepare the mind for the rushing things about them. They help along what people are pleased to term "the carnival spirit." This is the reason for the band. It has instructions to move about every hour playing, for the reason that it stirs up people and keeps them moving, which means, of course, potential success and money. For the first idea, the very basic idea of summer entertainment is to get people in good humor—and keep them there. When you can do that, success is an almost calculable proposition. . . .

Finally, and in brief, you must imagine your public—your grown-up human children —as a great clock which your experience and intuition enables you to wind up. The average man lives very largely the creature of conventions, the tragic victim of set and settled circumstances. Custom and habit force him to take life solemnly. This is your problem if you are going to be successful as a summer amusement promoter. You must wind that man up. You must wind up the clock that operates the other side of the average person. You must "get him going" as the saying has it. And to do this you must give him a tilt to get him started. Once started he'll do the rest himself.

Of course, all these things sound exceedingly foolish. They are. But it is their very foolishness which makes their chiefest success. Because these, our grown children, like to be foolish at the bottom of their hearts. They must be amused and thrilled. They will admit that it is all foolishness themselves afterward.

They laugh at themselves with perfect charity—and come again.

But the one great secret which the caterer in public amusement has learned and must learn well is that mankind never loses the heritage of its great mystery—the mystery of childhood.

Popular Responses

Coney Island was one of the few avenues of temporary escape available for the urban poor. Of all the large cities, New York had the highest proportion of recent immigrants; by the 1880s, four-fifths of the population were first-and second-generation Americans. East European Jews were the most numerous of the newcomers in the thirty years before World War One. In Anzia Yezierska's novel *Bread Givers* (1925), Sara Smolinsky is embarrassed when the women in the Lower East Side laundry tell ribald stories of unseemly behavior at Coney Island. In 1902, Sadie Frowne, a sixteen-year-old, orphaned Jewish immigrant from Poland, told her story to a weekly magazine interested in the lives of the "undistinguished." Industrial workers labored for long hours, about sixty a week, rather less for those in retail and the service trades, but generally had Saturday afternoons free. Frowne saw Coney's dance halls, like the melodramatic theater, as welcome relief from the tiring, foot-operated sewing machines in the Brooklyn garment sweatshop, relief that was just an hour's journey away.

The Life Stories of Undistinguished Americans as Told by Themselves, ed. Hamilton Holt (1906; New York: Routledge, 1990), 21, 86–87; originally published in the *Independent* 54 (September 25, 1902): 2279–82; 55 (September 24, 1903): 2261–66.

Sometimes we go to Coney Island, where there are good dancing places, and sometimes we go to Ulmer Park for picnics. I am very fond of dancing, and, in fact, all sorts of pleasure. . . . But a girl must have clothes if she is to go into high society at Ulmer Park or Coney Island or the theatre. Those who blame me are the old country people who have old-fashioned notions, but the people who have been here a long time know better. A girl who does not dress well is stuck in a corner, even if she is pretty, and Aunt Fanny says that I do just right to put on plenty of style.

In 1903, Agnes M., a twenty-year-old immigrant from Alsace-Lorraine, also told of her delight in enjoying social freedom as a single woman. As a nursemaid, she received twenty-five dollars a month, with additional food and clothing. She spent her two free afternoons a week in outings with German-speaking friends to local beaches, and in dancing.

I like Coney Island best of all. It is a wonderful and beautiful place. I took a German friend, a girl who had just come out, down there last week, and when we had been on the razzle-dazzle, the chute and the loop-the-loop, and down in the coal mine and all over the Bowery, and up in the tower and everywhere else, I asked her how she liked it. She said: "Ach, it is just like what I see when I dream of heaven."

Yet I have heard some of the high people with whom I have been living say that Coney Island is not tony [high-toned]. The trouble is these high people don't know how to dance. I have to laugh when I see them at their balls and parties. If only I could get out on the floor and show them how—they would be astonished.

Coney Island was a strange amalgam of order and disorder, the pretentious and the squalid. In 1905, in a snobbish guide to slumming celebrating the *flâneur* (the sophisticated observer who strolled through the city), Richard Hughes applauded the recent architectural glories but warned that Bowery "plebeiance at its worst" still lingered on the margins. Clustered haphazardly around the three walled parks remained scores of amusement enterprises. Roller coasters, switchback railways, and re-enacted narrative spectaculars, ranging from the classical Fall of Pompeii to the heroic Rough Riders, still mingled with fast-food counters, restaurants, beer halls, boxing booths, vaudeville shows, and cheap nickelodeons with the latest movies. Dance halls were especially popular with the young. The opening of Dreamland in 1904 provided O. Henry with a suitable setting to explore "New Coney" and Irish-American working-class subculture. Southern-born Henry (William S. Porter) was a prolific short-story writer with a close interest in class differences and the lives of New York's "four million." Those of Irish descent were, with Germans, the largest group of old-stock immigrants in the city and a subject for dialect humor.

O. Henry, "The Greater Coney," in *Sixes and Sevens* (New York: Doubleday, Page, 1911), 167–72.

Next Sunday, said Dennis Carnahan, I'll be after going down to see the new Coney Island that's risen like a phoenix bird from the ashes of the old resort. I'm going with Norah Flynn, and we'll fall victims to all the dry goods deceptions, from the red-flannel eruptions of Mount Vesuvius to the pink silk ribbons on the race-suicide problems in the incubator kiosk.

Was I there before? I was. I was there last Tuesday. Did I see the sights? I did not.

Last Monday I amalgamated myself with the Bricklayers' Union, and in accordance with the rules I was ordered to quit work the same day on account of a sympathy strike with the Lady Salmon Canners' Lodge No. 2, of Tacoma, Washington.

'Twas disturbed I was in mind and proclivities by losing me job, bein' already harassed in me soul on account of havin' quarrelled with Norah Flynn a week before by reason of hard words spoken at the Dairymen and Street-Sprinkler Drivers' semi-annual ball, caused by jealousy and prickly heat and that devil, Andy Coughlin.

So, I says, it will be Coney for Tuesday; and if the chutes and the short change and the green-corn silk between the teeth don't create diversions and get me feeling better, then I don't know at all.

Ye will have heard that Coney has received moral reconstruction. The old Bowery, where they used to take your tintype by force and give ye knockout drops before having your palm read, is now called the Wall Street of the island. The wienerwurst stands are required by law to keep a news ticker in 'em; and the doughnuts are examined every four years by a retired steamboat inspector. The nigger man's head that was used by the old patrons to throw baseballs at is now illegal; and, by order of the Police Commissioner the image of a man drivin' an automobile has been substituted. I hear that the old immoral amusements have been suppressed. People who used to go down from New York to sit in the sand and dabble in the surf now give up their quarters to squeeze through turnstiles and see imitations of city fires and floods painted on canvas. The reprehensible and degradin' resorts that disgraced old Coney are said to be wiped out. The wipin'-out process consists of raisin' the price from 10 cents to 25 cents, and hirin' a blonde named Maudie to sell tickets instead of Micky, the Bowery Bite. That's what they say—I don't know.

But to Coney I goes a-Tuesday. I gets off the 'L' and starts for the glitterin' show. 'Twas a fine sight. The Babylonian towers and the Hindoo roof gardens was blazin' with thousands of electric lights, and the streets was thick with people. 'Tis a true thing they say that Coney levels all rank. I see millionaires eatin' popcorn and trampin' along with the crowd; and I see eight-dollar-a-week clothin'-store clerks in red automobiles fightin' one another for who'd squeeze the horn when they come to a corner.

I made a mistake, I says to myself. 'Twas not Coney I needed. When a man's sad 'tis not scenes of hilarity he wants. 'Twould be far better for him to meditate in a graveyard or to attend services at the Paradise Roof Gardens. 'Tis no consolation when a man's lost his sweetheart to order hot corn and have the waiter bring him the powdered sugar cruet instead of salt and then conceal himself, or to have Zozookum, the gipsy palmist, tell him that he has three children and to look out for another serious calamity; price twenty-five cents.

I walked far away down on the beach, to the ruins of an old pavilion near one corner of this new private park, Dreamland. A year ago that old pavilion was standin' up straight and the old-style waiters was slammin' a week's supply of clam chowder down in front of you for a nickel and callin' you "curly" friendly, and vice was rampant, and you got back to New York with enough change to take a car at the bridge. Now they tell me that they serve Welsh rabbits on Surf Avenue, and you get the right change back in the movin'-picture joints.

I sat down at one side of the old pavilion and looked at the surf spreadin' itself on the beach, and thought about the time me and Norah Flynn sat on that spot last summer. 'Twas before reform struck the island; and we was happy. We had tintypes and chowder in the ribald dives, and the Egyptian Sorceress of the Nile told Norah out of her hand, while I was waitin' in the door, that 'twould be the luck of her to marry a red-headed gossoon with two crooked legs, and I was overrunnin' with joy on account

306

of the allusion. And 'twas there that Norah Flynn put her two hands in mine a year before and we talked of flats and the things she could cook and the love business that goes with such episodes. And that was Coney as we loved it, and as the hand of Satan was upon it, friendly and noisy and your money's worth, with no fence around the ocean and not too many electric lights to show the sleeve of a black serge coat against a white shirtwaist.

I sat with my back to the parks where they had the moon and the dreams and the steeples corralled, and longed for the old Coney. There wasn't many people on the beach. Lots of them was feedin' pennies into the slot machines to see the 'Interrupted Courtship' in the movin' pictures; and a good many was takin' the air in the Canals of Venice and some was breathin' the smoke of the sea battle by actual warships in a tank filled with real water. A few was down on the sands enjoyin' the moonlight and the water. And the heart of me was heavy for the new morals of the old island, while the bands behind me played and the sea pounded on the bass drum in front.

And directly I got up and walked along the old pavilion, and there on the other side of it, half in the dark, was a slip of a girl sittin' on the tumble-down timbers, and unless I'm a liar she was cryin' by herself there, all alone.

"Is it trouble you are in, now, Miss," says I; "and what's to be done about it?"

"Tis none of your business at all, Denny Carnahan," says she, sittin' up straight. And it was the voice of no other than Norah Flynn.

"Then it's not," says I, "and we're after having a pleasant evening, Miss Flynn. Have ye seen the sights of this new Coney Island, then? I presume ye have come here for that purpose," says I.

"I have," says she. "Me mother and Uncle Tim they are waiting beyond. 'Tis an elegant evening I've had. I've seen all the attractions that be."

"Right ye are," says I to Norah; and I don't know when I've been that amused. After disportin' meself among the most laughable moral improvements of the revised shell games I took meself to the shore for the benefit of the cool air. "And did ye observe the Durbar, Miss Flynn?"

"I did," says she, reflectin'; "but 'tis not safe, I'm thinkin', to ride down them slantin' things into the water."

"How did ye fancy the shoot the chutes?" I asks.

"True then, I'm afraid of guns," says Norah. "They make such noise in my ears. But Uncle Tim, he shot them, he did, and won cigars. 'Tis a fine time we had this day, Mr. Carnahan."

"I'm glad you've enjoyed yerself," I says. "I suppose you've had a roarin' fine time seein' the sights. And how did the incubators and the helter-skelter and the midgets suit the taste of ye?"

"I—I wasn't hungry," says Norah, faint. "But mother ate a quantity of all of 'em. I'm that pleased with the fine things in the new Coney Island," says she, "that it's the happiest day I've seen in a long time, at all."

"Did you see Venice?" says I.

307

"We did," says she. "She was a beauty. She was all dressed in red, she was, with—"

I listened no more to Norah Flynn. I stepped up and I gathered her in my arms.

"Tis a story-teller ye are, Norah Flynn," says I. "Ye've seen no more of the greater Coney Island than I have meself. Come, now, tell the truth—ye came to sit by the old pavilion by the waves where you sat last summer and made Dennis Carnahan a happy man. Speak up, and tell the truth."

Norah stuck her nose against me vest.

"I despise it, Denny," she says, half cryin'. "Mother and Uncle Tim went to see the shows, but I came down here to think of you. I couldn't bear the lights and the crowd. Are you forgivin' me, Denny, for the words we had?"

"'Twas me fault," says I. "I came here for the same reason meself. Look at the lights, Norah," I says, turning my back to the sea—"ain't they pretty?"

"They are," says Norah, with her eyes shinin', "and do ye hear the bands playin'? Oh, Denny, I think I'd like to see it all."

"The old Coney is gone, darlin'," I says to her. "Everything moves. When a man's glad it's not scenes of sadness he wants. 'Tis a greater Coney we have here, but we couldn't see it till we got in the humour for it. Next Sunday, Norah darlin', we'll see the new place from end to end."

George C. Tilyou's Steeplechase Park typified the "hurly-burly" park. In place of architectural grandeur it had a grotesque, grinning "Funny Face" at the entrance gate and clownlike gargoyles throughout. As the park's trademark, Tilyou imported from England the eight-lane, inclined steeplechase track equipped with two-person, mechanical hobby-horses that had been one of the features of the reconstructed Bastille amusement park at the 1889 Paris Exposition. A combination ticket of twenty-five cents gave admission and entrance to sixteen attractions housed within the vast glassed warehouse of the Pavilion of Fun built in 1907. Most of the rides were simple, brazen funfair ploys to encourage human interaction and male-female encounter; they temporarily disorientated visitors by spinning them round, or throwing them off-balance, or surprised them with sudden, hidden air-jets.

Steeplechase was among the parks that "Josiah Allen's wife," Marietta Holley's Samantha, visits in search of her foolish husband. Over a period of thirty years, Holley produced ten bestselling, humorous novels satirizing pretension in a male-dominated world. Josiah is so entranced by neighbor Serenus Gowdey's experiences at Coney that he sneaks off to sample the pleasures of that "frisky, frivolous spot" near big-city Brooklyn. The plump, homely Samantha brings the wise innocent's eye and Yankee common sense to bear on familiar, everyday experiences. The "Funny Place" had a reputation for hiding simple but ingenious devices that suddenly transformed staid country jakes like Samantha into figures "laughin' and bein' laughed at." Holley acknowledged the humor in the accidental encounters that Tilyou engineered but ignored completely the teasing physical contact between men and women for which Steeplechase was best known; she made the spectacle of middle-aged Samantha's raised skirts and lowered esteem comical but not titillating to the onlookers.

Marietta Holley, *Samantha at Coney Island and a Thousand Other Islands* (New York: Christian Herald, 1911), 251–55, 257–60, 263–66.

Steeple Chase Park is most as big as Luny Park, but is mostly one huge buildin' covered with glass, and every thing on earth or above, or under the earth, is goin' on there, acres and acres of amusements (so-called) in one glass house.

As I went in, I see a immense mirror turnin' round and round seemin'ly invitin' folks to look. But as I glanced in, I tell the truth when I say, I wusn't much bigger round than a match, and the thinness made me look as tall as three on me.

"Oh," sez I, "has grief wore down my flesh away like this? If it keeps on I shan't dast to take lemonade, for fear I shall fall into the straw and be drowned."

A bystander sez, "Look agin, mom!"

I did and I wuzn't more'n two fingers high, and wide as our barn door.

I most shrieked and sez to myself, "It has come onto me at last, grief and such doin's as I've seen here, has made me crazy as a loon." And I started away almost on a run.

All of a sudden the floor under me which looked solid as my kitchen floor begun to move back and forth with me and sideways and back, to and fro, fro and to, and I goin' with it, one foot goin' one way, and the other foot goin' somewhere else; but by a hurculaneum effort I kep' my equilibrium upright, and made out to git on solid floorin'. But a high-headed female in a hobble skirt, the hobbles hamperin her, fell prostrate. I felt so shook up and wobblin' myself, I thought a little Scripter would stiddy me, and I sez, "Sinners stand on slippery places."

"I see they do!" she snapped out, lookin' at me; "but I can't!"

I sez to myself as I turned away, "I'll bet she meant me." But bein' tuckered out, I sot down on a reliable-lookin' stool, the high-headed woman takin' another one by my side—there was a hull row of folks settin' on 'em—when, all of a sudden, I d'no how it wuz done or why, but them stools all sunk right down to the floor bearin' us with 'em onwillin'ly. . . .

And I hurried off till I come out into a kinder open place with some good stiddy chairs to set down on, and some green willers hangin' down their verdant boughs over some posy beds. Nothin' made up about 'em. Oh, how good it looked to me to see sunthin' that God had made, and man hadn't dickered with and manufactured to seem different from what it wuz. Thinks I, if I should take hold of one of these feathery green willer sprays it wouldn't turn into a serpent or try to trip me up, or wobble me down. They looked beautiful to me, and beyond 'em I could see the Ocean, another and fur greater reality, real as life, or death, or taxes, or anything else we can't escape from. . . .

SUMMER AMUSEMENT PARKS

I thought I would go upstairs into another part of the buildin' and mebby I might ketch a glimpse of my pardner in the dense crowd below.

And if you'll believe it, as I wuz walkin' upstairs as peaceful as our old brindle cow goin' up the south hill paster, my skirts begun to billow out till they got as big as a hogsit. I didn't care about its bein' fashion to not bulge out round the bottom of your skirts but hobble in; but I see the folks below wuz laughin' at me, and it madded me some when I hadn't done a thing, only jest walk upstairs peaceable. And I don't know to this day what made my clothes billow out so.

But I went on and acrost to a balcony, and after I went in, a gate snapped shet behind me and I couldn't git back. And when I got to the other side there wuzn't any steps, and if got down at all I had to slide down. I didn't like to make the venter, but had to, so I tried to forgit my specs and gray hair and fancy I wuz ten years old, in a pig-tail braid, and pantalettes tied on with my stockin's, and sot off. As I went down with lightnin' speed I hadn't time to think much, but I ricollect this thought come into my harassed brain:

Be pardners worth all the trouble I'm havin' and the dreadful experiences I'm goin' through? Wouldn't it been better to let him go his length, than to suffer what I'm sufferin'? I reached the floor with such a jolt that my mind didn't asnswer the question; it didn't have time.

All at once, another wind sprung up from nowhere seemin'ly, and tried its best to blow off my bunnet. But thank heaven, my good green braize veil tied round it with strong lute-string ribbon, held it on, and I see I still had holt of my trusty cotton umbrell, though the wind had blowed it open, but I shet it and grasped it firmly, thinkin' it wuz my only protector and safeguard now Josiah wuz lost, and I hastened away from that crazy spot.

As I passed on I see a hull lot of long ropes danglin' down. On top of 'em wuz a trolley, and folks would hang onto the handle and slide hundreds of feet through the air. But I didn't venter. Disinclination and rumatiz both made me waive off overtures to try it.

Pretty soon I come to a huge turn-table, big as our barn floor. It wuz still and harmless lookin' when I first see it, and a lot of folks got onto it, thinkin' I spoze it looked so shiny and good they'd like to patronize it. But pretty soon it begun to move, and then to turn faster and faster till the folks couldn't keep their seats and one by one they wuz throwed off, and went down through a hole in the floor I know not where. . . .

There wuz a tall pole in the middle of the Amaze, as they call it (well named, for it is truly amazin'), and the liebill on that pole read, "Climb the pole and ring the bell on it, and we will give you a prize."

I din't try to climb that pole, and wouldn't if I had been an athleet. How did I know but it would turn into a writhin' serpent, and writh with me? No, I thought I wouldn't take another resk in that dredful spot. And I wuz glad I thought so, for jest a little ways off, some honest, easy lookin' benches stood invitin' the weary passer-by to set down and rest and recooperate. And right there before my eyes some good lookin' folks sot down on 'em trustin'ly, and the hull bench fell back with 'em and then riz up agin', they fallin' and risin' with it.

I hastened away and thought I would go up into the second story agin and mebby ketch sight of my pardner, for the crowd had increased. And as I stood there skannin' the immense crowd below to try to ketch a glimpse of my lawful pardner, all to once I see the folks below wuz laughin' at me. I felt to see if my braize veil hung down straight and graceful, and my front hair wuz all right, and my cameo pin fastened. But nothin' wuz amiss, and I wondered what could it be. The balcony wuz divided off into little spaces, five or six feet square, and I stood in one, innocent as a lamb (or mebbe it would be more appropriate to say a sheep), and leanin' on the railin', and one sassy boy called out:

"Where wuz you ketched? Are you tame? Wuz you ketched on the Desert of Sara? Did Teddy ketch you for the Government?" and I never know'd till I got down what they wuz laughin' at.

The little boxes in the balcony wuz painted on the outside to represent animal cages. On the one where I had been wuz painted the sign Drumedary. Josiah Allen's wife took for a drumedary—The idee!

But the view I got of the crowd wuz impressive, and though it seemed to me that everybody in New York and Brooklyn and the adajacent villages and country, wuz all there a Steeple Chasin', yet I knowed there wuz just as many dreamin' in Dreamland and bein' luny in Luny Park. And Surf Avenue wuz full, and what they called the Bowery of Coney Island, and all the amusement places along the shore. And all on 'em on the move, jostlin' and bein' jostled, and bein' fooled, laughin' and bein' laughed at.

Two Critics of Coney's Banality

During his visit to the United States in 1906, the Russian socialist writer Maxim Gorky found Coney's tawdry amusements depressing beyond measure. From a distance the island at night was dazzling—as "a fantastic city all of fire," with "shapely towers of miraculous castles, palaces and temples," linked by necklaces of light bulbs. However, by day, once the glare of artificial illumination had faded, there was simply a cheap, "dull, gloomy ugliness." Only the spectacles of extreme danger or cruelty organized by greedy capitalists for profit roused the tired, jaded, pleasure-seeking conformists from their torpor.

Maxim Gorky, "Boredom," *Independent* 63 (August 8, 1907): 311–12.

The city, magic and fantastic from afar, now appears an absurd jumble of straight lines of wood, a cheap, hastily constructed toy-house for the amusement of children. Dozens of white buildings, monstrously diverse, not one with even the suggestion of beauty. They are built of wood, and smeared over with peeling white paint, which gives them the appearance of suffering with the same skin disease. The high turrets and low colonnades extend in two dead-even lines insipidly pressing upon each other. Everything is stripped naked by the dispassionate glare. The glare is everywhere, and nowhere a shadow. . . .

The people huddled together in this city actually number hundreds of thousands. They swarm into the cages like black flies. Children walk about, silent, with gaping mouths and dazzled eyes. They look around with such intensity, such seriousness, that the sight of them feeding their little souls upon this hideousness, which they mistake for beauty, inspires a pained sense of pity. The men's faces, shaven even to the mustache, all strangely like each other, are grave and immobile. The majority bring their wives and children along, and feel that they are benefactors of their families, because they provide not only bread, but also magnificent shows. They enjoy the tinsel, but, too serious to betray their pleasure, they keep their thin lips pressed together, and look from the corners of their screwed-up eyes, like people whom nothing can astonish. Yet, under the mask of indifference simulated by the man of mature experience, a strained desire can be detected to take in all the delights of the city. The men with serious faces, smiling indifferently and concealing the satisfied gleam of their sparkling eyes, seat themselves on the backs of the wooden horses and elephants of the merry-go-round and, dangling their feet, wait with nervous impatience for the keen pleasure of flying along the rails. With a whoop they dart up to the top, with a whistle they descend again. After this stirring journey they draw their skin tight on their faces again and go to taste of new pleasures.

The amusements are without number. There on the summit of an iron tower two long wings rock slowly up and down. At the end of each wing hang cages, and in these cages are people. When one of the wings rises heavily toward the sky the faces of the occupants of the cages grow sadly serious. They all look in round-eyed silence at the ground receding from them. In the cages of the other wing, then carefully descending, the faces of the people are radiant with smiles. Joyous screams are heard, which strangely remind one of the merry yelp of a puppy let to the floor after he has been held up in the air by the scruff of his neck.

Boats fly in the air around the top of another tower, a third keeps turning about and impels some sort of iron balloon, a fourth, a fifth—they all move and blaze and call with the mute shouts of cold fire. Everything rocks and roars and bellows and turns the heads of the people. They are filled with contented *ennui*, their nerves are racked by an intricate maze of motion and dazzling fire. Bright eyes grow still brighter, as if the brain paled and lost blood in the strange turmoil of the white, glittering wood. The *ennui*, which issues from under the pressure of self-disgust, seems to turn and turn in a slow circle of agony. It drags tens of thousands of uniformly dark people into its somber dance, and sweeps them into a will-less heap, as the wind sweeps the rubbish of the street. Then it scatters them apart and sweeps them together again.

James Huneker was a critic renowned for his wide-ranging art and music criticism and appreciation of modernism. Coney Island, however, aroused all

312

Two Critics of Coney's Banality

his middle-aged and middle-class prejudices. He was appalled: the "hideous symphony of noise" from the "savage horde of barbarians" was beyond redemption. It was "a disgrace to our civilisation." And the crowd: "half-child, half-savage," "simian gestures," "a disturbed ant-heap," "bedlam." This was commercial exploitation, not Art—a "monstrous debauch of the fancy."

James Huneker, *The New Cosmopolis: A Book of Images* (New York: T. Werner Laurie, 1915), 154–56, 161–62, 164.

[L]et me tell you of the joys I experienced after I had landed at the Steeplechase Park pier in company with some hundreds of fellow lunatics of all ages and conditions, for when you are at Coney you cast aside your hampering reason and become a plain lunatic. It was a great French writer who advised his readers to make of themselves beasts from time to time, to kick over the slow and painful step-ladder of moral restraint and revert to the normal animal from which we evolved. . . .

After the species of straitjacket that we wear in every-day life is removed at such Saturnalia as Coney Island, the human animal emerges in a not precisely winning guise. . . .

The barkers arouse us. We buy a string of parti-coloured tickets. They are so many keys that unlock to us the magic chambers of this paradise of secular joys and terrors. You may swim or guzzle; on the hard backs of iron steeds, to the accompaniment of bedlam music, you may caracole or go plunging down perilous declivities, swinging into the gloom of sinister tunnels or, perched aloft, be the envy of small boys. . . .

Every device imaginable by which man may be separated from his dimes without adequate return is in operation. You weigh yourself or get it guessed; you go into funny houses—oh, the mockery of the title!—and later are tumbled into the open, insulted, mortified, disgusted, angry, and—laughing. What sights you have seen in that prison-house, what gentlewomen—with shrill voices—desperately holding on to their skirts and their chewing-gum.

What I can't understand is the lure of the Island for the people who come. Why, after the hot, narrow, noisy, dirty streets of the city, do these same people crowd into the narrower, hotter, noisier, dirtier, wooden alleys of Coney? Is the wretched, Cheap John fair, with the ghastly rubbish for a sale, the magnet? Or is it just the gregariousness of the human animal? They leave dirt and disorder to go to greater disorder and dirt. . . .

But at Coney Island the cramped positions one must assume to stand or move, the fierce warfare of humanity as it forces its way along the streets or into the crazy shows—surely conceived by madmen for madmen—the indescribable and hideous symphony of noise running the gamut from shrill steam whistles to the diapasonic roar of machinery; decidedly the entire place produced the sensation of abnormality, of horrible joys grabbed at by a savage horde of barbarians, incapable of repose even in their moments of leisure. Some one has said that the Englishman takes his pleasures sadly, then we must take ours by rude assault. All Coney Island reminded me of

313

a disturbed ant-heap, the human ants ferocious in their efforts to make confusion thrice confounded, to heap up horrors of sound and of sight. . . .

Coney Island is only another name for topsyturvydom. There the true becomes the grotesque, the vision of a maniac. Else why those nerve-racking entertainments, ends of the world, creations, hells, heavens, fantastic trips to ugly lands, panoramas of sheer madness, flights through the air in boats, through water in sleds, on the earth in toy trains! . . . Mechanical waterfalls, with women and children racing around curving, tumbling floods; elephants tramping ponderously through streets that are a bewildering muddle of many nations, many architectures; deeds of Western violence and robbery, illustrated with a realism that is positively enthralling. . . . . .

Once en masse, humanity sheds its civilisation and becomes half child, half savage.

VAUDEVILLE

From the 1880s to the 1910s, vaudeville was the most popular form of entertainment in the country. Like the European musical hall, its essence was variety. It offered a fast-paced program of music, comedy, and drama, embellished with specialty and novelty acts of human skill and ingenuity, where the diverse acts seemed blended together into a package. Its virtues, *Cosmopolitan* noted in 1902, were "clean humor, nimbleness of action or fascinating originality."[1] Under its broad umbrella sheltered circus and minstrel acts but with a veneer of glamor and respectability that the dime museum never had. It retained much of the raw energy of the traditional traveling show but disciplined its asperities, introduced female star performers, and appealed to mixed, family audiences. More than its precursors in variety entertainment, vaudeville was managed as a business. Entrepreneurs attempted to apply rational principles, standardize a bill, and duplicate it in a circuit of regional theaters they controlled. They exaggerated vaudeville's refinement, for it never quite achieved gentility. Indeed, the tension among energy, enterprise, and edification gave it much of its vitality.

Before the Civil War, "vaudeville" was used occasionally to denote a show of comic songs or a short farce interspersed with songs; these were most common, as Charles Dickens found in the early 1840s, in that forging-ground of popular entertainment, New York's Olympic and Bowery theaters. A generation later, Tony Pastor redefined the variety show of "vaudevilles" and gave it an ambience of respectability. A circus comic and singer and minstrel clog dancer, Pastor opened his own Opera House on Bowery Street in 1865, moved closer to Broadway in 1875, and in 1881 established his New Fourteenth Street Theatre. From the beginning he adopted the tactic of the museum "lecture rooms," and, like Barnum, promised "Fun Without Vulgarity" —"all the latest gems of Opera, Comedy, Farce, and Minstrelsy, unalloyed by an indelicate act or expressions."[2] Pastor balanced his traditional Bowery audience's delight in robust comedy with the wishes of his increasingly middle-class clientele at Union Square. To differentiate his "refined" program from that of the nearby all-male concert-saloons, he banned the notorious "waiter-girls," offered premiums and prizes, and arranged matinees for women. Smoking and drinking were banned from the auditorium by 1881 and became less obtrusive elsewhere in the building. Pastor's topical songs—he wrote two thousand in a forty-year career—and his one-act sketches or "travesties," based loosely on popular musical comedies and spiced with allusions to local events, distinguished his entertainment.

But, apart from a brief annual tour, Pastor's enterprises were limited to greater New York. Others developed more fully his innovative strategy of lighthearted, family entertainment. In Boston, Benjamin Franklin Keith expanded the second-floor theater in his dime museum and presented low-priced, abridged versions of the British operettas popular in the city. Keith's theater also boasted a blameless moral atmosphere, with indecorous language forbidden, and with uniformed attendants ushering guests through the palatial lobby to luxurious plush seats. This polite music-hall entertainment was glamorized with the sophisticated French title of "vaudeville." In 1885 Keith introduced the "continuous" show, a sequence of nine or ten short acts in a program repeated from late morning to late evening. The format accommodated all in a twelve-hour cycle: suburban women shoppers, and mothers and children in the daytime, and men in the evening after work.

By the 1890s vaudeville was perceived to be the variety show best adapted to the modern city. It was the distilled essence of the major entertainments, lowbrow, middlebrow, even highbrow. With machinelike efficiency, an assortment of brief, fast-paced acts passed in rapid succession—acrobats and animal acts, ballerinas and boxers, clowns and comedians. It was an eclectic mix, a miscellany—magic tricks and technological innovations, one-act playlets and slapstick comedy, operatic arias and high-wire acrobatics. Almost any skill well-executed was included in the program. Arthur Ruhl described the performance of Barnold's Dogs in 1908. In a city street, "the dogs, dressed to represent various sorts of humans, march in on their hind legs and go about their business, especially that of patronizing the bar-room, as if no one else were there. . . . And especially you should see the astonishing animal who imitates a too-genial citizen. With unrepentant grin he starts across the street, zigzags uproariously, even falls and laboriously picks himself up, and finally after several wild and incredibly human attempts, makes the lamp-post on the other side and clings to it. Then the monkey policeman comes along, turns on the alarm, the patrol-wagon drives up clanging, and the unhappy bacchanalian is hauled to the station-house."[3]

Especially in "low-class," neighborhood vaudeville houses, stage sketches treated adjustment to the city—negotiations with officials, doctors, landlords, employers, school teachers, shopkeepers—and the everyday reality of courtship and marriage, parents and children, success and failure. Recognition had its charms for the inner-city poor. A third of the bill was devoted to fast-paced comedy that abandoned character development and narrative sequence and dwelt on ethnic peculiarities. "The backbone of vaudeville was low comedy," wrote Douglas Gilbert in 1940: "dialect, eccentric, and nut comedians in exaggerated costumes and facial make-ups predominated."[4] It was comedy stripped down to instant identification of stock types and quick-fire repartee. As well as the traditional blackface, "Irish," and "Dutch" (German) acts, it depicted recent arrivals to the city. Stage ethnicity was, Robert Snyder argues, "synthetic," a fiction based partly on reality and partly on theatrical stereotypes, and it was easily recognized by the audience. Cheap theaters were often more authentic. When John Corbin visited Italian and Jewish playhouses in the Lower East Side to see "How the Other Half Laughs," he found their plays "crude and often absurd," but "vital and spontaneous": "they treat the life and the history of the people who swarm to see them."[5]

Vaudeville prospered even during the economic depression of the 1890s. With tickets ranging from fifteen cents to a dollar, its prices were half that of the legitimate theater. When mainstream theater owners formed syndicates, dominated first by Marc Klaw and A. L. Erlanger, and later by the Shuberts, vaudeville also responded by consolidation. The most successful in the East was the circuit managed by Benjamin Franklin Keith and Edward F. Albee, who founded the United Booking Office in 1906. The aim of Keith and Albee and their rivals was to use a booking agency to regulate performers and theaters. This vision of neat bureaucratic order imposed centrally still left much discretion to the local manager. His responsibilities were numerous and onerous. He was required to discipline troublesome performers, make weekly reports on audience reaction to the acts, account for less-than-expected returns, and decide on the best order for acts on the bill, balancing the competing claims of cultural uplift and streetwise vitality. In a "refined" theater it was an almost impossible task to please the rowdy men in the gallery and balcony as well as the genteel in the boxes or women and children in matinee performances. Throughout the 1890s Sylvester Poli's strategy in New Haven, Connecticut, was to win over those of Irish and Italian descent with sympathetic and sentimental, but not demeaning, caricatures, and to entice the reluctant middle classes with more "refined," uplifting culture, while avoiding any hint of disreputable burlesque acts suited only for an all-male clientele. It required juggling and tightrope dancing as nimble as that of any acrobat on his Wonderland stage. Eventually, in the first decade of the new century, the emergence of Jesse Lasky's glamorous female performers, who deliberately sought publicity by defying convention and were popular with working-class women, made Poli's delicate negotiations much more difficult. In the Keith-Albee "Sunday-school circuit," the veneer of respectability wore thin by 1910.

"There must be something for everyone, and while the fastidious may be a little shocked (the fastidious rather like to be shocked sometimes)," Caroline

Caffin pronounced, "they must not be offended, while the seeker for thrills must on no account be bored with too much mildness."[6] The most prestigious "big-time" theaters had included some "name" players from the legitimate stage, particularly European actresses. Sarah Bernhardt, Lily Langtry, and Mrs. Patrick Campbell enlivened the bill, if only for their reputed beauty and elegance, to woo patrons of the legitimate stage. But vaudeville thrived on excitement and publicity, and even in the more genteel palaces, decorum had its limits. Younger, glamorous female singers, often immigrants like Gilda Gray and Sophie Tucker, who wore showy—and usually scanty—costumes, caused far greater problems for Poli and the Keith managers. Their stage routines were openly sensual and mocked the theater's highbrow pretensions. However, provided that flamboyant performers were restrained and doubles entendres qualified, they added an earthy raciness to the program. The "sex-personality" Mae West, however, was too uninhibited for Poli, and banned in 1912 for "that enchanting, seductive, sin-promising wriggle."[7]

The less expensive, "small-time" vaudeville theaters served the local neighborhood and a narrower-class clientele. By 1914 Marcus Loew built up a circuit of thirty-two vaudeville theaters in New York City alone. Low prices—five to twenty-five cents a ticket—made his theaters competitive with the cheapest melodrama house and even the nickelodeon, and with a change of bill twice a week, Loew hoped for repeat visits. He offered entertainment expressly suited to Jewish immigrants on the Lower East Side: combination film and vaudeville bills, amateur-night competitions for prizes, and a beauty contest at his Avenue B theater in June 1915. He showed shrewd business acumen. "When one of his emporiums of pleasure is opened in any city district, half the families within twenty minutes' walk are counted on for one visit a week," journalist Arthur Prill wrote.[8]

Stars were synonymous with turn-of-the-century vaudeville, even if there were few in Loew's cheap theaters. Of the popular "artistes," few were greater celebrities than Sophie Tucker. She graduated from Yiddish-language music hall and blackface to vaudeville where her strong voice and strong will made her a natural comedienne. She lacked the chorus girl's body and looks, but her vitality and evident hunger for success communicated almost intuitively with audiences. She spoke openly and uninhibitedly of her longing in "Some of These Days" (1910), her theme song, and questioned conventional gender roles, but as a "big fat mamma," she won sympathy. Even Sylvester Poli, who had great difficulties in curbing such aggressive, sensual New Women, promoted her in the press as "a personality that goes out straight over the footlights." She was the archetypal star performer-personality.[9]

Variety entertainers came in all shapes and forms, but the most successful, the critic Caroline Caffin noted in 1914, had "that feeling of good-fellowship that makes the audience love to be on confidential terms with the performer,

318

to be treated as an intimate." "They have learned, either by experience or instinct, so exactly the key in which to pitch their appeal, in order to evoke that answering vibration from their audience, that they can sound it at will, modulate it into what harmonies and expression they please, and ever be sure of the response." The highest-paid star of the vaudeville circuit—$3,500 a week in 1910—was Eva Tanguay, "The Queen of Perpetual Motion," "The Cyclonic One." Caffin was puzzled by her exceptional popularity. Tanguay was an enigma. She was not beautiful; she danced without grace; she sang poorly in a loud, high-pitched voice. Yet the audiences loved her, and screamed and shouted throughout her twenty-minute act. It was an "electrifying experience." Tanguay had "energy, not art," Caffin decided. She was restless, "alive, nervous, vital," with an "elemental dynamic buoyancy" and dashed across the stage in a "whirlwind of sound." Even her unruly hair had "electric vigor."[10] Her signature song, "I Don't Care," epitomized her untamed nature, her wild extravagant, physical gestures, and her off-stage reputation for tempestuous love affairs. Her other headline songs—"I Want Someone to Go Wild with Me," "It's All Been Done Before But Not the Way I Do It," and "Go As Far As You Like"—openly defied convention. Tanguay was a media-made celebrity who courted publicity and press gossip. Her eccentricity made her the quintessential vaudeville star—the individual as the primary creative force, the performer as personality.

Vaudeville Defined

In its first issue of October 1905, the *Midway*, the monthly periodical serving amusement park professionals, commented on vaudeville's ranking in the entertainment industry. It was "the acme of variegated theatrical entertainment," combining the best traditions of the popular theater with the latest technological innovations, and the model of good business sense for all showmen.

"In Vaudeville: A Short History of This Popular Character of Amusement," *Midway* 1 (October 1905): 27.

"Vaudeville," the word, is accepted generally as having been of Norman origin and dates back to the fourteenth and fifteenth centuries when Oliver Basselin, a fuller, living in the valley of the River Vire, composed and sang certain sprightly songs, which, in time, came to achieve a reputation throughout the country and inspired others to try their 'prentice hands. . . .

Vaudeville, the namesake of to-day, retains the spirit of these early troubadours, entertainers of the passing moment. Joyously, frankly absurd, it represents the almost universal longing for laughter, for melody, for color, for action and for wonder-provoking things. It strikes directly at the heart interests and the foibles of the day. Vaudeville is creative and progressive. The mind of the vaudeville creator runs, lightning-like, ahead of the public craving for the ever "new"; and his voyage of discovery leads him into strange haunts. Science yields her necromancy; the jungles give up their royal beasts and human nature parades all her eccentricities and moods, at his beck, for the delectation of legions of pleasure seekers.

Like all other forms of theatrical entertainment, it has had a bitter fight against hypocrisy and cant. The struggle would have been its undoing had it not possessed a vitality drawn from its relation to some of the strongest and most enduring instincts in our nature. It was called cheap by society; it was called vulgar by prudery; to-day it is triumphant in the affection of the people.

The women and children of America spend the greater part of $900,000 every week in proclaiming it the cleanest and most wholesome form of modern entertainment. No other theatre bears the same relation to the family circle. Cater to the women and children and the men will follow—it is a motto that has made millionaires of the great vaudeville caterers of the United States.

An investment of a little more than $26,000,000 in vaudeville is distributed among 300 theatres. More than 12,000 persons find their living in vaudeville and the public is sufficiently interested to expend nearly $1,000,000 a week in admission fees. The 12,000 employees may be divided as follows: Players or artists, 7,500; theatre attaches, 3,000; agents and assistants, 250; song writers, dramatists, etc., 350. The players have invested in wardrobe, scenery, music, plays and other necessary paraphernalia over $1,500,000 and pay the railroads of the country for their transportation over the various vaudeville circuits a sum in excess of $21,000 weekly.

The artistic work of the vaudeville stands on the highest plane, for when 12,000 persons lend their efforts to the promoting of one thing, it is evident at once that the thing must move ahead. Theatres devoted to vaudeville spend an enormous sum for providing their patrons with entertainment. Including the cost of operating the playhouses, this amounts to an expenditure of close to $600,000 every week that the theatre remains open—and a large number of them are running the year round. Some idea of the progressive quality of vaudeville may be gained when it is stated that there is an intense rivalry among the different managements for meritorious novelties; such a rivalry, in fact, as to require a weekly expenditure during the height of the season of $600,000.

The vaudeville bill, or program, consisting of six or eight to ten feature acts, costs considerably more than the average dramatic payroll of a first-class company. In many instances it is double or treble these salaries, although the prices usually are not more than one-half to one-third of those charged at the box office of the so-called "legitimate" theatres.

Formerly most of the novelties of the vaudeville were drawn from the "legitimate" stage; now the reverse is absolutely the case, and, indeed, nearly all the real "new" ideas embodied by the playwright are suggested from the thousands of clever things that have been used by the vaudeville managers. One time most of the big

320

names on the vaudeville stage were those of "stars" from the "legitimate" theatres; now quite the contrary rule applies. More new players are graduated from the vaudeville into the "legitimate" every year than the older stage has furnished vaudeville from its inception. Vaudeville has been the accepted test of younger players. Vaudeville managers do not hesitate still to snap up stars of the older profession, but they have turned their eyes into the field of newer discoveries for the things that astonish and make a "hit" or get a "laugh" from the public.

Vaudeville has become academic in its offerings—all that is best of scientific achievements and recent demonstrations in the theatres of the marvelous qualities of liquid air, radium, wireless telegraphy and kindred discoveries have done more to educate the public to the possibilities of modern scientific discovery and invention than a thousand popular lectures could have accomplished.

The birth of modern vaudeville—the perfect form of this immense field of entertainment—began with the idea that evolved in the brain of a New England country boy, B. F. Keith, who wandered into Boston in 1881. From a small start in an improvised storeroom the plan grew and prospered until on July 6, 1885, the present form of vaudeville entertainment had its inception. Its popularity was so immediate that to-day there is hardly a city of any consequence in the country that does not boast of its vaudeville house. From a mere "show" with no standing whatever, Mr. Keith has developed his "idea" into an entertainment that holds all that is best in the world of dramatic art.

Within the past five years a great change has come over this class of entertainment. The theatre, heretofore, has furnished such simple scenic appurtenances as the vaudeville performer needed. Now, however, the artist is becoming more ambitious, and is having built and is carrying with him, at his own expense, magnificent scenic equipment and electrical effects that hitherto have been considered the exclusive province of the regular theatre. At one time two or three persons were all that were required to constitute an act. Now it is no uncommon thing to find ten and even twelve players on the vaudeville stage, engaged in a twenty-minute turn.

When one can go to the theatre and see the best of dramatic, operatic, farce comedy and comic or music farce and even grand opera, with sprinklings of science, physical culture, some of the sawdust of the circus, marvelous children, wonderful training of wild animals, magic and illusion, all in one performance for the puzzlingly small price charged by the vaudeville theatre, the acme of variegated theatrical entertainment appears to have been reached.

Edwin Royle was a playwright and critic who appreciated the distinctively modern features of vaudeville, so peculiarly adapted to the American city. It was convenient and accessible. "It may be a kind of lunch-counter art," he noted in 1899, because, like the department store or the monthly-magazine story, it suited the quick tempo of modern life. Although serious art might have little place in this ruthlessly competitive and commercial forum, by

A New York vaudeville theater circa 1900, with a performing dog act on stage. From the Collections of the Henry Ford Museum and Greenfield Village.

1899, Royle observed, the "big-time" circuit was so well established that it was able to tempt stars from the conventional stage.

Edwin Milton Royle, "The Vaudeville Theatre," *Scribner's Magazine* 26 (October 1899): 485–95.

The vaudeville theatre is an American invention. There is nothing like it anywhere else in the world. It is neither the *café chantant*, the English music hall, nor the German garden. What has been called by a variety of names, but has remained always and everywhere pretty much the same—reeky with smoke, damp with libations, gay with the informalities of the half-world—is now doing business with us under the patronage of the royal American family.

Having expurgated and rehabilitated the tawdry thing, the American invites in the family and neighbors, hands over to them beautiful theatres, lavishly decorated and appointed, nails up everywhere church and army regulations, and in the exuberance of his gaiety passes around ice water. He hasn't painted out the French name, but that is because he has been, as usual, in a hurry. Fourteen years ago this may have been a dream in a Yankee's brain; now it is a part of us. The strictly professional world has been looking for the balloon to come down, for the fad to die out, for the impossible thing to stop, but year by year these theatres increase and multiply, till now they flourish the country over. . . .

Some of these theatres are never closed the year round. Some are content with three matinees a week in addition to their night performances. Others open their doors about noon and close them at 10:30 at night. These are called "continuous" houses. It is manifest, I think, that the vaudeville theatre is playing an important part in the amusement world and in our national life. Perhaps we should be grateful. At present it would seem that the moral tone of a theatre is in the inverse ratio of the price of admission. The higher the price, the lower the tone. It is certain that plays are tolerated and even acclaimed on the New York stage today which would have been removed with tongs half a dozen years ago.

So far as the vaudeville theatres are concerned, one might as well ask for a censorship of a "family magazine." It would be a work of supererogation. The local manager of every vaudeville house is its censor, and he lives up to his position laboriously, and, I may say, religiously. The bill changes usually from week to week. It is the solemn duty of this austere personage to sit through the first performance of every week and to let no guilty word or look escape. But this is precautionary only.

"You are to distinctly understand," say the first words of the contracts of a certain circuit, "that the management conducts this house upon a high plane of respectability and moral cleanliness," etc.

But long before the performer has entered the dressing rooms, he has been made acquainted with the following legend which everywhere adorns the walls:

NOTICE TO PERFORMERS

You are hereby warned that your act must be free from all vulgarity and suggestiveness in words, action, and costume, while playing in any of Mr.—'s houses, and all vulgar, double-meaning and profane words and songs must be cut out of your act before the first performance. If you are in doubt as to what is right or wrong, submit it to the resident manager at rehearsal.

Such words as Liar, Slob, Son-of-A-Gun, Devil, Sucker, Damn, and all other words unfit for the ears of ladies and children, also any reference to questionable streets, resorts, localities, and barrooms, are prohibited under fine of instant discharge.

GENERAL MANAGER

And this is not merely a literary effort on the part of the management, it is obligatory and final. When we have about accepted as conclusive the time-honored theory that "You must give the public what it wants," and that it wants bilge water in champagne glasses, we are confronted with the vaudeville theatre, no longer an experiment, but a comprehensive fact.

The funniest farce ever written could not be done at these houses if it had any of the earmarks of the thing in vogue at many of our first-class theatres. Said a lady to me: "They (the vaudeville theatres) are the only theatres in New York where I should feel absolutely safe in taking a young girl without making preliminary inquiries. Though they may offend the taste, they never offend one's sense of decency." The vaudeville theatres may be said to have established the commercial value of decency. This is

VAUDEVILLE

their cornerstone. They were conceived with the object of catering to ladies and children, and, strange to say, a large, if not the larger, part of their audiences is always men.

What I have said does not describe all theatres which may have "fashionable vaudeville" over their doors. Godliness has proved so profitable that there be here, as elsewhere, wolves masquerading in woollens, but the houses I have described are well known. Nor have the stringent regulations of these theatres exiled the "song and dance man" who was wont to rely on risque songs and suggestive jokes—they have only forced him to happier and saner efforts, and the result is not Calvinistic, on the contrary, nowhere are audiences jollier, quicker, and more intelligent, and the world of fashion even is not absent from these theatres primarily designed for the wholesome middle classes. . . .

A friend of mine was leaving a spacious vaudeville theatre, along with the audience, and was passing through the beautiful corridor, when one of the multitude of uniformed attachés handed him this printed notice:

> Gentlemen will kindly avoid carrying cigars or cigarettes in their mouths while in the building, and greatly oblige.
>
> THE MANAGEMENT

My friend was guilty of carrying in his hand an unlighted cigar.

How careful of the conduct of their patrons the management is may be seen from the following printed requests with which the employees are armed:

> Gentlemen will kindly avoid the stamping of feet and pounding of canes on the floor, and greatly oblige the Management. All applause is best shown by clapping of hands.
>
> Please don't talk during acts, as it annoys those about you, and prevents a perfect hearing of the entertainment.
>
> THE MANAGEMENT

. . . These are the chronicles of what is known among the vaudeville fraternity as "The Sunday-school Circuit," and the proprietor of the "The Sunday-school Circuit" is the inventor of vaudeville as we know it. This which makes for righteousness, as is usual, makes also for great and abiding cleanliness—physical as well as moral. I almost lost things in my Philadelphia dressing room—it was cleaned so constantly. Paternal, austere perhaps, but clean, gloriously clean!

The character of the entertainment is always the same. There is sameness even about its infinite variety. No act or "turn" consumes much over thirty minutes. Everyone's taste is consulted, and if one objects to the perilous feats of the acrobats or jugglers he can read his program or shut his eyes for a few moments and he will be compensated by some sweet bell-ringing or a sentimental or comic song, graceful or

324

Vaudeville Defined

grotesque dancing, a one-act farce, trained animals, legerdemain, impersonations, clay modelling, or the stories of the comic monologist. The most serious thing about the program is that seriousness is barred, with some melancholy results. From the artist who balances a set of parlor furniture on his nose to the academic baboon, there is one concentrated, strenuous struggle for a laugh. No artist can afford to do without it. It hangs like a solemn and awful obligation over everything. Once in a while an artist who juggles tubs on his feet is a comedian, but not always. It would seem as if a serious person would be a relief now and then. But so far the effort to introduce a serious note, even by dramatic artists, has been discouraged. I suspect the serious sketches have not been of superlative merit. Though this premium is put upon a laugh, everyone is aware of the difference between the man who rings a bell at forty paces with a rifle, and the man who smashes it with a club, and the loudest laugh is sometimes yoked with a timid salary. The man who said: "Let me get out of here or I'll lose my self-respect—I actually laughed," goes to the vaudeville theatres, too, and must be reckoned with.

So far as the character of the entertainment goes, vaudeville has the "open door." Whatever or whoever can interest an audience for thirty minutes or less, and has passed quarantine, is welcome. The conditions in the regular theatres are not encouraging to progress. To produce a play or launch a star requires capital of from $10,000 upward. There is no welcome and no encouragement. The door is shut and locked. And even with capital, the conditions are all unfavorable to proof. But if you can sing or dance or amuse people in any way, if you think you can write a one-act play, the vaudeville theatre will give you a chance to prove it. One day of every week is devoted to these trials. If at this trial you interest a man who is looking for good material, he will put you in the bill for one performance, and give you a chance at an audience, which is much better. The result of this open-door attitude is a very interesting innovation in vaudeville which is more or less recent, but seems destined to last—the incursion of the dramatic artist into vaudeville.

The managers of the vaudeville theatres are not emotional persons, and there were some strictly business reasons back of the actor's entrance into vaudeville. We do not live by bread alone, but by the saving graces of the art of advertising. It was quite impossible to accentuate sixteen or eighteen features of a bill. Some one name was needed to give it character and meaning at a glance. A name that had already become familiar was preferred. The actor's name served to head the bill and expand the type and catch the eye, and hence arose the vaudeville term—"Head-Liner."

This word is not used in contracts, but it is established and understood, and carries with it well-recognized rights and privileges, such as being featured in the advertisements, use of the star dressing room, and the favorite place on the bill; for it is not conducive to one's happiness or success to appear during the hours favored by the public for coming in or going out. The manager was not the loser, for many people who had never been inside a vaudeville theatre were attracted thither by the name of some well-known and favorite actor, and became permanent patrons of these houses.

At first the actor, who is sentimental rather than practical, was inclined to the belief that it was beneath his dignity to appear on the stage with "a lot of freaks," but he was tempted by salaries no one else could afford to pay (sometimes as high as $500 to $1,000 per week) and by the amount of attention afforded to the innovation by the newspapers. He was told that if he stepped from the sacred precincts of art, the door of the temple would be forever barred against him. The dignity of an artist is a serious thing, but the dignity of the dollar is also a serious thing. None of the dire suppositions happened. The door of the temple proved to be a swinging door, opening easily both ways, and the actor goes back and forth as there is demand for him and as the dollar dictates. Indeed, the advertising secured by association with "a lot of freaks" oiled the door for the actor's return to the legitimate drama at an increased salary.

Manifestly, it has been a boon to the "legitimate" artists. To the actor who has starred; who has had the care of a large company, with its certain expenses and its uncertain receipts; who has, in addition, responsibility for his own performance and for the work of the individual members of his company and for the work of the company as a whole, vaudeville offers inducements not altogether measured in dollars and cents. He is rid not only of financial obligation, but of a thousand cares and details that twist and strain a nervous temperament. He hands over to the amiable manager the death of the widely mourned Mr. Smith, and prevalent social functions, Lent and the circus, private and public calamities, floods and railroad accidents, the blizzard of winter and the heat of summer, desolating drought and murderous rains, the crops, strikes and panics, wars and pestilences and opera. It is quite a bunch of thorns that he hands over!

Time and terms are usually arranged by agents, who get five percent of the actor's salary for their services. Time and terms arranged, the rest is easy. The actor provides himself and assistants and his play or vehicle. His income and outcome are fixed, and he knows at the start whether he is to be a capitalist at the end of the year; for he runs almost no risk of not getting his salary in the well-known circuits.

It is then incumbent on him to forward property and scene-plots, photographs and cast to the theatre two weeks before he opens, and on arrival, he plays twenty or thirty minutes in the afternoon and the same night. There his responsibility ends. It involves the trifling annoyance of dressing and making up twice a day. In and about New York the actor pays the railroad fares of himself and company, but when he goes West or South, the railroad fares (not including sleepers) are provided by the management. . . .

When high-class musical artists and dramatic sketches were first introduced into vaudeville, I understand policemen had to be stationed in the galleries to compel respectful attention, but now these acts are the principal features of every bill, and if they have real merit the gallery-gods are the first to appreciate it. So it would seem that vaudeville has torpedoed the ancient superstition that the manager is always forced to give the public just what it wants. At first his efforts were not taken seriously either by the actor himself or the public, and many well-known artists failed to "make good," as the expression is, largely because they used "canned" or embalmed plays, that is, hastily and crudely condensed versions of well-known plays; but many succeeded, and the result has been a large increase in the number of good one-act farces and comedies, and a distinct elevation in the performance and the patronage of the vaudeville theatres. This has been a gain to everybody concerned.

It cannot be denied that the vaudeville "turn" is an experience for the actor. The intense activity everywhere, orderly and systematic though it is, is confusing. The proximity to the "educated donkey," and some not so educated; the variegated and motley samples of all strange things in man and beast; the fact that the curtain never falls, and the huge machine never stops to take breath until 10:30 at night; the being associated after the style of criminals with a number, having your name or number shot into a slot in the proscenium arch to introduce you to your audience; the shortness of your reign, and the consequent necessity of capturing your audience on sight—all this, and some other things, make the first plunge unique in the actor's experience. . . .

The man who arranges the program has to have some of the qualities of a general. To fix eighteen or nineteen different acts into the exact time allotted, and so to arrange them that the performance shall never lapse or flag; to see that the "turns" which require only a front scene can be utilized to set the stage for the "turns" which require a full stage, requires judgment and training; but there is very little confusion even at the first performance, and none thereafter.

Many of our best comedians, men and women, have come from the variety stage, and it is rather remarkable that some of our best actors have of late turned their attention to it. This interchange of courtesies has brought out some amusing contrasts. A clever comedian of a comic opera organization was explaining to me his early experience in the "old days," when he was a song-and-dance man. "The tough manager," he said, "used to stand in the wings with a whistle, and if he didn't like your act he blew it and a couple of stagehands ran in and shut you out from your audience with two flats upon which were painted in huge letters 'N.G.,' and that was the end of your engagement." Then he proceeded to tell with honest pride of his struggles, and his rise in the world of art. "And now," said he to me, "I can say 'cawn't' as well as you can." . . .

This unique and original world has its conventions, too, quite as hard and fast as elsewhere. The vaudeville dude always bears an enormous cane with a spike in the end of it, even though the style in canes may be a bamboo switch. The comedian will black his face, though he never makes the slightest pretense to negro characterization. The vaudeville "artist" and his partner will "slang" each other and indulge in brutal personalities under the theory that they are guilty of repartee; and with a few brilliant exceptions, they all steal from each other jokes and gags and songs and "business," absolutely without conscience. So that if a comedian has originated a funny story that makes a hit in New York, by the time he reaches Philadelphia, he finds that another comedian has filched it and told it in Philadelphia, and the originator finds himself a dealer in second-hand goods.

It is manifest, I think, that vaudeville is very American. It touches us and our lives at many places. It appeals to the businessman, tired and worn, who drops in for half an hour on his way home, to the person who has an hour or two before a train goes, or before a business appointment, to the woman who is wearied of shopping; to the children who love animals and acrobats; to the man with his sweetheart or sister, to the individual who wants to be diverted but doesn't want to think or feel; to the American of all grades and kinds who wants a great deal for his money. The vaudeville theatre belongs to the era of the department store and the short story. It may be a kind of lunch-counter art, but then art is so vague and lunch is so real.

And I think I may add that if anyone has anything exceptional in the way of art, the vaudeville door is not shut to that.

English-born Caroline Caffin was the one of the most articulate commentators on modern culture in the Progressive era. With her husband Charles Caffin, art critic and associate of Charles Stieglitz's *Camera Work*, she wrote *Dancing and Dancers of Today* (1912). Her book on vaudeville was both a series of elegant essays on individual performers and an extended discussion of how stars of the popular arts reflected audience tastes.
Caroline Caffin, *Vaudeville* (New York: Mitchell Kennerley, 1914), 9–10, 12–13, 15–17, 18–20, 21–23, 216–18, 221–23, 225–27.

"Our true intent is all for your delight." . . . The ability to recognize this answering vibration seems to call into play a sort of sixth sense, in response to which those whose "true intent is all for our delight" evolve for themselves an individual technique to accentuate the key in which they pitch their appeal. Into the discovery of this keynote and the creation of the technique it is inevitable that there will enter something of that mysterious quality which we call Art.

So little time is allowed to each performer that their appeal is necessarily frankly direct. It hides itself behind no subtleties but is personal and unashamed. It looks its audience straight in the face and says, in effect, "Look at ME! I am looking to astonish you!" It makes no claim to aloofness or impersonality, but comes right down to the footlights and faces the crowd and tells it "All for your Delight *We* are—here." . . .

To provide true delight for a Vaudeville audience you must have as a provoking cause some achievement apparently greater than that of the individuals in the audience. If the medium of the appeal be daring, the risk must be greater—or appear to be—than the man in front would care to face. If humor be the medium, not a single line must misfire. If it be vulgarity, it will be grosser than the audience, as individuals, would stand for. If it be skill, it must be proved as you watch it. You could never amuse an audience by displaying to it a specimen of skilful and minute engraving, the result of many years of toil. But let them see a cartoonist dash off a rough sketch in a few lines made before their eyes and he has secured their delight. In every case the effect must be vivid, instantaneous and unmistakable. . . .

Watch the audience trooping into a New York Vaudeville house. There is no more democratic crowd to be seen anywhere. It differs from a theatre crowd in the fact that usually more than half is composed of men. There are many reasons for this. One of them is the permission to smoke in parts of the house. Another is the familiar cry of the "tired business man" who doesn't want to be asked to think, or even to keep his mind continually on one set of characters. It is something of a mental effort to watch the development of a play that lasts the whole evening. Then there are many men who dislike continual conversation. I suppose no women object to this.

An excuse once offered to me by an habitué of the Vaudeville for preferring that form of entertainment to a play was that, in Vaudeville, if one turn be bad you always hope that the next will be good; whereas in a play, if the first act be bad, you know that the rest will continue to grow worse.

Anyhow, men of all degrees come trooping in; some, alone, some in batches, and some accompanied by women, or more often by one woman, wherein again is a difference from the theatre-going party. Meanwhile at the matinée women will arrive alone and in parties, especially at the uptown houses or in Brooklyn. There is a large proportion of non-New Yorkers, men in town on business trips, college boys come up for a lark, business men with an hour to spare before an appointment. . . .

There must be something for every one and, though the fastidious may be a little shocked (the fastidious rather like to be shocked sometimes), they must not be offended, while the seeker for thrills must on no account be bored by too much mildness.

It is, therefore, no easy task which confronts the manager. And added to his other worries is a demon of which he lives in fear. He seeks it out in every act. He gazes suspiciously at every visitor for fear the latter has it concealed somewhere. I do not know, but I strongly suspect him of holding a ceremony of exorcism every Monday morning, sprinkling every crevice and cranny, every bit of scenery, every prop, "sealing unto himself" against its baleful influence every sceneshifter, limelight man and orchestra leader, and even then being worried and haunted with dread of it.

And the name of this hideous demon—its dreaded name—is Highbrow! Of course it never has intruded. Occasionally some heretic manager has dared to take a chance and allow a suspect to appear on his boards. If the venture succeeded, we know for certain it was free from the taint. For it is the first law of the cult of Vaudeville that "Highbrow Stuff Never Pays."

With memories of Sarah Bernhardt still in our minds, we may doubt this theory. Highbrows have been known to claim kinship with her and with others who have appeared in Vaudeville. But NO! These cannot be Highbrow. These are Successes, and as such appeal to ordinary human beings. But the world moves, and sometimes a tremor indicates that even the firm-rooted prejudice against the Highbrow is being shaken by a suspicion that perhaps, after all, he too is a human being and appeals to other human beings.

Let us look again at our audience. There it sits, waiting for the show to begin, good-natured, eager to be amused, willing to accept its entertainers at their own valuation just so long as they are amused. It will applaud faintly even an unpopular turn from pure unwillingness to be hypercritical, but its genuine appreciation is unmistakable. I am not referring to "tryouts" or "amateur nights," where the baiting of the performer is as much a part of the show as the slaughter of horses at a bull fight. Those are another story. But I have frequently heard people speak slightingly of a performance and then applaud at its close from pure goodwill to the performer. . . .

But the manager knows that, good-natured and tolerant as the audience seems, its patience would soon be exhausted if he allowed it to be abused. It would make very little open demonstration, but it would cease to frequent his house, regardless of the fact that he too has his bread and butter to earn.

It is that feeling of good-fellowship that makes the audience love to be on confidential terms with the performer, to be treated as an intimate. It loves to have the actor step out of his part and speak of his dressing-room, or hint at his salary, or flourish a make-up towel. There are no secrets, no reserves between them, they know each other as man and man—or they think they do. For the actor has studied the little weaknesses of his audience, and plays up to them.

For he knows that, above all things, the audience is there to laugh. Give it an excuse for that, and it is his. It will seize any excuse to indulge in this, its favorite pastime, and, if it may not laugh with you, it will need very little to make it laugh at you. The slightest contretemps in the performance, and your audience is in a gale. The unexpected appearance of a cat on the stage and every chance of seriousness is gone. Even when laughter was intended, I have heard a queerly pitched laugh from the audience attract the amusement of the house from the performer to itself, and almost break up the show.

But there are performers to whom these interruptions would be well-nigh impossible. They dominate their audience and hold them enthralled under their spell. They have learned, either by experience or instinct, so exactly the key in which to pitch their appeal, in order to evoke that answering vibration from their audience, that they can sound it at will, modulate it into what harmonies and expression they please, and ever be sure of the response. . . .

[T]he most distinguishing trait of Vaudeville is its variety and, unless we recognise this, we ignore its most salient feature. . . . Anything that will amuse, interest, or satisfy the curiosity is welcome. But the welcome is easily outworn and, if the only claim to interest is that of novelty, it cannot expect to have more than a brief day. But novelty is one of the essentials, so that even acts having interest beyond that of curiosity, must be constantly refurbished to make them appear new. What wonder, then, if turns are sometimes incongruous or far-fetched?

Accordingly, we have every imaginable thing, animate or inanimate, keenly scrutinized with a view to their use for entertainment. The circus is freely borrowed from and animals of all sorts are pressed into service. We have bears on roller skates; ponies who ring out a tune on hand-bells; and cats, dogs, rabbits, pigeons, presenting episodes that imitate the doings of the dominant race—sometimes in a manner far from complimentary. We have monkeys who play billiards, ride bicycles, smoke and drink and behave generally in a manner so like an extremely ill-bred man that it is a wonder that some of the audience do not feel affronted.

Until the acts are actually tried out it is impossible for certain what will capture the fancy of an audience, and there are some which must rack the nerves of the local manager every Monday matinée, so narrow is the line on which they waver between success and failure. . . .

The desire to see a celebrity, or, unfortunately, a notoriety is the motive of certain turns. And for some reason it seems to make these celebrities more real and tangible if they appear in other than their wonted metiér. To hear a prizefighter talk, or a peer of England talk, or to see a baseball player act or an actor play baseball would seem to demonstrate that these people of whom we have read in the papers are just ordinary folks, not prodigies of tremendous achievement only, but capable of doing other things than those which have made them famous or which their names have become associated. It is not a very elevated attitude of mind, but it is very human and by no means confined to the unintelligent. . . .

The latest inventions of science, if sufficiently spectacular, find easy admittance on to the Vaudeville stage and gramophones, tel-electric and kinetophones are only some of the wonders here displayed. And, apropos of the kinetophone, it would seem as though the time were about ripe for the artistic genius of the moving picture to arise. For, in the case of the latter, we are, at present, in the anomalous condition of having an elaborate apparatus of wonderful mechanical possibilities but as yet no dramatic or artistic technique with which to develop their resources. Consequently, the effect of the voice being added to the motion picture, so far from rendering the presentations more interesting, has only given to them a weapon which they are not able to wield. For, to time voice and action in such a way as shall become natural and easy when represented on the screen has not yet become part of the actor's equipment, any more than to write dialogue which shall not impede the movement of the pictures has become part of the playwright's. We are, therefore, conscious that the two are constantly tripping over and impeding each other, and the slight but lively plots of the "movies" are being cumbered up with banal dialogue which makes them ponderous and tiresome. It is like having the joke explained to you, you don't enjoy it, neither does the joker.

Another combination of scientific mechanism with entertainment is found in those living pictures, shown with the aid of a stereopticon. In these a living model, clad in a full suit of white tights, poses before a white cloth, and the stereopticon playing on her makes her appear in varying guises, while the picture it throws, on the screen affords a suitable setting. Anything, from a mermaid to a lady in a winter suit with furs going to church, may be presented in this way and from these materials. Very ingenious and sometimes beautiful as they are already, there is no doubt that this idea is capable of being worked out to a higher degree of artistic merit. . . .

And so the curtain falls and the Show is over.

Did you like it? Some of it, yes, some of it, no. I suppose that would be the answer of ninety-nine out of every hundred of the dispersing audience.

Well! it is YOUR show. It is there because it is what is wanted by the average of you. If you want it different you only have to make the demand loud enough, large enough, persistent enough. For these figures you can see on the stage are but a reflection of what YOU, their creators want. They are the shadows cast on the screen by the actors in the old-time gallanty show. The figures may be dwarfed to insignificance or enlarged to preposterous size. Yet they are but the figures of you, yourselves, and represent, if not your actual appearance, some travesty of it made by the relation your own form bears to the source of its inspiration. More or less truly it throws upon its screen the current sentiment of the day. We cannot escape from its influence. The echoes of its songs are in our streets, our homes, our ballrooms, we hear them at our parades and public ceremonies and here, as I write these words, far from the busy streets, amid woods and hills, the sounds are borne to me over the water of young voices chanting in chorus, and the song is a song of Vaudeville. . . .

We have put our entertainers behind the frame of a proscenium arch and let down a curtain to mark the division between actor and audience. But the actor is still the reflection of his audience.

The Business

Benjamin Franklin Keith modernized variety theater. In 1883 he opened the storefront New York Dime Museum in a prime location on Washington Street in Boston's central business district. The improvised stage upstairs proved more attractive to downtown office workers and shoppers than the human oddities, and Keith found that abridged and burlesqued versions of Gilbert and Sullivan operettas were especially popular. It was the "continuous" show that he introduced in 1885 to give the impression of steady patronage that made his reputation. Keith and his general manager Edward Albee were not stage entertainers like Tony Pastor in New York City, but like Pastor they understood the importance of decency and morality in attracting those aspiring to middle-class status. Their target audience was the white-collar clerical and sales personnel who serviced the offices and retail stores in the expanding cities, a group that grew from less than 3 percent of the population in 1870 to 11 percent in 1920. Keith also hoped both to compete with the cheap amusements of the dance halls and trolley parks, and, at least occasionally, to tempt patrons of the legitimate theater to his variety halls with programs of high-quality music and drama.

The Business

Administration was Keith and Albee's forte, and they used sound management to build a small empire of theaters in New England. By 1893 they owned another theater in Boston and others in Providence, Philadelphia, and New York. In 1906 they founded the United Booking Office to administer a much larger business empire, which, in uneasy alliance with Martin Beck's Orpheum circuit on the West Coast, extended across much of the country. Their aim was vertical integration: to control every detail of vaudeville production from the salaries and schedules of major artistes to the conduct of performances in every theater in their circuit. As the most successful entrepreneur in the business, Keith explained his philosophy.

B. F. Keith, "The Vogue of The Vaudeville," *National Magazine* 9 (November 1898): 146–53.

It was clear that the majority of people would stay through an entertainment so long as they could, even sitting out acts that had to be repeated. The old form necessitated a final curtain at a specified time, and the emptying of the house. As a result the succeeding audience gathered slowly, the theatre was necessarily dreary as they came into it, and there was nothing going on. Did you ever notice the hesitancy on the part of early comers to a playhouse to assume their seats in the auditorium, how they hang back until reassured by numbers? Well, that is one of the things the continuous performance does away with. It matters not at what hour of the day or evening you visit, the theatre is always occupied by more or less people, the show is in full swing, everything is bright, cheerful and inviting. In this connection, I remember that in the days of my first shows (prior to the opening of the Bijou), I was always maneuvering to keep patrons moving up and down stairs in view of passersby on the sidewalk for the specific purpose of impressing them with the idea that business was immense. . . .

For the benefit of those who have never enjoyed a vaudeville show of the continuous order, I might explain that it is designed to run twelve hours, during which period performers appear two or three times, as it would be manifestly impossible to secure enough different acts to fill out the dozen hours. The best class of artists appear twice, just as at a matinee and evening performance in a dramatic theatre, and the balance do three "turns." . . .

Two things I determined at the outset should prevail in the new scheme. One was that my fixed policy of cleanliness and order should be continued, and the other that the stage show must be free from vulgarisms and coarseness of any kind, so that the house and entertainment would directly appeal to the support of ladies and children—in fact that my playhouse must be as "homelike" an amusement resort as it was possible to make it. While a certain proportion of the male sex may favor stage performances of a risqué order, none of them would care to bring the female members of their families to witness an entertainment of that description.

The advent of dramatic players into my theatres has been distinctly beneficial, in that it has added the element of novelty, which is the essence of vaudeville, and has attracted the attention of a desirable class of patrons whose previous knowledge of a variety entertainment had been very vague and largely governed by tradition. As to the sort of entertainment which seems to please most, light, frothy acts, with no particular plot, but abounding in songs, dances, bright dialogue and clean repartee, seem to appeal most to the vaudeville audiences of the present time. But, it is quite evident that a thoroughly good program, in its entirety, is what draws the public, rather than individual acts. . . . The most marked improvement is the tendency of artists to keep their acts clean and free from coarseness, and to do away with the ridiculous costumes which were formerly a glaring defect of nearly all vaudeville entertainments. Added to this is the closer attention paid to stage setting, and scenic embellishment generally.

The character of the vaudeville audience has notably improved in recent years, and the entertainment of today is freely patronized and enjoyed by the most intelligent and cultivated people, who flatter me by the assurance which their presence in my theatres brings that they have confidence in my pledge that therein nothing shall be given which could not with perfect safety be introduced to their homes.

Hartley Davis, a journalist experienced in writing on vaudeville, noted its efficiency and economy. Entrepreneurs were shrewd businessmen who saw a market for popular-priced entertainment and exploited it.

Hartley Davis, "In Vaudeville," *Everybody's Magazine* 13 (August 1905): 231, 238.

Hartley Davis, "The Business Side of Vaudeville," *Everybody's Magazine* 17 (October 1907), 529, 537.

There is a cheerful frivolity in vaudeville which makes it appeal to more people of widely divergent interests than does any other form of entertainment. It represents the almost universal longing for laughter, for melody, for color, for action, for wonder-provoking things. It exacts no intellectual activity on the part of those who gather to enjoy it; in its essence it is an enemy to responsibility, to worries, to all the little ills of life. It is joyously, frankly absurd, from the broad, elemental nonsense of the fun-makers to the marvellous acrobatic feats of performers who conceive immensely difficult things for the pleasure of doing them. Vaudeville brings home to us the fact that we are children of a larger growth, and this is one of the finest things about it. . . .

The great demand in vaudeville is for low comedy with plenty of action. Broad sweeping effects without too much detail are wanted. The artistic "legitimate" actor wastes too much time in working up to his points, but the skilled vaudevillist strikes them with a single blow and scores. A successful vaudeville sketch concentrates in one act as many laughs and as much action as are usually distributed over a three-act comedy.

In the good vaudeville, houses, the salary list of performers ranges from $2,500 to $4,000 a week, and the maximum is paid more often than the minimum. Occasionally the cost will run to $5,000 a week. The standard in practically every first-class vaudeville house in the country is $3,200 a week, and each manager tries to keep as close to that as possible. It has been found that this will provide an attractive bill and yet leave a fair margin of profit.

Now, by way of contrast, consider that the prices charged in these vaudeville theatres are just one-half, or oftener one-third, the prices of admission charged in the theatres presenting first-class attractions. In New York, for instance, the highest price for orchestra seats is one dollar, with box seats fifty cents more, and the downward range is to twenty-five cents. And this is the schedule of only a few houses. The usual rule for first-class vaudeville houses is fifty cents for the best seats, except those in the boxes, which are twenty-five and fifty cents more. Often the gallery seats are only ten cents, and when two performances a day are given, it is the universal custom to cut in half the higher prices for matinees.

The most popular acts are those that make people laugh, whether they be monologues, sketches, or acrobatic stunts, and to make vaudeville audiences roar, it is necessary to make a very simple, very direct appeal. . . .

The newest development in vaudeville is the presentation of elaborate ensemble acts with fine scenery and costumes. These have been so successful that there are regular producers of them, like Ned Wayburn, George Homans, and Lasky, Rolfe and Company. For "The Stunning Grenadiers," Lasky, Rolfe and Company imported a bevvy of strapping English girls, provided them with three changes of costume and three sets of scenery, as well as lighting effects. At least $5,000 was invested in this single act, which runs the usual twenty minutes. "The Pianophiends" cost nearby as much, for the young men and women who play six pianos in concert wear fashionable and expensive clothes and the scenery is as fine as can be painted. George Homans imported Italian opera singers for his Zingari troupe, and the stage setting, with its elaborate lighting effects, is as artistic as that seen in high-priced regular theatres. It takes twelve people to present "A Night with the Poets," including a male quartet that wears evening clothes costing $90 for each member, people who pose as living pictures, and an actor who can read poetry.

These big acts usually receive from $750 to $1,500 a week. The producer, who is also the manager, must pay the original cost, the salaries of the people he employs, and the transportation of the people and the scenery. His net profit on each act when it is playing averages about $100 a week. It's easier to book one of these big ensemble acts that costs a great deal than to book a cheaper one, because the vaudeville managers have found that audiences have been educated up to demanding the best that can be given them, and when people are pleased it means full houses. The managers make the audiences feel that they are receiving about double their money's worth. It's all business.

Brett Page, author of the most authoritative guide to the vaudeville profession, asserted that organizing the "diverse elements" of the weekly program to "combine to form a unified whole" required genius. To illustrate his point, Page quoted George A. Gottlieb, booking agent at Keith's Palace Theatre in New York, the most prestigious in the country. Gottlieb explained the art of devising the weekly program.

Brett Page, *Writing for Vaudeville: with nine complete examples of various vaudeville forms* . . . (Springfield, Mass.: Home Correspondence School, 1915), 6–12.

We usually select a "dumb act" for the first act on the bill. It may be a dancing act, some good animal act, or any act that makes a good impression and will not be spoiled by the late arrivals seeking their seats. Therefore it sometimes happens that we make use of a song-and-dance turn, or any other little act that does not depend on its words being heard.

For number two position we select an interesting act of the sort recognized as a typical "vaudeville act." It may be almost anything at all, though it should be more entertaining than the first act. For this reason it often happens that a good man-and-woman singing act is placed here. This position on the bill is to "settle" the audience and prepare it for the show.

With "number three" position we count on waking up the audience. The show has been properly started and from now on it must build right up to the finish. So we offer a comedy dramatic sketch—a playlet that wakens the interest and holds the audience every minute with a cumulative effect that comes to its laughter-climax at the "curtain," or any other kind of act that is not of the same order as the preceding turn, so that, having laid the foundations, we may have the audience wondering what is to come next.

For number four position we must have a "corker" of an act—and a "name." It must be the sort of act that will rouse the audience to expect still better things, based on the fine performance of the previous numbers. Maybe this act is the first big punch of the show; anyway, it must strike home and build the interest for the act that follows.

And here for number five position, a big act, and at the same time another big name, must be presented. Or it might be a big dancing act—one of those delightful novelties vaudeville likes so well. In any event this act must be as big a "hit" as any on the bill. It is next to intermission and the audience must have something really worth while to talk over. And so we select one of the best acts on the bill to crown the first half of the show.

The first act after intermission, number six on the bill, is a difficult position to fill, because the act must not let down the carefully built-up tension of interest and yet it must not be stronger than the acts that are to follow. Very likely there is chosen a strong vaudeville specialty, with comedy well to the fore. Perhaps a famous comedy dumb act is selected, with the intention of getting the audience back in its seats without too many conspicuous interruptions of what is going on the stage. Any sort of act that makes a splendid start-off is chosen, for there has been a fine first half and the second half must be built up again—of course the process is infinitely swifter in the second half of the show—and the audience brought once more into a delighted-expectant attitude.

Therefore the second act after intermisson—number seven—must be stronger than the first. It is usually a full-stage act and again must be another big name. Very likely it is a big playlet, if another sketch has not been presented earlier on the bill. It may be a comedy playlet or even a serious dramatic playlet, if the star is a fine actor or actress and the name is well known. Or it may be anything at all that builds up the interest and appreciation of the audience to welcome the "big" act that follows.

For here in number eight position—next to closing on a nine-act bill—the comedy hit of the show is usually placed. It is one of the acts for which the audience has been waiting. Usually it is one of the famous "single" man or "single" woman acts that vaudeville has made such favorites.

And now we come to the act that closes the show. We count on the fact that some of the audience will be going out. Many have only waited to see the chief attraction of the evening, before hurrying off to their after-theatre supper and dance. So we spring a big "flash." It must be an act that does not depend for its success upon being heard perfectly. Therefore a "sight" act is chosen, an animal act maybe, to please the children, or a Japanese troupe with their gorgeous kimonos and vividly harmonizing stage draperies, or a troupe of white-clad trapeze artists flying against a background of black. Whatever the act is, it must be a showy act, for it closes the performance and sends the audience home pleased with the program to the very last minute.

Now all the time a booking-manager is laying out his show, he has not only had these many artistic problems on his mind, but also the mechanical working of the show. For instance, he must consider the actual physical demands of his stage and not place next to each other two full-stage acts. If he did, how would the stage hands change the scenery without causing a long and tedious wait? In vaudeville there must be no waits. Everything must run with unbroken stride. One act must follow another as though it were especially made for the position. And the entire show must be dovetailed to the split seconds of a stop-watch. . . .

But there is still another problem the manager must solve. "Variety" is vaudeville's paternal name—vaudeville must present a *varied* bill and a show consisting of names that will tend to have a box-office appeal. No two acts in a show should be alike. No two can be permitted to conflict. "Conflict" is a word that falls with ominous meaning on a vaudeville performer's or manager's ears, because it means death to one of the acts and injury to the show as a whole. If two famous singing "single" women were placed on the same bill, very likely there would be odious comparisons—even though they did not use songs that were alike. And however interesting each might be, both would lose in interest. And yet, sometimes we do just this one thing—violating a minor rule to win a great box-office appeal.

Part of the many sides of this delicate problem may be seen when you consider that no two "single" singing acts should be placed next each other—although they may not conflict if they are placed far apart on the bill. And no two "quiet" acts may be placed together. The tempo of the show must be maintained—and because tragic playlets, and even serious playlets, are suspected of "slowing up a show," they are not booked unless very exceptional.

In 1913 two very experienced theatrical professionals joined forces to give a master class on the techniques of stagecraft. George M. Cohan was born into a vaudeville family, had thirty years' experience of writing, producing, and performing musical comedy, and had great success with songs like "Yankee Doodle Dandy" in 1904. George Jean Nathan was also youthful but already the leading critic and commentator on the popular theater. They advised close attention to formula. To "reach an audience's inmost recesses and cause it to collapse into tears, laughter, or horror," they wrote, was largely "a matter of mechanical preparation."

George M. Cohan and George J. Nathan, "The Mechanics of Emotion," *McClure's Magazine* 42 (November 1913): 70–77.

Given the average crowd in a theater, the experienced playwright, in the quiet of his study, can figure out in advance precisely what constituents in his play will produce particular effects.

In physiology there are certain familiar phenomena known technically as reflex actions. . . .

Reflex Emotions

Now, there are emotional reflexes as well as physical reflexes. There are certain outside stimuli, forces that will automatically make us, without much conscious action on our part, laugh, weep, or freeze with horror. Many of these emotional reflexes were at first unquestionably conscious acts. We laughed or cried because there was something in the stimulus that appealed to our human intelligence as being funny or pathetic. A constant repetition, however, has given these particular emotions the character of reflex actions. At first we roared or sobbed with our brains; now we do so largely with our spinal cords.

As a matter of fact the playwright has his audience at a distinct advantage. It comes to the theater for one definite purpose, to have its emotions played upon; this experience gives such exquisite delight and satisfaction, indeed, that the average citizen is willing to pay liberally for it. . . .

We All Laugh and Cry at the Same Things

It is a mistake to suppose that from the standpoint of the fundamental emotions we are not all alike. Emotionally we are essentially the same. Mere buffoonery has delighted many of the world's greatest minds. . . . The emotional lives of all men follow a fixed norm, precisely as do their physical lives. In the main, the same elemental ideas that "got a rise" out of our ancestors will do the same for us. Perhaps the permanence, through the ages, of the same type of humor is best illustrated by the circus clown.

If we are normal, we all cry at the same things, laugh at the same things, and these expedients are, for the most part, artless and simple—so simple that, under ordinary circumstances, we should indignantly repudiate the suggestion that they could move us. But the playwright knows exactly what they are. He has invented them; he has inherited them. His predecessors used them over and over again; his successors will use them to the end of time. In his own language he calls them his "bag of tricks," or, sometimes, more dignifiedly, his "tools of emotion." If produced at the right moment and with sufficient skill, they never fail to strike the audience in the midriff. They comprise the complete science of the "lump in the throat." They may be regarded as the germs or bacilli of emotions. He can inoculate audiences with them and get just as definite results as do the scientists when they inoculate their guinea-pigs with the microbes of disease. And he does so just as deliberately.

These emotion germs are hundreds in number, and they fall logically into three great classes: (1) Fears; (2) Laughs; (3) Thrills. . . .

Things that Act upon the Tear-Ducts

[Thirty examples of melodramatic situations or sentimental scenes with stereotypical characters.] Why is it that these simple expedients arouse the pathetic in us? This is a question for the psychologist. Probably stage tradition plays a considerable part. For generations the human family has been moved by situations of this kind, and has grown accustomed to them. The emotions aroused, as already said, are largely reflex in character. Fundamentally, however, these stage contrivances represent a transcript from nature. Most of them are "sad" in real life as they are "sad" upon the stage. A man driving an errant daughter out into a snow-storm—that much ridiculed episode of modern "mellerdrammer"—would unquestionably arouse our pity in real life. So, down at the core of what have become merely mechanical stratagems for the arousing of theatrical emotion, constant, immutable human nature declares itself.

But the theater must play upon other emotions than the pathetic. The playwright must make his audiences laugh, and here again his predecessors have laid down the essential formulas. Here again, the contrivances used are largely mechanical. For years, the playwrights have servilely depended upon them for "laughs," and will unquestionably always do so. And these devices are found not only in cheap farce and "slap-stick" plays, but in legitimate drama. . . .

Some Things Men Laugh At

[Fifteen examples, almost all involving non-verbal gestures.] All these "laugh-getters" are known to be experienced as "high class"; that is, they may all be used upon the legitimate stage. On the burlesque and vaudeville stage devices of a somewhat lower intellectual plane have established a permanent standing. . . .

The most successful tricks or jokes are all based on the *idea* of pain or embarrassment. Tacks made of rubber, matches that explode or refuse to light, exploding cigars or cigarettes, fountain-pens that smear ink over the fingers immediately they are to put to use, "electric" bells with pins secreted in their push buttons, and boutonnières that squirt water into the face of the beholder, are a few familiar examples.

"Thrill" and "Suspense"

[Twelve examples of the use of sound or lighting effects to produce dramatic tension.] We pass now to the spine and to that side of theatrical mechanics known as "thrill" and "suspense." In the secret ritual there are as many mechanical tricks wherewith to excite and thrill an audience and keep it in suspense as there are tricks to make it cry or weep. . . .

Every one of the different elements of thrill mechanics will be found to rest upon substantial grounds, even if the introduction of the thrill mechanics in certain parts of plays is made for mere trickiness. The reader must recall again that the audience is at the moment unaware that the thunder-clap or the mysterious locked door or the shadow against the wall, or whatever it is, has been utilized arbitrarily by the stage artificer, and that it may have absolutely nothing to do with what follows. The quality of suspense is shot into the audience on the spot. If, subsequently, the audience says to itself, "We were fooled," it does not matter. It will have been made to feel suspense— and that is all the trafficker in theatrical tricks has aimed for!

The secret of stage effectiveness rests in the impression of the moment. . . . All the "mechanics of emotion" are based, from the theatrical craftsman's point of view, on this one solid fact.

Routines

In his 1915 manual, Brett Page singled out Aaron Hoffman as unusually talented, and pronounced one of his vaudeville sketches "perhaps the best example of the pure monologue ever written." Hoffman's "The Horse Doctor" was a classic slapstick farce of mistaken identities, timed to fit a fifteen-minute spot in the program, and one of dozens that he wrote. In the early twentieth century, a "soubrette," the female character in this sketch, was a maid, but more generally in the theater, a young flirtatious woman who served as an attractive foil for the comic.

Aaron Hoffman, "A Comedy Sketch entitled The Horse Doctor" (manuscript, 1911, Rare Book and Special Collection Division, Library of Congress) [American Memory: The American Variety Stage: Vaudeville and Popular Entertainment, 1870–1920, http://memory.loc.gov].

Routines

A COMEDY SKETCH
entitled
THE HORSE DOCTOR
by
Aaron Hoffman

SCENE PLOT. C. D. F. [center door front] in three. Boxed set. *Doors R. and L. Furniture, bric-abrac, fireplace and mantle, etc., etc.*

Opening lively curtain music.

(*Enter* SOUBRETTE *at rise of curtain.*)

Well, this is the limit. The house is all upset. Yesterday one of our best horses was taken sick, we sent for a horse doctor, but he hasn't put in an appearance as yet, and now, poor Mr. Knight is sick in bed all day. His wife, Mrs. Knight, went down to the station to meet the doctor, and his young daughter, Miss Knight, left me here in charge of Lord How Poor. A young nobleman wants to marry her; she said he might come in some disguise, and she offered me fifty dollars to get rid of him, and you can just bet I will, because I need the money.

(*Bell rings outside.*)

I guess I'll go and see if Mr. Knight wants anything. I don't care what he wants as long as I get that fifty.

(*Exits door R.*)

(*Enter COMEDIAN.*) (C. D.)

Well, this is the place all right. No. 99 Spring, between Summer and Winter. I was an actor and a manager once, but ever since my play has failed I'm at liberty, or as they say in slang I'm dead broke, and when an actor or a manager is broke he'll do almost anything to make an honest dollar. A friend of mine told me there was a sick horse in this house; I know what I'll do, I'll just make him believe I'm a horse doctor, get some mizouma and Richard will be himself once again.

(*Enter SOUBRETTE from door R.*)

SOUBRETTE: Ah, stranger!

COMEDIAN: I beg your pardon.

SOUBRETTE: Well, sir, what do you want here?

COMEDIAN: I'm here on business. Even if I am poor.

SOUBRETTE: Did you say poor?

COMEDIAN: Yes, poor! P-u-r-e! Pure, poor, pure!

SOUBRETTE: (*Aside.*) That's him, Lord How Poor!

I beg your pardon, I knew you were coming, but I did not expect you.

COMEDIAN: Well, if you didn't expect me then I'm not here.

SOUBRETTE: I mean we did not expect you so soon.

(*Aside.*) Now to get rid of him.

But you are just as welcome as if you were in your own home.

COMEDIAN: (*Burlesquing her actions.*)

341

SOUBRETTE: Now if you'll excuse me, I'll go in the parlor and feed the cat.

COMEDIAN: Don't you keep the cat in the cellar?

SOUBRETTE: Of course not.

COMEDIAN: Why not?

SOUBRETTE: He's afraid of rats.

(*Exits with laughter; center door.*)

COMEDIAN: (*Pulls card out of his pocket.*) Well, this is the place all right. 99 Spring, between Summer and [W]inter. But it seems to me this girl has eagles in her skylight.

(*Enter SOUBRETTE C. D.*)

SOUBRETTE: Are you here yet?

COMEDIAN: Yes, I'm the same here yet.

SOUBRETTE: Now what do you want?

COMEDIAN: I want a glass of beer. No, no, no, I—I—want to go to work.

SOUBRETTE: Did you say work?

COMEDIAN: Yes, work.

SOUBRETTE: Hah, you ought to live in Cuba, over there everybody works. Everybody, everybody, everybody. (*Shakes her head in* COMEDIAN's *face.*)

COMEDIAN: (*Imitating her.*) Well, I'm from so so (*Local*) [w]here nobody works, nobody, nobody, nobody.

SOUBRETTE: Enough of this, Lord. I knew you the minute I saw you.

COMEDIAN: (*Surprised.*) Lord, I'm not a Lord.

SOUBRETTE: (*Jumping up and down.*) Oh, yes you are, yes you are, yes you are.

COMEDIAN: (*Imitating her jump.*) Oh, no I ain't, no I ain't, no I ain't. (*Bus. ad lib, etc.*)

SOUBRETTE: (*Puts her arms around* COMEDIAN's *neck.*) Now aren't you the Lord?

COMEDIAN: (*Half dazed.*) Yes, I'm the Lord. And the Lord knows who I am. And if I stay here much longer I'll be a lobster.

SOUBRETTE: Lord, I suppose when you left home, thousands of people saw you off.

COMEDIAN: Oh, yes, yes.

(*Aside.*) About fourteen sheriffs.

SOUBRETTE: And they all hopes you would soon return.

COMEDIAN: Oh, yes, yes.

(*Aside.*) If I'd ever come back they'd hang me.

SOUBRETTE: Oh, how forgetful I am. Will you have a little wine?

COMEDIAN: A little? Why, plenty.

SOUBRETTE: All you want. A hoop-la-la. (*Exits C. D.*)

COMEDIAN: (*Pulls card out of his pocket again.*) This is the place all right. 99 Spring between Summer and Winter. A little wine, will I have a little wine? Oh, say, I struck a cinch.

Routines

(*Enter* SOUBRETTE—*Tray in hand marching all around stage;* COMEDIAN *follows her, places tray and wine on small table; bus. explained.* COMEDIAN *grabs bottle.*)

SOUBRETTE: Allow me to help you. (*Pours wine into glass.* COMEDIAN *takes bottle by the neck and drinks from bottle.*) Lord, you are not afraid of spirits, are you?

COMEDIAN: Not while I've got 'em by the neck.

SOUBRETTE: (*Aside.*) Isn't the Duke lovely. What's the matter with me marrying him myself. I kind a like him. Lord, Lord, have you ever had an affair of the heart?

COMEDIAN: No, but I had malaria once.

SOUBRETTE: (*Acting rather shy.*) Have you never thought—of getting—getting—

COMEDIAN: Come on, come on, say something.

SOUBRETTE: Getting—married?

COMEDIAN: No, little one, I could never find anyone who would commit such a terrible crime. (*Lady acting very bashful and shy.*) Well, I beg your pardon, Miss, are you single or double?

SOUBRETTE: Why single, of course.

COMEDIAN: Single? Single, did you say? How dare you be single? When there are so many men in this town out of work?

SOUBRETTE: (*Lays her head on* COMEDIAN's *shoulder.*) Oh, this is so sudden.

COMEDIAN: There goes that old chestnut again. Now will you promise to support me?

SOUBRETTE: Sir?

COMEDIAN: I—I—mean, marry me?

SOUBRETTE: I will, but you'll have to give me time.

COMEDIAN: O, I'll give you time, I'll give you six months. And if you break your word I'll sue you for breech of breaches.

SOUBRETTE: Sir!

COMEDIAN: I mean breach of promise. But before we go any further, I want you to understand right now I'm not a Lord or a Duke. I'm a doctor.

SOUBRETTE: (*Surprised.*) The doctor? Oh, you wretch. I would not marry you in a thousand years.

COMEDIAN: Of course not. We'll both be dead by that time. But business before pleasure. So let's get to business.

(SOUBRETTE *sits on chair left;* COMEDIAN *chair to right; little book and pencil in* COMEDIAN's *hand.*)

COMEDIAN: Now where is the patient?

SOUBRETTE: (*Points to room L.*) In there.

COMEDIAN: (*To the audience.*) He must be an expensive horse. She keeps him in the parlor bedroom. (*To the* SOUBRETTE.) Now you must think a great deal of him.

SOUBRETTE: Yes, the family could not get along without him. He supplies all our wants.

COMEDIAN: (*Aside.*) He must be a race horse.

(*Aloud.*) Is he fast?

343

SOUBRETTE: (*Angry.*) Sir? He's not fast.

COMEDIAN: (*Ad lib.*) (*Bus. etc.*) Of course not, of course not. He must be one of those muts, that I went broke on more than once. (*To* SOUBRETTE.) Would you give me a few pointers?

SOUBRETTE: Why certainly.

COMEDIAN: How is his appetite?

SOUBRETTE: Very poor, doctor, very poor. All he ate this morning was two scrambled eggs and a cup of tea.

COMEDIAN: (*Falls off chair.*) (*Ad lib. Bus., etc.*) (*To himself.*) A cup of tea and two scrambled eggs for a horse. Now I wish I was a horse.

(*Aloud to her.*) But this will never do, Miss, you must give him some chopped hay mixed with oats.

SOUBRETTE: (*To the audience.*) Why this man is crazy.

(*Aloud.*) He could never chew that kind of food.

COMEDIAN: Well that will be all right. I'll file his teeth.

SOUBRETTE: (*Ad lib, bus., etc.*)

COMEDIAN: Has he ever had the heaves?

SOUBRETTE: (*Very angry.*) Certainly not.

COMEDIAN: That's good, that's good. Does he sleep well?

SOUBRETTE: No doctor, he kicks and tosses all night.

COMEDIAN: Oh, that's natural; he feels the oats.

SOUBRETTE: Yes, but it keeps us all awake nights.

COMEDIAN: Does anyone sleep with him?

SOUBRETTE: Why certainly.

COMEDIAN: Who?

SOUBRETTE: Why his wife[!]

COMEDIAN: (*Jumps up from the chair with a yell.*) His wife? (*Walks up and down stage.*) (*All excited, bus., ad lib, etc.*) This girl is daffy all right. Is he nervous?

SOUBRETTE: Yes, doctor, ever since he has been elected to Congress he sleeps very little.

COMEDIAN: (*Astonished.*) Well, I have heard of jackasses being elected to Congress, but this is the first time I have heard of a horse filling that position. Now tell me, Miss, what makes him so nervous?

SOUBRETTE: He worries about his children.

COMEDIAN: (*Up in the air again, all excited.*) Children, children?

(*To the audience.*) Oh, she means the colt.

Has he been harnessed lately?

SOUBRETTE: I don't understand you.

COMEDIAN: Is he well knuckled?

SOUBRETTE: (*Laughing.*) Oh, yes, yes, he does sometimes.

COMEDIAN: (*Business.*) He does sometimes. He does what sometimes?

SOUBRETTE: Why he plays pinochle.

Routines

COMEDIAN: (*Bus., pulling his hair, excited.*) Oh, he plays pinochle. Well he must be a game horse all right. Now tell me, what have you been doing for his nervousness?

SOUBRETTE: (*Aside.*) I'll make him believe Mr. Knight is my father.

(Aloud.) Why mother sings to him.

COMEDIAN: Mother sings to him? Mother sings to him? Oho, mama sings to a horse. And what does mother sing? Way Down on the Farm, or Mid the Green Fields of Virginia?

(*Rises from chair, makes a bluff to go to the room.*) Now could I see him?

SOUBRETTE: (*Stops him.*) Oh, no, no, no, doctor, he's fast asleep, and you might wake him up. Don't you think you had better wait?

COMEDIAN: Very well. What's his name?

SOUBRETTE: Summer's [Somers] Night [Knight], but they call him Sum for short.

COMEDIAN: (*Opens the little grip, takes out a large china egg.*) Well, Miss, I've another call to make, but before I go I wish you would give him this pill. (*Hands lady egg.*)

SOUBRETTE: (*Surprised.*) Why, what will this do?

COMEDIAN: Why this will help Sum.

SOUBRETTE: Why he could never swallow that.

COMEDIAN: Why of course not. You dissolve it, in a barrel of water. And give him a bucket full every hour.

SOUBRETTE: Why, I never heard of such a thing.

COMEDIAN: Well, you hear it now. And in the morning, have his shoes taken off, turn him out in the pasture, turn the hose on him and let him eat all the grass he wants.

SOUBRETTE: (*Frightened to death.*) Why this man is a lunatic. I mustn't oppose him. He might get violent. All right, doctor. All right, doctor.

(*Keeps on repeating all right, doctor, until off stage with pill in her hand looking at the doctor very much scared, exits to room L.*)

COMEDIAN: (*Looking after her, imitating her, all right, doctor, all right, doctor, etc.*) That girl is daffy all right. I think I better go in and have a look at him. (*Opens the door half way.*) Why there isn't a horse in there. Only an old man, asleep in bed. I knew that girl was kidding me all the time. Why, the idea of a horse in the parlor bedroom. Well, that's a horse on me all right. He must be out in the barn. Of course he's out in the barn. I better go out there and examine him. (*Picks up grip and all and exits C. D.*)

(*Enter SOUBRETTE from room L. looks in ver[y] scared.*)

SOUBRETTE: Doctor, Oh, doctor, he's gone. Thank goodness. I wish some of the family would return. If that crazy doctor comes back here again I will die of heart disease.

(*She looks in room L.*) Oh, I'm so glad Mr. Knight is asleep. I'm sure the rest will do him good. Now I'll go in the garden and pick some of his favorite flowers for his room. (*Exits*) (R. first entrance)

(*Bus. of crash on the outside, pistol shots, etc., etc.*)

345

(COMEDIAN *tumbles in on his head, hair mussed up, no collar on, black eye, etc., etc.*) (*Ad lib, bus.*)

Now I've done it. I went out in the barn and blew a pound of arsenic down that old plag's throat and he dropped dead. The best thing I can do now to get a piece of money is to bury him.

(SOUBRETTE *enters quickly from L.*)

SOUBRETTE: Oh, Doctor, have you seen him?

COMEDIAN: (*All excited.*) Oh, yes, I've seen him! I don't think he'll need any more medicine.

SOUBRETTE: Oh, I'm so glad he's out of pain.

COMEDIAN: Yes, he's dead.

SOUBRETTE: Dead? Dead, did you say? Oh, you murderer! (*Bus., crying, etc.*)

COMEDIAN: Now look here, Miss, don't you call me a murderer. But if that is the way you feel about him, I'll pay for him.

SOUBRETTE: (*Very angry.*) Pay for him? Pay for him? Oh, you wretch! Why all the money in the world couldn't pay for him, and replace him.

COMEDIAN: Oh, quit your kidding. Why, he was nothing but a bundle of skin and bones.

SOUBRETTE: He was not. He weighted one hundred and ninety pounds.

COMEDIAN: Well, it's a cinch he didn't weigh any more. The best thing you can do if you are so stuck on him is to have him skinned[,] and then have him stuffed and when you get tired of him you can kick th[e] stuffing out of him.

SOUBRETTE: Have him skinned? (*Aside.*) He wants to have poor Mr. Knight skinned. Oh you rascal, what do you mean?

COMEDIAN: Why, he's better off dead, poor beast.

SOUBRETTE: (*Screams at top of voice.*) Beast, beast[!] Oh, you wretch.

COMEDIAN: You ought to thank me for putting him out of his misery. (*Bus of taking off his coat and going to C. door*) I better skin him myself and then sell his carcass for soap grease.

(SOUBRETTE *stops him.*)

SOUBRETTE: You shall not skin the poor man.

COMEDIAN: (*Surprised*) Man? What man?

SOUBRETTE: Why, the man you killed in the other room. (*Points to room L*)

COMEDIAN: (*Laughing, bus, etc*)

SOUBRETTE: Laugh, you cold-blooded assassin.

COMEDIAN: Now this is a mistake, Miss. I haven't killed any man. I'm talking about a bum horse in the barn. He's dead.

SOUBRETTE: Then you have not killed Mr. Knight?

COMEDIAN: Not tonight, goodnight.

SOUBRETTE: Saved, saved! Doctor, catch me quick, I'm going to flop! (*Falls in a faint in doctor's arms*)

COMEDIAN: (*Bus., ad lib, etc.*) Now I'm in a nice fix. She has fainted and I haven't the faintest idea what to do. Oh, come on, come on, wake up. Why I must call for help. Assistance, assistance! This is getting serious—help, help!

(*Enter* PROPERTY MAN *C door*) Are you the help?

PROPERTY MAN: Yes.

COMEDIAN: Take a chair. (PROPS *takes chair and exits C Door*) Well, what to do now. I've got it. Rats.

(SOUBRETTE *comes to; jumps on chair, table, etc, bus explained*)

SOUBRETTE: Where are the rats? Where are the rats?

COMEDIAN: Why in the cellar.

SOUBRETTE: Oh, you rascal. You apology for a man. (*Chases* COMEDIAN *all over the stage*) How dare you scare a poor innocent little girl like me? (*Crying*)

COMEDIAN: Now see here—

SOUBRETTE: (*Still crying louder*) Don't you dare to talk to me, don't you dare touch me.

COMEDIAN: That's a nice way to treat your future husband.

SOUBRETTE: Husband, husband? I wouldn't marry an old bum horse doctor.

COMEDIAN: I am not a horse doctor.

SOUBRETTE: You are not a horse doctor? You are not the family physician, you're not a Duke, you are not a Lord—then what are you?

COMEDIAN: I'm an actor and manager.

SOUBRETTE: Why, a real live actor? Oh, I'd love to go on the stage.

COMEDIAN: Well, what can you do?

SOUBRETTE: I can do (*so and so whatever specialty may be*)

COMEDIAN: Well, I'm from Missouri and you have to show me.

SOUBRETTE: Will you wait here till I come back? I'll show you.

COMEDIAN: I certainly will.

(SOUBRETTE *exit[s] R first entrance*) (COMEDIAN *introduces his specialty*, SOUBRETTE *introduces her specialty, and both finish up th[ei]r act with double specialty in one.*)

Harry Newton was a prolific author of short sketches for performers, professional and amateur, and specialized in dialect speeches, minstrel and ethnic. Perhaps Newton's version of a miserable Jewish husband was inspired by Julian Rose's renowned "Levinsky at the Wedding," as well as by the well-worn theme of hen-pecked husbands.

"Abie Cohen's Wedding Day," in Harry L. Newton, *Some Vaudeville Monologues* (Minneapolis: T. S. Denison, 1917), 41–46.

Character: Abie Cohen is a ready conversationalist, when his hands are free.

Abie, seriously advises:

Take it away from me, I vouldn't tell you no lie, but double marriage is vorser than single cussedness.

VAUDEVILLE

Every time I think back ahead and think how happy I vas when I was it a single man, I get a headache in de head.

First, I asked de father from de girl dot I married, if I got married his daughter, vould I be happy.

He said it, "My boy, you vill never know true happiness until you are married."

Vell, by de time I found it out he was right, it was too late.

De girl I married said it she was a duchess in her own right. I found out she had a good vallop in her left, too.

I shall never forget it my vedding day.

De ceremony was called for five o'clock in the afternoon.

You see, nobody wanted to have it their whole day spoiled.

But I, like a chump, vas afraid I vould be late. So I hired a taxis cab. If I should know it then what I know now, I vould have valked.

De taxis cab went so fast we got a pinch from a cop policemans officer.

It made de taxis cab driver so mad he valloped the cop policemans officer in de jaw. Then two more cops came up and they brought us before de judge.

De judge looked at me and said, "Say, didn't I tell you de last time I never vanted to see you here again?"

I says, "Sure you did, judge. That's what I told de cops policemans officers, but they wouldn't believe me."

Then de judge said, "Can't this affair be settled out of court?"

De taxis cab driver said, "Your honor, that's what we was trying to do when them two cops butted in."

De judge says, "Vell, you are charged with breaking up de speed limits. Where was you going in such a hurry?"

I told de judge I vas on my vay to get married.

Then de judge says to de cop policemans officer:

"What do you mean bringing this man to me to be punished? If he was on his way to get married, ain't that enough punishment? Let him go and get it."

Vell, I had four hundred dollars saved up, and I put it in de bank. De next veek I drew it out again. Every time I vent in de bank de cashier had his hat on. He always looked like he was going avay out of town.

Vell, anyhow, when I go to de house de bride was vaiting for me. She vas afraid she would lose me otherwise.

All our friends and neighbors and a couple hundred members from de lodge was waiting, too.

But they was waiting to get a crack at de supper.

I'll bet them loafers had been saving up their appetites for a week.

Them members from de lodge go to a vedding on average once a day. On that account it don't cost them nothing to eat. They should vorry about de high cost of living. All they got to do is congratulate somebody. Somebody should congratulate them for not costing them any money to eat.

348

Routines

Everybody at de vedding congratulated me except de father from de bride. He was de only one who knew what I was getting.

One fellow said, "I think I shall congratulate you. You are going to be very happy." Oh, but he made a bum think.

Oi, I should be happy when I had to pay out my good money to feed all them loafers.

De father from de bride had de ring all ready, and de bride weighed in at de ringside at exactly 310 pounds.

Veepin' Rachel, she was a fat bride. She was so fat that when she went out at night she hung a red lantern on her to show that de street was blocked. But I thought a lot of her—310 pounds worth.

I think her age was somewhere between twenty-eight and her low-neck gown.

Nobody kissed de bride. They all wanted to hang on to their appetites.

One old lady looked at de bride de once-over and de up and down, and then she did de same to me and said: "I think he should be happy."

And a fellow said, "Vell, he's got a fat chance."

But I am gratified for one thing. I didn't pay de minister. De father from de bride paid him. I wouldn't pay no man for doing me a mean trick like he did. I don't know what de father from de bride paid de minister, but it should have been life.

When we left de house everybody threw old shoes at us.

Dot was all right except one fellow who forgot to take his foot out of his shoe.

When I think of it all, I could lie on de bed and blow out de gas. But de bill would be so big I couldn't afford it.

De bride and me vent to live in a six-room compartment.

Five rooms for her and de other one for me.

I think de landlord said it there was a bath room, with hot and cold running water. He was mistaken. De water was in no hurry—it didn't even walk.

De dining room is large. It would seat forty people—but I hope not.

De cost of living is so high that when we have steak all de neighbors come in and stand around and look at it.

De flats in de building are so close together that I can reach from our kitchen right into de next door neighbor's pantry. Take it away from me, that's a big saving.

De landlord wanted from me fifty dollars month rent. He said he thought he had that much coming to him. He has yet. I never paid him. De building was built in a hurry. After de first month it began to settle. De building settled, but I didn't.

After de first month de building had settled so much that de people on de third floor was living in de basement. Nothing stayed up but de rents.

De first Saturday I came home and from my six dollars wages I gave it my wife five dollars and kept one dollar for myself. De next Saturday I kept five dollars and give it to my wife one dollar. She hollered. She said, "Say, how do you expect me to make out on a dollar?" I says, "Vell, it is a tough job. I had a rotten time myself last veek."

NOTES

Introduction

1. See *Riot and Revelry in Early America*, ed. William Pencak, Matthew Dennis, and Simon P. Newman (University Park: Pennsylvania State University Press, 2002).

2. *Billboard*, December 26, 1925, in Joseph Csida and June Bundy Csida, *American Entertainment: A Unique History of Popular Show Business* (New York: Watson-Guptill, 1978), 269.

3. Olive Logan, *Apropos of Women and Theatres* (New York: Carleton, 1869), 151–52, 128; 110–53. A similarly broad definition, also critical of disreputable "low" elements, is J. J. Jennings, *Theatrical and Circus Life; or, Secrets of the Stage, Green-Room, and Sawdust Arena* (St. Louis: Sun Publishing, 1883).

4. Olive Logan, *Before the Footlights and behind the Scenes: A Book about "The Show Business" in all its branches* . . . (Philadelphia: Parmelee, 1870), 20; *Oxford English Dictionary*, 2d ed., 20 vols. (Oxford: Oxford University Press, 1989), 15:363–66; William A. Craigie and James R. Hulbert, *A Dictionary of American English on Historical Principles*, 4 vols. (Oxford: Oxford University Press, 1944), 4:2111.

5. See Richard Balzer, *Peepshows: A Visual History* (New York: Abrams, 1998), and Richard D. Altick, *The Shows of London* (Cambridge: Harvard University Press, 1978).

6. *Buffalo Bill's Wild West and Congress of Rough Riders of the World: Historical Sketches and Programme* (Chicago: n.p., 1893), 10; Jack Rennert, *100 Posters of Buffalo Bill's Wild West* (New York: Darien House, 1976), endpaper.

7. *Philadelphia Evening Bulletin*, 19 February 1858, and *National Intelligencer*, 27 April 1860, as quoted in David Carlyon, *Dan Rice: The Most Famous Man You've Never Heard Of!* (New York: Public Affairs Press, 2001), 226, 288.

8. *Oxford English Dictionary*, 7:295; George Crabbe, *English Synonymes* (New York: J. and J. Harper, 1831), 301; Noah Webster, *American Dictionary of the English Language* (New York: Harper and Brother, 1852), 921; Frederic W. Sawyer, *A Plea for Amusements* (New York: D. Appleton, 1847), 13; James L. Corning, *The Christian Law of Amusement* (Buffalo, N.Y.: Phinney, 1859), 10n.

9. David Jaffee, "Peddlers of Progress and the Transformation of the Rural North, 1760–1860," *Journal of American History* 78 (September 1991): 511–35. See also Jack Larkin, *The Reshaping of Everyday Life, 1790–1840* (New York: Harper and

Row, 1988), 205–31; Larkin, "From 'Country Mediocrity' to 'Rural Improvement': Transforming the Slovenly Countryside in Central Massachusetts, 1775–1840," in *Everyday Life in the Early Republic*, ed. Catherine E. Hutchins (Wintherthur, Del.: Winterthur Museum, 1994), 175–200; Richardson Wright, *Hawkers and Walkers in Early America* (Philadelphia: Lippincott, 1927), 178–208; Stuart Thayer, *Traveling Showmen: The American Circus before the Civil War* (Detroit: Astley and Ricketts, 1997); Timothy B. Spears, *100 Years on the Road: The Traveling Salesman in American Culture* (New Haven, Conn.: Yale University Press, 1995), chaps. 1–2; Alice C. Hudson and Barbara Cohen-Stratyner, *Heading West, Touring West: Mapmakers, Performing Artists, and the American Frontier* (New York: New York Public Library, 2001).

10. Quoted in Phyllis Kihn, "The Circus in Connecticut," *Connecticut Historical Society Bulletin* 22 (January 1957): 2.

11. Quoted in Paul McPharlin, *The Puppet Theatre in America: A History, 1524–1948. With a Supplement: Puppets in America since 1948, by Marjorie Batchelder McPharlin* (Boston: Plays, Inc., 1969), 150–51.

12. [Charles Farrar Browne], *Artemus Ward: His Works, Complete* (New York: G. W. Carleton, 1875), 25, 55; Nathaniel Hawthorne, *The American Notebooks*, ed. Claude M. Simpson [*The Centenary Edition of the Works of Nathaniel Hawthorne*, vol. 7] (Columbus: Ohio State University Press, 1972), 124, 130.

13. *The Memoir of John Durang, American Actor, 1785–1816*, ed. Alan S. Downer (Pittsburgh: University of Pittsburgh Press, 1966), 68–69.

14. *History of the Life, Travels and Incidents of Col. Hugh Lindsay. Written by Himself* (Philadelphia: n.p., 1859), 25; Elbert R. Bowen, *Theatrical Entertainments in Rural Missouri before the Civil War* (Columbia: University of Missouri Press, 1959), 17–21, 52, 113–14.

15. P. T. Barnum, *The Life of P. T. Barnum, Written by Himself* (New York: Redfield, 1855), 177, 210, 225.

16. Carlyon, *Dan Rice*, 44 (quotations).

17. Lawrence W. Levine, *Highbrow/Lowbrow: The Emergence of Cultural Hierarchy in America* (Cambridge: Harvard University Press, 1988), 56.

18. Rosemarie K. Bank, "The Boston Museum Company," in *American Theatre Companies, 1749–1887*, ed. Weldon B. Durham (Westport, Conn.: Greenwood Press, 1986), 72; Claire McGlinchee, *The First Decade of the Boston Museum* (Boston: Bruce Humphries, 1940), 80; Kate Ryan, *Old Boston Museum Days* (Boston: Little, Brown, 1915), 29; William B. Wood, *Personal Recollections of the Stage* (Philadelphia: Henry Carey Baird, 1855), 473–77.

19. See John Brewer, *The Pleasures of the Imagination: English Culture in the Eighteenth Century* (London: HarperCollins, 1997), chaps. 8–10; David Grimsted, *Melodrama Unveiled: American Theater and Culture, 1800–1850* (Chicago: University of Chicago Press, 1968), chap. 3.

20. Laurence Senelick, *Age and Stage of George L. Fox, 1825–1877* (Iowa City: University of Iowa Press, 1999), 143.

21. Marvin Carlson, "The Development of the American Theatre Program," in *The American Stage: Social and Economic Issues from the Colonial Period to the Present*, ed. Ron Engle and Tice L. Miller (Cambridge: Cambridge University Press, 1993), 107.

22. *New York Mirror*, 29 December 1832, 206, quoted in Stephen M. Archer, *Junius Brutus Booth: Theatrical Prometheus* (Carbondale: Southern Illinois University Press, 1992), 121.

23. *New York Tribune*, 14 December 1848, as quoted in William J. Mahar, *Behind the Burnt Cork Mask: Early Blackface Minstrelsy and Antebellum American Popular Culture* (Urbana: University of Illinois Press, 1999), 104. On the shared culture of opera and operatic burlesque, see Katherine K. Preston, *Opera on the Road: Traveling Opera Troupes in the United States, 1825–1860* (Urbana: University of Illinois Press, 1993), 312–17.

24. *Appleton's Journal* 1 (1869): 440, as quoted in Julian Mates, *America's Musical Stage: Two Hundred Years of Musical Theatre* (New York: Praeger, 1985), 140.

25. For connections between different musical styles, see Mates, *America's Musical Stage*.

26. Harlowe Hoyt, *Town Hall Tonight* (Englewood Cliffs, N.J.: Prentice-Hall, 1955); William L. Slout, *Theatre in a Tent: The Development of a Provincial Entertainment* (Bowling Green, Ohio: Bowling Green State University Press, 1972); William F. Condee, "*Hamlet*, Sunday School, and *Zarrow's Pig Revue*: Cultural Regulation in America's Opera Houses," *Journal of American Culture* 22 (summer 1999): 59–64.

27. N. T. Oliver (as told to Wesley Stout), "Med Show," *Saturday Evening Post* 202 (14 September 1929), quoted in James Harvey Young, *The Toadstool Millionaires* (Princeton, N.J.: Princeton University Press, 1961), 191; Brooks McNamara, *Step Right Up* (1976; rev. ed., Jackson: University Press of Mississippi, 1995), 92–95.

28. James Huneker, *The New Cosmopolis: A Book of Images* (New York: T. Werner Laurie, 1915), 162, 163; Dana Gatlin, "Amusing America's Millions," *World's Work* 26 (July 1913): 331.

29. Frederic Thompson, "Amusing the Million," *Everybody's Magazine* 19 (September 1908): 385; Frederick [sic] A. Thompson, "The Summer Show," *Independent* 62 (June 20, 1907): 1463. See also Rollin Lynde Hartt, *The People at Play* (Boston: Houghton, Mifflin, 1909), for a general survey of popular entertainment forms.

30. Q. K. Philander Doesticks, P. B. [Mortimer Q. Thomson], *Doesticks: What He Thinks* (New York: Edward Livermore, 1855), 255.

31. See Senelick, *Age and Stage*, chaps. 6, 7, 10; Richard Butsch, *The Making of American Audiences: From Stage to Television, 1750–1990* (Cambridge: Cambridge University Press, 2000), 44–61; Edwin G. Burrows and Mike Wallace, *Gotham: A History of New York City to 1898* (New York, 1999), 642–45, 752–59; Rosemarie K. Bank, "Hustlers in the House: The Bowery Theatre as a Mode of Historical Information," in *The American Stage*, ed. Engle and Miller, 47–64; Bank, *Theatre Culture in*

America, 1825–1850 (Cambridge: Cambridge University Press, 1997), chap. 2; Dale Cockrell, *Demons of Disorder: Early Blackface Minstrels and Their World* (Cambridge: Cambridge University Press, 1997), 30–32, and passim.

32. See Paul Schlicke, *Dickens and Popular Entertainment* (London: Allen and Unwin, 1985); Jim Davis and Victor Emeljanow, *Reflecting the Audience: London Theatregoing, 1840–1880* (Iowa City: University of Iowa Press, 2001).

33. William K. Northall, *Behind the Curtain; or, Fifteen Years Observations Among the Theatres of New York* (New York: W. F. Burgese, 1851), 91–92, quoted in Peter G. Buckley, "Paratheatricals and Popular Stage Entertainment," in *Cambridge History of American Theatre*, 3 vols., ed. Don B. Wilmeth and Christopher Bigsby (Cambridge: Cambridge University Press, 1998–2000), 1:460. See also Bruce A. McConachie, *Melodramatic Formations: American Theatre and Society, 1820–1870* (Iowa City: University of Iowa Press, 1992), chap. 5.

34. Josephine Harrop, *Victorian Portable Theatres* (London: Society for Theatre Research, 1989).

35. In 1890 the contrast remained: more than 60 percent of the population in England and Wales, but less than 28 percent in the United States, lived in cities of more than 60,000: Adna F. Weber, *The Growth of Cities in the Nineteenth Century: A Study in Statistics* (1899; Ithaca, N.Y.: Cornell University Press, 1963), 145–46.

36. See Mary C. Henderson, *The City and the Theatre* (Clifton, N.J.: James T. White, 1973); Peter G. Buckley, "Culture, Class, and Place in Antebellum New York," in *Power, Culture, and Place: Essays on New York*, ed. John Hull Mollenkopf (New York: Russell Sage, 1988), 29–52; William R. Taylor, "The Launching of a Commercial Culture: New York City, 1860–1930," in ibid., 107–33; Dell Upton, "Civilization and Urbanity in Antebellum New York," in *Art and the Empire City: New York, 1825–1861*, ed. Catherine Hoover Voorsanger and John K. Howat (New York: Metropolitan Museum of Art, 2000), 3–45.

37. "Shows and Showmen," *Chambers's Journal* 235 (July 3, 1858): 1–4; "Lord" George Sanger, *Seventy Years a Showman* (1910; London: MacGibbon and Kee, 1966), 141, 158.

38. *The Autobiography of Joseph Jefferson* (New York: Century, 1890), 394; review, *Atlantic Monthly* (1867), in *Famous Actors and Actresses of the American Stage*, 2 vols., ed. William C. Young (New York: R. R. Bowker, 1975), 2:981, quoted in McConachie, *Melodramatic Formations*, 238–39.

39. Clayton M. Hamilton, *The Theory of the Theatre* (1914; New York: Henry Holt, 1939), 187, quoted in Benjamin McArthur, *Actors and American Culture, 1880–1920* (Philadelphia: Temple University Press, 1984), 210; Harry James Smith, "The Melodrama," *Atlantic Monthly* 99 (March 1907): 327. For attitudes to popular amusements at the turn of the century, see Paul R. Gorman, *Left Intellectuals and Popular Culture in Twentieth-Century America* (Chapel Hill: University of North Carolina Press, 1996), chaps. 1 and 2.

40. Smith, "Melodrama," 327.

41. Smith, "Melodrama," 327; Edwin Milton Royle, "The Vaudeville Theatre,"

Scribner's Magazine 26 (October 1899): 495; Channing Pollock, *The Footlights Fore and Aft* (Boston: Gorham Press, 1911), 325; Sinow, quoted in Robert C. Snyder, *Voice of the City: Vaudeville and Popular Culture in New York City* (New York: Oxford University Press, 1989), 129.

42. George Jean Nathan, *The Popular Theatre* (New York: Knopf, 1918), 65, 232, 233, 220; George M. Cohan and George J. Nathan, "The Mechanics of Emotion," *McClure's Magazine* 42 (November 1913): 70–77.

43. Norman Hapgood, *The Stage in America, 1897–1900* (New York: Mac-Millan, 1901), 139.

44. Glenmore Davis, "The Moving-Picture Revolution," *Success Magazine* 13 (April 1910): 271, 239, 240.

45. William Allen Johnston, "The Moving-Picture Show: The New Form of Drama for the Million," *Munsey's Magazine* 41 (August 1909): 637, 636.

46. Robert Grau, *Business Man in the Amusement World: A Volume of Progress in the Field of the Theater* (New York: Broadway Publishing, 1910), 135. On illustrated songs and the fusion of vaudeville sound and machine-produced images, see Richard Abel, *The Red Rooster Scare: Making Cinema American, 1900–1910* (Berkeley: University of California Press, 1999), 40–46, 110–17; John Ripley, "Romance and Joy, Tears and Heartache," *Smithsonian Magazine* 12 (March 1982): 77–83; Patricia McDonnell et al., *On the Edge of Your Seat: Popular Theater and Film in Early Twentieth-Century America* (New Haven, Conn.: Yale University Press, 2002).

47. Linda Woal, "When a Dime Could Buy a Dream: Siegmund Lubin and the Birth of Motion Picture Exhibition," *Film History* 6 (1994): 152–65.

48. Kathryn H. Fuller, *At the Picture Show: Small-Town Audiences and the Creation of Movie Fan Culture* (Washington, D.C.: Smithsonian Institution Press, 1996), 12–13; Fuller, "Viewing the Viewers: Representations of the Audience in Early Cinema Advertising," in *American Movie Audiences: From the Turn of the Century to the Early Sound Era*, ed. Melvyn Stokes and Richard Maltby (London: British Film Institute, 1999), 123–26.

49. Gregory A. Waller, *Main Street Amusements: Movies and Commercial Entertainment in a Southern City, 1896 to 1930* (Washington, D.C.: Smithsonian Institution Press, 1995), 1–2, 25–27, 35–37, 43–45, 82–86, 94.

50. Ibid., 238; Charles Musser, *The Emergence of Cinema: The American Screen to 1907* (Berkeley: University of California Press, 1990), 444–47; Charles Musser with Carol Nelson, *High-Class Moving Pictures: Lyman H. Howe and the Forgotten Era of the Traveling Exhibition* (Princeton, N.J.: Princeton University Press, 1990).

51. Barton W. Curie, "The Nickel Madness," *Harper's Weekly* (August 24, 1907), in *The Movies in Our Midst: Documents in the Cultural History of Film in America*, ed. Gerald Mast (Chicago: University of Chicago Press, 1982), 50. See also Ben Singer, *Melodrama and Modernity: Early Sensational Cinema and Its Contexts* (New York: Columbia University Press, 2001), 145–220.

52. Tom Gunning, "From the Opium Den to the Theatre of Morality: Moral Discourse and Film Process in Early American Cinema," *Art and Text* 30 (September–

November 1988): 30–40; Lee Grieveson, "'A kind of recreative school for the whole family': Making Cinema Respectable, 1907–09," *Screen* 42 (spring 2001): 64–76.

53. Philip C. Lewis, *Trouping: How the Show Came to Town* (New York: Harper and Row, 1973), 10; Jack Poggi, *Theater in America: The Impact of Economic Forces, 1870–1967* (Ithaca, N.Y.: Cornell University Press, 1968), 29–30.

54. Thomas F. Gossett, *Uncle Tom's Cabin and American Culture* (Dallas: Southern Methodist University Press, 1985), 370, 385.

55. William L. Slout, "Tent Rep: Broadway's Poor Relation," in *American Popular Entertainment: Papers and Proceedings of the Conference on the History of American Popular Entertainment*, ed. Myron Matlaw (Westport, Conn.: Greenwood Press, 1979), 157. See also Slout, *Theatre in a Tent*; Landis K. Magnuson, *Circle Stock Theater: Touring American Small Towns, 1900–1960* (Jefferson, N.C.: McFarland, 1995).

56. Jere C. Mickel, *Footlights on the Prairie: The Story of the Repertory Tent Players in the Midwest* (St. Cloud, Minn.: North Star Press, 1974), 71–72.

57. Richard L. Poole, "Tent Rep vs. the Movies: The Dirty Business of Show Business," *Theatre History Studies* 17 (1997): 121–31.

58. Jack Burton, *In Memoriam: Oldtime Show Biz* (New York: Vantage, 1965).

The Dime Museum

1. Henry James, *A Small Boy and Others* (New York: MacMillan, 1913), 173.

2. Henry P. Tappan, *A Step from the New World to the Old and Back Again*, 2 vols. (New York: Appleton, 1852), 2:100, quoted in Neil Harris, *Humbug: The Art of P.T. Barnum* (Boston: Little, Brown, 1973), 33; Isabella Lucy Bird Bishop, *The Englishwoman in America* (1856), quoted in Bayrd Still, *Mirror for Gotham: New York as Seen by Contemporaries from Dutch Days to the Present* (New York: New York University Press, 1956), 157–58.

3. Quoted in Philip B. Kunhardt Jr., Philip B. Kunhardt III, Peter W. Kunhardt, *P. T. Barnum: America's Greatest Showman* (New York: Knopf, 1995), 234.

4. "Authentic Anecdotes of 'Old Zack,'" *Yankee Doodle* 2 (July 24–September 11, 1847), reprinted in *Piazza Tales and Other Prose Pieces, 1839–1860. The Writings of Herman Melville*, vol. 9, ed. Harrison Hayford, Alec A. MacDougall, Thomas Tanselle, et al. (Evanston, Ill.: Northwestern University Press, 1987), 225, 212–29.

5. Quoted in Peter G. Buckley, "Popular Entertainment before the Civil War," in *Encyclopedia of American Social History*, 3 vols., ed. Mary Kupiec Clayton, Elliott J. Gorn, and Peter W. Williams (New York: Scribners, 1993), 3:1622.

6. L. K. Philander Doesticks [Mortimer Thomson], *Doesticks: What He Says* (New York: Edward Livermore, 1855), 47, 46.

7. William Knight Northall, *Before and Behind the Curtain: or, Fifteen Years' Observations among the Theatres of New York* (New York: W. F. Burgess, 1851), 161.

8. *More Than Common Powers of Perception: The Diary of Elizabeth Rogers Mason*, ed. P. A. M. Taylor (Boston: Beacon Press, 1991), 54; *The Journals and*

Miscellaneous Notebooks of Ralph Waldo Emerson, vol. 11, 1848–1851 (Cambridge: Harvard University Press, 1975), 42.

9. *Catalogue or Guide Book of Barnum's Museum, New York, Containing Descriptions and Illustrations of the Various Wonders and Curiosities of That Immense Establishment . . .* (New York: Wynkoop, Hallenbeck and Thomas, n.d. [c.1863], 109.

10. Nathaniel Parker Willis, *Famous People and Places* (New York: C. Scribner, 1854), 441.

11. "A Word about Museums," *Nation* 1 (July 27, 1865): 113; "Popular Tastes and Amusements," *Christian Parlor Magazine* 2 (August 1845): 108.

12. *Catalogue or Guide Book of Barnum's Museum*, 102.

Minstrelsy

1. London *Times*, June 26, 1843, quoted in Hans Nathan, *Dan Emmett and the Rise of Early Negro Minstrelsy* (1962; Norman: University of Oklahoma Press, 1977), 137–38.

2. W. J. Lhamon Jr., *Raising Cain: Blackface Performance from Jim Crow to Hip Hop* (Cambridge: Harvard University Press, 1998), 158.

3. William J. Mahar, *Behind the Burnt Cork Mask: Early Blackface Minstrelsy and Antebellum American Popular Culture* (Urbana: University of Illinois Press, 1999), 154.

4. *Dwight's Journal of Music*, July 24, 1852, quoted in Charles Hamm, *Yesterdays: Popular Song in America* (New York: Norton, 1979), 109; [J. K.], "Who Are Our National Poets?" *Knickerbocker* 26 (October 1845): 332.

5. L. K. Philander Doesticks [Mortimer Q. Thomson], *Doesticks: What He Thinks* (New York: Edward Livermore, 1855), 214; William F. Stowe and David Grimsted, "White-Black Humor," *Journal of Ethnic Studies* 3 (1975): 95.

The Circus

1. *Letters of Emily Dickinson*, 3 vols., ed. Thomas H. Johnson (Cambridge: Harvard University Press, 1958), 2: 452.

2. James W. Barriskill, "The Newburyport Theatre," *Essex Institute Historical Collections* 41 (October 1955): 339–42, quoted in Peter Benes, "Itinerant Entertainers in New England and New York, 1687–1830," in *Itineracy in New England and New York*. The Dublin Seminar for New England Folklife Annual Proceedings 1984, ed. Peter Benes (Concord, Mass.: Boston University Press, 1986), 115.

3. Phyllis Kihn, "The Circus in Connecticut," *Bulletin of the Connecticut Historical Society Bulletin* 22 (January 1957): 14; Jon R. Sterngass, "Cities of Play: Saratoga Springs, Newport, and Coney Island in the Nineteenth Century" (Ph.D. diss., City University of New York, 1998), 73.

4. *Rochester Union & Advertiser*, August 24, 1868, quoted in Ruth Rosenberg-Naparsteck, "Big Free Street Parade: A History of the Circus in Rochester," *Rochester History* 49 (July 1987): 9, 10.

5. Hiram Fuller, *Belle Brittan on Tour: At Newport, and Here and There* (New York: Derby and Jackson, 1858), 160, quoted in Foster Rhea Dulles, *America Learns to Play: A History of Popular Recreation, 1607–1940* (New York: Appleton-Century, 1940), 134.

6. Edwin G. Burrows and Mike Wallace, *Gotham: A History of New York City to 1898* (New York: Oxford University Press, 1999), 642.

7. Henry David Thoreau, *Journal: The Writings of Henry David Thoreau*, 14 vols., ed. Bradford Torrey (1906; New York: AMS Press, 1968), 7: 461.

8. Circus courier quoted in A. H. Saxon, *P. T. Barnum: The Legend and the Man* (New York: Columbia University Press, 1989), 308.

Melodrama

1. Stephen Crane, *Maggie: A Girl of the Streets* (1893) in *Stephen Crane, Prose and Poetry* (New York: Library of America, 1984), 35, 36.

2. David Grimsted, *Melodrama Unveiled: American Theater and Culture, 1800–1850* (Chicago: University of Chicago Press, 1968), 232.

3. Michel Denning, "Cheap Stories: Notes on Popular Fiction and Working-Class Culture in Nineteenth-Century America," *History Workshop Journal* 22 (autumn 1986): 16.

4. Bruce A. McConachie, "'The Theatre of the Mob': Apocalyptic Melodrama and Preindustrial Riots in Antebellum New York," in *Theatre for Working-Class Audiences in the United States, 1830–1980*, eds. Bruce A. McConachie and Daniel Friedman (Westport, Conn.: Greenwood Press, 1983), 17–46; *Arcturus* (June 1841): 63, quoted in Bruce A. McConachie, *Melodramatic Formations: American Theatre and Society, 1820–1870* (Iowa City: University of Iowa Press, 1992), 114.

5. George L. Aiken, *Uncle Tom's Cabin* (1852), in *Dramas from the American Theatre 1762–1909*, ed. Richard Moody (Boston: Houghton Mifflin, 1966), 396.

6. James Parton, "Pittsburg," *Atlantic Monthly* (January 1868): 34–35, quoted in Francis G. Couvares, *The Remaking of Pittsburgh: Class and Culture in an Industrializing City, 1877–1919* (Albany: State University of New York Press, 1984), 39.

7. Charles M. Sheldon, *In His Steps: What Would Jesus Do?* (1896; London: Miles and Miles, n.d.), 194, 196 (chap. 9).

8. Herman Melville, *The Confidence-Man: His Masquerade*, eds. Harrison Hayford, Hershel Parker, and G. Thomas Tanselle (1857; Evanston, Ill.: Northwestern University Press and Newberry Library, 1984), 183.

9. Hartley Davis, "Tabloid Drama," *Everybody's Magazine* 21 (September 1909): 257; Owen Davis, "Why I Quit Writing Melodrama," *American Magazine* 128 (September 1914): 29; Harry James Smith, "The Melodrama," *Atlantic Monthly* 99 (March 1907): 323.

10. Marian Spitzer, "Ten-Twenty-Thirty: The Passing of the Popular-Priced Circuit," *Saturday Evening Post* (August 22, 1925): 40, 42, 48.

"Leg Show" Burlesque Extravaganzas

1. Rollin Lynde Hartt, *The People at Play* (Boston: Houghton Mifflin, 1909), 9.

2. New York *Clipper*, September 22, 29, 1866, quoted in Julian Mates, "The Black Crook Myth," *Theatre Survey* 7 (1966): 37.

3. *New York Tribune*, September 17 1866, quoted in Leigh George Odom, "*The Black Crook* at Niblo's Garden," *Drama Review* 26 (spring 1982): 22; *Spirit of the Times*, September 27, 1866, quoted in Kristina Gintautiene, "*The Black Crook*: Ballet in the Gilded Age (1866–1876)" (Ph.D. diss., New York University, 1984), 94.

4. Quoted in Laurence Senelick, *The Changing Room: Sex, Drag and Theatre* (London: Routledge, 2000), 263.

5. *New York Times*, November 8, 1868, quoted in Robert C. Allen, *Horrible Prettiness: Burlesque and American Culture* (Chapel Hill: University of North Carolina Press, 1991), 128.

6. Quoted in Lucinda Jarrett, *Stripping in Time: A History of Erotic Dancing* (London: HarperCollins, 1997), 10.

7. William R. Leach, "Transformations in a Culture of Consumption: Women and Department Stores, 1890–1925," *Journal of American History* 71 (September 1984): 329–30, and more generally, Linda L. Tyler, "'Commerce and Poetry Hand in Hand': Music in American Department Stores, 1880–1930," *Journal of the American Musicological Society* 45 (1992): 75–120.

8. *New York Tribune*, September 17, 1866, quoted in Laurilyn J. Harris, "Extravaganza at Niblo's Garden: *The Black Crook*," *Nineteenth Century Theatre Research* 13 (summer 1985): 11; *Spirit of the Times* 15 (September 26, 1866), 64, quoted in Deane L. Root, *American Popular Stage Music, 1860–1880* (Ann Arbor, Mich.: UMI Research Press, 1981), 87.

9. George G. Foster, *New York by Gas-light and Other Urban Sketches*, ed. Stuart M. Blumin (Berkeley: University of California Press, 1990), 81.

10. Louisa May Alcott, *Work: A Story of Experience* (1873; New York: Schocken, 1977), 40.

The Wild West Show

1. Quoted in Don Russell, *The Lives and Legends of Buffalo Bill* (Norman: University of Oklahoma Press, 1960), 195.

2. *Buffalo Bill's West and Congress of Rough Riders of the World. Historical Sketches and Programme* (Chicago: n.p., 1893), 4.

3. Ibid.

4. *The Wild West, Buffalo Bill and Dr. Carver, Rocky Mountain and Prairie Exhibition*, program (1883), quoted in Joy S. Kasson, *Buffalo Bill's Wild West: Celebrity, Memory, and Popular History* (New York: Hill and Wang, 2000), 55.

5. Letter of Commissioner Oberly to the Secretary of the Interior, March 20, 1889, quoted in Francis Paul Prucha, *American Indian Policy in Crisis: Christian Reformers and the Indian, 1865–1900* (Norman: University of Oklahoma Press,

1976), 318; *Seventeenth Annual Report of the Executive Committee of the Indian Rights Association* (1889), in *Americanizing the American Indians: Writings by "Friends of the Indian," 1880–1900,* ed. Francis Paul Prucha (Cambridge: Harvard University Press, 1973), 314.

Summer Amusement Parks

1. Joel Cook, *Brief Summer Rambles Near Philadelphia* (Philadelphia, 1882), 9, quoted in Jon R. Sterngass, "City of Play: Saratoga Springs, Newport, and Coney Island in the Nineteenth Century" (Ph.D. diss., City University of New York, 1998), 469.

2. Theodore Dreiser, *The Color of a Great City* (New York: Boni and Liveright, 1923), 119.

3. Reginald Wright Fauffman, "Why Is Coney? A Study of a Wonderful Playground and the Men That Made It," *Hampton's Magazine* 23 (August 1909): 215.

4. O. Henry, "Brickdust Row," in *The Trimmed Lamp, and Other Stories of the Four Million* (New York: McClure, Phillips, 1907), reprinted in *The Complete Works of O. Henry* (Kingswood, Surrey: Associated Bookbuyers', 1928), 1095.

5. *Coney Island To-day: The Only Authorized Publication on the World's Greatest Playground* 1 (New York: n.p., June 1911): 39, 37; Rollin Lynde Hartt, *The People at Play* (Boston: Houghton, Mifflin, 1909), 83, 81.

6. Richard Snow, *Coney Island: A Postcard Journey to the City of Fire* (New York: Brightwater Press, 1984), 78.

7. *Coney Island To-day,* 22.

8. Charles Belmont Davis, "The Renaissance of Coney," *Outing Magazine* 48 (August 1906): 514, 522.

9. Kauffman, "Why Is Coney?" 224.

10. Richard Le Gallienne, "Human Need of Coney Island," *Cosmopolitan* 39 (July 1905): 243.

Vaudeville

1. Charles R. Sherlock, "Where Vaudeville Holds the Boards," *Cosmopolitan* 32 (February 1902): 420.

2. Paterson *Daily Press,* March 22, 1865, quoted in Susan Kattwinkel, "Tony Pastor's Vaudeville: Serving the New York Community," *Library Chronicle of the University of Texas at Austin* 3 (1995): 55.

3. Arthur Ruhl, *Second Nights: People and Ideas of the Theatre To-Day* (New York: Scribner's, 1914), 10–11.

4. Douglas Gilbert, *American Vaudeville: Its Life and Times* (1940; New York: Dover, 1963), 393.

5. Robert W. Snyder, *The Voice of the City: Vaudeville and Popular Culture in New York* (New York: Oxford University Press, 1989), 110; John Corbin, "How the Other Half Laughs," *Harper's Monthly* 98 (December 1898): 30.

6. Caroline Caffin, *Vaudeville* (New York: Mitchell Kinnerley, 1914), 14.

7. Kathryn J. Oberdeck, "Contested Cultures of American Refinement: Theatrical Manager Sylvester Poli, His Audiences, and the Vaudeville Industry, 1890–1920," *Radical History Review* 66 (1996): 70.

8. Arthur Prill, "The 'Small-Time' King," *Theatre Magazine* 19 (March 1914), quoted in Robert W. Snyder, "Big Time, Small Time, All Around the Town: New York Vaudeville in the Early Twentieth Century," in *For Fun and Profit: The Transformation of Leisure into Consumption*, ed. Richard Butsch (Philadelphia: Temple University Press, 1990), 128.

9. New Haven *Union*, November 3, 1913, quoted in Oberdeck, "Contested Cultures," 67.

10. Caffin, *Vaudeville*, 37, 41, 19, 22–23.

BIBLIOGRAPHICAL ESSAY

General

There are many excellent introductions to nineteenth-century popular entertainment. The most wide-ranging are Robert C. Toll, *On with the Show: The First Century of Show Business in America* (New York: Oxford University Press, 1976); David Nasaw, *Going Out: The Rise and Fall of Public Amusements* (1993; Cambridge: Harvard University Press, 1999); and *American Popular Entertainment: Papers and Proceedings of the Conference on the History of American Popular Entertainment*, ed. Myron Matlaw (Westport, Conn.: Greenwood Press, 1979). Very useful for their excellent illustrations are Richard W. Flint, *Step Right Up! Amusement for All: Show Business at the Turn of the Century* (Rochester, N.Y.: Margaret Woodbury Strong Museum, 1977); and Donna R. Braden, *Leisure and Entertainment in America* (Dearborn, Mich.: Henry Ford Museum and Greenfield Village, 1988). The outstanding local studies are Roy Rosenzweig, *Eight Hours for What We Will: Workers and Leisure in an Industrial City, 1870–1920* (Cambridge: Cambridge University Press, 1983), on Worcester, Massachusetts; and Gregory A. Waller, *Main Street Amusements: Movies and Commercial Entertainment in a Southern City, 1896–1930* (Washington, D.C.: Smithsonian Institution Press, 1995), on Lexington, Kentucky.

Too often, discussion of the stage is divorced from that of the street. One exception is Peter G. Buckley, "Paratheatricals and Popular Stage Entertainment," in *The Cambridge History of American Theatre*, vol. 1, *Beginnings to 1870*, ed. Don B. Wilmeth and Christopher Bigsby (New York: Cambridge University Press, 1998), 424–81. Brooks McNamara has a similarly broad-ranging discussion in many essays, notably, "The Scenography of Popular Entertainment," *Drama Review* 18 (March 1974): 16–24; "Popular Entertainments," in *The Cambridge History of American Theatre*. vol. 2, *1870–1945*, ed. Wilmeth and Bigsby (New York: Cambridge University Press, 1999), 378–410; and "Defining Popular Culture," *Theatre History Studies* 18 (1998): 3–12. Outstanding books on entertainment and broader cultural change are Lawrence W. Levine, *Highbrow/Lowbrow: The Emergence of Cultural Hierarchy in America* (Cambridge: Harvard University Press, 1988), Michael G. Kammen, *American Culture, American Tastes: Social Change and the 20th Century* (New York: Knopf, 1999); and Richard Butsch, *The Making of American Audiences: From Stage to Television, 1750–1990* (Cambridge: Cambridge University Press, 2000). Similarly wide-ranging studies of Europe are Thomas Richards, *The Commodity Spectacle of Victorian England: Advertising and Spectacle, 1851–1914* (London: Verso, 1991); Charles Rearick, *Pleasures of the Belle Epoque: Entertainment and Festivity in Turn-of-the-Century France* (New Haven, Conn.: Yale University Press, 1985); and Tracy C. Davis, *The Economics of the British Stage, 1800–1914* (Cambridge: Cambridge University Press, 2000).

Don B. Wilmeth has the most complete bibliographies: *American and English Popular Entertainment: A Guide to Information Sources* (Detroit: Gale Research, 1980), and *Variety Entertainment and Outdoor Amusements: A Reference Guide* (Westport, Conn.: Greenwood Press, 1982), updated with more recent listings in *Theatre History Studies* 11 (1991): 151–65, and ibid., 18 (June 1998): 147–61. Wilmeth's *The Language of American Popular Entertainment: A Glossary of Argot, Slang, and Terminology* (Westport, Conn.: Greenwood Press, 1981) is an equally important work of reference.

Dime Museum

There are two comprehensive overviews: Andrea Stulman Dennett, *Weird and Wonderful: The Dime Museum in America* (New York: New York University Press, 1997); and especially Brooks McNamara, "'A Congress of Wonders': The Rise and Fall of the Dime Museum," *ESQ* 20 (1974): 216–32. The most notable studies are of Peale's educational museums in Philadelphia and Baltimore: Charles Coleman Sellers, *Mr. Peale's Museum: Charles Willson Peale and the First Popular Museum of Natural Science and Art* (New York: Norton, 1980); David R. Brigham, *Public Culture in the Early Republic: Peale's Museum and its Audience* (Washington, D.C.: Smithsonian Institution Press, 1995); and *Mermaids, Mummies, and Mastadons: The Emergence of the American Museum*, ed. William T. Alderson (Washington, D.C.: Smithsonian Institution Press, 1992).

For most of the century, museums made no clear distinction between education and entertainment. Important studies of the fascination with "curiosities" and "non-descripts" are Robert Bogdan, *Freak Show: Presenting Human Oddities for Amusement and Profit* (Chicago: University of Chicago Press, 1988); Rosemarie Garland Thomson, *Extraordinary Bodies: Figuring Physical Disability in American Culture and Literature* (New York: Columbia University Press, 1997); Leslie Fiedler, *Freaks: Myths and Images of the Secret Self* (New York, Simon and Schuster, 1978); Harriet Ritvo, *The Platypus and the Mermaid and Other Figments of the Classifying Imagination* (Cambridge: Harvard University Press, 1997); Jan Bondeson, *The Feejee Mermaid and Other Essays in Natural and Unnatural History* (Ithaca, N.Y.: Cornell University Press, 1999); and James W. Cook, *The Arts of Deception: Playing with Fraud in the Age of Barnum* (Cambridge: Harvard University Press, 2001). There are specific case studies of exhibits in *Freakery: Cultural Spectacles of the Extraordinary Body*, ed. Rosemarie Garland Thomson (New York: Columbia University Press, 1996); Ricky Jay, *Learned Pigs and Fireproof Women* (1986; New York: Farrar, Straus, and Giroux, 1998); and Joanne Martell, *Millie-Christine: Fearfully and Wonderfully Made* (Winston-Salem, N.C.: John F. Blair, 2000).

All scholars acknowledge P. T. Barnum's genius for publicity and the time, money and effort he spent in making his exhibits celebrities. His hoaxes were more transparent and more daring than the frauds of his peers and predecessors. He succeeded in molding his image as that of an amusing rogue rather than a scandalous charlatan, and his humorous approach to "humbug," as shown in his best-selling autobiography—*The Life of P. T. Barnum, Written by Himself* (1855; Urbana: University of Illinois Press, 2000)—caught the mood of the nation. David S. Reynolds, *Beneath the American Renaissance: The Subversive Imagination in the Age of Emerson and Melville* (Cambridge: Harvard University Press, 1988), explains the significance of comic irreverence in the late 1840s and 1850s. There are excellent studies: Neil Harris, *Humbug: The Art of P.T. Barnum* (Boston: Little Brown, 1973); A. H. Saxon, *P. T. Barnum: The Legend and the Man* (New York: Columbia University Press, 1989); Bluford Adams, *E Pluribus Barnum: The Great Showman and the Making of U.S. Popular Culture* (Minneapolis: University of Minnesota Press, 1997); and Benjamin Reiss, "P. T. Barnum, Joice Heth, and Antebellum Spectacles of Race," *American Quarterly* 51 (March 1999): 78–107, expanded in his *Showman and the Slave: Race, Death, and Memory in Barnum's America* (Cambridge: Harvard University Press, 2001). Philip B. Kunhardt Jr., Philip B. Kunhardt III, Peter W. Kunhardt, *P. T. Barnum: America's Greatest Showman* (New York: Knopf, 1995), is sumptuously illustrated and carefully researched, and the video *P .T. Barnum: America's Greatest Showman* (Discovery Channel, 1996) elaborates on themes in the Kunhardts' book. The video *P. T. Barnum: American Dreamer* (A & E, 1994) also has some excellent commentary. The American History Project has begun a virtual map of the second floor of Barnum's Museum (see web.gsuc.cuny.edu/ashp/LITBar), with an extensive file of contemporary documents.

Minstrelsy

Inside the Minstrel Mask: Readings in Nineteenth-Century Blackface Minstrelsy, ed. Anne-Marie Bean, James V. Hatch, and Brooks McNamara (Hanover, N.H.: Wesleyan University Press, 1996) reprints outstanding essays and brief primary sources and adds some new essays. Much of the early scholarship was descriptive: the best are Carl Wittke, *Tambo and Bones: A History of the American Minstrel Stage* (1930; Westport, Conn.: Greenwood Press, 1968); and Daily Paskman and Sigmund Spaeth, *"Gentlemen, Be Seated!": A Parade of the Old-Time Minstrels* (New York: Doubleday, Doran, 1928). Constance Rourke's elegant essay, "That Long-Tail'd Blue," part of her larger study, *American Humor: A Study of the National Character* (1931; Garden City, N.Y.: Doubleday, 1953), 70–90, noted the influence of southwestern folklore on slave songs reinterpreted by the two outstanding entrepreneurs, "Jim Crow" Rice and Dan Emmett.

Robert C. Toll was the leading scholar of the 1970s. His *Blacking Up: The*

Bibliographical Essay

Minstrel Show in Nineteenth-Century America (New York: Oxford University Press, 1974) remains the most detailed general account. Slavery and segregation created blackface, but minstrelsy was more than the simple expression of racial prejudice. The grinning black mask concealed whites' psychological needs: celebration of plantation anarchy obscured the reality of sectional strife and industrial urbanism, and images of ludicrous blacks reassured those troubled by the lack of freedom allowed to the largest minority. Sam Dennison, *Scandalize My Name: Black Imagery in American Popular Music* (New York: Garland, 1982), gives abundant details of prejudice, but little explanation. J. Stanley Lemons, "Black Stereotypes as Reflected in Popular Culture, 1880–1920," *American Quarterly* 29 (spring 1977): 102–16, traces minstrel images in ephemera and material culture. Joseph Boskin, *Sambo: The Rise and Fall of an American Jester* (New York: Oxford University Press, 1987), chaps. 3 and 4, sketches the lasting influence of the black fool.

Musicologists explored whether minstrelsy had genuine African American roots. *The Early Minstrel Show* (New World Records compact disk) provides performances of typical songs. Hans Nathan, *Dan Emmett and the Rise of Early Negro Minstrelsy* (Norman: University of Oklahoma Press, 1962), traces the connections between the Virginia Minstrels and the songs of the slaves. Others see the music as largely white invention. Charles Hamm, *Yesterdays: Popular Song in America* (New York: Norton, 1979), chaps. 6 and 10, shows that traditional Irish tunes were given new words. Robert B. Winans, "Early Minstrel Show Music, 1843–1852," in *Musical Theatre in America: Papers and Proceedings of the Conference on the Musical Theatre in America*, ed. Glenn B. Loney (Westport, Conn.: Greenwood Press, 1984), 71–98, also sees little evidence of slave authorship and argues that a creeping sentimentalism brought blackface music closer to the mainstream. Dale Cockrell, "Nineteenth-Century Popular Music," in *The Cambridge History of American Music*, ed. David Nicholls (Cambridge: Cambridge University Press, 1998), 158–85, surveys minstrelsy in context.

There were always critical voices arguing that Toll's liberal, civil-rights interpretation was incomplete. William F. Stowe and David Grimsted, "White-Black Humor," *Journal of Ethnic Studies* 3 (1975): 78–96, saw enjoyment in wit and genuine affection as well as derogatory comment. For Nathan Huggins, *The Harlem Renaissance* (New York: Oxford University Press, 1971), chap. 7, the blackface mask was liberating and allowed whites the freedom to express longings repressed by Victorianism. In "Blackface Minstrelsy and Jacksonian Ideology," *American Quarterly* 27 (March 1975): 3–28, modified in his *Rise and Fall of the White Republic: Class Politics and Mass Culture in Nineteenth-Century America* (London: Verso, 1990), 165–82, Alexander Saxton saw early minstrel songs as largely supporting the Democratic party and its alliance of New York's Tammany Hall and the proslavery South. For David Roediger in *The Wages of Whiteness: Race and the Making of the American Working Class* (London: Verso, 1991), chap. 6, blackface was a convenient unifying symbol for the poor to transcend ethnicity and forge a class alliance against privilege.

Eric Lott, *Love and Theft: Blackface Minstrelsy and the American Working Class*

(New York: Oxford University Press, 1993), is the most nuanced and sophisticated interpretation, blending cultural-studies theory with close attention to literary expression and social background. Representations, he argues, were ambiguous and ambivalent, revealing disgust and desire, jealousy and contempt. Although it has relatively little specifically on minstrelsy, Shane White and Graham White, *Stylin': African American Expressive Culture from Its Beginnings to the Zoot Suit* (Ithaca, N.Y.: Cornell University Press, 1998), traces white fascination with the black body. Two recent studies, based on the most extensive original research, explore the social context most thoroughly. W. J. Lhamon Jr., *Raising Cain: Blackface Performance from Jim Crow to Hip Hop* (Cambridge: Harvard University Press, 1998), and Dale Cockrell, *Demons of Disorder: Early Blackface Minstrels and Their World* (New York: Cambridge University Press, 1997), examine minstrelsy origins in New York City. William J. Mahar, *Behind the Burnt Cork Mask: Early Blackface Minstrelsy and Antebellum American Popular Culture* (Urbana: University of Illinois Press, 1999), is an extraordinarily wide-ranging study of its burlesque elements as portrayed in words and music. Philip F. Gura, "America's Minstrel Daze," *New England Quarterly* 72 (December 1999): 602–16, is a perceptive review of this new research.

E. J. Kahn Jr., *The Merry Partners: The Age and Stage of Harrigan and Hart* (New York: Random House, 1955), and Richard Moody, *Ned Harrigan: From Corlear's Hook to Herald Square* (Chicago: Nelson-Hall, 1980), are both rather descriptive accounts. The longer, three-act version of *The Mulligan Guard Ball* of the early 1880s is reproduced from manuscript with songs and music in *Irish American Theater*, ed. Katherine K. Preston (New York: Garland, 1994). The most incisive analysis is James Dormon, "Ethnic Cultures of the Mind: The Harrigan-Hart Mosaic," *American Studies* 33 (fall 1992): 21–40. Michael Rogin, *Blackface, White Noise: Jewish Immigrants in the Hollywood Melting Pot* (Berkeley: University of California Press, 1996), traces the decline of minstrelsy in the twentieth century.

The Circus

Of all the fields of popular entertainment, circus history is the least analytical. The best general studies are Helen Stoddart, *Rings of Desire: Circus History and Representation* (Manchester: Manchester University Press, 2000), and the forthcoming studies of the late nineteenth and twentieth centuries by Janet M. Davis, *The Circus Age: Culture and Society under the American Big Top* (Chapel Hill: University of North Carolina Press), and of Britain, by Brenda Assael, *The Circus and Victorian Society* (Charlottesville: University Press of Virginia). Richard W. Flint has three excellent essays: "The Evolution of the Circus in Nineteenth-Century America," in *American Popular Entertainment: Papers and Proceedings of the Conference on the History of American Popular Entertainment*, ed. Myron Matlaw (Westport, Conn.: Greenwood Press, 1979), 187–95; "The Circus in America: The World's Largest, Grandest, Best Amusement Institution," *Quarterly Journal of the Library of Congress* 40 (summer 1983): 202–33; and "Entrepreneurial and Cultural Aspects of the Early-Nineteenth-

Century Circus and Menagerie Business," in *Itineracy in New England and New York*, Dublin Seminar for New England Folklife Annual Proceedings 1984, ed. Peter Benes (Boston: Boston University Press, 1986), 132–49.

Stuart Thayer's very detailed investigations of local newspapers have made older descriptive accounts obsolete: *Traveling Showmen: The American Circus before the Civil War* (Detroit: Astley and Ricketts, 1997); *Annals of the American Circus, 1793–1860* (Seattle: Duven and Thayer, 2000); and, with William L. Stout, *Grand Entrée: The Birth of the Greatest Show on Earth, 1870–1875* (San Bernardino, Calif.: Borgo Press, 1998). David Carlyon, *Dan Rice: The Most Famous Man You've Never Heard Of!* (New York: Public Affairs Press, 2002), is a modern biography of the most renowned performer. Although P. T. Barnum entered the circus business seriously only in the 1870s and 1880s and left day-to-day administration to others, his career has generated some of the most perceptive discussions of the circus and society: Harris, *Humbug*, chap. 9; Saxon, *P. T. Barnum*, chaps. 11–14; and Adams, *E Pluribus Barnum*, chap. 4.

Melodrama

The standard general reference to the drama is *Cambridge Guide to American Theatre*, ed. Don B. Wilmeth and Tice Miller (New York: Cambridge University Press, rev. ed., 1996). The most useful introductions to major themes and genres are the essays in *The Cambridge History of the American Theatre*, vol. 1, *Beginnings to 1870*; vol. 2, *1870–1945*, ed. Don B. Wilmeth and Christopher Bigsby (New York: Cambridge University Press, 1998, 1999). Surveys of major dramatists and plays include Gary A. Richardson, *American Drama from the Colonial Period through World War I: A Critical History* (New York: Twayne, 1993); and two by Walter J. Meserve: *An Emerging Entertainment: The Drama of the American People to 1828* (Bloomington: Indiana University Press, 1977); and *Heralds of Promise: The Drama of the American People in the Age of Jackson, 1828–1849* (Bloomington: Indiana University Press, 1986).

Since the American theater imitated the style and content of foreign plays, the European context is especially relevant. The analytical studies of Michael Booth are outstanding, notably, *English Melodrama* (London: Herbert Jenkins, 1965), and *Theatre in the Victorian Age* (New York: Cambridge University Press, 1992). Martha Vicinus's brief and incisive essay, "'Helpless and Unfriended': Nineteenth-Century Domestic Melodrama," *New Literary History* 13 (autumn 1981): 127–43, is reprinted in *When They Weren't Doing Shakespeare: Essays in Nineteenth-Century British and American Theatre*, ed. Judith Fisher and Stephen Watt (Athens: University of Georgia Press, 1989), 174–86. Frank Rahill, *The World of Melodrama* (University Park: Pennsylvania State University Press, 1967); Peter Brooks, *The Melodramatic Imagination* (New Haven, Conn.: Yale University Press, 1976); *Melodrama: Stage, Picture, Screen*, ed. Jacky Bratton, Jim Cook, and Christine Gledhill (London: British Film Institute, 1994); and *Melodrama: The Cultural Emergence of a Genre*, ed.

Michael Hays and Anastasia Nikolopoulou (New York: St. Martin's Press, 1996), discuss modern critical perspectives.

Outstanding general studies of American melodrama are David Grimsted, *Melodrama Unveiled: American Theater and Culture, 1800–1850* (Chicago: University of Chicago Press, 1968), summarized in Grimsted, "Melodrama as Echo of the Historically Voiceless," in *Anonymous Americans: Explorations in Nineteenth-Century Social History*, ed. Tamara K. Hareven (Englewood Cliffs, N.J.: Prentice-Hall, 1971), 80–98; Bruce A. McConachie, *Melodramatic Formations: American Theatre and Society, 1820–1870* (Iowa City: University of Iowa Press, 1992), supplemented by McConachie, "Role-Playing and Authenticity in Midcentury Melodrama," *Journal of American Drama and Theatre* 4 (winter 1992): 45–62; A. Nicholas Vardac, *Stage to Screen: Theatrical Method from Garrick to Griffith* (New York: Benjamin Blom, 1968); and Jeffrey D. Mason, *Melodrama and the Myth of America* (Bloomington: Indiana University Press, 1993). The most informative on the late nineteenth century are Weldon B. Durham, "The Revival and Decline of the Stock Company Mode of Organization, 1886–1930," *Theatre History Studies* 6 (1986): 165–88; Jack Poggi, *Theatre in America: The Impact of Economic Forces, 1870–1967* (Ithaca, N.Y.: Cornell University Press, 1968); Alfred E. Bernheim, *The Business of the Theatre: An Economic History of the American Theatre, 1750–1932* (New York: Actors' Equity Association, 1932); and Ben Singer, *Melodrama and Modernity: Early Pulp Cinema and the Social Contexts of Sensationalism* (New York: Columbia University Press, 2001).

There is a large literature on the broader social context. Bruce A. McConachie, "Pacifying American Theatrical Audiences, 1820–1900," in *For Fun and Profit: The Transformation of Leisure into Consumption*, ed. Richard Butsch (Philadelphia: Temple University Press, 1990), 47–70; and Richard Butsch, *The Making of American Audiences: From Stage to Television, 1750–1990* (Cambridge: Cambridge University Press, 2000), explore the changing composition of "popular" audiences. Harlowe R. Hoyt, *Town Hall Tonight* (Englewood Cliffs, N.J.: Prentice-Hall, 1955), is a good local study of theater in Beaver Dam, Wisconsin. Also useful for understanding the appeal of melodrama are Christine Stansell, *City of Women: Sex and Class in New York, 1789–1860* (New York: Knopf, 1986); Timothy J. Gilfoyle, *City of Eros: New York City, Prostitution, and the Commercialization of Sex, 1790–1920* (New York: Norton, 1992); and Michael Denning, *Mechanic Accents: Dime Novels and Working-Class Culture in America* (1987; London: Verso, 1998), on popular novels with an urban theme. Francis Hodge, *Yankee Theatre: The Image of America on the Stage, 1825–1850* (Austin: University of Texas Press, 1964), discusses early national character.

There are good social-history studies of the theater. Rosemarie K. Bank, *Theatre Culture in America, 1825–1860* (New York: Cambridge University Press, 1997), examines the fit between dramatic representations and social reality. On the acting profession, see Benjamin McArthur, *Actors and American Culture, 1880–1920* (Philadelphia: Temple University Press, 1984); and Claudia D. Johnson, *American Ac-*

tress: Perspective on the Nineteenth Century (Chicago: Nelson-Hall, 1984). Faye E. Dudden, *Women in the American Theatre: Actresses and Audiences, 1790–1870* (New Haven, Conn.: Yale University Press, 1994), is wide-ranging and incisive.

Weldon B. Durham's edited *American Theatre Companies, 1749–1887* and *1888–1930* (Westport, Conn.: Greenwood Press, 1986, 1987) are essential references. George C. D. Odell's fifteen-volume *Annals of the New York Stage* (New York: Columbia University Press, 1927–49) is exceptionally thorough. The most wide-ranging collection of theatrical texts is *Dramas from the American Theatre, 1762–1909*, ed. Richard Moody (Cleveland: World Publishing, 1966). Among the more recent anthologies are *Early American Drama*, ed. Jeffrey Richards (New York: Penguin, 1997), and *Staging the Nation: Plays from the American Theatre, 1787–1909*, ed. Don B. Wilmeth (New York: Bedford, 1998). Readex Corporation's microfiche *Nineteenth-Century English and American Plays* is the only comprehensive collection; Chadwyck-Healey's CD-ROM *American Drama* series is much more selective.

"Leg Show" Burlesque

Michael Booth explains the nature of the European *féerie* and extravaganza in his edited *English Plays of the Nineteenth Century*, vol. 5, *Pantomimes, Extravaganzas and Burlesques* (Oxford: Clarendon Press, 1976). Claire McGlinchee, "The Marvellous in the Pantomimes: Spectacles and Extravaganzas in the 19C American Theatre," *Revue d'histoire du théâtre* 15 (January–March 1963): 63–70, sketches its introduction to the northeastern United States. Cecil Smith and Glenn Litton, *Musical Comedy in America* (1950; New York: Theatre Arts Books, 1981), 2–87, is succinct and comprehensive, but Deane L. Root, *American Popular Stage Music, 1860–1880* (Ann Arbor, Mich.: UMI Research Press, 1981), chap. 3, has the most detailed description of the spectacular stage shows. Laurence Senelick, *The Age and Stage of George L. Fox, 1825–1877* (1988; Iowa City: University of Iowa Press, 1999), is a pioneering study of midcentury pantomime.

The most detailed examination of "leg-show" burlesque in America is Robert C. Allen, *Horrible Prettiness: Burlesque and American Culture* (Chapel Hill: University of North Carolina Press, 1991); its main shortcoming is its failure to explore traditions before 1866 in America and Europe. Faye E. Dudden, *Women in the American Theatre: Actresses and Audiences, 1790–1870* (New Haven: Yale University Press, 1994), chap. 7; and Peter G. Buckley, "The Culture of 'Leg Work': The Transformation of Burlesque after the Civil War," in *The Mythmaking Frame of Mind: Social Imagination and American Culture*, ed. James Gilbert et al. (Belmont, Calif.: Wadsworth, 1993), 113–34, are excellent supplements. Two fine studies of women's fashion and attitudes toward the female body in the 1860s are Lois W. Banner, *American Beauty* (Chicago: University of Chicago Press, 1983), chaps. 6 and 7, and William R. Leach, *True Love and Perfect Union: The Feminist Reform of Sex and Society* (New York: Basic, 1981), chap. 9. Kurt Gänzl, *Lydia Thompson: Queen of Burlesque* (New York: Routledge, 2002), is a detailed biography of the major British star. Donna

Carlton, *Looking for Little Egypt* (Bloomington, Ind.: IDD Books, 1994) is an original study of "Oriental" dancing at the turn of the century.

The Black Crook has received far more attention than other extravaganzas. Julian Mates, "The *Black Crook* Myth," *Theatre Survey* 7 (1966), 31–43, argued very effectively that its influence on the development of musical comedy was limited. Kristina Gintautiene, "*The Black Crook*: Ballet in the Gilded Age (1866–1876)" (Ph.D. diss., New York University, 1984), discusses aspects of dance fully. Laurilyn J. Harris, "Extravaganza at Niblo's Garden: *The Black Crook*," *Nineteenth Century Theatre Research* 13 (summer 1985): 1–15, and Leigh George Odom, "*The Black Crook* at Niblo's Garden," *Drama Review* 26 (spring 1982): 21–40, explore its reception in the New York press. John Russell David, "The Genesis of the Variety Theatre: The *Black Crook* Comes to St. Louis," *Missouri Historical Review* 64 (1970): 133–49, deals with the franchised production of April–July 1867 in the city. *The Black Crook* play text— probably only a guide for improvisations by the many different productions of the 1860s and 1870s—is most conveniently available in *The Black Crook and Other Nineteenth-Century American Plays*, ed. Myron Matlaw (New York: Dutton, 1966), 319–74; this differs in minor respects from the 1866 original printed in Chicago by Rounds and James. The novel, *The Black Crook, A Most Wonderful History. Now being performed with immense success in all the principal theatres throughout the United States* (Philadelphia: Barclay, 1866), has illustrations from the show, but in all other respects bears no resemblance whatsoever to the play.

The Wild West Show

The broadest coverage of live stage shows of frontier life, from George Catlin's exhibitions of Indians in the 1830s to the demise of the last rodeo-circuses a century later, is Paul Reddin, *Wild West Shows* (Urbana: University of Illinois Press, 1999). One of the original features of the wild west shows was the demonstration of "cowboy fun" and skills associated with cattle-ranching. Lonn Taylor and Ingrid Maar, *The American Cowboy* (Washington, D.C.: American Folklife Center, 1983), and Don Russell, "The Cowboy from Black Hat to White," *Red River Historical Review* 2 (1975): 13–23, discuss the invention of the cowboy as a character in fiction and illustrated journalism in the 1870s and 1880s. Richard White surveys changing attitudes in the 1890s, and in particular, celebration of settlement of the land and conquest of the savages, in "Frederick Jackson Turner and Buffalo Bill," in *The Frontier in American Culture: Essays by Richard White and Patricia Nelson Limerick*, ed. James R. Grossman (Berkeley: University of California Press, 1994), 6–65.

Don Russell offers the most complete survey of Buffalo Bill, his competitors, and successors in *The Wild West; or, A History of the Wild West Shows* (Fort Worth, Tex.: Amon Carter Museum of Western Art, 1970), a book with excellent photographs and illustrations of posters. Jack Rennert, *One Hundred Posters of Buffalo Bill's Wild West* (New York: Darien House, 1976), has significant information on the evolution of show images. The outstanding commentary on representation is Joy S. Kasson,

Bibliographical Essay

Buffalo Bill's Wild West: Celebrity, Memory, and Popular History (New York: Hill and Wang, 2000). Kasson is acutely sensitive to the meaning of verbal and visual images, and to Cody's show as historical memory. She interprets the Wild West as high-brow/lowbrow, conveying both authenticity and nostalgia, with an emphasis on Indians, but has little on "cow-boy fun," manliness, and great-power posturing. *Buffalo Bill and the Wild West*, ed. David Katzive (Brooklyn: Brooklyn Museum, 1981), is an excellent collection of essays, with appropriate illustrations, on the major elements of the show. The show, and particularly the guns and ephemera associated with the shooting exhibitions, is described and illustrated in detail in R. L. Wilson with Greg Martin, *Buffalo Bill's Wild West: An American Legend* (New York: Random House, 1998). Richard Slotkin interprets the Wild West show in the context of America of the 1890s and the new ideology of expansion and rivalry with the major European powers; the staged reenactment of the conflict between white and red was the archetype for the struggle between the Anglo-Saxon "progressive" nations and the "primitive" races. Slotkin expounds this thesis in his essay in *Buffalo Bill and the Wild West* (1981), in "Buffalo Bill's'Wild West' and the Mythologization of the American Empire," in *Cultures of United States Imperialism*, ed. Amy Kaplan and Donald E. Pease (Durham, N.C.: Duke University Press, 1993), 164–68; and at length in his *Gunfighter Nation: The Myth of the Frontier in Twentieth-Century America* (New York: Atheneum, 1992), chap. 2. Jonathan D. Martin, " 'The Grandest and Most Cosmopolitan Object Teacher' ": *Buffalo Bill's Wild West* and The Politics of American Identity, 1883–1899," *Radical History Review* 66 (1996): 96–122, has similar conclusions, but more emphasis on Darwinism as an ideological influence.

Don Russell, *The Lives and Legends of Buffalo Bill* (Norman: University of Oklahoma Press, 1960), is the most thorough study of Cody's career, its mythical aspects, and his symbolic status. *The Life of the Hon. William F. Cody, Known as Buffalo Bill, The Famous Hunter, Scout and Guide: An Autobiography* (1879; Lincoln: University of Nebraska Press, 1978) is a reprint of the early "autobiography." Eric V. Sorg, *Buffalo Bill: Myth and Reality* (Santa Fe, N.M.: Ancient City Press, 1998), is a brief synthesis based on original archival research. The PBS video, *Buffalo Bill* (1992), dir. Donna Luistana, has interesting footage from the movie which Cody made in 1913 to re-create events a generation before. Roger A. Hall, *Performing The American Frontier, 1870–1906* (New York: Cambridge University Press, 2001), sketches the melodramatic vision of male dominance and violent contest.

Two articles by William E. Deahl Jr. trace the beginnings of Buffalo Bill's Wild West: "Nebraska's Unique Contribution to the Entertainment World," *Nebraska History* 49 (autumn 1968): 283–97, and "Buffalo Bill's Wild West Show, 1885," *Annals of Wyoming* 47 (fall 1975): 139–51. William Brasmer, "The Wild West Exhibition and the Drama of Civilization," in *Western Popular Theatre*, ed. David Mayer and Kenneth Richards (London: Methuen, 1977), 133–56, examines the influence of theater director Steele MacKaye in restructuring the show's program in 1886. Sarah J. Blackstone, *Buckskins, Bullets, and Business: A History of Buffalo Bill's Wild West* (Westport, Conn.: Greenwood Press, 1986), is largely descriptive. Blackstone's *Business of Being Buffalo Bill: Selected Letters of William F. Cody, 1879–1917* (New York: Praeger, 1988) deals more with his failing speculative ventures and has relatively little on his entertainment strategy.

Much more has been written on the Indian exhibits than on the cowboy. Jeffrey Steele, "Reduced to Images: American Indians in Nineteenth-Century Advertising," in *Dressing in Feathers: The Construction of the Indian in American Popular Culture*, ed. S. Elizabeth Bird (Boulder, Colo.: Westview Press, 1996), 45–64, is a careful study of popular depictions. In "The Indian Medicine Show," *Educational Theatre Journal* 23 (December 1971): 431–45, and more fully in *Step Right Up* (1976; Garden City, N.Y.: Doubleday, rev. ed. 1995), chaps. 5–8, Brooks McNamara illuminates small-town attitudes to fakelore, and, by implication, how Cody's show was understood. L. G. Moses in *Wild West Shows and the Images of American Indians, 1883–1933* (Albuquerque: University of New Mexico Press, 1993), and "Wild West Shows, Reformers, and the Image of the American Indian, 1887–1914," *South Dakota Quarterly* 14 (fall 1984): 193–221, is authoritative and argues that Cody was generally held in high esteem by the Indians. Louis Pfaller, " 'Enemies in '76, Friends in '85': Sitting Bull and Buffalo Bill," *Prologue: Journal of the National Archives* 1 (fall 1969): 16–31, explores the uses made of the Sioux chief's brief appearance.

Gender studies has only recently made much impact. Gail Bederman, *Manliness and Civilization: A Cultural History of Race and Gender in the United States, 1880–1917* (Chicago: University of Chicago Press, 1995), has broad relevance. Glenda Riley, *The Life and Legacy of Annie Oakley* (Norman: University of Oklahoma Press, 1994), replaces all earlier biographies. Two essays by Tracy C. Davis—"Shotgun Wedlock: Annie Oakley's Power Politics in the Wild West," in *Gender in Performance: The Presentation of Difference in the Performing Arts*, ed. Laurence Senelick (Hanover, N.H.: Tufts University/University Press of New Hampshire, 1992), 141–57, and "Annie Oakley and Her Ideal Husband of No Importance," in *Critical Theory and Performance*, ed. Janelle G. Reinelt and Joseph R. Roach (Ann Arbor: University of Michigan Press, 1992), 229–312—explore representations of the star second only to Cody.

Summer Amusement Parks

John F. Kasson, *Amusing the Million: Coney Island at the Turn of the Century* (New York: Hill and Wang, 1978), is a highly original discussion of the class and culture clash exemplified by the genteel beach hotels and the mass commercial amusements on Surf Avenue and the Bowery. Kasson explores the tension between the showmen-entrepreneurs who devised the most effective ways of form and function to make their parks profitable and the Progressive reformers and most intellectuals who preferred directed, uplifting recreation. His incisive reading of contemporary journalism and photographs informs his interpretation of the meaning of the amusements as a "moral holiday," offering exhilarating reprise from convention. Jon R. Sterngass disagrees. In *First Resorts: Pursuing Pleasure at Saratoga Springs, Newport, and Coney Island* (Baltimore: Johns Hopkins University Press, 2001), Sterngass argues that the significant commercial development took place in the 1880s before the separate parks were created. The amusement attractions in the parks were neither original nor did they pose a serious challenge to polite decorum.

Kathy Peiss, *Cheap Amusements: Working Women and Leisure in Turn-of-the-Century New York* (Philadelphia: Temple University Press, 1986), chap. 5, qualifies Kasson's argument significantly by introducing a gendered perspective. Lower-class women, often those employed in retail sales or offices, used disposable income in excursions to suburban resorts. Heterosexual interaction added excitement, for at the amusement parks women were both liberated and assertive, and they were objects of visual spectacle. Peiss distinguishes between the simple carnivalesque pleasures of unpredictable thrills and unplanned encounters at Steeplechase and the technological novelties and surreal fantasies at Luna Park and Dreamland. In *For the Love of Pleasure: Women, Movies, and Culture in Turn-of-the-Century Chicago* (New Brunswick, N.J.: Rutgers University Press, 1998), chap. 5, Lauren Rabinovitz explores the complexities of women as consumers and as commodity in movies depicting amusement-park encounters. There is little information on the perspectives of different ethnic groups, but Andrew R. Heinze, *Adapting to Abundance: Jewish Immigrants, Mass Consumption, and the Search for American Identity* (New York: Columbia University Press, 1990), sketches very briefly the responses of New York Jews.

Dutch architect Rem Koolhaas argues in *Delirious New York: A Retrospective Manifesto for Manhattan* (1978; New York: Monaceli Press, 1994), chap. 2, that Coney Island was an innovative "laboratory" for new building design and radical planning. Entrepreneurs exploited the "technology of the fantastic"—"fairy" towers and electric light—to create a futuristic city of illusion. Robert E. Snow and David Wright, "Coney Island: A Case Study in Popular Culture and Technical Change," *Journal of Popular Culture* 9 (spring 1976): 960–75, explore how enthusiastically the "parks" embraced mechanization. In "Disneyland and Coney Island: Reflections on the Evolution of the Modern Amusement Park," *Journal of Popular Culture* 26 (summer 1992): 131–64, Raymond M. Weinstein argues that Coney's success was a balance of shrewd and experienced showmanship and contrived visual spectacle. The most perceptive analysis of Frederic Thompson's aims is Woody Register, *The Kid of Coney Island: Fred Thompson and the Rise of American Amusements* (New York: Oxford University Press, 2001), chap. 3.

Ellen M. Snyder-Grenier, *Brooklyn! An Illustrated Social History* (Philadelphia: Temple University Press, 1996), is an excellent summary. Most studies of Coney are richly descriptive: Oliver Pilot and Jo Ransom, *Sodom by the Sea: An Affectionate History of Coney Island* (Garden City, N.Y.: Doubleday, Doran, 1941); Edo McCullough, *Good Old Coney Island: A Sentimental Journey into the Past* (1957; New York: Fordham University Press, 2000); Lucy P. Gillman, "Coney Island," *New York History* 36 (July 1955): 255–90; and Richard Snow, *Coney Island: A Postcard Journey to the City of Fire* (New York: Brightwater Press, 1984); and Michael Immerso, *Coney Island: The People's Playground* (New Brunswick, N.J.: Rutgers University Press, 2002).

Live shows of pageant scenes in exotic lands or reenactments of famous catastrophes and typical near-catastrophes were always popular within the parks and in specialized exhibition halls outside. Andrea Stulman Dennett and Nina Warnke, "Disaster Spectacles at the Turn of the Century," *Film History* 4 (1990): 101–11, explore the most renowned fire spectacles at Coney Island but ignore the re-creations of the Boer and the Spanish-American Wars; both live, staged action-melodramas and documentary-realistic battles at Coney Island influenced early movie-making. *Coney Island: A Documentary Film*, dir. Ric Burns (PBS, 1991, revised 2000), has excellent contemporary film of the beach and the parks at night.

On summer parks generally, the most wide-ranging analyses are Russel B. Nye, "Eight Ways of Looking at an Amusement Park," *Journal of Popular Culture* 15 (summer 1981): 63–75; Judith A. Adams, *The American Amusement Park Industry: A History of Technology and Thrills* (Boston: Twayne, 1991), chaps. 2 and 3; and David Nasaw, *Going Out: The Rise and Fall of Public Amusements* (1993; Cambridge: Harvard University Press, 1999), chap. 7. Charles E. Funnell, *By the Beautiful Sea: The Life and High Times of that Beautiful Resort, Atlantic City* (New York: Knopf, 1975), explores the most popular neighboring resort.

Vaudeville

The major interpretative study is Robert W. Snyder, *The Voice of the City: Vaudeville and Popular Culture in New York* (New York: Oxford University Press, 1989). Other significant studies are Douglas Gilbert, *American Vaudeville: Its Life and Times* (1940; New York: Dover, 1963), based on close observation of many of the stars; Albert F. McLean Jr., *American Vaudeville as Ritual* (Lexington: University of Kentucky Press, 1965); and John DiMeglio, *Vaudeville U.S.A.* (Bowling Green, Ohio: Bowling Green University Press, 1973). Useful brief analyses include Robert C. Toll, *On with the Show: The First Century of Show Business in America* (New York: Oxford University Press, 1976), chap. 6; Gunther Barth, *City People: The Rise of Modern City Culture in Nineteenth-Century America* (New York: Oxford University Press, 1980), chap. 6; and David Nasaw, *Going Out: The Rise and Fall of Public Amusements* (1993; Cambridge: Harvard University Press, 1999), chaps. 3 and 4.

Brooks McNamara, *The New York Concert Saloon: The Devil's Own Nights* (New York: Cambridge University Press, 2002), traces the origins of vaudeville in the 1860s and 1870s. There are fine studies of vaudeville managers: Robert C. Allen, "B. F. Keith and the Origins of American Vaudeville," *Theatre Survey* 21 (November 1980): 105–15; Parker Zellers, *Tony Pastor: Dean of the Vaudeville Stage* (Ypsilanti: Eastern Michigan University Press, 1971); Susan Kattwinkel, "Tony Pastor's Vaudeville: Serving the New York Community," *Library Chronicle of the University of Texas at Austin* 3 (1995), 50–75; and Kathryn J. Oberdeck, "Contested Cultures of American Refinement: Theatrical Manager Sylvester Poli, His Audiences, and the Vaudeville Industry, 1890–1920," *Radical History Review* 66 (1996): 40–91, expanded in her *Evangelist and the Impresario: Religion, Entertainment, and Cultural Politics in America,*

Bibliographical Essay

1884–1914 (Baltimore: Johns Hopkins University Press, 1999). Anthony Slide, *Encyclopedia of Vaudeville* (Westport, Conn.: Greenwood Press, 1994), has good, brief biographical sketches.

As ethnic pluralism gave American cities a social mix very different from European, so ethnic caricature distinguished American vaudeville from European music-hall variety theater. The most perceptive general study is James H. Dormon, "American Popular Culture and the New Immigration Ethnics: The Vaudeville Stage and the Process of Ethnic Ascription," *Amerikastudien* 36 (1991): 179–93. Lawrence E. Mintz, "Humor and Ethnic Stereotypes in Vaudeville and Burlesque," *Melus* 21 (winter 1996): 19–28, summarizes major interpretations succinctly. Of the ethnic groups in vaudeville, the significant studies are of Jews, immigrant and native: Armond Fields and L. Marc Fields, *From the Bowery to Broadway: Lew Fields and the Roots of American Popular Theater* (New York: Oxford University Press, 1993); Barbara W. Grossman, *Funny Girl: The Life and Times of Fanny Brice* (Bloomington: Indiana University Press, 1992); Kenneth Silverman, *Houdini!!! The Career of Erich Weiss, America's Self-Liberator . . .* (New York: HarperCollins, 1996); and Harley Erdman, *Staging the Jew: The Performance of an American Ethnicity, 1860–1920* (New Brunswick, N.J.: Rutgers University Press, 1997).

There are two outstanding studies of women in vaudeville: M. Alison Kibler, *Rank Ladies: Gender and Cultural Hierarchy in Vaudeville* (Chapel Hill: University of North Carolina Press, 1999); and Susan A. Glenn, *Female Spectacle: The Theatrical Roots of Modern Feminism* (Cambridge: Harvard University Press, 2000). Henry Jenkins, *What Made Pistachio Nuts? Early Sound Comedy and the Vaudeville Aesthetic* (New York: Columbia University Press, 1992), chaps. 2 and 3, considers the "new humor" in which gags tended to be dissociated from narrative continuity and intellectual appreciation.

There is no better illustration of vaudeville style than the video of early performers in *Vaudeville: An American Masters Special* (PBS, 1997), produced by Greg Palmer. There are several fine compilations of primary sources—*American Vaudeville as Seen by Its Contemporaries*, ed. Charles W. Stein (New York: Knopf, 1984); and *Selected Vaudeville Criticism*, ed. Anthony Slide (Metuchen, N.J.: Scarecrow, 1988)—but the resources of the Library of Congress's *American Variety Stage: Vaudeville and Popular Entertainment, 1870–1920* at the American Memory web site (memory.loc.gov/ammem/vshtml/vshome.html) and the New York Public Library's Performing Arts in America, 1875–1923, website (dlc.nypl.org/lpa/nypl/about/about_index.html) are outstanding. Brooks McNamara, *American Popular Entertainments: Jokes, Monologues, Bits and Sketches* (New York: Performing Arts Journal, 1983), has a representative selection of comedy from vaudeville, and he explains the context in "For Laughing Purposes Only: The Literature of American Popular Entertainment," in *The American Stage: Social and Economic Issues from the Colonial Period to the Present*, ed. Ron Engle and Tice L. Miller (New York: Cambridge University Press, 1993), 141–58.

INDEX

References to illustrations are in bold

Aaron Turner's Old Columbian Circus, 7, 117
Academy of Music, 193, 198
Act for the Suppressing of Mountebanks, 3
Adams, Nathaniel P., 189
Addams, Jane, 155
African Americans, 61, 67–68, 104, 287, 306; in circus audience, 113, 121, 123; as circus performers, 123; as minstrel performers, 69, 105–7; on minstrelsy, influence of, 66–70, 105; racial characteristics of, Doesticks on, 69–70, 183
Africans, 135–36, 240, 255, 281
Albee, Edward F., 317, 322–33
Alexander, Winthrop, 286
Alexis, Grand Duke of Russia, 238, 264
Ambrose Park, Brooklyn, 265, **266, 270**
American Indian performers: in Barnum's Museum, 137, 241; in George Catlin's show, 237; in circus sideshow, 137; in Wild West, 240, 244, 264, 266–72, 275–77. *See also* Kickapoo Indian Medicine Company
American Indians: bow as weapon, 264; in dime-novel stories, 257–58; in medicine show, 264–65; in Wild West programs, 250, 251, 254, 256, 259, 261–62. *See also* American Indian performers; Sioux
American Sunday-School Union, 110–12
amusements, evangelical opposition to: circus, 108–12, 114–15, 123, 125, 140;

"Continental" Sunday, 219; "leg show," 198, 217–18, 221; minstrel show, 92; mountebanks and itinerant showmen, 5; museums, 29, 58; theater, 8
An Old-Fashioned Girl (novel), 223–25
Appleton's Journal, 10
Astley, Philip, 109
Autobiography of Petite Bunkum (book), 50

Bailey, James A., 110
Baker, Benjamin, 157
Baker, Johnny, 252, 256
Barnold's Dogs, 316
Barnum, Phineas Taylor, 54–56, 168; autobiography, 50; circus, 7, 117, 129, 134–37; early career, 4, 6, 23; museum entertainment, 22, 28–29, 35–37; reputation as a showman, 15, 22, 23, 28, 46, 49, 50, 51, 58–60. *See also* Barnum's American Museum
Barnum and Bailey's Greatest Show on Earth, 110, 137, 140
Barnum's American Museum: advertising, 30–35, 57; family ambience, 31, 32, 34–35, 37, **52,** 57–58, 60; location, 49, 57; variety entertainment in, 4, 7, 22, 29, **30,** 173
Barnum's Grand Scientific and Musical Theatre, 7
Barras, Charles M., 195, 199, 200
Beecher, Henry Ward, 2
Belasco, David, and "Drama of Illusion," 18

377

Bigelow, Charles, 264–65
Billboard magazine, 1
Bird, Isabella, 23
Black Crook, The (play), 195–96, 198–218, **220**, 221–23; legacy, 217–18, 238
blackface disguise, 66–69, **70**, 75, 91, 92, 105–6, 327, 330–31
Booth, Edwin, 217, 218, 222
Booth, Junius Brutus, 10
Boston Museum, 8–9, 40
Boucicault, Dion, 9, 15, 158
Bouse, Sir Lyon. *See* White, Richard Grant
Bowery, 13–14, 16, 20, 37, 46, 49, 62, 67–68, 315
Bowery (Coney Island), 283, 284
Bowery Theatre, 9–10, 67–68, 155, 183–85
Boynton, Captain Paul, 280–81
Braham, David, 95
Brighton Beach, Coney Island, 280, 283–84
Bronner, Robert, 168
Brougham, John, 10
Brown, J. Purdy, 5
Browne, Porter Emerson, 185–87
Buckskin Bill's Wild West (Coney Island), 12
Buck Taylor, King of the Cowboys; or, The Raiders and the Rangers, A Story of the Wild and Thrilling Life of William L. Taylor (novel), 238–39
Buffalo Bill, 8, 238–40; celebrated in popular culture, 15, 237–38, 243–45, 257–58; and frontier stage melodrama, 237–38, 242–43, 246. *See also* Buffalo Bill's Wild West
Buffalo Bill, the King of the Border Men (novel), 237
Buffalo Bill's Wild West: celebration of American history, 237, 239, 260–62; claims for authenticity as "exhibition," 3, 238, 240, 250, 261–62. *See also* horsemanship; shooting
Buffalo Bill's "Wild West" Prairie Exhibition, and Rocky Mountain Show (1883), program, 249–56

Buffalo Bill's Wild West and Congress of Rough Riders of the World (1883), program, 258–64
Buntline, Ned, 237, 246
Burke, John, 239, 241, 247, 260–61
burlesque: in dime museum, 37, 39; "leg show" as, 2, 11, 196–98, 219, 225, 229–34, 236; literary parody, 5, 23, 50, 180, 183–85, 308–11; in minstrel show, 66, 67, 68, 73–75, 88, 92–94; theatrical parody, 10, 14, 95, 195, 213, 237, 316, 332
Burton, Jack, 21

Caffin, Caroline, 328; on audiences in vaudeville, 318–19, 328–29, 332; on successful performers, characteristics of, 317, 318–19, 330, 331; variety program, 321, 329–32
Cahn's *Official Theatrical Guide*, 20
Carver, "Doc" William Frank, 238, 242, 246–48, 263
Castello, Dan, 129, 134
Catlin, George, 66, 237
Cavendish, Millie, 212
Chambers's Journal, 13
Chang and Eng, the Siamese Twins, 26
Chesterton, G. K., 192–93
Christian Parlor Magazine, 58
Christy Minstrels, 14, 68
circus: advertising, 129, 130–31; audiences, 113, 116, 118, 125; English influence on, 117, 121; links with minstrelsy, 7; parade, 108, 109–10, 138, 148. *See also* menagerie
Clemens, Samuel. *See* Twain, Mark
Cline, Maggie, 234
Clipper (New York), 195, 229
Clofullia, Madame Josephine Boisdechene, **48**, 48–50
clown, in circus, 116, 117, 119, **120**, 121, 125–26, 150–51
Clum, John P., 241
"Coal Black Rose," 67, 76, **77**, 82
Cobb, Irvin S., 282
Cody, William F. *See* Buffalo Bill
Cohan, George M., 17, 338–40

Columbian Exposition, Chicago, 258, 281
combination companies, 20, 238
Coney Island, 11–12, 279–82. *See also* Brighton Beach; Dreamland; Luna Park; Manhattan Beach; Sea Lion Park; Steeplechase; Thompson, Frederic
Cook and Harris High Class Moving Picture Company, 19, 20
Cooper, James Fenimore, 237
Corbin, John, 317
Corning, James L., 3
Coup, William Cameron, 129–34
cowboys, 237, 238–39, 242, 244, 245, 248, 250, 254, 255–56; Cow Boy's Fun, 252, 256, 259
Crabbe, George, 3
Crane, Stephen, 155
cross-dressing, 26, 68, 71, 77, 91, 95, 123–24
cultural hierarchy: Bowery entertainments and the poor, 14, 65, 156, 160–61, 192; "highbrow" and vaudeville, 318, 320–21, 329–30, 333–34; opera and pan-class appeal, 10, 68–69, 315, 332, 335
curio hall (dime museum), 63–65
"curiosities," living, 22, 37, **52**, 53
Currie, Barton W., 20
Cushman, Charlotte, 162–68, **181**

Daly, Augustin, 158
Darwinism, 51, 240, 262; civilization and primitivism in Wild West, 240, 242, 243, 248, 254–55, 260, 262–64, 276–78; "savages" in sideshows, 135–37, 152, 281, 290. *See also* What Is It?; Wild Men of Borneo
Davis, Glenmore, 17–18
Davis, Hartley, 159, 334–35
Davis, Owen, 187–89, 190
Dayton, Abram C., 27–28
Denning, Michael, 156
department stores, 197–98
Dickens, Charles: burlesque extravaganzas, 222–23; and early "vaudeville," 315; and minstrel show, 69
Dickinson, Emily, 108
dime novels, 157, 168–69, 180, 186, 237–39, 246, 249, 256
Dixon, George Washington, 67–68, 72, 76
Doesticks (Mortimer Q. Thomson): Barnum's Museum, 29; and Bowery Theatre, 13, 183–85; comments on African Americans, 69–70, 183
Dreamland, Coney Island, 281, 290–93, 306–8
Drunkard, The (play), 11, 58
Dundy, Elmer, 281
Durang, John, 6

elephant, 114, 118, 119, 122, 139, 151, 286
Ellsler, Fanny, 71
Emerson, Ralph Waldo, 40, 73
Emmettt, Dan, 66, 68, 72
England: actors from, 10, 13–14; American entertainment in, 15, 37, 66, 239, 262, 272–75, 281; comments of visitors from, 14, 222; influence of theatrical traditions from, 22–23, 155, 159, 196, 198, 212, 231, 308; managers and showmen from, 13–14, 219; Adah Isaacs Menken in, 218; seaside resorts in, 279
English, William B., 169. See also *Rosina Meadows* (novel)
English Synonymes (Crabbe), 3
extravaganzas, 196–98

family audience, 8: and burlesque extravaganzas, 197, 217–18, 223–25, 233; and circus, 113, 115, 123, 125; and Coney Island, 284–85, 287, 291, 296–97, 299, 306, 312; and melodrama, 154–58, 181–83, 193; and minstrel show, 86, 89; and museum entertainment, 25–26, 27, 32, 40–41, 48, **52**, **63**; and vaudeville, 316, 323–24
Fejee Mermaid, 23, 59
Female Marine, The (novel), 26

Fern, Fanny, 49–50, 112–15
Ferree, Barr, 290–93
First Men in the Moon, The (novel), 286
Fisher, Sidney George, 53
Forrest, Edwin, 156
Foster, George G., 157, 219
Fox, George L., 9, 14, 196, 213
Fox, Richard Kyle, 115
France, influence on American theatrical entertainments, 18, 198, 223, 227, 316, 329
Frowne, Sadie, 304
Fuller, Hiram, 113

Garland, Hamlin, 146, 148–49
Gilbert, Douglas, 317
Gleason's Pictorial and Drawing-Room Companion (magazine), 57–58
Gorky, Max, 311–12
Gottlieb, George A., 336–38
Grau, Robert, 18
Greeley, Horace, 46
Greenwood, Ethan, 24
Griffin and Christy's Minstrels, 213; and *The Black Crook Burlesque*, 213–17
Grimsted, David, 155

Hamblin, Thomas S., 14, 155
Hamilton, Clayton, 16
Hapgood, Norman, 17
Happy Family, The, 61–62
Harrigan, Edward, 93; and *The Mulligan Guard Ball*, 95–102; and urban realism, 102–5
Hart, Tony, 95
Hartt, Rollin Lynde: on audiences, 65, 189–93, 195; on stress in cities, 282
Hawthorne, Nathaniel: on circus in Salem, 116–17; on itinerant showmen, 5–6; on melodrama, 180–83; on menagerie in western Massachusetts, 117–19; on sideshows, 25–27, 135
Healy, John, 264–65
Henry, O. (William S. Porter), 282, 286, 306–8
hippodrama, 109, 239
Hoffman, Aaron, 340–47

Hone, Philip, 40–41
horsemanship: chief attraction in circus, 108, 109, 110–12, 114, 122–24, 126, 132, 139–40, **141**, 149, 150–51; in Wild West, 239, 240, 245, 250–51, 252, 258–59, 267–70
Howe, Lyman, 20
Howells, William Dean, 63–64, 104–5, 149–51, 195, 229–31
Hughes, Richard, 305
Humpty Dumpty (play), 9
Huneker, James, 11, 313–14

illustrated songs, 18–19, 193–94
Ingraham, Prentiss, 238
In His Steps (novel), 158

Jaffee, David, 5
James, Henry, 22
James, Henry, Sr., 69
Jarratt, Henry C., 198, 199
Jefferson, Joseph, 15–16, 218
Jewett, Helen (Ellen), 26–27
Jim Crow, 26, 28, 67, 85, 86, 89
Johnston, William Allen, 18
June, Titus, Angevine, and Company, 17, 26–27, 118

Kauffman, Reginald Wright, 281
Keeler, Ralph, 90–92
Keene, Laura, 196
Keith, Benjamin F., 7–8, 316–18, 321, 332–34, 336
Kickapoo Indian Medicine Company, 11, 264–65
Kimball, Moses, 8, 35–37
Knickerbocker magazine, 69, 85–87, 121–24
Krausmeyer's Alley (play), 235–36
Kremer, Theodore, 159

Lasky, Jesse, 317, 335
Leavitt's Gigantean Minstrels, 69
Lecture Room, American Museum: early developments under Scudder and Peale, 27–29; praised by *Gleason's*, 57–58; promoted by Barnum as suit-

able for the family, 28, 29, 31, 32, 35, 57; variety entertainments in Barnum's, 7, 8, 58, 174, 241. *See also* Barnum's American Museum

Le Gallienne, Richard, 29

Levine, Lawrence W., 8

Lexington, Kentucky, 19–20

Lhamon, William T., Jr., 66–67

Life of P. T. Barnum, Written by Himself (book), 50

Lillie, Major Gordon W. (Pawnee Bill), 240

Lind, Jenny, 49, 57

Lindsay, Hugh, 6

Loew, Marcus, and small-time vaudeville, 316

Logan, Olive, 225; critical of the "leg business" and the "nude" actress, 225–29; on show business as commerce, 2–3

Lott, Eric, 69

Lubin, Siegmund, 18–19

Luna Park, Coney Island, 11–13, 281–82, 309, 311; as "new" park, 286–90, **288**, 291. *See also* Thompson, Frederic

M., Agnes, 304

MacKaye, Steele, 238

Maggie (novel), 155

Manhattan Beach, Coney Island, 280, 284

Mason, Elizabeth Rogers Cabot, 40

Mathews, Charles, 66

Mazeppa (play), 219, 222

McConachie, Bruce, 156

mechanical amusements, 16

Melville, Herman, 23, 158

menagerie: circus, wild animals in, 12, 108–9, 117, 120–22, **121**, 134, 138, 148–49, 154; display of exotic animals permitted in, 109, 112, 121–22; Wild West, American animals (buffalo, elk, mustangs) in, 242, 259. *See also* June, Titus, Angevine, and Company

Menagerie: A Reward for Good Children, The (book), 112

Menken, Adah Isaacs, 219, 222

Mexicans, in Buffalo Bill's Wild West, 238, 241, 242, 245, 248, 250, 255, 256, 259, 270

Midway: An Illustrated Magazine of Amusement Resorts and Attractions, 293, 319

Midway Plaisance, 281, 287

"Miss Lucy Long," 71–72, 91

Mitchell, William, 10, 14

model artists, 219, 220, 221

Morgan, J. Doug, 19

Morgan, Thomas Jefferson, 275; on Wild West shows as degrading, 275–77

Mose, 14, 56, 72, 157

moving pictures: competition with traditional shows, 155, 159, 189, 193, 194, 236, 240, 241; modernity of, 1, 16, 17–20, 331; as novelty in popular theater, 18–19, 193–94, 331. *See also* illustrated songs; nickelodeon

Mowatt, Anna Cora, 14–15, 157

Nathan, George Jean, 17, 338–40

National Intelligencer (Washington), 3

nationalism: circus, 123, 125; melodrama, 14–15, 159, 161–62, 188; minstrelsy, 68–69, 74, 85–86, 95, 105; museum entertainment, national heroes in, 28, 30, 33, 40; Wild West, celebration of American identity in, 237–39, 242, 259, 260–61, 272

National Police Gazette magazine, 115

Nation magazine, 58–60

Native Americans. *See* American Indian performers; American Indians

Nellie, the Beautiful Cloak Model (play), 187, 190

New England Museum and Gallery of Fine Art, 24

Newton, Harry, 347–49

New York Ledger magazine, 168–69

New York Sabbath Committee, 219–20

New York Tribune, 46–47, 89–90, 195–96

New York Zoological Institute, 113

Niblo's Garden, 198, 217, 221, 222, 233, 234

nickelodeon, 155, 159
Northall, William, 14, 37

Oakley, Annie, 239, 252, 256, 259
Oberly, John H., 275
Oliver, Nevada Ned, 11, 264–65
Olympic Theatre, 10
Osgood, Samuel, 217

Page, Brett, 335–36, 340
Palmer, Henry, 198, 199
Pan-American Exposition, Buffalo, 181, 189, 297
pantomime, 2, 3, 106–7, 181, 196–98
Parton, James, 157–58
Parton, Sara Payson Willis. *See* Fern, Fanny
Pastor, Tony, 7, 315–16, 332; and Pastor's Fourteenth Street Theatre, 315–16, **320**
Paulding, James Kirke, 159–62
Pawnee Bill's Historic Far West and Great Far East, 240
Payton, Corse, 158, 193–94
Peale, Charles Willson, 27, 51
Peale, Rubens, 27–28, 36
peepshow, 2–3, **4**, 16
Pelby's National Theatre, Boston, 180–83
Pinchbeck, William, 108–9
Plea for Amusements, A (Sawyer), 3
Po-ca-hon-tas, or, The Gentle Savage (play), 10
Poli, Sylvester, 317, 318
Pollock, Channing, 17
Pomeroy, Brick, 3, 261
Prill, Arthur, 318
Punch magazine, 46
Putnam's Monthly magazine, 87–89

railroads, 5, 129, 130, 133, 134–35, 140–45, 240, 280, 282, 284, 289
Ralph, Julian, 265–66; Coney Island, class cultures in, 282–85; Wild West Indians in Brooklyn, description of, 266–70
Rapp, Augustus, xi–xii
Red Right Hand: or, Buffalo Bill's First Scalp for Custer, The (play), 238

Remington, Frederick, 265, 267
Rice, Dan, 3, 7; circus in Brooklyn, 124–26
Rice, Thomas D., 10, 14, 67, 76, 87, 89
Ricketts, John Bill, 6, 109
Rigl, Betty, 212, **221**, 223
Ringling, Alfred T., 137–40
Rosina Meadows (novel), 169–73, **170**
Rosina Meadows (play), 173–79
Royle, Edwin Milton, 17, 321–28
Ruhl, Arnold, 234–36, 316
Ruskin, John, 197
Ryan, Kate, 9

Salsbury, Nate, 243, 245–47, 261, 266
Sandburg, Carl, 149–51
Sanger, "Lord" George, 15
Saunders, Charles H., 173. See also *Rosina Meadows* (play)
Sawyer, Frederic W., 3
Scouts of the Prairie; or Red Deviltry As It Is, The (play), 238
Scudder, John, 28–29
Sea Lion Park, Coney Island, 281
Sears, Roebuck, 19
Sheldon, Charles H., 158
shooting, 239, 247, 251–52, 253, 259, 263–64
Shoot-the-Chutes, 281
showbills, **12**, 110–12, 113, **120**, 122, 146–48, **147**, 185, **266**
show business: broad definition, 2–4, 15, 59; considered derogatory, 2, 3, 59; etymology of the phrase, 2–3; "show bizness," 5
sideshows: circus, 126, 135–37, 148–49, 150–53; city, 41; fairs, 25–27; Wild West encampments, 239, 240
Sioux, 244, 247, 250, 251, 257–58, 266, 271–75, 277, 284. *See also* American Indian performers; American Indians; Standing Bear, Luther
Slim Jack: or, The History of a Circus Boy, 110
Slosson, Edwin E., 294–95
Smith, Harry James, 16, 159
Smith, Sydney, 159

Smyth, Charles B., 198, 221
Snyder, Robert, 317
songs, illustrated, 18–19, 193–94
spectacle: public processions, 1; emphasis on visual splendor in theatrical productions, 15–16, 129, 155, 196, 199, 213, 218, 234, 240, 321, 335. *See also* street parades
Spirit of the Times (New York), 195, 200
Spitzer, Marian, 159
Spooner, Mary Gibbs, 193
Standing Bear, Luther, 272–75
Steeplechase Park, Coney Island, 281, 308–11
Stone, Augustus, 156
street parades, 21; circus, 108, 109–10, 138, **147**, 148; in Bowery theatrical shows, 10
Strong, George Templeton, 218–19
"Sunday-school Circuit," 317, 324
Surf Avenue (Coney Island), 280, 282, 293

Tanguay, Eva, 319
Tappan, Henry P., 22
Taylor, Bayard, 94–95
technology, 1, 18, 40; impact of electricity, 12, 129, 154, 280, 284, 288–89, 293–94; innovations in stagecraft, 154, 185, 198–99, 200, 239, 248, 306, 331; mechanical reproduction of sound and vision, 1, 18. *See also* moving pictures; railroads
tents, for traveling shows, 5, 7, 20, 109, 118, 120, 132, 134–35, 137–38
ten-twenty-thirty (cheap melodrama theaters), 158–59
Thalia Theater, 159
theater, evangelical opposition to. *See* amusements, evangelical opposition to
Thompson, Frederic A., 11–13, 15; design of Luna Park architecture, 297–99; on electricity as symbol of modernity, 285–86; experience at Pan-American Exposition, Buffalo, 181, 189, 297; on manufacturing "carnival spirit," 298, 302; on play as extended

childhood, 296–304. *See also* Luna Park, Coney Island
Thompson, Lydia, controversy surrounding "blonde burlesque," 2, 10–11, 196–97, 229–30, 233. *See also* Logan, Olive
Thomson, Mortimer Q. *See* Doesticks
Thoreau, Henry David, 120–21
Thumb, General Tom, 23, 35–41, 66
Tilyou, George, 281, 282, 308. *See also* Steeplechase
Times (London), 66
Trip to the Moon, A (Coney Island), 281, 289, 299
Trollope, Frances, 14
Trumble, Alfred, 116–18
Tucker, Sophie, 318
Twain, Mark: and Barnum, 61–62, 134–35, 241; and "Boney Part," 43–46; and "leg show," 220–22; and minstrel show, 90–94; and Wild Men of Borneo, 41–43; and Wild West, 249
Twenty Thousand Leagues Under the Sea (Luna Park), 286, 289–90

Uncle Tom's Cabin (play), 20, 156
United Booking Office, 3, 282, 333
urbanization: comparison with England, 13–14, 17, 354n35; significance for development of commercial amusements, 6, 8–9, 11, 279, 282, 313, 332. *See also* Bowery; Lexington, Kentucky

Van Amburgh, Isaac, 109, 118, 121
Van Elstine, W. E. "Doc," 153–54
Vanity Fair magazine, 3
variety entertainment, xi, 1, 4, 6–12, 14, 17, 20–21, 57, 59, 60, 68, 94, 184–85, 320–21, 330–32, 333–34
Vauxhall Garden (New York), 4, 7
Virginia Minstrels, 66, 68, 71, 72

Walker, George, 105
Wallace's Theatre, 9
Ward, Artemus (Charles Farrar Browne), 5, 180
Warren, William, 8

Watson, Billy, 234–36
waxworks, 5; Barnum's American
    Museum, 22, **30**, 31, 34, 51, 62;
    Daniel Lambert, 28; New England, 24;
    Salem, 25–27
Way of the Transgressor, The (play), 16
What Is It? 34, 51–53, **52**
Wheatley, William, 198, 199, 217
Wheeler, Silas O., 126–29
White, Charley, 68–69, 76
White, Richard Grant: on Barnum's
    giantess, 53–56; on burlesque extrava-
    ganzas, 231–34
Whitlock, Billy, 66, 71–72
Whitman, Walt, 69, 124–26, 168–69
Whitton, Joseph, 198–99
Wild Men of Borneo, 41–43, **42**, 126,
    152, 301
Wild West show: influence of circus on,
    239–41; invention of, 237–47; and
    national culture, 239, 242, 249–50,
    260–61; programs of, 239–41, 247–56,
    258–64
Williams, Bert, 105–7
Willis, Nathaniel Parker, 53
women performers, **48, 181, 220**; in

circus, 114, 115, 126, 135, 136, 140,
    151–52; in melodrama, 162–68, 169,
    180, **181,** 184–85, 186, 188; in minstrel
    show, 68, 71, 77, 91, 95, 123–24; in
    museum entertainment, 49–50, 63–
    64; in vaudeville, 318–19, 335, 340; in
    Wild West, 239, 240, 241, 259, 274. *See
    also* burlesque; Cushman, Charlotte;
    Logan, Olive; Menken, Adah Isaacs;
    Oakley, Annie; Thompson, Lydia
"wonders": Barnum's Museum as "Con-
    gress of Wonders," 22–23, **30**, 58; of
    nature, 24, 28, 32, 53. *See also*
    "curiosities"
Wood, William B., 9
Woolly Horse, The, 23, 59
Work: A Story of Experience (novel), 223
Wright, Mabel Osgood, 217

Yankee Doodle magazine, 23
Yellow Hand, 238, 251
Yellow Robe, Chauncey, 277
Yezierska, Anzia, 303

Ziegfeld Follies, 105, 197
"Zip Coon," 72

The New Languages

A RHETORICAL APPROACH TO THE MASS MEDIA AND POPULAR CULTURE

Edited by

Thomas H. Ohlgren
Purdue University

Lynn M. Berk
Florida International University

PRENTICE-HALL, Inc. Englewood Cliffs, N.J. 07632

Library of Congress Cataloging in Publication Data

Main entry under title:

The New languages.

    Includes bibliographical references.
    1. Mass media–Addresses, essays, lectures.
2. Popular culture—Addresses, essays, lectures.
3. English language—Rhetoric—Addresses, essays,
lectures.   I. Ohlgren, Thomas H., 1941–
II. Berk, Lynn M., 1943–
P91.N38   301.16′1   76–56432
ISBN 0–13–615104–3

PRENTICE-HALL SERIES IN ENGLISH COMPOSITION
James C. Raymond, *Series Editor*

Printed in the United States of America
10   9   8   7   6   5   4   3

Prentice-Hall International, Inc., *London*
Prentice-Hall of Australia Pty. Limited, *Sydney*
Prentice-Hall of Canada, Ltd., *Toronto*
Prentice-Hall of India Private Limited, *New Delhi*
Prentice-Hall of Japan, Inc., *Tokyo*
Prentice-Hall of Southeast Asia Pte. Ltd., *Singapore*
Whitehall Books Limited, *Wellington, New Zealand*

Contents

PREFACE   *ix*

INTRODUCTION TO THE RHETORIC OF MASS MEDIA   *xi*

RHETORICAL CONTENTS   *xv*

POPULAR CULTURE AND THE MASS MEDIA: THEORIES AND PRACTICES
Introduction   *1*

EDMUND CARPENTER, The New Languages   *4*
RICHARD KOSTELANETZ, Marshall McLuhan:
    High Priest of the Electronic Village   *14*
RUSSEL B. NYE, Notes for an Introduction
    to a Discussion of Popular Culture   *25*
ARTHUR ASA BERGER, Secret Agent   *32*
DWIGHT MACDONALD, A Theory of Mass Culture   *38*

Unit II

COMMERCIAL AND PUBLIC PROPAGANDA: THE MEDIUM IS THE BARRAGE
Introduction   51

VANCE PACKARD, The Ad and the Id   *59*
DANIEL HENNINGER, Worriers, Swingers, Shoppers "Psychographics"
    Can Tell Who'll Buy Crest, Who'll Buy Ultra Brite   *70*
JOHN R. CASHILL, Packaging Pop Mythology   *79*
HENRYK SKOLIMOWSKI, The Semantic Environment
    in the Age of Advertising   *91*
GEORGE G. KIRSTEIN, The Day the Ads Stopped   *102*
FAIRFAX M. CONE, Advertising's Response to Its Critics   *109*
Esquire's 3rd Annual Corporate Social Responsibility
    Advertising Awards   *115*
HUGH RANK, Learning about Public Persuasion:
    Rationale and a Schema   *118*
IRVING J. REIN, The Rhetoric of Popular Arts   *135*

Unit III

THE LANGUAGE OF PRINT
Introduction   143

MARSHALL McLUHAN, The Print: How To Dig It   *148*
EVERETTE E. DENNIS, The New Journalism: How It Came To Be   *155*
THE SOCIETY OF PROFESSIONAL JOURNALISTS, SIGMA DELTA CHI (1973),
    Code of Ethics   *173*
STEPHEN C. HOLDER, The Family Magazine and the American People   *176*
ROLAND L. WOLSELEY, The American Periodical Press and Its Impact   *185*
HARVEY COX, The Playboy and Miss America   *194*
The Stanford University Women's News Service,
    Guidelines for Newswriting about Women   *202*
TOM WOLFE, Pause, Now, and Consider Some Tentative Conclusions
    about the Meaning of This Mass Perversion Called Porno-violence:
    What It Is and Where It Comes from
    and Who Put the Hair on the Walls   *205*
SAUL BRAUN, Shazam! Here Comes Captain Relevant   *211*
Code of the Comics Magazine Association of America, Inc.   *228*
STEFAN KANFER, Editorial Cartoons: Capturing the Essence   *233*

Unit IV

THE LANGUAGE OF FILM
Introduction   239

WILLIAM JINKS, The Word and the Image   *243*
PETER P. SCHILLACI, Film as Environment   *255*

JOHN G. CAWELTI, Savagery and Civilization   *262*
X. J. KENNEDY, Who Killed King Kong?   *270*
SUSAN SONTAG, Science Fiction Films: The Imagination of Disaster   *278*
MARJORIE ROSEN, Popcorn Venus:
    Or How the Movies Made Women Smaller Than Life   *289*
MARSHA KINDER and BEVERLE HOUSTON, The Rhetoric of Film Propaganda:
    Triumph of the Will (1934–1936)   *303*

THE LANGUAGES OF TELEVISION AND RADIO
Introduction   *309*

HORACE NEWCOMB, Toward a Television Aesthetic   *314*
REED WHITTEMORE, The Big Picture   *323*
DANIEL MENAKER, Art and Artifice in Network News   *327*
NORA SCOTT KINZER, Soapy Sin in the Afternoon   *335*
STEPHANIE HARRINGTON, To Tell the Truth, the Price Is Right   *341*
MARTIN MAYER, If There Is No Answer, What Is the Message?   *353*
TIME MAGAZINE, No Time for Comedy   *360*
DAVID BLACK, How the Gosh-darn Networks
    Edit the Heck Out of Movies   *364*
PETER McCABE, Radio: Where Has All the Music Gone?   *370*
DON R. PEMBER, Radio: or "Come On,
    Let Me Show You Where It's At"   *378*
CLARK WHELTON, CB Radio Comin' at Ya:
    Running Down to Dirtytown   *386*

Unit
V

Preface

T his volume is designed to serve as a basic text for liberal arts courses in English composition and in mass communications offered by departments of speech and journalism in two- and four-year colleges. Although similar to other texts in that it is aimed at undergraduates who want to understand the impact of the mass media—advertising, magazines, newspapers, television, radio, and film—on contemporary popular culture, it differs from most texts for at least three significant reasons. First, factual, technical, and faddish selections have been avoided; instead, we have sought essays combining theory with clear, illustrative examples that have withstood the test of time. Second, critical apparatus have been carefully generated (a) to test readers' comprehension of the anthologized selections, (b) to encourage readers to discover parallels between persuasive strategies in the media and their own communication techniques, (c) to stimulate readers to analyze the rhetorical strategies of the essays themselves, and (d) to allow readers to apply their reading to their media environments. Third, the material in this volume grew out of a large program at a four-year state university; as a result, most of the essays and critical aids have been field tested by over six thousand undergraduate students in the past six years. Using a variety of measurements, including the Prentice-Hall Diagnostic tests, we discovered, in addition, that the mass media approach has had a significant impact on students' communication skills. By studying the media and popular culture, students learn not only to interpret, analyze, and evaluate the media environments in which they live but, more important, to realize the effectiveness of their own verbal skills in writing and speaking. Thus, this volume, along with the instructor's manual that accompanies it, can be used in both writing and speech courses.

Since this volume originated in an English composition program, largely taught by graduate teaching assistants, we would like to acknowledge the significant contributions of our colleagues, many of whom unselfishly supplied ideas, questions, and writing topics. Those deserving special mention are Joan Dean, Melinda Kramer, and Marilyn Horacek, who served as co-directors of the program; Melinda Kramer, who did the permissions and authored the instructor's manual; the late Robert A. Miller, former director of composition at Purdue, who encouraged this approach to composition from the beginning; John Daly, who devised the testing and measurement program; James Raymond, who served as academic consultant; and William Oliver, English editor at Prentice-Hall. We dedicate this anthology to Judy and Toby.

Introduction
to the Rhetoric of
Mass Media

The subtitle of this volume is "A Rhetorical Approach to the Mass Media and Popular Culture." *Rhetorical* is the key word here, but it is a word that is all too often misunderstood. To many, *rhetoric* has a negative connotation; when citizens accuse a politician of using "mere rhetoric," they are suggesting that the politician is making emotional appeals or doesn't really mean what he or she says; when students complain about teachers who ask "rhetorical questions," they are suggesting that the questions are not meant to be answered but are posed to achieve a certain effect. These, however, are not so much examples of rhetoric as illustrations of its abuse. Like biology, math, or philosophy, rhetoric is a field of study and in itself is neither good nor bad.

The Greek philosopher Aristotle defined rhetoric as the art of persuasion and suggested that a study of rhetoric would lead to a discovery of the tools of persuasion. Aristotle was primarily concerned with oratory, or the art of public speaking, but today the term rhetoric refers to the art of persuasion in all areas of communication. Speech departments concentrate on examining the rhetoric of public speaking; English departments study the rhetoric of the written word. As you will observe in this book, media critics often speak of the rhetoric of film, television, and advertising.

One of the principle focuses of this book is the rhetorical analysis of the anthologized prose selections. The essays were selected in part because they represent a variety of rhetorical modes. You will find that writers use many different techniques in communicating their messages, depending on the audience, purpose, and content of their writing. Although there are as many writing styles and techniques as there are writers, there are certain devices, certain ways of organizing material, that good writers use again and again. Although any essay will contain a combination of techniques, most can be categorized by one of four dominant rhetorical modes: exposition, argument, description, and narration. Since authors frequently mix modes, combining elements from several in one essay or article, the following Rhetorical Contents classifies the essays in *The New Languages* by major and minor modes: the major mode is the one that is predominant in an essay; the minor mode receives secondary (or sometimes nearly equal) emphasis.

An individual mode may be further broken down into its methods or strategies of organization. For example, an author using the expository mode may choose to explain his or her subject by means of definition, illustration, or comparison and contrast. A more complete discussion of the rhetorical strategies found in these essays is given in the Instructor's Manual.

You will notice that the majority of the essays in this anthology are broadly argumentative: that is, many of them contain a thesis the author tries to support by compiling evidence of one kind or another. This phenomenon is not too surprising, since for most people the act of putting pen to paper is analogous to mentally climbing on a soap box. Of the four modes cited in the Contents, argument is the only clearly persuasive rhetorical tool. Yet, it is important to recognize that almost all prose writing is ultimately persuasive. When, for example, you put ideas, people, or things into categories, you must convince your readers that those categories are valid; when you compare two different things, you must persuade your readers that you have established meaningful connections. Even description, which may seem to be the most objective sort of writing, is persuasive. Unlike the photographer, the writer cannot capture an event or scene in all its detail. The descriptive writer creates a certain mood or elicits a certain emotional response by the way he or she selects and arranges material. He or she persuades the reader to share one perception of the scene. A skillful descriptive writer might convince the reader that a hospital room was warm and comforting; another might make the same room appear cold and sterile. The essays in this volume will provide you with a wide variety of rhetorical modes, but remember that every essay is trying to persuade you of something. It is your task to determine how each writer achieves this goal.

Although the essays in *The New Languages* explore many aspects of the mass media and popular culture, many of them also examine the rhetoric of these phenomena. Some of the essays, like those on advertising and public propaganda, will address the question of persuasion directly. Others will explore the more subtle aspects of the rhetoric of the media—the carefully orchestrated spectacle of the network news, the underlying structure of the western movie, the propagandistic messages of song lyrics, and the surprising value system projected by *Playboy*. Some writers, like William Jinks in "The Word and the Image," highlight the similarities between the rhetoric of film and the rhetoric of prose writing. Others, like Edmund Carpenter in "The New Languages," suggest that contemporary mass media employ rhetorical devices antithetical to those of the printed word. Both positions, however, are useful in gaining a deeper understanding of the nature of rhetoric.

To help you appreciate the full implications of the selections in this volume, each essay is followed by a series of aids. The aids serve four basic purposes: (1) to test your comprehension of the selection; (2) to examine the rhetoric of the selection; (3) if applicable, to examine the rhetoric of the medium or aspect of popular culture under discussion; and (4) to explore some further implications of the ideas raised in the selection. Some of these aids will make good paper or speech topics. Others will be useful for class discussion. All of them should enhance your understanding of the forms, contents, and effects of the mass media.

Rhetorical Contents

Argument

Unit I

Carpenter, The New Languages (*exposition*)
Nye, Notes for an Introduction to a Discussion of Popular Culture
    (*exposition*)
Berger, Secret Agent (*narration*)
Macdonald, A Theory of Mass Culture (*exposition*)

Unit II

Cashill, Packaging Pop Mythology (*description*)
Skolimowski, The Semantic Environment in the Age of Advertising
    (*exposition*)
Cone, Advertising's Response to Its Critics (*exposition*)
Rank, Learning about Public Persuasion: Rationale and a Schema
    (*exposition*)
Rein, The Rhetoric of Popular Arts (*exposition*)

Unit III

Cox, The Playboy and Miss America (*description*)
Kanfer, Editorial Cartoons: Capturing the Essence (*exposition*)

Unit IV

Schillaci, Film as Environment (*exposition*)
Cawelti, Savagery and Civilization (*exposition*)
Kennedy, Who Killed King Kong? (*description*)
Sontag, Science Fiction Films: The Imagination of Disaster (*exposition*)
Rosen, Popcorn Venus:
    Or How the Movies Have Made Women Smaller Than Life (*narration*)
Kinder and Houston, The Rhetoric of Film Propaganda:
    Triumph of the Will (*description*)

Unit V

Whittemore, The Big Picture (*exposition*)
Menaker, Art and Artifice in Network News (*description*)
Mayer, If There Is No Answer, What Is the Message? (*exposition*)
McCabe, Radio: Where Has All the Music Gone? (*exposition*)

Exposition

Unit I

Kostelanetz, Marshall McLuhan: High Priest of the Electronic Village
    (*argument*)

Unit II

Packard, The Ad and the Id (*argument*)
Henninger, Worriers, Swingers, Shoppers (*narration*)

Unit III

McLuhan, The Print: How To Dig It (*narration*)
Dennis, The New Journalism: How It Came to Be (*description*)
Holder, The Family Magazine and the American People (*argument*)
Wolseley, The American Periodical Press and Its Impact (*argument*)

Unit IV

Jinks, The Word and the Image (*description*)

Unit V

Newcomb, Toward a Television Aesthetic (*description*)
Kinzer, Soapy Sin in the Afternoon (*description*)
Harrington, To Tell the Truth, the Price Is Right (*description*)
Time Magazine, No Time for Comedy (*argument*)
Black, How the Gosh-darn Networks Edit the Heck Out of Movies
    (*argument*)
Pember, Radio: or "Come On, Let Me Show You Where It's At"
    (*argument*)

Description

Unit III

Wolfe, Pause, Now, and Consider Some Tentative Conclusions about the
    Meaning of This Mass Perversion Called Porno-Violence:
    What It Is and Where It Comes from
    and Who Put the Hair on the Walls (*exposition*)
Braun, Shazam! Here Comes Captain Relevant (*exposition*)

Narration

Unit II

Kirstein, The Day the Ads Stopped (*argument*)
Whelton, CB Radio Comin' at Ya: Running Down to Dirtytown
    (*description*)

Photos/David Umberger

Unit I

Popular Culture and the Mass Media: Theories and Practices

The two photographs on the opposite page summarize the two major preoccupations of this volume: the mass media and popular culture. These concerns are inexorably connected, because the mass media are the vehicles of popular culture. The photograph of the stereo-radio-television section of a national discount store underscores the ubiquity of the electronic mass media—400 million radios are tuned to 7000 AM and FM stations, 75 million phonographs play the 480 million records sold annually, and 125 million TV sets receive programming from over 900 TV stations. The second photograph, which depicts plastic Walt Disney characters, symbolizes not only the pervasive influence of the media on popular culture but the contents, form, and esthetics of popular culture itself. The Disney phenomenon, with its innovative feature-length cartoons, its romanticized film sagas of American history, and its amusement parks, reflects if it does not help to shape the values of many Americans. Walt Disney is a touchstone for much of American popular culture.

The first pair of essays present important concepts about the form of the media. In "The New Languages," Edmund Carpenter introduces the metaphor that underlies the selection of essays in this anthology: the media —advertising, television, radio, film, music, and even today's changing print—are new languages of mass communication. Carpenter contrasts the lineality, causality, chronology, and spectator detachment of the old media with the nonlineality, simultaneity, and processor involvement of the new media. He suggests that the form of each medium is unique and "that a given idea or insight belongs primarily, though not exclusively, to one medium, and can be gained or communicated best through that medium." Thus, Carpenter's essay provides us with a theoretical introduction to the new languages of the media, eminently useful to students interested in understanding the unique biases of each medium of communication.

In the second selection, Richard Kostelanetz offers a lucid introduction to the salient concepts of the "High Priest of the Electronic Village," Marshall McLuhan. Kostelanetz notes that the ideas of McLuhan have had a profound influence on the communications industry and the intellectual community in general: "Not only do several notable advertising executives and businessmen enormously admire his work, but so do scholars, artists, educators, publishers, and critics, in addition to innumerable students (perhaps because his books define a reality perceived by them and yet invisible to their teachers and parents)." In his essay Kostelanetz explains and fully illustrates McLuhan's basic theories on the psychological and philosophical effects of informational technology. Since many of the writers in this anthology incorporate McLuhan's ideas in their interpretations of the new languages of the mass media, the reader should study Kostelanetz's essay carefully.

The next two essays not only focus on the contents of the new languages of the mass media, but offer surveys of approaches to the study of popular culture. In "Notes for an Introduction to a Discussion of Popular Culture," Russel B. Nye asserts that within the last decade or so there has been a significant shift in the attitudes of cultural historians and philosophers toward relationships among cultural levels and values. Nye gives five reasons for this new wave of interest in and recent reevaluation of the aims, audiences, conventions, and artifacts of popular culture. His essay helps us to understand that every age has its popular culture, but the popular culture of twentieth-century America is in many ways unique. Before the advent of modern technology, mass production, and political democracy, Western culture had two basic components—the high culture of the economic and social elite and the folk culture of the masses. Until the Industrial Revolution, these two levels remained relatively distinct. The advancement of modern technology and the subsequent growth of political democracy and popular education drastically changed the relationship between cultural levels. Suddenly, neither money nor education were a prerequisite for exposure to high culture. One need no longer be a collector or even go to a museum to enjoy Vincent Van Gogh, Pablo Picasso, or Salvador Dali; advances in color lithography have made quality reproductions available to almost everyone. One need no longer pay exorbitant prices to hear the Juilliard String Quartet or the Boston Symphony; quality stereo recordings of every performing group are available for only a few dollars. In the recent past, one had to live in a metropolitan area to experience good theater and film; now millions watch Keith Michell change from an eighteen-year-old Prince to a middle-aged monarch on the PBS TV series "The

Six Wives of Henry VIII,'' observe Kenneth Clark take us from the fall of the Roman Empire to the present day on the widely-acclaimed "Civilisation" series, and marvel at the way Jacob Bronowski traces the development of science and culture from the flint tool to Albert Einstein's theory of relativity. The masses now have front-row seats to a culture that was previously denied them.

An important assumption underlies Russel Nye's treatment of popular culture: "The study of popular culture has been demonstrably affected by the example of cultural anthropology and its belief that all parts of a culture are worth study." Arthur Berger, in "Secret Agent," echoes this view when he asserts that "Second-rate movies and other manifestations of mediocrity and 'bad taste' have a great deal to tell us about our society." To aid the reader in discovering the "hidden meanings and latent functions" of popular culture, Berger recommends that we ask certain questions of every cultural artifact or experience we encounter. He suggests that the pop culture critic is a "secret agent" who has the task of analyzing, interpreting, and evaluating the myths that form the basis of the American experience.

The essays so far have presented some essentially positive assumptions about the nature, value, and effects of the mass media and popular culture. Dwight Macdonald's essay, "A Theory of Mass Culture," however, is a classic attack on popular culture. A cultural historian, Macdonald reacts negatively to the industrialization and commercialization of high culture, claiming that the exploitative elements in our capitalistic society have transformed both high culture and folk culture into standardized, stereotyped, sentimentalized, and inferior kitsch products. Kitsch for Macdonald is a parasitic, cancerous growth on high culture. It is culture exhibiting "bad taste," which is synonymous with popular culture itself. Kitsch was created by certain economic and political developments, such as capitalism, which made art a commodity; democracy, with its emphasis on majorities; and technology, which precludes the care and craftsmanship that alone can create works of art.

What ultimately does all this mean? Who makes the distinctions between cultural levels? What esthetic, political, and economic biases are revealed by these cultural polarities? What roles do the media play in transmitting cultural values? These are some of the many questions dealt with by the essayists in this unit.

The New Languages
EDMUND CARPENTER

English is a mass medium. All languages are mass media. The new mass media—film, radio, TV—are new languages, their grammars as yet unknown. Each codifies reality differently; each conceals a unique metaphysics. Linguists tell us it's possible to say anything in any language if you use enough words or images, but there's rarely time; the natural course is for a culture to exploit its media biases.

Writing, for example, didn't record oral language; it was a new language, which the spoken word came to imitate. Writing encouraged an analytical mode of thinking with emphasis upon lineality. Oral languages tended to be polysynthetic, composed of great, tight conglomerates, like twisted knots, within which images were juxtaposed, inseparably fused; written communications consisted of little words chronologically ordered. Subject became distinct from verb, adjective from noun, thus separating actor from action, essence from form. Where preliterate man imposed form diffidently, temporarily—for such transitory forms lived but temporarily on the tip of his tongue, in the living situation—the printed word was inflexible, permanent, in touch with eternity: it embalmed truth for posterity.

This embalming process froze language, eliminated the art of ambiguity, made puns "the lowest form of wit," destroyed word linkages. The word became a static symbol, applicable to and separate from that which it symbolized. It now belonged to the objective world; it could be seen. Now came the distinction between being and meaning, the dispute as to whether the Eucharist *was* or only *signified* the body of the Sacrifice. The word became a neutral symbol, no longer an inextricable part of a creative process.

Gutenberg[a] completed the process. The manuscript page with pictures, colors, correlation between symbol and space, gave way to uniform type, the black-and-white page, read silently, alone. The format of the book favored lineal expression, for the argument ran like a thread from cover to cover: subject to verb to object, sentence to sentence, paragraph to paragraph, chapter to chapter, carefully structured from beginning to end, with value embedded in the climax. This was not true of great poetry and drama, which retained multi-perspective, but it was true of most books, particularly texts, histories, autobiographies, novels. Events were arranged chronologically and hence, it was assumed, causally; relationship, not being, was valued. The author became an *authority*; his data were serious, that is, *serially* organized. Such data, if sequentially ordered and printed, conveyed value and truth; arranged any other way, they were suspect.

The newspaper format brought an end to book culture. It offers short, discrete articles that give important facts first and then taper off to incidental details, which may be, and often are, eliminated by the make-up man. The fact that reporters can-

Excerpt from "The New Languages," by Edmund Carpenter, in *Explorations in Communication*, 1960, edited by Edmund Carpenter and Marshall McLuhan, pp. 162–174. Reprinted by permission of the Beacon Press. Copyright © 1960 by the Beacon Press.

[a]Johann Gutenberg, c. 1397–1468, German printer, believed to have been the first European to print with movable type. (eds.)

not control the length of their articles means that, in writing them, emphasis can't be placed on structure, at least in the traditional linear sense, with climax or conclusion at the end. Everything has to be captured in the headline; from there it goes down the pyramid to incidentals. In fact there is often more in the headline than in the article; occasionally, no article at all accompanies the banner headline.

The position and size of articles on the front page are determined by interest and importance, not content. Unrelated reports from Moscow, Sarawak, London, and Ittipik are juxtaposed; time and space, as separate concepts, are destroyed and the *here* and *now* presented as a single Gestalt.[b] Subway readers consume everything on the front page, then turn to page 2 to read, in incidental order, continuations. A Toronto banner headline ran: TOWN-SEND TO MARRY PRINCESS; directly beneath this was a second headline: *Fabian Says This May Not Be Sex Crime.* This went unnoticed by eyes and minds conditioned to consider each newspaper item in isolation.

Such a format lends itself to simultaneity, not chronology or lineality. Items abstracted from a total situation aren't arranged in casual sequence, but presented holistically, as raw experience. The front page is a cosmic Finnegans Wake.[c]

The disorder of the newspaper throws the reader into a producer role. The reader has to process the news himself; he has to co-create, to cooperate in the creation of the work. The newspaper format calls for the direct participation of the consumer.

In magazines, where a writer more frequently controls the length of his article, he can, if he wishes, organize it in traditional style, but the majority don't. An increasingly popular presentation is the printed symposium, which is little more than collected opinions, pro and con. The magazine format as a whole opposes lineality; its pictures lack tenses. In *Life*, extremes are juxtaposed: space ships and prehistoric monsters, Flemish monasteries and dope addicts. It creates a sense of urgency and uncertainty: the next page is unpredictable. One encounters rapidly a riot in Teheran, a Hollywood marriage, the wonders of the Eisenhower administration, a two-headed calf, a party on Jones beach, all sandwiched between ads. The eye takes in the page as a whole (readers may pretend this isn't so, but the success of advertising suggests it is), and the page—indeed, the whole magazine—becomes a single Gestalt where association, though not causal, is often lifelike.

The same is true of the other new languages. Both radio and TV offer short, unrelated programs, interrupted between and within by commercials. I say "interrupted," being myself an anachronism of book culture, but my children don't regard them as interruptions, as breaking continuity. Rather, they regard them as part of a whole, and their reaction is neither one of annoyance nor one of indifference. The ideal news broadcast has half a dozen speakers from as many parts of the world on as many subjects. The London correspondent doesn't comment on what the Washington correspondent has just said; he hasn't even heard him.

The child is right in not regarding

---

[b]Gestalt is a unified configuration having properties that cannot be derived from its parts. (eds.)

[c]*Finnegans Wake* (1939), by Irish novelist James Joyce, is a dream sequence representing the unconscious mind of one H. C. Earwicker, a Dublin tavern keeper, in the course of one night. (eds.)

commercials as interruptions. For the only time anyone smiles on TV is in commercials. The rest of life, in news broadcasts and soap operas, is presented as so horrible that the only way to get through life is to buy this product: then you'll smile. Aesop[d] never wrote a clearer fable. It's heaven and hell brought up to date: Hell in the headline, Heaven in the ad. Without the other, neither has meaning.

There's pattern in these new media— not line, but knot; not lineality or causality or chronology, nothing that leads to a desired climax; but a Gordian knot[e] without antecedents or results, containing within itself carefully selected elements, juxtaposed, inseparably fused; a knot that can't be untied to give the long, thin cord of lineality.

This is especially true of ads that never present an ordered, sequential, rational argument but simply present the product associated with desirable things or attitudes. Thus Coca-Cola is shown held by a beautiful blonde, who sits in a Cadillac, surrounded by bronze, muscular admirers, with the sun shining overhead. By repetition these elements become associated, in our minds, into a pattern of sufficient cohesion so that one element can magically evoke the others. If we think of ads as designed solely to sell products, we miss their main effect: to increase pleasure in the consumption of the product. Coca-Cola is far more than a cooling drink; the consumer participates, vicariously, in a much larger experience. In Africa, in Melanesia, to drink a Coke is to participate in the American way of life.

Of the new languages, TV comes closest to drama and ritual. It combines music and art, language and gesture, rhetoric and color. It favors simultaneity of visual and auditory images. Cameras focus not on speakers but on persons spoken to or about; the audience *hears* the accuser but *watches* the accused. In a single impression it hears the prosecutor, watches the trembling hands of the big-town crook, and sees the look of moral indignation on Senator Tobey's face. This is real drama, in process, with the outcome uncertain. Print can't do this; it has a different bias.

Books and movies only pretend uncertainty, but live TV retains this vital aspect of life. Seen on TV, the fire in the 1952 Democratic Convention threatened briefly to become a conflagration; seen on newsreel, it was history, without potentiality.

The absence of uncertainty is no handicap to other media, if they are properly used, for their biases are different. Thus it's clear from the beginning that Hamlet is a doomed man, but, far from detracting in interest, this heightens the sense of tragedy.

Now, one of the results of the time-space duality that developed in Western culture, principally from the Renaissance on, was a separation within the arts. Music, which created symbols in time, and graphic art, which created symbols in space, became separate pursuits, and men gifted in one rarely pursued the other. Dance and ritual, which inherently combined them, fell in popularity. Only in drama did they remain united.

It is significant that of the four new media, the three most recent are dramatic media, particularly TV, which combines language, music, art, dance. They don't, however, exercise the same freedom with

---

[d]Aesop was a Greek fable writer of the late sixth century B.C. (eds.)

[e]An intricate or exceedingly complicated problem. (eds.)

time that the stage dares practice. An intricate plot, employing flash backs, multiple time perspectives and overlays, intelligible on the stage, would mystify on the screen. The audience has no time to think back, to establish relations between early hints and subsequent discoveries. The picture passes before the eyes too quickly; there are no intervals in which to take stock of what has happened and make conjectures of what is going to happen. The observer is in a more passive state, less interested in subtleties. Both TV and film are nearer to narrative and depend much more upon the episodic. An intricate time construction can be done in film, but in fact rarely is. The soliloquies of *Richard III* belong on the stage; the film audience was unprepared for them. On stage Ophelia's death was described by three separate groups: one hears the announcement and watches the reactions simultaneously. On film the camera flatly shows her drowned where "a willow lies aslant a brook."

Media differences such as these mean that it's not simply a question of communicating a single idea in different ways but that a given idea or insight belong primarily, though not exclusively, to one medium, and can be gained or communicated best through that medium.

Thus the book was ideally suited for discussing evolution and progress. Both belonged, almost exclusively, to book culture. Like a book, the idea of progress was an abstracting, organizing principle for the interpretation and comprehension of the incredibly complicated record of human experience. The sequence of events was believed to have a direction, to follow a given course along an axis of time; it was held that civilization, like the reader's eye (in J. B. Bury's words), "has moved, is moving, and will move in a desirable direc-

tion. Knowledge will advance, and with that advance, reason and decency must increasingly prevail among men." Here we see the three main elements of book lineality: the line, the point moving along that line, and its movement toward a desirable goal.

The Western conception of a definite moment in the present, of the present as a definite moment or a definite point, so important in book-dominated languages, is absent, to my knowledge, in oral languages. Absent as well, in oral societies, are such animating and controlling ideas as Western individualism and three-dimensional perspective, both related to this conception of the definite moment, and both nourished, probably bred, by book culture.

Each medium selects its ideas. TV is a tiny box into which people are crowded and must live; film gives us the wide world. With its huge screen, film is perfectly suited for social drama, Civil War panoramas, the sea, land erosion, Cecil B. De-Mille spectaculars. In contrast, the TV screen has room for two, at the most three, faces, comfortably. TV is closer to stage, yet different. Paddy Chayefsky writes:

> The theatre audience is far away from the actual action of the drama. They cannot see the silent reactions of the players. They must be told in a loud voice what is going on. The plot movement from one scene to another must be marked, rather than gently shaded as is required in television. In television, however, you can dig into the most humble, ordinary relationships; the relationship of bourgeois children to their mother, of middle-class husband to his wife, of white-collar father to his secretary—in short, the relationships of the people. We relate to each other in an incredibly complicated

manner. There is far more exciting drama in the reasons why a man gets married than in why he murders someone. The man who is unhappy in his job, the wife who thinks of a lover, the girl who wants to get into television, your father, your mother, sister, brothers, cousins, friends —all these are better subjects for drama than Iago. What makes a man ambitious? Why does a girl always try to steal her kid sister's boy friends? Why does your uncle attend his annual class reunion faithfully every year? Why do you always find it depressing to visit your father? These are the substances of good television drama; and the deeper you probe into and examine the twisted, semi-formed complexes of emotional entanglements, the more exciting your writing becomes.[1]

This is the primary reason, I believe, why Greek drama is more readily adapted to TV than to film. The boxed-in quality of live TV lends itself to static literary tragedy with greater ease than does the elastic, energetic, expandable movie. Guthrie's recent movie of *Oedipus* favored the panoramic shot rather than the selective eye. It consisted of a succession of tableaux, a series of elaborate, unnatural poses. The effect was of congested groups of people moving in tight formation as though they had trained for it by living for days together in a self-service elevator. With the lines, "I grieve for the City, and for myself and you . . . and walk through endless ways of thought," the inexorable tragedy moved to its horrible "come to realize" climax as though everyone were stepping on everyone else's feet.

The tight, necessary conventions of live TV were more sympathetic to Sophocles in the Aluminium Hour's *Antigone.* Restrictions of space are imposed on TV as on the Greek stage by the size and inflexibility of the studio. Squeezed by physical limitations, the producer was forced to expand the viewer's imagination with ingenious devices.

When T. S. Eliot adapted *Murder in the Cathedral* for film, he noted a difference in realism between cinema and stage:

> Cinema, even where fantasy is introduced, is much more realistic than the stage. Especially in an historical picture, the setting, the costume, and the way of life represented have to be accurate. Even a minor anachronism is intolerable. On the stage much more can be overlooked or forgiven; and indeed, an excessive care for accuracy of historical detail can become burdensome and distracting. In watching a stage performance, the member of the audience is in direct contact with the actor playing a part. In looking at a film, we are much more passive; as audience, we contribute less. We are seized with the illusion that we are observing an actual event, or at least a series of photographs of the actual event; and nothing must be allowed to break this illusion. Hence the precise attention to detail.[2]

If two men are on a stage in a theatre, the dramatist is obliged to motivate their presence; he has to account for their existing on the stage at all. Whereas if a camera is following a figure down a street or is turned to any object whatever, there is no need for a reason to be provided. Its grammar contains that power of statement of motivation, no matter what it looks at.

---

[1]*Television Plays*, New York, Simon and Schuster, 1955, pp. 176–78. Reprinted by permission.

[2]George Hoellering and T. S. Eliot, *Film of Murder in the Cathedral*, New York, Harcourt, Brace & World, 1952, p. vi; London, Faber & Faber, 1952. Reprinted by permission.

In the theatre, the spectator sees the enacted scene as a whole in space, always seeing the whole of the space. The stage may present only one corner of a large hall, but that corner is always totally visible all through the scene. And the spectator always sees that scene from a fixed, unchanging distance and from an angle of vision that doesn't change. Perspective may change from scene to scene, but within one scene it remains constant. Distance never varies.

But in film and TV, distance and angle constantly shift. The same scene is shown in multiple perspective and focus. The viewer sees it from here, there, then over here; finally he is drawn inexorably into it, becomes part of it. He ceases to be a spectator. Balázs writes:

> Although we sit in our seats, we do not see Romeo and Juliet from there. We look up into Juliet's balcony with Romeo's eyes and look down on Romeo with Juliet's. Our eye and with it our consciousness is identified with the characters in the film, we look at the world out of their eyes and have no angle of vision of our own. We walk amid crowds, ride, fly or fall with the hero and if one character looks into the other's eyes, he looks into our eyes from the screen, for, our eyes are in the camera and become identical with the gaze of the characters. They see with our eyes. Herein lies the psychological act of identification. Nothing like this "identification" has ever occurred as the effect of any other system of art and it is here that the film manifests its absolute artistic novelty.
> . . . Not only can we see, in the isolated "shots" of a scene, the very atoms of life and their innermost secrets

revealed at close quarters, but we can do so without any of the intimate secrecy being lost, as always happens in the exposure of a stage performance or of a painting. The new theme which the new means of expression of film art revealed was not a hurricane at sea or the eruption of a volcano: it was perhaps a solitary tear slowly welling up in the corner of a human eye.

. . . Not to speak does not mean that one has nothing to say. Those who do not speak may be brimming over with emotions which can be expressed only in forms and pictures, in gesture and play of feature. The man of visual culture uses these not as substitutes for words, as a deaf-mute uses his fingers.[3]

The gestures of visual man are not intended to convey concepts that can be expressed in words, but inner experiences, nonrational emotions, which would still remain unexpressed when everything that can be told has been told. Such emotions lie in the deepest levels. They cannot be approached by words that are mere reflections of concepts, any more than musical experiences can be expressed in rational concepts. Facial expression is a human experience rendered immediately visible without the intermediary of word. It is Turgenev's "living truth of the human face."

Printing rendered illegible the faces of men. So much could be read from paper that the method of conveying meaning by facial expression fell into desuetude. The press grew to be the main bridge over which the more remote interhuman spiritual exchanges took place; the immediate, the personal, the inner, died. There was no longer need for the subtler means of ex-

[3]Béla Balázs, *Theory of Film*, New York, Roy Publishers, 1953, pp. 48, 31, 40; London, Denis Dobson, 1952.

pression provided by the body. The face became immobile; the inner life, still. Wells that dry up are wells from which no water is dipped.

Just as radio helped bring back inflection in speech, so film and TV are aiding us in the recovery of gesture and facial awareness—a rich, colorful language, conveying moods and emotions, happenings and characters, even thoughts, none of which could be properly packaged in words. If film had remained silent for another decade, how much faster this change might have been!

Feeding the product of one medium through another medium creates a new product. When Hollywood buys a novel, it buys a title and the publicity associated with it: nothing more. Nor should it.

Each of the four versions of the *Caine Mutiny*—book, play, movie, TV—had a different hero: Willie Keith, the lawyer Greenwald, the United States Navy, and Captain Queeg, respectively. Media and audience biases were clear. Thus the book told, in lengthy detail, of the growth and making of Ensign William Keith, American man, while the movie camera with its colorful shots of ships and sea, unconsciously favored the Navy as hero, a bias supported by the fact the Navy cooperated with the movie makers. Because of stage limitations, the play was confined, except for the last scene, to the courtroom, and favored the defense counsel as hero. The TV show, aimed at a mass audience, emphasized patriotism, authority, allegiance. More important, the cast was reduced to the principals and the plot to its principles; the real moral problem—the refusal of subordinates to assist an incompetent, unpopular superior—was clear, whereas in the book it was lost under detail, in the film under scenery. Finally, the New York

play, with its audience slanted toward Expense Account patronage—Mr. Sampson, Western Sales Manager for the Cavity Drill Company—became a morality play with Willie Keith, innocent American youth, torn between two influences: Keefer, clever author but moral cripple, and Greenwald, equally brilliant but reliable, a businessman's intellectual. Greenwald saves Willie's soul.

The film *Moby Dick* was in many ways an improvement on the book, primarily because of its explicitness. For *Moby Dick* is one of those admittedly great classics, like *Robinson Crusoe* or Kafka's *Trial*, whose plot and situation, as distilled apart from the book by time and familiarity, are actually much more imposing than the written book itself. It's the drama of Ahab's defiance rather than Melville's uncharted leviathan meanderings that is the greatness of *Moby Dick*. On film, instead of laborious tacks through leagues of discursive interruptions, the most vivid descriptions of whales and whaling become part of the action. On film, the viewer was constantly aboard ship: each scene an instantaneous shot of whaling life, an effect achieved in the book only by illusion, by constant, detailed reference. From start to finish, all the action of the film served to develop what was most central to the theme—a man's magnificent and blasphemous pride in attempting to destroy the brutal, unreasoning force that maims him and turns man-made order into chaos. Unlike the book, the film gave a spare, hard, compelling dramatization, free of self-conscious symbolism.

Current confusion over the respective roles of the new media comes largely from a misconception of their function. They are art forms, not substitutes for human contact. Insofar as they attempt to usurp speech and personal, living relations, they harm. This, of course, has long been one of the problems of book culture, at least during the time of its monopoly of Western middle-class thought. But this was never a legitimate function of books, nor of any other medium. Whenever a medium goes claim jumping, trying to work areas where it is ill-suited, conflicts occur with other media, or, more accurately, between the vested interests controlling each. But, when media simply exploit their own formats, they become complementary and cross-fertile.

Some people who have no one around talk to cats, and you can hear their voices in the next room, and they sound silly, because the cat won't answer, but that suffices to maintain the illusion that their world is made up of living people, while it is not. Mechanized mass media reverse this: now mechanical cats talk to humans. There's no genuine feedback.

This charge is often leveled by academicians at the new media, but it holds equally for print. The open-mouthed, glaze-eyed TV spectator is merely the successor of the passive, silent, lonely reader whose head moved back and forth like a shuttlecock.

When we read, another person thinks for us: we merely repeat his mental process. The greater part of the work of thought is done for us. This is why it relieves us to take up a book after being occupied by our own thoughts. In reading, the mind is only the playground for another's ideas. People who spend most of their lives in reading often lose the capacity for thinking, just as those who always ride forget how to walk. Some people read themselves stupid. Chaplin did a wonderful take-off of this in *City Lights*, when he stood up on a chair to eat the endless confetti that he mistook for spaghetti.

Eliot remarks: "It is often those writers whom we are lucky enough to know whose books we can ignore; and the better we know them personally, the less need we may feel to read what they write."

Frank O'Connor highlights a basic distinction between oral and written traditions:

"By the hokies, there was a man in this place one time by name of Ned Sullivan, and he had a queer thing happen to him late one night and he coming up the Valley Road from Durlas." This is how a folk story begins, or should begin. . . . Yet that is how no printed short story should begin, because such a story seems tame when you remove it from its warm nest by the cottage fire, from the sense of an audience with its interjections and the feeling of terror at what may lurk in the darkness outside.

Face-to-face discourse is not as selective, abstract, nor explicit as any mechanical medium; it probably comes closer to communicating an unabridged situation than any of them, and, insofar as it exploits the give-take of dynamic relationship, it's clearly the most indispensable human one.

Of course, there can be personal involvement in the other media. When Richardson's *Pamela* was serialized in 1741, it aroused such interest that in one English town, upon receipt of the last installment, the church bell announced that virtue had been rewarded. Radio stations have reported receiving quantities of baby clothes and bassinets when, in a soap opera, a heroine had a baby. One of the commonest phrases used by devoted listeners to daytime serials is that they "visited with" Aunt Jenny or Big Sister. BBC and *News Chronicle* report cases of women viewers who kneel before TV sets to kiss male announcers good night.

Each medium, if its bias is properly exploited, reveals and communicates a unique aspect of reality, of truth. Each offers a different perspective, a way of seeing an otherwise hidden dimension of reality. It's not a question of one reality being true, the others distortions. One allows us to see from here, another from there, a third from still another perspective; taken together they give us a more complete whole, a greater truth. New essentials are brought to the fore, including those made invisible by the "blinders" of old languages.

This is why the preservation of book culture is as important as the development

of TV. This is why new languages, instead of destroying old ones, serve as a stimulant to them. Only monopoly is destroyed. When actor-collector Edward G. Robinson was battling actor-collector Vincent Price on art on TV's *$64,000 Challenge*, he was asked how the quiz had affected his life; he answered petulantly, "Instead of looking at the pictures in my art books, I now have to read them." Print, along with all old languages, including speech, has profited enormously from the development of the new media. "The more the arts develop," writes E. M. Forster, "the more they depend on each other for definition. We will borrow from painting first and call it pattern. Later we will borrow from music and call it rhythm." . . .

Aids   *The New Languages*

1. Marshall McLuhan says, "Today we're beginning to realize that the media aren't just mechanical gimmicks for creating worlds of illusion, but new languages with new and unique powers of expression." According to Edmund Carpenter, what precisely are the "new languages"? What are the unique powers of expression of each medium? Why do you think McLuhan and Carpenter chose the analogy of language to describe the vehicles of mass communication?

2. For years a controversy has raged over the possible effects of the mass media. Many have claimed, for instance, that television dulls the mind, while others insist that it is highly educational. Most of these critics, however, have been concerned only with the *content* of the media. Edmund Carpenter in "The New Languages" maintains that the *form* of the media is even more important than the content. What, according to Carpenter, is the difference between watching a play in a theater, on television, and on film? What are the unique biases of each medium? What are the limitations of each?

3. Carpenter believes that changes in the technology of communication elicit profound alterations in our sensory balance and view of reality. What impact did the invention of the alphabet have on preliterate people? How did the invention of printing in the fifteenth century

complete this process? How do we, members of electronic culture, view reality differently from print people?

4.   Examine carefully the front page of a current newspaper, noting any differences between its form and that of a book. Do you agree with Carpenter that "The newspaper format brought an end to book culture"?

5.   Ads, according to Carpenter, constitute a new language. Examine a few ads from a major magazine, locating examples of the lack of chronology, lineality, and causality, and the presence of repetition and simultaneity.

6.   What effects have the new languages of the electronic media had on the old languages of print and photography? Consider the pictorial magazine and film as new extensions of print and photography.

7.   Writers often use metaphors in order to draw comparisons between unlike things. Carpenter develops a number of comparisons between difficult theoretical concepts and what he assumes is familiar to his audience. When discussing oral languages, for instance, he compares them to "twisted knots," creating a clear image in the mind of the reader. What may happen, however, when a writer compares a concept to something with which the reader is not familiar? What, for instance, does Carpenter mean by "The front page is a cosmic *Finnegans Wake*"? Locate some other examples of metaphors in the essay; do they help to clarify or to confuse?

8.   In attempting to distinguish film and television from theater, Carpenter asserts that the treatment of time in the electronic visual media has to be less sophisticated than in the theater: "An intricate plot, employing flash backs, multiple time perspectives and overlays, intelligible on the stage, would mystify on the screen." Test this assertion the next time you watch television or see a movie. Do you agree with Carpenter? Has he overstated the case for the purposes of contrast? For a treatment of time in film, see William Jinks' "The Word and the Image" in Unit IV.

9.   The careful writer and speaker looks for solid evidence to support assertions. There are at least four types of evidence: statistics, factual references to other studies, other appeals to authority, and personal opinion. What kinds of evidence does Carpenter use in "The New Languages"? Does he present personal opinion and judgment as fact? What evidence, for instance, does Carpenter enlist to support the following statement: "The film *Moby Dick* was in many ways an improvement on the book, primarily because of its explicitness"? Is it possible to prove such a statement?

Marshall McLuhan: High Priest of the Electronic Village

RICHARD KOSTELANETZ

What distinguishes McLuhan from other cultural prophets of recent years is the diversity of enthusiastic audiences his ideas have attracted. Not only do several notable advertising executives and businessmen enormously admire his work, but so do scholars, artists, educators, architects, publishers, and critics, in addition to innumerable students (perhaps because his books define a reality perceived by them and yet invisible to their teachers and parents). As McLuhan draws from knowledge accumulated in a multitude of disciplines, so he creates an intellectual mix resonant and various enough to influence practitioners in numerous fields. As the great books were scarcely advertised at first and even *Media* went generally unnoticed in the major reviewing journals, the enthusiastic response inevitably arose out of cracks in the pavement. Readers of all kinds must have been impressed by McLuhan, as well as, more important, recommending his work to all kinds of friends; to one book store manager in New York, the books' buyers were "people we've never seen before." Since McLuhan uses many words in very special ways and even popularizes several epigrams of his own creation—the medium is the message, for instance, as well as the massage—the diversified impact of his work suggests that conversation across various specialties, usually hampered by exclusive jargons, may soon be conducted in the common tongue of McLuhanese.

McLuhan's popular success is nothing but surprising for another reason, which is that his books contain little of the slick stuff of which best-selling sociology is usually made. As anyone who opens the covers

Richard Kostelanetz, "Understanding McLuhan." Reprinted from *Master Minds* (New York-Macmillan, 1969) by permission of the author. Copyright © 1967, 1969 by Richard Kostelanetz.

instantly discovers, *Media* and *Galaxy*[1] are horrendously difficult to read —clumsily written, frequently contradictory, oddly organized, and overlaid with their author's peculiar jargon. McLuhan reports that one of *Media's* editors, in dismay, told him, "Seventy-five per cent of your material is new. A successful book cannot afford to be more than ten per cent new." Even experienced readers, such as Ph.D.'s and literary critics, confess that they find McLuhan hard to read, although persistent effort is usually rewarded. One explanation of his stylistic sloppiness and self-indulgence is that everything he writes actually originates as dictation, either to his secretary or to his wife; and he is reluctant to rewrite, because, he explains, "I tend to add, and the whole thing gets out of hand." Moreover, some of his insights are so original that they evade immediate comprehension; indeed, some paragraphs may forever evade clarification. "Most clear writing is a sign that there is no exploration going on," McLuhan rationalizes. "Clear prose indicates the absence of thought."

The basic themes of these books seem impenetrable at first because the concepts are often as unfamiliar as the language; but on second (or maybe third) thought, the ideas are really quite accessible. In explaining the evolution of human history, McLuhan espouses a position one can only call "technological determinism." That is, whereas Karl Marx and other economic determinists suggest that the economic organization of a society shapes every important aspect of its life, McLuhan believes that crucial technological inventions are the primary influence. To justify his historiographical method McLuhan continually refers, for instance, to the work of the academic historian Lynn White, Jr., whose *Medieval Technology and Social Change* (1962) contends that the three innovations of the stirrup, the nailed horseshoe, and the horse collar created the Middle Ages. With the stirrup, the soldier could carry heavy armor and mount a charger; the horseshoe and harness brought more efficient tilling of the land and, thus, the feudal system of organized agriculture, which, in turn, helped pay for the soldier's more extensive armaments.

Developing this insight into technology's crucial influence, McLuhan focuses upon the role of media of communication, as he espouses the principle of informational technological determinism. This thesis holds that the chief technology of communication in a society has a determining effect on everything important in that society—not only politics and economics, but also the ways in which the representative individual's mind perceives and explains his experience. The corollary of this thesis is that a shift in informational media initiates decided and widespread social and psychological changes. In *The Gutenberg Galaxy*, he suggests that the invention of movable type crucially shaped the culture of Western Europe

[1]*Understanding Media: The Extensions of Man* (1964); *The Gutenberg Galaxy* (1962). (eds.)

from 1500 to 1900. For one thing, the mass production of mechanical print encouraged nationalism by allowing wider and more uniform spread of printed materials than was possible with handwritten messages. For another, the linear forms of print influenced music to repudiate the structure of repetition, as in Gregorian chants, for that of linear development as in a classical symphony. Also, print radically reshaped the sensibility of Western man; for whereas the medieval mind saw experience as individual entities—as a collection of separate segments—and assimilated his environment primarily by ear, representative man in the Renaissance emphasized the eye and saw life as he saw print—as a continuity, often with causal relationships. McLuhan even regards print as making Protestantism possible, because the printed book, by enabling people to think in isolation, encouraged individual revelation. Finally, "All forms of mechanization emerge from movable type, for type is the prototype of all machines."

In *Understanding Media*, the sequel to *Galaxy*, McLuhan suggests that electronic technologies of communication—telegraph, radio, television, movies, telephones, computers—are similarly reshaping civilization and sensibility in the twentieth century. Whereas print-age man visually perceived one thing at a time in consecutive sequence—like a line of type—contemporary man experiences numerous forces of communication simultaneously, sometimes through more than one of his senses. Contrast, for example, the way most of us read a book with how we look at a contemporary newspaper (a product of *wire* services). With the latter, we do not start one story, read it through and then begin another. Rather, we shift our eyes across the pages, assimilating a discontinuous collection of headlines, subheadlines, lead paragraphs, and pictures. "People don't actually read newspapers," McLuhan declares. "They get into them every morning like a hot bath." The form of a television news show is similarly segmented in form, rather than sequential—a series of moments, rather than a narrative exposition of events; modern movies like Federico Fellini's are more disconnected than nineteenth-century novels, or novelistic films like *High Noon*. Similarly, the structure of contemporary music, dance, and literature is more discontinuous than earlier works in those arts—as Stravinsky is to Tschaikovsky, so the Beatles's music is to Frank Sinatra's; as the watusi and frug are to the waltz, so Merce Cunningham and modernist dance are to traditional narrative ballet.

Furthermore, the electronic media initiate sweeping changes in the distribution of sensory awareness—in what McLuhan calls the "sensory ratios." A painting or a book strikes us through only one sense, the visual; both motion pictures and television, in contrast, hit us not only through the eye, but also the ear. The new media envelop us, asking us to participate, "moving us out of the age of the visual into the age of the aural and tactile." McLuhan believes that such a multisensory existence is bringing a return to the primitive man's emphasis upon the sense of touch, which he considers the primary sense, "because it consists of a meeting of the senses"; and not only is the television image, projected from behind the screen, more tactual than the cinema image, but color television, to Mc-Luhan's analysis, achieves greater tactility than black-and-white. Politically, he sees the new media as transforming the world into "a global village," where all ends of the earth are in immediate touch with one another, as well as fostering a "retribalization" of human life. "Any highway eatery with its TV set, newspaper and magazine is as cosmopolitan as New York or Paris."

In his grand scheme of human history, McLuhan sees four great stages, each defined by the predominance of a particular informational technology:

(1) totally oral, preliterate tribalism; (2) the codification by script that developed after Homer in ancient Greece and lasted two thousand years; (3) the age of print, roughly from 1500 to 1900; and (4) the age of electronic media, from 1900 to the present. This is, roughly, a dialectical scheme in which the first two eras are the thesis, the period of print the antithesis, and the current electronic age the synthesis that rehearses much of preprint culture; and for his remarks about the present and future, McLuhan continually draws upon traits characteristic of preprint, if not preliterate, peoples. This scheme of historical development is, as a dialectical form, analogous to classic Marxism; and like Marx, whose *Capital* portrays the emergence of capitalism, McLuhan writes most authoritatively not about the impending utopia, but the transition from the thesis to the antithesis—the emergence of the culture of print. In one of the more perspicacious negative critiques, the Canadian writer Gerald Taaffe detects a "medievalist, Catholic, corporatist bias. . . . It is in the Middle Ages that he (McLuhan) finds his spiritual home. He leaps from the time of St. Thomas Aquinas to the electronic age as though the intervening centuries were nothing but an unpleasant dream." McLuhan, in one of his rare evaluative cultural statements, confirmed this inference, when he remarked in a symposium, "Now we are moving back to what I would like to think perhaps a better orientation."

One of the presuppositions informing McLuhan's thought holds that art ultimately comes out of art—which is to say that just as artists are more profoundly influenced by the art that they see than by their extrinsic experience, so new ideas about man and his environment evolve out of previous ideas, as well as, of course, drawing freshly upon new developments in human experience. What is true for others is applicable to Mc-Luhan himself; for, in retrospect, his major ideas are not as original as they may at first have appeared to many readers. "Most of what I have to say is secondhand." McLuhan once admitted, with needless modesty, "gathered however from esoteric sources." . . . From these sources, as well as many others, McLuhan fashioned his own thought, which in turn has had and will have an immense impact on the thinking of others.

McLuhan's discussions of the individual electronic media move far beyond the previous comments of serious critics, most of whom complain about their content, generally arguing that if television, for instance, had more intelligent treatments of more intelligent subjects, its contribution to culture would be greater. McLuhan proposes that, instead, we think more about the character and form of the new media; and pursuing this bias, he offers an epigram—"The medium is the message"—which means several things. The phrase first suggests that each medium develops an audience of people whose love for that medium is greater than their concern for its content. That is, the TV medium itself becomes the prime interest in watching television; for just as some people like to read for the joy of experiencing print and a few find great pleasure in talking to just anybody over the telephone, so others like television primarily for its mixture of kinetic screen and relevant sound. Second, the "message" of a particular medium includes everything in Western culture that that medium has influenced. "The message of the movie medium is that of transition from linear connections to configurations." Third, the aphorism suggests that the medium itself—its intrinsic form—shapes its limitations and possibilities for the communication of content. One medium is better than another at evoking a certain experience. American football, for example, is invariably better on television than on radio or in a newspaper column; a bad football game on television is usually more interesting than a great game on radio (unless one has a sentimental interest in the fortunes of a particular team). Most United Nations hearings, in contrast, are less boring in the newspaper than on television. McLuhan's point is that each medium seems to possess a hidden taste mechanism which encourages some styles, subjects, and experiences while it rejects others.

To characterize these mechanisms, he devises the approximate categories of "hot" and "cool," which roughly analyze three crucial dimensions —the character of a communications instrument, the quality of the sensory experience it communicates, and its interaction with human response. A "hot" medium or experience has a "high definition" or a highly individualized character, as well as a high fidelity to the original model and a considerable amount of detailed information. "Cool" is low in definition, fidelity, and information; thus, it requires that the audience participate to complete the communication. McLuhan's own examples help clarify the distinction. "A cartoon is 'low' definition, simply because very little information is provided." Radio is usually a hot medium; print, photography, film and painting essentially are hot media. "Any hot medium allows for less participating than a cool one, as a lecture makes for less participation than a seminar, and a book for less than a dialogue." Television is cooler than movies, because a rough image of patterned dots, like that of cartoons, demands more intensive, participatory viewing than the photographic pictures of film. These unfortunately christened terms "hot" and "cool" McLuhan also applies to experiences and people; and unifying the multiple threads of his distinction, he suggests that while a hot medium favors a performer possessed of a strongly individualized presence, cool media prefer the nonchalant, "cooler" people. Therefore, just as the radio medium needs a voice of highly idiosyncratic [sic] that is instantly recognizable—think of Jean Shepherd or Westbrook Van Voorhees—television favors people of a definition so low that they appear positively ordinary; that perhaps explains why bland personalities, such as Ed Sullivan and Johnny Carson, are more successful on television: "It was no accident that Senator Joseph McCarthy lasted such a very short time when he switched to TV," McLuhan wrote in *Media*. "TV is a cool medium. It rejects hot figures such as Senator McCarthy and people from the hot media. Had TV occurred on a large scale during Hitler's reign, he would have vanished quickly." More recently, he added, "Anyone who looks as if he *wants* to be elected had best stay off TV. If Pierre Trudeau is a great TV image in politics, it is because he is indifferent to political power."

In his remarks on common phenomena, McLuhan possesses the most astonishing capacity to perceive what remains hidden from others—literally, to make the invisible visible. "As a rule," he says, "I always look for what others ignore," and *Media*, for instance, contains, among other things, some remarkably stimulating remarks on less considered modes of communication—telephones, typewriters, articulated spaces, clothing, games, clocks, and so on—while McLuhan's unusual criticisms continually suggest that we ought to rethink familiar concepts and problems. Much of his intellectual originality stems from a distinctly North American willingness to push his perceptions beyond conventional bounds into an unknown region where notions and perceptions seem "mad" before they are recognized as true. His ideas are neither as neatly nor as modestly presented as this summary might suggest, for McLuhan believes more in probing and exaggerating—"making discoveries"—than in offering final definitions, as well as raising the current critical discourse to a higher level of insight and subtlety. For this reason, he will in public conversation rarely defend any of his statements as absolute truths, although he will explain how he developed them. "I don't agree or disagree with anything I say myself" is his characteristic rationale. "For me," says an old friend, "the closest parallel to Marshall is Ezra Pound—a genius with words and phrases and insights, a ceaseless fox, though no hedgehog—jumping from point to point, taking this from here and that from there, throwing away huge ideas in pithy phrases, contradicting himself without concern, missing the daily trivia but identifying the bigger forces."

In conversation or on a stage, McLuhan evokes the impression of conjuring insights, largely because in drawing ideas from one realm and applying them to another, he makes spectacular, unfamiliar connections in propelling miscellaneous information through several comprehensive sieves of interpretative schemata, he produces a huge number of provocative remarks. Both these methods for producing insight demand a memory as prodigious as his curiosity, as well as an extraordinary shuffling mechanism in his head. More interested in similarities than differences, he frequently escalates a tenuous analogy into a grandiose generalization; and since "I use language as a probe," he particularly relishes making his points, if not conjuring a truth, through a pun: "When a thing is current, it creates currency." Or, "Type is the prototype. . . ." Or, "The medium is a massage; it works us over." He loves comic aphorisms, such as, "Money is the poor man's credit card." Some perceptions are considerably more tenable than others—indeed, many are patently ridiculous—and nearly all of his original propositions are arguable; so his books require the participation of each reader to separate what is wheat for him from the chaff. "Concepts," McLuhan admits, "are provisional affairs for apprehending reality; their value is in the grip they provide." In McLuhanese, his books offer a cool experience in a hot medium, even though McLuhan himself is indubitably an all but inflammatory presence. A reader's typical scorecard for *Understanding Media* might show that about one half is brilliant insight; one fourth, suggestive hypothesis; one fourth, nonsense. Given the book's purposes and originality, these are hardly discreditable percentages; for the reader, the price of insight is usually a dose of sludge. "If a few details here and there are wacky," the oracle rationalizes, "it doesn't matter a hoot."

All his books are unconventionally written, if not audaciously inventive in structure; for not only does McLuhan favor a particular use of esoteric words and a frustratingly casual attitude toward familiar ones, but he also eschews the traditional English professor's expository style— introduction, development, elaboration, and conclusion. Instead, McLuhan's books imitate the segmented structure of the modern media, as he tends to make a series of analytic statements, none of which become an explicitly encompassing thesis, though all of them approach the same body of phenomena from different angles or examples. These become a succession of exegetical glosses on a mysterious scriptural text, which is how McLuhan analogously regards the new electronic world—a definitive but mysterious reality. "I accept media," he once remarked in passing, "as I accept cosmos." He compiles his books with chapters of equal weight, set in a semiarbitrary order; and these embellish the major themes through similar insights, rather than develop an argument. He forms these chapters through a similarily discontinuous arrangement of paragraphs; for typically they start with an oblique example, conclude on a tangent, and represent a collection of glosses. Although a paragraph may often have a distinct topic sentence, its real point is usually buried in the text. In short, rather than straightforwardly set forth his points, McLuhan weaves a mosaic of meaning, where everything contributes, in unequal measure, toward shaping his themes.

This means that one should not necessarily read his books from start to finish—the archaic habit of print-man. True, the preface and first chapter of *The Mechanical Bride* (1951), an earlier work, really do *introduce* the themes and methods of the book; but beyond that, the chapters can be read in any order. The real introduction to *The Gutenberg Galaxy* is the final chapter, called "The Galaxy Reconfigured," even McLuhan advises readers to start there; and the book itself is all but a galaxy of extensive printed quotations. With *Media*, the introduction and the first two chapters form the most propitious starting point; thereafter, the reader is pretty much free to wander as he will, perhaps to the commentaries on more familiar territory, such as radio, television, and automation. Likewise, there is no need to read everything to understand these books. "One can stop anywhere after the first few sentences and have the full message, if one is prepared to 'dig' it," McLuhan once wrote of non-Western scriptural literature; but the remark is just as applicable to his own books. Similarly, McLuhan does not believe that his works have only one final meaning; for as a prober himself, he would encourage readers to let these books stimulate their own thinking on these matters. "My book," he declares, "is not a package but part of the dialogue, part of the conversation." Indeed, he evaluates other books less by how definitively they treat their subjects— the academic standard—than by how much thought they stimulate; therefore, a book may be wrong but great. (By his own standards, needless to say perhaps, *Media* is a masterpiece.) The point is that print-man, with his masochistic preference for, if not dependence upon, the successiveness of print (as well as a penchant for factual accuracy), will be a less adept reader of McLuhanese than the media-man with his awareness of configurations; these books are mosaics, rather than arguments. For that reason, perhaps the best way to coolly immerse oneself in McLuhan's hot thought would involve getting two paperback copies, cutting out all the pages and then pasting them around the walls and on the ceiling.

A continual preoccupation of McLuhan's explorations is the great modern question of whether technology is beneficial to man. Many intellectuals have argued, on the one hand, that technology stifles the blood of life by dehumanizing the spirit and cutting existence off from nature; more materialistic thinkers, on the other hand, defend the machine for easing man's burdens and providing desirable commodities at a reasonable price. McLuhan cuts across this dichotomous argument by exploring the psychological and philosophical effects of technology; and his comments stem primarily from pursuing Ralph Waldo Emerson's idea that "all the tools and engines on earth are only extensions of man's limbs and senses." That is, where a shovel is functionally an extension of the hand, the telephone is an extension of the ear (and the voice), and television extends our eyes and ears to a distant place as well as makes all current events both instantaneous and immediate. Our eyes and ears were live participants at the Kennedy funerals, although our bodies stayed at home. "Today, after more than a century of electric technology, we have extended our central nervous system itself, in a global embrace, abolishing both time and space as far as the planet is concerned." As extensions, the new media offer both possibility and threat; for while they lengthen man's reach into his existence, they can also extend society's reach into him, for both exploitation and control. To deflect this latter possibility, McLuhan insists that every man should know as much about the media as possible. "By knowing how technology shapes our environment, we can transcend its absolutely determining power," he says. "Actually, rather than a 'techno-logical determinist,' it would be more accurate to say, as regards the future, that I am an 'organic autonomist.' My entire concern is to overcome the determination that results from people trying to ignore what is going on. Far from regarding technological change as inevitable, I insist that if we understand its components we can turn it off any time we choose. Short of turning it off, there are lots of moderate controls conceivable." In stressing the importance of knowledge and man's capacity to shape his environment to his needs, McLuhan is trenchantly a humanist. To Harold Rosenberg, the books themselves represent "a concrete testimonial (illumi-nating, as modern art illuminates, through disassociation and regrouping) to the belief that man is certain to find his footing in the new world he is in the process of creating." . . .

Aids *Marshall McLuhan: High Priest of the Electronic Village*

1. According to Kostelanetz, the works of McLuhan are "horrendously difficult to read—clumsily written, frequently contradictory, oddly organized, and overlaid with their author's peculiar jargon." One barrier to understanding McLuhan is that he uses conventional words —*medium, message, sensory ratios, global village, probe, hot,* and *cool,* in rather special senses. As you read Kostelanetz's essay, make a list of these and other terms as they appear in context and define them. Would it have been better if McLuhan had chosen different words to express his ideas, or coined some new words?

2. Despite McLuhan's peculiar jargon and seemingly undecipherable one-liners, his basic themes and ideas, Kostelanetz suggests, are really quite accessible. What are McLuhan's basic ideas? You might want to define with examples each of the following:

    a. Informational technological determinism

    b. The three basic technological innovations

    c. The medium is the message/massage

    d. Hot and cool media

3. According to Kostelanetz, McLuhan's terms "hot" and "cool" characterize three dimensions of a medium: "the character of a communications instrument, the quality of the sensory experience it communicates, and its interaction with human response." The terms apply not only to media but to people and experiences. Keeping in mind that "hot" and "cool" are relative terms, categorize each of the following groups of media, people, and experiences, giving your reasons for each choice.

    a. Comic books, coloring books, advertising, telephone, television, film, traditional theater, living theater, newspapers, pictorial magazines

    b. Richard Nixon 1960, Richard Nixon 1972, George Wallace, Jimmy Carter; Janis Joplin, Ike and Tina Turner, Don Rickles, Lawrence Welk, Rolling Stones

    c. A lecture, a discussion class, a do-it-yourself project, playing pinball machines, making love

4. McLuhan uses the print medium to communicate his ideas. In view of what he says about the differences between print culture and electronic culture, do you find it paradoxical that he continues to communicate through written language? According to Kostelanetz, what techniques does McLuhan employ in his writing to simulate the nonlineality and simultaneity of the electronic media?

5. McLuhan maintains that cultures are shaped by their media. In what ways has the youth culture in America been shaped by the mass media? What are the roles of TV, film, and music? McLuhan also asserts that electronic media are returning us to a "tribal village." How does the youth culture conform to this notion?

6. Another provocative insight uttered by McLuhan is that "The youth of today reject goals. They want roles—R-O-L-E-S. That is, total involvement. They do not want fragmented, specialized goals or jobs." Do you agree with this assertion, which was made in 1967, about your ambitions? What political and cultural conditions in the late 1960s inspired McLuhan's observation? Is the insight valid today?

7. Although McLuhan's concepts and assertions are neither fully defined nor adequately supported with specific examples, they can be readily applied to and illustrated by our own experiences. Choose one or

more of the concepts listed below and write a paper or report in which you apply it to your own experience.

a. The electronic media far surpass any influence parents can bring to bear on their children.

b. In an electric information environment, minority groups can no longer be contained or ignored.

c. Far more thought and care go into the composition of any prominent ad in a magazine than go into the writing of its features.

d. When faced with a totally new situation, we tend always to attach ourselves to the objects, to the flavor of the most recent past. We look at the present through a rearview mirror.

8. McLuhan has much to say about education—its limitations and its possibilities. His comments center upon the question: where does the education of today's child *really* take place? In the classroom where information is scarce, ordered and structured by fragmented, classified patterns and schedules? Or does education occur by means of ceaseless exposure to and involvement in the mosaic of simultaneous, instantaneous electronic experiences—*outside* the classroom? Have you stopped your education by going to school, McLuhan asks? Describe an educational environment, real or imaginary, that implements some of McLuhan's concepts. In your description you might consider the following possibilities: (a) the classroom should demand involvement; (b) visual and audial aids should be used frequently; (c) students should be encouraged to probe, to explore, to search out their own points of view—participants in discovery and not passive recipients of neatly prepackaged linear learning; (d) learning should be individualized and self-paced—the responsibility for learning should be shifted from teacher to student; (e) even the seating arrangement in the classroom should reflect the "cool" learning environment; (f) bulletin boards should be dynamic, ever-changing mosaics of experience.

9. Kostelanetz comments specifically on McLuhan's writing style: he "eschews the traditional English professor's expository style—introduction, development, elaboration, and conclusion." How does McLuhan defend his unconventional style? Do you find his answer satisfactory given what you know as the basic rules of organization and documentation? Base your answer on a close reading of McLuhan's compositional style in "The Print: How to Dig It" in Unit III.

Notes for
an Introduction
to a Discussion
of Popular Culture

RUSSEL B. NYE

First, let us define terms. I use the word *popular* to mean that which is widely diffused, generally accepted, approved by the majority. *Culture,* an especially protean word, I use in the sense of Edward Tylor's definition as "that complex whole which includes knowledge, belief, art, custom, and other capabilities acquired by man as a member of society," a definition which, of course, needs to be focused more precisely, depending on the use of popular materials within particular academic disciplines. This is not the occasion to trace the history of popular culture, or of attitudes toward it; this has already been done with distinction by others.[1] I am more concerned at the moment with considering briefly recent trends in the study of popular culture, as observed by cultural historians, literary critics, historians of ideas, and philosophers of aesthetics. Within the last decade there has been, if I read the signs right, the beginnings of a significant shift in our attitudes toward relationships among cultural levels and cultural values. Artists and audiences seem to be crossing borders they shouldn't; critics are asking whether the lines that presumably separate "highbrow" from "lowbrow" or "elite" from "popular" (those classic terms never quite clearly established but traditionally and uncritically accepted) ought to be so sharply defined, or perhaps ought to be there at all. People who know Beethoven and Bartok listen to the Beatles; *Time* and *Newsweek* and Leonard Bernstein have approved California and Liverpool rock; even the *New York Review of Books, mirable dictu,*[a] has published an admiring article on popular music. *Peanuts* is written about by theologians and philosophers; there are articles on Marvel Comics and horror movies; John Lennon and Leonard Cohen are studied the way graduate students used to study Eliot and Pound. *Playboy* has a centerfold in the ancient and honorable *Police Gazette* tradition, and also publishes essays by Leslie Fiedler and

Russel B. Nye, "Notes for an Introduction to a Discussion of Popular Culture," from *Journal of Popular Culture,* spring 1971, pp. 1032–38. Reprinted by permission of *Journal of Popular Culture.*

[1]See, for example, Leo Loewenthal's essay, "An Historical Preface to the Popular Culture Debate," in Norman Jacobs, ed., *Culture for the Millions* (Princeton, 1961), 28–42.

[a]Latin. Wonderful to relate. (eds.)

Harvey Cox. There is a rock-opera and a folk-mass; painters use soup cans and high-way signs and hamburgers. Clearly, things are not what they used to be.

There are a number of reasons for this wave of interest in, and the recent re-evaluation of, the aims, audiences, conventions, and artifacts of popular culture. I should like to identify five which seem to me immediately operative, although there are probably others equally important. First, the attention given by social scientists to mass communications and media study has revealed serious limitations in the older concept of society as composed of a naive, maneuverable mass on the one hand, and a self-controlled, cultured elite on the other. The real relationships between the mass media and their various publics is proving to be much more complicated than the simplistic picture drawn by the critics of the thirties and forties. Social psychologists find that audiences resist manipulation in ways not earlier suspected; that mass communications do more than merely transmit information; that if the media do distort reality, people have compensatory built-in resistances, of which critics have never taken full account. Furthermore, it also seems clear that attempts to convince mass audiences that they ought to reject popular culture are ingenuous and ineffective, and that the critics of popular culture too may have their own biases and limitations. I do not think we can afford to overlook the importance of those explorations of popular culture now being made by the more alert social sciences.

Second, the study of popular culture has been demonstrably affected by the example of cultural anthropology and its belief that all parts of a culture are worth study. Cultural relativism, the idea that no

part of a culture has—for purposes of understanding it—innate superiority over another, has provided those who wish to study popular culture with a useful, viable methodology, as well as welcome scholarly and moral support. If it is permissible to study the songs of a Bantu tribe, or the marriage customs of a Polynesian sub-group, it seems equally permissible to study the songs of teeny-boppers in California or popular stories from *True Confessions*, and for the same reasons.

Third, the insights of Marshall McLuhan—scattered, confusing, but often brilliant—have attracted the attention of a number of younger critics who are putting together a new aesthetic which includes, rather than excludes, a wider range of cultural levels than before. McLuhan has made at least two suggestions which, in their reverberations, have deeply influenced the study of popular culture. His assertion that the medium is as important as, or more important than, the message, changed the focus of cultural criticism by shifting attention from content to medium, from *what* was said to *how* it was transmitted. "Concern with effect, rather than meaning," he wrote in *Understanding Media*, "is the basic change of our electric time"; or again, "When a medium becomes a depth experience, the old categories of classical and popular, or of highbrow and lowbrow, no longer obtain"; and again, "Anything that is approached in depth acquires as much interest as the greatest matters."

Deriving from McLuhan, critics such as Susan Sontag, for example, have opted for a "new sensibility," challenging all the old boundaries between scientific and artistic, high and low, mass and elite. In addition, another seminal idea has been McLuhan's concept of modern communications as a "mosaic"; that is, he suggests that information flows in upon the individual in a random "mosaic" pattern which is unified by the individual, who experiences and orders it. If life, as McLuhan says, has "discontinuous variety and incongruity," then art may reflect and interpret it by building similar mosaic, experiential structures in imitation of life. The Beatles' *Abbey Road* album, for example, a collection of separate songs in various styles and settings, gains full effectiveness only when the listener perceives the relationship among them all or simply experiences them all as a totality. To use the current popular phrase, "putting it all together" is a simplified version of McLuhan's idea of "mosaic" disconnection and reconnection. A novel like Leonard Cohen's *Beautiful Losers* asks the reader to do just that—to put together a discontinuous series of events and characters, separated by time and space, juxtaposed in a pattern that is no longer accidental as the reader imposes his own design on the experience.

Fourth, I think we are seeing the results of having lived for two generations with mass culture. We are not afraid of it any more, and we know how to find meaning and value in it. The dire predictions of the thirties and forties about the social disintegration and cultural decay that would inevitably follow movies, radio, comic strips, television, and jazz have simply not come true. The Canadian National Film Board calculates (and the figures no doubt hold true for the United States) that today's average 18-year-old has seen 500 feature films and 15,000 hours of television,[b] plus heaven knows how many commercials, advertisements, comics, or hours of disc-jockey music he has heard on his transistor. Yet he seems to be able to handle it with considerable sophistication and to respond to it in a number of interesting, subtle, and imaginative ways. We have lived for three-quarters of a century with mass culture, and we are culturally no worse off than before; in fact, there is reason to believe we may be better off.

Fifth, and this is important, popular culture and technology have made a unique merger, with interesting, powerful, and utterly new results. The customized car, to cite an example, is an authentic midcentury expression of the meanings of the automobile age; there are those who find similar technological and aesthetic validity in a Brabham taking the Thunder Valley esses at Elkhart Lake, or in the intricate kinetics of a freeway cloverleaf. The artist has become technician—sculptors are metallurgists, printmakers chemists, movie directors and editors highly skilled workmen in the use of cameras, lenses, lights, cutters, and other tools of the trade. Popular artists have taken eager advantage of technology, both its materials and techniques. Acrylic paints, welding torches, television cameras, and multitrack tape recorders (Apple Records uses as many as sixteen tracks) are as much cultural tools as commercial ones, and vice versa. Painters use real telephones and bathtubs; composers artificial noises; musicians instruments like the Fender bass and the Moog synthesizer. Popular music in particular has made imaginative use of electronic technology. The sound engineer's part in making music is as creative as the musician's, using reverberation, equalization, overdubbing and distortion techniques to create sounds and performances

[b]By the time the average person is a teenager he will have spent fifteen or twenty thousand hours, or about two full years, in front of the television set. (eds.)

that never existed; the amplifier alone has virtually transformed the character of much popular music. By using three amplifiers on a violin, for example, the engineer can select and combine sound frequencies and levels to produce quite new and striking sounds; to cite another example, the "wa-wa" pedal, developed recently for amplified guitar, for the first time gives a stringed instrument voice-like qualities. Certainly none of this bears resemblance to what were considered culturally acceptable techniques and subjects in the arts a short generation ago. This mutual absorption of culture and technology on the popular level is an outstanding characteristic of our contemporary world.

As a result of these and other factors, real doubts have been raised about the customary division of culture into brow-levels, and about ways of judging and investigating materials drawn from popular culture. I am not at all sure that the presumed dichotomy among "cultures" is real or natural. Do the culturally elite never search for entertainment, and the so-called "masses" never seek insight? Is culture *only* a matter of class, income, and education? If you stopped *Gunsmoke* next week, would there be larger audiences for *Oh Calcutta?* As for the argument that popular culture does not impart "genuine" values, how do you measure genuine-ness? Who can say that the TV watcher gets less "genuine" value—at *his* level of experience —than the professor reading James? I have never quite understood why, if a Ph.D. settles down with a Scotch and soda to read Ross MacDonald (who was recently favored with front-page *Times* and *Newsweek* reviews) it's sophistication, whereas a tool-and-die maker from Oldsmobile who watches *Mannix* on TV with a can of beer is automatically a slob. Whose values are the more genuine? These are some of the questions raised by the current explorations of the nature and uses of popular culture, and ones that should not only be raised but answered.

There are many more. What about standards of "good" and "bad," applied to the popular arts? Should we judge a popular novel as we would Faulkner?[c] Is Aristotle applicable to paperbacks, Northrop Frye[d] to television? Most of our critical standards are drawn from studies of eighteenth- and nineteenth-century fiction and poetry—what have they to do with twentieth-century media? As a result, what a good many critics are saying about popular culture is little more than that the aesthetic forms and aims that flourished in the nineteenth century do not satisfy the twentieth, a conclusion hardly profound. Furthermore, what do we mean by *popular,* in the critical sense? Is definition in terms of consumption, or economics, or sales, valid? Is a "good" book that millions of people read "popular" or not? What are we going to do with Charles Dickens? Or Charles Chaplin? Or *Hair?* I have no answers nor is it necessary here to make precise ones. The point is, that by continuing to ask questions the range of interest in the study of popular culture may be broadened, deepened, better understood, focused with greater precision.

The study of popular culture is still

[c]William Faulkner (1897–1962), American novelist, who won the Nobel Prize for Literature in 1950. (eds.)

[d]Northrop Frye is a Canadian literary critic. (eds.)

in the process of finding its methodology, primarily because it is a joint scholarly venture, involving several disciplines, borrowing and gaining something from each. I do not account this a weakness. It means, in effect, that in finding out what we want to know about the culture of a society at a given place and time, we can choose the most effective tools, whether they be sociological, psychological, historical, aesthetic, or philosophical. Popular culture can be considered as a point at which the investigative techniques of the social sciences and the humanities may converge. Where such interests draw together—in examinations of social behavior, cultural patterns, communications media, social and cultural values—the study of popular culture provides a common ground where different disciplines may combine. There is, then, no single, approved methodology for the study of popular culture, but several. Since many forms of popular culture depend for effectiveness on their collective appeal (and some, like contemporary popular music, are even collectively produced), any approach to the study of them almost necessarily must be eclectic. We should be able to choose that method of investigation which allows us to find out what we want to know. What works best is the best methodology.

Borrowing from a Wallace Stevens poem, I should like to suggest six ways of looking at popular culture, depending on what one wishes to find out and how one wants to define it. One way turns on the study of the means by which culture is transmitted. It assumes that popular culture includes those cultural elements which are not so complex and sophisticated that they cannot be effectively disseminated among a *majority* audience. This provides a useful distinction between popular and elite cultures—i.e., a painting versus a print—by focusing attention on the distributive process. A second way of approaching popular culture may be based on an examination of the differences in the production of popular cultural artifacts, distinguishing between the unique and the mass-produced—in other words, focusing on the creative *act*, and on whether or not it can be sustained or is reproducible. John Cawelti[e] has refined this approach by defining at least a broad portion of popular culture as that which is "characterized by artistic formulas which arise in response to certain cultural needs for entertainment and escape." That is, if there exists a majority cultural need, the popular artist evolves a formula for meeting it—the Western movie, the Sinatra song style, the McKuen poem, the *True Romance.*

Third, it may also be useful to examine the product of popular culture on the basis of its function—that is, to ask, What is it used for? Comics, B movies, "listening music," the detective story—is the point relaxation or cerebration? In recognizing the difference in function between Conan Doyle[f] and Tolstoy[g]—both masters at their craft—it is also recognized that one does

---

[e]An excerpt from Cawelti's book, *The Six Gun Mystique,* is reprinted in Unit IV. (eds.)

[f]Sir Arthur Conan Doyle (1859–1930) created the fictional character Sherlock Holmes. (eds.)

[g]Leo Tolstoy (1828–1910), a Russian novelist, wrote *War and Peace* (1865–69) and *Anna Karenina* (1875–77). (eds.)

not judge either by the other's standards. What this functional approach does, and very usefully, is to acknowledge gradations of aim among serious work seriously received, unserious work unseriously received, and all stages between. Basically, this view of cultural grades derives from Santayana's famous distinction between *work* and *play* as basic human activities, between what must be done and what is done by choice. While this approach is perhaps overly generalized, it is especially useful as a tool for studying popular culture before the appearance of the mass media—one cannot, I think, study pre-media and post-media popular culture in the same ways.

A fourth approach is that suggested by Marshall Fishwick's characterization of popular culture as "that part of culture abstracted from the *total* body of intellectual and imaginative work which each generation receives," which is not narrowly elitist or aimed at special audiences, and which is generally (but not necessarily) disseminated via the mass media. Popular culture thus includes everything not elite, "everything spoken, printed, pictured, sounded, viewed and intended for other than the identifiable few." Professor Fishwick's concept is particularly useful for its inclusiveness, and for its adaptability to sociological, historical, psychological, philosophical or critical investigation. Abraham Kaplan has suggested a fifth, somewhat related approach, pointing out that the distinguishing mark of popular culture is the *kind* of taste it reflects and satisfies, rather than how widely it is disseminated. Popular culture thus becomes not dependent for definition on numbers and profits, or for uniqueness or lack of it, but rather is defined on the basis of its own nature and aims. Sixth, Ray Browne

has suggested that differences among various levels of culture are to be considered matters of degree rather than of substance or audience. Culture, he has written, is not to be arranged vertically from "low" to "high," but in a kind of horizontal continuum, resembling a flattened lens or ellipsis, with Elite at one end, Folk at the other, and between, largest and most visible, Popular culture. Lines of demarcation are mobile, investigatory methods variable and pragmatically chosen, the purpose to treat culture in all its phases, to exclude none and include all. Although I cannot match Stevens' thirteen, these are six ways of approaching the study of popular culture, all valid for varying purposes, all useful and investigating what is, it seems to me, the most provocatively versatile field of academic study of our contemporary day.

The value of this pioneering conference, and of others which I hope will follow, lies in asking questions, testing boundaries, stretching conjectures. What the study of popular culture requires more than anything else at this point is this loosening of divisions and broadening of perspectives. The classic definition of culture as "the best that has been done or thought," or as "the upper ten-percent of a society's best accomplishments," has been valuable—and will always be—as a means of preserving and transmitting the cultural heritage. But on the other hand, to rule out the rest of the broad spectrum of human cultural activity as an area for exploration is a far too restrictive act. Certainly, the culture of the majority of society ought to be subjected to this kind of searching, intensive investigation by historians, literary critics, and humanists in general, if we are to know our modern, pluralistic, multileveled society.

Aids   *Notes for an Introduction to a*
Discussion of Popular Culture

1. Russel Nye notes that within the last fifteen years or so there have been the beginnings of a "significant shift of our attitudes toward relationships among cultural levels and cultural values." He offers evidence to support his thesis that artists are crossing the traditional categories of culture, i.e., rock operas, folk masses. Locate some current examples of popular culture that represent either a mixing of "popular" with "high" forms or a merging of the so-called brow levels (i.e., highbrow, lowbrow). You might consider, for instance, ABC's novel for television *Rich Man, Poor Man*, the rock opera *Tommy*, the film *The Great Gatsby*, or the recording "Switched On Bach." Are these blends a happy and successful merger? What traditional forms are these new combinations indebted to?

2. Nye enumerates five reasons for the recent interest in and reevaluation of the "aims, audiences, conventions, and artifacts of popular culture." Define each of the five reasons, providing examples whenever possible from current popular culture.

3. Culture can be defined in a number of ways, depending upon your point of view. At one extreme, culture strictly denotes the intellectual, esthetic, and philosophic side of civilization. At the other extreme, culture is the entire way of life of a society, without implication of refinement or advanced knowledge; it consists of the customs, ideas, and attitudes shared by a group. Which view of culture is promulgated by Russel Nye? According to Nye, why is it important that we adopt the anthropological view of culture?

4. Some critics have viewed the merger of culture and technology negatively, asserting that mass production has transformed legitimate culture into cultural trash. Russel Nye maintains, however, that "the dire predictions about the social disintegration and cultural decay that would inevitably follow movies, radio, comics, television, and jazz have simply not come true." One of the dire predictors is Dwight Macdonald, whose essay "A Theory of Mass Culture" appears in this unit. Examine Macdonald's 1953 essay and see if you agree with his negative assessment of popular culture.

5. Nye suggests that there are at least six ways of looking at popular culture. Assume you have been called upon to defend a popular culture artifact, such as a reproduction of a famous art work, a condensation of a literary work, or a recording of a popular song, against the attacks of Dwight Macdonald. Choose one or more of Nye's approaches and outline your defense.

Secret Agent

ARTHUR ASA BERGER

In which the author, illustrator, and collector of a
"monumentality of trivia" tells what is right (and wrong)
with the study of popular culture.

A friend once told me something that has been instrumental in my thinking. "When we are young," he said, "we have some larger purpose, some great thing we hope to do. But what happens is that we find a number of things that interrupt our pursuit of this goal. Before we know it we are old and we find that our life has been the interruptions and not the grand design we had originally set out to execute."

In my own case this is quite evident. I have been keeping a journal since 1954, and have written nearly thirty 300-page volumes of notes, impressions, and trivia. I do a great deal of my thinking "in" the journal: I list things I have to do, write people's names and addresses, draw pictures of things I've bought or hope to buy, draw cartoons.

If you were to look at the journals you would probably say, "My God, the guy has hardly had an idea in his life! All he does is write about trivial things. What junk!" Of course! That's what life is, for the most part. My life is a series of groceries bought at the supermarket, movies I've been to, minor repairs around the house, departmental meetings, with an occasional aside to wonder about something that has struck my attention.

Thus I "am" popular culture—and so are you! That is the base upon which any superstructure is built, and my life, like anybody's life, is an admixture of bits and pieces of popular culture and an occasional refinement.

What do I do with all that junk?

Years ago I had an embosser made for myself which reads: Arthur Asa Berger, Writer, Artist, Secret Agent. I stamp it on most of the letters I send to friends and everyone finds it amusing. Somehow the notion that a professor could be a secret agent is quite crazy; it is also absurd for secret agents to advertise themselves as such.

And yet . . . and yet, *I really am a secret agent!* Not the kind of secret agent who works for governments and steals plans for missiles. I am a self-employed secret agent who searches, relentlessly, for hidden meanings and latent functions. I like to think that, like all secret agents, I shake

From the *Journal of Communication*, spring 1974, pp. 70–74. Copyright © 1974 by the *Journal of Communication*. Reprinted by permission of the journal and the author.

the very foundations of society. For if society maintains itself on the basis of the unrecognized functions people engage in, when I point out these latent functions I make them recognizable (manifest), and the equilibrium in society is disturbed. The paradox of genuine sociological knowledge, as someone once explained it to me, is that the more we know, the worse off we are, for, in fact, it is the latent functions of our activities that maintain society.

Thus I am a secret agent who discovers secrets and broadcasts them (when I can get someone to publish my work) to the world.

The student of popular culture has the task of *analyzing, interpreting,* and *evaluating* whatever it is he is interested in. Since much of popular culture has an artistic or aesthetic component (no matter how dreadful this may be), it is important that we do not look upon popular culture and popular art as merely documents to be mined for incidents of violence, proportions of this or that, and so on. We must take into account the conventions of each popular art (and perhaps the popular arts in general) and other aesthetic considerations. For example, in many cases form has a "content" of its own, and to neglect formal and structural matters is simple-minded.

The problem with most of the work done in popular culture is that the social scientists have neglected aesthetic considerations and the literary scholars have neglected social scientific considerations. Second-rate movies and other manifestations of mediocrity and "bad taste" have a great deal to tell us about our society.

It may be best to think of our culture as something like an onion, and as we peel away the outer layers, we find, ultimately, a core of myth that has shaped everything else.

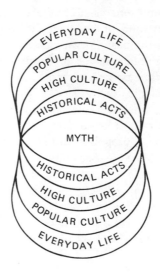

When we can see this mythical component in the things around us, we are equipped to probe our culture. It is also necessary to have a degree of familiarity with certain disciplines and areas, such as psychoanalysis, sociology, anthropology, literary criticism. For we must consider the following questions:

Historical Analysis: When did whatever it is you are investigating get started? Is it different now from the way it used to be? If so, why? If not, why not? When was it popular? Was it popular at a particular time for a particular reason? What does it tell us about the period in which it was popular?

Comparative Analysis: Is the same thing done the same way elsewhere? Do different cultures or countries have variations that are interesting? Can we get any statistical information that might be of value?

Psychoanalytical Investigation: Does whatever it is you are studying take care of certain needs we all have? Does it help us deal with anxiety or frustration or anger? Does it reassure us? Calm us? Excite us? What are its functions as far as our "unconscious" is concerned? Is there a difference between its meaning to our unconscious and to what we are conscious of?

Sociological Analyses: What class levels are appealed to? Does your subject have a racial or ethnic slant to it? Does it appeal to some groups (whether they be of a class, religious, racial, geographic, or other group) and not others? Does it have any political significance?

Myth-Symbol-Ritual Analysis: Can your subject be related in any way to important myths which have either universal or particular (to a country or group) significance? Does it have a symbolic dimension to it which makes it interesting? Can your subject be looked upon as a kind of (or part of a) ritual?

Content Analysis: How often (many times per minute, page, episode) is a given kind of behavior (violence, stereotyping of people) observed? What are the basic ideas, values, images, and beliefs that are to be found in some publication or program—generally speaking, which is part of a series? What patterns emerge?

Popular culturists lack an academic identity. (Someone once described me as an unclassifiable image.) You have to be a generalist and interdisciplinarian to be a good pop culturist and it is not easy work, by any means. But pop culturists have the most fun! My great heroes are the two Marxes—Karl and Groucho—as well as Sigmund Freud and James Joyce. I have developed my own "school" for sociological investigation which I describe as the Berger "stream of consciousness school of psycho-social analysis." A few nasty people have interpreted this to mean that I make my stuff up as I go along, and just throw charts and diagrams in to fool sociologists.

Question: *Aren't you really a cultural anthropologist?*
Answer: *Isn't everyone?*

Of course, as a secret agent, I face many problems. How do I know I haven't been lied to? How do I know I haven't read "too much" into things? How do I know that my analyses are not too subjective? partial? superficial? too profound? How can I be sure that my suspicions about the meaning of things to people's psyches are correct? How can I be sure that what I'm interested in is not atypical and unusual? How can I be sure that my secrets are worth anything?

The answer is that I can't. All I can do is build a case which will convince a reasonable person that my secrets are valuable and worth something. I don't claim infallibility. I am a secret agent and not the Pope!

For as long as I can remember I have been complaining to myself that I don't have any ideas and have been wondering what the future will hold. And somehow, in the midst of a monumentality of trivia, by a process of spontaneous generation, an occasional insight appears. It is on the basis of these lucky accidents and a few ideas borrowed from here and there that I have done my work in pop culture.

I lack what is often called "the higher seriousness," but I feel I am much more serious than many solemn souls around me. How can somebody who spends his time analyzing the meaning of comic strips or commercials or graffiti or joke cycles be solemn? It is possible but it would not be appropriate.

In which a man without ideas offers a
number of them to think about

- Do Freudians, with their passion for the Oedipus complex, have a natural affinity for *Pop* Culture? Do we think of the highway patrol, and police in general, as "father figures" who punish us for not playing with our toys the right way?
- Is the free-floating hostility that permeates our society a function of our individualism? Is it because we feel we are nobodies that we want to take part, even if as spectators, in "history?"
- Is romantic love connected with rugged individualism? After all, it is one of the few areas in which initiative counts.
- Is there a difference between a *lowest* common denominator and a *largest* common denominator?
- Clare Booth/Was Luce/But Martin/Was Luther.
  Aga/Khan/But Immanuel/Kant.
- What is the relation that exists between our economic system

and our cultural system? Is there such a thing as a "culture of capitalism?"

- All good things come to those Kuwait!
- Do Americans have a true sense of tragedy, or do we substitute irony for tragedy? An egalitarian society is not so much concerned with the fall of "great" men as with men making mistakes which are their undoing.
- Why is Popular Culture so unpopular?

Aids   *Secret Agent*

1. Arthur Berger informs us that he has been keeping a journal for over twenty years in which he has recorded his impressions about, among other things, popular culture and the mass media. He suggests, too, that we are surrounded by media which we accept as a natural part of the electronic landscape of the 1970s, often ignoring their "hidden meanings and latent functions." It is clear, then, that before we can analyze, interpret, and evaluate the aims, conventions, and effects of popular culture we must saturate ourselves in our environment and keep a record of our experiences. Emulate Berger's approach by keeping a detailed media log in which you record your investigations. Buy a small spiral notebook and carry it with you at all times. Divide it into sections for each of the following: advertising, propaganda, magazines, newspapers, comics, television, film, and music. For each entry, fill in the following information:

    a. Title and brief content summary
    b. Intended audience: Characterize by age, sex, race, socio-economic level, educational background.
    c. Purpose of the communication: Information, entertainment, persuasion, or a combination of the three.
    d. Stimulus factors: How is your attention attracted? How is it held? External stimulus factors include large size, loudness, intensity, isolation, repetition, contrast, movement, color, novelty, and humor. Internal factors include your interests, hopes, and fears; your basic and learned needs.
    e. Persona: How does the communicator present himself or herself to the audience?
    f. Characters: Roles and stereotypes.

2. Berger notes that every media form has "a 'content' of its own, and to neglect formal and structural matters is simple-minded." What

writers in this unit have neglected the forms of the media they are discussing? What writers have made form the central focus of their discussions? How does Berger himself define "content"?

3. Do you agree with Berger that "second-rate movies and other mani- festations of mediocrity and 'bad taste' have a great deal to tell us about our society"? What does this statement reveal about Berger's approach to popular culture?

4. Berger suggests that pop culture critics must have a familiarity with a number of disciplines before they can answer certain basic questions about contemporary culture and media. What are these disciplines? What questions should you always ask when dealing with popular culture artifacts? Apply some of the questions to an artifact of your choice, i.e., a song lyric, an advertisement, a film, a comic book, a popular novel or story.

5. The tone of Berger's essay is very personal, if not confessional and casual. How does it differ from the other essays in this unit in its use of authorities, allusions, and documentation? Do you find Berger interesting as well as informative? What effective writing strategies can be learned by studying Berger's tone?

A Theory of Mass Culture

DWIGHT MACDONALD

For about a century, Western culture has really been two cultures: the traditional kind—let us call it "High Culture" —that is chronicled in the textbooks, and a "Mass Culture" manufactured wholesale for the market. In the old art forms, the artisans of Mass Culture have long been at work: in the novel, the line stretches from Eugène Sue to Lloyd C. Douglas;[1] in music, from Offenbach to Tin-Pan Alley;[2] in art from the chromo to Maxfield Parrish[3] and Norman Rockwell; in architecture, from Victorian Gothic to suburban Tudor. Mass Culture has also developed new media of its own, into which the serious artist rarely ventures: radio, the movies, comic books, detective stories, science fiction, television.

It is sometimes called "Popular Culture," but I think "Mass Culture" a more accurate term, since its distinctive mark is that it is solely and directly an article for mass consumption, like chewing gum. A work of High Culture is occasionally popular, after all, though this is increasingly rare. Thus Dickens was even more popular than his contemporary, G. A. Henty,[4] the difference being that he was an artist, communicating his individual vision to other individuals, while Henty was an impersonal manufacturer of an impersonal commodity for the masses.

THE NATURE OF MASS CULTURE

The historical reasons for the growth of Mass Culture since the early 1800's are well known. Political democracy and popular education broke down the old upper-class monopoly of culture. Business enterprise found a profitable market in the cultural demands of the newly awakened masses, and the advance of technology made possible the cheap production of books, periodicals, pictures, music, and furniture, in sufficient quantities to satisfy this market. Modern technology also created new media such as the movies and television which are specially well adapted to mass manufacture and distribution.

The phenomenon is thus peculiar to modern times and differs radically from what was hitherto known as art or culture. It is true that Mass Culture began as, and to some extent still is, a parasitic, a cancerous growth on High Culture. As Clement Greenberg pointed out in "Avant-Garde and *Kitsch*" (*Partisan Review*, Fall, 1939): "The precondition of *kitsch* (a German term for 'Mass Culture') is the availability close at hand of a fully matured cultural tradition, whose discoveries, acquisitions, and perfected self-consciousness *kitsch* can take advantage of for its own ends." The connection, however, is not

Excerpt from Dwight Macdonald, "A Theory of Mass Culture," *Diogenes* (summer 1953), pp. 1–17. Reprinted by permission of the author.

[1]Eugène Sue (1804–57), French novelist, author of *The Mysteries of Paris* and *The Wandering Jew*, both widely translated; Lloyd C. Douglas, American novelist, author of *The Robe*. (eds.)

[2]Jacques Offenbach (1819–80), French composer of over a hundred operettas. (eds.)

[3]Maxfield Parrish (1870–1966), American painter and book illustrator. (eds.)

[4]George A. Henty (1832–1902), English journalist and author of eighty popular adventure books for boys. (eds.)

that of the leaf and the branch but rather that of the caterpillar and the leaf. *Kitsch* "mines" High Culture the way improvident frontiersmen mine the soil, extracting its riches and putting nothing back. Also, as *kitsch* develops, it begins to draw on its own past, and some of it evolves so far away from High Culture as to appear quite disconnected from it.

It is also true that Mass Culture is to some extent a continuation of the old Folk Art which until the Industrial Revolution was the culture of the common people, but here, too, the differences are more striking than the similarities. Folk Art grew from below. It was a spontaneous, autochthonous[5] expression of the people, shaped by themselves, pretty much without the benefit of High Culture, to suit their own needs. Mass Culture is imposed from above. It is fabricated by technicians hired by business; its audiences are passive consumers, their participation limited to the choice between buying and not buying. The Lords of *kitsch*, in short, exploit the cultural needs of the masses in order to make a profit and/or to maintain their class rule—in Communist countries, only the second purpose obtains. (It is very difficult to *satisfy* popular tastes, as Robert Burns'[6] poetry did, and to exploit them, as Hollywood does.) Folk Art was the people's own institution, their private little garden walled off from the great formal park of their masters' High Culture. But Mass Culture breaks down the wall, integrating the masses into a debased form of High Culture and thus becoming an instrument of political domination. If one had no other data to go on, the nature of Mass Culture would reveal capitalism to be an exploitive class society and not the harmonious commonwealth it is sometimes alleged to be. The same goes even more strongly for

Photo/David Umberger

[5]*Autochthonous:* native or indigenous. (eds.)
[6]Robert Burns (1759–96), Scottish lyric, descriptive, and narrative poet. (eds.)

Soviet Communism and *its* special kind of Mass Culture.

GRESHAM'S LAW IN CULTURE

The separation of Folk Art and High Culture in fairly watertight compartments corresponded to the sharp line once drawn between the common people and the aristocracy. The eruption of the masses onto the political stage has broken down this compartmentation, with disastrous cultural results. Whereas Folk Art had its own special quality, Mass Culture is at best a vulgarized reflection of High Culture. And whereas High Culture could formerly ignore the mob and seek to please only the *cognoscenti*, it must now compete with Mass Culture or be merged into it.

The problem is acute in the United States and not just because a prolific Mass Culture exists here. If there were a clearly defined cultural *élite*, then the masses could have their *kitsch* and the *élite* could have its High Culture, with everybody happy. But the boundary line is blurred. A statistically significant part of the population, I venture to guess, is chronically confronted with a choice between going to the movies or to a concert, between reading Tolstoy or a detective story, between looking at old masters or at a TV show; i.e., the pattern of their cultural lives is "open" to the point of being porous. Good art competes with *kitsch*, serious ideas compete with commercialized formulae—and the advantage lies all on one side. There seems to be a Gresham's Law in cultural as well as monetary circulation: bad stuff drives out the good, since it is more easily understood and enjoyed. It is this facility of access which at once sells *kitsch* on a wide market and also prevents it from achieving quality.

Clement Greenberg writes that the special aesthetic quality of *kitsch* is that it "predigests art for the spectator and spares him effort, provides him with a shortcut to the pleasures of art that detours what is necessarily difficult in genuine art" because it includes the spectator's reactions in the work of art itself instead of forcing him to make his own responses. Thus "Eddie Guest and the Indian Love Lyrics are more 'poetic' than T. S. Eliot and Shakespeare." And so, too, our "collegiate Gothic" such as the Harkness Quadrangle at Yale is more picturesquely Gothic than Chartres, and a pinup girl smoothly airbrushed by Petty is more sexy than a real naked woman.

When to this ease of consumption is added *kitsch's* ease of production because of its standardized nature, its prolific growth is easy to understand. It threatens High Culture by its sheer pervasiveness, its brutal, overwhelming *quantity*. The upper classes, who begin by using it to make money from the crude tastes of the masses and to dominate them politically, end by finding their own culture attacked and even threatened with destruction by the instrument they have thoughtlessly employed. (The same irony may be observed in modern politics, where most swords seem to have two edges; thus Nazism began as a tool of the big bourgeoisie and the army *Junkers* but ended by using *them* as *its* tools.)

HOMOGENIZED CULTURE

Like nineteenth-century capitalism, Mass Culture is a dynamic, revolutionary force, breaking down the old barriers of class, tradition, taste, and dissolving all cultural distinctions. It mixes and scrambles everything together, producing what might be called homogenized culture, after another American achievement, the homogenization process that distributes the globules of cream evenly throughout the milk instead of allowing them to float separately on top. It thus destroys all values, since value judgments imply discriminations. Mass Culture is very, very democratic: it absolutely refuses to discriminate against, or between, anything or anybody. All is grist to its mill, and all comes out finely ground indeed.

Consider *Life*, a typical homogenized mass-circulation magazine. It appears on the mahogany library tables of the rich, the glass end tables of the middle-class and the oilcloth-covered kitchen tables of the poor. Its contents are as thoroughly homogenized as its circulation. The same issue will contain a serious exposition of atomic theory alongside a disquisition on Rita Hayworth's love life; photos of starving Korean children picking garbage from the ruins of Pusan and of sleek models wearing adhesive brassieres; an editorial hailing Bertrand Russell on his eightieth birthday ("A GREAT MIND IS STILL ANNOYING AND ADORNING OUR AGE") across from a full-page photo of a housewife arguing with an umpire at a baseball game ("MOM GETS THUMB"); a cover announcing in the same size type "A NEW FOREIGN POLICY, BY JOHN FOSTER DULLES" and "KERIMA: HER MARATHON KISS IS A MOVIE SENSATION"; nine color pages of Renoirs plus a memoir by his son, followed by a full-page picture of a roller-skating horse. The advertisements, of course, provide even more scope for the editor's homogenizing talents, as when a full-page photo of a ragged Bolivian peon grinningly drunk on coca leaves (which Mr. Luce's conscientious reporters tell us he chews to narcotize his chronic hunger pains) appears opposite an ad of a pretty, smiling, well-dressed American mother with her two pretty, smiling, well-dressed children (a boy and a girl, of course—children are always homogenized in American ads) looking raptly at a clown on a TV set ("RCA VICTOR BRINGS YOU A NEW KIND OF TELEVISION—SUPER SETS WITH 'PICTURE POWER' "). The peon would doubtless find the juxtaposition piquant if he could afford a copy of *Life*, which, fortunately for the Good Neighbor Policy, he cannot.

ADULTIZED CHILDREN AND INFANTILE ADULTS

The homogenizing effects of *kitsch* also blur age lines. It would be interesting to know how many adults read the comics. We do know that comic books are by far the favorite reading matter of our soldiers and sailors, that some forty million comic books are sold a month, and that some seventy million people (most of whom must be adults, there just aren't that many kids) are estimated to read the newspaper comic strips every day. We also know that movie Westerns and radio and TV programs such as "The Lone Ranger" and "Captain Video" are by no means enjoyed only by children. On the other hand, children have access to such grown-up media as the movies, radio and TV. (Note that these newer arts are the ones which blur age lines because of the extremely modest demands they make on the audience's cultural equipment; thus there are many children's books but few children's movies.)

This merging of the child and grown-up audience means: (1) infantile regression of the latter, who, unable to cope with the strains and complexities of modern life, escape via *kitsch* (which in turn, confirms and enhances their infantilism); (2) "over-stimulation" of the former, who grow up too fast. Or, as Max Horkheimer well puts it: "Development has ceased to exist. The child is grown up as soon as he can walk, and the grown-up in principle always remains the same." Also note (a) our cult of youth, which makes 18–22 the most admired and desired period of life, and (b) the sentimental worship of Mother ("Momism") as if we couldn't bear to grow up and be on our own. Peter Pan might be a better symbol of America than Uncle Sam.

IDOLS OF CONSUMPTION

Too little attention has been paid to the connection of our Mass Culture with the historical evolution of American Society. In *Radio Research, 1942–43* (Paul F. Lazarfeld, ed.), Leo Lowenthal compared the biographical articles in *Collier's* and *The Saturday Evening Post* for 1901 and 1940–41 and found that in the forty-year interval the proportion of articles about business and professional men and political leaders had declined while those about entertainers had gone up 50 per cent. Furthermore, the 1901 entertainers are mostly serious artists—opera singers, sculptors, pianists, etc.—while those of 1941 are *all* movie stars, baseball players, and such; and even the "serious" heroes in 1941 aren't so very serious after all: the businessmen and politicians are freaks, oddities, not the really powerful leaders as in 1901. The 1901 *Satevepost* heroes he calls "idols of production," those of today "idols of consumption."

Lowenthal notes that the modern *Satevepost* biographee is successful not because of his own personal abilities so much as because he "got the breaks." The whole competitive struggle is presented as a lottery in which a few winners, no more talented or energetic than any one else, drew the lucky tickets. The effect on the mass reader is at once consoling (it might have been me) and deadening to effort, ambition (there are no rules, so why struggle?). It is striking how closely this evolution parallels the country's economic development. Lowenthal observes that the "idols of production" maintained their dominance right through the twenties. The turning point was the 1929 depression when the problem became how to consume goods rather than how to produce them, and also when the arbitrariness and chaos of capitalism was forcefully brought home to the mass man. So he turned to "idols of consumption," or rather these were now offered him by the manufacturers of Mass Culture, and he accepted them. "They seem to lead to a dream world of the masses," observes Lowenthal, "who are no longer capable or willing to conceive of biographies primarily as a means of orientation and education. . . . He, the American mass man, as reflected in his 'idols of consumption' appears no longer as a center of outwardly directed energies and actions on whose work and efficiency might depend mankind's progress. Instead of the 'givers' we are faced with the 'takers'. . . . They seem to stand for a phantasmagoria of world-wide social security—an attitude which asks for no more than to be served with the things needed for reproduction and recreation, an attitude which has lost every primary interest in how to invent, shape, or apply the tools leading to such purposes of mass satisfaction."

THE PROBLEM OF THE MASSES

Conservatives such as Ortega y Gasset and T. S. Eliot[7] argue that since "the revolt of the masses" has led to the horrors of totalitarianism (and of California roadside architecture), the only hope is to rebuild the old class walls and bring the masses once more under aristocratic control. They think of the popular as synonymous with cheap and vulgar. Marxian radicals and liberals, on the other hand, see the masses as intrinsically healthy but as the dupes and victims of cultural exploitation by the Lords of *kitsch*—in the style of Rousseau's "noble savage" idea. If only the masses were offered good stuff instead of *kitsch*, how they would eat it up! How the level of Mass Culture would rise! Both these diagnoses seem to me fallacious: they assume that Mass Culture is (in the conservative view) or could be (in the liberal view) an expression of *people*, like Folk Art, whereas actually it is an expression of *masses*, a very different thing.

There are theoretical reasons why Mass Culture is not and can never be any good. I take it as axiomatic that culture can only be produced by and for human beings. But in so far as people are organized (more strictly, disorganized) as masses, they lose their human identity and quality. For the masses are in historical time what a crowd is in space: a large quantity of people unable to express themselves as human beings because they are related to one another neither as individuals nor as members of communities— indeed, they are not related *to each other*

at all, but only to something distant, abstract, nonhuman: a football game, or bargain sale, in the case of a crowd, a system of industrial production, a party or a State in the case of the masses. The mass man is a solitary atom, uniform with and undifferentiated from thousands and millions of other atoms who go to make up "the lonely crowd," as David Riesman well calls American society. A folk or a people, however, is a community, i.e., a group of individuals linked to each other by common interests, work, traditions, values, and sentiments; something like a family, each of whose members has a special place and function as an individual while at the same time sharing the group's interests (family budget), sentiments (family quarrels), and culture (family jokes). The scale is small enough so that it "makes a difference" what the individual does, a first condition for human—as against mass—existence. He is at once more important as an individual than in mass society and at the same time more closely integrated into the community, his creativity nourished by a rich combination of individualism and communalism. (The great culture-bearing *élites* of the past have been communities of this kind.) In contrast, a mass society, like a crowd, is so undifferentiated and loosely structured that its atoms, in so far as human values go, tend to cohere only along the line of the least common denominator; its morality sinks to that of its most brutal and primitive members, its taste to that of the least sensitive and most ignorant. And in addition to everything else, the scale is simply too big, there are just *too many people*.

[7]Ortega y Gasset (1883–1955), Spanish essayist and philosopher, who believed that unless the masses can be controlled by an intellectual elite, chaos will result; T. S. Eliot (1888–1965), English poet and critic, whose major poem, *The Waste Land* (1922), expresses the anguish and barrenness of modern life. (eds.)

Yet this collective monstrosity, "the masses," "the public," is taken as a human norm by the scientific and artistic technicians of our Mass Culture. They at once degrade the public by treating it as an object, to be handled with the lack of ceremony and the objectivity of medical students dissecting a corpse, and at the same time flatter it, pander to its level of taste and ideas by taking these as the criterion of reality (in the case of questionnaire-sociologists and other "social scientists") or of art (in the case of the Lords of *kitsch*). When one hears a questionnaire-sociologist talk about how he will "set up" an investigation, one feels he regards people as a herd of dumb animals, as mere congeries of conditioned reflexes, his calculation being which reflex will be stimulated by which question. At the same time, of necessity, he sees the statistical majority as the great Reality, the secret of life he is trying to find out; like the *kitsch* Lords, he is wholly without values, willing to accept any idiocy if it is held by many people. The aristocrat and the democrat both criticize and argue with popular taste, the one with hostility, the other in friendship, for both attitudes proceed from a set of values. This is less degrading to the masses than the "objective" approach of Hollywood and the questionnaire-sociologists, just as it is less degrading to a man to be shouted at in anger than to be quietly assumed to be part of a machine. But the *plebs* have their dialectical revenge: complete indifference to their human *quality* means complete prostration before their statistical *quantity*, so that a movie magnate who cynically "gives the public what it wants"—i.e., assumes it wants trash—sweats with terror if box-office returns drop 10 per cent.

THE FUTURE OF HIGH CULTURE: DARK

The conservative proposal to save culture by restoring the old class lines has a more solid historical base than the Marxian hope for a new democratic, classless culture, for, with the possible (and important) exception of Periclean Athens, all the great cultures of the past were *élite* cultures. Politically, however, it is without meaning in a world dominated by the two great mass nations, U.S.A. and U.S.S.R. and becoming more industrialized, more massified all the time. The only practical thing along those lines would be to revive the *cultural élite* which the Avantgarde created.[8] As I have already noted, the Avantgarde is now dying, partly from internal causes, partly suffocated by the competing Mass Culture, where it is not being absorbed into it. Of course this process has not reached 100 per cent, and doubtless never will unless the country goes either Fascist or Communist. There are still islands above the flood for those determined enough to reach them, and to stay on them: as Faulkner has shown, a writer can even use Hollywood instead of being used by it, if his purpose is firm enough. But the homogenization of High and Mass Culture has gone far and is going farther all the time, and there seems little reason to expect a revival of Avantgardism, that is, of a successful countermovement to Mass Culture. Particularly not in this country,

[8]As Macdonald points out in an earlier section of this essay, the Avantgarde movement (1890–1930) was an attempt by the intellectual elite "to fence off some area where the serious artist could still function." (eds.)

where the blurring of class lines, the absence of a stable cultural tradition, and the greater facilities for manufacturing and marketing *kitsch* all work in the other direction. The result is that our intelligentsia is remarkably small, weak, and disintegrated. One of the odd things about the American cultural scene is how many brainworkers there are and how few intellectuals, defining the former as specialists whose thinking is pretty much confined to their limited "fields" and the latter as persons who take all culture for their province. Not only are there few intellectuals, but they don't hang together, they have very little *esprit de corps*, very little sense of belonging to a community; they are so isolated from each other they don't even bother to quarrel—there hasn't been a really good fight among them since the Moscow Trials.

THE FUTURE OF MASS CULTURE: DARKER

If the conservative proposal to save our culture via the aristocratic Avantgarde seems historically unlikely, what of the democratic-liberal proposal? Is there a reasonable prospect of raising the level of Mass Culture? In his recent book, *The Great Audience*, Gilbert Seldes argues there is. He blames the present sad state of our Mass Culture on the stupidity of the Lords of *kitsch*, who underestimate the mental age of the public; the arrogance of the intellectuals, who make the same mistake and so snobbishly refuse to work for such mass media as radio, TV and movies; and the passivity of the public itself, which doesn't insist on better Mass Cultural products. This diagnosis seems to me superficial in that it blames everything on subjective, moral factors: stupidity, perversity, failure of will. My own feeling is that, as in the case of the alleged responsibility of the German (or Russian) people for the horrors of Nazism (or Soviet Communism), it is unjust to blame social groups for this result. Human beings have been caught up in the inexorable workings of a mechanism that forces them, with a pressure only heroes can resist (and one cannot *demand* that anybody be a hero, though one can *hope* for it), into its own pattern. I see Mass Culture as a reciprocating engine, and who is to say, once it has been set in motion, whether the stroke or the counterstroke is "responsible" for its continued action?

The Lords of *kitsch* sell culture to the masses. It is a debased, trivial culture that voids both the deep realities (sex, death, failure, tragedy) and also the simple, spontaneous pleasures, since the realities would be too real and the pleasures too *lively* to induce what Mr. Seldes calls "the mood of consent," i.e., a narcotized acceptance of Mass Culture and of the commodities it sells as a substitute for the unsettling and unpredictable (hence unsalable) joy, tragedy, wit, change, originality and beauty of real life. The masses, debauched by several generations of this sort of thing, in turn come to demand trivial and comfortable cultural products. Which came first, the chicken or the egg, the mass demand or its satisfaction (and further stimulation) is a question as academic as it is unanswerable. The engine is reciprocating and shows no signs of running down.

Indeed, far from Mass Culture getting better, we will be lucky if it doesn't get worse. When shall we see another popular humorist like Sholem Aleichem, whose books are still being translated from the Yiddish and for whose funeral in 1916 a hundred thousand inhabitants of the Bronx turned out? Or Finlay Peter Dunne, whose Mr. Dooley commented on the American scene with such wit that Henry Adams was a faithful reader and Henry James, on his famous return to his native land, wanted to meet only one American author, Dunne? Since Mass Culture is not an art form but a manufactured commodity, it tends always downward, toward cheapness —and so standardization—of production. Thus, T. W. Adorno has noted, in his brilliant essay "On Popular Music" (*Studies in Philosophy and Social Science*, New York, No. 1, 1941) that the chorus of every popular song *without* exception has the same number of bars, while Mr. Seldes remarks that Hollywood movies are cut in a uniformly rapid tempo, a shot rarely being held more than forty-five seconds, which gives them a standardized effect in contrast to the varied tempo of European film cutting. This sort of standardization means that what may have begun as something fresh and original is repeated until it becomes a nerveless routine—*vide* what happened to Fred Allen as a radio comedian. The only time Mass Culture is good is at the very beginning, before the "for-

mula" has hardened, before the money boys and efficiency experts and audience-reaction analysts have moved in. Then for a while it may have the quality of real Folk Art. But the Folk artist today lacks the cultural roots and the intellectual toughness (both of which the Avantgarde artist has relatively more of) to resist for long the pressures of Mass Culture. His taste can be easily corrupted, his sense of his own special talent and limitations obscured, as in what happened to Disney between the gay, inventive early Mickey Mouse and Silly Symphony cartoons and the vulgar pretentiousness of *Fantasia* and heavy-handed sentimentality of *Snow White*, or to Westbrook Pegler who has regressed from an excellent sports writer, with a sure sense of form and a mastery of colloquial satire, into the rambling, coarse-grained, garrulous political pundit of today. Whatever virtues the Folk artist has, and they are many, staying power is not one of them. And staying power is the essential virtue of one who would hold his own against the spreading ooze of Mass Culture.

Aids   *A Theory of Mass Culture*

1. According to Macdonald, what are the historical reasons for the growth of mass culture?

2. What precisely does Macdonald mean by the term "mass culture"? Make a complete list of the defining terms as they appear throughout the essay. Locate some mass culture artifacts and explain how they differ from high culture or folk culture.

3. What is the difference between satisfying popular tastes and exploiting them?

4. At the beginning of his essay Macdonald makes a distinction between

"mass" culture and "popular" culture. Mass culture denotes impersonal, mass-produced commodities intended for mass consumption:
"It is fabricated by technicians hired by business; its audiences are
passive consumers, their participation limited to the choice between
buying and not buying." For Macdonald, popular culture, by contrast,
is not synonymous with mass culture. Although he does not offer
a full definition of popular culture, he clearly associates it with folk
art, "a spontaneous autochthonous expression of the people, shaped
by themselves, pretty much without the benefits of High Culture,
to suit their own needs." Thus, popular culture, as opposed to mass
culture, refers to democratically produced and shared art and entertainment. Locate some examples of popular culture in your own
environment. You might consider, for instance, the differences between the poetry in a local literary magazine and the poetry of
advertising or of greeting cards, the hand-thrown pottery of a local
potter and the mass-produced versions in the corner giftshop, or your
own efforts at patching and fringing your denim jeans with the
ready-to-wear products at a clothing store.

5. Compare Macdonald's conception of popular culture with those of
   Russel Nye and Arthur Berger. Do they make the same distinction
   between mass culture and popular culture or do they treat the
   two terms as being synonymous? Are their positions weakened by
   their blurring of this important distinction?

6. Examine Macdonald's use of analogy in defining mass culture, i.e.,
   Gresham's law in culture and homogenized culture. Do these comparisons help us to understand otherwise difficult concepts?

7. How does Macdonald's view of esthetics (the branch of philosophy
   that provides a theory of beauty, good taste, and of the fine arts)
   differ from that of Arthur Berger in "Secret Agent"? Under what
   very different assumptions are the two writers operating? With
   which view do you sympathize? why?

8. What precisely is "the problem of the masses"? What is the "mass,"
   and how does it differ from a "community of individuals"? Who
   creates the "mass"? Is it simply a sociological construct by the
   Lords of Kitsch?

9. Macdonald cites a 1943 study by Leo Lowenthal on the high proportion of media space given over to mass culture heroes, such as
   movie stars, pop singers, and sports figures. Is this observation still
   valid today? Examine a current magazine, such as *Time, Sports
   Illustrated,* or *People,* and estimate the proportion of serious versus
   popular idols of consumption. Who are today's culture heroes? What

values do they represent? What is the difference between a person and a personality?

10. What, according to Macdonald, is the future of high culture in America? Keeping in mind that his essay was published in 1953, do you think that Macdonald's dire predictions have been confirmed in the 1960s and 1970s?

11. What, according to Macdonald, is the future of mass culture? Is mass culture today "a debased, trivial culture that voids both the deep realities (sex, death, failure, tragedy) and also the simple, spontaneous pleasures"?

12. All writers make use of connotative language, but political writers tend to be especially conscious of this tool. Dwight Macdonald was known as a radical in the 1930s. What does his use of language in "A Theory of Mass Culture" reveal about his political and social attitudes in 1953 when the essay was published? Reviewing what you know about propaganda devices (see p. 118), locate some examples of the techniques in Macdonald's essay. That is, does he attempt to manipulate the attitudes of his audience by using name calling, glittering generalities, card stacking, and transfer? Do you agree with Macdonald's view of mass culture?

13. Abstractions are usually difficult to define because they depend on no concrete referents. In order to define an abstraction, one must depend on comparison and contrast, common usage, examples, and other devices. Such definitions are called extended definitions. Macdonald provides us with an extended definition of mass culture in "A Theory of Mass Culture." Emulating Macdonald's approach, write your own extended definition of an abstract term like high culture, folk art, or popular culture.

14. The term *kitsch* appears throughout Macdonald's essay. *Kitsch*, a German or Russian word for mass culture, belongs to all the arts, to all human forms of expression on every level of society—from the plaster reproductions on the marble coffee tables of the rich to the plastic Walt Disney characters on the lawns of the masses. According to Gillo Dorfles, a kitsch artifact may include some or all of the following characteristics: (a) sensationalism (focus on sex or violence); (b) sentimentalism (appeal to the heart, not the head); (c) stereotyping (simplistic and overgeneralized types); (d) expendability (planned obsolescence); (e) escapism (arrests thought, seeks to avoid ugliness); and (f) an element of a legitimate work of art transferred from its real ethos to another and used for a different purpose (reproductions and condensations—for example, the plastic

copies of great monuments, paintings, or statues transformed into paperweights, designs on fabric, ashtrays, and souvenirs). Kitsch, then, transforms the authentic creation into something inferior, false, sentimental, and no longer genuine. The greatest repositories of kitsch in the United States are undoubtedly the national discount stores. Make a pilgrimage to one of these meccas of kitsch, and write a paper or report in which you describe in vivid detail the object's kitschness, making sure to incorporate the brand name and advertising claims into your description. Next, formulate a precise thesis about the subject of kitsch, and using everything in your description, write an argumentative paper or speech on the effects and value of kitsch.

15. Before the advent of mass culture, there were, says Dwight Macdonald, two cultures, one composed of a minority of wealthy, well-educated aristocrats, the other of the majority of the common people. Homogenized mass society developed by borrowing from the preceding high and folk cultures, "extracting its riches and putting nothing back." Beginning in the eighteenth century, writers, artists, and intellectuals have attacked the sterility, tastelessness, and conformity of the middle classes, but the theme reaches its climax in twentieth-century American literature, music, and film. Examine one or more of the following works and determine what attributes of mass man are being criticized. What literary vehicle (exposition, description, argument, polemic, satire, science fiction) does your work employ? Do you feel that the attack is justified? (Poetry: T. S. Eliot's "The Waste Land," Hart Crane's "The Bridge," Allen Ginsberg's "A Supermarket in California," Richard Brautigan's "The Pill versus The Springhill Mine Disaster." Fiction and essays: Nathanael West's *Miss Lonelyhearts* and *The Day of the Locust;* Terry Southern's *The Magic Christian;* Ray Bradbury's *Fahrenheit 451;* Jerzy Kosinski's *Being There;* Evelyn Waugh (British), *The Loved One;* Tom Wolfe's *The Electric Kool-Aid Acid Test, The Pump House Gang,* and *Radical Chic & Mau-mauing the Flak Catchers;* Douglas M. Davis, ed., *The World of Black Humor;* and Bruce Jay Friedman, ed., *Black Humor.* Film: *The Graduate, A Clockwork Orange, Carnal Knowledge, Diary of a Mad Housewife, Petulia, Divorce American Style, Dr. Strangelove, Tommy,* and *Nashville,* to name only a few. Music: Simon and Garfunkel, the Beatles, Bob Dylan, and so on.

Photo/David Umberger

Unit II

Commercial and Public Propaganda: The Medium Is the Barrage

B oth advertising and public propaganda are types of persuasive communication; as such, their techniques and goals are those of persuasion in general: to reach a defined audience, through specified media, for a specific purpose. Commercial and public propaganda, however, differ from persuasion based on rational discourse by appealing mainly to the emotional, irrational hopes, fears, and anxieties of our natures. A relatively heavy emphasis on deliberateness, manipulativeness, and distortion also distinguishes some advertising and propaganda from the free and easy exchange of ideas, let us say in rational argumentation or in responsible education. Unlike the educator, who attempts to present fairly all sides of an issue, the propagandist and, in some cases, the ad man try to divert attention from the truth by a conscious manipulation of language, logic, and emotions. The important word in the last sentence is *try*. Most recent authorities on public persuasion agree that advertising and propaganda cannot actually control our behavior. Recent studies have also shown that the traditional model of a passive audience exploited by the media ignores the fact that mass communication, given large and diverse audiences, varies greatly in its impact.[1] Advertisers and propagandists, nevertheless, continue to attempt to influence our behavior in a number of ways.

Advertising is big business in America. This year alone $40 billion is being invested in the creation and dissemination of advertising messages in the six major media: newspapers, television, direct mail, magazines, radio, and outdoor displays. Thus, for each man, woman, and child in the United States, the merchandisers are investing about $200 a year for advertising. The consumer, consequently, is being barraged with up to 1600 advertising messages, slogans, symbols, and trademarks a day; of these, only 80 ads engage the consumer's attention. Why is all this money and energy expended on advertising? Clearly, advertising is one of the most important economic and cultural forces in a capitalistic, profit-oriented society. It plays a crucial role in the distribution of products from popsicles to politicians, in influencing people to want better products and services, and in elevating the standard of living. It functions to inform and to persuade. It informs consumers about new products and services. It stimulates and creates wants. It indicates differences between various products and services. It shows how stirred-up wants and desires can be fulfilled by particular products.

Advertisers attempt to influence our buying in a number of ways. In the beginning, ads were an effective means to attract the consumer's attention for the purpose of transmitting information. The earliest known advertisement, for instance, is a 3000-year-old papyrus sheet offering a reward for the return of a runaway slave. With the development of printing, the increase in trade, and the rising literacy of the consumer, more attention was paid to the medium or language of communication itself. An examination of eighteenth- and nineteenth-century ads reveals that merchandisers were becoming increasingly aware of stimulus factors, such as large size, color, isolation, repetition, and contrast. The ad people learned, however, that to attract the consumers' attention was not enough; some means had to be devised to hold their attention. Thus, ad people became interested in consumers themselves—their socioeconomic characteristics, such as age, sex, race, income, and occupation. Market research, which has become an essential part of every advertising campaign, collects and analyzes data bearing on the distribution of the product to be advertised. Not content to probe into socioeconomic categories, after World War II the merchandisers began to enlist the services of psychologists and sociologists, who developed techniques for probing into the psyches of the consumers in order to reach the subconscious mind. As Vance Packard points out in "The Ad and the Id," motivational research, or simply MR, provided the ad person with another source of human data—the hopes, fears, ideologies, and myths of consumers. The assumption of the MR people, Packard asserts, is that people do not buy products, they buy psychological satisfaction. Women don't buy soap, they buy the promise of beauty and immortality. Men don't buy automobiles, they buy sexual power. The MR people also assume,

[1] See, for instance, Raymond A. Bauer's "The Obstinate Audience," *American Psychologist* (May 1964), pp. 319–28.

perhaps incorrectly as some recent research claims,[2] that the most effective ad is the one that best manipulates these hidden desires, dreams, beliefs, symbols, and myths. These so-called "hidden persuaders" have been isolated and described by Vance Packard, who, as you will see, is a vehement critic of the depth approach in advertising. The ad people, Packard concludes, in attempting to merchandise such basic needs as emotional security, reassurance of worth, ego gratification, and love objects, invade the privacy of our minds.

Whether this *psyche sell* is effective or not is one of the questions raised by Daniel Henninger in "Worriers, Swingers, Shoppers." Essentially updating Vance Packard's 1957 analysis of advertising practices, but now in television, Henninger outlines how computers have supplemented the psychiatric couch in targeting potential segments of consumers. In spite of these efforts, however, many consumers develop perceptual screens to block out the attempts at hard sell, soft sell, and psyche sell.

In addition to stirring up basic human cravings, which the ad people then attempt to assuage with particular products, the depth manipulators also deliberately exploit the cultural myths inherent in American life. According to John R. Cashill in "Packaging Pop Mythology," a cultural myth is a pattern of beliefs, assumptions, and knowledge assimilated by a group of people. These myths, which help to explain or interpret unexplainable or unknown events and persons, permeate the mass and exist on a largely subconscious level. Myths that are characteristic of American cultural life are (a) the myth of manifest destiny, (b) the racial myth of "white makes right," (c) the myth of success and the Puritan ethic, (d) the myth of democratic brotherhood, (e) the middle landscape myth, (f) and the myth of the West as the promised land. The myth of the American West, Cashill points out, is seen not only in a famous advertising campaign for Marlboro cigarettes, but, more important, in the basic pattern of suburban life— the archetypal suburbanite buys a quarter-acre ranchette on Old Farm Road, builds a one-level ranch-style house, surrounds it with corral fencing from Sears, and parks his Mustang, Pinto, or Maverick in the driveway. This phenomenon has also been analyzed by Marshall McLuhan as an attempt by urban man, when confronted with a totally new situation (the electronic revolution), to attach himself to the objects and flavor of the most recent past: "We look at the present through a rear-view mirror. We march backwards into the future. Suburbia lives imaginatively in Bonanza-land."[3]

So far we have seen how advertisers attempt to manipulate our psyches and our myths for a very precise material goal: to sell products and services. The vehicle of this attempted manipulation is, of course, language, and no introduction to advertising would be complete without some attention

[2]According to William A. Yoell, in "The Abuse of Psychology by Marketing Men" (*Marketing/Communications,* August 1970, pp. 42–44), MR men have misused and abused psychological theories that have been repeatedly disproved: "No one has yet proved that psychological techniques designed to uncover causes of irrational behavior, emotional or psychotic behavior, traumatic experiences, personality defects, neuroses can and do determine why consumers buy automobiles, floor waxes."

[3]Marshall McLuhan, *The Medium Is the Massage* (New York: Bantam Books, 1967), p. 75.

to the linguistic artistry and tyranny of ads. Henryk Skolimowski, in "The Semantic Environment in the Age of Advertising," probes into the hidden force of language in shaping our consumer behavior. His thesis is that since advertisers have made some important discoveries about the power of language, we as consumers should know about these techniques in order to acquire some immunity. The linguistic techniques surveyed include these: (a) the use of an adjective vocabulary, with such words as *free, new,* and *soft,* which presumably have a hypnotic effect on us; (b) the use of performative utterances or imperative clauses, such as "Get a box today," "Buy now!" and "Try it, you'll like it," which command us to perform actions; and (c) the creation of pseudopoetry, complete with meter, rhyme, alliteration, and figurative language (similes and metaphors), whose ritualistic qualities have subconscious effects on listeners. These and other techniques, Skolimowski asserts, involve the distortion of language, the violation of logic, and the corruption of values; advertising, in short, constitutes Orwellian doubletalk. The author is alluding to the futuristic novel, *1984,* by George Orwell. In Orwell's Oceania, all media are controlled by the totalitarian government, which manipulates peoples' minds through a new language, Newspeak. The purpose of Newspeak, Orwell explains, is "not to extend but to diminish the range of thought."

For George Kirstein, however, the fictional future projected by George Orwell will never become reality because, as he points out in "The Day the Ads Stopped," consumer groups, led by militant women, successfully lobbied to have advertising banned by the Senate of the United States. Kirstein speculates that although newspapers and magazines would become more expensive and radio and television would have to be subsidized by listener/viewer subscriptions, the overall effect of the ban would be beneficial to society. Consumer products such as cosmetics, razor blades, and appliances would be reduced in price from 5 to 25 percent. In addition, urban blight would be eradicated by the removal of all outdoor display advertising. Mental blight would be cured by raising the educational and esthetic standards of television.

Kirstein's fictional speculation is not to be taken literally; it is a warning to advertisers of what may happen if they continue to ignore the public demand for responsible advertising. A decade ago the ad industry would have responded to these and other charges with utter contempt, but as the excerpt from Fairfax M. Cone's *With All Its Faults* makes clear, the ad industry, reeling from a two-pronged offensive by consumer groups and the Federal Trade Commission, is undergoing a period of intense self-examination. Pointing out that it is impossible to sell a bad product twice to the same person, Cone refutes the criticism that the majority of ads are dishonest and deceptive. If there is a problem in the industry, Cone maintains, it is the questionable taste of some ads. Most of the ads for the dreadful Ds—detergents, deodorants, dentifrices, and depilatories— would fall into the tasteless category. Cone blames this crudeness on the permissiveness of our times; he emphasizes that advertising always follows, never leads. Cone concludes his mandate by leveling three challenges to the American industry he helped to shape: (1) ads should never make odious comparisons between competitive products; (2) advertisers should play a personal role in community affairs; and (3) advertising should be used as an educational force in society. Although a growing number of advertisers are taking advertising beyond the mere hustling of consumer products and services, Cone argues that more advertisers need to put the public welfare ahead of corporate profits by explaining, attacking, or defending all manner of good and evil in our society. Some excellent examples of public service advertising, which Cone would like to see become the rule rather than the exception, can be seen in "Esquire's 3rd Annual Corporate Social Responsibility Advertising Awards." These ads clearly demonstrate that effective, responsible advertising does exist in America; they constitute counterevidence to the sweeping condemnation of all advertising by its severest critics.

In spite of the efforts at self-regulation and self-improvement, commercial as well as political persuaders are under attack from yet another flank— academe. In late 1971 a Committee on Public Doublespeak was formed by some teacher-members of the National Council of Teachers of English; the aims and goals of the committee are reflected in the following two resolutions passed by NCTE in 1971:

Resolved, That the National Council of Teachers of English find means to study dishonest and inhumane uses of language and literature by advertisers, to bring offenses to public attention, and to propose classroom techniques for preparing children to cope with commercial propaganda.

Resolved, That the National Council of Teachers of English find means to study the relation of language to public policy, to keep track of, publicize, and combat semantic distortion by public officials, candidates for office, political commentators, and all those who transmit through the mass media.

According to Hugh Rank, original chairman of the NCTE Committee on Doublespeak, we are experiencing today a propaganda blitz unequaled in human history:

In our daily, unnoticed environment we Americans are subjected to more ads and more political persuasion than ever generated in the supposedly "classic" propaganda campaigns of Nazi Germany. Granted, it's easy for us to recognize the overt, blatant propaganda machinery of Red China, with its blunt ballets, slogans, and posters. It's more difficult for us to be aware of our own environment, saturated with propaganda urging us to buy this product or that policy. [From the Introduction to *Language and Public Policy* (Urbana, Ill.: National Council of Teachers of English, 1974), edited by Hugh Rank.]

The term *propaganda,* which Rank applies to both commercial and political persuasion, is one of those protean words; depending on your point of view, it can take many different shapes and forms. The origin of the word is the Latin verb *propagare,* which denotes the gardener's practice of placing the fresh shoots of a plant into the earth in order to reproduce new plants. The term was first used in the sociological sense by the Roman Catholic Church to describe the work of the Congregatio de Propaganda Fide

(Congregation for the Propagation of the Faith), an organization of Catholic cardinals founded in 1622 to spread Christianity by preaching and by example. In its missionary and ecclesiastical sense, then, the word *propaganda* has beneficent connotations—at least to the proponents of Catholicism.

The word has yet another meaning in the Soviet Union; it is the reasoned use of historical and scientific arguments to indoctrinate the educated and enlightened. For the Russian, the term is closely associated with *agitation,* which is the use of slogans, symbols, and parables to exploit the grievances of the uneducated. The use of propaganda in this sense would be commendable and honest to a Russian. To the opponents of communism, however, this propaganda would be seen as vile, dangerous, ugly lies. Thus, there is a tendency for the average person to perceive his or her own attempts at influencing others as being "logical," "honest," or the "truth," whereas the persuasive efforts of others, which contradict his or her own beliefs, are perceived of as being "dirty propaganda." Indeed, truth is in the eye of the beholder.

Until recently, the analysis of propaganda has been based upon the work of the Institute for Propaganda Analysis, founded in the 1930s to enable Americans to recognize the propaganda devices used by Adolph Hitler. To this end, the institute formulated what became a widely accepted list of devices:

1. Name calling—giving the opposition a bad label, i.e., "Fascist," "honky," "racist pig."
2. Glittering generality—associating your program with "virtue words," such as *freedom, honor, the American way.*
3. Transfer—associating your program with the authority, sanction, and prestige of something or someone respected and revered; symbols, such as the cross, the flag, and Uncle Sam, are constantly used.
4. Testimonial—having some respected or hated person testify that a program or product is good or bad.
5. Plain folks, or the *ad populum* fallacy—equating yourself with "the common man," "the little guy," or the "ordinary taxpayer."
6. Card stacking—the use of facts or falsehoods, logical or illogical assertions to give the best or worst possible case for an idea, program, person, or product.
7. Band wagon—a device to convince us that all members of a group to which we belong accept a program and that we must therefore follow the crowd.

As Hugh Rank, in "Learning about Public Persuasion," points out, however, the IPA list is too limited: "the list simply doesn't have the scope or flexibility to deal with contemporary propaganda." As chairman of the NCTE Committee on Public Doublespeak, Rank devised new schemes for the analysis of commercial, political, and cultural propaganda. The schemes, which have broad application to all types of public persuasion, isolate two basic patterns in human communication: people communicate by *intensifying* or *downplaying.* The three major categories of intensifying are *repetition, association,* and *composition.* The three most common ways to downplay are *omission, diversion,* and *confusion.* Rank suggests, in addition, that people manipulate communication to (1) intensify their own "good"; (2) to intensify others' "bad"; (3) to downplay their own "bad"; and (4) to downplay others' "good." These schemes offer eminently useful approaches to the study of the messages of the mass media: political speeches, campaign strategies, public relations, and commercial advertising. To this list may also be added some extremely subtle, if not insidious, manifestations in the popular arts—television programs, popular song lyrics, comedy routines, cartoons, film, and theater. As Irving J. Rein aptly points out in "The Rhetoric of the Popular Arts," one of the functions of art has always been to persuade: "Whether a comedy by George Bernard Shaw or a waltz by Johann Strauss, a Western by Howard Hawks or a comic monologue by Will Rogers, they have worked attitude changes."

In sum, advertising and public propaganda are, to use Edmund Carpenter's analogy, new languages of communication, whose grammars as yet are unknown. The selections in this unit, together with the aids, were chosen with the intent of helping you to discern the form, contents, and effects of commercial advertising and public propaganda; in short, of helping you to generate a grammar for the subtle manipulation and hidden linguistic persuasion of ads, political speeches, and the popular arts. Many of the techniques of the ad writer, the politician, and the propagandist are valuable, in a negative if not in a positive way, in helping you realize the effectiveness of your own attempts at communication.

The Ad and the Id

VANCE PACKARD

The early nineteen fifties witnessed the beginnings of a revolution in American advertising: Madison Avenue became conscious of the *unconscious*. Evidence had piled up that the responses of consumers to the questions of market researchers were frequently unreliable—in other words, that people often don't want what they say they want. Some years ago, for instance, a great automobile company committed one of the costliest blunders in automobile history through reliance on the old-style "nose counting" methods. Direct consumer surveys indicated that people wanted a sensible car in tune with the times—without frills, maneuverable and easy to park. A glance at today's cars—elongated, fish-finned and in riotous technicolor—shows how misleading were the results of the survey. Errors of this sort convinced manufacturers and advertisers that they must take into account the irrationality of consumer behavior—that they must carry their surveys into the submerged areas of the human mind. The result is a strange and rather exotic phenomenon entirely new to the market place—the use of a kind of mass psychoanalysis to guide campaigns of persuasion. The ad is being tailored to meet the needs of the id.

The so-called "depth approach" to selling problems is known as motivational research, or simply M.R. Social scientists by the hundreds have been recruited for this massive exploration of the consumer's psyche, and hundreds of millions of dollars are being spent on it. Two-thirds of the nation's leading advertising agencies have been using the depth approach (along with the more conventional methods), and one major agency resorts to it for every single product it handles, to detect possible hidden appeals and resistances.

A number of factors have contributed to the rapid growth of motivational research. By the mid-nineteen fifties, American producers were achieving a fabulous output. This meant that we must be persuaded to buy more and more to keep the wheels of the economy turning. As the president of National Sales Executives exclaimed: "Capitalism is dead—consumerism is king!" Another formidable obstacle that faced the mer-

From *Harper's Bazaar*, August 1957, pp. 8–14. Copyright © 1957 by Vance Packard. Reprinted by permission of the author.

The secret of advertising

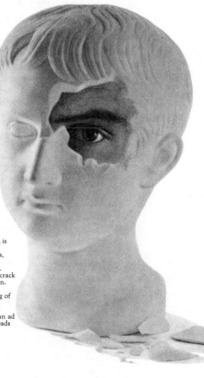

The secret of advertising

We have often been reminded, not only by businessmen but even by a doctor and a minister, that our Campbell-Ewald philosophy is pertinent wherever people really want to communicate with people, in every business and profession.

And so it is. And so it may be that you'd like to tear out the page and put it on your mirror, or send it to a friend, or even an enemy.

One beauty of the printed page is that you *can* save it, or show it, or send it, or paste it on a mirror.

We'd like to thank TIME for the gift of a very valuable page. And writer Harvey Bailey and art director Paul Grissom for expressing our philosophy as they have here.

Detroit, New York, Chicago,
Los Angeles, Dallas, Washington,
Cincinnati, San Francisco, Atlanta,
Pittsburgh, Kansas City

Each of us wears a Halloween mask all year long.

We have to, to keep our nerve endings hidden. To keep our hopes, and needs, and hangups, our fears and prides and prejudices, our irrationalities and our cry-buttons from hanging out for everyone to stare at.

Or step on.

We wear these shells to work, to lunch, to meetings, and to church. We always keep them handy for when friends drop in. And adjust them for *which* friends drop in.

It's this shell, whether it be button-down, Edwardian, or denim, that confuses a lot of us in advertising. If we're not careful, we find ourselves writing to the mannequin, instead of to the man inside, which often makes our ad cute but not convincing, beautiful but not believable, "swinging" but without substance.

Shell-talk forgets that inside each of us, no matter how old or young we are, is a person who is worried about his money, his age, his looks, his health, his happiness, his family, and whether people like him. Or hate him. Or worse, simply ignore him.

The secret of advertising, then, is to crack the shell, to talk to the man inside the man.

Simple it is, but easy it isn't.

It takes an uncommon understanding of people, great sensitivity and skill, and the discipline to use them every single time.

But it means the difference between an ad someone skips over and an ad someone reads all the way to the end.

Campbell-Ewald Company
Advertising

chandisers in our advanced technology was the increasing similarity of competing products. While it might still be possible for people of discrimination to distinguish between brands of cigarettes, whiskey, detergent, and so on, it became increasingly difficult to teach them to do so on any rational basis. Still, loyalty to a particular brand had to be created, and it was done in many instances by "building a personality"—playful, conservative or showy—into the brand. In this way, Procter and Gamble's image makers have projected a living personification for each of their brands of soap (Ivory is mother and daughter on a sort of pedestal of purity; Camay a glamorous woman), and a Chicago chain of food stores decided that the image which would give it the edge over its competitors should have "the traits we like in our friends"—generosity, cleanliness, etc.

What the depth researchers are looking for, of course, are the hidden *whys* of our behavior—why many people are intimidated by banks, why men are drawn into showrooms by convertibles but emerge with sedans, why women go into a trance-like state at the supermarket and why junior likes noisy cereal. The principal tools of M.R. are the techniques of psychiatry—interviews "in depth" (but without the couch, which might make the consumer guinea pig wary); Rorschach (ink blot) tests; stress tests, in which the rate at which you blink your eyes is recorded by hidden cameras; lie detectors; word association tests; and finally the group interview, which, surprisingly, has the effect of breaking down inhibitions. (One candid statement prompts another and presently a roomful of people are freely discussing laxatives, deodorants, weight reducers and athlete's foot.)

The efforts of the persuaders to probe our everyday habits for hidden meanings are often fascinating purely for the revelations—some amusing, some rather appalling—which they offer us about ourselves. The average American likes to think of himself as a rugged individualist and, above all, a thoughtful, hard-headed consumer of the products of American enterprise. But in the findings of the motivational researchers, we are apt to emerge as comic actors in a genial if twitchy Thurberian world—bundles of daydreams, secret yearnings and curious emotional quirks.

In learning to sell to our subconscious, the persuaders soon discovered unsuspected areas of tension and guilt. Self-indulgent and easy-does-it products are a significant sector of the total American market, yet Americans, it seems, have in them a larger streak of Puritanism than is generally recognized. For instance, the hidden attitude of women toward labor-saving devices is decidedly surprising. Working wives can accept them, but the full-time housewife is liable to feel that they threaten her importance and creativity. The research director of an ad agency sadly explained the situation as follows: "If you tell the housewife that by using your washing machine, drier or dishwasher she can be free to play bridge, you're dead!—the housewife today already feels guilty about the fact that she is not working as hard as her mother. Instead, you should emphasize that appliances free her to have more time with her children." Makers of ready-mixes and foods with "built in maid service" ran into the same sort of problem. In the early days, the packages promised to take over all the work, but wives were not grateful for this boon. A leading motivational analyst, James Vicary, has stated the reason. Cake-making, he finds, is steeped in creative symbolism for women—it is, in fact, "a traditional acting out of the birth of a child." This feeling shows up in our folklore in such jokes as the one which says that brides whose cakes fall obviously can't produce a baby yet. (A Chicago analyst has noted that gardening, too, is a symbolic "pregnancy activity" and thus is particularly popular with women past the child-bearing age who need creative outlets.)

Subconscious tensions about food also rose to plague the makers of Jello a few years ago. Jello had become known to millions of households as a quick dessert, simple and shirt-sleeved in character. Then the ad-men, trying to make it more captivating, started showing it in beautiful, layered,

You can take a White Horse anywhere

lavishly decorated concoctions. The ads were not a success, and the Institute for Motivational Research was able to tell why. Many women, looking at these feats of fussy preparation, wondered if they could duplicate them, and often concluded that if they had to go to all that work, they would much rather make their own dessert without someone standing over their shoulder telling them how to do it. The Jello people, alerted, went back to showing simple mounds of the stuff, and added to their attraction largely by such simple devices as fairy-tale drawings.

The whole area of food, in fact, would seem to be booby-trapped with hidden problems for women. Mr. Vicary noticed, for instance, that young wives in particular tended to avoid the smaller, clerk-manned grocery stores in favor of the supermarket. He was able to isolate the explanation: newly married women are more ignorant about food than older women and are afraid the clerk will find them out. A Midwestern grocery chain found that this state of fearfulness centered around butcher clerks in particular. Faced with a discussion of cuts of meat, where their lack of knowledge is often profound, many women feel anxiety. After "depth-probing" the situation, the chain began training its butchers to exhibit extraordinary patience and garrulity with younger women, and the strategy has paid off by turning the chain into a haven for innocents.

Supermarkets, on the other hand, are so tension-free as to make many women fall into a state bordering on hypnotic trance. Anxious to trace the reasons for the enormous rise in so-called impulse buying in American supermarkets (today seven out of ten purchases in supermarkets are made on impulse—the shopping list of old is becoming obsolete), Mr. James Vicary made a remarkable test. He had assumed that some special psychology must be at work to put women in an impulsive state when they got into supermarkets, possibly the tension of confronting so many products and having to make rapid decisions. Since our blink rate is one rough index of our inner tension, Mr. Vicary installed hidden cameras to record the blink rate of women shoppers. Normally, we blink about thirty-two times a minute, and he expected to see the rate go up as the ladies faced their decisions. Nothing of the sort occurred. The rate went down, down, down to a subnormal fourteen blinks a minute for the average woman—a condition of hypnoidal trance. Many of the women collided with boxes or passed the whirring cameras without noticing them. But when they approached the checkout counters with their loaded carts, their blink rate would start rising back toward normal; and when they heard the bell of the cash register, the rate shot up to the abnormal figure of forty-five a minute, a symptom of acute anxiety. Mr. Vicary's explanation of the trance: the woman feels herself a queen in a fairyland filled with lovely, accessible objects, unimaginable in former years and all whispering "buy me, buy me."

The calorie consciousness which swept the country, beginning a few years ago, created other psychological troubles for foodmakers. A number of brewing companies, who had thought to capitalize on the phenomenon, tried to outdo one another in plugging low-caloried beer, and for a time sales did go up. But M.R. hoisted warning flags. Dr. Ernest Dichter, head of the Institute for Motivational Research, warned that calorie consciousness is a sort of psychological penance. People go on diets because they are trying to punish themselves for past indulgence. Hence, low-calorie diets are not supposed to be pleasant. What the brewers were conveying in effect, was that real beer must be fattening and that low-calorie beer was somehow denatured. "Thus," said the Institute, "when a beer advertises itself as low in calories, the consumer reacts by feeling the beer has a poor taste." Perhaps this cautionary note was responsible for one brewer's recent clarion call: "Made by people who like beer for people who drink beer, and plenty of it!"

Another product which found its market temporarily constricted because of too much harping on calories was Ry-Krisp, which ran advertisements containing calorie tables and showing very slim people nibbling the wafers. Motivational analysts found that Ry-Krisp had developed for itself a self-punishment image as a food that was "good" for people—an image which drove away people not in a self-punishing mood. Corrective action was taken: in advertisements, Ry-Krisp began appearing with tempting foods and was described as delicious and festive. This more permissive approach nearly doubled sales in test areas.

Even in travel we have hidden anxieties which marketers find it profitable to take into account. A number of years ago, an airline became disturbed by the fact that so many passengers flew only when pressed for time, and it hired a conventional research firm to find out why. The simple answer came back that they didn't fly because they were afraid of being killed, but an intensive advertising campaign emphasizing safety yielded disappointing results. At last Dr. Dichter was called in. His answer, based on picture tests which encouraged potential travelers to imagine themselves involved in airline crashes, was different and astonishing. What the traveler feared was not death but a sort of posthumous embarrassment. The husband pictured his wife receiving the news and saying, "The damned fool, he should have gone by train." The obvious answer was to convince wives of the common sense of flying, which would bring their husbands home faster from business trips, and to get them in the air (to get their feet wet, as it were) with tempting family flying plans.

Still other subconscious fears, and not always the obvious ones, relate to money. Motivational studies have proved, for example, that it is not guilt about owing money which makes people hesitate to approach the bank for a loan. The fear is of the bank itself, which is seen as an angry father-figure who will disapprove of our untidy financial affairs. Many people would rather go to a loan company, in spite of the higher interest rate, simply because the moral tone associated with it is lower; in fact, there is a complete shift in moral dominance in which the borrower becomes a righteous fellow, temporarily forced into low company, and the higher cost of the loan is a small price to pay for such a changed view of ourselves. It is worth noting that a good many banks today are trying to mellow the stern image of themselves by removing the bars on teller windows, making wider use of glass fronts and staging folksy little exhibits which depict them—at worst—as rather crusty but charming old gentlemen in Scotch hats.

It will surprise nobody to learn that sex plays an enormously important part in selling. But how it works *is* frequently surprising. Sex images have, of course, long been cherished by ad-makers, but in the depth approach sex takes on some extraordinary ramifications and subtleties. A classic example is the study of automobiles made by Dr. Dichter which became known as "Mistress Versus Wife"—a study responsible for the invention of the most successful new car style introduced to the American market for several years. Dealers had long been aware that a convertible in the window drew the male customer into the showroom. They also knew that he usually ended by choosing a four-door sedan. The convertible, said Dr. Dichter, had associations of youth and adventure—it was symbolic of the mistress. But the sedan was the girl one married because she would make a good wife and mother. How could an automobile symbolically combine the appeals of mistress and wife? The answer was the celebrated hardtop, which Dr. Dichter's organization takes full credit for inspiring.

A company advertising a home permanent wave ran into another sexual problem, which was solved by M.R. They had thought it would be a brilliant idea to picture a mother and daughter with identical hairdos captioned: "A Double Header Hit with Dad." Wives, interviewed at the conscious level, said they didn't object at all to the implied idea of competition for the husband-father's admiration, but the company was still apprehensive—rightly, as it turned out. Depth interviews revealed that women would indeed deeply resent the "hit with dad" theme, and it was hastily dropped.

As for the American male, he stands in equal need of sexual reassurance, particularly as women continue to invade the traditional strongholds. The fact that cigar makers have been enjoying their greatest prosperity in twenty years has been credited by many to the man-at-bay, and at least one ad agency disagrees with the efforts of the Cigar Institute of America to draw women into the picture. This agency, puzzled by the failure of a campaign which had pictured a smiling woman offering cigars to a group of men, ordered a depth survey to uncover the reason. The conclusion was that men enjoy cigars precisely because they are objectionable to women; nor is the man sincere who politely asks if the ladies

COMBINING THE BEST OF THE PAST AND PRESENT IS THE GANT ATTITUDE. THIS GINGHAM CHECK GETS OUR FITTED HUGGER® BODY, EARL COLLAR, AND A 65% DACRON® POLYESTER, 35% COTTON BROADCLOTH FABRIC. BY GANT SHIRTMAKERS, NEW HAVEN, CONN. 06509.

THE GANT ATTITUDE

mind his lighting up. As the head of the agency put it: "He knows . . . he is going to stink up the room."

Motivational analysis has even discovered certain products to be sexually "maladjusted," and it is responsible for several spectacular cases of planned transvestitism. When the cancer scare drove millions of men to try filter tips, the makers of Marlboro cigarettes decided to cash in by changing the sex of a cigarette originally designed for women. The ads began to show a series of rugged males, engaged in virile occupations and all of them, by an extraordinary coincidence, tattooed. The tattoo motif puzzled a good many people, since the tattoo is a common phenomenon among delinquents in reformatories. Marlboro, however, decided it was exactly what was needed to give its men a virile and "interesting past" look—the same look arrived at, by other means, in the one-eyed man in the Hathaway shirt.

When Lloyd Warner published his book, *Social Class in America*, in 1948, it created a respectful stir in academic circles; but in later years it was to create an even greater one among merchandisers. Like David Riesman in his classic, *The Lonely Crowd*, or Russell Lynes, whose famous dissection of high-, middle-, and low-brows charted the social significance of such items as tossed salad and rye whiskey, Warner defined social classes less in terms of wealth and power than criteria of status, and merchandisers have begun to give considerable thought to his conclusions. Burleigh Gardener, for example, founder of the M.R. firm of Social Research, Inc., has taken Warner's concepts as his guiding thesis. Social Research has put a class label on many sorts of house-furnishings: the solid color carpet, it appears, is upper class; the "knickknack" shelf lower class; Venetian blinds are upper middle class.

Chicago's Color Research Institute (a psychoanalytically minded group) ran into some of the intricacies of class structure when it was asked to design two candy boxes, one intended to sell to lower class buyers at $1.95, the other to an upper class clientele at $3.50. The Institute's researchers led it to a curious recommendation: the box for the cheaper candy would be in vermilion metal tied with a bright blue ribbon, and it would have to cost fifty cents; the box for the expensive candy could be made of pale pink pasteboard at a cost of no more than nine cents. The reason? Candy-giving is an important rite in the lower class, and the girl is likely to treasure the box, whereas the upper class girl will ignore the box (the candy is what counts) and will probably throw it away.

Many advertising men have filled the air above their Madison Avenue rookeries with arguments over the validity and potency of M.R. And the researchers themselves have added to the confusion by disagreeing with each other's methods and results. Of more concern, however, to the average citizen are the possibilities for mass manipulation opened up by motivational research. Disturbing examples of such manipulation have, unfortunately, appeared in politics, industrial relations (a California engineering school boasts that its graduates are "custom-built men") and even in the church, where ministers are being advised how they can more effectively control their congregations. The manipulative approach to politics is not, of course, new—Machiavelli[1] was perfectly familiar with it. But the manipulation of the people by a tyrant is an infinitely simpler problem than that of dealing with the citizens of a free society, who can spurn your solicitations if they want to. Now, however, mass persuasion in this kind of situation has been greatly reinforced by the techniques of the symbol manipulators, who have drawn on Pavlov and his conditioned reflexes, Freud and his father images, Riesman and his concept of modern American voters as spectator-consumers of politics. In the 1956 election, both parties tried to "merchandise" their candidates by commercial marketing methods, using on billboards slogans of scientifically tested appeal, hammering out

[1]Niccolo Machiavelli (1469–1527), Italian statesman and author of *The Prince*, which describes the means by which a prince gains and keeps power. (eds.)

key messages until the public was saturation-bombed, and grooming their candidates to look "sincere" in front of the TV cameras. As one advertising man put it: "I think of a man in a voting booth who hesitates between the two levers as if he were pausing between competing tubes of tooth paste in a drugstore. The brand that has made the highest penetration in his brain will win his choice."

What are the implications of all this persuasion in terms of morality? The social scientists and psychiatrists have a workable rationale for explaining their co-operation with, say, the merchandisers. They are broadening the world's knowledge of human behavior; and knowledge, as Alfred Whitehead has said, keeps no better than fish. But there remains the disturbing fact that by scientifically catering to the irrational, the persuaders are working toward a progressively less rational society. We may wonder if, in a few decades when it becomes technically feasible, we will be ripe for biocontrol, a brand new science for controlling mental processes, emotional reactions and sense perceptions by bio-electrical signals. Already, rats with full bellies have been made to feel ravenously hungry, and to feel fear when they had nothing to be afraid of. As one electronic engineer has said: "The ultimate achievement of biocontrol may be the control of man himself. . . . The controlled subjects would never be permitted to think as individuals. A few months after birth, a surgeon would equip each child with a socket mounted under the scalp and electrodes reaching selected areas of brain tissue. . . . The child's sensory perceptions and muscular activity could either be modified or completely controlled by bioelectric signals radiating from state-controlled transmitters." He added that the electrodes would cause no discomfort.

I'm sure the persuaders of 1957 would be appalled by such a prospect. Most of them are likeable, earnest men who just want to control us a little bit, to maneuver us into buying something that we may actually need. But when you start manipulating people, where exactly do you stop?

Aids   *The Ad and the Id*

1. According to Vance Packard, ad people attempt to create brand loyalty by building personalities into consumer products. Examine the identities they have created for one or more of the following product lines: automobiles (Cadillac, Lincoln, Capri, Honda Civic, Volkswagen); beer (Michelob, Miller High Life, Schlitz, Pabst Blue Ribbon); cigarettes (Marlboro, Viceroy, Salem, Benson & Hedges, True); toothpaste (Crest, Gleem, Ultra Brite, Close Up, Macleans); soft drinks (Coca Cola, Pepsi-Cola, Seven-Up, Dr. Pepper, Royal

Crown Cola). Note any attempts to endow the inanimate product with human sensibilities or emotions; this is called personification.

2. Most Americans, Packard asserts, aspire to enhance their status. The most effective ways to sell status symbols to American strivers are the three advertising strategies: bigness, high price tag, and testimonials from status personages. Locate some specific examples of the three strategies in current ads. How is social striving encouraged in each of the ads? What emotions are being manipulated? Are there status products for young people as well as for adults?

3. Packard advances the notions of "sexual reassurance" in advertising —women yearning for evidence that they are still feminine and men yearning for masculine confirmation. Find ads that make bold masculine or feminine statements such as "Want him to be more of a man? Try being more of a woman." Do the details—colors, backgrounds, and accessories—help to reinforce the "gender" of the ads?

4. In ads that give sexual reassurance, locate particular words that are used to connote feminine images (are women ever labeled "handsome"?) and masculine images (are men ever called "beautiful"?) Make a list of words that emphasize either masculinity or femininity. Are these the words you would use to describe males and females?

5. Look at the brand names of products which are, for the most part, directed exclusively at either male or female audiences. What correlations, if any, do you find between the brand names and the intended audience?

6. Because Packard is exploring the hidden whys of our behavior, he makes assertions that may seem strange to most readers. Would most readers, for instance, readily accept the proposition that cake-making symbolically acts out the birth of a child? You should note, however, that Packard does not take personal responsibility for many of his assertions about consumer behavior; he cites authorities. It is "a leading motivational analyst" who draws the conclusion about cake-making. The citing of authorities is a useful tool in writing and speaking. It allows a communicator to bolster an argument or thesis with supporting evidence from experts. The credibility of an authority is important. Do you think the MR researchers are credible authorities? Although Packard takes his supporting documentation from them, does he draw his own conclusions? Does he cite their findings and then attack them? Does his approach depend on the credibility of his authorities?

7. In his essay Packard proceeds by defining the technique he is exploring (motivational research) and then analyzing how it works to

provide handles by which advertisers may "grab" a reader's psyche for promotional purposes. Finally, he evaluates the technique he has defined and illustrated, suggesting its danger. Write a theme or prepare a report in which you define and analyze a ploy used in an ad you have selected from the examples included in this unit. Then evaluate the overt and implied values the ploy suggests—are these values healthy or distorted?

8. Packard asserts that some ads attempt to play upon the consumers' hidden cravings, needs, and fears. The typical approach in such ads is to (a) stir up the hidden fear, (b) promise that a particular product will ease or assuage these psychological feelings, and (c) threaten the consumer in some way (usually withdrawal of love) if he or she decides not to buy the product. Locate some ads in which the technique of product therapy is used. You might begin by looking at ads for the so-called *dreadful d's:* dentifrices, deodorants, depilatories, and dandruff shampoos. What specific fears are being manipulated? What are you promised if you buy the products? Do you take these kinds of ads seriously? How many of these products do you buy?

9. As we have seen, Packard suggests that many ads function by probing into psychological feelings and states of mind and by making subtle associations. Some re-enact dream-like states and even employ dream colors (pinks, blues, and cloudy whites) or blurry photography to induce a dream-like trance in the viewer. Look carefully at the ad for White Horse on page 61. Describe what is taking place in the ad. What is the thesis of the ad? What psychological feelings are being explored? What does it promise the consumer? Why do you think an ad for scotch whiskey might choose a dream-like setting?

10. Look closely at the ad for Gant shirts on p. 65. The ad is very subtle. Very little explicit information is provided. Look at the setting and the clothing. What do you think is happening between the man and woman? If the man embodies the "Gant Attitude," what precisely *is* the "Gant Attitude"? To what sort of person would this ad appeal? Would it appeal to women?

Worriers, Swingers, Shoppers 'Psychographics' Can Tell Who'll Buy Crest, Who'll Buy Ultra Brite

DANIEL HENNINGER

Scene: A typical American family—father, mother, and teen-aged daughter—is watching "The Every Night Movie" on television. A commercial appears showing a beautiful young girl walking through a rainstorm. A close-up reveals tears in her eyes. She stops and from her shoulder bag takes a small canary-yellow cylinder of "Can Dew" mouth spray. She pumps a few jets into her mouth and turns to greet a handsome young man. He smiles. She smiles. They embrace, kiss, and depart into the misting rain, followed by a deep male voice: "When you can't, Can Dew. Always."

Sitting with the family is a research specialist in "psychographics," an increasingly popular marketing science that uses psychology, sociology, and computers to help advertisers sell their products. He asks each family member's reaction to the commercial.

Daughter: "It looks pretty good. I've never used a mouth spray, but I think I'll try Can Dew."

Mother: "It's awful. Ads like this are the work of a bunch of subliminal sneaks who are teaching our kids aerosol emotions."

Father: "What commercial?"

The psychographics man is thrilled: All responded just as his computer predicted. He knew that the ad might enrage Mom and miss Dad. But the commercial sold its "target," their daughter. Although Can Dew is a fictional product, the ad is based on reality. The girl is a "target" because she belongs to a specific group of consumers identified by the computer as "a segment of the youthful population which has an active, socially oriented life style, is inclined to accept changing values and mores, and prefers personal-care products that promise cosmetic appeal rather than personal hygiene."

IDENTIFYING LIFE STYLES

All that in a 30-second commercial? Yes, say the psychographics researchers. They maintain that the current TV audience, or "consumer market," has split into many disparate "segments." General com-

Daniel Henninger, "Worriers, Swingers, Shoppers," *The National Observer*, June 10, 1972, pp. 1, 19. Reprinted by permission of the publisher.

70

mercial appeals to "the average consumer" are now less than successful, they say. What appeals to one segment of the market may annoy or disinterest other segments.

Psychographics (which has other imposingly murky names, such as "segmentation research" and "activity and attitude variables") tries to identify the personal values, attitudes, emotions and beliefs—the life style—common to a particular market segment. It then directs that seg-

ment, through finely tuned advertising, to a product that fits the group's psychographic portrait.

For example, everyone expects his tooth paste to prevent cavities, but people choose specific brands for other reasons. Russell Haley of Appel Haley Fouriezos, Inc., New York City, is a leading proponent of segmentation research. He describes four possible psychographic segments in the tooth-paste market: Worriers, Sociable, Independents, and Sensory.

"It's time women got their own American Express Card and started taking me to dinner."

Lee Musachio, Designer and former Male Chauvinist

"As a former Male Chauvinist Pig, I'm glad to see women are finally making their own decisions. It takes a lot of the strain off me.

"So for purely selfish reasons, I'd like to urge every woman to get her own American Express Card.

"I've found it works wonders at hotels, restaurants, nightclubs and stores in every city I've ever been to.

"I've used it to pay for airline tickets from New York to London, car rentals in San Francisco, and car repairs in Westport.

"Anyway, all I can tell you is how I use the Card. Once you get your own, maybe you can teach me

a thing or two—over dinner."

If you'd like an American Express Card of your own, fill out the attached "Women Only" application (no discrimination intended against men—the application is the same for both men and women. However, 5 times as many men have the Card, and we'd like to start evening things up).

A few more pertinent facts: you're never liable for more than $50 if the Card is lost or stolen; you get descriptive statements at the end of every month that show exactly where you've spent your money (a handy record come income-tax

time); and you get optional extended payment plans for airline tickets and vacation packages. Have fun.

AMERICAN EXPRESS

The Money Card

Haley says the Worriers contain "a disproportionately large number of families with children." They are concerned about cavities and prefer fluoride tooth paste. "This is reinforced by their personalities," he says. "They tend to be a little hypochondriacal and, in their life styles, they are less socially oriented than some of the other groups." Their brand is Crest, whose ads portray a Responsible Father dedicated to his son's healthy teeth.

The Sociables, Haley says, "is where the swingers are." They are young marrieds, active, and probably smoke a lot. To assure teeth that are Ali MacGraw white they use Plus White, Macleans, or Ultra Brite, which "gives your mouth—sex appeal!"

'VOYEURS INTO THE PSYCHE'

Price-conscious men dominate the Independents. They "see very few meaningful differences between brands," says Haley. They think for themselves, trust their judgment when buying, and shop for tooth paste on sale.

The Sensory segment prefers tooth paste pleasing in flavor and appearance. Most Sensories are children who choose Stripe and Colgate.

Haley suggests that advertising for the Sociable and Sensory segments should be light; for the Worriers, serious; for the Independents, "rational, two-sided arguments."

Shirley Young, director of research services for Grey Advertising, Inc., New York City, says psychographic analysis includes "attitudes about the product category, about brands, as well as attitudes which reflect personality and attitudes about life style. The personality and life-style data, of course, are what's relatively

new. They provide the juicy stuff that captures the imagination of the researcher and marketer alike. They allow us to become voyeurs into the psyche of the consumer."

Are we really that tough to sell, or is Madison Avenue substituting psychographics for its failed imagination? Long-time TV viewers may recall an old commercial in which a band of pixies hopped around the bathroom sink and tub, polishing and singing: "So use Ajax, bum, bum, the Foaming Cleanser. Floats the dirt right down the drain." That commercial first appeared in 1948, but it still sticks in the minds of many people.

It is possible, though, that no one would notice or remember that ad if it appeared for the first time today. The pixies would fall victim to the ad world's worst nemesis, the "perceptual screen." Americans watch endless hours of television, and to survive the accompanying commercial flood they have developed perceptual screens: They watch the ads without letting them register. Dad's perceptual screen was up when he answered "What commercial?" to the Can Dew mouth-spray ad.

Researchers have shown volunteers a 30-minute film of a drama or comedy broken by three commercials. The next day many of the volunteers could not recall seeing any commercials. The Quaker Oats Co. recently telephoned several hundred viewers of six popular programs one day after they appeared and found only 3 per cent remembered brands advertised on specific shows.

CONFOUNDING THE DEMOGRAPHERS

In the past advertisers tried (and some still try) to penetrate the screens by tailoring ads to broad population segments sharing common demographic characteristics—income, sex, age, and residence. But advertisers often find demographic data to be unreliable or incomplete.

For example, many middle-aged fathers still conform to a demography of high income and conservative taste in fashion and leisure interests. But today several men on the same block—the conservatives' demographic peers—may have adopted their children's fashions. The kids in turn throw away *their* bright clothes, resurrect dad's GI jacket, and all wear blue denim. Yet the young spend $9 a week on gas, one survey shows, and 50 per cent of them use mouthwash.

This family defies conventional demography. How do I reach such people? the advertiser wonders. More importantly, how and where do I find them?

Enter the psychographics researcher carrying a market basket full of sharply defined "segments."

OF CARS AND POTIONS

A psychographics study by MPI Marketing Research, Inc., for American Motors Corp. found that new-car buyers worry most about having problems during the first year of ownership. American Motors' Guaranteed Car Campaign resulted, guaranteeing the free repair or replacement of any defective part, except tires, for one year or 12,000 miles.

Benton and Bowles, Inc., a New York City ad agency, did a psychographic study of housewives' attitudes and divided the drug market into four categories:

Realists "view remedies positively, want something that is convenient and works, and do not feel the need for a doctor-recommended medicine."

"Authority Seekers are doctor- and prescription-oriented" and "prefer the stamp of authority on what they do take."

"Skeptics have a low health concern, are least likely to resort to medication, and are highly skeptical of cold remedies."

Conversely, Hypochondriacs "regard themselves as prone to any bug going around and tend to take medication at the first symptom."

Translating their findings into possible advertising strategies, Benton and Bowles said that Realists "could be reasoned with on practical terms" and "should not be depicted as either overly sick or overly concerned." Authority Seekers "would be receptive to claims that specify doctor's approval, laboratory testing, to advertising with an ethical aura or prescription look." Admen sometimes call this "man-in-the-white-coat information."

Authority Seekers. The Sociables. Psychographics. It sounds as if the Viennese psychologists are still mixing their motivational theories with the daily horoscope. "You are buying a red convertible because you can't afford a mistress."

In fact, psychographics is the product of statisticians, sociologists, and psychologists trying to figure out how a shifting market of finite consumption capacity can absorb an endless proliferation of goods and services. For them, computers have replaced the couch.

Psychographics researchers obtain their information from large population samples through personal interviews or mail questionnaires. Motivational researchers such as Ernest Dicter [The National Observer, Nov. 13, 1971] rely on in-depth interviews with individuals or small groups. Proponents of psychographics admit that the motivational people can sometimes identify market segments similar to theirs, but they say large-sample statistical analysis is more reliable than a psycholo-

DEWAR'S PROFILES
(Pronounced Do-ers "White Label")

SHEILA ANN T. LONG

HOME: Hampton, Virginia

AGE: 28

PROFESSION: Physicist

HOBBIES: Ballet, Sailing, Car Racing, Chess

LAST BOOK READ: "Beyond Freedom and Dignity"

LAST ACCOMPLISHMENT: Member of the team of international scientists who are mapping earth's electromagnetic field for the first time

QUOTE: "Scientific research in all fields has been a prime contributor to America's greatness. Let us not forget this in our concern for the dying environment, for Technology holds the very means to save it."

PROFILE: Brilliant, beautiful, in love with life. Involved, and unintimidated by difficult challenge. Saluted by *New Woman* magazine as one of the 26 women who "made it big in their twenties."

SCOTCH: Dewar's "White Label"

BLENDED SCOTCH WHISKY · 86.8 PROOF · © SCHENLEY IMPORTS CO., N.Y. N.Y.

Authentic. There are more than a thousand ways to blend whiskies in Scotland, but few are authentic enough for Dewar's "White Label." The quality standards we set down in 1846 have never varied. Into each drop goes only the finest whiskies from the Highlands, the Lowlands, the Hebrides. *Dewar's never varies.*

gist's judgment, which may be influenced unintentionally by subjective factors.

'CONSCIENTIOUS VIGILANTS'

Benton and Bowles mailed questionnaires to 2,000 housewives for its study of their product attitudes. A computer analysis of the 1,600 responses received classified some of the women, for example, as Conscientious Vigilants who tend to be "conscientious, rigid, meticulous, germ-fighting, with a high cleanliness orientation." They have "sensible attitudes about food. They have a high cooking pride, careful shopping orientation, tend not to be convenience-oriented."

In a TV commercial this Conscientious Vigilant might be portrayed sniffing out household odors, killing them with disinfectant spray. Her war on bacteria might amuse some women, but it might also draw other Vigilants to the product.

WHAT SORT OF MAN READS PLAYBOY?

A man who exercises the same skill and knowledge in shopping for exotic foods as he does in preparing the intimate dinner that will follow. And as a guide to home entertaining as well as an authority on all aspects of his lifestyle he looks to PLAYBOY. Fact: He and millions of young men like him pay more attention to the features and advertising in PLAYBOY than in any other major magazine. That's why advertising gets maximum results in PLAYBOY. (Source: *Media Insight, 1974.*)

New York · Chicago · Detroit · Los Angeles · San Francisco · Atlanta · London · Tokyo

Correctly identifying distinct consumer segments such as the Conscientious Vigilant is acutely important because many product categories—analgesics, breakfast cereals, toiletries, deodorants—are filled with products that all do pretty much the same thing. What imposes order on product chaos is "positioning."

If brands A, B, and C are almost identical, they must establish some product distinction in the consumer's mind. They must assume different "positions" in the market and appeal to specific segments of it. Otherwise there may be little basis for customer loyalty to any of the products. Avis, for example, "positioned" itself in the car-rental market by saying, "We're Number Two."

SEEKING HOLES IN THE SCREEN

In seeking open positions a company may turn to the psychographics people, whose research chops up the market and tells the company what segments are available. Sometimes the studies turn up a previously unidentified segment. "That's the ideal," says the market-research director of a large analgesic manufacturer. "Take one of your established brands and tap that market or come up with another product and go after that group."

Some years ago, while at Grey Advertising, Russell Haley made a psychographic study of the cigaret market for the P. Lorillard Co., whose brand sales had leveled off. Haley discovered a segment of highly independent smokers, and an ad campaign stressing independence was developed for Old Gold cigarets. In one ad, says Haley: "A guy driving on a crowded throughway would turn off and drive on another road by himself. That was for the man who likes to make up his mind." Old Gold sales increased.

It is estimated that the "average consumer" encounters about 300 commercial

messages of all types daily. Day after day these commercial suitors pour out their promises to millions of unnervingly fickle consumers. Like a computerized dating service making matches less by love than logic, the psychographics man rummages through the market place, searching with his questionnaires and computers for consumer segments statistically compatible with his client's product. For his services the psychographics researcher may charge between \$30,000 and \$300,000. We segments are expensive.

Aids   *'Psychographics' Can Tell Who'll Buy Crest, Who'll Buy Ultra Brite*

1. What is "psychographics"?

2. What is a "perceptual screen"? Does this device prove that some ads won't work no matter how much time and money is spent on them?

3. What are the moral implications of using psychographics? Does Henninger reveal his attitude toward this approach in advertising?

4. What is "positioning"? Locate three different ads for the same type of product and show how each assumes a different "position" in the market.

5. Locate examples of toothpaste ads that illustrate the four possible groups of consumers. What argument does each type of ad employ? Are the arguments based on fact or fantasy?

6. What is the rhetorical purpose of Henninger's essay? description? argument? definition?

7. What specific compositional strategies can be learned from studying the techniques of advertising? How does a good writer, for instance, "target" his or her intended audience?

8. As Henninger points out, ads may provide us with valuable information concerning the particular audience to whom a magazine or TV program is directed. Select a few mass-circulation magazines or TV programs and deduce from the ads the intended audiences. Construct a hypothetical portrait of the typical reader or viewer for each example. Compare the image of humanity as presented in the ads with that of the TV program or periodical. Do the images match? If not, how do you explain the differences?

9. Using your knowledge of market research and the *depth approach* in advertising, formulate a hypothetical ad campaign for one of the

following categories of products and services: (a) an electric-powered automobile, (b) condominium apartments on the moon, (c) a nicotine-and-tar-less cigarette or legal marijuana cigarette, (d) a woman or minority-group person for President of the United States, and (e) wall-size TV sets.

10. Look closely at the ads for American Express, Dewar's scotch, and Virginia Slims that accompany Daniel Henniger's essay. All are clearly targeted at women. What is the thesis of each ad? Create a psychographic profile of the women to whom each ad is aimed. How does each ad exploit the feminist movement? Which ad, if any, comes closest to the actual ideology of that movement? Which ad (or ads) is least influenced by that ideology? Are drinking alcohol and smoking cigarettes conducive to the success pictured in the scotch and cigarette ads? Locate other ads that manipulate social movements or alternative life-styles to sell consumer products.

11. Look closely at the ad for *Playboy* magazine. Show how it is an explicit psychographic portrait of the intended readers of the magazine. Discuss how the ad illustrates the claim by Harvey Cox in "The Playboy and Miss America" (pp. 194) that *Playboy* fills a special need for insecure young men, ages 18 to 35, by supplying them with a comprehensive and authoritative guidebook to manhood: "It tells him not only who to be; it tells him how to be, and even provides consolation outlets to those who secretly feel that they have not quite made it." *Playboy* is, of course, a magazine that plays heavily upon sexuality. Examine the ad closely for sexual imagery. Do you think that readers are aware of the sexual imagery when they view the ad? Is it an example of Packard's not-so-hidden persuaders?

Packaging
Pop
Mythology

JOHN R. CASHILL

In all societies mythology makes the cosmos somehow more comprehensible. Myths narrate sacred history, explain sacred origins, elucidate the relationship of human beings to the whole of their reality. They are, in short, a series of beliefs that have a very real force in the life of a people. In contemporary America, however, most everything has been explained away by science, communications, social engineering, and the like. Within limits, though, there is imagination. We are not automatons quite yet. There still exists a mass of beliefs, values, fears, and dreams which may not decipher Americans' relationship to the universe, but which do shape the gritty clay of their everyday existence. We cannot exist without myths, and Americans are no exception. Theirs may be less profound and more profane than those of their ancient ancestors, but they are no less real.

Regardless of the origin of the myth, be it indigenous or borrowed, American mass media have been willing to turn the energy of the myth to work, to make it pay its own way. The temptation, in fact, is to say that the mass media exploit American beliefs. American mythology, some media detractors claim, is pasteurized, processed, packaged in cellophane, and pushed off on the American public like so much Velveeta. There is, of course, truth to this claim. After all, some of America's most revered culture heroes, from Davy Crockett to Ronald McDonald, have been used to sell such items as T-shirts, wallpaper, soft drinks, movies, hamburgers, beach towels, vitamins, wastepaper baskets, and underwear.

But we are what we eat. Either the American public consumes its own mythology, or it consumes an alien, artificial, and perhaps dangerous mythology of someone's devising. Of course, America's mythocultural diet might be more palatable were it not so bland, were it not all served with the same supposedly "special" sauce, but such are the drawbacks of democracy.

Things are, though, the way things are. Thus, this essay will not attempt to prescribe or editorialize, but rather to probe an almost indefinable area: the relationship between myth and media.

Let us begin with the myth of manifest destiny. Historically, manifest destiny meant that God himself had decided that America should push its western boundary to the Pacific, but it has come to be a belief that America is, and should be, the most blessed and powerful nation in the world. This myth is so intrinsic a part of the national makeup, even in this era of antinationalism, that it goes fundamentally unquestioned. We take it for granted that Clark Kent should have grown up in Smallville U.S.A. and should have fought for "truth, justice, and the American way." But what would have happened had Clark come to perch in Tijuana or Toronto? Could Americans have acknowledged a Superman whose blue leotard sported a maple leaf instead of stars and bars? I doubt it.

Advertisers usually appeal to manifest destiny when their product needs good press. If, for example, the price of a commodity has grown extremely high, pitchmen quell would-be consumer rebellion by reminding their customers that a purchase contributes to national greatness. In other words, don't buy Blandco gasoline for quality or price—everyone knows it's ordinary and expensive—but to keep America strong, to keep foreign interests out; so the advertisers tell us. Moreover, the consumer is reminded of the by-products of petroleum which are responsible for a miraculous upturn in the civilization: men on the moon, heart valves made of plastic, increased agricultural production, and cures for acne. For sure, more than bicentennial gewgaws have been sold by appealing to national prestige. "God," as Kate Smith has reminded us for years, may indeed "bless America."

A second myth and a corollary one is that of racism: the myth that white people are and always will be superior to their black brethren. For years, the American movie industry notoriously championed this view by playing blacks only in stereotypic, demeaning roles too numerous to list. Indians fared little better. Portrayed usually as howling subhumans, they barely even began to speak in the movies until the 1950s. In the early movies, white men showed more compassion shooting squirrels than they did red men. This is especially evident in the "Eastern" westerns of the thirties such as *Northwest Passage, Drums Along the Mohawk,* and *The Last of the Mohicans.*

On TV racism is sold subtly and subliminally to the allegedly sex-starved housewives of America. Advertisers have decided that sex can sell only if it does not scare. Black sex can scare. Hence, a phalanx of super-white supermen is dredged up to do battle in the kitchens, laundries, and bathrooms of America. First, Mr. Clean, exotic but oddly avuncular, charmed the ladies in his white duds; then the White Knight charged through their backyards clutching his utterly phallic white lance and riding his equally phallic white horse; next, Big Wally popped out of their walls with a few household hints and a knowing smile. Cleanliness does have something to do with the whiteness of these fellows, but no such rationalization can be offered for the Man from Glad, the whitest white man of them all. Women's ads, one will notice, are often littered with white horses, white swans, white fog as well as white men.

In contemporary America old-line racism has yielded to an even more pervasive race consciousness. No longer excluded from TV portrayal, blacks are now carefully spaced throughout. If we were to gauge American race relations solely from what we saw on TV commercials, we would have to conclude that in every group of three or more people there is exactly one black person. Indeed, advertisers tread very, very delicately when dealing with race relations. If, for example, a track meet is staged for a commercial, the ad people make sure that the black will come out no worse than second—but usually no better either (although ties are nice). Blacks are no longer cruelly stereotyped on TV; the current stereotype is much more benign.

In the movies racism is turning in on itself. The white man has become the villain, the loser. In *Little Big Man, Billy Jack, Soldier Blue,* and *Tell Them Willie Boy Is Here,* whitey catches it from the Indian; in *Walkabout* from the aborigine; in *White Dawn* from the Eskimo. What he catches is not so much destruction as guilt. In the post-*Shaft* rash of black adventure films, whitey catches both and is asked to like it. Perhaps he does.

The frontier represents another source of American mythic strength. Despite the fact that it officially closed nearly a century ago, the frontier West conjures up an image of freedom, virility, and ruggedness that continues to captivate the American fantasy.

Little need be said about the "western" movie as genre save that it has kept John Wayne in oats for the past forty years (and 200 movies). TV, likewise, has given extensive air to the "Western." In 1960, in fact, 30 percent of all prime time was farmed out to horse operas of one breed or another. The TV western has more or less died in the seventies, but the western mentality continues to thrive on the many police shows—the most obvious example of this phenomenon being NBC's "McCloud."

Nowhere can the effect of the West be seen more distinctly than in the advertising industry. A man can easily gain that western macho touch by hopping in a Mustang or a Maverick or a Pinto or a Cougar or an El Dorado and driving off into the sunset. Or perhaps, dressed in his Wrangler jeans and Dingo boots, a funny little Winchester cigarette hanging sinisterly from his lower lip, he can stroll out to the country kitchen of his ranch-style house and grab himself a can of Colt 45. No effete suburbanite is the man who can chuck the kids into his ranchero station wagon and drive them down to the Ponderosa Steak House (or will it be the Bonanza tonight) for some grub.

Furthermore, the West is used as a backdrop for numerous car, beer, gasoline, tire, and cigarette commercials. The appeal of the West in these commercials is decidedly masculine, as evidenced particularly by the

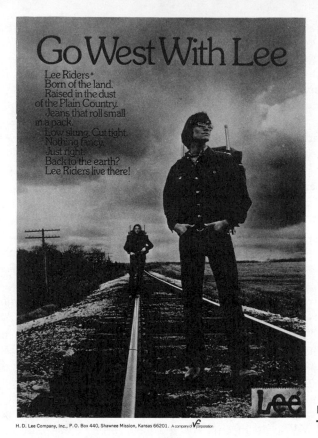

Go West With Lee

Lee Riders®
Born of the land.
Raised in the dust
of the Plain Country.
    Jeans that roll small
in a pack.
    Low slung. Cut tight.
Nothing fancy.
Just right.
Back to the earth?
Lee Riders live there!

Lee

H. D. Lee Company, Inc., P. O. Box 440, Shawnee Mission, Kansas 66201. A company of V corporation

Reprinted by permission of
The H.D. Lee Company, Inc.

Marlboro advertising campaign with its sprawling western vistas, epic
frontier macho music (lifted from the movie *The Magnificent Seven*), and
men who seem to have been hewn out of old leather.

One very successful by-product of the western mystique is Coors
beer. Sold only in the West, Coors is immensely popular in the East
despite the obvious difficulty and expense of obtaining it. Some people
attribute its popularity to its taste; others to the Rocky Mountain spring
water allegedly used in its concoction; others still to its beguiling unavail-
ability. Another possibility is that Coors is prized so dearly because it is
directly associated with the West; western *mana* is that strong.

The frontier pitch, as one might note, has little to offer women. The
media tell us that women have had little to do with the West. Their roles
usually fall into one of two confining categories: the not-so-nice lady
with the heart of gold and the so-called nice lady who is fearful, possessive,
restrictive, and small-minded. In *High Noon*, Grace Kelly demands that
Gary Cooper forsake gunfighting for marriage. True to his code, Coop

Come to where the flavor is.
Come to Marlboro Country.

forsakes marriage for gunfighting. Only a few women thrive in the western, and they, like Gunsmoke's Kitty, must be prepared to hang loose.

The woman as confiner, as castrator, is a type not limited to the western. This type, in truth, dominates the so-called "funny" pages. Blondie, Lois, Mrs. Wizard (of Id), Maggie (Jiggs' wife), Mrs. Dithers, Mrs. Halftrack, Mrs. Mitchell, Daisy Duck, Dotty Dripple—all delight in restricting their husbands' wanderlust. This limiting function, the comics tell us, must come naturally to women since little girls are its ace practitioners. Nancy is forever chiding Sluggo for his lack of civilization, and Margaret does the same to Dennis the Menace. Lucy, however, goes beyond criticism and indulges herself in the complete humiliation of the woeful Charlie Brown. Fittingly, the only truly tolerant woman in the comics is British: Flo Capp. She not only forbears Andy's indolence and drunkenness but his obvious adulteries as well (can one even imagine Dagwood philandering).

Although the feminist movement is changing the images of men in ads, many advertisements still portray the American male the way he would like to see himself portrayed: not as Dagwood but as Davy Crockett or Joe Namath. Man becomes mythic man, the American Adam. This archetypal hero—personified in the movies by Shane, by Billy Jack, by McMurphy in *Cuckoo's Nest*, by Kowalski in *Vanishing Point*, by Nobody (Terrence Hill) in the movie series bearing that name, and by the Man with No Name (Clint Eastwood) in *Fistful of Dollars* and other spaghetti westerns—is called the American Adam because of his absolute rootlessness and his essential innocence, his lack of moral dilemma. In many men's advertisements there is pictured but one man alone in the wilderness, rugged, unrefined, unbothered by women and the claims of civilization. The Marlboro ad campaign, based on just such a theme, has been the most successful in advertising history. Bel Air has run an extremely similar campaign in men's magazines, but in women's magazines Bel Air peoples its wilderness with a woman and a man as coequals. Clearly, advertisers believe more in money than in myth.

For companionship the Adamic man will turn to another man or blood brother before he turns to a woman. Schlitz reminds the American male that since he can "only go 'round once in life" he had better go in the company of his fellow man, at least if he wants to do it with "gusto." Often the Adamic hero will have a sidekick who is somehow marked as an inferior either through race, age, or intelligence. The Lone Ranger has his Tonto, Superman has Jimmy Olsen, the Cisco Kid his Pancho. Whatever the nature of the relationship, this man-man alliance continues to crowd women out of the picture in recent movies. *Scarecrow, Midnight Cowboy, Butch Cassidy, Papillon, The Sting, Brian's Song, Cuckoo's Nest, Jaws, The Man Who Would Be King*, and even *Blazing Saddles* all center on the near love between men. The woman movie star, in fact, has become an endangered species in America.

The frontier is not the only alternative to urban mass society. The media offer the public another escape, albeit a more low-keyed and homely one, the middle landscape. From Tom Jefferson to Andy Taylor, Americans have often expressed a distaste for the city as well as a certain dread of the frontier and its concomitant barbarity. The answer is the middle landscape, the mythic place where sanity and compromise prevail, the "country," a down-home Shangri La which remains unaffected by progress and the passage of time: Mayberry RFD, if you will.

Mayberry represents the quintessential middle ground. A dry town, Mayberry annually receives the award for being the most crime-free community in the USA. If any crime does occur, its perpetrator is almost always an alien: the big city criminal or the backwoods rowdy. Once exposed, however, to Andy's natural wisdom and Aunt Bea's cooking, these criminals usually forswear the life of crime. Everything still makes sense in the mythic heart of the country.

"The Real McCoys," "The Beverly Hillbillies," "Gomer Pyle," "Green Acres," "Petticoat Junction," "The Farmer's Daughter," "Apple's Way,"

FOLKS WHO WORK AT JACK DANIEL'S go out of their way to drink the cool limestone water coming from our Cave Spring.

We only have two fountains. But folks could be working at the farthest warehouse and still find an excuse for getting by one of them. So, we know it's good for drinking. We also know it's good for Jack Daniel's. You see, it runs at 56° year-round, and it's completely iron-free. (Iron is murderous to whiskey; a nail dropped in a barrel would ruin every drop.) A sip of our whiskey, we feel, will tell you why we all appreciate our spring.

CHARCOAL
MELLOWED
◊
DROP
◊
BY DROP

© 1972, Jack Daniel Distillery, Lem Motlow, Prop., Inc.
TENNESSEE WHISKEY · 90 PROOF · DISTILLED AND BOTTLED BY JACK DANIEL DISTILLERY · LYNCHBURG (POP. 361), TENNESSEE

By permission of Jack Daniel Distillery.

"The Waltons," and "Little House on the Prairie" all offer or have offered variations on the Mayberry theme. Most of these shows are consciously anachronistic, returning in either place or time to that happy amalgam of nature and moral civilization so characteristic of the American middle landscape tradition.

The country theme also gets extensive play in advertising. Whereas the West suggests isolation and contemplation, the country suggests companionship—male and female, young and old—and overt happiness. Ironically, too, the country also implies a distinctly nonurban purity: a good place to smoke one's cigarettes. The country also evokes a strong sense of nostalgia, a theme that is exploited by concerns as diverse as cameras, soft drinks, cereals, sleeping pills, and laxatives. The country is a tranquil place peopled largely by folks old enough to be hooked on Geritol. Many grandparents live there too.

The Puritan ethic is as ubiquitous a belief as manifest destiny, and it too is an intrinsic part of the American mythic structure. Simplified, the Puritan ethic translates, "God helps those who help themselves." For the Puritans, work was a way of praising God; for Ben Franklin, work became a virtue in itself; for Horatio Alger, it became a way of making money; and for the modern American it seems a way to accumulate material possessions. The manifestations of this drive for success and goods are everywhere: Dagwood occupies his time thinking of new ways to ask for a raise; Blondie spends her time thinking of ways to translate that raise into hats and dresses. Material accumulation, the public is led to believe, represents *the* sign of success.

Advertising strongly and perhaps subconsciously urges the consumer to "keep up with the Joneses" be it with big cars or electric toothbrushes. Liquor companies, for example, are often wont to chip away at the security of one's social status. The trappings in the liquor advertisement are always glittery, the people beautiful, and the booze acknowledgedly expensive. But, say the ads implicitly, one has not really made it unless he drinks the proper brand of liquor. The result, of course, is half a nation of people who choose their liquor not for its taste, nor even for show, but rather out of fear of seeming gauche and low class.

Big car salesmen have a cunning way of pushing big car glamor. The "West," they imply, may be adequate for blue-collar honchos, but if one really has taste, he must look to Europe for satisfaction. Thus the "Europeanized" American car becomes *de riguer*.[1] The Continental, the Riviera, the Le Mans, the Regent, the Grand Prix, the Granada, the L'etoile, the Volaré, the Coup de Ville, and the Torino among others all are named and advertised to evoke some mystical European essence. In truth, none of them have anything to do with Europe, but truth is about as popular in Detroit as safety or economy. What matters is that these cars all ooze that certain *je ne sais quoi*,[2] that look of money misspent.

A key to the paradoxical nature of American materialism is *Playboy* magazine. The true *Playboy* male drinks the right liquor, listens to the right jazz on the right stereo, wears the right clothes, drives the right car, and consumes the right women. All of these goods are, of course, irrationally expensive. The irony is that *Playboy* also supports the right causes. One article might bemoan the plight of the hungry and unclothed while the next insists on fourteen sets of color-coordinated silk underwear for the fall wardrobe. But materialism and egalitarianism have always coexisted in America, however uneasily.

Another strong mythic force abounding in the land might better be called an anti-force, and that is the distrust and resentment of anything intellectual. One is forced, for example, to wonder why Spock, an intellect and a genius, remains second in command to Kirk, an everyday Joe, on

[1]French for indispensable or obligatory. (eds.)
[2]French idiom for "indescribable something." (eds.)

Confidence. It is what any fine automobile gives you. And what you get in full measure from Cordoba. Here is the confidence of knowing your car has a look of great dignity. And the feel of great quality. Here, too, is the confidence of knowing your car controls the road, handling both curve and straightaway with marked assurance. In Cordoba, you will enjoy much more than great comfort at a most pleasant price. You will enjoy great confidence. For which there can be no price.

Reprinted by permission of Chrysler Motors Corporation, Ricardo Montalban, and Young and Rubicam, Inc.

the good ship *Enterprise*. Popular American lore it seems, has always preferred the man of action to the man of thought.

Although this anti-intellectual inclination has not had significant impact on product advertising, it has had a very real impact on political advertising. Campaigning out of the old Populist tradition, George Wallace made great headway with the American voter by promising to throw all the "pointy heads" (translate: intellectuals) into the Potomac. Likewise, Spiro Agnew scored well in the polls by denouncing academicians as "effete intellectual snobs." Similarly, the term "egghead," when applied to Adlai Stevenson, was probably pejorative enough to secure his presidential losses in both 1952 and 1956. "Plain folks" campaign propaganda, from Andy Jackson's[3] day to the present, has assured many a politician his votes.

[3]Andrew Jackson (1767–1845), seventh President of the United States. (eds.)

The final myth to be covered may well be the most frivolous, but it might also be the one for which the media are most responsible, and this is the compelling American need for absolute cleanliness.

This cult of hygiene, intensified by an ad-induced insecurity, has become a national neurosis. Americans would scrub themselves to death lest they be thought unclean. Ten years ago, for example, no one had ever heard of vaginal deodorant; today, many women would not be without it. Advertising pressure can and does work.

"Aren't you glad you use Dial," Mr. Voice-Over asks some otherwise insignificant mass-man. "Don't you wish everyone did?" This Dial-scrubbed fellow suspects that maybe there are cretins out there who don't use Dial. After all, he has seen people lose customers, friends, and lovers because of white speckles ("tell-tale" signs of dandruff) on their shoulders. He has seen girls who will never be kissed again because they "did not make certain with Certs." He has heard of husbands abandoning wives over chronic "ring-around-the-collar" or because of cherry stains on their shirts. He has seen grandmothers hopelessly alienate grandchildren by looking grumpy from constipation. He has seen hardy youths win big games but strike out on dates because of unsightly blemishes. He has known of housewives who have dismayed their neighbors with the waxy yellow buildup on their kitchen floors. He has learned of bosses upsetting employees, teachers offending students, and maiden aunts estranging relatives all because they failed to use Scope. He has seen ladies hands turn into unsightly lobsters. He has had sure intuition about ladies' and he isn't even a hairdresser. Sometimes he has been able to tell mothers apart from their daughters. And yes, he has even smelled bad breath in dogs. What, he asks, can the world be coming to?

H. L. Mencken once claimed that no one ever went broke under-estimating the intelligence of the American public. For sure, Mencken speaks some truth, but he does so a bit too harshly. True, the American can be counted on to respond to a series of mythic suggestions, sometimes even if the myths are manipulated by the most blatant of hucksters. But there will always be a healthy stock of Americans too ornery and too independent to yield to the dictates of the mass media. Individualism, you see, is also an integral part of the nation's mythic heritage.

Aids   *Packaging Pop Mythology*

1. According to John Cashill, what are the popular myths in American society? How is each of these myths exploited by advertisers? Locate one ad from current media that clearly illustrates each myth.

2. Although Cashill's thesis focuses on myths and advertising, he provides examples of these myths from other arenas of popular culture. Why does he do this? Is it effective?

3. In order to emphasize the effect of the western myth on American culture, Cashill creates a hypothetical scenario in which a man dressed in Wranglers hops into his Ranchero and drives to the Ponderosa for some grub. Cashill has crammed into this scenario as many references as possible to western artifacts, language, and styles. The point is clearly and humorously made. Choose another of Cashill's myths and create a mock scenario that illustrates the prevalence of that myth in American society.

4. Establishing tone is an essential part of writing an essay. A reader's attitude toward a subject may be greatly conditioned by the writer's tone. Cashill uses a number of devices to establish his special tone:

    a) His omission of authorities and scholarly references contributes to the informality of the essay.
    b) The informality is heightened by his use of conversational language (hopping into a Mustang, grab himself a can of Colt 45) and his use of slang (gewgaws, whitey, honchos).
    c) His verbal humor prevents us from taking the essay too seriously —he turns an old cliché, "you are what you eat," into an extended metaphor on the consumption of popular culture; he uses language to heighten the absurdity of a situation, i.e., the White Knight does not simply ride through suburbia, he *charges* through backyards; he creates anticlimaxes when he lists together "men on the moon, heart valves, increased agricultural production, *and cures for acne.*"

    How do these devices condition your attitude to the subject of the essay? What do they reveal about Cashill's attitude? Does he at times substitute clever verbal fireworks for clarity and precision?

5. According to Arthur Berger in "Secret Agent," "It may be best to think of our culture as something like an onion, and as we peel away the outer layers, we find, ultimately, a core of myth that has shaped everything else." Look for examples of Cashill's myths in media other than advertising. Do political speeches, TV programs, films, and popular song lyrics exploit any of these myths? Are these myths unique to the American experience? Can you think of any myths that Cashill neglected?

6. According to Cashill, what is the appeal of the Marlboro Man? What myths does the ad for Marlboro exploit? Do you agree with Bruce A.

Lohof, who says, in "The Higher Meaning of Marlboro Cigarettes (*Journal of Popular Culture*, Winter 1969, pp. 441–450), that "The higher meaning of this Marlboro Man and the wilderness he faces down cannot be written in terms of tobacco. Not cigarettes but metaphors—or in this case *a* metaphor—are being merchandised. The Marlboro image is a cultural symbol which speaks to the collective imagination of the American people. It speaks of the virgin frontier, and of the brutal efficacy and constant vigilance which the frontier exacts from its residents. It speaks, as did Frederick Jackson Turner three-quarters of a century ago, of that 'coarseness and strength combined with acuteness and inquisitiveness; that practical, inventive turn of mind, quick to find expedients; that masterful grasp of material things, lacking in the artistic but powerful to effect great ends; that restless, nervous energy; that dominant individualism, working for good and for evil, and withal that buoyancy and exuberance which comes with freedom . . .' "?

7. The ad for Lee Riders also utilizes the Western myth, but how does it differ from the Marlboro ad? What other myths or cultural values does the Lee ad exploit? To what audience is this ad aimed? Does the woman in the ad contradict Cashill's claim that the "frontier pitch has little to offer women"?

8. What myth is celebrated by the ad for Jack Daniels? Why does the ad employ language like "folks" and "it's"? Is this ad an exception to Cashill's claim that the "trappings in the liquor advertisement are always glittery, the people beautiful, and the booze acknowledgedly expensive"?

9. Look at the other ads in this unit. Can they be categorized according to Cashill's myths? Do the men in the ads for Gant shirts, American Express, and Playboy illustrate the American Adam? What about the women in the ads for White Horse, Dewar's, and Virginia Slims? Do they fall neatly into one of Cashill's categories?

The Semantic Environment in the Age of Advertising

HENRYK SKOLIMOWSKI

David Ogilvy is a very successful advertising man. In addition, Mr. Ogilvy has turned out to be a successful writer. His book, *Confessions of an Advertising Man,* was a best-seller in 1965. His confessions are in fact intimate whisperings of one adman to another. These whisperings, however, turned out to be interesting enough to make his book one of the most readable and lucid stories of advertising ever written. What is so fascinating about this book is not the amount of linguistic contortions which he advocates, but the amount of truth which is expressed there incidentally. There is nothing more comforting than to find truth accidentally expressed by one's adversary. *Confessions of an Advertising Man* provides a wealth of such truths.

Mr. Ogilvy tells us that "the most powerful words you can use in a headline are FREE and NEW. You can seldom use FREE," he continues, "but you can always use NEW—if you try hard enough." It is an empirical fact that these two words have a most powerful influence upon us. This fact has been established by scientific research. Whenever these words appear, they are used deliberately—in order to lull and seduce us.

The word FREE is especially seductive. Whether we are aware of this or not, it has an almost hypnotic effect on us. Although we all know "nothing is for nothing," whenever the word FREE appears, it acts on us as the light of a candle acts on a moth. This is one of the mysteries of our language. And these mysteries are very skillfully exploited by advertising men.

Apart from the words FREE and NEW, other words and phrases "which make wonders," as Mr. Ogilvy's research has established, are: "HOW TO, SUDDENLY, NOW, ANNOUNCING, INTRODUCING, IMPORTANT, DEVELOPMENT, AMAZING, SENSATIONAL, REVOLUTIONARY, STARTLING, MIRACLE, OFFER, QUICK, EASY, WANTED, CHALLENGE, ADVICE TO, THE TRUTH ABOUT, COMPARE, BARGAIN, HURRY, LAST CHANCE." Should we not be grateful to Mr. Ogilvy for such a splendid collection? Should we not learn these "miraculous" phrases by heart in order to know which particular ones drive us to the marketplace? To this collection I should like to add some of the phrases which I found: SIMPLE, SAVE, CONVENIENT, COMFORT, LUXURY, SPECIAL OFFER, DISTINCTIVE, DIFFERENT, RARE.

Having provided his collection, Ogilvy comments upon these words that make wonders (and this comment is most revealing): "Don't turn up your nose at these clichés. They may be shopworn, but they work." Alas! They work on us. What can we do about their merciless grip? Nothing. Language and its workings cannot be controlled or altered through an act of our will. The cumulative process of the development of language used as the instrument of tyranny or as the bridge to God through prayers; as a recorder of everyday trivia or as a clarion trumpet announcing new

From *ETC: A Review of General Semantics*, March 1968, pp. 17–26. Reprinted by permission of the International Society for General Semantics.

epochs in human history; as an expression of private feelings of single individuals or as a transmitter of slogans to the masses—this process has endowed some words with incredible subtleties and others with irresistible power. The only thing we can do about the influence of language on us is to become aware of it. This awareness may diminish the grip language has on us.

It is very gratifying to know that nowadays advertising is so punctilious, so systematic, and so scientific in its approach to the customer. Mr. Ogilvy in *Confessions* relentlessly repeats that "research has shown" so and so, "research shows" this and that, "research suggests" that, "research has established" that, etc. This constant reference to research is not an advertising humbug. It is through systematic research that we are "hooked" more and more thoroughly. With perfect innocence Ogilvy informs us that "Another profitable gambit is to give the reader helpful advice or service. It hooks about [was this a slip of the tongue, or intentional, plain description?] 75 per cent more readers than copy which deals entirely with the product."

Madison Avenue has, above all, established that through words we may be compelled to perform certain acts—acts of buying. This conclusion is not to be found in Ogilvy. Whether it is an historical accident or not, it is a rather striking fact that, independent of semanticists and logicians and linguistic philosophers, advertising men have made some important discoveries about language. And they have utilized these discoveries with amazing success. They are probably not aware of the theoretical significance of their discoveries and are no doubt little interested in such matters.

J. L. Austin, one of the most prominent linguistic philosophers at Oxford during the 1950's, developed a theory of what he called *performative utterances*. He observed that language is systematically employed not only for stating and describing but also for performing actions. Such utterances as "I warn you to . . ." or "I promise you x" are performances rather than descriptions. They function not only on a verbal level, but also as deeds, as concrete performances through words. The discovery and classification of performative utterances is an important extension of ordinary logic—that is, logic concerned with declarative utterances. On the other hand, it is an important finding of the hidden force of language in shaping our social and individual relationships.

Quite independently, advertising men have developed and successfully applied their own theory of performative utterances. They may be oblivious to the logical subtleties involved; however, they are not oblivious to the power of their medium—that is, the verbal utterances through which they induce our acts of buying. Again, there is very little we can do about it. This is the way language works. We can only recognize this fact. But once we recognize it, we acquire some immunity.

Now, we all know that advertising messages are conveyed in words. Usually, there are not only words, but pictures and images which suggest appropriate associations to the person reading the words. The images are projected to be psychologically appealing. Psychologically appealing images are those which appeal to our seven deadly sins: sexual urges, vanity, snobbery, gluttony, greed, etc.

Many analyses of advertising have shown the mechanism of psychological associations built into the ad message. In particular they showed that the level of most of these appeals is that of sheer brutes, of ultimate half-wits whose only desire is to satisfy their most rudimentary biological urges. However, not many analyses of advertising, if any at all, show how frail the link is between the picture set to evoke emotional reactions and the linguistic utterance which, in the final analysis, is the message of the ad. We must remember that it is the verbal message which ultimately draws us to the marketplace. The analysis of this verbal or linguistic level of the ad is our main concern here.

Language is, of course, basically a medium of communication. To be an adequate medium, language must be flexible. But to be flexible is one thing; to be entirely elastic and malleable is another. These other two characteristics, extreme elasticity and malleability, are required from the language which is set to infiltrate people's minds and contaminate their mental habits. It is in this latter capacity that admen want to employ language. And consequently, they do everything conceivable, and sometimes inconceivable, to make language infinitely flexible and as malleable as plasticene.

The point is very simple. If language is made a plasticene, the meaning of concepts is so stretched that words are deprived of their original sense and end up with whatever sense the wild imagination of the admen equips them. Since the language of ads often departs radically from ordinary language, advertisements could in one sense be regarded as pieces of poetry.[1]

A piece of poetry should have a nice ring to its words, pleasant or extraordinary association of ideas, unusual combinations of meanings. The factual content is not important. For communication, as I shall use the term here, the factual content is most important. It is the content that we wish to communicate, and this is conveyed in messages. Consequently, messages must contain factual information. If there is no factual information in the message, the message does not communicate anything. Usually the actual content of the message may be expressed in many different ways. What is important is the content, not the manner of expression. If the manner of expressing a message is more important than its content, then the message does not serve the purpose of communication. It may serve many other purposes, but it does not serve the purpose of conveying factual information.

And this is exactly the case with advertising. The advertising messages are pseudo-messages, not genuine messages. They do not contain factual information. At any rate, this is not their main purpose. Their main purpose is not to inform but to force us to buy. It is clear that if the content of advertising were of any importance, then the same message worded differently would serve the same function; namely, of informing us. This is obviously not the case with advertising: the over-

---

[1]The idea that advertising is a kind of bad poetry was first forcibly and tellingly expressed by E. E. Cummings in his "Poem, or Beauty Hurts Mr. Vinal" (1926). See also "Poetry and Advertising," Chapter XV of Hayakawa's *Language in Thought and Action* (rev. ed., 1964). See also "Advertising as a Philosophical System," Chapter 3 of Jules Henry's *Culture Against Man* (1963). (eds.)

She came on softly.
There was something so silky
about the way she looked.
I wanted so much to get close to her.
And as I did, she smelled so fresh,
so real, so gentle.

JOHNSON'S *Baby Powder*.
When a woman wants to make a gentle impression.

Johnson & Johnson

whelming majority of ads would have little effect, if any, if they were phrased differently.

In art, our emotional involvement is the source of our delight. It is the uniqueness of the form that inspires our thoughts and arouses our emotions. The meaning and significance of the work of art hinge upon the uniqueness of its form. Once the form is destroyed or altered, the work of art does not exist any more. If the validity of advertisements depends on preserving their form intact, then they pretend to be pieces of art, but not the carriers of factual information. The trouble is that they *do* pretend to give factual and objective information—but in a rather peculiar way: in such a way that the "information" would force us to acquire the product which is the substance of the message.

Communication is for humans. It is the mark of a rational man to grasp the content of a message irrespective of the form of its presentation—that is, irrespective of its linguistic expression. The nature of any communication in which the actual information conveyed is less significant than the manner of its presentation is, to say the least, illogical. The illogical man is what advertising is after. This is why advertising is so anti-rational; this is why it aims at uprooting not only the rationality of man but his common sense; this is why it indulges in exuberant but deplorable linguistic orgies.

Distortion of language, violation of logic, and corruption of values are about the most common devices through which advertising operates. This is particularly striking in endless perversions of the word FREE. Since this word has such a powerful impact on us, there is no limit to its abuse. In his novel *1984*, George Orwell showed that what is required for establishing a "perfect" dictatorship is perhaps no more than a systematic reform of language. The condition is, however, that the reform must be thorough and complete. "Doubletalk" as a possible reality has, since Orwell's novel, been viewed with horror, but not with incredulity. The question is whether doubletalk has not already become part of our reality, has not already been diffused in our blood stream through means different from those Orwell conceived of. Isn't it true that advertising has become a perfect Orwellian institution?

Nowadays there is in operation a doubletalk concept of freedom according to which protecting the public from fraud and deceit and warning people about dangers to their health is but "an erosion of freedom." This concept of freedom is, needless to say, advocated and defended by advertising agencies. In the opinion of admen, "freedom" for people means protecting people from their common sense

and ability to think. For many admen "freedom" means freedom to advertise in whatsoever manner is profitable, freedom to force you to buy, freedom to penetrate your subconscious, freedom to dupe you, to hook you, to make a sucker of you, freedom to take away your freedom. Anything else is for them but an "erosion of freedom." Hail Mr. Orwell! Hail doubletalk!

Now to turn to some concrete illustrations:

MUSTANG! A CAR TO MAKE WEAK MEN STRONG, STRONG MEN INVINCIBLE.

Do not say that we do not believe such obvious blusterings. We do. It seems that the art of magicians—according to which some incantations evoke events, bring rain, heal wounds; some amulets bring good luck, prevent bad luck or illness—has been re-established by contemporary advertising. Motor cars in particular are the amulets of the atomic age. They possess all the miraculous qualities you wish them to possess—from being a substitute for a sweetheart (or mistress, if you prefer) to being a soothing balm to a crushed ego. Dictionaries usually define an automobile as a self-propelled vehicle for the transportation of people or goods. The car industry and car dealers are of a quite different opinion. Perhaps lexicographers are outdated in their conception of "automobile."

Roughly speaking, motor cars are advertised to be amulets of two kinds. The first casts spells on us and makes us happy, or builds up our personality, or adds to our strength, or makes us invincible if we are already strong; the second casts spells on others and, while we drive this magic vehicle, makes other people see us as more important, more influential, more irresistible. As yet, there are no cars which, being driven by us, would bring punishment upon our enemies. Perhaps one day this will come to pass. The question is how many of us can really resist the incantations of car dealers and remain impervious to the "magical" qualities allegedly embodied in the modern automobile. How many of us can remain uninfluenced by the continuous flow of messages, in spite of our ability to see the nonsense of each one individually?

Our civilization has often been called the motor-car civilization. But in no less degree, it is the drug civilization; it is also the detergent civilization. Each of these elements is apparently essential to the well-being of our society. But it is by no means only detergents, cars, or drugs that offer us full happiness "at a reasonable price." Nowadays, practically any product can give you happiness.

Happiness Is To Get (or Give) a Bulova

The only problem is to believe it. Whether Bulova is a yellow canary, a black watch, or a green giraffe, it unfortunately takes a bit more to achieve happiness than getting or giving a Bulova. But of course the counter-argument can go, "happiness" in this ad was not meant literally but only figuratively. Admen today are like poets; we must allow them poetic license. But must we? And how figuratively would they really like to be taken? It seems that they (and the producers of the products they advertise) would be very unhappy if we took all their messages figuratively. On the contrary, they want their messages to be taken as literally as

possible. It is precisely their business to convince us about the "loveliness" of soaps, "happiness" in Bulovas, and "delights" of a cigarette puff. The poetic language they use is meant to break our resistance, to produce desirable associations which we usually associate with poetry.

The sad part of the story is that in the process of serving advertising, poetry has gone down the drain. Poetic expressions are poetic so long as they are in the context of poetry; so long as they evoke unusual emotional reactions, serve as a substance of an esthetic experience—the experience of delight. In its exuberant development, advertising has debased almost the entire poetic vocabulary. And advertising seems to be responsible for a decline of the poetic taste and for a considerable indifference, if not hostility, of American youth toward poetry.

The nausea which one experiences on being bombarded by the pseudo-poetry of advertising may recur when one approaches genuine poetry, unless one has developed love for poetry *before* becoming aware of advertising—which is impossible for young people nowadays. It is quite natural that such a reaction would develop. We are not likely to seek nausea deliberately, and so we would rather avoid whatever reminds us of it. It seems that if the process of debasing and abusing language by advertising is carried further, we may discover a new value in absolute simplicity of language. Perhaps one day, when the traditional poetry is completely ruined, we shall count as poetry some simple and concrete descriptions like this: "There is a table in the room. The table is brown. There are three chairs at the table. A man is sitting on one of the chairs."[2]

The main point is more significant. By applying highly charged emotional terms like "lovely" to soaps, and "bold" and "proud" to automobiles, advertising pushes us to consider objects as if they were human beings. Through the language of advertising, we participate in the process of constant personification of objects which we should "love," be "enchanted by," be "delighted with," and "be happy with." Unconsciously we have developed emotional attachments to objects surrounding us. We have become worshippers of objects. Advertising has been a powerful force in this process.

My thesis is that the semantic environment has a more profound influence on our behavior and our attitudes than we are aware. If this thesis is correct, it may throw some light on the phenomenon which we usually attribute to the population explosion and the mechanization of our lives; namely, the depersonalization of human relations. I should like to suggest that perhaps a transfer of attitudes through the change of the semantic environment has taken place. Previously, highly emotional expressions were applied to human beings. Nowadays, they are constantly and massively applied by the admen to objects. We have thus developed loving fondness for objects which we worship. Dehumanizing of human relations seems to be the other part of this process. It is quite natural that when we become more and more emotionally involved with objects, we tend to be less and less involved with people. As a consequence, attitudes traditionally reserved for objects are now displayed toward people. In love, in friendship, and in the multitude of other human relations, detachment, lack of interest, and coldness seem to prevail. Human beings are treated like objects.

To summarize, the success of advertising and our failure to defend ourselves against it result mainly from our obliviousness to some of the functions of language. We think that language is a tool, an indifferent piece of gadgetry which simply serves the process of communication and that the only relation we have to language is that *we use language*. We do indeed use it. But this is only part of the story. The other part, which is usually overlooked, is that *language uses us*—by forming our personal and emotional habits, by forming our attitudes. Language is thus not only our servant; it is also our master. No one knows this better than the adman!

The relation between language and us is more complicated than we usually are prepared to admit. To escape the tyranny of language, we have to recognize the double role of language in human relations, (1) as a carrier of messages we send, and (2) as a shaper of the content of human relations. We cannot reduce or nullify the influence of language on us by simply denying the existence of this influence. The only reasonable thing we can do is to recognize the force of language: its strength, the way it works, its theater of operations. By identifying the traps of language, by identifying the linguistic

---

[2]Perhaps some poets have discovered this principle already. Here is the complete text of "The Red Wheelbarrow" by William Carlos Williams: "so much depends / upon / a red wheel / barrow / glazed with rain / water / beside the white / chickens." (*Collected Poems 1921–1931*, Objectivist Press, 1934.)

strategies of the admen and other propagandists, we shall be able to cope with the
semantic environment much more effectively than we have done hitherto.

Aids   *The Semantic Environment
in the Age of Advertising*

1. According to Skolimowski, certain words when used in ads have
    a seductive, almost hypnotic effect upon consumers. Make a list
    of these words, locating specific examples in current ads and
    commercials.

2. What can we do about "the merciless grip" of these seductive words?
    What specific defenses should we develop to combat the powerful
    influence of these words?

3. What are some of the important discoveries that ad people have
    made about the power of words?

4. What, according to the author, is the "double role" of language in
    human relations?

5. What are "performative utterances"? Locate some specific examples
    from current ads.

6. Do you agree that pictorial images in ads appeal to "our seven
    deadly sins"? Locate examples of ads that appeal to our sexual urges,
    vanity, snobbery, gluttony, and greed. Can you add some additional
    "sins" to the list?

7. The author maintains that the language of ads is "pseudo-poetry."
    What precisely is pseudo-poetry? How does it differ from genuine
    poetry? What are the effects of pseudo-poetry upon us and upon
    our appreciation of genuine poetry?

8. Each word in the special language of advertising, Skolimowski
    suggests, attempts to tap a particular yearning and hunger in the
    consumer. Conduct a study of the language of ads, focusing on a
    particular line of products (e.g., cosmetics, automobiles, liquor).
    Examine the brand names, slogans, and copy for (a) their persuasive
    power, (b) their manipulation of connotations, (c) their use of
    mood phrases, (d) their use of sensuous and suggestive similes, and
    (e) their use of performative utterances. You might begin by exam-
    ining the following copy from an ad for Revlon's Pango Peach:
    "From east of the sun . . . West of the moon. Where each tomorrow

dawns . . . 'Pango Peach' the new color creation by Revlon. A many-splendoured coral . . . pink with pleasure. What a *volcano* of fashion color! It's a full ripe peach with a world of difference . . . born to be worn in big juicy slices. Succulent on your lips. Sizzling on your fingertips. *Go* Pango Peach . . . *your* adventure in paradise."

9. The pseudo-poetry of advertising may be further characterized by rather special devices. Locate additional examples of each of the following in current ads:

   a) Informal and utilitarian usage ("Hey Charger! Where'd you get that racy look?")

   b) Fresh idioms ("You've come a long way, baby"; "Sock it to me"; "I bet you can't eat the whole thing.")

   c) Unconventional spellings (Duz, E-Z Off, Kool, Kleen)

   d) Puns and double meanings ("You AUTO buy now"; "Look what Oldsmobile hatched. Two sporty new hatchbacks"; Hiram Walker's "Alexander the Greats.")

   e) Inventive new compounds ("Sheer Ribbed Control-Top Panty-hose"; "Introducing Robin's-Egg-Blue, Bunny-Rabbit-Pink, Baby-Chick-Yellow, Pretty-Pastel-Purple and Jelly-Bean-Green Easter L'eggs"; "Whipped Creme Enriched Eye Shadow")

   f) Hyperbole ("Pulsar continues to change the way the world tells time"; "Now the world takes MASTER CHARGE")

   g) Blends (native neologisms, such as Triscuit, Vaporub, Eversharp, Duracell, Philco)

   h) Functional shifts, especially idiomatic verb phrases ("to tough it through," "to stonewall," "to impact on," "to run rampant," "to hunker down," "to strike out")

10. Skolimowski also suggests that ads employ a special logic, the goal of which is not the *truth* but contamination of our mental habits. Truth in advertising is what sells, what you want people to believe, and that which is not legally false. It would seem then that distortion and misrepresentation are features deliberately incorporated into some ads in order to sell the image of humanity to which the consumer aspires. Conduct a study of the logic of advertising, locating examples of some of the following flaws in asserting and arguing: (a) ambiguity, (b) vagueness, (c) misleading statement, (d) exaggeration or understatement, (e) overgeneralization, (f) oversimplification, (g) irrelevance, (h) tautology, (i) equivocation, (j) misuse of etymology, (k) large numbers, (l) begging the question, (m) ad hominem ("to the man"), (n) false analogy, (o) post hoc, ergo propter hoc, (p) ad populum ("to the people"), (q) tu quoque ("you're another"),

(r) black/white argument, (s) red herring, (t) genetic fallacy, (u) begging the question, and (v) inductive leap.

Inductive leap, for instance, occurs in most ads for personal grooming products. In an ad for Casaque perfume, a sophisticated, handsome young man is shown embracing a beautiful woman in a typical Parisian setting. Above the couple, the caption reads, "The exciting, igniting world of Casaque." The ad seems to be formulating the following implausible argument: any woman who buys Casaque perfume will be guaranteed an exciting world of romance. The argument of the ad *leaps* from partial evidence (a woman buying perfume) to a conclusion that goes well beyond the evidence (the promise of romance).

11. Assumptions play a role in all reasoning. They are what we take for granted before we begin our arguments. Since we usually *assume* that others make the same assumptions we do, we do not feel obliged to make them explicit. All ads make assumptions about their intended audiences. Choose one or more of the assumptions that follow and locate specific examples from current ads: (a) cleanliness is next to godliness, (b) a picture is worth a 1000 words, (c) sex sells, (d) pets are people, (e) smoking cigarettes is natural and desirable, (f) drinking alcohol is romantic, (g) consumers have an insatiable appetite for newness, (h) housewives need a fairy god*father* in the kitchen, laundry, and bathroom, (i) men don't buy automobiles, they buy masculine virility—or more recently, they buy sporty economy, (j) women don't buy cosmetics, they buy the *promise* of love, youth, and immortality, (k) children don't buy toys, they buy miniaturized adult worlds, (l) pleasure seeking is everything.

12. As we have seen, Skolimowski asserts that ad people employ deplorable linguistic habits in order to uproot "not only the rationality of man but his common sense." Another type of language manipulation in advertising and public persuasion is called the *weasel word*, "a word used in order to evade or retreat from a direct or forthright statement or position." According to Paul Stevens in *I Can Sell You Anything* (Ballantine Books, 1972), weasel words can do anything: "They can make you hear things that aren't being said, accept as truths things that have only been implied, and believe things that have only been suggested." Locate examples of the following weasel words in current advertising:

a) The word *help* is the one single word that has done the most to say something that couldn't be said: Helps stop . . . , Helps fight . . . , Helps you feel . . . , Helps you look . . .

b) Ads use *like* to get you to transfer your thinking from the product being advertised to something that is bigger or better. According to Paul Stevens, "Cleans like a white tornado" is a copywriter's dream, because no one has to substantiate the claim.

c) Ads that use *virtual* or *virtually*, as in "virtually trouble-free," are not saying "almost or just about the same as . . . ," but "in essence or effect, *but not in fact.*"

d) If an ad cannot say "cures" or "fixes," it will probably say "acts like" or "works against."

e) According to Stevens, ads also claim results that may not be achieved by everyone by using the following weasels: "can be," as in "Crest can be of significant value when used in . . ."; "up to," as in "cured for up to eight long, lazy weeks"; and "as much as," as in "as much as 20% greater mileage." All three weasels promise the ideal, *but qualify it.*

13. Like words, ads have the potential to work us over on several levels. On the literal, or denotative level, a cigarette ad, for instance, declares that smoking is dangerous to our health, but on the connotative level, the young, tanned couple standing there in their tennis costumes *visually* suggests health, vitality, energy, and good times. Locate some additional examples in current ads of *visual connotation.*

The Day the Ads Stopped

GEORGE G. KIRSTEIN

The day the advertising stopped began just like any other day—the sun came up, the milk was delivered and people started for work. I noticed the first difference when I went out on the porch to pick up *The New York Times*. The newsdealer had advised me that the paper would now cost 50¢ a day so I was prepared for the new price beneath the weather forecast, but the paper was thinner than a Saturday edition in summer. I hefted it thoughtfully, and reflected that there really was no alternative to taking the *Times*. The *News* had suspended publication the day before the advertising stopped with a final gallant editorial blast at the Supreme Court which had declared the advertising prohibition constitutional. The *Herald Tribune* was continuing to publish, also at 50¢, but almost no one was taking both papers and I preferred the *Times*.

As I glanced past the big headlines chronicling the foreign news, my eye was caught by a smaller bank:

> 1 KILLED, 1 INJURED IN
> ELEVATOR ACCIDENT AT MACY'S.

The story was rather routine; a child had somehow gotten into the elevator pit and his mother had tried to rescue him. The elevator had descended, killing the woman, but fortunately had stopped before crushing the child. It was not so much the story as its locale that drew my attention. I realized that this was the first time in a full, rich life that I had ever read a newspaper account of an accident in a department store. I had suspected that these misfortunes befell stores, as they do all business institutions, but this was my first confirmation.

There were other noticeable changes in the *Times*. Accounts of traffic accidents now actually gave the manufacturers' names of the vehicles involved as, "A Cadillac driven by Harvey Gilmore demolished a Volkswagen operated by. . . ." The feature column on "Advertising" which

Reprinted from *The Nation* (June 1, 1964), pp. 555–57. Reprinted by permission of the publisher.

used to tell what agencies had lost what accounts and what assistant vice president had been elevated was missing. As a matter of fact, the whole newspaper, but particularly the Financial Section, exhibited a dearth of "news" stories which could not possibly interest anyone but the persons mentioned. Apparently, without major expenditures for advertising, the promotion of Gimbels' stocking buyer to assistant merchandise manager was not quite as "newsworthy" as it had been only yesterday. Movies and plays were listed in their familiar spot, as were descriptions of available apartments in what used to be the classified section. The women's page was largely a catalogue of special offerings in department and food stores, but no comparative prices were given and all adjectives were omitted. One could no longer discover from reading the *Times*, or any other paper, who had been named Miss National Car Care Queen or who had won the Miss Rheingold contest.

Driving to work, I observed workmen removing the billboards. The grass and trees behind the wall of signs were beginning to reappear. The ragged posters were being ripped from their familiar locations on the walls of warehouses and stores, and the natural ugliness of these structures was once more apparent without the augmenting tawdriness of last year's political posters or last week's neighborhood movie schedules.

I turned on the car radio to the subscription FM station to which I had sent my $10 dues. The music came over the air without interruption, and after awhile a news announcer gave an uninterrupted version of current events and the weather outlook. No one yet knew which radio stations would be able to continue broadcasting. It depended on the loyalty with which their listeners continued to send in their subscription dues. However, their prospects were better than fair, for everyone realized that, since all merchandise which had previously been advertised would cost considerably less on the store counter, people would have funds available to pay for the news they read or the music or other programs they listened to. The absence of the familiar commercials, the jingles, the songs and the endless repetition of the nonsense which had routinely offended our ears led me to consider some of these savings. My wife's lipsticks would now cost half as much as previously; the famous brand soaps were selling at 25 per cent below yesterday's prices; razor blades were 10 per cent cheaper; and other appliances and merchandise which had previously been nationally advertised were reduced by an average of 5 per cent. The hallowed myth that retail prices did not reflect the additional cost of huge advertising campaigns was exploded once and for all. Certainly these savings should add up to enough for me to pay for what I listened to on my favorite radio station or read in the newspaper of my choice.

After parking my car, I passed the familiar newsstand between the garage and the office. "*Life* $1," the printed sign said. "*Time* and *Newsweek*, 75¢." Next to these announcements was a crayon-scrawled message!

"*Consumer Reports* sold out. Bigger shipment next week." I stopped to chat with the newsie. "The mags like *Consumer Reports* that tell the truth about products are selling like crazy," he told me. "*Reader's Digest* is running a merchandise analysis section next month." I asked about the weekly journals of opinion. He said, "Well now they are half the price of the news magazines—*The Nation* and *The New Republic* prices have not gone up, you know, but I don't think that will help them much. After all, a lot of magazines are going to begin printing that exposé-type stuff. Besides, people are buying books now. Look!" He pointed across the street to the paperback bookstore where a crowd was milling around as though a fire sale were in progress.

I walked over to the bookstore and found no special event going on. But books represented much better value than magazines or newspapers, now that the latter were no longer subsidized by advertisements, and the public was snapping up the volumes.

Sitting in my office, I reviewed the events and the extraordinary political coalition that had been responsible for passing the advertising prohibition law through Congress by a close margin. The women, of course, had been the spearhead of the drive. Not since the Anti-Saloon-League days and the militant woman-suffrage movement at the beginning of the century had women organized so militantly or expended energy more tirelessly in pursuit of their objective. Their slogans were geared to two main themes which reflected their major grievances. The first slogan, "Stop making our kids killers," was geared mainly to the anti-television campaign. The sadism, killing and assorted violence which filled the TV screens over all channels from early morning to late at night had finally so outraged mothers' groups, PTAs and other organizations concerned with the country's youth that a massive parents' movement was mobilized.

The thrust of the women's drive was embodied in their effective two-word motto, "Stop lying." Women's organizations all over the country established committees to study all advertisements. For the first time in history, these common messages were analyzed in detail. The results were published in anti-advertising advertisements, by chain letter and by mouth. The results were devastating. No dog-food manufacturer could claim that pets loved his product without having the women demand, "How in the name of truth do you know? Did you interview the dogs?" No shampoo or cosmetic preparation could use the customary blandishments without having the women produce some witch who had used the particular product and who had lost her hair, developed acne or had her fingernails curl back.

Women led the attack, but the intellectuals soon joined them, and the clergy followed a little later. The intellectuals based their campaign largely on the argument that the English language was losing its usefulness, that word meanings were being so corrupted that it was almost impossible to teach youth to read to any purpose. One example commonly cited was the debasement of the superlative "greatest." The word had come to mean anything that didn't break down; viz., "the greatest lawn mower ever," interpreted realistically, was an instrument that, with luck, would cut grass for one summer. The clergy's campaign was geared simply to the proposition that it was impossible to teach people the virtues of truth when half-truths and lies were the commonly accepted fare of readers and viewers alike.

Opposition to the anti-advertising law was impressive, and at the beginning it looked as if all the big guns were arrayed against the women. Spokesmen for big business contended throughout the campaign that elimination of advertising meant elimination of jobs. The fallacy of this argument was soon exposed when all realized that it was not men's jobs but simply machine running time that was involved. By this decade of the century, the cybernetic revolution had developed to a point where very few men were involved in any of the production or distribution processes. No one could feel much sympathy for the poor machines and their companion computers because they would be running only four hours daily instead of six.

Some merchants tried to blunt the "stop lying" slogan by telling the absolute truth. One San Francisco store advertised:

> 2,000 overcoats—only $12. Let's face it—our buyer goofed! These coats are dogs or you couldn't possibly buy them at this price. We're losing our shirt on this sale and the buyer has been fired. But, at least, many of these coats will keep you warm.

The trouble with this technique was that it backfired in favor of the women. The few true ads, by contrast, drew attention to the vast volume of exaggeration, misrepresentation and outright lies that were printed as usual. The advertising industry published thirteen different editions of its "Advertisers Code" in the years preceding the law's passage, but few could detect any difference from the days when no code at all existed.

The press, of course, was the strongest opponent and loudest voice against the advertising prohibition. Its argument was largely legalistic, based on the First Amendment to the Constitution, for the publishers had decided at the outset of their defense not to emphasize the fact that if advertising stopped, readers would actually have to pay for what they read, rather than have America's largest corporations pay for the education and edification of the public. However, the words "Free Press" came to have a double meaning—both an unhampered press and a press that charged only a nominal fee for the publications.

The constitutional argument was really resolved in that final speech on the floor of the Senate before a gallery-packed audience, by Senator Thorndike of Idaho. His memorable oration, certainly among the greatest in the Senate's distinguished history, concluded:

> And so, Mr. President, the opponents of this measure [the advertising prohibition] claim that the founders of this republic, our glorious forefathers, in their august wisdom, forbade the Congress to interfere with the freedom of the press to conduct itself in any way it found profitable. But I say to you, that the framers of our Constitution intended to protect the public by permitting the press, without fear or favor, to examine all of the institutions of our democracy. Our forefathers planned a press free to criticize, free to analyze, free to dissent. They did not plan a subsidized press, a conformist press, a prostitute press.

The applause was thunderous and the bill squeaked through the Senate by four votes. Three years later, the Supreme Court upheld Senator Thorndike's interpretation. That was two days ago, and today the advertising stopped.

All morning I worked in the office, and just before noon I went uptown for lunch. The subway cars were as drab as ever and seemed a little less bright because of the absence of the familiar posters. However in one car the Camera Club of the Technical Trades High School had "hung" a show of New York City photographs chosen from student submissions. In another car, the posters on one side carried Session I of a course in Spanish for English-speaking riders, while the opposite side featured the same course in English for those speaking Spanish. This program was sponsored by the Board of Education which had subcontracted the administration of it to the Berlitz school. A poster in both languages in the middle of the car explained that the lessons would proceed on a weekly basis and that by sending $1 to the Board of Education, review sheets and periodic tests would be available upon request.

On Madison Avenue, the shopping crowds were milling around as usual, but there was a noticeable absence of preoccupied and hatless young men hurrying along the street. The retirement plan that the advertising industry had worked out through the insurance companies was fairly generous, and the majority of key personnel that had been laid off when the agencies closed were relieved not to have to make the long trek from Westport or the nearer suburbs each day. Some of the copywriters who had been talking about it since their youth were now really going to write that novel.

Others had set up shop as public relations counselors, but the outlook for their craft was not bright. Without the club of advertising, city editors looked over mimeographed press releases with a new distaste, and it is even rumored that on some newspapers the orders had come down to throw out all such "handouts" without exception. On the magazines, the old struggle between the editorial staff and the advertising sales staff for dominance had finally been resolved by the elimination of the latter. There were even some skeptics who believed that public relations counseling would become a lost art, like hand basket weaving. So most former advertising copywriters planned to potter about in their gardens, cure their ulcers and give up drinking. They were not so many. It was a surprise to most people to learn that the advertising industry, which had had such a profound effect on the country's habits and moral attitudes, directly employed fewer than 100,000 people.

Outside 383 Madison Avenue, moving vans were unloading scientific equipment and laboratory accessories into the space vacated by Batten, Barton, Durstine & Osborn. The ethical drug industry had evolved a plan, in the three-year interim between the passage of the advertising prohibition and the Supreme Court's validation of it, to test all new drugs at a central impartial laboratory. Computers and other of the latest information-gathering machinery were massed in the space vacated by this large advertising agency to correlate the results of drug tests which were being conducted in hospitals, clinics, laboratories and doctors' offices throughout the world.

The Ford Foundation had given one of its richest grants, nearly three-quarters of a billion dollars, to the establishment of this Central Testing Bureau. The American Medical Association had finally agreed, under considerable public pressure, to take primary responsibility for its administration. It was pointed out to the doctors that when the drug companies could no longer make their individual claims through advertisements in the AMA bulletin or the medical society publications, a new and more reliable method of disseminating information would be required. At the outset, the AMA had joined the drug companies in fighting bitterly against the prohibition, but the doctors now took considerable pride in their centralized research and correlation facilities. The AMA bulletin, once swollen to the bulk of a small city's telephone directory, was now only as thick as a summer issue of *Newsweek*. Doctors no longer would find their mail boxes stuffed with throw-away material and sample pills; but they would receive the weekly scientific report from Central Testing Bureau as to the efficacy of and experience with all new preparations.

Late in the afternoon, I began to hear the first complaints about the way the new law worked. One of the men came in and picked up a folder of paper matches lying on my desk. "I'm swiping these; they're not giving them out any more, you know." Someone else who had been watching TV said that the two channels assigned to the government under a setup like that of the B.B.C., were boring. One channel showed the ball game, but the other had been limited to a short session of the Senate debating the farm bill, and a one-hour view of the UN Security Council taking up the latest African crisis. My informant told me the Yanks had won 8 to 0, and the Senate and the UN weren't worth watching. I reminded him that when the channel that was to be supervised by the American Academy of Arts and Sciences got on the air, as well as the one to be managed by a committee of the local universities, things might improve. "Cheer up," I told him, "At least it's better than the Westerns and the hair rinses."

Oh, there were some complaints, all right, and I suppose there were some unhappy people. But personally I thought the day the advertising stopped was the best day America had had since the last war ended.

Aids   *The Day the Ads Stopped*

1. Why were the ads stopped?

2. Who initiated the attack against advertising? In what ways is this group the principal victim of deceptive advertising?

3. What impact did the moratorium on advertising have on (a) the print and broadcast media, and (b) American culture?

4. What ultimately is the author's attitude toward advertising? Does the story have an implied thesis?

5. Using Hugh Rank's schema in "Learning About Public Persuasion," show how Kirstein intensifies the "badness" of advertising, while downplaying its "good." Is the story propagandistic?

6. What other attack is explicit in the slogan "Stop making our kids killers"? What assumption about the influence of the media on its viewers is implicit in this slogan?

7. Do you think that Kirstein has considered the full implications of his fantasy-scenario? Where does advertising stop, after all? Would the government have to regulate political speeches, song lyrics, television programs, labeling on consumer products, and the classified section of the daily newspaper?

8. "The Day the Ads Stopped" is an example of narration. The author is telling a story. He is answering the question: *what happened* the day the ads stopped? Using the story as a model, write your own story in which you narrate what happens *to you* when (a) the ads stop, or (b) media violence is banned.

Advertising's Response to Its Critics*

FAIRFAX M. CONE

The principal challenge to advertising people everywhere is to move toward professional status. Technically, this may be something they can never achieve, but they can observe professional rules and they can maintain professional standards. Obviously, this begins inside the business, for whatever may be done outside it will not make up for any lack within.

Once upon a time it would have been challenge enough simply to clean up advertising, to make it truthful and to make it useful. But as most people now know, dishonest advertising has become a small part of the total. The requirement of most advertised products to produce results as promised is inherent in the economics of the marketplace; it is not a matter of the advertiser's morals. It is virtually impossible to sell a bad product twice to the same person, and the number of products that can succeed as a result of one-time sales is limited almost entirely to products of infrequent purchase such as automobiles, heating systems and major appliances

that are sold, for the most part, in person-to-person confrontation by live salespeople and not by advertising.

But if honesty in advertising has become the accepted standard, the question of good taste continues to plague the industry. I am referring to the extremely poor taste of a great deal of book and moving picture advertising and to political advertising that oversteps what I consider to be the bounds of decency. I should mention also the excesses that occur in the advertising of health and beauty products. Almost all of these are matters of tasteless presentation. Somehow there must be a better way to present a mouthwash on television than to show a distraught, tearful teenager screaming at her escort at a party "You said I had . . . *bad breath!*" Or a frantic woman reporting to a friend that her husband insisted that her "breath was a major cause of air pollution."

Obviously there is nothing immoral about this kind of thing. Nor was it advertising that first brought it forth. It is part of the permissiveness of our times, and the crudeness that filters into advertising from books, movies, plays and television entertainment where no subject is too intimate or too delicate to be exploited for laughs or for tears.

Under the circumstances of a general breakdown in the authority of schools and the church to preserve social standards, it can hardly be expected that advertising will pick up the pieces and put them together again. But it can, and it *should*, be made with the obligation in mind to raise the standards of our manners and our conduct and not to accept these at the scornful level of a rude and frequently vulgar generation. This is not to say that I believe the hippies and their fellow travelers have been responsible for the breakdown. On the contrary, I hold them to be a result of it. But they are also its clearest manifestation.

Advertising always follows, it never leads. Nevertheless, it should be used in the best traditions of our society and not the very questionable postures that evolve from time to time. One of the worst of the offenses of advertising in this area of bad manners is the denigration of competitive products through the use of odious comparisons, sometimes joking, sometimes deadly serious. I am perfectly aware that depreciation is the basis of both nightclub humor and many a salesperson's strongest ploy. But this doesn't alter my view that advertising should never stoop to conquer. To see that it doesn't is the second charge that I would make to the successors.

It ties closely to the first, to play a personal part in community affairs; and it leads directly to the third, which is to use advertising as an educational force.

For sixteen years the *Saturday Review* has made awards to a growing number of advertisers and agents who have taken advertising beyond the call of duty to explain and argue and defend and attack all manner of good and evil aspects of our life and times, and some of their efforts have been so successful that the critics' failure to note them can only be put down as calculated and irresponsible.[1]

Much of what I am talking about is called institutional advertising, and it appears in several forms. One of them is public relations advertising and another is public service advertising. The longtime Weyerhauser campaign in magazines (now also on television) which explains the company's program of reforestation is a prime example of the first, for it is a direct answer to the charge of lumbermen's contemptuous destruction of national resources. The Caterpillar Tractor Company has used its advertising to explain reclamation projects in which its products are engaged and to point out ways in which other communities and municipalities can look forward to public improvements of a similar nature. This I would call public service.

In neither of these instances (and there are many more) is there any direct connection between the advertiser and his audience. He sells to someone else. The advertising is a matter of education and elucidation and the climate in which the advertiser's business is done.

Institutional advertising of a slightly different cast has been carried on for many years by the Metropolitan Life Insurance Company in the interest of better health; by Warner & Swasey, toolmakers in Cleveland, who have attacked inflation in all

---

[1]For the past four years, *Esquire* has published the winners of their Corporate Social Responsibility Advertising Awards Program; see pp. 115–16 for their third annual awards. (eds.)

its many guises; and by the Container Corporation, which has presented the wisdom of the ages in a long series of brief quotations embellished with brilliant illustrations or even more remarkable abstractions. These campaigns serve as strong backgrounds for the salesmen who must approach the advertisers' best prospects, very few of whom ever telephone an insurance company, a lathe maker or a manufacturer of paper cartons.

Advertising as a public service is another variation. It comes closer to the Advertising Council concept. There is no direct connection between the advertising and the advertiser's products, but the subject of the advertising is strongly connected with the advertiser's interests. Thus the Mobil Oil Company publishes powerful appeals to the public to drive safely so that they may continue to be customers. The Better Vision Institute of the American

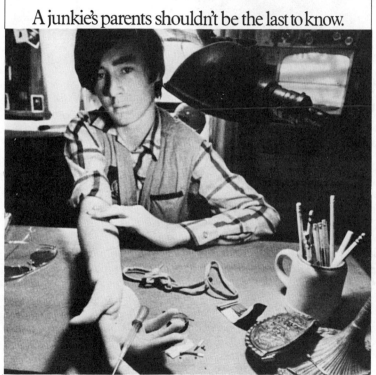

A junkie's parents shouldn't be the last to know.

More and more kids are letting the temptation of drugs get to them. And a lot of them are the kind of kids you'd least expect to become addicts.

If you're a parent and you're frightened, you should be.

Some authorities say that of all the many young people who start experimenting with drugs out of curiosity, one in every three will become a regular user. Totally dependent on drugs to get through life.

You could talk to your kids about drugs, but your kids would know more than you do.

Because even if they're not into taking drugs, drugs are a very real part of young people's lives. And all you know are a parent's fears.

Metropolitan Life would like to tell you the facts about drugs you don't know, but definitely should.

We've written a booklet. A parent's primer. What drugs are. What they do. How drug use starts. What to do when you see it.

It's called "To Parents / About Drugs." If you'd like a copy

for yourself or copies for your community group, write "Drugs," Metropolitan Life, 1 Madison Avenue, New York, N.Y. 10010.

It's only a booklet. But if you learn from it, it might be a help.

You can't help solve a problem if you don't know what the problem is.

Or that the problem is there. Possibly even closer than you think.

Metropolitan Life
We sell life insurance.
But our business is life.

Optical Company and associated optical goods manufacturers warns against failing sight and blindness, and suggests how these may be avoided. General Electric explains the Pacemaker, the electric heart stimulant that is surgically implanted under the skin. International Paper Company presents both the joys and the lifetime values in reading. Seagram's distilling company advertises so that teenagers and their parents will understand that drinking is a pleasure that should be reserved for adults.

One may hope, and I do, that institutional advertising is just now getting its second wind, after the hiatus that followed the return to product selling in the aftermath of World War II. Except for their contributions to the Advertising Council, most advertisers took a hard-nosed look at anything not directly connected with

Seven million Americans find love, security, escape, adventure and an early death in this bottle.

They're the seven million alcoholics in this country. But most of them aren't the skid row drunks you're thinking of.

They're the ordinary people who abuse alcohol. Most of them are people you'd never suspect.

The bright, young man who works with you. The housewife next door with two nice kids. The president of your company. Your secretary.

The point is, it could be anyone. It could even be you. The price we pay for alcoholism is frightening.

Last year, it cost our economy more than $75 billion. In absenteeism. Loss of productivity. Lost sales. Court costs. And law enforcement.

But alcoholism eats up more than just profits. It eats up people.

It destroys families. Health. Friends. Careers. Dreams. And often, life itself.

Alcoholics can get well. But there's something better than treatment. It's prevention.

The more you know about alcoholism the better you'll be able to guard yourself and your family against its dangers.

That's why Blue Shield has published a fully illustrated booklet on alcoholism entitled "The Alcoholic American." It's available from your local Blue Shield plan.

If you drink at all, you should have a copy.

What you don't know about the misuse of alcohol could hurt you. It could even kill you.

 Blue Shield®

How many minutes in a cocktail hour?

When most Americans entertain at home, serving drinks before dinner is a gracious custom. But an invitation to dinner at seven should not mean cocktails until ten.

Common sense in this respect is a mark of the considerate host.

And just as he has enough alcohol beverages on hand for guests who drink, he has a variety of soft drinks for those who don't.

We, the makers and sellers of distilled spirits, hope that you show as much care in using our products as we do in making them.

If you choose to drink, drink responsibly.

DISTILLED SPIRITS COUNCIL OF THE UNITED STATES
1300 Pennsylvania Building, Washington, D.C. 20004

Reprinted by permission of the Distilled Spirits Council of the United States.

product selling. When the *Saturday Review* began to make its awards, there was barely enough such advertising to fit a single category.

Now that institutional advertising is established as good public relations, I expect it to be used increasingly as an extension of private relations—which, after all, are where public relations begin. The only danger that I foresee is in overenthusiasm. This is something that the successors should watch out for.

Aids   *Advertising's Response to Its Critics*

1.   The excerpt from *With All Its Faults* attempts to answer some of the charges made against the advertising industry. What are the charges leveled at advertisers? How does Fairfax M. Cone answer the critics? Is his response supported by empirical evidence?

2. According to Cone, what are the main functions of advertising?

3. Do you agree with Cone that "Advertising always follows, it never leads"? *What* does advertising always follow? Is Cone's assertion an adequate justification for the existence of some dishonest and tasteless advertising?

4. Cone criticizes ads that make odious comparisons with competitive products. Does this practice exist in current ads? Do advertisers still stoop to conquer?

5. According to Cone, a growing number of advertisers and their clients have taken advertising beyond mere hustling of consumer products and services. They have put the public welfare ahead of corporate profits by explaining, arguing, defending, or attacking all manner of good and evil in our culture. Look closely at the three ads that accompany this essay and answer the following questions:

   a) Using Cone's categories, which ad (or ads) is an attempt at *public relations?* Which ad (or ads) performs a *public service?*
   b) What is the thesis of each ad?
   c) Which ad is the most self-serving?
   d) Which is the most effective?
   e) What kinds of associations are evoked by each?

6. Persona refers to the role that a communicator plays for his audience; the term derives from the Latin noun for the masks worn by Greek actors in classical drama. It is an appropriate term to describe the identity assumed by a writer, speaker, or corporation, such as a lumber and building supply conglomerate that curiously calls itself "The Tree Growing People." Examine the three corporate ads that accompany Cone's essay, locating the personae created by the ads. Do you find any discrepancies between the assumed persona and the actual product or service offered by the company?

Presenting the winners of

Esquire's 3rd Annual Corporate Social Responsibility Advertising Awards

Exxon Corporation: A TV spot dealing with pipeline burial in Alaska meets directly some of the most persistent arguments against construction. Fine use of graphics.

IBM: TV spot dealing with computer applications to air pollution documents, in a brief period of time, how machine-based analysis can be used to help clean up the atmosphere.

St. Regis Paper Company: Clear explanation of company's efforts to reduce waste in growth and harvesting of forest resources. One TV spot shows particularly effective use of animation.

Texaco Inc.: A lovely and imaginative TV adaptation of a well-known fable which utilized the medium to the fullest.

Kellogg Company: An outstanding TV spot shows preschoolers dramatizing the effects of poor-nutrition breakfasts. The message is clearly presented and avoids unnecessary product enhancement.

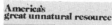

American Can Company: A modestly executed but informative series of magazine ads making the case for better utilization of disposed waste.

Atlantic Richfield Company: An imaginative and well-organized print campaign that combines whimsy and seriousness to put public transportation on the public agenda.

Blue Cross of Western Pennsylvania: TV spots aimed at children are simple, compelling, and make singular use of Mr. Rogers' appeal to preschoolers. These are backed up by explanatory messages to parents via attractive print.

If there is one clear message to be gleaned from Esquire's 3rd Annual Corporate Social Responsibility Advertising Awards Program, it seems to be this: despite continuing—even mounting—pressures of inflation, recession and general uncertainty, American business is firmly committed to advertising that demonstrates its concern for the public welfare.

The number of entries in this year's competition was substantially greater than in either of the two previous years. Equally significant, the entries were, in the words of our panel of judges, "much stronger overall." We think these are two very encouraging signs...for business...and for the public interest.

Those of you with photographic memories, or good files, will recognize some repeats among the winners. ARCO (Atlantic Richfield Co.) and IBM both grace these pages for the third straight year; and Eastman Kodak and Metropolitan Life Insurance Company are back after having won awards in the first year.

To the judges at the Department of Journalism of The University of Michigan—Peter Clarke, Chairman, Department of Journalism; John D. Stevens, Associate Professor of Journalism; Chauncey R. Korten, Professor of Art; Alfred H. Sloate, Associate Professor of Television Broadcasting Service; William E. Porter, Professor of Journalism—our special gratitude for the sensitivity they have exhibited in selecting this cross-section of what's good with America and American business.

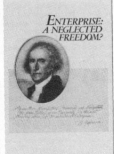

Swissair: Some clear, fundamental teaching on the facts of air travel and shipping costs. These newspaper ads are attractively laid out and fun to read.

Eastman Kodak Company: Judges were particularly impressed with "Excel! Excel!" which not only carries a strong message but a fine demonstration of what photography is all about.

Continental Oil Company: A topical and informative discussion of free enterprise that combines clear copy and effective graphics.

WLS-TV: Vivid and effective promotion of timely news topics which directs the reader's attention to feature content of TV news and local enterprise reporting.

Central Telephone & Utilities Company: Art and words harmonize to encourage parents to teach children to use the telephone properly in emergency situations.

Commuter Computer: Joyous and effective approach to a subject that has usually been handled with threats and cajoling—the forming of car pools to save energy and urban clutter.

Metropolitan Life Insurance Co.: An instructional ad about water safety without being pedantic. Gives the reader practical help and is well suited to the medium in which it appears, *Readers Digest.*

First National City Bank: Arresting radio and print messages showing one bank's commitment to public safety in its city. Sponsor should be commended for including version in Spanish.

The Babcock & Wilcox Co.: Clear exposition of some fundamental applications of science and technology in the social setting. Good copy is enhanced by handsome art and layout in this trade magazine campaign.

Phillips Petroleum Company: Excellent ad and TV spot—both of which do honor to the company's long-standing support of excellence in American athletics. Entries show progression from novice to championship swimming

The Standard Oil Company of Ohio: A practical rather than rhetorical exhortation on how to save gas and enjoy your vacation. Ingenious art makes maximum effective use of space in print. Skillful use of sound in radio spots.

Caterpillar Tractor Co.: Ads conclude with effective statement: "There are no simple problems, only intelligent choices." Copy and art demonstrate competing choices about compelling ecological problems in America today.

Aids   *Esquire's 3rd Annual Corporate Social*
             Responsibility Advertising Awards

1.   Look carefully at the award-winning ads in the *Esquire* contest. According to the ads, what are some of the important issues facing us in the second half of the 1970s? What are we, as responsible citizens and consumers, being asked to do?
2.   From the captions under the ads, deduce the criteria for the awards. That is, what makes for an effective ad?
3.   What connections, if any, can be found between the message of each ad and the interests of the company sponsoring these ads?
4.   According to D. G. Kehl, in an essay entitled "The Electric Carrot," "the secret of effective, responsible writing is essentially the secret of effective, responsible advertising." From a close examination of the captions under the ads and the ads themselves, deduce some effective techniques that might be emulated in your writing or speaking. You might consider the ways in which the ads (a) formulate precise thesis statements, (b) target their intended audiences, and (c) offer clear, illustrative examples.

Learning about Public Persuasion: Rationale and a Schema

HUGH RANK

RATIONALE

In the mid-1930s, Adolph Hitler began exploiting the fears and hopes of the people by means of a propaganda blitz, an unprecedented organized campaign of persuasion, using new media—radio and motion pictures—and traditional persuasion devices to such a degree that it transformed modern propaganda. In America, some scholars and teachers recognized early that Hitler's propaganda blitz had serious consequences for the world and that "something ought to be done." Thus, a small group of concerned people joined together, formed a group which called itself the Institute for Propaganda Analysis, and managed to publish a few pieces, including what became a well-publicized and widely used list of what they considered to be the seven most common propaganda devices: glittering generalities, name-calling, transfer, testimonial, plain folks, card-stacking, and bandwagon.

Since the 1930s, the world has changed. On the international scene, population has almost doubled; whole new cities of people are being born each day. Two, then three, massive superpowers have emerged in world politics. A dozen nations have gained the power to destroy, with one weapon, more than all previous wars in human history.

But, in a world of change, some things haven't changed. Despite the growth of commercial advertising from a cottage industry in 1945 to a $31 billion a year industry in 1976; despite the increase in the sophistication of modern persuasion and the development of technological aids to persuasion (from color TV to computers); despite the growth of the Pentagon into the world's largest, richest, most sophisticated propaganda machine; despite the fantastic changes in American political campaigning

Revised and adapted from the script of a slide show first presented at the 1974 NCTE convention in New Orleans. The original version, "Teaching Counter-Propaganda Techniques" is available on audio cassette, NCTE #74035. Copyright © 1976 by the National Council of Teachers of English. Excerpts reprinted by permission of the publisher and author.

since the first awkward use of television by Eisenhower; despite all these changes, some things haven't changed. For example, after 40 years of the most significant changes in communications, in persuasion techniques, and in propaganda, the most commonly used item to analyze such propaganda is still the old list of the Institute for Propaganda Analysis.

Very few textbooks discuss propaganda analysis, and more than half of those textbooks which even deal with it still rely upon the IPA list as their basic teaching device. Though the IPA list has been of value in the past, it is too limited for the complexities of modern propaganda. . . . [T]he list simply doesn't have the scope or flexibility to deal with contemporary propaganda.

We've experienced a significant change in persuasion during the past twenty years; we are now in a state of gross inequality. The professional persuaders have the upper hand: money, media access, sophisticated personnel utilizing scientific techniques, aided and abetted by psychologists and sociologists skilled in analyzing human behavior. All of that on one side. On the other side, the persuadees: the average citizen and consumer. Who trains the citizen? Not the schools. There is no coherent, systematic effort in the schools today to prepare our future citizens for a sophisticated literacy. In many schools there is more attention given to a minor nineteenth-century writer than to the major language developments of the twentieth century. . . . Perhaps schools should shift their emphasis in order to train the larger segment of our population in a new kind of literacy so that more citizens can recognize the more sophisticated techniques and patterns of persuasion.

We have sixty million children in our schools, millions more on their way during the next decade, and we do very little about the real facts of life and language today. These kids are growing up in a propaganda blitz unparalleled in human history. By the time they enter school at the age of five or six, they've watched thousands of skillfully devised commercials. John Wilpers estimates that by the time children are 16, they have seen over 640,000 commercials. Thus, while the schools do little to instruct and to inform the persuadees, the persuaders continue; the propaganda blitz intensifies. Will the advertisers and political persuaders of 1980, or 1984, be less sophisticated, less informed, less funded than they are today? If we close our eyes, will they go away?

If one accepts the premises of an accelerating propaganda blitz and of an increasing imbalance between the professional persuaders and the average untrained persuadee, then it would seem reasonable in a democratic society to seek as a goal a systematic method within the schools to inoculate future citizens, to immunize them from the potential dangers of organized public persuasion.

*   *   *

To replace the IPA list (and subsume 25 other random lists I've come across) and to expand the scope so that it includes a wider range of human communication—including nonverbal and verbal languages both spoken and written, and other symbolic communication (such as mathematics)—I devised a chart, or schema, working from the following criteria:

1.   It should be a *simple* explanation of a complex reality; simple enough to be understood by very young children, and by adults not keenly interested in reading scholarly papers about language.

2.   It should be *flexible* enough to be a common denominator and thus useful within the diverse disciplines which actually exist in the schools today, in departments of English, speech, language arts, communications, media, journalism, psychology, and so on. And it should be flexible enough to be used at all educational levels, from kindergarten to graduate school.

3.   It should be *accurate*. To avoid promulgating error, it must have an inner consistency, and must avoid contradiction of known truths.

4.   It should be *useful*, practical, teachable, reproducible in many forms.

SCHEMA: INTENSIFY/DOWNPLAY

Intensify/Downplay focuses attention on a simple pattern useful to analyze communication, persuasion, and propaganda techniques. Binary computers, working on a very simple two-part positive/negative $(+/-)$ basis, can generate very complex combinations. So also, one way of looking at human communication is to see that we can produce an almost infinite number of variations and combinations by intensifying or downplaying the various parts, or bits of information, communicated.

Sometimes this pattern is very easy to recognize: people *intensify* by raising their voice, shouting, making certain gestures, using certain words or patterns of words. People *downplay* by silence, and by other kinds of words (e.g., euphemisms) and gestures. Downplaying is often harder to recognize. Some very sophisticated techniques (e.g., satire, irony, concessive arguments) are often very difficult to analyze. But, people do not need to be "experts" to recognize the *most common ways* in which we all intensify or downplay.

The three most common ways to intensify are *repetition, association,* and *composition*. Their counterparts, the three most common ways to downplay, are *omission, diversion,* and *confusion*.

Each of these subdivisions can be further broken down into parts. Before such analysis, a warning is useful: avoid rigidity or confining things into one category. Recognize that these categories and terms may be useful, but are arbitrary (created by observers); recognize that many parts often function simultaneously.

REPETITION

Intensifying by repetition is a simple, but very effective, way to persuade. Some scholars believe that certain redundancy is essential in all communication simply because there are so many distractions that messages would get missed unless our languages had a built-in repetition factor. Other experts emphasize the psychological comfort we get from repetition. We love the familiar, the known. As children, we want to hear the same stories over and over. Later, we listen to our "favorite" songs, watch "favorite" programs, read "favorite" kinds of books, play "favorite" sports and games, and so on.

Commercial advertising recognizes the effectiveness of repetition. Every American knows that Budweiser is the King of Beers, Miller is the Champagne of Bottled Beers, Coke is the Real Thing, and that you can double your pleasure, double your fun with Doublemint, Doublemint, Doublemint gum. The *last* singing commercial for cigarettes was aired on TV in 1970, none since; yet most people today can still sing or whistle the Salem commercials: "You can take. . . ."

Thus, slogans, signs, symbols, logos, brand names are repeated often to intensify. All education, training, indoctrination, conditioning, propaganda is largely based on repetition, and is concerned with the receiver's memory; the ability of the receiver to identify or recognize and *respond* appropriately.

Politicians know the importance of repetition. In the early 1976 primaries, for example, a critical problem in the Democratic party was the lack of recognition of the names of the many candidates. Simple repetition of names (posters, bumper stickers) to identify the candidates became important. Naturally, incumbent politicians who have a high visibility have an advantage over the unknowns. Repetition of politicians' names and slogans is not a new technique; Kenneth Clark, in *Civilisation*, describes the ancient Egyptian hieroglyphics as the first recorded "propaganda" based on repetition. But, even before that, most primitive cultures had established religious and social customs involving verbal repetition (chants, prayers, litanies) and nonverbal repetition (dances, rituals). The repeated pleas of cheerleaders today (Hold that Line! Hold that Line!) have their ancestral roots far back in human history.

Technology—ranging from the invention of the printing press to the most modern Xerox machine or videocassette recorder— makes repetition a lot easier to disseminate to mass audiences. But the basic patterns of verbal repetition (assonance, alliteration, anaphora, etc.) were cataloged by the Greek rhetoricians. Although random repetition is possible, it's much more likely that repetition will have some kind of *patterning*—in time or space.

INTENSIFY

Repetition

Intensifying by repetition is an easy, simple, and effective way to persuade. People are comfortable with the *known*, the *familiar*. As children, we love to hear the same stories repeated; later, we have "favorite" songs, TV programs, etc. All cultures have chants, prayers, rituals, dances based on repetition. Advertising slogans, brand names, logos, and signs are common. Much education, training, indoctrination is based on repetition to imprint on *memory* of the receiver to identify, recognize, and *respond.*

Association

Intensifying by linking (1) the idea or product with (2) something *already loved/desired by -or hated/feared by* (3) the intended audience. Thus, need for **audience analysis:** surveys, polls, "market research," "consumer behavior," psychological and sociological studies. Associate by *direct* assertions or *indirect* ways: metaphoric language, allusions, backgrounds, contexts, etc. Terms describing common *subject matters* used to link: *Flag-Waving, God-on-Our Side, Plain Folks, Band-Wagon, Testimonials, Tribal Pride, Heritage, Progress,* etc.

Composition

Intensifying by pattern and arrangement uses *design, variations in sequence* and *in proportion* to add to the force of words, images, movements, etc. How we put together, or compose, is important: e.g. in verbal communication the choice of words, their level of abstraction, their patterns within sentences, the strategy of longer messages. **Logic,** inductive and deductive, puts ideas together systematically. **Non-verbal** compositions involve *visuals* (color, shape, size); *aural* (music); *mathematics* (quantities, relationships) *time* and *space* patterns.

Omission

Downplaying by omission is common since the basic selection/omission process *necessarily omits* more than can be presented. All communication is limited, is edited, is slanted or biased to include and exclude items. But omission can also be used as a *deliberate* way of concealing, hiding. Half-truths, quotes out of context, etc. are very hard to detect or find. Political examples include *cover-ups, censorship, book-burning, managed news, secret police activities.* Receivers, too, can omit: can "filter out" or be closed minded, prejudiced.

Diversion

Downplaying by distracting focus, diverting attention away from key issues or important things; usually by intensifying the side-issues, the non-related, the trivial. Common variations include: *"hairsplitting," "nit-picking," "attacking a straw man," "red herring";* also, those emotional attacks and appeals (*ad hominem, ad populum*), plus things which drain the energy of others: *"busy work," legal harassment,* etc. Humor and entertainment (*"bread and circuses"*) are used as pleasant ways to divert attention from major issues.

Confusion

Downplaying issues by making things so complex, so chaotic, that people "give up," get weary, "overloaded." This is dangerous when people are unable to understand, comprehend, or make reasonable decisions. Chaos can be the accidental result of a disorganized mind, or the deliberate flim-flam of a *con man,* or the political *demagogue* (who then offers a "simple solution" to the confused.) Confusion can result from *faulty logic, equivocation, circumlocution, contradictions, multiple diversions, inconsistencies, jargon* or anything which blurs clarity or understanding.

DOWNPLAY

ASSOCIATION

Intensifying by association is a technique of persuasion which links (1) the idea, person, or product with (2) something already loved or desired—or hated or feared—by (3) the intended audience. Thus, it is very important to know the audience. Aristotle, 2500 years ago, devoted a major portion of his *Rhetoric* to audience analysis; today, millions of dollars are spent by advertisers in such "market research" ranging from simple polls, surveys, questionnaires, and contests to sophisticated psychological and sociological research. Politicians have advisors, and governments have agencies, whose function it is to provide such "target audience" information so that political persuasion campaigns can be based on an assessment of the audience.

Verbal association can be done by direct statements, allusions, or a wide variety of metaphoric language: direct comparisons (metaphors), indirect comparisons (similies), etc. Many English teachers have great ability in analyzing metaphoric language in "poetry" as commonly taught in literature courses. Perhaps these insights can be expanded or applied by analyzing the mundane metaphoric language of everyday life: viewing commercial advertising as the "poetry of the corporation" and clichés as the "poetry of the people."

Nonverbal association techniques follow the basic pattern of putting the item into a *context* which already has emotional significance for the intended audience. Consider, for example, the *visual* background settings and *musical* accompaniment in television commercials.

Although there are an almost infinite number of possible combinations of subject matters and intended audiences, some patterns of human behavior are predictable (for example, attitudes toward God, country, nature etc.) and are commonly exploited by the persuaders. Variations occur in different cultures, different eras, but essentially the subject matter of the association technique extends to all of the pleasures and ideals for which people live and die. In contemporary American culture, for example, any listing of the most common favorable associations as seen in commercial advertising and political persuasion would include: God (God-on-our-side) Flag (Flag-waving); Tribal Pride (ethnic groups, alumni, sports fans, etc.) Ideals (virtues or movements); Heroes and Experts (testimonials); Foll Sayings; the Most People ("bandwagon"); the Best People ("status"); th Average Person ("plain folks"); Heritage ("good old days"); Progres ("exciting, new"); Science; the Arts; Domestic Pleasures (Ma, apple pie dogs, babies); Sensual Pleasures (especially sex). Some of these appeal contradict each other; what would delight one person would offend another. Compare the ads in *Playboy* with those in *Good Housekeeping:* different strokes for different folks.

COMPOSITION

Intensifying by patterns and arrangements uses design and order, variations in sequence and in proportion to add to the effectiveness of words, images, movements, etc. Choice of words, their level of abstraction, and their patterning within sentences are important; in longer messages, overall strategy is involved in planning patterns (grouping, structure, divisions, sequence, climax, etc.). Logic, both inductive and deductive, deals with the systematic patterns of linking ideas together. Nonverbal patterning includes visual aspects (color, size, shape), aural (music), mathematics (quantities, relationships, etc.), and time and space patterns in relation to whole context.

In verbal communication, diction (word choice) and syntax (arrangement within the sentence) are both basic in patterning. The words we choose will either intensify or downplay the information transferred and the emotional associations of our communication. In old fashioned terms, all adjectives and adverbs are intensifiers, adding some information to the nouns and verbs which they modify. All nouns and verbs have a level of abstraction or specificity. We have options, as we speak and write, of choosing not only the linear sequence of words following after each other, but also selecting the "vertical" level of specificity of the nouns and verbs, and whether or not we'll add more information.

While there is no such thing as a neutral transfer of information from one person to another, we commonly use the terms "denotation" and "connotation" to indicate the relative degree of emotional associations involved in the diction. What a word connotes or suggests is not intrinsic to the word, but relative to the situation and the experience of both the speaker and audience.

In written languages, we often use certain customs or conventional patterns to signify when we want something intensified; we use CAPITALS, underlining, some punctuation marks! Sometimes we can intensify, attract attention, by violating standard conventions: Cummings' poetry is a good example of the conscious artist doing this; but consider also the protestors' banners which deliberately misspelled Nixxon (or used a swastika for the x) and U$A.

In spoken language, we can intensify by raising our voice, by changing the patterns of the tone, pitch, stress, or by pausing; by differing these things from what is "normal" for the situation, we can change the meaning conveyed. Using the same words, we can be sweet or sarcastic. The subtle nuances of languaging here are very intricate; certainly, foreigners wouldn't catch all the subtle implications which native speakers pick up. And, even within a homogenous "native" group, some people simply "can't take a hint." That is, some people are not aware or do not understand the non-verbal communication which contradicts and overrides the verbal message.

*   *   *

In contrast to the rather overt techniques of *intensifying* elements of communication (by repetition, association, composition) we have extremely limited awareness of the techniques of *downplaying*, of the tactics of omission, the strategy of silence. We don't even have an adequate vocabulary to label or to identify the variations of downplaying which are more obscure, more subtle, more difficult to analyze. It's much easier to spot examples of intensification: there's something out there to analyze. But, it's extremely difficult to know when things are being withheld, hidden, or omitted. Much more attention must be paid by scholars and analysts, by teachers and students, to the whole problem of downplaying as a form of communication, because it has such importance to us in terms of political life (secrecy and censorship, classified documents, and cover-ups) and corporate advertising (half-truths, confusing claims, etc.), as well as in our daily affairs with others.

Omission, diversion, and *confusion* are suggested here as three major categories of downplaying. If one intensifies by repeating things frequently, then one can downplay by omitting them. If one intensifies by association, which brings things together, then one can downplay by diversion, which splits things apart. If one intensifies by composition, which lends order and coherence, then one can downplay by confusion, which creates disorder and incoherence.

OMISSION

The basic selection/omission process *necessarily omits* more than can be presented. Thus, all communication is edited, is limited, is biased or slanted to include and exclude items. But, omission can be used deliberately, as a calculated and systematic strategy of silence. As such, it is the most difficult aspect of communication to analyze, since we must attempt to detect that which is withheld, concealed, hidden, or omitted. Political examples would include many forms of governmental *censorship, book-burning, cover-ups, managed news,* and activities involving *secret police* and *secret diplomacy.*

Euphemisms—words which downplay the unpleasant or unpopular —are a form of omission, a substituting of a more socially acceptable word for one which is "offensive." Forbidden words (especially concerning death and deities, sex and bodily functions) are common in many cultures. Euphemisms downplay; in contrast, one can intensify, can shock an audience, by using the "forbidden" words: profanity, vulgarity, cursing, etc. Euphemisms are frequently condemned as being "bad" *per se*; but, here too, one must make value judgments in relation to the situation. To comfort a grieving friend, it may well be humane to use "passed on" rather than "died." But, the euphemism "nuclear device" may be inhumane if it disguises reality.

DIVERSION

Downplaying by diverting attention, distracting focus away from key issues or important things; usually by intensifying, emphasizing, the side-issues, the unimportant, the trivial, the nonrelated. Common variations have been called *"red herring," "straw man," "hairsplitting," "nit-picking"*; also, emotional attacks and appeals (*ad hominum, ad populum*), plus activities which drain the energy of others (*"busy work,"* legal harassment). Humor and entertainments (*"bread and circuses"*) are often used as pleasant tactics to draw attention away from significant issues.

CONFUSION

Downplaying key issues by making a situation so complex, so chaotic, so unintelligible that people often weary, get "overloaded," "drop out," "give up." This can lead to dangerous situations if people are unable to understand, comprehend, take necessary actions; or if people follow leaders offering a panacea, a simple solution. Chaos can be the accidental result of a disorganized, confused mind, or it can be the deliberate flim-flam of the con man or the demagogue. Confusion can result from *faulty logic, shifting definitions, equivocation, circumlocution, multiple diversions, contradictions, inconsistencies, jargon,* or anything which obscures clarity or understanding.

To avoid confusion, or cut through the maze, one should seek careful definitions, precise diction, clear syntax, strong structure, exact logic: in brief, all of those ideals of the counterpart, composition. Yet, such clarity is difficult in real situations when everything seems to demand our attention at once and leads us to the feeling of weariness, chaos, overload. Confusion is a strategy of some persuaders who think, "If you can't convince 'em, confuse 'em." Anything we can do to slow down the speed and sort out the junk, any kind of outlining, listing, or chart-making may be helpful to avoid that very common feeling of being overwhelmed by the "information explosion."

Thus far, this Intensify/Downplay schema is *static*, an analysis breaking some concepts into parts for clarity. In reality, communication is a *dynamic*, fluid, ever-changing process with many things going on at once, always in a wider context.

Based on observation, it would seem that people manipulate communication: (1) to *intensify* their own "good"; (2) to *intensify* others' "bad"; (3) to *downplay* their own "bad"; and (4) to *downplay* others' "good." "Good" and "bad" are in quotation marks here deliberately to suggest the qualifications and reservations needed in order to avoid setting up rigid dichotomies. An assumption: All people, in all eras, in all countries, intensify or downplay elements of communication as a natural human activity.

The moral and ethical judgments which have to be made about any human activity, including language manipulation, must be made in the

INTENSIFY OWN "GOOD"	INTENSIFY OTHERS' "BAD"
"Glittering generalities" and *"purr words"* are often used to mean the superlatives, hyperbole, favorable associations, etc. used to praise, brag, boast, show off the "good" aspects of one's own *self* (or *group, product, idea*, etc.) In advertising: "puffery."	*"Name-calling"* and *"snarl words"* are used to mean the *attacks* and *aggressive* communication toward others. To blame, criticize, nag, scold, find fault, etc. In politics: "mudslinging," "smear campaign," "character assassination."
DOWNPLAY OWN "BAD"	**DOWNPLAY OTHERS' "GOOD"**
Deliberate cover-up: to hide, omit, conceal, suppress, censor, disguise, mask, bury, screen, etc. Also, the *alibi*, the excuse, to avoid guilt or responsibility by *downplaying importance* ("it's only...") or *shifting blame* to circumstances or to others or to lesser faults.	The Put-Down: the *sarcastic* or mocking "So what!" or "Big deal!" To ignore, slight, neglect, deny, undervalue, disregard, forget the value or merits of the other.

context of specific situations: *who is saying what to whom, with what intent, with what result.* Such moral issues are complex, and important, but they are *distinct* from an analysis of how the elements of communication can be intensified and downplayed. As Cardinal Newman said: "Knowledge is one thing, virtue is another; good sense is not conscience. . . ." For further discussion of the moral issues involved, see my concluding essay in *Language and Public Policy* (Urbana, Ill.: NCTE, 1974, pp. 216–223). In this schema, the focus is on *how* communication can be manipulated.

These ideas are not new. This is simply a resorting, a translation into a simple language and a simple pattern. It's quite probable that you already accept these basic ideas, and that you are already familiar with many of the metaphoric words and labels currently in use to describe the parts of this schema. For example, focus on the top section of Figure 2. Depending on the textbooks you've already used, you've read other authors who discuss the intensification process, labeling concepts usually in paired terms: "glittering generalities" and "name-calling," "purr words" and "snarl words," "god words" and "devil words," "cleans" and "dirties," and so on.

When communication is intensified to focus on the others' "bad," we already have a vocabulary to describe such attacks: catty, snide remarks, mud-slinging, smear campaigns, and confrontation tactics. Such attack language would include not only verbal insults—shouted obscenities and scrawled graffiti—but also a whole cornucopia of intensified nonverbal communication: fist-shaking, teeth-clenching, sneering and smirking, ranging from the silent malice of the "hate stare" to the actual use of physical violence.

In our era, in our country, Watergate may well be the classic example of downplaying: omission, secrecy, deletions, half-truths, concealment, and cover-up. If we were to analyze Watergate language manipulation using the four-part pattern, certainly it would be reasonable to emphasize one area: downplay own "bad."

Yet the Watergate affair provides a good illustration of how all aspects of language manipulation can work together simultaneously. By recognizing such multiplicity and simultaneity, we may be able to avoid the trivial, hair-splitting arguments of previous techniques of propaganda analysis which sought to pigeonhole things into single categories, attempting to force a complex reality into simplistic packages. While Watergate was primarily a "downplaying own 'bad'" by the Nixon conspirators, at the same time some things were being intensified—such as the emphasis on Nixon's successful foreign relations with China and Russia, and the intensified attacks on the press, and on other politicians for being "biased" and "partisan."

Many Americans have been frightened by the abuses of power as

Intensify Own "Good"	Intensify Others' "Bad"
Stress foreign affairs, detente, peace, end of war, return of POWs.	Attack on press, on "leaks" as being treasonous, dangerous to national security.
Image building: protestations of innocence ("I am not a crook"); Operation Candor.	Attack on any factual press errors, misquotations.
Appearance of disinterest in matter—too busy with important affairs of state.	Attack on Democrats as being partisan, biased.
	Attack on credibility of witnesses (untrustworthy, disloyal "squealers").
Downplay Own "Bad"	**Downplay Others' "Good"**
In general, the whole cover-up conspiracy; some specifics: 1700 "inaudibles" and "unintelligibles" on the tapes; 150+ "expletives deleted" and "characterizations deleted"; 18-minute gap in tape; key tapes missing; documents withheld, shredded; silence of witnesses; evasive answers; perjury, etc.	Denying, ignoring, not responding to opponents' true claims.
	Denying valid motives, good intent of others.
	Denying competency of others (e.g., of the judge, the jury, the evidence, the tape experts, etc.).

evidenced in the Watergate affair, in the CIA involvement in foreign assassination plots, and in the FBI record of illegal domestic spying. Many investigators (e.g., David Wise in *The Politics of Lying*) have documented the systematic deceptions, the overclassification of government documents, the growing web of secrecy, censorship, concealment in recent years in the United States. Such fears of a totalitarian police state are reasonable fears. We have seen other nations in this century so abuse power. For example, the brutal history of the Soviet Union has been so revised by Kremlin historians as to downplay their own bad: to omit, to delete references, to ignore those whole ethnic groups and millions of political enemies who were purged, murdered, or enslaved by the USSR during the past half century. Today, it is not fashionable in an era of detente, or in an academic atmosphere of polite liberalism, to allude to the Gulag Archipelago. But I'm simply pointing out that the Soviet leaders are downplaying their own bad, concealing that which is not favorable, while they intensify the glories of their space programs, industrial and technological progress.

If you accept this four-part pattern as being a reasonable way of describing human behavior; if you accept the premise that all people in all eras for all kinds of motives, good and bad, intensify and downplay certain elements of communication; and if you recognize the recent growth in organized corporate persuasion, the concentration of power, money, and media access, then you may see some of the possible political and social implications resulting from a widespread use of this pattern as a teaching device, and from some of the axioms which can be inferred from it for use in analyzing public persuasion.

For example, assuming that any concentrated propaganda blitz in the future will come from governments or corporations, one might recommend to the citizen: *"When they intensify, downplay."* That is, when we recognize the propaganda blitz, we should be cool, detached, skeptically alert, not only to the inflated puffery of advertising with its dreams and promises, but also to intensified attack propaganda, the threats and the exploitation of fears by a demagogue or a government.

Conversely, we could recommend to our fellow citizens and to our students, our future citizens, that when a government or corporation hides or suppresses something, citizens should intensify and seek out: *"When they downplay, intensify."* Obviously, not everyone can be an expert investigative reporter, nor do we all have access to materials closely guarded, covered up, or concealed. But a whole citizenry can be taught in the schools about the need for openness in government, the need for a free press if we are to retain our democratic freedom.

People trained in recognizing the intensify/downplay patterning might even start seeing this pattern in the apparently random efforts of those various consumerists and reformers who urge a variety of *disclosure* laws (truth-in-lending, truth-in-packaging, truth-in-advertising, etc.), political campaign reforms, and corporate reporting practices designed to make public that which has been hidden in the past. Today, after a decade of consumerism and highly visible reformers, relatively little progress has been made because of the general randomness of the reformers and the confusion of the public. Such confusion works in favor of those who wish to conceal. With training, future citizens might be better able to recognize patterns and to see the implications of various "Shield Laws," full disclosure laws, standardized systems, clear record keeping, and reporting of data.

Thus far, I've emphasized verbal communication, but have made some allusions to the importance of nonverbal communication. The intensify/downplay pattern is also a useful way to analyze many elements of spacing and distancing, gestures, clothing, and ornamentation. It's also very probable that those who are concerned with visual literacy, especially with the analysis of photography and the cinema, will recognize the intensify/downplay elements involved in lighting, in audio techniques, in background setting, in camera angles, in pacing and timing, and so on.

For the average person, perhaps the most complicated kind of intensifying and downplaying occurs in our system of symbolic communication, mathematics. For most people, the manipulation of numbers, figures, and statistics is very confusing, as it takes special training and aptitude to understand how to intensify and downplay the various elements involved.

The language of business is the language of money. Most people are not able, or do not wish, to be expert in this form of human languaging. But it would be valuable to have a larger population of citizens and consumers who have a basic "liberal education" in the intricacies of this language. We need more "common people" or "non-experts" who are able to recognize the basic ways of manipulating figures and statistics; how governments or corporations can intensify—inflate—certain figures to give favorable illusions (seeking votes, selling stock), and can downplay other items to conceal losses and income. "Juggling the books" is not a new human activity, but, with the advent of the computer, it's going to be an increasingly complex one—with the odds favoring the rich, the powerful, the huge corporations and governments.

If we are to seek equity and balance, the citizenry should recognize some of the basic problems, and some of the possible solutions: laws and lawmakers intent on counterbalancing power; and an educational system "of the people, by the people, and for the people," which seeks to train future citizens in a more sophisticated literacy in order to cope with the propaganda blitz of today, and of tomorrow.

Aids   *Teaching about Public Persuasion*

1. What, according to Hugh Rank, are the seven most common propaganda devices? Define each device and provide a brief example. For definitions of some of these devices, see the Introduction to this unit.

2. What specific social-political conditions inspired the work of the Institute for Propaganda Analysis?

3. What, according to Rank, are the limitations of the old IPA list of propaganda devices in the 1970s? How did the Watergate affair change our views about the nature and scope of propaganda?

4. What precisely is Rank's new approach to the study of propaganda?

Define with brief examples each of the six devices: repetition, association, composition, omission, diversion, and confusion.

5. Why do you think Rank refers frequently to advertisements and commercials for his examples of the six devices? What does this reveal about his attitude toward advertising? Is advertising a form of propaganda?

6. What, according to Rank, are some of the moral and ethical implications of using persuasion? Look closely at the distinction he makes between the moral issues involved and the objective study of how communication can be manipulated. Does Rank consider the six techniques as intrinsically wrong or morally neutral? Is Rank suggesting that it is the *use* of these techniques that determines their "goodness" or "badness"?

7. How does Rank protect himself from the charge that his six categories of language manipulation represent only an oversimplified, static scheme? Look closely at his discussion of communication as a "dynamic, fluid, ever-changing process."

8. Writers often use charts and diagrams not only to supplement their words but to summarize their ideas. Look closely at the three diagrams in Rank's essay. How useful are they as summaries of his ideas? Write a paper or report in which you include at least one diagram.

9. According to Rank, what specific compositional/rhetorical strategies can be learned by studying public persuasion? What uses of these devices should you emulate in your writing? What uses should you avoid? Why?

10. All writers use evidence to support their assertions. From what fields does Rank draw most of his illustrative examples? Does he present both good and bad uses of language manipulation? Is he using the very devices he decries in his treatment of the Watergate affair? Should he have also included a "positive" example of downplaying?

11. Locate a political speech in the current media or in *Vital Speeches of the Day*. Apply Rank's schema to the speech, isolating examples not only of the six categories of language manipulation but of the four-part pattern as exemplified in Figure 3. Draw some conclusions about the speaker's *use* of these strategies; that is, is the speaker's use of the devices morally questionable or morally unquestionable?

12. Try your own hand at writing propaganda. Choose a controversial topic, such as school busing, abortion, or decriminalization of mari-

juana, incorporating as many of Rank's techniques of language manipulation as you can. You might write two versions. In the first version, make a deliberate attempt to *misuse* the devices; that is, mislead, distort, and lie outright. In the second version, using the same devices, make a deliberate effort to present the same issues fairly and rationally. What are the major differences between the two versions? Which version is the most effective?

The Rhetoric of Popular Arts

IRVING J. REIN

The popular arts always have been persuasive. Whether a comedy by George Bernard Shaw or a waltz by Johann Strauss, a Western by Howard Hawks or a comic monologue by Will Rogers,[1] they have worked attitude changes. In extreme cases, such an art may have effected change in a political belief; more often, it has created an alteration in a personal view or conviction. What is noteworthy about persuasion-in-art today is that through technological innovation one presentation—a single song, a single dramatic performance—can be appreciated by millions of people. Before the introduction of electronic media, the opportunity for the masses to witness a play or hear a musical concert was slim. Such enjoyment was a luxury which the average wage earner could not afford; attendance was generally limited to the critics and wealthy patrons.

Inventions of the twentieth century drastically reshaped the purpose and thrust of the popular arts. Radio made it possible for music to be aired, playscripts to be dramatized and heard, and sketches of comedic art to be broadcast. Motion pictures that could "talk" added another exciting and significant dimension. And, in a few short years, television projected art forms of all kinds—oral, aural, and visual—into myriad living rooms around the world. Concurrently, due to the invention of the phonograph, the public could experience over and over again the hearing of a chosen piece of music; and the refinements of tapes and cassettes facilitated the handling and the playing of an even broader and more personal selection of music and of recordings of great dramas and great speeches. Innovations to speed the processes of printing dramatically raised the output and allowed the introduction of the mass-produced paperback book. The same production breakthroughs enabled small-circulation magazines to focus upon and specialize in single art forms. Because of these and other technological inventions, like the computer and the earth-circling communication satellite, millions of the world's exploding populations have been exposed to and significantly influenced by the persuasive power of the popular arts. In addition, the older forms of art and media have interacted and combined to produce ancillary effects which are, in fact, entirely new presentational forms. Elvis Presley performing on television is not Presley in "live" performance. A videotape can "telescope" time, rescheduling signifi-

Irving J. Rein, "The Rhetoric of Popular Arts," in *Rudy's Red Wagon: Communication Strategies in Contemporary Society*, pp. 72–79. Copyright © 1972 by Scott, Foresman and Company. Reprinted by permission of the publisher.

[1]Shaw (1856–1950), Irish playwright and critic, whose play, *Pygmalion* (1913), is his most successful work as a play, a film and the basis for the musical *My Fair Lady*; Johann Strauss (1825–99), famous Viennese musician and composer of more than 400 waltzes, including the "Blue Danube"; Howard Hawks (1896–   ), American film director, famous, in part, for such westerns as *The Big Sky*, *Rio Bravo*, and *Red River*; Will Rogers (1879–1939), American humorist and social commentator, who was widely known as the "cowboy philosopher." (eds.)

cant events and entertainment for maximum viewing at a more convenient moment. And consider what such technological innovations as slow-motion film, split screen, and instant playback have done to revolutionize and popularize athletic contests (which in turn help to sell beer, automobiles, razors, and shaving lotions).

ART AS PERSUASION

What makes art an effective instrument of persuasion is the viewer's unique perception of the artistic event as he experiences it. All audiences, when they are about to attend or experience an event—whether "live" or electronic—have certain expectations about the *content* of that event. When the event is a political rally, the audience anticipates discussion and exhortation. When the event is a concert—a Presley concert, for instance—the concert-goer would expect to hear, among other old favorites, "You Ain't Nothin' but a Hound Dog."

In addition to expectations regarding content, audiences also have anticipations as to the *form* and *intent* of the presentation. The form of a political rally is primarily a succession of public speeches, with perhaps some preliminary and "transitional" music designed to attract attention and add a pleasurable, but secondary, dimension. The political spectator knows that, above all, the public-address form is designed to maintain or change his attitudes and beliefs. He naturally, therefore, comes to the event prepared for a verbal onslaught on his political attitudes; and he sharpens his critical senses in order to analyze the ideological arguments with which he knows he will be bombarded. He

will be alert to anything that accords with his views and can be applauded, and equally ready to reject claims and assertions contrary or inimical to those views.

If the popular arts have so much persuasive potential why aren't they being exploited? Or are they?

In contrast, the concert-goer, anticipating a full evening of music intended solely for the purpose of providing esthetic enjoyment, does not expect his attitudes to be challenged, his beliefs to be threatened. In music, usually, he anticipates no persuasiveness as such; and so, of course, he does not mentally brace himself to counter arguments or to refute ideas, even if some were to be embedded or disguised in the song, the opera, or the festival. Similarly, a poem often may be enjoyed for reasons other than its ideological content; frequently it may be appreciated for such stylistic elements as its rhythm, its imagery, the precision and compactness of its phrasing, the delicacy of its structural balance, and for its power to evoke mood and emotion. Generally speaking, those who read poetry do not become argumentative about its substantive ideas or disqualify a poet's work because of his political beliefs. Similarly, with regard to the lyrics of a song, a listener can enjoy "Puff, the Magic Dragon" without buying into its alleged exaltation of smoking marijuana; he can appreciate the music without feeling prompted to debate the legalization of grass.

What is important to remember is that, although the auditor is appreciating the poem or song for its literary or musical qualities, he is nevertheless absorbing the *content*. Since he perceives the form as being pleasurable rather than persuasive, he may listen to the piece many times. Thus, even though the message may be subtle, the fact that it is repeated over and over—on radio, television, stereo, and cassette—means that millions of people will hear it. This repetition makes the potential power of the piece enormous. While the Federal Communications Commission may limit the broadcast or televised speeches of political figures, it has not similarly restricted the singing of Neil Young or the sarcastic comedy routines of Don Rickles. We may quite correctly conclude, then, that when members of an audience witness or experience an artistic performance, they often suspend judgment or make no critical evaluation of the *persuasive* effect of the work.

ARTISTIC LICENSE

That a viewer suspends or abrogates judgment of controversial content is an acknowledged part of artistic license. There is an unstated assumption between artist and audience that political or moral biases are to be discounted to allow the artist freedom of creation or of expression. This assumption would probably be subject to reexamination when applied to such an obviously political play as *MacBird!*[2] or to some of the more blatant revolutionary songs and poems. But generally the assumptions of artistic license stand unchallenged. There are few rhetorical analyses of the revolutionary strategies of Donovan. The fact of the matter is, however, that the strategies *are present*—and virulent.

Rock music was born of a revolt against the sham of Western culture: It was direct and gutsy and spoke to the senses. As such it was profoundly subversive. It still is.

Jonathan Eisen, *The Age of Rock*

That the popular arts are considered essentially *entertainment* gives them a decided advantage over other and more direct forms of verbal expression. They are normally pleasurable, and at the same time they lower the receiver's resistance to whatever subtle persuasion may be embedded in them. At a distinct disadvantage in this respect are such directly communicative forms as the lecture, the public address, and the personal encounter. Their direct form proclaims their obvious intent. Even if these forms are intended to be informative or inspirational in their impact, audiences do not view them as entertainment. On the other hand, as we have noted, most of our music, film, and nightclub routines are perceived almost entirely as pleasurable, esthetic events utterly devoid of subtle or sinister "impurities" of persuasion against which we must defend ourselves. The "lively" arts, being entertaining, encourage us to attend and pay attention. We may eagerly buy a ticket to a Joan Baez concert and listen entranced to her singing. But a lecture or a public address is another matter. Unless we have a special or vested interest in the subject or the sociopolitical stance of the speaker, we may be reluctant to attend even if the event is admission free. If we do decide to go, we start with a defensive frame of mind, anticipating that at best the experi-

[2]Barbara Garson's shocking 1966 parody of Shakespeare's *Macbeth*, in which she parallels Lyndon Johnson with Macbeth, John F. Kennedy with Duncan, and Robert Kennedy as a combination Malcolm-Macduff. (eds.)

ence will be boring. Potentially, the speech —and certainly the lecture—proffers more intellectual justification, but it is Baez' music which generates repeated applause and quite frequently the audience's insistence upon an encore.

The so-called stand-up comedy act—whether staged in a nightclub or on television—illustrates even more strikingly the peculiar advantage of the entertainment form as a vehicle of persuasion. Many comedians induce audiences to laugh at political jokes even though these jokes reflect sentiments which the same audience would find objectionable in a speech or formal address.

> I have to fly to Kansas City, Missouri, right after the show. This white cat moved into an all colored neighborhood and some colored bigots burned a watermelon on his lawn.
>
> Dick Gregory, comedian

The late Lenny Bruce was famous for his blackly humorous attacks on sacred targets. People who laughed at his comedy routine about Eleanor Roosevelt's fabulous breasts probably would find the idea repulsive or at least offensive if Bruce had presented it in the form of a straight speech and without the shield of humor.* But given the nightclub/entertainment surroundings, most of the audience—even though they may have downgraded the comedian as being foul—tended to discount the grossness and to laugh. Using the format of comedic commentary, Bruce forced an alternate view of the dignified former First Lady upon them. By tossing his darts amid a milieu of liquor and laughter, the comedian was able to disguise his attack and achieve a tolerant audience reception.

Of course, the tactic of comedic commentary can backfire, especially if the target happens to be an extremely influential or powerful politician. Mort Sahl, who used humorous license to comment upon the foibles and fallacies of the presidency, regardless of the party which happened to be in power, purportedly found his contracts cancelled and the number of his engagements drastically curtailed after he tried to "take on" the Kennedy clan.

THE PURITY OF ART FORMS

Another factor which enables popular art forms to be unobtrusively but powerfully persuasive is the audience's perception of the "purity" of these forms. The artist is not considered the arch manipulator as is, for example, the public speaker. There have been too many lies and too many unfilled promises delivered in the form of speeches. As communication, public speaking has been somewhat discredited. Because, in the public mind, artistic creativity is not as closely associated with business and politics as is public speaking, art forms are traditionally considered as rather unbiased and unsullied outlets of expression. You can trust a folksinger. When has a balladeer seriously extolled the virtues of General Motors?

As a people, however, we are becoming increasingly—and, perhaps, uneasily—aware that we cannot consistently perceive

---

*In his routine, which is reprinted in *The Essential Lenny Bruce*, ed. John Cohn (New York: Ballantine Books, 1970), p. 239, Bruce spoke about a friend of his who supposedly walked in on Mrs. Roosevelt while she was dressing.

all art as being above manipulative intent. Many television programs which in themselves are highly artistic and unbiased nevertheless enjoy commercial sponsorship. It is not unusual for a too creative piece to be censored by a queasy company willing to sponsor only art that is consistent with its conception of an easily offended public. That, in fact, has come to be the prevailing practice, the essential economic fact of life for television. And in the films also we find some straightforward, unabashed propaganda. One example is *Battle of Algiers*, a how-to-do-it guide for revolution.[3] Obviously, the appeal of this kind of film—and its employment of persuasion—is more direct than, say, an Ingmar Bergman film, which is often vague and mystical. *Algiers* assaults the spectator with violent action and patriotic speeches; Bergman's *Wild Strawberries*, through its mood and pacing, works more subtly on the viewer.[4] However, even if we use the extreme example of *Battle of Algiers*, our initial assertion is still valid: the filmic format makes its theme more acceptable to far larger groups than would be the same theme expressed in a public speech.

MUSIC AS PERSUASION

[P]opular music is potentially one of the most persuasive of all of the arts. Clearly, its advantages in this respect are unique and varied: (1) Thematically, modern popular music is relatively simple. When it is coupled with the insistent repetitiveness of today's rock lyrics, listeners need exert very little effort to grasp the ideas, persuasive or otherwise, that the song is trying to communicate. (2) Even more important, perhaps, is the fact that the listeners themselves—thanks to the easy availability and relatively low cost of records, record-players, and cassettes—can play the same song over and over, scores or even hundreds of times. Not beyond belief is the estimate that an admirer of Bob Dylan's music may play his "Blowin' in the Wind" fifty times in a single evening. In contrast, very few people will play a recording of a speech, much less purchase a recording of one. Consider, then, how much greater are the opportunities for the singer of popular songs to make repeated and persuasive impressions upon a listener. (3) Since an infectious beat or a simple lyric has a way of embedding itself in our conscious and subconscious minds, the subliminal persuasiveness of the song is always with us. Once our thinking has been impregnated with the idea, we multiply its effect manyfold and perpetuate it within ourselves—and by ourselves.

Would it make sense for a teacher to write his lecture in poetry or rock lyrics?

In total effect, while as yet there may be no scientific proof that popular music can influence conversion to ideas, political and cultural, it dins into our ears so constantly and bombards our minds so heavily that the possibility of such influencing cannot be shrugged off. Nor can we dismiss an even stronger possibility that repeated

[3]Directed by Gillo Pontecorvo, *The Battle of Algiers* (1967) is a starkly realistic reenactment of the violent rebellion of the Algerians against the French in 1954. (eds.)

[4]Written and directed by the Swedish filmmaker Ingmar Bergman, *Wild Strawberries* (1959) concerns the dream experiences of an aging scientist, played by Victor Seastrom, who is on his way to the university at Lund to be honored. (eds.)

playings of music and lyrics *when coupled with more direct forms of persuasion*—a political speech, for example—will produce significant attitude change.

> Two thousand college students riot after hearing attorney William Kunstler discuss the Conspiracy Trial of the Chicago Seven.
>
> *Question:* What caused the riot?
>   Kunstler's speech?
>   The trial?
>   Society?
>   Bob Dylan?
>   *Rolling Stone?*
>   All of the above?

That a single speech by a middle-aged militant or that any other similar communicative event can in and by itself produce mass conversion to an idea is both implausible and improbable. What is much more likely is that a *combination* and *repetition* of speechmaking, popular music, comedic acts and commentary, and "guerrilla" movies have *all* contributed to the attitudinal shifts which are taking place in our society. Kunstler's speech may have sparked what *appeared* to be riot-oriented conversion,

but years of "softening up" by Phil Ochs, the Beatles, the comic strips of R. Crumb, and polemic films like *Algiers* and *Z* made it possible.

Significantly, the popular arts have not been in the hands of the Establishment (a condition which prevailed in earlier eras). If anything, the rock musician, the stand-up comedian, or the modern poet is an outsider who attacks Society's conventions. Since the marriage of the popular arts with the mass media, much of America—much of the world, in fact—has been steadily exposed to alternate life styles. In matters of civil rights, Vietnam, and ecology, for example, the popular arts have exerted steady pressure on a number of major governmental policies during the past decade. There are few folk songs defending the notion of racial or economic inferiority, and very few poems glorifying the backlash. These negativistic, reactionary stances rarely are taken by musicians, poets, and other artists. And this may very well be an important reason why the popular arts remain highly articulate antagonists of twentieth-century bias and bigotry.

Aids *The Rhetoric of Popular Arts*

1. According to Irving Rein, what technological developments accelerated the persuasive potential of the popular arts?

2. What are our expectations regarding the form and content of the popular arts? Do we expect to be exposed to persuasive messages when we listen to a song or watch a television program? Does Rein feel that there is cause for alarm?

3. Rein insists throughout his essay that the popular arts are persuasive. What concrete evidence does he provide to support his thesis? Do you think his comment about the music of Donovan qualifies as supporting evidence? Look for other unsupported assertions in the essay.

4. It is clear from the format of the essay that Rein is not writing a conventional essay. What is the purpose, for instance, of the various inserted remarks and quotations?

5. Why does Rein feel that popular music is "potentially one of the most persuasive of all the arts"? Examine some current song lyrics for their persuasive messages. Does each song have a thesis? To what audience is each song directed? What political or cultural beliefs is each songwriter assuming? Do any of the songs represent exceptions to Rein's contention that songwriters are outsiders who attack society's conventions? Are any of the songs propagandistic? Using Hugh Rank's essay as a guide, locate some specific propaganda devices. Listen to recordings of the songs; does the music reinforce the persuasive content of the lyrics?

6. Examine a television comedy show for its persuasive qualities. What, for instance, do shows like "I Love Lucy" and "I Dream of Jeannie" suggest about women? What do shows like "The Brady Bunch" and "Family Affair" suggest about family life in America? For more detailed treatments of persuasion in the popular arts, see the aids in the other units in this anthology.

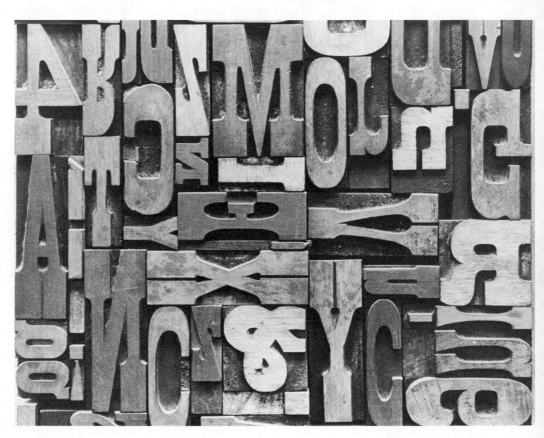

Photo/David Umberger

The Language of Print

The print media today encompass the popular forms of fiction, nonfiction, newspapers, magazines, poetry, comicbooks, and even greeting cards. Despite Marshall McLuhan's claim that the oldest mass medium, which began in fifteenth-century Europe with Gutenberg's printing press, is being superseded by the electronic media, the print merchants continue to churn out 80,000 books, 360 million comicbooks, 10,000 different periodicals, and 11,000 different newspapers yearly. The total daily newspaper circulation in 1975 was over 65 million. The ten best-selling magazines distribute a total of 97 million issues monthly. Print is here to stay, but it is changing.

The changes in the print media have been noticed by several commentators, including Edmund Carpenter, whose essay "The New Languages" appears in Unit I, and Marshall McLuhan. According to McLuhan in "The Print: How to Dig It," electric means of communicating information are altering our typographic culture as sharply as print changed medieval manuscript culture. This does not mean that print is being replaced by radio, TV, or film, but that print is changing to accommodate our rearranged sense ratios in the electric age. Print culture is primarily visual in orientation, whereas electronic culture requires us to participate tactilely:

"People don't actually read newspapers," McLuhan asserts, "they get into them every morning like a hot bath." Newspapers, magazines, and even books will continue to employ the printed word, but their formats are becoming more nonlinear, more nonsequential, and more involving. As Edmund Carpenter points out in "The New Languages," the newspaper, with its "short, discrete articles that taper off to incidental details," avoids chronology and lineality for simultaneity. This format changes the reader from mere spectator to active processor of the news. The magazine also opposes lineality, juxtaposing instead unrelated articles, photographs, and ads in a visual mosaic. The format of the comics, too, according to McLuhan, is electric. Because they offer so little data about any object, the viewer is compelled to participate in completing the few hints provided by the colored dots. Thus, although print is one of the oldest languages, it is adopting the electric formats of the new languages of television, radio, and film.

The changing form of print is best exemplified by the new journalism, which, as Everette E. Dennis points out in "The New Journalism: How It Came To Be," manifests itself in newspaper columns, magazine articles, and books. In addition to outlining how new journalism "came to be," Dennis shows us how the new forms of journalistic writing differ from the traditional who-what-where-when approach of news reporting. The major difference is that the new journalists, such as Tom Wolfe, Jimmy Breslin, Gay Talese, Norman Mailer, and Truman Capote, are as much interested in *how* they say it as in *what* they say. That is, the form, style, and language of their writings is their message. They have adopted the literary techniques of the short story and novel—the dramatic scene-setting, the overheard dialogue, the narrator as participant in the action, the photographic effects, and the impressionistic language—and applied them to news reporting. The result, as Gay Talese suggests, "is, or should be, as reliable as the most reliable reportage although it seeks a larger truth than is possible through the mere compilation of verifiable facts, the use of direct quotations, and adherence to the rigid organizational style of the older form." Although the term "new journalism" is usually reserved for the new style of nonfiction writing, Dennis expands the definition to include alternative journalism, whose purpose is to expose and attack wrongdoing in government and business, and advocacy journalism, or "the new propaganda," which makes no pretense of hiding its commitment to a particular point of view. These new forms of journalistic expression, then, represent a dramatic break from the traditional news format and style.

If the form of the print media is important for an understanding of the ways in which media shape our modes of perception, an awareness of the *contents* of the print media is essential for an evaluation of American popular culture. According to Russel B. Nye, author of *The Unembarrassed Muse* (required reading for any serious student of popular culture), today's popular print media owe their action, sensationalism, violence, sex, adventure, and sentimentalism to genres in Colonial America: the sensational travel journals, the historical and didactic accounts of witchcraft, exotic Indian customs and legends, adventures spawned by the Revolutionary War, and sentimental domestic romances. These were the stuff that tears, terror, and titillations were made of—and still are. The modern counterparts of these mass-appeal publications are the family magazines, women's magazines, adventure stories, confessional romances, detective fiction, comics, and science fiction.

Every magazine in the United States, as pointed out by Stephen C. Holder in "The Family Magazine and the American People," is directed at a certain audience, a certain segment of the populace that comprises that magazine's readership. More particularly, a magazine must establish "an accurate sense of its identity and must communicate that identity to the public in such a way that the public can readily recognize certain future issues." To ensure this recognition, every magazine develops a basic formula. For most family magazines, for instance, the broad goal is to reflect many aspects of the American experience. This broad goal can be analyzed according to six basic roles: (1) information, (2) entertainment, (3) escape, (4) assistance in forming opinions, (5) reinforcement of moral values, and (6) provision of a consumer's showcase. Although Holder's specific illustrative examples are such family magazines as *Collier's, Look,* and *The Saturday Evening Post,* his categories of goals can be readily applied to virtually all magazines if not to all media. Holder's essay also makes it clear that every magazine is directed to certain assumptions common to that audience—its interests, moral values, and dreams. This direction is basic to the persuasive appeal a magazine must make in order to sell itself and the products it advertises. Without effective appeals, magazines such as *Collier's, Life* and the weekly *Saturday Evening Post* die of neglect.

In spite of the failure of these widely read American magazines, the health of the periodicals industry, Roland L. Wolseley points out in "The American Periodical Press and Its Impact," is quite sound because some of the giant magazines like *The Reader's Digest* and *Ladies' Home Journal* have successfully adjusted to the "new competition, new tastes, new climates of opinion, and a changing economic order." In addition to outlining the economic complexities of magazine publishing today, Wolseley attempts to assess the social impact of the periodical press. He briefly surveys the contributions made to American life by a broad range of magazines, from *The Reader's Digest* to *Playboy.* He summarizes, too, the various arguments made by critics who claim that magazines pander to public tastes, deprive their audiences of full disclosure, fail to provide leadership in problem solving, and stimulate irrational desires for material possessions.

Another criticism is that some magazines offer spurious models for popular consumption. The images of humanity projected by some consumer magazines are often narrow, misleading, or false. Such is the position taken by Harvey Cox, who in "The Playboy and Miss America" offers an illuminating analysis of the Adonis and Aphrodite of our leisure-consumer society. Although published in 1966, this essay is still relevant given the plethora of magazines like *Cosmopolitan, Seventeen, Playgirl, Playboy, Penthouse,* and *Oui* that glut the newsstands. By means of religious imagery, Cox ironically undercuts the deities of our time—the Playboy and Miss America, who together encapsulate a false vision of life in America.

Another subject that has generated much discussion by critics is violence in the media. Considerable concern has been voiced about the excessive violence and aggression depicted in newspaper columns, magazine articles, film, and television and their effects on Americans, especially young people. One critic has estimated that adolescents are exposed to some 18,000 televised murders by the age of fourteen. Fictionalized violence is only one part of the problem, however; the news media constantly provide information about assassinations, bombings, riots, mass murders, and police brutality. Since the media are the vehicles for carrying news of violence, they are often associated in the minds of the public with violence itself. The excessive depiction of violence in the media is the focus of Tom Wolfe's essay, "Pause, Now, and Consider Some Tentative Conclusions About the Meaning of This Mass Perversion Called Porno-violence: What It Is and Where It Comes From and Who Put the Hair on the Walls." Wolfe asserts that the old violence has been superseded by a new "pornography of violence," wherein the vantage point is never that of the victim but of the aggressor: "What you get is . . . the view from Oswald's rifle. You can step right up here and look point-blank through the very hairline cross in Lee Harvey Oswald's Optics Ordnance four-powered Japanese telescopic sight and watch, frame by frame by frame by frame by frame, as that man there's head comes apart." Wolfe concludes that television has schooled us in the view from Oswald's rifle and made it a normal pastime.

A survey of the contents of the print media would not be complete without a consideration of the comic, which is either a comicbook, comicstrip, or cartoon. The enduring popularity of comics is evident: six out of every ten readers read newspaper comics every day; over 100 million people read the Sunday comicstrips; and over 300 million comicbooks are sold annually. Despite continuing complaints about them as junk art, escapist literature, and puerile entertainment, comics are a dynamic force in American popular culture. At their best they compress information, entertainment, and persuasion into a single pictorial image. This image encapsulates the changing human comedy and tragedy. Now more than ever, the comics provide us with a visual commentary on the wacky and wicked ways of the world. Indeed, as Saul Braun asserts in "Shazam! Here Comes Captain Relevant," comics have turned toward relevance and social commentary and away from simplistic good versus evil plots and unimaginative, wooden characters. Topics now treated by comics include civil rights, women's liberation, drug abuse, the search for the self, and misuse of power by government, business, and the media. Braun not only compares the new breed of comics with the old, but analyzes the various sociopsychological appeals made by each generation of comics. The comics as overt political and social commentary is the subject of Stefan Kanfer's *Time* essay, "Editorial Cartoons: Capturing the Essence." According to Kanfer, the best editorial cartoons still manage "to encapsulate crises, expose pretensions and eviscerate swollen egos—all with a few well-drawn strokes." Kanfer mentions some of the leading practitioners of the art—Herbert Block, Jules Feiffer, Bill Mauldin, and, most recently, Garry Trudeau, creator of

"Doonesbury." As the cartoons depicting Megaphone Mark Slackmeyer, Michael Doonesbury, and Calvin illustrate, Trudeau has brought ideological climates of opinion back to the comicstrip.

In sum, this unit attempts to introduce you to the changing language of print media. The topic is obviously broad, and the essays included here represent only a small fraction of the material available on print. They should, however, not only introduce you to some of the basic concepts and issues involving print but, more important, provide you with the critical tools to examine newspapers, magazines, new and old journalism, and comics.

The Print:
How To Dig It

MARSHALL McLUHAN

The art of making pictorial statements in a precise and repeatable form is one that we have long taken for granted in the West. But it is usually forgotten that without prints and blueprints, without maps and geometry, the world of modern sciences and technologies would hardly exist.

In the time of Ferdinand and Isabella[1] and other maritime monarchs, maps were top-secret, like new electronic discoveries today. When the captains returned from their voyages, every effort was made by the officers of the crown to obtain both originals and copies of the maps made during the voyage. The result was a lucrative black-market trade, and secret maps were widely sold. The sort of maps in question had nothing in common with those of later design, being in fact more like diaries of different adventures and experiences. For the later perception of space as uniform and continuous was unknown to the medieval cartographer, whose efforts resembled modern nonobjective art. The shock of the new Renaissance space is still felt by natives who encounter it today for the first time. Prince Modupe tells in his autobiography, *I Was a Savage*, how he had learned to read maps at school, and how he had taken back home to his village a map of a river his father had traveled for years as a trader.

> ...my father thought the whole idea was absurd. He refused to identify the stream he had crossed at Bomako, where it is no deeper, he said, than a man is high, with the great widespread waters of the vast Niger delta. Distances as measured in miles had no meaning for him. ... Maps are liars, he told me briefly. From his tone of voice I could tell that I had offended him in some way not known to me at the time. The things that hurt one do not show on a map. The truth of a place is in the joy and the hurt that come from it. I had best not put my trust in anything as inadequate as a

[1]Ferdinand II (1452–1516), king of Spain, Sicily, and Naples; under his auspices Christopher Columbus discovered America. (eds.)

map, he counseled. . . . I understand now, although I did not at the time, that my airy and easy sweep of map-traced staggering distances belittled the journeys he had measured on tired feet. With my big map-talk, I had effaced the magnitude of his cargo-laden, heat-weighted treks.

All the words in the world cannot describe an object like a bucket, although it is possible to tell in a few words how to *make* a bucket. This inadequacy of words to convey visual information about objects was an effectual block to the development of the Greek and Roman sciences. Pliny the Elder reported the inability of the Greek and Latin botanists to devise a means of transmitting information about plants and flowers:

> Hence it is that other writers have confined themselves to a verbal description of the plants; indeed some of them have not so much as described them, even, but have contented themselves for the most part with a bare recital of their names . . .

We are confronted here once more with that basic function of media —to store and to expedite information. Plainly, to store is to expedite, since what is stored is also more accessible than what has to be gathered. The fact that visual information about flowers and plants cannot be stored verbally also points to the fact that science in the Western world has long been dependent on the visual factor. Nor is this surprising in a literate culture based on the technology of the alphabet, one that reduces even spoken language to a visual mode. As electricity has created multiple nonvisual means of storing and retrieving information, not only culture but science also has shifted its entire base and character. For the educator, as well as the philosopher, exact knowledge of what this shift means for learning and the mental process is not necessary.

Well before Gutenberg's development of printing from movable types, a great deal of printing on paper by woodcut had been done. Perhaps the most popular form of this kind of block printing of text and image had been in the form of the *Biblia Pauperum,* or Bibles of the Poor. Printers in this woodcut sense preceded typographic printers, though by just how long a period it is not easy to establish, because these cheap and popular prints, despised by the learned, were not preserved any more than are the comic books of today. The great law of bibliography comes into play in this matter of the printing that precedes Gutenberg: "The more there were, the fewer there are." It applies to many items besides printed matter —to the postage stamp and to the early forms of radio receiving sets.

Medieval and Renaissance man experienced little of the separation and specialty among the arts that developed later. The manuscript and the earlier printed books were read aloud, and poetry was sung or intoned. Oratory, music, literature, and drawing were closely related. Above all, the world of the illuminated manuscript was one in which lettering itself was given plastic stress to an almost sculptural degree. In a study of the art of Andrea Mantegna, the illuminator of manuscripts, Millard Meiss mentions that, amidst the flowery and leafy margins of the page, Mantegna's letters "rise like monuments, stony, stable and finely cut. . . . Palpably soled and weighty, they stand boldly before the colored ground, upon which they often throw a shadow. . . ."

The same feeling for the letters of the alphabet as engraved icons has returned in our own day in the graphic arts and in advertising display. Perhaps the reader will have encountered the sense of this coming change in Rimbaud's sonnet on the vowels, or in some of Braque's paintings.[2] But ordinary newspaper headline style tends to push letters toward the iconic form, a form that is very near to auditory resonance, as it is also to tactile and sculptural quality.

Perhaps the supreme quality of the print is one that is lost on us, since it has so casual and obvious an existence. It is simply that it is a pictorial statement that can be repeated precisely and indefinitely—at least as long as the printing surface lasts. Repeatability is the core of the mechanical principle that has dominated our world, especially since the Gutenberg technology. The message of the print and of typography is primarily that of repeatability. With typography, the principle of movable type introduced the means of mechanizing any handicraft by the process of segmenting and fragmenting an integral action. What had begun with the alphabet as a separation of the multiple gestures and sights and sounds in the spoken word, reached a new level of intensity, first with the woodcut and then with typography. The alphabet left the visual component as supreme in the word, reducing all other sensuous facts of the spoken word to this form. This helps to explain why the woodcut, and even the photograph, were so eagerly welcomed in a literate world. These forms provide a world of inclusive gesture and dramatic posture that necessarily is omitted in the written word.

The print was eagerly seized upon as a means of imparting information, as well as an incentive to piety and meditation. In 1472 the *Art of War* by Volturius was printed at Verona, with many woodcuts to explain the machinery of war. But the uses of the woodcut as an aid to contemplation in Books of Hours, Emblems, and Shepherds' Calendars continued for two hundred years on a large scale.

It is relevant to consider that the old prints and woodcuts, like the modern comic strip and comic book, provide very little data about any particular moment in time, or aspect in space, of an object. The viewer, or reader, is compelled to participate in completing and interpreting the few hints provided by the bounding lines. Not unlike the character of the

[2]Arthur Rimbaud (1854–91), French poet; Georges Braque (1882–1963), French painter who used typographical letters in his paintings. (eds.)

woodcut and the cartoon is the TV image, with its very low degree of data about objects, and the resulting high degree of participation by the viewer in order to complete what is only hinted at in the mosaic mesh of dots. Since the advent of TV, the comic book has gone into a decline.

It is, perhaps, obvious enough that if a cool medium involves the viewer a great deal, a hot medium will not. It may contradict popular ideas to say that typography as a hot medium involves the reader much less than did manuscript, or to point out that the comic book and TV as cool media involve the user, as maker and participant, a great deal.

After the exhaustion of the Graeco-Roman pools of slave labor, the West had to technologize more intensively than the ancient world had done. In the same way the American farmer, confronted with new tasks and opportunities, and at the same time with a great shortage of human assistance, was goaded into a frenzy of creation of labor-saving devices. It would seem that the logic of success in this matter is the ultimate retirement of the work force from the scene of toil. In a word, automation. If this, however, has been the motive behind all of our human technologies, it does not follow that we are prepared to accept the consequences. It helps to get one's bearings to see the process at work in remote times when work meant specialist servitude, and leisure alone meant a life of human dignity and involvement of the whole man.

The print in its clumsy woodcut-phase reveals a major aspect of language; namely, that words cannot bear sharp definition in daily use. When Descartes[3] surveyed the philosophical scene at the beginning of the seventeenth century, he was appalled at the confusion of tongues and began to strive toward a reduction of philosophy to precise mathematical form. This striving for an irrelevant precision served only to exclude from philosophy most of the questions of philosophy; and that great kingdom of philosophy was soon parceled out into the wide range of uncommunicating sciences and specialties we know today. Intensity of stress on visual blue-printing and precision is an explosive force that fragments the world of power and knowledge alike. The increasing precision and quantity of visual information transformed the print into a three-dimensional world of perspective and fixed point of view. Hieronymus Bosch,[4] by means of paintings that interfused medieval forms in Renaissance space, told what it felt like to live straddled between the two worlds of the old and the new during this revolution. Simultaneously, Bosch provided the older kind of plastic, tactile image but placed it in the intense new visual perspective.

[3]René Descartes (1596–1650), French philosopher and scientist, who is said to be the father of modern philosophy and analytical geometry. (eds.)

[4]Bosch (c. 1450–1516), Flemish painter, whose works, such as *Garden of Earthly Delights,* illustrate the depth of human depravity. (eds.)

He gave at once the older medieval idea of unique, discontinuous space, superimposed on the new idea of uniform, connected space. This he did with earnest nightmare intensity.

Lewis Carroll[5] took the nineteenth century into a dream world that was as startling as that of Bosch, but built on reverse principles. *Alice in Wonderland* offers as norm that continuous time and space that had created consternation in the Renaissance. Pervading this uniform Euclidean world of familiar space-and-time, Carroll drove a fantasia of discontinuous space-and-time that anticipated Kafka, Joyce, and Eliot. Carroll, the mathematical contemporary of Clerk Maxwell, was quite *avant-garde* enough to know about the non-Euclidean geometries coming into vogue in his time. He gave the confident Victorians a playful foretaste of Einsteinian time-and-space in *Alice in Wonderland*. Bosch had provided his era a foretaste of the new continuous time-and-space of uniform perspective. Bosch looked ahead to the modern world with horror, as Shakespeare did in *King Lear*, and as Pope did in *The Dunciad*.[6] But Lewis Carroll greeted the electronic age of space-time with a cheer.

Nigerians studying at American universities are sometimes asked to identify spatial relations. Confronted with objects in sunshine, they are often unable to indicate in which direction shadows will fall, for this involves casting into three-dimensional perspective. Thus sun, objects, and observer are experienced separately and regarded as independent of one another. For medieval man, as for the native, space was not homogeneous and did not *contain* objects. Each thing made its own space, as it still does for the native (and equally for the modern physicist). Of course this does not mean that native artists do not relate things. They often contrive the most complicated, sophisticated configurations. Neither artist nor observer has the slightest trouble recognizing and interpreting the pattern, but only when it is a traditional one. If you begin to modify it, or translate it into another medium (three dimensions, for instance), the native fails to recognize it.

An anthropological film showed a Melanesian carver cutting out a decorated drum with such skill, coordination, and ease that the audience several times broke into applause—it became a song, a ballet. But when the anthropologist asked the tribe to build crates to ship these carvings in, they struggled unsuccessfully for three days to make two planks intersect

[5]Lewis Carroll, pseudonym of Charles Dodgson (1832–98), English mathematician and author; he is chiefly remembered as the author of *Alice's Adventures in Wonderland* (1865) and its sequel *Through the Looking Glass* (1872). (eds.)

[6]Alexander Pope (1688–1744), English poet, whose *The Dunciad* (1728–43), a scathing attack on literary dunces, social follies, and political corruption, ends with a vision of the disintegration of civilization. (eds.)

at a 90-degree angle, then gave up in frustration. They couldn't crate what they had created.

In the low definition world of the medieval woodcut, each object created its own space, and there was no rational connected space into which it must fit. As the retinal impression is intensified, objects cease to cohere in a space of their own making, and, instead, become "contained" in a uniform, continuous, and "rational" space. Relativity theory in 1905 announced the dissolution of uniform Newtonian space as an illusion or fiction, however useful. Einstein pronounced the doom of continuous or "rational" space, and the way was made clear for Picasso and the Marx brothers and *MAD*.

Aids   *The Print: How To Dig It*

1. According to Richard Kostelanetz in the excerpt from "Marshall McLuhan (pp. 14–22), McLuhan is a "technological determinist." He believes that changes in the technology of communication have had profound effects on societies. According to "The Print: How To Dig It," what precisely were the effects of the invention of the printing press on Renaissance Europe?

2. McLuhan believes that a change in the technology of communication also has a direct and lasting impact on the psyches of the people in a culture. What specific changes did the invention of print elicit in the minds of people—their sensory perspective, their distance from first-hand experience, and their education?

3. One of the psychic manifestations of print, McLuhan contends, is the noninvolvement or detachment of the reader. Print is, to use McLuhan's term, "hot"—well filled with information and low in participation. Television, by contrast, is a "cool," low-definition medium that provides a minimum of information but involves all the senses. Do you agree with McLuhan that reading a fictional story with interesting content is less involving than watching it on television? And why is radio "hot" instead of "cool," like television? Do you find these apparent inconsistencies exasperating?

4. According to McLuhan, when an old medium, such as print, meets a new medium, such as TV, striking changes take place in the old medium. This clash of technologies produces transitional media forms. Using pictorial magazines, newspapers, and "nonbooks" as your

examples, demonstrate what results when an old medium confronts a new medium.

5. Do you find it paradoxical that McLuhan uses the printed word to describe the downfall of the printed word?

6. Analyze the prose style of McLuhan. Include a consideration of his academic style, his use of reference material, his creation of metaphors and aphorisms, his fascination with puns and other word games, and his use of the "probe." Speaking about his writing style, McLuhan says: "Most clear writing is a sign that there is no exploration going on. Clear prose indicates the absence of thought."

7. McLuhan focuses exclusively on the form of print. Why do you think he ignores the *content* of the medium that caused so many social and psychic changes in Renaissance Europe? If print, for instance, caused universal education, how is education possible without the knowledge and insights—that is, the content—of print?

8. The careful writer and speaker look for solid evidence to back their assertions. There are at least four types of evidence: statistics, factual references to other writers, appeals to authorities, and personal opinion. What types of evidence does McLuhan marshal in "The Print: How To Dig It"? Does he present personal opinion as fact?

For additional questions on the impact of print on society, see the essays by Edmund Carpenter and Richard Kostelanetz in Unit I.

The New Journalism: How It Came To Be

EVERETTE E. DENNIS

It was a time when old values were breaking down; new knowledge exploded all around us; people worried about drugs, hippies, and war. We talked of violence, urban disorder, turmoil. New terms like polarization, credibility gap and counterculture crept into the language. It was during *this* time, somewhere between 1960 and 1970, that the term "new jouralism" also began to appear in the popular press. Almost as rapidly as the term became a descriptive link in the vernacular, it was used and misused in so many contexts that its meaning was obscured. First accepted and used by its practitioners, the term found its way into older, more established publications by the mid-Sixties. *Time* called former newsman turned author Tom Wolfe "the *wunderkind* of the new journalism," while *Editor & Publisher* described Nicholas von Hoffman of the *Washington Post* as an "exponent of the new journalism." And there were others: Lillian Ross, Jimmy Breslin, Norman Mailer, Truman Capote, Gay Talese, and Pete Hamill, all were designated "new journalists" by one medium or another. At the same time a number of different forms of communication, from nonfiction novels to the underground press, were being labeled "new journalism."

By 1970 few terms had wider currency and less uniformity of meaning than new journalism. Yet one wonders whether this curious mix of people, philosophies, forms and publications has any common purpose or meaning. To some the term had a narrow connotation, referring simply to a new form of nonfiction that was using fiction methods. Other critics were just as certain that new journalism was an emerging form of advocacy in newspapers and magazines which previously had urged a kind of clinical objectivity in reporting the news. Soon anything slightly at variance with the most traditional practices of the conventional media was cast into the new journalism category.

While the debate over definition

From Everette E. Dennis, "The New Journalism: How It Came To Be," in Everette E. Dennis, ed., *The Magic Writing Machine*, 1971, pp. 115–32. Reprinted by permission of the University of Oregon School of Journalism, and the author.

droned on, it began to obscure any real meaning the term "new journalism" ever had. The scope and application of new journalism was not the only point of contention, though. Some critics looked peevishly at the jumble of writers, styles, and publications and suggested that "there is really nothing very new about the new journalism."

And it was true. One could trace every form and application of the new journalism to an antecedent somewhere, sometime. The underground press, for example, was said to be a twentieth century recurrence of the political pamphleteering of the colonial period. "And isn't the alternative press simply muckraking in new dress?" And on it went.

Although much of the criticism of new journalism has concentrated, unproductively I believe, on whether or not it is new, no attempt will be made here to resolve this question. Perhaps we should think of the new journalism as we do the New Deal or the New Frontier. No one argues that using these terms means one believes there was never before a deal or a frontier. So it is with the new journalism.

What began as a descriptive term for a kind of nonfiction magazine article has been mentioned previously. As one who is viewing these journalistic developments, I know that a number of dissimilar forms are called "new journalism." This is the reality of the situation. I will not argue with this commonly used and loosely-constructed definition of new journalism, but will look instead at its various forms, outlets, content and practitioners. Much of what is regarded as new journalism can be judged only by the most personal of standards. It is, after all, a creative endeavor of people seeking alternatives to the tedium of conventional media.

Carl Sandburg used to say every generation wants to assert its uniqueness by

---

Guidelines for Straight News Reporting

Compiled by the editors

1. The reporter should clearly state the 5Ws (who, what, when, where, and why) and the H (how) in the lead paragraph.
2. The structure of the news story should be the inverted pyramid; the facts are arranged in descending order, the most important coming first.
3. Accuracy is the key word in straight news reporting; no conjecture, no opinion, no editoralizing.
4. The reporter should be impersonal and detached; should not participate in the story; should avoid using the first-person pronoun; should not delve beneath the surface for a human interest angle.
5. The reporter's style should be clear, concise, and to the point; no trace of the writer's individual style should emerge.

crying out, "We are the greatest city, the greatest nation, nothing like us ever was." If this is so, one might conclude that every generation will have its own "new journalism" or at least that it will regard its journalistic products as new. Creative journalists have always tried to improve upon existing practices in writing and gathering news. The history of journalism chronicles their efforts. But even when one accepts the notion of each generation having its own new journalism, the decade of the Sixties still stands out as an unusually productive and innovative period.

Magazines and newspapers, having felt the harsh competitive challenge of the electronic media, realized that the public no longer relied upon them for much entertainment in the form of short stories and longer fiction. As the public demanded something new, the *new nonfiction*, an attempt to enliven the traditional magazine article with descriptive detail and life-like dialog, emerged.

Newsmen who tired of the corporate bigness of metropolitan dailies and their unwillingness to challenge establishment institutions, founded their own papers. We will, they said, offer an *alternative* to traditional journalism, the chain papers and their plastic personnel.

Other newsmen, who stayed with the conventional papers, were arguing against the notions of balanced news, objectivity, and stodgy use of traditional sources of news. They sought and were granted opportunities for open *advocacy* in the news columns.

The alienated young constructed a counter-culture which would reject most of the underlying assumptions of traditional society. Needing communications media that were equally alienated from the straight world, they created the *underground* press which was, as one

writer said, "like a tidal wave of sperm rushing into a nunnery."

Still other journalists found the impressionistic newsgathering methods of the media to be crude and unreliable measures. They would apply the scientific method and the tools of survey research to journalism, thus seeking a *precision* before unknown in media practice.

Any look back at the Sixties and the swirl of journalistic activity has the appearance of a confused collage of verbal and visual combatants, seeking change in the *status quo* but not knowing quite what or where in all that was happening; a concern for form, for style often seemed to supersede content. John Corry, who worked with the *New York Times* and *Harper's* during this period, offers this recollection:

It happened sometime in the early 1960's and although no one can say exactly when, it may have begun in that magic moment when Robert Frost, who always looked marvelous, with silver hair, and deep, deep lines in his face, read a poem at the inauguration of John F. Kennedy, and then went on to tell him afterwards that he ought to be more Irish than Harvard, which was something that sounded a lot better than it actually was. Hardly a man today remembers the poem, which was indifferent, anyway, but nearly everyone remembers Frost, or at least the sight of him at the lectern, which was perhaps the first sign that from then on it would not matter so much what you said, but how you said it.

With similar emphasis on form, Tom Wolfe recalls his first encounter with the new journalism: "The first time I realized there was something new going on in journalism was one day in 1962 when I picked up a copy of *Esquire* and read an article by

Gay Talese entitled 'Joe Louis at Fifty.' "* Wolfe continues, " 'Joe Louis at Fifty' wasn't like a magazine article at all. It was like a short story. It began with a scene, an intimate confrontation between Louis and his third wife:

'Hi, sweetheart!' Joe Louis called to his wife, spotting her waiting for him at the Los Angeles airport.
She smiled, walked toward him, and was about to stretch upon her toes and kiss him—but suddenly stopped.
'Joe,' she snapped, 'where's your tie?'
'Aw, sweetie,' Joe Louis said, shrugging. 'I stayed out all night in New York and didn't have time.'
'All night!' she cut in. 'When you're out here with me all you do is sleep, sleep, sleep.'
'Sweetie,' Joe Louis said with a tired grin, 'I'm an ole man.'
'Yes,' she agreed, 'but when you go to New York you try to be young again.'

Says Wolfe, "The story went on like that, scene after scene, building up a picture of an ex-sports hero now fifty years old."

Talese, who gained little recognition until the late Sixties, in the introduction to *Fame and Obscurity* cautions those who deceptively regard the new journalism as fiction:

"It is, or should be, as reliable as the most reliable reportage although it seeks a larger truth than is possible through the mere compilation of verifiable facts, the use of direct quotations, and adherence to the rigid organizational style of the older form."

To Talese the new journalism "allows, demands in fact, a more imaginative approach to reporting, and it permits the writer to inject himself into the narrative if he wishes, as many writers do, or to assume the role of detached observer, as other writers do, including myself."

In the search for a definition of new journalism, Tom Wolfe explains "it is the use by people writing nonfiction of techniques which heretofore had been thought of as confined to the novel or the short story, to create in one form both the kind of objective reality of journalism and the subjective reality that people have always gone to the novel for." Dwight MacDonald, one of Wolfe's severest critics, disagrees, calling the new journalism "parajournalism," which he says, "seems to be journalism—the collection and dissemination of current news—but the appearance is deceptive. It is a bastard form having it both ways, exploiting the factual authority of journalism and the atmospheric license of fiction. Entertainment rather than information is the aim of its producers, and the hope of its consumers."

Dan Wakefield finds middle ground suggesting that writers like Wolfe and Truman Capote have "catapulted the reportorial kind of writing to a level of social interest suitable for cocktail party conversation and little-review comment. . . ." He continues:

Such reporting is "imaginative" not because the author has distorted the facts, but because he has presented them in a full instead of a naked manner, brought sight, sounds and feel surrounding those facts, and connected them by comparison with other facts of history, society and literature in an artistic manner that does not diminish, but gives greater depth and dimension to the facts.

*Wolfe's memory betrayed him. The correct citation is Gay Talese, "Joe Louis—The King as a Middle-Aged Man," *Esquire*, June, 1962—Ed.

Each of the other forms of new journalism mentioned previously (alternative, advocacy, underground and precision) have also sparked vigorous criticism, related both to their content and their form. If there is one consistent theme in all the criticism, it is probably the McLuhanistic "form supersedes content." The real innovative contribution of the new journalism has been stylistic. This theme will be expanded later as we examine examples of new journalism.

The theory of causality is of little use in chronicling the development of new journalism. Most of the innovations in form and approach have occurred simultaneously. Some were related to each other; some were not. The new journalism is an apparent trend in American journalism which involves a new form of expression, new writers and media, or an alteration in the patterns of traditional media. It has been suggested that this trend can be traced to the early 1960's and is related to (a) sociocultural change during the last decade, (b) a desire by writers and editors to find an alternative to conventional journalism, and (c) technological innovations such as electronic media, computer hardware and offset lithography.

Rarely has any decade in American history seen such drastic upheaval. Beyond the immediate surface events—rioting, student unrest, assassinations, and war—lies a pervasive youthful alienation from traditional society and the beginnings of a radical rejection of science and technology. Calls for a new humanism were heard. Young people, rejecting the materialistic good life, sought new meaning through introspection, drugs, and religion. The decade witnessed the beginnings of what some would call a counter culture: "a culture so radically disaffiliated from the mainstream assumptions of our society that it scarcely looks to many as a culture at all, but takes on the alarming appearance of a barbaric intrusion."

The new journalism, especially the new nonfiction and the writing of underground editors, seemed to respond to youthful needs. The practitioners of reportage attempted to bring all of the senses to bear in their journalistic product—with special attention to visual imagery. Thus Norman Mailer gave us sight, sound, and inner thoughts as he sloshed through great public events and issues. It is probably too early to determine how much the social upheaval and its resulting influence on the young affected the organizational and perceptual base that the new journalists would use. Writers like Jimmy Breslin and Studs Terkel would go to the periphery of an event, calling on a spectator instead of a participant to summarize the action. Tom Wolfe thought the automobile and the motorcycle were better organizing principles than war or race relations. Ken Kesey, the central figure in Wolfe's *The Electric Kool-Aid Acid Test*, introduces the reader to the Age of Acid, while a small town in western Kansas is a vehicle with which Truman Capote orchestrates a nonfiction novel about violent crime and its effects.

Journalism would also be influenced by television. Technological change in communications has always meant new functions for existing media. With television bringing electronic entertainment into our homes, we had less need for the *Saturday Evening Post's* short stories. The ratio of fiction to nonfiction in magazines would change as would the nature of the package of the newspaper. The days when newspapers serialized books blended into the distant past. Even the traditional comic strip seems at times to be threatened. Television changed the programming habits of radio, just as it changed magazines and newspapers.

The technological innovation of greatest importance to the new journalism was probably offset printing. It suddenly became possible to produce a newspaper cheaply, without having to invest in typesetting equipment or presses. The rapid reproduction of photo-offset meant that a single printer could produce dozens of small newspapers and that the alternative or underground paper could be produced rapidly at limited cost. Offset also allowed for the inclusion of freehand art work without expensive engravings, thus permitting efforts of psychedelic artists to merge with the underground journalists.

Although "new journalism" is used most often to describe a style of nonfiction writing, the definition has been further expanded to include alternative journalism and advocacy journalism. Although the reiteration of these terms may be following the fads, they do provide some shades of meaning which contribute to an understanding of the richly expansive scope of new journalism. These descriptive categories are offered more as a tool for analysis than a definitive up-to-the-minute classification of the rapidly proliferating output of the new journalists. Through an examination of a few of these new journalistic developments it is hoped that there will be fuller appreciation and awareness of what may be an important trend in the evolution of the mass media.

REPORTAGE

In the early 1960's it occurred to Truman Capote, who already had a reputation as a writer of fiction, that "reportage is the great unexplored art form." While it was a metier used by very few good writers or craftsmen, Capote reasoned that it would have "a double effect fiction does not have —the fact of it being true, every word of it true, would add a double contribution of strength and impact." Some years after Lillian Ross used a nonfiction reportage form in the *New Yorker*, Capote and other writers had experimented with reportage in magazine articles. *Picture* (1952), a nonfiction novel by Miss Ross, had been hailed as a literary innovation. "It is," one critic said, "the first piece of factual reporting to be written in the form of a novel. Miss Ross' story contains all the raw materials of dramatic fiction: the Hollywood milieu, the great director, the producer, the studio production chief and the performers." Another of the new nonfiction reportage innovators was Gay Talese, whose articles in *Esquire* "adapted the more dramatic and immediate technique of the short story to the magazine article," according to Tom Wolfe. Wolfe says it was Talese's "Joe Louis at Fifty" that first awakened him to the creative potential of reportage.

Some of the best early examples of the new nonfiction, in addition to the writing of Miss Ross and Talese, are articles by Wolfe collected in an anthology with an unlikely title: *The Kandy-Kolored Tangerine Flake Streamline Baby* (1965). Wolfe, like Talese, used scenes, extended dialog, and point of view. A few years later Wolfe described this period of his life as a time when he broke out of the totem format of newspapers. He had worked as a reporter for the *Washington Post* and *New York Herald Tribune* but later found magazines and books a better outlet for his creative energies. Another new journalist, Jimmy Breslin, was able to practice the

A Schematic Look at the New Journalism

Form	Medium	Content	Practitioners
The new nonfiction, also called reportage and parajournalism	Newspaper columns Books Magazine articles	Social trends Celebrity pieces The "little people" Public events	Tom Wolfe, Jimmy Breslin, Gay Talese, Norman Mailer, Truman Capote, others.
Alternative journalism, also called "modern muckraking"	Alternative newspapers New magazines	Exposes of wrongdoing in establishment organizations, attacks on bigness of institutions	Editor and writers for *San Francisco Bay Guardian, Cervi's Journal, Maine Times, Village Voice.*
Advocacy journalism	Newspaper columns Point-of-view papers Magazines	Social change Politics Public issues	Jack Newfield, Pete Hamill, Nicholas von Hoffman, others
Underground journalism	Underground papers in urban areas, at universities, high schools, military bases	Radical politics Psychedelic art The drug culture Social services Protest	Editors and writers for LA, New York and Washington *Free Presses, Berkeley Barb, East Village Other,* many others.
Precision journalism	Newspapers Magazines	Survey research and reporting of social indicators, public concerns	Editors and writers the Knight Newspapers, other newspapers, news magazines.

new journalism in a daily newspaper column. Breslin, whom Wolfe calls "a brawling Irishman who seemed to come from out of nowhere," is a former sportswriter who began using a reportage style in a column he wrote for the *New York Herald Tribune.* Breslin breathed life into an amazing assortment of characters like Fat Thomas (an overweight bookie) and Marvin the Torch (an arsonist with a sense of professionalism). Breslin met many of his characters in bars and demonstrated conclusively that the "little people of the street" (and some not so little) could say eloquent things about their lives and the state of the world. More important, Breslin brought the expectations and intuitions of these people to his readers in vivid, almost poetic style. In doing so, he as much as anyone else added the nonauthority as a source of information to the concept of new journalism.

Truman Capote tried the experimental reportage form on two articles in the *New*

Yorker (one on the "Porgy and Bess" tour of Russia and the other on Marlon Brando) before writing his powerful *In Cold Blood* (1966). As Capote describes it: "I realized that perhaps a crime, after all, would be the ideal subject for the massive job of reportage I wanted to do. I would have a wide range of characters, and more importantly, it would be timeless." It took Capote nearly seven years to finish the book which he himself described as "a new art form."

Contributing yet another variation on the new nonfiction theme during the 1960's was Norman Mailer, who, like Capote, had already established himself as an important fiction writer. To new journalism reportage Mailer contributed a first-person autobiographical approach. In *Armies of the Night* (1968), an account of a peace march on the Pentagon, Mailer ingeniously got inside his own head and presented the reader with a vivid description of his own perceptions and thoughts, contrasting them with his actions. This was a variation on the approach Talese had used earlier in describing the thoughts of persons featured in his articles and books. He called this description of one's inner secrets "interior monolog."

Examples of nonfiction reportage, in addition to those previously mentioned are: Breslin's *The World of Jimmy Breslin* (1968), Miss Ross' *Reporting* (1964), Talese's *The Kingdom and the Power* (1969), and *Fame and Obscurity* (1970), Wolfe's *Electric Kool-Aid Acid Test* (1969), *The Pump House Gang* (1969), and *Radical Chic and Mau-mauing the Flak Catchers* (1970). Frequent examples of new nonfiction reportage appear in *Esquire, New York* and other magazines.

ALTERNATIVE JOURNALISM

While Tom Wolfe would like to keep the new journalism pure and free from moralism, political apologies and romantic essays, increasingly the term "new journalism" has been broadened to include the alternative journalists. Most alternative journalists began their careers with a conventional newspaper or magazine but became disillusioned because the metropolitan paper often got too big to be responsive to the individual. Certain industries or politicians become sacred cows, the paper gets comfortable and is spoiled by economic success. At least this was the view of one of the most vigorous of alternative journalists, the late Eugene Cervi of Denver. In describing *Cervi's Rocky Mountain Journal*, he said,

> We are what a newspaper is supposed to be: controversial, disagreeable, disruptive, unpleasant, unfriendly to concentrated power and suspicious of privately-owned utilities that use the power with which I endow them to beat me over the head politically.

Alternative journalism is a return to personal journalism where the editor and/or a small staff act as a watchdog on conventional media, keeping them honest by covering stories they would not have touched. The alternative journalists are in the reform tradition. They do not advocate the elimination of traditional social, political, or economic institutions. In their view the institutions are all right, but those who run them need closer scrutiny.

Little has been written about the contribution of the alternative journalists who have established newspapers, newsletters, and magazines which attempt to provide an alternative to conventional media. "The traditional media simply are not covering the news," says Bruce Brugmann, editor of San Francisco's crusading *Bay Guardian*. Brugmann, a former reporter for the *Milwaukee Journal*, asserts that the kind of material produced by his monthly tabloid is "good, solid investigatory journalism." The *Bay Guardian* has been a gadfly for San Francisco, attacking power companies, railroads, and other establishment interests. One crusade of long standing is a probe with continuity of the communications empire of the *San Francisco Chronicle*, which Brugmann calls "Superchron." The *Bay Guardian* is a lively tabloid with bold, striking headlines and illustrative drawings which are actually editorial cartoons. *Cervi's Journal*, for years a scrapping one-man operation, is being continued by the late founder's daughter. Cervi, sometimes called the LaGuardia of the Rockies, was a volatile, shrill, and colorful man who, while providing news of record to Denver's business community (mortgages, bankruptcies, etc.), fearlessly attacked public and private wrongdoing. *Cervi's Journal* has taken on the police, local government, business, and other interests. Unlike the *Bay Guardian*, which has been in financial trouble almost since its founding, *Cervi's Journal* seems to have found a formula for financial success.

Other publications operating in an alternative-muckraking style are *The Texas Observer* in Austin, *I.F. Stone's Bi-Weekly* in Washington, D.C., Roldo Bartimole's *Point of View* in Cleveland, and the *Village Voice* in New York City. All of these publications (including the *Village Voice*, which began as an early underground paper in 1955), are read by a middle and upper-middle class audience, although all espouse a decidedly left-of-center position on social and political issues. Brugmann and several of his fellow alternative editors agree that their function is to make the establishment press more responsible. While conveying a sense of faith in the system, the alternative press has little tolerance for abuse or misuse of power.

Also a part of alternative journalism are a little band of iconoclastic trade publications—the journalism reviews. Shortly after the Democratic National Convention of 1968 when newsmen and students were beaten by police in the streets of Chicago, a number of working journalists organized the abrasive *Chicago Journalism Review*, which confines most of its barbs to the performance of the news media in Chicago. Occasionally, other stories are featured, but usually because one of the Chicago dailies or television stations refused to run the story first. The journalism reviews are perhaps the most credible instrument of a growing inclination toward media criticism. The writers and editors of the reviews continue as practicing reporters for traditional media, at times almost daring their bosses to fire them for revealing confidences and telling stories out of school. Other press criticism organs include *The Last Post* in Montreal, the *St. Louis Journalism Review*, and *The Unsatisfied Man: A Review of Colorado Journalism*, published in Denver.

A talk with the editors of the various alternative press outlets makes one wonder whether they wouldn't secretly like to put themselves out of business. As Brugmann puts it: "In Milwaukee, a *Bay Guardian* type of publication could never make it because the Milwaukee *Journal* does an adequate job of investigative reporting." Perhaps if the San Francisco media had such a record, the *Bay Guardian* would cease to exist.

ADVOCACY JOURNALISM

The alternative journalist sees himself as an investigative reporter, sifting through each story, reaching an independent conclusion. He does not openly profess a particular point of view, but claims a more neutral ground. The advocacy journalist, on the other hand, writes with an unabashed commitment to a particular viewpoint. He may be a New Left enthusiast, a professed radical, conservative, Women's libber or Jesus freak. The advocacy journalist defines his bias and casts his analysis of the news in that context. Advocacy journalists, usually though not always, suggest a remedy for the social ill they are exposing. This is rarely the case with the alternative journalist who does not see the development of action programs as his function.

Clayton Kirkpatrick of the *Chicago Tribune* says advocacy journalism is really "the new propaganda." He continues, "Appreciation of the power of information to persuade and convince has been blighted by preoccupation and is a primary influence in the activist movement that started in Europe and is now spreading to the United States. It threatens . . . a revolution in the newsroom." John Corry, writing in *Harper's* says, "the most important thing in advocacy journalism is neither how well you write or how well you report, but what your position in life is . . . " Corry sees advocacy journalists as persons who are not concerned about what they say, but how they say it. The advocacy journalists "write mostly about themselves, although sometimes they write about each other, and about how they all feel about things," Corry says.

Advocacy journalism is simply a reporter expressing his personal view in a story. "Let's face it," says Jack Newfield of the *Village Voice*, "the old journalism was blind to an important part of the truth . . . it had a built-in bias in its presentation: Tom Hayden *alleges*, while John Mitchell *announces*." In the old journalism, Newfield continues, "authority always came first. The burden of proof was always on minorities; individuals never get the emphasis that authorities get." Central to advocacy journalism is involvement. Writers like Newfield, who is an avowed New Leftist, are participants in the events they witness and write about. They debunk traditional journalism's concern about objectivity. "The Five W's, Who Needs Them!", declares an article by Nicholas von Hoffman of the *Washington Post*. Von Hoffman, a community organizer for Saul Alinsky's Industrial Areas Foundation in Chicago before joining the *Chicago Daily News*, has established a reputation as an advocacy journalist who shoots from the hip and calls shots as he sees them, according to *Newsweek*. His coverage of the celebrated 1970 Chicago conspiracy trial likened the courtroom and its participants to a theatrical production. Von Hoffman produces a thrice-weekly column, "Poster," which is syndicated by the *Washington Post-Los Angeles Times* News Service. In his search for advocacy outlets, Von Hoffman has written several books: *Mississippi Notebook* (1964), *The Multiversity* (1966), *We Are The People Our Parents Warned Us Against* (1968), and a collection of his newspaper columns, *Left at the Post* (1970).

Jack Newfield, who writes regularly in *New York* as well as in the *Village Voice*, has produced *A Prophetic Minority* (1966), and *Robert Kennedy: A Memoir* (1969), said to be the most passionate and penetrating account of the late Senator's life. Another of the advocacy journalists is Pete Hamill of the *New York Post*. Hamill, who seems at times to wear his heart on his sleeve, writes about politics, community problems, and social issues for the *Post* and a variety of magazines ranging from *Life* to *Ladies Home Journal*. He also writes regularly for *New York* where his concern for the unique problems of urban crowding show through in articles like "Brooklyn: A Sane Alternative."

Publications such as *Ramparts* and *Scanlan's* are examples of advocacy journalism. The *Village Voice* seems to fit into both the alternative and advocacy categories as do a number of other publications. Many of the social movements of the recent past and present needed organs of communication to promote their causes. Thus Young Americans For Freedom established what is regarded as a new right publication, *Right-On*. Jesus freaks have a publication with the same name. The Women's Liberation movement has spawned a number of newspapers and magazines. Ecology buffs also have their own publications as do the Black Panthers and other groups too numerous to mention.

THE UNDERGROUND PRESS

While the literature about underground journalism is growing rapidly—even in such staid publications as *Fortune* —a clarifying definition is rarely offered. Underground journalism has its psycho-social underpinnings in the urban/university counter-culture communities of the 1960's. The underground newspaper is a communications medium for young people who are seeking alternative life styles. Often these persons feel alienated from the message of conventional media. The *Los Angeles Free Press* is regarded as the first underground. Editor Arthur Kunkin explains, "the underground press is do-it-yourself journalism. The basis for the new journalism is a new audience. People are not getting the information they desire from the existing media. The LA *Free Press* is aimed at the young, Black, Mexicans and intellectuals." Kunkin says his paper is open to "anyone who can write in a comprehensible manner." He believes the underground press serves as a "mass opposition party." He urges his contributors to "write with passion, show the reader your style, your prejudice."

Some critics, however, are not as generous in their descriptions of underground journalism. Dave Sanford, writing in *New Republic* said:

> There is nothing very underground about the underground press. The newspapers are hawked on street corners, sent to subscribers without incident through the U.S. mails, carefully culled and adored by the mass media. About three dozen of them belong to the Underground Press Syndicate, which is something like the AP on a small scale; through this network they spread the word about what is new in disruptive protest, drugs, sex. Their obsessive interest in things that the "straights" are embarrassed or offended by is perhaps what makes them underground. They are a place to find what is unfit to print in the *New York Times*.

Early examples of the underground press were the *East Village Other*, published in Manhattan's East Village, not far from that latter-day Bohemian, the *Village Voice*, the *Chicago Seed, Berkeley Barb, Washington Free Press*, and others. The undergrounds are almost always printed by offset. This "takes the printing out of the hands of the technicians," says editor Kunkin, a former tool and die maker. The undergrounds use a blend of type and free hand art work throughout. They are a kind of collage for the artist-intellectual, some editors believe. The content of the undergrounds ranges from political and artistic concerns (especially an establishment v. the oppressed theme), sexual freedom, drugs, and social services. Much of their external content (that not written by the staff and contributors) comes from the Underground Press Syndicate and Liberation News Service.

In addition to the larger and better known undergrounds, there are underground papers in almost every sizable university community in the country. Most large cities have a number of undergrounds serving hippies and heads in the counterculture community. Newer additions to the underground are the high school undergrounds and the underground newspapers published on and adjacent to military bases, both in the U.S. and abroad. Some critics foresee the end of the underground press, but the large undergrounds are now lucrative properties. This, of course, raises another question about how long a paper can stay underground. Can a paper like the *Los Angeles Free Press* with a circulation of 90,000 stay underground? When does an underground paper become a conventional paper? These are among the many unresolved questions about the under-

ground press. The undergrounds have been called the most exciting reading in America. Even David Sanford reluctantly agrees: "at least they try—by saying what can't be said or isn't being said by the staid daily press, by staying on the cutting edge of 'In' for an audience with the shortest of attention spans."

PRECISION JOURNALISM

Perhaps the persons least likely to be classified as new journalists are the precision journalists, yet they may be more a part of the future than any of their colleagues in the new journalism ranks. Richard Scammon and Ben Wattenberg, authors of *The Real Majority*, a 1970 analysis of the American electorate, declare: "we are really the new journalists." They are concerned with an analysis of people that is as precise as possible. Or, at least as precise as the social survey research method allows. These men try to interpret social indicators and trends in prose that will attract the reader and are doing something quite new in journalism.

A leading practitioner of precision journalism is Philip Meyer, a Washington editor for the Knight Newspapers. Meyer, who has written a book which calls for application of behavioral science methodology in the practice of journalism, conducted a much-praised study of Detroit Negroes after the 1967 riot. Meyer and his survey team interviewed hundreds of citizens of Detroit to probe the reasons behind the disorder. His study, *Return to 12th Street*, was one of the few examples of race relations reporting praised by the Kerner Commission. Meyer is a prolific writer with recent articles in publications ranging from

Public Opinion Quarterly to *Esquire.* Whenever possible he uses the methods of survey research, combined with depth interviews to analyze a political or social situation. For example, early in 1970 a series of articles about the Berkeley rebels of 1964 appeared in the *Miami Herald* and other Knight newspapers. An editor's note explained the precisionist's approach:

> What happens to college radicals when they leave the campus? The whole current movement of young activists who want to change American society began just five years ago at the University of California's Berkeley campus. In a landmark survey, Knight newspapers reporters Philip Meyer and Richard Maidenberg located more than 400 of the original Berkeley rebels, and 230 of them completed detailed questionnaires. Of the respondents, 13 were selected for in-depth interviews. The results, based on a computer analysis of the responses, are provided in a series beginning with this article.

Says Meyer, "When we cover an election story in Ohio we can have all the usual description—autumn leaves, gentle winds—but in addition we can offer the reader a pretty accurate profile of what his neighbors are thinking." The precision journalists combine the computer with vivid description. Meyer and his colleagues at the Knight newspapers are also planning field experiments in which they will use the methods of experimental psychology to test public issue hypotheses in local communities. Of the future Meyer says, "We may never see a medical writer who can tie an artery, but a social science writer who can draw a probability sample is not unheard of."

"I like to think," Ben Wattenberg says, "that we are the new journalism—journalism which is not subjective but which is becoming more objective than ever before. We've got the tools now—census, polls, election results—that give us precision, that tell us so much about people. Yet, at precisely the time when these tools become so exact, the damn New Journalists have become so introspective that they're staring at their navels. The difficulty is that when you put tables in you bore people. Yet when I was in the White House, [he worked for L.B.J.] knowing what was going on, reading the new journalists was like reading fairy tales. They wrote political impressionism."

There are an increasing number of precision journalists—some of them are writers and editors who are integrating social science research into stories for news magazines and other mass circulation periodicals. They are, at present, the unsung heroes of the new journalism. Yet, their work is so boldly futuristic that they cannot long remain in the background. The work of precision journalists differs from the traditional coverage of the Gallup or Harris polls in the amount of information offered and the mode of presentation. The precision journalists extract data, add effective prose and attempt to interpret trends and conditions of concern to people.

HOW IT CAME TO BE

The various forms of new journalism —new nonfiction, alternative, advocacy, reform, underground and precision—all grew up in the 1960's. The reasons for these developments are not easily ascertained in the short run. However, there were coincidental factors—a break away from traditional news format and style; bright, energetic journalists on the scene; established literary figures who wanted to experiment with reportage; urgent social issues and the advancement of technology. But it was more than all this. There was a mood and a spirit which offered a conducive milieu for new journalism.

In the late Fifties and early Sixties those on the management side of the American press were worried. Enrollments in schools of journalism were not increasing at the same rate as other areas of study in colleges and universities. This was only one manifestation of the tired, staid image of the American press. One editor on the speaking circuit in those days used the title, "You Wonder Where The Glamour Went," trading on a toothpaste advertising slogan in an address rebutting the notion that American journalism had lost its glamour. Such a defensive posture says something about the journalism of the day. It was true that youthful enthusiasm for journalism had waned considerably since the time when foreign and war correspondents had assignments any young person would have coveted. The glamour and excitement simply were not there. Journalism was increasingly being viewed as stodgy by many young people. Economic pressures had reduced the number of newspapers in the country. One-newspaper towns, without the lusty competition of another day, were becoming commonplace. Journalism—both print and broadcast—had taken on a corporate image. Personalities of days past gave way to teams of little gray men, and it was a foregone conclusion that starting your own paper was next to impossible. This image may not have represented the reality of the situation, but it was the dismal picture in the minds of college students at the dawn of the Sixties.

To many bright, young writers the form of journalistic writing itself seemed to constrict creativity. The inverted pyramid, which places elements of a news story in a descending order of importance, and the shopworn "five w's and the h" seemed to impose a rigid cast over the substantive issues and events of the day. Many writers, especially those like Wolfe and Breslin, found the traditional approach to journalism impersonal and dehumanizing, at a time when there was little debate in the trade journals about the concept of objectivity, an ideal to which every right-thinking journalist adhered.

The new journalists' assault on objectivity is displaced, press critic Herbert Brucker believes:

> . . . critics of objective news are not as much against objectivity as they make out. What they denounce as objectivity is not objectivity so much as an incrustation of habits and rules of news writing, inherited from the past, that confine the reporter within rigid limits. Within those limits the surface facts of an event may be reported objectively enough. But that part of the iceberg not immediately visible is ruled out, even though to include it might reveal what happened in a more accurate—indeed more objective—perspective.

It is probably too early to assess all of the elements of the Sixties that set the stage for the development of the new journalism. Yet, one might cite as factors the verve and vitality of the early days of the Kennedy Administration, the ascendency of the civil rights movement, the evolution of a counter-culture, the drug scene, the war in Southeast Asia, student unrest, riots, and urban disorder. The media were affected by these events.

Historian Theodore Roszak speaks of the uniqueness of the Sixties in *The Making of a Counter Culture:*

> It strikes me as obvious beyond dispute that the interests of our college-age and adolescent young in the psychology of alienation, oriental mysticism, psychedelic drugs, and communitarian experiments comprise a cultural constellation that radically diverges from values and assumptions that have been in the mainstream of our society at least since the Scientific Revolution of the seventeenth century.

Reporters who covered the turbulence of the Sixties were wont to maintain traditional objectivity or balance, and few claimed to have the necessary detachment. At the same time the dissent abroad in the land pervaded the newsrooms so that by 1969 even reporters for the *Wall Street Journal*, the very center of establishment journalism, would participate in an antiwar march. Today, the traditional news format is under fire. Subjective decision-making at all stages of the reportorial process is evident. As one reporter put it: "Subjective decisions confront reporters and editors at the stage of assignment, data collection, evaluation, writing, and editing." "Who," the reporter asks, "decides what events to cover, which ones to neglect? When does the reporter know he has gathered enough information? What if there are fifteen sides to a story—instead of the two usually acknowledged by the theory of objectivity? Finally, writing and editing are purely subjective acts."

Certainly the turmoil over objectivity has touched conventional media and enhanced the climate for the new journalism.

The critics, however, had justifiable concern about some of the practices of new journalists. The work of writers like Breslin involves a good deal of literary license. Some new journalists are simply not as concerned with accuracy and attribution as are their more conservative colleagues. Some say the new journalism is simply undisciplined, opinionated writing. But it is difficult to determine whether the new journalism threatens any semblance of fairness the media has developed in the four decades since the era of jazz journalism, when sensationalism and embellishment were in full force. Many who criticize the new journalism are simply not ready for the diversity now available in the marketplace. Even a writer like Jack Newfield, perhaps the most strident advocacy journalist in America, says many of the new approaches including his own must serve as part of a total continuum of information which would include many of the traditional approaches to news gathering and dissemination.

As others have pointed out, most of the new journalists developed their style after learning the more conventional newspaper style. They are breaking the rules, but they know why. Even the most forceful advocates of the new journalism praise the organizing principles of the old journalism, in much the same way that Hemingway hailed the style book of the *Kansas City Star*. They part ways on matters of substance and content, but in the early organizing stages, nothing, they say, is better discipline. The inverted pyramid and the fetish for objectivity may have been too rigid, but these methods do offer something in terms of succinct treatment and synthesis of complex, inter-related facts. Perhaps the ideas and actions of the

Seventies are too complex for such simplistic treatment.

The new journalism offers rich detail and what Tom Wolfe calls "saturation reporting." The new journalism in all its forms is a more sophisticated kind of writing aimed at a more highly educated populace than that which gave life and readers to the old journalism. The new journalism is in its earliest stages of development. It has not yet arrived. It is not yet—and may never be—the dominant force in American journalism. Perhaps, like minority parties in American politics, it may suggest opportunities for innovation and thoughtful change. The media will do well to listen to the sounds of the new journalism and the resultant response of the new audience. It may be the stuff that the future is made of.

Aids   *The New Journalism: How It Came To Be*

1. Dennis's essay may be considered an extended definition of the term "new journalism." Make a list of the defining terms used by Dennis. Make a parallel list of the terms used to define "conventional" journalism.

2. How did new journalism "come to be"? Discuss the roles played by television, the war in Vietnam, the sixties, the counterculture, and underground newspapers.

3. Define with examples each of the five types of new journalism.

4. In what ways is new journalism propagandistic?

5. The journalist as advocate makes no pretense at objectivity; the new journalist openly reveals his subjectivity and bias. Conventional journalists, as the Guidelines for Straight News Reporting make clear, are supposed to be free from opinion or bias of any kind. Conduct a study of bias in television news broadcasting. Do you detect a bias, positive or negative, on the following issues: (a) gun control, (b) abortion, (c) prayer in school, (d) busing to achieve racial integration, (e) defense spending, (f) ecology, (g) deficit spending for health, education, and welfare? Can this bias be identified with a political point of view? Do you agree with some critics that the press corps and broadcasters reflect an Eastern, liberal, Democratic bias? If you discovered a bias, does it undermine the credibility of the press? How can the media return to the goals of objectivity, balance, and nonadvocacy?

6. Examine one or two pages of your local newspaper and make a list of all the value-loaded words such as adjectives, adverbs, and verbs.

What value judgments do these words imply? What impact might the continued exposure to value-loaded words have on our attitudes about current issues?

7. Throughout his essay Dennis invokes the name of Tom Wolfe as one of the leading practitioners of new journalism. Indeed, Wolfe not only explores the genre in his collected essays [*The Kandy-Kolored Tangerine Flake Streamline Baby* (1965), *The Pump House Gang* (1968), *Radical Chic and Mau-mauing the Flak Catchers* (1970), and *The Electric Kool-Aid Acid Test* (1969)], but analyzes its form, content, and goals in several prefaces and in "The New Journalism," from the anthology *The New Journalism* (Harper & Row, 1973), edited by Tom Wolfe and E. W. Johnson. As Everette Dennis asserts, the distinguishing feature of new journalism is style. Examine Tom Wolfe's style in "Pause, Now, and Consider Some Tentative Conclusions About the Meaning of This Mass Perversion Called Pornoviolence" in this unit. Locate examples of each of the following techniques: (a) The writer either injects himself into the narrative or assumes the role of detached observer; (b) the writer adopts the literary techniques of the short story and novel—the dramatic scene-setting, the extended dialog, the subjective point of view where the writer enters directly into the mind of a character; the full description of gesture, posture, and facial expression; the creation of whole scenes; and (c) the innovative typography—the lavish uses of dots, exclamation points, italics, unusual punctuation—and the use of interjections, shouts, nonsense words, coined words, onomatopoeia, alliteration, extended similes, and oxymoron. Do you find Wolfe's style entertaining? effective? How does Wolfe's style help to reveal his attitude toward his subject matter?

8. The techniques and goals of new journalism may be found in media other than those described by Everette Dennis. What, for instance, are the goals of such a magazine as *Time*? to convey the news? to editorialize? to make the news "interesting"? or a combination of all three goals? To appreciate the complex interplay of goals, one might focus on the way in which language is used, sometimes covertly, to reveal the political, cultural, and esthetic biases of the magazine. Examine a current issue of *Time*, locating examples of each of the following stylistic devices. What bias, positive or negative, is implied by the use of such devices?

    a. Alliteration ("frozen frivolities," "medal mania," "the tumbles along with the triumphs," "sex and sorrow")

    b. Similes ("The soaps are like Big Macs—a lot of people who won't admit it eat them up"; "The annual proliferation of decorations has led critics to observe that the government selects winners with the same skill as the blindfold player in a game of pin-the-tail-on-the-donkey")

c. Play on words and literary allusions ("Since selling his Kentucky Fried Chicken business for $2 million in 1964, Colonel Harland Sanders has not found the finger lickin' so good"; "Threescore years ago, Jerome Kern and Guy Bolton brought forth on Broadway a thoroughly beguiling musical"; "The Glass Menagerie is Williams' portrait of the artist as a young man")

d. Coined words ("Jawsmania," "meritocracy," "pop-psych")

e. Use of absolute numbers ("Most of the victims were taken to Elmhurst Hospital, 2.3 miles away"; "To solve the mystery, the FBI assigned 300 men and the New York Police 200 to the case")

Code of Ethics

THE SOCIETY OF PROFESSIONAL JOURNALISTS, SIGMA DELTA CHI

The Society of Professional Journalists, Sigma Delta Chi, believes the duty of journalists is to serve the truth.

We believe the agencies of mass communication are carriers of public discussion and information, acting on their Constitutional mandate and freedom to learn and report the facts.

We believe in public enlightenment as the forerunner of justice, and in our Constitutional role to seek the truth as part of the public's right to know the truth.

We believe those responsibilities carry obligations that require journalists to perform with intelligence, objectivity, accuracy, and fairness.

To these ends, we declare acceptance of the standards of practice here set forth:

RESPONSIBILITY

The public's right to know of events of public importance and interest is the overriding mission of the mass media. The purpose of distributing news and enlightened opinion is to serve the general welfare. Journalists who use their professional status as representatives of the public for selfish or other unworthy motives violate a high trust.

FREEDOM OF THE PRESS

Freedom of the press is to be guarded as an inalienable right of people in a free society. It carries with it the freedom and the responsibility to discuss, question, and challenge actions and utterances of our government and of our public and private institutions. Journalists uphold the right to speak unpopular opinions and the privilege to agree with the majority.

ETHICS

Journalists must be free of obligation to any interest other than the public's right to know the truth.

Code of Ethics of The Society of Professional Journalists, Sigma Delta Chi, (1973). Adopted by the 1973 national convention. Reprinted by permission.

1. Gifts, favors, free travel, special treatment or privileges can compromise the integrity of journalists and their employers. Nothing of value should be accepted.

2. Secondary employment, political involvement, holding public office, and service in community organizations should be avoided if it compromises the integrity of journalists and their employers. Journalists and their employers should conduct their personal lives in a manner which protects them from conflict of interest, real or apparent. Their responsibilities to the public are paramount. That is the nature of their profession.

3. So-called news communications from private sources should not be published or broadcast without substantiation of their claims to news value.

4. Journalists will seek news that serves the public interest, despite the obstacles. They will make constant efforts to assure that the public's business is conducted in public and that public records are open to public inspection.

5. Journalists acknowledge the newsman's ethic of protecting confidential sources of information.

ACCURACY AND OBJECTIVITY

Good faith with the public is the foundation of all worthy journalism.

1. Truth is our ultimate goal.

2. Objectivity in reporting the news is another goal, which serves as the mark of an experienced professional. It is a standard of performance toward which we strive. We honor those who achieve it.

3. There is no excuse for inaccuracies or lack of thoroughness.

4. Newspaper headlines should be fully warranted by the contents of the articles they accompany. Photographs and telecasts should give an accurate picture of an event and not highlight a minor incident out of context.

5. Sound practice makes clear distinction between news reports and expressions of opinion. News reports should be free of opinion or bias and represent all sides of an issue.

6. Partisanship in editorial comment which knowingly departs from the truth violates the spirit of American journalism.

7. Journalists recognize their responsibility for offering informed analysis, comment, and editorial opinion on public events and issues. They accept the obligation to present such material by

individuals whose competence, experience, and judgment qualify them for it.

8. Special articles or presentations devoted to advocacy or the writer's own conclusions and interpretations should be labeled as such.

FAIR PLAY

Journalists at all times will show respect for the dignity, privacy, rights, and well-being of people encountered in the course of gathering and presenting the news.

1. The news media should not communicate unofficial charges affecting reputation or moral character without giving the accused a chance to reply.

2. The news media must guard against invading a person's right to privacy.

3. The media should not pander to morbid curiosity about details of vice and crime.

4. It is the duty of news media to make prompt and complete correction of their errors.

5. Journalists should be accountable to the public for their reports and the public should be encouraged to voice its grievances against the media. Open dialogue with our readers, viewers, and listeners should be fostered.

PLEDGE

Journalists should actively censure and try to prevent violations of these standards, and they should encourage their observance by all newspeople. Adherence to this code of ethics is intended to preserve the bond of mutual trust and respect between American journalists and the American people.

The Family Magazine and the American People

STEPHEN C. HOLDER

No doubt the longevity of our mass media depends in large measure on their efficacy as producers' commodities. That is, the continued success of a medium is closely related to how well it meets the needs of advertisers and how competitive it is economically with other media. It is equally true, however, that a medium cannot rise unless there is a demand for it great enough to make its production feasible; continued demand is a requisite of continued success. The general, family magazines performed certain functions for the mass audience. *This is the unique position occupied by the family magazines in our cultural history: the peculiar relationship they enjoyed with readers.* Popular taste can be a demanding mistress; it vacillates wildly and rapidly in some areas at the same time it remains relatively constant in others. That the family magazines wooed popular taste successfully for many years is obvious. We shall see how they came to have a happy relationship with popular taste and the present utility of the magazines as reflections of that taste. We shall also see ways that readers' faith in their magazines was violated.

A major problem faced by any magazine is establishing the public role it is to occupy, both for itself and for its readers. To be successful, a magazine must have an accurate sense of its identity and must communicate that identity to the public in such a way that the public can readily recognize future issues. Accordingly, virtually all magazines adopt a basic formula.[1] The initial formula success is heavily dependent on the success of the formula the editors arrive at.

In deciding on a formula, the editors need to consider many factors.[2] A comparison of almost any issue of any of the big family magazines with almost any issue of another will show that *the formulas of the family magazines were nearly identical.* One reason for this similarity is the homogeneity of readership, as has been demonstrated by many studies.[3] Having decided on the group he wants to reach, the publisher must decide what he wants to reach them with. The general, family magazines were extremely inclusive in deciding this function. Basically, *they attempted to reflect all aspects of the American experience, current concerns and*

Excerpts from Stephen C. Holder, "The Family Magazine and the American People," *Journal of Popular Culture*, fall 1973. Reprinted by permission of the publisher.

[1] Roland E. Wolseley, *The Magazine World: An Introduction to Magazine Journalism* (New York: Prentice-Hall, Inc., 1951), 137.

[2] Wolseley, 139–40.

[3] For an example, see *Nationwide Magazine Audience Survey, Report No. 3—Families* (New York: MAB, 1948), ii.

general concerns. More specifically, the broad goal breaks down into some six realizable goals: (1) information, (2) entertainment, (3) escape, (4) assistance in forming opinions, (5) reinforcement of moral values, and (6) provision of a "consumer's showcase." The continued success of a popular magazine is dependent upon the magazine's ability to establish a personal relationship with its readers, acting as a unique companion in a majority of these areas. The following paragraphs offer an examination of each of these, both as roles of all media and as specific roles of the family magazines.

The family magazines shared their informational function with the other media. Of course, they were never able to compete effectively in the up-to-the-minute news arena, but informational articles could be current. Moreover, the greater leisure inherent in magazines allowed them to be broader in their scope, more complete in their explanations and, frequently, better at putting current events items into perspective than the other media. There was a large area in which the family magazines did not duplicate the news coverage of the other media—items of generally current interest, but not especially newsworthy. For example, the July 2, 1949 issue of Collier's carried a story about Rudolph Valentino, "The Actor Who Won't Stay Dead." Valentino died twenty-three years before. This is an area that television has since developed with "Specials" and "Spectaculars," but it was a major source of magazine material for years.

Most of the informational material in the family magazines was about some aspect of the American experience. There was a great deal of information; generally speaking, at least half of the tables of contents of the family magazines was devoted to this fare. And the range of the articles themselves was tremendous; frequently the juxtaposition of articles touching the ends of the social and economic spectrum was striking. The July 2, 1949 Collier's carried informational articles on "A One-Shot Cure for Syphilis," "Charlie Brannan and his Wonderful World," and "Who Said Promised Land?" The September 21, 1971 issue of Look, the penultimate issue, carried "Julius Rudel: Washington's Music Man," and an article on the poverty area "Where Vida Blue Grew." The June 11, 1960 Post carried "Adventures of the Mind, '54: The U.S. Presidency," and "The Face of America: The Grandeur That Was." Similar examples are found in almost every issue of every one of the family magazines. These articles were generally high in quality and accuracy. They took full advantage of the magazine format; that is, they used the comparative leisure of the magazine to be complete and offer background information, and they were often generously illustrated.

Author Tom Wolfe, speaking recently at the Midway campus of the University of Chicago, indicated that writers for magazines in the 1950s and 1960s were generally regarded as second class by the rest of the literary world. But he could not have been speaking of the family magazines, for they went out of their way to print articles by well-known authorities. Look's last issues, for example, featured articles by Walt W. Rostow, Christopher S. Wren and Allen Drury. Post's contents for April 1, 1961 show articles by Bill O'Hallaren, Stephen Spender and Dean Acheson. Collier's contents for November 27, 1948 contain articles by Virginia Leigh, Francis Cardinal Spellman and J. D. Ratcliff. These, of course, are just a few of hundreds of examples.

In terms of their historic interest, collections of old family magazines are well worth preservation. The articles in them offer a far more textured picture of American life than we are apt to find in any history text. Factually the articles are accurate, at least as the world was able to understand the facts when they were printed; the family magazines were too big and too prestigious to risk their reputations with the half-truths seen occasionally in "pulp" magazines. The articles offer more than facts; they represent the *way* Americans saw and understood those facts in any given moment of history. That is, *the family magazines put the facts into social context by the juxtaposition of articles about all sorts of things going on at the same time which drew the interest of the American public.* No other popular medium does this so well. Granted, there are huge libraries of videotapes made of old TV shows and mountains of tapes of old radio shows . . . but they are inaccessible to the general public. *The inherent impermanence of the broadcast media makes them of limited value for the historian.* Comparatively few books have been written so far about television as popular cultural history. Many have been written about TV technologically, sociologically or psychologically, but the books that catch the flavor of the early days of TV are few.[4]

Side by side with the articles was the fiction printed by the big magazines. Again speaking in terms of historical interest, the fiction carried by the family magazines represents at least as much about the American people as the articles do. As is pointed out in greater detail later in this article, the family magazines were generally *conforming*, rather than *transforming* in their treatment of the American experience. In his book, *Mass Entertainment*, Harold Mendelsohn notes,

> by its very preoccupation with the middle class, . . . mass entertainment reinforces the values and life-ways of the middle class and as a by-product no doubt helps to maintain the middle class status quo of American society. This latter function in turn must serve as still another source of reassurance for the middle classes.[5]

In addition to the political and technological tenor of a given time, then, the family magazine fiction offers new dimensions: the prevailing moral standards and popular literary taste. This can be seen in the fiction of both *Post* and *Collier's*; *Look*, of course, carried almost no fiction. Of the two magazines, *Post's* fiction was generally of superior literary quality. For this reason, and because the general moral values of the fiction in *Post* and *Collier's* were essentially the same, it seems unnecessary to offer an examination of both. Instead, there follows a short analysis of *Post* fiction. Moreover, *Collier's* died before the real impact of the recent moral revolution was felt across America.

The editors of the *Saturday Evening Post*, the *Ladies Home Journal, Country Gentleman*, and even *Jack and Jill* had all been born and bred in the Middle West. They

---

[4]One of the best books on the subject is Tedd Thomey, *The Glorious Decade* (New York: Ace Books, 1971), which does manage to portray some of the glamour and excitement of early TV. The book is, however, dependent upon the reader's remembering from actual experience "how it was." The coming of another generation or two will render the book mere history.

[5]Harold Mendelsohn, *Mass Entertainment* (New Haven: College and University Press Services, Inc., 1966), 68.

retained their freshness, honesty, and innocence, their belief in the simple virtues, and their distrust of Yankee shrewdness, big business, big labor, big government, and the big world that menaced the United States. This was correct, for they were editing for the great American middle class to which they belonged. They had an unconscious rapport with their readers which was stronger than their deliberate attempts to give them what they thought they wished.[6]

Post's fiction was essentially a reinforcement of traditional American values. All of the things held dear for generations appeared on *Post*'s pages . . . from Apple Pie to the Girl Next Door.

* * *

Many of the characteristics of magazine fiction apply equally to the family magazines' regular, humorous features. In addition to humorous stories, there were generous assortments of cartoons. Many favorite cartoonists appeared regularly: *Post* carried Ted Key's "Hazel." *Look* included Chon Day's "Brother Sebastian," *Collier's* regularly featured Virgil Partch drawings on a variety of subjects. The cartoons probably appealed to all readers of the family magazines, not only to the less educated, as we might expect. A 1960 study by Edward J. Robinson and David Manning White of the readers of newspaper comics showed very wide readership among the well-educated.[7] It seems entirely reasonable to make the extension of their conclusions to cover magazine comic reading as well. Generally speaking, the cartoons were sprinkled throughout family magazines; even the non-reader of newspaper comics was apt to have read magazine cartoons . . . he would have had a hard time avoiding them.

We should note some other things about family magazine humor. As did the rest of the magazine, cartoons reflected American family life. Typical subjects might include the neighborhood "gossip" mimeographing her news, the little boy with his hand in the cookie jar, etc. To appreciate a joke, we must be able to understand it from our own experience in some way.[8] General cartoons in family magazines treated experiences so broad that there could be almost no problem with understanding. By way of contrast, the family magazine cartoons were not "racy" humor of the type featured in *Playboy*, *Rogue*, etc. Sex was not treated humorously. And family magazine cartoons were not the "hard" cartoons of *The New Yorker* variety, which often depend on literary or philosophical allusion.

The family magazines reflected the American experience editorially as well. Most of the editorials were bland and of conforming nature. Of the big magazines, *Post* was the most outspoken. But *Post* editorials were most frequently of general appeal. The April 16, 1960 issue, for example, carried three editorials in this order: "One Item Omitted from Tests for Drivers —Character!" "Can Red China's Cringing Bureaucrats Hold on Forever?" and "An

[6]James Playsted Wood, *The Curtis Magazines* (New York: The Ronald Press Co., 1956), 204.

[7]Edward J. Robinson and David Manning White, *An Exploratory Study of the Attitudes of More Highly Educated People Toward the Comic Strips* (Communications Research Center, Report No. 1, September, 1960), 94.

[8]This is the same idea expressed in Henri Bergsen's classic study, *Laughter*, in which he discusses the inherent "complicity of laughters."

Educated Man Should Have the Dictionary Habit." *Collier's* was equally bland, with such editorials as "Entertainment Is Here to Stay," in the July 2, 1949 issue. *Look* carried no editorials.

Another function filled by the family magazines was escape for the reader from the problems of his everyday life. Mendelsohn indicates the need for this cathartic experience:

> Man repairs the deficiencies in his life and experience by creating and enjoying art, music, drama, poetry, and fiction— and contemporaneously—mass entertainment.[9]

* * *

As noted by Patricke Johns-Heine and Hans H. Gerth, the trend has been away from titans and superstars as heroes of magazine fiction. In their place are the small businessman, the farmer, the industrial worker.[10] This is not to say, of course, that magazine fiction was made "cheap" literarily; rather, it was made more accessible to the reader.[11] The adjustment was in the direction of reality . . . perhaps in the same sense that Arthur Miller's *Death of a Salesman* can be regarded as legitimate tragedy. To be sure, the "happy ending" remained a feature of much magazine fiction—and readers wanted it in their magazines. But the plot resolution was much less apt to be in the form of success via achievement, marriage or luck; it was

likely to be the solving of some human problem.[12]

Not only did the editors of the family magazines conform to generally held convictions and moral values, they were careful to let the public know that they were conforming. They told us how good they were at reflecting the broad American scene.[13] For instance, *Look* ran a two-page editorial in the March 23, 1965 issue, listing all the "Major Awards" bestowed on the magazine by various national groups. This, of course, was only good business.

The family magazines served still another function for the reader and, by extension, still serve the same function for the historian. Through magazine advertising readers became educated consumers. Without leaving the comfort of his living room, the reader could find out all about the newest appliances, automobiles, insurance plans, etc. More important for the consumer in a material society, he could judge his own standard of living in terms of new items on the market. He could see, for example, that his bathroom fixtures were sadly dated. One advertisement in 1960 demonstrated with color pictures the off-the-floor toilet, the off-center design bathtub and the single lever faucet. (*Post,* April 16, 1960, 20–21). In the same issue he could learn about no-defrost refrigerators, nylon tires, wide-track automobiles, polyester fiber, permanent auto radiator

---

[9]Mendelsohn, 90–91.

[10]Patricke Johns-Heine and Hans H. Gerth, "Values in Mass Periodical Fiction, 1921–1940," in Bernard Rosenberg and David Manning White, *Mass Culture: The Popular Arts in America* (New York: Macmillan, 1957), 230–31.

[11]Rosenberg and White, 231.

[12]Rosenberg and White, 230.

[13]Robert S. Brustein, "The New Faith of the *Saturday Evening Post,*" *Commentary,* Vol. 16, 1953, 367–69.

fill, new designs in telephones, "detergent-action" shoe polish, poison ivy pills, and a vacuum cleaner that "dances out deep down dirt" . . . plus a lot more. The family magazines had an important function as "consumers' showcases."

The real interest for us in family magazine advertising lies in what it reveals about changing trends in American taste. We can take almost any ad for a large durable good, put it in the context offered by the rest of a magazine (including other advertisements) and understand the forces operating on the consumer at that moment. For example, the same issue of *Post* mentioned above carried a double-page spread in full color for the 1960 Chrysler. The car featured a pushbutton transmission, a trend for at least three auto makers (Chrysler, American Motors, Ford), but a gadget that never caught on. Influenced by the recent space-craze, the car carried enormous tail-fins, ostensibly to promote high-speed stability (there was never any real evidence for this). The car had huge expanses of glass fore and aft, another trend of the sixties that has since died. The point here is that we can learn a great deal about American manufacturing history and American consumer tastes from back issues of family magazines. They are best suited for this kind of study because of their very broad range.

Naturally, it is possible to take a dim view of the role of the advertiser.[14] We should remember, however, that the *advertisements are just as much a part of the magazines as the articles or fiction. They become increasingly useful as history.* Even if, as Mr. Handlin suggests, the commodities sold are not worth study (although it

seems highly unlikely), the selling job itself is worth a close look. The development of formulas for the family magazines was largely a product of the magazines' advertising function. Once again, we are struck by the fact that the real manipulators of the popular media are those with financial interests. The point is that the formulas worked for producers, advertisers and consumers. And, in the case of the consumer in an increasingly visual society, the habit factor was most important in keeping the family magazines alive.

We have seen the magazines' obligations to consumers under the formulas they adopted to meet their roles. The formulas themselves were highly similar due to the similarity of the consumers reached. One role has dominated all of the others: the reinforcement of moral values is an integral part of information, entertainment and escape in family magazine fiction. It is also readily apparent in the bland editorial sections of *Collier's* and *Post* and is implicit in the magazines' function as "consumers' showcases."

The fulfillment of all of these roles led to an increasingly ritual-oriented audience for the general, family magazines. Subscription lists remained relatively constant for all the family magazines—probably representing a high percentage of ritual readers. Moreover, these readers felt a close relationship with the magazines and did not hesitate to voice approval or disapproval. Had nothing else changed, these ritual readers might still be sitting down weekly or bi-weekly with their favorite magazines.

It was on the basis of the six goals discussed in this article that the family

---

[14]Oscar Handlin, as found in Norman Jacobs, ed,. *Culture for the Millions?: Mass Media in Modern Society* (Toronto: D. Van Nostrand Co., Inc., 1959), 69.

magazine's peculiar relationship with the American people was built. None of these areas, by itself, could produce a love affair of such huge proportions—and a love affair it was. The coldness of the newsmagazine does not invite the closeness Americans had with *Collier's, Look* and *Post*. Our needs for short fiction of the family magazine type are now being met by television. The American people would hardly stand still for a magazine with nothing in it but editorials and advertisements for new products, much less for a magazine of morals. Escape, by itself, does not really offer sufficient base for a magazine, except of the very sensational variety. Yet all of these items in correct proportion and covered with a protective moral shield offered the American people an irresistible package for many years. The recent success of the *Post* is evidence that the package is still a sound one, if uneconomical on a weekly or bi-weekly scale. America still has no one popular medium that fills our multiple needs as well as the family magazine did. Television has now taken over the role—but its success is due to a combination of technological and economic factors, not to a sudden shift in American mass values.

Aids   *The Family Magazine and the American People*

1. According to Stephen Holder, most magazines adopt a basic formula in order to sell themselves to the public. What formula was adopted by such general family magazines as *The Saturday Evening Post* and *Collier's*? What are the six broad goals of such magazines? Locate some back issues of one of these magazines and provide examples for each of the six goals.

2. Using Holder's approach as a guide, locate the formula adopted by one of the following types of magazines:

    a) Digests (*Reader's Digest, The Intellectual Digest*)
    b) Black magazines (*Black World, Ebony, Jet Magazine*)
    c) Detective magazines (*Master Detective, Police Gazette*)
    d) Science fiction (*Analog, Galaxy, Amazing Science Fiction*)
    e) Satire (*Mad, Cracked, National Lampoon*)
    f) Family (*Family Circle, Family Journal, Woman's Day*)
    g) Romance (*Your Romance, Personal Romances*)
    h) Teen (*Ingenue, Seventeen, Teen Magazine*)
    i) TV and film (*Screen Secrets, Daylight TV, TV Dawn to Dusk*)

    Can you deduce the goals of the magazine? Provide examples for each of the goals.

3. Apply the following statement by Holder to one or two issues of a

family magazine: "In terms of their historical interest, collections of old family magazines are well worth preservation. The articles in them offer a far more textured picture of American life than we are apt to find in any history text."

4. According to Holder, the fiction in family magazines is "generally conforming, rather than transforming in [its] treatment of the American experience." Examine a fictional story in one of the family magazines, showing how it reinforces the values, tastes, and life styles of the intended audience. How does the story offer reassurance? How many of Holder's six goals does it illustrate? Do your conclusions hold true for the fictional stories in the other types of magazines enumerated in question 2? Compare and contrast a story from a family magazine with one in another type of magazine.

5. Many magazines contain cartoons. Examine the cartoons in one or two issues of a family magazine. Do they reinforce the values projected by the articles and fictional stories? What kinds of topics are taboo in family magazine cartoons? How do these cartoons differ from those in men's magazines, such as *Playboy* or *Penthouse,* or in magazines like *The New Yorker*?

6. Determine the success formula of such magazines as *Family Circle,* and *Woman's Day.* Consider the ways in which these magazines portray the housewife and mother as hero, glamorize her daily chores, advocate economy, practicality, and self-improvement, and perform for their readers the important psychological function of reaffirming the role of the housewife and mother in today's changing society. Are these magazines female counterparts to *Popular Mechanics?*

7. Another function of magazines is to serve as a consumers' showcase for the newest products and services. Advertisements, Holder reminds us, are just as much a part of the magazine as the articles and fiction. Examine the ads in one issue of a magazine. How do they reinforce the values, tastes, and life styles of the intended audience? Can you deduce the demographics (i.e., age, sex, race, income level) of the audience from the ads? Can you deduce the psychographics (hopes, fears, dreams) of the audience from the ads? Does the image of humanity revealed in the ads match that of the articles and fiction?

8. Much of the writing done by college students is *analysis*—the process of dividing something into its component parts, then examining the ways in which those parts relate to one another. Stephen Holder is interested in isolating the "formula" of the family magazine. His documentation consists of the contents of various family magazines.

Without some way of arranging his data, the essay would be a mass of undifferentiated examples. How does Holder organize his material into component parts? How, according to Holder, are these parts related? Can you think of other ways Holder might have organized his material?

9. Another purpose of Holder's essay seems to be to *define* the family magazine as a unique mass medium in American society. Definition does not normally occur in isolation except in dictionaries. It usually fits into a larger rhetorical plan or pattern of argumentation. What is Holder's larger rhetorical purpose? What is he saying about the value of studying family magazines?

The American Periodical Press and Its Impact

ROLAND L. WOLSELEY

While this article was being written the world of the periodical press in the U.S.A. was the maker of front-page news. One of the country's oldest and most famous magazines, *The Saturday Evening Post*, died of malnutrition, i.e., of lack of advertising revenue. At its death, almost its 150th birthday anniversary, it had more than three million subscribers and newsstand buyers; a few months before it had in excess of six million, but half the subscription list was dropped in an economy move that was unsuccessful.

Too much circulation is a disease from which a number of American magazines have suffered in the past two decades. On the surface it appears to be a paradoxical situation. Generally speaking, in all print journalism it has for years been the rule that the higher the circulation the higher the advertising rate and consequently the greater the income. This formula still is followed, by and large. But an enormously expensive magazine to manufacture and distribute by the millions of copies each week (in recent years every other week), as was the *Post* and as were such other giants of circulation that succumbed at mid-century (*Collier's*, *Coronet*, *American*, and *Woman's Home Companion* were among them) must enlarge the formula to include 'if costs of production and distribution are kept in ratio'.

Once, too, magazines and newspapers could take for granted that if they offered an advertiser the readers he wanted they could count on him to buy the space to reach those readers. But today there is a new type of competitor: broadcasting, and particularly television. It can tell an advertiser that he can reach the mass of the people through television sets, of which in the U.S. there now are more in use than there are motor cars or telephones. Since television's arrival as an advertising competitor, two decades ago, magazines of mass circulation have had problems.

All this about the failure of widely-known American magazines may leave the impression that the periodical press is in an unhealthy state. But

From *Gazette*, 1969, 15, No. 1, p. 1. Reprinted by permission of *Gazette* and the author.

this conclusion has no basis in fact. On the contrary, the health of this industry as a whole is sound. The animal kingdom was not destroyed, centuries ago, when the dinosaurs, and almost all other huge animals, died out. Similarly, some of the giant magazines have not been able to adjust to new competition, new tastes, new climates of opinion, and a changing economic order. But there are at least 20,000 periodicals in the U.S.A., and the handful of huge-circulation publications is only a small, if widely-publicized, minority.

To understand the American periodical press and its impact it is necessary to see it whole. Only a few generalizations can be made about the entire industry, for it is in many segments. In fact, neither the industry itself nor the public at which it is aimed agrees on what that industry includes. To most Americans the word *magazine* (the term *periodical* is not much used) connotes a publication, weekly or monthly, intended either for all persons, as is the *Reader's Digest,* or for a large portion of the population, as is *McCall's* or *Ladies' Home Journal*, both multi-million circulation periodicals for women. And many persons employed in this consumer or general area of magazinedom take the same narrow view. In fact, the most widely used reports and studies of the industry usually cover only the consumer books (in the jargon of the publishing business a magazine often is called a *book*, to the utter confusion of outsiders), as if the thousands of small periodicals did not count. This situation came about, of course, because the bulk of the dollar investment in advertising space is in the consumer area: these magazines have been the big money makers. Actually, the majority of the consumer magazines do not have large circulations despite their broad content.

Just what kind of publication the others are considered by the owners of the consumer magazines is not clear. Those others exist, just the same, and are far greater numerically and in the long run have a different and perhaps greater impact.

Depending upon how you count them, the consumer magazines may number as few as three and as many as 900. Perhaps the *Reader's Digest*, with 27,000,000 circulation, is the only true American consumer magazine left. The figure 900 is reached by including those that attempt to reach a wide public. The majority have small circulation and little advertising. They print trivia. They include sensational, sexy adventure magazines for boys and men, various fan publications for the worshippers of cinema idols, sports stars, and other entertainers; various collections of thin articles about hobbies, and numerous attempts to catch the teen-agers' coins with magazines telling the girls how to apply cosmetics and the boys how to become a professional football player.

The remaining 19,100 are for the most part the actual core of the magazine press. That figure, in round numbers, includes about 10,000 known as industrial periodicals but more commonly called house organs or company magazines, and are ignored by the entrepreneurs in the business because they do not accept advertising and are given to readers, who are employees of a company, its customers, its dealers, or its prospects. Also, in the 19,100 are 2,500 business magazines, that is, commercially-published periodicals catering to the business world and ranging from the austere *Fortune,* published by Time Inc., to the highly specialized *Roads and Streets,* issued by the Reuben H. Donnelley Corp., which has 17 others equally specialized. And it also includes about 400 published by associations, embracing the *National Geographic* and the *Journal of the American Medical Association,* two of the most profitable enterprises in the business.

To these can be added about 1,500 that deal with religion, 300 magazines of education at different levels, 200 about labor, and the remaining thousands that are devoted to such subjects as science, specialized sports, all of the arts, and various juvenilia.

In America, it appears, if three or more people get together their first act is to form a committee and their second is to launch a publication; generally it is a magazine.

The periodical press in the U.S. therefore is overwhelmingly composed of specialized journals. Yet those who trace the press's current fortunes insist upon judging it by the fate of a minority of large periodicals hardly typical of the entire industry.

The situation is made even more complicated by the realization by some of the larger publishing companies that issue consumer magazines that the specialized field is a less risky one and that a mixture of operations is desirable. Cowles Communications, Inc., for example, is a widely diversified firm that issues several mass magazines (including *Look* and *Family Circle,* with 7,750,000 and 6,000,000 circulation, respectively) but also has a clutch of business periodicals which it calls 'Magazines for Industry'; these include *Candy Marketer, Food & Drug Packaging, Bottling Industry* and nine others. Another large firm, Condé Nast, is best known for its popular *Vogue, Mademoiselle,* and *Glamour.* But only insiders realize that it also issues *Analog,* a science fiction periodical, and *House and Garden,* whose function is obvious from its title. Similarly, the Hearst firm, one of the ancients of American magazine journalism, has *Good Housekeeping* as well as *Motor* and *American Druggist,* among others, in its group of more than a dozen.

The picture of the industry must include certain trends. One relates to advertising. In each of the past four years the gross income from advertising has exceeded one billion dollars. Year by year the intake was higher. Actually it is more, for those who do the adding include mainly the consumer magazines. But at the same time the number of pages of advertising sold has decreased, the decline in 1968 from 1967 amounting to 2 per cent, for example. There has been some question about the soundness of an industry where such a situation exists. But it is a debatable situation and of concern, perhaps, largely to businessmen who insist on quantity, who measure success by numbers: number of subscribers, number of readers, number of advertisers, numbers of pages of it sold, and numbers of dollars brought in. They are so fascinated by numbers that they neglect quality and fail to see the danger of the numbers game, as did *The Saturday Evening Post* and several other magazines, before it is too late. Within the bitterly competitive consumer magazine business however, the worry about losses in amounts of advertising sold is justified, if for no other reason than that buyers of general advertising space tend to place their orders with periodicals already swollen with copy. They give little thought to any obligation to support a publication that may be in temporary distress so as to keep competition alive, if not a voice heard. In other words, the successful publication becomes still more successful and its rivals are killed off by advertisers who flock to the leader.

The worshippers of numbers stand in strong contrast to one of the great American editors, Frederick Lewis Allen, who was at the helm of *Harper's*, for many years a leading serious magazine. Writing in his magazine in 1950, Allen said: "Our circulation . . . is a practically microscopic figure when set alongside the circulations of the monster slicks and digests. But it includes so many people who write, speak, teach, edit, manage, and govern that we may perhaps be permitted to remind you that the ignition system is a very small part of an automobile."

The American periodical press is an industry which is fundamentally sound so long as printed communication is vital and has not been replaced by electronic means of communication. It also is a highly segmented and diversified industry. Few generalizations therefore can be made about its impact as a whole. Easier to point out are the effects of the various types of periodicals. The main obstacle to a clear, broad answer is that tools or techniques for the measurement of effect or influence still are rudimentary. Some progress has been made in noting the effect of single elements that can be isolated: certain advertisements or specific articles, for example, but little reliably beyond that. Some studies have been made which indicate effects within the segments, however, and these can be put on the record for what they may be worth.

The impact of the American periodical press also has been technological and social. The large, mass-circulation magazines have influenced the smaller magazines, which in many instances seek to imitate their appearance and to emulate the high quality of their printing, layout, and makeup. They also have influenced magazines around the world. Europe, for example, is given to publishing magazines resembling *Life* and *Look,* and almost no heavily industrialized country is without its imitator of *Time* (*The Link* in India, *Elseviers* in the Netherlands, *Tiempo* in Mexico, *Der Spiegel* in Germany, and *L'Express* in France, for example).

The social effect has to do with the discharge or failure to discharge its social responsibilities. These responsibilities the magazine press shares with all communications media, printed or electronic. They include the obligation, in a political democracy such as is the U.S.A., to provide the people with a fair presentation of facts, with honestly held opinions, and with truthful advertising. All but the subsidized periodicals hold—or seek to hold—to these goals within a certain framework; that of the business order, the private initiative, profit-making system.

As business institutions, commercial magazines, consumer and specialized alike, have influenced the progress of the business world by stimulating the desires for products and services on the part of readers through advertising and editorial content. This result has in turn affected the living standards of readers, influencing their decisions about how they dress, what they eat, and how they use their spare time. The enormous consumption of cosmetics by American girls and women is in part due to the years of commodity advertising in magazines for those readers. The sale of motor cars is heavily influenced by the advertising and special editorial content about new models.

What might be considered the official concept of the influence of the general magazines has come from the Magazine Advertising Bureau of the U.S.A. Placed first among general effects is the shaping of public opinion. 'The national magazine does not have the spot news function of either the newspaper or the radio,' MAB said. 'But being edited with deliberation, it is read with equal deliberation, and therefore has the unique ability to form a *mature* public opinion, nationally.' It also is a reflector of American life or what the owners think is American life. Said the MAB: 'Life is not the daily headlines of the newspaper, nor is it the artificial dramatics thrown out daily, hourly by radio. The solid values of the lives of millions of American families are reported by the national magazine, unsensationally but vividly and accurately, in articles and fiction, in pictures and illustrations.' The contrast with television, even sharper, might have been added.

James Playsted Wood, a magazine official and writer of several books on periodicals, reminds us that the magazine is read more persistently than any other medium, is less perishable, and is read attentively. It provokes results, receives reactions. Much magazine material later goes into books and motion pictures; reprints are made.

'The character of a given magazine limits its audience,' he says, 'thus, to some extent, the spread of its influence, its educational force, its persuasion to belief, and possibility to individual or social action.'

Wood properly qualifies his generalization by using the word *given*. The effects of the comic magazines are unlike those of the literary, and within the specialized magazine world the effects of one technical journal only in a superficial way resemble those of another.

Led by the *Reader's Digest*, condensed material and pocket-size magazines have stimulated popularized reading by the middle-class public, have spread certain social positions and attitudes, and have increased demand for short, quickly-read publications. The digest made the portable magazine among the most popular of those published, one of them being of world influence.

With magazines of seven and eight million circulation setting the pace, the women's group, with which may be associated the service and shelter books (*Woman's Day* representing service, with its many recipes, and *Better Homes*, the shelter group), has been principally responsible for influence wielded by advertising departments on homes and families of the middle class. They have to some extent standardized housekeeping tools, widened the variety of cookery, introduced or popularized certain habits, such as more frequent bathing and shaving, use of deodorants, and hair coloring, and called attention to books, motion pictures, and art works, considerably broadening their effect. Not a minor result has been the introduction of fictional stereotypes; most heroes and heroines of fiction in women's magazines seldom are realistic, although there is a trend away from that in a few. Consumer magazines try to exert influence through their advertising and editorial policies. *Esquire* in 1968, after the assassinations of Dr. Martin Luther King Jr. and Senator Robert F. Kennedy, adopted a policy of accepting no gun advertising of any kind. This decision came after a campaign against gun advertising launched by *Advertising Age,* a business weekly. *McCall's,* with a circulation of more than eight million, on the day of Senator Kennedy's assassination, stopped its presses and inserted a two-page editorial calling on its women readers to support stronger gun-control legislation, help stop excessive violence on broadcasting programs and in films, boycott certain toys, and follow other policies.

The confession magazine, more and more an imitator of the slick ones in content, has had a changing influence. In its early days it played a psychological role: it offered spiritual release for uneducated or immature readers (whether adults or adolescents) enabling them to experience adventures of the more daring and unorthodox without personal risks. Now, except for a surviving group offering stories of sex adventures and crime detection, it is achieving on its own economic level a standardization in reader habits and practices similar to the women's slicks.

The circulation and advertising leaders among men's magazines have turned away to some extent from tales of wartime bravery to tales of bedroom exploits, holding as admirable man's sexual domination of women and gratification of his dreams of wealth, power, and comfort. They encourage their readers to a hedonistic philosophy of life and to be primarily patrons of entertainment.

The religious magazines, less given than they once were to regularizing moral concepts, now are influencing their readers to apply their religious principles to social concerns as well as to personal conduct. Some have helped bring social movements into existence, such as the civil rights groups, and mustered support for social legislation in various areas of human activity: conscientious objection to war, better housing, and employment opportunities for minorities, for example.

American literary magazines have started movements, erected critical standards, and founded schools of criticism, introduced new writers, maintained the following of older ones, and provided an outlet for work not marketable to the public through general or consumer periodicals.

Magazines for juveniles have had definite effects, since their readers are in formative years. A youngster's heroes once were provided almost solely by books and magazines; today radio, television, cinema, and recordings also have strong influence, perhaps stronger. The religious juvenile publications have built concepts of right and wrong in human conduct and of individual responsibility at home and in the church or temple. They have aroused loyalties. The secular juveniles in more recent times have been simplified versions of magazines for grown-ups. Their effect has been at once to create little adults and to encourage youthful independence and also standardization of mores among adolescents. The comics have appealed to childish imaginations so effectively, and with so much questionable content, that they have been treated as social phenomena to be studied as seriously as are educational practices.

The effects of specialized magazines are vertical rather than horizontal. A clothing publication or a food magazine affects the profession, industry, business, or other group it serves by conveying news created by the group, evaluating trends within, providing an outlet for ideas, and stimulating business through advertising. Business periodicals have taken dramatic stands to correct what they consider evils. The company magazine (house organ, as often dubbed) has established itself as a bulwark or dam against ideas that its publishers deem undesirable or has helped to stimulate business.

These influences and effects have not escaped criticism. The adverse critics say that the magazines, particularly the consumer type, are too much inclined to give the public what it wants, they deprive the public of the fullest knowledge of facts and ideas; through advertising content they stimulate desires for possessions that cannot be gratified by the average reader's income. Nor is that all the criticism. The critics go on to say that the periodicals present only conventional or ultra-conservative viewpoints, that they evade their duty to provide leadership in solving social problems, that they are time-wasting, distracting the reader from more valuable uses of his leisure, and that they knuckle in to advertisers.

The favorable critics, on the other hand, counter that magazines have helped produce the high standard of living in the U.S.A. through their advertising content, have helped to stimulate mass consumption of goods and, thereby, mass production; have therefore contributed toward the lowering of the cost of living; that they have merchandised, as one proponent has put it, new ideas; and that they have played a part of importance in every national crisis, whether it be flood, war, depression or recovery from such disasters.

As with so many arguments, this collection is not a clear case for either pro or con. To begin with, most critics of either side are talking exclusively about the consumer magazine, and, as usual, overlooking all the rest, which as we know are in the U.S.A. fifty times as numerous, and in some instances just as influential. Accepting the consumer scope, some parts of each set of criticisms may be accepted as true.

A business society such as that of the U.S.A. prevents the majority of the magazines, consumer or specialized, from fulfilling the role of the institution wholly devoted to the welfare of society as are, for example, the church, school, and the professions of medicine and nursing. It is left for the periodical press to play a part short of full devotion to the commonweal.

Aids   *The American Periodical Press and Its Impact*

1. According to Roland Wolseley, what were the causes of the demise of such family magazines as *The Saturday Evening Post* and *Life*?

2. Wolseley asserts that the periodical press is sound "so long as printed communication is vital and has not been replaced by electronic means of communication." What print media have been replaced by electronic media? What print media have changed their form and function in order to survive?

3. According to Wolseley, what are the social responsibilities and effects of magazines?

4. Do you agree with the following statement by the Magazine Advertising Bureau: "Life is not the daily headlines of the newspaper, nor is it the artificial dramatics thrown out daily, hourly by radio. The solid values of the lives of millions of American families are reported by the national magazine, unsensationally but vividly and accurately, in articles and fiction, in pictures and illustrations."

5. In his survey of magazines, Wolseley asserts that the *Reader's Digest*, with a monthly circulation of at least 27 million, is the only remaining true American consumer magazine. The *Digest's* contribution to American life is that it has stimulated popularized reading by the middle class public and has spread certain social positions

and attitudes. To gain an appreciation of these two contributions, compare a condensed article from an issue of the *Reader's Digest* with the original source. What changes in content, style, and language have been made? How do you account for the differences? If the changes also include significant deletions and omissions, can this practice be called censorship?

6. Wolseley also notes the contributions to American life made by the various women's magazines. One effect has been to introduce fictional stereotypes: "Most heroes and heroines of fiction in women's magazines seldom are realistic, although there is a trend away from that in a few." Examine one issue of a women's magazine, such as *Woman's Day*, *McCalls*, and *Ladies' Home Journal*, for its presentation of the American woman. What images of women are offered by the articles, fictional stories, regular features, cartoons, and advertisements? By looking closely at the types of situations depicted in the advertisements (social setting, quality and value of the products, and the sophistication of the appeals), you should be able to generalize about the ad person's image of the typical reader. The same approach should be used for the articles. If there are fictional stories, who are the heroines, the villains? What values do they represent? Do the articles sell certain values, goals, or life styles? Are the stories didactic or moralistic? Do you agree with the accuracy of the images of humanity being sold by the magazine?

7. Locate "The Best Markets for Fiction and Non-Fiction" in *The Writer's Yearbook*, which gives advice to aspiring magazine-story writers. Choose one of the magazines listed, and compose a paper or report in which you compare the contents, format, and style of a recent issue of the magazine with the editor's requirements as stated in *The Writer's Yearbook*.

8. Examine closely one of the other types of magazines cited by Wolseley: confession, men's, religious, literary, and juvenile.

9. Wolseley uses the term "consumer magazine." Is this a common term? Does the author adequately define it? Is an understanding of this term important to your understanding of the essay?

10. Like Stephen Holder, in "The Family Magazine and the American People," Wolseley is writing an analytical essay. How does he divide his material? What relationships does he perceive among the component parts? What is the larger rhetorical purpose of the essay?

11. How would you assess Wolseley's objectivity in the essay? Does he favor a particular point of view? Does he adequately present opposing points of view?

The
Playboy
and
Miss America
HARVEY COX

Let us look at the spurious sexual models conjured up for our anxious society by the sorcerers of the mass media and the advertising guild. Like all pagan deities, these come in pairs—the god and his consort. For our purposes they are best symbolized by The Playboy and Miss America, the Adonis and Aphrodite[1] of a leisure-consumer society which still seems unready to venture into full postreligious maturity and freedom. The Playboy and Miss America represent The Boy and The Girl. They incorporate a vision of life. They function as religious phenomena and should be exorcised and exposed.

Let us begin with Miss America. In the first century B.C., Lucretius wrote this description of the pageant of Cybele.[2]

> Adorned with emblem and crown ... she is carried in awe-inspiring state. Tight-stretched tambourines and hollow cymbals thunder all round to the stroke of open hands, hollow pipes stir with Phryg-

ian strain. . . . She rides in procession through great cities and mutely enriches mortals with a blessing not expressed in words. They straw all her path with brass and silver, presenting her with bounteous aims, and scatter over her a snow-shower of roses.

Now compare this with the annual twentieth-century Miss America pageant in Atlantic City, New Jersey. Spotlights probe the dimness like votive tapers, banks of flowers exude their varied aromas, the orchestra blends feminine strings and regal trumpets. There is a hushed moment of tortured suspense, a drumroll, then the climax—a young woman with carefully prescribed anatomical proportions and exemplary "personality" parades serenely with scepter and crown to her throne. At TV sets across the nation throats tighten and eyes moisten. "There she goes, Miss America—" sings the crooner. "There she goes, your ideal." A new queen in Amer-

[1]In Greek mythology, Adonis is the beautiful youth beloved by Aphrodite. (eds.)
[2]The Phrygian goddess of nature. (eds.)

ica's emerging cult of The Girl has been crowned.

This young woman—though she is no doubt totally ignorant of the fact—symbolizes something beyond herself. She symbolizes The Girl, the primal image, the one behind the many. Just as the Virgin appears in many guises—as our Lady of Lourdes or of Fatima or of Guadalupe—but is always recognizably the Virgin, so with The Girl.

The Girl is also the omnipresent icon of consumer society.[3] Selling beer, she is folksy and jolly. Selling gems, she is chic and distant. But behind her various theophanies she remains recognizably The Girl. In Miss America's glowingly healthy smile, her openly sexual but officially virginal figure, and in the name-brand gadgets around her, she personifies the stunted aspirations and ambivalent fears of her culture. "There she goes, your ideal."

Miss America stands in a long line of queens going back to Isis, Ceres, and Aphrodite.[4] Everything from the elaborate sexual taboos surrounding her person to the symbolic gifts at her coronation hints at her ancient ancestry. But the real proof comes when we find that the function served by The Girl in our culture is just as much a "religious" one as that served by Cybele in hers. The functions are identical —to provide a secure personal "identity" for initiates and to sanctify a particular value structure.

Let us look first at the way in which The Girl confers a kind of identity on her initiates. Simone de Beauvoir says in *The Second Sex* that "no one is *born* a woman." One is merely born a female, and "*becomes* a woman" according to the models and meanings provided by the civilization. During the classical Christian centuries, it might be argued, the Virgin Mary served in part as this model. With the Reformation and especially with the Puritans, the place of Mary within the symbol system of the Protestant countries was reduced or eliminated. There are those who claim that this excision constituted an excess of zeal that greatly impoverished Western culture, an impoverishment from which it has never recovered. Some would even claim that the alleged failure of American novelists to produce a single great heroine (we have no Phaedra, no Anna Karenina)[5] stems from this self-imposed lack of a central feminine ideal.

Without entering into this fascinating discussion, we can certainly be sure that, even within modern American Roman Catholicism, the Virgin Mary provides an identity image for few American girls. Where then do they look for the "model" Simone de Beauvoir convincingly contends they need? For most, the prototype of femininity seen in their mothers, their friends, and in the multitudinous images to which they are exposed on the mass media is what we have called The Girl.

To describe the mechanics of this complex psychological process by which the fledgling American girl participates in the life of The Girl and thus attains a

---

[3]An icon is an image created as a focal point of religious veneration. (eds.)

[4]Isis was the Egyptian goddess of fertility; Ceres was the Roman goddess of agriculture; Aphrodite was the Greek goddess of love and beauty. (eds.)

[5]In Greek mythology, Phaedra is the second wife of Theseus; when her stepson, Hippolytus, rejected her love, she accused him of raping her and hanged herself. Anna Karenina is the Russian heroine in the nineteenth-century novel by Leo Tolstoy. (eds.)

woman's identity would require a thorough description of American adolescence. There is little doubt, however, that such an analysis would reveal certain striking parallels to the "savage" practices by which initiates in the mystery cults shared in the magical life of their god.

For those inured to the process, the tortuous nightly fetish by which the young American female pulls her hair into tight bunches secured by metal clips may bear little resemblance to the incisions made on their arms by certain African tribesmen to make them resemble their totem, the tiger. But to an anthropologist comparing two ways of attempting to resemble the holy one, the only difference might appear to be that with the Africans the torture is over after initiation, while with the American it has to be repeated every night, a luxury only a culture with abundant leisure can afford.

In turning now to an examination of the second function of The Girl—supporting and portraying a value system—a comparison with the role of the Virgin in the twelfth and thirteenth centuries may be helpful. Just as the Virgin exhibited and sustained the ideals of the age that fashioned Chartres Cathedral, as Henry Adams saw, so The Girl symbolizes the values and aspirations of a consumer society. (She is crowned not in the political capital, remember, but in Atlantic City or Miami Beach, centers associated with leisure and consumption.) And she is not entirely incapable of exploitation. If men sometimes sought to buy with gold the Virgin's blessings on their questionable causes, so The Girl now dispenses her charismatic

favor on watches, refrigerators, and razor blades—for a price. Though The Girl has built no cathedrals, without her the colossal edifice of mass persuasion would crumble. Her sharply stylized face and figure beckon us from every magazine and TV channel, luring us toward the beatific vision of a consumer's paradise.

Besides sanctifying a set of phony values, The Girl compounds her noxiousness by maiming her victims in a Procrustean bed of uniformity.[6] This is the empty "identity" she panders. Take the Miss America pageant, for example. Are these virtually indistinguishable specimens of white, middle-class postadolescence really the best we can do? Do they not mirror the ethos of a mass-production society, in which genuine individualism somehow mars the clean, precision-tooled effect? Like their sisters, the finely calibrated Rockettes, these meticulously measured and pretested "beauties" lined up on the boardwalk bear an ominous similarity to the faceless retinues of goose-steppers and the interchangeable mass exercisers of explicitly totalitarian societies. In short, *who* says this is beauty?

The caricature becomes complete in the Miss Universe contest, when Miss Rhodesia is a blonde, Miss South Africa is white, and Oriental girls with a totally different tradition of feminine beauty are forced to display their thighs and appear in spike heels and Catalina swim suits. Miss Universe is as universal as an American adman's stereotype of what beauty should be.

The truth is that The Girl can*not* bestow the identity she promises. She forces

---

[6]An allusion to Procrustes, the cruel highwayman in Greek myth, who sawed off the legs of his victims to make them fit on a short bed. (eds.)

her initiates to torture themselves with starvation diets and beauty-parlor ordeals, but still cannot deliver the satisfactions she holds out. She is young, but what happens when her followers, despite added hours in the boudoir, can no longer appear young? She is happy and smiling and loved. What happens when, despite all the potions and incantations, her disciples still feel the human pangs of rejection and loneliness? Or what about all the girls whose statistics, or "personality" (or color) do not match the authoritative "ideal"?

The Playboy, illustrated by the monthly magazine of that name, does for the boys what Miss America does for the girls. Despite accusations to the contrary, the immense popularity of this magazine is not solely attributable to pinup girls. For sheer nudity its pictorial art cannot compete with such would-be competitors as *Dude* and *Escapade*. *Playboy* appeals to a highly mobile, increasingly affluent group of young readers, mostly between eighteen and thirty, who want much more from their drugstore reading than bosoms and thighs. They need a total image of what it means to be a man. And Mr. Hefner's *Playboy* has no hesitation in telling them.

Why should such a need arise? David Riesman has argued that the responsibility for character formation in our society has shifted from the family to the peer group and to the mass-media peer-group surrogates. Things are changing so rapidly that one who is equipped by his family with inflexible, highly internalized values becomes unable to deal with the accelerated pace of change and with the varying contexts in which he is called upon to function. This is especially true in the area of consumer values toward which the "other-directed person" is increasingly oriented.

Within the confusing plethora of mass media signals and peer-group values, *Playboy* fills a special need. For the insecure young man with newly acquired free time and money who still feels uncertain about his consumer skills, *Playboy* supplies a comprehensive and authoritative guide-book to this forbidding new world to which he now has access. It tells him not only who to be; it tells him *how* to be, and even provides consolation outlets for those who secretly feel that they have not quite made it.

In supplying for the other-directed consumer of leisure both the normative identity image and the means of achieving it, *Playboy* relies on a careful integration of copy and advertising material. The comic book that appeals to a younger generation with an analogous problem skillfully intersperses illustrations of incredibly muscled men and excessively mammalian women with advertisements for body-building gimmicks and foam-rubber brassière supplements. Thus the thin-chested comic-book readers of both sexes are thoughtfully supplied with both the ends and the means for attaining a spurious brand of maturity. *Playboy* merely continues the comic-book tactic for the next age group. Since within every identity crisis, whether in teens or twenties, there is usually a sexual identity problem, *Playboy* speaks to those who desperately want to know what it means to be a man, and more specifically a *male*, in today's world.

Both the image of man and the means for its attainment exhibit a remarkable consistency in *Playboy*. The skilled consumer is cool and unruffled. He savors sports cars, liquor, high fidelity, and book-club selections with a casual, unhurried aplomb. Though he must certainly *have* and *use* the latest consumption item, he must not permit himself to get too attached to it. The style will change and he must always be ready to adjust. His persistent anxiety that he may mix a drink incorrectly, enjoy a jazz group that is passé, or wear last year's necktie style is comforted by an authoritative tone in *Playboy* beside which papal encyclicals sound irresolute.

"Don't hesitate," he is told, "this assertive, self-assured weskit is what every man of taste wants for the fall season." Lingering doubts about his masculinity are extirpated by the firm assurance that "real men demand this ruggedly masculine smoke" (cigar ad). Though "the ladies will swoon for you, no matter what they promise, don't give them a puff. This cigar is for men only." A fur-lined canvas field jacket is described as "the most masculine thing since the cave man." What to be and how to be it are both made unambiguously clear.

Since being male necessitates some kind of relationship to females, *Playboy* fearlessly confronts this problem too, and solves it by the consistent application of the same formula. Sex becomes one of the items of leisure activity that the knowledgeable consumer of leisure handles with his characteristic skill and detachment. The girl becomes a desirable—indeed an indispensable—"Playboy accessory."

In a question-answer column entitled "The Playboy Adviser," queries about smoking equipment (how to break in a meerschaum pipe), cocktail preparation (how to mix a Yellow Fever), and whether or not to wear suspenders with a vest alternate with questions about what to do with girls who complicate the cardinal principle of casualness either by suggesting marriage or by some other impulsive gesture toward a permanent relationship. The infallible answer from the oracle never varies: sex must be contained, at all costs, within the entertainment-recreation area. Don't let her get "serious."

After all, the most famous feature of the magazine is its monthly foldout photo of a *playmate*. She is the symbol par excellence of recreational sex. When playtime is over, the playmate's function ceases, so she must be made to understand the rules of the game. As the crew-cut young man in a *Playboy* cartoon says to the rumpled and disarrayed girl he is passionately embracing, "Why speak of love at a time like this?"

The magazine's fiction purveys the same kind of severely departmentalized sex. Although the editors have recently improved the *Playboy* contents with contributions by Hemingway, Bemelmans, and even a Chekhov translation,[7] many of the stories still rely on a repetitious and predictable formula. A successful young man, either single or somewhat less than ideally married—a figure with whom readers have no difficulty identifying—encounters a gorgeous and seductive woman who makes no demands on him except sex. She is the prose duplication of the cool-eyed but hot-blooded playmate of the foldout.

Drawing heavily on the fantasy life of all young Americans, the writers utilize for their stereotyped heroines the hero's

---

[7] Ernest Hemingway (1899–1961), American novelist and short-story writer, who won the Nobel Prize in Literature in 1954; Ludwig Bemelmans (1898–1962), Austrian-American writer of whimsical and witty books; Anton Chekhov (1860–1904), Russian short-story writer and dramatist. (eds.)

schoolteacher, his secretary, an old girl friend, or the girl who brings her car into the garage where he works. The happy issue is always a casual but satisfying sexual experience with no entangling alliances whatever. Unlike the women he knows in real life, the *Playboy* reader's fictional girl friends know their place and ask for nothing more. They present no danger of permanent involvement. Like any good accessory, they are detachable and disposable.

Many of the advertisements reinforce the sex-accessory identification in another way—by attributing female characteristics to the items they sell. Thus a full-page ad for the MG assures us that this car is not only "the smoothest pleasure machine" on the road and that having one is a "love affair," but most important, "you drive it —it doesn't drive you." The ad ends with the equivocal question "Is it a date?"

Playboy insists that its message is one of liberation. Its gospel frees us from captivity to the puritanical "hatpin brigade." It solemnly crusades for "frankness" and publishes scores of letters congratulating it for its unblushing "candor." Yet the whole phenomenon of which *Playboy* is only a part vividly illustrates the awful fact of a new kind of tyranny.

Those liberated by technology and increased prosperity to new worlds of leisure now become the anxious slaves of dictatorial taste makers. Obsequiously waiting for the latest signal on what is cool and what is awkward, they are paralyzed by the fear that they may hear pronounced on them that dread sentence occasionally intoned by "The Playboy Adviser": "You goofed!" Leisure is thus swallowed up in apprehensive competitiveness, its liberating potential trans-

formed into a self-destructive compulsion to consume only what is *à la mode*. *Playboy* mediates the Word of the most high into one section of the consumer world, but it is a word of bondage, not of freedom.

Nor will *Playboy*'s synthetic doctrine of man stand the test of scrutiny. Psychoanalysts constantly remind us how deepseated sexuality is in the human being. But if they didn't remind us, we would soon discover it ourselves anyway. Much as the human male might like to terminate his relationship with a woman as he would snap off the stereo, or store her for special purposes like a camel's-hair jacket, it really can't be done. And anyone with a modicum of experience with women knows it can't be done. Perhaps this is the reason *Playboy*'s readership drops off so sharply after the age of thirty.

Playboy really feeds on the existence of a repressed fear of involvement with women, which for various reasons is still present in many otherwise adult Americans. So *Playboy*'s version of sexuality grows increasingly irrelevant as authentic sexual maturity is achieved.

Thus any theological critique of *Playboy* that focuses on its "lewdness" will misfire completely. *Playboy* and its less successful imitators are not "sex magazines" at all. They are basically antisexual. They dilute and dissipate authentic sexuality by reducing it to an accessory, by keeping it at a safe distance.

Freedom for mature sexuality comes to man only when he is freed from the despotic powers which crowd and cower him into fixed patterns of behavior. Both Miss America and The Playboy illustrate such powers. When they determine man's sexual life, they hold him in captivity. They prevent him from achieving maturity.

Aids   *The Playboy and Miss America*

1. According to Harvey Cox, what precisely are the characteristics of The Girl? Are these traits still celebrated in today's print and electronic media?

2. What values does The Girl represent in our society? Do you agree with these values?

3. Why does Harvey Cox use such words as "icon," "theophanies," "sanctify," and "beatific vision" to describe The Girl in American society?

4. Why do you suppose there have been no black, Chicano, or Oriental Miss Americas?

5. What ultimately is Cox's attitude toward The Girl? How does his writing style reinforce his point of view?

6. Read the following excerpt from Evelyn Waugh's *The Loved One:* "With a steady hand Aimeé fulfilled the prescribed rites of an American girl preparing to meet her lover—dabbed herself under the arms with a preparation designed to seal the sweatglands, gargled another to sweeten the breath, and brushed into her hair some odorous drops from a bottle labelled: 'Jungle Venom'—'From the depth of the fever-ridden swamp,' the advertisement had stated, 'where juju drums throb for the human sacrifice, Jeannette's latest exclusive creation Jungle Venom comes to you with the remorseless stealth of the hunting cannibal.' "
   What aspects of American culture are being satirized by Waugh? Would Harvey Cox agree with Waugh's view of The Girl? Using the passage above as a model, create your own parody of The Girl or The Playboy. You might consider incorporating actual quotations from magazine advertisements and articles.

7. According to Cox, what exactly are the psychological appeals of The Girl? How do advertisers and magazine publishers allow the fledgling American girl to participate in the life of The Girl and thus attain a woman's identity? Does the Miss America type actually "personify the stunted aspirations and ambivalent fears of her culture"?

8. The Girl, Cox also points out, is the omnipresent icon of consumer society. We seem to demand, too, that all of them be exactly alike. How does the following statement by Marshall McLuhan help to

explain this phenomenon? "No culture will give popular nourishment and support to images or patterns which are alien to its dominant impulses and aspirations. . . . There will be many variations, but they will tend to be variations on certain recognizable themes. And these themes will be the 'laws' of that society, laws which will mould its song and art and social expression." (From "Love-Goddess Assembly Line," pp. 93–97 in *The Mechanical Bride*)

9.   In what ways is the Playboy the exact male counterpart to The Girl?

10. What, according to Cox, is the *Playboy* image of a man? Keeping in mind that Cox's essay was published in 1966, has the image changed in recent years?

11. What special needs does *Playboy* provide male readers from seventeen to thirty? Is it simply a guidebook to the good life or does it satisfy more complex social and psychological needs?

12. Do you agree with Cox that, despite its nudity and suggestive ads, *Playboy* is basically an antisexual magazine?

13. According to Hugh Rank in "Learning about Public Persuasion" (see Unit II), a writer intensifies his argument by associating or linking his idea with something already loved, desired, or revered by his intended audience. Look closely at Harvey Cox's use of metaphoric language and allusions in his essay. What effect does he achieve when he compares the Playboy and Miss America to Adonis and Aphrodite? What effect does he achieve when he frequently links his subject matter with anthropological terms related to religion, such as icon, taboo, and fetish? What kind of comment is Cox making by using these comparisons?

Guidelines
for Newswriting
About Women[*]

THE STANFORD UNIVERSITY WOMEN'S NEWS SERVICE

1. Prefixes indicating marital status should be avoided. First reference should include a person's title (if any) and given name; later references should include LAST NAME ONLY. For example: Secretary of State Henry Kissinger held a news conference . . . Kissinger stated. Rep. Edith Green (D-Ore.) said today . . . Green stated. Use of Mr. and Mrs. is limited to discussions which include a married couple, where the last-name-only rule might cause confusion. Miss and Ms. are not to be used at all. First names alone are also not appropriate for adults.

2. Females over the age of 18 are "women." They are not "girls," "gals," "ladies," "chicks," "broads," "blondes," "lovelies," "honeys," or any similar term. Words like "homemaker" and "housewife" are also not synonyms for "woman"; check carefully for accuracy before they are used. "Co-ed" does not mean "woman" any more than "ed" means "man"; persons who attend school are "students."

3. Gratuitous physical description, uncommon almost to the point of absence in news stories about men, should also be eliminated from such stories about women. If you would not say, "Slim, attractive Sen. Howard Baker announced today . . ." do not say, "Slim, attractive Gloria Steinem announced today . . ." This rule does not apply with equal force to feature writing, especially profiles, in which physical description is often an essential aspect. However, care should be taken to avoid stereotypical descriptions in favor of describing an individual's unique characteristics or mannerisms.

4. Similar considerations apply to the mention of an individual's spouse and family. In a news story about a man, his wife and family are typically mentioned only in passing and only when relevant; the same

*These guidelines were developed by Wendy Quinones, Amy Sabrin, Iris Yang, and Terri McDonald, all members of the Stanford University Women's News Service. Reprinted by permission.

practice should apply to news stories about women. If you would not say, "The gray-haired grandfather of 3 won the Nobel Prize," do not say, "The gray-haired grandmother of 3 won the Nobel Prize." Again, the practice is slightly different for feature stories and profiles, but the test of relevance should always be applied.

5.   Most achievements do not need sexual identification; those which do should be so identified for both men and women. If you would not say, "Dan Rather is a male reporter," do not say "Helen Thomas is a female reporter." Instead of "Arthur Ashe is one of the best American tennis players and Billie Jean King is one of the best American women tennis players," say "Arthur Ashe and Billie Jean King are two of the best American tennis players," OR "Arthur Ashe is one of the best American male tennis players and Billie Jean King is one of the best American female tennis players."

6.   Avoid sins of omission as well as those of commission. If, for example, an expert is sought in a given field, or if an example is needed to make a point, women should be used in these cases as a matter of course —not simply as "oddities" or representatives of "a woman's viewpoint."

7.   "Man," used alone and in words like "chairman," is a sexually exclusive term and should be avoided when at all possible. "Man-on-the-street," for instance, can easily be changed to "person-on-the-street," or "ordinary person"; "chairman" to "chairperson." The U.S. Bureau of the Census has begun officially changing its occupation titles to eliminate this problem: "salesmen" are now "sales workers" or "sales agents," "newsboys" are "newspaper carriers and vendors," and "airlines stewardesses" are now "flight attendants."

8.   Women's professional qualifications or working experience should always be acknowledged, to forestall the common (and incorrect) expectation that most women are full-time housewives.

9.   "Feminist" is the correct term to describe a woman committed to equal rights for women. "Women's libber" is an unacceptable pejorative.

10.   Headlines seem to be particularly susceptible to the use of stereotypical, simplistic language. As in other areas, play on these stereotypes is to be avoided.

11.   When you have completed a story about a woman, go through it and ask yourself whether you would have written about a man in the

same style. If not, something may be wrong with the tone or even the conception of your article. Think it through again.

Aids   *Guidelines for Newswriting About Women*

1. Although the feminist movement has been in evidence for about the last ten years, the Stanford Guidelines clearly suggest that Man-glish is still the language disseminated by media today. As one feminist has put it, the English language continues to force women to view themselves through a male mirror that distorts and insults them. What specific recommendations are contained in the Stanford Guidelines? Locate examples of sexist uses of language in current media, beginning with your local newspaper.

2. Divide the guidelines into two categories: (1) those referring to obvious male chauvinist attitudes, such as the derogatory synonyms for women, and (2) those that are a result of linguistic tradition, such as masculine office titles (chairman). Do you agree with Stefan Kanfer, who in "Sispeak: A Msguided Attempt to Change Herstory" (*Time*, August 13, 1973), argues that changing the words without changing the values they represent is a crime against reason, meaning, and civilization itself: "Changing chairman to chairperson is mock doctrine and flaccid democracy, altering neither the audience nor, in fact, the office holder. . . . Chairman is a role, not a pejorative. Congressman is an office, not a chauvinist plot. Mankind is a term for all humanity, not some 49% of it"? [For some other treatments of this controversy, see Israel Shenker, "Is It Possible for a Woman to Manhandle the King's English?" (*The New York Times*, August 29, 1973); Ann Bayer, "A Women's Lib Exposé of Male Villainy" (*Life* Magazine, August 7, 1970.)]

Pause, Now, and Consider Some Tentative Conclusions About the Meaning of This Mass Perversion Called Porno-violence: What It Is and Where It Comes From and Who Put the Hair on the Wall

TOM WOLFE

Keeps His Mom-in-law in Chains, meet *Kills Son and Feeds Corpse to Pigs*. Pleased to meet you. *Teenager Twists Off Corpse's Head . . . To Get Gold Teeth*, meet *Strangles Girl Friend, then Chops Her to Pieces*. Likewise, I'm sure. *Nurse's Aide Sees Fingers Chopped Off in Meat Grinder*, meet. . . .

In ten years of journalism I have covered more conventions than I care to remember. Podiatrists, theosophists, Professional Budget Finance dentists, oyster farmers, mathematicians, truckers, dry cleaners, stamp collectors, Esperantists, nudists and newspaper editors—I have seen them all, together, in vast assemblies, sloughing through the wall-to-wall of a thousand hotel lobbies (the nudists excepted) in their shimmering grey-metal suits and Nicey Short Collar white shirts with white Plasti-Coat name cards on their chests, and I have sat through their speeches and seminars (the nudists included) and attentively endured ear baths such as you wouldn't believe. And yet some of the truly instructive conventions of our times I seem to have missed altogether. One, for example, I only heard about from one of the many anonymous men who have labored in . . . a curious field. This was a convention of the stringers for *The National Enquirer*.

The Enquirer is a weekly newspaper that is probably known by sight to millions more than know it by name. In fact, no one who ever came face-to-face with *The Enquirer* on a newsstand in its wildest days is likely to have forgotten the sight: a tabloid with great inky shocks of type all over the front page saying something on the order of *Gouges Out Wife's Eyes to Make*

Her Ugly, Dad Hurls Hot Grease in Daughter's Face, Wife Commits Suicide After 2 Years of Poisoning Fails to Kill Husband. . . .

The stories themselves were supplied largely by stringers, i.e., correspondents, from all over the country, the world, for that matter, mostly copy editors and reporters on local newspapers. Every so often they would come upon a story, usually via the police beat, that was so grotesque the local sheet would discard it or run it in a highly glossed form rather than offend or perplex its readers. The stringers would preserve them for *The Enquirer*, which always rewarded them well and respectfully.

In fact, one year *The Enquirer* convened and feted them at a hotel in Manhattan. It was a success in every way. The only awkward moment was at the outset when the stringers all pulled in. None of them knew each other. Their hosts got around the problem by introducing them by the stories they had supplied. The introductions, I am told, went like this:

"Harry, I want you to meet Frank here. Frank did that story, you remember that story, *Midget Murderer Throws Girl Off Cliff After She Refuses To Dance With Him.*"

"Pleased to meet you. That was some story."

"And Harry did the one about *I Spent Three Days Trapped at Bottom of Forty-foot-deep Mine Shaft and Was Saved by a Swarm of Flies.*"

"Likewise, I'm sure."

And *Midget Murderer Throws Girl Off Cliff* shakes hands with *I Spent Three Days Trapped at Bottom of Forty-foot-deep Mine Shaft*, and *Buries Her Baby Alive* shakes hands with *Boy, Twelve, Strangles Two-year-old Girl*, and *Kills Son and Feeds Corpse to Pigs* shakes hands with *He Strangles Old Woman and Smears Corpse with Syrup, Ketchup and Oatmeal* . . . and. . . .

. . . There was a great deal of esprit about the whole thing. These men were, in fact, the avant-garde of a new genre that since then has become institutionalized throughout the nation without anyone knowing its proper name. I speak of the new pornography, the pornography of violence.

Pornography comes from the Greek word *porne*, meaning harlot, and pornography is literally the depiction of the acts of harlots. In the new pornography, the theme is not sex. The new pornography depicts practitioners acting out another, murkier drive: people staving teeth in, ripping guts open, blowing brains out and getting even with all those bastards. . . .

The success of *The Enquirer* prompted many imitators to enter the field, *Midnight, The Star Chronicle, The National Insider, Inside News, The National Close-up, The National Tattler, The National Examiner*. A truly competitive free press evolved, and soon a reader could go to the newspaper of his choice for *Kill the Retarded! (Won't You Join My Movement?)* and *Unfaithful Wife? Burn Her Bed!, Harem Master's Mistress Chops Him with Machete, Babe Bites Off Boy's Tongue*, and *Cuts Buddy's Face to Pieces for Stealing His Business and Fiancée*.

And yet the last time I surveyed the Violence press, I noticed a curious thing. These pioneering journals seem to have pulled back. They seem to be regressing to what is by now the Redi-Mix staple of literate Americans, plain old lust-o-lech sex. *Ecstasy and Me (By Hedy Lamarr)*, says *The National Enquirer*. *I Run A Sex*

Art Gallery, says *The National Insider.* What has happened, I think, is something that has happened to avant-gardes in many fields, from William Morris and the Craftsmen to the Bauhaus group. Namely, their discoveries have been preempted by the Establishment and so thoroughly dissolved into the mainstream they no longer look original.

Robert Harrison, the former publisher of *Confidential,* and later publisher of the aforementioned *Inside News,* was perhaps the first person to see it coming. I was interviewing Harrison early in January of 1964 for a story in *Esquire* about six weeks after the assassination of President Kennedy, and we were in a cab in the West Fifties in Manhattan, at a stoplight, by a newsstand, and Harrison suddenly pointed at the newsstand and said, "Look at that. They're doing the same thing *The Enquirer* does."

There on the stand was a row of slick-paper, magazine-size publications, known in the trade as one-shots, with titles like *Four Days That Shook the World, Death of a President, An American Tragedy* or just *John Fitzgerald Kennedy (1921–1963).* "You want to know why people buy those things?" said Harrison. "People buy those things to see a man get his head blown off."

And, of course, he was right. Only now the publishers were in many cases the pillars of the American press. Invariably, these "special coverages" of the assassination bore introductions piously commemorating the fallen President, exhorting the American people to strength and unity in a time of crisis, urging greater vigilance and safeguards for the new President, and even raising the nice metaphysical question of collective guilt in "an age of violence."

In the three and a half years since then, of course, there has been an incessant replay, with every recoverable clinical detail, of those less than five seconds in which a man got his head blown off. And throughout this deluge of words, pictures and film frames, I have been intrigued with one thing. The point of view, the vantage point, is almost never that of the victim, riding in the Presidential Lincoln Continental. What you get is . . . the view from Oswald's rifle. You can step right up here and look point-blank right through the very hairline cross in Lee Harvey Oswald's Optics Ordnance four-power Japanese telescopic sight and watch, frame by frame by frame by frame, as that man there's head comes apart. Just a little History there before your very eyes.

The television networks have schooled us in the view from Oswald's rifle and made it seem a normal pastime. The TV viewpoint is nearly always that of the man who is going to strike. The last time I watched *Gunsmoke,* which was not known as a very violent Western in TV terms, the action went like this: The Wellington agents and the stagecoach driver pull guns on the badlands gang leader's daughter and Kitty, the heart-of-gold saloonkeeper, and kidnap them. Then the badlands gang shoots two Wellington agents. Then they desist because they might not be able to get a hotel room in the next town if the word got around. Then one badlands gang gunslinger attempts to rape Kitty while the gang leader's younger daughter looks on. Then Kitty resists, so he slugs her one in the jaw. Then the gang leader slugs him. Then the gang leader slugs Kitty. Then Kitty throws hot stew in a gang member's face and hits him over the back of the head with a revolver. Then he knocks her down with a rock. Then the gang sticks up a bank. Here comes the sheriff, Matt Dillon. He shoots a gang member and breaks it up. Then the gang leader shoots the guy who was guarding his daughter and the woman. Then the sheriff shoots the gang leader. The final exploding bullets signal The End.

It is not the accumulated slayings and bone-crushings that make this porno-violence, however. What makes it porno-violence is that in almost every case the camera angle, therefore the viewer, is with the gun, the fist, the rock. The pornography of violence has no point of view in the old sense that novels do. You do not live the action through the hero's eyes. You live with the aggressor, whoever he may be. One moment you are the hero. The next, you are the villain. No matter whose side you may be on consciously, you are in fact with the muscle, and it is you who disintegrate all comers, villains, lawmen, women, anybody. On the rare occasions in which the gun is emptied into the camera —i.e., into your face—the effect is so startling that the pornography of violence all but loses its fantasy charm. There are not nearly so many masochists as sadists among those little devils whispering into your ears.

In fact, sex—"sadomasochism"—is only a part of the pornography of violence. Violence is much more wrapped up, simply, with status. Violence is the simple, ultimate solution for problems of status competition, just as gambling is the simple, ultimate solution for economic competition. The old pornography was the fantasy of easy sexual delights in a world where sex was kept unavailable. The new pornography is the fantasy of easy triumph in a world where status competition has become so complicated and frustrating.

Already the old pornography is losing its kick because of overexposure. In the late Thirties, Nathanael West published his last and best-regarded novel, *The Day of the Locust*, and it was a terrible flop commercially, and his publisher said if he ever published another book about Hollywood it would "have to be *My Thirty-nine Ways of Making Love by Hedy Lamarr*." *Ecstasy and Me* is not quite that . . . but maybe it is. I stopped counting. I know her account begins: "The men in my life have ranged from a classic case history of impotence, to a whip-brandishing sadist who enjoyed sex only after he tied my arms behind me with the sash of his robe. There was another man who took his pleasure with a girl in my own bed, while he thought I was asleep in it."

Yawns all around. The sin itself is wearing out. Pornography cannot exist without certified taboo to violate. And today Lust, like the rest of the Seven Deadly Sins—Pride, Sloth, Envy, Greed, Anger and Gluttony is becoming a rather minor vice. The Seven Deadly Sins, after all, are only sins against the self. Theologically, the idea of Lust—well, the idea is that if you seduce some poor girl from Akron, it is not a sin because you are ruining her, but because you are wasting your time and your energies and damaging your own spirit. This goes back to the old work ethic, when the idea was to keep every able-bodied man's shoulder to the wheel. In an age of riches for all, the ethic becomes more nearly: Let him do anything he pleases, as long as he doesn't get in my way. And if he does get in my way, or even if he doesn't . . . well . . . we have *new* fantasies for that. *Put hair on the walls.*

Hair on the walls is the invisible subtitle of Truman Capote's book, *In Cold Blood*. The book is neither a who-done-it nor a will-they-be-caught, since the answers to both questions are known from the outset. It does ask why-did-they-do-it, but the answer is soon as clear as it is going to be. Instead, the book's suspense is based largely on a totally new idea in detective stories: the promise of gory details, and the withholding of them until the end. Early in the game one of the two murderers, Dick, starts promising to put "plenty of hair on them-those walls" with a shotgun. So read on, gentle readers, and on and on; you are led up to the moment before the crime on page 60—yet the specifics, what happened, the gory details, are kept out of sight, in grisly dangle, until page 244.

But Dick and Perry, Capote's killers, are only a couple of lower-class bums. With James Bond the new pornography has already reached dead center, the bureaucratic middle class. The appeal of Bond has been explained as the appeal of the lone man who can solve enormously complicated, even world problems through his own bravery and initiative. But Bond is not a lone man at all, of course. He is not the Lone Ranger. He is much easier to identify than that. He is a salaried functionary in a bureaucracy. He is a sport, but a believable one; not a millionaire, but a bureaucrat on expense account. He is not even a high-level bureaucrat. He is an operative. This point is carefully and repeatedly made by having his superiors dress him down for violations of standard operating procedure. Bond, like the Lone Ranger, solves problems with guns and fists. When it is over, however, the Lone Ranger leaves a silver bullet. Bond, like the rest of us, fills out a report in triplicate.

Marshall McLuhan says we are in a period in which it will become harder and harder to stimulate lust through words and pictures—i.e., the old pornography. In an age of electronic circuitry, he says, people crave tactile, all-involving experiences. The same thing may very well happen to the new pornography of violence. Even such able craftsmen as Truman Capote, Ian Fleming, NBC and CBS may not suffice. Fortunately, there are historical models to rescue us from this frustration. In the latter days of the Roman Empire, the Emperor Commodus became jealous of the celebrity of the great gladiators. He took to the arena himself, with his sword, and began dispatching suitably screened cripples and hobbled fighters. Audience participation became so popular that soon various *illuminati* of the Commodus set, various boys and girls of the year, were out there, suited up, gaily cutting a sequence of dwarves and feebles down to short ribs. Ah, swinging generations, what new delights await?

Aids *Pause, Now, and Consider Some Tentative Conclusions About the Meaning of This Mass Perversion Called Porno-violence*

1. Look closely at the full title of Tom Wolfe's essay. Implicit in the title are three questions: what is porno-violence? where did it come from? who put the hair on the walls? Answer each of the questions.

2. "The point of view—the vantage point—is almost never that of the victim. . . . You live with the aggressor, whoever he may be." Test this assertion through your own personal observation of the print and electronic media.

3. What, according to Wolfe, is the "new pornography"? How does it differ from the old pornography?

4. Wolfe says that the discoveries of the Violence press "have been preempted by the Establishment and so thoroughly dissolved into the mainstream they no longer look original." What specific type of periodicals constitute the "Violence press"? What evidence does Wolfe offer to support his assertion that the Establishment media have usurped the role of the tabloids? Is Wolfe's observation still valid today? In other words, is there excessive violence in the media today?

5. Why do you think we have more and more violence in the media?

6. Wolfe makes no real distinction between violence in print and violence in television and films. Is there a difference? Does one medium have a greater (or more damaging) effect than the others?

7. Wolfe begins the essay by repeating the observations of a news reporter covering a convention of stringers for *The National Enquirer*. Does the essay, however, represent conventional news reporting? In what specific ways is this essay an example of "new journalism"? For an account of the goals, content, and techniques of new journalism, see the essay by Everette E. Dennis on pp. 155–70.

8. What other roles does Wolfe assume in his essay? Does he, like the cultural historian, jump outside the massive details of his subject and make a perceptive observation about it? Are his findings objective or laudatory? What, in short, is his attitude toward his subject matter?

9. Is Wolfe's essay based primarily on personal opinion? How does he attempt to support his opinions? Does he ever present opinion as fact?

10. What stylistic devices does Wolfe use to hold the attention of the reader? Do you find his style interesting and effective?

Shazam! Here Comes Captain Relevant

SAUL BRAUN

Envision a scene in a comic book:

In Panel 1, two New York City policemen are pointing skyward with their jaws hanging open and one is saying, "Wha . . .?" They are looking at four or five men and women, shown in Panel 2 plummeting through the air feet first, as though riding surfboards. The dominant figure has a black long coat thrown over his shoulders, wears a peaked, flat-brim hat and carries a cane. As the group lands on the street and enters the "Vision Building," Panel 3, a hairy hip figure on the sidewalk observes to a friend: "Fellini's in town."

In Panel 4, an office interior, the man with the cape is saying to the secretary, "I am Federico Fellini, come to pay his respects to . . ." Turn the page and there is the Fellini figure in the background finishing his balloon: ". . . the amazing Stan Lee." In the foreground is a tall, skinny man with a black D. H. Lawrence beard, wearing bathing trunks, long-sleeved turtleneck sweater and misshapen sailor hat. Stan Lee stands alongside a table that has been piled on another table, and on top of that is a typewriter with a manuscript page inserted in it that reads: "The Amazing Spiderman. In the Grip of the Goblin! It's happening again. As we saw last. . . ."

This visit, in more mundane fashion, actually took place. Stan Lee has been writing comic books for 30 years and is now editor-in-chief of the Marvel Comics line. His reputation with *cognoscenti*[1] is very, very high.

Alain Resnais is also a Lee fan and the two are now working together on a movie. Lee has succeeded so well with his art that he has spent a good deal of his time traveling around the country speaking at colleges. In his office at home—which is currently a Manhattan apartment in the East 60's

The New York Times Magazine, May 2, 1971, pp. 32–55. © 1971/1975 by The New York Times Company. Reprinted by permission.

[1]Italian for persons of superior taste. (eds.)

—he has several shelves filled with tapes of his college talks. An Ivy League student was once quoted as telling him, "We think of Marvel Comics as the 20th century mythology and you as this generation's Homer."

Lee's comic antiheroes (Spiderman, Fantastic Four, Submariner, Thor, Captain America) have revolutionized an industry that took a beating from its critics and from TV in the nineteen-fifties. For decades, comic book writers and artists were considered little more than production workers, virtually interchangeable. Now Lee and his former collaborator, artist Jack Kirby of National Comics, Marvel's principal rival, are considered superstars—and their work reflects a growing sophistication in the industry that has attracted both young and old readers.

"We're in a renaissance," says Carmine Infantino, editorial director at National Comics, and he offers as proof the fact that at Brown University in Providence, R.I., they have a course, proposed by the students, called "Comparative Comics." A prospectus for the course sets out the case for comic books as Native Art:

> Comics, long scorned by parents, educators, psychologists, lawmakers, American Legionnaires, moral crusaders, civic groups and J. Edgar Hoover, have developed into a new and interesting art form. Combining "new journalism" with greater illustrative realism, comics are a reflection of both real society and personal fantasy. No longer restricted to simple, good vs. evil plot lines and unimaginative, sticklike figures, comics can now be read at several different levels by various age groups. There are still heroes for the younger readers, but now the heroes are different—they ponder moral questions, have emotional differences, and are just as neurotic as real people. Captain America openly sympathizes with campus radicals, the Black Widow fights side by side with the Young Lords, Lois Lane apes John Howard Griffin and turns herself black to study racism, and everybody battles to save the environment.

As for Fellini, his interest in American comic books, and Stan Lee's work in particular, is no passing fancy. For an introduction to Jim Steranko's "History of the Comics," he wrote the following lines:

> Not satisfied being heroes, but becoming even more heroic, the characters in the Marvel group know how to laugh at themselves. Their adventures are offered publicly like a larger-than-life spectacle, each searching masochistically within himself to find a sort of maturity, yet the results are nothing to be avoided: it is a brilliant tale, aggressive and retaliatory, a tale that continues to be reborn for eternity, without fear of obstacles or paradoxes. We cannot die from obstacles and paradoxes if we face them with laughter. Only of boredom might we perish. And from boredom, fortunately, the comics keep a distance.

For an industry that wields considerable influence, comic-book publishing has only a small fraternity of workers. There are something like

200 million comic books sold each year, a volume produced by less than 200 people, including writers, artists and letterers. The artists fall into two categories, pencilers and inkers. Pencilers are slightly more highly reputed than inkers but, with few exceptions, nobody in the business has much of a public reputation, and most are poorly compensated. Most are freelancers, paid at a page rate that the various publishers prefer not to divulge. A rate of $15 a page, however, is said to be not uncommon.

"This is a fiercely competitive business," says Infantino. "After Superman clicked in 1935 everybody jumped in; there were millions of outfits. Then one by one they all slipped away. When World War II ended, then came survival of the fittest and, boom, they died by the wayside."

As in other industries, power gradually became concentrated during the nineteen-fifties and sixties, and now the industry consists of perhaps half a dozen companies with annual sales of about 200 million. National, the leader, sells about 70 million. Marvel sells 40 million, Archie 35 million, and the next three firms—Charleton (Yogi Bear, Beetle Bailey, Flintstones), Gold Key (Bugs Bunny, Donald Duck, Mickey Mouse) and Harvey (Casper the Friendly Ghost, Richie Rich, Sad Sack) each sell about 25 million. That is a great many copies, but doesn't necessarily reflect profitability. The index of profit and loss is not sales but the percentage of published copies that are returned unsold from the store racks. A book that suffers returns of more than 50 per cent is in trouble.

Martin Goodman, president of the Magazine Management Company, which puts out the Marvel line, recalls that the golden age of comics was the war years and immediately afterwards. By the late forties, he says, "everything began to collapse. TV was kicking the hell out of a great number of comics. A book like Donald Duck went from 2¼ million monthly sale to about 200,000. You couldn't give the animated stuff away, the Disney stuff, because of TV. TV murdered it. Because if a kid spends Saturday morning looking at the stuff, what parent is going to give the kid another couple of dimes to buy the same thing again?

"Industrywide," says Goodman sorrowfully, "the volume is not going up. I think the comic-book field suffers from the same thing TV does. After a few years, an erosion sets in. You still maintain loyal readers, but you lose a lot more readers than you're picking up. That's why we have so many superhero characters, and run superheroes together. Even if you take two characters that are weak sellers and run them together in the same book, somehow, psychologically, the reader feels he's getting more. You get the Avenger follower and the Submariner follower. Often you see a new title do great on the first issue and then it begins to slide off . . ."

Goodman recalls with avuncular diffidence the arrival of Stan Lee at Marvel, then called Timely Comics. "Stan started as a kid here; he's my wife's cousin. That was in 1941, something like that. He came in as an apprentice, to learn the business. He had a talent for writing. I think when Stan developed the Marvel superheroes he did a very good job, and he got a lot of college kids reading us. They make up a segment of our readership, but when you play it to them you lose the very young kids who just can't follow the whole damn thing. We try to keep a balance. Because I read some stories sometimes and I can't even understand them. I really can't!"

Today's superhero is about as much like his predecessors as today's child is like his parents. My recollection of the typical pre-World War II child (me) is of a sensitive, lonely kid full of fantasies of power and experiencing, at the same time, a life of endless frustration and powerlessness. Nobody knew, of course, about the hidden power, the supermuscles rippling beneath the coarse woolen suits I had to wear that itched like crazy. How I longed to rip off that suit. Shaz . . .

Comic book buffs will not need to be reminded that Shazam is the magic name of a mysterious bald gentleman with a white beard down to his waist, which, when spoken by newsboy Billy Batson, turns Billy into Captain Marvel. The book didn't last long, due to the swift, self-righteous reprisals of National Comics, which took Captain Marvel to court for impersonating Superman. It lasted long enough to impress upon my memory, however, that "S" stood for Solomon's wisdom, "H" for Hercules's strength, "A" for Atlas's stamina, "Z" for Zeus's power, "A" for Achilles's courage and "M" for Mercury's speed. I always had trouble remembering the last two; like many another man, I have gone through life saying "Shaz" to myself and getting nowhere.

So my childhood was one of repressed anger and sullen obedience and scratching all winter long, together with an iron will that kept me from lifting my all-powerful fist and destroying those who threatened me: Nazis, Japs, Polish kids (mostly at Easter time), older kids, teachers and parents. My personal favorite was Submariner. He hated everybody.

Actually, all of the early comic-book heroes perfectly mirrored my own condition, and even provided pertinent psychological details. The parents of superheroes were always being killed by bad men or cataclysmic upheavals over which the heroes—let me make this one thing perfectly clear —had absolutely no control. However, they then embarked on a guilty, relentless, lifelong pursuit of evildoers. So many villains in so many bizarre guises only attested to the elusiveness and prevalence of—and persistence of—superhero complicity.

Secretly powerful people, like the superheroes and me, always assumed the guise of meekness; yet even the "real" identities were only symbols. All-powerful Superman equaled all-powerful father. Batman's costume disguise, like the typical parental bluster of the time, was intended to "strike terror into their hearts." For "their" read not only criminal but child.

Infantino, whose National Comics publishes, among others, the long-run superhit of the comic-book industry, Superman, believes that power is the industry's main motif:

> The theme of comic books is power. The villain wants power. He wants to take over the world. Take over the other person's mind. There's something about sitting in the car with the motorcycles flanking you back and front and the world at your feet. It motivates all of us.

For three decades, the social setting was an America more or less continuously at war. At war with poverty in the thirties, with Fascism in the early forties, and with the International Red Conspiracy in the late forties and in the fifties. During these years there existed simultaneously, if uneasily, in our consciousness the belief that we were uniquely strong and that nothing would avail except the unrelenting exercise of that strength. From wanting or being forced to take the law into our own hands during the thirties, we moved swiftly towards believing that our security depended on taking the whole world into our hands. That carried us from the Depression to Korea and, eventually, in the sixties, to a confused war in which it was impossible to tell whether we were strong or weak, in which irresponsible complacency existed comfortably with political and social atrocities that could spring only from secret weakness masquerading as strength.

It is not irrelevant to note that the Vietnamese war developed without hindrance—with some few exceptions—from a generation of men flying around the world on a fantasy-power trip, and was resisted in the main by their sons, the generation that began rejecting the comic books of the fifties with their sanitized, censored, surreal images of the world: a world in which "we" were good and "they" were bad, in which lawlessness masqueraded as heroism, in which blacks were invisible, in which, according to a survey taken in 1953 by University of California professors, men led "active lives" but women were interested mainly in "romantic love" and only villainous women "try to gain power and status." A world in which no superhero, whatever his excesses, ever doubted that he was using his powers wisely and morally.

During this time the industry was adopting a self-censorship code of ethics in response to the hue and cry raised by a Congressional look into the industry's excesses of gore and by the appearance of "Seduction of the Innocent," a shrill piece of psycho-criticism by a psychiatrist named Fredric Wertham, who supported his view that the comics were a pernicious influence on children with stories like: "A boy of 13 committed a 'lust murder' of a girl of 6. Arrested and jailed, he asked only for comic books."

While it is true some publishers were printing stories with grisly and violent elements, I must confess that I to this day find myself unable to believe that the worst comic books could have corrupted the child's mind as much as the knowledge that in his own world, the world he was being educated to join, 6 million men, women and children had only recently been killed in gas ovens for no very good reason, and large numbers of others had died at Hiroshima and Dresden, for only slightly better reasons. Two of my own strongest memories of the time are of my father, who owned a candy store, denying me the treasure trove of comics ("They'll ruin your mind"), and of my father, after receiving a telegram telling him that his family had been wiped out in some concentration camp somewhere, turning ashen and falling to his knees. So, Superman, where were you when we needed you? My mind was corrupted, yes, and so were those of countless other children of the forties and fifties.

During this time, the only comic that held its own commercially was none other than William M. Gaines's "MAD." Gaines's defense of one of his horror comics was the high point at hearings of the Senate subcommittee on juvenile delinquency. The cover, depicting the severed head of a blonde, said Gaines, would have been in bad taste "if the head were held a little higher so the neck would show the blood dripping out."

The industry response was the comics code,[2] including provisions forbidding horror, excessive bloodshed, gory or gruesome crimes, depravity, lust, sadism and masochism; an authority to administer the code was created, with power to deny the industry seal of approval to any comic book violating its provisions. This satisfied parents and educators, but only intensified the sales slide for seal-of-approval comic books. The turnabout came in 1961, when Stan Lee metamorphosed the Marvel line and very likely saved comic books from an untimely death.

"Our competitors couldn't understand why our stuff was selling," Lee recalls. "They would have a superhero see a monster in the street and he'd say, 'Oh, a creature, I must destroy him before he crushes the world.' And they'd have another superhero in another book see a monster and he'd say 'Oh, a creature, I must destroy him before he crushes the world.' It was so formularized. I said to my writers, 'Is that what you'd say in real life? If you saw a monster coming down the street, you'd say, 'Gee, there must be a masquerade party going on.'

"Because sales were down and out of sheer boredom, I changed the whole line around. New ways of talking, hangups, introspection and brooding. I brought out a new magazine called 'The Fantastic Four,' in 1961. Goodman came to me with sales figures. The competitors were doing well with a superhero team. Well, I didn't want to do anything like what they were doing, so I talked to Jack Kirby about it. I said, 'Let's let them

---

[2]For the latest version of the Code of the Comics Magazine Association of America, see p. 228. (eds.)

not always get along well; let's let them have arguments. Let's make them talk like real people and react like real people. Why should they all get superpowers that make them beautiful? Let's get a guy who becomes very ugly.' That was The Thing. I hate heroes anyway. Just 'cause a guy has superpowers, why couldn't he be a *nebbish,* have sinus trouble and athlete's foot?"

The most successful of the Stan Lee antiheroes was one Spiderman, an immediate hit and still the top of the Marvel line. Spidey, as he is known to his fans, is actually Peter Parker, a teen-ager who has "the proportionate strength of a spider," whatever that means, and yet, in Lee's words, "can still lose a fight, make dumb mistakes, have acne, have trouble with girls and have not too much money."

In Parkers' world, nobody says, 'Oh, a creature.' In an early story, Spiderman apprehends three criminals robbing a store, and the following dialogue ensues:

Spidey: "If you're thinking of putting up a fight, brother, let me warn you . . ."

Crook: "A fight? The only fight I'll put up is in court. I'm suin' you for assault and battery, and I got witnesses to prove it."

Second crook: "Yeah, that's right."

If it is not already perfectly clear that the last vestiges of the nineteen-forties have fallen away from the world that Spiderman inhabits, it becomes so two panels later when one crook says, right to his face, "Don't you feel like a jerk paradin' around in public in that get-up?"

After overhearing a conversation in another episode between two men who also apparently consider him a kook, Parker goes home and, unlike any superhero before him, does some soul-searching. "Can they be right? Am I really some sort of crackpot wasting my time seeking fame and glory? Why do I do it? Why don't I give the whole thing up?"

The 48-year-old Lee may very well have asked precisely these questions at some point in his career. He's been in the business since 1938 when, as a 16-year-old high school graduate, he held some odd jobs (delivery boy, theater usher, office boy). Then he came to Timely Comics with some scripts and was hired by editors Joe Simon and Jack Kirby.

For the next 20 years, he labored professionally, but without any special devotion, to what he thought of as a temporary job. When Simon and Kirby left, Lee took over as editor as well as writer, and all during the forties and fifties, mass-produced comic books, 40 or 45 different titles a month.

The top sellers varied from month to month, in cycles. Romance books, mystery books. We followed the trend. When war books were big, we put out war books. Then one day my wife came to me and said, 'You've got to stop kidding yourself. This is your work. You've got to put yourself into it.' So I did. Joanie is the one you really ought to interview. She's beautiful and talented. And my daughter, Joanie, who's 21, she's also beautiful and talented. I'm a very lucky guy.

His wife, he says, is exactly the dream girl he'd always wanted, and he decided to marry her the first time he saw her. At the time she was married to another man, but that hardly deterred him. For something like 25 years, the Lees lived a quiet domestic life in Hewlett Harbor, L.I., before recently moving back into town. Lee is nothing if not a devoted family man. Among his other self-evident qualities: he enjoys talking about his work. He is in the office Tuesdays and Thursdays, editing, and at home the other five days of the week, writing. "I'm the least tempermental writer you'll ever know," he says. "I write a minimum of four comic books a month. Writing is easy. The thing is characterization. That takes time. The thing I hate most is writing plots. My scripts are full of X-outs [crossed-out words]. I read them out loud while writing, including sound effects, 'Pttuuuu. Take that, you rat!' I get carried away."

The comic industry has treated Lee very well. He is now, he says, in the 50 to 60 per cent income tax bracket, and he has a very high-paying, five-year contract with Cadence Industries, which bought Magazine Management Company from Goodman some 2½ years ago. When the contract expires, he says, he's not sure what he'll do. He has the vague discontent of a man looking for new fields to conquer, or, to use another simile, the look of a superhero adrift in a world that no longer wants him to solve its problems.

Last year he solved a recurring problem for industry workers by helping to form the Academy of Comic Book Artists:

> I felt that the publishers themselves weren't doing anything to improve the image of the comic books, so I thought, why don't we do it? Also I wanted to leave it as a legacy to the industry that has supported me over 30 years.

The academy now has as members about 80 writers, artists and letterers. I attended one of their recent meetings, held at the Statler-Hilton Hotel in the Petit Cafe, a barren, pastel-blue and mirrored room with about 200 gray metal folding chairs with glass ashtrays on them, and a gray metal long table with glass ashtrays and a lined yellow pad on it.

Around the room, leaning on gray folding chairs, were "story boards" from comic books that have been nominated for this year's awards, which are to be called Shazams.

Sketches of the proposed designs for the Shazams were being passed around, most of them serious renderings of the jagged bolt of lightning that accompanied Billy Batson's transformation. One, however, represented a side of comic book artistry that the fans rarely see: A naked young woman, bent forward at the waist, stands upon the pedestal, while the airborne Shazam lightning bolt strikes her in the rear. She has a look of unanticipated delight upon her face.

There were about 30 men present, and one or two young women. Among the artists and writers I spoke to, there was general agreement that working in the comic-book industry was not all magic transformations of unworthy flesh. Problems mentioned as organic included the lack of economic security, the inability of the artists to keep control over their material, insufficient prestige and a catch-all category that is apparently the source of abiding resentment: publishers who do not treat them as serious artists.

As for the censorship of the Comics Code Authority, virtually everybody agreed they wanted more freedom. Younger writers, in fact, are bringing fresh ideas into the field. But, as 33-year-old Archie Goodwin, who writes "Creepy Comics" for Jim Warren Publishers, wryly observes, the real problem is self-censorship: "The truth is, maybe half the people here wouldn't do their work any different if they didn't have censorship."

It did seem to me as I observed the crowd that there was perhaps more than a random sample of serious-purposed people who spoke haltingly, with tendentious meekness. The meeting began with nominations for A.C.B.A. officers for the coming year. I gleefully anticipated some earth-shaking confrontations between good and evil, but none developed. Nobody slipped off to a telephone booth to change. The two nominations for president, Neal Adams and Dick Giordano, by coincidence, jointly draw the Green Lantern-Green Arrow book for National. Lantern and Arrow have been squabbling lately, but Adams and Giordano were not at all disputatious.

In the entire group I was able to uncover only a single secret life.

"This is my secret life," Roy Thomas admitted. "Or rather it was, when I was a teacher at Fox High School in Arnold, Mo." Thomas, a bespectacled 30-year-old who wears his corn-silk hair straight down almost to the shoulders, edits at Marvel. "After school hours, I was publishing a comics fanzine called Alter Ego. I spent all my time at night working on Alter Ego."

"The people in this business," Lee said to me after the meeting, "are sincere, honorable, really decent guys. We're all dedicated, we love comics. The work we do is very important to the readers. I get mail that closes with, 'God bless you.' Most of us, we're like little kids, who, if you pat us on the head, we're happy."

All in all, add a little touch of resentment, discontent and a pinch of paranoia to Lee's description and you have the modern-day comic book superhero. Lee himself has only one frustration in a long, satisfying career:

> For years the big things on campus have been McLuhan and Tolkien, and Stan Lee and Marvel, and everybody knew about McLuhan and Tolkien, but nobody knew about Marvel. Now our competitor is coming out with

"relevant" comics and he has big public relations people, so he's been easing in on our publicity.

Relevance is currently such a lure that even industry classics like Archie are having a stab at it. John Goldwater, president of Archie Comics, says that Archie definitely keeps up with the times, and offers as evidence Xerox copies of a silver print, which is an engraver's photographic proof of an original drawing. It was of a recent six-page Archie story entitled, "Weigh Out Scene."

"This is a civil-rights story," Goldwater said. "It's done subtly. It has to do with a fat boy who comes to town who can't fit into the mainstream with the teen-agers in town. Because of his obesity, he's taunted and humiliated. You know how kids are. Then one night Archie has a dream. And in this dream he is obese and fat and everybody is taunting him and ridiculing him and now he finally realizes what happened to this poor kid. So then there is a complete turnaround. But we don't say, remember, this kid is black. We don't say that. But the subtlety is there."

Goldwater, who is also president of the Comics Code Authority, is convinced that "comics don't ruin your mind." He says: "I wouldn't be in this business unless it had some value, some educational value. If you can get a kid today to read, it's quite some victory—instead of him looking at the boob tube, you know?"

Recently there were some ruffled feelings in the industry when Marvel issued a comic book without the authority seal, which was denied because the subject of drugs was alluded to in one story that showed a stoned black kid tottering on a rooftop. Goldwater felt that hinted a bit of sensationalism, and Infantino believes the subject calls for a more thorough and responsible treatment. Lee scoffs. Black kids getting stoned isn't exactly a biannual occurrence, he suggests. Goodman calls the fuss a tempest in a teapot. Goldwater, at any rate, is not inclined to be harsh:

> Goodman came before the publishers and promised not to do it again. So we're satisfied. Anybody with 15 solid years of high standards of publishing comic books with the seal is entitled to one mistake.

Subsequently the publishers agreed to give themselves permission to deal with the subject. "Narcotics addiction," says the new guideline, "shall not be presented except as a vicious habit."

Goodman is not so sure relevance will continue to sustain sales, but Infantino is elated at National's success with social issues.

National turned toward relevance and social commentary for the same reasons Marvel had a decade earlier. "I'd like to say I had a great dream," says Infantino, "but it didn't happen that way. Green Lantern was dying. The whole superhero line was dying. Everything was sagging, everything.

When your sales don't work, they're telling you something. The front office told me, get rid of the book, but I said, let me try something, just for three issues. We started interviewing groups of kids around the country. The one thing they kept repeating: they want to know the truth. Suddenly the light bulb goes on: Wow, we've been missing the boat here!"

In the first of National's relevant books, which came out in the fall of 1970, Green Lantern comes to the aid of a respectable citizen, besieged by a crowd, who turns out to be a slum landlord badly in need of a thrashing. Lantern is confused to discover his pal Green Arrow actually siding with The People. "You mean you're . . . defending . . . these . . . ANARCHISTS?" he says.

Following a tour of the ghetto, Green Lantern is finally brought face to face with reality by an old black man who says: "I been readin' about you, how you work for the Blue Skins, and how on a planet someplace you helped out the Orange Skins . . . and you done considerable for the Purple Skins. Only there's Skins you never bothered with. The Black Skins. I want to know . . . how come? Answer me that, Mr. Green Lantern."

This story, written by 28-year-old Denny O'Neil, is one of the nominees for the writing Shazam, and the consensus of opinion, even among rival nominees, is that he'll win it. In the following months, O'Neil had the superheroes on the road discovering America and taking up such provocative current issues as the Manson family, the mistreatment of American Indians, the Chicago Seven trial, and, finally, in a forthcoming issue, the style and substance of the President and Vice President.

Mr. Agnew appears as Grandy, a simpering but vicious private-school cook whose ward is a certain ski-nosed child-witch named Sybil. A mere gaze from Sybil can cause great pain; one look from her and even Arrow and Lantern double over in agony. That certainly is making things clear. Grandy is constantly justifying his nastiness: "Old Grandy doesn't kill. I simply do my duty. Punish those who can't respect order. You may die. But that won't be my fault."

"What we're saying here," says Infantino, "is, there can be troubles with your Government unless you have the right leaders. Sure, we expect flak from the Administration, but we feel the kids have a right to know, and they want to know. The kids are more sophisticated than anyone imagines, and we feel the doors are so wide open here that we're going in many directions.

"You wouldn't believe whom I'm talking to. Big-name writers—and they're interested. We have innovations in mind for older audiences, and in graphics we're going to take it such a step forward, it'll blow the mind." He was so excited during our talk that he stood up. "We're akin to a young lady pregnant and having her first baby." He grinned shyly.

The artist who has produced the most innovative work for Infantino is 53-year-old Jack Kirby, about whom Stan Lee says: "He is one of the giants, a real titan. He's had tremendous influence in the field. His art work has great power and drama and tells a story beautifully. No matter what he draws it looks exciting, and that's the name of the game."

Unlike the "relevant" comic books, Kirby's new line eschews self-conscious liberal rhetoric about social issues and returns to the basic function of comic books: to describe in an exciting, imaginative way how power operates in the world, the struggle to attain it by those who lack it and the uses to which it is put by those who have it.

Kirby began to conceive his new comic books when he was still at Marvel, but felt he might not get enough editorial autonomy. He left his $35,000-a-year job at Marvel and took his new books to National. He also moved from New York to Southern California, where he edits, writes and draws the books.

His new heroes are the Forever People, whom he describes as "the other side of the gap—the under-30 group. I'm over 50. I've had no personal experience of the counterculture. It's all from the imagination."

The Forever People arrive on earth through a "boom tube," which is an attempt to offer approximate coordinates for an experiential conjunction of media wash and psychedelic trip. They are said to be "In Search of a Dream." There are five of them: one is a relaxed, self-assured, young black man who, probably not by accident, carries the group's power source, known as the "mother box"; another is a shaggy-bearded giant who overwhelms his small-minded taunters with a loving, crushing bear hug; the third, a beautiful saintly flower child named Serafin is called a "sensitive"; the fourth, a combination rock star-football hero transmogrified into one Mark Moonrider; and the fifth, a girl named Beautiful Dreamer.

The mother box, which warns them of impending danger, also transforms them—not into five distinct, ego-involved superheroes but into a single all-powerful Infinity Man, who comes from a place where "all of natural law shifts, and bends, and changes. Where the answer to gravity is antigravity—and simply done."

These new heroes, unlike the characters of the sixties, are brash, confident youngsters whose superpower lies in their ability to unify. They are also, says Kirby, "basically nonviolent."

Infantino has been asked up to Yale to talk about Kirby's new books, and to Brown, for the new course in Comparative Comics. Students in Comp. Com. I will doubtless relish Kirby's toying with words like "gravity" (and other mild Joycean puns sprinkled elsewhere) to suggest elements of his parable of culture vs. counterculture. Suffice it to say here that the Forever People are from New Genesis, where the land is eternally green and children frolic in joy, and their enemy is Darkseid, who serves "holocaust and death."

The story of New Genesis is also told in another new Kirby book called "New Gods." When the old gods died, the story goes, the New Gods rose on New Genesis, where the High-Father, who alone has access to The Source, bows to the young, saying, "They are the carriers of life. They must remain free. Life flowers in freedom."

Opposed to New Genesis is its "dark shadow," Apokolips, the home of evil Darkseid and his rotten minions. Darkseid's planet "is a dismal, unclean place of great ugly houses sheltering uglier machines." Apokolips is an armed camp where those who live with weapons rule the wretches who built them. Life is the evil here. And death the great goal. All that New Genesis stands for is reversed on Apokolips.

Darkseid has not, of course, been content to rule on Apokolips. He wants to duplicate that horror on, of all places, Earth, and he can do this if he manages somehow to acquire the "antilife equation." With it, he will be able to "snuff out all life on Earth—with a word."

Thus is the battle drawn, and the Forever People, notably, are not going to waste their time hassling with raucous hardhats who don't understand the crisis. When a hostile, paranoid, Middle-America type confronts them, they arrange it so that he sees them just about the way he remembers kids to have been in his own childhood: Beautiful Dreamer wearing a sensible frilly dress down to her knees, the cosmic-sensitive Serafin wearing a high-school sweater and beanie, Moonrider with hat and tie and close-cropped hair.

"What's going on here? You kids look so different—and yet so familiar."

"Why sure," says Beautiful Dreamer soothingly. "You used to know lots of kids like us. Remember? We never passed without saying hello."

In the titanic struggle against Darkseid, the Forever People have lots of help, and they are beginning to populate four different comic books: "Forever People," "New Gods," "Mister Miracle" and "Superman's Pal Jimmy Olsen." Both Superman and Jimmy Olsen are being altered to fit the evolution of Kirby's Faulknerian saga of the difficult days leading to Armageddon. Already identified in the Kirby iconography on the side of the good are the newly revived and updated Newsboy Legion, so popular in the nineteen-forties; various dropout tribes living in "The Wild Area" and "experimenting with life" after harnessing the DNA molecule; and a tribe of technologically sophisticated youths called "Hairies," who live in a mobile "Mountain of Judgment" as protection against those who would destroy them. "You know our story," says one Hairy. "We seek only to be left alone—to use our talents, to develop fully."

On the other side, in support of Darkseid are middle managers and technocrats of the Establishment, like Morgan Edge, a media baron who treats his new employee Clark Kent—now a TV newscaster—abominably.

Darkseid's lousy band also includes an assortment of grotesque super-villains. Among them are DeSaad and his terrifying "Fear Machine," and a handsome toothy character named Glorious Godfrey, a revivalist. Godfrey is drawn to look like an actor playing Billy Graham in a Hollywood film biography of Richard Nixon starring George Hamilton.

"I hear you right thinkers," Godfrey says to his grim, eyeless audience of true believers, "You're shouting antilife—the positive belief."

In the background acolytes carry signs: "Life has pitfalls! Antilife is protection!" And, "You can justify anything with antilife!" And, "Life will make you doubt! Antilife will make you right!"

"I have no final answers," Kirby admits. "I have no end in mind. This is like a continuing novel. My feeling about these times is that they're hopeful but full of danger. Any time you have silos buried around the country there's danger. In the forties when I created Captain America, that was my feeling then, that patriotism. Comics are definitely a native American art. They always have been. And I'm feeling very good about this. My mail has been about 90 per cent positive, and sales are good."

Infantino adds:

> The kids at Yale think Kirby's new books are more tuned in to them than any other media. They're reading transcripts from 'New Gods' over their radio station. The Kirby books are a conscious attempt to show what things look like when you're out where the kids are. The collages, the influence of the drug culture. We're showing them basically what they're seeing. We're turning into what they're experiencing.

If that is true—and I am not so sure it isn't—then perhaps the rest of us had better begin choosing sides. New Genesis anyone?

Aids   *Shazam! Here Comes Captain Relevant*

1. According to Saul Braun, what are the differences between the "old" and the "new" comics?

2. How did Stan Lee, editor of Marvel Comics, save comicbooks from an untimely death in 1961? What factors were threatening comics in the 1950s?

3. Some comics, not content with simple humor and escapist entertainment, are attempting to deal with such realities of our social and political world as racial and sexual discrimination, governmental corruption, poverty, drug abuse, and ecology. Examine some current comic books, locating the specific social concerns. Do these "relevant" comics have a social, cultural, or political bias? Can some of these comics be called propagandistic?

4. Braun mentions a whole new generation of comicbook readers that didn't exist in years past—the high school and college crowd. What are some of the dangers inherent in attempting to appeal to several audiences at the same time? Can some comics, like some "childrens' classic novels," be read on several levels simultaneously?

5. Comment on the following quotation by Carmine Infantino, editorial director of National Comics: "Superman was created in the Depression as an icon, a Nietzche superman. At that time, people needed a perfect being."

6. Comment on the following quotation by John Culhane: ". . . the kind of heroes the comic page offers no longer provides us with images of aspirations. We no longer believe in the hero as soldier, as fighter pilot, as astronaut: Television has shown them all too close up. . . . We no longer confuse the man with the role, and we believe in the man only as long as he acts ethically. . . . What we need now is not heroes but lots of citizens with a respect for truth, a sense of balance and a sense of humor."

7. Stan Lee, in his Prologue to *Origins of Marvel Comics* (1974) calls Marvel Comics "a pictorial tonic to relieve the awesome affliction that threatens us all: the endlessly spreading virus of too much reality in a world that is losing its legends—a world that has lost its heroes." Does this statement contradict in any way Saul Braun's thesis that the comics are now relevant?

8. One serious student of comics has said: "We think of Marvel Comics as the 20th century mythology and you [Stan Lee] as this generation's Homer." Focusing on adventure comics like "Tarzan," "Prince Valiant," "Superman," or any of the Marvel group, locate some examples of the heroic experience. The following patterns in mythology, taken from Joseph Cambell's *Hero with a Thousand Faces*, may be helpful:

    I. Separation or departure
        a. Call to adventure
        b. Supernatural aid
        c. Crossing the threshold
        d. Passage into the unknown
    II. Trials and victories of initiation
        a. Dangerous confrontations with monsters or villains
        b. Meeting the goddess, who sometimes takes the form of a temptress
        c. Atonement with the godlike father
        d. Apotheosis (hero becomes godlike and powerful)

      e. Hero receives the "message" (the truth or mission)

III. Return and reintegration into society

    a. Hero cannot stay in Nirvana

    b. He must use his message or gift to save the world

9. What American myths, discussed by John Cashill in "Packaging Pop Mythology" in Unit II, are evident in comics? Locate examples of "manifest destiny," the "American Adam," and "the woman."

10. Illustrate with specific examples from current comics the assertion by Carmine Infantino that "The theme of comic books is power."

11. Braun mentions that Brown University has a course in comicbooks. If you were to organize such a course at your school, what would you include? What would you state as the goals and educational values of the course?

12. The term "relevance" is central to Braun's thesis. What precisely does he mean by the term? Is it the same as the denotative dictionary definition?

13. What ultimately is Braun's attitude toward comics? Do you agree with his view?

14. According to Stan Lee, comics should be seen as an art form in the same way as film. In addition to judging comics by their contents, their transmitted values, and their sociological messages, we can evaluate comics as an artistic medium. Examine a current comic for its artistic effects. How is the story told in picture and text? Do the linguistic and pictorial elements work together or does one element dominate the other? That is, is the text too wordy where a picture would be more effective? It is no coincidence, too, that many artists have studied film techniques. Look for examples of camera positioning —the long and medium shot, the closeup. Look also at the way in which the pictorial narrative, or montage, is structured. Does the artist adhere to the traditional six-panel layout or does he vary the format? Does the artist create a visual tension paralleling the conflict or crisis in the story?

15. Writers, especially journalists, sometimes begin their essays with dramatic scenarios. What is the function of such an introduction? How does it serve to introduce what follows? Is this technique effective?

16. Articles from *The New York Times Magazine* tend to have a distinctive journalistic style. They often cite many facts and figures, quote the observations of notable personalities and authorities, pro-

vide succinct historical surveys of their subject matters, and "take us behind the scenes" to show personalities at work and at play. Is Braun's essay typical of this kind of journalism? Do you find this type of writing effective?

17. The thesis of Braun's essay is never explicitly stated, although it is summarized by the title. What is the implicit thesis of the essay? Do the components of the essay (the many quotations and personal reminiscences) support the thesis? Would it have been better if Braun had stated his thesis more openly?

Code
of the
Comics Magazine
Association
of America, Inc.

APPROVED
BY THE
COMICS
CODE
(CA)
AUTHORITY

PREAMBLE

The comics magazine, or as it is more popularly known, the comic book medium, having come of age on the American cultural scene, must measure up to its responsibilties.

Constantly improving techniques and higher standards go hand in hand with these responsibilities.

To make a positive contribution to contemporary life, the industry must seek new areas for developing sound, wholesome entertainment. The people responsible for writing, drawing, printing, publishing and selling comic books have done a commendable job in the past, and have been striving toward this goal.

Their record of progress and continuing improvement compares favorably with other media. An outstanding example is the development of comic books as a unique and effective tool for instruction and education. Comic books have also made their contribution in the field of social commentary and criticism of contemporary life.

Members of the industry must see to it that gains made in this medium are not lost and that violations of standards of good taste, which might tend toward corruption of the comic book as an instructive and wholesome form of entertainment, will not be permitted.

Therefore, the Comics Magazine Association of America, Inc. has adopted this Code, and placed its enforcement in the hands of an independent Code Authority.

Further, members of the Association have endorsed the purpose and spirit of this Code as a vital instrument to the growth of the industry.

To this end, they have pledged themselves to conscientiously adhere to its principles and to abide by all decisions based on the Code made by the Administrator.

CODE FOR EDITORIAL MATTER

General Standards—Part A

1. Crimes shall never be presented in such a way as to promote distrust of the

Originally adopted in 1954, and revised in 1971 to meet contemporary standards of conduct and morality, the enforcement of this Code is the basis for the comics magazine industry's program of self-regulation. Reprinted by permission.

Photo/David Umberger

forces of law and justice, or to inspire others with a desire to imitate criminals.

2. No comics shall explicitly present the unique details and methods of a crime, with the exception of those crimes that are so far-fetched or pseudo-scientific that no would-be lawbreaker could reasonably duplicate.

3. Policemen, judges, government officials and respected institutions shall not be presented in such a way as to create disrespect for established authority. If any of these is depicted committing an illegal act, it must be declared as an exceptional case and that the culprit pay the legal price.

4. If crime is depicted it shall be as a sordid and unpleasant activity.

5. Criminals shall not be presented in glamorous circumstances, unless an unhappy end results from their ill-gotten gains, and creates no desire for emulation.

6. In every instance good shall triumph over evil and the criminal be punished for his misdeeds.

7. Scenes of excessive violence shall be prohibited. Scenes of brutal torture, excessive and unnecessary knife and gun play, physical agony, gory and gruesome crime shall be eliminated.

8. No unique or unusual methods of concealing weapons shall be shown, except where such concealment could not reasonably be duplicated.

9. Instances of law enforcement officers dying as a result of a criminal's activities should be discouraged, except when the guilty, because of their crime, live a sordid existence and are brought to justice because of the particular crime.

10. The crime of kidnapping shall never be portrayed in any detail, nor shall any profit accrue to the abductor or kidnapper. The criminal or the kidnapper must be punished in every case.

11. The letters of the word "crime" on a comics magazine cover shall never be appreciably greater in dimension than the other words contained in the title. The word "crime" shall never appear alone on a cover.

12. Restraint in the use of the word "crime" in titles or subtitles shall be exercised.

General Standards—Part B

1. No comic magazine shall use the word "horror" or "terror" in its title. These words may be used judiciously in the body of the magazine.*
2. All scenes of horror, excessive bloodshed, gory or gruesome crimes, depravity, lust, sadism, masochism shall not be permitted.
3. All lurid, unsavory, gruesome illustrations shall be eliminated.
4. Inclusion of stories dealing with evil shall be used or shall be published only where the intent is to illustrate a moral issue and in no case shall evil be presented alluringly nor so as to injure the sensibilities of the reader.
5. Scenes dealing with, or instruments associated with walking dead, or torture shall not be used. Vampires, ghouls and werewolves shall be permitted to be used when handled in the classic tradition such as Frankenstein, Dracula and other high calibre literary works written by Edgar Allen Poe, Saki (H. H. Munro), Conan Doyle and other respected authors whose works are read in schools throughout the world.
6. Narcotics or drug addiction shall not be presented except as a vicious habit.
   Narcotics or drug addiction or the illicit traffic in addiction-producing narcotics or drugs shall not be shown or described if the presentation:

(a) Tends in any manner to encourage stimulate or justify the use of such narcotics or drugs; or
(b) Stresses, visually, by text or dialogue, their temporarily attractive effects; or
(c) Suggests that the narcotics or drug habit may be quickly or easily broken; or
(d) Shows or describes details of narcotics or drug procurement, or the implements or devices used in taking narcotics or drugs, or of the taking of narcotics or drugs in any manner; or
(e) Emphasizes the profits of the narcotics or drug traffic; or
(f) Involves children who are shown knowingly to use or traffic in narcotics or drugs; or
(g) Shows or implies a casual attitude towards the taking of narcotics or drugs; or
(h) Emphasizes the taking of narcotics or drugs throughout, or in a major part, of the story, and leaves the denouement to the final panels.

General Standards—Part C

All elements or techniques not specifically mentioned herein, but which are contrary to the spirit and intent of the Code, and are considered violations of good taste or decency, shall be prohibited.

Dialogue

1. Profanity, obscenity, smut, vulgarity, or words or symbols which have ac-

---

*The Board of Directors has ruled that a judicious use does not include the words "Horror" or "Terror" in story titles within the magazine.

quired undesirable meanings—judged and interpreted in terms of contemporary standards—are forbidden.
2. Special precautions to avoid disparaging references to physical afflictions or deformities shall be taken.
3. Although slang and colloquialisms are acceptable, excessive use should be discouraged and wherever possible good grammar shall be employed.

Religion

1. Ridicule or attack on any religious or racial group is never permissible.

Costume

1. Nudity in any form is prohibited. Suggestive and salacious illustration is unacceptable.
2. Females shall be drawn realistically without undue emphasis on any physical quality.

Marriage and Sex

1. Divorce shall not be treated humorously nor represented as desirable.
2. Illicit sex relations are not to be portrayed and sexual abnormalities are unacceptable.
3. All situations dealing with the family unit should have as their ultimate goal the protection of the children and family life. In no way shall the breaking of the moral code be depicted as rewarding.
4. Rape shall never be shown or suggested. Seduction may not be shown.
5. Sex perversion or any inference to same is strictly forbidden.

CODE FOR ADVERTISING MATTER

These regulations are applicable to all magazines published by members of the Comics Magazine Association of America, Inc. Good taste shall be the guiding principle in the acceptance of advertising.
1. Liquor and tobacco advertising is not acceptable.
2. Advertisement of sex or sex instruction books are unacceptable.
3. The sale of picture postcards, "pinups," "art studies," or any other reproduction of nude or semi-nude figures is prohibited.
4. Advertising for the sale of knives, concealable weapons, or realistic gun facsimiles is prohibited.
5. Advertising for the sale of fireworks is prohibited.
6. Advertising dealing with the sale of gambling equipment or printed matter dealing with gambling shall not be accepted.
7. Nudity with meretricious purpose and salacious postures shall not be permitted in the advertising of any product; clothed figures shall never be presented in such a way as to be offensive or contrary to good taste or morals.
8. To the best of his ability, each publisher shall ascertain that all statements made in advertisements conform to fact and avoid misrepresentation.
9. Advertisement of medical, health, or toiletry products of questionable nature are to be rejected. Advertisements for medical, health or toiletry products endorsed by the American Medical Association, or the American Dental Association, shall be deemed acceptable if they conform with all other conditions of the Advertising Code.

THE COMICS CODE AUTHORITY

The Code Authority of the Comics Magazine Association of America, Inc. was established at the same time the Code was adopted, to ascertain compliance with the terms of the Code. It is headed by a Code Administrator, who has no connection with any publisher, and who exercises independent judgment to determine whether the material intended for publication meets Code standards.

Publisher-members of the CMAA are required to submit their original text and art-work to the Code Authority, *in advance of publication*. The staff carefully checks each panel of art and every line of text, ordering such changes or deletions as in the judgment of the Administrator violates any tenet or the over-all principle of the Code. Being an industry self-regulation program, the publisher may appeal the decision of the Administrator to the CMAA's Board of Directors, but in nearly two decades of operation, this privilege has been rarely used. In almost every instance, the decision of the Administrator has prevailed.

Finally, each individual page must receive the stamp of approval of the Code Authority, or authorization from the Board of Directors, before the publisher may place the official Seal of Approval on the upper right-hand portion of the comics magazine's cover.

Editorial Cartoons:
Capturing the Essence

STEFAN KANFER

"Boss" Tweed, corrupt Tammany chief of the 1860s, raised little objection when muckraking reporters prowled city hall. What the papers wrote had no meaning, Tweed liked to boast; his constituency was illiterate. The only criticism that ever bothered or threatened him, the Boss confessed, was "them damn pictures."

Thomas Nast's editorial cartoons were worth fearing; the savage caricatures showed Tweed variously as a vulture, a bag of money and, when Nast had sufficiently aroused the civic conscience, a felon in prison stripes.

A century of history has brought little change. Corruption is still ubiquitous—but so, happily, is the editorial cartoon, grinning out from banks of gray prose. In about 16 square inches, that journalistic institution still manages to encapsulate crises, expose pretensions and eviscerate swollen egos—all with a few well-drawn strokes. Two new paperback editions underscore the point. On the far side of history, *Thomas Nast: Cartoons & Illustrations* (Dover) reveals a mature artist whose work could exhibit the bite of Daumier and the mordant wit of Twain.[1] His meticulous crosshatching created three ineradicable symbols: the Democratic Donkey, the Republican Elephant and the Tammany Tiger. Nast's gentler conceptions of John Bull, Uncle Sam and even Santa Claus are the ones that most artists still sedulously ape. On the near side, *Herblock's State of the Union* (Viking/Compass) presents the dean of contemporary cartoonists, Herbert Block, drawing—and quartering—his favorite quarry: Government waste, pomposity, fat-cat lobbyists, and last and by all means lost, the Nixon Administration.

Between these two masters, a hundred years' worth of artists have passed in review. A few remain in the memory because of a Pulitzer Prize or an anthologized work; the bulk have been forgotten. Yet anyone who peruses ancient journals knows that if nothing is as old as yesterday's news, nothing seems fresher than its editorial cartoon. In satirizing events and event makers, the cartoon refines material until only the ridiculous essence

Stefan Kanfer, "Editorial Cartoons: Capturing the Essence," from *Time*, February 3, 1975, pp. 62–63. Reprinted by permission of Time, Inc.

[1]Honoré Daumier (1808–79), French caricaturist, painter, and sculptor, who was imprisoned for six months for his cartoon of Louis Philippe, King of France, as Gargantua; Mark Twain, pseudonym of Samuel Clemens (1835–1910), American humorist and social observer. (eds.)

remains. Circumstances impossible in the real world are staged upon the cartoonist's proscenium: the politician comes face to face with his broken promises, hypocrisy assumes a human face, fingers are pointed, blame is fixed, responsibility attached to recognizable figures.

Such onslaughts have their liabilities. The cartoon's first obligation is to be pithy; faces and facts may be stretched to fit a gag. Editorial artists work best against rather than for something, and not every issue is as black and white as the drawing proclaims. That lack of shading and subtlety obviously influenced New York *Times* Founder Adolph Ochs when he kept sketches from his paper's editorial page—a tradition that is maintained today. "A cartoon," Ochs is said to have complained, "cannot say 'On the other hand.'"

On the other hand, a cartoon can do what prose cannot. It can sometimes elicit action by overstating—and overheating—an issue: Daniel R. Fitzpatrick's unsubtle smog-laden cartoons helped clean up St. Louis' air back in the 1950s. It can provide a graphic perspective on this or any other time: Thomas Nast's cartoon of the U.S. contending with inflation might have been inked yesterday instead of in 1876. And the cartoon can provide a time capsule for the historian. New York *Times* Columnist William V. Shannon offers a sound, if witsful, prophecy when he foresees that "a hundred years from now, Herblock will be read and his cartoons admired by everyone trying to understand these strange times."

In fact, cartoons help illuminate *all* strange times. Of all the publications of the Foreign Policy Association, none enjoys the immediacy of its *A Cartoon History of United States Foreign Policy Since World War I.* In an introduction, Political Analyst Richard H. Rovere acknowledges the ability of certain cartoons to provide "flashes of extraordinary insight and political prescience." In this category he places a David Low cartoon of 1939. Hitler bows to Stalin: "The scum of the earth, I believe." Stalin returns the courtesy: "The bloody assassin of the workers, I presume." Recalls Rovere: "It took most of us more than 20 years to catch up with the truth captured by Low—that where ideology and national interest are in conflict, national interest prevails."

Low was the last of the great British cartoonists. But even at his apogee he seldom surpassed the best of his American colleagues. *A Cartoon History* offers compelling work of artists representing the whole ideological spectrum. On the political left are some superlative efforts from the World War II years: William Gropper's fascists, consuming the globe for dinner, and Saul Steinberg's Hitler, portrayed as a constipated hen. The progressives are matched in temper and tone by conservatives of the '50s: Joseph Parrish's conception of the U.N. as a Trojan horse, brimming with "alien spies"; Reg Manning's portrayal of General MacArthur's hat hemmed in by toppers belonging to The Appeasing Diplomats.

It would be the grossest distortion to pretend that editorial cartoonists are all Goyas in a hurry. Nothing inspires bromides like a deadline. Artists against the clock have too often relied on labels and fatigued metaphors to make their point. Back in 1925, *The New Yorker* lampooned the journeyman cartoonist with his crayoned clichés: the literalized Sea of Public Indignation; the bearded Radical; the masked thief with his tag of Crime Wave; the debt-ridden Commuter.

Happily, such pictures are beginning to find less favor with readers— and with cartoonists. Says Bill Mauldin, at 53 a 35-year-veteran of the editorial page: "Cartoons are getting better, more and more away from labels. Readers are more savvy. It is less and less necessary to put names on things. The trend is more interesting drawing, less complicated captions." To sharpen his point, Mauldin spent last semester teaching a course in his profession at Yale. "I deliberately started with a nondrawing bunch," recalls the most technically proficient cartoonist of his generation. "What counts is the thinking. A drawing with authority helps give authority to an idea, but there's no way a weak idea can make a good cartoon." Don Wright, Pulitzer-prizewinning cartoonist of the Miami *News,* agrees: "The editorial cartoon has become a welcome relief from some of the ponderous, elitist, overwritten poopery that typifies so many editorial pages today."

Wright's judgment has been accepted by many editors who know that, of all features, the editorial cartoon is the least imitable by TV. Cartoonists have been encouraged to explore new forms: Jules Feiffer's psychiatric monologues have spawned a generation of imitators; Garry Trudeau's campus favorite, *Doonesbury,* is bringing politics back to the comic strip. Moreover, because cartoons are a major journalistic attraction, editors are often tolerant of artistic statements that would not be welcome in a prose piece. Says Herblock: "A lot of newspapers run my stuff even though they don't agree with me. They feel it's a signed piece of work, an example of personal opinion." This liberty has brought U.S. editorial cartooning to something of a rebirth. It is a renaissance with too few galleries; the great epoch of newspapers is gone and with it, many of the journals that carried the art of the great cartoonists. Yet the work somehow finds space in the surviving dailies, in magazines and in student publications. At its frequent best, contemporary cartooning in the U.S. steadily outshines work anywhere else in the world. No country now produces corrosive lampoons equal to Patrick Oliphant's vaudeville sketches or Paul Conrad's acidulous critiques. The competition for attention may have reduced the impact of graphic art everywhere. Yet the cartoon seems to be gaining influence. No photograph damaged Lyndon Johnson so much as David Levine's waspish drawing of L.B.J. lifting his shirt to reveal a gall bladder scar—in the shape of Viet Nam. Richard Nixon once admitted, "I wouldn't start the morning by looking at Herblock." Even President Ford, gazing forlornly at a gallery of U.S. political cartoons, recently conceded, "The pen is mightier than the politician."

It is likely to remain so. The mood of the nation is skepticism, not credulity. The appetite for the cartoon is whetted. International and local tensions call for caricature, not portrait. Today, more than a score of editorial cartoonists answer that demand—and answer it with astonishing quality. These artists fulfill the difficult prerequisites that Historian Allan Nevins lays down for their work: "Wit and humor; truth, at least one side of the truth; and moral purpose." After 100 years, the nation that nurtured Nast can be proud of his successors.

That, of course, is an ambiguous compliment. If U.S. cartoonists are nonpareil, might it be because they never lack for objects of derision? Is it because shortages, recession, political scandals and assorted other follies provide a perpetual festival for anyone with a grease pencil and a sense of humor? Whatever the reasons, the editorial cartoon is one of America's liveliest and most permanent art forms. As Watergate proved, politics cannot eradicate or even tame journalism. As subsequent events have demonstrated, the reverse is also true. Them damn pictures are likely to enliven the next hundred years—and more.

Aids   *Editorial Cartoons: Capturing the Essence*

1. What are editorial cartoons? Are not all cartoons in some respects "editorial"?

2. According to *Time,* what can cartoons do that prose cannot? In other words, what are some of the differences between verbal language and pictorial language?

3. Apply the following statement to some current editorial cartoons: "Editorial cartoons are cartoons with a message. They mean to sway public opinion. The weakest of them merely restate the news in graphic form. The strongest depict a political, social, or economic problem and, by implication, offer some solution."

4. Select an editorial cartoon from the editorial page of your local newspaper and answer the following questions:

   a. What characters are depicted? What do they represent? Look closely for identifying attributes such as hair styles, clothing, and symbols.

   b. What social or political issue is being commented upon?

   c. What is the message of the cartoon; that is, what attitude is being expressed about the issue?

d. Does the editorial view in the cartoon correspond to the political bias of the newspaper in which it appears?

e. What techniques does the cartoonist use to make his point? Techniques include analogy, symbolism, caricature, hyperbole, understatement, play on words, allusions to well-known sayings, song titles, or advertising slogans.

Write an editorial paper or speech in which you restate the message of the cartoon.

5. One of the functions of editorial cartoons is to satirize events and event makers, refining material "until only the ridiculous essence remains." Apply each of the following characteristics of satire to some current cartoons:

   a. Its purpose is to rebuke the failures, foibles, and ill manners in our present society.

   b. It adheres to the "doctrine of the golden mean" by attacking vices, which outnumber their respective virtues (the mean) by two to one; that is, every virtue has two corresponding vices, one of which is an excess, the other a deficiency. An excess of courage (the virtue), for instance, is recklessness, while the deficiency is cowardice.

   c. It demands a double view: the discrepancy between "what is" and "what should be."

   d. It varies greatly in tone: some satire, called Horatian, aims to correct by gentle, sympathetic laughter; another type, called Juvenalian, is bitter, angry, and biting, pointing with contempt and moral indignation at the corruption of institutions and men.

   e. It is based on rhetoric: a form of discourse speaking to a specific audience to bring out a specific end.

   f. It describes type characters and follows the rule: to pass over a single foe to charge whole armies.

   g. It uses the techniques of irony, exaggeration, understatement, and puns to achieve its ends.

6. Examine the structure and style of the *Time* essay. How does the essay begin? Where is the thesis? What kinds of evidence are used to support the thesis? How does the style reinforce the theme of the essay? Does the essay itself exhibit the pithy, concise quality of the editorial cartoons it is describing?

Unit IV

The Language of Film

The movies are in the awkward position of straddling that invisible line between popular culture and high art. Film has, of course, always been considered a genuine artistic medium by some intellectuals, especially Europeans. But in America in recent years movies have gained a new respectability, as evidenced by the prominence of film courses in the college curriculum and by scores of new books being published on the subject. Fifteen years ago the only "movie" magazines one could find on the newsstands were tabloids featuring lurid stories about the private lives of movie stars; now such publications have to share the rack with more serious enterprises like *The Film Journal*. Popular periodicals regularly feature articles on filmmaking; the techniques used in *The Exorcist* and *Jaws* have been widely discussed, for instance. Even small town newspapers publish regular film reviews. No popular art is accorded so much attention in print.

But how does one take a "serious" look at the movies? How does one evaluate its artistic merits? Describe its form? Account for its popular appeal? The emergence of a relatively new artistic medium seems to require a new vocabulary, a new language. Unfortunately, a new vocabulary is difficult to generate. Interestingly, in the search for a language with which to discuss film, many filmmakers and critics have seized upon language itself as the appropriate metaphor. Sergei Eisenstein, a Soviet filmmaker of the 1920s, wrote at length about "the grammar of cinema." In an essay, "Verbal and Visual Languages," Robert Richardson maintains that

> . . . the elements of film narrative, as they have existed since the mid-twenties, form not a figurative but an actual language. Language consists of vocabulary, grammar, and syntax. Vocabulary consists of words, which represent things or abstractions, while grammar and syntax are the means by which the words are arranged. The vocabulary of the film is the simple photographed image; the grammar and syntax of film are the editing, cutting, or montage processes by which the shots are arranged.[1]

In "The Word and the Image," William Jinks takes Richardson's language analogy one step further and likens film to the novel where the frame, the shot, the scene, and the sequence parallel the word, the sentence, the paragraph, and the chapter. Jinks's analysis is an obvious one. Marshall McLuhan has often pointed out that the old medium is frequently the content of the new, and many of our most popular films have been based on novels— *Love Story, Catch 22, The Exorcist,* and *Jaws.* English teachers often joke about the student who says, "Oh, I didn't need to read that book; I've seen the movie." Movie buffs argue about whether the book was better than the film or whether the movie did justice to the novel. Like Jinks, many critics and teachers of film use the language and assumptions of literary study in discussing movies. Film books and reviews are full of terms like plot, narrative, epic, and poetry.

Despite this emphasis on literary analogs, film and literature are vastly different media and some films (*8½, 2001, Tommy*) do not lend themselves to Jinks's framework. These are the films that interest Peter Schillaci, who in "Film as Environment" tries to capture the special quality of this sort of "film experience." The essay is very McLuhanesque in tone; he attempts by his choice of diction to convey the nonlinear, nonstructured quality of a movie like *2001: A Space Odyssey.* He sees in contemporary cinema reflections of television commercials and the format of "Laugh In" (or its British cousin, "Monty Python"). Schillaci perceives film neither as language or literature, but as environment.

Whatever our view of film and esthetics, we need to remember that the movies are popular culture and as such are big business. It is hard to make a feature-length film for less than a million dollars, discounting drive-in fare of the Kung Fu and soft core variety, and thus even independent filmmakers create with one eye on the box office. Of course, the filmmaker who is interested in selling the product must have some knowledge of the market. Thus, O. B. Hardison, a writer with a long-time interest in the cinema, regards the commerical filmmaker as a rhetorician. He says:

> The purpose of art is to give pleasure . . . the sort that comes from learning. . . . Rhetoric, on the other hand, is oriented toward the market place. Its purpose is not illumination but persuasion and its governing concept is that the work produced must be adjusted to the mind of the audience. . . . Rhetorical art

[1] Robert Richardson, *Literature and Film* (Bloomington: Indiana University Press, 1960), p. 65.

succeeds by saying what the audience has secretly known (or wanted to know) all along . . . professional entertainment goes according to formula. A formula is simply a way of doing things that work.[2]

It is difficult to deny the formulaic quality of many American films. Once the *Poseidon Adventure* proved a box office hit, the movie public was inundated with disaster films. *Variety,* an entertainment trade magazine, assures us that the success of *Jaws* will (and, in fact, has) generate "more shark thrillers, as well as scripts about killer bears, crocodiles, alligators, and even piranha fish."[3]

Some formulas, however, are more enduring than others. The western, the science fiction film, and the horror/monster movies have been around as long as the cinema itself. Maybe such films touch something special in our psyches, maybe they tap our most deep-seated fears and desires. This is the position taken by the author of an essay on the western film. John G. Cawelti, in "Savagery, Civilization and the Western Hero," uses the term "epic" to describe that brief moment in history in which "heroic individual defenders of law and order without the vast social resources of police and courts stand poised against the threat of lawlessness or savagery." Cawelti also shows how the epic formula is reinforced by geographic setting, which helps to dramatize the tripartite division of characters—the threatened townspeople, the lawless Indians/outlaws, and the hero—and by costume, which helps to reflect character and theme. Like the western, the science fiction film also has great appeal. Susan Sontag, in "The Imagination of Disaster," feels that our age labors under two fearful destinies—"unremitting banality and inconceivable terror." Fantasy, particularly that discovered in science fiction films, helps one deal with these horrors by both reflecting them and allaying them. Sontag maintains that these films are one of the most accomplished art forms. Her thesis is that science fiction films are not about science but disaster and in confronting absolute destruction on the screen viewers are better able to cope with the twin horrors of their own lives.

For a deeper analysis of the sociological implications of the science fiction/horror film we turn to X. J. Kennedy, who in "Who Killed King Kong?" tries to determine why the forty-year-old monster movie still appeals to large audiences. He concludes that we identify with Kong. We share his compulsion to destroy the machinery of our urban culture, and he reflects our reactions as captives of the industrial order. Kennedy's essay, too, is valuable in providing points of departure for discussions of more recent horror and disaster films.

Film genres, of course, are reshaped as public tastes change. During the 1960s the traditional horror film, for instance, was supplemented (though not replaced) by the psychological horror film. Films like *Psycho* and *Repulsion* used many of the standard conventions (ghostly apparitions, strange noises, dark passages, screams in the night) but in the end the horror could be

---

[2]O. B. Hardison, "The Rhetoric of Hitchcock's Thrillers," *Man and the Movies* (Baton Rouge: Louisiana State University Press, 1939), p. 138.
[3]*Variety,* July 30, 1975, p. 7.

explained away as the workings of a deranged mind. Interestingly, more recent films have returned to a more traditional explanation for such goings-on. In *Rosemary's Baby* and *The Exorcist* only the existence of evil and the supernatural can account for what transpires.

So the movies sell us formulas; they sell us what we want. But many filmwriters feel that the movies also tell us what we should want, or be. This is the point Marjorie Rosen makes in "Popcorn Venus: Or, How the Movies Have Made Women Smaller Than Life." Rosen maintains that for decades women have been manipulated by an image on the screen, an image which may have shaped their perceptions of themselves and others. Until recently, too, the image of the American Indian projected by Hollywood was the only image many Americans had. Blacks have seen themselves as so many mammies and maids, superstuds and Superflies, but rarely have they seen themselves in positive or realistic roles. Hopefully, films like *Sounder* and *Claudine* are the harbingers of a new image for black Americans in the movies. As Teena Webb, a political filmmaker says:

> All films, all art works for that matter, comment on society, either explicitly or implicitly. Often it's the implicit statements that are the most powerful and most of these are statements for support of the status quo. . . . To over-simplify, if the heroes in our movies are all rich, handsome, and white, whatever the plot may be, a statement is being made about the importance of being rich, handsome, and white.[4]

Some films, of course, take an explicit social or political position. *The Green Berets* and *Billy Jack* represent vastly different social and political views, but each depends on a rather stock set of stereotypes and symbols with which the sympathies of the audience are manipulated. Some films are openly propagandistic. Governments and political movements have long recognized the manipulatory potential of film. Hitler quickly brought the German film industry under his control, and scores of films glorifying Nazism were made under his direction. He commissioned Leni Reifenstahl to make *Triumph of the Will,* one of the most terrifyingly brilliant propaganda films ever made. Its subtle powers are described in the Kinder and Houston article. The techniques described in this essay (juxtaposition of scenes, camera angles, use of artifacts and symbols, stereotyping) are the stock devices of the propagandist. A filmmaker who uses these devices clumsily will leave his/her audiences unmoved; a skillful filmmaker, however, might affect the course of history.

In sum, the movies sell us images, they manipulate us, they assault our senses; but they also move us, excite us, and above all entertain us. The movies are a vast and complex topic. The selections in this unit represent only a small fraction of the material available on film. But these essays should familiarize you with the basic issues and questions regarding film and provide you with some of the tools you will need to take a serious (and sometimes not-so-serious) look at the movies.

4Teena Webb, "Political Filmmaking," *Women in Film* (summer 1975), p. 25.

The Word and the Image

WILLIAM JINKS

What follows is an extended analogy between the basic structural units of the novel—the word, sentence, paragraph, and chapter—and the elemental building blocks of the film—the frame, shot, scene, and sequence. And though Ezra Pound is very right in asserting that "you can *prove* nothing by analogy. [It] is either range-finding or fumble,"[1] the analogy can sometimes make the unfamiliar more accessible by relating it to the familiar. Thus, it is possible to recognize that—even though film is essentially a visual experience and literature a linguistic one—these two "languages" share a remarkable number of similarities.

The word and the image are similar in that they are both visual phenomena—they must both be perceived with the eye. On one hand, the string of letters that make up *farmhouse* demands that the reader convert the lifeless and yet suggestive word into an approximation of what the author intended. Transposing a word to an internalized image will necessarily evoke a highly individualized response, because everyone's experience of a farmhouse differs. To a boy raised in a city slum, *farmhouse* might mean "health," "contentment," "peace"; to a country boy who left home, it might mean "chores," "boredom," "endless, mindless drudgery." In short, the word "farmhouse" will be interpreted by the reader for himself.

On the other hand, it would seem that the film maker is able to exert a greater degree of control over his medium than the writer, since the picture of a farmhouse is much more explicit than the word itself. That is, it is not necessary to *translate* a picture into a mental image —film is literal, concrete, and explicit. The film maker is able to show precisely the farmhouse he has in mind—he doesn't have to trust that the reader will "see" the same farmhouse.

Yet, because his medium is so explicit, the film maker cannot utilize the kinds of ambiguities inherent in language that enable the novelist to suggest more than he says. For example, a novelist might write: "The weathered red barn in back of the house somehow always gave me a comforting feeling of security whenever I looked at it." The film maker can present a barn that is visually attractive, solid in appearance, but he cannot depend on his viewer to perceive the barn as an emblem of security unless he is willing to have an off-camera voice blatantly announce: "Please view this barn as a symbol of security." Yet despite the different degrees of explicitness and connotative control, both artists must work with "languages" that function in a remarkably similar fashion.

For the writer, the most integral unit of creation is the *word*. It is from the word that he creates his sentences, paragraphs, chapters, and ultimately, his book. For the film maker, the basic building block is the *frame*—a single transparent picture on a strip of film. Isolated, both the word and the frame have meaning, but that meaning

[1] Ezra Pound, *ABC of Reading* (New York: New Directions, 1960), p. 84.

243

is imprecise—the word and frame must be set in a context to clarify their meaning.

The word "quiver," for example, could be a reference to either a case for holding arrows—in which instance it would be a noun—or it might describe a particular kind of action as a verb. Even if the reader is able to assume that what he is dealing with is a verb rather than a noun, the ambiguity is still unresolved, for the reader is still unclear as to the nature of the verb. The verb could be indicating the movement that an arrow describes when it comes to rest, or simply the nature of a motion like a shaking movement—a tremor. Even if the reader is further advised that the verb is not describing the motion of an arrow, he still isn't quite sure as to how to perceive the essential character of the quivering movement—the tremor. If this motion, for example, describes a leaf, it is one thing; if it describes, on the other hand, a girl, it is something else again, for the tremor could be simply a reaction to the cold, or perhaps even the reaction to a fright—there even exists the possibility that it might be a combination of both fear and inclement weather.

Again, it might appear that with film, no such problem would exist because of the explicitness of the frame—it provides far more information than the single ambiguous word. And yet notice what happens when a viewer is confronted with the single frame. . . . The viewer sees the image of a cabin. The cabin appears to be unpainted pine with a wood-shingled roof, and from the outside the cabin appears to be a single large room. A simple chimney runs up the side of the windowless cabin. The background appears to be bean fields. The image might represent a sharecropper's house during the early depression days; but even if it does, despite the viewer's assurance of *what* he is seeing, there is still some doubt as to *how* to see the cabin. With only the single frame from which to work, it is very difficult to decide in what kind of context the picture needs to be placed, because several possibilities exist.

Perhaps the viewer is supposed to perceive the house as a nostalgic memory of a less complicated, less anxiety-ridden past. In this case, the frame takes on the kind of hard and simple beauty that James Agee[2] captured so well in his *Let Us Now Praise Famous Men*.

The house may appear in a documentary concerning the conditions of poverty in the United States. In this instance, the house is not a remnant of the past, but an eyesore in the present. It is a testimony to the discrepancies that exist between the "Haves" and the "Have-nots." Here the viewer would see the "shack" in the house, would probably feel sympathy or sorrow, perhaps even indignation.

The house may also appear in another kind of documentary—one produced by a government bureau, concerning the history of farming in the United States. Now the cabin represents only a survival of the historic past—an artifact. In this instance, the house (no longer a shack, notice) may well evoke pleasure on the part of the viewer. In comparing the contemporary farm dwellings with the cabin,

---

[2]James Agee was one man who was at home both with the novel and the film. His *A Death in the Family* was posthumously awarded the Pulitzer Prize in 1957. He also found time to write five screenplays, the most famous of which was John Huston's *The African Queen* (1952). In addition, he was a film critic for *Time* and *The Nation*, and many people consider him one of the most perceptive critics who ever wrote.

the viewer is even made to feel proud that the standard of living has been raised so substantially. Just as the reader would need to see "quiver" in the context of a sentence before he could be clear about the meaning of the word, the viewer would need to see the single frame of the farmhouse within the context of the shot.

A sentence typically clarifies the meaning of an individual word, sets it in a more meaningful perspective. In a complete sentence the word "quiver" would attain a more explicit meaning: *She quivered slightly at the coolness of the night air, then proceeded alone up the deserted street.* From this sentence, it is clear that the girl's quivering is the result of the night air, that the motion is a sign of physical discomfort. At the same time, the sentence is colored slightly by the phrase *then proceeded alone up the deserted street.* The additional information—that she is alone, that it is dark, quiet, and chilly—suggests a feeling of fear, of foreboding. Thus, in this sentence the word "quivered" seems to convey both physical discomfort and fear.

In order to provide the same degree of clarity for the film viewer, it would be necessary for him to see a *shot*—a fragment of a film which has been taken, either actually or apparently, in one uninterrupted running of the camera. The shot, in other words, serves the same function for the film maker that the sentence does for the novelist. For example, if a film maker were shooting an important tennis match and wanted to indicate the tension of the contest to an audience, it is very unlikely that he would follow the exchanges of the match like a spectator. That approach would not only be repetitive, monotonous, and dizzying to follow, but it would probably also be completely devoid of tension —the viewer would be so caught up in the very mechanics of watching that the excitement of the match would be lost. To evoke the feeling of tension inherent in the match, the film maker would probably cut extensively during the event. (A *cut* is an instantaneous transition from one shot to another and is usually easy to spot in a film because it is invariably accompanied by a shift of camera position.) He might open with a long shot of the two antagonists facing each other, then cut to a medium shot of the player who was serving, then perhaps to a close-up of the taut face of the player waiting to return the ball. In this instance, the slowing down and breaking up of the action—converting it into shots—has helped to convey the tension involved in the contest.

* * *

For the viewer, then, a shot of the farmhouse discussed above is clearly easier to "read" than the single frame—like the sentence, the shot provides an enlarged context. For example, the viewer might first see the farmhouse at a distance of fifty feet or so, then perhaps the camera begins to zoom* in toward the house and stops only when the doorway of the house nearly fills the entire screen (both the establishing shot of the house and the succeeding zoom would be considered one shot). Perhaps the camera remains focused on the doorway for a moment, and soon a woman comes to the door carrying a bucket. She wears a torn, ill-fitting cotton dress, and though her body looks young,

*A zoom lens is a lens whose focal length can be changed, thus altering the magnification of the image.

her face appears drawn and haggard, and her shoulders seem to bend forward slightly. She leans against the doorframe and, for a moment, looks rather vacantly in the direction of the horizon. There is something about her stance that suggests a "bone-tired" kind of weariness. The shot concludes with her standing in the doorway.

This single shot might be as short as ten seconds; yet notice how much information it conveys. First, it becomes apparent that the house and its occupant are not being romanticized—the stark, weary figure of the woman precludes that kind of an interpretation. Second, although it is not impossible, it is unlikely that the footage represents an excerpt from a documentary concerning this nation's farming history. There are clues within the shot itself that suggest what the film maker is doing. The establishing shot (a shot that sets the scene) seems to remain with the house only long enough to suggest location: then it quickly moves to the doorway of the house, implying that it is the occupant or occupants of the house who are the real focus of attention. Also, the woman in the doorway is presented in a very special way. There is the contradiction between her youthful body and prematurely aged face; there comes the realization that she carries the water to the door because she probably has no plumbing; there is pathos in the sudden knowledge that she continues to wear what is clearly a rag because she has nothing to replace it with. These carefully selected details shape the response of the viewer just as surely as the phrase *then proceeded alone up the deserted street* alters and implements the verb *quiver*. Though the question of *what* the word or shot refers to is answered in part by the context, other questions in the reader's and viewer's minds remain to be solved. But expectations of answers have been raised, and these answers can be provided through referring to a broader context.

A paragraph, a series of closely related sentences, typically gives the reader additional information about a particular "key" sentence in it, as in the case of the sentence about the solitary girl:

> The car seemed to be in the throes of death, the way it jerked and stalled. She looked at the gas gauge and discovered the source of her problem—it read empty. She was in a section of town where even the residents stayed behind carefully locked doors at night, and her face showed apprehension as she let the car drift to the curb. After securing the car doors, she stepped out onto the sidewalk. She quivered slightly at the coolness of the night air then proceeded alone up the deserted street.

This paragraph, it should be noted, is set up much as a film maker might conceive a five-shot scene—an interior close-up shot of the girl being jostled about in the car; an extreme close-up of a gas gauge reading empty, followed by a shot of her tense face; a medium shot of the car drifting toward the curb; a medium-close shot of the girl locking the car and walking up the street of the deserted neighborhood. In this instance, the paragraph has revealed how the girl came to be in this particular predicament, and the paragraph also confirms the implications of fear that previously were only suggested.

A *scene* is ordinarily an action which is unified around a specific action or event and, normally, is also united by considerations of a time and place. The following three-shot scene of the sharecropper's cabin would remove most of the aforementioned ambiguity as to the type of film the audience is seeing:

Shot #1: Medium shot of the cabin; a slow zoom shot stopping when the doorway of the cabin fills the frame. A woman, walking from the interior, appears in the doorway holding a pan of water. She looks toward the camera.

cut to:

Shot #2: Long shot of a man, perhaps a quarter of a mile away, walking along a dirt road that is lined sparsely with pines. His feet set up small, barely discernible puffs of dust as he walks.

cut to:

Shot #3: The woman, as she was before, looking toward the camera. Abruptly she tosses the water into the yard and returns to the darkened interior of the house.

With this scene, the viewer's speculations are, in part, resolved. No longer is it necessary for him to guess how he should "read" the information he is witnessing. The hardship, the weariness of the people's lives has become readily apparent. It is also apparent, from this three-shot scene, that the film maker is able to exert the kind of artistic control that is ordinarily associated only with the novelist.

* * *

Eventually the novelist combines his paragraphs into larger units—chapters. In many respects, the chapter resembles an expanded paragraph; it is usually unified by one central focus. A chapter could derive its unification from a single incident or event; it might cover the events of a particular period of time—an hour, day, year, or even a generation. A chapter

could limit itself to a description of a single character. Sometimes unity can be achieved by means of a physical setting: a room, a town, or a country.

In the example of the stranded girl, the episode of her running out of gas might be just one of many similar unpleasant occurrences in the same chapter. Earlier, she may have been threatened over the telephone. Sometime later, an inexplicable fire takes place in the kitchen of her house while she is asleep. While crossing the street, she narrowly averts being run over by an automobile. Finally, she runs out of gas in a dangerous neighborhood. All of these incidents might have one thing in common: the deliberate terrorizing of the girl. Thus, the incidents form a common thread that unifies the chapter into a coherent whole.

Chapters, like paragraphs, are distinct divisions of a novel and are usually characterized by coherence, unity, and completeness. It is difficult, however, to say *exactly* what it is that distinguishes a paragraph from a chapter. Typically, the chapter is much longer than a paragraph, but there are instances of chapters in novels being no longer than a couple of sentences (Laurence Sterne's innovative *Tristram Shandy* and Ken Kesey's *One Flew Over the Cuckoo's Nest* are two obvious examples). The problem is even more complicated when the *sequence*—the film's equivalent of the chapter—is considered.

The film, for example, does not have its narrative neatly divided into chapters (although British film maker Lindsay Anderson, in a film entitled *If . . .* [1969], did utilize an eight-part chapter-like division). The sequence—a series of closely related scenes—is subject to precisely the same criteria as the chapter: namely, unity, coherence, and completeness. In some instances, such as Anderson's *If . . .*, or Stanley Kubrick's *2001: A Space Odyssey* (1969) with its three-part division, the separation between sequences is apparent. In most films, however, it is more difficult to recognize and define the divisions.

The previously described scene of the sharecroppers would, most likely, represent a part of a sequence. The entire film might be composed of three thirty-minute sequences. This scene would be part of the first sequence, depicting the poverty and deprivation of a single family in the rural South. This first sequence might conclude with the family's decision to move north to a large city, and hopefully, a better life. The second sequence might describe their journey to the North, while the third could reveal the protagonists in their new environment. As with chapters in a novel, the possibilities for creating sequences are virtually unlimited; the artist need merely establish the relationship of one scene to another.

In order to compare the language of film with the language of literature, it was necessary to ignore, for the most part, the very striking dissimilarities of the two genres. Although a metaphor and a simile can enlarge perception by comparing the familiar with the unfamiliar or by examining something in a slightly altered perspective, it is essential to consider the peculiarities of each of the genres in order to determine how they differ from each other.

To begin with, film is a multi-sensory communal experience emphasizing immediacy, whereas literature is a mono-sensory private experience that is more conducive to reflection. A film is usually viewed in the presence of others who necessarily become part of the total gestalt of the film experience. Ideally, each member of the audience

respects the presence of others and opens himself to the film. A tall hat, a noisy popcorn chewer, or a self-appointed narrator can adversely affect the impact of the film. The responses of the audience can also affect the perception of a film—an inappropriate laugh can provoke irritation, while infectious laughter can increase delight.

A novel, however, is typically a private experience, in which the relationship between the author and the reader is relatively direct and immediate. The responses of others do not impinge on the novel as they do on the film. The novel is also conducive to reflection, as the reader can pause and consider an important passage or mull over a particular phrase. This convenience, of course, is denied the viewer because the film moves unceasingly toward its conclusion (though developments in cassette television may soon change this).

But the film and the novel are alike insofar as their order is typically linear. For the most part, the movement in the novel as well as the film could be described as sequential—events and scenes are ordered in direct relation to each other. The exception, of course, would be a film like Alain Resnais' *Last Year at Marienbad* (1961), which deliberately eschews causality as well as psychological motivation. However, whether the order be A, B, C or C, B, A, the progression is usually straightforward. This tends to be true even if a film or novel opens with a conclusion (Orson Welles' *Citizen Kane* [1940] or Thornton Wilder's *Bridge of San Luis Rey* come to mind—both open with the protagonist's death); and even though the normal order has been reversed, the narrative will still tend to follow a relatively predictable, sequential path.

One of the exciting features of the film experience is its immediacy—the fact that the film is occurring *right now* before the audience's eyes. Although immediacy tends to promote greater involvement, it also creates certain problems for the film maker. Most of them center around considerations of time.

In order to describe a peculiar habit of one of his characters, a novelist might simply write: "Every day for six months at precisely eleven thirty-two, he would seat himself at a park bench on 27th Avenue and count the buses that passed." The reader unquestionably accepts the suggested duration of time; in other words, to the reader, it seems credible. For a film maker, this sentence would pose a problem. He would have to portray, visually and convincingly, the passage of six months in a relatively short segment of film. This would entail a number of shots of the man on the bench counting busses; it would also be necessary to indicate, within the shots, the passage of time. Typically, this would be accomplished by use of the background: trees blooming, leaves falling, then, finally, the stark, leafless, skeletal trees of winter. The changing attire of the man—short-sleeved shirt to jacket to overcoat—would also support this impression.

Conversely, a novelist might well devote an entire chapter to an event that actually took only seconds to transpire. A man nearly drowns. As he struggles to the surface and subsequently sinks again, the events of his life flit through his mind. Despite the fact that it might take an entire chapter to describe what thoughts race through his mind during this crisis, a reader would have no problem in accepting this chapter as credible. The film maker, however, cannot take advantage of this particular convention. If he moves the scene too rapidly, the viewer loses the density of the experience. If he takes too

much time with the scene, its credibility is called into question. Robert Enrico, in his Cannes Film Festival Award-winning short film, *Occurrence at Owl Creek Bridge* (1961), does manage to successfully "stretch" the passage of a second or two into seventeen minutes. In order to do so, he has to introduce some ambiguities that make the viewer realize that time is being altered—but not why. The viewer believes that he is witnessing the miraculous escape of a man who was almost hanged, when in fact he is witnessing the internalized fantasy of a condemned man at the gallows.

It is a relatively easy task for the novelist to manipulate time. He can, for example, employ a narrator who tells a story from two vantage points simultaneously. The narrator can relate events that happened to him when he was seventeen as though he were again experiencing those same events in the present. The narrator, however, is now twenty-seven and the distance from the experience is ten years. Nevertheless, the writer can alternate between these two mentalities, the seventeen-year-old and the twenty-seven-year-old (as, for instance, John Updike does in his highly praised short story, *Flight*), with little difficulty. The film maker, however, will usually select one or the other (though not always, as in Ingmar Bergman's *Wild Strawberries* [1957]). Although it is possible to accompany the earlier scene with the voice of the older narrator, a strikingly different effect than the novelist's dual narrator is produced. The "voice over" (off-camera narration) tends to undermine the immediacy of the earlier scene.

There is, in addition, another curious feature that distinguishes time in a film: technically speaking, film time is always present tense. For example, open a conventional novel to a passage that deals with the past and the verbs alone will signal you that these events occurred some time ago. On the other hand, walk into a theater while a contemporary movie is in progress and try to determine whether you're watching past, present, future, or fantasy. Certainly, given enough time you would figure it out, but the point is that without the additional context, you'd have no way of knowing.

Not only is time employed differently in a film, but space is as well. In the novel, the reader brings his own experience to bear on the novelist's suggestions. If the novelist describes a building, the reader, having had the experience of visualizing a building, will tend to see a structure that conforms not only to the novelist's description but also to his own accumulated experience. Much of Wallace Stevens' poetry, for instance, is "about" or at least deals directly with this convention. In a film, however, the camera sees differently from the eye itself or the mind's eye, and the viewer tends to be more passive than the reader since the *conceptualization* of a scene is provided by the film.

This raises the entire question of conceptualization in the novel and the film. By its very nature, the film tends to be concrete and literal. The novel, on the other hand, is abstract and suggestive. The distinction is an important one, for it means that it is very difficult for the film to deal with abstractions. A brief example might serve to point up this distinction. In one of Macbeth's most famous speeches, he exclaims:

Tomorrow and tomorrow and tomorrow
Creeps in this petty pace from day to day,

To the last syllable of recorded time;
And all our yesterdays have lighted fools
The way to dusty death. (Act V; sc. 5)

In the first two lines, Shakespeare has made use of personification; he describes an abstraction—tomorrow—as having the ability to creep, an activity that is usually limited to something animate. Similarly, in the following lines, he suggests that yesterdays (again, an abstraction) have "lighted fools the way to dusty death." The unusual juxtaposition of the abstract with the concrete produces a striking literary trope. A film maker obviously could have an actor deliver Macbeth's speech, but could not possibly film the kind of tropes that the speech includes. How, for example, could a film maker render the following in visual terms: a sea of troubles, a dusty nothing, liberty plucking authority by the nose, a dagger of the mind? The film, of course, through metaphors, similes, and symbols, does deal with abstractions, but it must necessarily render them in concrete images.

The literal-mindedness of the camera also produces other problems. Many writers (Nathaniel Hawthorne in *Young Goodman Brown*, Herman Melville in *Bartleby, the Scrivener*, and Franz Kafka in *The Trial*)[3] have successfully created characters who are representative figures of mankind. In each of these tales, there is little physical description of the central character, with the result that he becomes "universalized," an Everyman. The camera, however, produces the opposite effect; it tends to wed the character and the role forever. It is very difficult to imagine *La Strada* (1954) without Giulietta Masina; *The Seventh Seal* (1957) without Max Von

---

[3]Kafka's *The Trial* was brought to the screen in 1962, script and direction by Orson Welles.

Sydow; *The Graduate* (1968) without Dustin Hoffman; and *Cries and Whispers* (1973) without Ingrid Thulin, Harriet Andersson, Liv Ullman, and Kari Sylwan. Likewise, it is not enough for a character to experience a particular scene as beautiful or threatening. In order to convince the viewers, the scene must actually be filmed as beautiful or threatening.

Finally, it should always be recognized that the film is a multi-dimensional experience; it combines sight and sound with movement. A film maker who is too "literary," who relies too heavily on dialogue, will produce a film that is "talky." In fact, at times there seems to be a basic conflict between literate or complex language and visual imagery. In Anthony Harvey's *The Lion in Winter* (1968), James Goldman's witty, literate screenplay provides the players with sparkling dialogue, yet the film itself seems almost totally devoid of any memorable images. Cartoonist Jules Feiffer, who wrote the screenplay for Mike Nichols' *Carnal Knowledge* (1971), created a script that was excessively talkative; in order to prevent the audience from being distracted from the characters' speeches by competitive visuals, Nichols was forced to constantly employ darkened and semi-darkened lighting for the interior shots and extreme long shots for the exteriors.

Likewise, a film maker who doesn't understand the languages of vision and movement may end up producing a film that is visually static. Some film makers attempt to avoid this by "opening up" the play with exterior shots and scenes that take place away from the primary setting. Mike Nichols did this in *Who's Afraid of Virginia Woolf?* (1966) with the opening shots of the college campus and later, the roadhouse scene. William Freidkin's *Boys in the Band* (1970), similarly, opened with a montage of short scenes showing what the main characters were doing just prior to their arrival at Michael's apartment.

The dramatist, of course, must confine his action to a relatively small area and restrict the movements of his characters because of the spatial limitations of the stage. In a film, however, "all the world's a stage," and the film maker who ignores this creates a film that seems to the viewer to be unnecessarily restricted and confined.

Aids   *The Word and the Image*

1. The main body of Jinks's essay consists of two parts. In the first part he develops an extended analogy between a literary form, the novel, and film. Analogy is essentially a comparison between two things that are alike in certain respects but unlike in other respects. What are the individual components of Jinks's analogy? In what respects are these components similar? In what respects are they different? Using Edmund Carpenter's essay, "The New Languages" (in Unit I), discuss the difficulties inherent in comparing different media, each of which is a separate language with a unique bias. Does Jinks's analogy succeed in making the "unfamiliar more accessible by relating it to the familiar"?

2. Every writer makes assumptions about the educational background, experience, and verbal ability of his audience; to ignore one's audience is to risk being misunderstood and, hence, ignored. What assumptions is William Jinks making about his audience? Does he assume that you have a working knowledge of basic literary terms, such as "characterization," "structure," "theme," "point of view," "metaphor"? Is an understanding of these terms essential to an understanding of the essay? Where would you go to find out the meanings of such terms?

3. William Jinks, as we have seen, chooses the analogy of literature to describe the basic structural units of film; the word, sentence, paragraph, and chapter are likened to the frame, shot, scene, and sequence. It is clear, too, that the making of a film parallels the writing of a paper or report. Our knowledge of film techniques, in fact, may be useful in helping us to learn as well as to remember some principles of effective composition. Both a film and a paper, for example, require a central idea or thesis; without one the result would be a boring tour through the miscellaneous. Assume that your topic was "visual pollution." As a filmmaker you would have to decide what you wanted to say *about* the subject: i.e., it makes your city ugly; it is a health and safety hazard; every citizen should do his or her share to prevent it; and so forth. Second, you would have to decide what examples you needed to support your thesis, and if you were actually filming, you would be forced to focus on select, representative examples; i.e., to support the thesis that commercial signs and billboards are unsightly, you would have to film a brief sequence of shots showing rows of signs for fast food restaurants, car dealerships, and discount stores. And third, like the writer, you would no doubt collect more data than you actually need to make your point and, as a result, you would need to edit your documentation and, if necessary, reshoot or revise some of the scenes. What other parallels exist between filmmaking and writing?

4. In filmmaking the distance of the camera from the object or person being filmed is important. If the camera is far from the subject, the result will be a long shot; a long shot would typically include a lot of background. If a camera is brought in closer, the result would be a medium shot; the same subject would seem closer to the viewer and if the subject were a person, the shot might show that person only from the knees up. If the camera is brought in closer still, the result would be a closeup which would show only the person's face. Moving from a long shot to a closeup in the same scene is a common device in filmmaking. When the filmmakers do this, they are doing just what

the good writer does—moving from the general to the specific. Consider this paragraph from Carson McCuller's novel, *The Heart Is a Lonely Hunter*. Jake, a character in the book, is walking down the street. "Weaver's Lane was dark. Oil lamps made yellow, trembling patches of light in the doorways and windows. Some of the houses were entirely dark and the families sat on the front steps with only the reflections from a neighboring house to see by. A woman leaned out of a window and splashed a pail of dirty water into the street. A few drops of it splashed on Jake's face." If you were a filmmaker how would you shoot this scene? Examine it sentence by sentence and ask yourself what each sentence requires—a long shot, a medium shot or a closeup.

5. Good writers provide their readers with verbal cues when they are about to move into another topic, make another point, provide a new piece of information. Transitional words and phrases like "furthermore," "on the other hand," and "however" tell the reader that he or she is about to move into new territory. Filmmakers, too, provide signposts when they are about to change the subject. Look for the transitional devices used in film—fade-out fade-in sequences to suggest the passage of time, a wavering screen image to tell us we are about to witness a flashback. What other transitional devices do filmmakers use?

6. As Jinks points out, film is a very concrete medium. Writers have at their disposal many shades of language from the most concrete to the most abstract. A writer can easily communicate the terror of a young girl who confronts an assailant alone at night; she or he can describe the beating of the girl's heart, allude to her sweating palms, even tell us of her thoughts and feelings. How would a filmmaker handle the same situation? To get a feel for the difficulties a filmmaker faces, try the following exercise: write a passage in which you describe an emotional state (love, hate, fear) from a totally subjective point of view; you might want to verbalize the scene of the terror-stricken girl mentioned earlier. After completing this version, then rewrite the same scene from a totally objective point of view, allowing yourself to *see* no more than a movie camera would see. Examine the language you have used in the two passages. How is it different?

7. Like writers, film directors often develop a characteristic film *style*, a style you might recognize after viewing three or four of his or her films. A director's style might be characterized by use of color (Ken Russell), editing (Kubrick or Penn), or themes (Peckinpah's violence, Walt Disney's sanitized view of life). If you have the opportunity,

view two or three films directed by the same person. Try to characterize the director's style. Style will, of course, depend on more than one
dimension. You may have to talk about different aspects of the film
to capture your director's "uniqueness."

8. Although William Jinks explores film by comparing it to the written
word, he is careful to point out that film and literature are two very
different artistic media. It is literally impossible to translate a piece
of fiction to the screen, or a movie into a short story. Each medium
has its own strengths and weaknesses. Watch your local theater and
television listings for a film that is based on a novel or story you have
read. Decide in advance that you will focus your attention on one
major scene or episode. How does the film treatment differ from the
literary treatment? How is set handled in each? How are thoughts
and feelings revealed? Has the dialog been changed? Is there more
dialog? less? Do you feel that the changes made by the director were
necessary given the medium in which he/she was working? Do you
think the changes strengthen or weaken the scene?

9. Jinks points out that there is a difference between *literary* language
and *visual* language. The movies were meant to move and a filmmaker who relies too heavily on dialog may produce a film that is
"talky." In order to avoid tedium in "talky" scenes, some directors
will try to introduce visual variety in such scenes—medium shots
moving to closeups, change of camera angle, use of unusual lighting
or lighting changes. If you happen to watch a film that is heavily
dependent on dialog, watch closely and note any attempt on the director's part to introduce visual variety in the scene.

Film as Environment

PETER P. SCHILLACI

The better we understand how young people view film, the more we have to revise our notion of what film is. Seen through young eyes, film is destroying conventions almost as quickly as they can be formulated. Whether the favored director is "young" like Richard Lester, Roman Polanski, and Arthur Penn, or "old" like Kubrick, Fellini, and Buñuel,[1] he must be a practicing cinematic anarchist to catch the eye of the young. If we're looking for the young audience between sixteen and twenty-four, which accounts for 48 per cent of the box office today, we will find they're on a trip, whether in a Yellow Submarine or on a Space Odyssey. A brief

Abridged from Peter P. Schillaci, "Film as Environment," *Saturday Review*, December 28, 1968. Copyright © 1968 by Saturday Review, Inc. Reprinted by permission of the publisher and the author.

[1]Richard Lester, director of *A Hard Day's Night* and *Help*; Roman Polanski, director of *Repulsion* and *Rosemary's Baby*; Arthur Penn, director of *Bonnie and Clyde* and *Little Big Man*; Stanley Kubrik, director of *Dr. Strangelove* and *2001*; Federico Fellini, director of *8 1/2* and *Amacord*; Luis Buñuel, director of *Viridiana* and *Belle de Jour*. (eds.)

prayer muttered for Rosemary's Baby and they're careening down a dirt road with Bonnie and Clyde, the exhaust spitting banjo sounds, or sitting next to The Graduate as he races across the Bay Bridge after his love. The company they keep is fast; Belle de Jour, Petulia, and Joanna are not exactly a sedentary crowd. Hyped up on large doses of *Rowan and Martin's Laugh-In*, and *Mission: Impossible*, they are ready for anything that an evolving film idiom can throw on the screen. And what moves them must have the pace, novelty, style, and spontaneity of a television commercial.

All of this sounds as if the script is by McLuhan. Nevertheless, it is borne out by the experience of teaching contemporary film to university juniors and seniors, staging film festivals for late teens and early adults, and talking to literally hundreds of people about movies. The phenomenon may be interesting, and even verifiable, but what makes it important is its significance for the future of film art. The young have discovered that film is an environment which you put on, demanding a different kind of structure, a different mode of attention than any other art. Their hunger is for mind-expanding experience and simultaneity, and their art is film.

Occasionally a young director gives us a glimpse of the new world of film as environmental art. The optical exercise known as *Flicker* came on like a karate chop to the eyes at Lincoln Center's Film Seminar three years ago. One half-hour of white light flashing at varied frequency, accompanied by a deafening sound track designed to infuriate, describes the screen, but not what happened to the audience. As strangers turned to ask if it was a put-on, if they had forgotten to put film in the projector, they noticed that the flickering light fragmented their motions, stylizing them like the actions of a silent movie. In minutes, the entire audience was on its feet, acting out spontaneous pantomimes for one another, no one looking at the flashing screen. The happening precipitated by *Flicker* could be called the film of the future, but it was actually an anti-environment that gives us an insight into the past. By abstracting totally from content, the director demonstrated that the film is in the audience which acts out personal and public dramas as the screen turns it on. The delight of this experience opened up the notion of film as an environmental art.

Critics have noted the trend which leaves story line and character development strewn along the highways of film history like the corpses in Godard's[2] *Weekend*. The same critics have not, in general, recognized that the growing option for nonlinear, unstructured experiences that leave out sequence, motivation, and "argument" is a vote for film as environment. Young people turn to film for a time-space environment in which beautiful things happen to them. The screen has, in a sense, less and less to do with what explodes in the audience. This new scene could mean either that film

[2]Jean-Luc Godard, a contemporary French director. (eds.)

is plunging toward irrelevant stimulation, or that there is a new and unprecedented level of participation and involvement in young audiences.
I prefer to think the latter is the case. Young people want to talk about
Ben's hang-up, why Rosemary stayed with the baby, or what it feels like
to be in the electronic hands of a computer like Hal. They do not forget
the film the minute they walk out of the theater.

The attention given the new style of film goes beyond stimulation
to real involvement. A generation with eyes fixed on the rearview mirror
tended to give film the same attention required for reading—that is, turning
off all the senses except the eyes. Film became almost as private as reading,
and little reaction to the total audience was experienced. As the Hollywood
dream factory cranked out self-contained worlds of fantasy, audiences
entered them with confidence that nothing even vaguely related to real
life would trouble their reveries. As long as one came and left in the middle
of the film, it was relatively noninvolving as environment. When television
brought the image into the living room, people gave it "movie attention,"
hushing everyone who entered the sacred presence of the tube as they
would a film patron who talked during a movie. One was not allowed to
speak, even during commercials. It took post-literate man to teach us how
to use television as environment, as a moving image on the wall to which
one may give total or peripheral attention as he wishes. The child who
had TV as a baby-sitter does not turn off all his senses, but walks about
the room carrying on a multiplicity of actions and relationships, his
attention a special reward for the cleverness of the pitchman, or the skill
of the artist. He is king, and not captive. As McLuhan would put it, he
is not an audience, he *gives* an audience to the screen.

The new multisensory involvement with film as total environment has
been primary in destroying literary values in film. Their decline is not
merely farewell to an understandable but unwelcome dependency; it means
the emergence of a new identity for film. The diminished role of dialogue is
a case in point. The difference between *Star Trek* and *Mission: Impossible*
marks the trend toward self-explanatory images that need no dialogue.
Take an audio tape of these two popular TV shows, as we did in a recent
study, and it will reveal that while *Mission: Impossible* is completely unintelligible without images, *Star Trek* is simply an illustrated radio serial,
complete on the level of sound. It has all the characteristics of radio's
golden age: actions explained, immediate identification of character by voice
alone, and even organ music to squeeze the proper emotion or end the
episode. Like *Star Trek*, the old film was frequently a talking picture
(emphasis on the adjective), thereby confirming McLuhan's contention that
technologically "radio married the movies." The marriage of dependence,
however, has gone on the rocks, and not by a return to silent films but a

new turning to foreign ones. It was the films of Fellini and Bergman, with their subtitles, that convinced us there had been too many words. Approximately one-third of the dialogue is omitted in subtitled versions of these films, with no discernible damage—and some improvement— of the original.

More than dialogue, however, has been jettisoned. Other literary values, such as sequential narrative, dramatic choice, and plot are in a state of advanced atrophy, rapidly becoming vestigial organs on the body of film art as young people have their say. *Petulia* has no "story," unless one laboriously pieces together the interaction between the delightful arch-kook and the newly divorced surgeon, in which case it is nothing more than an encounter. The story line wouldn't make a ripple if it were not scrambled and fragmented into an experience that explodes from a free-floating present into both past and future simultaneously. *Petulia* is like some views of the universe which represent the ancient past of events whose light is just now reaching us simultaneously with the future of our galaxy, returning from the curve of outer space. Many films succeed by virtue of what they leave out. *2001: A Space Odyssey* is such a film, its muted understatement creating gaps in the action that invite our inquiry. Only a square viewer wants to know where the black monolith came from and where it is going. For most of the young viewers to whom I have spoken, it is just there. *Last Year at Marienbad*[3] made the clock as limply shapeless as one of Salvador Dali's watches, while *8 1/2* came to life on the strength of free associations eagerly grasped by young audiences. The effect of such films is a series of open-ended impressions, freely evoked and enjoyed, strongly inviting inquiry and involvement. In short, film is freed to work as environment, something which does not simply contain, but shapes people, tilting the balance of their faculties, radically altering their perceptions, and ultimately their views of self and all reality. Perhaps one sense of the symptomatic word "grooving," which applies to both sight and sound environments, is that a new mode of attention—multi-sensory, total, and simultaneous—has arrived. When you "groove," you do not analyze, follow an argument, or separate sensations; rather, you are massaged into a feeling of heightened life and consciousness.

If young people look at film this way, it is in spite of the school, a fact which says once more with emphasis that education is taking place outside the classroom walls. The "discovery" that television commercials are the most exciting and creative part of today's programming is old news to the young. Commercials are a crash course in speed-viewing, their intensified sensations challenging the viewer to synthesize impressions at an ever increasing rate. The result is short films like one produced at

[3]Film by French director Alain Resnais. (eds.)

UCLA, presenting 3,000 years of art in three minutes. *God Is Dog Spelled Backwards* takes you from the cave paintings of Lascaux to the latest abstractions, with some images remaining on the screen a mere twenty-fourth of a second![4] The young experience the film, however, not as confusing, but as exuberantly and audaciously alive. They feel joy of recognition, exhilaration at the intense concentration necessary (one blink encompasses a century of art), and awe at the 180-second review of every aspect of the human condition. Intended as a put-on, the film becomes a three-minute commercial for man. This hunger for overload is fed by the television commercial, with its nervous jump cuts demolishing continuity, and its lazy dissolves blurring time-space boundaries. Whether the young are viewing film "through" television, or simply through their increased capacity for information and sensation (a skill which makes most schooling a bore), the result is the same—film becomes the primary environment in which the hunger to know through experience is satisfied.

Hidden within this unarticulated preference of the young is a quiet tribute to film as the art that humanizes change. In its beginnings, the cinema was celebrated as the art that mirrored reality in its functional dynamism. And although the early vision predictably gave way to misuse of the medium, today the significance of the filmic experience of change stubbornly emerges again. Instead of prematurely stabilizing change, film celebrates it. The cinema can inject life into historical events by the photoscan, in which camera movement and editing liberate the vitality of images from the past. *City of Gold*, a short documentary by the National Film Board of Canada, takes us by zoom and cut into the very life of the Klondike gold rush, enabling us to savor the past as an experience.

Education increasingly means developing the ability to live humanly in the technological culture by changing with it. Film is forever spinning out intensifications of the environment which make it visible and livable. The ability to control motion through its coordinates of time and space make film a creative agent in change. Not only does film reflect the time-space continuum of contemporary physics, but it can manipulate artistically those dimensions of motion which we find most problematic. The actuality of the medium, its here-and-now impact, reflects how completely the present tense has swallowed up both past and future. Freudian psychology dissolves history by making the past something we live; accelerated change warps the future by bringing it so close that we can't conceive it as "ahead" of us. An art which creates its own space, and can move time forward and back, can humanize change by conditioning us to live comfortably immersed in its fluctuations.

* * *

[4]See also Pyramid Film's *An American Time Capsule* and *The Sixties*. (eds.)

Aids   *Film as Environment*

1. Schillaci has obviously been influenced by the ideas of Marshall McLuhan. How are McLuhan's ideas of participation, simultaneity, and the nonlinear nature of the electronic media reflected in Schillaci's essay? (If you are unsure about McLuhan's views, reread the essay on McLuhan in Unit I). What examples of "McLuhanesque" language can you find in this essay?

2. Peter Schillaci's thesis hinges on a rather abstract idea. What is Schillaci's thesis? Note how he uses metaphors to take his argument from the abstract to the realm of concrete experience. Do his metaphors help you understand the point he is making? Examine Schillaci's first paragraph. How does his use of language there suggest the immediacy of the experience he is describing?

3. Schillaci uses a few metaphors that have become rather stock among media people—Hollywood Dream Factory, the rear view mirror. Are these metaphors clichés? How can you tell when a metaphor or any sort of figurative expression has become a cliché?

4. Schillaci's essay is full of action words like *explode* and *plunging*. How does his use of such words support his thesis?

5. Schillaci says that "When you groove, you do not analyze, follow arguments, or separate sensations; rather you are massaged into a feeling of heightened life and consciousness." Does this definition make sense to you? Have you had the experience he describes? Is Schillaci's essay meant to be analyzed or grooved?

6. Jinks notes that the narrative ordering of events in literature is typically linear and sequential, i.e., things tend to happen chronologically. Schillaci, however, maintains that in modern films literary values such as sequential narrative "are in a state of advanced atrophy." Many films employ nonsequential narrative techniques; that is, the chronological time is distorted or rearranged by dream sequences, fantasies, flashbacks or flashforwards. For example, a middle-aged hero who is going through a crisis in his life might think back to certain scenes in his youth; those flashbacks would appear on the screen as if the events were happening in the present. Nonsequential narration is often used when a director wishes to explore a character's mental state. The next time you go to the movies or watch a film on television, note how the filmmaker manipulates time. If the film contains nonsequential techniques, consider

the ways in which the handling of the narrative contributes to mood and the themes of the film. Television commercials are a good source of nonsequential narration. When you find nonsequential narration in a commercial, ask yourself how the narration contributes to the effectiveness of the commercial.

7. Schillaci stresses the multisensory involvement of film. Sound is a very important and often overlooked component of this multisensory involvement. Music, for example, can have a profound effect on an audience. Often it simply sets the mood—romance, excitement, tension. Sometimes it is used to evoke a particular time or place (the Scott Joplin music in *The Sting*). Sometimes the music actually undercuts the action on the screen and thereby modifies our responses to that action. (The bluegrass music in *Bonnie and Clyde* makes the robbing and killing seem somehow less real.) Next time you watch a film, listen carefully to the sound track. Try to evaluate the music's effect on you and on the audience. Be aware of when music is simply used as background and when it is trying to affect the audience's responses.

Savagery and Civilization*

JOHN G. CAWELTI

The Western formula emerged as American attitudes toward the frontier gradually underwent significant change around the middle of the nineteenth century. It was possible for Americans in the early nineteenth century to treat the frontier as a symbol of fundamental moral antitheses between man and nature, and, consequently, to use a frontier setting in fiction that engaged itself with a profound exploration of the nature and limitations of man and society. However, the redefi-

*Editors' title. From John G. Cawelti, *The Six Gun Mystique* (Bowling Green, Ohio: Bowling Green Popular Press, 1971), pp. 38–47. Reprinted by permission of the publisher. This edited version appears in *Focus on the Western*, Jack Nachbar, ed. (Englewood Cliffs, N.J.: Prentice-Hall, 1974), pp. 57–63.

nition of the frontier as a place where advancing civilization met a declining savagery changed the frontier setting into a locus of conflicts which were always qualified and contained by the knowledge that the advance of civilization would largely eliminate them. Or, to put it another way, the frontier setting now provided a fictional justification for enjoying violent conflicts and the expression of lawless force without feeling that they threatened the values of the fabric of society.

The social and historical aspects of setting are just as important in defining the Western formula as geography. The Western story is set at a certain moment in the development of American civilization, namely at that point when savagery and lawlessness are in decline before the advancing wave of law and order, but are still strong enough to pose a local and momentarily significant challenge. In the actual history of the West, this moment was probably a relatively brief one in any particular area. In any case, the complex clashes of different interest groups over the use of Western resources and the pattern of settlement surely involved more people in a more fundamental way than the struggle with Indians or outlaws. Nonetheless, it is the latter which has become central to the Western formula. The relatively brief stage in the social evolution of the West when outlaws or Indians posed a threat to the community's stability has been erected into a timeless epic past in which heroic individual defenders of law and order without the vast social resources of police and courts stand poised against the threat of lawlessness

or savagery. But it is also the nature of this epic moment that the larger forces of civilized society are just waiting in the wings for their cue. However threatening he may appear at the moment, the Indian is vanishing and the outlaw about to be superseded. It is because they too represent this epic moment that we are likely to think of such novels as Cooper's *Last of the Mohicans*, Bird's *Nick of the Woods*, or more recent historical novels like Walter Edmonds' *Drums Along the Mohawk*[1] as Westerns, though they are not set in what we have come to know as the West.

Why then has this epic moment been primarily associated in fiction with a particular West, that of the Great Plains and the mountains and deserts of the "Far West" and with a particular historical moment, that of the heyday of the open range cattle industry of the later nineteenth century? Westerns can be set at a later time—some of Zane Grey's stories take place in the twenties and some, like those of Gene Autry, Roy Rogers or "Sky King," in the present—but even at these later dates the costumes and the way of life represented tend to be that of the later nineteenth century. Several factors probably contributed to this particular fixation of the epic moment. Included among these would be the ideological tendency of Americans to see the Far West as the last stronghold of certain traditional values, as well as the peculiar attractiveness of the cowboy hero. But more important than these factors, the Western requires a means of isolating and intensifying the drama of the frontier encounter between social order and lawlessness. For this purpose, the geo-

[1]James Fenimore Cooper (1789–1851), American novelist, author of *The Leatherstocking Tales*; Robert Bird (1806–54), American playwright and novelist; Walter Edmonds (1903–   ), American historical novelist. (eds.)

graphic setting of the Great Plains and adjacent areas has proved particularly appropriate, especially since the advent of film and television have placed a primary emphasis on visual articulation. Four characteristics of the Great Plains topography have been especially important: its openness, its aridity and general inhospitability to human life, its great extremes of light and climate, and, paradoxically, its grandeur and beauty. These topographic features create an effective backdrop for the action of the Western because they exemplify in visual images the thematic conflict between civilization and savagery, and its resolution. In particular, the Western has come to center about the image of the isolated town or ranch or fort surrounded by the vast open grandeur of prairie or desert and connected to the rest of the civilized world by a railroad, a stagecoach, or simply a trail. This tenuous link can still be broken by the forces of lawlessness, but never permanently. We can conceive it as a possibility that the town will be swept back into the desert—the rickety wooden buildings with their tottering false fronts help express the tenuousness of the town's position against the surrounding prairie; nonetheless we do not see the town solely as an isolated fort in hostile country, like an outpost of the French foreign legion in *Beau Geste*, but as the advance guard of an oncoming civilization. Moreover, while the prairie or desert may be inhospitable, it is not hostile. Its openness, freshness and grandeur also play an important role in the Western. Thus, the open prairie around the town serves not only as a haven of lawlessness and savagery, but as a backdrop of epic

magnitude and even, at times, as a source of regenerating power.

This characteristic setting reflects and helps dramatize the tripartite division of characters that dominates the Western pattern of action. The townspeople hover defensively in their settlement, threatened by the outlaws or Indians who are associated with the inhospitable and uncontrollable elements of the surrounding landscape. The townspeople are static and largely incapable of movement beyond their little settlement. The outlaws or savages can move freely across the landscape. The hero, though a friend of the townspeople, has the lawless power of movement in that he, like the savages, is a horseman and possesses skills of wilderness existence. The moral character of the hero also appears symbolically in the Western setting. In its rocky aridity and climatic extremes the Great Plains landscape embodies the hostile savagery of Indians and outlaws, while its vast openness, its vistas of snow-covered peaks in the distance, and its great sunrises and sunsets (in the purple prose of Zane Grey,[2] for example) suggest the epic courage and regenerative power of the hero. Thus, in every respect, Western topography helps dramatize more intensely the clash of characters and the thematic conflicts of the story.

The special openness of the topography of the Great Plains and western desert has made it particularly expressive for the portrayal of movement. Against the background of this terrain, a skillful director can create infinite variations of space ranging from long panoramas to close-ups and he can clearly articulate movement

[2]Zane Grey (1875–1939), American writer of western stories; in his lifetime over 13 million copies of his books were sold. (eds.)

across these various spaces. No matter how often one sees it, there is something inescapably effective about that scene, beloved of Western directors, in which a rider appears like an infinitely small dot at the far end of a great empty horizon and then rides toward us across the intervening space, just as there is a different thrill about the vision of a group of horses and men plunging pell-mell from the foreground into the empty distance. Nor is there anything which quite matches the feeling of suspense when the camera picks up a little group of wagons threading their way across the middle distance and then pans across the arid rocks and up the slopes of a canyon until it suddenly comes upon a group of Indians waiting in ambush. Moreover, the western landscape is uniquely adaptable to certain kinds of strong visual effects because of the sharp contrasts of light and shadow characteristic of an arid climate together with the topographical contrasts of plain and mountain, rocky outcrops and flat deserts, steep bare canyons and forested plateaus. The characteristic openness and aridity of the topography also makes the contrast between man and nature and between wilderness and society visually strong.

Perhaps no film exploits the visual resources of the western landscape more brilliantly than John Ford's 1939 *Stagecoach*.[3] The film opens on a street in one of those western shanty towns characterized by rickety false fronts. By the rushing motion of horses and wagons along the street and by the long vista down the street and out into the desert we are immediately made aware of the surrounding

wilderness and of the central theme of movement across it which will dominate the film. This opening introduction of the visual theme of fragile town contrasted with epic wilderness will be developed throughout the film in the contrast between the flimsy stagecoach and the magnificent landscape through which it moves. Similarly, the restless motion of the opening scene will be projected into the thrust of the stagecoach across the landscape. This opening is followed by several brief scenes leading up to the departure of the stagecoach. These scenes are cut at a rather breathless pace so that they do not slow down the sense of motion and flight generated by the opening. Visually, they dwell on two aspects of the town, its dark, narrow and crowded interiors and its ramshackle sidewalks and storefronts, thus establishing in visual terms the restrictive and artificial character of town life. Then the stagecoach departs on its voyage and we are plunged into the vast openness and grandeur of the wilderness with the crowded wooden stagecoach serving as a visual reminder of the narrow town life it has left behind. Ford chose to shoot the major portion of the stagecoach's journey in Monument Valley, a brilliant choice because the visual characteristics of that topography perfectly embody the complex mixture of epic grandeur and savage hostility that the film requires. The valley itself is a large, flat desert between steep hills. Thrusting up out of the valley floor gigantic monoliths of bare rock dwarf the stagecoach as it winds across this vast panorama. This combination of large open desert broken by majestic upthrusts of rock

[3]John Ford (1895–1973), American film director of nearly 200 films, including *Stagecoach* (1939), *Rio Grande* (1951), and *The Horse Soldiers* (1959); he established John Wayne as the definitive western hero. (eds.)

and surrounded by threatening hills creates an enormously effective visual environment for the story, which centers around the way in which the artificial social roles and attitudes of the travellers break down under the impact of the wilderness. Those travellers who are able to transcend their former roles are regenerated by the experience: the drunken doctor delivers a baby, the meek salesman shows courage, the whore becomes the heroine of a romance and the outlaw becomes a lover. By stunning photographic representation of the visual contrasts of desert, hills and moving stagecoach, Ford transforms the journey of the stagecoach into an epic voyage that transcends the film's rather limited romantic plot.

Costume—another feature of the Western setting—has also contributed greatly to the Western's success in film. Like topography, Western costume gains effectiveness both from intrinsic interest and from the way writers and filmmakers have learned how to make it reflect character and theme. In simplest form, as in the B Westerns, costumes symbolized moral opposition. The good guy wears clean, well-pressed clothes and a white hat. The villain dressed sloppily in black. The importance of this convention, simple-minded as it was, became apparent when, to create a more sophisticated "adult" Western, directors frequently chose to dress their heroes in black. However, the tradition of Western costume also contains more complex meanings. An important distinction marks off both hero and villain from the townspeople. The townspeople usually wear the ordinary street clothing associated with the later nineteenth century, suits for men and long dresses for women. On the whole this clothing is simple as compared to the more elaborate fashions of the period and this simplicity is one way of expressing the Westernness of the costume. However, in the midst of the desert, the townspeople's clothing has an air of non-utilitarian artificiality somewhat like the ubiquitous false fronts on the town itself. It is perhaps significant that even in Westerns purportedly set at a later date, the women tend to wear the full-length dresses of an earlier period.

The costumes associated with heroes and outlaws or savages are more striking. Paradoxically, they are both more utilitarian and more artificial than those of the townspeople. The cowboy's boots, tight-fitting pants or chaps, his heavy shirt and bandana, his gun, and finally his large ten-gallon hat all symbolize his adaptation to the wilderness. But utility is only one of the principles of the hero-outlaw's dress. The other is dandyism, that highly artificial love of elegance for its own sake. In the Western, dandyism sometimes takes the overt and obvious form of elaborate costumes laid over with fringes, tassels and scrollwork like a rococo drawing room. But it is more powerfully exemplified in the elegance of those beautifully tailored cowboy uniforms which John Wayne so magnificently fills out in the Westerns of John Ford and Howard Hawks.

The enormous attraction of this combination of naturalness and artifice has played a significant role in both popular and avant-garde art since the middle of the nineteenth century. Baudelaire's[4] fascination with the dandyism of the savage which he described as "the supreme incarnation of the idea of Beauty transported into the material world," is just one indi-

---

[4]Charles Baudelaire (1821–67), French poet and critic. (eds.)

cation of the nineteenth century's fascination with the mixture of savagery and elegance which has been implicit in the costume of the Western hero from the beginning. Cooper's Leatherstocking even gained his name from his costume, suggesting the extent to which this particular kind of dress excited Cooper's imagination. Like later cowboys, Leatherstocking's costume combined nature and artifice. His dress was largely made of the skins of animals and it was particularly adapted to the needs of wilderness life. Yet at the same time it was subtly ornamented with buckskin fringes and porcupine quills "after the manner of the Indians." Still, it is important to note that Leatherstocking's costume is not that of the Indians, but rather a more utilitarian wilderness version of the settler's dress. Thus, costume exemplified the mediating role of the hero between civilization and savagery. Later the formula cowboy's costume developed along the same lines. In its basic outlines it resembled town dress more than that of the Indian, yet it was more functional for movement across the plains than that of the townspeople. At the same time, the cowboy dress had a dandyish splendor and elegance lacking in the drab fashions of the town and based on Indian or Mexican models. In later Westerns, the hero shared many of these qualities with the villain, just as Leatherstocking had a touch of the Indian, despite his repeated assurances that he was "a man without a cross," i.e., actual Indian kinship. But the hero's costume still differentiated him from the savage, whether Indian or outlaw, both by its basic resemblance to civilized dress and by its greater restraint and decorum. Thus costume, like setting, expressed the transcendent and intermediate quality of the hero. By lying between two ways of life, he transcended the restrictions and limitations of both. Or, to put it another way, the Western setting and costume embody the basic escapist principle of having your cake and eating it too.

As already indicated, there are three central roles in the Western: the townspeople or agents of civilization, the savages or outlaws who threaten this first group, and the heroes who are above all "men in the middle," that is, they possess many qualities and skills of the savages, but are fundamentally committed to the townspeople. It is out of the multiple variations possible on the relationships between these groups that the various Western plots are concocted. For example, the simplest version of all has the hero protecting the townspeople from the savages, using his own savage skills against the denizens of the wilderness. A second more complex variation shows the hero initially indifferent to the plight of the townspeople and more inclined to identify himself with the savages. However, in the course of the story his position changes and he becomes the ally of the townspeople. This variation can generate a number of different plots. There is the revenge Western: a hero seeks revenge against an outlaw or Indian who has wronged him. In order to accomplish his vengeance, he rejects the pacifistic ideals of the townspeople, but in the end he discovers that he is really committed to their way of life (John Ford's *The Searchers*). Another plot based on this variation of the character relations is that of the hero who initially seeks his own selfish material gain, using his savage skills as a means to this end; but as the story progresses, he discovers his moral involvement with the townspeople and becomes their champion (cf. Anthony Mann's film *The Far Country*). It is also possible, while maintaining the system of relationships, to reverse the conclusion of the plot as in those stories where the townspeople come to accept the hero's savage mode of action (cf. John Ford's *Stagecoach* or, to a certain extent, Wister's *The Virginian*). A third variation of the basic scheme of relationships has the hero caught in the middle between the townspeople's need for his savage skills and their rejection of his way of life. This third variation, common in recent Westerns, often ends in the destruction of the hero (cf. the films *The Gunfighter* or *Invitation to a Gunfighter*) or in his voluntary exile (*Shane, High Noon, Two Rode Together*). The existence of these and many other variations suggests that the exploration of a certain pattern of relationships is more important to the Western than a particular outcome, though it is also probable that they reflect different components of the mass audience, the simpler variation being more popular with adolescents and the more complex variations successful with adults. In addition, changing cultural attitudes have something to do with the emergence of different variations, since variation two is clearly more characteristic of early twentieth century Westerns, while variation three dominates the recent "adult" Western.

Aids   *Savagery and Civilization*

1. According to Cawelti, at what precise moment in history is the western actually set? Why is it set at this period? Why does the western typically take place on the Great Plains or in the Far West? What three types of characters dominate the action in a western?

2. Cawelti's thesis hinges on a contrast between savagery and civilization in the western and his organization reflects this contrast. However, instead of first discussing all the elements of savagery in the western, then all the elements of civilization, Cawelti divides his topic into manageable pieces. He first contrasts savagery and civilization in the set, then savagery and civilization in the characters, then savagery and civilization in the topography. What other contrasts does Cawelti provide? Do you think he organizes his series of contrasts coherently?

3. An extended example is a useful tool because it allows a writer to work out a thesis in some detail. As Cawelti works out his various contrasts, he provides a few examples from films; however, to tie his contrasts together he provides one extended example— the movie *Stagecoach*. Does Cawelti apply all his previous generalizations to this film? Does the extended example generate any new generalizations?

4. The word *stereotype* denotes a metal printing plate cast from a

mold; from this mold unvarying copies can be endlessly produced. The term also and more commonly refers to a person, group, or event considered to typify or conform to an unvarying pattern, lacking any individual identity. In the traditional western, the forces of savagery and civilization tend to be stereotypical—the ruthless and inscrutable Indian versus the hardworking, moral townspeople and the brave, resourceful hero. But the western depends on more specific stereotypes as well. A common source of conflict in the western is the antipathy between the rugged western hero and the "refined" easterner. As you watch old westerns look for the easterner. Ask yourself what role he plays in the western. How is he stereotyped? Are women stereotyped in the western? (Look at Cashill's discussion of women in the western in "Packaging Popular Mythology" in Unit II). If so, do the stereotypes conform to any of Marjorie Rosen's categories in "Popcorn Venus"? Historians have carefully documented the fact that many of the plains cowboys were black men, yet blacks are seldom seen in the western. Why not? As you watch old westerns on television or new westerns at your theatre, look for black characters and ask yourself how they are treated. Are they stereotyped?

5.   Because the western hero is caught between civilization and savagery, he often finds himself in a morally ambiguous situation, i.e., he is often a killer of men. Watch some old westerns on television. How do they deal with this ambiguity? How do they make heroic an individual whose behavior might not be acceptable in contemporary society?

6.   Do you think Cawelti's thesis and his three basic plot types work for the new westerns?

Who Killed King Kong?

X. J. KENNEDY

The ordeal and spectacular death of King Kong, the giant ape, undoubtedly have been witnessed by more Americans than have ever seen a performance of *Hamlet, Iphigenia at Aulis,* or even *Tobacco Road.*[1] Since RKO-Radio Pictures first released *King Kong,* a quarter-century has gone by; yet year after year, from prints that grow more rain-beaten, from sound tracks that grow more tinny, ticket-buyers by thousands still pursue Kong's luckless fight against the forces of technology, tabloid journalism, and the D.A.R. They see him chloroformed to sleep, see him whisked from his jungle isle to New York and placed on show, see him burst his chains to roam the city (lugging a frightened blonde), at last to plunge from the spire of the Empire State Building, machine-gunned by model airplanes.

Though Kong may die, one begins to think his legend unkillable. No clearer proof of his hold upon the popular imagination may be seen than what emerged one catastrophic week in March 1955, when New York's WOR-TV programmed *Kong* for seven evenings in a row (a total of sixteen showings). Many a rival network vice-president must have scowled when surveys showed that *Kong*—the 1933 B-picture—had lured away fat segments of the viewing populace from such powerful competitors as Ed Sullivan, Groucho Marx, and Bishop Sheen.

But even television has failed to run *King Kong* into oblivion. Coffee-in-the-lobby cinemas still show the old hunk of hokum, with the apology that in its use of composite shots and animated models the film remains technically interesting. And no other monster in movie history has won so devoted a popular audience. None of the plodding mummies, the stultified draculas, the white-coated Lugosis[2] with their shiny pinball-machine laboratories, none of the invisible stranglers, berserk robots, or menaces from Mars has ever enjoyed so many resurrections.

Why does the American public refuse to let King Kong rest in peace? It is true, I'll admit, that *Kong* outdid every monster movie before or since in sheer carnage. Producers Cooper and Schoedsack crammed into it dinosaurs, headhunters, riots, aerial battles, bullets, bombs, bloodletting. Heroine Fay Wray, whose function is mainly to scream, shuts her mouth

From *Dissent,* spring 1960. Reprinted by permission of the journal.

[1]*Iphigenia at Aulis,* a classical Greek drama; *Tobacco Road,* a steamy novel by Erskine Caldwell. (eds.)

[2]Reference is to Béla Lugosi, a film actor who specialized in horror films. (eds.)

for hardly one uninterrupted minute from first reel to last. It is also true that *Kong* is larded with good healthy sadism, for those whose joy it is to see the frantic girl dangled from cliffs and harried by pterodactyls. But it seems to me that the abiding appeal of the giant ape rests on other foundations.

Kong has, first of all, the attraction of being manlike. His simian nature gives him one huge advantage over giant ants and walking vegetables in that an audience may conceivably identify with him. Kong's appeal has the quality that established the Tarzan series as American myth—for what man doesn't secretly imagine himself a huge hairy howler against whom no other monster has a chance? If Tarzan recalls the ape in us, then Kong may well appeal to that great-granddaddy primordial brute from whose tribe we have all deteriorated.

Intentionally or not, the producers of *King Kong* encourage this identification by etching the character of Kong with keen sympathy. For the ape is a figure in a tradition familiar to moviegoers: the tradition of the pitiable monster. We think of Lon Chaney in the role of Quasimodo,[3] of Karloff in the original *Frankenstein.* As we watch the Frankenstein monster's fumbling and disastrous attempts to befriend a flower-picking child, our sympathies are enlisted with the monster in his impenetrable loneliness. And so with Kong. As he roars in his chains, while barkers sell tickets to boobs who gape at him, we perhaps feel something more deep than pathos. We begin to sense something of the problem that engaged Eugene O'Neill in *The Hairy Ape*: the dilemma of a displaced animal spirit forced to live in a jungle built by machines.

King Kong, it is true, had special relevance in 1933. Landscapes of the depression are glimpsed early in the film when an impresario, seeking some desperate pretty girl to play the lead in a jungle movie, visits soup-lines and a Woman's Home Mission. In Fay Wray—who's been caught snitching an apple from a fruitstand—his search is ended. When he gives her a big feed and a movie contract, the girl is magic-carpeted out of the world of the National Recovery Act. And when, in the film's climax, Kong smashes that very Third Avenue landscape in which Fay had wandered hungry, audiences of 1933 may well have felt a personal satisfaction.

What is curious is that audiences of 1960 remain hooked. For in the heart of urban man, one suspects, lurks the impulse to fling a bomb. Though machines speed him to the scene of his daily grind, though IBM comptometers ("freeing the human mind from drudgery") enable him to drudge more efficiently once he arrives, there comes a moment when he wishes to turn upon his machines and kick hell out of them. He wants to hurl his combination radio-alarmclock out the bedroom window and listen

[3]Quasimodo, the hunchback in *The Hunchback of Notre Dame.* (eds.)

Pravda snaps at 'Jaws'

MOSCOW (AP) August 27, 1975. — The Soviet Union's most influential newspaper told its readers today that "Jaws" is one of a "flood of movie horrors" inundating America.

"Horror movies have been put on an assembly-line basis," said Pravda, the Communist party newspaper.

Correspondent G. Vasilyev writes that films showing mass destruction or horror are successful in the United States because they "exploit a sense of fear, do not demand great intellectual effort and promise good profits."

But Vasilyev said American writer Gore Vidal provided the chief reason for the success of such movies. He quoted Vidal:

"That which I call the second act of the greatest economic depression the world has ever known has given birth to this tendency of relishing all kinds of troubles and cataclysms."

According to Pravda, Vidal said it reminded him of ancient Rome where "to let off steam they had a show of lions eating people and gladiators killing each other. Such movies distract people from their thoughts of the robbery and deceit to which they are subjected daily by oil companies, politicians and banks."

"Progressive movie critics warn Americans, 'Beware of sharks,' " Pravda concluded.

to it smash. What subway commuter wouldn't love—just for once—to see the downtown express smack head-on into the uptown local? Such a wish is gratified in that memorable scene in *Kong* that opens with a wide-angle shot: interior of a railway car on the Third Avenue El. Straphangers are nodding, the literate refold their newspapers. Unknown to them, Kong has torn away a section of trestle toward which the train now speeds. The motorman spies Kong up ahead, jams on the brakes. Passengers hurtle together like so many peas in a pail. In a window of the car appear Kong's bloodshot eyes. Women shriek. Kong picks up the railway car as if it were a rat, flips it to the street and ties knots in it, or something. To any commuter the scene must appear one of the most satisfactory pieces of celluloid ever exposed.

Yet however violent his acts, Kong remains a gentleman. Remarkable is his sense of chivalry. Whenever a fresh boa constrictor threatens Fay, Kong first sees that the lady is safely parked, then manfully thrashes her attacker. (And she, the ingrate, runs away every time his back is turned.) Atop the Empire State Building, ignoring his pursuers, Kong places Fay on a ledge as tenderly as if she were a dozen eggs. He fondles her, then

'Horror Films Soothe Psyches In Hard Times'

Minneapolis, July 22.

New York psychologists Mildred and Bernard Berkowitz claim the current spate of terror films serve a useful function, reassuring people that despite their own problems, things could be worse. Here last week on a book promotion tour, the husband and wife team pointed out that "horror films are very popular in very hard times when people have a lot of anxiety in their own lives."

Mrs. Berkowitz told Minneapolis Star reporter Gordon Slovut that exciting films provide a kind of relief for filmgoers. "Whatever is going on in your own life, (what you see in such pictures) is worse," she said. "You go to the movie, whether it's a 'Towering Inferno,' an 'Earthquake' or a 'Jaws,' you scare yourself, you have a terrible time, and you come home to relative safety." Patronizing horror films is an unconscious effort to sublimate one's own worries, she feels.

"You have to assume that some important psychological needs are being served." Berkowitz added. "People are shelling out an awful lot of money. It comes under the rubric of entertainment."

The couple noted that nerve tingling pictures have been around for years, serving a therapeutic purpose. They cited such vintage nail biters as "Phantom of the Opera," "P s y c h o" and "Godzilla Meets Frankenstein."

From *Variety*, Wednesday, July 23, 1975. Reprinted by permission.

turns to face the Army Air Force. And Kong is perhaps the most disinterested lover since Cyrano.[4] His attentions to the lady are utterly without hope of reward. After all, between a five-foot blonde and a fifty-foot ape, love can hardly be more than an intellectual flirtation. In his simian way King Kong is the hopelessly yearning lover of Petrarchan convention.[5] His forced exit from his jungle, in chains, results directly from his single-minded pursuit of Fay. He smashes a Broadway theater when the notion enters his dull brain that the flashbulbs of photographers somehow endanger the lady. His perilous shinnying up a skyscraper to pluck Fay from her boudoir is an act of the kindliest of hearts. He's impossible to discourage even though the love of his life can't lay eyes on him without shrieking murder.

The tragedy of King Kong, then, is to be the beast who at the end of the fable fails to turn into the handsome prince. This is the conviction that the scriptwriters would leave with us in the film's closing line. As Kong's corpse lies blocking traffic in the street, the entrepreneur who

[4]Cyrano de Bergerac (1619–55), a writer of French romances who was later satirized by Edmond Rostrand in his play *Cyrano de Bergerac* (1897). The fictionalized Cyrano is a great lover with a huge nose. (eds.)

[5]Refers to Italian poet Francesco Petrarch (1304–74), who "modernized" the love poem. (eds.)

brought Kong to New York turns to the assembled reporters and proclaims: "That's your story, boys—it was Beauty killed the Beast!" But greater forces than those of the screaming Lady have combined to lay Kong low, if you ask me. Kong lives for a time as one of those persecuted near-animal souls bewildered in the middle of an industrial order, whose simple desires are thwarted at every turn. He climbs the Empire State Building because in all New York it's the closest thing he can find to the clifftop of his jungle isle. He dies, a pitiful dolt, and the army brass and publicity-men cackle over him. His death is the only possible outcome to as neat a tragic dilemma as you can ask for. The machine-guns do him in, while the manicured human hero (a nice clean Dartmouth boy) carries away Kong's sweetheart to the altar. O, the misery of it all. There's far more truth about upper-middle-class American life in *King Kong* than in the last seven dozen novels of John P. Marquand.[6]

A Negro friend from Atlanta tells me that in movie houses in colored

---

[6]John P. Marquand (1893–1960), American novelist, famous for *The Late George Apley.* (eds.)

neighborhoods throughout the South, *Kong* does a constant business. They show the thing in Atlanta at least every year, presumably to the same audiences. Perhaps this popularity may simply be due to the fact that Kong is one of the most watchable movies ever constructed, but I wonder whether Negro audiences may not find some archetypical appeal in this serio-comic tale of a huge black powerful free spirit whom all the hard-working white policemen are out to kill.

Every day in the week on a screen somewhere in the world, King Kong relives his agony. Again and again he expires on the Empire State Building, as audiences of the devout assist his sacrifice. We watch him die, and by extension kill the ape within our bones, but these little deaths of ours occur in prosaic surroundings. We do not die on a tower, New York before our feet, nor do we give our lives to smash a few flying machines. It is not for us to bring to a momentary standstill the civilization in which we move. King Kong does this for us. And so we kill him again and again, in much-spliced celluloid, while the ape in us expires from day to day, obscure, in desperation.

Aids   *Who Killed King Kong?*

1. X. J. Kennedy maintains that *King Kong* has been a popular film because viewers identify strongly with Kong. According to Kennedy, *why* do viewers identify with this fifty-foot ape? In what specific ways does his behavior appeal to moviegoers?

2. What is Kennedy's attitude toward the "industrial order"?

3. There is a great deal of subtle and not-so-subtle humor in "Who Killed King Kong?" One of Kennedy's favorite humorous devices is to create an incongruous series of items—"Kong's luckless fight against the forces of technology, tabloid journalism, and the D.A.R." or "such powerful competitors as Ed Sullivan, Groucho Marx and Bishop Sheen." It is, of course, the last item in the series that makes it humorous. What is the D.A.R.? Who was Bishop Sheen? Kennedy also wrings humor from unlikely phrases like "good, healthy sadism" or "Kong may well appeal to that great-granddaddy primordial brute from whose tribe we have all deteriorated." Look for other examples of humor that depend on surprise or incongruity.

4. Kennedy's essay is full of "unprovable" generalizations—urban man "wants to hurl his combination radio-alarmclock out the window and listen to it smash" or "What subway commuter wouldn't love— just once—to see the downtown express smash head-on into the

uptown local?" What purpose do such statements serve? Does it matter that they may not be literally true? Do such assertions weaken Kennedy's argument?

5. In his attempts to humanize King Kong, Kennedy provides his readers with an extended metaphor in which Kong becomes a medieval knight. His metaphor, however, depends on his reader knowing the conventions of the medieval romance. What is chivalry? Who is Cyrano? What is Petrarchan convention? Do you think the metaphor works for readers who are unfamiliar with these terms?

6. Toward the end of his essay, Kennedy quotes a friend who describes the reaction of black audiences to *King Kong*. Kennedy's essay was written in 1960, just as the civil rights movement was getting under way. Do you think Kennedy would use words like "Negro" and "colored" today? How do you feel about Kennedy's explanation regarding the response of black viewers? Do you accept it? Do you find it offensive?

7. X. J. Kennedy asserts that Kong is treated with sympathy in the original 1933 version of the film. Several years ago, however, three minutes of film, excised when *King Kong* was edited, were discovered in the attic of the RKO editor. In the first brief scene, Kong is shown cautiously stripping away Fay Wray's clothing and running his fingers over her body. In the second scene, we are shown a full-face closeup of Kong crunching islanders in his giant jaws. Do these scenes change Kennedy's interpretation of King Kong as a chivalric gentleman and "pitiable monster"? Why do you think the two scenes were removed from the film in the first place?

8. Sound effects are especially important in horror films (although there are some magnificent silent horror films). Sound effects in horror films are rather predictable—bloodcurdling screams (Fay Wray provides this in *King Kong*), creaking doors, mysterious footsteps. Natural sounds can be used to advantage as well. Marsha Kinder and Beverle Houston discuss the use of sound in the film *The Exorcist* (*Cinema*, No. 34, 1974, p. 25): "The sound track is extremely loud, providing a cacophony of noises that keeps the audience tense and edgy: the devil's poundings, the clanging hammers of the archaeological dig; the city noises . . ., the roaring subway trains; the intolerable screech of the medical instruments." As you watch a horror movie, note how the director uses sound to manipulate your reactions. Ask yourself whether the director uses predictable devices or is creative in his/her use of sound.

9. The horror film, even an atypical sample like *King Kong,* is related to the eighteenth- and nineteenth-century gothic romance in literature. In *Nathaniel Hawthorne and the Tradition of Gothic Romance* (New York, 1964), Jane Lundblad outlines the principal traits of the gothic novel: (1) the story is often told secondhand or in a flashback; (2) the background is a gloomy castle containing secret passages and subterranean passages; (3) there is usually a character connected with religion; (4) the villain is deformed; (5) there are ghosts; (6) magic is common; (7) works of art have mysterious properties; (8) suits of armor, helmets, and shields abound; and (9) there is plenty of blood. Watch your television listings for old horror movies. Examine a horror film for traces of the gothic novel. Sometimes an element will be transformed slightly—magic, for instance, often becomes "science."

10. That the story of King Kong is still capturing the imagination of moviegoers is seen by the 1976 remake of the 1933 classic. Is Kennedy's interpretation of the original *King Kong* applicable to the current version? What social, political, and economic conditions might account for the appeal of the 1976 remake?

Culver Pictures

Science Fiction Films:
The Imagination of Disaster

SUSAN SONTAG

Science fiction films are not about science. They are about disaster, which is one of the oldest subjects of art. In science fiction films disaster is rarely viewed intensively; it is always extensive. It is a matter of quantity and ingenuity. If you will, it is a question of scale. But the scale, particularly in the wide-screen Technicolor films (of which the ones by the Japanese director Inoshiro Honda and the American director George Pal are technically the most convincing and visually the most exciting), does raise the matter to another level.

Thus, the science fiction film (like that of a very different contemporary genre, the Happening) is concerned with the aesthetics of destruction, with the peculiar beauties to be found in wreaking havoc, making a mess. And it is in the imagery of destruction that the core of a good science fiction film lies. Hence, the disadvantage of the cheap film—in which the monster appears or the rocket lands in a small dull-looking town. (Hollywood budget needs usually dictate that the town be in the Arizona or California desert. In *The Thing From Another World* [1951] the rather sleazy and confined set is supposed to be an encampment near the North Pole.) Still, good black-and-white science fiction films have been made. But a bigger budget, which usually means Technicolor, allows a much greater play back and forth among several model environments. There

is the populous city. There is the lavish but ascetic interior of the spaceship—either the invaders' or ours—replete with streamlined chromium fixtures and dials and machines whose complexity is indicated by the number of colored lights they flash and strange noises they emit. There is the laboratory crowded with formidable boxes and scientific apparatus. There is a comparatively old-fashioned-looking conference room, where the scientists unfurl charts to explain the desperate state of things to the military. And each of these standard locales or backgrounds is subject to two modalities—intact and destroyed. We may, if we are lucky, be treated to a panorama of melting tanks, flying bodies, crashing walls, awesome craters and fissures in the earth, plummeting spacecraft, colorful deadly rays; and to a symphony of screams, weird electronic signals, the noisiest military hardware going, and the leaden tones of the laconic denizens of alien planets and their subjugated earthlings.

Certain of the primitive gratifications of science fiction films—for instance, the depiction of urban disaster on a colossally magnified scale—are shared with other types of films. Visually there is little difference between mass havoc as represented in the old horror and monster films and what we find in science fiction films, except (again) scale. In the old monster films, the monster always headed for the great city, where he had to do a fair bit of rampaging, hurling buses off bridges, crumpling trains in his bare hands, toppling buildings, and so forth. The archetype is King Kong, in Schoedsack's great film of 1933, running amok, first in the African village (trampling babies, a bit of footage excised from most prints), then in New York. This is really no different in spirit from the scene in Inoshiro Honda's *Rodan* (1957) in which two giant reptiles—with a wingspan of 500 feet and supersonic speeds—by flapping their wings whip up a cyclone that blows most of Tokyo to smithereens. Or the destruction of half of Japan by the gigantic robot with the great incinerating ray that shoots forth from his eyes, at the beginning of Honda's *The Mysterians* (1959). Or, the devastation by the rays from a fleet of flying saucers of New York, Paris, and Tokyo, in *Battle in Outer Space* (1960). Or, the inundation of New York in *When Worlds Collide* (1951). Or, the end of London in 1966 depicted in George Pal's *The Time Machine* (1960). Neither do these sequences differ in aesthetic intention from the destruction scenes in the big sword, sandal, and orgy color spectaculars set in Biblical and Roman times—the end of Sodom in Aldrich's *Sodom and Gomorrah*, of Gaza in De Mille's *Samson and Delilah*, of Rhodes in *The Colossus of Rhodes*, and of Rome in a dozen Nero movies. Griffith began it with the Babylon sequence in *Intolerance*, and to this day there is nothing like the thrill of watching all those expensive sets come tumbling down.

In other respects as well, the science fiction films of the 1950s take up familiar themes. The famous 1930s movie serials and comics of the adventures of Flash Gordon and Buck Rogers, as well as the more recent spate of comic book super-heroes

with extraterrestrial origins (the most famous is Superman, a foundling from the planet Krypton, currently described as having been exploded by a nuclear blast), share motifs with more recent science fiction movies. But there is an important difference. The old science fiction films, and most of the comics, still have an essentially innocent relation to disaster. Mainly they offer new versions of the oldest romance of all—of the strong invulnerable hero with a mysterious lineage come to do battle on behalf of good and against evil. Recent science fiction films have a decided grimness, bolstered by their much greater degree of visual credibility, which contrasts strongly with the older films. Modern historical reality has greatly enlarged the imagination of disaster, and the protagonists—perhaps by the very nature of what is visited upon them—no longer seem wholly innocent.

The lure of such generalized disaster as a fantasy is that it releases one from normal obligations. The trump card of the end-of-the-world movies—like *The Day the Earth Caught Fire* (1962)—is that great scene with New York or London or Tokyo discovered empty, its entire population annihilated. Or, as in *The World, The Flesh, and The Devil* (1957), the whole movie can be devoted to the fantasy of occupying the deserted metropolis and starting all over again, a world Robinson Crusoe.

Another kind of satisfaction these films supply is extreme moral simplification —that is to say, a morally acceptable fantasy where one can give outlet to cruel or at least amoral feelings. In this respect, science fiction films partly overlap with horror films. This is the undeniable pleasure we derive from looking at freaks, beings excluded from the category of the human. The sense of superiority over the freak conjoined in varying proportions with the titillation of fear and aversion makes it possible for moral scruples to be lifted, for cruelty to be enjoyed. The same thing happens in science fiction films. In the figure of the monster from outer space, the freakish, the ugly, and the predatory all converge—and provide a fantasy target for righteous bellicosity to discharge itself, and for the aesthetic enjoyment of suffering and disaster. Science fiction films are one of the purest forms of spectacle; that is, we are rarely inside anyone's feelings. (An exception is Jack Arnold's *The Incredible Shrinking Man* [1957].) We are merely spectators; we watch.

But in science fiction films, unlike horror films, there is not much horror. Suspense, shocks, surprises are mostly abjured in favor of a steady, inexorable plot. Science fiction films invite a dispassionate, aesthetic view of destruction and violence —a *technological* view. Things, objects, machinery play a major role in these films. A greater range of ethical values is embodied in the décor of these films than in the people. Things, rather than the helpless humans, are the locus of values because we experience them, rather than people, as the sources of power. According to science fiction films, man is naked without his artifacts. *They* stand for different values, they are potent, they are what get destroyed, and they are the indispensable tools for the repulse of the alien invaders or the repair of the damaged environment.

The science fiction films are strongly moralistic. The standard message is the one about the proper, or humane, use of science, versus the mad, obsessional use of science. This message the science fiction films share in common with the classic horror films of the 1930s like *Frankenstein,* *The Mummy, Island of Lost Souls, Dr. Jekyll and Mr. Hyde.* (George Franju's brilliant *Les Yeux Sans Visage* [1959], called here *The Horror Chamber of Doctor Faustus,* is a more recent example.) In the horror films, we have the mad or obsessed or misguided scientist who pursues his experiments against good advice to the contrary, creates a monster or monsters, and is himself destroyed—often recognizing his folly himself, and dying in the successful effort to destroy his own creation. One science fiction equivalent of this is the scientist, usually a member of a team, who defects to the planetary invaders because "their" science is more advanced than "ours."

This is the case in *The Mysterians,* and, true to form, the renegade sees his error in the end, and from within the Mysterian spaceship destroys it and himself. In *This Island Earth* (1955), the inhabitants of the beleaguered planet Metaluna propose to conquer earth, but their project is foiled by a Metalunan scientist named Exeter who, having lived on earth a while and learned to love Mozart, cannot abide such viciousness. Exeter plunges his spaceship into the ocean after returning a glamorous pair (male and female) of American physicists to earth. Metaluna dies. In *The Fly* (1958), the hero, engrossed in his basement-laboratory experiments on a matter-transmitting machine, uses himself as a subject, exchanges head and one arm with a housefly which had accidentally gotten into the machine, becomes a monster, and with his last shred of human will destroys his laboratory and orders his wife to kill him. His discovery, for the good of mankind, is lost.

Being a clearly labeled species of intellectual, scientists in science fiction films are always liable to crack up or go off the deep end. In *Conquest of Space* (1955), the scientist-commander of an international expedition to Mars suddenly acquires scruples about the blasphemy involved in the undertaking, and begins reading the Bible mid-journey instead of attending to his duties. The commander's son, who is his junior officer and always addresses his father as "General," is forced to kill the old man when he tries to prevent the ship from landing on Mars. In this film, both sides of the ambivalence toward scientists are given voice. Generally, for a scientific enterprise to be treated entirely sympathetically in these films, it needs the certificate of utility. Science, viewed without ambivalence, means an efficacious response to danger. Disinterested intellectual curiosity rarely appears in any form other than caricature, as a maniacal dementia that cuts one off from normal human relations. But this suspicion is usually directed at the scientist rather than his work. The creative scientist may become a martyr to his own discovery, through an accident or by pushing things too far. But the implication remains that other men, less imaginative—in short, technicians—could have administered the same discovery better and more safely. The most ingrained contemporary mistrust of the intellect is visited, in these movies, upon the scientist-as-intellectual.

The message that the scientist is one who releases forces which, if not controlled for good, could destroy man himself seems innocuous enough. One of the oldest images of the scientist is Shakespeare's Prospero,[1] the overdetached scholar forcibly retired from society to a desert island, only partly in control of the magic forces in which he dabbles. Equally classic is the figure of the scientist as satanist (*Doctor Faustus*, and stories of Poe and Hawthorne).[2] Science is magic, and man has always known that there is black magic as well as white. But it is not enough to remark that contemporary attitudes—as reflected in science fiction films—remain ambivalent, that the scientist is treated as both satanist and savior. The proportions have changed, because of the new context in which the old admiration and fear of the scientist are located. For his sphere of influence is no longer local, himself or his immediate community. It is planetary, cosmic.

One gets the feeling, particularly in the Japanese films but not only there, that a mass trauma exists over the use of nuclear weapons and the possibility of future nuclear wars. Most of the science fiction films bear witness to this trauma, and, in a way, attempt to exorcise it.

The accidental awakening of the super-destructive monster who has slept in the earth since prehistory is, often, an obvious metaphor for the Bomb. But there are many explicit references as well. In *The Mysterians*, a probe ship from the planet Mysteroid has landed on earth, near Tokyo. Nuclear warfare having been practiced on Mysteroid for centuries (their civilization is "more advanced than ours"), ninety percent of those now born on the planet have to be destroyed at birth,

---

[1]Prospero, a character in Shakespeare's *The Tempest*. (eds.)

[2]*Doctor Faustus*, a play (1589) by Christopher Marlowe about the scholar-scientist Faustus who sells his soul to the devil for 24 years of absolute power; also a 1947 novel by German author Thomas Mann. Edgar Allan Poe (1809–49), American poet and short-story writer; Nathaniel Hawthorne (1804–64), American novelist and short-story writer. (eds.)

because of defects caused by the huge amounts of Strontium 90 in their diet. The Mysterians have come to earth to marry earth women, and possibly to take over our relatively uncontaminated planet. . . . In *The Incredible Shrinking Man*, the John Doe hero is the victim of a gust of radiation which blows over the water, while he is out boating with his wife; the radiation causes him to grow smaller and smaller, until at the end of the movie he steps through the fine mesh of a window screen to become "the infinitely small." . . . In *Rodan*, a horde of monstrous carnivorous prehistoric insects, and finally a pair of giant flying reptiles (the prehistoric Archeopteryx), are hatched from dormant eggs in the depths of a mine shaft by the impact of nuclear test explosions, and go on to destroy a good part of the world before they are felled by the molten lava of a volcanic eruption. . . . In the English film, *The Day the Earth Caught Fire*, two simultaneous hydrogen bomb tests by the United States and Russia change by 11 degrees the tilt of the earth on its axis and alter the earth's orbit so that it begins to approach the sun.

Radiation casualties—ultimately, the conception of the whole world as a casualty of nuclear testing and nuclear warfare—is the most ominous of all the notions with which science fiction films deal. Universes become expendable. Worlds become contaminated, burnt out, exhausted, obsolete. In *Rocketship X-M* (1950) explorers from the earth land on Mars, where they learn that atomic warfare has destroyed Martian civilization. In George Pal's *The War of the Worlds* (1953), reddish spindly alligator-skinned creatures from Mars invade the earth because their planet is becoming too cold to be inhabitable. In *This Island Earth*, also American, the planet Metaluna, whose population has long ago been driven underground by warfare, is dying under the missile attacks of an enemy planet. Stocks of uranium, which power the force field shielding Metaluna, have been used up; and an unsuccessful expedition is sent to earth to enlist earth scientists to devise new sources for nuclear power. In Joseph Losey's *The Damned* (1961), nine icy-cold radioactive children are being reared by a fanatical scientist in a dark cave on the English coast to be the only survivors of the inevitable nuclear Armageddon.

There is a vast amount of wishful thinking in science fiction films, some of it touching, some of it depressing. Again and again, one detects the hunger for a "good war," which poses no moral problems, admits of no moral qualifications. The imagery of science fiction films will satisfy the most bellicose addict of war films, for a lot of the satisfactions of war films pass, untransformed, into science fiction films. Examples: the dogfights between earth "fighter rockets" and alien spacecraft in the *Battle of Outer Space* (1959); the escalating firepower in the successive assaults upon the invaders in *The Mysterians*, which Dan Talbot correctly described as a non-stop holocaust; the spectacular bombardment of the underground fortress of Metaluna in *This Island Earth*.

Yet at the same time the bellicosity of science fiction films is neatly channeled into the yearning for peace, or for at least peaceful coexistence. Some scientist generally takes sententious note of the fact that it took the planetary invasion to make the warring nations of the earth come to their senses and suspend their own conflicts. One of the main themes of many science fiction films—the color ones usually, because they have the budget and resources to develop the military spectacle—is this UN fantasy, a fantasy of united warfare. (The same wishful UN theme cropped up in a recent spectacular which is not science fiction, *Fifty-Five Days in Peking* [1963]. There, topically enough, the Chinese, the Boxers, play the role of Martian invaders who unite the earthmen, in this case the United States, England, Russia, France, Germany, Italy, and Japan.) A great enough disaster cancels all enmities and calls upon the utmost concentration of earth resources.

Science—technology—is conceived of as the great unifier. Thus the science fiction films also project a Utopian fantasy. In the classic models of Utopian thinking—Plato's Republic, Campanella's City of the Sun, More's Utopia, Swift's land of the Houyhnhnms, Voltaire's Eldorado—[3]society had worked out a perfect consensus. In these societies reasonableness had achieved an unbreakable supremacy over the emotions. Since no disagreement or social conflict was intellectually plausible, none was possible. As in Melville's *Typee*, "they all think the same." The universal rule of reason meant universal agreement. It is interesting, too, that societies in which reason was pictured as totally ascendant were also traditionally pictured as having an ascetic or materially frugal and economically simple mode of life. But in the Utopian world community projected by science fiction films, totally pacified and ruled by scientific consensus, the demand for simplicity of material existence would be absurd.

Yet alongside the hopeful fantasy of moral simplification and international unity embodied in the science fiction films lurk the deepest anxieties about contemporary existence. I don't mean only the very real trauma of the Bomb—that it has been used, that there are enough now to kill everyone on earth many times over, that those new bombs may very well be used. Besides these new anxieties about physical disaster, the prospect of universal mutilation and even annihilation, the science fiction films reflect powerful anxieties about the condition of the individual psyche.

For science fiction films may also be described as a popular mythology for the contemporary *negative* imagination about the impersonal. The other-world creatures that seek to take "us" over are an "it," not a "they." The planetary invaders are usually zombie-like. Their movements are either cool, mechanical, or lumbering, blobby. But it amounts to the same thing. If they are non-human in form, they proceed with an absolutely regular, unalterable movement (unalterable save by destruction). If they are human in form—dressed in space suits, etc.—then they obey the most rigid military discipline, and display no personal characteristics whatsoever. And it is this regime of emotionlessness, of impersonality, of regimentation, which they will impose on the earth if they are successful. "No more love, no more beauty, no more pain," boasts a converted earthling in *The Invasion of the Body Snatchers* (1956). The half-earthling, half-alien children in *The Children of the Damned* (1960) are absolutely emotionless, move as a group and understand each others' thoughts, and are all prodigious intellects. They are the wave of the future, man in his next stage of development.

[3]Tommaso Campanella (1568–1630), Italian Renaissance philosopher; Sir Thomas More (1478–1535), English statesman executed by King Henry VIII for refusing to accept Henry as head of the Church; Jonathan Swift (1667–1745), English satirist; the Houyhnhnms appear in his most famous work, *Gulliver's Travels*; Voltaire, pen name of François Marie Arout (1694–1778), French philosopher, famous for his satire *Candide*. (eds.)

These alien invaders practice a crime which is worse than murder. They do not simply kill the person. They obliterate him. In *The War of the Worlds*, the ray which issues from the rocket ship disintegrates all persons and objects in its path, leaving no trace of them but a light ash. In Honda's *The H-Man* (1959), the creeping blob melts all flesh with which it comes in contact. If the blob, which looks like a huge hunk of red Jello and can crawl across floors and up and down walls, so much as touches your bare foot, all that is left of you is a heap of clothes on the floor. (A more articulated, size-multiplying blob is the villain in the English film *The Creeping Unknown* [1956].) In another version of this fantasy, the body is preserved but the person is entirely reconstituted as the automatized servant or agent of the alien powers. This is, of course, the vampire fantasy in new dress. The person is really dead, but he doesn't know it. He is "undead," he has become an "unperson." It happens to a whole California town in *The Invasion of the Body Snatchers*, to several earth scientists in *This Island Earth*, and to assorted innocents in *It Came From Outer Space, Attack of the Puppet People* (1958), and *The Brain Eaters* (1958). As the victim always backs away from the vampire's horrifying embrace, so in science fiction films the person always fights being "taken over"; he wants to retain his humanity. But once the deed has been done, the victim is eminently satisfied with his condition. He has not been converted from human amiability to monstrous "animal" bloodlust (a metaphoric exaggeration of sexual desire), as in the old vampire fantasy. No, he has simply become far more efficient—the very model of technocratic man, purged of emotions, volitionless, tranquil, obedient to all orders. (The dark

secret behind human nature used to be the upsurge of the animal—as in *King Kong*. The threat to man, his availability to dehumanization, lay in his own animality. Now the danger is understood as residing in man's ability to be turned into a machine.)

The rule, of course, is that this horrible and irremediable form of murder can strike anyone in the film except the hero. The hero and his family, while greatly threatened, always escape this fate and by the end of the film the invaders have been repulsed or destroyed. I know of only one exception, *The Day That Mars Invaded Earth* (1963), in which after all the standard struggles the scientist-hero, his wife, and their two children are "taken over" by the alien invaders—and that's that. (The last minutes of the film show them being incinerated by the Martians' rays and their ash silhouettes flushed down their empty swimming pool, while their simulacra drive off in the family car.) Another variant but upbeat switch on the rule occurs in *The Creation of the Humanoids* (1964), where the hero discovers at the end of the film that he, too, has been turned into a metal robot, complete with highly efficient and virtually indestructible mechanical insides, although he didn't know it and detected no difference in himself. He learns, however, that he will shortly be upgraded into a "humanoid" having all the properties of a real man.

Of all the standard motifs of science fiction films, this theme of dehumanization is perhaps the most fascinating. For, as I have indicated, it is scarcely a black-and-white situation, as in the old vampire films. The attitude of the science fiction films toward depersonalization is mixed. On the one hand, they deplore it as the ultimate horror. On the other hand, certain characteristics of the dehumanized invaders, modulated and disguised—such as the ascendancy of reason over feelings, the idealization of teamwork and the consensus-creating activities of science, a marked degree of moral simplification—are precisely traits of the savior-scientist. It is interesting that when the scientist in these films is treated negatively, it is usually done through the portrayal of an individual scientist who holes up in his laboratory and neglects his fiancée or his loving wife and children, obsessed by his daring and dangerous experiments. The scientist as a loyal member of a team, and therefore considerably less individualized, is treated quite respectfully.

There is absolutely no social criticism, of even the most implicit kind, in science fiction films. No criticism, for example, of the conditions of our society which create the impersonality and dehumanization which science fiction fantasies displace onto the influence of an alien It. Also, the notion of science as a social activity, interlocking with social and political interests, is unacknowledged. Science is simply either adventure (for good or evil) or a technical response to danger. And, typically, when the fear of science is paramount—when science is conceived of as black magic rather than white—the evil has no attribution beyond that of the perverse will of an individual scientist. In science fiction films the antithesis of black magic and white is drawn as a split between technology, which is beneficent, and the errant individual will of a lone intellectual.

Thus, science fiction films can be looked at as thematically central allegory, replete with standard modern attitudes. The theme of depersonalization (being "taken over") which I have been talking about is a new allegory reflecting the age-old awareness of man that, sane, he is always perilously close to insanity and unreason. But there is something more here than just a recent, popular image which expresses man's perennial, but largely unconscious, anxiety about his sanity. The image derives most of its power from a supplementary and historical anxiety, also not experienced *consciously* by most people, about the depersonalizing conditions of modern urban life. Similarly, it is not enough to note that science fiction allegories are one of the new myths about —that is, one of the ways of accommodating to and negating—the perennial human anxiety about death. (Myths of heaven and hell, and of ghosts, had the same function.) For, again, there is a historically specifiable twist which intensifies the anxiety. I mean, the trauma suffered by everyone in the middle of the 20th century when it became clear that, from now on to the end of human history, every person would spend his individual life under the threat not only of individual death, which is certain, but of something almost insupportable psychologically—collective incineration and extinction which could come at any time, virtually without warning.

From a psychological point of view, the imagination of disaster does not greatly differ from one period in history to another. But from a political and moral point of view, it does. The expectation of the apocalypse may be the occasion for a radical disaffiliation from society, as when thousands of Eastern European Jews in the 17th century, hearing that Sabbatai Zevi had been proclaimed the Messiah and that the end of the world was imminent, gave up their homes and businesses and began the trek to Palestine. But people take the news of their doom in diverse ways. It is reported that in 1945 the populace of Berlin received without great agitation the news that Hitler had decided to kill them all, before the Allies arrived, because they had not been worthy enough to win the war. We are, alas, more in the position of the Berliners of 1945 than of the Jews of 17th century Eastern Europe; and our response is closer to theirs, too. What I am suggesting is that the imagery of disaster in science fiction is above all the emblem of an *inadequate response*. I don't mean to bear down on the films for this. They themselves are only a sampling, stripped of sophistication, of the inadequacy of most people's response to the unassimilable terrors that infect their consciousness. The interest of the films, aside from their considerable amount of cinematic charm, consists in this intersection between a naïve and largely debased commercial art product and the most profound dilemmas of the contemporary situation.

Ours is indeed an age of extremity. For we live under continual threat of two equally fearful, but seemingly opposed, destinies: unremitting banality and inconceivable terror. It is fantasy, served out in large rations by the popular arts, which allows most people to cope with these twin specters. For one job that fantasy can do is to lift us out of the unbearably humdrum and to distract us from terrors— real or anticipated—by an escape into exotic, dangerous situations which have last-minute happy endings. But another of the things that fantasy can do is to normalize what is psychologically unbearable, thereby inuring us to it. In one case, fantasy beautifies the world. In the other, it neutralizes it.

The fantasy in science fiction films does both jobs. The films reflect worldwide anxieties, and they serve to allay them. They inculcate a strange apathy concerning the processes of radiation, contamination, and destruction which I for one find haunting and depressing. The naïve level of the films neatly tempers the sense of otherness, of alien-ness, with the grossly familiar. In particular, the dialogue of most science fiction films, which is of a monumental but often touching banality, makes them wonderfully, unintentionally funny. Lines like "Come quickly, there's a monster in my bathtub." "We must do something about this." "Wait, Professor. There's someone on the telephone," "But that's incredible," and the old American stand-by, "I hope it works!" are hilarious in the context of picturesque and deafening holocaust. Yet the films also contain something that is painful and in deadly earnest.

There is a sense in which all these movies are in complicity with the abhorrent. They neutralize it, as I have said. It is no more, perhaps, than the way all art draws its audience into a circle of complicity with the thing represented. But in these films we have to do with things which are (quite literally) unthinkable. Here, "thinking about the unthinkable"— not in the way of Herman Kahn,[4] as a subject for calculation, but as a subject for fantasy—becomes, however inadvertently, itself a somewhat questionable act from a moral point of view. The films perpetuate clichés about identity, volition, power, knowledge, happiness, social consensus, guilt, responsibility which are, to say the least, not serviceable in our present extremity. But collective nightmares cannot be banished by demonstrating that they

[4]Herman Kahn is a futurist. (eds.)

are, intellectually and morally, fallacious. This nightmare—the one reflected, in vari- ous registers, in the science fiction films— is too close to our reality.

Aids   *The Imagination of Disaster*

1. "The Imagination of Disaster" is rich in ideas, but it is a sophisticated essay that requires close scrutiny. As you reexamine the essay, ask yourself the following questions: (a) According to Sontag, what attitudes toward science and scientists are expressed by science fiction films? (b) What is the role of machinery in these films? (c) What attitudes toward war emerge in science fiction? (d) How is "dehumanization" practiced in these films? Sontag says that in these films attitudes toward depersonalization are mixed. What does she mean? (e) What *is* the imagination of disaster? Why does it exist? What makes its modern manifestation unique?

2. What does Sontag mean when she says ". . . we live under continual threat of two equally fearful, but seemingly opposed destinies unremitting banality and inconceivable terror"? How does fantasy help us cope with these twin specters?

3. According to Sontag, what are the basic differences between very old science fiction films and those made in the 1950s and early 1960s?

4. In what ways are science fiction films and horror films alike? In what ways are they different?

5. Sontag uses concrete examples from films to support her generalizations. Many of the films she cites may be unfamiliar to you. Does she provide enough information in her examples to make them useful? (Although it is not always necessary to choose examples familiar to your readers, it is necessary to somehow make your examples meaningful to them.)

6. Sontag says that "Science fiction films can be looked at as thematically central allegory." What is an allegory? How are science fiction films allegorical? Do you think X. J. Kennedy would agree or disagree with Sontag on this point?

7. Sontag states that science fiction films in the 1950s registered the collective nightmare about the improper uses of technology. Technology meant the atom bomb and destruction. Television is a good source of old science fiction films. Watch, if possible, a 1950s film and examine the way technology is treated. Observe not only the

characters' attitudes toward technology, but also the ways in which technological devices are actually treated by the director. (Technology in monster movies, for example, is often housed in damp, dark caverns; tubes bubble mysteriously, electrical connections spark inexplicably. The equipment itself is rendered mysterious and somewhat sinister.) Does the treatment of technological devices in 1950s films suggest imminent destruction?

The 1960s brought manned space travel and the first landing on the moon—exciting adventures that appealed to the pioneering instincts of many Americans. Filmed shots of the moon landing rendered that event almost poetic—soft pastel colors, men walking gracefully in slow motion. To many Americans technology became beautiful, exciting, and promising. Do you find this new attitude reflected in the science fiction films of the 1960s? in contemporary science fiction films?

8. In an article entitled "The Science Fiction Film" (*Film Journal*, vol. 2, 1974), Fred Chappell notes five types of incongruity found in science fiction films: (1) anachronisms (objects displaced from their normal historical contexts), (2) scale (giantism or pygmyism), (3) displacement of faculties or sympathies (intelligent machines, benevolent monsters), (4) violent collision of natural and artificial objects (space ship in the wilderness), (5) inaccuracy of detail (factual error displayed out of ignorance or out of concern for visual effect). Test Chappell's categories against an old science fiction film. Which sorts of incongruity are most common in the film you chose? Do you think incongruity is an important ingredient in the "imagination of disaster"?

9. According to Gerald Jonas, a critic of science fiction, the stylistic barrier that separates most science fiction from "mainstream" literature is the pseudotechnical jargon devised by science fiction writers "who want to pay homage to modern science without letting it hinder their wilder flights of fancy." Examine the style (diction, structure, imagery, symbolism) of a science fiction story or novel, and determine the effect of the technical language on your appreciation of the work. Does the language separate you from the story in particular and science fiction in general?

10. The skills of prediction, speculation, and extrapolation used by science fiction writers are extremely popular in our future oriented society. Try your hand at science fiction, and write a story based on some technological development or social and cultural change. In addition to creating a realistic portrait of a future society, develop one of the themes discussed by Susan Sontag in her essay.

Popcorn Venus:
Or How the Movies
Have Made Women
Smaller Than Life

MARJORIE ROSEN

Movies have always been a form of popular culture that altered the way women looked at the world and reflected how men intended to keep it. Money, entertainment, and morality were inextricably intertwined, yet often they worked at cross-purposes, creating a Cinema Woman who has been a Popcorn Venus, a delectable but insubstantial hybrid of cultural distortions.

First came Edison's Kinetoscope, on April 23, 1896, and among his images was a prophetic one of a girl performing a hula. Within 10 years, five-minute movies had become the great escape, and sometimes even the bridge between life and death. Witness the following:

MOVED BY MOVING PICTURES
(special to *Variety*)

Denver, Colorado; February 22, 1906: It developed at the inquest on the body of the woman who committed suicide on the stage of the Crystal Theater Monday that she was moved to the act by a motion picture subject which showed the suicide of a criminal at its climax. The woman had been in a bad mental state for some time, and was taken to the theater in the hope that the entertainment would cheer her up. Instead, the showing of the picture brought on acute suicidal mania and she stepped to the stage and shot herself.

If movies at this primitive stage could have such an effect, think of the potent fantasies that would be given shape by strong plots, sophisticated techniques and hard-sell ideas and images, images which at first would preserve man's cherished girl-child.

Enter Mary Pickford. With her, the film industry would develop its first real star. Known as "The Girl with the Curl," she couldn't have happened at a better time to stultify the growth of women's self-image. It's no coincidence that her screen credits read like a child's garden of verses: "In the Sultan's Garden," "Little Red Riding Hood," "The Little Princess." By 1917 she made $350,000 a year; her star was still rising.

Only her age was diminishing—on screen. Mary made "Rebecca of Sunnybrook Farm" (1917) when she was 24, "Pollyanna" at 26, "Little Lord Fauntleroy" at 28; she played 12-year-old Annie Rooney at 32. Even into the Roaring Twenties, audiences clamored for her feisty girl-children and innocent waifs. For two decades she and the public played on each other's fears and fantasies. But her myth was an insult. In abhorring age and repressing sexuality she had created a freak who denied—in fact made repugnant—all womanhood.

If Mary Pickford was the Eternal Child of Victorian fantasies, D. W. Griffith[1] was the embodiment of the male conscience that idealized her. Griffith not only surrounded himself with nubile teenage actresses (Lillian Gish, Pickford, Blanche Sweet, Mae Marsh), but at the age of 61 realized his fantasy by marrying Evelyn Baldwin, a woman 35 years his junior whom he'd known since she was 13. His movies continually focused on females as love objects, females as children who had no identities other than sexual, yet who were rarely allowed to fulfill their sexuality without negative consequences. In "The Birth of a Nation," the coming of age of the new medium, Lillian Gish is rescued from near-rape, but not before the audience is on the edge of its seat rooting for the safety of her hymen. In "Broken Blossoms" (1919) a Chinese lusts after a 12-year-old girl, and because he hasn't the courage to act out his desires, Griffith deceptively assures us: "his love remains a pure and holy thing—even his worst foes say this." If Griffith's incipient nymphophilia was in tune with the nation's Victorian conscience, it drastically clashed with the approaching twenties' morality. The director was to falter, then fade into oblivion as sex took a different, more nonchalant turn on the silver screen.

The 19th Amendment, ratified in January, 1919, finally granted women the right to vote. The number of workingwomen had virtually doubled since the turn of the century so that women represented more than one-fifth of the total working population. For the first time the flapper had money of her own. She could choose how and where to spend it. Films were reflecting her new situation, reinforcing the chic and high spirits of the time: "In Search of Sinners," "Jazzmania," "The Flappers," "Our Dancing Daughters," "Dancing Mothers," "Wine of Youth." But the cheeky flapper only got her man *if she deserved to*. Shopgirl Clara Bow snared her wealthy

[1]D. W. Griffith directed Mary Pickford in a number of successful movies. (eds.)

boss because she had IT ("*It*," 1927), while Joan Crawford exploited the love of a millionaire and got her comeuppance by dying in an automobile wreck in "Sally, Irene, and Mary" (1925).

It is interesting, too, that flappers were always shopgirls and blue-collar workers on screen. Although more women than ever before were going to college in the twenties (the percentage earning Ph.D.'s was higher than it is today), the prevailing attitude toward education was summed up by Calvin Coolidge when he called women's colleges "hotbeds of radicalism." Movies glorified women who were young, beautiful, highly moral, and ready to drop job and glitter for a good man.

The most suitable genre to the needs of the industry was that of the chorine. Chorus Girl films—"Broadway Lady," "Queen of the Chorus," "Peacock Alley"—not only appealed to girlish fantasies, but also moralized endlessly. If a chorine "fell," she was disposed of during the final reel; but if, like the flapper, she overcame temptation, she was rewarded by a handsome hero's proposal. The sound of babies, not applause, would fill her ears and satisfy her ego.

As the decade closed, films held a tight rein on their "liberated" heroines. And in real life, too, women were forced to wonder about the contradictions of their partial freedom. Where would their education take them if men required them to stay home and have babies? What would a decade of working do for them if their take-home pay barely covered expenses, and employers refused to equalize it with male salaries for similar jobs?

Was liberation worth anything, after all?

Women became the sacrificial lambs of the Depression; but amid the collective pain of the nation's bellies they scarcely felt the knife. Mass despair was reflected in Tin Pan Alley's dreamy ironies like "Time on My Hands," or "Brother, Can You Spare a Dime?" In marathon dances, trials of endurance. By the end of 1930, with the worst of hard times yet to come, one-fifth of the 10 million workingwomen were jobless. Schools drafted regulations making married women ineligible to teach and firing single women who married during the term of employment. Professional women, whose ranks had doubled, tripled, quadrupled during the Jazz Age, were now fighting simply to maintain their status quo. But Hollywood expediently ignored reality.

The "talkies" created a new dynamic on the screen. Characters, now vocal, were also more real. Brittle edges fascinated. Depression movies focused on women living by their wits. A curious conglomeration of detectives, spies, con artists, private secretaries, molls, and especially reporters constituted the new genre. Audiences saw the calm and elegant Myrna Loy, whose cool common sense graced "The Thin Man" (1934) and its five sequels; Bette Davis as stenographer in "Three on a Match," political campaigner in "Dark Horse" (both 1932), copywriter in "Housewife" (1934), insurance probator in "Jimmy the Gent" (1934), and cub reporter in "Front Page Woman" (1935).

But the genre really belonged to Jean Arthur, whose best-remembered films, "Mr. Deeds Goes to Town" (1936) and "Mr. Smith Goes to Washington" (1939), cast her as a captivating but nosy go-getter who orders men's lives and smoke-screens her astuteness in a cloud of dizzy offhand conversation. She's a good deal freer than her flapper predecessors. But she's also meddlesome and manipulative, a warning from Hollywood of the dire consequences of womanpower.

In the name of escapism, such films were guilty of extravagant misrepresentations, exuding a sense of well-being to the nation in general and women in particular. Studios, purporting to ease the anguish of Depression reality, transformed movies into the politics of fantasy, the great black-and-white opiate of the masses. And along the way stars had become larger than life—and more memorable.

It was the era of Greta Garbo and Marlene Dietrich. Each casts a shadow as eerie as the mythological Circe. Each inscrutable. Each haunting in her embodiment of the yin/yang of opposites. Aloof, but inviting. Passionate, but impassive. Direct though elusive. Extravagantly beautiful—almost masculine.

Garbo and Dietrich shared the fame they gained as enigmatic incarnations of all that is mysterious to man—all that he wants to conquer, subjugate, destroy. Divinely untouchable, often unworldly, their allure lay in their denial of that humdrum destiny reserved for real-life woman. Rarely did they seek or want love, perhaps because it would be their ruin or demystification. For, once a man imposed himself on them, he consumed them.

But even though there was this sameness, they were distinctly different from each other.

Garbo excelled at conveying with exquisite precision the complexities of her emotions at the crushing devastation that would follow. She made love as if her partner were invisible; as if she were caught up on the crest of autoerotic intimacy. She was elusive, and at the same time all things to all men. "There is nothing in me, nothing of me; take me, take me as you desire me," she tells her lover in "As You Desire Me" (1932).

Dietrich was not so pliable. Much of what Garbo suggested, Dietrich carried to extremes. She could be more sultry, more seductive, more masculine. More warmhearted, more deadly. She remained from the first —with her cajoling Lola in "The Blue Angel" (1930)—the calculating serpent, ever aware of the men, their follies and weaknesses. Ever ready to spring. It evolved into a game: Who would subjugate whom? Who would crack the whip? Whose will would break first? In "Morocco" (1930), she and Gary Cooper at first evade each other, but finally, shoes in hand, she joins the women following the legionnaires into the desert.

If the Mysterious Woman was one thirties' opiate warding off the Depression's reality, another was the earthy blonde bombshell; Jean Harlow, Mae West, Carole Lombard, Joan Blondell, Ginger Rogers, Alice Faye, Marion Davies.

Of them, the most interesting of course were Jean Harlow and Mae West. Brash, brassy, and brittle, Harlow's voice echoed with worldliness and commonness simultaneously. This vocal equalizer humanized her. For men, the goddess proved fallible and not as aloof as her image threatened. For women, the voice made the image at once humorous, vulgar, and trashy enough, dumb enough to be touchingly human. Harlow, who originally scored as the tough, wisecracking gun moll of "Hell's Angels" (1930), "The Secret Six" (1931), and "The Public Enemy" (1931) under M-G-M's tutelage, finally graduated to the improbable roles of socialite ("Dinner at Eight," 1933, "Saratoga," 1937), smart secretary ("Suzy," 1936), and star ("Bombshell," 1933); the delectable heroine was often abused, misused, and misled by men, but never relinquished her feistiness.

West, on the other hand, swaggered from one artificial costume epic to another, writing her own scripts, and emanating her brand of vulgarity and ribald comedy. She made nine films between 1932 and 1943—enough to create a lasting legend. And enough to convulse the censors, the Hays Office,[2] the Catholic Church, the Episcopalian Committee on Motion Pictures, and William Randolph Hearst himself, who accused her of being a "monster of lubricity."

It was not her physical appearance that elicited such vehemence from her detractors; actually West was a self-styled drag queen, boned and corseted and looking uncomfortably like a turn-of-the-century sausage, barely able to move because her skirt was too tight and heels too high. Nor were her hilarious one-liners like "I used to be Snow White, but I drifted" enough to anger them so. The more likely explanation is that she, as author and star, controlled plots and manipulated males with the deftness of a puppeteer. In "She Done Him Wrong" (1933), as in her other movies, she sets up harmless situations in which appointed admirers are directed to exalt her. At the end she tootles off with Cary Grant, not out of passion but convenience. It was for her boldness rather than for her innuendo that Mae West was punished.

Of the two bombshells, Harlow's impact was the happier. Without the West wit or studied style, Harlow was spontaneously willful, going after the money or man she wanted with commitment. Her desires mattered. West, although she had chutzpah, took nothing seriously. But the tart directness of Mae West and Jean Harlow were to go soft and

[2]Hays Office, the movie industry's self-censorship board, created in 1922. (eds.)

saccharine as the Depression and the production of escapist movies wore on.

Hollywood, seeing a good thing with its explosive bombshells, converted sass to sugar and taught the blonde to dance. Joan Blondell's Depression Dollies in "Footlight Parade" (1933) and "Gold Diggers of 1933." Ginger Rogers paired with Fred Astaire,[3] a delicate hint of sex hovering in the air, made all the more intricate by his taut hardness flowering under her fleshy blonde femininity. Songstress Jeanette MacDonald, whose cloying courtships-over-high-C with Nelson Eddy[4] earned them the titles of "The Iron Butterfly" and "The Singing Capon." And Little Miss Alice Faye in "That Night in Rio" (1941) and later "The Gang's All Here" (1943), always blubberingly earnest and in love, with a strikingly adolescent ardor for so mature a woman.

Then on December 7, 1941, the Japanese bombed Pearl Harbor. Johnny got his gun. America mobilized. And social roles shifted with a speed that would have sent Wonder Woman into paroxysms of power pride. With the men at war, by 1943 more than 4 million women were employed in munitions work alone. An additional 15 million joined the labor force, doing such formerly "masculine" jobs as coal mining, operating machines, and firing and cleaning antiaircraft guns. At the beginning, nobody, not even the women themselves, imagined they might want to make it permanent.

Hollywood could therefore afford to be temporarily indulgent in the name of patriotism. So Rosie the Riveter, the lower-class working girl, queened it in forties movies. Women in combat and nurses on the front idealized female bravery and participation. But the most affecting and meaningful films were the simpler, perhaps overly sentimental and trite "woman's pictures" in which workers came to grips with their manless existence. Bitchiness and frivolity on the screen gave place to female strength; strength and love and support between mother and daughter, woman and woman. Ginger Rogers in "Tender Comrade" (1943) setting up house with three other women who later comfort her and her newborn after she receives a telegram of her husband's death. Greer Garson in "Mrs. Miniver" (1942) defending her bombed-out house from a wounded Nazi, joining forces with her teen-age daughter-in-law Teresa Wright. Stoical Bette Davis watching her husband, then her sons, risk their lives for the underground in "Watch on the Rhine" (1943).

Since women workers had fallen into an abyss of obedience during the Depression, it is not surprising that at the beginning of the war, they unanimously expressed their intent to work only temporarily. By 1944,

---

[3]Ginger Rogers and Fred Astaire, a famous movie dancing team of the 1930s and 1940s.

[4]Jeanette MacDonald and Nelson Eddy sang together in musical romances.

however, more than 85 percent had reconsidered and wanted to keep their jobs. Industry, though, had other ideas.

With 11 million veterans coming home, massive layoffs began. By 1947 more than 3 million women had resigned or been fired from their positions (more than during the Depression dip). Movies during the forties were no more reflective of the societal shift than those of the thirties. Movies, heretofore stressing female strength, now began to distort it.

A peculiar strain of suspense film preyed on alleged female doubts and infirmities. The most obvious method of undermining was physical. Deafness, and maniacs, plagued Dorothy McGuire in "The Spiral Staircase" (1945) and Jane Wyman in "Johnny Belinda" (1948). Plain deafness plagued Loretta Young in "And Now Tomorrow" (1944), and plain maniacs plagued Barbara Stanwyck in "The Two Mrs. Carrolls" (1944) and Teresa Wright in "Shadow of a Doubt" (1943). Then there was the mental undermining. Ingrid Bergman in "Gaslight" (1944), Olivia de Havilland in "The Snake Pit" (1947), Joan Fontaine in "Suspicion" (1941), and Ginger Rogers in "Lady in the Dark" (1941). When Rogers takes her private demons to a shrink, his diagnosis of the problem is: "You've had to prove you were superior to all men; you had to dominate them." "What's the answer?" she begs. "Perhaps some man who'll dominate you," replies the eminent doctor.

The female-victim genre emerged simultaneously with that of the Evil Woman. It may be no coincidence that at the same time women were acquiring economic and social power in real life. Hollywood simplistically interpreted this shift in the only terms it could understand: power, the quest for love or money.

By the time the Evil Woman genre had played itself out, and Hollywood had given us Mary Astor's Brigid in "The Maltese Falcon" (1941), Lana Turner in "The Postman Always Rings Twice" (1948), Bette Davis in "In This Our Life" (1942), the greedy duplicity and vicious rampage wrought by these women was inextricably intertwined with their allure. As Fred MacMurray says of murderer Barbara Stanwyck in "Double Indemnity" (1944): "How could I know that murder sometimes smells like honeysuckle?"

But honeysuckle wasn't the only peacetime blossom. The war had sanctified the idea of the pinup, and though the movies had concentrated on wholesome family entertainment (since the majority of the audiences were women), men plastered their barracks with inviting photos of film stars. Most popular of all were Rita Hayworth kneeling on an unmade bed and Betty Grable in a skintight swimsuit. The peaches-and-cream wholesome sexuality of these women in wartime musicals—Grable in "Song of the Island" (1942), Hayworth in "Cover Girl" (1944) and "You Were Never Lovelier" (1942)—soon took a back seat and with the return of the men, pure, isolated screen sex escalated like mercury on a hot summer day.

Accordingly, Hayworth, in a black strapless sheath, sang "Put the Blame on Mame" in "Gilda" (1946), and her overt sexuality pulled out all the stops that had been plugged since the demise of the Marlene Dietrich sultriness. Hayworth's sexuality was a very physical one, without mystery or pretense. The golden girl, the beautiful all-American hooker, reverberated in the public imagination, dispelling with her ripe pleasure the intense ephemeralism of the thirties' siren.

That same year marked the brief release of "The Outlaw." A rather ordinary Western made in 1941 but held up by censors because of the film's obsession with Jane Russell's cleavage, it hit a new low in advertising and exploitation. "What are the two great reasons for Jane Russell's rise to stardom?" went an advertising slogan. Almost as tasteless were rulings such as that of a judge who complained that her breasts "hung over the picture like a thunderstorm spread out over a landscape."

Simultaneously, Esther Williams was dipping in and out of the water in "On an Island with You" (1948) and Jennifer Jones was arching her back and quivering her nostrils as the spitfire Pearl in "Duel in the Sun" (1947). Even Joan Crawford had left behind the strength of "Mildred Pierce" (1945) and "Daisy Kenyon" (1947) to be decked out as a cylindrical-breasted tempest in "Flamingo Road" (1949). And in movie-magazine back pages Frederick's of Hollywood was having a mail-order bonanza by advertising the pointy bosoms and clover behinds that every wistful housewife and movie-mad teenager was being told were truly "sexy." Hollywood, however, was not content to dictate exteriors alone. Johnny was home from the war. And by the fifties the industry was reaffirming male dominance and female subservience.

One of the few constants during that decade was the direction women were heading: backward. They married younger than at any previous time during this century; in 1951 one in three had found a husband by the age of 19. And movies reflected this with: *women trapping men* in "Three Coins in the Fountain" (1954), "Gentlemen Prefer Blondes" (1953), "How To Marry a Millionaire" (1953), "Seven Brides for Seven Brothers" (1954); *women preparing for the wedding* in "Father of the Bride" (1950), "High Society" (1955), "The Catered Affair" (1956); *romancing widows* in "The Magnificent Obsession" (1954), "Love Is a Many-Splendored Thing" (1955). *Woman alone* was portrayed as a desperate and needy neurotic— recall the *oeuvre* of Tennessee Williams, Katharine Hepburn's spinsters in "Summertime" (1955) and "The Rainmaker" (1956), or Bette Davis's Margo Channing in "All About Eve" (1950). Marriage was the be-all and end-all. Women's films divorced themselves from timely plots and controversial subjects and became "how-to's" on catching and keeping a man. Veneer. Appearance. Sex Appeal.

Hollywood descended into mammary madness. Monroe, Mansfield, Bardot, Loren, Ekberg were all elevated to fame in the thrust of Russell's

Culver Pictures

original largesse. Men ogled. And women emulated. While they were going off to colleges to find their man (because the G.I. Bill was sending more men to college than ever before), they were also allowing themselves to be molded and beautified.

But despite Hollywood's enthusiasm for the (highly profitable) Mammary Woman, the industry was still unable to shake off a depression. So, as early as 1950, Hollywood began thinking young; the movies intrepidly went to work on America's daughters.

Daddy's little girl would merge with Everyman's ideal, and precocious teenager Debbie Reynolds, clowning around in Dick Powell's oversized pajamas in "Susan Slept Here" (1954), froze the frame on the archetypal teenager of the decade. Reynolds led a gaggle of girls-next-door—Doris Day, Pier Angeli, Terry Moore, Janet Leigh, Natalie Wood. Pretty, amusing, and childish, they enjoyed marvelous popularity among fans who could relate to them as they never had to the haughty sophistication of Joan Crawford, Bette Davis, Lana Turner. Movie magazines boomed.

Who could dislike Audrey Hepburn's fawnlike elegance in "Roman Holiday" (1953) and "Sabrina" (1954), or Leslie Caron's pouting Mademoiselle in "An American in Paris" (1951), her girl-woman in "Gigi" (1958) and "Fanny" (1961)?

A good many fifties' notions about little girls and burgeoning sexuality were embodied on screen by Sandra Dee. While Dee presented the most passive fluttery pink-and-white-ribbons perfection, her ample mouth recalled the petulance of an adolescent Bardot. By scaling down this image of feline sexuality for the high school set, Dee wove the transition between the fifties' naiveté and the sixties' nymphet, exhibiting a provocative self-awareness, almost a fear of her own sexuality. She enjoyed a swift and sweeping success, giving new dimensions to such teenage fantasy films as "Gidget" (1959) and later "A Summer Place" (1959), in which even youthful motherhood and a hasty marriage couldn't upstage the fact of teenage eroticism, which had never been explored so directly.

And kids responded to it. "A Summer Place" grossed more than $1.9 million in its first two months in movie theaters. The heroine's pregnancy was almost immaterial, for the picture was tied up in such an attractively passionate package that nobody cared.

Change, however, was hovering at the edge of the sixties. By the close of the decade middle-class girls were *expected* to attend college. And while a good percentage were hunting for husbands, others picked up degrees and career ambitions. Also, as divorce rates skyrocketed, the first generation brought up on "happily ever after" Hollywood endings discovered that reality delivered something else.

The sixties' woman possessed a unique problem: she was single, and often self-supporting. Movies reduced her "problem" to one question: *Will she or won't she?* Love stories—starring Natalie Wood, Connie Stevens, and most obviously Doris Day—focused on this dilemma to the exclusion of most other plot or character conflicts.

At the same time, offscreen, the Pill had happened. And off the American screen, so had "La Dolce Vita" (1961), the Beatles, LSD, galumphing "Georgy Girl" (1966), glamorously amoral "Darling" (1965), and David Hemmings, romping on colored paper with two nude "birds" in "Blow-Up" (1966). Audiences traded in Doris Day for Julie Christie, and Sandra Dee for Twiggy. Teenagers were sexually mobilized.

Meanwhile back in Hollywood moviemakers were offering "Mary Poppins" (1964), "The Sound of Music" (1965), and "The Group" (1966); they seemed unwilling or unable to reflect the tapestry of the youth culture. Yet the English heroines, for all their freewheeling carryings-on, were at best unable to get a grip on their lives, only on their libidos. And a new kind of sex object was born—the amoral nymphet. Exemplified by Genevieve Waite in "Joanna" (1968), she was baby-faced, reed-slender; her emotional lineage may have been that of "Darling," but physically her family tree revealed a bit of Hayley Mills's childish faun, a good deal more of "Baby Doll" (1956) and "Lolita" (1962). Most significant about this new gamine was the elevation to an ideal of her helplessness and little-boy body—an almost violent reaction to the breasts-and-buttocks fetishes of the Monroe period. "Joanna" is the sixties' sex symbol. Waite's heroine, as nonthreatening and pure as a nine-year-old, signified a futuristic trend: woman as androgyne.

Movieland sex used to go with romance, but as profits sagged and theater audiences dwindled, male moviemakers began to dissect the sex act itself—as men fantasize it.

And so we have "Deep Throat" (1972), with Linda Lovelace's shaved pubis and carefully guarded secret—how to control her gag reflexes while giving head. We have "The Killing of Sister George" (1968) and "X, Y, and Zee" (1972)—sensational exploitation of lesbianism (hasn't it always been an erotic turn-on for men, from the old stag-movie days?). We have, with Andy Warhol's films "Trash" (1970), "Women in Revolt" (1972), and "Heat" (1972), contemptuous exploitation of femininity. We have women getting gang-banged, as in "Straw Dogs" (1971), and liking it.

And we have films that don't even need women at all: "Bullitt" (1968), "2001" (1969), "Patton" (1970), "The French Connection" (1971), "Dirty Harry" (1971), "Prime Cut" (1972), "Deliverance" (1972), "Papillon" (1973).

It is ironic that sixties' and seventies' women have seized on a more productive lifestyle than ever before, but the industry has turned its back on reflecting it in any constructive or analytical way. Is there any hope for intelligent portrayals of women as productive and emotional beings, as intriguing protagonists and heroic models? Have movies, since women have united to raise their own consciousness and society's, produced anything worthwhile for us?

A few do exist. Joanne Woodward's lonely and aching spinster in "Rachel, Rachel" (1968); Shirley MacLaine, nicely manipulating a happy husband and happy lover in "The Bliss of Mrs. Blossom" (1968); Jane Fonda's gritty and needy call girl Bree in "Klute" (1971); Ellen Burstyn and Cloris Leachman in "The Last Picture Show" (1971). And perhaps the most gloriously intelligent film of the past few years, "Sunday Bloody Sunday" (1971), in which Glenda Jackson emerges from an unsatisfactory affair, alone, but with her integrity intact. "I used to believe anything was better than nothing," she tells her lover. "Now I know that sometimes nothing is better."

Think, too, of the dignity black women are finally gaining on screen —Diana Ross's lovely and agonizing portrait of Billie Holiday in "Lady Sings the Blues" (1972), and Cicely Tyson's watchful, proud, and loving mother in "Sounder" (1972). With the exception of a few rare movies— "Porgy and Bess" (1959), for one—Hollywood's attitude toward blacks has historically been shamelessly racist. From the first pickaninnies dancing in the streets, their mouths full of watermelon, in Griffith's "The Birth of a Nation," through Mae West's shuffling, yassum maids and King Vidor's fetching but disloyal and dumb temptress Nina Mae Kinney in "Hallelujah!" (1930), to Butterfly McQueen's lazy featherhead Prissy in "Gone with the Wind" (1939), black women have been herded into the most abominably simplistic and offensive molds.

But the Chicana has yet to appear on the screen. The closest Hollywood came to acknowledging her presence was in the Latin Spitfire, the exoticism of Dolores Del Rio in "Bird of Paradise" (1932), Lupe Velez in "Cuban Love Song" (1932) and "Mexican Spitfire" (1939), and Maria Montez in "Gypsy Wildcat" (1944) and later Katy Jurado in "High Noon" (1952) and "One-Eyed Jacks" (1961). All were merely sultry sex objects, "wildcats" in need of taming.

Women filmmakers with a sense of their own history and a political perspective on the future must become integrated into the fabric of commercial moviemaking. Until then, it's up to us to vocalize loudly about what *we* want, to support it when it comes along, and to boycott those movies which disregard or do injustice to the image of woman. There's no excuse for the insubstantial Popcorn Venuses that have embodied and distorted our fantasies and shaped false realities. If movies unconsciously or consciously define and reflect us, we must *demand* substance as well as chimera.

Aids   *Popcorn Venus*

1. In "Popcorn Venus" Marjorie Rosen traces various female stereotypes in American movies. (For a definition of stereotype, look at question 6 following John Cawelti's essay, "Savagery and Civilization.") Discuss the changing stereotypes of women in American film from 1896 to the present. Locate from the essay or from your own experience examples of each of the following types:

girl-children	female as victim
mystery woman	evil woman
blonde bombshell	mammary woman
Rosie the riveter	girl next door
gold digger	amoral nymphet

   How does each type represent an oversimplification? Are feminists, such as Marjorie Rosen, justified in their criticism of the sexual subject-master relationship as portrayed in film? Have filmmakers become more sensitive to this problem? Locate if you can some current films in which women are depicted realistically.

2. In choosing to treat her material historically, Rosen is committed to organizing her essay chronologically. Histories, biographies, and autobiographies are usually organized chronologically. However, "Popcorn Venus" is not merely a history of the movies. At each step in this chronology Rosen carefully analyzes her data. What does Rosen conclude as a result of her analysis? Can you isolate a single thesis?

3. Rosen provides many examples of each of her film stereotypes. Many of the movies and movie stars she cites may be unfamiliar to you. Does this diminish the impact of her essay? Do you think presenting a reader with masses of evidence is an effective means of illustrating a problem of social injustice?

4. According to Haig A. Bosmaijan, in "The Language of Sexism" [*ETC: A Review of General Semantics*, XXIX, 3 (1972)], "our identities, who and what we are or think we are, how others see and define us, are greatly affected by language." Watch some films made in the 1940s and 1950s on television, noting uses of what is considered today as sexist language. What words are used to describe women? What are the connotations of such words as *chicks, dish, broad,* and *honeys?* What do they suggest about the image of women during this period? Can the same be said for language used to describe (a) men, (b) blacks, (c) youth, and (d) other minority groups in the media during these decades?

5. Although Rosen's essay deals specifically with female stereotypes, it would be difficult to deny that men too have been stereotyped by the film industry. Locate examples of the following types:

American Adam	effete intellectual
blood brother	father knows best
macho male	Superfly

6. Media stereotyping is, of course, not limited to unrealistic portrayals of women and men. Black people have been much abused by the American movie industry. Old movies are full of offensive stereotypes —Stepin Fetchit, who shuffled his way through Shirley Temple movies; Prissy, the simpering houseslave in *Gone with the Wind.* Although the 1960s brought positive black characters to the screen, these characters were often so good as to be oversimplified and unrealistic. What is the current status of blacks in film? Do movies continue to perpetuate old stereotypes? Are realistic films about

blacks being made? What kinds of roles do black actors play? How are black women treated on the screen?

7. American Indians have been part of American cinema since the beginning, yet no group has been more maligned by the film industry. We are all too familiar with those countless westerns in which a tribe of bloodthirsty, screaming "savages" attacks the wagon train, scalps the men, and carries off the women. The movies have created most of our widely held stereotypes of our native Americans—they all speak pidgin English (Ugh, me go now), they can't be trusted with alcohol, and they kill for the sake of killing. Do you think the rise of a militant Indian movement, groups like AIM, and the recent confrontation at Wounded Knee have influenced Hollywood's treatment of the Indian? Do the Billy Jack films break down old stereotypes or reinforce them? How are Indians depicted in current westerns?

The Rhetoric of Film Propaganda: Triumph of the Will (1934-1936)

MARSHA KINDER

BEVERLE HOUSTON

When the Nazis came to power in 1933, they immediately took over the film industry. Goebbels[1] foresaw that films could do for Germany what *Battleship Potemkin*[2] had done for the Soviet Union. In *Mein Kampf* Hitler recounts how he "experienced a mass demonstration of the Marxists," with "a sea of red flags, red scarves, and red flowers," which gave to the demonstration "an aspect that was gigantic from the purely external point of view." He concludes, "I myself could feel and understand how easily the man of the people succumbs to the suggestive magic of a spectacle so grandiose in effect." *Triumph of the Will* tries to achieve this "suggestive magic." Ironically, though it supposedly documents the Nazi party congress at Nuremberg, the huge extravaganza was actually staged for the film.

The goal of the film is to unify the German people. The congress is a massive public relations event, as Hitler observes, "a demonstration of political power for millions." Many of director Leni Riefenstahl's techniques are designed to reveal the variety of groups and national elements participating in this gigantic effort.

During the first parade, the camera reveals soldiers saluting Hitler, women and children offering him flowers, office workers cheering from windows, old people watching him more quietly, and even a cat, under a Nazi flag, silently observing. During the rallies, Hitler addresses groups of men and boys whom we see cleaning, eating, dressing, competing in games, playing in bands, marching. Women and children dance, cheer, and parade in national costumes. He addresses a variety of official groups like the SA, the SS, the Labor Servicemen, and the Hitler Youth. Occasion-

[1] Joseph Goebbels, Hitler's propagandist; Goebbels had complete control over the mass media in Nazi Germany. (eds.)

[2] *Battleship Potemkin*, Sergei Eisenstein's famous film about the abortive 1905 revolution in Russia. (eds.)

ally a dissolve juxtaposes two contrasting images to show their contribution to the unified purpose. For example, the picturesque towers of the old city buildings dissolve into the orderly rows of tents erected to house all the participants in the congress, uniting the old and the new, the permanent and the temporary.

The emphasis on review of troops, both marching and standing in formation, exposes the great range of subtle variations between the kinds of people and activities that will contribute to the unified effort. The Labor Servicemen shoulder their spades like weapons. Marchers carry band instruments, flags, swords, packs, and guns; they wear helmets, officer's hats, and caps. They march in a variety of styles including, of course, the famous goosestep; they offer various military salutes, including the "Heil" with arm extended.

Although the film shows this variety, its emphasis is on unity as it focuses always on groups rather than on individuals, with the single exception of Hitler, who is seen as the living symbol of the entire German nation. His person is frequently intercut with other visual symbols such as the swastika, the eagle, and the iron cross. Speakers underscore his symbolic role with statements like, "You are Germany. When you act, the people act; when you judge, the people judge." "The party is Hitler and Hitler is the party. Germany is Hitler, and Hitler is Germany." Hitler has a variety of functions. He is performer and audience, creator and judge, all-perceiving and perceived by all. The opening titles announce that this film was produced "by order of the Führer" and immediately direct attention to his action: "Adolf Hitler flew again to Nuremberg to review his faithful followers." To strains of music, a plane moves silently across lightly clouded skies. God's airplane does not need engines. We get an aerial view of the town from Hitler's omniscient perspective, which is continued in the parade as the camera shoots over his left shoulder. It is slow to give us a shot of Hitler's face, as if reluctant to offer his full glory too quickly. Later, however, the camera shows not Hitler's perspective but a view of him as the symbolic center of attention. It shoots his face from upward-angle close-ups against fluffy clouds or with other people out of focus. His double role as performer and audience is perhaps best seen in the review of the "52,000 Labor Servicemen." The men put on a stunning performance for Hitler—huge masses chanting, singing, and moving in unison, alternating with occasional soloists, who, when asked by the group, "Where are you from?" tell their points of origin. The camera pans their ranks, reviewing them as Hitler is doing. They dramatically lower their flags as the battlefields of past German defeats are named and then on cue suddenly thrust them upward to show that Germany is alive and powerful. This mass ritual is preparation for Hitler's solo number, a powerful speech that stresses that "work will bind us together." The sequence ends with a cross-dissolve of the troops singing and marching in unison across a gigantic close-up of Hitler's face. This shot anticipates the final image of the film: a close-up of a swastika dissolving to an upward-angle shot of the troops marching, with puffy clouds in the background. When we recall the opening sequence, these visuals equate Hitler with God, with the swastika, and with the German nation. It is not that God is on the German side, or that he is German, but that God is Germany.

The film's handling of time supports this view of the transcendental sources and potentialities of the new state. Events are followed chronologically through morning, afternoon, and evening. In one sequence, we watch the passage of time as the light changes from late afternoon through evening. This handling of time gives to the film the illusion of documenting the congress in an objective way: All time is accounted for; nothing is left out. The huge numbers of people and great sweeps of space require a lot of slow panning intercut with close-ups and demand that the camera remain focused for an extended period on single events in order to get their full effect, creating slow-paced camera work that heightens the illusion of nonselective documentary-like recording.

However, the reliance on chronological development enhances another quite different quality: the film's mythic and religious dimension. The movement of the film through time implies that the energy and resources of the people participating in this great rally defy the limitations of time. The film can run on (in its original version) for the full three hours without exhausting the financial resources of the producer, the physical energy of the persons being photographed, or the patience and enthusiasm of its intended audience. The national fervor also transcends distinctions between night and day. The inclusion of night scenes allows for visual effects that further intensify the mythic quality. The evening rallies are dramatically heightened by the abstract beauty of flickering torches and bonfires, the explosive light of fireworks, and the mysterious effects of billowing smoke. In the second evening rally, this quality is strengthened by effective cutting carefully synchronized with the music, giving the impression that the nation is supported not only by the clear purpose and discipline of the daytime events but also by the dark sources of raw energy and symbolic allegiance revealed at night. Goebbels emphasizes the importance of the recurring smoke and fire imagery as he says, "May the flame and light of our enthusiasm never fail." The night sequences also permit visual effects that develop the analogy between national goal and religious belief. The final night rally takes on the appearance of a religious ceremony as the hall, darkened by shadows, becomes like a cathedral and the camera cuts to the twisted cross of the swastika as Hitler says of the party, "Its total image will be like a holy order."

The mythic dimension of the film is further enhanced by the Germans' own conception of time as an infinite commodity that can nevertheless be controlled, shaped, and absorbed into the national vision. The film's emphasis on youth, expressed in the crowd shots, the youth rallies, and the recurring theme of training and indoctrination, implies the desire to transcend mortality itself. Hitler suggests that the youth can unite past and present in flesh and spirit. He says, "We will pass away, but in you Germany will live." The state, too, must transcend time, as Hitler prophesies that it will "endure for thousands of years." Time itself is shown as pregnant with the possibilities of Germany's destiny as the very opening locates the congress in time's movement toward this destiny. We are told that it took place on September 5, 1934, twenty years after the First World War, sixteen years after Germany's "crucifixion," and nineteen months after its "renaissance." In the first morning sequence, time is presented as poised and waiting for Germany to make use of it. We see, in the early light, overhead shots of the quiet city, windows open, flags waving, streets empty as the day and the city awaken expectantly. In his closing speech at the final night rally, Hitler announces, "We are happy to *know* that the future belongs to us entirely."

Thus in this film the techniques of documentary are used to create the appearance of objective recording where the explicit purpose is to create a sense of group unity to which the individual is subjugated. In fact, these techniques help to create a mythic conception of national destiny.

Aids   *Triumph of the Will*

1. One of the most skillful film propagandists of all time is Leni Riefenstahl, who was employed by Hitler to produce *Triumph of the Will*. The film techniques discussed by Kinder and Houston have been used not only by Riefenstahl, but by all effective propagandists in the cinema. One of the most important tools of the propagandist is the visual symbol—the flag, the emblem, the salute. How, according to Kinder and Houston, does Riefenstahl combine the use of national symbols with mood symbols of mythic dimensions like clouds, fire, and smoke?

2. Camera technique is also an important tool of the propagandist. Riefenstahl consistently shot the Nazi party officials from below so that they would appear to loom larger than life. Hitler, a short man, was photographed so that his head seemed to be in the clouds. According to Houston and Kinder, what other examples of camera techniques does Riefenstahl employ?

3. Editing is another tool to organize and juxtapose experience, but in propaganda it can suggest relationships and analogies that compel viewers to draw conclusions that might be false. In a 1968 campaign film supporting Lyndon Johnson, we hear Barry Goldwater's voice discussing military preparedness while a scene of a small girl picking flowers suddenly cuts to a picture of an atomic mushroom cloud. What examples of propagandistic editing do Kinder and Houston provide? Look for additional examples of these techniques in campaign films and in television commercials.

4. "The Rhetoric of Film Propaganda" originally appeared in a film textbook, and Kinder and Houston frequently use the specialized language of filmmaking. Find out the meanings of the following film terms: *pan, shot, close-up, cutting, dissolve*. A good desk dictionary (like the *American Heritage Dictionary of the English Language*) will

contain most of these terms. William Jinks's essay (the first in this Unit) will also help.

5. Note the propaganda devices discussed by Hugh Rank in Unit II. Test these and the devices described by Kinder and Houston on a movie. You might choose a full-length documentary like *The Sorrow and the Pity* or the campaign film of a national or local politician. Even entertainment films are full of such visual rhetoric. Movies like *The Green Berets, Billy Jack*, and a host of 1940s war films would make fruitful studies.

Photo/David Umberger

Unit V

The Languages of Television and Radio

Television is the newest of the new languages and in terms of audience the most popular. Few periodicals, best sellers, or movies ever get the exposure of a prime-time television series; 100 million people watched "All in the Family" during its first year on the air. Researchers estimate that ninety-six households out of one hundred have at least one television set and that the average American watches television approximately seventeen hours a week.

Yet, although television is our most popular medium, many Americans are uneasy about the quality and impact of the television experience. Television is seldom accorded the status of high art, and the shows that do receive kudos for artistry are usually one-shot specials or Public Broadcasting productions. Critics complain about the dramatic quality of television programming; parents and educators worry over the effects of television viewing on children. Avid TV watchers sometimes apologize for their addiction, and other viewers disclaim any interest: "Oh, I really watch very little TV" or "I only watch the news." Americans are embarrassed and even worried about their love affair with television. It is an infatuation they do not fully understand. The television articles in this unit address this ambivalence and attempt to explain television's massive appeal and assess its impact on our lives.

Horace Newcomb is one of a growing number of critics and scholars who believe that TV is far more than a worthless pastime, that it deserves to be taken seriously. In "Toward a Television Aesthetic" Newcomb acknowledges the tremendous appeal of television and attempts to account for it by an examination of the form rather than the content of this medium. He suggests that one of the most important and unique aspects of television is its quality of "intimacy." The television set itself is small; it is usually part of the living room and often functions as furniture, as an intimate part of our lives. Television programs heighten this sense of intimacy by their use of set, camera work, and visual images. Newcomb is not critical of this aspect of television. He simply points out that this is one quality that has made television our most popular art.

Reed Whittemore makes a similar point when he suggests that television is appealing because it provides us with the familiar. Whittemore, however, turns his analysis into invective. Viewers "wanted big time football . . . they wanted friendly middle class faces with predictable accents telling them at enormous length about the weather." Whereas Newcomb focuses on the unique aspects of television, Whittemore dwells on the derivative qualities of the medium. He feels that nearly everything "that now comprises the TV scene first had its innings in movies and radio. TV made more effective what it borrowed, but it was as a borrower that it grew." Whittemore is far less sanguine than Newcomb about what he sees, and he predicts television will give us more of the same for the next thirty years.

Daniel Menaker's attitudes toward television seem to fall somewhere between those of Newcomb and Whittemore. Menaker shares Newcomb's interest in the form and esthetics of television. He is especially interested in network news, which he perceives as a carefully orchestrated piece of "art/entertainment." Like Whittemore, however, Menaker is uncomfortable with the results of his analysis. He suggests that instead of attempting to reflect reality, the network news is a series of funhouse mirrors which "shrink, elongate, widen, narrow, lighten or exaggerate what stands before them."

According to Nora Kinzer, soap operas pose almost the reverse problem; the soaps have no obligation to mirror reality, yet some viewers become so wrapped up in the drama that they find it difficult to distinguish the character from the actor and the plot from real life. Although this is an extreme response, Kinzer is also worried about the effects of soap operas on the average viewer. She is uncomfortable with the cultural and moral values reflected by the soaps and uneasy about impact the soaps might have on a female viewer's perception of her own life: "While soap operas may make housewives feel safe, soap-opera settings may make those same viewers dissatisfied with their own dull lives. And as long as they watch the soaps, things will never be right."

Stephanie Harrington suggests that viewers delight in game shows precisely because they brighten their own dull lives. She quotes game show producer Mark Goodson, who says that the game show is the type of drama "that allows you to sit home and watch actual people involved in actual situations . . . and you can say 'I could be there myself.' " Harrington, however, is torn between Goodson's rather benign assessment and producer Chuck Barris's contention that "audiences are being entertained whether in awe or shock, or horror, or joy over someone going bananas in public."

Martin Mayer moves the discussion from television's impact on the individual viewer or groups of viewers to its impact on the society as a whole. He is not concerned with specific TV shows or even types of shows but with the medium itself. His results are fascinating. According to Mayer, television has altered the very fabric of our cultural life. It has changed the face of the city, affected racial perceptions, destroyed local entertainment, weakened education, and unified the nation culturally. Mayer points out that in the process of precipitating these massive changes, television drastically altered the roles of the other mass media and destroyed certain segments of the magazine industry altogether. Mayer is not happy with television, but he understands that "it is a phenomenon of unmeasured but clearly major importance in the conduct of all the world's business" and that as such, it must be studied and understood.

Questions about the psychological and social impact of the mass media ultimately lead to the question of censorship. If television is such a potent force, it is not surprising that there are those who would wish to control it. Interestingly, media experts agree that most actual media censorship comes not from the government, but from the networks themselves (although sometimes networks censor in anticipation of government censorship). Nicholas Johnson, a former member of the Federal Communications Commission, suggests that "the networks are keeping off your television screen anything they find inconsistent with their corporate profits or personal philosophies."[1]

Johnson's remark underscores the fact that television is a commercial venture. Although occasionally a well-rated show like "The Smothers Brothers" will be taken off the air for political reasons, most shows are removed or altered because of their ratings. The Nielsen rating is at the very heart of network television programming. According to Joan Hanaur in "Why So Much Emphasis on the Ratings":

> There are 69.9 million television households in the U.S. Each tenth of a rating point represents 69,600. Time is money to networks and they sell to prime-time sponsors at the rate of roughly $5 per thousand households per commercial minute. . . . If a network gets an extra tenth of a rating point it earns an extra $348 per commercial minute. . . . In the course of a 22 hour prime-time week, networks sell approximately 134 commercial minutes. That means that a tenth of a rating point is worth about $46,632 per week and that comes out to just over $2.4 million per year for a tenth of a rating point—or $24 million per point.[2]

In "How the Goshdarn Networks Edit the Heck Out of Movies" David Black suggests that it is this paranoia over the Neilsen ratings (coupled with the fear of government censorship) that is responsible for the networks

[1]Nicholas Johnson, "The Corporate Censor," *T.V. Guide*, July 5, 1969, p. 174.
[2]*Miami Herald T.V. Preview*, March 14, 1976, p. 3.

editing violence and (more often) sex out of commercial movies before they are aired on television. *Time* Magazine has more difficulty accounting for the de facto censorship of "family time." *Time* quotes producer Norman Lear, who says that "sex and violence are a smokescreen. There are interests in this country that don't care to have fun made about the problems existing in society." Although it is unclear whether or not *Time* shares Lear's particular view, *Time* does lament the loss in prime time of "the fresh, funny irreverence of the sitcoms that for only a brief span of time has lit the wasteland."

For better or for worse (or more likely for better and for worse) television is here to stay. As Martin Mayer quips, "it is embedded in the culture now, like frozen lasagna." Television has had and will continue to have an important impact on us individually and collectively, and it is important that we understand the nature of that impact. The television essays in this unit present a variety of points of view and a range of attitudes toward television. They should help you come to your own conclusions about your own television experience.

But what about radio? It once played many of the roles we now ascribe to television. The content of contemporary television *is* in fact that of old radio—westerns, detective shows, sitcoms, and soaps. Many shows moved intact from radio to TV—"Gunsmoke," "The Jack Benny Show," "The Lone Ranger," "The Guiding Light." When television usurped radio's entertainment functions, radio was forced to carve out a new media role for itself.

As Don Pember points out in "Radio: or 'Come On, Let Me Show You Where It's At' " radio's response to this challenge was to narrow the content and style of its programming. Contemporary radio generally broadcasts news, talk shows, public affairs shows, and music. Individual stations tend to appeal to a fairly narrow group of listeners. In any city you will probably find soul stations, country western stations, jazz stations, and a whole range of rock stations—something for everyone.

As television programming came under the control of the networks, radio programming became increasingly local. Today radio, unlike television, consistently covers local events and local news, and features local personalities. Some stations feature live call-in shows that allow the listener to talk back to the station. During an emergency, radio becomes the primary source of information and instruction.

But although we may tout radio's community and service functions, music is the primary content of contemporary radio, and music means records. The relationship between the radio stations and the recording companies has been a checkered one. The music industry very quickly realized that a disc jockey could make or break a record, and the payola scandals of the 1950s were the result. (DJs were paid, either in goods or cash, to promote certain records and recording artists.) In "Where Has All the Music Gone?" Peter McCabe discusses a new problem in the relationship between the radio stations and the record industry. The demise of the listening booth in the record store means that radio is one's only means of hearing the latest records, and the demise of the concert tour means that the artist must become increasingly dependent on radio to market his or her wares. The radio stations, however, have become very conservative in what they are willing to air, and as a result innovative artists find it difficult to get the necessary exposure. McCabe suggests that the Beatles might never have made it had they hit the music scene in 1976.

Although McCabe's article exposes a negative aspect of radio broadcasting, it does underscore the fact that radio is still a potent media force. In fact citizens band radio transceivers have recently become the most-wanted item on everyone's gift list. Originally used for emergency and service communication by police and fire departments, rescue squads, and repairmen, limited-range radio is now the small-talk medium of truck drivers, business executives, and housewives. C. W. McCall's popular recording hit "Convoy" brought to national attention the special lingo generated by truckers for their mobile conversations on CB. Since then thousands have been getting into the act. As Clark Whelton's article "CB Radio Comin' At Ya: Running Down to Dirtytown" illustrates, "Everybody's got a CB these days. . . ." CB operators must be licensed by the FCC, but a 1976 federal government study speculates that by 1979 the FCC will have virtually abandoned efforts to enforce its rules. By 1986 an estimated 10 million CB radios will be jamming the airways.

Television did not kill radio; it simply transformed it. Television may be our most popular art, but in point of fact more adult Americans tune in a radio sometime during the week than turn on a television. They may turn that radio dial for only a few minutes a day—to catch the news or the weather—or they may drive miles engaged in CB small talk. Whether they spend minutes or hours, whether they send or merely receive, radio lovers assure the potency of their chosen medium. Television and radio seem to have carved out mutually exclusive pieces of media territory, and neither is a threat to the other; both play significant roles in our lives.

Toward
a Television
Aesthetic

HORACE NEWCOMB

Defining television as a form of popular art might lead one to ignore the complex social and cultural relationships surrounding it. In his book *Open to Criticism*, Robert Lewis Shayon, former television critic for *The Saturday Review*, warns against such a view.

> To gaze upon this dynamic complexity and to delimit one's attention to merely the aesthetic (or any other single aspect of it) is to indulge one's passion for precision and particularity (an˙undeniable right)—but in my view of criticism it is analogous to flicking a piece of lint off a seamless garment.
>
> The mass media are phenomena that transcend even the broad worlds of literature. They call for the discovery of new laws, new relationships, new insights into drama, ritual and mythology, into the engagement of minds in a context where psychological sensations are deliberately produced for nonimaginative ends, where audiences are created, cultivated and maintained for sale, where they are trained in nondiscrimination and hypnotized by the mechanical illusion of delight. When the symbols that swirl about the planet Earth are manufactured by artists who have placed their talents at the disposition of salesmen, criticism must at last acknowledge that "literature" has been transcended and that the dialectics of evolutionary action have brought the arts to a new level of practice and significance. [Boston, 1971, pp. 48–49]

. . . [H]umanistic analysis, when used to explore aesthetic considerations in the popular arts such as television, can aid directly in that "discovery of new laws, new relationships, new insights into drama, ritual and mythology," which Shayon calls for. In doing so it is necessary to concentrate on the entertaining works themselves, rather than on the psychological effects of those works on and within the mass audience. In those areas the social scientific methodologies may be more capable of offering meaningful results. But we should also remember that most of the works we have dealt with are highly formulaic in nature, and if we think of formula, in John Cawelti's words, as "a model for the construction of artistic works which synthesizes several important cultural functions," then it is possible to see how the aesthetic point of view and the social scientific point of view might supplement one another in a fuller attempt to discover the total meaning of the mass media.

Television is a crucially important object of study not only because it is a new "form," a different "medium," but because it brings its massive audience into a direct relationship with particular sets of values and attitudes. [Even when we examine] works that are less formulaic, we should still be able to recognize the direct connection, in terms of both values and the techniques of presenting them, with more familiar television entertainment. In those newer shows, where the values may become more ambiguous, more individualized, we find an extension and a development of popular television rather than a distinct new form of presentation. The extension and development have demonstrated that even in the more complex series, popularity need not be sacrificed.

To the degree that the values and attitudes of all these shows are submerged in the contexts of dramatic presentation, the aesthetic understanding of television is crucial. . . . In approaching an aesthetic understanding of TV the purpose should be the description and definition of the devices that work to make television one of the most popular arts. We should examine the common elements that enable television to be seen as something more than a transmission device for other forms. [One of these is intimacy.] . . .

The smallness of the television screen has always been its most noticeable physical feature. It means something that the art created for television appears on an object that can be part of one's living room, exist as furniture. It is significant that one can walk around the entire apparatus. Such smallness suits television for intimacy; its presence brings people into the viewer's home to act out dramas. But from the beginning, because the art was visual, it was most commonly compared to the movies. The attempts to marry old-style, theater-oriented movies with television are stylistic failures even though they have proven to be a financial success. Television is at its best when it offers us faces, reactions, explorations of emotions registered by human beings. The importance is not placed on the action, though that is certainly vital as stimulus. Rather, it is on the reaction to the action, to the human response.

An example of this technique is seen in episode twelve of Alistair Cooke's "America: A Personal History." In order to demonstrate the splendor of a New England autumn, Cooke first offers us shots of expansive hillsides glowing with colored trees. But to make his point fully he holds a series of leaves in his hand. He stands in the middle of the forest and demonstrates with each leaf a later stage in the process from green to brown, stages in the process of death. The camera offers a full-screen shot of Cooke's hand portraying the single leaves. The importance of this scene, and for the series, is that Cooke insists on giving us a personal history. We are not so much concerned with the leaves themselves, but with the role they play in Cooke's memories of his early years in America. To make his point immediate, he makes sure that we see what he wants us to see about the autumnal color. The point about the process of death is his, not one that we would come to immediately, on our own, from viewing the leaves.

Commenting on the scene, Cooke praised his cameraman, Jim McMillan. It was McMillan, he said, who always insisted on "shooting for the box," or filming explicitly for television. Such filming is necessary in the series if Cooke's personal attitudes are to be fully expressed visually as well as in his own prose. (Alistair Cooke, concluding comments at a showing of episode twelve of "America: A Personal History" at the Maryland Institute College of Art, Baltimore, Maryland, April 1973)

Such use of technique is highly self-conscious. More popular television, however, has always used exactly the same sense of intimacy in a more unconscious fashion. It is this sense that has done much of the transforming of popular formulas into something special for television. . . . [T]he iconography of rooms is far more important to television than is that of exterior locations. Most of the content of situation comedies, for example, takes place in homes or in offices. Almost all that of domestic comedy takes place indoors, and problems of space often lead to or become the central focus of the show. Even when problems arise from "outdoor" conflicts—can Bud play football if his mother fears for his safety—are turned into problems that can be dealt with and solved within the confines of the living room or kitchen.

Mysteries often take us into the offices of detectives or policemen and into the apartments and hideouts of criminals. In some shows, such as "Ironside," the redesigning of space in keeping with the needs of the character takes on special significance. Ironside requests and receives the top floor of the police headquarters building. In renovating that space he turns it not only into an office but into a home as well. His personal life is thereby defined by his physical relationship to his profession and to the idea of fighting crime. He inhabits the very building of protection. He resides over it in a godlike state that fits his relationship to the force. The fact that it is his home also fits him to serve as the father figure to the group of loyal associates and tempers the way in which he is seen by criminals and by audience. Similarly, his van becomes an even more confined space, also a home, but defined by his handicap. It is the symbol of his mobile identity as well as of his continued personal life.

Such observations would be unimportant were it not for the fact that as we become more intimately introduced to the environment of the detective we become equally involved with his personality. It is the character of the detective, as we have seen, that defines the quality of anticrime in his or her show. The minor eccentricities of each character, the private lives of the detectives, become one of the focal points of the series in which they appear. It is with the individual attitudes that the audience is concerned, and the crimes are defined as personal affronts to certain types of individuals.

Nowhere is this emphasis more important than in the Westerns. In the Western movie, panorama, movement, and environment are crucial to the very idea of the West. The films of John Ford or Anthony Mann consciously incorporate the meaning of the physical West into their plots. It may be that no audience could ever visually grasp the total expanse of land as depicted in full color, but this is part of the meaning of the West. The sense of being overwhelmed by the landscape helps to make clear the plight of the gunfighter, the farmer, the pioneer standing alone against the forces of evil.

On television this sense of expansiveness is meaningless. We can never sense the visual scope of the Ponderosa. The huge cattle herds that were supposed to form the central purpose for the drovers of "Rawhide" never appeared. In their place we were offered stock footage of cattle drives. A few cattle moved into the tiny square and looked, unfortunately, like a few cattle. The loneliness of the Kansas plains, in the same way, has never properly emerged as part of the concept of "Gunsmoke."

What has emerged in place of the "sense" of the physical West is the adult Western. In this form, perfected by television, we concentrate on the crucial human problems of individuals. One or two drovers gathered by the campfire became the central image of "Rawhide." The relationship among the group became the focus. Ben Cartwright and his family were soon involved in innumerable problems that rose out of their personal conflicts and the conflicts of those who entered their lives. Themes of love and rebellion, of human development and moral controversy, were common on the show until its demise. On "Have Gun—Will Travel" Paladin's business card was thrust into the entire television screen, defining the meaning of the show as no panoramic shot could. This importance of the enclosed image is made most clear in "Gunsmoke." The opening shots of the original version concentrated on the face of Matt Dillon, caught in the dilemma of killing to preserve justice. The audience was aware of the personal meaning of his expression because it literally filled the screen, and the same sorts of theme have always dominated the program content. Even when landscape and chase become part of the plot, our attention is drawn to the intensely individual problems encountered, and the central issue becomes the relationships among individuals.

This physical sense of intimacy is clearly based in the economic necessities of television production. It is far more reasonable, given budgetary restraints, to film sequences within permanent studio sets than on location, even when the Western is the subject. But certainly the uses of intimacy are no longer exclusively based on that restriction. The soap operas, most financially restricted of all television productions, have developed the idea from the time when audiences were made to feel as if they were part of a neighborhood gossiping circle until today, when they are made to feel like probing psychiatrists. Similarly, made-for-television movies reflect this concern and are often edited to heighten the sense of closeness. A greater sense of the importance of this concept is found in those shows and series that develop the idea of intimacy as a conceptual tool. It becomes an object of study, a value to be held. In such cases the union of form and content leads to a sense of excellence in television drama.

The situation comedies such as "All in the Family," "Maude," "Sanford and Son," and "M*A*S*H" have turned the usual aspects of this formula into a world of great complexity. . . . [T]heir themes are often directed toward social commentary. The comments can succeed only because the audience is aware of the tightly knit structures that hold the families together. It is our intimate knowledge of their intimacy that makes it possible. Objects, for example, that are no more than cultural signs in some shows become invested with new meanings in the new shows. In the Bunker home a refrigerator, a chair, a dining table, and the bathroom have become symbolic objects, a direct development from their use as plot device in more typical domestic comedy. They have become objects that define a particular social class or group rather than the reflection of an idealized, generalized expression of cultural taste. They are now things that belong to and define this particular group of individuals. Similarly, our knowledge of the characters goes beyond a formulaic response. Jim Anderson, of "Father Knows Best," was a type, his responses defined by cultural expectation. Archie Bunker is an individual. Each time we see him lose a bit of his façade we realize that his apparently one-dimensional character is the result of his choice, his own desire to express himself to the world in this persona. With his guard down we realize that he cares about his wife, in spite of the fact that he treats her miserably most of the time.

In the mini-series of the BBC the technical aspects of this sort of intimacy have been used to explore the idea itself and have resulted in moments of great symbolic power. In the adaptation of Henry James's *The Golden Bowl*, for example, we begin with a novel crucially concerned with problems of intimacy. The series is then filled with scenes that develop the idea visually. Such a sequence occurs during the days before Adam Verver asks Charlotte to be his wife. Though he does not realize it, Charlotte had at one time been the mistress of his daughter's husband, the Prince. She is considerably younger than Verver, and in order to establish a claim for her marriage, he suggests that they spend time together, in the most decorous manner, in his country home and in Brighton. In the midst of rooms filled with candles, furniture, paintings,

Jean Stapleton and Carroll O'Connor in "All in the Family," a CBS Television Network program.

and ornaments, the camera isolates them. Even in the huge ornate rooms they are bound together, the unit of our focus. One evening as Charlotte turns out the lamps, pools of light illuminate them, circled in the large dark rooms.

In one of the most crucial scenes of this sequence the camera moves along the outside of an elegant restaurant. Through the rain, through the windows, couples are framed at dining tables. A waiter arrives at Verver's table as the camera stops its tracking motion. The couple begins to laugh; we hear them faintly as if through the actual window. Then, apparently at Verver's request, the waiter reaches across the table and closes the drapes. We are shut out of the scene, and we realize how closely we have been involved in the "action." We are made more aware of private moments. In the closing scene of the episode the camera movement is repeated. This time, however, Charlotte has agreed to the marriage and the couple is celebrating. Again we are outside. But as the episode ends, we remain with Verver and Charlotte, participating in their lamplit laughter.

Finally, this same motif is used in another episode. Charlotte and the Prince have again become lovers. They meet for a last time, realizing that their secret is known. The camera frames their hands, meeting in a passionate grip. It is like an embrace and it fills the entire screen. Suddenly the camera pulls back and the two people are shown in an actual embrace. Again, suddenly, the camera zooms out and the couple is seen from outside the window. It is raining again, as it was in Brighton, and a rapid torrent of water floods over the window, blurring the picture in a powerful sexual image.

Clearly, in the adaptation of a novel so concerned with matters of intimacy, the attempt has been to convey that concern with a set of visual images. In "The Waltons," however, we are reminded that this visual technique parallels a set of values that we have found operating in popular television throughout our survey of formulas. Intimacy, within the context of family, is a virtue, and when "The Waltons" uses specific techniques to make us aware of intimacy, it is to call our attention not to the form, but to the ideas, of the show.

In that series each episode closes with a similar sequence, John Boy sits in his room writing in his journal. He has learned the requirement of solitude for his work, and his room has become a sacred space into which no one else intrudes. Other children in the family must share rooms, but he lives and works alone in this one. At the close of each story he narrates for us the meaning that he has drawn from the experience. We see him through a window as his voice comes over the visual track in the form of an interior monologue. As he continues to talk, the camera pulls back for a long shot of the house. It sits at the edge of the forest like a sheltered gathering place. It conveys the sense of warmth and protection, and even when there has been strain among the members of the family, we know that they have countered it as they counter their social and financial problems and that they will succeed. John Boy's window is lighted, usually the only one in the otherwise darkened home. As his speech ends, his light also goes out. We are left with the assurance of safety and love, as if we have been drawn by this calm ending into the family itself.

Aids   *Toward a Television Aesthetic*

1. Esthetics is the study of those elements that contribute to our sense of beauty and pleasure when we experience a work of art. In other words, esthetics tries to explain why art "appeals" to us. Newcomb maintains that intimacy is an important element in the esthetics of television. What does he mean by "intimacy"?

2. Why does Newcomb feel that the physical qualities of television suit it for the handling of intimacy? How are television sets used to foster intimacy?

3. Newcomb says that "Television is a crucially important object of study . . . because it brings its massive audience into a direct relationship with particular sets of values and attitudes." What values and attitudes is he talking about? How are they related to intimacy?

4. When Newcomb asserts that intimacy is an esthetic quality in television programming generally, he has presented a thesis which must

then be supported. On how many different types of television shows does Newcomb test his thesis? Do you think he examines the most important (or at least the most popular) types of shows? Do you find his analyses convincing?

5. Newcomb's notion of intimacy in television is a complex one. In order to explain it, he provides detailed illustrations from actual television programs. One such illustration involves Alistair Cooke's discussion of a New England autumn, another is from the BBC's adaption of *The Golden Bowl*, while a third is a typical sequence from "The Waltons." How does each of these scenes illustrate a *different* aspect of television intimacy?

6. In "Savagery and Civilization" (Unit IV) John Cawelti discusses the use of landscape in the western film. Newcomb discusses landscape and set in the television western. Compare their discussions, then test their observations. Watch a television western and an old western film. (Weekend television is a good source for these.) Ask yourself the following questions: (1) Which medium depends most heavily on outdoor shots? (2) Which medium depends most heavily on action, as opposed to dialog? (3) Which medium uses the most long shots and panoramic shots (very long shots in which the camera moves from side to side, taking in the whole view)? What do the answers to these questions tell you about the nature of the two media?

7. Newcomb maintains that the family is the "central symbol of television." Certainly most situation and domestic comedies revolve around the family—"Family Affair," "Bewitched," "All in the Family," "Sanford and Son," "Good Times"; many television dramas focus on family life—"The Waltons," "The Little House on the Prairie"; even an occasional western includes the family—"Bonanza." The very titles of many of these shows reflect their preoccupation with the family unit. Why do you suppose the family is such a staple ingredient in television programming? (Reed Whittemore's essay may give you some ideas.) Newcomb suggests that "M*A*S*H" and other programs succeed as social commentary "only because the audience is aware of the tightly knit sanctions that hold the family together." In what ways do the characters in "M*A*S*H" constitute a family? Can you assign familial roles (mother, father, adolescent son, etc.) to the central characters? Newcomb also suggests that the detective Ironside is a father figure. Do you think the characters on this show interact as a family? Can you detect family patterns on other nonfamily shows like "Mod Squad," "Medical Center," or "Mary Tyler Moore"?

8. Newcomb seems to believe that movies made for TV are designed to exploit that sense of intimacy he feels is crucial to the television esthetic. This suggests that movies made for TV may have more in common with television programs than they do with movies. Watch a movie made for TV and ask yourself how it would look on a large movie theater screen. You might apply some of the questions raised in question 4 above to the movie made for TV.

9. Elsewhere in his book *Television: The Most Popular Art,* Newcomb maintains that in shows like "All in the Family," "Our sense of class and economic reality, the distinctions among groups of persons within American society allows us to confront problems directly." Unlike comedies with built-in gimmicks like "Bewitched" (in which the heroine is a suburban witch) or comedies that depend heavily on slap-stick like "I Love Lucy," the newer situation comedies sometimes address contemporary social issues. Do these shows, as Newcomb suggests, "confront problems directly"? How, for example, does "All in the Family" confront the problem of bigotry? How realistically does "The Jeffersons" portray the difficulties of an upwardly mobile black family and the problems of interracial marriage? Does "Mary Tyler Moore" address the problems of the single working woman? How are social issues handled within a framework of intimacy? How often, for example, are social problems raised outside the context of the television family?

The Big Picture

REED WHITTEMORE

TV has been with us about 30 years, and has changed our culture as much in that time as the movies and radio did in the 30 years before it. It has reduced reading and literacy, it has increased thumb-sucking and the glassy stare, and it has destroyed what little was left of the American community. What more could one ask of it? We can knock it but not ignore it. It is big, it stirs the multitudes in their slumbers, it sits in our parlors steadily steaming with its importance. And indeed it *is* important—and sometimes even good.

Yet what has it given us that is distinctively its?

Videotape, that's what. It has given us the grand privilege of watching every football play at least twice.

Oh yes, and it has given us "Sesame Street," a novel educational aid of considerable (once) punch that can still stir sleepy pedagogues to argument.

And that is all. Everything else that now composes the TV scene first had its innings in movies and radio. TV made more effective what it borrowed but it was as a borrower that it grew; it was an exploiter of the already known, rather than as an innovator, that it blossomed into over-ripeness before our eyes.

Radio had covered events live before TV but TV came along and made them liver.

Radio had created the Soap, but TV came along and learned to use radio Soap's most extraordinary contribution to the dramatic unities to make its *own* pile. The contribution?—time broken up into half hour blocks, and then broken up again into segments between which occurred the dropping of Alka Seltzer tablets into water glasses.

As for the movies, the movies had produced a drama that favored the close-up and featured careening horses rather than static parlor scenes framed by a proscenium arch. TV came along and grabbed both the proscenium arch *and* the careening horses—plus squad cars. It was able to straddle the world of both stage and film, and able to bring the two together into the parlor.

By the time that TV was through with its meddling, the forms and materials it meddled with were themselves changed—for TV cast a spell on everything it touched—yet the changes that it brought about were not so much due to its own creative ingenuity as to the simple enormity of its presence in American private life. Chiefly it brought public matters, national matters *into* the private life as nothing before it ever had. It brought into the parlor for example congressional hearings and big-time sports, and did so with a relentless-ness that changed the whole character of these events, yet it created no new sport and devised no novelties in the hearing line (except perhaps the close-ups of victims trying to talk privately with their lawyers, or of senators thinking suddenly they might make a run for the White House). TV remained content to play along with the genres and conventions around it. It did not even breed a new kind of critic but was satisfied with being battered about by traditionally patronizing high-brows (like this one) who earned their miserable wages being nasty about pop art.

In other words TV was, from the beginning, a conservative medium, experimenting rarely and discovering, when it did experiment, that experimenting was costly and that the critters watching in all the parlors didn't seem to *want* experiments. Instead they wanted what they knew already. They wanted bigtime football, but more of it, and every play twice. They wanted detective stories and Westerns and Soaps. They wanted friendly middle class faces with predictable accents and predictable neckties telling them, at enormous length, about the weather. And they wanted commercials every 10 minutes so that they could go to the kitchen and make a sandwich and clean up the dog vomit. All in all they wanted TV to help them achieve in their parlors the condition described in the old song, "Ain't Misbehavin." In that song the hero does not stay out late but sits abstemiously at home saving himself for a certain "you."

Who have our TV watchers been saving *them*selves for? Each viewer will have his own answer to that one, but from the evidence available about why people do plant themselves in the parlor and grow roots there, it seems likely that most of them would like to alter the question and say not who (or what) they are saving themselves for, but from. For TV is at heart a protective medium, keeping the watcher from mother, wife, husband, housework, homework, bills, thought, self. It is perfect in its demand-lessness, perfect for those interested in neither misbehaving nor behaving, but just vegetating. Is such an interest bad? If so, most of us are bad at least part of every day. Anyway, TV's demandlessness has been, and remains, its chief vice.

But also, maybe, its chief virtue. The conservatism of TV requires of it that it give us the familiar, and the familiar has had a bad press for so long from the world of art and literature that the poor thing does need a medium of its own. TV is that medium and TV does not, or not always, do wickedly by it. TV not only does formula stuff to extinction but it moves in without embarrassment on materials sufficiently elevated to be graced by a grander word: the traditional. The traditional on TV may either be something incredibly cultural like three hours of "The Taming of the Shrew" to the beating of promotional drums, or something vaguely goody-goody for children like "The Swiss Family Robinson," but it can be good even when cultural, even when goody-goody. Also there is much to be said for having TV feel guiltily obligated to help the species it has itself endangered. So let us not complain about these ventures.

Then too, beyond the uplifting shows, and beyond the shows for children that the earnest campaigners against TV's violence and moronism can be called up about and urged to watch, there is another kind of essentially conservative, traditional show that TV is well capable of exploiting, and of exploiting well while remaining its old mean mercenary self, not trying self consciously to do any good at all but just make a buck. "Batman" was such a show, and now "Mary Hartman, Mary Hartman" seems to be such a show. Parody, farce, flimflam, camp—whatever the genre should be called (and what it should be called varies because the shows tend not to *know* what they are) it is a genre that is only workable within a familiar world. It cannot be novel, it has to be about the known, the mundane, the everyday because its job is to ridicule some segment of the known, the mundane, the everyday. "Batman" went after a certain kind of inescapably, boringly available comic strip; "Mary Hartman, Mary Hartman" is going after "All My Children" and the like. Neither show could have come into existence without their targets, and they are automatically limited by their targets' limits. "Batman" did all it could with its impoverished target in a relatively small number of shows (now being endlessly, sporadically repeated) and "Mary Hartman, Mary Hartman" may similarly be expected to run out of steam fast unless it gets *serious* (or is it serious *now*? the question keeps coming up); but despite the limitations of each they do credit to, and well represent, their medium. Let us not complain about them either.

Other instances of TV's not always villainously conservative conventional heart could be hauled out here—and not complained about—but the point here is not to give instances but to mumble that for the next 30 years TV will probably have to continue to be judged, if it is to be fairly judged, largely by the conservative and conventional shows upon it, since they are the shows that best represent its role in our living rooms. The centrist role is the role we clearly *want* it to play, and it is the role that it therefore has to play, and it is a role that is needed among us, even though it sometimes shows us up with our shoes off and our minds let out for the night. Those who dream of TV giving itself over to a nest of gloriously imaginative innovators, or even of TV working to become a medium with its own distinct integrity, will have to keep dreaming. For better or worse the American parlor is still more ready for "Robin Hood" and "The Little House on the Prairie" than "Ulysses" or even "Sesame Street."

Aids   *The Big Picture*

1. Whittemore seems to feel that television is a derivative medium, that television derives its form and its content from the other mass media. What specific examples does he cite to support this observation? Are his examples convincing? What, according to Whittemore, are television's two unique contributions to the popular arts? Do you think he is serious about this?

2. Why does Whittemore regard television as a conservative medium? What does he mean when he says that television gives the "familiar"? What does he mean by the "traditional" on television?

3. Whittemore says: "As for the movies, the movies had produced a drama that favored the close-up and featured careening horses rather than static parlor scenes framed by a proscenium arch. TV came along and grabbed both the proscenium arch and the careening horses." (The proscenium arch separates the stage from the audience in the theater.) What does Whittemore mean by this? Do you think Newcomb would agree with this analysis?

4. One of the first things you notice when you read an essay is the author's tone. Tone, as the word suggests, is the way something *sounds*. We use a variety of tones in speaking. By modulating our voice inflections, we can make the same statement sound angry, flippant, sarcastic, or sincere. Sometimes, as in the case of sarcasm, our tone will belie our words—"I just *love* going to the dentist!" Tone, then, exposes our attitude toward our subject. Writers, of course, cannot depend on voice inflection to establish tone; they must depend on word choice and the arrangement of words. How would you characterize the tone of Whittemore's essay? Provide examples of words and sentences that you think are important in establishing his tone.

5. What kinds of assumptions is Whittemore making about his audience? Is he trying to convince his audience of his point of view or does he assume his audience shares his point of view? This article originally appeared in *The New Republic*. What kind of readership does *The New Republic* have and what does this tell you about Whittemore's audience?

6. Whittemore identifies "Batman" and "Mary Hartman, Mary Hartman" as parody, filmflam, or camp. Do these three words mean the same thing? Do they have the same connotations? Discuss either "Batman" (if it is available in your area) or "Mary Hartman, Mary Hartman" as parody. Watch two or three episodes of the show and ask yourself what aspects of the original genre are being parodied. Nora Kinzer's article on the soap opera should help you analyze "Mary Hartman, Mary Hartman."

7. Whittemore feels that television appeals because it gives us the familiar. Unfortunately, one familiar commodity on television is the stereotype. Older situation comedies often depend on extremely stereotypical characters. "Amos and Andy" was finally removed from the air because of its cruel racial stereotyping; "I Love Lucy" capitalized on the notion of the pretty but rather feather-brained young woman. "The Beverly Hillbillies," a more recent show, depends on a narrowly stereotyped view of mountain people. What about the newer, socially relevant situation comedies? Is Archie Bunker a complex character or is he a stereotype of the ignorant, bigoted hard-hat? In 1975 the cast of "Good Times" complained that the characters on that show were being oversimplified and that J. J. had been turned into a caricature of the "jive" black teenager. Is this criticism still valid? Is Chico of "Chico and the Man" in any way a stereotype of Mexican-Americans?

Art and Artifice in Network News

DANIEL MENAKER

You may never have cared to analyze the literary aspects of the television ad in which Fat Ralph sits on the edge of his bed and keeps his wife awake by groaning, "I can't believe I ate that whole thing!" But the ad is not without poetry and drama. It has a chorus (in almost perfect iambic pentameter), physical suffering, character contrast, marital conflict, and a comedic resolution generated by patient wifely wisdom and a deus-ex-tinfoil.[1]

Three factors militate against our regarding the Alka-Seltzer ad as art. First, most everyday happenings are relatively poor in artistic quality. Fat Ralph's dyspeptic insomnia falls far nearer zero on the aesthetic scale than does, say, Macbeth's lament over "sleep that knits up the ravel'd sleave of care." Second, we approach very few experiences with an attitude that makes us receptive to their aesthetic value. It would be pointless, although perhaps amusing, to explicate every phone call we make. Finally, even if it were pragmatically possible to view our ordinary actions and circumstances as artifacts, it would soon become tiresome to do so. The experience of art gains part of its psychological value from its very extraordinariness: we turn to music, films, or literature because they "take us out" of ourselves and our jumbled surroundings for a while.

Nevertheless, for the past twenty years or so, an increasing number of artists and critics have been directing our attention toward the aesthetic potential of the commonplace: Warhol[2] gave us Brillo boxes and soup labels; serious architects have begun to celebrate gas stations and pizza parlors; poets "find" poetry everywhere; composers have incorporated

[1]Deus-ex-tinfoil, a play on *deux ex machina*, meaning literally "god from the machine." This refers to those moments in Greek theater when the gods intervened to make everything turn out all right. (eds.)

[2]Andy Warhol, a contemporary pop artist and filmmaker. (eds.)

The real
The news media, both broadcast and print, continue ,
to be the center of controversy. Have they gone
too far or aren't they going far enough?

The very heart of a democracy is an open free-flow
of information. Without it, our system of government
cannot exist. A non-informed electorate is no
electorate at all. Without freedom to investigate
and report the news from every angle, the members
of the press become corporate and government
spokesmen. We must keep the channels of
communication open to all, even when it hurts.

The ideal
An open society in which information is passed
freely back and forth.
The more we know, the better off we are.

AtlanticRichfieldCompany ◇

"real" noises into their works; underground films show us long segments
of unedited reality.

One would expect that commercial-television programming and
advertising should be a major subject for this new, iconoclastic aesthetic
scrutiny. After all, approximately forty million Americans watched *Marcus
Welby, M.D.* each week last season. But, because of vestigial academicism
or because it bears too strong a resemblance to "real" film and drama,
"shlock" TV remains the disowned daughter of Pop Culture. This neglect
is lamentable because it keeps TV in a cultural doghouse, where, I believe,
it has never belonged. More important, in at least one area—documentary

and news programming—failure to apprehend the artifice in what we see on television may have practical implications for our "real" lives. It is crucial that we understand how TV producers mingle art and reality in their news shows so we can at least try to separate the two elements.

Approximately fifty million people watch Cronkite, Chancellor, or Reasoner and Smith every weekday evening. I hazard the guess that an overwhelming majority of this audience believes that network news keeps them "in touch" with the world at large. But I suggest that even if network news fulfills this presumed purpose of accurate communication, it simultaneously and contradictorily functions as art/entertainment—and that this second function vitiates the first.

Each of the evening network news shows begins with a scenario. On CBS Walter Cronkite, often scribbling copy up to the last second, is first seen in profile. An announcer, speaking somewhat loudly over the exciting chatter of teletype machines, introduces the show and Cronkite; he then recites the name and location of each correspondent, as the same information is superimposed in white printing over the opening shot. On NBC John Chancellor sits to the side of an oversize calendar month, with today's date circled, and tells the audience about the stories to be covered, often suggesting interrelationships among them. On ABC the opening format is a bit more complicated, but Reasoner and Smith do make use of pictures for the lead stories and a listing for the less important ones.

On each network the ritual opening establishes the theme of the entire program: excitement governed by order. The announcer projects intensity (as do Chancellor and Smith); the listing of events to be covered conveys control and structure. A pattern of decreasing importance

CBS Evening News with Walter Cronkite, CBS Television Network.

strengthens the audience's sense of structure: all three news organizations almost invariably start with what they consider the "biggest" story and then proceed to matters of smaller and smaller dimension. On many evenings, the first few reports deal with international affairs—the South Vietnamese Army staging one of their patented dramatic comebacks, another agreement handed down from a Summit, Britain overcoming the thirteenth in a seemingly interminable series of procedural obstacles to joining the Common Market—and the anchormen present them with appropriately grave mien and in serious tones. The middle distance is littered with more fragmentary national news—the House-Senate squabble over the antibusing amendment to the higher-education bill, another Ford or GM recall (this one occasioned by the discovery that for a week mayonnaise was inadvertently substituted for transmission fluid at a Detroit plant), the Republican governors' conference—which anchormen and correspondents report more chattily, unless, of course, they are dealing with some local disaster. The conclusion of many network-news programs strives for humor or lightness, justified by Broader Social Significance. CBS occasionally ends with a report by Charles Kuralt "On the Road," examining, say, the efforts of a Menominee, Wisconsin, senior citizens group to form a semipro jai alai team. Chancellor or Reasoner may finish up with a funny marijuana story or an all-of-us-are-human anecdote (Chief Justice Burger gets a traffic ticket).

This thirty-minute diminuendo, especially when it ends on a cheerful note, promotes an illusion of hard work accomplished. It implies that simply watching a news program is a meaningful task and that if we see the whole thing through, we deserve a reward, a little fun. The show's overall structure also tends to cancel out or modify whatever urgency informs its content and belies the radical messiness of reality.

Network-news shows routinely use highly structured film or tape reports from correspondents in the field as building blocks in their total edifice. These reports generally follow a formal, almost ritualized dramatic pattern, of which the following is a hypothetical example:

CRONKITE: Zanzibar's Grand Satrap Mustafa Kelly visited the White House today for talks with President Nixon. Dan Rather has a report. [Cut to shot of White House lawn, followed by Satrap's debarkation from limousine, followed by shots of Nixon and Kelly shaking hands and grinning in the Trapezoidal Room and then disappearing into privacy. Rather narrates the pictures.]

RATHER: Satrap Kelly, a man well known for his blunt, outspoken frankness, was expected to have some harsh words for Mr. Nixon concerning the President's plan to use Zanzibar, a tiny island republic, for Navy target practice, and to resettle its inhabitants in Joplin. The two leaders greeted each other warmly and joked about jet lag, but many observers feel that the smiles may fade once serious talks begin. [Cut to a full-length shot of Rather standing in front of White House, microphone in hand.] It is impossible to predict what the outcome of Kelly's visit will be, but one thing is certain: no one knows how—or whether—the issue will be resolved. Dan Rather at the White House.

This facetious example illustrates the stylized construction of filmed news coverage. It has a beginning (Cronkite's introduction and site-fixing pictures), middle (greetings and verbal exposition), and, most typically, end (Rather's on-camera summary statement). Whether it concerns a Vietnam counteroffensive, a German-Russian treaty agreement, or a Washington peace demonstration, each report is a self-contained subunit of a self-contained half hour. The most predictable element of the filmed report—the correspondent's on-camera summary—embodies the pervasive atmosphere of controlled excitement mentioned earlier: it serves simultaneously as emotional denouement (concern over what will happen next, in our example) and formalistic completion. In most cases, the structural coherence dominates and, again, cancels out the open-endedness of the actual content. The appearance of the correspondent on camera and the "Dan Rather at the White House" jerk our attention away from the news and back to the news *program*. The reporter's donation of his name and location has come to sound like an incantatory *pax vobiscum*,[3] a formulized placebo.

Our imaginary White House visit also exemplifies the news shows' efforts to inject excitement into merely symbolic events—signings, arrivals, departures, press conferences, briefings, government announcements, speeches, appointments, and so forth; in fact, much of TV news consists of ersatz verbal and visual drama masquerading as the drama that in the real world lies behind a resignation, say, or an increase in the cost of living. Eyewitness stories about unplanned action are unusual fare (except for the relentless battle reports from Vietnam). And even when the networks are "lucky" enough to have a camera crew and newsman on hand at a spontaneous event (as NBC did for the shooting of George Wallace), they inevitably edit the film and wrap it up in smooth prose, if they have the time, so as to maintain as much consistency of product and packaging as possible.

The instinct to control crisis by structural technique rules the network-news program's settings, sounds, and graphics, as well as its copy and film. I have already remarked on the associate sense of urgency created by the teletype clatter audible during the opening of the *CBS Evening News*. Other examples abound: again on CBS, the calm and spacious cerulean behind much of Cronkite's reporting works as a visual antagonist to concern and

[3]Latin for "peace be with you." (eds.)

involvement. (NBC favors darker background colors, like navy or black, which lend intimacy as well as coolness, whereas ABC uses red or orange settings, which are hot and sensational.) Although these studio backgrounds have a basic color scheme, they are also used in other ways. All three networks supplement their anchormen's words with various kinds of rear-screen graphics—maps, drawings, still photographs, organization logos, and so forth. Many of these devices (such as the jagged Expressionist silhouette of a fist clenching a rifle, which ABC has used to illustrate guerrilla news) are distractingly noninformational in themselves, but their most striking general aesthetic quality is the magical ease with which they are summoned forth. Chancellor says, "In Vietnam today," and presto! a bright red map of that beleaguered nation appears behind him. "U.S. B52s carried out more heavy bombing raids on Hanoi," he continues, and Shazam! little white planes appear on the map over North Vietnam with little white sunbursts representing bomb explosions. The newsmen never even take notice of these light shows; they conjure them up and coolly ignore them. The anchormen skip by map, satellite, telephone, and film all over the world, dipping into one crisis after another, but always keeping their emotional distance, like master magicians who perform sensational feats in a detached, almost routine manner.

These men perform as consummate actors, even if they are simply being themselves. Walter Cronkite's paternal persona has been the subject of much analysis. Roger Mudd, Cronkite's heir apparent at CBS, sounds and looks substantial. He is a relatively young man, but his folksy Southern solidity makes him seem widely experienced. Mudd's speech inflections constantly hover on the edge of irony, as if he were saying, I am stable and serious and will tell you a down-home kind of truth, but let's none of us lose perspective and get too *serious*. John Chancellor is less the father and more the friend—the friend who knows a lot and lets you in on it. Harry Reasoner often appears open and vulnerable—an innocent, impressionable man-child. His colleague, Howard K. Smith, is prudent and authoritarian, though his high voice offsets the firmness a little. David Brinkley is smart-alecky, cynical, impish; he habitually asks barbed rhetorical questions and seems to treasure his opportunities to make trouble. Eric Sevareid always looks and sounds weary; he represents pure reason besieged by irrational extremism. Most of the players in the three troupes are physically attractive and aurally elegant. An obese, ugly, or squeaky-voiced newsman, though he might be professionally qualified, could not meet the nonjournalistic requirements of a network correspondent's job. The competition for ratings, one assumes, must lead the three organizations to seek reporters with stage appeal, which, like dramatic structure and entertaining graphics, to some degree blurs the audience's vision of reality.

One may argue that coherent structure and dramatic delivery constitute precisely the right kinds of bait for luring an apathetic TV viewer toward interest in what is going on in the world outside of his personal concerns. That argument may be valid, but it misses the point: the methods used to capture the viewer's interest in a news program are simultaneously diverting and entertaining in themselves; unlike Cleopatra, the news shows satisfy where most they make hungry. And while it may be true that *any* successful attempt to distill reality into dramatic order becomes to some extent self-contained and "unreal," most such efforts—films, paintings, well-told stories, novels, musicals—are at least in part *presented* as works of art and entertainment.

The three network-news programs are for many Americans the only available mirror of the world at large. And they are fun-house mirrors: they shrink, elongate, widen, narrow, lighten, or exaggerate what stands before them. I do not know whether these images could be corrected or even that they ought to be corrected. I do know that we must see them for what they are, for we do not live in a fun house.

Aids   *Art and Artifice in Network News*

1. Menaker maintains that the network news functions as art/entertainment. What does he mean when he says the second function *vitiates* the first?

2. Menaker says, "On each network the ritual opening establishes the theme of the entire program: excitement governed by order." How is the opening on each network's news *ritualistic?* What does Menaker mean by "excitement governed by order"? According to Menaker, how are all network news programs structured?

3. Like the writer, the broadcaster must choose a tone appropriate to the subject. Language, voice quality, even facial expressions will vary with the content of the story. According to Menaker, how does the reporter's tone and manner reflect the content of the script? What special tone is reserved for disaster and tragedy? Do you think writers dealing with the same kinds of content would (or should) adopt the same tone as the newscaster?

4. In his brief discussion of the Alka-Seltzer ad as literature, Menaker refers to a resolution by "deux-ex-tinfoil." A deux-ex-machina is the use of some unlikely incident in the plot that makes everything turn out in the end. (The term literally means "god from the machine" in Latin and it refers to a time in ancient Greek theater when the gods came down from machinery in the ceiling to intervene.) Menaker's joke assumes an understanding of this term. What other Latin phrases

and literary allusions appear in this article? How do they contribute to the author's style?

5. Menaker feels that newscasters are "consummate" actors and that each has a slightly different persona. How do the looks and style of each anchorperson contribute to his or her mystique? Examine the newscasters on your local stations. How would you characterize them as physical types? What sort of image does each project?

6. Menaker's discussion of the image projected by the network anchormen may explain why there are so few women newscasters. A newswoman expressed the view that for women newscasters "There's still a subtle difference in approach, a tightrope to be walked. . . . I had to carry all the heavy equipment on an assignment but not overdo it, be aggressive but not overaggressive, if you get the distinction!" (*Miami Herald*, March 15, 1976, p. 5–B). Examine the images projected by women newscasters. Does their sex in any way affect their style or delivery? Do you respond any differently to a woman newscaster?

7. Compare the physical qualities and style of a local newscaster, weathercaster, and sports announcer. How do the differences reflect the content with which they deal and our attitudes toward that content?

8. Although Menaker is critical of the form of the network news, many have been critical of its content. In 1969 Vice-President Spiro Agnew raised a blistering attack on the network newsmen. "Is it not fair and relevant to question concentration [of power] in the hands of a tiny, enclosed fraternity of privileged men elected by no one" (*The New York Times*, November 14, 1969). He goes on to suggest that because network newsmen live in the "unrepresentative" northeast, they do not represent "the views of America." Herbert Gans suggests that "newsmen are on the whole more liberal than their total audience" ("How Well *Does* TV Present the News," *The New York Times Magazine*, January 11, 1970). One evening compare a network news broadcast with a local broadcast. Note how each newscaster handles the same events, the same issues. Can you detect a difference in attitude? a difference in political or social bias? Do you think network newscasters *should* have the same attitudes and ideologies as their viewers?

Soapy Sin in the Afternoon

NORA SCOTT KINZER

Nearly eight million Americans know that the finest neurosurgeon in the United States is Dr. Nick Bellini, that the greatest internist is Dr. Matt Powers, and that they both work at Hope Memorial Hospital located on the NBC channel. But as a veteran of many years of viewing the tragedy-laden episodes of *The Doctors*, I have my doubts. Hope's staff is so busy with illicit affairs, premarital pregnancies, and contested divorces that I worry about their ability to deliver good medical service. In fact, my fear has reached such proportions that I wear a metal identification bracelet which reads not "Diabetes" or "allergic to Sulfa," but "Don't take me to Hope Memorial Hospital!"

FLIGHT IN TERROR

Far fetched? Hardly. Millions are intimately involved with the lives and problems of their favorite assortment of soap-opera heroes, heroines, villains, and villainesses. They write letters to fan magazines anxiously inquiring about the personal lives of the stars, threatening mass defection should Mark marry Susy and leave Mamie, weeping over the death of a special character, and pouting about an actor who has been replaced. Sometimes their passions even spill over into real life. Eileen Fulton, who plays the bitchiest of all the soap-opera bitches—Lisa Shea of *As the World Turns*, once fled in terror from the appliance section of a large department store after watching a taped segment of her show and listening to women customers mutter how much they hated Lisa and wanted to kill her. On another occasion a woman asked her if she was Lisa Shea. When she said "yes" and began searching for a pencil to write an autograph, the fan began cursing Lisa and beating Fulton with her purse.

How do the soap operas entice such audience involvement? To answer this, I have developed a typology of soap-opera characters—no article written by a sociologist is complete without at least one two by two table of some sort. Here is mine:

Eileen Fulton and James Douglas in "As the World Turns," a CBS Television Network program (produced by Procter & Gamble Productions, Inc.).

	good	bad
good	good–good	good–bad
bad	bad–good	bad–bad

In most soap operas the good-good is usually a motherly-grandmotherly type to whom all the other characters tell their respective tales of woe. In *The Doctors*, good, kind, fatherly Matt Powers is the pivotal character who spends more time listening to his staff's tales than he does operating, or balancing Hope Memorial's budget. Nurse Kathy Ryker is a typical bad-bad. She is an out-and-out thoroughly mean bitch who always causes trouble and ruins the lives of the other characters.

While a bad-bad like nurse Ryker is easy to spot, the viewer has to be adept to pinpoint the switcheroo character: the good-bad or the bad-good. Nick Bellini of *The Doctors* is a typical good-bad, a baddie who turns out to have a good side, while John Morrison is a typical bad-good, a goodie with a bad side. Part of the fun of soap operas lies in the fact that the audience usually knows that the supposed bad-bad is really a bad-good or a good-bad long before the good-goods realize what is happening.

But the immense popularity of the soaps is a complex affair. While their lusty plots titillate fans' daydreams, their chaos and affliction make the viewer's dull life seem well-ordered and safe by comparison. On *General Hospital*, for example, out of seventeen major characters there are four divorces, two premarital pregnancies, four illicit affairs, two male drug addicts, one male alcoholic, one male amnesiac, one male in prison, and one female incarcerated in a mental hospital.

SUDSVILLE HEROINES

These afternoon sagas of sin and woe are played out against a lily-white, middle-class WASPy backdrop, or at least the

WASPy setting as the writers imagine it and the viewers want it to be. Silver services and booklined libraries are sure symbols of upper-middle-class status. Sudsville heroines arise in the morning fully clothed with their eyelashes on straight and their Saks dresses unmussed. Good-good husbands spend hours over the breakfast table talking to their wives. The moral, of course, is that if every wife looked like the good-good soap-opera heroines, her husband would stick around too.

Male sex appeal is just as necessary. Bad-bads like Dr. Stephen Aldrich of *The Doctors* and Doug Williams of *Days of Our Lives* spent a good deal of their on-camera time talking on the telephone in bed with a sheet tucked around their respective chests, and soon had to be transformed into good-bad because of their swift rise in the popularity polls.

ADA AGONISTES[1]

Actresses playing minor roles often achieve overnight stardom because the audience identifies so closely with them. Ada Clark of *Another World* and Lahoma Reynolds of *Somerset* are relatively uneducated, lower-middle class, blue-collar women maneuvering in a middle-class world. Their vocabularies are filled with expressions such as *sumpin'*, *walkin'*, *talkin'*, *he don't*, and sometimes *ain't*. Ada is the long-suffering mother of an ungrateful but beautiful daughter, Rachel, and every mother in the audience who feels betrayed by her daughter agonizes alongside Ada. Lahoma married her lawyer-

husband Sam when he was only a garage mechanic, and poor Lahoma's fumbling mistakes symbolize doubts felt by every woman whose husband has risen in status. No matter what their difficulties, Lahoma and Ada do quite well. They are both female Horatio Algers[2] who hold their own with the country-club crowd, and best of all, periodically tell off those hoity-toity bastards and effectively put snobs in their place.

SIN IN THE AFTERNOON

Lahoma, Ada, Doug and Stephan are unmistakably white and Protestant. Ethnics such as Chicanos, Hungarians, Greeks, or Czechs don't appear on the afternoon soaps. Of the 333 characters listed in the 1972 Afternoon TV Yearbook, only twenty-one had non-Anglo surnames, and five of those played members of the same family. *Somerset* has two blacks: one is a kind, intelligent lady lawyer, and the other is a gentlemanly crook, now reformed. Both are in the genre of the super-black Sidney Poitier. The soaps do not tackle problems of race prejudice or exclusionary clauses in country clubs; that's for the evening news. Sin is the serious business of the afternoon.

WASPy in format, Protestant in intent, and Puritanical in morality, the afternoon soaps grind out their ethical message: all crimes will be punished; retribution will strike down the most secretive and recalcitrant of sinners. Subjects such as homosexuality, lesbianism, and cannibalism are taboo, and although the soaps are sado-

[1]A parody on *Samson Agonistes* (*agonistes* means "contestant" in Greek), a tragic drama by John Milton. (eds.)

[2]Horatio Alger (1834–99) wrote boys' books and specialized in rags-to-riches stories. (eds.)

masochistic, the whip and chain crowd never appear on camera. Drug addiction among teenagers is a common theme, but the soap operas just reinforce popular misconceptions. Anyone who takes drugs will go crazy, have hallucinations in the most inappropriate circumstances, and give birth to deformed children.

PREGNANCY: THE ULTIMATE RESULT

Whether any of soapland's characters means to commit his crime (or sin) has no bearing on the final outcome; disaster always follows. Nowhere is this rule followed more explicitly than in the case of sexual transgression. All women and girls who engage in premarital or extramarital sex even once, through seduction, stupidity, or rape, will end up pregnant (that's just what my mother told me would happen). Dr. Karen Werner, Nurse Ryker, and Nurse Simpson of *The Doctors*, and poor unfortunate Dr. Laura Horton (who was raped by her brother-in-law, Dr. Bill Horton) are testimonials that pregnancy is the ultimate result of illicit intercourse. We can only wonder why so many doctors and nurses are seemingly ignorant of basic contraceptive techniques and hope that these same doctors and nurses never work in a Planned Parenthood clinic. But to viewers who have had unplanned babies, it must be comforting to know that lady doctors and nurses get caught too. Sudsville heroines give rise to a birthrate on afternoon TV that is eight times as high as the U.S. birthrate as a whole, and higher than the birthrate of any underdeveloped nation in the world. Fifty percent of these babies are conceived either before marriage or with someone other than the mother's husband. This frantic rabbitlike reproduc-

tion underscores the pronatalist attitude of TV writers and reinforces the very worst of a female value system. The afternoon soaps foster an ideology based on female passivity, ineptness, and subservience. Even independent women of the highest professional stature manage to get themselves in the damnedest messes, from which only strong, brave, intelligent males can extricate them. The soap-opera heroines are always acted *upon*. They are raped, divorced, abandoned, misunderstood, given drugs, and attacked by mysterious diseases. More females than males go mad, have brain tumors, and die.

WOMAN'S PLACE

TV commercials follow the same pattern and treat women as even more stupid and incapable. As Judith Hennessee and Joan Nicholson reported, nearly all the ads show women inside the home, 43 percent of the time involved in household tasks, 38 percent of the time as adjuncts to men, and 17 percent of the time as sex objects. Earth-shattering problems such as cleaning the toilet bowl, keeping leftover food palatable, or making dishes shiny are solved by an off-camera male voice or a man who flies through the window. With a booming, deep voice like Zeus atop Mt. Olympus or Wagner's Siegfried passing through the Ring of Fire, an omnipotent male rescues a befuddled female from her dilemma and advises, "Use Zappo to clean your toilet bowl, keep your food fresh and your dishes gleaming." And if the soap heroine never seems to be cleaning *her* toilet or washing her dishes, it must be because she uses Zappo.

When the heroines aren't getting pregnant or wrecking someone's marriage, they are getting sick. And the female "sick role" with all its assorted bag and baggage of hypochondriacal symptoms is portrayed with antiseptic frequency. Leading ladies never suffer from simple influenza, but from obscure diseases like syringomyelia, myasthenia gravis, sub-acute bacterial endocarditis, meningitis, and sundry brain tumors, not to mention the perennial favorite, amnesia, or its close runner-up, partial amnesia. While amnesia is a diagnostic rarity, its incidence on afternoon television is astronomical. Partial amnesia, which means that you remember your name, address and profession but forget little things like whom you married and why, is not even found in the medical textbooks.

The TV writers deliberately select the most exotic illnesses from the *Merck Manual*, not only to awe their viewers, but also to keep from alienating them. Soap-opera heroines do not have hysterectomies, don't have jejunal bypasses, and never endure kidney dialysis. There is, after all, a limit to how much involvement a fan can have with a heroine. The average viewer can enjoy a certain amount of vicarious suffering over subacute bacterial endocarditis, which few of the actors can pronounce, but God forbid that anyone say "cancer."

If things are tragic in Sudsville, they are miserable in Lubbock. Every day the television set contrasts Louis XIV with Penney's best, Saks with Robert Hall's, Cartier's with K-Mart, the svelte heroine with the housewife, and the handsome hero with her husband. When the housewife turns off the TV, looks around her home, glances into the mirror, and greets her husband, the comparison is not pleasant.

While soap-opera plots may make housewives feel safe, soap-opera settings may make those same viewers dissatisfied with their own dull lives. And as long as they watch the soaps, things will never be right.

Aids   *Soapy Sin in the Afternoon*

1. As a spoof on sociological charts, Nora Kinzer provides her readers with a chart that outlines the primary character types in the soap opera. Are the distinctions she makes useful? Test them on your favorite soap opera.

2. What does Kinzer mean when she says "this frantic rabbitlike reproduction underscores the pronatalist attitude of TV writers and reinforces the very worst of a female value system"? What images of women are projected by soap operas? Do any of the stereotypes Rosen discusses in "Popcorn Venus" (Unit IV) appear in the afternoon soap opera?

3. According to Kinzer, what kinds of ads accompany the afternoon soaps? Why are the soaps seldom, if ever, sponsored by companies selling automobiles, life insurance, or beer? (Reexamine the articles by Packard and Henninger in Unit II.)

4. Kinzer says that soap operas are "WASPy in format, Protestant in intent, and Puritanical in morality." What does each of these labels mean? WASP is, of course, simply an acronym (a word made out of initials) for White, Anglo-Saxon, Protestant. But what are the connotations of the word WASP? Is Kinzer depending on stereotyped views of WASPs, Protestants, and Puritans? Where do you think such stereotypes come from?

5. The title of an article or essay is more important than many readers realize. What kinds of expectations does Kinzer's title raise? What does her title suggest about her attitudes toward soap operas? How does it set the tone for her article?

6. Kinzer says that "the afternoon soaps foster an ideology based on female passivity, ineptness, and subservience." In his essay "Life Can Be Beautiful/Relevant" (*The New York Times Magazine*, March 25, 1975), Anthony Astrachan points out that "Classical soap-opera convention says that women are stronger than men. The women create and solve the majority of the problems. . . . They discern the moral imperatives through the dramatic haze and forgive masculine sins." Are these two views compatible? If so, how do they reinforce one another? If not, which do you think most accurately describes the role of women in the typical soap opera?

7. Although Nora Kinzer maintains that soaps are largely populated by white, middle-class characters, she does point out that "Another World" and "Somerset" include blue-collar characters. Anthony Astrachan notes that "One Life to Live" includes both working class and black characters. Examine a soap opera that portrays working class and/or black characters and evaluate their roles. Are such characters taken seriously? Is their class, ethnic background, or race made fun of in any way? Do these characters have important roles in the series?

8. Why do you think soap operas typically avoid discussions of common illnesses like cancer or heart disease?

9. Kinzer sees the afternoon soaps as traditionally moralistic: "all crimes will be punished; retribution will strike down the most secretive and recalcitrant of sinners." As you watch the soaps be aware of their treatments of such issues as abortion, birth control, drug abuse, and extramarital sex. "One Life to Live" has been touted as a more liberal, socially conscious soap opera. You might compare its treatment of sensitive social and moral issues to their treatment in one of the more traditional soaps—"The Guiding Light," "Search for Tomorrow," "Love of Life."

To Tell the Truth,
the Price Is Right

STEPHANIE HARRINGTON

To critics, game shows are a vulgar expression of American material-ism. To an enthusiast, they are a passion that drives someone in its throes to appear on national television dressed as a baked Alaska in hopes of winning a Vega Hatchback or a color TV or, at least, a nuclear-powered potato masher by AEC, Inc., and a week's supply of Blue Luster Carpet Shampoo. To broadcasters, this low-budget format is such an inexpensive schedule filler that, during daytime and early evening hours, they have given viewers little else to choose from. And the game shows' ratings are more than healthy enough to indicate that millions of viewers seem to find them an entertaining way to pass the time.

So, on ABC you are apt to find Leslie and Larry on "Let's Make a Deal," biting their lips and flushing with the intensity of their effort to win a car by guessing the price of a jar of Orville Redenbacher's Popping Corn, or catch Ray and Jay jumping up and down and clapping for a Puerta Vallarta vacation they did *not* win. And earlier, on NBC, you might have seen Shelia crying all over the set of "Celebrity Sweepstakes" over $1,341 she *did* win. You might also find yourself becoming surpris-ingly absorbed in shows that involve engaging tests of mental agility—like the word-association games. "The $25,000 Pyramid" and "The $10,000 Pyramid." (One virtue of these games is that they are played for straight cash, so concentration is not broken by run-on commercials for Staley's Syrup or a real Vendome fashion necklace, "the closest thing you can get to gold.") Meanwhile, back on NBC, Sheila has upped her winnings to $11,686 and is crying harder than ever.

Anyone who has missed all this action and may still labor under the illusion that we left those dishwashers and pieces of matching luggage and Bill Cullens and Monty Halls back in the Eisenhower era with the Kingston Trio and the Great Game Show Scandals should note that the three TV networks are currently enriching our weekdays with 17 half-hour audience-participation programs. ("Audience participation" is a category covering quiz, game and panel shows.) In the New York City area, between 10 A.M. and 4:30 P.M. weekdays, one or two audience-participation net-work shows are on every half hour. Additional syndicated game shows,

Wink Martindale and Elaine Stewart in "Gambit," a CBS Television Network program.

independently produced, are run during the day by the local stations, which offer another 11 syndicated (independently produced) audience-participation shows in the evening. It all adds up in a single week to 31 different shows within antenna reach of New York on which just plain folks overdose on millions of dollars' worth of cash prizes and merchandise. (Last year $12-million was the approximate total doled out on the network game shows. About another $5-million was given away on nationally syndicated nonnetwork shows.)

How did a phenomenon of such proportions manage to sneak up on us? Actually, audience-participation shows never went away. The scandals of the nineteen-fifties merely chased them out of the prime-time evening hours into the wasteland of daytime TV. (Prime time—when 60 per cent of the nation's sets are in use, the wage earners who buy expensive consumer goods are home, and the networks, consequently, can get as much as $70,000 for a one-minute commercial—consists in the Eastern and Pacific time zones of the four hours from 7 to 11 P.M.; in the central and mountain time zones, it's 6 to 10 P.M.) Between 1958 and 1970, the number of the networks' audience-participation shows in prime time fell from 16 to two. In the same period, however, daytime audience-participation shows remained relatively steady: 12 in 1958, nine in 1970.

So there was still an audience for game shows, and financially they were a format the networks couldn't refuse. On daytime TV, when fewer sets are in use and the wage-earning consumers aren't home, the networks can get only $10,000 to $13,000 for a one-minute commercial. Ideal fillers for this less profitable time period are game shows, which are less expensive than just about any other kind of program except reruns. Game shows don't require expensive stage sets, high-priced script writers or casts of actors, and five half-hour shows can be taped in one day. So, in recent years game shows have remained very much with us. However, since the daytime audience is only one-fourth to one-third as big as the prime-time audience, most Americans passed through the nineteen-sixties in blissful quarantine from all those dishwashers and waffle irons and cases of Sue Bee Honey.

Then, during the 1971-72 broadcast season, the Federal Communications Commission put into effect its new prime-time access rule. Up until then, programs supplied by the networks had filled all four prime-time hours on network-owned or affiliated stations. Under the new rule, local stations in the top 50 TV markets are prohibited from running more than three hours of network programs during prime time. The other hour is thus made accessible to the stations' own programs or their choice of independently produced shows.

Today most stations allocate all or half of the less profitable first hour of prime time to such "local access" programs. There is a waiver to the rule that allows them to give half of this hour to network news, provided it runs next to an hour of local news. So, in a market like New York, where local news runs from 5 to 7 on NBC and from 6 to 7 on CBS and ABC, the network news runs from 7 to 7:30, leaving half an hour—7:30 to 8—for local access programming.

The rationale behind the access rule (which has been challenged in the courts and modified and may be further appealed) was that it would weaken the networks' increasing stranglehold on program development and distribution and provide a market for independent producers, who employ a variety of creative people not connected with the networks. It was argued that this would bring about greater diversity in programs and also give local stations an opportunity to offer shows especially created to serve their communities. But local stations do not have the kind of money networks have for big-budget programs in prime time, and the rule actually seems to have been nothing more than an effort to protect the market interests of independent producers and distributors. "Economics," according to Dean Burch, former chairman of the Federal Communications Commission, "is really what this rule is all about."

And its effect has been to deliver the public, which F.C.C. is supposed to serve, from "My Mother the Car," "Camp Runamuck," "The Monkees," "Gilligan's Island" and "The Ugliest Girl in Town" (the networks' contributions to the 7:30-to-8 time slot when they controlled it) to the independently produced "Name That Tune," "Let's Make a Deal," "Hollywood Squares" and "The New Treasure Hunt." According to an F.C.C. report made after its rule had been in effect for three seasons, during the sample week beginning Sept. 21, 1974, 41.6 per cent of all local-access time, or a total of 844 half hours in 48 of the top television markets, was devoted to audience-participation shows. The rule, as F.C.C. Commissioner Glen O. Robinson has observed, "has not caused the wasteland to breed lilacs."

Again it is a matter of economics. It costs only about $25,000 to produce a half-hour game show for the 7:30-to-8 time slot. Other types of prime-time shows cost an average of $105,529 per half hour. Independent producers say they might make a greater investment in developing programs for the access-time slot if the F.C.C. assured them their market by declaring that the access-time rule would be retained for a minimum of five years. But legal challenges still loom and it is not certain that local stations would pay more for an alternative type of access-time program. As it is, they have been making good money on access-time game shows because they retain more of the commercial fees from independently produced programs than they do under network arrangements. So, if the public is once again aware of game shows, it is because the local-access rule has given them entree to prime time when most of us are home to observe the spectacle.

But why do so many of us observe it? What is the appeal of game shows? One of the least charitable explanations has been offered by a man who has made millions from some of the most exploitive examples of the genre, independent producer Chuck Barris, who has given us "The Newlywed Game," "The Dating Game" and "The New Treasure Hunt." Barris, an assiduous *enfant terrible*, who has referred to himself as "the King of the Slob Culture," told a TV Guide interviewer that the elements of a game show are "emotions and tensions . . . you must bring out those hidden hostilities in your contestants. You can actually watch them temporarily lose their sanity on the air. We prompt them to do that. Thus, audiences are being entertained, whether in awe or shock or horror or joy, over someone going bananas in public."

A more benign view is subscribed to by Mark Goodson, game-show elder statesman, whose firm, Goodson-Todman, has produced "What's My Line?", "To Tell the Truth," "Password," "Concentration," "Now You See It," "The Price Is Right," "Match Game" and "Tattletales." "There are two types of drama," says Goodson, "the type that is written and done with actors for laughs or suspense, and the type that allows you to sit home and watch actual people involved in actual situations with actual emotions and you can say, 'I could be there myself.' These dramas are unwritten and the endings cannot be planned. That is the drama of actuality, and that is all a game show is about. The Miss America Contest and the Academy Awards are game shows. . . . There are enormous stakes for the people involved, you know they're going to cry, and you want to see that happen."

If there's nothing at stake, of course, there is no tension and, therefore, no context for emotional release. So, Goodson says, "when planning a game show, we ask, 'How do you establish risk?' " But he also insists, and network people and other producers agree, that "the stakes [prizes] are put on by the producers, the packagers, the networks," not for the contestants, but "to make it more important for the viewers, to give them an empathetic interest. The reason people go on game shows," Goodson maintains "is ego. If we suddenly reduced all the money stakes, we would still get contestants. In the early days of television, stakes were low—the top prize on 'What's My Line?' was $50—and people would write to us asking to get on. Most of us lead lives where we have no chance to be a hero, to be known . . . the instinct to wave at the camera is so overwhelming."

And contestants do talk offstage about how much they enjoyed just being on a game show—the excitement of being on television, the camaraderie among contestants. One educated, middle-aged, middle-class mother, who had always been contemptuous of game shows but, at her children's urging, went on a computerized riddle show called "Jackpot," said it was fascinating to watch herself on television (the taped performance), to see herself reacting to a situation in which she never expected to be. And she said she was pleased to see herself respond emotionally to the tension and the excitement.

However, only three of 10 contestants I talked to—she was one of them—said they would go on a game show even if there were no prizes. Indeed, contestants seem much less unwilling than producers or programers to say that they go on game shows for the prizes. "Greed," says Barris, "is a horrendous emotion . . . but if it's orchestrated properly, it can be dramatic. It can be orchestrated without excess, so that the participant and the viewer enjoy it. In the end, if it's done correctly on a game show . . . everyone will walk away happy—the person who's been manipulated, the people who have watched him being manipulated."

But perhaps the most profoundly manipulative aspect of the game-show business is the kind of financial calculation that leads broadcasters and producers not just to offer enough game shows to satisfy audiences who enjoy them but to blanket certain stretches of viewing time with game shows to the point that television consumers have little other choice. As one former network programer, who now works for an independent producer, observed, "It isn't really a public demanding a trend, but responding to a trend in offerings." And what is being offered is:

"Wheel of Fortune," on which contestants spin a roulette wheel to win guesses at the letters in a word puzzle, and winners must use their cash earnings to "shop" among "showcases" of prizes. Richard, winner of the *largest three-day total* in the program's *history* (more than $16,000), is beaming and rubbing his hands and saying, "I gotta go shopping." "That video cassette is really fabulous," volunteers host Chuck Woolery, who has been pushing the video cassette as if his brother-in-law had manufactured it. "Or do you want another car?" "For $170 I'd love the camera," says Richard, "and the wine and cheese for $50 and the Tiffany gift certificate for $1,000." Losers go home worse than bankrupt, with the consolation promise of a generous supply of Days Ease Air Freshener and Tabby Treat, "every meal a banquet for your cat."

Then there are the celebrity game shows, designed to capitalize on the American public's seemingly unshakable addiction to the glamour fix. And it doesn't even seem to matter whether the celebrity is anyone whom anyone, besides his or her agent, has ever heard of. The top-rated of *all* daytime shows, "Match Game," offers neither a challenging game nor a celebrity you could recognize without a scorecard, let alone pick out of the crowd at the Academy Awards. What passes for a game is the simple hope that a contestant's choice of a word to complete a silly sentence will be matched by one or more of the celebrity panelists.

Self-inflicted gossip with sexual undertones is the premise of "Tattletales," which purports to let us know how well a celebrity husband and wife know each other by finding out if, out of each other's hearing, they give the same answer to the same question. And 24 per cent of the viewing public at 11 A.M. weekdays does seem to care that Milton and Ruth Berle would *not* attend a premiere of a hard-core pornographic film and that Orson and Carol Bean *would* and Orson *knew* he knew she would but *they* weren't invited, although Amanda Blake and her husband *were* but didn't go because *he* wouldn't even though *she* would. And if Milton Berle had known that, *he* would have gone with Amanda Blake.

And then there is the hard-core experience of fun and games in the consumer society, "The Price is Right," which demands neither more nor less than precise knowledge of the famous Spiegel mail-order catalogue, containing more than 50,000 quality items. If, as sociologist David Riesman observed, childhood in America is being a consumer trainee, "The Price Is Right" is the final exam.

On this show, contestants compete to see who can come closest to guessing the retail value of merchandise without guessing higher than the exact price. Here, the chance to win a front-loading portable dishwasher, a refrigerator-freezer with activated-charcoal air filter and "meat keeper" temperature control, and a heavy-duty garbage compactor-disposer with one-half-horsepower motor depends on the contestant's certain knowledge that the retail price of four sets of "thick and thirsty famous St. Mary's towels," plus the retail price of a craft set plus the retail price of 15 cans of Lucite paint add up to more than the retail price of a Sunbeam 1,000-watt hair dryer with four speed settings and styling stand plus the retail price of a Schick Fresh Air Machine plus the retail price of a leather bag plus the price of a pollinium-proof pollywog terrarium with infrared heating device and southern exposure. With this kind of information, you can price your way to a shot at pricing—and thereby *winning*—the Don

Quixote Showcase! Which includes "a trip to the land of Don Quixote," where you will stay in the *Eurobuilding Hotel* "in the heart of Madrid's Generalissimo Quarter!"

This side of that supershowcase in the sky, what could match this brand of Dionysian transport, except maybe a weekend at Friendly Frost, or dressing up like a macaroon to be sure you will be noticed and picked out of the studio audience to be a contestant on "Let's Make A Deal," which is such a big deal that admission to the studio audience is booked up for the next two years and host-producer Monty Hall was elected honorary Mayor of *Hollywood*. Here you can compete with the couple dressed in matching his and hers Lhasa Apso skins and the guy in the skirt who is supposed to be a cheerleader and the couple impersonating a pair of shoes and waving a sign that says, "Let's lace up a deal." Here you can experience the ecstasy of selling Monty the contents of your grungy old handbag for $150 and then agreeing to spend the $150 on a box, the contents of which you do not know, but which turns out to be . . . a *$759.95 refrigerator-freezer stocked with $25 worth of Breakstone's Cottage Cheese! And a $479.75 sewing machine!* Which means that you've traded *$150* and an old purse for a *deal*, the total retail value of which is *$1,264.70!* And you can compound your ecstasy by being smart enough *not* to trade it all back for your old purse and whatever amount of money Monty has put in it (which turns out to be a measly 27 bucks), or for the solid wall of frozen chopped chives from Armanino and the real clunker of a prize behind it. And then, after all this . . . the *agony* of *not* knowing when to stop and trying for the really *big* deal by agreeing to trade your $1,264.70 deal in for whatever is behind Door No. 3. Which turns out to be three bicycles and a $50 gift certificate to Dairy Queen.

But when it comes to sheer sado-masochism, the master of the medium is Barris, whose "The New Treasure Hunt" opens with the boast that it is the show that offers "more prizes and more cash than any other show in the world." (It is also a show that, according to Barris, grosses at least $2-million a year.) A stripped-down witless version of "Let's Make A Deal," "New Treasure Hunt" reached a pitch of manipulative frenzy with one contestant who traded in a prize of $1,850 for one clunker after another (each related to the word "tire")—a unicycle, a bicycle, the humiliating experience of being tied up on stage by four human *ti-ers*. Her emotions were pushed and pulled until she was crying and pleading like a victim in a trap. When at last she was presented with a Rolls-Royce, she fainted. (Later she had to sell the Rolls to pay the taxes on it.)

Then there is Donna, who begins shaking and holding her face and giving nervous little jumps the moment she comes on stage. Her first lucky guess wins her an envelope containing $1,120. She decides to trade that in for a surprise. That turns out to be a World-War-I-flying-ace getup

—flight helmet, flight jacket, scarf—which host Geoff Edwards puts on her because, as he announces in the promising cadence of someone about to give away an airplane, "You are going to fly your own . . . Treasure Hunt Kite!" Having planted the knife firmly in the middle of Donna's expectations, Edwards then turns it with the information that "the retail value of this clunk is $4.95." Then he turns it a little more by reminding his victim that, "Donna, you gave up $1,120!"

"Well," says Edwards, moving from the tease into the humiliation, "let's see if you can make it fly." And she really tries. "Donna, that's terrible!" laughs Edwards. "Run a little bit." And the trembling, overweight woman in the flight helmet and flight jacket and scarf actually runs around the small stage, trying to fly a kite indoors. Finally Donna is rewarded for her suffering. Edwards tells her she can tie her kite string to the bumper of her brand-new car, which with the golf equipment in the trunk, adds up to a retail value of $6,129.40.

"New Treasure Hunt" is an object lesson in what can happen when someone like Barris who is contemptuous of game-show contestants and viewers decides to profit from them. "That lady [on "Treasure Hunt"] can," he told a lecture audience, "be hit over the head with a chicken-salad sandwich or a Rolls-Royce. . . . When that lady is disappointed we're ecstatic; when she's ecstatic, we're nauseous." In an interview at the Plaza Hotel, where the bellhops knew his name, Barris asserted that game-show contestants "want to be manipulated. . . . They've watched the show for eight years. They know what's going on. And in 90 per cent of the cases, they're going to leave saying they had a good time." "Everybody," he says, "thinks: 'Those poor women!' But I find they don't find it humiliating. They find it exhilarating, considering where they're coming from. They're coming from a drab existence. . . ." Barris concedes, however, that, once people get into the studio, with the lights, the pressures, the interaction with the audience, things happen to them emotionally that they can't anticipate.

Barris amuses himself with fantasies about a game show he would call "Greed." "As I see it," he explains, "you would have this horrendous situation in which an arthritic 85-year-old man would come in on crutches and contestants would bid down to see how little money they would take to kick the crutches out. . . ." But he is not beyond turning irony on himself. He is writing a novel in which a failing game-show producer, in a desperate effort to boost his ratings, figures out a way to kill contestants on the air.

Contestants can, of course, pick their shows. And on those that emphasize playing a game rather than acting out, contestants are treated with, if not dignity, at least courtesy. And whatever degree of emotional manipulation comes into play is inherent in the kind of studio pressures Barris describes. But how are contestants picked? Many of them are drawn from game-show studio audiences. Some viewers write in and say they would like to be on. Some contestants are recommended by former contestants, some are picked out of ticket lines for other shows and some are just approached on the street by free-lance "contestant coordinators."

Pleasant-looking extroverts are given appointments for further screening, which often means a test of their ability to play the game and of how they respond emotionally during the course of the game. The one out of every 10 or 15 who is accepted usually participates in a preshow run-through with practice questions to familiarize himself or herself with the set, the experience of playing the game before an audience and even of jumping up and down and cheering and clapping on a stage. Often, contestants who have proved bright and entertaining on one show are invited to be on another. As a result of the 1958 scandals, however, CBS and ABC limit contestants to one appearance a year on any game show on any network; NBC limits them to one a year and no more than two in a lifetime.

And, as entrepreneurial proof of Parkinson's Law, the game-show business has spun off a profitable suboccupation for middlemen who call themselves "merchandise consultants" and who broker the mutual needs of give-away shows and manufacturers. Many manufacturers designate a percentage of their yearly advertising budget for promotional time on game shows, and some of them keep merchandise consultants on retainer (1974-75 was the best business year to date for Edward E. Finch & Co., one of the best known of the handful of merchandise-consultant firms in the country). The networks also have their own merchandise departments.

It is the manufacturers of less expensive items, like air freshener and after-dinner mints and chicken dip or small appliances, who pay the $250 fee for promotional time as well as donate a prize. Merchandise in the $350 to $1,500 range (major appliances and furniture) is simply traded for time. For more expensive shills, like cars, the networks have to pay dealers' costs. However, about $1,400 is deducted for every 10 seconds a car is shown on an evening show and about $300 for every 10 seconds on a daytime show. So, if a car is not won too quickly, it can end up half-price or an even trade. Hotel accommodations are donated in exchange for 10 seconds of promotional time, but the networks have to buy airline tickets since it is against the law to give them away. Money is the most coveted prize. But, mindful of the scandals, CBS has a $25,000 limit on the amount of money and/or prizes a contestant can win, and ABC has a $30,000 limit. Winnings in excess of these ceilings must be forfeited. NBC has no prize limit.

With prizes, come problems. The biggest, which grows with the winnings, is that all prizes—money and merchandise—are taxed as income, and merchandise is taxed according to its "fair market value," which is what it would sell for at a discount store. And all prizes, even five cans of cat food, have to be reported by the recipients. Winners cannot exchange unwanted prizes for either money or other merchandise. But if companies cannot deliver prizes because they are low in stock, they substitute checks for the retail value of the items.

Winners of vacations are allowed a year from air date to take their trips by CBS and ABC, and a year and a half by NBC. But NBC trippers cannot travel during peak periods or holidays. Winners of cars receive vouchers, which they take to a local dealer. The network pays the basic price of the car and the sales tax; the winner pays for extras, like air-conditioning or white walls. Contestants can forfeit their prizes within one week of the air date of the show if they do not want to pay the taxes, or if they want to avoid graduating to a higher bracket. Or, prizes like $25 worth of Eskimo Pies can be donated to a charity and treated as a deduction. According to a TV Guide follow-up on prize-winners, about 5 per cent to 10 per cent of game-show winnings are forfeited or donated.

As a result of the 1958 scandals, the networks strictly monitor game shows to be sure they operate in a manner that satisfies Federal law and public morality. They supervise the signing of forms and affidavits by game-show employes and contestants; they review game-show material; they station people in control rooms and in studios to be sure there is not even an opportunity for cheating; and they chaperon contestants all the time they are in the studio, even to the bathroom. They enforce the ceilings on prizes, they see that contestants receive their prizes in working order, and they keep files on contestants to be sure they do not exceed their limit of game-show appearances. And at NBC, the Compliance and Practices Department is responsible for the disclaimer run at the end of the celebrity show "Hollywood Squares" that informs viewers in unintelligible gobbledygook that, while panelists are not briefed on specific questions before show time, many of their seemingly quick-witted ad libs are pre-packaged, rehearsed responses.

But then, calculated spontaneity is the name of the game-show business. And if game shows as a native American art form do not rank up there with jazz or modern dance or even musical comedy, they still have their legion of viewers. (One network's demographics show that most of its game-show viewers are from households in which the income is less than $15,000 a year and the level of education is four years of high school or less.) While most people don't believe they could be Miss America or Robert Redford, they can identify with game-show contestants, most of whom are pleasant-looking if not stunning; intelligent if not brilliant; at an income level at which they could really use some prize money or a new car; and as anxious as anyone would be about winning or losing and about keeping a handle on their composure.

And no matter what happens to the contestant, the viewer always wins: If the contestant does well, the viewer can identify with him or her. And if the contestant loses or makes a fool of himself, the viewer can say,

"I could have done better." So maybe one thing game shows are doing is dragging Aristotle into that Vega Hatchback with the rest of us, and, whether they mean to or not, offering modern American Everyman a shot of low-risk catharsis between commercials.

Aids   *To Tell the Truth, the Price Is Right*

1. Why, according to Harrington, did game shows suddenly appear on prime-time television? What is the prime-time access rule? How many game shows are aired between 7 and 8 P.M. in your area?

2. A number of times Harrington alludes to the quiz show scandals of the 1950s. Can you infer from her article some of the issues involved in these scandals? How have the producers of the current game shows protected themselves against similar scandals?

3. Harrington quotes producer Chuck Barris as saying: "You must bring out those hidden hostilities in your contestants. You can actually watch them temporarily lose their sanity on the air. We prompt them to do that." Watch a game show (preferably "The New Treasure Hunt" or "Let's Make a Deal") and look for devices designed to make people lose their sanity. Notice the ways in which excitement and tension are generated.

4. Harrington gives us a great deal of background on quiz shows; she explains the laws regarding prime time and provides facts and figures as to the popularity of various shows, costs of production, and methods for choosing contestants. Why does Harrington provide this sort of information? How does it help her accomplish her purpose? What is her purpose? Journalists are not required to provide footnotes and bibliography for their data; thus, Harrington does not cite her sources. Do you think most readers will accept her data as valid? How does her tone and style affect her reliability? How readily do you accept Nora Kinzer's assertion that "Sudsville heroines give rise to a birthrate on afternoon TV that is eight times as high as the U.S. birthrate as a whole"? (See p. 338.) Why? Is the accuracy of this statistic important to Kinzer's argument?

5. As Harrington discusses each of the game shows, she provides a short scenario. What is the effect of each of these scenarios? What is their cumulative effect?

6. In describing "The Price is Right," Harrington condenses the game into one very long, convoluted sentence. Generally speaking, such

sentences are bad rhetorical form. Why does Harrington use this sentence where she does? Can you think of other situations in which a writer might deliberately construct an overlong sentence?

7. How well does the prime-time access rule work in your area? Examine the network listings for prime time. How many local shows appear during prime time on any given weekday? Saturday? Sunday?

8. In her article Harrington often balances one observation regarding game shows with an opposing point of view. After she quotes Chuck Barris on the manipulation of contestants, she includes Mark Goodson's "more benign" view. After she quotes Goodson, who suggests that contestants are not after the money, she notes that the contestants she interviewed were very interested in the prizes. Why do you think Harrington presents these opposing viewpoints? Do they increase her own credibility? Do they make the article more objective?

If There Is No Answer, What Is the Message?

MARTIN MAYER

. . . [T]elevision will not go away; it is embedded in the culture now, like frozen lasagna, golf carts and sociology departments. Those who would deny that it has been a boon to individuals in their private lives can be brushed aside: there is simply no question that television has answered the most desperate of human needs, the need for escape from boredom, escape from self. Traditionally, heaven has always been seen as a place of pretty continuous entertainment. For those multitudes who cannot escape through their work or their reading or the experience of art, television has been about as close as they could hope to come to a heaven on earth.

But men do not live as individuals: they are sustained by each other in a society. Television has been so pervasive a presence in American society that one cannot imagine what American life would be like without it. Still, some influences can be claimed for it on no better authority than obviousness and observation:

1. People go out less at night. The diminishing need for places to congregate has been a contributing factor in the flight to the suburbs and the decay of the city. The fact that the home has become the prime locus for entertainment has changed the nature of home and family in ways nobody has yet been bright enough to explore. Among the real differences between today's young and the young of previous generations is the fact that as children today's young shared more of their parents' entertainment—and less of every other aspect of their parents' lives —than the young of any previous generation in any social class except the very rich.

2. People have acquired a new kind of relationship with large numbers of total strangers who come into their homes on a picture tube. Every television entertainer (including newsmen) has had the experience of being greeted on the street by people they do not know at all, who then suddenly withdraw on the realization that this person who was indeed in their home cannot know he has been there. In America the fact that many of these visitors have been Negro is a social event of prime importance but sometimes ambiguous meaning. Several surveys have strongly indicated that Negroes themselves believe television to be the American institution that cares most about what happens to them and is most on their side; certainly, Negroes have been more prominent on television—in sports, entertainment and public-affairs programs—than anywhere else in the large society. But the effects of the entertainment programs have probably been far more positive than the effects of the most well-meaning (*especially* the most well-meaning) public-affairs shows. The inescapable bias of news qua news has too often impaled black Americans as a class in the butterfly case of trouble, *interesting* trouble, on the short-time horizon. The

experience of color on color television has been most important, and sometimes most disturbing, for Negroes themselves. "If you live in a black community," Albert Murray wrote recently, commenting on what he called the Minority Psyche Fallacy, "the world looks black." True once; but no longer.

Politically, the common statement that the constant presence of an electronic specter has made "image" substitute for reality is as simple-minded as the earlier insistence that television somehow revealed "the truth" about people. No political figure today has the "image" that a Warren G. Harding or Andrew Jackson or Caesar Augustus commanded in times prior to television. But the feeling of familiarity is new.

3. The work of establishing a unified culture in a country the size of a continent has been accomplished (apparently in the Soviet Union as well as in the United States), completing a job the national magazines began three generations ago (and thereby, though I write as one with strong personal reasons to wish 'tweren't so, making the mass magazine obsolete in terms of social function). This final Americanization of the community has greatly weakened in fact the particular institutions of a heterogeneous society (the Sokol, the Knights of Columbus, the Negro church, the trade-union meeting hall, the DAR, the neighborhood political club, the KKK). As a prime mover in the downgrading of local phenomena and the elevation of national phenomena in the consciousness of ordinary people, television has contributed to the feeling of "powerlessness" that does afflict fair numbers of people.

4. The speed and ease of introduction of novelty have biased both con-sumption and production toward new—or arguably new—products; the nature of television advertising has biased industrial research toward the creation of products that yield a demonstrable, surface improvement. But the idea that television advertising is itself a major cultural influence (apart from the pressure for maximum audience that advertising creates) cannot be seriously supported in the 1970s. All the stigmata of Americanization, from snack bars on superhighways to dishwashers to supermarkets to snotty kids, have come rapidly to Europe despite the much slighter presence of television advertising there. The triumphant ad campaigns of the 1950s, which built new markets for detergents and headache remedies and life insurance and hair sprays and air travel and other estimable economic goods, were not to be found in the latter 1960s; advertising on television like advertising in print had become part of the wallpaper for most people most of the time, proving, probably, that one can become conditioned to anything.

No doubt television advertising continues to sell merchandise, probably at unit costs lower than those attributable to other general-audience media, and its pervasiveness makes it an indispensable tool for forcing new products onto already crowded shelves in the stores. Moreover, because the arrival of quality inexpensive videotape equipment enabled local stations to make professional-looking advertising for local retailers at about the same time that the 1970 recession pushed down the price of minutes, food chains and department stores have begun to do price-oriented broadcast advertising, taking the money out of their newspaper budgets. This advertising has been effective in drawing customers into the stores, and as a class it grew rapidly even in the recession years 1970 and 1971. During this decade, local television will probably cripple the big metropolitan newspapers as network television in the 1950s and 1960s crippled *Collier's*, the *Saturday Evening Post* and *Look*.[1] Painfully little attention has been paid to this erosion of support for the newspapers, which are in fact the only possible medium for the expression of diversity to the entire community. Typically, the FCC picked precisely the wrong moment to move against newspaper ownership of television facilities: for the 1970s, it would have been much wiser public policy to encourage the ownership of local stations by local papers.

While it remains true that a man who advertised a cancer cure on television could sell a lot of snake oil (which means that some regulation is always going to be necessary), ordinary advertising for ordinary products ought not to be taken so seriously as most academic critics seem to take it. At present, it seems more significant in shifting market shares from one brand to another than in encouraging increases in total consumption of any product. In 1971 cigarette advertising was ruled off the air completely—and sales of cigarettes in the United States *increased*. Continuing to argue that the tube makes people buy buy buy what they would otherwise shun shun shun, as J. K. Galbraith does, is like spinning prayer wheels: it may get you good marks Somewhere, but it doesn't much help you understand what's going on.

    5.   The universal instant availability of entertainment to a national professional standard has severely reduced the demand for entertainment to regional or local standards. "The trouble with show business today," Jack Benny told Tom Sloan of the BBC, "is that there is nowhere to go to find out how bad you can be." In sports, television killed off the minor leagues; in the cities, it killed off the night clubs. It has seriously diminished the demand for touring companies of all Broadway shows other than those that offer a look at the pubic hair of actors and actresses. (The increasing nudity in films is also a by-product of television, because that's what television can't supply.) Here, of course, television merely continues and accelerates a trend begun by the talking picture and the phonograph record. Certainly in proportion to the population and maybe in absolute numbers, there are fewer people making a living in America today as entertainers and artists—though those few who do make a living probably live a good deal better than their ancestors.

Television itself, in America, has been extremely inhospitable to all artistic effort that is designed to remain in the memory. It is more than possible—though far from certain—that television will end up diminishing the pool of trained talent from which significant artists can be drawn, and that any reduction in this pool produces a reduction in the number of artists. Setting out on an artistic career is a bad gamble at best; if there are to be rewards only for big winners, some who could have made important contributions may be rational enough to decide that the risks are too great. Whatever the social values of ama-

[1]See the essays by Stephen Holder and Roland Wolseley in Unit III for a discussion of television's impact on magazines. (eds.)

teurism, the fact is that significant contributions to an art form can be made only by those who dedicate to it full time and energy. A diminution of their numbers would endanger the history of mankind.

6. Increasing proportions of people have received increasing proportions of what they think they know from the vicarious experiences of television. This, too, extends and accelerates a trend, which John Dewey was the first to remark more than seventy years ago. Civilization is a coin with two sides; people who live in cities know a great deal less about the natural world than people who live on farms; thus, Dewey argued, education in the cities should be careful to provide as much experience as possible, even at some sacrifice of abstract reasoning. The growth of electronic media, especially television, has vastly expanded the extent to which people learn (or think they learn) at second hand, without employing the trial-and-error, reward-and-punishment, successive approximation processes which are the basic human equipment for learning. Moreover, the apparent data base is shared by young and old, neither of whom have experienced much of what they think they know.

When Spiro Agnew was riding around on his charger denouncing the young, the *New York Times* reacted angrily in an editorial acclaiming the new generation as "the best-informed in history"—but all that was really meant by the praise was that the young talked about the same currently fashionable ideas and stories that bemused their elders. To the extent that the conflict between generations in the 1960s was exacerbated by differences in perception, the cause was not a great difference in experience between the two groups (which has always been the case and never makes the real trouble: people honor each

other's different experiences) but a great similarity in the vicarious experience which had become the base of knowledge for both. Of knowledge, but not of wisdom; for the consciousness of ignorance is the beginning of wisdom, and the media mask the consciousness of ignorance.

We touch here, daintily, on the McLuhan problem. Much of what McLuhan has written is simply ignorant and wrong (especially the widely accepted argument that sequence is obsolete: the heart of the television experience is remote control of the viewer's time, and the fundament of the computer, McLuhan's other example, is the rigorously sequential flow chart). The urgent statement that the medium is the message means no more (probably much less) than the old saw that the style is the man. The hopelessness of the "hot" and "cool" stuff as tools for analysis becomes obvious after about two sentences. Page after dreary page the reader is forced to observe the antics of a popular college lecturer of real but limited scholarly attainment who keeps the class hopping by saying the first thing that comes to the surface in his ragbag of a mind. But McLuhan's instinct that something new has happened with the introduction of television—a widely shared instinct, accounting for his sales and reputation—cannot be dismissed so easily.

The viewing experience *does* seem more of-a-piece than the reading experience—that is, the differences between reading a newspaper and reading a novel seem greater than the differences between looking at a televised movie and looking at a documentary. This homogenization of what ought by rights to be different experiences is the strangeness of television. The prattle about media and messages hides the truth, because it reduces complex experience to simple statement and because it falsely proclaims that other media have similar characteristics. They do not. Content changed the nature of the radio experience drastically: the Philharmonic, Jack Benny, The Shadow and Elmer Davis offered very different experiences indeed. And the content of television is nearly as varied as that of radio in the 1940s (there is much less good music)—but everybody feels that somehow it's "all the same."

A possible explanation of this almost universal attitude is that different radio programs demanded very different levels of attention. A few were really absorbing; most could be heard while doing the dishes or school homework or while daydreaming; some could be satisfactory background for reading a book. But watching television is an activity that excludes doing anything else except eating and knitting. The requisite minimum level of attention is fairly high. At the same time, unlike films or plays in a properly designed theatre, televised pictures do not absorb the peripheral vision; and it may be that the attainable maximum level of attention is fairly low. At best, the spread between minimum and maximum is much reduced from that experienced in the use of other media.

In such an atmosphere individuality must carry greater burdens than it can manage. Thus people and issues burn themselves out with unprecedented speed. Worst of all, perhaps, television becomes ineffective at performing what has always been seen as the most important social and political role of any medium: powerful at creating celebrity, it cannot legitimate leadership or attitude. There is a spurious equality of stimuli. It should not be forgotten, of course, that radio gave legitimacy to some queer and dangerous characters, among them Adolf Hitler, Father Coughlin and Huey Long.[2] ("I'm not going to have anything very important to say for the first few minutes, so you can call up your friends and neighbors and tell them that Huey P. Long is talking at you—United States Senator from Louisiana.") The normative quality of television —the tendency of initially impressive personalities or ideas to wear out quickly— probably limits the damage as well as the good that can be done through the use of the medium. But the subject is worth much greater attention than it has yet received.

7. Men, women and children have all been given the notion that life can be entertaining all the time. As Daniel Boorstin pointed out in *The Image*, "There was a time when the reader of an unexciting newspaper would remark, 'How dull is the world today!' Nowadays he says, 'What a dull newspaper!' " A great deal of current societal misfortune that is investigated under political and psychological headings more probably traces to this pervasive attitude. In England, where people pay for their television service with a set tax, the matter may be stated directly: "What I want is a funny programme at 6 P.M. each day while I am eating my evening meal," a man wrote to the BBC. "I pay you six pounds a year." Similarly, John Leonard of the *New York Times Book Review* demands a news service that will make him scream (though he doesn't want a news service that might make him chuckle). . . . Most comment about the

[2]Father Coughlin, a Detroit priest who aired his right-wing views over the radio in the 1930s; Huey Long (1893–1935), governor of Louisiana impeached on charges of bribery and gross misconduct. (eds.)

contents of the medium is suffused with a fear of being thrown back on other resources, by which one can achieve only with effort, or maybe not at all, the pleasures gained from television. A very high fraction of the world's population— probably as much as a quarter of it—has become addicted to the box. It is a phenomenon of unmeasured but clearly major importance in the conduct of all the world's business.

Aids *If There Is No Answer, What Is the Message?*

1. What does Mayer mean when he says "as children, today's young shared more of their parents' entertainment—and less of every other aspect of their parents' lives—than the young of any previous generation in any social class except the very rich"?

2. Mayer notes that television has brought black Americans into the homes of white Americans and vice versa. He feels, however, that public affairs shows have done blacks a disservice. What does he mean when he says, "the inescapable bias of news qua news [news as news] has too often impaled black Americans as a class in the butterfly case of trouble, interesting trouble, on the short-time horizon"? Do you agree?

3. Mayer takes pains to compare the experience of television watching with that of watching a movie or listening to the radio (old radio which included dramatic and entertainment programs). What does he say about the attention required for each of these activities? Why, according to Mayer, does the degree of attention required for television viewing turn it into a "homogenized experience"? Observe your family or friends as they watch TV. Does attention seem to vary with the program? Do younger people seem less or more attentive than older people?

4. Why does Mayer feel that television advertising should not be taken seriously? Do you agree with him? Would Vance Packard or Daniel Henninger agree with him? (See Unit II).

5. An unlikely simile will usually grab a reader's attention. Mayer begins his essay by maintaining that television "is embedded in the culture now, like frozen lasagna, golf carts and sociology departments." What does this unusual comparison suggest about Mayer's attitude toward television? What does it suggest about his attitude toward sociology departments?

6. Mayer's purpose is to identify at least some of the influences television has had on American society. He isolates seven influences

which he says "can be claimed on no better authority than obviousness and observation." Do you agree that all seven are obvious
and can be tested by observation? If not, does Mayer provide
adequate evidence as to the validity of his assertions? Which of
Mayer's assertions are the easiest to support? Which are the most
difficult?

7. Mayer maintains that "The work of establishing a unified culture
    in a country the size of a continent has been accomplished." He
    feels that television has "downgraded local phenomenon and elevated
    national phenomenon." Network stations have special times in which
    no network shows are programmed so that local programs can be
    aired. Those slots, however, are frequently occupied by reruns or
    independently produced shows (like the game shows). Examine one
    day's offerings of a network channel in your area; how many locally
    produced shows were aired? Most areas also have a nonnetwork
    local channel on which many local programs could be aired. Examine
    your own local station for programs that have local appeal or
    address local problems and issues. What percentage of the station's
    total broadcast day is devoted to local programming?

8. Mayer maintains that television, "powerful at creating celebrity . . .
    cannot legitimate leadership or attitude." To your mind, what celebri-
    ties have been created by television? Do you think, for example, that
    Joe Namath and Muhammad Ali would have become superstars
    without television? Can you think of any political leaders whose
    powers have been "legitimized" by television?

9. Does Newcomb's notion of an esthetic that underlies all television
    programming help explain Mayer's feeling that television viewing is
    "homogeneous"?

No Time for Comedy

TIME MAGAZINE

Will the new TV season feature the same old guns, rape, murder and arson? Yup. But with a difference. This fall the networks have agreed that between 7 p.m. and 9 p.m. Eastern Time (6 to 8 Central Time) is to be "family time," when Mom, Pop, the kids and Rover can cluster round the tube assured that they are not going to be shocked or scared. The very notion summons up classic adventure stories and young people's concerts. Is TV finally beginning to grow up?

Not a bit of it. Family time is a cynical compromise reached by the FCC and the networks to deflect mounting protests, in and out of Congress, about the rising tide of TV violence. Criticism peaked last fall when NBC aired at 8 p.m. a seamy story (*Born Innocent*) about a rebel teen-ager who was raped with a broom handle. With a glow of virtue, the networks "voluntarily" agreed to police themselves with their own censors and wrote into the National Association of Broadcasters' television code what amounts to a rule clearly intended to ban sex and violence from the air between 7 and 9. For audiences this simply means that most cops and robbers are now pushed back to 9 p.m. In their place the networks are busy emasculating the medium's most promising genre, the situation comedy, into appropriate pap.

CHUCKLES CURTAILED

"It's like a knee in the groin of social criticism," says Norman Lear who only 5½ years ago launched TV's new wave of frankness with *All in the Family*. Since then, sitcoms have laughed at almost everything: there was Maude's abortion, Archie's bigotry, and Rhoda and the Pill. The family laughed with them. Now it will find its chuckles curtailed. *All in the Family*, TV's No. 1 show last season in its 8 p.m. slot on Saturdays, has been moved to Monday at 9 p.m. Lear has been told that most of last year's episodes were not family fare. *Rhoda*, scheduled for family time, is feeling the censor's breath. Says *Rhoda* Executive Producer Allan

Burns: "Rhoda and Joe may give the impression that although they are newlyweds, sex is a thing of the past." Another family-time show, M*A*S*H, has for the first time in three years had trouble with the word virgin. CBS censors took it out, saying, "A parent might be asked to explain what it means to a younger member of the family."

New shows are having an even tougher passage. *Phyllis*, starring Cloris Leachman, and *Fay*, with Lee Grant, came close to never getting on the air at all. *Phyllis* Executive Producer Ed Weinberger almost choked when CBS meddled with the pilot, in which the widowed Phyllis suspects her 17-year-old daughter of having an affair. Says Phyllis, as she ends an explanatory phone conversation with her daughter: "Nothing happened —if she is telling the truth." CBS cut the tag line.

NBC objected to a romantic situation merely implied in *Fay's* pilot. Says Grant, who plays a divorcee with three kids, "I can't have affairs, only serious relationships." But even they are risky. In another episode, Fay goes out with a man who has no sexual interest in her. The network had a fit. Says one frustrated scriptwriter: "They want to return to shows like *Leave It To Beaver*—except that that title would never get past the censors."

STEAMY CLIMATE

With a double standard worthy of Hollywood's old Hays Office, the networks have apparently raised few objections to the season's seven new crime shows. They start at 9, which is shown by Nielsen to be almost as much of a children's viewing hour as family time. There is no indication either that the censors so much as raise an eyebrow at the lubricious exchanges that enliven family-time game shows like *Hollywood Squares*.

Norman Lear suggests that "sex and violence are a smokescreen. There are interests in this country that don't care to have fun made about the problems existing in society." He has another problem too. He stood to make a bundle when *All in the Family* finally went off network TV and was sold for syndication to local stations. Now he may make a good deal less. The prime hour for syndicated shows is 7 p.m. to 8 p.m., when networks and their affiliates air news and local programs. That is the only time when independents feel they are competitive, and they are willing to pay a lot for a show. But *All in the Family* is ineligible for that time slot. So are crime series. Quinn Martin, who produces *The Streets of San Francisco* and *Cannon*, predicts: "It's going to force the networks into giving producers more money to make these shows if we can't make any money from syndication."

That threat raises the faint hope that a few years of family time might drive some crime shows off the air. What is more likely, however, is that local stations will simply abandon the optional N.A.B. code. After all, cops and robbers are the most popular enduring fare. Now, in the steamy climate of lost tempers, producers of all kinds are discussing lawsuits. One approach is on constitutional grounds: family time violates the First Amendment. The second involves an antitrust action that the networks' agreement to ban violent shows from early prime time amounts to collusion. In the fuss, the original issue of violence on TV has been lost. Another loser may well be the fresh, funny irreverence of the sitcoms that for only a brief span of time has lit the wasteland.

Aids   *No Time for Comedy*

1. Why does *Time* call "family time" a cynical compromise?

2. What has been the effect of the FCC ruling on situation comedies?

3. What does *Time* mean by the "lubricious exchanges that enliven family-time game shows like the *Hollywood Squares*"? Examine this show for "lubricious exchanges."

4. What points does *Time* raise about the networks' scheduling of crime shows? What is *Time*'s attitude toward crime shows?

5. Norman Lear is quoted as saying that "sex and violence are a smokescreen. There are interests in this country that don't care to have fun made about the problems existing in society." Does *Time* ever explain what those interests are? What interests do you think Lear is talking about? What other reasons does Lear have for opposing "family time"?

6. *Time* Magazine is known for its breezy, irreverent style. How does *Time* achieve this effect? How would you characterize the tone of this article? How does *Time*'s tone compare to that of Reed Whittemore in "The Big Picture"? Note the way *Time* uses quotations not only to bolster an argument, but also to enliven the presentation. The most sexual joke in the article is contained in the remarks of a "frustrated" script writer. Look for other examples of lively quotations. Does *Time* use slang? Look for words and phrases that are decidedly informal.

7. Do you think "family time" is a valid concept? What kinds of shows would you like to see scheduled during these hours? Do you think that the networks have a responsibility not to air shows that might

be damaging to children? Do you think shows like "All in the Family" or "M*A*S*H" are damaging to children? Do you think parents should monitor childrens' television viewing?

8. Nicholas Johnson, a former Federal Communications Commission commissioner, writes that "it . . . is a form of censorship to so completely clog the public airwaves with tasteless gruel that there is no time left for quality entertainment and social commentary" ("The Corporate Censor," *T.V. Guide*, July 5, 1969, p. 179). What shows do you consider quality entertainment? What kind of criteria do you use in making such a judgment? How do you feel about Johnson's statement?

How the Gosh-darn Networks Edit the Heck Out of Movies
DAVID BLACK

Harvey Korman, playing the evil Hedley Lamarr in Mel Brooks's movie "Blazing Saddles," loses patience with Madeline Kahn, a sham Marlene Dietrich, and, in a fury, screams at her, "You Teutonic *twivit!*"

"Twivit"? That is definitely not what Korman called her when the film played in movie theaters. But that is what he will say in the CBS version of the film now in the process of being re-edited for television, a medium that has the power to transform the obscene into the coy and to change savagery into humdrum violence.

"Twivit" may vanish before the film reaches the home screen—the editors at CBS are also considering replacing the original obscenity with "twirp"—but equally peculiar epithets and expletives have found their way into other movies that have been sanitized to conform to network standards. In CBS's soon-to-be-broadcast version of "The Great White Hope," when James Earl Jones is about to leave for Mexico with his new mistress, he is told he had better not go off with that "sneaky little wax-faced *love'em!*" And, in the TV-edited version of Francis Ford Coppola's "The Godfather," which NBC broadcast last November, James Caan calls someone "a son of a *buck!*"

Why do the networks tamper with theatrical films prior to broadcasting them? First, they are in constant fear of offending the sensitivities of even a small number of viewers whose dissatisfaction might be reflected in lowered Neilsen ratings. And second, they prefer to police themselves rather than have others do it for them—a state of affairs they fear might come to pass if raciness on the TV screen were ever to prompt a public outcry.

Accordingly, all three networks have created their own in-house staffs of censors—departments that enjoy a virtually unchallengeable veto power over all programs. These TV censors rule out a great many "dirty" words and expressions and also numerous scenes. The relaxation of similar standards in the movie industry in recent years is keeping them quite busy.

For instance, in James Caan's death

From *The New York Times*, January 26, 1975, pp. 1, 33. Copyright © 1975 by The New York Times Company. Reprinted by permission.

scene in "The Godfather," gunmen appear at a highway toll booth and blast at Caan through the window of his car. He staggers out onto the road and is about to be hurled back by another blast. In the television version, the shots come, but Caan's chest does not erupt into a fountain of blood. The horrifying scene—Caan arched back, blood pouring from his wounds, an underworld St. Sebastian[1]—is missing.

The cuts in that scene, only a few minutes of scrapped action, may be noticed by only those who are very familiar with the film. But sometimes the material deleted from a movie is needed for a full understanding of the plot—as in the case of "Klute," a thriller in which Jane Fonda plays a prostitute and which NBC broadcast last fall. By cutting a crucial moment from a scene involving the discovery of a pair of Miss Fonda's panties, only vague references were left to what had been an important clue leading to the apprehension of the sex maniac who had been stalking her throughout the film.

Sometimes what is cut is the very heart of the film, as in the case of "Midnight Cowboy," which was also aired last fall and in which Jon Voight plays a male prostitute. ABC deleted all scenes of homosexual encounters.

The network prohibitions are not confined to the obscene and the violent. Even when dramatically useful and not at all lewd, frontal nudity is considered unacceptable. For example, in NBC's version of "The Godfather," just before a woman sheds her dress . . .

. . . cut to the office of Herminio Traviesas, Vice-President of Standards and Practices at NBC, the network on which

"The Godfather" was shown, who is saying, "We had to drop that scene even though it was not erotic." Feet up on the desk, occasionally slicing the air as though he were cutting film, he explains, "In adapting movies for television, you must address yourself to language, sex and violence. When a supplier offers us a film, we look at the picture and make notes, explaining why certain scenes may not be acceptable. We then send the notes back to the supplier, who has the responsibility for making changes. Sometimes we'll work with the director of a film. Last year, I went west before the deal on 'The Godfather' was finalized, and I sat down with Coppola at a Movieola. We went over the entire movie scene by scene. Out of three hours of film, there were only ten minutes of violence. We took out less than one minute. In the total show, there were only 35 things we changed with Mr. Coppola. A lot were words. We changed some of the obscenities to 'you lousy *rat*' or 'you lousy, cold-hearted *monster*.'

"Coppola caught Caan in Europe," Traviesas says, sweeping his arm toward a window, as though Europe were somewhere below him in Rockefeller Plaza, "and Caan did the new words himself. In only one case did Coppola fail to use the voice of the original actor in redubbing a line. You never notice it.

"He also caught John Marley," Traviesas continues, "and had him redo some words." Marley, who plays the head of a movie studio in the film, describes a woman (in NBC's version) as being "the greatest piece of *stuff*" instead of the more familiar obscenity . . .

. . . cut to CBS, where Tom Swafford,

Vice-President of Program Practices, is leaning over a circular desk, saying, "Our department looks at approximately 500 feature films each year. This year we rejected about 40 per cent because of sex, violence, nudity or language which in our judgment would be uneditable or not worth editing."

Considering his position of responsibility, Swafford is admirably candid, a man who seems to have an appreciation of the difference between the ribald and the pornographic, which allows him to make intelligent distinctions when deciding what to cut and what to leave in a film doomed to a diminished life on television.

"One of my worst mistakes," Swafford is saying, "was to think we could edit 'The Damned.' Visconti's style tends to be kaleidoscopic. He jumps from one scene to another. We edited 32 minutes out of it. It was difficult to understand in its original form. When we got done, it was incomprehensible."

In "The Graduate," which CBS first aired a year and a half ago, the important scene in which Ann Bancroft, naked, corners Dustin Hoffman in a bedroom—a scene that launches the plot—proved to be a problem to Swafford and his staff. It could not be dropped, but the quick cuts to her breast and belly could not be left in. A compromise was worked out. The shots of the naked breast and belly were replaced with shots of the room's doorknob—which logically worked since Hoffman was intent at that moment on getting out of the room.

According to Swafford, his toughest editing job was on "Who's Afraid of Virginia Woolf?" which most recently appeared on television last spring. The obscenities that peppered the original film defined character—particularly between co-stars Elizabeth Taylor and Richard Burton—and were therefore vital to many scenes. The edited-for-TV version, in which many of the saltier words were either simply cut or replaced with less pungent ones plucked from elsewhere on the soundtrack, suffered accordingly.

In the television version of "Patton," which was first broadcast on ABC in 1972, this same technique—looting the soundtrack for safe words to replace unacceptable ones—was used. ABC (like CBS) usually does its own re-editing on the films it is going to broadcast, but in the case of "Patton" the network consulted the film's producer, Frank McCarthy. According to Grace Johnson, Vice President of Broadcast Standards at ABC, "The producer and I sat down together. We went over the script, and I indicated what edits we desired. There was one scene where he [Patton, played by George C. Scott] was full-face, and it was very difficult to get the language changed." In the edited-for-TV version of the movie, "dirty bastard" became "despicable coward."

Such magical shuffling of words from frame to frame is done by dividing the finished film, which has the soundtrack running in a ribbon along one edge, into two components: the film itself, with the images on it, and the soundtrack. The soundtrack can be further separated into three parts—voice, background music, and sound effects—and remixed. An offending word can thus be drowned out by raising the volume of the music or the sound effects in the scene. Or a word can be replaced by another word—either newly recorded as was done in "The Godfather" or lifted from elsewhere on the soundtrack as in "Virginia Woolf" and "Patton"—without disturbing the continuity of the background noises or music.

"I once made a word from parts of other words the actors said in other places in the movie," Jay Sherman, a film editor at CBS, explains as he hits the stop button on an editing console. On the small screen of the console, Roger Bowen, the actor who played the colonel in "M*A*S*H," freezes with his mouth open. "He said 'Goddamn,' which was unacceptable. I decided to make it 'Gosh-damn.' So I took the 'ga' sound from 'God' and the 'sh' sound from something Elliott Gould had said, mixed them together and came out with 'gosh.' People thought it still gave the impression he was saying 'Goddamn,' so we never used it. But it was a good technique to try."

Re-editing the image in a film is rarely as complicated as weaving a word together from vagrant sounds. When there is no dialogue, offending scenes can be easily cut. In the version of "Bonnie and Clyde" that was originally shown on CBS a year and a half ago, 16 of the goriest seconds of the blood ballet at the end of the movie were cut. The only sound was that of guns firing—which did not have to be synchronized with the images.

If there is an offending detail—for example, a random breast along the edge of a scene, the film can be adjusted by blowing the picture up and cropping it. In the version of "The Heartbreak Kid," shown last weekend on ABC, a close-up of Jeannie Berlin was blown up and her naked breast cropped out of the picture.

If there is no way to get rid of the detail, a reaction shot—someone looking shocked or (depending on the plot line) blasé—can be substituted. Or, since it takes approximately two to three seconds

for an image to register completely on the human eye, the problem scene is sometimes merely flashed on the screen for an instant.

"In a scene in 'M*A*S*H,'" Jay Sherman says, while winding the film to the appropriate point on his editing machine, "I got the image down to less than one second." He slows the film to the specific scene. Sally Kellerman has just entered a tent to take a shower. Everyone on the base gathers in front of the shower tent. The side of the tent lifts, exposing . . .

. . . cut to reaction shot of reporter scribbling notes as he watches the screen.

Since the techniques used in adapting films for television are becoming more sophisticated, there is an increasing threat to the integrity of the original films. A substituted image could change the meaning of a crucial scene. Trading an obscenity for a safer word could violate a character by making a phrase suggestive instead of vulgar, smutty instead of colloquial, polite instead of rowdy—as in a scene in the version of "M*A*S*H" that CBS broadcast last fall, when a replaced word had Elliott Gould saying, uncharacteristically, "Get me a nurse who can work in close without getting her *chest* in the way."

To protect their films, more directors and producers than ever before are exercising their option—recently negotiated by the Directors' Guild—to be consulted during the editing of a movie for television. And many of them seem relatively satisfied with the arrangement. For example, Frank McCarthy, the producer of "Patton," has said that he feels the television version of that film "worked out very well." And, after "Virginia Woolf" appeared on television, Ernest Lehman, screenwriter and producer of the film, wrote to CBS's Tom

Swafford to tell him how much he "admired the care, the taste, the skill and the intelligence with which you edited and presented the film on your network last night. . . . Your decision to preserve the integrity of the work as completely as you did was courageous."

Other moviemakers, however, aware of how often films are damaged in re-editing for television, still distrust the networks. As Robert Altman, the director of "M*A*S*H," sees it, network censorship, no matter how benign, is still censorship. "If the networks sincerely said they were willing to work together," Altman recently said, "I'd do it. But they don't care. You only have an option to make the cuts they want you to make. They won't let you really work on the editing for TV. The networks still have total control."

Determined to ward off possible government regulation, the networks will doubtless continue to exert their control. But some loosening-up is likely. As Tom Swafford explains, "Theater was always ahead of motion pictures. Movies are now ahead of TV. And things are changing a little. In 'Guess Who's Coming to Dinner,' there's a scene in which Spencer Tracy looks right into the camera, works his jaw muscles and says, 'I'll be a son-of-a-bitch.' We left it in, and got only eighteen letters. We left it in because it was so right. Almost anything is acceptable, if it's dramatically right. Almost."

Aids   *How the Goshdarn Networks Edit the Heck Out of Movies*

1.   According to Black, why do the networks edit theatrical films? What sorts of things are edited out? Why does Black object to the networks' editing of movies?

2.   How does Black's title set the tone for his article?

3.   Consider the subtle ways in which Black communicates his annoyance with network censors. How, for example, does he turn the standard film editing direction "cut to . . ." into a satiric comment? What do the quotation marks around the adjective suggest when Black says "These TV censors rule out a great many 'dirty' words. . . ."?

4.   Although Black is annoyed with the network censors, he is interested enough in their techniques to describe them to us. The passage in which he describes "such magical shuffling of words" is an example of "process analysis," i.e., dividing a process into steps and discussing the relationship between steps. (A writer would use the same technique in describing how to build a treehouse or how to fix a sewing machine.) Does Black do a good job of analyzing the process of film editing? Is his discussion of this process clear?

5.   If you have the opportunity, watch the televised version of a movie you have seen in a theater. Can you tell whether or not the movie has

been edited? If so, what was cut out or altered? Did the editing change the movie in any important way—did it alter the plot, change characters, or affect impact?

6. Do you think theatrical films should be edited for television? Is this censorship? Can you think of alternative ways of handling the sex and violence shown in movies?

7. Both the *Time* article on "family hour" and Black's article suggest that the networks worry most about sex and violence on the air. What other elements in television programming might be offensive to viewers? What aspects of television programming are most offensive to you? Do you think these aspects should be censored in any way?

8. Both *Time* and Black suggest that the networks sometimes engage in censorship themselves because they fear government censorship of television programming. Have you read or heard of any recent instances of such government censorship? If so, what sorts of things were censored? Do you think the government is ever justified in censoring entertainment programming? news programming?

Radio:
Where Has
All the Music Gone?

PETER MCCABE

It's late and Larry and I still have 50 miles to go. We need some music to keep from dozing off. Since Larry has had two tape decks ripped off in the last six months, the only choice is the AM-FM radio. So he starts punching buttons.

He tries AM first, and works his way through "Rhinestone Cowboy," "Get Down Tonight," "Mr. Jaws," "Please, Mr. Please," and an appalling version of "Help Me Rhonda" by Johnny Rivers. He snarls, switches to the FM band, and this time uses the tuner to work his way back down the dial, hoping for a cut from Dylan's *Basement Tapes*, something by Rod Stewart, Eric Clapton or the Grateful Dead, maybe some Reggae, Joe Cocker's new single—hell, he'll settle for the Eagles or a first-rate disco song. He strikes out. Larry gives a Bronx cheer and turns the radio off. "Do you remember," he says, "there was a time when you could hear *music* on this thing?"

Larry has just made the discovery I made three months ago while driving across country: that America has become an endless highway of Top 20 tunes. There still exist good country and soul stations and a few pockets of varied programming such as CKLW out of Windsor, Ontario, KSAN in San Francisco and WNEW-FM in New York, but these are isolated islands in an ocean of homogeneity. What's happened here is total capitulation to that old enemy of American media, the rating game. Radio playlists are now down to fewer than 20 songs, repeated roughly every two hours, sometimes more, and program directors choose music based on statistics. At most large rock stations the making up of a playlist has always been an internal struggle for the program or music director. On one side, the love of novelty; on the other, fear of risk. Victory for "fear of risk" is now almost total.

Take the case of WABC, the AM station which dominates New York City. Rick Sklar is the director of operations for WABC, as well as director of program development for all ABC-AM stations. WABC may just be the most important radio station in the country. When a record lands on WABC's playlist it sells 100,000 extra copies, says one record company. WABC is probably one of the most awful screamers you will ever hear.

Rick Sklar has been at WABC for a long time, but he has never "broken" (popularized) a record in his life. His playlist is made up only of what he considers the finest blue chips (those songs that are already proven hits across the country), and a few records that are selling especially well in New York because of regional tastes. The director's playlist is like a conservative mutual fund that leaves the "new" and the "interesting" to others. The reason for this is simple: The fellow is very conscious of ratings. He couldn't care less about the exposure of new records. His heart is hardened to the pleas of promotion men. Rick Sklar is only concerned with obtaining a greater share of the market than such rivals as WNBC. That is why WABC is a 20-tune jukebox. That is why WABC uses a timer, like a kitchen timer, for its number one record of the week; every time it goes off, it cues the disc jockey to play the record.

One thing that Rick Sklar perhaps does not consider is what this means for music. The director is not beloved in the record business, just as radio as a whole is not. The feeling is that the record industry has grown too dependent on radio (which for years has offered free exposure of new products) and that it is now paying the price. Many record executives who have been twisted around radio's finger for too long not to feel any resentment, would be secretly delighted if the disco trend in the big cities spread out across the entire country and could be used as a way of introducing new records to the mass public. But this is a long way off and it is questionable if it will ever happen, so in the meantime radio maintains its whip hand and the record industry has to live with it.

The record industry understands what radio either doesn't or cares not to see, that it is much harder, i.e., expensive, to introduce new artists to the public now than it was, say, five years ago. The main reason for this is that FM radio has gone the way of AM. It, too, now follows in most cases a programming format, the difference being that it plays "hit album cuts" as opposed to hit singles (though in many cases these may be the same) and its disc jockeys speak rather than shriek.

Joe Smith, president of Warner-Reprise Records, yearns for the days when FM radio offered an alternative.

"When FM stations began in the sixties, they were losers," said Joe Smith. "The owners left things to the disc jockeys, who played great album cuts and gradually drew listeners. Suddenly the FM stations were no longer selling time to the local gas station and Freddie's hardware store but to big advertisers. The station owners woke up. They saw these FM stations had good demographics. What did they do? They looked at the formats of AM stations and considered it would make good business sense to formatize their own FM stations, without ever thinking that maybe one of the reasons for the success of FM was the lack of format. What this means is that the pipeline for good music has narrowed."

How the battle between formatized and free-form FM radio will resolve is still undecided, although the trend is toward the former. Scott Muni, program director of WNEW-FM in New York, a free-form station, believes that the young adult listener wants to be treated with more respect than Rick Sklar would advocate, and points to the continued success of KSAN-FM in San Francisco as an example of free-form holding its own. Sklar on the other hand, considers that the kid who grew up on the tight playlist will continue to adhere to it as he becomes a young adult. It may eventually boil down to whom the advertisers believe, since one of the criticisms leveled at the rating services is that they don't accurately reflect the complete listening audience.

One person the advertisers did believe, although he was supported by the rating services, was Bill Drake. The concept of formatized radio was largely his brainchild. Drake was vice-president of programming at RKO General Stations. The phrase "much more music" is his. Drake has now gone exclusively into the programming of automated radio, where there are no live personalities, just tapes introducing songs, and giving time checks.

Drake started his experiment at a small station in Fresno, California, which future generations of music lovers might come to think of as the musical equivalent of White Sands, New Mexico. Drake eliminated a lot of disc jockey conversation, announcements of record titles, etc. and cut the playlist to the super hits and those songs that were about to become super hits (in some cases because of the tremendous exposure they received on his stations—Catch 22). It meant that listeners could count on hearing the top-selling records over and over again. Bearing out one of H.L. Mencken's[1] more memorable observations about vulgarity, the policy proved successful, and the audiences of the Drake-programmed stations have increased substantially.

The rest of AM radio had no choice. It was forced to go along or lose ratings—and advertisers. And over the years the Drake format spread, with the competition between stations becoming cutthroat. Radio-station thinking was that any mistake, any variation from this formula, could cause what is known in the business as a tuneout. Before FM radio began to move in the same direction, the record companies could at least hope for exposure by non-best-selling artists on FM stations. Consequently, throughout the late sixties and early seventies, they maintained wider rosters of recording artists. Now they're cutting these back.

---

[1]H.L. Mencken (1880–1956), an American journalist noted for his attacks on complacency and convention. (eds.)

The consequences of modern radio policy for recorded music are inevitable, given the enormous costs of recording and promoting a new artist: the record companies are only going to release records by musicians of the highest commercial potential, and the rest of the roster will be dumped overboard. To some extent this is already happening. These days the release of a record is much less a hit-or-miss business. Before the record company promotion men even get their hands on a new 45 rpm single, the record company will have scrutinized the appeal of its product in the same way Procter and Gamble will gauge the charms of a new soap it is about to market. What's even more ominous is that there is now a rating service that uses computers to predict a record's chances of winding up in a given chart position.

Clive Davis, former president of Columbia Records and now president of Arista Records, understood how business practice should be applied to the merchandising of records. Once a week Davis used to meet with about 100 of his staff at Columbia. This was the singles meeting—45 rpm singles that is—and its purpose was to evaluate which records had the quality that would translate into upward progress in the charts. Davis had refined the singles meeting, a record business tradition, into a Noh play.[2]

The reason, of course, for all this hoopla is to cater to the absurdities of radio. Radio sets the guidelines to which music must conform. If J.S. Bach were writing music today, he might be wise to try and write a three-minute single if he wanted to keep eating. The record companies, through means fair and sometimes foul, try to release singles that will find a place on the playlist of a radio station somewhere in the country. With most station playlists consisting of 20 records or less a week, this isn't easy. So radio, especially AM radio, may be viewed as a bottleneck, where huge amounts of vinyl pile up—representing thousands of dollars in investments and countless hours of energy—all waiting to get on the air. Once a record finds a place on one of these playlists, the record company has won a free three-minute advertisement for one of its products. The free ad will be repeated several times throughout the day. Of course the real item being advertised is not the single, but the album from which the single has been taken. Albums are where the real money lies. But the only way to sell an album (and this applies even if you're an established artist) is to have a single from the album played regularly on the radio. This will enable it to climb in the music trade charts, which in turn means it will be played on more radio stations, which means it will be requested in more stores, which gets the salesmen off their butts, and means that in the end a lot of records get sold. Certainly is a complex little business, isn't it?

It is an oft-repeated cliche of the music business that nobody ever bought a record without hearing it first. Now that the listening booth has

[2]Noh, slow-paced, ritualized Japanese theater form. (eds.)

vanished totally from the record store, the only way to hear a record is on the airways. Hence, the power of radio. (Some record executives are so disgusted with the current state of affairs that they would like to see the listening booth make a comeback.) If this is so, I asked one record executive, why does the record industry advertise in music magazines? Partly it's image building, I was told, partly to simply satisfy an artist's ego, but radio is really all that sells records. You can't hype records like you can movies, where that effete bunch—Simon, Reed, Kael and Crist[3]—determine what will play in the backwoods. In the record business it's the hinterland radio stations that decide what will play in New York, Chicago and Los Angeles. So after a record company releases a single, it's up to the promotion men to try and get it played—anywhere.

Now there was a time when promotion men had a real function. They could justify their gig by convincing a program director that they had so much belief in a record that if he would only give it a few spins, he would see for himself the response. The phones would come off the walls. And this happened many times; the record nobody thought had a chance touched a chord with the audiences. "Sounds of Silence" by Paul Simon and Art Garfunkel broke and made them one of the biggest recording acts ever, only because some obscure program director gave their "weird" record a spin. But these days every radio station is looking over its shoulder to see what its neighbor is playing. Fear of risk is becoming the bane of the record industry, and promotion men are being turned into drones.

The only hope for a new record by a new artist is that someone, somewhere, takes a chance. Where is not that important, though certain towns may be considered significant in the progress of a record. Detroit, for example, which has what the record industry calls a "good salt and pepper" situation or "an ideal balance of R&B and pop." Once a record breaks out, the promotion men can "spread" it. This means they can march into a station in Chicago and New York and say that CKLW (a station in Canada) is playing it, after hearing that WCOL in Columbus had been playing it.

* * *

. . . Freedom of choice for disc jockeys has all but been eliminated in this country, largely due to the payola scandals that have rocked the music business twice in the last 15 years. DJs these days are little more than automatons. They no longer exercise the role of opinion-makers. Judith Sims, former Los Angeles editor of *Rolling Stone:* "They know absolutely nothing about the music they are playing. They have no involvement whatsoever with their audience. I have never seen one at a concert or a

---

[3]John Simon, Rex Reed, Pauline Kael, and Judith Crist are all influential film critics. (eds.)

club in L.A. How can one have any admiration for the world of radio when it's so completely divorced from what's happening in music?"

And it is the music that has suffered as a consequence. "There are lots of critics saying that the music just isn't as vital anymore," says one part-time disc jockey and music reviewer. "That's simply not true. The recording techniques that are available now are better than they were ten years ago. The kind of people who make rock and roll records are better educated musically than they were. The stuff that is good just gets buried. It doesn't get on the airwaves like it should, and so only a limited aware group knows about it. That's what's hurting rock. We've got to get back to a time of knowledgeable disc jockeys and stop worrying if some DJ somewhere is doing a little grass on the side because a promo man gave it to him.

"The FM DJs are not only restricted by playlists now, they're restricted to which particular cut they should play from an album. Can you imagine who would want a job like that? It hasn't happened at the station I work at, but it's happening at many others. When it happens at mine, I'll quit. If I can't turn people on to several tracks from Joe Cocker's *Jamaica Say You Will*, which is a great album that isn't getting played a lot, then they can shove it."

Aside from limiting what its listeners hear, how else does radio hurt music? was a question I asked one producer I know.

"Let me put it this way," he said. "In the sixties you had this tremendous outpouring of great music. The music became too sophisticated to be slotted into "the top 20 tunes," and who cared about that stuff anyway? Everyone knew who the bands were. You'd go see the Dead or the Airplane, whether they had a hit single that week or not. You knew their album cuts from FM and from concerts. It seemed like such a total victory for music that nobody noticed that radio was fighting this all the way. I remember Clive Davis saying in the early seventies: 'Don't underestimate the importance of the hit single; it's making a comeback.' This was in the days when it was almost considered uncouth to release a single. And that's what happened. Now I'm always aware when I go into a studio of the need for a hit single. It's a necessary evil. Now I like good singles, don't misunderstand me, but I try not to let a band know that I'm listening for the potential single. It gets in the way of their music."

It is sometimes forgotten how fast the music business grew. It has grown ten times in terms of record and tape sales in the last 20 years. Sales of records and tapes are now $2 billion a year, more than the entire gross receipts from movies and professional sports combined. With the record industry making vast profits year after year, and benefiting from all the free advertising, it was no wonder it considered itself special. It never did consider that a day might come when its interests did not coincide with those of radio. Consequently it never lobbied for a whole review section in newspapers such as the book business gets from the

New York Sunday *Times*. It never bothered to hold on to its customers when they began slipping toward jobs, marriage and babies. It never envisaged a day when radio, doing the best for itself, might not be doing the best for music and the record industry.

Now the grumbles over radio grow louder. "They say Elton John is a phenomenon," says one executive, "but that's not really true. He's just the biggest we've got right now. But what concerns me is if a real phenomenon came along, and phenomena are always good for music, I don't think radio would know what to do. When the Beatles first came to the U.S. in 1964, radio stations played all their album cuts back to back. That was radio responding to exactly what was happening in the way radio should. Now they're so twisted up in their damn formats they wouldn't know how to respond."

So how can you know what's happening in music if you're not learning it from the radio? Well, there are at least three music papers that will help clue you in on what you're not hearing. *Rolling Stone* is the largest. It offers informed articles on new acts, and it has a tolerable review section which can be faulted because it tries to review everything. The problem with the magazine is that it is not fast at picking up new music trends. It took *Rolling Stone* 18 months to discover there was a disco-dancing craze in New York and about the same amount of time before it realized that Reggae ought to be on its front pages. But it does have some knowledgeable contributors and writers, and occasionally they'll pick up on some album or artist that everybody's overlooked.

Crawdaddy magazine is less widely distributed than *Rolling Stone*, and the quality of writing is more adolescent, but it might be sharper in terms of keeping in touch with what's happening musically.

Country Music is the best magazine available if you're into country. Its review section rarely leads with the left, but the information is all there and the features are well-written. Also, the turnover of new acts is much slower in country music, so when something new happens, you're likely to read about it right away.

Of all the other magazines, the new *Village Voice* probably offers the best music review section. It is being run by Bob Christgau, who's as fanatical in his opinions as the John Birch Society, but at least it's nice to read brutally honest reviews that speak knowledgeably.

If you still feel you're not being sufficiently informed, you could do what my friend Larry did. Being sufficiently masochistic, he gave up on radio altogether, and bought another tape deck. Then he invited all his musical friends to compile an hour of their favorite music on cassette, music that he might not be familiar with. His friends, all being frustrated disc jockeys, were happy to oblige, and Larry now drives in a state of bliss . . . and doesn't leave his tapes in the car.

Aids *Radio: Where Has All the Music Gone?*

1. According to McCabe, what is the relationship between the radio stations and the recording industry?

2. What is "formatized" radio? What is "free-form" radio? Does McCabe adequately define these terms?

3. What have been the historical differences between AM and FM radio? How does McCabe view the future of FM radio?

4. Every profession, every trade has a special linguistic shorthand—a jargon. Jargons take a variety of forms; some are very technical, others tend to be slangy. Students use jargon when they speak of "acing a test," "cribbing notes," or "taking a gut course." McCabe is using the jargon of the record industry when he writes, "Once a record breaks out, the promotion man can 'spread' it." What does this mean in standard English?

5. McCabe's article was originally printed in *Argosy*. *Argosy* is a man's magazine full of articles on hunting, weaponry, and adventure. Does McCabe's style reflect the biases of the magazine? Is his use of language designed somehow to appeal to male readers?

6. McCabe suggests that one of the consequences of the rating system is that the top-ranked records are played again and again. Listen to a rock station and note how many minutes elapse before a record is played a second time.

Radio
or "Come On, Let Me
Show You Where It's At"

DON R. PEMBER

Announcer: The Columbia Broadcasting System and its affiliated stations present Orson Welles and the "Mercury Theater of the Air" in *The War of the Worlds* by H. G. Wells. Ladies and gentlemen, the director of the Mercury Theater and star of these broadcasts, Orson Welles.

Welles: We know now that in the early years of the twentieth century this world was being watched closely by intelligences greater than man's . . .

Jingle: More muuuuuuuuuuusic, K*O* Mmmmmm

DJ: Welcome back to boss radio number one, the top sound in the top city. Cousin Brucie layin' 'em on you til seven when brother Jack B. Nimble rocks in with more of the hits on the big eleven. (Cue music) And now more outtasight sounds, far-reaching wails and good vibes with Dental Floss and the Cavities, the first of eighteen nonstop hits in a row from your man Bruce.

American radio has changed dramatically in the past 30 years. And all the important changes can be discovered just by reading closely the two passages above. The first contains the opening lines of Orson Welles' famous production of *The War of the Worlds*. The second represents what might be heard on at least one radio station in almost any American city today.

The differences are striking. The Welles' production was a dramatic presentation given in an era when radio was filled with drama, comedy, and variety programs. As Cousin Brucie says, recorded music is about all that's programmed on modern radio. *The War of the Worlds* originated in New York City and was broadcast to millions of Americans over a radio network—a linking of several hundred stations. In the seventies nearly all radio programming is produced (if that word is accurate) locally by individual radio stations.

The Welles' production was broadcast in the evening hours, prime radio listening time, to a vast audience of all ages. Nighttime radio today is generally regarded as the domain of young people. Prime radio time is early in the morning and late in the afternoon as millions of commuters, momentary captives of their radio hosts, wend their way along crowded freeways to and from their jobs. Finally, the quality of radio broadcasting has shifted dramatically from what was once considered a fairly high-class entertainment medium to a barren desert of commercial messages, dotted here and there with musical oases. . . . "The public eloped with a brazen but seductive hussy called television and radio suddenly became an abandoned orphan," former ABC commentator Edward P. Morgan said in a speech entitled "Who Forgot Radio?" at American University in 1965. . . .

THE SHAPE OF THE BUSINESS

There are about 7,000 commercial radio stations broadcasting in the United States. They can be heard on the more than 330,000,000 radio receivers in the nation, nearly a third of which are in automobiles. According to studies, radio ranks third as a source of news, and is the third "most believable" medium in most persons' opinion. Faced with a choice of having a single medium, more people would select television or newspapers than radio. Yet radio is the most immediate medium, the one that people turn to first in an emergency. When the East Coast was blacked out for many hours in November of 1965, portable radios constituted the chief source of information for the confused and often frightened populace. But except for those rare emergencies, radio has abdicated its role as an information medium to become an entertainment medium. For listeners—and radio has twice the popularity among teenagers as adults—the medium has moved from the foreground of their interests to the background. Radio is something you can listen to while you are doing something else. Television is generally tied to the electrical wall socket. Newspapers and magazines are bound by an overland distribution system. But, like the ubiquitous crushed styrofoam cup and the empty beer can, wherever you go, there's radio.

It will probably come as news to most of you, but radio plays a far less important role in our society than it does in the rest of the world. On that two-thirds of the planet that is economically and socially underdeveloped, radio is a vital part of the communications and information process. It can transcend the physical distances wrought by mountains and jungles as well as the intellectual distances shaped by illiteracy. In some of the remotest parts of the world a visitor will see inhabitants walking down dusty roads with small transistor radios clasped over their ears. Social scientists call it the "transistor revolution" and some pin great hopes of human improvement on it. Most of these foreign broadcasting stations are not privately owned and hence are not concerned about profits and commercial advertising. The government subsidy that funds them usually insures that they will be information-oriented rather than entertainment-oriented.

Because of its ability to travel almost anywhere, and because of the great number of radio receivers in use—about one and a half for every person in America—radio has the appearance of being the "massest" of the mass media, and it is. But strangely enough, it also has the physical and economic structure needed to become a fragmented medium, serving smaller and smaller segments of society; "narrowcasting," if you will, instead of broadcasting.

Because radio costs less to operate than television, it can afford to pick out a segment of society—a small subgroup—and make an appeal to it. Some newspapers and magazines can do this as well, and many small publications are reaching out to special interest groups today. But when print media seek to appeal to a small subgroup, they tend to lose the quality of mass media (that is, media that appeal to a large heterogeneous audience.) The publisher who seeks to prepare a newspaper for left-handed billiard players faces economic limitations on his distribution. With as few as 1,500 copies he can reach all the left-handed billiard players on his subscription list. But no one else will see the newspaper. However, radio can program for the same 1,500 left-handers without diluting its essence as a mass medium, for anyone else in the community can eavesdrop.

THE AM DIAL

The two kinds of radio sets you might most likely find in a home or car are AM receivers and FM receivers. AM is the most common and the most commercial, and really is the heart of the radio system in this country. Two-thirds of all broadcasting stations are AM and there are far more AM receivers than FM ones.

AM stands for *amplitude modulation.* This term has to do with the way the radio waves are sent from broadcaster to receiver, and that's all we're going to say about it. For decades American AM radio was dominated by the radio networks—NBC, CBS, and later ABC and the Mutual Broadcasting System. Programs that originated in New York, for example, were sent to your local stations via cable and then broadcast over the airwaves to your receiver. The decades of the thirties and forties are known variously as the golden era, big-time radio, or the heyday of broadcasting. Compared to radio in the seventies there is some accuracy in all these labels, although as radio historian Jim Harmon has written, those days of radio will always seem a little better than they were.

Television was developed by the same men who controlled network radio. It didn't make much economic sense to these men to promote television viewing in the evening on one hand and at the same time offer a full slate of network radio programs at night as well. It would only tend to confuse advertisers. So slowly, but surely, network radio began to disappear. The first shows to go were the big-budget evening programs that conflicted with evening TV time. (Television began by broadcasting primarily in the evening.) Next went the daytime shows as television expanded its daytime hours. Weekend radio services faded out as well as sports began to dominate the tube on weekends. And the story goes on.

Well, this was fine for radio networks —but what about all those stations that had been broadcasting network radio programs? What were they to do? Music programming seemed to be the most logical answer. Production of drama or comedy or variety was too expensive for most local stations to undertake. Music programming was cheap. All you needed was a turntable and some phonograph records. Oh, yes, and a man to play them and read commercial messages, the disc jockey.

* * *

VARIATIONS ON A THEME

The music format remains the most common programming scheme in American radio today. Radio is well suited to broadcast music, especially FM radio where fidelity is of high quality. Some broadcasters who own or have access to both AM and FM frequencies as well as a television channel have even experimented with simulcasting music on all three media. If the listener positions his receivers according to instructions from the station, he will literally be surrounded by music.

Other stations use recorded music as a supplement to a richer format that in a small way attempts to fill the void left when network radio died. WJR in Detroit, for example, which many persons consider the nation's best radio station, offers listeners a variety of music and non-music fare. The station features the standard personality disc jockey during drive times and in the midnight to dawn slot. But during the remainder of the day it concentrates heavily on live music, recorded classical music with intelligent commentary by an expert on fine arts, humor and commentary from both network and local personnel, 15-minute news segments throughout much of the day with an hour and a half of news and comment in the dinner hour, and scripted music programs in which a carefully written narrative accompanies a series of thematically similar recordings. But stations like WJR, "The Great Voice of the Great Lakes," are indeed rare.

Stations that do rely on the music format generally also offer listeners capsulized editions of news, weather, and sports on the hour or half hour. Sometimes these ingredients are added in a true spirit of public service, but other times they are included only as fillers between commercial messages. The typical broadcaster today relies heavily on the news wire and the special five-minute summaries prepared hourly by the wire services especially for radio. An announcer (generally called a *newsman* because he reads the news) will rip off the copy minutes before newstime and present the headlines in stacatto fashion—often without having looked at them previously. Sometimes this "rip and read" formula backfires. On the day Black Muslim leader Malcolm X was murdered in New York, one Iowa announcer flashed

the bulletin to his listeners that "Malcolm Ten was shot today."

PUT ANOTHER NICKEL IN

A tight program scheme or format dictates what music will be heard on most radio stations. And within the music format genre there are a wide variety of different approaches, ranging from classical to hard rock on a musical scale. Yes, there are a few AM stations that still play classical music—about a dozen at last count. FM has become the new retreat of classical music. This represents a distinct change in American broadcasting for there was a time, not too long ago, when AM radio not only broadcast classical music but supported it financially as well. NBC, CBS, and Mutual all supported respected symphony orchestras at one time. But radio has gotten out of that business, at least in the United States. The respected British Broadcasting Corporation still has its own widely renowned symphony orchestra. And the Japanese broadcasting network, NHK, financially supports three symphonies as well as several light orchestras. In fact, NHK has succeeded in a little more than a generation in giving a large portion of the Japanese people an appreciation for Western classical music. In the United States, radio tends to play music, but not directly support it.

Moving down the musical spectrum from the classics, one encounters the *good music* stations that tend to steer away from the heavier rock sounds. This kind of format rarely attracts large numbers of listeners, but those that do listen tend to be better educated and more affluent, which gives the station an edge in advertising rates, because it appeals to an audience that is more likely to buy. WJR in Detroit, for example, counts among its listeners many of the major executives of the automobile industry and carries commercial messages aimed specifically at them. Ads for roller bearings and for tool works companies, for example, are often aired. There aren't many people in the market for roller bearings, but purchasing agents at Ford, GM, and Chrysler do buy millions of them. Few cities can support more than one or two "good music" stations.

The *middle-of-the-road* or "MOR" station falls between the good music and the rock categories. The MORs play the softest of the rock and the loudest of the "good" music. This kind of station frequently attempts to build up a personality cult around its record spinners, and sometimes it appears that music is secondary. These friends of the housewife and buddies of the commuter often carry high ratings during drive time, 6 to 10 A.M. and 3 to 7 P.M., when adult radio listening is at its peak. The MOR station sounds a lot like radio sounded when the disc jockey first emerged—unplanned and rather hectic at times. But usually it is as tightly programmed as the prototype rock stations.

The contemporary sound in radio (that's what the programmers like to call it) is the *rock* station, the battleground for the jingle warfare of the airwaves. Within the rock format there are variations, but they appear important only to those who know and love radio. Critics call the stations "screamers" and describe the format as one "with an extreme foreground treatment, playing only the top tunes with breathless and witless striplings making like carnival barkers."

The heart of the rocker is the chart— top 30, top 40, top 50, and so forth. Record sales, or jukebox plays, are charted each week. These are songs with proven appeal:

someone has paid money to hear them. The records are scheduled in sequence and played over and over during the week. A few album cuts are sometimes thrown in, and a few new songs are featured as well. But the charted records are the heart of the scheme.

One variation in the rock format is the *personality rocker* which is a station like the MOR mentioned earlier that attempts to create listener interest in the disc jockey himself. WMCA in New York rode the crest of popularity for years with the "Good Guys" format, and at KHJ in Los Angeles the "Real Don Steele" captured the ears of teenyboppers throughout Southern California. The most successful prototypes for this kind of personality appeal were Alan Freed and Murray the K, both of whom broadcast from New York in their heyday.

Some rock stations have successfully integrated tunes that were formerly popular—golden oldies, blasts from the past— into their format and capitalized on the nostalgia craze of the early seventies. Often the format is one of half oldies, or two to one from the "vault of gold." In 1972, stations like WCAU in Philadelphia, WIXZ in Pittsburgh, KWIZ and KNEW in Southern California, and KUUU in Seattle all significantly boosted their ratings with the "where have all the good songs gone" format.

Other "contemporary" radio stations have attempted to capture a soul sound, with heavy emphasis on blues and ethnic music. Scores of AM radio stations in America are programmed primarily for black audiences, although they frequently have listeners outside this group. (Tragically, most of the soul stations aren't owned by blacks. Surely one of the great dilemmas facing the electronic media is the lack of the means to increase black and other minority-group economic participation in broadcasting.)

Some AM stations have even successfully programmed "hard rock" or "acid rock" or "underground rock." The audience for this kind of pure rock is small; the heavy sounds turn off most listeners. The greatest success for such a format has been in the FM field. KDAY in Santa Monica, California, first succeeded with this format on AM. It featured a long play list (meaning that it played lots of different records), limited commercials to eight minutes each hour, and tried to create personality DJs who were knowledgeable about the music they played but not "jivers" like those on the screamer stations. The successful format was quickly copied elsewhere.

Perhaps the most interesting concept in rockers is the *more music* format, first promulgated in the sixties by men like Bill Drake. Drake was born Philip Yarbrough in 1937 and cut his teeth in radio spinning country and western tunes on backwater southern radio stations. In 1961 the owner of KYA radio in San Francisco gave Drake a chance at overhauling his rock station, which was at that time running behind the pack in the ratings sweepstakes. When he began work at KYA it was the prototype rocker, with music coming last, after the commercials, DJ chatter, jingles, air horns, and gongs. Drake's formula was to clean up the station and clear away the clutter on the airwaves. He toned down the station's rock image and began playing softer—but still popular—music. His theory was if you don't like it, don't play it. He depersonalized the disc jockey and emphasized music instead. Split-second timing was the key to his format, with a plethora of mini-jingles announcing what was coming up next. Disc jockeys were instructed to talk over

both the intros and endings of records and often commercials were spaced to allow two and three record sweeps. Time was told only with numbers—it was 12:30, not half past the hour. And news was used to gain a strategic advantage in the battle for listeners. Drake's theory was that many listeners will tune out news. If station KOMM carried its five minutes of news at twenty-five minutes after the hour, a Drake station would carry the news at twenty minutes after the hour. Listeners would switch their dial when the news came on KYA at 12:20, but switch back when KOMM news came on at 12:25 and then stay with KYA until the next news cycle began. A Drake trademark was 20/20 news, twenty minutes before and after the hour.

The Drake format is a superslick sound. Most disc jockeys hate it and say that Drake is turning his back on what's really happening in music—progressive rock and soul. (But although the criticism may be valid, we must remember these are the same DJs Drake told to stop talking and play more music.) And the formula has been successful. In the early seventies there were at least forty stations that had the Drake sound and paid the young man more than $100,000 annually for his programming service, which includes weekly play lists and predictions of new records. He has attained such importance in the record industry that many recording companies don't feel a record has a chance to succeed if the song doesn't appear on the Drake play list. Drake's success with the AM format has pushed him into even more programming in FM. . . .

Probably the one remaining important subgroup in the variety of music formats is the country and western station, or what many people used to call "hillbilly" music. Following a decrease in the number of

C & W stations during the past ten years, a renaissance of sorts has taken place and new "country" stations are popping up in many parts of the nation, including some large sophisticated eastern urban centers such as New York City. Country music is adult music, and its popularity might be a reaction to the youth orientation of pop music in the past three decades. Bill Sherrill at Columbia records calls it humanitarian music, music that talks about human problems at a very mundane level—about love and cheating, about drinking and the daily frustrations most people share. Rock, on the other hand, confronts issues on a grander scale—war, ecology, and racism are popular themes. One reason the number of country music stations have decreased is because country and western sounds have begun to infiltrate popular music. . . . The remaining "barefoot" radio stations have adopted a top-forty kind of format, using C & W charts rather than pop music play lists.

Although music remains the basic AM format, it is not the only one. In recent years two innovations have been introduced, neither of which has been an overwhelming success. Phone-in programming was very popular for a while. Some stations went almost exclusively to this scheme, while others just used it an hour or two each night. This kind of format adopts two of America's basic rural pastimes as its attractions—listening in on the party line and talking at the town meeting. The premise is simple: the average citizen probably has something to say about most issues, so let him call the station and give his ideas over the air. A fairly glib host is required, as well as some special tape recording equipment that permits the station to broadcast the callers on a five- or eight-second tape delay (to give the station the chance to censor obscenity, libel, or other noxious remarks). But the program still retains the spontaneity of a live broadcast. With a good host and a good topic, this kind of programming was often popular. But after a while listeners got tired of hearing generally uninformed people, most of whom had a petty complaint or a plan to save the world. Also, the same callers tended to monopolize the lines. In any case, the format began to fade.

But it didn't die completely. In fact, in 1973 call-in radio was given a new breath of life when several stations shifted the flavor of the telephone discussions from social, political, and economic issues to more earthy subjects—mainly sex. During discussions that the radio hosts described as "frank and honest but not dirty," listeners were asked to give their views on extramarital relations, premarital sex, group sex, and so forth. Many listeners have responded favorably to a limited amount of this kind of programming, especially when the phoned-in comments are interspersed between records.

The other innovation was kind of a throwback to early radio as many large-city stations went to a 24-hour all-news format. Although it sounds exciting, public interest-oriented and all those good things, in fact it was usually a bore. The idea was fine, but most stations refused to put out the cash to hire enough newsmen to do the job. So listeners would hear about the same news with maybe twenty minutes of new material, in one-hour cycles. The first hour was great, the second hour was even okay, but by the third hour listeners began to know the news headlines as well as the readers at the radio station. Only large cities can support such stations, and few all-news stations still exist.

Music remains as the staff of life for the AM radio station, and there is nothing to suggest that this will change in our lifetimes. If we begin with the premise that the medium of radio tends to be background rather than foreground, music is an inexpensive, noncontroversial, and usually profitable programming concept. In the years to come we will probably see program formats play an even more significant role. The old-timers of radio despise the format; it means a loss of freedom to them. But the younger generation of radio hands understand it, have a feel for it. As Arnold Passman wrote in his book, *The DeeJays*, "It speaks their language. If they have a sense of freedom, and they are no way near their politically active and socially experimenting peers, it may be in the vocal furor they are asked to create. The medium's message (any medium's) seems to be: Out of passion comes chaos, and out of chaos comes order." In contemporary radio it is often the listener who creates the order.

Aids   *Radio: Come On, Let Me Show You Where It's At*

1. Why, according to Pember, did network radio disappear with the rise of television?

2. In describing the fragmented quality of radio programming, Pember uses an analogy to left-handed billiard players. Do you think this analogy is successful? Think of an alternative analogy.

3. In classifying stations by their musical format, Pember establishes a number of different categories—good music, middle-of-the-road, rock, soul, hard rock. Is each of these categories adequately defined? Are these categories adequately differentiated from one another?

4. Pember's article is excerpted from a textbook on mass communications for undergraduates. How is his intended audience reflected in his tone? in his style?

5. Listen to seven or eight radio stations in your broadcast area and try to categorize them by music format. How do the DJs' styles reflect the format? Do you see any correlation between the products advertised and the kinds of music played?

6. Most of us listen to the radio a lot more often than we realize. Because it plays a secondary role in our lives—it accompanies other activities like studying, driving, cleaning house—we tend to be less aware of it than other forms of the media. For two or three days keep close track of all your radio listening. (Don't forget to count the piped-in FM at the supermarket and dentist's office). The next few days log your television viewing. Compare the results. (Of course, your results may be misleading because you will be *aware* of your media activity. Nevertheless, you will get some insights into your media habits.)

CB Radio Comin' At Ya: Running Down to Dirtytown

CLARK WHELTON

I kicked the clutch, jammed the gears into number one position, whirled the wheel around to the left, and put the pedal to the metal. It was 120 miles down to Dirtytown and this time I was going to make it home in two hours or under. If the Smokies wanted to talk business along the way, they'd have to catch me first. For sure.

I reached down under the dash and fired up my CB. I wanted to put the good numbers on my CB buddies up in that Connecticut state. I clicked the crystal selector over to channel six. There was nobody on the air so I just jumped right in.

"Breaker six, breaker-by. How about ya, Cookie Jar? You got ears for this Doctor W?"

"Hey there, Doctor W. You got the Cookie Jar coming at you from her East Hartford base. Where be ya?"

"We be southbound on the Silas Deane Highway in Wethersfield. We just about to climb onto Interstate Ninety-One at the Two-Four Exit. We're heading ourselves back to our home twenty in New York City, how about it?"

"That's a big ten-four in there, Doctor W, for sure. We definitely going to miss you up here on channel six. It's been nice modulating with you these last couple of days. Sorry we didn't get to eyeball this time around, but maybe we'll catch you on the flip-flop for coffee."

"Breaker-by break."

"That's a definite ten-four on eyeballing for coffee on our next trip through this twenty, Cookie Jar. But stand by. We got a breaker in there. Pick it up, breaker."

"Ten-four, thanks for the break. How about ya, Doctor W? You got a copy on this Dragon Lady in Glastonbury?"

From *The Village Voice*, June 28, 1976, pp. 105–6. © 1976 The Village Voice Inc. Reprinted by permission.

"That's a big ten-four there, Dragon Lady. You're wall to wall and treetop tall. You're really making the trip. You're giving me a solid ten-pounder on the meter."

"Right back at you, Doctor W. You're doing a fine job yourself. You're hitting me hard over here. We just wanted to give you the good numbers before you got out of range. It's been nice having you up here. You couldn't drag me down to Dirtytown with an eighteen-wheeler, but I guess some people like New York."

"That's a definite ten-four, Dragon Lady. Dirtytown is our home twenty. We like it there, for sure. We going to break our own record for the run down there. Under two hours."

"Well, you keep an eyeball peeled for those Picture Takers up there on the Nine-One or you'll be feeding the Bears for sure. So threes and eights on ya, Doctor W. You got the Dragon Lady and we clear and on the side."

"How about it, Doctor W.? You still got ears for this Cookie Jar?"

"Go, Cookie Jar."

"For sure. We just wanted to repeat what that Dragon Lady told you. Drive safely. Keep the shiny side up and the greasy side down. Give us a shout on the flip-flop. This is the Cookie Jar and we be ten-ten on the side."

"Threes on ya, Cookie Jar. Have a good day today and a better day tomorrow. You got one Doctor W and we southbound and down."

I turned onto the entrance ramp, merged into Interstate 91, and took my white Dart right up to the Double Nickle. But you can't make time at 55 miles an hour. So before I took it up to 70, I wanted a Smokey report. I switched over to channel 19. It was crowded as usual with truckers and four-wheelers. I wanted for a clear spot and keyed my mike.

"Breaker, breaker one-nine for a ten-thirteen on that Nine-One southbound, how about it?" I got a comeback right away.

"You got a northbounder here, guy. I climbed onto the Nine-One down in that New Haven town, and you definitely got Smokey Bears in Tijuana Taxis sitting off to the side on that southbound side at Exit Seventeen. I think they're taking pictures."

"We definitely thank you for that comeback, guy. We be keeping an eyeball peeled at Exit Seventeen, for sure. What's the handle over there?"

"You got Mr. Wonderful here, guy."

"A big ten-four there, Mr. Wonderful. You got one Doctor W. coming at you from the southbound side and we going down to Dirtytown."

"That's a ten-four, Doctor W. We're taking our eighteen wheels up to that Beantown. How we looking up that way?"

"Can't help you out there, Mr. Wonderful. We just climbed on the Nine-One at Exit Twenty-Four. But you have yourself a safe trucking trip and we'll catch you on the flipper, for sure. You got the Doctor W. putting the good numbers on you and we going south."

"Seventy-thirds right back on ya, Doctor W. You got one Mr. Wonderful and we northbound and down."

No Smokies until Exit 17. I stamped on the ramp and took it up to 65. I didn't want to hit 70 just yet. Sometimes the Smokies shift their Picture Takers around real quick to beat the CB warning network. But they wouldn't get me. My CB would see to that. I looked down at it, sitting there under the dash. A Lafayette Telsat 50, all 23 channels crystal controlled with AGC, a 455 kHz ceramic filter, a dual conversion superhet receiver, a tuned RF stage at 0.7 uV for 10 dB S+N/N, with a monitor to catch the state police signals on the 30-50 MHz band. When I plugged in my D-104 power mike and pushed heat through my trunk-mounted 40-inch wire whip Hellcat antenna, there isn't a mobile in the East that can walk on my signal. For sure.

"Breaker for that Doctor W." Somebody was shouting for me.

"You got the Doctor W. Who's looking for him?"

"Hey there, Doctor W. You got one Bionic Beaver coming at you. We heard you in there with that Mr. Wonderful and we thought we'd give you a shout. We're going south on the Nine-One, too, so it looks like we be on your front door down here by the Two-Three Exit, how about it?"

"That's a definite ten-four, Bionic Beaver. We just climbed on at the Two-Four Exit. You're a couple of miles ahead of us. Where you bound?" It's always nice to hear a woman's voice in there.

"We bound for that Keystone state, guy. Did I hear you telling Mr. Wonderful that you were bound for Dirtytown, how about it?"

"That's a big ten-four, so it looks like we'll be running convoy for a while. We definitely keep the back door shut tight for you. You shake the bushes and I'll rake the leaves."

"That's a ten-four, Doctor W. I'll shake 'em, you rake 'em. We got the old eyeball peeled for those Smokies down at the One-Seven Exit, for sure. This is the Bionic Beaver and she's on the side."

"Break for that Doctor W."

"You got him."

"Ten-four, thanks for the break. I heard you in there with that Bionic Beaver. The handle here is the Missing Link. I'm just passing Exit Twenty-Five southbound for that Bridgeport town. So it looks like I'll be at your back door for a while, how about it?"

"That's a ten-four, Missing Link. That puts me right in the rocking chair between you and the Bionic Beaver. We got a report of Picture Takers on the southbound side down by the One-Seven Exit."

"Ten-four on those Picture Takers, Doctor W. We heard about them all the way back in that Springfield town. But I'll check with my back door to make sure he knows they're there. How about it, Captain Kirk, you copy that Smokey report on the Picture Takers down at Exit Seventeen?"

There was a hunk of dead air. Wherever that Captain Kirk was, he was too far off for me to copy his signal.

"That's a ten-four," I heard the Missing Link say. "How about it, Doctor W? Captain Kirk is back by the Two-Eight Exit and he's going to pass on the Smokey report to his back door, so the word is definitely out."

I gave him a 10-4, pulled on my deerskin driving gloves, settled in behind the wheel, and watched the Connecticut countryside roll by. The needles on my oil pressure, alternator, fuel and temperature gauges were all pointing in the right direction. I was holding steady at 70 and really laying 'em down. I figured to catch the Bionic Beaver in a few minutes and take the front door myself. I checked my watch. I'd make it down to Dirtytown in record time if I could hold this speed.

"Break break break."

"Go, break break break," I said. I always keep my mike laying across one leg so I can get at it real quick when somebody asks for a break. I'm usually the first one in there.

"Thanks for the break. The name here is Sky Rider. What's your name and where are you?" Whew. If there's one thing that puts my ears on edge it's modulating with somebody who doesn't know how to talk CB. I could tell by the heavy signal he was hitting me with that this breaker was a base station somewhere nearby. I could also tell that he was a hot-dogging high school kid with a new birthday present, trying to shout up some action on the mobile channel. Everybody's got a CB these days but not everyone knows how to use them.

"Breaker on channel nineteen. This is the Sky Rider speaking. Does anybody hear me?"

I could see that nobody was going to give this kid a comeback, but that didn't damp down his eagerness any. He kept on keying his mike and hollering for someone to modulate with. Only one way to deal with a case like this one. I picked up my mike.

"That YL shouting for a break in there. Go ahead."

"I'm not a YL," the kid said. "Who are you?"

"The handle here is the Cherokee," I told him. I didn't want to hit him with my real handle because this kid sounded like a handle thief to me. He probably picked up his "Sky Rider" handle from some passing trucker. Handle thieves are everywhere today. I used my former handle of "Cherokee" for three years, until there were so many other "Cherokees" on the air that I had to hunt myself up a new handle.

"Ten-four, Cherokee," the kid said. "How am I doing?" His signal was crashing in on me, of course, but I wasn't about to tell him that.

"I can hardly hear you," I said. "You're giving me a two."

"A two?" the kid said. "Gee, you're hitting me with a solid ten. Where are you?"

"My ten-twenty is three feet off the ground and six inches behind the steering wheel."

"What?"

"I said I'm down here by Exit Twenty-one."

"Gee," the kid said. "That's right down the road from me. Are you sure that I'm only giving you a two?" He sounded kind of worried. The worst thing that can happen to you in CB is to get hit with a stronger signal than you're putting out.

"I can hardly hear you," I said.

"Wait a minute. Let me adjust my antenna. There. Is that any better?" He was yelling into the mike.

"What?" I said. "You're getting stepped on by static."

"I said, is that any better. Better!"

"Did you say your handle is Betty? Listen, Betty, let's not choke up channel nineteen. Take it down to fifteen."

"Gone to fifteen," the kid said. Of course I didn't go with him.

"Break for that so-called Cherokee." It was the Bionic Beaver.

"This is the Doctor W."

"That's the way to handle those hot-doggers, Doctor W," she said. "Listen, I coming up on the One-Seven Exit right now. We definitely going to back it down to the Double Nickle. I can see Tijuana Taxis off to the right with blue gumball machines on the roof, and a couple of plain brown wrapper chase-em-up cars waiting to give out bad marks. You better back it down or smile pretty as you go by. They definitely taking pictures, for sure."

"We thank you, Bionic Beaver. How about it, Missing Link. Did you copy that Smokey report from the Bionic Beaver?"

"That's a big ten-four," the Missing Link said. "We'll pass it on back to the Captain Kirk. Hey, Doctor W. I went down to fifteen with that kid. He's still shouting for the Cherokee down there."

I came up over a rise in the road, past the one-mile warning marker for the One-Seven Exit, and there they were. Tijuana Taxis setting up a sweet little radar trap. I backed it down to the Double Nickle.

"Break for the Missing Link," I said. "I definitely got the eyeball on those Smoke-em-ups at Exit Seventeen. Don't let the Bears bite. They got their electric teeth turned on, for sure."

I put my mike back in my lap as I rolled past the State Troopers doing 55. It's against the law in that Connecticut state to talk on your CB while you're moving, and the Smokies all got CB ears themselves these days. They don't like the CB alert system and if they see you with a mike in your hand they sometimes pull you over. It's hard to prove that you were actually talking, of course. That's the thing about CB. It's anonymous. Nobody knows who or where you are unless you want to tell them. But the Smokies flag you down now and then when they see your CB antenna. They just want to let you know that they know.

"Break for that Doctor W. This is the Bionic Beaver, guy. We just had a shout from a northbound eighteen-wheeler. Once you get by those Picture Takers at Exit Seventeen you're clean and green all the way down to New Haven, how about it?"

I gave her a ten-four and took it back up to 70. I kept my eye on the rearview mirror in case the Smokies sent a Tijuana Taxi after me before my back door could get into position, but I didn't see a thing. I settled down for some serious driving, tuning up the CB to listen to the Smokey reports, the traffic conditions, and the people gabbing away with each other. CB means "Citizens Band," and that's what it is. For sure. One of the best things about CB is that there's never anything new to talk about. It's always the same. Smokey reports, signal strength, the weather, and coffee. It's real comfortable. Once you learn the language, you fit right in.

Just south of Exit 16 I saw a four-wheeler off to the side. I thought it might be a Plain Brown Wrapper but it was just a YL with a flat tire. She was sitting there behind the wheel waiting for help. I changed channels until I found a base station and asked them to put in a land line to the Smokies and tell them where the YL was waiting, and kept on going. I made it down to New Haven in good time, made the merge into that Interstate 95 southbound, and kept the hammer down hard. I thought sure that I'd have caught up with that Bionic Beaver by now, but she was driving hard herself. I couldn't gain ground to put the eyeball on her. She gave me a shout as she hit the first Donation Station on the Green Stamp.

"We're dropping our quarter in the Piggy Bank right now, Doctor W. Haven't seen a thing so bring it on down. You can really do it to it!"

I gave her a ten-four, reached for my wallet and pulled out some Green Stamps. Like to have them ready when I reach the Donation Station. Then it was time for the best part of the trip. I keyed my mike and shouted for my favorite YL, the neatest little beaver in the East.

"How about that Super Skirt one time? How about it, you got your ears on, Super Skirt?"

"Who's hollering for the Super Skirt?" a voice said. It wasn't her.

"You got the Doctor W coming at you. Who we got on that end?"

"You got the Sweet Sheets over here, guy. That Super Skirt went ten-seven on us about twenty minutes ago. I think she's still off the air. Stand by and I'll give her a shout on the land line and tell her you're looking. We gone."

I waited. I sure hoped that Super Skirt would give me a shout before I drove out of range. It just wouldn't be the same running the big Nine-Five without modulating with the Super Skirt. She's got the sexiest CB voice I ever did hear. You've probably given her a shout yourself on your way through her home 20 near New Haven. She's almost always on channel 19, night and day. I've been meaning to stop by and have coffee one of these days, but so far I haven't done it. You know how it is on CB. Everybody has their own CB personality. Everyone gets along on how compatible their voices are. It's a matter of sound, not looks. So when you eyeball your CB buddies, you're always taking a chance. There's no telling what will happen when you see the face behind the voice. Beautiful CB friendships have come to a quick end that way. For sure.

"Breakity-break one-nine. How about that Doctor W?" It was the Super Skirt.

"A big ten-four, Super Skirt. Hey, it's fine to hear you in there. Thought we might miss you this time through."

"That's a ten-four, there, Doctor W. We were making ourselves a sandwich. Hey, it's always nice to hear my favorite four-wheeler in there. What do you say we take it up to two-one so we don't jam up the one-nine channel, how about it?"

"We gone to twenty-one," I clicked over.

"How about ya, Doctor W?" What a voice. Smooth, soft, sexy.

"You got him."

"Hey, we definitely glad to hear your voice in there again. Which way you bound?"

"Back to our home twenty in Dirtytown."

"That's a ten-four. You must like that town, guy. You keep going back to it. You'd never get me in there, for sure."

"Come on, Super Skirt. You can't live forever. What do you say one of these days I stop by for coffee and run you down to Dirtytown with me?"

"A big ten-four on the coffee, Doctor W. But I don't know about leaving our home twenty. We like it where we are."

"Know what you mean there, Super Skirt. But who knows, one of these days. . . ."

"That's a ten-four, Doctor W. One of these days. In the meantime, I've always got the coffee hot for you."

"Hey, we'd sip your coffee any time we could, Super Skirt, for sure. But we trying to break our record for the run down to Dirtytown."

"Ten-four. Know what you mean. We thought you had the hammer down hard. You're starting to fade out on us fast. You were banging me hard with a ten-pounder. Now you're giving me a six." She was right. Our signals were getting weaker. Mobile CB is only effective within a five-mile radius.

"Okay, Doctor W," she said. "We real glad that the Sweet Sheets told us you were shouting for us. So you have yourself a safe one down to Dirtytown. Keep that tin side up and the rubber side down. You got one Super Skirt pulling the plug. We clear. We gone. Byeee."

I went back to channel 19. Suddenly I heard a trucker jump in with a Smokey report. A Tijuana Taxi coming onto the Green Stamp at Exit 38. I looked around. There he was, in the right lane. I slowed down quick to the Double Nickle.

"Come on, Smokey," somebody said. "I got to make time. Get off the Green Stamp or I'll push you right through the guard rail." I looked over at the Smokey. He had a CB antenna. Oh oh.

"So you want to push me right through the guard rail, do you, white Dart? Well, I'll keep that in mind." White Dart? Hey, the Bear thought I was the one who had made that remark. I grabbed my mike to set him straight, but of course I couldn't give him a shout without breaking the law. That's what he was waiting for. He pulled into position behind me and I waited for him to turn on his gumball machines, but he didn't. He just followed me, while I stayed at the Double Nickle. I switched off my CB set. If he pulled me over, I'd tell him that my CB hadn't even been on. Go ahead, I'd say. Feel how cool it is.

He stayed on my tail for 25 minutes. No hope of breaking my record now. I just sat there behind the wheel, plunged back into all the isolation of the pre-CB world. Wondering what the other drivers are thinking about. Wondering where they're going. Counting white lines and telephone poles to make the time go by.

Finally the Smokey jumped off the Green Stamp in Greenwich. I went back on the air. I tried for the Bionic Beaver, but I was sure she'd have run out my front door by now. But no, she had stopped for coffee with a trucker and was only a little ways ahead of me. I asked her if she was taking the GW Bridge.

"Negatory, Doctor W. We going to take the Throg's Neck over to that Interstate Two-Seven-Eight through Queens and Brooklyn and then take the Guinea Gangplank into Staten Island and over to Jersey by the back door."

"I'm going the other way," I told her. "Down the Bruckner to Dirtytown."

"Well, it's been nice," she said.

"For sure. I thought I'd catch you back there and put the eyeball on you."

"The Bionic Beaver often catches, but is never caught," she said. "But maybe we'll eyeball one of these days for coffee."

"That's a definite ten-four," I said. I headed up the Bruckner. Off to my left I could see the city, sheathed in sooty air. Home again. City CBers were jamming up the channel with shouts. The Iguana Man. The Ghetto Cowboy. The Six Pack. Pretty quick they'd be walking on the Bionic Beaver's signal. I keyed my mike.

"We going to put the good numbers on you, Bionic Beaver," I said. "Give me shout if you ever come into Dirtytown. We'll definitely have coffee."

"That's a big ten-four, Doctor W," she said. Her signal was fading fast. "Keep the Bears off your back and the YLs on your lap. You got the Bionic Beaver heading south. We going to do it to it. Sorry we didn't eyeball but we'll definitely catch you on the flipper. Three's and eight's on you, for sure. You got one Bionic Beaver and we gone. We clear. We down. Byeee."

I crossed the Third Avenue Bridge, swung around and connected with the FDR southbound. Two hours and 20 minutes. Not so good. But next time down I'd break the record. For sure.

Aids   *CB Radio Comin' At Ya: Running Down to Dirtytown*

1. Linguists who study the influence of jargon on American English have found that terms from the underworld of crime, jazz music, space technology, and the drug culture have become a permanent part of our language. Using Whelton's article alone, make a brief glossary of CB slang. Are all the terms clear from their context? Try to formulate definitions for those that are not. Which terms are particularly imagistic, i.e. paint word-pictures of what they denote? Which terms are currently used by others besides CB buffs? Have any of their meanings been changed by popular usage?

2. What is the appeal of CB communication? Why does CB ownership cut across age, income, and occupational barriers? As a student of popular culture, can you attribute sociological significance to the CB phenomenon?

3. Why do you think Dr. W. gives the "hot-dogging high school kid" such a hard time? Does his remark about the kid's not knowing how to talk CB refer simply to the boy's CB language skills, or is Whelton's attitude based on something else?

4. Whelton writes: "One of the best things about CB is that there's nothing new to talk about." What does he mean? How much real information is being communicated in CB radio exchanges? *Webster's Seventh New Collegiate Dictionary* defines "phatic" as "revealing or sharing feelings or establishing an atmosphere of sociability rather than communicating ideas." How does this definition apply to CB radio?

5. Truckers spend long monotonous hours on the road. Do you see a

possible cause-and-effect relationship between CB radio and the "endless highway of Top 20 tunes" referred to by Peter McCabe?

6. Clark Whelton's article is based on his own true adventures as Dr. W. He is practiced and proficient at the slang he records in the article's dialog. Many social groups have their own language, speech idioms, or dialects. Write a narrative in which you carefully reconstruct the actual speech of a group which you have observed or to which you belong. The conversation of participants in sports events is one of many possibilities. You may want to use a tape recorder to capture live dialog for later transcription.

7. What is the purpose of Whelton's article? Does it have a thesis— either explicit or implicit?

8. Would Marshall McLuhan categorize CB radio as hot or cool? CB radio allows high participation, but how personal is it?

9. Whelton notes the dangers of eyeballing CB buddies. What are the psychological implications of "handles" and other aspects of the CB personality?

THE
WEIGHT
OF
LOVE

JOHN HERMAN

THE
WEIGHT
OF
LOVE

 NAN A. TALESE

DOUBLEDAY

New York

London

Toronto

Sydney

Auckland

PUBLISHED BY NAN A. TALESE
an imprint of Doubleday
a division of Bantam Doubleday Dell Publishing Group, Inc.
1540 Broadway, New York, New York 10036

DOUBLEDAY is a trademark of Doubleday, a division of
Bantam Doubleday Dell Publishing Group, Inc.

All of the characters in this book are fictitious,
and any resemblance to actual persons, living or dead,
is purely coincidental.

Book design by Ronnie Ann Herman

Library of Congress Cataloging-in-Publication Data

Herman, John, 1944–
The weight of love / John Herman.—1st ed.
p.   cm.
I. Title.
  PS3558.E6815W45   1995
  813'.54—dc20   94-39555
                    CIP

ISBN 0-385-47815-1
Printed in the United States of America
June 1995
First Edition

10   9   8   7   6   5   4   3   2   1

For R, of course.

"My weight is my love;
by it I am borne whithersoever I am borne."

—AUGUSTINE, *Confessions*

BOOK
ONE

Yesterday, as I walked out into the day, I saw the cold blue sky above the beautiful island of Manhattan. A few clouds hovered in the air and then disappeared. The sky was a dome . . . an arena . . . a fish tank—while all about people hurried off on their business or loitered about doing nothing. The city was dying—and at a rate so that a middle-aged man could catch the breath of its passing: and this was sad and was common. Sometimes when I walk in the city I think of the women I have loved, and where they lived, and what we did together; and often I am struck by my utter uselessness on the face of the earth. The old Hebrews taught that the one thing needful was faith in God, and I think they were right, though I am incapable of it. As I walked out under the sky on a beautiful day in Manhattan, dreams and nightmares and hallucinations were put aside. Even regrets were put aside. All things were as they should be, or as they had to be, or as they were.

I married Barbara Grotton in 1970 when I was twenty-four and she twenty-two. I met her during my senior year at Yale, when she was a sophomore at Vassar and she was dating an acquaintance of mine named Toby DeWulfe. I remember thinking the first time I saw her that she was too good for Toby. Toby was a well-heeled guy with a prominent nose and dark skin and he seemed always to be sporting a beauty on his arm. He enjoyed the reputation of being a playboy. Barbara was billowy, with long reddish brown hair that she threw over her shoulder when she laughed, and she wore one of those fluffy angora sweaters that made you want to get your hands on her right away. She had flawless skin and long peerless legs, and it takes my breath away to think how young we were.

It was spring then and everything smelled of lilacs. Wherever I went there was the odor of lilacs.

"Your sweater tickles my nose," I said.

"Oh? Maybe you're standing too close."

"I wish I could stand closer."

We were waiting in line to buy drinks between acts at the repertory theater, and we knew each other by then. When she laughed she threw her hair over her shoulder. She too smelled of lilacs, it was as if she were enveloped in a bank of lilacs, and when she laughed something went funny in my stomach.

Later, on our first date, on a balcony overlooking the Connecticut River with the sound of music drifting to us from the restaurant, I said, "I've been wanting to do this since the first time I saw you."

"Have you?" There was an edge to her voice that made the funny thing happen again in my stomach.

"Here," she said. "You can put your hand here."

"I love the way it feels."

"I love it too," she said.

There was something bohemian about Barbara that appealed to me immediately. She came from an old-line Long Island family, but she set no store by that and hung out with the literary and dramatic crowd. She had dated Bob Weaver, a big man on campus who went on to have a career on Broadway, and she was likely to be seen at poetry readings or at offbeat literary functions from New York to Boston or at amateur theatrical events. She was full of wry offbeat humor and she was very beautiful and she wasn't afraid of anything.

When I started dating Barbara I found she was a well-known figure on campus and soon I wanted her to date only me.

I had no telephone in my room and I used to call her every night from the Woolworth's on the corner. I would put through the call and hang up after one ring, and Barbara would call back immediately and reverse the charges. Then I'd accept the call from the pay phone. I don't know whether this scam would still work, but it worked for us in the spring of 1968 and it amused us greatly.

One evening after we had been seeing each other for a while she said to me, "I can't see you Saturday."

"What's happening Saturday?"

"Oh, nothing really."

"Then why can't you see me?"

"Because I promised Toby ages ago that I'd go with him to the opening of Pirandello at Circle in the Square. He already has the tickets."

"Does he? Well, bully for Toby."

"Please be serious, David. What am I supposed to do?"

"Why don't you tell Toby to take his mother? Don't you think it would be nice if Toby took his mother?"

"Why won't you be serious?"

"I am being serious. I don't want you going to Pirandello with Toby DeWulfe. I don't want you going *any*place with Toby DeWulfe. If you'll agree not to go to Pirandello, I'll take you anyplace you want to go. Okay?"

"Okay what?"

"Okay you won't go out with Toby DeWulfe."

She hesitated for only an instant.

"Okay," she said. "Okay, I won't go out with Toby DeWulfe."

And she didn't.

* * *

"Where are you going?" Gordo Tate asked me that Saturday as I prepared to drive to Poughkeepsie. My roommate took an avuncular interest in my amorous life, which he considered exiguous.

"If you don't watch out, Smith," he would say, "you will fall into the habit of self-abuse. Hasn't your mother warned you against the habit of self-abuse? It's an epidemic, Smith, a national epidemic. You should see more young ladies, they're the only known cure for the habit of self-abuse. Take it from me. That's why I date so many ladies. They're the only cure, Smith, the only known cure."

Now I said to him, "I'm seeing Barbara Grotton."

"Are you really? What a remarkably good idea! I wouldn't have thought it of you. Did you come up with that idea all on your own?"

Gordo had dated Barbara once or twice himself, but I had never heard him talk much about her.

"We're seeing a lot of each other," I said.

"Oh yeah?" Gordo swung his bulk around on the bed and sat up to look at me. He was a dark rugged man from Pittsburgh, where he had inherited a fortune from his grandfather. He played varsity football and dated many marvelous-looking girls and generally remained one step ahead of mayhem; and we had roomed together since our freshman year and had become the best of unlikely buddies.

"So you're seeing a lot of each other, huh?"

"That's right, Gordo."

"Well, I'll tell you what—she's a great girl. If she likes you, Smith, I'd hold on tight."

"Would you?"

"Yeah."

"Well, Gordo, that's what I intend to do."

I became restless if I was away from Barbara for a week. I associate that time with the oversweet fragrance of fresh-cut grass, which was in evidence wherever we went, in the restaurants where we ate, by the roadsides where we drove, billowing in the rooms where we now lay next to each other in the heavy summer heat. By the end of August we were engaged.

My father ran a nursery in Connecticut. He was a cultivated, knowledgeable man, and he ended up making money doing land-scape architecture for the suburbanites as they pushed out into the state during the fifties. I had two siblings, an older brother and a younger sister, and we had a loose-limbed, knockabout childhood with a few significant quirks.

At some point during his adolescence it became apparent that my brother was brilliant and given to bouts of melancholia. He taught himself to play the piano, set up a laboratory in the attic, built himself a shortwave radio—and stopped talking to anyone in the family for long periods of time. My parents were educated people and consulted a doctor, who told them not to worry, he would grow out of it.

After a while my brother took to curling up in his room with the lights off and not coming out for days. Even my mother, a hearty New Englander, was upset, but my father was distraught. He would stand outside my brother's door with his head down like an official waiting for an important appointment; if my brother discovered him there, he would start screaming at him.

It was at this time that I began my lifelong habit of reading whatever I came across. My father possessed a good collection of the English classics and I read my way through them, not just Thackeray and Dickens and Trollope, but Meredith and Hakluyt and Peacock and Macaulay and Walpole—anything I could find. I used to go into the nursery behind the row of baby linden trees and settle down in a patch of sunlight, and there I'd stay for hours, sheltered from responsibility while I inhaled the odor of sweet fern and slowly ate my way through English lit.

One day while I was reading in the nursery behind the bed of lindens I looked up to see my sister Karin playing below me at the edge of the stream. Karin must have been seven then, an elfin magical child with orange-gold hair that deliquesced like a lemon drop into the pale sunlight. I was seven years older than Karin and felt for her the passionate bewildered affection of an older brother for a beloved superior object of little definable use.

I got up and meandered over to where she was crouched in the wet soft weeds by the side of the stream.

"What are you doing, Karin?"

"I'm planting."

"Planting?"

I bent down to see where she had scooped out the rich earth in little palm-size holes about four inches deep, in the bottom of which she had deposited four round whitish stones, smooth and glaucous as eyeballs.

"Are those your seeds?"

"No."

"Oh? What are they, then?"

"They're stones," she said matter-of-factly.

"Do you think you can plant stones, Karin?"

"Yes."

This surprised me, since Karin had grown up around plants and knew perfectly well the difference between stones and seeds. I looked at her closely but her face was as serious and impenetrable as an undisturbed pool of water.

"What happens if you plant stones?" I asked. "Do they grow?" I sat facing her cross-legged on the ground.

"Of course not."

"What *does* happen, then?"

"They bring good luck."

"They do? Who told you that?"

She pursed her lips and looked at me seriously.

"They do, David. Please believe me."

I thought about this for a while. I was quite certain that planting stones wouldn't bring *me* any luck, but I couldn't be so sure about Karin. I already knew she possessed a fund of knowledge foreign to me. I decided to try a different tack.

"And why do you need good luck?"

"For Warren." She said it as if it were the most obvious thing in the world, which in fact it was.

After a while she asked, "Do you think Warren will commit suicide?"

"Jesus, Karin! What are you talking about?"

She regarded me thoughtfully.

"Did I frighten you?" she asked.

"Yes, as a matter of fact you did."

"I'm sorry."

I waited for her to continue but she had returned to contemplating her stones.

"So?" I said after a while. "Do *you* think he's going to . . . you know. What you said."

Again she regarded me steadily.

"I don't know," she said. "I don't want him to. That's why I'm planting stones."

I don't know whether or not it was the stones, but Warren didn't commit suicide. He was a weird guy and for many years we didn't have much to say to each other, but he did get better and after a while he went to Harvard and eventually became a prominent astrophysicist.

One result of these events was that in some manner peculiar unto himself my father became religious. He started attending the local Methodist church, though no one in our family had ever been Methodist; but it was the nearest place of worship, and as my Dad used to say, all religions are equal: equally inadequate.

Dad and Karin had always been tight, but now they became even tighter. It didn't surprise me when Karin insisted on being confirmed in the Methodist church. Warren and I had performed our perfunctory obeisance in the local family Presbyterian quarters in deference to our mother's wishes; but in her own unfathomable, imperturbable manner, Karin took the ceremony seriously.

After leaving Yale I spent two years working for my father while I waited for Barbara to graduate from Vassar. These were happy carefree years with my arms immersed in soil. On weekends I would take the car to Poughkeepsie and Barbara and I would head for the city, the Mecca of our dreams. I remember the happy hours spent visiting friends in the Village or drinking in plush hotel bars on the East Side or careening to the theater in taxis; but mostly I recall the long heat-sodden afternoons spent making love with Barbara with her nonpareil legs wrapped tight around me.

We had a large wedding on Park Avenue and Barbara's picture appeared prominently in the social column of the *New York Times*. We had gone round and registered at Tiffany's and Bloomingdale's and Jensen's, and Barbara had a beautiful white dress made for her by her mother's seamstress. Indeed, Mrs. Grotton took the whole thing very much in hand. My parents made less of a fuss about such events; I think my mother rather looked down her nose at the Grottons. Gordo Tate was my best man.

I remember issuing into the early summer heat of June after the ceremony and, as I surveyed the rows of bright-colored flowers that bloomed down the center of Park Avenue, thinking to myself, Well, boy, now you've really done it! I'm not sure what I meant by that. I was wearing a morning coat that was slightly too tight, and throughout the morning I was aware of its pinch like a toothache one tries to ignore.

We spent the wedding night in the Pierre and flew to Paris the next morning on Air France. Barbara had sent a trunk packed with enough clothing to relieve one of the smaller Balkan states, and I, under the watchful auspices of my fiancée and her mother, had purchased a pair of white ducks.

The cost of the trip was footed by my in-laws.

Barbara already knew Paris, and Paris was another thing she gave me. We dined at Taillevent, went to the races at Clichy, climbed Montmartre, explored the *bouquineries* on the Left Bank, visited the Jardin des Plantes, twisted along the rue Mouffetard, and watched the girls dance topless at two A.M. at the Crazy Horse. And when in the heat of afternoon we returned to our hotel after lunch at the Méditerranée, Barbara closed the shutters on our lofty cavernous room and there in the penumbral cool she danced like that for me.

After a week we rented a Peugeot and drove south from Paris, passing through the Loire Valley and past Bordeaux to les Landes and then skirting the Pyrenees to the Mediterranean. One day we paused to catch our breath in one of the small fishing villages along the Côte d'Azur between Marseilles and Nice.

Our hotel faced the harbor, which extended in either direction for a good half-mile toward the shimmering sea. We stopped early that day so that Barbara could have her hair coiffed, an operation that proved onerous and time-consuming and somehow fell below Barbara's expectation, and the afternoon found her in a foul temper. She refused to go out. The harbor lay below us in clamorous echoing activity; the small streets wound back like so many waiting secrets; the Mediterranean flashed from the horizon like a great warning light urging us to seize the day; but Barbara wanted to stay in her room and have a boiled egg.

Now, I detest the very thought of a boiled egg, and so we finally decided that we should try a few hours of separation, Barbara so that she could tease her hair, I so that I could explore the promise of the harbor.

I had a precise image of what I would do. I would walk to the end of the harbor, where I would discover a small restaurant facing the water. There I would order a local variety of fish and a bottle of inexpensive dry white wine, which I would consume in leisurely isolation, after which I would smoke a cigar and then return by some circuitous route to the hotel; and if this adventure consumed all afternoon, that was all right with me, and I cannot swear that some unspoken reproach was not intended.

I remember setting off with a kind of jaunty insouciance, trying with exaggerated consciousness to appreciate the colorfulness of the scene: the iridescent slicks of oil that bobbed on the water, the flutter of clothing hanging on back lines, the caterwaul of fishermen as they emptied their bilge or started up the sput-sput of their motors or called to each other in heavy incomprehensible guttural; but in fact I was aware from the first of an underlying unsettling excitement, as on a day when inclement weather hangs in the air.

The farther I proceeded, the seedier the city became. It soon appeared that the harbor stretched for over a mile and not the half-mile I had assumed. Though I continued doggedly, the harbor front came to a mysterious end far short of the elusive breakwater; access to the Mediterranean was impeded by a series of fetid and apparently untraversable canals; and though I followed one of these back into the moldering town, I could discover no bridge but only an increasing warren of side streets and alleyways.

In my turnings I found myself in what I took to be a small park, and loath to retrace my steps, I kept pushing forward until, in frustration and annoyance, I began jogging down the small pebbled lane in search of an exit.

Suddenly from nowhere there appeared a dour, flush-faced Frenchman dressed in a seedy blue workingman's smock.

"Eh, diable, qu'est-que vous faites là? Où allez-vous à cette vitesse dans un cimetière?"

I understood his imperious manner better than his words, and looking about, I realized that I was indeed in a cemetery.

I apologized in broken French.

"Ah, les boches, toujours les boches," he muttered. *"Qu'est-ce qu'ils font dans un cimetière français, les vaches?"*

I tried to explain that I wasn't a German but he would have nothing of it; I only succeeded in igniting an incomprehensible tirade that became more alarming as it proceeded. He advanced upon me until I was afraid he would bump me with his vast protruding belly, and I began to sweat profusely in the intense Mediterranean sunlight.

But he didn't bump me, he relented, he pointed a way out. Even so, as I retreated he loosed upon me an unstoppable series of expletives in an ever deepening growl.

I found myself sweating in the street.

Any pleasure I had taken in this outing had long since evaporated. I was considering what next to do when someone called me from a doorway.

"Qu'est-ce que tu as, mon gars?"

Looking up, I saw a young woman of coarse attraction, her dyed black hair piled on top of her head, her body bound in a tight yellow sweater and short black leather skirt.

"Rien, rien."

"Eh!bien, mon petit homme, tu es perdu, n'est-ce pas?"

Now, I stood at five-eleven and had been on my high school boxing team and was in no mood to be addressed as *"petit homme."*

"Pas du tout, Madame," I insisted. *"Je cherche quelque chose à boire, c'est tout."*

And this was true, I was dying of thirst.

"Tu veux quelque chose à boire?"

"Ah, oui, Madame—je crève de soif."

And so it came about that I found myself drinking watery beer at a small round marble-topped table in a flea-bitten bar with a French *fille* dressed in a leather skirt.

After a while she put her hand on mine.

Later, in her room, after the cramped flight of stairs, sitting on the broken bed with the crease down its center like a loaf of dough indented with the side of a hand, I could not make out what was happening. I fondled her breasts. She removed her sweater, and it seemed I was swimming under water. She had fine breasts, slightly brownish, with one nipple that protruded farther than the other.

When I reached to stroke her hair she stopped me with a short, practiced gesture.

"Pas ça, mon chou."

"Mais pourquoi?"

"Pas les cheveux," she repeated. *"Ça, c'est ma profession."*

While still on top of her I thought, This is all meaningless.

It was as accurate an epiphany as life was ever to vouchsafe.

Afterward, rushing back through the noisome streets of that now detested little town, my actions already seemed to me as unreal and gratuitous as an automobile accident. Barbara let me into our room. She embraced me, she apologized for our not having spent the day together; and as I kissed her, as I made love to her, I knew beyond question that here was absolute center, the axis on which I turned, and that anything that stretched beyond was wasteland—mere outer space.

We returned from our honeymoon on a sticky bleary afternoon in late August of 1970, flying into Kennedy above the sparkling towers of Manhattan. My in-laws set us up in a little apartment on East 87th Street in one of those new white-brick high rises that were beginning to disfigure the city like giant mushrooms.

Frank and Marilyn Grotton were presentable examples of the Long Island moneyed drinking set. Marilyn was a Huntsford and might as well have been the queen of France. She had never been without money and had little more idea of its value than she did of the quantities of Latin syllables. I came to doubt whether she was inherently stupid, but she had such little need for the brain, had found such infrequent cause to make its acquaintance, that its fate had come to resemble that of the small bones in the coccyx, which we are told represent the vestigial remains of a tail. She was inordinately fond of her looks and was indeed a fine-looking woman in a fleshy, high-colored, boozy sort of way; there was even a place in her heart for kindness; but her life was so tyrannized by her infantile egotism that in the end she made everyone around her miserable, including herself.

Francis Grotton had made a lot of money on the stock market, and as is the wont of men who make a lot of money on the stock market, he thought well of himself. He regularly played handball at the Athletic Club, dined at Pen and Pencil, and took a drink standing at the bar at the 21 Club before repairing to his spacious home on Park Avenue. He had rubbed shoulders with men of stature—Stimson, McCoy, Nitze—but all that notwithstanding, I never heard him utter an original comment on any subject what-soever. We both liked to drink and to eat at expensive steak restaurants, and on this our relationship was founded. When Frank started speaking on any subject, I stopped listening and ordered another Wild Turkey.

Barbara had been given a conventional upbringing as a rich kid in New York: she attended Chapin, took dancing lessons in little white gloves with Mrs. Dubois, went ice skating at Rockefeller Center dressed in wool tights and a short navy blue wool skirt and afterward ate ice cream at Rumpelmayer's. When she was older she attended dances with the boys from Trinity and Collegiate and for a year dated a boy named Albert Gibbon who was at school at Choate. When she was sixteen she allowed herself to be deflow-ered by a drunken Dartmouth sophomore at a weekend-long party on Long Island. She had her coming-out party at the Waldorf in the fall of 1965 and a year later she matriculated at Vassar.

To conclude this familial gallery: Barbara's younger sister, Annette, had been more of a rebel than Barbara, though less intelligent. She went to the University of Pennsylvania, where after five months Barbara had to intercede to arrange for her first abortion. During the early seventies she continued to play the hippie with a tie-dyed bandanna about her head and so many boyfriends that she often couldn't remember when introduced to a boy whether she had already slept with him. Toward the end of that decade she suddenly recalled her status as a true blue-blooded Daughter of the American Revolution, and discarding her disreputable practices and accommodating herself to the perquisites of affluence, she married an investment banker named Charles Phillips and retired to the bars and well-plushed watering holes of the Upper East Side.

I liked Annette—for ten minutes at a time. For inscrutable reasons she always assumed that I agreed with her opinions, whether in their liberal or their conservative guise, and she was forever assuring someone that she and I saw "eye to eye"; but since Annette was the soul of conventional platitude, this flattered me less than she supposed, since it was unclear where her opinions ceased and the great blank chatter of the world began.

But I've anticipated. In 1970 I was still a young man of twenty-four casting about for a way to earn a living. As I indicated, the Grottons had set us up on the East Side in a manner they thought befitting to their daughter, though Barbara and I both considered it a mere makeshift; neither of us had any intention of living off the Grottons, much less of domiciling in a jerry-built apartment of pseudo elegance where the walls shook every time the neighbor flushed the toilet.

I had set myself a few rules concerning my employment, which boiled down to this: I refused to work for someone else. I had no intention of laboring in an office, a corporation, a bureaucracy, of being tied down for years doing someone else's dirty work, of pretending to be a "team player" or to give a damn about somebody else's "bottom line." Not only did such considerations bore me to tears; I was certain I would be no good at them.

And so I cast about for something else, and here I had a guiding instinct. I had been impressed by the success my father had enjoyed in servicing the new suburbanites as they pressed ever deeper into the green and pleasant land of Connecticut; and so the inspiration of the "service economy" dawned on me long before it became a catchphrase. I'd let my industrious peers generate new wealth and somehow I'd skim off part of the cream.

At first I thought I might open a travel service. Taking stock of my qualifications, I found they did not include patience, applicability, *sitzenfleisch,* or even an unusual measure of utilitarian intelligence. (The "gentleman's C" was invented for a guy like myself; I would have made a lousy lawyer and would rather dig a ditch than be an accountant.) Rather, I am courteous, curious, restless, and love to travel. And between Barbara and myself I could get to every blue-blooded, moneyed family on the East Coast—nothing to sneeze at by way of a business asset.

I spent about a month talking to people and investigating the possibility of getting a travel license and of finding an office, but somehow I couldn't get this travel idea off the ground. In my heart I couldn't see myself as a travel agent.

"I never saw you as one either," Barbara said. "I always thought it was a crummy idea."

"Gee, thanks for telling me now. So what do you see me as?"

"Anything you want," she said breezily. "You can be anything you want."

"What if I don't want to be anything?"

"Oh, pooh! Go have a drink with Gordon—that'll cheer you up."

So I went and had a drink with Gordo Tate in the Oak Bar at the Plaza while outside the November twilight congealed like frost in the naked trees of Central Park.

"So, Dave," Gordo said to me. "How's the travel business?"

Gordo had never been high on this enterprise, and unlike Barbara, he had not been chary of his opinion.

"Great," I said peevishly as I swished the bourbon around in

my glass (a true whiskey glass and not—God forbid!—the dese-
cration of a *wine*glass) and listened to the comforting crack of the
ice melting.

"You're out of your mind!"

"Oh? What's wrong with a travel service?"

"Too many clients," Gordo said. "Too many phone calls from
old ladies."

"Is that right? I take it you've given this much thought. I
mean, I take it that a travel service is one of the subjects you've
studied intensely."

"Don't believe me if you don't want to," Gordo said. Then we
sat morosely and studied our whiskey.

Though Gordo had been endowed with impeccable credentials
and stood to inherit a fortune from his Pittsburgh robber-baron
forebears, he had a streak in him that worried people. Gordo
wasn't mean and was as loyal as a large sheepdog, but he went
through mood swings that could be abrupt and that carried him
from rowdy heights to morose, dyspeptic lows, and at either extreme he could get out of hand. Once in an argument with a New
Haven cop Gordo broke the cop's jaw, and believe me, it takes a
lot of high-powered finagling to unscramble the mess that follows
from breaking a cop's jaw.

Gordo had adopted an attitude toward me that I never fully
fathomed but that consisted in part of good-humored condescension and in part of proprietary enthusiasm, as if I were a gold
mine in which he had invested against much sober advice. Once
during our junior year when I threatened to transfer to pre-med,
Gordo announced that being a doctor wasn't good enough for me.
"Smith," he said, "is the type of guy who if you lock the door will
go out the window, if you close the window will go up the chimney." "And what," I asked, "if you plug up the chimney?"
"Then," he said, "he'll knock down the wall."

These were apparently compliments.

After graduating from Yale, Gordo shunned the paternal hills
of Pittsburgh in favor of the bars of Manhattan, where he commenced drinking up his sizable trust fund.

"He's going to get himself into trouble," Barbara said to me.

"Gordo was made to get himself into trouble."

Now as we sat at the bar in the Plaza staring at our whiskey I could discern the shape of trouble in the heavy outline of Gordo's stooped shoulders.

"So what's *your* idea?" I asked. "What do *you* plan to do with this fine specimen of manhood—other than drink it to death?"

"I don't know," Gordo said. "But I'll tell you this. If you can figure a way to let me drink myself to death, I'll go in with you halves. It just can't be a travel service, that's all."

"What do you mean, halves?"

"I mean I'll go into business with you. I'll advance half the money. But I don't want to run a travel service."

"Are you serious?"

"Why shouldn't I be serious? Didn't you tell me I needed to *do* something with myself? Isn't that what you and Barbara are always lecturing about? Okay, wise guy, I'll *do* something with myself—whatever you say. Only not a travel service."

After this we both remained silent while Gordo commandeered another round of drinks.

"Do you mean all this?"

"Absolutely."

"Okay," I said. "Done!"

Gordo put out his hand and we shook portentously in the Oak Bar.

"Partners!"

"Partners!"

Then more silence.

"So *now* what?" Gordo asked after a while.

"Now what *what?*"

"Now what do we *do?* I mean, now that we're partners, what kind of partners *are* we?"

"I don't know," I said.

"Great," said Gordo. "What a genius!"

I sat cogitating—but not for long.

"Okay, Gordo," I said. "I know what we'll do."

"Oh, yeah?"

"Yeah. You and I are going to be wine merchants."

"*Wine* merchants?"

"Yeah, wine. You know—booze."

"Ah, booze! Yeah, I've heard of that. Well, why not?" He shrugged his heavy shoulders like Samson settling down for a haircut. "I like booze just fine."

And that's what we became.

Barbara and I had stayed in a small hotel along the Ebro where every day we were served a wine I had never heard of, a Rioja *negra* they called it, tangy, resinous, light-bodied, with a sweet grapy aroma; and even then it occurred to me that someone could make his fortune by introducing this inexpensive beauty to the American public. It was just at the beginning of the wine craze in the United States, and somehow Gordo's challenge dovetailed in my mind with the recollection of those pleasant days in Spain under the heady influence of Rioja *negra* until, like Gibbon on the ruins of Rome, the epic of my future hove into view.

Gordo and I incorporated under the name of Stendhal & Fils, an utterly fictitious appellation chosen for its euphonious literary connotations: Gordo put up half the money, Barbara the other. My job was to make the business work.

I lit out immediately for Spain. We enjoyed a remarkable run of good luck, starting with my introduction in Madrid to Señor Juan Hermano, a wine merchant of congenial wit and disposition who became my cicerone in the European wine business and eventually a silent partner. He was a great bulging boisterous man, generous and shrewd and knowledgeable about human nature, a European in the best sense, skeptical but humane, and he took us under his wing with genuine affection and prudent calculation. He arranged for us to buy a sizable shipment of Rioja *negra* at an advantageous price, and this became the foundation of our success. Renamed Gracianos Noches and decked out in an elegant label designed for the purpose, the stuff sold like lemonade in July, not just to the matrons up and down Park Avenue but to the country clubs and catering establishments of Long Island, which Gordo now began to work like a Cadillac dealer with a franchise in Dutchess County.

Gordo and I ran at a small loss for the first two years, broke even on the third, and have made money ever since—eventually quite a lot of money. Gordo turned out to have an entrepreneurial flare, an ability to drive hard bargains, maneuver shrewdly in the liquor business, expand wisely when the moment was right and hold the line in between, sometimes in the teeth of my enthusiasm. Ultimately we owned three stores in Manhattan and a wholesale business on the Island run almost entirely by Gordo.

We are now talking about a business it took us over fifteen years to build, and of course it wasn't all fun and games, but in fact this part of my life ran remarkably smoothly and I enjoyed it. I got to travel, to dabble in foreign cultures, to stutter in foreign languages, to get to know the wine business, which is a fascinating one, to drink a lot of wine, and—no small pleasure—to make a lot of money. After five years Barbara and I moved out of the nouveau dump on 87th Street into the beloved prewar building we still inhabit on Park Avenue in the lower eighties, a spacious apartment with ten rooms, fourteen-foot ceilings, a working fireplace, and a doorman who has been with the place as long as we have. I took to dressing nattily and driving a Mercedes leased through Stendhal & Fils.

Many significant things happened to me that will find small place in this narrative. I taught myself German and read Fichte and Schlegel and Schleiermacher. I fell in love with the operas of Verdi, Puccini, and Strauss and sat up in my study listening to my records late into the night.

Barbara and I had four children: Jenny and Alexandra and the twins, Mat and Timmy. Sometimes when the children were very young I would enter their rooms at night, and seeing them sleeping in their small beds, I would be seized by a wrenching intensity that for us poor mortals is the very definition of love.

Barbara made a career of raising our four kids. Thanks in part to her money, we enjoyed a lot of perks—skiing in Colorado, the weekend house in Connecticut, trips to Europe—and I imagine we presented an energetic close-knit family à la Bobby Kennedy's. The family was Barbara's form of religion and she worked at it with the dedicated perseverance of a believing Catholic, not only organizing trips and holidays and weekend excursions but attending to the slogging day-to-day affairs of clothing, food, homework (when Jenny was having problems with algebra, she bought herself a textbook and worked through it cover to cover), teacher appointments, play dates, rivalries, fights, romances, heartaches—the works.

She was invariably an attentive, loving wife, and if, in our busy upper-middle-class Manhattan existence, I could not always tap her fund of warmth, I always assumed it was there. Throughout these fifteen years I was a true and faithful husband. I never stopped loving Barbara. She never bored me—and that's a mouthful. I'm not sure I never bored her.

Yet sometimes when I looked at this thriving family I had helped to create, these strong-willed independent creatures all somehow yoked together, a feeling of helplessness would possess me, as if the whole thing were a species of dream, a beautiful, inspiring, insubstantial dream.

My father died in 1985. Barbara and I left the children in New York and drove to Connecticut in the Mercedes. It was autumn, and as I drove up the Merritt I watched the extravagance of the maples wagging outside the window in the mild, sweet-smelling air.

When we got to the nursery there were unfamiliar cars parked in the driveway. Warren had already arrived, as well as Mr. and Mrs. Booth. Karin, who had prepared coffee, was talking to Mrs. Booth when I came in. Warren stood by himself looking moodily out the window.

"I'm so sorry," Mrs. Booth said, taking my hand. "He was such a wonderful man." I could see she had been crying. Barbara kissed her.

Someone touched me from behind, and, turning, I saw it was Karin. I didn't want to see anyone but Karin and I took her in my arms. Then I heard our mother talking in the farther room.

Mom had gotten herself up in an outlandish fashion with a gardenia pinned to her lapel, and she seemed to have put her makeup on aslant like a comic actress. I could not tell whether she was drunk. She kept on repeating, "I was married to Gil for forty-five years, do you understand that, for forty-five years." It was impossible to determine whether she was boasting or complaining.

Dad's funeral was in the Methodist church. There were lots of people and everyone was very respectful and quiet; then the minister appeared and shook hands and said something consoling to Mother. He was a new minister, younger than me, and his lashes and eyebrows were so blond that they disappeared into his blond serious face like clouds into a white sky. I tried to imagine what would prevail upon anyone to become a Methodist minister in a small community in Connecticut, but without success.

"I was married to Gil for forty-five years," Mother said.

We sat in the front pew, and Mother sat next to Warren and gripped his hand while she stared ahead fiercely and without deviation, as if trying to perceive an oncoming disaster through thick fog.

The minister read from the Bible. Then he said some words about my father, whom he had hardly known. He said what a good man my father had been and what a pillar of the community and what a pillar of the Methodist church. Then he said some consoling words about heaven.

I didn't give a damn about what a good man my father had been or whether he had been a pillar of the community or of the Methodist church. I missed the shape of my father's hands.

Then Karin spoke. She looked very small standing in the pulpit and she looked very much like my father, and as she spoke I had to watch my emotions.

Karin said some words about growing up with Dad and some words about what he had been like as a father and as a gardener, and I believed everything she said. Then she said something like this. She said that Essence was greater than Existence. She said that somehow, however, Essence didn't fully share in Existence. She said that God was the essence of Being, yet there was some question about whether God existed. The essence of Dad, she said, could not be touched by death—and yet Dad had ceased to exist! How was this possible? The belief, she said, in Essence constituted the Ontological Argument. The Ontological Argument, she said, was self-evidently true for those with eyes to see.

That's what Karin said. Neither Warren nor I chose to say anything.

After the service we returned to the rectory for something to eat. It was easy to perceive that Dad had been well liked: people kept pulling me aside to share anecdotes, many of them unknown to me.

"After our Joey committed suicide, your dad stood beside me and the missus like nothing you ever saw. Gil was always there for us, Dave, I can tell you that. We're gonna miss him."

"He was a wonderful man, your dad," Mrs. Oaks said to me. Mrs. Oaks had a wart by the side of her nose and as a child I found it uncomfortable to talk to her because I was afraid I would stare at her wart. Even now I found it uncomfortable to talk to her. "We owed your father money after our barn burned to the ground," Mrs. Oaks said, "but when Herbert came down sick your father forgave the debt till we could get on our feet again."

When I was a kid I was afraid of the dark. There were years when I lay awake every night counting the hours until daylight. As long as I could hear my father moving in the house, my fear was contained. I knew things were all right as long as he was there. It seemed to me that nothing could hurt my dad. He was a kind of mythical figure, I suppose; but more than that, it was just that I knew he loved me. Whatever happened, I knew Dad would intervene to help me—and that knowledge seemed sufficient to face the dark.

Now I could see Barbara standing across the room talking with some of the guests. Her figure had filled out slightly and even at this distance I could feel the fullness of her as if I were caressing her through the softness of her clothing. I wanted to bite her and hold her and enter her and it seemed that without her I would fall through the floor and disappear; yet I also wanted to make love to every woman in the room. It seemed that without the love of women I would die.

We came outside into the fragrant autumn air and the wind was blowing. I knew many of the people who had come to the funeral but I didn't feel like speaking to any of them. I recognized some of the kids I had gone to high school with, now grown to adulthood, and I looked for Paula Light, but I didn't see her.

Barbara drove us back to the house.

"Are you okay?" she asked.

"Yes, I'm okay."

"Are you sure?"

"Yes. I'm fine."

There were many people at the house and pretty soon the cars stretched down the driveway and onto the front lawn. I didn't want to be there but I stayed because of Mom.

For a long time I wandered from room to room talking to people, though I don't remember anything I said. At one point Karin came up to me and squeezed my arm and looked hard into my eyes. Karin had pellucid blue eyes and when you looked into them it was like looking into perfect pools of water.

"Don't be like that," she said. She sounded sad.

"Like what?"

"You know what," she said. "Just don't be like that."

Later I spoke briefly with Warren.

"When can we go?" I said.

Warren looked at me out of his cold crazy inscrutable eyes and I could see he was eager to seize the high ground. "This is for Mother," he said.

"It sure isn't for Dad."

"It's Mother who needs us now. She wants us to stay." It was peculiar hearing Warren preach family cohesion.

When everyone had gone the family gathered in the living room for drinks. The Booths stayed as surrogate family members. Barbara sat next to me on the arm of the couch and I could feel her breast press against me.

"Someday I'm going to marry you," I said.

"Are you?"

"Yes. I'm going to marry you and we're going to have four kids."

"How enterprising," she said. "That sounds wonderful. Just for the record, who's going to have them, you or me?"

"We'll decide that later," I said. "I haven't worked out all the details. But the main thing is, it will be marvelous."

"Isn't that wonderful," she said. "When are we going to get started?"

"Any minute now. You'll be amazed and surprised. I've got it all figured out."

"It sounds very exciting," she said. "Please let's love each other forever."

My mother announced, "I won't have that flower in my house."

"They meant well," Warren said from across the room, where he sat in a brown three-piece suit, an expression of his incumbency at Princeton as an associate professor of astrophysics. His voice sounded unconvincing as a medium of prudent accommodation.

"Their intentions be damned," my mother said. "I won't have that object in my house. Karin, please put it out the back door."

Karin removed the offending vegetable, a bird of paradise plant, expensive and as ugly as the shorn neck of a goose, sent by two of my father's oldest friends, a couple who had not attended the funeral because of their presence in Europe. The hideous offering enraged my mother.

"Out of the house," she called. "I want it out of the house!"

"Wasn't the service beautiful," Peggy Booth observed, trying to change the subject. She was a large organdy woman, a perpetual peacemaker, sweet beyond honey and molasses, and she had adored my father for many years. Karl Booth nodded and pulled on his pipe but my mother eyed her balefully.

"That's beside the point," my mother said. "I have something I want to say. Tell Karin to come back," she ordered Warren. "I have something I want her to hear."

Warren got up and started toward the door but Karin met him before he reached the threshold.

"You two sit down," my mother said. "I have something I need to say to you."

Barbara put her hand on my shoulder and squeezed.

My mother was sitting on the far couch with a glass of whiskey in her hand. She had run the nursery for twenty-five years and it had flourished under her authority, for she was a shrewd business-woman and nothing could be done on the place without her approving the plans. Her way of conducting affairs invariably proved the best way, and she enforced her intentions with an iron will; but I think she had come to hate the nursery. She now surveyed the room with what we called her Lord Nelson stare.

"I've decided to sell the nursery," she said.

"What do you mean?" Warren asked. "What do you mean, you decided to sell the nursery?"

"Sell the nursery," my mother said. "Sell the nursery. What does it sound like?"

"It sounds like nuttiness," I said.

"Well, it isn't nuttiness," my mother said haughtily, looking at me. "And I'll thank you to keep your flippancies to yourself."

"But what about Karin?" I said. "Karin lives here too."

"I've already spoken to Karin about this. Karin is a full-grown woman and has to look out for herself. It was one thing when your father was alive and you children were young. I had no choice. But you're all grown up now, and if you think I'm going to run this place just to satisfy your nostalgia, you have another think coming." She uttered her familiar sarcastic snort.

"No one has suggested anything like that," Warren said.

"Well, I don't know," I said. "I can't imagine us without the nursery."

"You are invited to come and run it if you feel that way," my mother said.

"I'd like to run it," Karin said. She hadn't said anything until then. We all looked at Karin.

"Where will you get the money?" my mother asked.

"What money?" I said.

"The money to buy the place," my mother said, turning to me again. "I don't mean to sound mercenary, but I intend to sell the place and I intend to sell it for top dollar. It's the only money I'll have. You know I've always wanted to live where it was warmer. I begged your father for years to sell the place so we could move. Well, now he's dead and I intend to do it. I was married to your father for forty-five years and now I intend to do something *I* want."

Barbara's hand tightened on my shoulder. Warren stared blankly out the window.

"I don't know where I'll get the money," Karin said. "But I want to try. I think it's what Dad would have wanted."

"I do too," I said. "I don't think he would have wanted us to sell the place."

"Well, that's not really for us to say," Warren said. There was silence for a moment. "I think Mom has to have the opportunity to do what she thinks is best for *her*. This is no time to be sentimental."

"Do you call it being sentimental?" Barbara inquired. Warren looked at her coldly but didn't say anything.

"I just don't want to see you fight," Mrs. Booth said. "This is no time for you to fight."

"We're not fighting," Warren said.

"I'll raise the money," Karin said. "I don't know how, but I'll raise the money."

"Well, that's fine," my mother said. "If you want to run the nursery, that's fine. But I want my position to be clear. I don't want there to be any room for misunderstandings. I was married to your father for forty-five years and they were the best years of my life but they are over now and I've got to go on. And I'll be darned if I'm going to continue to run this nursery just to suit you children."

"No one is asking you to, Mom," Warren said. "We don't need to settle all this right now."

"For me it *is* settled," Mother said. And then, turning to Karin, "And please make sure that infernal plant is out of my house."

On the way home Barbara said, "I'll buy the nursery."

"What are you talking about?"

"Just what I said. I've got the money and I'll buy the nursery. It shouldn't be out of the family. We'll let Karin run it."

"No you won't," I said. "You're not getting into the middle of this scrap. There'll be no winning, Barbara. It's my family and you're not getting caught in the middle of it—and neither am I."

That wasn't the end of my father's death—it was *never* the end of my father's death—but somehow I had to make peace with the fact that he was gone. I didn't know what his death meant, but I sure knew it was a fact. And that's life: a succession of facts whose meaning is . . . well, anyone's guess. My dad took whatever secrets he had with him to the grave. I had to discover my own for myself.

Sometime that fall shortly after my fortieth birthday we attended a party of Yale cronies at Dick and Jeannie Simon's on the Upper East Side. These were all people I had known at Yale, people I liked, and we were now in our middle years, married and prospering, with kids and mortgages and headaches, but happy and in good health, and we had gathered to drink and chew the fat for the evening and to have a good time.

Dick Simon was in real estate and doing very well, thank you. Jeannie, his *gemütlich* wife, was buxom and vivacious and from time to time my hand would stray from her waist to the top of her butt and give her a little squeeze. Tom Brichett and Elbert Mc-Pherson were both in money in some capacity, stocks or banking or something—I didn't care enough to discriminate between these enterprises—and William Dix and his wife Marion were lawyers.

We sat in Dick Simon's study while Dick mixed drinks and Jeannie sat on the arm of Tom Brichett's chair and fussed at him playfully while he tried to tell us about a business deal he had recently concluded.

"This trickle-down economics is just fine by me," Tom said.

"I think we call it 'supply side,' " Marion Dix said ironically. "Our side gets supplied and somebody else gets trickled on."

"That's not entirely fair," her husband, Bill, a bluff red-faced man who made money as counsel to large corporations, observed.

"It's what in pornography we call the 'golden shower,' " Jeannie added naughtily. "Somebody else gets pissed on and they're supposed to like it."

"My wife is an expert on such matters," Dick said. "Here, Jeannie, give Dave another drink."

Barbara was trying to explain to Fanny Brichett a dilemma concerning a nanny who Barbara thought was acting irresponsibly.

"I don't know whether to tell Elizabeth," Barbara said. "I don't know her that well and I'm afraid she'll think I'm meddling. But I'll never forgive myself if something happens to the children. Little Danny was halfway across the park before that girl so much as lifted her head."

"Did I ever tell you about the time we came home and found the baby-sitter in our bed with her boyfriend?" Jeannie said. "I mean, *our bed!*"

"I'd stay out of it if I were you," Fanny said to Barbara. "Elizabeth's a bitch—you won't get any thanks."

"I couldn't disagree more," Gail McPherson said. "I think the whole nanny situation is a nightmare. How do we know what they are up to when we're not there? I'd be thankful if someone told me what was going on behind my back."

"In all seriousness," Bill Dix said, "there is something wrong with a civilization that can't supply a respectable class of nannies."

"What are you talking about?" Marion Dix said. "You don't even have *children.*"

"Did you ever see that movie *Peau Doux?*" Jeannie asked. "The one where the baby-sitter leaves the baby to go fuck her boyfriend?"

"Who wants another drink?" Dick asked.

"Well, that's *you,* Gail," Fanny said. "Of course we'd tell *you.* But that Elizabeth Stuart is such a bitch that all I can do is advise you, Barbara, to stay away. You can do what you like, of course, but I've known Elizabeth a long time and my advice is to stay away."

"Has anyone heard that the Finklesteins are getting divorced?" Tom Brichett asked. "Isn't that what you told me, Fanny—that the Finklesteins are getting divorced?"

"How's the wine trade, ol' buddy?" Elbert McPherson asked, looking at me out of boozy indifferent eyes and turning his back on the women.

"Not bad, El, not bad. I can't say that I have anything to complain about."

"I bet you don't," Dick Simon said. "I think Château Margaux has become the national drink."

"Have you heard that Coca-Cola is getting into the wine business?"

"No, I haven't heard that."

"Well, that's the scuttlebutt on the Street. That's the poop."

"No kidding."

"But what do you think of this real estate market, eh? Unreal, don't you think? Dix told me his place is going co-op and the *insider's* price is two mil."

"It's a beautiful place," Bill Dix said gravely, leaning toward us.

"That's not even that expensive," Dick said. "I'm moving properties now for five or six mil that once wouldn't have gone for half that. It's a go-go market, that's for sure."

"Yeah, well, it's all fine and good for you," Elbert said, "but it's crazy money, crazy money."

After the conversation had continued for a while I excused myself and left the room. It took me some time to locate the head and then I found I was in no hurry to return to the others. Instead I loitered in the long cool hallway, finishing my drink and contemplating the paintings on the wall.

Jeannie painted, but there was something gay and meretricious about everything she did. It was as if she hadn't sorted out the difference between painting and decoration. I paused for a while before a picture of a young woman naked from the waist up, which bore a striking resemblance to a younger, idealized Jeannie repackaged to look like a large-eyed, large-breasted lobotomy case.

I could hear the voices from the study, the men discussing money and the women the pros and cons of private schools, and suddenly I felt a weight of boredom descend so palpably that it took my breath away. For the life of me I could not reenter that room. I knew that these were decent and well-intentioned people, my friends and companions, but the prospect of rejoining them was suddenly intolerable. I had no idea what misunderstanding had brought me to this pass, but for a panic-stricken moment I did not see how I could go forward with my life.

In October Barbara and I attended a parents' evening at Jenny's school. We had sent the girls to different schools, for they were very different children: Alexandra had from early on exhibited a quiet scholarly bent, but Jenny was a rebel.

Jenny was a beautiful, difficult child with long rust-colored hair and skin so pale that sometimes it seemed translucent. From an early age she had loved to sing and draw, and there was something fay and wayward about her that refused to be disciplined. She was a strong-willed, self-directed kid and as she got older— she was now fourteen—she proved a handful.

Jenny fought with her mother. In her late thirties Barbara was still a beauty, slightly full in hip and bosom but only in a tantalizing way, tall and long-throated, with tawny hair ablaze with only a dab of artificial encouragement. I'm not sure what she had expected from her eldest daughter but it certainly wasn't Jenny; and these two formidable females could tangle like cats.

On this particular evening Jenny and Barbara had quarreled over whether we should go to this event at all. Jenny took the position that school was an authoritarian imposition of the adult world inflicted on kids for sadistic purposes; the only way we could show solidarity would be to eschew the institution entirely. This came on the heels of a bad report card.

Barbara was not amused.

It was a damp autumn night and as we entered the school from the gloom of the street I was seized by one of those irrational moments of elation that must underpin the notion of grace. Barbara was still carrying on about Jenny, trying to analyze her from every which-way; and as we entered the light I experienced a disjunctive sense of alienation, not unpleasant, as if this grand, beautiful, rather imposing woman at my shoulder were not my beloved wife but an utter stranger, a mystery.

The school was crowded and muggy and exuded that peculiar

odor of steel locker and stone stair that seems to be the monopoly of high school corridors. Barbara seemed to know everyone, while I fixed on my face the idiot grin of complaisant uncomprehending greeting.

I had noticed Anne Stokowski before, not only because she had been pointed out as the wife of Bob Stokowski, one of the richest men in the city, but because of her own regal bearing, the haughtiness of her prominent Bourbon nose—which in fact she had inherited from the Jewish side of her family—the silkiness of her golden hair, the *froideur* of her ice-blue eyes.

Anne sat across from us in Jenny's English class, where I found myself studying her well-heeled composure, her pearls and gold earrings and pale flawless skin, while the young teacher discoursed on the nature of the journals the kids were supposed to be keeping and the exact weight he assigned to the surprise quizzes he gave as opposed to the three formal tests.

Anne reappeared in Jenny's math class, and again in her history class.

Just sitting in these classes made me feel trapped and reduced and revived my ineradicable distaste for school, and to escape my boredom I rested my eyes on Anne Stokowski's long elegant neck. Once she raised her eyes briefly, impatiently, as if to say, What do you want? But also, inadvertently, I see you. I know you are there.

The haughtiness of her eyes enchanted me.

After classes the parents milled in the dining room while they drank watery coffee out of Styrofoam cups and exchanged animated impressions concerning the world of adolescent pedagogy.

"I don't think Jenny's *keeping* a diary," I heard Barbara say to another mother, a pudgy woman who, to judge by her complexion, must have been suffering from a form of carotenemia. "The *rat!* Sometimes I could just *murder* that child!"

I drifted away into the bright shoal of parents, and veering to the left to escape the notice of someone I recognized, I saw standing in a corner, her back half turned while she blew on a cup of coffee, the elegant Anne Stokowski.

"These events remind me how lucky we are not to be in school anymore."

She looked at me over the steam.

"Do you think so?"

"Decidedly. Would you be an adolescent again? Not for all the money in the world, am I right?"

She smiled briefly.

"Is that what you are going to tell your child?"

"Jenny? I don't have to tell Jenny anything. I'm sure she could tell me a thing or two. Incidentally, our kids seem to share a number of classes."

"Yes, so I noticed. I'm Ben Stokowski's mother."

She put out her hand.

"Yes, I know," I said. Her hand was long and cool and delicate-boned between my fingers. "I'm Jenny Smith's dad."

"Ah, so you are Jenny Smith's father." Again she smiled.

"Do you know Jenny?"

"I know *of* her. I think my Ben may have something of a crush on her, actually. I think he admires her independent spirit."

"Is that what he calls it?" I laughed. "I'm not sure what name her mother would give it."

"Really? I'd love to have a daughter like that. I only have sons."

"I have sons and daughters, and daughters are better. Not that I have anything against the boys. I prefer girls, that's all. I mean as a general statement—females. It's a piece of advice my father passed on to me. Son, he said, no matter how famous the man, the woman in any couple will be more interesting. And he was right."

"Oh? You've had occasion to notice this?"

"Countless times. Look around you here. Would you care to wager that the men are more interesting than the women?"

We surveyed the large echoing dining room filled with the lumpy middle-aged figures of lawyers, stockbrokers, business executives, advertising people, and other examples of our generation dressed in business suits or in the expensive sporting outfits that Madison Avenue was beginning to promote as acceptable wear.

Anne Stokowski snorted.

"You're not very generous to your own sex," she said.

"Why should I be? What have they ever done for me?"

"And what about your wife? Is she more interesting than you?"

"Absolutely. And what about your husband? Which one is he?"

"Bob isn't here. But you're wrong about him. He's *much* more interesting than I."

"Am I allowed to doubt it?"

"We shouldn't talk this way."

"Oh, I don't mean to cast aspersions on your husband. It's all part of my theory, that's all. And in my eyes, you see, he'd need to be *awfully* interesting to be more interesting than you."

That week I went to Boston for a seminar on the burgeoning wine business in New England, and finding myself bored and restless, on the third day I rented a car and drove to Walden Pond to pay homage to the ghost of Henry Thoreau. It was difficult, however, to recapture any of the beauty or excitement that that strange man had recorded in his masterpiece. The pond seemed small and undistinguished; and though in the gathering autumn I had the shore almost to myself, it was chewed by previous feet and marred with the scrofula of America. It was hard to believe that Thoreau had found the landscape pristine and solitary just over one hundred years ago.

I was still restless when I returned to New York. Indian summer had arrived and the air was warm and unhealthy. That Wednesday I took the car out of the garage and drove up the West Side Highway. It was a moisture-soaked day, dropsical and intemperate, and I put the window down and let the wind whip over my face and arms.

After the Spuyten Duyvil bridge I turned off the highway and drove west toward the river. I was unfamiliar with the area and for a while I was lost amid narrow streets with large stately houses set back on well-tended lawns.

The Stokowski residence, a white Colonial-style mansion, was surrounded by manicured grounds adorned with towering beeches and Japanese maples and an English garden that meandered in the back. I parked my car by the hedge that fronted the property and mounted the paving stones.

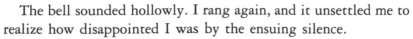

The bell sounded hollowly. I rang again, and it unsettled me to realize how disappointed I was by the ensuing silence.

Then Anne opened the door.

She looked surprised—but also, I thought, pleased. Then she frowned.

"Hello," I said, and the word sounded foolish to my ears. "I was passing and thought I'd drop in. I should have called, I know, but—I didn't know what to say. So I thought I'd just ring your bell. I hope you don't mind."

"No, no," she said, gathering herself. "I'm surprised, that's all. I mean, you're the last person I expected."

"Am I? Well, here I am. May I come in?"

"Of course. How stupid of me."

She stepped back and I entered the foyer.

The house had a distinctive odor of sunlight and polished wood, and also an evanescent something that struck me as a distillation of Anne herself, as if something of Anne's essence floated in these elegant rooms, something expensive, elusive, desirable, and distant. She was dressed in beige riding trousers and an eggshell-white Oxford shirt with a blue paisley scarf across her forehead and tied at the back of her neck. Her blond short-cut hair was glossy and slightly mussed and she held a garden trowel in her hand.

"Excuse me," she said. "I'm something of a mess."

"You look lovely."

"Do I?"

"We have an affiliate in the area," I said. "And since I was done early with my business and don't need to be back in Manhattan until after lunch, I thought I'd take a chance on your being in."

"That's very nice." She had regained the poise of a society woman but I thought she watched me with genuine curiosity, her head tilted back so that she looked down her nose at me in what I came to recognize as a habitual stance.

I followed her into the sun-filled living room. The great windows wimpled the oncoming light so it swam over the backs of the chairs like water and onto the Persian carpet. The room was appointed in elegant simplicity with modern but comfortable furniture and the gleam of polished brass. Beyond the windows stretched the garden, now dunned with autumn.

"What a beautiful house!"

"Thank you. May I get you something? Tea perhaps?"

"No, I'm fine. I don't want to put you out. Have you been gardening?"

"Yes, a bit. I'm starting to get things ready for winter. Do you garden?"

"Well, my dad was a gardener. I grew up around gardens. *In* them, really. My father ran a greenhouse in Connecticut. At one time I couldn't get the dirt out from under my nails."

"That must have been nice."

"Do you think so?"

"Yes. I'd love to be a gardener. I think it would be much more satisfying than most of the things we do. Why didn't you become a gardener?"

"I don't know. It's a calling really—like everything else. My father had it, and my sister Karin. But not me. But I can always *tell* a real gardener. You, for example. I can smell it."

"*Smell* it?" She wrinkled her nose at the word *smell,* though she smiled, intrigued.

"Yes. Some instinct picks it up—perhaps the slight odor of something green, something life-enhancing."

"And that's what you think I *smell* like?"

I laughed. "Well, at any rate like *something* good. But maybe I'd better have that tea."

"Yes, maybe you'd better."

She left me while she prepared the tea. I wandered about the room studying its objects: a picture of Bob Stokowski dressed in a naval lieutenant's uniform, a picture of the two Stokowski children, valuable African and Mesoamerican statuary, a photograph of Anne looking stately and slightly distracted, like some beautiful wild creature caught in a headlight. The books on the shelves were predictable and mediocre.

A bird came and fluttered persistently at the window, wanting to get in. He would fly against the glass, his wings beating double time, then fly away. But a moment later he would be back.

"There," Anne said. She set down the tray with the tea things. "It's the maid's day off."

"Is it? I'm glad."

"Are you? What brings you here, Mr. Smith—besides of course your affiliate in the Bronx?"

"I don't know exactly." I got up and paced to the window. Outside the sparrows in the golden-rain tree were burrowing into the sunlight, shaking their feathers in a small Dionysian dance in the autumn heat.

"After seeing you the other night, I felt I wanted to see you again. I don't myself know why. Instinct, maybe. I don't mean you any harm—quite the opposite. Can you understand?"

She was watching me closely, not without sympathy.

"I'm not sure I can," she said. "I'm not a very sophisticated woman."

"Sophisticated?" I shrugged impatiently. "What does that have to do with it? I'm not talking about sophistication."

"What *are* you talking about? Are you making love to me?"

That brought me up for a moment. Again I watched the sparrows luxuriating in the October air.

"If I said I was making love to you, would you turn me out? Would you chase me away?"

She hesitated above her tea things, frowning as she sat and stared at the rug.

"This has never happened to me before," she said presently.

"To me neither," I said.

She looked at me sharply. "Don't lie to me!"

"I'm not lying. Do I look as if I'm lying?"

At that she looked at me for a long time. Then she slowly shook her head.

"This is all very strange."

"Listen," I said. "Let me take you to lunch. I'm not trying to harm you in any way."

"I can't," she said. "I have things I have to do."

"Tomorrow, then. Or the next day. Just let me take you to lunch."

Again she considered me with her hooded blue eyes, and now I noticed that a flush colored her long lissome neck and was lost in the V of her open shirt.

"All right," she said gravely after a pause. "But I can't do it until Monday. You'll have to wait until then."

I spent that weekend in a blaze of energy, playing the devoted father with Mat and Timmy. We took a football to the park and bought frankfurters and then we walked to the zoo and watched the polar bears.

"Would they eat you if you fell in?" Timmy asked.

"Don't be stupid," Mat said. "How could you fall in?"

"I dunno," Timmy said. "But if you *did,* would they eat you if you *did?*"

"Of course not," Mat said.

"They might."

Both boys looked at me seriously.

"You mean they might *eat* you?"

"They might."

Timmy and Mat pressed their noses against the railing and stared at the polar bears.

"Maybe we should go watch the seals," I said.

"I don't want to watch the seals," Timmy said. "I want to watch the polar bears."

"Me too," Mat said. "Let's just watch the bears."

That evening Barbara asked me, "So how was your day with the boys?"

"Great."

"What did you do?"

"We played football and ate frankfurters and communed with the polar bears."

"That sounds jolly."

"What about you and your daughters?"

"We fought."

"That sounds less jolly."

"Yes, it was," she said. And then, "Lucky you," she added. "Surrounded by little boys and adoring females."

* * *

"I thought you wouldn't come," I said to Anne Stokowski.

I had seen her as soon as she entered the restaurant. I was seated at a banquette toward the rear, which Grégoire knew I preferred, and as I sipped my whiskey I kept my eyes on the front door so I wouldn't miss her if she came.

She was wearing a fur-trimmed blue coat and I watched her shy, slightly awkward gesture as Grégoire helped her remove it. They exchanged a few words and as he ushered her into the room, I observed the furtive glance she bestowed in the mirror as she advanced toward me.

She colored when she saw me.

I rose to meet her.

"I didn't think you would come."

"I wanted to come." It was simple, straightforward, without any coquetry.

"Good! Grégoire, let's have some wine. A bottle of Pouilly-Fuissé—very cold, please. Will that be good for you?"

"Whatever you say."

She sat next to me on the banquette and again I caught the distinctive aroma of her perfume.

"I saw you the minute you came in."

"Did you?"

"I really didn't think you'd come."

"Why not?"

"I don't know. But I'm very glad you did. I didn't know how glad until I saw you come in in your blue coat."

"I thought about you all weekend," she said matter-of-factly.

We drank the wine and talked about inconsequential matters: our children, my job, places we had visited, things we would like to see. She had the veal, I ordered striped bass.

"I realize I knew your sister," I said. "She was at Smith when I was a senior at Yale. She dated a guy named Morgan Cox. I used to see them at Houlighan's. I thought her very attractive. She was the kind of woman who doesn't realize she is pretty, and that can be wonderfully attractive—especially when she really is."

"Is that what you see in me?" Again it was matter-of-fact.

"Not at all. You remind me of your sister—maybe that's what first caught my attention. No one could overlook that you are sisters. But you are not really very much like her, are you? You carry yourself like a beautiful woman."

"Is that a compliment?"

"It's just a fact. Both that you are beautiful and that—well, that you carry yourself in a certain way. Perhaps imperious is too strong a word. But like somebody who . . . knows her own worth."

"Maybe it's the wine, but I don't know quite what to make of all this. In fact I've looked up to Jessica all my life. She's a much more serious person than I. You may think me imperious, but actually I have only the vaguest idea who I am. Perhaps that's why I came today."

"I'm trying to define how you strike me. Because, you see, you strike me as . . . quite wonderful."

"Do you speak this way to all your women?"

"I don't have women."

"You don't have women? But surely that can't be." She seemed genuinely perplexed. "Surely you've had other women before. I don't really care, you see. I'm just trying to figure out what the procedure is. Because . . . I've never done this before."

"The procedure?" I said. "I don't know about the procedure. I guess it's very simple. I guess it's just that . . . I'm smitten with you. It sounds ridiculous, but there you have it."

Again she sat thinking about what I had said.

"You should watch what you say to me," she said after a pause. "Right now I'm very vulnerable."

"Vulnerable?"

"Yes. I might as well tell you, something has gone wrong with my marriage. I'm not quite sure what. I suppose we don't love each other anymore. You see, for a long time we were a kind of team. It was all very romantic and exciting, I suppose. I met Bob when I was an undergraduate at Radcliffe. He was a graduate student at Harvard, and already everyone knew he would be someone. I mean, he was terribly brilliant and ambitious and all that.

He wanted to be rich. Not just wealthy but *rich*—with fame and power and all the trappings. He had the brilliance and dash, and I —well, I had the money. To get him started, I mean. And the connections, and so forth. Oh, I was a good 'package.' "

"Were you in love with him?" I asked.

"In love with him? Oh, I suppose I was, in a way. We were so very young. We've been married now for over fifteen years. And— well, we just don't seem to have much in common. I seem to get on his nerves."

"I'm sorry."

"Sorry? Why should you be sorry? It has nothing to do with you. It's just that you came along at . . . an opportune time, I suppose. For you. Or maybe for me. I really don't know. You've just got to be careful about what you say."

"Well . . . I stand by everything I said."

"Do you? Well, it's all very flattering, I suppose—your being *smitten* with me. Isn't that what you said? You see I won't let you off the hook. That's what I mean about being careful."

"I don't want to be off the hook. In fact, if it comes to that, I want to be very much *on.*"

Again she was silent, as if gathering her thoughts. Her long elegant hands rested by the side of her plate. When she spoke she didn't lift her eyes.

"But why the sex?" she asked. "Why does there have to be sex?"

I too paused before answering.

"Well, I don't know," I said. "I suppose it's something men and women *give* to each other. A kind of grace, maybe. If you are lucky. I mean, we are very much alone out here."

That seemed to make sense to her.

"Yes, I suppose. Because, you see, I've never done this before. In fifteen years I've never been unfaithful to Bob."

The first time I made love to Anne was on the fifteenth floor of the Regency Hotel overlooking Park Avenue.

At first she was shy. Then I stroked her and she drew in her breath sharply and seized hold of me as if she were about to fall. After a moment she began to moan and her head beat back and forth on the pillow. She came quickly in a long shuddering gasp hardly distinguishable from pain.

She lay in my arms and I stroked her face and she moved against me again. She had small breasts like upturned thumbs and when I caressed them she commenced again to moan. She opened her legs wide and I caressed her and then I entered her, and she wrapped her legs around me and locked her feet in the small of my back. Now she was moving under me. She pressed up against me, crying out, and we came together in one long desperate moment as if we were falling locked together like that.

"My God," she said. It was another of her matter-of-fact statements. She lay on her back and pressed my hand against her small breasts. "Do you always do that?"

"Do what?"

"Do you always make love like that? You're very good at it."

"*You're* very good."

"No, I'm not good. I'm just hungry."

And it was true, there was a hunger in Anne—a hunger that belied her cool exterior. Sometimes later when we were in public together, I would marvel at the contrast between the tall aristocratic woman with the short blond hair and prominent nose and the hooded blue eyes who seemed to draw back slightly when being introduced to a stranger and the passionate woman who wrapped her legs around me and cried out in the heat of love. Perhaps it was this contrast that drove me on.

Annette bought tickets for *Les Misérables*. It had just opened and already everyone was touting it as the great new Broadway musical.

"I'm curious," Annette said, as if to indicate she was above such manifestations of popular enthusiasm but owed it to her anthropological interests to investigate such phenomena. "I'm curious to see what it's all about."

"I'm not," I said to Barbara in the privacy of our study. She had just informed me of the event.

"Well, we've got to go. I wish you'd try to be a better sport about my sister."

"I'm a fine sport about your sister. Did I complain when you flew down to Pennsylvania for the fifteenth time? It's just *Les Misérables* that I'm not a fine sport about." Broadway musicals bored me.

"It will be okay."

"Like hell it will."

"Well, I'm asking you to come—and I'm asking you to be pleasant about it. Is that so much to request?"

"Oh, of course I'll come, Barbara. And of course I'll be pleasant. When am I ever not pleasant?"

We dined at Sardi's, where we hadn't eaten in years, though clearly the Phillipses ate there regularly. We sat at a front table under a cartoon of Elizabeth Taylor by Al Hirschfeld and I ordered duck with green grapes.

"I expect this will be a very boring evening," Charles Phillips observed. He was a phlegmatic banker of great self-importance who, like many of his peers, had taken to affecting braces.

"Why do you say that, old bean? I think it will be great."

"Do you?" He looked at me quizzically, as if to determine whether I was pulling his leg.

"Of course I do. Don't you know this took all London by storm?"

"By hurricane, no doubt."

"Oh, I think it will be fascinating," Annette said, looking around excitedly. "I loved *Les Misérables* when I read it in high school—and I'm sure David did too. I'm sure we'll see eye to eye on this, David."

In fact the performance was great stupid fun, full of energy and noise. I sat in the second row, between Barbara and Annette, and Annette took my arm. She was really a sweet needy girl who deserved better than the stuffed shirt Charles Phillips.

Just before the lights went down Annette said to me, "Isn't that Peter O'Toole sitting in the front row?"

I looked and saw a phthisic, dried-out-looking man the color of an old orange chamois cloth slouched in his seat next to a stunning dark-skinned woman half his age aglitter with diamonds. He looked more like Death than like Peter O'Toole, though after a moment I recognized he was indeed the formidable actor.

It shocked me to see Lawrence of Arabia looking like a dried tobacco leaf.

"My God," I said. "He must be dead of dysentery."

"Barbara!" Annette hissed, leaning across me. "Barbara, it's PETER O'TOOLE!"

"Where?" Barbara said, and the two women's faces turned in unison like figures on a cuckoo clock.

As the lights went down Annette clutched at my arm as if to say, I *told* you this would be some evening!

At intermission the sisters sprang up to indulge in O'Toole gazing while Phillips and I wandered back through the crowd to get a drink.

"Well, what do you think?" I asked.

"A little loud, wouldn't you say?"

"It's *supposed* to be loud. That's the whole point."

"Isn't that like saying it's supposed to be boring?"

Well, what do you know, Charles Phillips had committed a witticism!

Waiting at the bar among the surging crowd of theatergoers, I turned and saw—Anne Stokowski. She was standing with her husband in the midst of a group of people, and she created about her a calm, as the moon creates a calm among windy trees.

She hadn't seen me, and as she leaned back listening to the others her laughter was no more than a smile. She was as tall as the men and she wore at her throat a brooch of diamonds while her blond hair shimmered in the light.

Bob Stokowski was a well-knit, medium-size man of dark features and hawklike nose. He was a famous man by now—I had seen him before, in the papers—immensely rich, a former member of the Reagan administration who had left to run one of the great stock emporia in the city. With his dark lively intelligent eyes he was clearly the center of his little group; and as he spoke he touched Anne on the elbow from time to time as if to establish proprietorship.

Anne's figure was hardly visible beneath her evening dress, but I could imagine the small of her back, the flare of her hips, the flatness of her stomach, the upturn of her small hungry breasts. She regarded her companions through blue hooded distant eyes, and when Stokowski touched her she drew back instinctively, as from a draft of unwanted air.

The lights went on and off in the lobby.

"I'm going back to the girls," Charles Phillips said to me.

"That's fine."

As Anne preceded me, I kept my eyes fixed on the small of her back, as if something of great value were centered there that I alone could discern.

During the second act I knew Anne was somewhere behind me and I couldn't concentrate on the stage. It was as if I could feel her eyes on me. I kept picturing the way she had appeared standing with her friends and then as I knew her in the moments of our intimacy, her knees tucked up to her ears and her small mouth biting mine.

At the conclusion of the play everyone started clapping loudly and Annette sat up and started clapping too. Her clapping caused a strange painful echoing in my ears, as if even this about her was excessive and out of balance. Then the lights went on and everyone stood up and started milling about.

"Do you think we should go and say hello to him?" Annette asked Barbara. They were still O'Tooleing.

"Let's leave the poor man alone," Barbara said. "I don't think he looks very well."

I offered to get the coats.

There was a great press in the aisles as people filed slowly toward the back of the theater. I kept looking for Anne Stokowski, though I wasn't certain whether I wanted to see her.

"I thought it was *mar*velous," a woman in front of me exclaimed. "Simply *mar*velous."

For a while I couldn't see anything but the backs of people's heads. A great crowd eddied about the cloakroom, where men and women pushed and jostled one another as they waited for their coats. Then I saw Anne leaning against a wall with her back to me. She looked very graceful like that, and with her dress pulled taut, I could see the curve of her body.

I went up behind her and touched her in the small of her back.

She turned swiftly, her mouth half open as if in exclamation; but when she saw me her eyes opened wide and I saw fear and pleasure.

"David!"

My hand slipped further down her back until it was on her rump, and then I patted her, and then I turned and, swiftly, I left.

On a Saturday Anne and I drove to Long Island to watch our children play high school athletics. It was a blustery day with autumn clouds scudding across the flawless blue sky, and when we got out of the car I could see the girls clustered on the playing field, running and shouting, while parents congregated in a knot along the sidelines.

I had no idea where we were.

Anne departed to watch her son Ben play football and I walked toward the girls' hockey field and the parents who seemed to represent our school. So far as I could tell I didn't know any of them. Then I saw Jenny and waved.

My Jenny was a demon at field hockey, the captain of the junior varsity team, and had expressed complete indifference to my presence at the game. Nonetheless, I could detect her pleasure when she saw me. She kept throwing glances toward me and then tossing her head with feigned nonchalance.

Dressed in kilts and jerseys, the girls looked like long-legged colts as they ran and called to one another, their hair and skirts whipping in the wind. The wind tasted of copper in the autumn air and from this distance it carried the girls' voices but not their words as it gusted and fell.

The referee started the game with a blast of his whistle and the girls ran down the field hitting the ball. I couldn't tell which one was Jenny. Then I saw her on the far side of the field and my heart gave a sudden lurch as when a car leaps forward when left in gear.

A small group of adults huddled along the sideline. As I approached I was surprised to recognize Leslie Salt, a woman I had known in young adulthood, when she was a beauty. For a while she had been engaged to Michael Daniel, one of my Yale friends, but she had declined to marry him on the grounds that he was insufficiently devoted to the acquisition of money. Instead she had married a sweet nebbishy guy from Brown. For a while we had seen a bit of Leslie and Walt, until Barbara, refusing to be bored further, put her foot down. Since then Walt and Leslie had separated and I heard she was engaged to a TV producer.

"Well, hel-*lo,* David!" I had forgotten how Leslie leaned backward when greeting you, her green eyes growing larger with feigned excitement. In the sharp light it pained me to observe that there were now crow's-feet at the corners of her eyes.

"Hello, Leslie."

"I was *won*dering whether you and Barbara would be here. You know, Sara tells me *all* about Jenny." And she offered me a significant look by way of tentative humorous commiseration.

"Yes, that's right, Sara must be on the team too."

"Yes, there she is. The lumpish one. Do you see? She's not a beauty like your Jenny."

She pointed across the field and I made out a heavy-legged girl with dirty-blond hair who seemed even at this distance to radiate a kind of stolid ill humor.

"But where is Barbara?" Leslie inquired.

"Oh, she's with the boys. We split up the parental duties. I came by myself."

"Oh, what a shame. I'd so love to see Barbara. Let me introduce you to Jerry, my significant other." She wrinkled her nose to indicate her disdain for the plebeian phrase.

Jerry, who had been standing idly by, now put out his hand in a firm manly sort of way. Leslie seemed to have a predilection for nondescript men.

I shook Jerry's hand.

"We'd *so* love to get together with you," Leslie said. "It's been ages."

"Yes, that would be great," I lied. I became aware of Anne standing by the sideline about fifty feet away and I wanted to go over and take her arm.

"Can I call Barbara? Would she mind?"

"Of course not. Why should she mind?"

"Oh, I don't know. People act so strange after a divorce, that's all. Sometimes it gets a little . . . lonely. Is that silly?"

"Of course you should call," I said. "Barbara would love to hear from you."

"Who was that?" Anne asked when I was standing as close to her as I dared, staring out at the playing field, where the girls were maneuvering up and down like sailboats driven before the wind.

"An old acquaintance. I had no idea she'd be here."

"One of your old girlfriends?"

"No, don't be silly. Just someone we used to know."

"I don't care, David. I wouldn't blame her. I wouldn't blame any girl."

"Is that how it is?"

"Yes, that's how it is—very much so."

"I want to kiss you."

"You can't kiss me now."

"Yes, I know that. We'll get out of here as soon as the game is over."

At halftime I sought out Jenny to tell her I was leaving. She was sitting with the other girls at the end of the field listening to the coach, but when she saw me she jumped up and ran to meet me. Then, remembering her dignity, she slowed to a walk.

"Gee, Dad," she exclaimed. "At least you could stick around to drive me home!"

"I thought you'd want to go home in the bus with the other kids."

"Why should I want to do that? What gave you that idea? Would *you* like to go home on the bus with all those creeps?"

"Come on, Jenny."

"Well, would you?"

"That's not the point. You're supposed to be the *captain*."

"Yeah, yeah, yeah."

"You *wanted* to be the captain, Jenny. Don't you remember? It was between you and Beth Larkin."

"The cow."

"See? So there you have it. You made your bed and now—"

"Yes, yes, yes. Another piece of profundity from the pater." And then quickly, appeasingly, she pecked me on the cheek.

I drove fast in the Mercedes with Anne beside me. I loved the feel of the car, with its large slick motor and its well-appointed interior, and when we reached the Long Island Expressway I turned east toward the tip of the island. I was taking Anne to see the ocean.

But somehow we got lost. I took a wrong turn and then another and finally we emerged into a small community of lower-middle-class houses painted white and all as identical as shoeboxes. Ultimately we discovered a kind of dirty cove where the water lapped like coffee grinds against the blackened sand.

When we got out of the car the wind tasted of chemicals.

"At least we have it to ourselves," Anne said.

The sand was brackish and striated with twisted strands of kelp, and I could detect the traces of teenage love trysts: empty bottles of beer, sodden pieces of charred wood, an old condom, and, crumpled and blanched almost white, a pair of discarded pink panties.

Across the bay a factory winked blankly in the afternoon sun.

"I always wanted to live by the sea," Anne exclaimed. "Even as a child I thought how wonderful it would be to live by the ocean and watch it change with the seasons. I've seen sharks and whales off the shore right here on Long Island."

"Really."

"Yes. Once when I was with my father out in his sailboat we followed a school of whales for about an hour. It was thrilling. I've never forgotten."

"Why don't you get Bob to buy you a house by the ocean?"

"Bob? Bob doesn't care about the ocean—unless perhaps it

were to buy a fleet of tankers. If Bob were to buy a place by the ocean it would be a mansion on Martha's Vineyard where he could invite State Department officials for cocktails . . . Oh, David, sometimes I feel I can't stand it any longer! Why don't we run away together someplace? Can't we run away to—Darjeeling?"

"Darjeeling?"

"Yes! Where is Darjeeling, anyway?"

"Darjeeling? Damned if I know. I thought Darjeeling was a kind of tea."

"Oh, David—don't be silly."

"Well, I don't quite see how we can run away to Darjeeling. *This* will have to be our Darjeeling."

"I thought this was New Jersey."

"No, darling. This is condom heaven."

"Well, kiss me in condom heaven."

I leaned over and kissed her and felt her small tongue lick at my mouth.

"How'd you get to be such a randy lady?"

"You made me that way. I was never that way before. You see what you've done? I want you to make love to me now."

"Here, in teenager heaven?"

"No, not here. Come with me."

When we got to the car she leaned against the door and I kissed her hard on the mouth. There was nobody around and I put my hand on her.

"Please do more of that," she said.

After a while she said, "I'm going to fall down. Let's get into the car."

But before we entered she bent down, and swiftly, with easy grace, she removed her panties.

I would meet Anne in the afternoon for a drink or to visit a gallery, and there was invariably something cool and collected about her that pleased me. She dressed with taste and elegance, unostentatiously but expensively, like a beautiful woman who had never been without money. Sometimes, however, the inevitable string of pearls, the small exquisite diamond, the tailored clothing from Bergdorf or Saks, got on my nerves.

But we never argued; diplomatists of accommodation, we skirted those subjects that might cause a row, and so about many things we never knew what the other really thought. I never knew what she really thought about her husband, of whom she remained in some ways proud and protective.

"Bob thinks the boys should be sent to boarding school," she told me.

"Oh? Are you having trouble with them?"

"No, not at all. But he thinks it's good training—good for their character. And then they'll have the opportunity to meet so many boys from their own class."

"Class?"

"Well, you know what I mean—background. Bob never had those opportunities."

"It doesn't seem to have done him any harm."

"Well, it's only natural that he should want to give his boys the advantages he never had."

"I thought you said he didn't pay any attention to them."

"Well, all the more reason for him to want to do well by them like this, don't you think?"

"I don't know what I think. What do *you* think? Won't you miss them when they're away?"

"Oh, I'll miss them horribly. I can't stand to think about it."

"Then why do it? Why send them away?"

"I don't know, it's just an idea Bob had. Let's not talk about it anymore. Bob will have to make up his mind what he wants to do."

I let it go at that; there was no point in pushing the matter. Later she mentioned in passing that both boys had been enrolled at Exeter.

Then later she told me she was accompanying Bob to Washington to attend an economic convention given by the President.

"You don't have to apologize," I said.

"I'm not apologizing. Bob asked me to go and I don't see how I can refuse. We used to go to these things together all the time.

When we were living in Washington it was an endless round of such affairs. I couldn't stand it. You can't imagine how mindless they are—at least for the wives. Standing about in large hotel rooms holding a highball in your hand while the men talk to each other about the gross national product of Venezuela."

"It sounds pretty ghastly."

"Oh, it is. Ghastly is the word. Still, if Bob asks me I can't say no. I owe it to him as his wife."

As Anne had said, I had caught her at a vulnerable moment when she had been unhorsed in the great tournament of life, and she remained thankful to me for having picked her up.

"What do you see in me?" I asked her once, curious to know what she would reply.

"Oh—I like the way you look!" She laughed. "No, seriously," she said. "You bring me things. Bob doesn't bring me things anymore."

"*Bring* you things? What do I bring you?"

"Oh, I don't know. All sorts of things. Let's see. You bring me knowledge and insight and experience and excitement. We can talk about all sorts of things together. We can *do* all sorts of things together. We can go to the art galleries. We can do all the things we do in bed."

"Didn't you do those things with Bob?"

"Oh, I don't know. Maybe long ago—I can't remember. But not the way we do. That's something you've given me."

And in bed Anne's beautiful hooded eyes would half close and her eyeballs would roll up into her head. In bed she would start to come as soon as I touched her breasts. In bed she would hold my head between her legs and groan until it was almost a scream.

Christmas arrived and the kids were out of school and the house was filled with tumult and fragrance. Barbara was preoccupied with the holiday, organizing the shopping, wrapping the presents, preparing for the Christmas meal. I took the twins to buy the Christmas tree and we set it up in the living room and put on Christmas music and we all decorated it together. Later, when everyone was in bed, I went into the living room and put out the lights except for the Christmas lights and sat in the big chair drinking whiskey and watching the colored lights play against the wall.

Anne was away with her family skiing in Europe and for a while it was as if she didn't exist. I was very happy. We called Warren and Karin on Christmas day, and we called my mother in Santa Fe, where she now lived. The Grottons and the Phillipses came for Christmas dinner and we drank champagne punch and after dinner Annette played the piano while the children sang Christmas carols.

"We shouldn't forget that today is the birthday of baby Jesus," Alexandra, my eleven-year-old, said.

"No, darling, we haven't forgotten."

"Are you sure, Daddy? Are you sure we haven't forgotten?"

"I'm sure, darling, *I* haven't forgotten. But it's nice that you reminded us anyway."

It was past one before everyone left and then Barbara and I cleaned up the kitchen together.

"You know, I could find it in my heart to be glad that Christmas is over," she said.

"Don't say that, darling."

"Well, it's just so much work. Do you think it's worth it?"

"Of course it's worth it! The children love it, we all love it—and it's all thanks to you."

"You can say that again!"

"I do! Do you think I don't know that? You're just tired."

"I am tired. But it was fun, wasn't it?"

"It was wonderful. It's the best time of year."

At two o'clock Barbara sat at the edge of our bed brushing her luxuriant hair. She was in her negligee now and she looked tired but relaxed. She turned to me and smiled.

"Show me that you love me, Charlie Brown."

I showed her.

* * *

After Christmas Barbara was occupied with finding a new camp for the boys. Through her extensive network she had discovered a number of possibilities, including some that were rather recherché: an adventure camp where the kids bushwhacked through the rain forests of Zaire, a wilderness camp where the children lived solo for two weeks off the fruit of the land, a boating camp where they kayaked to Newfoundland.

She finally settled on a sports camp, and a few days after Christmas the owner, a Mr. Thomas Mixer, arrived to show us slides. Thomas Mixer sported a cowboy hat and tooled leather boots and when Mat called him Mr. Mixer he rubbed the boy's hair with excessive zeal and insisted on being called Uncle Tommy.

"Wonderful lads, wonderful lads," Uncle Tommy exclaimed, turning to Barbara, who visibly softened under such suasion. "Just the kind of boys we want at Iquopoowo. What's your name, sonny?"

"I'm Timmy."

"Well, Timmy, I'm Tommy!" And he laughed boisterously until everyone joined in bewildered unison.

The promotional demonstration included color brochures and elaborate slides that depicted small kids hiking up the sides of mountains or playing tournament tennis or riding large horses or sailing swift sailboats through the blue waters of Vermont. Timmy and Mat were enthusiastic, especially about the tennis and baseball programs, and Barbara, who kept leaning forward to punctuate Uncle Tommy's presentation with excited oohs and ahs, was clearly captivated by the multidimensional possibilities of Camp Iquopoowo.

"Oh, can we go, Daddy? Can we go?"

"Please, Daddy, *please!*"

"Whatever your mom says, kids. It's up to her."

"Are you sure you don't want to look at a few more camps?" Barbara asked for propriety's sake.

"No, Mommy, no. This is just *perfect.*"

"All right, then," Barbara said, smiling broadly. "Camp Iquopoowo it will be."

* * *

That was Christmas vacation. Then Anne came back and I started seeing her again and then my life was again divided. I was less happy now than I had been when Anne was away, but despite my unhappiness I didn't or I couldn't stop.

One afternoon Anne accompanied me to a wine tasting at the Hilton on Sixth Avenue. I attended many of these functions but I had never taken Anne before. We stopped at the Dorset for a drink before the party.

Anne was dressed that afternoon in a purple suit with a pale lemon blouse that heightened the color of her hair, and her long shapely legs showed to good effect in her expensive high-heeled shoes. She ordered a Campari and soda.

"I shouldn't be going with you," she said.

"Why not?"

"It's too public. If we become careless . . ."

"What?"

"I don't know. It's just not smart."

"I never said I was so smart."

"What is it you see in me?" she asked, almost exasperated. "I've never understood why you came swooping down like that and picked me out of the blue."

"Oh, that's easy. I see the length of your skillful fingers. I see the elegance of your stylish mind. I see the ironic humor of your laugh. I see the improbable luck of our being together having a drink here in this marvelous city while under your expensive clothing there awaits the high adventure of your body."

"Don't talk that way."

"Why not?"

"Because it makes me want you. It makes me ache."

"Should we go upstairs?"

"Don't be stupid. I thought you had to go to this party."

"I do, alas. It's a bore, but it can't be helped. But I'll tell you what I want you to do. Go to the ladies' room and take off your panties."

"What do you mean?"

"Just what I said. Take off your panties. I want you to go to the party without panties."

"You're mad."

"So what? You already know I'm mad. I want you to go to this party without panties."

She gave a snort of laughter.

"Does that excite you?"

"Yes. Yes, it does. Thinking about it now excites me. Here, put your hand under the table."

"You really are crazy." She laughed. She pushed back from the table.

"Where are you going?"

"To the ladies' room, of course." She looked at me and smiled.

Whenever I looked at Anne during the party my blood raced. From across the room I observed the thin tapering of her waist and the unimpeded grace of her thighs and buttocks. Once our eyes met and Anne's face colored deeply.

"It's going to be a good year for the Bordeaux," one of the distributors said. "I'm stocking up on the petits Graves, which are as good as the expensive stuff and much easier to sell."

"That's a mistake in my market. My people want quality and they'll pay the extra bucks to get it."

"It doesn't make any difference what you stock from France, its day is over. Mark my words, California will push everything else off the shelves."

"Never."

"Just mark my words. You heard it first from me."

Impulsively I crossed the room to where Anne was standing.

"Come with me."

"No."

"Why not?"

"Because I don't trust you. I don't trust that look in your eye."

"Just come with me."

"Where are we going?"

"I don't know. Just come!"

I led her out of the party.

"You really are crazy."

"I know. Just follow me."

We took the elevator to the sixth floor. I had no idea where I was going. I followed the corridor until we came to a door that said ROOM SERVICE. The room contained two carts piled with fresh towels, small bars of soap, and other bathroom accessories. In one corner stood a hamper for dirty towels.

I touched her breasts through her blouse. I kissed her neck. She closed her eyes, raised her chin, and now she was breathing heavily.

"David!"

Someone passed in the corridor; then there was silence.

I reached under her suit and touched her where she was without panties.

"David!" This time it was only a whisper.

"Lift up your skirt."

"Not here."

"Lift up your skirt!"

She lifted her skirt and the skirt bunched about her waist. She was naked now from the waist down except for the high-heeled expensive shoes.

"David, David—this is crazy."

I thought I heard someone in the corridor. Then I no longer heard anything—not even the sharp intake of her breath.

Later I found the dark welts where her nails had bitten my shoulder.

One day Anne said to me, "I don't see how this can go on."

It was April and we had been seeing each other since October.

"Why not?" Her words didn't surprise me.

"Because it's no good for anyone. It's not good for you, it's not good for the children . . . It's tearing me apart."

"What's wrong with the children?"

"It's what's wrong with *me*. I feel split in two. I'm no longer a whole person. I'm angry at Bob—and I'm guilty about him. I'm angry at you. I'm angry at myself."

"Should we stop seeing each other?"

"I don't know."

We tried not seeing each other and I too felt better. But then the restlessness started again; I called her, she called me; we saw each other for a drink; we made love.

We frequented a small hotel on the East Side where the proprietors had come to recognize us and where they treated us with restrained ironic humor, as if we were a private joke they had contrived for their own amusement. At first we were a part of the joke, but after a time their discreet officious humor became a bore.

"I hate this place," Anne said. "It's something out of a stupid French farce. We should have gone to one of those large towering antiseptic places where you can walk in and out and no one is any the wiser."

"Would you have liked that better?"

"Oh, I don't know. That would have been horrible also."

"You're in a fine mood."

"Oh, I'm sorry. I'm sorry I'm sorry I'm sorry. Just make love to me, all right? I'm fine when you make love to me."

A number of times Anne couldn't meet me because of obligations with Bob—parties, meetings, another conference out of town. There was a story about him in the *Wall Street Journal* and a party given in his honor at the Waldorf and Anne was afraid she would cause a scandal and damage his career.

"I've done him enough harm without appearing on page six of the *Post.*" She said this with a frown though the idea made her laugh.

"What harm have you done him?"

"Don't you call this harm?"

"Who's to say? Does he know about it?"

"Of course not. He doesn't care enough to notice."

"So who has harmed whom?"

"You're a Jesuit, David—but I know what I mean."

Then she left for a week to attend the flower show in London, a yearly ritual, and then Bob met her there for a few days at the end of the show.

"He has a conference," she explained to me. "He wouldn't come to London just for me—not anymore."

"More's the pity for Bob."

"Bob's not like you," she said. "Bob's life is making money." She didn't say it with special disapproval, just matter-of-factly, the way you might observe that someone was a Dutchman rather than French.

When she came back she seemed distant and we didn't see each other until mid-week. We had drinks at the St. Regis and she wore a large-brimmed straw hat she had bought in London, very English and becoming but nothing I would have imagined on my woman.

We talked politely about London and the flower show and about her children, and with her haughty beauty and with the tentative hidden gentleness that lay underneath, it was easy to remember why I admired her.

"I missed you," I said.

"I missed you too."

"Did you? I thought you had forgotten me."

She offered her little ironic laugh. "I could never forget you, David."

"Well, I thought maybe you had."

"No, it's not that."

"What is it, then?"

"You know."

"Yes, I suppose I do. So I don't suppose you want to go upstairs."

"Did you book a room?"

"Of course I did. Didn't you know I would?"

She hesitated before answering. "Of course I knew, David. Why are you such a bad boy?"

"Is that what I am? Am I a bad boy?"

"Yes—yes and no." And I could follow the blush that I knew so well as it traveled down her neck.

Later, when we were upstairs, I made her wear her hat when she was in bed; and if she looked good before, she was unforgettable like that.

*   *   *

That spring Gordo became engaged to a society girl named Pamela Stokes. Pamela was fifteen years younger than Gordo and I heard much about how rich and beautiful she was and how she played tennis and vacationed at Palm Beach and how her father was a wealthy industrialist with a large house in the Hamptons.

Barbara and I went out with Pamela and Gordo to celebrate the engagement. Pamela was a large bouncy girl with a red strapless evening dress that offered her shapely shoulders and the tops of her shapely breasts. Her young flesh was firm and rich-colored and she revealed it with accustomed ease.

Gordo had made a reservation at Ondine's, the in place of the moment, but when we arrived our table wasn't ready and we had to wait for twenty minutes at the crowded bar.

"I don't see why they can't seat us," Pamela said. "Gordon, did you remember to make a reservation?"

"Of course I made a reservation."

"Well, what name did you use?"

Gordo looked at her but didn't reply.

"Well, did you use my father's name?"

"Of course I didn't use your father's name."

"You didn't? Didn't I tell you to use my father's name?"

"Come on, kids," Barbara said. "Let's have another drink."

"I don't want another drink," Pamela said. "I think this is disgraceful. I'm going to speak with the maitre d'."

"Why don't you just stay where you are," Gordo said.

"Here," I said. "I'll get some drinks."

I waved my hand but I couldn't attract the bartender's attention. We were crowded at one end of the bar, and since there weren't enough chairs for us to sit on, I was standing above the ample descent of Pamela.

The truth was that I too was becoming annoyed. I hated places like this, with their chichi in crowd and their flashy noisy vulgarity, precisely as elegant as an expensive hotel lobby; and I hated being ignored by slick-haired young bartenders biding time between nonexistent acting jobs. I started down the bar to see if I could negotiate the fellow's attention.

In my passage I inadvertently bumped against a square-jawed red-faced man dressed in expensive evening clothes.

"Hey, just wait your turn, buddy."

He stared at me with bleary, hostile intent.

"Sorry about that. You'll get your soda water."

"You being funny?"

"What do you want, Hank?" his girl said sharply.

At that moment the bartender appeared. Hank turned his back but he kept hunching his shoulder in some atavistic minatory gesture like the pawing of a water buffalo. I gave my order behind Hank's glowing linebacker neck.

When I returned to our seats Pamela had disappeared and Barbara was speaking to Gordo in a low earnest voice.

"Where is Pamela?"

"She went to speak to the owner."

"Ah! Well, who can tell—maybe she'll get results."

"She's more likely to get us thrown out," Gordo said.

"I'd like to see them try."

"Would you two men stop acting like children?" Barbara said. "Did we go out to fight or to have a good time? Let's just go somewhere else. David, what's the name of that little Italian place on Second Avenue? You know the one."

"No I don't."

The drinks arrived and I downed the whiskey in a gulp, standing behind Barbara.

"I don't want you to drink too much of that stuff," she said.

"Please don't tell me what to do."

"Please don't act like an ass."

Pamela returned and I could see she was in a fluster.

"I've never been so insulted in my life!"

"What did you say?" I asked.

"Never been so insulted!"

"Isn't that a line from a movie?"

Barbara hit me hard in the thigh.

"What did I tell you?" Gordo said, starting to laugh. "What did I tell you? Well, did you use your *father's name?*"

"Let's get out of here," Barbara said.

Much later we found ourselves in the Italian restaurant on Second Avenue, with its soiled checked tablecloths and its plastic vine leaves, and we had been drinking much red wine. Barbara was looking disgusted.

"I wanted to be a tap dancer," Pamela said. "I always wanted to be a tap dancer."

"A tap dancer?"

"Yes, a tap dancer. What's wrong with that? What's wrong with being a tap dancer?" She turned to me. "Gordon is always trying to put me down. Whatever I do, he is always trying to make me look stupid. Aren't you, Gordon? Aren't you always trying to make me look stupid?"

"You don't need me for that," he said.

"That's right," Pamela said. "That's not what I need you for. I need you to *love* me."

"Why don't you kids tell us about the wedding?" Barbara suggested.

"It's going to be a June wedding," Pamela said.

"It's going to cost her old man one hundred grand. Isn't that right, Pam? Isn't that what you told me? That it would cost your father one hundred grand?"

"I don't think it's in good taste to talk about money," Pamela said with dignity.

"No? Well, we won't talk about money then. But isn't that what you told me? That the wedding will cost one hundred grand?"

"Something like that, I suppose."

"You suppose, nothing. He's inviting his entire law firm. The old woman is inviting the entire Episcopal church. Isn't that right, Pamela?"

"I think it's very exciting," Barbara said.

Pamela turned to Barbara and gave her a stony stare.

"You don't have to condescend to me," she said.

"What are you talking about?" Gordo said. He sounded genuinely shocked. "Barbara is not condescending to you."

"Oh yes she is. You think I'm so stupid, but I'm not. I know when someone is condescending to me. She thinks she has to humor me. She thinks I'm some sort of a child. But I'm not."

I looked at Pamela and I saw she was dead drunk. She was sitting upright and talking but all the while she was dead drunk.

"Barbara is not *humoring* you," Gordo said. "That's called being nice. That's called being considerate. It's something you wouldn't know anything about."

"That's all right," Barbara said, but I could hear she was hurt. "I think it's time we all went home."

"You see?" Pamela said. "You see what I mean?"

"Oh, shut up," Gordo said.

In the taxi going home I said to Barbara, "Why in hell is he marrying her?"

Barbara was sitting very straight at the other side of the cab.

"Maybe she will make him a fine wife," she said after a moment. I recognized the tone of voice: she was being "fair."

"A fine wife? What are you talking about?"

"She has very nice shoulders," she said. "They will have a fine time together in bed. She's very rich. They come from the same background. They both like to drink. He can play around a little, she can play around a little, it won't be a big deal. They can fight and make up, it's a way to pass time."

"You've thought it all out," I said.

"He won't have to pay her much attention," Barbara said. "Have you ever thought that Gordon doesn't *want* to pay anyone much attention? He wants to be left alone? . . . In truth, Gordon shouldn't marry anyone. It's unfair to the girl. She'll just drink herself to death."

"So now you're worrying about *her?*"

Barbara gave an involuntary shudder.

"Ugh," she said. "She was *horrible.*"

"What are you laughing about?" she said after a moment. "You weren't so great yourself."

"Me?"

"Yes, little ol' you. If you don't watch out you're going to turn into a drunk."

"No, I'll never turn into a drunk."

"Well, sometimes I worry about you. Sometimes it's not easy to tell the difference between you and any horse in the stable."

"You didn't think that once."

"Once was once."

"Oh yeah?"

"I'm not going to fight with you," she said. "There has been quite enough fighting for one evening." And she turned her back and stared out the taxi window.

At the end of May one of our suppliers gave a party on a pleasure boat in New York Harbor, and since Anne and I were seeing each other again, I asked her to come. Though she didn't at first want to join me, I insisted and finally she agreed.

It was a sticky heavy evening and the sounds of New York billowed in the heat as we rattled downtown in a taxi. Anne's hair was held in a ribbon and her blue silk suit accentuated the cool blueness of her eyes. I was very worked up and kept touching Anne's knee and then peering out the window at the whizzing city. With its immense breathing life Manhattan seemed to me sinister and marvelous, an endless shifting phantasmagoria like some fantastic movie run at the wrong speed. To participate in its brilliant *louche* life seemed to me the very essence of being alive.

A great milling crowd waited at the pier, part glitterati, part hoodlum. There were lots of pretty women, some dressed in elegant black silk evening dresses, some in designer jeans. I didn't recognize anyone. I took Anne's elbow as we ascended the gangplank.

"I shouldn't have come."

"Why not? Aren't you having a good time?"

"Oh, David, that's not the point. People will know us here."

"I don't care. I don't give a damn."

"Yes you do. You know you do. And what about me? Bob is a well-known man."

"If that's all you're worried about, relax. Not in this crowd he's not. Imelda Marcos is the only public figure anyone in this crowd ever heard of."

I kissed her impulsively on the neck.

"So, Davey, glad you could make it."

It was our host, Charlie Krumpf, sweating profusely, the folds of his neck protruding over the starched collar of his tailored shirt, his rings glistening in the yellow electric light of the deck like gold fillings.

"Hi, Charlie. Good to see you."

"And who's this? Introduce me to your enchanting guest."

"This is Anne Stokowski, an old friend and investor. Anne, meet Charlie Krumpf."

Anne smiled and put out her hand and leaned backward as if from a piece of malodorous cheese.

"Good t' meet you, Anne. You make this guy show you a good time, y' hear?"

"Who was *that?*" Anne asked when we had moved away.

"Some liquor distributor. Some nouveau riche thug. One of my partner's playfellows. A new Croesus of the Reagan era."

She gave a snort of laughter. "Where in the world have you brought me now?"

"See, I told you. No one here is going to know Bob Stokowski."

We went to the railing and I leaned over and stared into the brown swirling water. The boat was still docked and the water eddied against its side in turbulent whirlpools the color of muddy coffee. The river looked sluggish and powerful, as heavy as mercury, and I remembered a story I had read in the *Times* about a man drowning in its lethargic shrug.

Anne leaned against the brass railing and I moved my hand so it rested against her rump.

"You're high on this," she said.

"Why shouldn't I be? It's great being here like this."

"No it's not, David. We shouldn't have come. We shouldn't even be seeing each other."

"Let's not start all that again. I'll get you a drink."

"Yes. You'd better make it a double."

I looked back and saw her standing by the railing looking isolated and haughty and very beautiful.

The bar was crowded. Through a window I could see down a side street into Manhattan and it seemed weird to be standing on a boat in the middle of the city. I wanted to share my excitement with someone but I didn't know anyone there.

"An Absolut on the rocks and a Black Label and soda," I said to the bartender. He was dressed in a white jacket and appeared to be another actor out of a job. "Make them doubles," I said.

Just then I felt the boat lurch and we pulled away from the pier.

"Hey, isn't that Lauren Hutton?"

A young man standing next to me addressed me excitedly. He was a handsome young man sweating copiously in the heat, and his eyes were lit up with confused anticipation, as if someone had hit him on the back of the head and stood him up again too quickly. He wore a double-breasted blue sports jacket with polished brass buttons and affected the general appearance of an advertisement in *Vanity Fair.*

"Where?"

"There. Over there. The one in green."

"I dunno. Could be."

"Yeah, I'm sure it is."

I looked again. I didn't think it was Lauren Hutton, though the woman did indeed look like her, but I didn't say anything.

"Hey, listen," the young man said. "Can I get you a drink?" He smiled insistently and I noticed a trickle of perspiration that started at his temple and traversed the length of his face, pale and sinuous as a river seen from the height of an airplane.

"I just got a drink. I have to take this back to my companion. She's waiting on deck."

"Well, maybe we could have a drink later. I don't really know anyone on board, you see. I don't know why I was invited."

"That's true for many of us." I laughed. "I'll be on the port side by the railing. Why don't you look for me in a little while?"

"Fabulous! Hey, listen, my name is Terry White."

"Great to meet you, Terry. Let's have a drink later."

I threaded my way back to the deck. Outside, the air, heavy

and unbreathable, smelled of perfume and bilge. The black water glittered with reflected light.

Anne still stood by the railing where I had left her.

"Where have you been? I thought you'd gotten lost."

"I was waylaid by Terry White, who wanted to show me all the pretty landmarks. Here, bottoms up."

"Who in the name of God is Terry White?"

"I dunno. Some kid I met at the bar. He kept pointing out celebrities so I invited him to have a drink with us."

"Very ingenious. You're as high as a kite, David."

By the time we were past the Statue of Liberty we were both a bit to windward and Anne had relented sufficiently for me to take her hand. It was a cloudy night, suffused with the phosphorescent glitter of the city, and music floated up to us from the lower deck.

Charlie Krumpf found us at about ten o'clock.

"So how's the boy, Davey? You having a good time?"

"Just fine, Charles, just fine. Nifty little boat you've got."

"You like it, huh? Well, she's all yours, Davey. All yours and my other friends'. But tell me, where's Gordo? Why don't I see Gordo here tonight?"

"Gordon couldn't make it, Charles. He sends his regrets. I'm here instead. You'll just have to put up with second best."

"Second best? Don't talk that way! Naw, it's just I thought you looked after the fine spirits and Gordo looked after the rougher trade."

"Well, it does sort of work out that way, but really we're inter-changeable commodities. Partners, the greatest word in the French language!"

"How's that?"

"Nothing. Pay me no heed, Charles. I'm just being frivolous."

"Yeah? But did Gordon talk to you about this new dealership I told him about?"

"He mentioned it, Charles, but I dunno. *Beaucoup de fric,* eh?" And I rubbed my fingers together under his nose.

"Yeah, whatever you say. But I'm telling you, this could be sweet. You ought to talk to Gordon about it—seriously. It's no business for a joker."

"No, absolutely. Absolutely. That's what I said to Gordo. Gordo, I said, this is no business for a joker. No business at all."

"You're a comedian, that's what. You go back to your lady. I'll deal with Gordo."

"What was that all about?" Anne asked.

"Nothing. I can't stand these liquor hoodlums, that's all."

"You're a snob, David. You just don't like the common man."

"You know, you may be right."

"Of course I'm right. You're hardly American. There should be someplace where you could be reported."

"What about the bar?" I said. "Let's go report me to the bar."

The bar was less crowded now and we stood in the corner of the cabin drinking whiskey and vodka.

"My God!" Anne said. "Look at that strange man over there."

"Which one?"

"That strange one with all the rings. Who in the name of God do you think he is?"

The ship was crowded with the most unlikely characters, part Mafia from the Island, part wine buffs from the city, with a powdering of Hollywood. Anne's guy was middle-aged with a matted toupee, a bottle-green coat, and large gold rings on each finger. He had with him a striking young woman considerably taller than himself, dark-skinned and almond-eyed, wearing spiked high heels.

"He's probably Mafia," I said.

"Mafia? Do you mean really *Mafia?*"

"Well, probably not. Just a punk, a wise guy."

"You do hang out with the funniest crowd."

"Oh, this is more Gordo's crowd than mine. He gets a kick out of these types. He handles them very well."

"I'd like to meet this Gordo."

"Oh, I don't think that would be a good idea. Gordo's kind of a diamond in the rough. Besides, I don't think he'd approve of us."

"Well . . . I don't blame him."

"C'mon, Anne, you're not going to start that again, are you? I mean, Jesus, what ships have my sighs drowned? Not this one, for sure. Not this ship of fools."

"If it's a ship of fools, David, maybe we shouldn't be on it."

"There's no choice about that, Anne. It's the voyage we embarked on. The ship's put out to sea. C'mon, let's have another drink."

Just then Terry White came running over to us.

"They just threw a man overboard, into the water!"

"No, that can't be true."

"Swear to God! They threw a man overboard into the East River."

"Did you see it happen?"

"No, but I heard about it from someone who did."

There was indeed a pushing crowd of people halfway up the deck on the starboard side. People kept craning their necks and looking into the water.

"What do you think we should do?" Terry White asked. His face was drained of color.

"Why don't we have a drink?" I said. "There are enough people up there watching the fireworks. Here, Terr, ol' boy, I want you to meet Anne Stokowski."

Anne and Terry shook hands while I looked on approvingly.

"This is a funny party," Terry White said, shaking his head. "A funny party."

"Really?"

"You know, I don't think that was Lauren Hutton we saw before. But David Bowie is here. I saw him just a while ago in the other cabin."

"David Bowie? No kidding! That's great."

The dance floor on the lower deck slowly filled as people drifted back from the excitement on the starboard side. Dancers jostled up against one another, sweating in the late-night heat. Three scraggly musicians led by a dark, sinister guitarist, an Alain Delon look-alike, beat out a ragtime tune.

When Anne danced her small rump wriggled back and forth in time to the music and her shoulders shimmied. She was a fine dancer and the flush on her face spread downward from her neck and disappeared down her suit. I could feel the heat from her body, and dancing with her now, dizzy with the whiskey and the heat and with the lateness of the hour, I thought again how strange it was to be here with this beautiful distant woman on this pleasure boat under the heavy impenetrable Manhattan night sky—and it seemed to me that all life was like that, strange and dangerous and improbable.

The ship didn't put into berth until after three. The music was slow now with the slow movement of the ship and Anne rested her head in the crook of my neck and uttered small catlike noises. Her face was flushed and the hair at her ears stood out in small golden ringlets like small splashes of water frozen in time. We were almost the last on board.

Then the music ceased and the musicians were putting away their instruments.

"Where can we go?"

"David, you're bad."

"Here, wait here till they go."

"Not here."

"Why not? There's no one here. Let me kiss you."

We stood in the galleyway at the foot of the stairs that led to the upper deck, and no one else was around. I kissed her and I could feel her body press against mine. From the distance came the sounds of the city. I put my hand under her skirt.

"Here," she said. "Do that."

Then for a while we just made love.

"Do you want me?" I whispered.

"Just don't stop!"

Then over Anne's shoulder I saw something. A woman was watching us. She was standing halfway down the stairs and watching us.

Anne began to shake. She couldn't see the woman and my hand continued what it was doing, but over Anne's shoulder I was watching the other woman.

"Oh, God!" Anne said. "Oh, God!"

The woman looked straight into my eyes. Her eyes were deep brown and she did indeed look like Lauren Hutton though of course she wasn't, she was someone I had never seen before that night. Her eyes were so intense that for a moment I didn't know whom I was making love to. Then Anne stopped shaking.

I looked down. Anne was standing with her head buried in my shoulder and I thought perhaps she was crying. Then I looked at the other woman, the one still watching me, and it was as if those eyes, haunted and lost and beautiful, would be watching me forever.

BOOK TWO

I remember waking early in the morning in love with Hélène. It would come to me just as I opened my eyes; then, with my eyes open, the world would come rushing back and I would look around and everything would be slightly out of place. Even the objects on the desk seemed slightly out of place, vibrant, as if trying to tell me something.

When I walked outside I could feel the energy in my legs. Everything looked new, the children with their skateboards and roller skates, the young women walking their dogs, the men in business suits with their newspapers under their arms. It all filled me with wonder, the great improbability of being alive here at this moment surrounded by these people walking down Park Avenue—and in love with Hélène.

When I saw Hélène at an exhibition of paintings by Hans Hofmann I knew her instantly. The gallery was suffused with sunlight and a tangy, salty odor as of blood, and the great vibrant rectangles of color—red and blue and orange—dazzled me with their tactile excitement as if I were drinking strong coffee.

"What do you think of them?" I asked her.

She was almost as tall as I, and as she passed from canvas to canvas the swoop of her spine was catlike and assured, as poised and graceful as a sailboat. Her movements possessed the skill and certainty of a small craft maneuvering on deep water.

"I'm not sure I know how to look at them." She spoke with a clean American accent with only the slightest hint of a foreign elongated *a.*

"There's no special way to look at them. You look at them the way you look at trees or flowers or beautiful human beings."

"They give me courage," she said.

Her flawless skin was a subdued pink, the color of health, and it radiated a vibrance that was itself a sort of light, and this came to possess for me a spiritual quality, as if it disclosed something permanently significant about Hélène. Her eyes were dark brown and her eyebrows were dark and heavy so that they almost touched across her brow, but otherwise her hair was light brown and sandy and her skin was ruddy and high-colored with Gallic good health.

I was not sure where to take her to have coffee. I could not imagine her in the greasy atmosphere of a coffee shop, and so we settled for the Carlyle, with its rundown little bar like the salon at a brothel.

She told me she was writing a book.

"A book? I would have guessed you were a movie star."

"A movie star?" She gave a laugh. "I suppose that's a compliment. No, I have no desire to be a movie star. I'm writing a book about my family—one of my ancestors, a general in the Napoleonic wars."

"Then you're French. That's as good as being a movie star."

"My father is French. My mother was American. I spent my early adolescence in Connecticut."

"Then we both grew up in Connecticut."

"I wish I could say as much. In fact I moved back to France when I was fourteen, after my mother died. I'm not entirely French—and I'm certainly not American. I'm something in between, something mid-Atlantic—not exactly the most comfortable position in the world. Perhaps I'm only that Eurotrash you read about in *New York* magazine."

"I don't think so."

"You're sweet—but I have to be going."

"Is there someplace you have to be?"

"Not really. But I have to be there anyway."

But she agreed to see me in a few days for another drink.

Hélène's father was a vintner who owned an estate in the Loire Valley. The family was an ancient one ennobled by Napoleon, and when Hélène spoke of her father her voice changed tone.

"Poppie is a very gentle person," Hélène said. We were sitting in a bar on Second Avenue and we had been talking for over an hour.

"It's as if Poppie doesn't quite understand the twentieth century. The telephone confuses him. When I call, he can never quite make out what's happening. He'll say, 'Where are you? Are you calling from Paris?' He thinks it a miracle that I'm calling from New York."

"Well, it is, isn't it?"

"I suppose."

"He sounds wonderful to me."

"He is wonderful."

The lines in her throat rippled as she talked and her fingers, long and surprisingly sturdy, rested on the table in tense repose.

"Do you miss France?"

"Yes, of course. But it seems . . . far away. It seems like my childhood—something very dear but very far away that I can't return to. When I was a child my father took me to the public gardens in Tours. There is a picture of me in a little white dress riding in a pony cart. My cheeks are fat and red and I am frowning ferociously. I can almost remember the day. I remember the quality of the light in the garden and the excitement and pride of being out alone with Poppie. I was afraid he was going to walk alongside the pony cart and ruin my independence, and that's why I was frowning.

"Later, when I was living in Connecticut, I missed France terribly. I made up a myth about it, really. I wouldn't make friends with the American kids and that only made things worse. I blamed my mother for taking me away from Poppie. They had never been happy together. Poppie is shy and reclusive and my mother was much more social. She never really fit in in France. You can go so far with the French, and then you come up against an invisible wall. It's not chauvinism exactly. It's really just the tenacity of the culture, its own self-referring nature. Mama never got used to it. She was proud and sensitive and always . . . well, *American. Un peu vulgaire.* I'm the same really. Americans are just . . . *larger* than the French. At any rate, then my parents separated and Mama took me back with her. I don't blame her anymore—it was the only thing she could do. But they never got divorced. They were both Catholics and they didn't believe in divorce."

"And then your mother died?"

"Yes. She died of cancer. I was fourteen and we weren't close. It makes me sad to think of it. All I wanted was to run away, to return to France. When I think of her now it's as if there is this large emptiness. Not pain, not sorrow, just emptiness. I never mourned for her and now it's too late and it's as if there were nothing left but emptiness."

When I was away from Hélène I thought about her constantly. I would wake at night thinking about her. When I called she was distant, friendly, slightly on guard—but she agreed to see me for another drink.

Anne had called to say she couldn't see me anymore. I hadn't argued. She cried on the phone and I told her how wonderful she was and how she would be fine without me.

When I hung up I went outside and it was as if everything had been rinsed in benzene, brilliant and white and stinging to the eyes.

"Didn't you ever marry?" I asked Hélène. Again we were in the bar on Second Avenue and we had been conversing for an hour.

"No—not yet." Her laugh was easy and self-mocking. "We marry later in Europe. Sometimes we don't marry at all. First I was too busy taking care of Poppie. Then I had my studies. I studied American literature at the Sorbonne—it was a way to keep in touch with the American part of my life. Then I became interested in writing this book on Général de Compière. That's how I came here. Many of the papers are at Columbia and at the Berg collection in the public library."

"Don't you have a boyfriend?"

"A *petit copain?* Oh, no, no." She laughed. "Not a boyfriend."

"That's hard to believe. What's wrong with the men in New York?"

"What men?" Again she laughed.

"What do you do for companionship?"

"I write letters to Poppie."

I dreamed that Hélène and I were in a large house and became separated and that I lost her, and I awoke with a panic so great that I felt dizzy.

We started doing things together, going to galleries, walking in the park, having lunch in out-of-the-way restaurants. She was a beautiful woman whose looks meant nothing to her and she was always exciting to be with.

I told her about my family and about my brother Warren.

"He teaches at Princeton at the institute. He's a physicist and a mathematician, and he's exceedingly strange. I'm told that often he won't look at his students. He invented a device used in the commercial cutting of metal and it's made him quite rich, but he lives in a rooming house and donates most of his money to charity. He also bought my father's nursery for my sister, though she insists on paying him back. It's quite a strange family. I only see Warren two or three times a year and we say little to each other. Often we sit silently at a coffee shop over a cup of coffee. But I love him."

"You are lucky," she said. "I envy you your large family. I really have no one at all."

We went to the zoo in Central Park, surrounded by young women with babies with colored balloons, and the Technicolor made me feel lightheaded and happy. I couldn't imagine anything better than being with Hélène. We watched the seals slither and play and then the great cats lying listlessly in their too-small cages.

"Do you know the poem by Rilke about the panther?" I asked. "He says of the panther, For him it was as if there were a thousand bars, and behind those thousand bars there was—nothing at all!"

"That doesn't sound very cheery."

"Oh, it's a beautiful poem!"

We watched the baboons in their outside cage with their beetling, humanoid faces and their absurd boiled behinds, and one of the large males kept insistently mating with the obliging females. It might have been embarrassing but Hélène only laughed and took my hand, and it was the first time we had held hands like that.

"I have to go," she said.

"Oh?"

"A friend of my father's, Walter Straus, is in town and I promised I'd meet him for tea."

"Lucky Mr. Straus."

"Actually, it's something of a bore. It's just that he promised my father he'd look after me, so I have to keep my end of the bargain."

"Well, I certainly wouldn't want to interfere with your father's wishes."

I had to fly to Chicago to attend an independent retailers' convention. Usually Gordo went—he was "growing" the business, he explained—but he had another commitment and he asked me to go instead.

"I'd just as soon not fly to Chicago," I said.

"I'll go myself if you can't attend," he said testily, lurching about the office and knocking papers off the desk.

"I didn't say I wouldn't go, Gordo. Just explain what I'm supposed to do when I get there."

"Make contacts. Talk up customers. Network. Take the pulse of the country."

"I don't know how to network, Gordo. I thought it was a kind of knitting."

"Cute, Smith. I see I'll have to go myself. I don't know what I'll say to Pamela, but I'll figure out something."

"No, no—I'll go. I don't want to be responsible for any hullabaloo with Pamela."

For much of the trip I stared out the plane window. We passed over the canyons of Manhattan, above the towns and shopping malls of New Jersey, crisscrossed with a veinwork of highways, then westward over forest reaches. I ordered a whiskey from the attendant and tried to read the newspaper. When I again looked down the landscape had flattened and we were over farmland laid out as far as one could see in rectangular symmetry.

At the horizon the sun needled off a distant plane.

From O'Hare I took a taxi and checked into the Palmer House with its faux ducal oak and purple wainscoting. My room gave onto Michigan Avenue and I could see out to the park and beyond to Lake Michigan shimmering in the afternoon.

I spent the remainder of the day in the cavernous convention hall under blank neon lighting, listening to people talk about racking and shipping and wholesale discounts. The men were dressed in rayon and polyester and the women in floral dresses with large pins affixed to their bosoms.

After a few hours I retreated to the bar at the end of the hall where I ordered a whiskey and sat chewing pensively on a plastic swizzle stick as I contemplated the spectacle of bustling mercantile America.

I did not return to my room until late that evening. Standing by the window watching the lights from the boat basin as they rocked under a small wind, I was suddenly struck by the thought that I might have invited Hélène to join me. Perhaps I needn't have been there alone, observing that vast and landlocked body of water stretching coldly like a slab of slate under the dark midwestern sky. Perhaps I could have been there with Hélène.

This thought stabbed me with excitement and alarm.

* * *

"Would you have come with me?" I asked.

We were sitting in the Oak Bar in New York City by the great tinted windows that frame Central Park South and I was leaning across the table to talk to her. She wore a beige French silk scarf at her neck that highlighted the intangible glow of her skin, and her dark heavy eyebrows were pulled into a frown.

"Would you?" And I took her hand.

"David—I don't know what you are asking."

"I am asking you to try to love me."

She smiled slightly. "Do you think that's so very hard?"

"Then say you would have come."

"Are you asking me to go away with you? What about your wife?"

"I'm not talking about my wife. I'm talking about *us*. I'm talking about what has been between us since the moment we saw each other on that boat. Do you remember?"

Again she laughed. "I'm not likely to forget. If I remember correctly you were making love to another woman."

"From that moment when our eyes met I've been thinking about no one but you. And it's the same for you, Hélène. You know it is."

She lowered her head. I had forgotten I was sitting in the middle of a fashionable bar in the middle of Manhattan; all I could see was Hélène.

Hélène raised her head and looked at me. "Are you a scary person?"

I started to laugh. "I'm not a scary person, Hélène. I'm not at all a scary person."

"Well . . . you scare me."

I kissed her on the way home in the taxi. At first she wouldn't open her lips, but then, after a moment, she did, though only a little. Then she pushed me away.

"Do you know that expression 'not safe in taxis'? We used to use it in school."

"I'm forty, Hélène. I don't remember anything about school. When can I see you again?"

"Not for a while. I have to go away."

"Because of me?"

"Of course not. I have to go to Atlanta to visit the archives for my book. I'll be gone for five days."

"I'll die," I said.

"No you won't."

"Can I see you when you get back?"

"Of course. Of course you can."

I kissed her again before she got out of the taxi, and this time she parted her lips and I kissed her properly. Then she got out and I saw her walk away; but she turned once before she disappeared and waved to me. Then she turned the corner.

On the third day after her departure Hélène called me at the office.

"It's some dame," Gordo said.

He put the call on hold and I could see the yellow light blinking at the base of the telephone. I turned my back so Gordo couldn't hear.

"David, is that you?"

"Yes."

"David, I miss you terribly. I think I'm going crazy."

"Me too," I said. My voice sounded unsteady in my ear.

"Do you remember that question you asked? The one about Chicago?"

"Yes, of course."

"Well, the answer is yes."

"Really and truly?"

"Yes. I can't stand it here without you . . . David, I think I'm in love with you."

I lowered my head until it was almost between my knees.

"I am too," I said. "I'm in love with you." Then, after a moment, "Can you cut your trip short?"

"No. But it's only another two days."

"*Only?*"

"God, David, I know! Don't talk to me that way or I'll die. Hearing your voice makes me *sick*. Is that bad to say?"

"No, darling. I love it. Your voice has a different effect on my anatomy."

"God, David, don't!"

"Should I book a hotel for us?"

"Yes, please. For the minute I get back. The minute!"

After I hung up I sat for a moment with my elbows on my knees. When I looked up Gordo was watching me.

"Who was that?"

"No one, Gordo. A friend. Just a dame."

Gordo was having trouble with Pamela. He said, "I'm not going to marry her."

"That's the second time you've called it off."

"Is it? Well, this time I mean it. She's a cow, David, do you understand, a cow."

"So, what's wrong with a cow? They give good milk."

"Don't be profane."

"Listen, *I* didn't break off this engagement."

"But what do you think? What do you think about Pamela?"

"Think? I don't think nuthin'."

"You're some help. But what does Barbara think? That's more to the point. What does Barbara think about my engagement?"

"I dunno. Why don't you ask her?"

"I think I will. I think I'll ask Barbara."

That evening I said to Barbara, "Gordo says he's breaking off his engagement to Pamela."

"Good."

We were sitting across the dining room table after the children had left and Barbara was correcting Alexandra's French homework. She didn't bother to look up.

I regarded her for a moment with curiosity and something approaching trepidation.

"He says he's going to ask your opinion."

"Is he? Then I'll tell him what I think."

"Not so fast, Barbara. He's liable to do what you say."

Now finally she looked up at me, but only for a moment.

"Is he?"

"Yes, he is."

"Yes," she said. "I know."

After I checked into the Plaza I sat in the Oak Bar drinking whiskey. The whiskey had no effect on me and I was about to order another when I saw Hélène enter the room. She was wearing a brown leather skirt and a light brown blouse and as she came toward me I thought I was the luckiest man in the world.

As we rode up in the elevator Hélène stood close to me and I could smell her perfume and the clean odor of her hair. Halfway up I took her arm above the elbow and held her tight.

The room was spacious and light and we could see out the window up Central Park. I overtipped the bellboy to make him leave. Hélène stood by the window and when I approached I could see the park rippling below us in the heat. She turned to me and I took her in my arms and then a great wave took me and rolled over me and pulled me down and I was lost.

Afterward I lay studying the contours of her face. The more I regarded her the lovelier she became until I had to look away. It was not that I was unmindful of her small imperfections—the thinness of her upper lip, the slight pockmark on her forehead, the right front tooth that didn't align with the left. But these only enhanced her beauty.

"I didn't know I loved you," she said. "It was those days away from you, not being able to see you, not being able to touch you. I thought I would go mad."

"I love you," I said, and when I heard the words I knew they were true.

"Don't say that," she said. She rolled on her side and touched my lips with her finger and I could smell the sweet heaviness of our lovemaking.

"It's true," I said. "God help us but it's true."

*   *   *

For many months I spoke with Hélène every day and saw her almost every day and we slept with each other two or three times a week. I came to know her apartment as if it were my own—the cupboard where she kept the tea and sugar, the small bathroom with the yellow tiles, the desk where she piled the manuscript she was working on, the double bed with the hand-sewn quilt and the pillows lined against the wall. After a time I knew everything in the apartment and where everything belonged and entering the apartment was like entering home.

And now I recall the way Hélène would lounge against a wall waiting for me, her chin down and her hair tousled in the wind. I would turn a corner and my heart would skip as I saw her at the end of the block, her face lost in thought, one leg crossed casually over the other, her long body relaxed in a graceful reversed S curve as she waited. Then she would see me and her eyes would light and she would lift her head and wave.

Or she would enter a restaurant late, her cheeks flushed, her brow drawn in a frown; the maitre d' would rush to her, a man would lift his head in admiration, I would recognize the fullness of her breasts, the glitter of the sequins on her vest, the stride of her long legs as she hurried forward; and again my heart would leap, my hand clutch, I would jump up to greet her, my chair tipping back, my napkin cascading to the floor.

One remembers the way a woman walked and talked and how her voice sounded on the telephone and the clothing she wore and the jewelry and the perfume she wore. You remember the things you discussed and the places you went and how she laughed and how she reached out impulsively and touched your hand. You remember the way her breast grazed your arm as you walked together and the way she left her clothing in a heap to come to you in a rush. You remember smells and sounds and the intimacies of the night or of the afternoon, and these things you have always and you carry them with you always and they will last, you suppose, as long as you do—even, perhaps, when you no longer care for them to last.

We would meet in the evening for a drink at the Oak Bar. Hélène would order white wine and I would have whiskey and she would press her knee against mine under the table and tell me about what she had done that day and whom she had seen and how she was progressing on her book. Outside in the gathering sky the winter twilight was the color of bourbon.

I was very happy then, being in love with Hélène, and I thought of her as beautiful and funny and life-giving and high-spirited and full-blooded and thoughtful and truthful and loyal and mine.

"I wish you could come to Compière. Poppie has fixed the first floor so it isn't cold, and now with winter there would be a large fire and the mist would come in from the Cher and lick against the window. There is a copse behind the château and then the hills rise steeply and from the top of the hills you can see out across the river. The sides of the hills are planted with grapevines and the vineyards stretch away for miles to the south. The family has cultivated the fields for centuries. In my research I've come across a sixteenth-century de Compière who fought with Henri IV."

"I would love to come," I said. "It's strange that both your father and I are involved with wine."

"Oh, I believe in coincidences like that. *Correspondances.* Don't you?"

That evening I looked up Compière in the atlas and stared at it a long time, trying to imagine that distant foreign place and trying to apply to it what I knew of Hélène.

It is strange, the stages by which you realize you are in love with a woman. At first you think you could always break off, yet somehow you never do. If you don't see her for a day you grow restless and fidgety. You begin to take chances you thought you would never take, and when you ask yourself why you do this you have no answer; yet you do it anyway. Then one day you realize it is too late, you have swallowed the hook. You couldn't extract it even if you wanted. But you don't. You are in love.

And so it came about that I was in love with two women at the same time.

* * *

On the day Hélène and I left for Philadelphia I thought I would be late. I hurried about the apartment dropping things, unable to get out the front door.

"Do you have your electric razor?" Barbara asked.

"I don't know. Let me check."

"Money?"

"Yes, yes, money I have."

"Well, what else do you need?"

"I don't know . . . I'll call tonight."

"I'll be here."

Then I was out the door and Patrick was helping me with my luggage while I stood in front of the apartment waiting for a taxi and gulping the bright morning air.

Hélène was not downstairs. I rang her bell and her voice came over the intercom.

"I'm sorry," she said and she sounded squeaky and disembodied. "I'll be down immediately."

I went outside and stood in a patch of winter sunlight and suddenly I felt entirely at ease just waiting for her to come down.

We held hands in the taxi and she put her leg against mine while I looked out the window and felt my heart beat with excitement. It was ten to nine when we reached Penn Station. Our train was scheduled to depart at 9:07.

"We'll never make it," I said.

"Yes we will. Everything will be fine."

I threw some bills at the driver and we ran into the station. Hélène ran in front of me with her valise tucked clumsily under her arm; she was surprisingly strong and wouldn't let me help her. It took me a minute to find the ticket window. My nerves raced and then the light blinked above the window and it was our turn.

"Two round trips to Philadelphia on the 9:07," I said. "Are we going to make it on time?"

The man behind the window barely glanced at me from under

his brow as he collected the tickets. Then he gestured toward the announcement board with his thumb.

Hélène looked at the board and her forehead wrinkled as she tried to make out what it said.

"Delayed," she said. "The train is ten minutes delayed."

We stood in the center of the great soiled waiting room and watched for the gate to be posted. Businessmen in overcoats and businesswomen in tailored suits and scarves and gold stickpins jostled about us, all of them carrying leather rectangular cases of various colors. A black man with swollen whitish hands that looked as if they had been dipped in flour begged with a dilapidated paper coffee cup.

The rows of tattered scoop-bucket seats accommodated the retinue of the poor; pasty-faced overweight women with ratty-looking children dressed in cheap electric colors cheek by jowl with homeless men with smudged faces and glazed indifferent eyes.

The information board whirred and our train was twenty minutes delayed.

"I'm going get some magazines for the train." Hélène's tall figure disappeared into the crowd.

I stood observing a young woman twist her hair into a knot at the base of her neck. She was an unwell-looking young woman, delicate-boned and thin-nosed, and her skin was absolutely ashen, as if you were seeing through it to some underlying source of decay. Her hands were long-fingered and delicate and even at this distance I could discern the blueness of her veins. She couldn't arrange her hair to her satisfaction and kept putting it up and letting it down again; and this alternately transformed her from a sickly, unexceptional-looking woman to a woman of grave, startling beauty, like a Virgin in van Eyck.

Again the board whirred and now our train was scheduled to arrive at gate ten in seven minutes.

I considered trying to move the baggage to gate ten, but there was too much to move by myself and I was concerned lest Hélène not find me; then I saw her coming from the opposite direction with a bundle of magazines under her arm.

"I'm sorry," she said. "I wanted to find *Le Monde* and they sent me all around Robin Hood's barn. Isn't that what you say—Robin Hood's barn?"

"Well, some people say it. I'm surprised you could find *Le Monde* at all."

Hélène picked up a heavy bag and when I tried to help she pulled away. A strand of hair had worked loose and lay like a ripple of water across the smoothness of her forehead. We jostled past the entry and down the escalator to the platform.

We boarded the smoking car and lumbered through the aisles, our bags jolting against the seats, until we found four unoccupied places where we swung in, and taking Hélène's baggage, I swung it up onto the rack above us. Then we sat and she snuggled against me.

"Kiss me," I said. I felt her lips and the heat from her body and smelled the perfume that enveloped her sweater.

Hélène placed her magazines on the opposite seat: *Vanity Fair, Cosmo, Elle, The New Yorker, Le Monde,* the *New York Times.* Then she spread out a variety of candy bars.

"My goodness! Do you read *all* of those?"

"Of course. If I weren't inhibited by my heavyweight intellectual boyfriend I'd buy the *Inquirer* and the *Star.* I keep up on all the gossip."

"Do you really?"

She laughed. "You're so easy to tease!"

"Am I?"

"Yes you are. You believe whatever I tell you."

"Well, shouldn't I?"

"Of course you should." She laughed again. "Now should you believe that or not?"

The train slipped away from the station and at first I couldn't see anything out the window because of the darkness of the tunnel. I could hear the clickety-click of the wheels over the rails and could see reflected in the darkened window the compartment behind me and Hélène's face at my shoulder; then we came out into sunlight into New Jersey and the train was moving faster and Hélène pressed her thigh against mine.

"New Jersey!" she exclaimed. "Now we are international travelers."

A thin dusting of snow mantled the industrial landscape. We came to Newark and I tried to tell Hélène about the riots of the 1960s and about Amiri Baraka and Allen Ginsberg and Philip Roth and about anything else I could think of to lend some semblance of interest to the blighted fume-darkened urban disaster we were traversing.

"Have you ever actually *been* to Newark?" she asked.

"No, that far I've never gone. I can't say there is anything actually to see in Newark. I'd like to go to Paterson sometime and see where William Carlos Williams lived."

"Why don't we do that?"

"Or we could go to Baltimore when the crabs are running and stay in a hotel by the harbor and eat crabs and drink white wine."

"That sounds wonderful," she said.

"I wish we were going to Compière," she added after a moment. "We could have a picnic overlooking the Cher. Poppie and I often had picnics in the summer. There is a hill with the river running below it and to the south the fields of vines and in the distance the château of Bellac."

"It sounds good to me."

"It's the most beautiful place in the world!"

"Even more beautiful than Newark?"

"Well . . . maybe not more than *Newark.*"

"*Chère comtesse,*" I said, "I'm in love with you."

She put her head on my shoulder and I stroked her beautiful hair.

"Tell me," I asked. "Are your people very grand?"

She smiled. "Poppie's not grand at all," she said after a moment. "Anyway, I came away to escape all that."

"Why did you leave?"

"Oh," she said, shrugging, "you know. You can't go home again."

I tried to tell her about Windflower and about the mint that my father grew by the stream and about how as a boy I sat by the stream reading Dickens and Trollope and later Conrad and Henry James.

"And you too," she asked. "Why did you leave?"

"Oh, I couldn't stay at Windflower. First my father was there, and then after my father died my mother sold it to my sister. Then my mother moved to Santa Fe and now my sister lives at Windflower and runs it very effectively."

"Somehow it sounds a little sad."

"No, it isn't sad. It's just the way things are. I couldn't go back to Windflower any more than you to Compière. But it makes me happy to think of my sister there."

"All that talk about picnics makes me hungry," Hélène said.

She drew out of her straw satchel some French cheeses wrapped in white paper and some cold meat and a loaf of crusty French bread with a bottle of Chablis and real wineglasses and a silver corkscrew.

"You French are remarkable." I laughed. "Even on a commuter train you manage to provide a gourmet picnic."

"Mais bien sûr, mon chéri. Même en chemin de fer on n'est pas des sauvages."

She spread the food out carefully on the adjacent seat and cut the bread and cheeses while I uncorked the wine.

"May I pour you some?"

"Of course!"

Then we sat side by side and were very happy while we ate Hélène's picnic and watched the poor scarred debased landscape of the urban Northeast click by outside our window.

After we finished the bottle of wine I took my overcoat from the rack and placed it around our shoulders and Hélène put her head on my shoulder and slept while I sat very still and looked out the window and didn't think about anything.

Hélène gave a little yawn and woke up. She stretched. Then she turned to me and her face was still fuzzy with sleep.

"Did I fall asleep?"

"Yup."

"Poor you! I'm not much of a companion, am I! Was it very long?"

"Just long enough."

"Just long enough for what?"

"Just long enough for my shoulder to fall asleep."

"Oh, pooh! That's not very romantic." And she kissed me.

"Now I'm going to read my magazines," she said. "I need to keep up with all the gossip for my friend Caroline. Now, *Caroline* is very grand. I'm rather afraid of Caroline. I need to read all these magazines so Caroline won't think me *provincial.*"

"That sounds like a horrible thing to be. I'd like to meet this Caroline."

"Oh no you wouldn't." Hélène laughed. "You wouldn't approve of Caroline. Caroline is a society girl from San Francisco. Now I'm going to go use the loo, and when I come back I'm going to read all my magazines."

We gathered our baggage in the aisle as the train pulled into Thirtieth Street Station. Then the platform ceased moving and I could see passengers debouching from the train, and lifting the heavy valise in front of me, Hélène exited onto the platform.

"Here we are," she said. And when she turned to me she was smiling.

We hailed a taxi outside the station and instructed the driver to take us to Rittenhouse Square. Hélène kept craning forward to look out the window.

"Is this fun?" I asked.

"It's wonderful!"

The large potted plants that filled the hotel lobby had the air of abandoned maiden aunts drooping in corners. The concierge bowed solemnly as he accepted my credit card.

"I believe this is your first visit with us, Mr. Smith. I trust you and Mrs. Smith will enjoy your stay. May we send anything up to the room for you?"

They had given us a suite on the fifteenth floor overlooking the square, and from the window I could see down into the naked treetops and onto the automobiles parked at the curb. From this height the square appeared sedate and Old Worldish.

We made love in the large saggy double bed.

I never stopped being amazed by the act of love, which was

never just a "natural" act, certainly not with these high-strung, delicate, beautiful women who gave themselves with such trust and abandon like trapeze artists who let go into space, confident you will be there to catch them.

"Do you think I am a nymphomaniac?"

"Why do you say such a thing?"

"Because I want to make love with you all the time. I want you all the time."

"You're not a nymphomaniac. You're a dear sweet lovely girl and I'm in love with you."

Afterward we wanted to go out and see the city.

"Let's hurry," Hélène said. "I hate to waste even a minute when I'm with you."

The weather had turned cold and the sky had a drear centerless look as if it had been drained of all content. Few pedestrians were out except for some poor wandering destitute blacks. Our reflections distorted in the green corporate glass of the skyscrapers as we passed eastward. Then we rounded a corner and we could see Independence Square.

We visited the colonial buildings with their narrow rectangular rooms and saw where the cooking had been done in the large open fireplaces and where in the narrow uneven beds the lovemaking and the birthing had been accomplished, and our feet trod the fitted planks where our eighteenth-century forerunners had trod and where in an unlikely, unrepeatable miracle the Constitution had been hammered out.

"I love the Americanness of the place," Hélène said.

"Do you? It must seem very ungrand to you."

"That's a horrible thing to say! It seems very grand indeed. Grand in spirit. It makes me proud to be American."

"*Are* you American?"

"Well—don't be horrid!"

When we went outside, occasional flakes of snow floated like ash through the gray air. I consulted my map and we started for the Franklin house.

Franklin's home was a handsome rectangular four-story red brick building with white trim and an interior court for horse-

drawn carriages. We visited his study and workshop and the upstairs rooms where he and his voluminous family had resided. It
was cold when we left and the winter light was draining from the
sky.

We managed to get lost walking back to the hotel; somehow I
took a wrong turn, and then another.

"I thought you were good at this navigating business."

"Well, usually I am."

"Why don't we just take a taxi?"

"No, no. Never say die."

"Well, my feet are killing me. Why don't we at least say
drink?"

We located a bar on a side street where we sat at a darkened
table sticky with other people's beer while the friendly slovenly
waitress swabbed down the top with a reeking cloth. I ordered a
Heineken and Hélène a glass of white wine.

"Here's to the City of Brotherly Love," I said. "It's from here
that the Good Ship Lollipop set out over two hundred years ago to
bring to the huddled masses the good tidings of mass democracy
and entrepreneurial capitalism."

"Do you say all that for my benefit?" Hélène inquired. "Because you don't have to. I couldn't ask for a bigger adventure, a
more thrilling or unlikely adventure, than to be sitting here with
you drinking wine in this funny bar in the city of Philadelphia."

"You're a generous-hearted woman."

"No. I'm just a woman in love."

As we made love on the large crumpled hotel bed, I seemed to
reach a place with Hélène beyond where I had ever been before, a
spot I literally touched such that, shuddering, lost together, we
were fused in that heat like metals in a single flame.

Afterward we lay next to each other like spent swimmers.

"Oh!" Hélène said. "How do you *do* that? It feels as if I've
never made love before. Not even long ago, with my husband."

I had been tracing the mole under her left breast but I stopped
now and looked at her.

"Your husband?"

She shifted her weight so she could face me.

"I thought you said you had never been married."

"It was many years ago, when I was very young."

"Who was he? Tell me about it."

"He was just a boy."

"What happened to him?"

"He went away. It's not important."

"But why didn't you tell me? I want you to tell me everything."

She laughed drily. "I'm telling you now, though really there's nothing to tell. He was just a boy who lived in the village. There were no suitable boys and I was very young, so we got married. But there was nothing between us, nothing to keep us together. We were like two leaves that come to rest next to each other on a wall. Then the wind rises and they are blown away."

I was very moved by what she said and again I took her in my arms. It seemed I could not get enough of her. When I entered her she cried out and I stayed with her a long time. Afterward she buried her face in my shoulder.

"Oh, David," she said, and tears smudged her cheeks. "It feels as if I'd never made love before."

In the night when I woke Hélène wasn't in bed. I tried to wait for her to return but after a while I drifted off and when I woke again I could hear her breathing softly next to me. I lay for a long time listening to her and watching the movement of the light on the ceiling until finally, at some point, with the dawn coming up outside the window, I fell back to sleep.

I had to spend the next day with clients. Hélène had purchased a guidebook to Philadelphia and was eager to see more of the city and to visit the Museum of Art and see the Duchamps.

"Are you sure you don't want to catch an early train without me? I hate to think of you hanging around all day."

"Don't be silly. I would hate to go back without you. You

think I can't spend a day alone? How do you think I spend my life?"

Sometime during the morning I had to call the office, but when I phoned Gordo wasn't there. It wasn't like Gordo not to be in the office without telling me, and it worried me. I called Barbara.

"Hi, darling. Is everything okay?"

"Everything's fine. But I'm a little worried about Gordo. I called the office and he wasn't there."

"Well, that's nothing to be concerned about."

"Maybe not. But I can count the number of days Gordo has stayed away from the office."

"Maybe he had something to do that he forgot to tell you about."

"Well, maybe. And how is Jenny? Is she behaving herself?"

"Oh, she doesn't talk to me anymore. She just goes in her room and closes the door and talks on the telephone. It's like not having a daughter. Thank God for Alexandra! I want you to speak to Jenny when you get home."

"Well, I'll be back for dinner unless something comes up, and I'll speak to her then."

"I don't envy you that. Just call if there's a change in plans."

"Okay. I love you."

"Yes, I love you too."

That day I ordered a shipment of Montrachet from France and a new effervescent Spanish wine suggested by Juan Hermano (who, curiously enough, knew Hélène's father) and discussed a possible depot storage arrangement in Camden. The day was busy and productive and by four-thirty I was ready to meet Hélène at the station for a drink.

When I came into the bar I saw her sitting with her back to me in the far corner and I felt my heart skip; then she turned and she saw me and her face lit with a smile.

"Hi!"

"Darling!" And I kissed her.

"What are you drinking?"

"White wine. But you have a whiskey. Did you have a good day?"

"*This* is the best part of the day."

"Yes, for me too. I love it when you call me darling. No one has ever called me darling before!"

That was our trip to Philadelphia. It lasted only one night—less than forty-eight hours—and it was over before we knew it; but I remember it now in every detail. And I think I always will.

It was at about this time that I first noticed Gordo's limp. At first I thought he must have twisted his leg playing racketball. Gordo had accumulated weight with the years but he was still a keen sportsman of considerable prowess and undaunted aggression, and if he couldn't beat you fair and square he'd beat you otherwise.

Gordo had become restless with our entrepreneurial achievements. These were the Reagan go-go years and he wanted a piece of the action. He had started to buy up real estate, little lots here and there; but clearly he had grander ambitions.

"This is baby shit," he'd say to me. "All this is baby shit."

"What do you mean, Gordo? What do you mean, baby shit? Do you know how much money we made last year?"

"Yeah, yeah. Big deal. You're a goof-off, Smith."

"It makes me nervous when you start thinking, Gordo. You have no talent for it, no calling. There's something unseemly about it, if you don't mind my saying. It's uncomfortable to observe, like a fat man in tights."

"I don't give a fart for your opinion, ol' boy. You're a goof-off. Just follow ol' Gordie and we'll all get rich."

He meant it, too. Much of the initiative for the business had in fact passed into Gordo's hands. He had a kind of genius for making a deal, for negotiating, for bullying a distributor or outmaneuvering a rival. Gordo had already established three new stores on the Island and had bought up a distributor in the five towns that serviced lower-middle-class family restaurants.

"Why are you limping, Gordo?"

"Whaddaya mean, limping?"

"I mean limping. You know. I noticed it the other day."

"Well, I don't consider this a limp."

"No? What is it, then? Some kind of new affectation? Something you read about in the 'His' column?"

Suddenly Gordon turned on me in anger.

"Why don't you mind your own business, Smith? Do I go poking around in your business? If I started poking around, you might hear things you didn't care to hear."

"Oh, yeah? What are you talking about? What is it I wouldn't care to hear?"

"Nothing. Nothing at all. I just don't want you snooping around in *my* affairs, okay? That's all I'm saying."

"I just asked about your leg."

"Well, don't."

Hélène and I made the Oak Bar our bar, where we would meet for a drink at the end of the day before I dropped her off in a taxi. She was supposed to be working on her book, but the circle of her acquaintance proved large and she would often arrive late from some social appointment.

Though the least pretentious of women, Hélène in fact knew everyone; I had to remind myself that she was, after all, a countess. If you mentioned Henry Kissinger, it would emerge two months later that Hélène had spent a weekend with him at Compière or had dined next to him at a party in Georgetown. She was filled with amusing anecdotes about the people she had known, which she would recount in high good humor.

"Did I ever tell you about the time Harold Acton got stuck in the loo? It was just awful! Sir Harold is a great friend of Poppie's and we used to visit La Pietra when Poppie was working on his book on Pico. Harold is a dear and the most punctilious of men but once at Compière he got tight and locked himself in the loo and couldn't get out. He refused to say anything so we didn't know where he was for the longest time. Then we kept hearing this sort of rattling from upstairs and I went up to see. I understood immediately what it was, but I knew Harold would be too embarrassed if a *girl* found him like that so I had to go back downstairs and tell Poppie. Well, Poppie *hates* any mention of the loo, it turns him scarlet with embarrassment, so he refused to understand what I was getting at. They had both been tippling quite a bit of sherry, you understand."

"What did you do?"

"Oh, he got the point after a while. Poor Poppie. I don't know which of them was more upset. And the worst of it was that I couldn't stop laughing!

"I used to see a great deal of the comtesse de la Pole when I was a young woman in Paris. She was a collateral relation of Poppie's and I kept hoping she'd put me in her will. Well, she was a frightful old bag. She had been a beautiful young woman, you know, and quite a courtesan. Jean Gabin was her lover, and so was Maurice Chevalier. She wrote scurrilous memoirs. But now she lived by herself in an enormous flat on the boulevard Montaigne and kept dogs. She must have had forty chows running around like rats under your feet."

"Forty!"

"Well, ten, at any rate. But this is the point. No men were allowed in her apartment. She said she'd had enough of men. But the chows were let in her bed. You'd be talking to her and the chows would crawl up under her bedclothes and under her nightie! Ugh! I have no idea what they were doing there but whatever it was, it was disgusting!"

"You make me laugh."

"Yes? Well, *la comtesse* would may you *cry!*"

"How come we never quarrel?" she said. "We just *get* each other. We just *click.* We're on the same wavelength. We're on the same *cloud.*"

"The same cloud?"

"Yes. Can't you say that?"

"Well, I've never heard it."

"Well, now you have. It's us. It's what we are."

She would arrive late from shopping with her friend Caroline or from visiting with Brooke Astor or Coco Peking or from seeing her father's friend Walter Straus—whose name I occasionally encountered in the pages of *Vanity Fair*—her hair slightly fussed and her eyes aglitter with conspiratorial excitement, as if we were spies meeting to exchange important surreptitious information.

"Tell me about this Walter Straus," I asked her.

"Oh, he's a friend of my father's, a rich American. I'm afraid you wouldn't like him much. He's a jeweler who's made himself immensely rich and I'm afraid somewhat ostentatious, but Poppie admires him. He admires his worldly know-how and success. Walter wears Armani suits so Poppie thinks he's European. If he were a Frenchman he'd see through him immediately, but because he's American—well, he doesn't get it. But this must be boring."

"You couldn't bore me if you tried. Besides, I want to know everything about you."

"Well, I'm afraid you already do. There's nothing else to know —except that I love you."

In fact the only fight Hélène and I had that year had to do with Walter Straus. One evening as we went home in a taxi Hélène said to me, "I have to go out to a dinner party tonight."

"Oh? What party is that?"

"Well, actually it's with Walter Straus. I promised I'd accompany him to a party at Mort Klein's."

"Isn't Straus that nouveau chap you were telling me about— that friend of your father's?"

"Oh, he isn't really a *nouveau* chap. That's not really fair. Let's just say he's an old friend of the family."

"Isn't he one of these absurd socialites? I mean, *Mort Klein!* Give me a break!"

"You are frightful."

"Am I? I just don't admire that collection of Wall Street hustlers and real estate manipulators with their pouffed-up wives who get celebrated in our chichi journals."

"Well, that's really not the point. The point is I promised Walter Straus."

"Well, you shouldn't have. I don't want you going out to dinner with other men."

She looked at me, half amused, half alarmed.

"But David, it's just a dinner party."

"I don't care what you call it. It comes to your going out with another man."

"I'm not sure you have the right to ask that of me."

"It's not a right. There are no rights in love. I never said any of this was right. I just don't want you going out with anybody else. I mean, my God, Hélène, think what's between us! If we don't have that much commitment to each other, what are we doing?"

"I shouldn't have mentioned it," she said. "But I've got to go out with Walter tonight. I promised him."

"You've *got* to go out with Walter? What are you talking about? Call him and tell him you're sick."

"I can't do that."

"No? Then let me out of here." And I leaned across her and started to open the door to the cab.

"What are you doing?" There was real panic in her voice as she pushed me back.

"I'm going. I'm leaving right now." Suddenly I was furious. "What do you mean, you shouldn't have told me? What else don't you tell me?"

"Nothing, for God's sake. I tell you everything."

"Apparently not about your dinner dates with Walter Straus. I mean, my God, I just took all this for granted. If you are not my woman, then all this is a farce."

"Of course I'm your woman."

"Then I don't want you going out with this Walter Straus. If you are my woman, then you don't go out to dinner parties with other men. It's as simple as that."

"Okay, okay—I won't go out with Walter Straus. I'll call him and tell him I'm sick. Is that what you want?"

"Yes—that's very much what I want."

That was the only time we fought, and it was over before it began. As Hélène said, we *clicked*. She must have been right—we were on the same cloud.

That's the way the winter passed, and then the spring, and then in June we had known each other for a year.

I wanted to buy her something. I didn't like anything I saw at Tiffany's and I ended up buying her a ring from Russia in worked gold with a diamond inlay that I found in an antique shop. She wore it on her wedding finger and I was proud whenever I saw it or thought of it.

To mark our anniversary we went for a picnic in the country. We drove up the West Side Highway across the Spuyten Duyvil bridge, up the Saw Mill River past Hawthorne, and turned onto the Taconic. We drove deep into New York. It was a windy, sun-filled day—the air was soft with early summer—and we drove with the windows down and the wind blowing through our hair.

Hélène was wearing a summer dress, and as we drove I could see her radiant skin across the top of her breasts. Reaching over, I touched her breasts—and she took my hand and pressed it to her.

"I can't believe my luck," I said.

"Me too. I thought such love only existed in books."

"I never want anyone else to touch you."

She laughed good-humoredly.

"That's greedy of you, David."

"Well, I'm greedy."

"They are just breasts, you know. Rather too large, really."

"Too large for what?"

"Well, too large to wear T-shirts without a bra."

"Is that what you'd like to do?"

"Yes. Don't you think that's chic?"

"Isn't that the name of the magazine you worked at?"

"Yes—once upon a time."

"Well, you're chic all the time."

"If we lived together would you make love to me every day?"

"Every day if we wanted. We could make love whenever we wanted."

"And wouldn't you get sick of it?"

"Would you?"

"Me? I would never want to get out of bed. I need to make up for all the time I've lost."

"I'm glad you haven't been with all sorts of men."

"Are you?"

"Yes. I don't care what other women do, but with you it's different. The thought of someone else even holding your hand fusses me."

"Well, you don't need to worry. I'm not like that. I'm the monogamous type, David. I truly don't think I could make love with another man. The thought disgusts me. And, frankly, I don't think it would *work*. Maybe you think that's naive, but that's who I am. I truly believe what I say. The thought makes me physically sick."

"Here," I said. "Lean over to me."

"What are you doing?"

"Kiss me."

"Not while you're driving, silly!"

"Yes, kiss me now, while I'm driving. Make my day!"

We drove along a two-lane road that wound through trees beside a swollen river. The trees cast shadows that filled the car with dampness, but when we emerged into sun the air was instantly hot, as if someone had opened a stove door, and there were banks of flowers by the side of the road which I could see as I drove through the sunlight.

I came up behind a slower car and tried to pass.

"Don't be so impatient, David. You are going to get us killed."

"Ssh!"

I pulled out into sunlight and for a moment I was blinded as the car veered into the oncoming lane. We were racing toward a sharp curve. Then the car beside me dropped behind and, gunning, I careened over and took the curve as the car swerved back into its lane.

"Whee!"

"Macho man!"

And leaning over, she bit me, hard, on the biceps.

We turned off the road into the state park onto a potted lane, and the shadows were large pools that blotted the sun. No one was at the visitors' station and I drove another hundred yards over the ruts and pulled off onto the moist, matted, ill-looking grass and turned off the motor.

I got out of the car and the sunlight was warm on my back. For

a moment I was dizzy. I smelled the odor of the damp earth like
wet moldering leaves, and the sharp evaporating odor of gasoline,
and I heard from below the hill the sound of rushing water.

Hélène stretched, and I could detect beneath her clothes the
strong lines of her body, like an ax handle that fits the hand.

"I'm going to use the loo."

"Good idea."

As I pissed into the tin trough with its ball of ill-smelling
camphor, I thought of Hélène sitting just beyond me beyond the
plywood partition; and I longed to be with her and to plunge my
hand into the warm stream of her body and to rub her friendly
beautiful light-haired cunt which I knew so well.

When we met by the car I kissed her hard on the lips. It was
warm in the pool of sunlight where we stood, but where the path
ran down into hemlocks beyond the small field the shadows lay
like cold water. I opened the trunk and took out the picnic.

"What did you bring to sit on?" she asked.

"Oops! I forgot."

"It's not important. We can sit on my sweater."

"It will be ruined."

"Oh, it doesn't matter."

At first the path looked chewed and spat out where the earth
had been ground to fine powder underfoot, but when we reached
the edge of the meadow the earth firmed and the air smelled of
pine needles and fern. It was cold in the forest and we walked
briskly and moved our arms.

We encountered a group of Germans in khaki knee-length
shorts setting up camp, three handsome dour men who regarded
us grimly as we passed as if we were intruders in their private
domain.

The path turned right and forded the stream and then we began to climb along the steep side of the ravine. Hélène went first,
and from behind I could admire the strength of her legs and of her
haunches as she climbed. Deep in the forest the sunlight, descending through the treetops, formed long shafts smoky with motes of
dust. Here and there white three-petaled trilliums poked through

the groundcover, and a growth of skunk cabbage dankened the air.

After twenty minutes I was sweating. To our left the hill fell away to where the stream churned; to our right the mountain, its side studded with oak and fir through which sunlight made difficult progress, towered precipitously. Then the path descended and we wound down to the stream and to a small clearing where the sunlight lay unimpeded by a fallen log.

"Should we stop to eat?"

"Sure. It's as good a place as any."

I swung the knapsack down by the log where the air was pungent with pine.

"I love being here with you," she said.

"Isn't it great?"

"Everything we do together is great."

I clambered down to the stream. The ground was slippery and I almost fell on a piece of wood slickened to the consistency of glass. Kneeling, I wedged the bottle of wine in the freezing water between two stones.

Far away I could see the sky, indigo blue, and passing lazily through it, a single cloud.

I picked my way carefully up the bank.

"Oh, this is good!" she said. "This reminds me of all things good. Here, sit close to me."

"Let me put the sweater down. Your bottom will get wet."

"Oh, I don't care. Just sit next to me and kiss me."

I kissed her for a long time. "There, that's better," she said. "Now let's eat. I'm as hungry as . . . a sheep!"

"A sheep? Are sheep particularly hungry?"

"Oh, I don't know. *This* sheep is. Let's see what we have."

I sat beside her on the wet ground while she laid out the things to eat. She had strong purposeful hands, skillful lovemaking hands, and the pinky on her right hand was set slightly crooked.

"Do you think that wine might be ready?"

"It would be better if we gave it another few minutes."

"I'm not sure I can. This is a thirsty sheep."

Again I negotiated the descent to the stream. The water was

steel blue, the color of cold winter light, but where in the shallows the bottle lay the water was colorless and I could see to the bottom where the water magnified the clean coppergold sand. Hélène waited above in the circle of sunlight.

Again I sat beside her on the wet ground and we began to eat.

"Pour me some wine, my macho man."

"*Pour la comtesse!*"

The cork came out true.

"There's only one glass."

"How stupid of me!"

"It doesn't matter. I can drink out of the bottle."

Tipping the bottle back, I felt the cold wine in my throat. Somewhere in the forest a bird sounded, first a note, then another, then a third—distinct and repeated, as if in secret message.

"Have some more wine."

"Yes, pour me another glass. Let's drink all the wine."

Again I drank out of the bottle, and as I drank, I could see overhead the bright sky, cold and very distant.

"I love being a part of your life," she said. "Sometimes, before you, I felt . . . I don't know. Totally adrift. Do you know that feeling when you wake in the morning and you feel forlorn? As if you were utterly lost? I mean as if your life were essentially—lost? It's the worst feeling in the world! Well, since I've known you, I don't feel it anymore. I have you to thank for that, David."

She kissed me and I put my arm around her while she laid her head on my shoulder.

The young trees cast a feathery froth of shadow. We were caught in the elbow of the hill, surrounded by the murmur of the forest. Pale light brightened beside us, focused through the masts of the trees. When I lowered my eyes, Hélène was smiling.

"Here," she said. "Touch me here."

She lay back on the wet earth.

"What if someone comes?"

"Let them," she said. "I don't care."

When I touched her I felt the wine in my head. She slipped her hand under my shirt and a great wind came and blew away the top of my head. I was aware of her body and of her legs wrapped around me. Her hand was on me as I loosened her clothes. Then I was aware of nothing. When she cried out her cry was blown away and lost in the forest.

After a long while I was again aware that someone could come up the path.

"No," she said. "Don't move."

I lay on top of her while high above me the wind soughed in the trees.

"It's bliss," she said simply. "I don't want you ever to move."

We lay there a long time. I was aware of her breathing and of the wetness of the earth against my thigh. After a time I was no longer in her.

She sighed. "I wish we could stay like that forever."

Then I rolled over, but the earth was too wet and I sat up. She remained lying on her back on the wet earth so that I could see her breasts where I had loosened her dress. She was relaxed and entirely beautiful lying half naked on the ground.

"What we have is so *huge!*" she said.

"Isn't it, darling? Isn't it huge?"

"Yes. Yes it is. Come on top of me again."

"You'll catch cold. It's too wet like that."

"I don't care. I'll warm the earth!"

But after a moment she stirred and sat up.

"Oh, God," she said. "Wasn't that *wonderful?*"

"It was grand," I said. "Huge and soaring and grand."

"Is there any more wine?"

"No. We drank it all."

"Too bad. I'd like some more wine."

Then she stood up. I took her in my arms, and beyond her the world moved out farther and farther in concentric circles, as when you throw a pebble into a pond, until, holding her, I could no longer think where it might end.

We packed our few things and then it was time to go.

"Here," she said. "Feel how wet I am."

I felt her bottom and we laughed.

We descended the trail and though the sun was still bright, the air was chilly now and the forest stirred with the first hint of evening. The Germans were still pottering in their camp as we crossed the meadow. Again they regarded us in sober disapproval.

"They could have come up the trail," Hélène said. And she laughed gaily.

"I didn't care."

"Neither did I!" And again she laughed, as if I had entirely missed the point of her observation.

Sometime that summer Gordo ended his engagement to Pamela Stokes. I was too taken up with my own affairs to notice when; one day I looked up and Pamela was no longer there.

"So how are you and Pamela getting along?" I asked.

"What?"

"You know, Pamela—the girl you're engaged to. I asked you how you're getting along."

"Nice of you to ask. Actually, I broke up with her a long time ago."

"I'm sorry to hear that," I said, and I was. I had counted on Pam to straighten Gordo out—maybe even to make him happy.

"Are you? I didn't know you admired her so. Last time I heard she was on your shit list."

"She was never on my shit list, Gordo. I don't care who you marry. I was happy that *you* were happy."

"Well, I wasn't."

After that he didn't say anything for a while. I watched him blunder about the office, and suddenly it struck me that something was wrong. There was something wrong about this persistent sense of *blundering* in a man who had been a consummate athlete.

"Are you all right, Gordo?"

"Yeah, sure. What do you mean?"

"I don't know. I just want to hear that you're all right."

"You mean about Pamela?"

"Yeah, that. And whatever."

"Well, whatever's just fine."

He went to the refrigerator and poured himself a tall glass of water. Gordo had become a great believer in the salubrious effects of water and he consumed great quantities of the stuff throughout the day—whether in preparation for or as consequence of the evening's intemperance, I didn't know.

"Since we're having a little heart-to-heart," he said to me now, "how are *you* doing?"

"Me? What's wrong with me?"

"I dunno. I'm just asking."

"Well, I haven't broken off my engagement recently."

"No? I thought maybe you had."

"Oh? What's that supposed to mean?"

"Nothing. It doesn't mean anything. The world surprises me, that's all. The world is forever surprising me."

"Well, it's gratifying to know that you retain your faculty for wonder. That's a great gift, Gordo. It's worth more than the Eiffel Tower. It will keep you young and it's also good for your complexion."

"Fuck you, Smith."

Just then, and for no apparent reason, Gordo's glass of water fell to the floor. It just seemed to drop out of his hand.

The glass shattered at his feet and the water splashed over his legs and shoes. Gordo didn't move. He stood staring at me out of his dark, intelligent eyes, and his brow puckered in concern. For a long moment we remained looking at each other.

I thought of many things to say but I didn't say any of them and Gordo didn't say anything either. After a moment he turned away and started mopping up the water.

Sometimes the closeness between Hélène and myself seemed unsurpassable. I remember once, when we were making love in the afternoon, she cried out beneath me in the moment of her coming. Then, without intercession, I rolled her over, and the awkward abandon of her cry as she came again in long shuddering spasms on top of me seemed even more intimate than anything we had shared before.

We agreed we would have dinner that evening and she kissed me as we parted.

Later she called me at the office.

"I'm sorry, darling, but I'm afraid I won't be able to make dinner after all."

"Oh? What's up?"

"It's Caroline. She's having a party tonight and she wants me to come to keep up her spirits. She's been such a good friend, David —I don't see how I can refuse."

"Well, I suppose not. But we had been planning this."

"Yes, I know, it's such a bore. But you don't really want me to say no to Caroline, do you? I mean, that just wouldn't be right."

"Well, I don't know about that."

"Well, not *right* exactly. But I mean, we can go out to dinner *any*time."

Walking home that evening I felt forlorn. I bought a cigar and smoked it as I wandered up Madison Avenue. There had been a time, I reflected, when Hélène would have dropped anything to have dinner with me. I felt certain of her love. But when I thought of us in bed that afternoon, I could not understand why six hours later she was at somebody else's party instead of dining with me.

It must have been at this time that Hélène started telling me about Alexander Pitt.

"Do you know that Caroline is going out with Alex Pitt?" she asked one day.

I had never heard of Alex Pitt.

"You've never heard of Alex Pitt? Of course you have. You know—Pitt, the anchorman with the long hair on the evening news. You must have seen him."

"I never watch the evening news."

"But you must have *some*time."

"No, never."

"You're impossible. Well, Alex Pitt is just *it*. You know, for the in crowd. *Vanity Fair* did a profile on him recently. He was married to Thelma Furr and had a wild affair with Katrina Uberding."

"He sounds like a wonderful guy."

"Well, he wouldn't be your type, but *People* thinks he's *it*—and so does Caroline."

That evening I asked Barbara if she had ever heard of Alexander Pitt.

"Oh, God!" she said.

"Is it that bad?"

"I'm afraid it's worse. He's the greasy long-haired person on the evening boob tube."

"Is he some kind of big society figure?"

"Well, not the society I come from."

"He's dreamy," Jenny said dryly. She was standing by the counter making herself a peanut butter sandwich forty minutes before dinner. "You know, Dad—a Gucci Gucci, Pucci Pucci kind of guy, the kind of guy you'd like to bring home to Mother."

"On a chain," Barbara said. And the two women laughed.

Later that week Hélène said to me, "Caroline is going to Paris for the weekend. She's flying there with Alex."

"*Alex?*"

"Yes. Don't be horrid about Alex. I may be the bridesmaid someday."

"He doesn't strike me as the marrying type."

"Oh, don't underestimate Caroline."

"Why, has she set her sights on marrying Mr. Pitt?"

"I wouldn't put anything past Caroline."

I took Hélène to a concert one evening and I felt her stiffen as we held hands during the second movement of the Mozart Piano Concerto in E-flat, K. 482. During intermission we moved unheeding among the crowd.

"What utterly amazing music!"

"Yes, yes! That's exactly what it is!"

I was intensely pleased that she had been so moved by the Mozart.

"This is another thing you've given me," she said. "Music and friendship—and sex! You know," she added, "I really had no idea about sex, I didn't know what people were carrying on about. I would read about lovers or see things in the movies, but it was like listening to a foreign language."

"You are a wonderful lover."

"Well, you did it. It's you who showed me what was there."

"Do you think these other people know about it?" she asked after a minute. "All these other people? Sometimes I feel so smug. I can't believe they have what we have."

And it was true, it often seemed to me—though I knew this was ridiculous—that we had invented the act of love and that no one else had ever done what we did, as if the things we committed were our own unique creations, reserved for us alone, unknown to anyone but us.

"I don't believe they do have what we have," I said.

"There, do you think that fat lady with her husband does what we do?"

"God forbid!" And we both laughed.

"Sharing the music is the same," she said. "Everything we do together is the same. Don't you see that? Don't you see that we just . . . click?"

"I see that I'm very much in love with you," I said.

But there came a time when Hélène and I saw less of each other. "I'm not worth seeing," she would say on the phone. "You don't want to see me when I'm in a funk like this. I'll just be a bore."

"You're never a bore," I said. "I want to see you."

"Really?" She always sounded surprised when I said this, as if someone's wanting to see her was unexpected.

"Let's just have lunch."

"No, I can't do lunch, David. I promised to see Caroline."

I did not question why she could see Caroline but not me. There was a point beyond which I did not wish to push the matter.

"You know, I don't quite understand how you manage your life," she said to me one day. "I mean, you love your family very much."

"Yes, I do."

"Well . . . what about me?"

"I love you too!"

"I see. It's very big-hearted of you."

"Well, I'm a big-hearted guy."

"The Big Two-Hearted Guy."

"Is it really so impossible to love two people at the same time?"

"I don't know. I think it would be for me. Sometimes I wonder what we even mean by love."

"Well, I know what I mean."

"Do you?"

"Yes, I do. Love is the willing of the other person's existence. The willing of it as you will your own."

"That's very ambitious, David. I wonder if that could possibly be right."

"What do you think love is?"

"That's simple. In loving you I want you. Love is selfishness."

"I don't agree. It might look that way, but in fact love is the opposite. Love is the attempt to escape the self. It is the attempt to escape loneliness."

Much of the time during this period Hélène sounded depressed and disoriented. She was in a funk, she said. It had nothing to do with me, she said. It was better just not to see her, she said. And so for a while I didn't.

But these periods never lasted long. I would call her in the morning as soon as I got to the office, and again late in the afternoon.

"How are you, darling?"

"Oh, I'm fine! It's so good to hear your voice."

"Is it?"

"Yes, truly. I miss you terribly, David. I'm sorry to be so beastly. You're an angel to me! I do love you."

"Do you, darling?"

"I love it when you call me darling. I ache for you. Your voice makes me ache."

"Let me come to you now."

"No, not now. Come to me in the morning."

"I'll be there at nine."

"Yes, come to me at nine. The earlier the better. I ache for you."

That August Barbara and I went to visit the twins at camp. It was high summer and the thruway was jammed with Americans seeking retreat. We passed station wagons pulling powerboats with motorcycles strapped to the back. Every car seemed to carry a message for its fellow citizens: Elevator Men Keep It Up, I'd Rather Be Fishing, Jesus Is Your Friend, I Love a Goose.

We drove up the New York side of Lake Champlain through the Adirondacks toward Port Kent, where we'd take the ferry to Burlington. Barbara hated air conditioning so we kept the windows down though the day was hot and the swollen air buffeted us. There was a great deal of traffic and I kept the radio on and drove fast as I wove in and out among the lanes.

"If Timmy hates the camp, perhaps we should bring him home."

"I don't think that's a good idea," Barbara said. "You'll make a sissy of him. Besides, what is Mat going to do without Timothy?"

"If they're such buddies, why is Timmy so unhappy in the first place?"

"That's not the point. I don't want them to think they can back out of things once they've started. You remember how excited they were going to camp."

"Yeah, well, they were all excited as they marched off to Bull Run."

"So should they have run away?"

"I don't know. I just can't stand to think of Timmy unhappy."

"Oh yes? Do you have a formula to make him happy? If he can't stand a little unhappiness at camp, what's he going to make of the world?"

"The world be damned, Barbara. When did you get to be such a Calvinist?"

"I'm not a Calvinist. The word you're looking for is *realist.*"

And it was true, Barbara understood the world better than

anyone I knew and I relied on her judgment implicitly. But I never observed that this knowledge made her happy.

We drove through the Adirondacks and the mountains were craggy and dark green and we were surrounded by wilderness.

"God, I wish we could live here. Why don't we live here, David? Why do we live in the middle of Manhattan with its bus fumes and its dog shit and its shitty people? That's never where I wanted to live."

"No? Where did you want to live? In a cabin by the sea?"

"I wouldn't mind that. I wouldn't mind living right here in the Adirondacks. I'd like to live where I could garden all year."

"Well, that's not the Adirondacks. In the Adirondacks you dig snow all year. Except when you're slapping deerflies. When did you get so restless, anyway? I don't think of you as the restless type."

"Oh, no? What do you think of me as—the Earth Mother? Someone who sits home all day and knits?"

"What are you talking about, Barbara? I think of you as the most accomplished woman I've ever known."

"Oh yes? Shouldn't you say the most accomplished forty-year-old woman?"

"Are you forty? You could have fooled me."

"What a line you have, David Smith . . . But I like it."

We waited at Port Kent for the ferry. The sun was bright and Barbara put on her dark glasses and leaned against the railing. With her rich full color bronzed from gardening and with her long simple skirt and white sleeveless shirt with the collar turned up, she looked terrific.

"Do you want a Coke?"

"Yes, that would be nice."

I bought two Cokes and I brought them back and gave her one where she was waiting by the dock. I could see the ferry approaching in the distance.

"I always love ferryboat rides," she said as she sipped her Coke through a straw. "Do you remember the ferry we took to Block Island and the kids who came out on those speedboats and followed alongside?"

"And the gulls that swooped down and took food from your hand."

"From *your* hand, you mean. I was too scared."

"No you weren't. You did it after a while."

"And the ferry that time when Jenny was a toddler and we had been camping and her face was covered with mosquito bites as if she had the measles."

"God, I was exhausted!"

"I finally went and slept in the car."

"You were pregnant then, weren't you?"

"Yes, I was pregnant with Alexandra."

"And the ferry across the Channel to Copenhagen with the students who started to dance and the old folks who joined in until pretty soon everyone was dancing."

"And the ferry to Cape May when the storm came up and I took the kids out into the storm and you were sure everyone was going to be washed overboard and wouldn't speak to me for an hour."

"God, that was crazy! I still think that was crazy! With the boat listing like the *Titanic* and those tiny kids out there on the deck and you fearless out there with them and me cowering in the cabin praying you wouldn't be washed away!"

"You big idiot."

"Yes, that's what I suppose I am."

And we both laughed.

We stood in the stern of the ferry and ate ice cream cones and made plans about how we would handle Timmy the next day.

"Do you think I don't want to baby him as badly as you do?" she said. "But he's got to grow up. Do you know he was the only kid who wouldn't go on the class sleep-away this spring?"

"Is that right?"

"Yes, it is. God, David, it's time the kid shaped up!"

"Well, I'm sure you're right. You always are."

The ferry nosed into the dock and the slight concussion sent a tremor through the ship. We got into the car and Barbara drummed her fingers impatiently against the dashboard as we waited our turn to leave. Then we drove into Burlington.

"Should we stay here for the night or drive north?"

"Let's drive north. I'd like to get there."

The countryside was poverty-stricken and beautiful as we drove northward, with small rundown cabins tucked back from the road like pockets of mold surrounded by forest and rusting auto fenders.

"*Appalachia redivivus,*" Barbara said.

We reached the town by four P.M. The "hotel" the camp had recommended turned out to be a double-decker motel set fifty feet back from the main road, within easy reach of the gas stations and fast-food establishments that were the century's chief contribution to the area. We checked into a room the size of a large closet smelling of Lysol and stagnant air.

"Good God!"

"Come on. You can put up with anything for Timmy."

"Now what do we do?"

"Let's go find the camp."

We drove out of town and the countryside by the lake was beautiful. A large sign at the entrance to the camp read CAMP IQUOPOOWO, NO TRESPASSING. We weren't allowed to visit until the next day.

We dined at a restaurant overlooking an old mill and separated from the millpond by a road; on the other side of the road there stood a bar. We both had the fresh fish of the day, which tasted strongly of refrigeration.

After dinner Barbara and I walked down to the pond. The ground was covered with goose shit and the geese had eaten the grass until it was as patched as a mangy dog. A white wrought-iron bench sat by the side of the pond, and near it there stood a sign that informed us FOR THE USE OF BAR CUSTOMERS ONLY!

When we got to the edge of the pond a man came out from the bar and waved at us vigorously with both arms over his head. He didn't look friendly.

"What do you think he wants?"

"I don't care," Barbara said.

"He seems in quite a snit."

"That's his problem."

"Can't you people read the sign?" the man called.

Barbara looked at the sign and then she looked at the man. He was a large red-faced man in a plaid shirt, and his hair resembled the grass by the pond.

"What do you think he wants?" she repeated.

"I think he wants us to go away."

"Why should we go away? We're not hurting anyone."

The man came halfway down the yard. "Hey, can't you people *read?*"

Barbara turned and looked at him steadily. "What's wrong with you?" she said. "We're just looking at the pond."

"This is private property," the man said. "It's for my customers only."

"That's not very friendly," Barbara said.

The man looked at her and didn't say anything.

"Let's go," I said. "We can live without this Shangri-La."

"I just want to look at the pond," Barbara said.

The man glowered at us. He was a big ugly-looking man, and it looked to me as if his life had been made up of a lot of disappointments.

"Come on, Barbara," I said. "Let's get out of here."

I touched her on the elbow and she started reluctantly up the bank.

The man didn't say anything. He just stood there and watched us leave.

"I've half a mind to tell him what I think."

"What's the point? Leave him to his goose shit."

We got into the car.

"What is this place?" Barbara asked. "Redneck heaven?" And with that we both began to laugh.

"Come on," I said. "Let's go back to the Ritz-Carlton."

When Barbara went to the local pit stop for provisions, I called Hélène.

"Are you having a marvelous time?" she asked.

"I wouldn't say that."

"Well, I hope you're having a marvelous time."

"Don't be like that."

"Why? I'm not being facetious. I mean it, I hope you're having a marvelous time. I know what a great dad you are. I envy you, that's all. I'm jealous. I hope Barbara appreciates what she has."

For reasons beyond calculation the small town's television offered a remarkable supply of good movies: *Giant* on one channel, *A Touch of Evil* on another, and then *The Guns of Navarone.* Barbara broke out the goodies she had bought and we sat propped in bed together, switching back and forth between channels and eating junk food late into the night.

The bed was too small, and when long after midnight we turned off the lights I curled up next to Barbara and we slept curled up next to each other like that, like two spoons curled in a drawer.

Uncle Tommy greeted us the next morning when we arrived at the camp at nine. He was the same old dude wrangler we knew and loved, sporting a cowboy hat and tooled leather cowboy boots and looking like a character in a children's cartoon.

"Well, howdy, Smiths! Good to have you aboard."

"How are you, Mr. Mixer?"

"It's Uncle Tommy to the boys, and it's Uncle Tommy to the dads and moms as well."

"Well, Uncle Tommy, how's the summer going?"

"Hunky-dory, Barbara, hunky-dory! The little rascals are having a whale of a time."

"Timothy writes that he's homesick."

"Nonsense. Don't believe a word of it. It's just what little boys write home to their moms."

We walked down toward the bunks and the boys charged uphill to greet us. They were funny knock-kneed little boys with long sandy hair and missing teeth, and though they were twins they were quite distinct. Mat was a competent, tough-spirited kid, good at sports and studies and emotionally standoffish. Timmy was softer-edged, high-spirited, easily hurt, uncertain of himself, sweet-tempered and emotionally needy. Because I was fearful on his behalf, I babied him—sometimes to Barbara's annoyance.

"Hi, Dad."

"Hi, Mat. How are you, son?" I rubbed Mat on his head.

Timmy had buried his face in his mother's lap and I knelt down to wait my turn.

"Hi, Daddy!" And he threw himself into my arms.

"Hi, Timmy. Hi, darling."

"I don't think he should cry like that," Mat said under his breath. I glanced at him and I felt a spasm of irritation.

"Mat, when I need your advice about Timmy I'll ask for it."

"They'll just think he's a sissy," Mat said.

"Why don't you come with me?" Barbara said to Mat, holding out her hand. "I want you to show me around."

"I want to go too," Timmy said.

"Then get ahold of yourself," Barbara said mildly. "You don't want the other boys to see you crying."

The boys spent the morning showing us the camp. The facilities were fine and the lake was clean and beautiful and at eleven o'clock we took a family swim together and I splashed and played with the twins.

"What's wrong with Timmy?" I said to Mat when I had him alone for a moment on the dock.

"Aw, he's all right."

"Is he?"

"Some of the kids are nasty."

"Oh yeah? Which kids?"

"Oh, just some of the kids. I've told them to stop."

"Have you? I'm proud of you for that."

He looked at me gravely from under his brows.

"I'll look after Timmy," he said. "But you've got to tell him not to be a sissy. It's embarrassing, Dad."

"You don't need to be embarrassed for your brother," I said, and my voice sounded too harsh.

Mat looked at me carefully and then looked away.

"You're a good kid," I said, tousling his hair, trying to compensate for my partiality.

After the family swim there was a barbecue. Uncle Tommy served spareribs and bug juice and everyone sat on the great lawn while the kids milled about and grew restless.

I pulled Timmy onto my lap.

"Timmy, I don't want you to be homesick, do you hear?"

"But Daddy, I *am* homesick."

"Listen to what I'm saying, Timmy. You've got to work at it. You're not a baby anymore. There's no cause for you to feel homesick. Mommy and Daddy love you, you'll be home before you know it. But you can't just run away from your problems. That's not right. You've got to deal with them. If you're a little homesick, you've just got to put it aside and not lend it too much attention, the way you do when you have a skinned knee. Do you understand?"

"I think so."

"Good. Now tell me, are the other kids being mean?"

"I dunno."

"Well, are they?"

"Maybe one or two sometimes."

"Do you want me to talk to Uncle Tommy?"

"Aw, Uncle Tommy's not good for anything."

"That's what I think too. Do you want me to talk to the kids?"

"No, Daddy—please. I'd rather *die.*"

"So what are we going to do?"

"I'll be okay."

"Will you?"

"Yes, Daddy. I promise."

"That's my boy. You'll make your mama proud."

At four we said goodbye and Barbara kissed the boys and there were a few teary moments, even for Mat. Barbara hated to leave them and for a while as I drove she sat in the car and dabbed at her eyes.

"How was your little talk with Timmy?" she asked.

"He'll be okay," I said. "He's a good kid."

"God, I hope you're right. I can't stand to think of him unhappy."

Though it was a long way home we decided to make a run for it.

"We'll be there by eleven," Barbara said. "What difference does it make? At least we won't have to put up with another motel!"

Barbara drove for an hour and then I took over and drove into the evening while Barbara slept. As I drove I thought about Mat and Timmy and about Barbara, and I tried not to think about Hélène. My life made sense only from hour to hour and I needed to serve each hour as best I could and not lose it all and ruin everybody's life. I wasn't sure I could do it. I didn't know how I had allowed everything to get so balled up and I was ashamed of myself for allowing it to happen. I had thought I was smarter.

One day Gordo came into the office with a gold-headed cane. He put up an elaborate pretense of indifference. I didn't say anything though I watched out of the corner of my eye. Finally, pushing back from my desk, I crossed my arms and stared.

"Okay, okay—I'm limping."

"So I see."

"It's no big deal."

"Who said it was? What did you do, pull a muscle?"

"I don't think so."

Gordo heaved himself into a chair. He was playing with the cane, twirling it between his hands while resting its tip on the floor.

"It doesn't feel like a pulled muscle," he said. "I have this funny tingly feeling."

"Have you been to a doctor?"

"Why should I go to a doctor?"

"Because you are limping around with a gold-headed cane and a funny tingly feeling. Do you *have* a doctor?"

"Sure I have a doctor—I suppose. I mean, I haven't been to a doctor in five years—and I'm not going now. Just don't worry your head about it, ol' bean. You've got your *own* things to worry about."

And he lumbered out of his chair and, leaning ever more pronouncedly on his cane, buffaloed out of the room.

That evening I mentioned the incident to Barbara.

"I'm worried about Gordo."

"Why—is he drinking?"

"No, it's not that. He's limping around on a gold-headed cane. He's been limping for over a month."

"Has he been to a doctor?"

"Of course not. He says he hasn't seen a doctor in five years."

"Well, he probably doesn't need a doctor. Gordon is as strong as an ox."

"Yes, but he says his leg is tingling. And the other week he dropped a glass of water as if it had been greased."

"What does that mean?"

"Damned if I know. But I can tell Gordo is worried about it. I can tell by the way he pretends he *isn't* worried."

"I see. Well, do you want me to talk to him about it?"

"Yes, if it keeps up I think you'd better. *Some*one has got to look after Gordo. And he'll listen to you."

Again I had to go to Chicago and this time I asked Hélène to accompany me. We were supposed to catch the five o'clock plane from La Guardia, but when I spoke with her at eleven that morning she said she had a cold.

"That's terrible, darling."

"I hate to disappoint you," she said, "but I'm really feeling awful. Maybe I'd better not come."

"Really?"

"I wouldn't be any fun like this."

"Well, you know I'd love to have you. But you have to do what you think best."

"I'm not going to come, darling. I'm really sorry. It's such lousy luck."

I worked hard all morning and had a sandwich at my desk and called Hélène at two. She wasn't in. I felt an inadvertent spasm of annoyance. If she was so sick why wasn't she at home in bed?

She called me back fifteen minutes later and in fact she did sound as if she had a cold.

"I'm sorry, darling. I went out to get some medicine."

"That's okay. I was worried about you, that's all. I just want to know you're okay."

"Well, you can hear, can't you?"

"Poor you."

"Poor *us*. We'll just have to take a raincheck."

I flew to Chicago and again my room overlooked the dark waters of Lake Michigan. I spoke to Barbara and to the children and had dinner by myself, and I was sitting in my room drinking whiskey when Hélène called at eleven-thirty.

"Hi, you."

She sounded slightly drunk.

"Why aren't you here with me?"

"I don't know. I don't know why I'm not there."

"Well, you should be."

"I know. I know I should."

"How's your cold?"

"It's nothing. It's all gone."

"So you could have come after all."

"Don't be angry with me, David. I *did* have a cold. Oh, I don't know. It just all seems so hard."

"What have you been doing?"

"Nothing. Sitting home and watching television. Pining for you. Drinking white wine."

"Don't drink too much of that stuff."

"I'm not. I'm not drinking too much. I'm just pining for you, that's all."

"Well, you could have come."

"I know that. You think I don't know that. I could have been there with you in bed. All night with you in bed. What heaven!"

I didn't say anything.

"Don't be angry with me," she repeated.

"I'm not angry," I said, but my voice didn't sound convincing.

"I want to be there with you in bed. I want you to be making love to me."

"What's the point of that?" I said, and I couldn't suppress my annoyance. "What's the point of saying that when we are a thousand miles apart?"

"I don't know," she said, and her voice sounded so sad and

small that my heart went out to her and I felt how much I loved her and how I wanted her.

"I wish you were here too," I said. "I wish I were holding you in my arms."

I went to her as soon as I returned. Her rooms were decorated with things I had given her, things we had bought together. I had come to think of her apartment as ours.

Afterward she nestled in the crook of my arm.

"Wouldn't it be lovely if we could start every day like this?"

"Yes, it would be lovely."

I rolled over and kissed her on the nose. I loved the way she smelled, a combination of flesh and the warm sweetness of her breath, of sex, perspiration, perfume, and the sweetish whiff of excrement that love entails. I would carry this odor on my person for the day.

"What if I stopped taking the pill?"

"What do you mean?"

"Just that. Just what I said. What if I stopped taking those things and became pregnant?"

"Go ahead."

"Really?"

"If that's what you want to do."

She thought about that for a moment.

"I guess we can't," she said.

"It's not such a great idea."

"You don't want to have a baby?"

"That's not what I said."

"No? It sounded that way from here."

"That's unfair, Hélène. It's you who said we shouldn't. I'm not stopping you from having a child. How could I?"

"You could insist that I have one of those things."

"An abortion?"

"I would never have one, you know. You'd better know that. And it's not because I was brought up a Catholic."

"You can't scare me, Hélène. I never said anything about an abortion."

I was obsessed with Hélène. I kept trying to imagine an act of

such intimacy that its performance would bind us together forever. We would emerge from lovemaking with our bodies
drenched, our minds dazed with the chemistry of love.

"My God, David—what are you *doing* to me?"

"I'm making you mine."

"I'm so utterly yours, David. How can you doubt that I am
yours?"

Nonetheless she would call the next day to say she couldn't see
me for lunch. Indeed, it seemed there was a kind of rhythm to our
relationship, the more intimate our lovemaking, the more certain
the swing in the opposite direction, though Hélène denied this.

"No, David. My moods have nothing to do with you. You are
what's *right* about my life. I just wish there could be more of it."

"What do you mean?"

"I mean I wish I could be with you all the time."

"But think how much time I do spend with you."

"How much? An hour, two hours, four hours? Then you go
home to your family. I'm just a good fuck."

I was profoundly shocked by this. Hélène never swore.

"Don't talk that way!"

"Why not? It's true, isn't it?"

"It's utterly not true. It's absurd."

"Well, why don't you make an honest woman of me?"

I was deeply moved by what she had said. I was deeply moved
by the thought that she wanted me to marry her. I wondered
whether it was entirely true.

"I would if I could," I said. I didn't myself know for certain
what that meant.

"That's what all men say to their mistresses," she said.

"That doesn't sound like you, Hélène. Who told you that,
Caroline?"

"It has nothing to do with Caroline."

These tiffs ended in bed. Afterward I couldn't believe I had
fought with Hélène; it must have been a different woman. Then,
in another week, the quarreling started again.

* * *

One night that fall when I called Hélène at eleven she wasn't in. I couldn't imagine where she was. It wasn't like her to be out at eleven without letting me know.

I called again at twelve and she still wasn't there.

I called again at one.

I sat by the phone and was incapable of explaining how this disaster had come to pass. The large apartment filled with the sleeping people I loved seemed to echo emptily around me. I had no idea where Hélène might be.

"I went out with Caroline," she said the next day.

We were sitting at lunch at the back of a small restaurant and I thought she had never looked more beautiful. The image came back to me of when I had first seen her on the boat in New York Harbor, when I thought she must be a movie star.

"Where would you be with Caroline until two in the morning?"

"Don't you believe me?"

"Of course I believe you," I said.

It was impossible for me not to believe her, though something about her story didn't ring true, perhaps that she hadn't told me her plans in advance, for we told each other everything.

She smiled, and it was impossible not to believe her smile.

"Who do you think I am?" she asked. "Do you think I am a party girl like Caroline? David, you've got to believe me, I'm not like that."

"I do believe you."

And I did. I felt ashamed of my doubt.

Later we went to her apartment and made love.

In the heat of lovemaking I hoisted her onto her knees so that her fine buttocks were in the air and her head down and her large breasts hung down so that her nipples grazed the sheets. She groaned as I entered her. And longing for there to be something irrevocable between us, something sacramental that could never be taken away, I removed myself and, finding her again, I thrust myself up her ass.

Afterward she sat at her mirror and chatted about Caroline. She was naked, and her long elegant legs were crossed and one foot with its red painted nails beat time idly as she spoke.

"She's gone utterly bonkers. She's decided she's too fat for Alex and has gone on a crash diet consuming nothing but water and— dog food. She keeps a supply of the stuff in her pocket and nibbles on it throughout the day; it's nutritious, she says, and it keeps her sufficiently nauseated so she doesn't crave anything else. She prefers something called 'Lassie' and orders it by the boxful the way you might order Evian water. She says it's proof positive she is a bitch.

"She's convinced that if she becomes pregnant Alex will marry her. He's told her as much. He's fifty and never had a child and apparently he promised to marry Caroline if she becomes pregnant. The only problem is he's said the same thing to Katrina Uberding and three or four other women to Caroline's knowledge, so they're all in a race to see who can throw her diaphragm away the fastest. Last night her dress was so low you could see the tops of her nipples. She powdered them so they wouldn't be so visible. I think she has lost her mind."

I did not understand why we were talking about Caroline and I had to suppress a wave of irritation. I tried to hold in my mind an image of how Hélène had appeared ten minutes ago, groaning and abandoned. No matter how intimate the act, she always escaped. I could never entirely penetrate the polish of her worldly prattle.

"Poor Caroline," I said. "She sounds a little nuts."

"Does she? Well, we're all a little nuts."

"Not as nuts as Caroline. I'm afraid she's an idiot."

"You think everyone is an idiot. You look down your nose at everyone."

"No I don't."

"Well, tell me someone you don't look down your nose at."

"You."

"That's not fair. You are not allowed to include the woman you are fucking."

"Is that what we do?"

"Making love, if you prefer. But yes—fucking. Wouldn't you say that we were just fucking?"

"I suppose, if you want."

"I do want. I do want very much, thank you."

And she came and sat on my lap. She put her hand on my nipple and kissed me with her tongue.

"I can't get enough of you," she whispered. "Do you see what you've done to me?"

And then we didn't see each other for a week. "I'm not worth seeing," she said. "I'm just in one of those moods."

"What moods? I don't understand these moods. Tell me about them. Let me try to help."

"How can you help? Why don't you just go back to Barbara and help her? You are too busy helping too many women."

"Why are you saying these things, Hélène? I don't understand you. I thought everything was fine between us."

"Did you? Did you think that?"

"Don't you love me anymore?"

"Love you? Of course I love you. I love you too much."

When she said this a weight lifted from me and I could breathe again.

"And don't you believe that I love you?"

"Oh, I suppose you do. And Barbara. And Jane and Jill and Joan. You're a great lover, aren't you, David? A great lover of women. A great cocksman."

"Don't talk that way."

"No? Well, then don't talk to me. I told you I'm not worth talking to. I'll get over it. You've just got to leave me alone when I get like this. Lock me in a closet and throw away the key."

But she called the next day.

"When are you coming to me?" she asked. It was as if there had never been a problem between us.

"I don't like it when you take me from behind," she said later. "I like it when you are on top of me and deep in me and we come together. That's the best," she said.

"Oh, God!" she said. "I can feel it when you touch my center, way deep inside me. I want you to stay like that forever!"

When she was like this it was impossible not to believe that everything was right between us. Anything seemed worth it for this.

When we walked side by side her breast often brushed my arm and she appeared to me the most desirable woman in the world.

She said, "If you left me I would go back to being celibate. I was celibate for years. I'd just go back to being celibate."

"You've changed," I said. "You couldn't go back to being celibate."

After a while she said, "Maybe you are right."

"I think of you as my wife," I said.

"You shouldn't call me your wife."

"But I feel you are."

"You have a wife, David."

"Yes. But it seems to me you are my wife also."

"But I'm not. I wish I were but I'm not. You are just confused."

And it was true, it seemed to me I was married to Hélène. How I managed this I cannot say, for I never doubted I was married to Barbara, so I suppose I thought I was married to two women at once. Perhaps when one is in love one is doomed to relive the entire epic of the heart in all its chapters, as if forging it for the first time.

One weekend we went to the country and Barbara planted hundreds of bulbs. She was out in the garden by nine in the morning, and she worked all morning without surcease. Whenever I looked out the window she was on her hands and knees planting bulbs. At about eleven I went outside and stood near her, watching. She glanced at me once but didn't say anything.

"Can I help?"

"If you want."

"What should I do?"

"See these? Plant them around the tree."

"Will they thrive over there?"

"Just do as you're told."

I planted the bulbs around the pine tree. There were about twenty of them and I had to scoop out the earth and put down enriched soil and bone meal and then plant and cover the bulbs. It was easy monotonous work and after a while I enjoyed it.

"Aren't you two *ever* going to be finished?" Mat called. Barbara didn't bother to answer.

Alexandra made lunch. We had soup and bread and I had a beer. Then we went back to planting.

"Don't bend over like that," Barbara called to me. "You'll get a stiff back."

"I have one already."

"Well, quit if you want."

"No, I can do some more."

We weren't done until four o'clock. We both stood, and Barbara put her hands on the small of her back and stretched. She surveyed her work and I could tell she was pleased.

"Why do you let me buy so many?" she said.

"Do you think I could stop you?"

"Every year I swear I'm going to buy fewer."

"And every year it's more beautiful. It wasn't such a big job, really."

She looked at me and shielded her eyes from the sun.

"Not when you have help. Thanks."

"I enjoyed it."

"Well, soon we'll have to mulch the garden for winter."

"Ugh."

"You don't have to do that," she said. "I can get Hogan in to do that."

"Whatever you want," I said. "It's good when we do it together."

"Yes," she said. "That's what I think."

And then again I didn't know where Hélène was. I waited up past two calling her, but all I received by way of answer was her voice on the answering machine, friendly and serene and slightly scented with its untraceable foreign accent.

"Hi! I'm not here right now. But if you'd like to leave a message, I'll get back to you as soon as I can." Click.

What message did I want to leave? That I didn't know where she was? That my life was coming apart? That I was going crazy?

"Where the hell *are* you?" I hissed into the phone at two A.M., and immediately I knew it was a mistake.

I hung up and lay on the couch in the dark, and as I watched the unidentifiable lights move like outlandish submarine creatures across the ceiling, I tried vainly to piece together the parts of my shattered life.

I did not call her the next morning and she did not call me, but she called at the office at three that afternoon.

"It's Hélène," Marie, the secretary said, and I could hear the disapproval in her voice. Gordo shifted so his back was to me.

"I'll take it in the other room," I said, and I shut the door behind me.

"Hello," I said.

"Hi!" Her voice was cheery and friendly, as if nothing had happened, as if I hadn't left the message on the phone, and my heart sickened, for even with that "Hi!" I knew I couldn't resist her.

"Where were you last night?" I said. "Where the hell were you till three A.M.?"

"Please don't speak to me like that. I'm not used to being spoken to like that."

"I don't care about that," I said, though in fact her words made me check myself. "I want to know where you were until three A.M."

"It wasn't three."

"Well, I called you at two."

"Yes, I remember your message, David. *Très poli.*"

"Please don't play games with me. Don't give me that French bullshit."

"I'm sorry you think it is bullshit. It happens to be who I am. Under the circumstances I don't see there is anything more to say."

And she hung up.

I sat shaking with fury and despair, staring at the telephone, waiting for it to ring again. But it didn't. Finally I called her back.

"What are you doing?" I said, and I could hear my voice shaking. Somehow I managed to scream and whisper at the same time. "What in the name of God do you think you are doing?"

"I don't like being a mistress," she said. "It isn't my style."

"What are you talking about?"

"Just what I said. Being a mistress isn't my style. I don't like the secrecy, the deceit. It isn't worthy of us, David. Not of you and not of me. You should go back to your wife."

"You don't mean that," I said. "You know you don't mean that. Think of how we were just two days ago. Think of what we did with each other."

"Yes, I know. I'm just an easy lay, someone you sneak off to between breakfast and dinner with your wife and family."

"Oh, God, Hélène—you're not going to start that again. You know that's not how it is. You know I love you."

"Do you? Well, maybe you do, David. How should I know? But it doesn't change anything, does it? It doesn't change the way things are."

"Well, I don't see that the way things are is so terrible. I don't say it's ideal, but I don't see that your life suddenly becomes so wonderful the moment I leave the scene. What do you do then? What do you do by way of a man, Hélène? Which brings me to last night. I still want to know where you were last night."

"I went out with Walter Straus, if you want to know. I could tell you some story—that I was out with Caroline, for example—but why should I? What's so criminal about my going to a party with Walter? He happens to be an old friend of the family, as you know. An old friend of my father's. And why shouldn't I go to a party with him from time to time? Why should I sit at home doing nothing while you watch television with your forty children, or whatever it is you do?"

"No reason," I said, and I felt a lump rise in my throat, a dryness, as if something had gotten caught halfway down. "No reason, except you said you wouldn't. We had an agreement. If you wanted to change the agreement you should have told me. You should have. I mean, I was up waiting for you until two o'clock, Hélène. I had no idea where you were."

"It's because you don't trust me," she said.

"Of course I trust you."

"No you don't, or what would you be doing waiting up until two o'clock?"

"Because I call you every night, Hélène. What are you talking about? What fairy tale are you spinning? I called you the way I do every night and you weren't there. And you weren't there and you *still* weren't there. What was I supposed to assume?"

"That I had gone to bed with Walter Straus, right? That I was making love with some sixty-five-year-old friend of my father's."

"Hélène, no! That's not what I'm saying. I'm just saying that if you wanted to go out with Walter Straus you should have told me. You owed it to me, Hélène. Not just because we agreed, but because I love you. There can't be the degree of intimacy that exists between us without our at least telling each other what we're doing."

There was silence after that.

"That's all fine and good for you," she said. "But it's not working for me."

"What's not working?"

"The whole thing, David. The whole thing. I can't go on being a . . . *mistress!* It will kill me."

I tried to convince her that she wasn't a mistress, but I could discover no word in English to substitute for it. There was no noun to describe what we were.

"If you want me to be your wife I'll be your wife," she said. "I'll marry you in a shot. But you've got a wife, David, so that's not what I am. I'm your mistress."

We tried not to see each other. This attempt lasted exactly five days. During that time we did not speak to each other and it was the longest we went in two years without speaking.

One morning as I walked in Central Park I saw how badly I had misled my life and an immense wave of relief lifted me as I reflected that now I could put it back into shape. I recognized that the only way to lead one's life was in accordance with some moral order—which I had violated.

But as I pursued these reflections I observed two dogs bound across the frozen meadow. A clutch of sparrows wheeled into the sky like a handful of pebbles and flew away. Light beat like thunder against the adjacent buildings. And a young woman with her afghan slouched past, both gliding with the same undulant nonchalant grace, the woman leaning backward from her waist, her slender shoulders together, her smooth flanks moving, rhythmic and dazzling.

The next day found me by the telephone.

"Why don't you get down to work and do something productive," Gordo said. He was wearing a brown corduroy sports coat and he looked strangely scrunched-up and old, like a piece of wrapping paper thrown into a corner. His face had assumed a scruffy appearance, as if he weren't shaving properly, and his lower jaw trembled even when at rest like a glass jar left on top of a motor. But his eyes were a deeper shade of brown and bored into me with a loony prophetic intensity.

"What are you, some sort of inquisitorial magistrate, Tate? How do you know, maybe I'm waiting for my bowels to work."

"Yeah, you have that constipated, squinched-up appearance, it's true. What you need, ol' boy, is a mountainload of prunes to clean out your fucked-up soul."

I went out to lunch and wandered up and down the streets and felt abandoned. I could see no remedy for this aloneness. It was as if I were trapped in a small air pocket in absolute darkness under the ground—only the air pocket was the entire world.

That afternoon she called.

"I love you," I said. It was the first thing out of my mouth and it was as instinctive as drawing breath after being long under water. I said it too loud and I saw Marie shift her back so it was to me. I too shifted my back, but I didn't care.

"I love you too," she said.

"God, it's sweet to hear that!"

"We can't fight like this," she said. "It will kill me."

"Yes," I said. "I thought I was going to drown."

"Me too. Caroline is pregnant," she added. "She's going to have a baby." She sounded strangely shaken.

"Is that good?"

"I don't know. I hope it's good. David, I don't care if I'm your mistress as long as I have you. You're all I have in the world. Do you understand that? I'm completely alone in the world."

"You'll always have me," I said.

We started seeing each other again. I called her three or four times a day and we saw each other for a drink at the end of every day. I went to her almost every morning and Hélène would have made love every day except I could not keep up with her.

She said to me, "I have nothing in the world but you. I have lost my country, my mother, my father, my husband. I have no one else but you."

I stroked her hair, her breasts, her cunt.

"I love it when you touch me," she said. "I *love* it!"

But later she said, "I've done the stupidest thing in the world. I've fallen in love with a married man."

Caroline lost her baby. It was winter now and cold and when she started spotting her doctor ordered her to bed; but she got up anyway to do some shopping and was doubled over with cramps on Madison Avenue. She lost the baby as soon as she got home. She called the doctor but it was too late. Afterward he sent her back from the hospital to rest at her apartment.

Hélène spent every day with her. I was surprised how deeply she identified with the crisis. She wept repeatedly when she spoke of the lost child.

"Would you give me a baby if we could?" she asked.

We were lying together in the still, afternoon light.

"Of course I would."

"No, don't just say that. I'm being serious. Would we have a child together?"

"You know we would. Nothing would be a greater pleasure—a greater privilege."

She started to cry. At first I wasn't sure what was happening but then I saw her shoulders shaking. I had never seen Hélène cry before and it moved me deeply. I took her in my arms.

"Don't talk," she said. "Just please don't say anything."

"It's the worst thing that could have happened," she said about Caroline. "Now she'll never have a baby."

"You don't know that," I said. "She's not old."

But Hélène insisted. "No," she said. "She is forty, that was her last chance. She says so herself. Now she'll never have a baby. She'll die without a child."

And she said to me, "I'm not going to die without a child."

One morning at about eight o'clock I was sitting in the kitchen drinking coffee and catching up with the *New York Times* when Jenny said, "Dad, why is America rich when the rest of the world is poor?"

She was leaning against the pantry counter, and when I looked at her I felt a mixture of pleasure and pride tempered by trepidation, for it was no easy job answering this fiery independent sixteen-year-old.

"Well, let me see. First of all it's not quite true that the rest of the world is poor."

Jenny wrinkled her nose. "You know what I mean, Dad. *Most* of the world. Is it because America is greedy?"

"Well, yes, in part. But I don't think that's the crux of the matter."

"Well, then, what is the *crux* of the matter?"

"Some cultures are good at creating wealth. That's what they do."

"What's that mean? I don't understand."

"Wealth doesn't just grow on trees like oranges. It has to be created. It requires a certain kind of organization. Other cultures have different organizations, different disciplines. They create different things. Think of each society as a kind of machine. Well, some of these machines create wealth. Others create other things."

"Such as what?" Jenny asked. She was watching me attentively.

"Well, let's see. Religious cohesion. Civic pride. Military prowess. Maybe human happiness. Maybe many of these other societies, these Third World societies, were significantly happier than we before we came along and began squeezing wealth out of them. Maybe they were wiser than we. Who's to say? It doesn't seem unlikely to me. But the point is this: the wealth wasn't just there lying around waiting for us to steal it. Without us, no wealth. Happy harmonious societies, for all I know. But no wealth."

"So that's what we do?"

"Yes, in part. In great part."

"I think I prefer other machines."

I snorted with amusement. "That doesn't surprise me, Jenny. After all, you're my daughter. But it's the machine that gives us this coffee to drink, this paper to read."

As I said that my eye glanced down and alighted on a photograph in the society page of a back issue of the *New York Times.* It was of Hélène.

An electric shock passed through me. I grew very still. It was as if an accident had occurred and I was afraid to see what injury had been inflicted.

The caption read, "The comtesse de Compière was accompanied last night to the Highland Ball by the prominent social figure Walter Straus."

I looked at Straus carefully: a short, balding, heavyset man, powerful in appearance, with a curly gray beard and a haughty nose that listed to the right. His eyes sparkled in the picture and his mouth was twisted at the corner in the simulacrum of a grin.

Dressed in a low-cut evening gown, Hélène looked beautiful even in the grainy news photo. She wore a diamond collar at her throat.

"Well, I still think it's greed that makes us so rich," Jenny said. "I mean, it's obscene, when Africa and China are the way they are."

"What?"

"China, Dad. Think about China."

"Yes, whatever you say. But why don't you run along for a while, Jenny, okay? I mean, I'm sorry, darling, but I just don't want to debate China and Africa first thing in the morning."

"Well, thanks for being so interested in what I'm saying, Dad. Thanks a whole bunch!"

I tried not to look at the photograph. Hélène was smiling brightly; she looked as if she were having the time of her life. I felt a tremor or rage pass through me which I subdued, but I could not banish the taste of despair.

Barbara came into the kitchen.

"What did you say to Jenny to put her into such a huff?"

"Nothing. She wanted to debate Third World politics."

I closed the paper.

"Well," Barbara said, "you've been called a fascist for your pains. As in, Why don't you have breakfast with my fascist father?"

"The self-righteous little prig."

"Now you know what it feels like. She's on my case twenty-four hours a day."

"Poor you!" I kissed her on the cheek.

"Where are you off to?"

"I need to make a phone call."

I went to the study and closed the door. My hands were shaking and I felt short of breath. It was insane to call Hélène from the apartment like this in the morning.

"Hello," she said, and her voice almost made me desist. It was impossible for me to associate anything sinister with the sound of her voice.

"I see your picture in the *New York Times.*"

"What?" She sounded genuinely surprised, and for a moment I thought perhaps there was some mistake.

"In the *New York Times,*" I repeated. "In the social page."

"Oh, *that!* Yes, isn't it ridiculous?"

"What are you doing on someone else's arm in the social page of the *New York Times?* What's going on?"

"Nothing's going on. Nothing."

"It doesn't look like nothing. It doesn't look like nothing when I open the social page of the *Times* and find a picture of you in evening dress on someone else's arm at a prominent social event. It doesn't feel like nothing when this is the first I hear of it. I don't usually read the social page of the *New York Times,* Hélène. This one is almost a week old. Clearly I wasn't supposed to know anything about this."

"There is nothing to know about. I went to the Highland Ball with Walter, that's the beginning and the end of it. I didn't tell you because I knew you would make it into a big deal."

"You're damn right I will make it into a big deal. Didn't we explicitly agree that you weren't going to do this? It makes me wonder what else is going on."

"Nothing. Nothing is going on."

"Who is this Walter Straus, anyway?"

She paused for an instant. "I told you, he is a friend of the family. An old friend of the family."

"A close friend, it would seem."

"You are not going to be jealous of *Walter?*"

"I wasn't jealous of him, Hélène. It's you who have done this, not me. It's not I who put your picture in the *New York Times.*"

"Big deal," she said, and her tone had taken on an edge of exasperation. "So I went to a dance with Walter. I'll go to a dance with fourteen men if I want to."

"What are you saying? What in God's name are you saying?"

"I don't know," she said, and her voice sounded genuinely bewildered. "What am I saying?"

"You said you'd go out dancing with fourteen men." In my excitement it seemed to me possible that she had actually misunderstood her own words and I seized on this as if they had been a mistake.

"Did I say that? Well, I don't know what I'm saying. Walter's been so good about Caroline," she added. "He's really been magnificent. A crisis brings out the best in him."

"Yes? Like invitations to the Highland Ball?"

"That's not what I mean," she said.

"Well, that's great. That's dandy that he's so nice to Caroline. But what does that have to do with your turning up on the social page on his arm? That doesn't have anything to do with Caroline, Hélène. That has to do with *us.*"

"Walter's very nice to me," she said. "He takes me out places.

He's a friend. I used to have a social life, you know, before I devoted my life to waiting around for you."

"Are we going to start all that again?"

"What do you mean, start? When did it ever stop? The three nights a month when you can sneak away to some hole-in-the-wall restaurant where no one will recognize us? Or to some hotel in a distant city where you can check me in as your wife? Is that what you mean? But the other nights, believe me, it's going on—the nights when I sit around waiting for you alone in my apartment with nothing to do but to think and be lonely and watch my life slip away. All my friends think I'm crazy. They think I'm out of my mind."

"Is that what Walter Straus tells you?"

"Yes, it is, if you have to know. He thinks I'm crazy to be tied up with a married man who will never leave his wife. And he's right. I'm nothing but an easy lay."

"What did you say?" I felt as if I were choking.

"Just what I said. I'm nothing but an easy lay. That's all I am to you. So I go out dancing one night with Walter Straus. Big deal. Big fucking deal!" And she slammed down the receiver.

I was shaking with fury, fear, despair. It was entirely unlike Hélène to slam down the phone like that. It was entirely unlike her to swear.

I looked around but for a time I couldn't take in where I was. Slowly the room came into focus. A picture frame. My desk. I was still in my study. I had been carrying on like this in my study.

Through the closed door I could distinguish the sound of the twins preparing to leave for school.

I thought to myself, You are losing your mind.

I sat down and my heart was pounding so violently I was afraid I was going to have a heart attack. How in the name of God had I reduced myself to this? The thought of losing her was intolerable. Her picture in the *Times* made me sick.

I picked up the receiver and called her back. I didn't know what I would say but the silence between us was unbearable.

I got a busy signal. She had taken the phone off the receiver.

I stood up slowly. My head was spinning. You are panicking, I thought. Unless you are careful you will do something stupid.

"Are you all right?" Barbara asked. I was in the foyer. I couldn't remember walking down the long hall.

"Yes, yes. It's nothing at all. It's just—oh, nothing. I was talking with Gordo, that's all."

"Is Gordon all right?"

"Yes, yes. It was about a business deal. You know Gordo. You know how exasperating he can be."

"Poor Gordon! I don't want you fighting with him, David. He's not well. And he's your oldest friend."

"Yes, yes, I know. I'm not fighting. I just have to go to the office, that's all."

"Well, call me later. Let me know that everything is all right."

"Daddy, don't forget the tickets," Mat called.

"Tickets?" I turned to Barbara for help.

"For the Knicks," she said. "You promised to take them to the Knicks."

"Oh, God!"

"Do you want me to pick them up?"

"Would you?"

"Of course. Just tell me where to go."

"The Garden, I think—but I don't really have the slightest idea."

"Well, don't worry about it. I'll find out. Daddy will know."

"Yes, that's a good idea. Call your father. He'll know."

I went out into the sunlight. The doorman was at the corner hailing a cab and I turned abruptly uptown to escape his greeting. I needed to find a pay phone.

The air still held its early-morning promise before the city smudged it with fumes.

"Don't be angry at me," she said.

Again her voice, plaintive and small, constrained me to belief.

"Let me come to you," I said.

"Yes," she said. "Yes."

Later, when I was holding her, when her full breast with its large pinkish areola like a delicate fruit stain was pressed against my arm, later she whispered, "Save me."

"What do you mean?"

"Just save me, save me. Oh, David, you must marry me and make me yours. Don't you see it? Don't you see that that's all I want? David, I'm so frightfully alone."

I took her to dinner and we tried to examine what was happening to us.

"I'm obsessed with you," I said.

"Yes," she said. "And I with you. We are totally in love. I don't think there can be many loves like ours."

"No, of course not."

"Have you ever been in love like this?"

"No, never."

"I never even knew it existed," she said. "I thought it was only something you read about in books."

"But what are we going to do?"

"You've got to marry me. Don't you see that? Don't you see that otherwise it is all wasted? It will all come to nothing."

"But I can't marry you, Hélène. I have four children. I have a wife who loves me."

"And what do I have? What about me? David, I'm no good at being alone. I want you. I want you for me. I want to have a child with you. I don't want to end up like Caroline. I don't want to be a society girl in the pages of the *New York Times*. Save me from that, David. You've got to save me from that."

It was literally as if the ground were falling from under me, as when you stand on the beach and the waves cut the sand from under your feet and suddenly you are pitched off-balance by the incoming waves.

"But Hélène, this is crazy. How does it make your life better to go to parties with Walter Straus? It's you who do this to yourself, to us. I beg you, Hélène. Don't get all fussed. Why can't you hold on to what we have? It's imperfect, I know—but isn't it preferable to our *not* having it? I no longer can imagine life without you. When I try to imagine it, it's as if I were suffocating, as if I were being forced into a narrow box. I can't live without you, Hélène.

And I can't see your life without me. What would that solve? You'd be thrown into a world where you'd drown."

"Yes, very likely," she said.

"So why must we do this? Why can't we hold tight to one another? I don't care what it looks like to the world. Except for hurting Barbara I don't care about any of it. I don't care what the world thinks. Its opinion isn't worth our love. But I can't continue if you are going to go out with other men behind my back. I just can't do it. It's too painful, Hélène. It's not in me."

"Yes, I know that. I don't want to hurt you, David. It's not as if I did anything so terrible, is it?"

"Of course not. Of course you didn't do anything so terrible. I don't say you did. I don't think it for a minute. I would put my life on your honor. If you don't love me, if I'm mistaken about that, I don't know anything, I might as well say I'm not sitting in this chair."

"Well, you are," she said. "You are sitting in the chair. And I do love you."

"Well, then can't we stand by each other? Listen, darling, I give you my love to carry, it's like water in a beaker. If you fall, it's my love you spill. Do you get it? Do you see what I'm trying to say?"

"I don't really understand about the beaker," she said. "But I know this. I'm no good at being left alone. We've got to work something out. You've got to give me something more. I want you to marry me, David. I want you to think about that."

After this I was perpetually off-balance. For almost two years Hélène had seemed completely mine, and even now it was impossible when we were together to doubt the strength of her love; but henceforth throughout that spring there was always an undercurrent, a sense that once I left the room, all bets were off.

"Tell me you are mine," I said as we lay on her crumpled sheets after making love.

"Yes," she said, but then her eyes clouded over. "But it's more complex than that, isn't it, David? Marry me and I will be completely yours."

A chill passed over me. The thought of her with another man sickened me.

I actually began to consider whether I could marry her.

In May I had to go to Boston for two days. I couldn't get out of the commitment and Barbara said she wanted to go. She had a school chum in Boston she wanted to visit.

I was afraid to tell Hélène.

"Let me go with you," she said.

"You can't. Not this time. I'm sorry, Hélène. I'll make it up to you."

"Barbara is going."

"Yes. She has a school friend she wants to visit."

"Why doesn't she visit her another time?"

"I can't say that to her."

"No, of course not. You couldn't hurt Barbara. Barbara always comes first."

"It's not a question of coming first, Hélène."

"No? What is it, then?"

"I have no way of telling Barbara she can't come. I just can't work it out."

"So where does that leave me?"

"Please, darling, don't be like that. I hate it as much as you."

"Really? As much as I? How extraordinary!"

"But I do, Hélène. You've got to believe me."

"Then why do it at all?"

I was afraid to ask her what she would do when I was away.

"Will you go out with Straus?" I asked.

"No, I won't go out with Straus," she said impatiently. "I won't go out with anyone. I don't know who you think I am. I'm completely faithful to you. Stupidly so. Disgustingly so. I'll just sit around and moon and stare at the walls."

"No, I don't want you to do that," I said. "Go out with Straus if that makes you happy. I don't care. Just don't forget you are mine."

"As if I could forget that," she said.

But I was delighted when she told me Straus would be out of town. I trusted her implicitly—but I was delighted she wouldn't be going out.

I could not call her until eleven-thirty at night, but when the phone rang she picked up immediately.

The sound of her voice made me shiver.

"Hi, darling!"

"Hi!"

"Are you okay?"

"I'm fine. I'm just fine. I'm missing you is all."

"Did you go out?"

"I just had dinner with Caroline. Nothing special. Just to cheer her up."

"Alone?"

"No, with Mick Jagger and Sting."

"Are you serious?"

"God, you're silly. Alone, stupid, alone. I had dinner with Caroline alone. Two old maids."

"Two beautiful young women."

"Two middle-aged women."

"One middle-aged woman and one beautiful young woman."

"Now which one could that be?"

But two days later she said, "The other night Walter asked Caroline and me to go out with him to the Hamptons."

"Oh? The other night?"

"Yes."

"When you were having dinner with Caroline?"

"What? Oh no, no. It was another time. The point is he invited me to the Hamptons."

The point was I had caught her out—or maybe I had.

"So Walter was with you the other evening?"

"No . . . Yes, he stopped around at Caroline's for fifteen minutes. He came to see Caroline. David, you are getting to be a bore."

"Am I? I wouldn't be if you just told me the truth."

"That's a horrible thing to say! I *do* tell you the truth. You just get all fussed, is the problem. But from now on I'll tell you every little itty-bitty piece of the truth, okay? So here: the other day when *you were away in Boston with your wife* and I went out till *ten o'clock* to have dinner with *Caroline, Walter Straus* stopped around for *fifteen minutes* to invite the two of us to join him two weekends from now in the Hamptons. Okay? Now the question is, do you mind if I go?"

"Of course I mind," I said, and I could hear I was already losing control. "I thought we settled all this—I don't want you going out with Walter Straus, whoever he may be. I don't want you going out with anybody. Jesus, Hélène! I just don't get it. Think of what we were doing half an hour ago. Think of that. And now you ask me, cool as anything, whether I object to your going out to the Hamptons with another man. I just don't understand that, Hélène. I don't understand why you *want* to go."

"Why I want to go? Because I'm lonely, that's why. I'm lonely and I'm jealous. I'm thirty-two years old without a husband without a child living in a country that isn't really my own in love with a married man who won't leave his wife and who demands complete loyalty from me—loyalty which by the way I gladly give but for which all I get is more loneliness. I don't want to go to the Hamptons with Walter. I hate the Hamptons. I hate that whole scene. Do you think I want to hang out with Walter Straus? Is that what you think? So I won't go for the weekend. I don't want to anyway. But I'll tell you what I *do* want. I want to go away with you. I want us to go away and I want us to go away for the whole weekend. I want it to be ours. That's not asking too much, David, is it? I don't want to go away with Walter Straus, but I do want to go away with you. So work it out. Please work it out. I don't mean to be threatening you, but please work it out."

I did not see how I was going to get away for a whole weekend, but I did not see how I could not. I saw that if I did not, Hélène would go to the Hamptons with Straus.

"Okay," I said. "Okay, I'll work it out. We'll find a weekend and I'll work it out."

"What's wrong with that weekend?"

"Nothing. Nothing's wrong with that weekend. I'll work it out and we'll go away for that weekend. Okay? Does that make you happy?"

"Of course it makes me happy, David. It makes me ecstatic. I'd like to spend *every* weekend with you. I'd like to be *married* to you!"

I could think of nothing to tell Barbara. I watched her the next weekend watering the flowers in the garden, and I remembered how we had laid out the garden together when we had bought the house over fifteen years ago. We had paid for the house with Barbara's money but it had been bought in both our names.

I knew I could never leave Barbara.

When she picked up the hose to drag it to another location she leaned forward, causing the muscles in her calves to tighten, and I remembered how her legs had looked when I first knew her. I recalled an afternoon of flawless sunlight when I found her sitting on a rock taking the sun, and as I approached I saw up her dress along the curve of her thighs all the way to the soft triangle of her panties. She had been one of the most sought-after girls at Vassar, and the sight of her thighs and of her panties beneath her dress had taken my breath away; and now twenty years later I recalled that moment perfectly.

Again I had a sense that I was losing my mind.

I decided not to say anything to Barbara about the coming weekend until I had worked things out in my head.

Once or twice during the week I attempted to raise the subject, but without success.

"I may have to go away next weekend," I said tentatively.

"Oh, not next weekend. Don't you remember the gutters are being done on the roof? I want you here for that. We need to decide about the windows on the front porch and I don't want to make that decision without you."

"Oh, yes, that's right," I said. Barbara's voice had assumed its no-nonsense tone.

"Where shall we go this weekend?" Hélène asked.

"Where would you like to go?"

"No, you decide. Baltimore? Should we go to Baltimore? You once spoke of our going to Baltimore. But at any rate, someplace nice. Someplace near the water. I want to sit on the beach with you. I want to make love on the beach."

I was to pick Hélène up at her apartment early Saturday morning.

I wrote Barbara a letter.

My dearest B:

I love you. I have loved you since I first saw you. I will always love you.

I am going away this weekend. It's not worth going into the details since you with your keen mind and instincts would find them stupid and boring. They have nothing to do with you, nothing to do with the fact that I love you, which remains untouched, inviolable.

For the first forty years of my life I always felt older than I was. I wasn't tempted by the mistakes that tripped up my contemporaries and made a mess of their lives. It was as if I had lived before. Well, I must have died at thirty-nine. Everything since then has been terra incognita. This is the second life.

You didn't approve when I told you about my boxing in high school, but I loved it. At first I loved winning. I didn't have a knockout punch, but I was fast and could outpoint most of my opponents. I bloodied many noses. What I now remember is losing.

I remember one particular bout with a guy named Gerald Roving. He hit me early and I knew I was in trouble. He put me on the seat of my pants in the first round. After that all my skills were dedicated to losing well. I knew he could beat me up. He put me down again in the fifth but I got up quickly. I had pulled back just in time to slip the punch. He didn't put me down again. Of course he won the decision. I remember later someone saying to me, Too bad about the fight. Actually it was the best fight I ever fought. It's what I now remember about having been a boxer. It's what makes it worth having boxed.

We all lose, my darling. Only you never deserved to.

I love you.

I sealed this letter and put it in my top drawer. I still hadn't decided what I would do. I had agreed to pick Hélène up between eight and nine. Barbara wanted to be on the road by eleven.

When nine-thirty passed I thought the phone would ring but it didn't.

At ten I called Hélène. No one answered. A wave of panic went through me. I told Barbara I would be back soon.

"Well, make it *very* soon." I could hear the irritation in her voice.

I put the letter to her on the Louis XV table by the front door, then I went round to the back hall, where I had placed my suitcase. I was sick with nerves.

I felt steadier when I went outside. I took a cab to Hélène's.

It was after ten and I was an hour late. I rang her from downstairs. No one answered. I let myself in with my key and went up.

No one was there. It looked as if no one had been there that night. The air conditioning was off and the windows were closed and the apartment was stuffy and swollen with heat. I sat in the hot cloistered air and tried to think. I had no idea where she could be.

I got up and looked around the apartment. Everything was in its place waiting to be picked up, to be used, but frozen, frozen and motionless, as if in a frozen, motionless slice of time. I saw the records I had given her, the books. A message was written in oil pen on the top of her desk and then partially wiped out. The pages of the manuscript she was writing sat in a pile in a corner.

I picked up an article of her clothing and held it to my face as I wandered absently about. Its odor clung to me.

When I sat down again I was perspiring heavily. The apartment was stifling. The entire place had the air of waiting, of waiting for life to start again. I felt sick.

I let myself out the front door. And as the door closed I felt a weight drop from me palpably, as when a fever breaks and suddenly the exhaustion is a palpable relief.

When I got home the letter was still on the front table where I had left it. I picked it up and put it in my pocket.

"There you are," Barbara called. "Kids, your dad is home. Come on, it's time to go."

I called Hélène repeatedly that weekend but no one answered. She had gone, I didn't know where. When I tried her on the phone I felt mad with apprehension; when I worked in the garden my mind went numb. At night I lay and stared at the ceiling.

I didn't hear from Hélène on Monday. I kept calling the apartment but still no one answered. On Tuesday I called Caroline but she wasn't home. Then on Wednesday someone picked up at Hélène's.

It was Caroline. Something terrible had happened. Hélène had been struck by a taxi on Madison Avenue. It had happened Monday afternoon. She had been killed instantly. Hélène was dead.

BOOK THREE

S he had decided to end her affair with Tony.

She went to the library to continue her research on her book but instead she opened the most recent letter from Poppie and read it while she sat among the American students in the cold-smelling hall. The letter was in French.

Compière, March 12, 1986

Dearest Hélène:

 Yesterday I dined at Mme. Follenvie's together with the ambassador and his wife, the comtesse de Grieux, Tiddy and Dianne, and a host of others. The comtesse looks like a great orange cake that has been sat upon. I sat next to an American lady from Arkansas, very lively and talkative, who had read my books and wanted to discuss God. The Americans are a delightful people but incorrigible. But you know my opinion. We were served truffles, and there ensued a great discussion concerning whether they were real, *for it seems a brisk trade is now carried on with home-grown varieties that can lay no claim to the proper venue. At any rate, they were delicious. Again, you know what I think about "delicacies."*

My eyes are not much improved but this cannot be helped. You are please not to worry. I spoke with Father Lathes, who sends his greetings. He asked whether you were coming home. Compière is beautiful now with the first buds of spring and the morning air still biting. It misses you, as do we all. But enough of that.

Dearest child, I hope you are happy. I pray for you daily. I also hope that the research is progressing and that soon you will be able to commence the actual writing. I will write again in a few days. The Tallyrands will be coming for the weekend and I have invited David and Agnes and their teenage boys to join us for dinner on Saturday. I hope this won't prove imprudent. I shall let you know. In the meantime, dearest child, be sure that you retain the full affection of

> *your husband,*
> *Armand, comte de Compière*

Hélène, comtesse de Compière, folded the letter and put it back into her purse and sat staring at the long wooden table in front of her marked with pencil scratches and knife-like indentations. After a while she rose and left the library.

She exited into the bland March sunlight of Manhattan. Though officially still a graduate student at Columbia, she had not attended classes in over two years.

She could hear the traffic on Broadway, and as she hesitated at the top of the stairs, the wind, which was cold, caught at her skirt and troubled it. Goosebumps prickled along her arms.

She had absolutely nowhere to go.

She struck out northward up Broadway. Though she had lived in Manhattan for more than four years, she had never ventured in this direction. The sidewalk ran downward into the trough at 125th Street beneath the elevated train, but when she ascended the other side into Harlem she was in a different world.

Protected from the wind, she found the air warm and she began to perspire. Children were playing on the sidewalk, their voices strident and as high-pitched as sparrows'. The sidewalk smelled of laundromats and of the heavy odor of fried food. Young black men loitered in tight knots at the corners. A Hispanic lurched sideways toward her, then veered away.

Working well now, her body shook off the emptiness of the library. A Puerto Rican woman escorted her daughter to the bakery, the little girl dressed in yellow finery with shiny gold studs in her ears. A handsome black woman laughed at something a young man said. Two middle-aged men, their skin cocoa and coffee respectively, worked on a dilapidated Buick propped on cinder blocks at the curb.

The sky had cleared to a milky blue. Hélène removed her sweater and pushed her sleeves up her forearms. Her nostrils filled with a faint odor of dust and excrement. Overhead an airplane passed, its boom rattling the windows. Sun smudged the sides of automobiles. She heard the drone from the West Side Highway; a bus wheezed by, filling the block with black ill-smelling exhaust.

She entered a pizzeria and ordered a slice of pizza with pepperoni and a diet Coke and ate the pizza from a piece of greasy white paper. The pizzeria smelled of fresh pizza dough. The young man behind the counter was dressed in a red-striped uniform with a greasy apron and she watched him position a fresh pizza pie in the oven with a long wooden spatula. He was a young Hispanic man with a soft black mustache and she could discern the play of muscles in his forearms as he maneuvered the pizza.

After she left the pizzeria she hesitated at the corner. Again she realized she had nowhere to go. It had been months since she had accomplished anything on her book. For an instant she felt dizzy and thought she was going to fall down. She fought an urge to call Tony.

A bus approached up the block. She opened her purse and fumbled for a token; she could see the overseas envelope that contained her husband's letter. Then she climbed into the bus and sat in a seat with a window.

She sat for a long time without paying attention. Lulled by the motion of the bus, she managed to lose herself without thought or requirement. When she roused herself she was amazed to see how little progress they had made.

She climbed the hill at 207th Street and the wind chilled her.

A sinister emptiness invested the park. The trees seemed eaten by the winter; irregular patches of bark had been bitten away like ugly sores. The sticks by the side of the path looked waterlogged, as if the entire park had been immersed in dirty water.

The Cloisters reminded her painfully of Europe. The spring when she had been pregnant with Eve, Poppie and she had traced the pilgrimage route to Compostella across southern France. She had slept in the back seat of their Citröen while Poppie stopped at Souillac and Moissac to study the Romanesque statuary; when she awoke the flamelike figures seemed to swirl and sway at her out of the moving stone. It had been hot in the car and they had paused at a little hotel by the Lot and had eaten trout and drunk the local white wine and then she had fallen back to sleep while Poppie drove. He had been invariably kind, with his long white face and white hands, and he had ordered separate rooms for them in the hotels when they stopped for the night.

Now however she sat in the Cloisters in New York City in the United States of America in the small lower garden with the espaliered trees that overlooked the Hudson and thought about Tony. She wished she could erase him from her mind forever.

When she married Poppie she had been only nineteen years old and he was thirty-five years her senior. Poppie was the younger son of one of the old vintner families of France, and her father, then dying of throat cancer and much concerned for the welfare of his only daughter, was delighted by the match. Hélène's mother, a Catholic from America, had separated from her husband when Hélène was ten; but upon the mother's death, when Hélène was fourteen, the girl had been shipped back to Paris and the care of her adored father. Eager to set her father's mind at rest, she had acquiesced to the marriage proposal pressed upon her with gentle effete ardor by her father's friend.

Her father had been a French diplomat of the old school and had known Armand de Compière all his life. He saw nothing strange in passing his daughter on to a man his own age. He knew the count to be a man of honor and rectitude, an author of scholarly disposition like himself, and he could imagine no more suitable guardian for his beloved daughter as she entered adulthood bereft of mother and father.

The mother had been a different kettle of fish, and it would take Hélène years to articulate to herself the suspicion that she had been something of an adventuress: sedate, to be sure, cautious and with an eye to propriety, but when all was said and done, on the make. She was a woman of great beauty, with high delicate features and a petite waist and full womanly breasts; and though her husband had been a good catch, it was a disappointment when he proved less worldly than an elegant woman of her appointment might have desired. Not that her tastes were recherché. She liked parties. She liked to be admired. And there were many in Paris willing to oblige. When the marriage broke up there was a hint of scandal.

She returned to America to regroup, with her ten-year-old daughter in tow. They had been great buddies when Hélène was young, companions in the great adventure of life, and Hélène had wished for nothing more than to be like her mother. But she could not countenance the abandonment of her father, and it was from this event that she dated the dawn of independent consciousness. She began to observe her mother with a new eye, and what she saw gave her food for thought for the rest of her life.

Then her mother was diagnosed with cancer.

Hélène returned to Paris just before her fifteenth birthday. Her mother became someone she did not care to think about. She settled down to be her father's little wife. And thus in turn the marriage to Armand seemed as natural as inheritance.

Country life demanded some adjustment after her Parisian adolescence, during which she had been coddled and spoiled by her father. She had played hostess at the parties he gave and had acquired a taste for the grand world. His death, however, left her deeply shaken, and she was content to shelter in the regard of the older man into whose hands she had been entrusted.

She soon came to love Compière, with its vast fields of grapes and its gentle rolling mists that came in from the Cher and its early mornings with the odor of tillage and the stirrings of small-town life. Her bedroom opened onto a terrace overlooking the valley, and there in the heat of day the bees would come and at night the village owl would swoop past in the dark. In winter she would lie in the narrow bed and watch the frost bite into the windowpanes, and in the heat of summer she bathed in the river.

Poppie was a tall shy refined man with a prominent Gallic nose and gentle watery blue eyes. He looked like a Norman warrior gone slightly effete. He had served bravely in the war, first at the front and then in North Africa with the Free French. Later he had been an ardent Gaullist, representing Compière in parliament. He was a devoted Catholic, an expert on Port-Royal who had written lives of Pascal and Fénelon and often contributed articles to *Le Figaro* which proved as whimsical as they were astute. His brother had been a socialist and the mayor of Compière, but the two bachelors had lived together amicably all their lives. Upon the elder brother's death, Armand had inherited the estate.

Nothing surprised his friends so much as his marriage.

Poppie's devotion to Hélène was apparent. He had known the beautiful young woman since she was a little girl and her orphanhood moved him deeply.

Compière was windy and cold and disheveled and only the ground floor was suitable for habitation. Poppie moved his study upstairs and had a living room prepared for his young bride. He decorated a bedroom and a sitting room for her and installed modern plumbing. He was invariably deferential and considerate and *vous*-ed Hélène when they were together in public. She quickly came to depend upon him.

To her surprise Armand did not approach her on their wedding night. It was winter then at Compière and cold, and they routinely retired early to their separate rooms. Then one night at nine he knocked at her boudoir.

His knock startled her.

She found him in no way disgusting, though he was thirty-five years her senior and balding. They seemed equally virginal. But though she helped him, the encounter was a muddle, with no adequate response at first and then a sudden blinding spurt that left her sticky but intact and him shaken and apologetic. She might have laughed save for his discomfiture. It seemed scandalous to see Poppie in that condition. After that they desisted.

There were no neighbors, no young women in the area to befriend, and Hélène was thrown on her own resources. Poppie was unalteringly polite and considerate but absorbed in overseeing the château and keeping up with his writing, and for much of the day there was no one to talk to. She didn't mind. She had been an only child and she had grown accustomed to being alone. But sometimes, despite her mild contentment, it struck her that something, she hardly knew what, was lacking.

In summer she swam in the Cher. Often she would go in the morning and then again in the afternoon. She went whether it rained or the temperature fell—it made no difference. To miss even a day depressed her.

She loved to push out into the tepid, slightly muddy water and feel its current nudge her waist. The stream was strong toward center. Sometimes she would float downstream watching the osiers by the shore and the large willows that bent riverward and trailed their long fluttering leaves in the water. Flycatchers darted out from the branches, and from the banks the sweetish odor of manure floated in sultry invisible clouds on the air.

Once she saw a group of young men swimming. She paused in the bushes to watch; she recognized some of them from the village. They must have been eighteen or nineteen, younger than she, just country boys playing and splashing. It pleased her to watch. It pleased her to observe the sun on their shoulders and flanks. When they splashed the spray wheeled out like knives. Their shouting and laughter made her smile. One of the young men raised himself out of the water, the sun beating off his breast like gold. And it came to her with a shock that the male body was beautiful.

After that she was less at ease. Sometimes she would catch herself looking at Armand, wondering about him. She realized she didn't know him at all.

She went frequently to church and tried to talk to Father Lathes but she had the feeling he didn't want to hear her problems. He was a dark, well-knit man with heavy eyebrows, much devoted to the house of Compière.

"Your husband is a beautiful man," he said. "A gentleman of the old school. There are not many like him left."

She shrugged her shoulders impatiently. She didn't need lessons on the value of her husband.

She was more and more troubled by restlessness. Her dissatisfaction reminded her of her mother, but this only angered her, for it was her father she had loved.

She confused her restlessness with a desire to return to the United States, which she invested with all manner of excitement. The friends she had known in junior high school troubled her dreams. She wondered what had become of them. Their lives seemed to her infinitely desirable and they returned to her imagination charged with erotic intensity.

She started a friendship with a boy in the village, the wayward unkempt son of the local police magistrate. It began with a case of arson in one of the outlying buildings on Compière. When M. Flange arrived to investigate, Hélène accompanied him to the site of the fire. As she approached the charred ruins she saw Louis standing to one side poking with a stick in the dark earth.

There was a fair that evening in a village thirty kilometers distant, an annual *kermesse* she wanted to attend, and since Poppie wouldn't drive at night, Louis offered to take her. He appropriated his father's police car and they drove at breakneck speed through the gathering dusk, tearing down hills into pockets of mist and veering round bends. Her heart pounded as they careened through the countryside, but she said nothing.

After that he would pick her up in the evenings and they would go driving. Poppie encouraged her to go; he thought it healthy for her to have a friend her own age. In fact Louis was a year younger than she.

He had failed his *bac,* not through lack of intelligence—she quickly saw that he was intelligent enough—but through utter lack of interest. He wanted to be a rock star. She got him to sing for her: he had a sweet weak high-pitched voice, and when he sang something moved in her as if he had touched her belly with his hand. She was attracted to the bad boy in him.

He talked about going to America. America was the home of rock 'n' roll. It was only in America that he could achieve himself. He wanted to hitchhike to Memphis and visit Graceland.

She told him everything she could remember about the United States, and the more she talked, the more mythic it appeared to both of them. It bound them together, it was their secret. Once while she was talking he reached out in his excitement and touched her hair.

Armand and she went to Paris for a week to see Armand's publisher and when they returned Louis was sullen and withdrawn. He didn't come at night to take her driving and when he saw her in the village he *vous*-ed her and called her Comtesse.

She dreamed of him and when she awoke she thought she would cry. She couldn't believe she had become dependent on a scruffy nineteen-year-old village boy.

They went driving again and he stopped by the Cher and kissed her on the mouth. He put his hands on her breasts and she didn't see how she could summon the strength to stop him. Nothing in her life had ever felt so good.

She gave him her virginity on the bank of the river. It seemed to her that she was rising up and up; she pushed herself against him so hard that her buttocks were off the ground. She did not realize that the cries she heard were her own. Later he wiped her thighs with damp leaves.

But soon she came crashing to ground. The guilt and shame were so severe that she didn't see how she could live. She dropped Louis. She determined never to see him again. She told Armand she wanted to have a child.

Poppie was a gallant and persistent lover but she soon understood that he harbored some fundamental repugnance for the body, with its strange insistence and awkward demands; and this saddened her, for they might have been happy together. She loved his kindness and his innate tact. And she loved the body. When he entered her—and he was still a strong and imposing man—she felt a warmth that suffused her to the crown of her head.

When she told him she was pregnant he ceased coming to her room.

At first she was sick with the pregnancy, but after the second month she felt fine.

She studied herself in the full-length mirror in the old oak armoire in her bedroom and she was pleased with what she saw— pleased with her breasts, which had now swollen out so the nipples protruded and there were stretchmarks along the sides; pleased with the meniscus swell of her belly and the bushy prominence of her pubis, which she touched lightly with her hand. She had never felt healthier.

Nothing had seemed right since the death of her father, but now it was as if the world had settled back into place. She wasn't afraid. Pregnancy seemed to her like a country to which she was returning after a long and troubled voyage. She couldn't wait to be a mother.

It was at this time that Poppie conceived the trip to southern France. He had been approached to write an article about the pilgrimage route to Compostella, and she slept in the back seat of the car while he drove from Tours to Toulouse, the voyage a pleasant dream of movement and long sojourns in village squares and of half-seen landscapes and dappled warming sunlight moving across her sleeping face.

The labor started at midnight and continued for twelve hours. She kept calling out to Poppie as if he were her father. Sometimes she thought she would drown in the waves of pain. But she was never demoralized.

Eve Marie Denise de Compière was born at 12:37 P.M. on June 9, 1978. She weighed five pounds, four ounces and she had congenital heart disease.

The child was beautiful but of a slightly bluish color, and as she lay in Hélène's arms, her little mouth gasping for air, she seemed to Hélène as if she were a delicate creature from some other element unable to breathe the coarse atmosphere into which she had been plunged.

The doctors were not hopeful.

As Hélène nursed the baby she knew she would gladly give her life so the child might live. "Please, God," she prayed, not bothering to finish her sentence. "Please, God . . ."

For two weeks they kept Eve in the hospital. Hélène would spend the day with the baby or in the waiting room. The infant was losing weight. Hélène had to abandon breastfeeding and for days her swollen breasts hurt so it brought tears to her eyes.

When she came home at night Poppie would silently take her hand. When he had first learned of the baby's condition he had wept.

Then they were allowed to take Eve home. If she lived they would operate on her. The valves of her heart were damaged.

They had prepared the baby's room in the south corner of the château and a nurse had been hired, but Hélène would not allow anyone else to touch the child. She carried her daughter from the car up the front stairs across the parquet floor into the nursery and laid her in the bassinet. Armand kneeled by the side of the bassinet and prayed.

Then began a struggle that would last for nearly a year, a fight that she perceived she could not win but that she stubbornly refused to lose.

Eve did not gain weight. Hélène would nestle her daughter in her arm, willing her to take the bottle the nurse had prepared. Eve watched her mother out of large slate-blue eyes and wrinkled her small face into a frown. Her little hands clenched and unclenched like sea anemones.

Then for a time Eve improved. She was a good baby, *pas sauvage, très sage.* She slept through the night, she took her bottle, she smiled at the strangers who came to admire her frail beauty.

When Hélène entered the baby's room at night and saw the child sleeping on her back in the bassinet, her small diaphragm rising and falling, her dark hair matted with perspiration, her entire being clenched with something that was more pain than joy and that, not being translatable into any other emotion, constituted the root signification of love.

Sometimes she accompanied Armand to mass on Sunday in the ancient rain-soaked church with its worn porticoes and mullioned stained-glass windows, and the damp-smelling silence filled her with rebellion. Armand's tall shoulders stooped as he prayed and the thin candles guttered and flared, and she wondered what she was doing there and longed to be back with her baby.

The doctors assured her that when Eve gained another three pounds they would be able to operate. Hélène would put her ear to the narrow chest and listen to the small pit-pat of the damaged heart; and Eve would grasp her mother's thick unruly hair in her hands and laugh.

But before the day of surgery arrived Eve succumbed to the first of a series of viral attacks that reduced her little organism to feverish hacking.

Hélène spent her nights crouched beside her daughter's crib listening to the congested wheezes and coughs of the nine-month-old. It was impossible not to pray. She had lost all conception of whom or what she was praying to; but the tension of waiting was too great for her to bear alone. She was open to any deal, any connivance, so long as her daughter survived.

Eve weathered the first of these bouts and even seemed to improve. She was a loving child who laughed and cooed and played with her mother. She recognized her father and her nanny and was actively experimenting with sounds. She would lie on her back for forty minutes talking to herself with the little chortles and articulations of the newborn. She seemed delighted to be alive.

It was May now, and the heat of the day would carry the sweet odor of talcum and unmortified flesh throughout the rooms. When Hélène entered the baby's quarters the sun lay over the furniture like shellac. Everything assumed a still slow gravity in her eyes, as if she were trying to commit it all to memory.

Eve came down with another virus.

In the heat, the doctors were especially concerned about dehydration. The tiny form seemed to be sweating into inexistence. Hélène could feel the heat of the fever when she placed her hand above the crib. She spent her nights by the infant trying to induce her to drink. Finally Armand insisted that she get some sleep. He took her place by the baby's side.

Then the baby could hardly move. She lay like a drowned puppy at the bottom of the crib, a small doll crushed by the weight of being. Hélène looked at her for a moment and then looked away. On the sixth night Armand took her aside.

"*Ma chérie,* it's no good. You have got to let her go."

"What do you mean? What do you mean?"

"My dear! Please. I can't see you like this."

"But what are you trying to say?"

"It is you who are keeping her alive, Hélène. With your will. It is not fair to the *bébé.* It is not fair to yourself."

"Ooh! How can you say that? How?"

"Because it is true. You know it yourself. You must let go. You must trust in God."

"In God? In God, you say? I hate your God! I only wish He existed so I could tell Him how I hate Him."

"Please, Hélène. You don't know what you are saying."

"I know what I am saying. I know exactly what I am saying."

Two days later Eve died. By now she was just a small sack of bones. When Hélène lifted her she seemed no heavier than the stuffed dolls Hélène had slept with as a child.

They buried her in the family crypt overlooking the Cher where Hélène had swum. Poppie and she held hands. But she refused to attend the mass held that evening for the child's soul.

Then there started a bad time for Hélène. She tried to interest herself in the viniculture of Compière, but wherever she looked she saw emptiness. Pointlessness. It was a taste in her mouth. The look of barren afternoons when the sky has no center and hangs behind the naked trees like a stupid idea. It was a long voyage that she did not want to take toward no destination whatever.

It was at this time that she began to call Armand Poppie. He demonstrated toward her an infinite patience and kindness. When she looked at him he seemed to have aged, to have grown balder, with only a few gray hairs flying discordantly from the top of his head. He was a tall, well-built man with stooping shoulders and a long, rather sad face, ugly by modern standards but aristocratic, with refined prominent features whose lineage could be traced in family portraiture back to the seventeenth century; and when she looked at him she felt a combination of love, pride, and impatience.

That winter she walked between the long, frozen rows of vines and it seemed to her that they formed a net in which she was trapped. Once she thought she saw Louis standing at the far end of a field, but she turned away. All that was dead in her. Besides, it couldn't have been Louis, he had fled to America leaving his native village of Compière behind.

If she could think of a place to go, she would go there herself, but there was nowhere, the world was contained where she was, at Compière, trapped among the frozen fields.

A year passed, then two. In the evenings Poppie poured sherry and pottered in the kitchen. In the winter Hélène watched the crimson light low against the western horizon, a ribbon of fire beneath the black kettle of descending night.

She noticed that Poppie was drinking too much sherry.

He went every Sunday to mass and said his prayers at night on his knees. His belief, whatever it was—and she never inquired—was apparently as naive and immediate as the colors of the landscape.

Then one spring she decided to write a book. It was the first idea she had had since the death of Eve. It came to her as a kind of hope, a dull stirring like a sluggish motor trying to turn over.

She would write a book about the de Compières, it would be a tribute to Armand, a way of telling him that she loved him; and it would serve as a memorial to Eve, the last of the line.

She spent evenings interviewing Poppie about his ancestors, about his memories of his parents and grandparents and the legends surrounding the family. The family had been local gentry for centuries; Napoleon had conferred the present title on Général de Compière after the battle of Austerlitz. Armand's mother's line, the Lingers, was one of the oldest families in the country, descended from the Normans and much grander than the de Compières.

Armand was delighted with Hélène's project. Though the least pretentious of men, he was intensely proud of his lineage and proved a storehouse of information not only about the de Compières but about the history of the region and of France in general, for he was a good historian, with an encyclopedic knowledge of the minutiae of the ruling class of the last three centuries. Hélène's research gave the two of them something to share.

Hélène spent hours reading documents in the local *mairie* and *société d'histoire.* For the first time in years her attention was concentrated on something other than herself. Sometimes she would lift her head from the annals she had been reading and stare up into the blond warm light streaming in from the large dirty window onto the table where she sat, and it would come to her with surprise that for three hours she had been utterly absorbed in what she was doing.

Her research came to center on the Napoleonic general, the first comte de Compière. She saw him as a kind of alter ego to her husband, a dashing figure who represented what Armand might have been had he not found himself tied down Gulliver-fashion by the inhibitions and punctilios of an ancient line running to seed at the conclusion of the modern era.

The first de Compière had been a man of the Enlightenment who at eighteen had sailed to America like his friend Lafayette to fight with the colonists against perfidious Albion. An adjunct to General Greene, he had been present at Yorktown and had seen action throughout the southern campaign, where he had received the first of the fourteen wounds he would boast of before his death at eighty-two. During the revolution he had served with Lafayette in Belgium, had avoided the Terror by a blade's edge, and then had distinguished himself in the Italian campaign. It was at the battle of Austerlitz that he won Napoleon's loyalty. When ordered against great odds to turn the flank of the Austrians, de Compière jauntily replied, *"Je m'en fiche de cette enfilade de fillettes, mon général,"* whereupon he led the charge that decided the day.

The more Hélène read about de Compière, the more fascinated she became. It seemed to her that in marrying Armand and bearing Eve she had affiliated herself across the generations with the Général in some intimate ineffable manner that implicated both of them in a desperate impossible struggle, so that if somehow she could extract from the dusty annals the essence of de Compière's dashing forgotten compromised existence, if she could make them surrender the shape of that elegant and superfluous biography and

could resurrect it, then he in turn, with a careless shrug of benediction across the centuries, would confer on her own growing and
panic-stricken confusion the form and outline of a meaning.

She soon discovered that many of the relevant papers were in
the National Archives in Paris and that there she must go if she
intended to pursue her studies. Poppie was entirely supportive.
And so it came about that Hélène began spending three or four
days a week in the capital, catching the Monday train to Paris and
returning on Wednesday or Thursday. Her days were passed at the
Bibliothèque Nationale and she roomed in a modest pension on
the rue Jacob.

She was not lonely. Though Poppie pressed upon her the names
of his abundant acquaintanceship, she rarely accepted the invitations that ensued; she hadn't the time to be bothered with the
elderly aristocrats and right-wing intellectuals and ladies of society who constituted Armand's circle. She knew she was adrift in a
small skiff surrounded by heavy fog far out at sea, and there was
nothing for it but to set her oars in the locks and start rowing—
though she had no idea where she was headed.

So she plugged away at her biography of de Compière, her
quasi-relative, biting her nails, neglecting her hair, developing
hemorrhoids from her long hours of sitting on the hard benches at
the *bibliothèque.*

A young man who worked at the library sometimes brought
her the books she requisitioned. His hands were narrow and
white, with long delicate fingers and pinkish handsome fingernails, and they held objects with a kind of nervous attentiveness,
as if they possessed an intelligence of their own, cunning and
gentle. Sometimes at night Hélène thought about this young
man's hands, the delicacy of their touch and how they would feel
on her neck; and this simple desire appeared to her comely,
wholesome, and utterly unattainable.

And so eight months passed, and then nine. She spent more
time now in Paris; she attended more of the cocktail and dinner
parties to which Armand's friends invited her. Her notes on de
Compière collected in bunches and began to seem a little incoher-

ent. Sometimes, sitting in the library, she would read a volume that had nothing to do with her work at all.

It was at this time that she met Walter Straus. He was an acquaintance of Anna Troy, an American widow of a certain age who kept a kind of salon in Paris and New York and who had known her father as well as Poppie.

Straus was a short, rotund American in his fifties with a powerful stomach and chest and a prominent nose that veered to the right, hooded intelligent gray eyes, and a weak chin disguised beneath a gray curly beard. He spoke correct French in a careful high-pitched voice while he kept time by pinching his fingers together in a strange rhythmic gesture. Eager to speak English as well as to hear of the United States, Hélène was delighted to meet Straus, whose practiced and elaborate politeness amused her; and soon they were conversing in his native tongue.

Straus was a jeweler who moved freely between New York, London, and Paris. His stores on Madison Avenue and the Faubourg St. Honoré catered to the moneyed on both sides of the Atlantic, and Straus, whose name frequently appeared on the society pages of the *New York Times* and *Vogue,* counted among his intimates such notables as the duchesse de Bobo, Mr. and Mrs. Eucalyptus Swoon, Carter B. Carter, the Abraham Baumbergs, Coco Peking, Sir Harold Fat, and Lord Weinreb.

"My dear countess," Straus said, "you must allow me to take you to lunch. I know you must be overwhelmed by invitations, but you can't imagine the pleasure it would give me to spend some time with a woman like you who can appreciate the inconvenience of my position. I flatter myself that we have something in common, what with your being part American, I mean. Perhaps only you can imagine how isolated and lonely one can become with one foot on one side of the Atlantic and one, as it were, on the other. The posture, I assure you, is precisely as comfortable as it sounds."

Perhaps it was the word *lonely* that touched her, for there was indeed something lonely about the gray eyes that watched her so intently. She found herself agreeing to have lunch with him.

The morning before their luncheon he sent round a dozen long-stemmed roses. It was a piece of extravagance, but one that she found she could countenance. The flowers seemed to light her small room like flames.

"I would have sent two dozen," he told her as he arranged his linen napkin, "but I was afraid you would balk at that."

"Quite right," she said, laughing. "I wouldn't have any idea what to make of *two* dozen roses. Indeed, I don't quite know what to make of one, but somehow my modesty can accommodate that moderation."

"It's a token of my friendship," he said. "Of my thankfulness, countess, for your being here with me. I know what an honor it is."

"What silliness. I'm really just an American girl—or at any rate *half* American."

"Really? Well, I've known many Americans, but none like you."

They ordered trout and she allowed him to pour her a glass of white wine. She found to her surprise that she was having a good time. She wanted to talk about America.

"You must return and see for yourself," Straus said. "It would give me the greatest pleasure to show you New York. It's truly quite wonderful these days, quite the capital of the world."

"I don't think Poppie would care much to visit America. He has the friendliest feelings for Americans—as long as he is safely on this side of the Atlantic. But as for visiting New York . . . well, frankly I can't imagine it!"

"Perhaps you could come sometime by yourself."

"Oh, I don't think so. I could never leave Poppie."

"Well, then it's too bad he entertains the feelings he does. I say nothing about your husband, who by all accounts is the most agreeable of men, but as for the French in general, though they are a people whom I love and admire, they seem incapable of thinking straight on the subject of Americans. Though clearly fascinated by our culture, everything from Levi's to rock 'n' roll to the layout of our weekly magazines, they habitually speak of the United States as a place of cowboys and red Indians and quite look down their noses at us as so many barbarians."

"Oh, the French look down their noses at everyone." She laughed. "You can't take that seriously. The French *like* America."

"Yes, yes, I know all that. It's just this isolation that makes me dyspeptic. It's such a relief to have someone to *talk* to. Someone, I mean, who *understands.*"

"But you are not isolated at all," she protested. "You know everyone in Paris."

"Ah, dear countess, but everyone is not *you!*"

The next day he sent her another dozen roses.

She began to see Walter Straus regularly. They would walk in the Tuileries in the late afternoon among the bursts of afternoon sun, or he would accompany her to the Jeu de Paume or procure tickets for the opera in the evening.

She liked him. She thought of him as elderly; but unlike her father or Poppie, he was a worldly man, wealthy by reason of his own exertions, at home in London and New York and Paris, acquainted with the new international moneyed society which he cultivated assiduously, adept at the maneuvers of success. She enjoyed the opportunities he provided, the restaurants, the acquaintances whose names she encountered in the newspapers, the gossip. It was as if she could see her mother blowing kisses in benediction from beyond the clouds.

And so, without quite noticing, she began running with that strange amalgam of playboys, aristocrats, movie stars, society girls, call girls, screenwriting novelists, female journalists, and yuppie bankers which, when translated to the cis-Atlantic, earns the well-deserved moniker of Eurotrash.

He took her to lunch at the Café Voltaire and they sat in one of the banquettes in the side room with the bust of Voltaire leering down at them from the end of the room. Jacques, the maitre d', looked after them and they ordered expensive red wine and expensive white wine and ris de veau and a fresh sole which Jacques said they must try. Outside the window was the quai Voltaire and the Seine and people from the art world or from the diplomatic world passed by on the quai or came in for lunch.

"Now, my dear, Coco Peking is giving a party next Wednesday evening and I insist that you come. I know you say you don't like these things but I just can't manage without you, and I know you and Coco will be such good friends. She's dying to meet you, and to tell the truth, the party is really in your honor."

"But Walter, why should she give a party in my honor?"

"You're entirely too modest, my dear. You can't imagine how an American woman like Coco would love to make the acquaintance of a countess. But that's beside the point. You must believe me, my dear Hélène, I would never permit such an event if I didn't just *know* that you and Coco will hit it off. It's you I'm thinking of."

"Of course I will come if that will make you happy."

"It makes me immensely happy! I can't tell you how gratified I am by our friendship."

"You are a dear sweet man."

Just then there was a great bustling and a woman accompanied by two younger men swept into the restaurant and settled herself, with the ministrations of the maitre d' and two auxiliary waiters, in the banquette facing them across the room.

The woman was loud and pretty and raucous and middle-aged and white-skinned and she wore a large black hat and she was Joan Collins.

"My dear Joan!" Walter cried.

"Oh! Is that you? Walter! Walter Straus. How *divine*. How positively *divine*."

Walter was already struggling to release his bulk from the grip of gravity and the confines of the banquette to pay his respects to the television celebrity who found his presence so vociferously divine. He waddled across the room with alarming celerity.

"But you know Jeremy," Ms. Collins said, indicating the young suntanned gentleman who sat to her right. "And Mr. Bath, the producer—of course you know Mr. Bath."

There was bowing and scraping and laughing and guffawing and then Hélène's turn arrived.

"Allow me to introduce the comtesse de Compière."

"*Enchanté.*"

"*Enchanté, madame.*"

And the two women bowed to each other across the small room.

"How delightful, how delightful," Walter said as he regained his seat. He was smacking his hands and lips simultaneously in excitement. "Dear Joan is such a friend."

Then he had another idea. "Do you think she'd like to come to the party on Wednesday? Coco would be so pleased! Remind me to ask her when we are ready to go. I don't want to intrude, but remind me to ask her when we leave."

The fish arrived and the ris de veau and Hélène was well amused. Walter was really a dear friend.

"But I must meet your husband," Walter said over his food. "I won't rest content until I have met the comte."

This was an *idée fixe* with Walter, though Hélène greeted it with apprehension. She would not answer for how Poppie might react to Walter; for whereas Armand considered himself the least judgmental of men, he was in fact a fearsome snob with an elaborate code of do's and don'ts derived in part from his class and upbringing and in part from a private system that he had concocted out of his own fancy.

"Doesn't he ever come up to Paris?" Walter asked.

"Very infrequently."

"Well, then, we'll just have to go down to Compière. Would that be an imposition? Surely you could arrange such an outing."

"Well, of course, Walter—if that's what you really want."

"But it is, my dear countess. It is. By all accounts he's such a charming man!"

They went down to Compière in late March when the weather was blustery, and Straus hired a chauffeured car to drive them. It was, she thought, very American.

She dreaded Poppie's reaction, but she needn't have bothered. The plush limousine pulled into the pebbled drive of the château, and as they disembarked she could see Poppie waiting for them at the top of the stairs in a ring of sunlight. He had put on his *other* jacket—the one he wore for special occasions, the one that didn't smell—and she observed the amazement and satisfaction that lit his face as he saw the automobile.

To hire a limousine lay far beyond Armand's powers of worldly contrivance and he was impressed and delighted. He admired everything about the venture: the sleek vehicle, the accomplishment with which the transaction had been conducted, the ingenuity of the inspiration, the thoughtfulness of the intention.

And Straus was equally impressed by *le comte.* He was enough of a connoisseur to recognize the real thing when he saw it. It was as if he had finally soft-shoed his way into the presence of the *ancien régime.*

"My dear count," he said in his correct precise pedantic American French, pinching his fingers together, "I am honored to make your acquaintance. *La comtesse* has told me so much about you. She has kindly allowed me to share with her some of the charms of Paris, but now that I see Compière I have an awakened sense of all that she forgoes in my company."

"My dear fellow, you mustn't speak that way. It is we, truly, who owe you thanks, and especially I for all the solicitude you have showered on my poor Hélène. She works too hard, and if it weren't for the entertainment you kindly afford, I would worry for her health."

Hélène stood aside and let the two men compliment each other in this courtly manner. Their mutual admiration amused and relieved her.

Straus was even impressed by the aristocratic frugality of the meal: a single slice of roast beef, a new cheese, a bottle of the château red. He had brought the champagne himself, and Hélène soon had reason to fear that Poppie was slightly inebriated. She worried increasingly about his bibulousness.

After lunch the two men went out to examine the estate while she followed at a distance. Though it was cold, neither man permitted an overcoat, and with the blood suffusing his cheeks, with his large frame animated by unselfconscious excitement, Armand, as he strode between the vine rows, his long arms demonstrating some future improvement, appeared to her like the aging Vercingetorix imparting instructions to a minor chieftain.

On the drive back to Paris, Walter expostulated on his admiration for Poppie and for Compière. He seemed unduly mindful of

Poppie's condescension in extending to him, a mere American (for so he expressed it), such cordial hospitality. Hélène was relieved at the success of the visit and she sat back in the limousine and relinquished Walter to his newfound enthusiasm.

Armand had been unable to locate a craftsman to repair the stained-glass windows in the small chapel at Compière, and Straus had volunteered to locate a suitable person in Paris. He did indeed find such an artisan, and it was the first in a series of services that he rendered to Armand and Compière. He assumed a kind of proprietary interest in the estate and its liege, and his friend le comte de Compière was soon as frequently on his lips as previously Walrus von Schnecken or the baroness Tofu had been.

It was at this time that his letters to Hélène began. He had been in the habit of sending her small gifts: a pair of gloves, opera glasses, tickets to La Salle Pleyel, the habitual dozen roses. But accompanying these there now commenced a stream of epistolary confessions.

> *My dearest Hélène:*
>
> *I know you will not deny me the intimacy of my salutation, since in this as in all else I can depend upon the generosity of your kindness. I express nothing short of the truth—and you yourself must know this to be the case—when I confess how utterly you have changed my life. I, who in my middle years had given up the expectation, nay, the dream of encountering a friend like you; I, who had felt my life wasting away in frivolousness, in despair, how can I express the astonishment, the joy I feel when, on my knees before you, I proclaim: my life is changed, utterly changed, you have changed me utterly! Dearest countess, dearest Hélène! I ask nothing —I swear it! Only to continue as we are—with this one alteration: that you permit me the expression, in the intimacy of these letters, of my innocent, of my utter devotion. Do not, dearest woman, suppose me to presume on that kindness and generosity I hailed above. No! (Though were I less certain of your kindness, this heart, these poor lips, would be locked in silence.) Rather, consider these words the*

*outpouring of an affection that can no longer restrain itself within
the decorum of a mere tacit understanding but which, in irrepressible
tribute to who and what you are, must call forth for your dear eyes
alone the witness of my newfound, my undying love!*

Hélène was astounded by this letter, the first of many she received. Its ornate rotundity amused and astonished her and for a
long time she held the missive in her lap, staring vaguely at the
floor. The flattery of his attention was unwanted, but neither had
she any wish to hurt him. She was touched by his loneliness, his
need, and she had no desire to incarnate the rejection of his middle age. She had grown fond of him.

She said nothing. They met that afternoon and took tea as if
nothing had transpired, and the next afternoon she received another letter.

From this time forward they saw more of each other. Often in
the taxi returning home at night she would allow him to take her
hand. Thus spring turned into summer.

She took tea at Coco Peking's and Coco Peking said to her, "You
and Walter are quite the thing."

She wasn't entirely certain what the colloquialism implied—
though she feared she did, and she colored deeply. Coco Peking
only continued to look at her with sly impertinent conspiratorial
significance, as if they were old friends sharing an understanding.

Coco took Hélène's hand and held it in her own as if it were an
expensive glove she had bought for the opera. She was a withered
anorexic woman with high arching eyebrows and sharp nervous
eyes which reflected in their darting tremor the duration of her
attention.

Hélène withdrew her hand.

"Walter has been very kind to me," she said somewhat primly.
"He's a great friend of my husband's," she added, though immediately thereafter she felt herself blushing, she couldn't say why.
This infuriated her, and she sat scowling at her hostess across the
petits fours.

"Indeed," Coco Peking said, and bestowed another of her significant smirks. "Walter is of course very charming. Many women, dear countess, have found him very charming."

Hélène decided to spend August in Compière. She wanted to escape from Paris. She wanted to escape from the insufferable Coco Peking. She wanted to think.

She had hit a kind of impasse in her book. Because of the Général's participation in the American Revolution, a significant portion of his papers were now housed at Columbia and in the New York Public Library. These papers covered what she had come to think of as the decisive decade.

Further, she wanted to spend an extended period with Poppie. It wasn't that her affections had become alienated from him. Her work on the Général had if anything made her feel closer to her husband, to the essence of who and what he was; but it was a closeness that did not entail proximity, and sometimes she would wake in the night with the anxiety that her marriage had ceased.

Before she left for Compière, Walter gave her a small diamond pin. She did not wish to accept the present, but when she tried to return it Walter's disappointment was so apparent that she acquiesced. Why should she deny him this pleasure? Besides, the pin was beautiful.

She had now been married to Armand for more than seven years and in that time Compière had become home. She loved the play of light on its yellowish stone, the odor of the earth under her window, the stand of cypresses that lined the dilapidated garden, the murmur of the Cher in the distance at night. She loved the very sound of the pebbles on the driveway under her feet.

Poppie was delighted to welcome her. He treated her with the consideration of an honored guest. He had become stuck in his ways. He rose early, took breakfast in his room, then repaired to chapel to say his prayers. Afterward he worked in his study throughout the morning. Lunch was frugal. The afternoon was devoted to the estate. At five he returned to the château, washed, attended to his correspondence, read the papers, and started his sherry. By the time dinner was laid he was quietly potted. He retired to bed at nine-thirty.

Hélène's presence effected no alteration in his routine. Poppie was delighted to see her, but he continued about his business with the polite undeviating insistence of a stationmaster keeping to schedule.

She wasn't lonely. She couldn't even say that she felt neglected. She respected Poppie, she respected his work, she had no desire to interfere. But it came to her with sadness and force that her presence was supererogatory. Their lives were set on adjacent, nonconverging tracks.

Again she took to swimming in the Cher. She hadn't had an opportunity to swim in Paris, and the renewed pleasure made her wonder how she had gone without it. The water filled her with buoyant exhilaration, as if it were trying to tell her something simple and gravely important.

As she walked the banks of the Cher she found she was thinking of Louis; and whereas in the past the thought had caused her pain, she now remembered the boy with an affection that made her smile.

She also thought of Walter and of her life in Paris and of her book, and these reflections filled her with unease. It surprised her how much she missed Walter's letters. She undertook long restless walks on the country lanes, as if these would resolve her distemper. At night she stared out the window into blackness while she listened to the frogs and to the heavy chur of the insects.

So the month passed, and the thought of returning to Paris held no appeal. Then one morning she received a letter from Straus.

August 24, 1983
Paris

Dearest girl:
　　Though we agreed I would not write while you were away, something has occurred to change my plans in a manner I must share with you. I am returning to the States. I will not trouble you with the particulars. Suffice it to say that one of my associates in

*New York is in need of my counsel. I leave in three days and
cannot predict when I shall return.*

*I cannot however hide from you that our relationship has weighed
heavily on my mind since your departure and that it has played
some part in my decision to—I almost wrote flee. Since you have
gone I have been good for nothing. It has been borne in upon me in
the most forceful and painful way how much you mean to me, how
little I mean to you. In saying this I do not mean to complain. I
merely mean to state the facts as both of us know them. The thought
of seeing you again fills me with a pleasure that is indistinguishable
from pain.*

*In short, dear woman, I must take action if I am to save myself
alive. I leave behind my love—all of it, for whatever good it will
do. Knowing you, countess, has been the great event of my middle
years.*

This letter shook her deeply. The thought of not seeing Walter
again filled her with unaccountable despair.

It required the remainder of the day while she paced back and
forth across her room to reach a decision: she could not allow
Walter to leave without seeing him again. She went downstairs
and told Poppie that she would depart for Paris immediately.

Poppie took the news with surprise, disappointment, and equanimity.

"My dear child, do wait until the morning. The evening trains
are insalubrious and there will be no time to have your room
prepared for your arrival."

"No, it's quite all right, Armand. You can call ahead about the
room if it will make you easier, but really it makes no difference.
I've got to get back to Paris, I can't explain why. I know I'm
acting foolishly, but . . . it's just something I have to do."

"Not at all, not at all. I quite understand. But I will call ahead
about the room. It will put my mind at rest. We can't have you
inconvenienced!"

He bustled about attending to various arrangements, his thin
grayish hair flying above his head like a tarnished halo. He

wouldn't say how much he would miss her, though she knew he would.

In the last half-hour before Poppie drove her to the station she ascended the hill to Eve's grave.

She had avoided the site in the three weeks she had been at Compière. It was toward the front of the family plot overlooking the Cher, and when she reached the small mound she fell to her knees.

She found she was sobbing. It seemed her heart had never mended, it was shattered beyond repair. The clouds had opened in the west and the sun, descending, released against the horizon a golden column of light, lofty and motionless, such that, as she knelt above her daughter's grave, this sunburst appeared to her like the very epiphany of God, like Godhead itself—distant and beautiful and utterly useless.

At the station before she boarded the train Poppie kissed her on the forehead, as if in benediction, and she experienced a surge of love for this gentle unworldly man who loved her and into whose hands she had been entrusted. And it seemed to her that whatever she touched came to grief.

"Take care of yourself, dear child. I must come up to Paris next month and then everything will be better. We will have lunch and you will tell me all about your work."

"Yes, Poppie, yes. Take care of yourself, dear Poppie."

"Until next month, then. Bye-bye. The room should be ready by the time you arrive."

In the small compartment speeding toward Paris she could no longer remember why she had wanted to return. Her mind was completely blank. She kept putting her book aside in anticipation of some momentous insight; but the next instant her mind was again empty and she could not even remember why she had stopped reading.

It was raining when she reached the Gare d'Austerlitz and a dank mist licked the surrounding buildings. She took a taxi directly to Straus's flat. Staring out the rain-soaked window at the darkened streets of Paris, she felt that she had entered a nightmare. At any moment she would come to her senses, turn around,

go home to Poppie, and her life would resume its familiar contours. But even as she thought this she knew it was impossible:
she could not turn back. There was no place to go.

As she mounted the stairs to Walter's apartment she was covered in cold perspiration. She was caught in a strange and momentous dream.

"My dear Hélène!" Straus exclaimed. He seemed genuinely surprised—and he was a man who did not like surprises.

As he retreated before her down the long hall, she had a sudden
half-articulated intuition that he might in fact care for her less
than his asseverations suggested.

"Walter, forgive me. I have come directly from the station."

"But my dear, I'm delighted to see you. Come in, come in. I'm
surprised, that's all."

"I couldn't have you go without saying goodbye."

"I'm deeply touched. But here, you must dry yourself. You are
wet through and through."

He helped her off with her coat. All this time he was watching
her carefully.

His flat had a particular odor, formal and slightly florid, as if it
had been sprayed with some cheap eau de cologne. It oppressed
and offended her and she had an instinct not to breathe through
her nose. She knew she was not thinking clearly.

"I received your letter."

"Yes?"

"I couldn't let you go like that."

"Oh?" He regarded her, she thought, with a kind of ironic
condescension, as if he found her disheveled plight slightly dis-
tasteful. "Why not?"

What, she suddenly thought, if I hate him?

But it was too late to retreat.

"Walter, I don't know. With your brains you probably know
better than I. You've probably thought it all through. I just know
that . . . I can't let you go. I can't let you out of my life. You are
my last chance."

"My dear countess—what do you mean?"

"No, don't! What can I say?" She had a blinding insight. "All those letters . . . were they then . . . nothing?"

"Dear girl!"

"Well, how was I to know? I mean—how? I'm just a poor mixed-up woman. An American countess! I know it sounds ridiculous! Walter, for God's sake, don't abandon me! Take me with you. Can't you see I'm drowning?"

"My dear countess, I don't know what to say. Here, let me get you something to drink."

It gave him a moment to gather his wits, but she had stopped caring. She had burned her bridges.

When he gave her a glass of champagne she drank it straight off.

"I am astounded, dear girl. I am deeply touched. Have you discussed this with Poppie?"

"Walter, please!" She said it with exasperation, with resignation. "Leave all that alone. I want to go to America. I can't let you go without me."

With that they stood staring at each other for an instant. She was shaking with shame and determination.

"Perhaps," he said, and his voice had changed, had acquired a note of weariness, "perhaps you would like another drink."

"Yes. Why not?"

He gave her the fluted long-stemmed glass as if it held medicine, and again she drank it off.

"My dear countess, you surpass my every wish."

"Do I? Ah, Walter—I can't play this game any longer."

"Game?"

"Please, Walter, let me come."

It hung between them for a moment.

"But of course you can come," he said. "If that is what you want, then of course you can come."

She thought she was going to weep with nerves.

"My dear countess, here—come to me."

She went and knelt by the side of the voluminous chair to which he had retreated.

"Dear countess!" He stroked her hair and she could hear the

sound of his breathing and of something in his voice that was still tentative. Slowly he bent and kissed her.

And she was thankful. She was thankful to have it come to something as simple as that. There, she thought. So that's what it's all been about.

He kissed her for what seemed to her a long time. He caressed her full bosom. Then, after a while, he fumbled for something in his lap until she perceived he had attained what he desired.

"Please," he said, and he still sounded tentative, almost apologetic. He was directing her head downward.

But there was no turning back. She found she wasn't even disgusted. It was all so simple, really. She hardly even cared.

Now, three years later in the Cloisters in New York City, the weather had turned cold. It was four o'clock and March had not yet escaped the grip of winter. Hélène stood up and shivered.

The atmosphere in the high-vaulted subway station was fetid and penetrating. Water had collected between the tracks and the accumulated debris had rotted into a mush. Only a few other passengers occupied the platform.

The warmth of the train calmed her. Now that she was moving she was again enveloped in the mindless contentment she had experienced that morning on the bus, as if the secret of life consisted in locomotion without the impertinence of destination.

A middle-aged man across the train looked at her until, with a cold practiced stare, she caused him to turn away. The man's eyes made her feel unclean.

She decided to go to Brentano's to see if she could purchase a volume of Chateaubriand that Poppie had mentioned in a recent letter. She had no interest in Chateaubriand, but she thought it might be a way to keep in touch with Poppie.

She stood in the middle of the elegant bookstore inhaling the odor of affluence. She fingered a volume by Bernanos. The language affected her like the voice of a dear lost friend speaking long-distance over a telephone. She had a sudden vision of the entire city moving about her with purpose and decision while only she remained superfluous.

When she went outside it had started to rain. She hesitated, watching the taxis and passing cars as they swerved through the gathering evening, and again she was shaken by a sense of purposelessness. There was still time to go to Bloomingdale's. She would buy a raincoat, a hat. At least her father had left her well provided.

She browsed among the scarves, fingering their silk while a crowd milled vaguely about her. The people smelled of the rain. A salesclerk with a scar on his chin inquired if he could be of assistance. His eyes were gray and he smelled unpleasantly of onions.

She took a scarf and tried it around her neck and put it back and selected another. She liked the texture and color of the silk, and again she held it between her fingers, unable to explain why it affected her so.

She tried on a raincoat but the sight of herself in the mirror depressed her; she felt she was suffocating and decided to leave the store.

As she passed through the exit she was dimly aware of an alarm. Then someone had taken her by the elbow.

" 'Scuse me, ma'am, would you please stop a moment?"

"What?"

A black man in a light blue uniform was holding her by the arm.

"What do you want?"

"I'm afraid I needs to ax you to show me what's in dat bag."

He spoke mildly, with great decorum, his voice tinged with sadness, and she felt for him an instant rapport, as if they were both conspirators in some melancholy tawdry drama; but she had not yet taken in what he wanted.

"My bag?"

"Yes. The alarm went off when you passed dat door."

"The alarm?" She became aware of a small knot of people watching them. "You don't think I—"

"Please, ma'am—yo bag."

She began rummaging through the larger bag she carried, trying to balance it on her knee. It slipped and she feared for a moment that everything was going to fall onto the ground.

"But I . . . I . . ."

She avoided the scarf at the bottom of her bag while she tried to figure out what to do, but she could think of nothing.

"I don't know how this got here," she said, pulling out the scarf. The black man looked at her unhappily.

"Really, you've got to believe me. I have no recollection of how this got here. I must have done it inadvertently. It was an accident."

"I's sorry, ma'am. You're going to need to come with me."

"But it was an accident," she said. "I swear it!"

"Ma'am, I believe you. It's jus' my job. You're going to need to come."

She followed him into the store. The afternoon had dissolved into nightmare.

Upstairs she was ushered into the office of an assistant manager, a prissy little man from whom she foresaw no possibility of mercy. She tried to explain that it had been an accident while he listened with his eyebrows cocked.

"I'm sorry, madame," he said. "We have an inflexible store policy. We cannot allow ourselves to be taken advantage of."

"Yes, but what about *truth?*" she pleaded. "Don't you know that things aren't always the way they appear?"

"I don't concern myself with such speculations. You passed through the door, the alarm went off, the scarf was in your possession."

"For God's sake, can't you show a little understanding? What's gained by all of this? Do you think I am a *thief?*"

"It's not for me to say what you are, madame. I abide by the facts."

She thought she was going to weep. Simultaneously she became angry, though she hardly knew at what. She hated the prissy little man.

"Here. Here's my credit card," she said. "I'll buy the scarf, all right? I'll buy ten of the scarves. Look up my credit rating. I don't go around stealing things from Bloomingdale's."

"There are other considerations."

"What considerations? There are no other considerations. It's a case of misunderstanding. An accident. Don't you ever have accidents?"

"Our policy is quite explicit."

"Oh, please, please!" Suddenly she was rocked by a wave of weariness. "Do you want me to beg? Is that what you want? Do you want me to get down on my knees? What good is served by all of this? Can't you see I'm telling the truth? Just let me buy the scarf and leave!"

It was dark by the time she quit the store. Traffic was heavy on Third Avenue and the lights were streaked in the rain. Her forlornness was a poison.

She called Tony from a corner phone.

"Well, long time no see," he said. His voice was sarcastic and cold. "I was just about to go out."

"I need to see you." As she spoke she leaned her forehead against the dirty interior of the phone booth, wet now from the rain. She told him what had happened.

He thought it a joke.

"So you've been shoplifting again."

"Tony, I'm all beat up."

"Because of some prick like that? Don't be ridiculous."

"Can I come over?" Even as she said it she knew it was a mistake.

"I told you I'm going out."

"Just for a little while? I don't want to be alone."

"I'm not stopping you. Come over if you want."

She took a taxi downtown. She felt she would die if she did not see someone—if she did not see Tony. She tried not to remember the tone of his voice.

Tony lay on his bed. He had propped himself up with pillows and she could discern the dark hair at the base of his neck as it rose and fell with his breathing. He was dressed in black jeans and a dirty T-shirt.

"So!" he said. "The countess. She walks in beauty like the night."

"I'm exhausted," she said.

"Take off your things and stay a while." He didn't make a move to help her.

The room looked exactly the same—the same dirty clothes over the chair, the same guitar and amplifier in the corner. The walls were adorned with the same pictures: Tony with Jerry Garcia; Tony looking stoned with Jimi Hendrix. There was the same dog-eared photograph of Tony from *Vanity Fair*. Everything made her shudder.

She sat at the end of the bed while they considered each other. When she touched his foot he let her hand remain for a moment before moving his leg away.

"Poor countess! The Big World isn't treating you nice."

"I think I'm losing my mind. I swear I don't remember putting that scarf in my bag."

Again he laughed.

"Fuck the scarf," he said.

"Tony—oh, Tony!"

"What's that supposed to mean?"

"I don't know. I've missed you."

"Yeah? Well . . . I've missed you, too."

"Have you?"

"Yeah. Big surprise. What did you think?" There was anger in his voice. She felt her stomach go cold with his anger.

"This was your idea," he said. "Remember?"

Again she felt dizzy.

"I couldn't take it anymore, Tony. It hurt."

"It hurt? It hurt? You like being hurt!"

"No, I don't. Don't say that. I don't like being hurt."

"You don't? Then what are you doing here?"

"I'm lonely," she said. "I can't take the loneliness."

For a while there was silence between them. Then he smiled.

"Why don't you take your blouse off?" he said.

"My blouse?"

"Yes, your blouse. What are you, deaf? Do what I say."

It was hard for her to swallow. Slowly she took off her blouse.
"Now take off the bra."

"Tony!"

"The bra!"

He remained smiling while she removed her bra. Then he sat
and looked at her for a while.

She moved toward him up the bed but he pushed her away.

"Tony, please!"

"Do you want to stay?"

"You know I do."

"Then do as I tell you. Get down on the floor!"

"Please, Tony." It was hardly more than a whisper. "Come to
me, Tony."

"When I'm ready. First get down on the floor."

She slipped off the edge of the bed until her knees touched the
floor and for a moment she was kneeling with her forehead against
the side of the mattress. Then she was on all fours.

She remained like that for what seemed to her a long time. She
could no longer tell whether the roar she heard was the city or the
sound of her own blood in her ears. Then she felt him.

When he took her he seized her by the scruff of the neck.

She first saw David Smith on a boat in Manhattan harbor at one of
Tony's gigs. Tony was high and had abandoned her to wander
among the guests while he played. It was a hot sticky night and
she had worn the green dress that he favored and had walked
among the crowd accepting their notice as her due. She dressed up
for Tony, who was proud of her looks, but he was also jealous and
she had to exercise caution.

She had stared down into the whirling black water of the harbor while the fat ship labored forward and the early summer heat
of New York slammed into her. She was quite drunk.

It was at the conclusion of the evening that she saw the two
lovers clasped at the bottom of the passageway, the woman tall
and slender with her elegant arms around him and her head

thrown back, and the man, so far as Hélène could make out, diddling her with his hand.

Precisely at that moment the man had looked up, and as their eyes met, she felt pass between them some species of electric recognition, she didn't know what else to call it, as if his eyes had locked upon whatever it was that knitted her together as a person; and for a prolonged instant she knew herself joined to him inexorably, as if somehow complicit in the mystery of his being, whether tawdry or exalted.

When she saw David Smith again she recognized him immediately. It was in a gallery on Madison Avenue, and when he spoke to her, as she knew he must, she thought, Destiny, for she never went to galleries.

He discussed the pictures in a cool American accent while she stood before the canvases attending to none of his words but astounded by the reds and blues that shouted at her in some barely apprehended dialect that filled her with excitement and hope.

After that they began seeing each other.

He would meet her in bars or coffeeshops and they would talk. He said he thought she must be a movie star. He told her about his family and while he talked she studied his hands. They were handsome hands, strong and delicate, and she could make out that he was a handsome man, though not really her type, too American, too sandy-haired and even-featured, as if life had somehow passed him by.

She told him about her father and mother and about Poppie and about Compière, but she confounded Poppie and her father and covered her tracks. She had an instinct to lie, a habit of duplicity imbibed from her mother. She wanted to keep her options open, as if she could remake herself and forge for herself one more chance in this New World.

During these months she finally dropped Tony. Tony had been a mistake she acquired while free-lancing for *Chic.* For two or three seasons he had been a hot item in the jet set, his brooding unshaven visage a presence in the pages of *GQ* and *Vanity Fair,* his band swinging at all the prominent clubs in London and New

York. It had been a gas being his girlfriend, a trip, it provided kudos around the halls of *Chic*. Besides, he reminded her of Louis —a Louis gone rotten. No one knew about the bad stuff with Tony, she kept that to herself.

She met Walter Straus at his special table at the Regency. Walter was a fussy exacting patron and two waiters hovered nearby.

"Well, my dear, how have you been?"

"I'm fine, Walter." She tried to hide the weariness in her voice, but he looked at her quizzically.

"Are you? Because you look a bit peaked. Have you lost weight?"

"Not that I'm aware of. I don't pay attention to my weight."

"Well, it's nothing to boast of," he said. "A fine-looking girl like you should keep herself up. Speaking of which, Anna Troy is giving a party tomorrow evening and I'd be thankful if you would accompany me."

"Oh, God, Walter!"

"None of your 'Oh, God' business, please. I'm afraid I'm going to have to insist. Anna Troy is really quite important, you know, and Caroline is already spoken for."

"You mean you've already asked Caroline?"

"That's neither here nor there, Hélène. I know you don't like these events, and so naturally I turn first to Caroline. The point is that she can't make it, and so I'm afraid you'll have to come—and I don't want any of your sulking, either."

"I never sulk, Walter. I've known Anna Troy longer than you."

"Well, perhaps you have. All the more reason for you to attend her party. But let's not quarrel, my dear girl. We have so much to discuss. Waiter, bring us some more rolls."

With the years Walter's features were being pushed ever more aslant, like a ship that was badly listing. Sometimes Hélène wondered how long it would take before they foundered entirely. But such thoughts were idle: Walter was the quintessential survivor. He was a fixed point in the social circles of New York, and his silk shirts and white linen suits had become, if possible, even more sumptuous than before. As he spoke, Hélène studied his manicured nails with their clear glossy polish.

"I bring word from Poppie," Walter said. "He's quite fine. I had a look into the heating system at Compière, and I think I've put that on an even keel, which will be a blessing for Poppie come winter. He is a dear man, but the least practical soul alive, as you know. I sometimes wonder what would happen to him without me. Which brings me to my point. He says nothing, of course, but I know he misses you sorely. I think you really ought to give thought to going home—at least for an extended visit."

Hélène cradled her forehead in her hand before looking up with asperity.

"Please, Walter, can we not discuss this again? You know my position."

"Well, I know it, I suppose, but that doesn't mean I agree with it."

"I don't care whether you agree with it," she said. "I mean, really, Walter, isn't it somewhat odd for you to be setting yourself up in this matter as the champion of my husband?"

Straus glanced down at his plate and his face flushed slightly.

"I don't know what you mean," he said. "Your husband and I are dear friends, as you know. I am uniquely situated, it seems to me, to look after the welfare of the family, which is all I mean to do. If you mean to suggest otherwise, I must say I take it amiss."

"Oh, Walter, Walter," she said, resting her hand on his. "Let's not fight. It's too late in the day for that. I can't go back to Poppie, and that's all there is to it. I'd die of shame."

"There, there," he said, patting her hand in turn. "You are too hard on yourself. Well, we'll have to leave it as you think best, though I must say I think your attitude peculiar. But let's say no more about it. The main point is this—I'll pick you up tomorrow at eight in a limousine."

After Anna Troy's she lay on her bed and wondered why she drank so much white wine. She considered calling David Smith, though it was two in the morning. The thought filled her with excitement, as if it brought news of a powerful new restorative.

She leapt out of bed but her movement was too precipitous and she felt she was going to be sick.

Then David went away to Chicago and she missed him terribly. Something about him scared her but filled her with hope.

"Would you have come with me?" he asked her. They were sitting in the Oak Bar upon his return.

On their way home in the taxi she let him kiss her.

In her bedroom she lay on her bed fully clothed and stared at the ceiling. Now that she was alone she savored the kiss; it was as if she were allowing him entrance for the first time. It amazed her how much she liked it.

She felt herself begin to shake.

Walter wanted her to accompany him to Atlanta, where there was to be another party, and though the prospect filled her with dread, she supposed she would end by accepting. Why should she not be of use to Walter, since she seemed to be of none to anyone else?

They stayed in a hotel called the Atlanta Candy on Peachtree and the temperature outside was one hundred degrees. The lobby was spacious and elegantly appointed in glass and steel with beige furniture constructed from light-colored wood, and the air-conditioning was so cold that Hélène had to wear a sweater. While enjoying a glass of wine by herself in one of the plush cushioned lobby chairs, she observed that all the large green plants were made of plastic.

Outside the heat dazed her; even with dark glasses it was difficult to see. She walked down Peachtree and it was as if she were negotiating in a dream. She had no associations with this city, only an oppressive sense of dread and phony elegance. No one else was out, only a few loitering, ratty-looking men with nowhere to go.

The downtown area consisted of two streets lined with hotels and surrounded by broken-down edifices interspersed with macadamized parking lots. She turned a corner and she was nowhere. Where, she wondered, was the Atlanta in Atlanta? She returned to her hotel room and took a shower.

The next evening Walter escorted her to a party near the Governor's Mansion. They took a taxi from the hotel and sped along the freeway at eighty miles an hour while the wind from the driver's window beat feverishly at Hélène's hair. Walter had extracted a cigar from his case, which he fingered nervously but did not light.

"Well, are you having a good time?" he inquired irritably.

"Lovely, Walter."

"If you had accompanied me to Nancy Kidder's tea this afternoon you might have enjoyed yourself more. You're getting to be petulant, Hélène. It's not becoming."

"I'm sorry," she said. "I don't mean to be petulant."

He looked at her but he didn't say anything. Then he put the cigar in his mouth.

They turned off the freeway and onto a narrow two-lane road lined with high bushes and heavily trafficked.

"Where you goin'?" the driver asked. He was a middle-aged black man of sickly complexion with a bandanna tied around his neck, and he sucked periodically at the air from his window as from a respirator. Walter read him the address for the second time.

"Uh-huh. That be the udder side of de gov'nor's mansion. You sure that's the address?"

"Of course I'm sure."

"Okay, boss. Whatever you say. Ah jus' don't wanna drive all that distance an' then turn round."

A stoplight turned red and the driver stamped on the brake. Hélène, glancing in the rearview mirror, saw a car approaching too fast. She braced herself before the car slammed into the back of the taxi.

Walter, thrown forward, caught himself with his hands against the back of the driver's seat. The driver lurched forward and struck his chest against the wheel, though not hard.

"My God!" Walter said.

Hélène rubbed the back of her neck, but the collision had not been severe and she knew she was all right. She turned and looked out the back window and saw the occupants of the other car: two blond kids, a man and a woman, each perhaps twenty-four. They looked scared.

"Are you all right?" Walter asked her.

"Yes, I'm fine."

"This is unbelievable. Now we'll never make it to the party."

"I feel sick," the driver said.

He began to get out of the car.

"Where are you going?" Walter demanded in consternation. "We need to get to our party." But the driver got out of the car. He went over to the side of the road and sat down in the ivy.

The blond boy who had been driving the other car stuck his head in the back window.

"Are you okay?" he asked. "Is anyone hurt?"

"We're all right," Walter said. "But we're expected somewhere."

"Thank God no one is hurt," the boy said. He seemed genuinely relieved. "It was all my fault, I didn't see the red light. I don't think I hit you very hard."

"Hardly at all," Walter said. "I don't see why we can't continue on our way."

"That's what I thought. There's no dent in the car."

"I don't think the driver is well," Hélène said. He was lying in the ivy by the side of the road.

"What? The driver? What happened to him?"

"I think he hit himself against the wheel."

"Against the wheel? Impossible. I hardly hit you at all."

It was true the concussion had been nothing, but there nonetheless lay the driver curled up in the ivy. Hélène got out of the car and walked over to him.

The boy walked over too. He touched the driver with his foot and the man groaned. The boy looked at Hélène and smiled.

"He's faking," he said happily.

"Why do you think he's faking?"

"Of course he's faking. I hardly touched your car. You need to know these boys. He'll get the rest of the night off with pay."

Hélène leaned over and tried to decide whether the driver was faking. He didn't appear changed, but he hadn't looked very well to begin with.

"Are you all right?" she asked.

The driver groaned and clutched at his chest.

"He might not be well," she said. "I think we'd better call an ambulance."

"Sure," the blond boy said. "Do you have a phone?"

The driver sat up and looked at them. "There be a phone in de car," he said. Then he lay back down in the ivy and pulled up his knees.

The boy looked at Hélène and smiled happily.

Hélène went over to the taxi. Walter had parked it halfway on the ivy, and he was standing now, frowning and smoking his cigar.

"What a disaster," he said. "We'll never make it to the party."

"We need to call an ambulance," Hélène said.

She leaned into the car and took out the phone. It was a brown, much-used-looking object and she wasn't certain she knew how to operate it. After a while she managed to dial 911.

The fire department arrived almost immediately. They appeared in a chartreuse fire engine and spilled out onto the road, where they milled around looking at the two cars and at the driver, who was lying with his legs pulled up. Seven or eight fit-looking firemen were now wandering about smiling at one another as if enjoying an outing.

"Where you all headed?" the fire chief inquired.

"We are expected at a party," Walter said. "It's very important that we get there."

"No problem!"

Walter showed the fireman the engraved invitation with the address where they were going.

"Is there any way we could get there?" he asked. "Could we walk?"

"I don't know about that," the fire chief said. "That's quite a piece."

Just then a police car drove up and a large black policeman got out of the car. He must have been six-two and his neck was the size of an average man's thigh and his limbs could hardly be accommodated by his clothing. He looked around at the milling white men and then he strode over to the two cars and began taking notes.

The driver still lay in the ivy with his legs tucked up to his chin. Every once in a while one of the firemen would ask him a question and then would look at his fellow firemen and smile happily.

Hélène walked over to the policeman and spoke to him in a low voice.

"I think someone should attend to the driver," she said. "He might really be hurt."

The policeman looked at her and suddenly his eyes were filled with fury.

"Ah you suggesting that ah'm not doin' mah job?"

Hélène was taken aback.

"Do you think you can do mah job better than ah can? Is that what you think?"

"I don't think anything of the sort."

"Then ah you tryin' to interfere with an awficer in the explication of his duty?"

"I'm not trying to interfere with anyone," she said. The fierceness of the man alarmed her. "I just think someone should look at the driver."

"Do you wanna come down to the precinct and register a complaint?"

"No, I have no interest in registering a complaint."

"Then ah think you just makin' trouble."

"What seems to be the problem, officer?" Walter asked. He was standing next to her though she hadn't seen him approach.

"This lady fahnds reproach with the explication of mah professional duties." He had worked himself into a towering rage.

"I just think someone should look at the driver," Hélène said, her own temper beginning to flare.

"I'm sure the officer will attend to the driver in good time," Walter said. "She's a foreigner," he confided to the policeman. "We're just trying to get to a party."

He drew Hélène aside.

"For goodness' sake, don't start an altercation with the police! Are you mad?"

"I'm not starting an altercation, Walter. I just want someone to look after the driver."

"What business is that of yours? Besides, one of the firemen told me he was faking."

"How do they know he's faking? Maybe he's really sick."

"Oh, for goodness' sake, don't be ridiculous. Look, there are fifteen officials here. What business is it of ours? We just need to get to the party."

In the end they were driven to the party in the emergency van. The firemen had trussed the driver onto a dolly, where he lay perfectly still in the back of the van, contemplating the ceiling. Hélène could see him whenever she looked in the rearview mirror.

Walter and she disembarked at the end of a long drive in front of a great mansion and Walter shook the dust from his clothes.

"This is the most inauspicious way to begin a party!"

Then they hiked up the graveled drive.

The party was hosted by a friend of Anna Troy's, and the mansion, filled with people overdressed in the summer heat, had the aspect of a pleasure liner marooned on a golf course.

Walter's humor was quickly restored. "This is the countess de Compière," he kept saying. "The countess de Compière."

"Whah, countess, ah'm just thrilled to make yo acquaintance! Welcome to Gawgiah!"

Hélène was soon in need of a drink. She made her way to the bar and obtained a white wine spritzer, which she drank in a gulp, the perspiration starting at her forehead and enveloping her body in a riptide. She took another glass of wine.

Standing a few feet away, Walter was recounting to a buxom woman and her tall emaciated husband the misadventure of the taxi ride, which he had transformed into low comedy.

"And then the driver," she heard him say, "went over to the side of the road and lay down in the ivy as if it were a private bed."

"Land sake's alive!" the buxom woman exclaimed.

Walter looked up and saw Hélène and his face lighted as if he had spied an especially valuable cufflink he had misplaced.

"Come here, countess!" And then, turning to the other two, "I want you to meet the countess de Compière."

Hélène went as she was bid and was introduced to Jack Sprat and his wife.

"I'm jus' so *humilified* by that accident," the wife kept repeating. "I'm jus' so *humilified.*"

"Ah hope you don't conclude that misadventures like that happen of-ten in this town, countess," the tall man said, leaning solicitously toward Hélène.

"I suppose that accidents happen everywhere," Hélène said.

"Now ain't that the truth!"

"I'm afraid we'll seem very provincial to you after Paris, countess."

"New York is really my home. I've lived there for four years now."

"Ah, New York! Ah suppose you're used to all sorts of happenings in New York."

"Not exactly like this," Hélène said. "I had the feeling that nobody cared about the driver."

"Well, that's jus' shocking! But don't y' imagine, countess, just between the two of us, that he was fakin'?"

By now others had joined the conversation, which became ever more animated and amusing. Many guests aspired to the acquaintanceship of the comtesse de Compière. Hélène kept drinking white wine spritzers until her skin felt as if it had turned to quicksilver. She feared she was becoming ill.

"You must allow us to show you the *real* Georgia," a man said, bending close to Hélène as in a dream. His weather-beaten skin had a leathery alligator-like quality that at this proximity struck her as strangely nonhuman, as if a piece of bark or rawhide should presume to address her.

"Here, George," the man said. "I want you to meet the countess Compière. She's People Like Us." And they laughed conspiratorially.

In her hotel room Hélène lay on her bed and sweated. She had only the vaguest idea where she was or how she had gotten there. She knew she was sick but she didn't know with what. Was it the wine she had drunk? Was it the heat? Perhaps it was her mind.

She thought of David Smith and suddenly her sickness and her longing for David seemed one. She was lovesick. She was literally lovesick. She groaned in her fever and cried out, and it seemed that what she cried out for was David Smith.

The next day she called David at his office.

"David, do you remember what you asked me about Chicago?"

"Yes."

"Well, the answer is yes."

"Really?"

"Yes, yes! David, I think I'm in love with you."

"Yes, I am with you too. Can't you cut your research short and come home early?"

"No—but it's only two more days."

"Only?"

"I know. Don't talk to me that way. Just hearing your voice makes me shake."

"It has a different effect on my anatomy."

"Don't! Book a hotel for the minute I come back. The *minute!*"

On the plane to New York she tried to analyze what she was doing, but it was too late. All she wanted was to lie in David Smith's arms. She realized she knew almost nothing about him. She liked his hair and his hands and the softness of his skin and the firmness of his body and the youthfulness of his face. Especially she liked how much he liked *her.* For some reason she could not fathom he had swooped down into her life and given it fresh meaning and direction.

The recollection of Walter Straus filled her with nausea.

David took her to the Plaza and they kept the shades open as they made love so they could see the tops of the trees swaying in Central Park.

There, she thought. A new start!

"I didn't know I loved you," she said. "It was those days away from you, not being able to see you, not being able to talk to you. I thought I would go mad."

She moved onto him again. The lovemaking was a revelation to her. She kissed his neck, bit his nipple—and he rose into her like a spear.

In December David Smith and she went to Philadelphia. They took the train and held hands while she watched the smudged urban landscape slide by outside the window. He talked to her about the cities they passed and she held his hand and pretended to listen.

She looked at his fingers while he talked and marveled at what they could do to her.

He took her to dinner that evening at a small French restaurant and they ordered *moules* and a bottle of Chardonnay and she held his hand while they waited for the *moules* to be served.

The couple next to them could not decide what to order. The woman was a schoolmarmish-looking thing with a wen by the side of her nose who was on a diet and kept asking the waiter to detail the ingredients of each dish. David, amused, kept eaves-dropping and looking at Hélène significantly, and when he laughed it had a boyish, infectious sound. It was easy, she found, to love him.

"Everything between us clicks," she said.

"Clicks?"

"Yes. Like we were made to fit—just like that. I don't have to explain to you what I mean. You get me—we get each other."

"Here," he said. "Drink your wine."

"Why do you want me to drink my wine? Do you want me to be drunk?"

"Yes," he said. "I want you to be drunk, and then we will go back to the hotel and make love."

"I don't need to be drunk," she said.

When they returned to the hotel he had to telephone his wife. Hélène sat silently on the edge of the bed while he spoke into the receiver. He seemed at ease, and he spoke with affection to this woman to whom he had been married for many years. Hélène listened as they spoke about one of their daughters and some kind of difficulty she had caused.

She realized she had not factored the wife into the equation.

As they made love, it was as if a circle had been closed and had brought her back to where she had begun with Louis, only now she was no longer a child.

"Oh!" she said when they were done. "How do you *do* that? It feels as if I'd never been touched before—not even by my husband."

He had been stroking the mole under her breast, but she could feel his fingers stop now in mid-course.

"Your husband? I thought you said you had never been married."

"It happened long ago, in France, when I was very young."

"Who was he? Tell me about him."

"He was just a boy."

"What happened to him?"

"He went away. It's not important."

He turned on his side and propped his head on his palm to watch her.

"But why didn't you tell me?" he asked. "I want to hear everything."

She laughed without humor. "There's nothing to hear. He was a boy who lived in the village. There were no other boys and I was very young and so we got married. But there was nothing between us, nothing to keep us together. We were like two leaves that come to rest next to each other on a wall. Then the wind rises and they are blown away. He went to America to be a rock star."

After that they were silent. She wanted to tell him about Eve but she was afraid. She was afraid she would no longer be able to control herself. She was afraid her life would come unraveled here in this dilapidated hotel in a foreign city with a man she hardly knew.

Later, when he was asleep, she went into the bathroom and stood naked in front of the full-length mirror that was on the back of the door. She saw that she was still beautiful. She observed, however, that there were delicate lines at the corners of her eyes; and she knew that these were the ends of a large net that had already ensnared her and that would slowly drag her to the ground.

Turning away, she rested her hand against the cool tile of the wall. If only I can love him! she thought. Maybe, she thought, it's not too late.

She wrote a letter to France.

Dearest Poppie:

Thank you for telling me about the poplars. Now as I write I can see them standing in rows along the drive and glowing in the winter sun. I miss them and love them and it seems to me that they represent what you are and what Compière is and always will be. For myself, however, I have come to feel ever more American—or at any rate identified with America. In many ways this saddens me, for it puts more than the Atlantic between myself and dear Compière, and I regret that I cannot return in kind the lovingness and surety that you and Compière have given. But I cannot share that surety, I can only love it and admire it from a distance like some beggar girl in a story by Andersen. This is American, I think —this rootlessness, this at-loose-endedness, as if we were stones kicked along the road. But what is also American is this sense that one can start over, that a new start is possible, and it is this that I cling to and claim as my heritage and which offers a portion of hope and even, if I dare, of happiness!

I woke the other morning at five, something I rarely do, and I saw the sun coming up over Manhattan in a great booming chorus, an outrageous apocalyptic fountain of light, and I thought to myself, How remarkable that this happens every day and that every day we sleep through it, as if a god daily delivered the newspaper but we were too preoccupied to greet him! All that is saved for us are the gray dregs of the day! I express myself poorly, but I know you will understand what I am trying to say, dear Poppie, and will extend

your wise forbearance. I write in haste but with all love and
abiding affection. Your wife,

Hélène, comtesse de Compière

And now there was a time when she was happy. She was in love
with David and it was her first true love affair, the first time she
could give herself without restraint. She bought him presents,
wrote him letters, thought about him constantly. In a lingerie
shop she feared she would swoon with excitement, so eager was
she to purchase a black low-cut bra and diaphanous panties so that
David could remove them.

When he touched her it was always as if for the first time. She
was bashful when she had her period and didn't want to make
love; but when she told him she had the curse, he only laughed at
her European euphemism.

"I don't care about that," he said.

"Don't you?"

"Not in the slightest."

They made love with a towel under them and she bled onto the
towel, but now she didn't care. She wanted to share everything
with David, she didn't want any secrets between them. Afterward
she said, "It was like being a virgin again."

She was satisfied, she thought, with only a portion of his life.
Her relationship with David filled her with energy and happiness
and she continued the rest of her existence with renewed zest: she
dined with her acquaintances from *Chic,* shopped with her friend
Caroline, and even did a little work on her book.

At first Caroline was amused by the love affair, but as it continued for two and then three and then six months, her attitude
changed.

"You are crazy to be mixed up with a married man," she said.
"They are nothing but trouble. I suppose he tells you he is misunderstood by his wife."

"No, he doesn't. He tells me he loves his wife."

"He *loves* his wife! Well, isn't that fancy. Are you sure this guy
isn't nuts?"

"No, he isn't nuts."

"Well, then you are. He sounds like poison to me. It's the oldest trap in the book. He'll tie you up in knots, and when he's through he'll drop you like a dirty diaper. Get rid of him now, Hélène."

"I can't get rid of him. I'm in love with him."

"Love, love, love. Phooey! Love is a kind of food poisoning—an overwhelming spasm that moves you beyond all modesty. Stay away from it."

Caroline was a blowzy experienced woman whose good looks had run to seed. A beauty when younger, she now flaunted extra weight in her breasts and hips and face, which, of a reddish hue, full-cheeked and full-jowled, was topped with a profusion of red hair encouraged by chemical persuasion.

"The problem is there are no good men left," Caroline explained. "The nice ones are gay or married. So what's a girl to do?"

"Please don't feed me all sorts of platitudes, Caroline, it doesn't help. I know as well as you the problems with a married man. The fact remains that this particular woman, me, is in love with that particular man, David. It's not a question of whether it's a good idea, like endorsing some new product."

"Well, don't say I didn't warn you. Something like this *can't* work. It's like indulging in rancid mayonnaise."

But Hélène paid Caroline no heed. She was in love. When David called her darling she thought she would do anything for him. Sometimes she did worry about the sex, for truly it had never felt like that before; but she knew it wasn't "just" sex. They clicked. They could do anything, talk about anything. Everything she did was in some manner oriented to him.

"What do you think I should do about Jenny?" he asked her one evening while they sat together at the Oak Bar, as they did at the close of almost every day. "She is driving Barbara mad. She won't speak a civil word to her. She spends her time talking on the telephone with the door shut."

"Do you think she knows about us?"

"No, that's not possible."

"Children are funny that way. They come to know things in mysterious ways."

"Yes, but I don't think that's the case, thank God. She isn't particularly angry at me. It seems to be Barbara. And of course it's damnably unfair, because Barbara is a superlative mother."

"Maybe that's the reason. Adolescent girls are funny creatures, you know. I wouldn't be fourteen again for anything."

"But of course your parents were separated."

"Yes, indeed—by the Atlantic Ocean. And all I wanted was to be with my father. I held it against my mother that we were here and that I was unhappy and that my father was far away. I think I imagined she could make it all right if she wanted to, could put all the pieces back together, and so my unhappiness was really her fault, not just because she had caused the situation—which of course was itself unfair—but because she perpetuated it, to spite me."

"Jenny must feel something the same. When she was little she was so close to Barbara that when she fell down she would get angry at her. Somehow Barbara should have saved her from falling down. And I fear that something of that magical thinking still persists."

She loved it that David came to her for advice about his daughter. But in the night when she thought about the conversation something in her stirred and she sat up in bed.

Eve, she thought, would have been eight.

She said to David, "My father's friend Walter Straus is back in town. He's asked me to accompany him to dinner at Mort Klein's."

"Oh?"

"Yes. It's one of those social affairs. Do you mind?"

"Do I mind what?"

"Do you mind if I go? With Walter Straus."

They were riding home in a taxicab. He looked at her for a moment, trying to assess what she was saying.

"Should I mind?"

"I really can't say," she said, laughing. He looked at her with alarm.

"I thought you said he was just some old fogey, some friend of your father's."

"Yes, he is—though not really that old. Walter must be fifty-five."

David frowned. He looked away. "I don't know what you are saying to me. Does this guy have eyes for you?"

"Walter? Don't be silly."

"Then what's this all about? What is it you're trying to convey?"

"Nothing. I just don't want to do anything behind your back, that's all. After all, it *is* a party."

"What the hell does *that* mean?"

"Please don't raise your voice, David."

"Please don't raise my voice? What's this Walter Straus stuff? Where's this coming from?"

"It's coming from exactly nowhere. It's you who are making it into a big deal."

"Well, let's say I don't want you to go to the party with Walter Straus. What then?"

"Is that quite fair? I mean, given your situation. Do you think you have the right to ask me not to go to some party with an old friend of the family?"

"I don't know whether I have the right or not. It was you who brought up the question, Hélène. Apparently you wouldn't have brought it up unless there was some reason. I mean, who *is* this Straus?"

"He's nobody. He's nobody at all. I'm sorry I even mentioned him."

"But you are going to go to the party?"

"Yes, I am. I promised him and now I have to go."

David Smith leaned across her and started to open the door to the cab.

"What are you doing?" she asked in alarm. She wished she had never mentioned the subject.

"I'm leaving. I'm leaving right now."

She saw that he was furious. "David, don't be silly. Don't be stupid. I won't go to the idiot party."

"If you do go to that party with Walter Straus, then we are through. I mean, I took that much for granted. Think of what's between us, think of the intimacy. If you are not my woman, then all this is a farce."

"Let's not fight, David—please." She took him by the forearm. "You know if I were yours I'd never go out with another man. Never."

"If you were mine? I thought you *were* mine."

"How can I be? How can I be yours when you are happily married to Barbara with no intention of ever leaving her? I mean, I love you, David, but how can I be yours?"

"You *are* mine," he said fiercely. "And I won't have you going out to dinner parties with other men. It's as simple as that."

"This is silly," she said after a moment. "Walter Straus means nothing to me. Nothing. If you don't want me going out, I won't go out. Okay? Is that what you want?"

She saw the look of relief that came into his face, and she thought, How easily I could crush him. And thinking this, she felt how much she loved him.

"I won't go out with other men—not even Walter Straus," she said. "I promise you I won't."

And she didn't. She stopped seeing Walter. She didn't go that May to his house on the Island as she always had previously. He was disgruntled but she didn't care. She didn't go to Coco Peking's spring bash or to the much-touted spring gala at *Chic*. She hardly even saw Caroline. She sat at home and thought about David, or met him at the end of the day at the Oak Bar, or went to dinner with him when he could arrange it. And in June they had been in love with each other for a year.

To mark the event they had a picnic in the woods and made love under the trees, and as she lay with him on the damp forest-scented ground, she felt she was as close to him as she had ever been to anyone—as close as two people could ever be.

But as the summer wore on she began to change. She found she wanted more of David. The thought of him lying next to his wife tortured her. She struggled with these feelings, but when she was alone she was increasingly assailed by jealousy and rage.

Often she felt that all she wanted was to hear his voice on the telephone. She spent hours trying to will him to call. Sometimes she drank alone at night, but this only produced tears and hysteria. As the hours passed her anxiety settled blankly. Dawn brought leaden unhappiness, or stupefied sleep.

She was desperate when she saw how her resources had dwindled. She had given up on the book, given up on returning to France. The thought of Tony sickened her. Walter had lost interest in her, took her for granted, had made his peace with the limits of their relationship—limits that she herself had imposed —and picked her up and put her down like a glove.

And yet she was still a beautiful woman. When she walked in the street men's eyes fluttered about her like shadows or burned on her like sun. Often she was possessed by restless energy. She walked in the city and the world seemed to her beautiful and potent, full of opportunity, and she chided herself for the waste of her life and told herself it was still not too late.

Then she would turn listless, she would fall into despair, nothing seemed worthwhile—not even David. She might as well be dead.

She played the traffic game. It was something she had contrived during the bad years, with stern rules and observations that demanded strict adherence; but though the danger was great, the recompense was greater, filling her with energy for many days, as shoplifting had done when she was younger.

She stepped off the curb and, without looking, she proceeded toward the other side. Brakes screeched, a bicycle swerved, the wind from a bus lifted her skirt. Eyes down, she plodded forward unheeding. Then, finally, she was on the farther side.

And she was shaking. She looked up, and everything seemed new-made, as if her eyes were new-minted. Her throat constricted, her head spun. Her breath came in gulps. And she was extraordinarily excited, extraordinarily elated to be alive.

The game was very bad, but the high it afforded was worth it. It was a secret she had, something she had invented that no one else knew about. She had to reserve it for special occasions, special emergencies. But it worked!

Caroline took her out on the town and for the first time in months she enjoyed herself. They went shopping at Bergdorf's, had drinks at the Pierre while they gossiped about the men sitting across the way and Caroline arranged her legs so they showed to good effect under the table.

"Come out to dinner," she said to Hélène. "We'll go to the Quilted Giraffe and have a party."

"I'm supposed to see David."

"David shmavid! Come with me tonight, you can see David anytime. Besides, I have something I need to talk to you about."

"All right," Hélène agreed. "I'll call David and cancel. Let him have dinner with his wife!"

They had soft-shell crabs and a bottle of French wine and Caroline told Hélène about her new beau.

She was dating Alex Pitt, a notorious playboy and well-known figure on the five o'clock television news who was yearly voted one of the ten most eligible bachelors by *Women's Wear.* He had told Caroline he would marry her if she bore him a child.

"Are you mad?" Hélène said. "What makes you think he will marry you if you become pregnant? You'll be forty with a child and no husband."

"I don't care," Caroline said. She was picking at her salad as if she had lost something valuable among its greenery. "At least I'll have a child. This is my last chance, Hélène. My last chance to put my life into some kind of shape."

"But Caroline, what kind of shape is that? Where will you get the money to raise the child?"

"Oh, the money will come. I'll stick him for the money whether he marries me or not. He's rolling in money, the bastard."

"I wouldn't be so confident," Hélène said. "I wouldn't be so sure I could handle this guy. You're not the first, you know."

Caroline emitted a sarcastic laugh.

"Thanks for reminding me. I'm not the only one *now.*"

"What do you mean?"

"I mean I know for a fact he is seeing at least one other woman."

"At the same time as you?"

Again Caroline laughed. "Well, not quite at the same time—not yet, at least. Usually we are separated by a few hours."

"And you want to marry this creep?"

"Yes. Yes, I do. I love him. And besides, he's my last hope. My great white hope." And she uttered her peculiar laugh.

Hélène shook her head. The two women ordered another bottle of wine and Caroline expostulated on her philosophy of men.

"Listen, all men are pricks, they can't help it, they're programmed that way. When a woman is pregnant she's pregnant for nine months, but a man can impregnate a different woman every afternoon—that's why they made lunch hours so long. To this day a man doesn't know how many children he's sown—how could he? One two three and it's over. I mean, if you have a *considerate* lover we're talking about forty-five minutes to an hour, so figure it out for yourself. What's the proportion of forty-five minutes to nine months? That's the ratio God established in heaven. So what's a girl to do? The answer is she's got to look out for herself. Every man wants to own you and screw other women—they can't help it, it's the way they're made. Well, you can't let it happen. I mean, you can't get into that mindset for a moment. It's mere lunacy. It will never work out and you're the one left with the short end of the stick. And when it comes to that, if you're just talking about *screwing,* why, we can outscrew any man alive. The way I see it, they are there for impregnating *us,* that's their job, that's what those little things they are so proud of are *for.* Not for owning us. Not for making us theirs. All that is their bullshit for keeping us on a shelf. No, all their one-two-three stuff is just a little way nature has for us to get pregnant—when we're good and ready. What it comes down to is this—men are there for us to use. Really and truly. And the funny part is, they think it's the other way around. Har, har!"

"Do you really believe all that?" Hélène asked.

"Do I believe it? Just watch me!"

Once when Hélène was lying in David's arms she said to him impulsively, "Would you give me a child? If other things were different would you give me a child?"

They were in her apartment on her large double bed and suddenly she could see how it would be if they lived together.

"I'd love to give you a child."

He was lying on his side propped on his elbow and she could see the tautness of his muscle and the smooth skin across his shoulders and breast.

"Would you marry me?" She had never gone this far before, and her words filled her with sickness and longing, part desire, part self-disgust.

He moved uneasily.

"Don't ask that, Hélène."

She felt a spurt of anger, both for having asked and for his having responded so.

"But would you? Would you marry me? If you could, would you marry me?"

"Yes, of course I would—if I could."

She laughed bitterly. "What a bourgeois farce," she said. She rolled onto her back. "Here," she said. "Do this." And she took his hand. "At least you can do this."

Hélène began frequenting parties again. She hadn't gone out for many months—not since David and she had quarreled over Walter Straus—but Caroline helped convince her that there was no point in her moping at home waiting for the telephone to ring while David cultivated domestic harmony every evening with his wife and children.

Caroline traveled with the socialites favored by Walter, a world that overlapped with the fast set Hélène had known when she worked for *Chic;* and they were all delighted to welcome back the comtesse de Compière.

"My dear comtesse," Coco Peking exclaimed. "Where have you

been keeping yourself? I'm so delighted to see you. You must allow me to give a little party in your honor—just a luncheon for some of the girls. I'll invite Erica Crone and dear Mrs. Steinberg and of course Laetitia Small, who is quite recovered from the divorce and looking divine. And I'll want you at my table at the dance at the Met next month. Also, the duchess of Kent is coming to town, and I know she'll be eager to see you. By the way, do try the macaroons, they come all the way from Venice." And suddenly she emitted a small yawn, like a sailboat that is overtaken by a lull.

At first Hélène was uncomfortable as a single woman on the town, but after a time she found that the parties and dances distracted and even amused her. She told David nothing about any of this. And why shouldn't I see other men, she said to herself defiantly. I don't sleep with them, I don't kiss them, I don't even hold their hand. I'm allowed to have a social life, aren't I? I'm not just his *mistress!* The word enraged her.

She began to divide her life into separate compartments which she kept jealously isolated from one another. It wasn't exactly that she was duplicitous. She meant the promises she made to David— when she made them. But later, when she was alone, her relationship with him didn't seem entirely real. The commitments she made to him didn't seem binding to her, as if they were something said in a dream, so that when she recalled what she had promised, she recoiled in confusion, frustration, disbelief—and anger.

She began to act like two different people, a woman who craved a stable relationship with David and a fun-loving, flirtatious, adventurous, wine-drinking young woman who loved a good time.

She refused to go with David to Chicago. She had a slight cold which she used as an excuse. Then she was overcome with regret. She longed to be in his arms and raged at the difficulties that separated them.

She saw more of Caroline. It amused her to go out with her, to listen to her sharp bitter gossip, to follow the vagaries of her affair with Alex Pitt.

"I'm writing a book, *How to Get Pregnant in Four Easy Lays,*"

Caroline said in her unbuttoned manner. "You know, they say there's more chance of getting knocked up in the doggie position. Do you believe that?"

"I wouldn't know," Hélène said, coloring but laughing.

"No? Well, it makes sense if you think about it. I mean, that's the way animals do it, right? And they're not crazed sex machines like us. All their fucking has a point—to make babies. And so does mine! I'm going to stick it to this bastard, just watch and see. And if that means getting down on all fours every afternoon and wagging my ass in the air, well, so be it!"

Again Hélène laughed.

"Caroline, I wish I could make you stop. Can't you see this is going to end in a crack-up?"

"What crack-up? The worst that can happen is that I have a baby—but that's exactly what I want. And who are you to be giving me lessons, anyway? Your relationship with David is worse than mine with Alex. At least Alex isn't married. Because if you think your David is ever going to leave his wife, you are crazy. I mean bonkers, baby. Out to lunch."

Subtly and then not so subtly Caroline encouraged Hélène to see other men.

"Why don't you ever see Walter anymore?" Caroline asked. Straus was her kind of fellow—sophisticated, elderly, and wealthy. "You don't have to love the guy," she said. "You don't have to marry him. He'll take you around on his arm, he'll show you a good time. That's what men are for, for chrissakes! To spend money."

"I can't start all that again," Hélène said.

"Why not?"

She didn't have an answer—not one Caroline would understand.

She encountered Walter wherever she went. He was a regular feature with Coco Peking and the charity ball set. Everyone seemed to know and approve of Walter.

And he was kind to her. He didn't seem to hold her past coldness against her. Once he asked about David and she treated the question lightly, as if David Smith were no longer a part of her life. The next week Walter called to invite her to accompany him to a dinner at Odette Ford's, and she agreed. Why shouldn't she? It was just like old times.

But halfway through the dinner she was overtaken by vertigo. A tall thin man on her right whom she had never seen before kept pressing his knee against her. Across the way a fat small woman with bright feral eyes talked hysterically about Ronald Reagan and AIDS. The room was unusually dark for a dinner party and the walls were coruscated with what she had been assured was an inlay of real gold. She excused herself and went to the bathroom.

She locked the door and sat on the lowered lid of the toilet with her head in her hands.

What would it be like, she thought, if she were married to David? She shivered. David would never take her to a place like this. Together they would laugh about Odette Ford and her gold-plated walls. She felt she was falling into an abyss.

Someone knocked at the door.

"Hélène? Are you all right?" It was Walter.

She looked up. More time had elapsed than she had realized.

"Yes. Yes, I'm all right."

She stood up and straightened her dress. She unlocked the door.

Walter stood considering her for a moment.

"Do you want to leave?"

A great swell of thankfulness buoyed her, as if he had offered her his place on a lifeboat on the *Titanic.*

"Oh, Walter, yes. Yes!" She rested her head against his shoulder.

But they didn't leave. Not then. Walter became engaged in a conversation with a well-known financier from which he wouldn't extract himself. She watched him from across the room as his solid rotund figure inclined in sympathetic humorous attention to whatever it was the financier was saying. Straus had aged with the years and his gray curly hair receded up his forehead, but he was still a striking man of his kind, his nose listing badly to the side, his gray eyes arched and intelligent, his lips pouting in sensuous accommodating scorn.

What destiny, she thought, attached her with bands of steel to Walter Straus?

At the door to her building Straus detained her for a moment.

"My dear countess, you must decide who you want to be."

She lowered her head.

"I know, Walter. You're right. That's just the problem. I don't know who I am."

He held her shoulder with some delicacy. "I see that."

"But what am I to do?"

"You must let your friends help you to see clearly."

"Must I? But who *are* my friends?"

He shook her slightly. "I am."

"Are you?" She looked up, and it was as if there were hope in her voice.

"Yes," he said. "Yes, I am."

But it was David she wanted. They held hands on Fifth Avenue though she felt him tense with the public display. But she persisted. She could demand this much of him.

"You don't take me to the galleries anymore."

"I'd take you every day if I could."

"Yes—if you could. Well, we won't continue in that strain. We'd only quarrel."

"We never quarrel. You say it yourself." And he squeezed her hand.

If I could live with him, she thought, I'd never be confused. I'd wake up every morning and be happy.

She thought about that for a moment and so far as she could determine it was true.

"I wouldn't hurt Barbara for the world," she said.

He looked at her with his ironic boyish good humor and she thought, He knows nothing of the world. For all his intelligence he doesn't truly get anything.

"What do you mean?"

"I mean I wouldn't hurt her. I don't want to hurt her."

"I know that. I never thought otherwise."

"Yes, well . . . what do *you* know?"

He laughed. "My goodness, you are Delphic today."

"Am I? Then keep in mind that you know nothing."

"Oh, that's easy to keep in mind. I rarely forget that. I just want to love you, that's all. I want to love you and hurt no one."

"Yes? Well, I want to leave my feet on the ground while I jump up the stairs."

He regarded her thoughtfully.

"David," she said. "You do know, don't you, that I'm not Barbara? I'm not a well-heeled member of the American upper middle class with children and husband and parents living on Long Island. I'm a French countess with a father who still imagines he is a member of the *ancien régime* living in a château on the other side of the Atlantic, myself a rootless half-American adrift without profession or family in New York City in love with a married man who won't leave his wife. I have no clear vision of who or what I am or what I should do or be or how I should behave or what my life will be like in a week, much less a year. I say all this not to frighten you but simply as a statement of fact, since sometimes I think you don't quite understand what you have taken on."

He frowned. "What's wrong, darling? Why are you saying all this?"

"Don't call me darling."

He looked at her carefully. "Why not?"

"Because no one has ever called me darling. No one but you. When you call me darling I can no longer think straight. It's not fair."

"Well, what's the big advantage in thinking straight?"

"Oh, that doesn't sound like you. Not like the David Smith I know. The David Smith I know is a deep thinker, a student of Heidegger or some such person."

"Is he? Well, more power to him. I wonder where it ever got him, all this deep thinking. Deep thinking can stunt your growth." And he laughed.

"I love you for your deep thinking, David. When you ask what is the advantage of thinking straight, I know there is something you don't want to think."

"Well, what would that be?"

"That you can't be married to Barbara and love me at the same time."

He scowled deeply. "Why not? Who says I can't? Where is it written in the stars?"

"It's written right here," she said, and she touched him on the breast.

"I love you," he said.

"I know you do, David. But we're not talking about that."

"Why do you have to be so smart?" he said. "I love your intelligence."

"Pooh! I set no store by my intelligence. But I've thought about this a lot."

"So have I. But what conclusion do you reach? I should never have fallen in love with two women. It was a bad, a stupid thing to do. It's not worthy of my intelligence, and all that. But who says I *want* to be so intelligent? Who even says I am? Life is— what? A kind of passion, the way Christ's life was a passion. On an infinitely smaller scale, of course, but the same word, the same concept. It runs much deeper than mere intelligence. It's a primal process that we're enmeshed in, though most of us don't see it. It's much more like—God forgive me—like the movement of the bowels. I say this in all sobriety. We are all caught up in some-thing vastly larger than we, something about which there can be no question of mere intelligence or of ultimate control."

"Oh, David, David," she said. "You are marvelous. And of course I love you. In fact I adore you. But even you can control your bowels."

She received a letter from Poppie.

My dear Hélène:

Walter wrote to tell me about the party at Mrs. Ford's. I must say it all sounds very elegant. Sole à la dieppoise indeed! You must thank Mrs. Ford for me when you next see her. Walter mentioned she was coming to France and would "simply die" for an invitation to Compière, and of course I will write to say that Mrs. Odette

Ford would be more than welcome after the kindness she has shown my dear girl. Indeed, it turns out she is a dear friend of the Roco Joneses, who, you may recall, came to stay with the ambassador last summer. So it is all en famille, *even if—between us—a trifle* vulgaire.

I am delighted to hear that you and Walter are social companions again. I know you entertain mixed feelings about Walter, but he has been a faithful friend to me, and to you as well. Even if he is not entirely our sort—and again I say this strictly entre nous—*his heart is in the right place, and that is what ultimately counts. It is my belief that even a black African is not that different under the skin, if you share the same convictions about life.*

My book on Lamartine draws to a close. It has been a long and hard pull, and I have often lost sympathy with my subject; but in the final analysis he was a great poet and a majestic personality, and the modern world could learn much from his example. Do not lose heart on your book. I often think the good Lord puts obstacles in our way for a purpose, not only to test our resolve but to close off avenues that in our myopia would only lead us astray. The pleasures of friendship, of social intercourse, and of productive work are perhaps all any rational creature can expect from this world.

But I do not mean to end on a note of solemnity. I merely wish to convey what little wisdom I have accumulated in nearly seventy years of life. Be happy, dear child. Trust in God's love. Rely on the fellowship of your friends and the sturdiness of your own convictions. With that, and with this kiss, I part from you for this evening.

Your loving husband,
Armand de Compière

That night she woke at three A.M., sweating. All she wanted was David. If she lost him she felt she would die. She determined that henceforth she would live by her promises to him. When Walter asked her to accompany him to the St. Luke's Charity Ball, she put him off with excuses.

But when the event arrived, Caroline was in an uproar. Alex Pitt had told her he would be out of town and wouldn't attend the dance, and consequently Caroline hadn't arranged to go. She now learned, however, that Alex was going, and that he was to be accompanied by Nancy McPhane, the stunning young anchor who had replaced that old battleax Darcy McDrew on the national news.

Sick with anger, Caroline scurried about all day trying to procure an invitation to the ball, calling Coco Peking and Tina Brown and finally Bianca Jagger, who used her influence to obtain two tickets. Caroline was to be accompanied by Craig Dice, the well-known gossip columnist and companion about town who often escorted Caroline on her late-night forays.

"You've *got* to come," Caroline insisted to Hélène. "I *need* you." She was trying to smooth her back into the silk stricture of her strapless dress, casting concerned glances over her shoulder at the ripple of excess flesh that obtruded whenever she moved; and she spoke to Hélène with a mixture of impatience and disbelief that might have suited a lady of the court enduring a younger sister's scruples concerning the disposition of her virginity.

"Why do you need me?"

"Oh, don't you see? Do I have to explain *everything?* This is a crisis, Hélène, for chrissakes! Don't you see the position he has put me in?"

"Well, it's beastly, Caroline, I know. But what did you expect?"

"Don't start preaching to me, please! What I need is a little help from my friends."

"Yes. But I promised David I wouldn't go out."

"Who? David? How dare you mention that man's name to me at a time like this? Let David Smith take his wife to *The Mikado.* Let them have mint tea at the Waldorf. What do I care about David Smith?"

"But I care about David Smith."

"I don't want to hear about your dementia right now. I've got enough problems of my own. Put David Smith out of your mind, he has nothing to do with this. I mean, it's only your best friend here who is having a nervous breakdown and asking for a little support, that's all that's going on. Nothing important."

Hélène sighed. In fact she was curious to witness the encounter with Alex Pitt, a prospect that promised considerably more stimulation than waiting all evening in her flat for a call from David.

She dressed carefully, as Walter liked; she even donned the diamond choker that Poppie had given her, an heirloom from his grandmother.

The dance was held in the Temple of Dendur and *tout New York* was present. Mickey Spine accompanied Onassis Fudge. Hamilton Hamilton took the beautiful Dorothea Pop. The Carmichaels were there and the Darmichaels, the Steinbergs and the Steinfelds and both sets of the Steinwalds. The lights in the great hall were dimmed so that one could barely discern beyond the sloping glass walls the ripple of Central Park and the ongoing life of the city.

Halfway through the dinner Hélène felt Walter rest his hand on her back. He was talking to a man across from him while Hélène leaned to her left to discuss an article in *Vanity Fair* with a woman dressed in green tulle who kept frowning and sucking in her lower lip; and although Walter's was the simplest gesture, its unconscious act of proprietorship froze her blood.

When the music commenced Caroline wheeled onto the dance floor and started strutting her stuff. She was a fine athletic dancer and she had taken Bernard Owen as her partner. The band was playing "ABC" and soon many were watching Caroline. Her face was flushed and she kept tossing her mane of red hair—a shade brighter, Hélène observed, than the previous day—and glancing haughtily in the direction of Alex Pitt and Nancy McPhane.

Hélène danced with Walter. He was light-footed and Hélène loved to dance. After a while she changed partners and danced with Bernard Owen. Then she danced with Anthony Puck and then with Cy Renning and then with Buddy Schutz and then with Peter Mark-Fitzby. Then they played something slow and she danced again with Walter.

"You appear to be having a good time." He spoke with irony but not without affection.

She rested her head against his shoulder—he was exactly her height. For a moment she closed her eyes and tried to stop the swirling in her head.

"Yes," she said. "I am having a good time."

"You see," he said, and he pulled her closer. "You must trust to your friends."

Alex Pitt approached Caroline and there was some sort of altercation.

"Keep your fucking hands off me," Caroline hissed. She batted at his hands as if they were flies.

Pitt backed away, embarrassed. The couples around Caroline had stopped dancing and were looking at her.

Hélène went up to Caroline and took her by the shoulder. Caroline looked at her and Hélène could see that she was drunk. Her eyes didn't register anything.

"Come along, Caroline. Let me help you out of here."

"Don't touch me," Caroline hissed.

Walter Straus stepped to Caroline and put his arm around her. He looked about him with sangfroid.

"Go ahead and dance," he said in a mild voice to the curious couples. Then he led Caroline from the floor.

In the hall Caroline wept on Hélène's shoulder. She smelled of heat and white wine and fading perfume. Hélène held her while over her shoulder a Ming statue regarded them with perfect refined equanimity.

"I hate him," Caroline sobbed. "I hate him. The bastard *knows* I'm pregnant."

Walter looked at Hélène and lifted his eyebrows.

They took Caroline home in a taxi. She had calmed down, and her cheeks, sallow in the mortuary light of the streetlamps, were smudged with mascara and tears.

"Are you really pregnant?" Hélène asked.

"Yes. I've known now for a week. The bastard promised he'd marry me if I got pregnant."

Walter looked at her in disbelief. They sat in silence while the taxi hurried down Fifth Avenue.

"Do you want me to come up?" Hélène asked.

"No, I'll be all right. Just call me in the morning."

"She seems like a zombie," Walter observed when they were alone.

"Can you blame her?"

Straus shrugged his shoulders. "You girls are a mystery to me. It's incomprehensible that a girl of Caroline's experience should take a man like Pitt at his word. Incomprehensible!" Again he shrugged and looked away in distaste.

They walked for a few blocks so Walter could smoke a cigar and after a time he took her arm. She felt the night come over her like a great weariness, a powerful drug urging her toward some ultimate oblivion. He stopped outside her apartment.

"May I come up?"

She had to look away. "Not tonight, Walter, please. Not after Caroline."

He tried to master his impatience.

"Caroline is a sloppy girl."

"She's my friend, Walter."

He looked at her severely. "You're all of you sloppy girls."

"Yes," she said. "Very likely you are right."

There was a message from David on her answering machine. "It's two A.M.," the message said. "Where the hell *are* you?"

She lay on her bed fully clothed and stared at the ceiling. Her head was dizzy with wine and music and she could feel the dizziness seeping into her blood. She could not understand why she was consistently denied the simplest things: a bit of happiness, a decent man, someone to lie next to her at night.

Perhaps she should have let Walter come up after all. It seemed such a waste, lying here like this with the city rustling outside the window and her blood astir. David was angry at her, Walter was angry at her, she was alone.

After a while she sat up. She rested her head in her hands and tried to recount the images of the evening. She kept returning to insignificant details: the leathery neck of Amanda Billings seen from across the table, the tight backside of Bernard Owen doing the monkey, the smudged mascara on Caroline's swollen face. She thought again of David, but the reflection filled her with misery and incoherent anger and she fought it off.

Then she thought of Tony. She hadn't seen Tony for almost two years. She went and sat by the phone and stared at it as if it were a moving flame. It wasn't too late to call Tony, no hour was too late to call Tony.

She could imagine the conversation. "Hi, Tony! I just thought I'd call to say hello."

The thought of it made her sick with excitement and despair. All that stopped her from calling was her recollection of his parting words. "You'll call me," he had said. "Just wait and see, you'll call me."

She felt dizzy and ill. She had an urgent desire to touch herself, something she never did. Finally she went back to her bed and lay down and cried.

Later she dreamed she was on top of a hill. Below her was the Cher. Behind her stood Poppie, though she couldn't see him; and, strangely, she knew that Poppie was David—they were distinct and yet somehow the same. All this made sense in the dream and filled her with happiness. Then she turned and saw below her the family cemetery. She gave a cry and awoke; and when she woke she was flooded with a sense of nostalgia so powerful that she thought she would drown.

For the next weeks she avoided David: she told him she was in one of her moods—a phrase they used when she got into a funk.

"Sometimes it's too much for me," she explained. "You have Barbara while I have . . . nothing. Sometimes I'd just rather be alone."

"Just tell me you love me," he said.

"I love you."

"Okay, darling. That's all I need to know. I'll call you again tomorrow."

Caroline began spotting and the doctor ordered her to her bed until the bleeding stopped. Hélène visited her daily, delivering books, magazines, chocolate truffles, eau de cologne, turkey sandwiches with honey mustard, the newest Rolling Stones release— whatever she could conceive of to entertain her friend.

Caroline sat in bed holding court on the telephone. Though she affected to despise television she kept it on all day in the background, and at five she invariably watched Alex Pitt, accompanying his appearance with a running commentary of obscenities and execrations.

"There he is, Long John Pencil Prick, the Pasha of the Bimbos. They need to strap his cock down with duct tape so it won't wag on prime time. He's been known to mount the water cooler when his secretary of the week is away from her desk."

After a few days Hélène found herself resisting these visits. Everything about Caroline's room depressed her—the crumpled tissues on the floor, the pile of soiled clothing on the chair, the empty candy wrappers stuffed in the half-eaten box, the long strands of hair depending from the teeth of the comb. But it wasn't only that Caroline was a slob. It was the thought of the child. Hélène was jealous.

It smote her with terror and disgust to admit that her life had disintegrated to the point where she was jealous of Caroline, but so it was. She too wanted a child.

She called David at his work and got his partner; the man's voice was gruff on the phone. David had told her that his partner was ill, but that wasn't the problem. He didn't approve of her—and Hélène didn't blame him.

She told David to meet her at her apartment—immediately.

As soon as he kissed her she felt herself change; it was some sort of chemical metamorphosis. The rest of the world ceased to exist, she was possessed by insensate desire.

"It's such bliss!" she mumbled as he stroked her.

She heard herself cry out as she came, a sound alien, forlorn, and slightly mad.

It was impossible to be closer to a man than she had just been to David, yet a moment later she felt stir between them the pathos of separation. She struggled with her irritability, but she was too tired to resist for long.

"I don't think your partner likes me very much."

"Oh?"

His insouciance galled her. She had a vision of him as the Golden Boy of America, the born winner to her eternal foil.

"Isn't he your partner?" she asked in subdued petulance. "Don't you even care what he thinks?"

"What Gordo thinks? I couldn't care less."

"Don't you give a damn for the respectable opinion of mankind?"

He regarded her with amusement.

"Not a damn."

"Well, it's a mistake," she said, moving away from him.

He sat up and frowned. Something in her movement alarmed him.

"I don't care about anyone's opinion but yours and Barbara's."

"Yes? But oil's and water's, you mean. But Pat Robertson's and the Communists'."

"Are we going to start this again?" he asked. "I don't know what you want me to say."

"Yes, you do. You know what I want. I want *you,* David. I want you to love me. I want you to commit to me."

He made a small movement of desperation. "But I *do* love you, Hélène. How can you doubt that? I *am* committed to you."

"How can you be committed to me?" she said in exasperation. "How? What am I but your mistress?" She spat out the word with scorn. "But I don't *want* to be someone's mistress. It's not my *scene.*"

He tried to touch her but she pulled away.

"You're not my mistress," he pleaded.

"No? What would you call me, then?"

He looked about in some confusion. "My wife," he said. "I'd call you my wife."

She let the air escape from her lungs in a puff. For a time there was silence between them while she continued to lie flat on her back on the bed.

"I'm not your wife, David."

"There's no word for what you are," he said. "There's no word in the language."

She turned to him and touched the top of his hand lightly. When she spoke her voice had changed, had become gentler.

"David, what if I told you I'd stopped taking my pills?"

He looked at her interrogatively. "Your pills?"

"My birth control pills. What if I told you I had thrown them away?"

He seemed to weigh his words. "Don't you think that is something we should discuss first?" He watched her carefully. "Have you?" he asked. "Have you thrown them away?"

"No," she said after a moment. "I forgot to take one yesterday. That's all."

"So you might just have gotten pregnant."

"Oh, I didn't get pregnant," she said quietly. "No such luck. But I'd like to, David. I'd like to have your child. I'm thirty-two, David, and I want to have a child."

"I'd like that too," he said.

"Would you? Well . . . it's impossible."

"Impossible? That's a big word."

"Please, David. You're a dreamer. You live in a dream world."

"Well . . . yes, I suppose I do."

"And I love you for it. It's the secret of your eternal youth. But some of us don't have this option, this proclivity for the interior landscape. I can't live in a dream forever."

"What do you mean?"

"I mean just what I said. Nothing more and nothing less. I'm thirty-two, David. Somehow I've got to move my life off point zero."

"We've discussed this before, Hélène, but what's the option? I *love* you. I don't want to be without you. And what about you? What are you going to do? Take a string of lovers? Throw yourself into the great sexual melting pot of America? What advantage is there in that? Besides, I thought you were in love with me."

"Oh, God, David, I am! Can't you see that I am? But this is killing me. Can't you see this can't go on?"

After that a glacial weight settled on Hélène's spirit. She felt as if something had died inside her, something she had not previously taken cognizance of but that had supplied her with light and hope. Again she tried not seeing David.

During this time she permitted herself the indulgence of Walter Straus. He distracted her from herself. Besides—why shouldn't she admit it?—she enjoyed the social life he afforded. Walter's tastes were not necessarily the best, but they were the most expensive, and he provided her with opportunities that distracted if they did not satisfy.

Increasingly, however, she had difficulty keeping Walter at bay. He was a cosmopolitan of various taste who much appreciated social intercourse, and he genuinely desired Hélène's company; but she knew that sooner or later he would require payment in a different currency.

She had elaborated for his confusion a tale of celibacy, and though she remained uncertain to what degree she was believed, the fiction served its end.

"My dear girl," he observed, "you puzzle me. It is not as if we were strangers to each other. I don't mean to intrude where I don't belong, but I consider your attitude unhealthy."

"I'm grateful for your solicitude." She smiled, tapping him on the hand. "But surely this is one area where a woman can be allowed to decide for herself."

"Perhaps," he said pensively. "But I am inclined to think it the area where one is least likely to perceive oneself properly. Just consider your absurd attachment to that—what's his name?—David Smith."

That made her look down. She was afraid to give herself away. She still could not hear his name with equanimity.

"We must agree to disagree about David," she said. "But at any rate that's all in the past."

"Precisely. That's why your attitude is so . . . unhealthy. I don't care what you say, you can't continue in it for long. I will indulge you in this as in all things, but it's against my better judgment."

During her depression she considered according him the pleasure he desired. In itself it was such a simple act, so purposeless and absurd, that she could not bestow on it the significance that men in their possessiveness claimed to discern. It was only her fear of sullying her experience with David that stopped her.

But she was thankful to Walter. He took her to the Quilted Giraffe and Le Cirque and the Pierre and the Union Square Café;

they attended balls and cotillions and dined regularly at the Jackie
Jacksons' and with Coco Peking. Once to her amusement her
picture appeared in the *New York Times* social section after she had
attended the Highland charity ball.

All of these were palliatives. She would wake the next morning
exhausted, with a hangover and a sense of loneliness that afflicted
her like nausea.

Caroline lost her baby.

She had gotten up to go to the store and had started bleeding
on her way home. The bleeding hadn't stopped and after an hour
her doctor told her to go to the hospital, but she had lost the baby
before she could depart.

Hélène spent the night with her. She had rarely seen anyone so
distraught. It was not just the loss of the baby; Caroline felt her
life had come to an end.

"I'll never have a baby, Hélène. I'm forty—this was my last
chance. Don't you understand? I'll never have a child."

Hélène understood only too well. She calmed Caroline as best
she could. When she returned to her apartment she flushed her
contraceptive pills down the toilet.

Her lethargy of the previous months seemed to her shameful
and foolish, a failure of nerve. She perceived it was her duty to
make David come to her so they could complete their lives together. It was too absurd for people to love each other as they did
and remain separated, like islands cut by a running channel.

She tried to explain to David what had befallen Caroline, but
every time they discussed it she was overwhelmed by tears.

"It's the worst thing that could have happened," she said.
"Now she'll never have a baby."

"You can't be sure. She's not so old."

"No, she's forty and that was her last chance. Oh, David—
she'll die without a child."

Then, when she was in his arms, "I'm not going to die without
a child."

* * *

For a number of days they were supremely happy. Hélène felt she had made a new commitment to David. She had not worked out the details—there remained the immense fact of Poppie—but she knew she wanted David as a permanent part of her life.

"I've never been more in love with you," David said.

Then he called her on Thursday.

"What's this picture of you in the paper?"

"What paper?"

"In the *New York Times*. I was going through the old papers and I found you on the social page at some charity ball. It says you were accompanied by 'the well-known socialite Walter Straus.'"

"But I told you Walter was a social butterfly."

"Yes. But you didn't tell me you accompanied him on his flights."

"Don't be ridiculous, David. I accompanied Walter to this party because at the last moment his date, the woman he's all but engaged to, came down ill and he asked me as a favor to take her place. I couldn't say no. What would be the point? I suppose I forgot to tell you—or didn't want to tell you because you get all worked up over nothing. And now you inform me my picture has ended up in the *Times*. How very silly."

"Yes, but didn't you tell me you *weren't* going out with Straus? Didn't we have an agreement?"

"Oh, I knew you'd work this up into something! That's why I didn't tell you. I mean, it's nothing. Precisely nothing. Walter asked me as a favor to go to some party. Do I have to call to get your permission to do that? Is that what you're saying?"

"That's not the point. The point is, we had an agreement."

"What's the agreement, David? That I sit home night after night doing nothing while you play with Barbara?"

"What do you mean by that?"

"Nothing. I don't mean anything. I don't want to fight. But the truth is, I am free to go out with Walter Straus whenever I want."

"Is that the truth? Is that the truth?"

She was appalled at how quickly their relationship had come to this. He was almost screaming into the phone.

"David, let's not fight," she repeated.

"But what I don't understand is why you *want* to go out with Walter Straus. I mean, don't you know what kind of a slimeball he is? All of those people. Don't you have a nose? Those creepy car salesmen. Those shoe salesmen. Dressed up in thousand-dollar tuxedos with their done-over wives or girlfriends on their arms. My God, they make the robber barons look like the guardians of good taste."

"I'm sorry you don't approve of my friends."

"Your *friends?*"

"Yes. Walter is my friend, David. He's a friend of my father's. He's been kind to me in the past. I'm indebted to him. I owe him, if you will, a party once a year."

"Well, not anymore. I don't want you seeing him anymore. I don't want to wake up and see you on somebody else's arm in the *New York Times.* Is that so very strange?"

She took a deep breath. "It wouldn't be so very strange if I were your wife. But I'm not. I'm not your wife. If you want me to marry you, I will. I'll marry you today. Say the word and I'll meet you at Town Hall, in Reno—wherever."

"Hélène, for chrissakes! You know that's impossible."

"All right. Then it's impossible. But don't tell me I can't go to some stupid innocent party with Walter Straus."

There was a prolonged silence on the phone.

"David, don't you get it? Don't you get it at all? I don't *want* to be with Walter Straus. I don't want to be with anyone but you. But I can't have my life come to a complete standstill. It's not fair. It's not *fair!*"

She could hear him breathing. She tried to make out whether she was sorry or pleased to have hurt him.

"Tell me what you want," he said, and his voice sounded tired. "Tell me what you want within the confines of the possible, and I will do it."

"You know what I want."

"Hélène, I can't leave my wife and children. It would be dastardly. You wouldn't want me to."

"Oh, I wouldn't want you to do something *dastardly,* David!"

When she hung up she sat for a long time, thinking. She saw clearly how she could put him over the barrel of his jealousy and break him. And it made her shudder.

She went to a party at Lord Weinreb's and was seated next to an art dealer named Ulrik, whom she had met before. Ulrik was a tall handsome German with a stunning wife and two blond stunning children, and he was reputed to be a homosexual. He was witty and risqué and Hélène liked to be with him because he was fun.

Ulrik was unaccompanied this evening and he immediately caressed Hélène's throat and chucked her behind the ear.

"Haf I told you the story about the man whoz ear was turnt into a fagina?"

"His ear?"

"Yez, yez—it is all true. Von't you haf some vine?"

Ulrik proceeded to relate the story about the man and the errant pudendum. The tale was long and complicated and included various references to dogs and horses, and it struck Hélène as highly amusing. Here, she thought, was a clever man! This was more fun than sitting at home alone.

"I like parties," she explained to Ulrik after she had drunk a few glasses of wine.

"Do you?"

"Yes, I do. They are part of who I am."

"Vunderful, countess! Vunderful! Allow me to pour you more vine."

Everyone was laughing and having a fine time. Ulrik put one arm across the back of Hélène's chair and the other hand he put palm down in her lap over her womb; and for some reason this arrangement struck Hélène as sophisticated and natural and she would have considered it uncouth and even ill-bred to complain of Ulrik's gesture.

"I love dirty stories," she confessed to the handsome German.

"Do you? I'm zo glat. Haf some more delicious vine!"

Later in the evening Hélène went to the bathroom and studied herself in the bathroom mirror, and her eyes struck her as particularly bright and attractive. I look wonderful! she thought. This is me! Another me. The evening seemed to her gay and adventurous, the way she imagined her mother's young life in Paris. David should stay at home with his wife, she thought. She is *safer!* And impetuously she removed her ring, the gold fretted one from Old Russia that David had given her, and placed it in her purse.

Ulrik helped her back into her seat. He was beaming at her as if they had struck up a special understanding, and Hélène found she was beaming back, though she wasn't entirely sure what this understanding was supposed to be.

"You have a vunderful figure," Ulrik said to her. He was leaning toward her and smiling and he put one arm around her shoulder and put his hand on the top of her breast where it was exposed because of the dress.

"Do I?"

"Deep-breasted, yes? As Homer says. Vunderful cleafage!"

He's one of those homosexuals, she thought, who likes to put his hands on women. And then she thought, What difference does it make? I'm not going to go to bed with him. I don't go to bed with men. This seemed to settle something for her and afterward she relaxed and had more wine.

But when she woke the next morning with a terrible headache the recollection of Ulrik appalled her. She had actually said that she liked dirty stories!

I'm just like my mother, she thought. I'll end up a drunkard. If David doesn't save me I'll end up a drunkard.

Throughout that spring men seemed to be buzzing at her from all directions and she couldn't resist them properly—it was a kind of dizziness, she didn't understand it herself. She seemed to have lost her footing and she couldn't regain it again and she wasn't even sure she wanted to.

A man named Fitzsimmons called her up. She had met him at a party and had agreed to go yachting with him on a Saturday. He was sixty and tall and elegant-looking and she had thought it would be fun and above reproach to go sailing with him on his yacht on Long Island Sound.

"You're the kind of gerl I like," he said to her on the phone in what she had learned to think of as a Yale accent, hardened to brutality through the exercise of arrogance. "And when I say like, I mean *like*."

"That's very—"

"And I don't like many gerls. I'm very choosy about that, very discriminating."

"I'm very—"

"I'm intrigued by the colah of your hair—that reddish hue. I bet that's natural, am I right? I bet that's the colah all the way down the line!"

"Mr. Fitzsimmons!"

"No false modesty, please! I know what I'm dealing with."

"Mr. Fitzsimmons, I have to ask you—"

"Ask anything, honey. You can have anything you want. Why don't we have dinner together Friday night? How would that suit you?"

She was shaking when she hung up the phone. Why, she thought, the man's fucking me on the telephone!

He was abusive when she called to say she wouldn't see him.

"Oh, that's just Ed Fitzsimmons." Caroline laughed when she told her about it. "Why don't you go out with him? You'll have a good time."

"I don't think so," Hélène said, though in truth she had almost gone, he had just come on too strong, it wasn't her style.

"I don't go to bed with men," she repeated to herself, though she didn't ask herself why she needed to repeat this talisman.

She played the traffic game again. It was against all rules, but she didn't care. She felt drugged, angry, indifferent.

The moment she stepped off the curb she was shaking with excitement. It required all her nerve not to lift her eyes. This time it seemed she would never reach the farther side. She was dizzy with fear, the adrenaline pounding through her veins. She plodded forward, trapped in a nightmare of terror and exhilaration.

Then, once more, she was on the other side. A taxi had stopped and the driver, leaning out, was screaming at her. She thought she was going to faint. She staggered to one of the benches and sat down and put her head between her knees.

Slowly she caught her breath. When she lifted her head—O brave new world!—everything was dazzling. It was as if the air had thinned, or maybe her blood, as if she had arisen from a sickbed. The world was new-made and beautiful. She was wonderfully excited.

When she arrived home she was violently ill.

In May David went to Boston with his wife leaving Hélène alone for two days. Heat had come early to New York and when she opened the window the sounds of the city floated to her elongated and blurred. She tried not to think of David.

Walter called and she agreed to take an early dinner with him Saturday night. She *allowed* herself Walter. She allowed herself all sorts of things. Of course she wouldn't tell David.

"My dear girl," Walter said to her. "Permit me to observe that you are again looking . . . shopworn."

"Shopworn?"

"Well, tired. I mean no offense. Quite the opposite. I tell you how it is: I'm going out to the Hamptons and I think you should join me. It will do you a world of good. Just like old times, what do you say?"

She didn't say anything. She wasn't ready to decamp to the Hamptons with Walter Straus.

But she did mention the invitation to David later, when he had returned from Boston. She knew it would set him off.

"Of course I don't want you going to the Hamptons," he said heatedly. "I just don't understand you, Hélène. I don't understand why you *want* to go."

"I don't want to go to the Hamptons with Walter Straus. I hate the Hamptons. But I'll tell you what I *do* want. I want to go away with you. I want a weekend to ourselves. Just us. And I want it *soon.*"

David agreed, but he called on Tuesday to say that the weekend they had chosen wasn't good after all. It had to do with one of his daughters. She was in some play he had promised to attend and he couldn't get out of the commitment. She listened in silence.

"Well, that's very nice for you and your daughter. I'm not being sarcastic, David. I know how much your children mean to you. But what about me? Where do I fit in in all of this? I'm just dessert, something sweet to have at the end of the meal, a platter of delicious calories."

"That's not fair, Hélène. You know I was looking forward to this as much as you. We'll just have to put it off for a week, that's all. Don't make a big deal out of nothing."

"Well, it's nothing to you, perhaps, but not to me. If you can't make it, then perhaps I'll go with Walter to the Hamptons."

"Why are you doing this, Hélène? I'm not running off to see another woman. It's my daughter, for chrissakes! I gave her my word."

"And I wouldn't want you to break it. Not to your daughter. Break it to me instead. It's just another instance of what I've been saying for a long time. You can't love your family and me. Someone's got to take the back seat."

"But it isn't so, Hélène. It isn't a question of whom I love more. There are different kinds of love. If I had my druthers I'd go with you."

"I don't even want you to, David. Not under these circumstances. You go with your daughter and I'll go with Walter. It's better that way."

"Better? Better for whom?"

"Frankly, for me. I've reached this conclusion painfully, but I've got to have some other choices in my life."

"And Walter is another choice? Is that what you're saying?"

"I don't know what I'm saying, David. I don't know what I'm saying."

"I won't go to the play, Hélène. I'll think of some excuse. We'll go away as planned."

"No, I don't want that."

"Yes. I insist. I won't have you seeing another man—not in that way. What you don't seem to take in is that I love you."

"I do take it in, David. I do. What you don't take in is that it's hopeless."

It was concluded that they would go away together that weekend. It was a victory of sorts, but it didn't feel like one. She tried to pretend she was happy. Instead she felt guilt, shame, and anger.

All she wanted was to live her life with David.

They were to meet on Saturday morning. On Friday she found herself sitting in Central Park reading a letter from Poppie.

9 June 1988

Dearest child:

Today I went to visit Eve's grave. As of course you know, it is the tenth anniversary of her birth. I do not allow myself the luxury of thinking how different our lives might have been had she lived. I want to assure you that she is resting peacefully in her little plot above the Cher. I also want to assure you, dearest Hélène, that our Eve's soul has been gathered to God and is happy. As I grow older I am ever more convinced of certain simple things I was taught in childhood: that it is God's universe, that he watches over us throughout our lives, that we are gathered to him after death. Our Eve is an angel in heaven—I believe that with the simple faith of a child. Not to believe is to be lost without recourse. I say this to you, my dear wife, because I would protect you, even at this distance. I know you will never be coming home. And yet God's ways are mysterious. Who can tell? Whatever befalls, you remain, now and unto eternity, my wife. And the three of us—you, myself, and our dear Eve—will be gathered together in heaven after death. This thought gives me solace and strength, and I trust it will you, too. Know also that in dedication to the memory of Eve I have resolved to write a life of the Abbé de Saint-Cyran of that Jansenist movement which had such a profound influence on French letters. I feel small sympathy for Saint-Cyran, but this only makes the undertaking more agreeable in my eyes. I know you will wish me well on this venture. With that I conclude for the present, though my thoughts are with you now and forever. Your loving husband,
                    Armand, comte de Compière

She sat for a long time with the letter between her hands. Overhead the leaves rustled and from a neighboring bush a songbird twittered in the sunlight. She was certain that neither she nor David nor anyone else had breath to continue this game much longer.

Looking up, she saw Barbara. She recognized her instantly though she had only seen her once before. She was a large handsome woman with high cheekbones and flowing chestnut hair, and though older than Hélène had recalled, she was still beautiful.

She looked, Hélène thought, like David's wife.

She was with her two daughters, the three talking earnestly as they walked hurriedly, paying no attention to what was about them. The girls were handsome girls and Hélène marveled at how much they looked like their parents: it was impossible to say which they resembled more. They passed without seeing her.

Hélène sat for a long time. She felt a great resistance to getting up. She wished she could sit there forever. Finally she folded her letter and put it away.

It's all so very simple, she thought. So very obvious. How have I ever been so very dumb?

Jack Hamilton's house in East Hampton was not on the water, but it was large and spacious, situated on grounds protected from its neighbors by high luxuriant bushes, and provided in the back yard with an ample black-bottomed swimming pool. The house was constructed of Finnish teak and from the attic on the fourth story one could sight out to the bay. Here Hamilton had set up a telescope focused on the nest of an osprey.

When Hélène looked through the apparatus it took her a moment to locate the bird.

"Here, let me take a look," Hamilton said. He leaned against her and she inhaled the odor of his eau de cologne.

Hamilton was living in the house alone since his wife had taken the children to California, and though it was unclear whether the couple had formally separated, the spring months had clearly consisted of a seamless succession of houseguests who more or less occupied the space of his bachelorhood.

"There he is," Hamilton said, and he took her shoulders to position her correctly.

Again Hélène peered through the telescope, and this time she was startled by the proximity of the haughty predatory beak framed in the small circle almost as if she could touch it.

"Got it?" Hamilton inquired.

"Yes." She was breathless with the strange beauty of the thing. Its golden liquid eye and humped sinister shoulder recalled Richard III.

"It's a young one," Hamilton explained. "You can tell by the feathering."

Hélène had met Jack Hamilton a number of times and she didn't like him. He was a handsome athletic man with excess beef on his shoulders and belly, and his oblong face with its even, somewhat heavy features was perpetually tanned, as if his skin had been cured and dyed like a particularly valuable trophy. He was some species of writer, successful at whatever it was he did, and he habitually regarded the world out of gray, bored, scornful, intelligent eyes.

"How thrilling!" She couldn't help expressing her excitement, which, she noticed, amused him.

"Yeah? You think so?"

"Yes, I do. He's marvelous."

"Well, he's a lot better than most of us," Hamilton said. "My wife and I used to go to the Andes to see the condors. Now there's a bird!"

"How wonderful!" Hélène said. "I would love to do that."

"Would you?" And he smiled strangely at her, partly in admiration, partly in condescension, as if she were a handsome dog that had learned a trick.

There were seven of them sitting around the black pool: Walter, Hélène, Jack Hamilton, Doe Peter, the Coopers (Freddie and Marge), and one of Hamilton's young retainers, a handsome sinister-looking boy whom Hamilton called Cousin Tom and employed as a general gofer.

Cousin Tom was the only one in the pool. He would hoist his lean body up onto the side to keep abreast of the conversation, then spiral back like a seal into the emerald water.

"What I can't understand is why they buried the bodies on their own property," Marge Cooper said. They were discussing a particularly outlandish set of murders that had occurred not distant from where they now sat.

"That's the beauty of it," her husband, Freddie, explained. "It's like Dostoevsky, don't you think? I'm putting through the movie deal now. You should get a piece of it, Jack."

Jack Hamilton turned up his lip in distaste. "It's not my kind of thing," he said.

"Really? When it's literally in your own back yard? That's spurning the hand of chance, Jackie. That's spurning the hand that feeds you."

"Yeah? I thought you were the hand that feeds me."

Cousin Tom smiled as if Hamilton had said something witty. Then he dove back into the water with a sudden splash. But he was up on the farther side and out in a single movement, his black sleek hair plastered back from his forehead.

"Oh, Jack, don't write about anything as ghoulish as that," Doe Peter exclaimed. She was a well-built girl wearing a very brief bikini with high-heeled mules and three or four gold chains around her neck. She came over and sat on the edge of Jack Hamilton's lounge chair.

"I'm not going to write about anything," Jack Hamilton said. "I'm on sabbatical."

"What exactly *do* you write about?" Hélène asked from across the pool. Her words were greeted with a moment of silence.

"That's a good question," Jack Hamilton said, and he smiled at her unpleasantly. "I used to write novels, didn't I, Fred? But recently I write for the magazines."

"Didn't you see Jack's piece on scuba diving in the Turks?" Marge Cooper asked. "It was the cover piece for *Traveler.*"

"I'm sorry," Hélène said. "I must have missed it."

"Well, you didn't miss a lot," Hamilton said. "It was a piece of shit."

"How can you say that!" Marge Cooper said. "Jack is his own worst critic."

"What I thought," Walter Straus said, "is that the countess and I would run into town and pick up some lobsters for dinner. How does that sound?"

"That sounds dandy," Fred Cooper said. "But I'd like to contribute to the wherewithall."

"Don't worry about dinner," Jack Hamilton said. "We'll cook some steaks on the grill. Relax and let's have some drinks while the sun is up. Cousin Tom here can mix the sauce. Unless of course the *countess* wants to go to town." He uttered her title with derision.

"Oh, I'm quite content," Hélène said. "Don't worry about me."

The men went to the bar to gather the drinks while the women clustered by the pool.

"Now we can talk girlie talk," Marge Cooper said. "Let the men fix the problems of the world."

Doe Peter looked at her and blinked her eyes.

"I mean," Marge said, "I'd rather talk about men and sex, wouldn't you?" And she giggled self-consciously.

"Frankly," Hélène said, "I feel better qualified to fix the problems of the world."

She got up to find the bathroom.

Hamilton stopped her in the hall on her way back. He had obviously followed her.

"So tell me," he said. "What's this countess bit? Where'd you get the title?"

"My husband is the comte de Compière," Hélène explained simply. "The family was ennobled in the early nineteenth century."

"Oh," he said. "I see." She observed her value shoot up like some venture stock on the market. She could divide the world between those who were and those who were not impressed by her title. It had meant nothing to David.

"I apologize," Jack Hamilton said, and he touched her tentatively on the wrist. "It's just, you know, most people you meet are such phonies."

They returned to the pool and he fetched her a glass of white wine.

Later the sun was orange and was coming almost straight at her eyes. Hélène had switched to vodka and she had donned a straw hat to protect her from the sun.

Doe Peter had ventured into the pool, where she and Cousin Tom sported like sleek young otters. Now their bodies glistened as they lay drying.

Walter was discussing the stock market with Freddie Cooper. Walter's entire capacious torso—stomach, shoulders, back—was covered with long gray hair like a pelt. He wore some variety of gold medallion about his neck that nestled in his hair like an animal.

Marge Cooper was trying to entertain Jack Hamilton. He had surrendered his hand to her as he reclined in the lounge chair, and she was reading his fortune in its lines. In his other hand he held a tall glass of whiskey.

"You have a wonderful life line," Marge said. "It runs right off your hand like a highway."

"Yeah? What does that mean? That I'm going to live till I'm eighty?"

"At least. But your love line is more conflicted."

"Conflicted? No shit. Tell me something I don't know."

"Well, I see a major change in your life."

"I bet," Hamilton said, looking at Hélène. "Like what? That I'm going to drive off the edge of a cliff?"

"Be serious, Jack," Marge said. "You've got to be serious about this."

"Yeah? Or what happens? My life line expires like Tinker Bell?"

"Oh, Jack," Marge said. "You're such a card!" She turned to Hélène for confirmation. "Don't you think Jack is a card?"

"Jack is surely a card," Hélène said dryly. Jack Hamilton looked at her and smiled.

"So tell me," he asked her, "do you believe in all these things, these gypsy tricks, these haruspications?"

"There was an old woman in my village of Compière who could

tell fortunes," Hélène said. She looked at Hamilton and saw that his lips were moist and slightly swollen, as if peeled in the sun. She averted her gaze.

"No josh," Hamilton said. He removed his hand from Marge and sat up. "What could she do?"

"I don't think it was a question of doing. She seemed to enjoy some degree of second sight."

"Madame Compière, countess—whatever you're called. I don't believe it."

"It wasn't a question of belief," Hélène said. "It seemed to be something of a fact."

"Something of a fact?" Hamilton said. "Do facts come in degrees?"

"She wasn't always accurate," Hélène said quietly.

"Did you have your fortune told?"

"No."

"Why not?"

Hélène looked at him again and saw that he was genuinely interested. "I was afraid," she said.

Jack Hamilton laughed. Surprisingly, it was a nice sound, clear-toned and manly. "I bet," he said. "I bet you were. I would be too."

"Against all the odds," Hélène said, "I like to believe in freedom."

"Don't we all. But do you succeed? Do you believe in freedom?"

Hélène shook her head and smiled. "It's such a big word."

"Yes, but do you believe in it? Do you believe, for example, that I could change my life?"

"I've changed mine," she said.

Hamilton looked at her as if he were again sizing her up. "When was that?" he asked.

"Today." As she said this it became clear to her that she was drunk.

Jack Hamilton lay back in his lounge chair and whistled. "Today? As of right now?"

"Not exactly right now," Hélène said. She took another sip of the vodka.

Marge Cooper called out to the rest of the company. "Listen to this," she cried. "Did you know, Walter, that your friend Hélène has just changed her life?"

Walter looked at Hélène and lifted an eyebrow. An expression of concern crossed his bearded features.

Hélène looked around her at the other faces. "That's right," she said in an even voice after a moment had elapsed. "As of today my life is changed."

There was silence around the pool. The light of evening fell on the pool with violence. Where it caught a ripple, it shot back like fire.

"Is changed?" Hamilton said, and his voice had resumed its irony. "That's not the same as your changing it."

Hélène looked at him pensively. "I suppose not," she said. "For our purpose, however, it comes to the same thing."

"What are you talking about?" Walter inquired, a tone of annoyance in his voice. "Is this some sort of party game?"

"Not really," Hélène said. "I just offered it as an observation."

"A bulletin," Hamilton amended. "A public pronouncement."

"I'm thinking of going back to France," Hélène said. She was speaking to Walter. Her head felt dizzy.

"My dear Hélène," Walter said, "whatever are you talking about? You can't go back to France. You don't belong there anymore. You belong here with your friends."

Hélène looked around at Marge and Freddie Cooper and suddenly she felt overwhelmed with weariness. Doe Peter was leaning so far forward that her cleavage was like a strange circus mouth pursed at Hélène in fascination. Cousin Tom's black eyes darted about like a radar gun.

"I suppose you must be right," Hélène said wearily. "You always are."

"I'll tell you what," Jack Hamilton said, sitting up with renewed energy. "If you can't go to France you can come with me to the Andes. We'll go see the condors together."

Hélène looked at Hamilton and saw that he was smiling at her. To her increasing sadness she realized that he was good-looking.

"That's nice of you," she said.

"You're damned right it's nice of me. So it's decided, then. I'll take Hélène here to the Andes to see the condors to celebrate the fact that she changed her life. It's an inspiration to all of us."

The assembled company seemed to think this a fine idea. The announcement was conducive to general hilarity. More drinks were provided; Hamilton poured Hélène another vodka. Only Walter looked out of sorts as he squatted on his lounge chair like a great hirsute deity discomfited by the tidings of a newer god.

The night had come down, and the charcoals in the barbecue hissed and spluttered where the grease oozed from the steaks. Jack Hamilton was wearing khaki shorts, and he staggered slightly as he called to his guests, "Party time!"

The participants were dressed informally for the cookout. Freddie Cooper wore a Hawaiian shirt open at the neck. Walter, always the dresser, sported white slacks and an ascot atop his pink silk shirt. Doe Peter had arranged her blouse so that her navel was apparent and her handsome cleavage was still available.

Hélène wore a simple white dress with sandals. She had lain down in her room for half an hour but the silence ended by depressing her and she mixed herself another vodka. The thought of calling David passed through her mind but she forced it aside.

When she had left the poolside to change, Hamilton had followed her into the house.

"I didn't know whether you'd want to be put in Straus's room," he said.

"No, my own room, please."

"Good."

"Why good?"

"I don't know. Just . . . good."

Now she could see he was watching her as he attended to the steaks.

Cousin Tom slipped diagonally across the patio toward Hamilton. Appareled in Levi's and a black T-shirt, he moved with feline unnerving grace, a sinister new James Dean.

"So, boss, we goin' to score tonight?"

"Just watch me, son," Jack Hamilton said solemnly. "Just watch me."

Hélène approached Walter Straus and took his arm.

"My dear countess," he said, walking her up and down in the shadows and speaking to her in French while he pinched his fingers together in his peculiar fashion. "I take your resolution to change your life as a good omen. *La vita nuova,* and all that."

"*La vita nuova,* indeed. *Nel mezzo del cammin di nostra vita.*"

"I've ceased to inquire too closely into your personal life," Straus continued, "but I suspect you wrapped yourself up in some sort of impossible situation."

"That's me," Hélène said. "The Impossible Situation girl."

"Well, it's high time you disengaged yourself," Walter said.

"Oh, I mean to. Indeed, I intend to do just that. I intend to disengage myself from all impossible situations."

"That's excellent, that's excellent. But as for France, why, it's too late for that. You'd suffocate now in Compière."

"What are you two chitchatting about?" Jack Hamilton asked. He had approached them without Hélène's noticing.

"We're discussing impossible situations," Hélène said.

"Oh, yeah?" Hamilton smiled. "I'd like to hear about some of those."

"Oh, they are less interesting than you might think. Most of them turn out to be just . . . impossible."

He placed her next to himself at the table. It was a hot night and all of them were now drunk. It was a long time since Hélène had been drunk on vodka and the experience came as a revelation.

"Someone should have reminded me about this," she said to Hamilton. "About vodka, I mean."

"You're not a vodka drinker?"

"No. Strictly white wine."

"I wouldn't take you for a party girl," he said.

"Oh? Is that a compliment? What would you take me for?"

"A classy dame."

"A classy dame? Is that a special American species?"

"It's an endangered species, countess. Perhaps you think I wouldn't know the difference, but I assure you that's not the case. My wife was a classy dame. Top drawer. I have a special facility for lousing up relations with classy dames."

"I take that to be some sort of warning," Hélène said.

"I suppose it's some sort of proposal," Jack Hamilton replied.

We're both drunk, Hélène thought. This is the Gay Life one reads about in the chronicles of the inebriate. A joke once told her floated through her mind. It was the Hollywood equivalent of a Polish joke and the punchline was "She slept with the writer."

Later she observed that the Coopers were quarreling; she couldn't make out what it was about. Marge had been crying and Freddie was poking at her with a straw.

The night had assumed a heavy fulgurant quality, weighted and overripe, as if from some odor from the sound.

"So tell me, countess," Doe Peter asked, leaning forward across the table. "Where did you acquire your title?"

Walter Straus looked sad and heavy. Hélène noticed he had placed his hand in Doe Peter's lap.

"Doe, there's no cause to be jealous," Jack Hamilton said. "Everyone at this table's got a title. I mean, she's a countess, you're a cunt, right?"

After a while Hélène observed that Jack Hamilton had abandoned them. It came to her that he had done this a number of times. She put her napkin down and followed him into the house.

For a while she could not find her way and stumbled about in the spacious rooms, unable to give herself any account of what she was doing. Finding Jack was all that seemed to present itself to her mind.

Then she found him. He had left the bathroom door ajar and was bent over the sink. She noticed a row of bright yellow lights above the medicine chest. As she approached she saw he was snuffing dope.

He straightened up and looked at her.

"I didn't know where you were," she said.

"Well, now you do."

He leaned over and took another snort. Then he tilted his head so it was facing the ceiling. His eyes were closed and watering. When he lowered his head he turned toward her slowly.

"Here," he said. "Have some."

"How do you do it?"

"You mean you've never done dope?" He snorted. "Some princess!"

The dope slammed into the back of her nose. It took her breath away. For a moment she wasn't certain whether she was still breathing. Then she saw that Jack Hamilton was holding her and they were sitting on the edge of the bathtub.

"My God!" she said.

"Here," Jack Hamilton said. "Wipe your nose." He gave her a piece of tissue. He didn't remove his arm from around her waist.

"My God," she repeated.

"You like that?" He smiled.

It took her a moment to locate her words.

"Yes."

Jack Hamilton took down the top of her dress and kissed her breasts.

"Not here," she said.

He hoisted himself up and stood above her. "C'mon," he said. He was still smiling.

They were moving through a long dark corridor. She didn't let go of Jack Hamilton's hand. She felt fine.

They emerged onto the patio and she could see the black rectangle of the pool. Someone had extinguished the patio lights, but light still filtered through the canopy of thick leaves. Walter was lying on a lounge chair with Marge Cooper. Then she saw that Doe Peter was swimming naked in the pool with Cousin Tom. Freddie Cooper was nowhere to be seen.

"Let's get out of here," Jack Hamilton said.

In his room she could see the lights blinking in the bay. Then she was naked and Jack Hamilton had his hands upon her. He was making love to her, but in her head she was far away.

She was startled to hear herself cry out.

David, she thought. David.

*   *   *

Heavy morning light flooded the room. For a long while she couldn't move. She was alone in the bed with only the most tentative idea where she was.

La vita nuova, she thought.

After a time she sat at the edge of the bed and felt sick. Her entire system was drugged. She rose unsteadily and made her way to the bathroom.

When she returned she felt better. She lay back in the large bed and stared at the ceiling. Hot liquid light wove patterns against the plaster. Slowly the events of the previous night floated back to her.

"Mi ritrovai per una selva oscura," she said out loud. The beauty of the Italian caused her to smile ruefully.

"I'm sorry," she said, speaking to she hardly knew whom—to Poppie, to David, to Général de Compière. Then she again sought unconsciousness.

When she awoke she was still alone but the light had changed. It was thinner now, less oppressive, and she could breathe more easily.

You must get up, she thought, you must leave, you must . . .

And then she thought, But there *is* no you. There is only a series of different rooms through which you passed like a country air. Or if there was a you, it was lost so long ago that now it is little more than a memory, a nostalgia, with no more substance than those poor dried bones that were your daughter. And the men you knew, the boys—what were they but so many branches you caught at as you fell, mere bending boughs as you plummeted on your way, rushing earthward?

BOOK FOUR

indflower descends in tiers toward the stream. My father devised a system of irrigation sluices, still in operation, whereby the water, which mounts in the hills, is diverted through the descending tiers to regain its course below the flower beds at the foot of the hill; and here among the aroma of monarda and yarrow I repaired as a boy to read and to elude as best I could the responsibilities of the day.

My mother named the nursery Windflower. The small white anemone was among her favorite flowers, and the euphony of the name pleased her. She had been the backbone of our success at the nursery, keeping the books, fulfilling the orders, dunning the creditors; and when my father died she sold the place to my sister Karin and decamped with never a look behind, and this too was typical.

Though my father sold anything green—shrubs, trees, grass— the center of the business was the tiers of flowers: foxglove, lythrum, malva, sedum, bleeding heart, the names as seductive as the bright flickering flames that delighted my boyhood and that, like fairy gold, underpinned the family's welfare. I never took these flowers for granted: spring meant the return of their vivid surprise. First witch hazel and the pale forsythia; then tulips, bleeding hearts, forget-me-nots. Full summer brought lilies, hollyhocks, red monarda. Then asters, dahlias, and of course chrysanthemums at summer's end, never my favorites but rich with the association of cicadas and the lumbering, thumb-size, late-summer bees.

Karin changed things very little. She gave up the trees, since she did not desire the heavy work of planting, but she made up for this by extending the beds of flowers, which now stretched beyond the greenhouse to the road. Her skills as a gardener were considerable and she could easily have earned her living as a landscape architect without ever selling a flower.

I was staying in my old room. I could hear Karin downstairs early in the morning the way I had once heard my mother.

"Don't mind me," Karin said. "I have things to do. You stay in bed as long as you want." She afforded me the latitude of the crack-up.

I took her at her word, which was always the best policy with Karin. I wasn't sleeping well, I was much perplexed in spirit and sometimes feared for my grasp on things, and I would often be up when everyone else was asleep.

It was strange to be back in my room. Throughout my adulthood I had periodically waked, and with my eyes still shut, I had been unable to piece together the geography of the room where I lay, even in my own bedroom, so strong remained the association of my childhood surroundings.

As a boy I rose early to see the dew on the grass. The green world was always my choice, although even then something about it struck me as unreal; it remained a luxury, all the more beloved for being fugitive.

At early light I'd watch the groundhogs on the lawn. The dogs were supposed to scare them off but they were too lazy to be up at that hour and the creatures had the run of the place. Sometimes I'd get Karin up and we'd watch together.

We had a childhood agreement to share with each other whatever we found that was out of the ordinary, though groundhogs hardly qualified. It was just the excitement of getting up early.

Mom wanted Dad to shoot the groundhogs. She loved the natural world but was utterly unsentimental about it and hated what the rodents did to her lawn.

Dad wasn't about to shoot groundhogs just because they had the impertinence to trespass on his grass. He looked at Mother and looked away, and that was the end of that.

Later I shot groundhogs in the hills with my .22. Shooting made me feel uneasy, but I did it anyway and kept at it for a number of weeks when I was fifteen. I was a good shot and something about the stalking and bagging of the critters was hypnotic; but afterward I felt uneasy, as if in the grip of a compulsion stronger than I. It was a relief when I gave up the shooting. I never shot anything again.

For the first few days at Windflower I didn't do anything. I revisited my old haunts, especially the sylvan nook where I had read Plutarch and Trollope. I took the car into town and paid my compliments to the library and to the secondhand bookstore. I sat in a lawn chair and read the *New York Review of Books*.

By the third day, however, I was restless and asked Karin how I could be of use.

"You can stake up the hollyhocks," she said. "You can dig out the swale at the edge of the second field. You can check the roof of the barn where the shingles are falling off."

I started with the hollyhocks.

I worked down a row, tying up the long clumsy flowers and trying not to think of anything in particular. It was the kind of job I hated; gardening bored me.

Dad had always called hollyhocks stupid flowers. He invested flowers with personalities and spoke of them in light of a theory known only to himself. He preferred fine-petaled things like anemones, cosmos, and poppies, and disparaged hardier breeds. Dad would have considered Nietzsche a crackpot.

After a while the sun dizzied me and I was glad when I finished the row.

The greenhouse smelled of sphagnum and dill and of the familiar odor of wetted concrete. Paul, Karin's hired hand, was working in the far corner, but he ceased what he was doing when he saw me and came over.

"I saw you tying the hollyhocks," he said.

"That's right."

"It must feel good to be doing that. I mean, after the city and all."

I was tempted to tell him that tying the hollyhocks bored me silly but I resisted.

"It feels fine," I said.

"So how does it feel to be back on the old homestead?"

"It feels just fine."

"I guess you can see how Ms. Smith has changed the place."

"Has she?"

"Oh, yes. Look at all that phlox. You didn't have them banks of phlox before."

"No, I guess that's true."

"And the cosmos. You see them cosmos?"

"Yes. I was admiring that."

"I should think you were. You don't see cosmos like that any-place else in the state. That's Ms. Smith's doing."

"I bet it is."

"You betcha. She's a fine lady, Ms. Smith. A holy lady."

"A what?"

"A holy lady."

"Oh, *holy.* Yes, yes she is."

It took me aback to hear my sister described this way. Though everyone was mindful of Karin's religious convictions, it was star-tling to hear her described as holy.

After dinner that evening I said to her, "Paul tells me you are very holy."

Karin smiled.

"Dear Paul," she said. "It's he who is holy. He is really a kind of holy fool."

"Well, I'm more certain of the noun than the adjective."

Karin frowned. "You hardly know him" was all she said.

I respected Karin too much to press the conversation, though for the life of me I couldn't imagine what she saw in Paul. He was

another broken-winged bird she had taken home to mend. Karin
was the slightest of us, with a neat boyish figure, glossy blond
short-cut hair, and the upturned nose of the Smiths. Her eyes
were sharp blue and humorous but could turn serious quickly,
like pools of water that still to show their depth.

I had always had a special feeling for Karin, an earnest, intelligent person with her own take on the world. She had attended
Radcliffe for two years and had partaken in some sort of political
turmoil, and Dad had had to go up there to fetch her home. After
that she started working at the nursery.

I was cheered by Karin's religious beliefs, whatever they were;
cheered by the recognition that a person of her intelligence could
hold them. We never spoke about her convictions, though I had
heard her quote Emerson to the effect that God enters each person
through a private trapdoor, a sentiment I admire but do not share.

I hadn't seen much of Karin in the last years and I found her
subtly changed. There was still something elfin about her, but she
had gained in gravity. I observed her working—steadily, silently
—among her flowers, and I thought she must be the better genius
of our family, a kind of guardian of the earthly hearth.

At dawn Karin meditated. At ten she stopped in the fields for a
silent cup of tea. The frugal midday meal was served at one. At
vespers she read from the Book of Common Prayer or some ecu-
menical holy tract. She retired early and rose early. As she said,
she set her clock by the sun.

I admired the beauty of her routine—but from afar, like a
landscape from an airplane window. She had crafted her life into
something handsome and admirable, but its shape wasn't mine
and its heft would never accommodate the grip of my hand.

"Warren won't let me repay him for the nursery," Karin said.

"That doesn't surprise me."

"He pays Mother directly, though the deed is in my name."

"What would Warren want with the nursery?"

"That's not the point."

"Well, it's something Warren wants to do. What else is he to
do with all his money?"

"But the nursery makes money. It's quite self-sufficient."

"I bet it is," I said. "I didn't doubt it for a moment."

"So why shouldn't Warren let me pay?"

"You know the answer as well as I."

"Yes," she said. "I suppose I do."

That night I lay awake for a long time. At about two I let myself out the front door and wandered toward the upper field. Pete, the old hound, offered a growl but I ordered him to shut up.

My eyes adjusted to the dark. The moon was setting and the stars quivered with benzene whiteness. But the bushes hulked in darkness, and when I stepped off a small hillock I lost my balance and almost fell.

I stood by the uncut grass by the fence that bordered the field and inhaled the deepness of the night. Far across the field I could see the tops of the trees tolling softly. The air was heavy with the fragrance of the flowers and I could hear the night frogs calling from the pool near the barn.

I stood by the fence for a long time. For a while I heard an animal thrashing in the forest. It sounded larger than any animal I could account for—presumably some badger or weasel intent upon the blood sport of the night. I pissed into the heavy grass. The stars lay close overhead, and as I watched, a shooting star tore loose and, arching through the darkness, disappeared like a torch thrown into water.

After a time my sense of communion with the night faded. I could no longer account for what I was doing standing by the grasses under the night stars. Violently, inadvertently, my body shivered. It seemed a long distance back to the house.

After the first day of working in the garden I gave up and took to hiking in the woods. I would take a book with me, but generally I tried to wear myself out walking.

The forest was wooded with yellow birch and sugar maple, black cherry and hickory and red oak, eastern hemlock and white pine and spruce. I knew from childhood the flowers with their vivid unexpected names: harebell, foxglove, Indian pipe. Fern sprouted among the shrubs: elderberry, hazel, honeysuckle, and the ubiquitous suburban rhododendron that was overcrowding all. The birds too were familiar: jays, warblers, woodpeckers, mourning doves, the red-tailed hawk, the turkey vulture with its high, lazy swoop and V-tipped wing. Wild turkey had returned to the area along with the habitual grouse and pheasant. I happened upon a glen where an abundance of goldfinches threaded the sunlight with startling, audacious brilliance.

I loved the rocks of the region, with their graceful frozen waves of time. The Wisconsin glacier had crept through the area, scoring and strewing boulders. Much of the rock was hard igneous stone from one of the oldest formations in the world, but this was interspersed by sedimentary upcroppings layered like bakery cake and as obvious to interpretation as a simple Latin inscription.

Karin informed me that coyotes had returned to the area; they could be heard sometimes at night, howling like strange demented spirits. I saw a group of creatures in a far field that resembled nothing so much as wild dogs, with humpbacks and moon-ringed, feral eyes. I had no idea what they might be. There was also a multitude of foxes; I observed one at close range that watched me with unhaste, its head swaying back and forth like a metronome before it turned and trotted into the forest.

At night I took the car out and raced along the blacked-out backcountry roads, a species of unglamorous thoughtless exhilaration that recalled the delinquent excitement of adolescence.

Karin always had people working with her, usually young folk she had befriended in some manner, a mixture of ecology mavens, back-to-earthers, and religious enthusiasts. At present there were three such persons, Agnes and Berthe and a young man named Edgar Charles, a gawky individual of an angular variety with a protruding Adam's apple and slow, ponderous eyes. The two young women, attractive in their own way though militantly unkempt, were doctrinally innocent of bras and carried about them a persistent reminder of the farm.

Agnes prepared the food, undercooked vegetables in some glutinous brown sauce which she ladled out of a brown earthen pot onto earthen plates.

During the silence that ensued we all bowed our heads and the

two young women clasped hands in earnest subdued ardor, a posture we retained for a full minute and a half by my reckoning,
until Karin lifted her head.

"So," she said. "Let's see what Agnes has provided tonight."

"It's vegetable stew," Agnes said bashfully. "I'm afraid it's all I
know how to make."

"It's delicious," Karin said, while Agnes wriggled with delight.

"We received another large order for phlox," Edgar announced
from his side of the table. There was something slow and inarticulate about him, as if the syllables blundered up against that sizable pharynx and couldn't find their way around.

"That's wonderful!" Karin said. "We'll have to dig another bed
to have enough for next year. Edgar, could you turn over the bed
behind the barn? You know, the one where we used to grow
tomatoes."

"Maybe David would like to help," Edgar said, turning to me
with slow earnest scrutiny. I was at a loss how to respond until
Karin rescued me.

"I don't think David wants to dig up a flower bed," Karin said,
"though God knows"—turning to me—"it might do you good."

"Yes, very likely," I said. "Me and Count Tolstoy and Henry
George."

"You could have worse company."

"That's very true. I didn't mean it otherwise. It's just that
whatever good it might do my soul, it would play the devil with
my hands."

The three disciples looked at me sternly though Karin only
smiled.

"Have you become so soft, David?"

"Pretty soft."

"Well, you ought to harden yourself up."

"We'll need some more manure," Berthe observed. "We're just
about out of what we had."

"That's no problem," Karin said. "Someone can drive over to
Ted Donnell's farm and see what he has."

"Is that the Ted Donnell I know?" I asked. "The one who
married Paula Light?"

"Yup, the same one."

"Well, manure is my style," I said. "If it's just a question of driving over, I'll go—though I'm not in the market for carting loads back."

"Well, it's *matured* manure, after all, David. But I won't ask you to do it anyway. Just drive over and see what they have."

"You can use the pickup if you want," Edgar added, presumably implying that I needn't use my Mercedes.

"We must give some thought to the Sunday festival," Berthe said. The Congregational church was holding a Sunday bazaar and the nursery had been chosen to provide the floral decoration.

"That's right," Karin said. "Why don't you and Agnes start thinking about a pattern? I want it to be simple and elegant, appropriate for a religious occasion. I have some ideas myself, but I'd like you to set the basic design."

"I'd like to use lilies," Agnes said. "They were St. Francis's favorite flower."

"Would that be appropriate for a Congregational church?" I asked. "Aren't they descendants of the Puritans?"

"That doesn't make any difference," Karin said. "I think your suggestion is fine," she said to Agnes.

Dessert was a fruit compote cooked to the consistency of paste.

"This is delicious," Berthe said.

"Very nice," said Karin.

"I'm going to work on the shrine while it's still light," Edgar Charles announced.

"Good idea. Agnes and Berthe, why don't you help Edgar while the heat is down? We'll meet in an hour for meditation."

Karin and I stopped outside the dining room in the long hall that extended the length of the house. It was already dark, and in the flickering evening, the scene reminded me of when we were children and my mother was still a slender young woman.

"What's this shrine?" I asked.

"We need to clear the stones in the lower pasture and Edgar is gathering them into what he calls a shrine."

"Isn't it all a bit sacerdotal?"

"It could have been a wall. It could have been a sheepfold. Anything is a shrine that is sanctified by its intention."

"Well, I suppose you're right, Karin. I wouldn't argue with you about such things. It could have been an outhouse."

Karin laughed. "Well, it could have been. And what's wrong with an outhouse? You're becoming a mite prideful in your middle years."

"Am I? Well, maybe you're right again."

"You know, David, the Prince of Heaven didn't fall. Heaven withdrew from him, the way clean flesh withdraws from an astringent."

"Is that a parable?"

"Yes, it is. God exists—but mostly now in Silence."

"And in the babble of Edgar Charles."

Karin only smiled and shook her head.

The next day I took the pickup truck and drove to the Donnell farm. I had known Ted when I was growing up, and Paula I had known well.

The farm was large and well tended—apparently the Donnells were thriving. I turned up the drive and passed between a lawn and garden and, on the right, a large paddock with sheep and enormous lazing muddy big-teated pigs.

When I got out of the truck I could smell the odor of the farm.

Paula was working in the garden. She wore jeans and a man's tattered blue Oxford shirt rolled up at the sleeves; I recognized her immediately.

"Hello, Paula."

"Who is that?"

"It's David Smith."

"David!"

She advanced toward me shading her eyes with one hand. The sun was in her eyes and her face was screwed up against its brightness. Her skin was tanned and weather-beaten and there were lines at her eyes and forehead and at the corners of her mouth, but she was still a handsome woman.

"David!" she said again, with what seemed to me genuine enthusiasm.

"Hi, Paula. It's good to see you."

"I won't shake hands," she said. "I'm an absolute mess." She rubbed her hand vigorously against her butt to clean it.

"I don't care about that," I said. And I leaned forward and kissed her on the cheek. "Where's Ted?"

"He's in town. He'll be hoppin' mad he missed you! But what brings you this way? You staying with Karin?"

"Yup. And she sent me over for . . . a load of manure."

We both laughed. I had forgotten her laughter, which came back immediately.

"Cow shit," she said. "You see the business I'm in."

"Well, I'm in bullshit."

Again she laughed.

"Really," I said. "The place looks beautiful. You always wanted to be a farmer's wife."

"Yes, I did. And I got my wish—in spades. And what about you, David? What did you want to be?"

"I can't remember. Maybe I just wanted to sit under the cork tree and smell the flowers."

"Well, I don't have any cork trees. But there is a whole orchard of apples."

The screen door slammed and a boy of about fifteen exited into the sunlight in a houndlike slouch, his eyes darting furtively in our direction.

"That must be your boy."

"That's Mike," she said brightly. "Mike, come over and say hello to Mr. Smith. Mr. Smith grew up on Windflower, over by Smithfield, and went to school with your dad and me."

"Hello, Mike," I said, and I shook his hand. "You look just like your dad."

Mike smiled shyly and his features suddenly assumed a sweet winsome appearance, as if a mask had fallen from his face.

"Your dad and I were on the track team together," I said, and a picture of Ted as an earnest, musclebound adolescent flashed into my mind. He had been the class president, a straight-backed, straight-arrow kid, diligent, handsome, and serious, and I wondered what twenty years of marriage to him could have been like.

"Dad and I are putting in the fence out by the south pasture," Mike said, and it was clear that his dad was a big deal to him.

"That must be hard work."

"Nah. It gets a little hot sometimes, that's all."

"Ted and Mike are great companions," Paula said.

"I bet," I said.

"Didn't you have any daughters?" I asked when Paula and I were walking toward the barn. I admired from behind her taut country-girl physique.

"I had a daughter who died."

"I'm sorry, Paula. I didn't know."

"Oh, it was ten years ago. She just died in her crib, just up and died. She couldn't have been very healthy. However, I'd rather not talk about it. I was sorry to hear about your dad. He was a fine gentleman."

"Thank you. I was fond of him myself. Karin now owns the place, you know."

"Of course."

"Of course—the manure!"

The barn smelled of hay and cool height. I too could have been a farm boy, I thought, and smelled all day the clean odor of hay and the strong odor of cow urine. I ordered the manure for Karin.

Paula walked me back to the truck.

"It's good seeing you, David. Do you get up here often?"

"Not often. I'm just here for a week or so."

"Well, I'm glad you came over. Ted will be sorry he missed you."

"Yeah, me too. Well, I've got to be going now."

I looked at Paula for a moment. She had light gray eyes with small gold flecks at the rim of the iris, and this too I now remembered. Then I swung up into the truck.

"It's good seeing you, Paula."

"You, too, David. Goodbye."

I drove home slowly, contemplating the hills and listening to the sound of the fields outside the open window.

* * *

That evening I spoke with Barbara on the phone.

"You've got to come home soon," she said, and I detected a note of hysteria beneath her cool exterior. "I can't run this family without you. Jenny is impossible, she won't do anything I say, the twins have come down with a cold, Virginia is leaving on vacation so there's no one to clean, and I don't see how I'm supposed to cope."

It wasn't like Barbara to complain.

"I'll be home soon," I said.

"Will you? Well, I hope so. I don't know what sort of a crisis you're having, David, but whatever it is, it's time for it to stop. I don't know what you want from me."

"Nothing. Did I ever say I wanted anything else from you? You've given me everything anyone could ask for."

"Have I? Well, you've got a wife who is beginning to come apart."

"I'll be home soon, I promise."

When I hung up I stood for a long time staring at the phone. It sickened me to realize how little I wanted to return home.

"Was that Barbara?" Karin asked.

"Yes. She doesn't sound so good."

"Maybe you ought to go home."

"That's what she thinks."

"And you?"

"I don't know, Karin. I mean, of course I'll go home but . . . I don't know. It isn't that I am unhappy," I found myself saying to my sister. "It's only that I wanted . . . something more."

"Something more?"

"Yes. I don't quite know what I mean but . . . something *more.* Do you remember those fairy tales we used to read, the ones in which one would enter a cave and the cave would contain another world? Or where there was a door at the back of a closet that opened into a completely different realm? Well, it's something like that, only . . . I never found the door."

"Of course you didn't," Karin said.

"Why didn't I?"

Karin only smiled. We stood looking at each other. I wanted to ask Karin for help, but I've never asked anyone for help in my life —not like that. Then Karin did something strange. Slowly she put her finger to her lips as if she were saying hush. She looked at me like that for a while and continued to smile.

It took me a day to realize that Karin had stopped talking to me. In fact she had stopped talking entirely. When she passed she would smile and look at me with her blue humorous eyes and put her finger to her lips.

"What's going on?" I asked.

She simply smiled and shook her head and passed on. She made it clear she considered me with affection, but she had stopped talking.

"What's going on with Karin?" I asked Edgar Charles.

"She's taken a vow of silence."

"How do you know that?"

"Well, do you hear her talking?" He looked at me as if I were a dummy. "It must be in preparation for Sunday," he continued. "She's a very holy person. Isn't it amazing how families produce such different types? Don't you find that amazing? Well, nature is a marvelous thing. It takes all kinds. God works in mysterious ways."

I didn't think her silence was in preparation for Sunday; I was pretty certain it was meant for me.

When I woke on Saturday I could see the four of them already in the garden, working. I went downstairs and had a cup of coffee and went out the back door. It had been a rough night.

I thought I would inspect the shingles on the barn roof. They had been coming loose and Karin had asked me to have a look. I wanted to do something for Karin.

I couldn't find a ladder.

I circled the barn in the sunlight, studying it from various angles. It was a large, handsome barn and it figured prominently in my childhood. Sometimes Warren would stand on one side and I on the other and we would play catch over the roof. We had various ways of climbing it. Sometimes we would jump from the roof. We could swing from a rope from the hayloft. We could jump from the loft into the new hay.

Now I circled the barn, studying it carefully. The memory of the things I could once perform with this barn amazed me. It seemed larger to me now, which was not the way it was supposed to be.

Finally I circled to the back and followed the fence to the back shed. It was easy to climb the shed and from there I could maneuver onto the top of the fence that led to the barn. At one time Warren and I could run along the top of this fence, but now I straddled it carefully and inched my way forward. When I reached the end of the fence I stood.

I was about ten feet from the ground; by leaping I could reach the edge of the roof. I stood and eyed the distance. Something told me not to do it.

Then I leapt and caught the barn roof and gripped it with my arms and grappled my way forward, pulling myself onto it.

Looking down, I knew I couldn't leap back onto the fence; if I missed, I would brain myself on the concrete below.

I worked my way carefully to the top of the roof, where it flattened. The shingles were loose all right; I pried them up easily with my toe. The entire roof needed to be reshingled.

I stood and surveyed the horizon. I could see the tops of the trees moving in the wind. From the garden the flowers were flames, now flickering singly, now in banks of fire. The grass was green and the wind ran over it like water, creating paths and erasing them. All the colors were intensely bright: blue sky, white clouds, green grass, green leaves. The world was immeasurably beautiful.

I started working around the edge of the roof. I had no way to get down. I could stand and walk and as I moved I watched the grass and the green paths that formed and disappeared; I would have liked to have stayed up there forever but I knew I couldn't. A still small voice said, Jump.

I knew the front of the barn was the longest drop—over thirty feet—and I steered away from it. I went to the right side and peered down into the thick grass; we had jumped here as kids, it couldn't be more than sixteen or seventeen feet.

It was too far.

I worked my way back up to the top of the barn, where I could see the garden. The four distant people seemed very small, like figures in a painting by Brueghel. There was no way to get down.

You could call Karin.

But I knew I wouldn't do that.

Jump, the voice said.

If you go back to the edge, I warned, you will jump.

I started to work my way down the face of the roof.

I could see the grass at an angle far below me and it seemed very thick and lush and beautiful. Again the wind moved, bending the grass. The edge of the roof drew nearer.

Jump!

I sat down on the roof and tried to think but there was nothing to think about. Overhead the sky was deep blue. My mind was completely empty; I seemed to have reached the end of my mind. I got up and again moved slowly forward.

When I got to the edge of the roof I rose to my full height. I didn't allow myself time to hesitate.

I jumped.

I lay in my bed running a fever. I had taken the painkiller when Karin drove me home, but after that I didn't use it although the pain was intense. When I got up I was exhausted immediately. I lay in bed sleeping.

"I'll be all right," I told Barbara through the pain. "Don't make a big deal about it."

"Don't make a big deal about it? You could as easily have snapped your spine. They might have brought you home a paraplegic."

"Well, they didn't. I'll be up and around in a week."

"A week! You'll be lucky if you are all right in six months."

She set me up in bed, fussing about me angrily. I could see the fear in the children's eyes; they had never seen their dad hurt before. Barbara was angry, resentful. She wanted me to admit to some extraordinary stupidity. When they x-rayed the foot she said to the doctor, "It's his head you should x-ray."

Yet I could not unthink the jump. It had served its purpose.

"Don't you think I have enough to look after?" Barbara said. "Do you always have to be center stage?"

The doctor had plastered the leg up to the knee and given me crutches. I couldn't carry a glass of water from one room to another; it was difficult bringing the paper in from the front door. I couldn't then know I had destroyed my right foot forever.

I made myself go to work.

"We make a fine pair," Gordo said.

His hands turned down now at the wrists as if they were broken. Sometimes he drooled from the corner of his mouth. Barbara would tidy him up, bring him lunch, make sure the car service picked him up on time.

"What kind of a jerk are you, anyway? You know what you remind me of? Remember that joke about the American, the German, and the Frenchman in an airplane crash with only two parachutes? And the Frenchman jumps out holding his sleeping bag?"

"What was I supposed to do?" I said. "Call and let the girls get me down?"

"I've heard of stupider ideas."

"Well, let's not talk about it. We used to do that jump all the time."

"Yeah? And I used to play football at Yale."

In fact I don't remember much about the next six weeks. It seemed that all I saw was emptiness. It wasn't only the buildings, the streets, the cars, which floated past like thoughts deflated of all content. No, people themselves, their words, their thoughts—my thoughts—all seemed like emptiness, as if the world were just emptiness turned inside out like a mitten to show a variegated surface. It was as if one were watching a movie with the sound turned off so that faces floated up like gray, etiolated balloons and then again floated away; and all the time one heard nothing except, vaguely, the whir of some broken machine.

*   *   *

When the cast came off after six weeks and I could hobble about with a cane, Barbara insisted that I start physical therapy.

"I'm not going to live with a cripple," she said.

I started going three times a week to a place on Madison Avenue owned by two smart brassy young women, the Mses. Kenner and Stein, who were clearly minting money out of the physical therapy trade.

"So, Mistah Smith," Ms. Kenner drawled with ironic indifferent humor in her Bronx accent. "What did yuh do to yourself?" She was a tall sloe-eyed young woman dressed in a blue laboratory coat, and she stood above me manipulating my damaged foot as I lay prone and all but naked in one of the small examining rooms.

"Can you bend it to me?" she asked.

I tried to bend my foot to her but I couldn't. Ms. Kenner made a note of this in her book.

"Let's see if we can rotate to the right," she said. "There, that's good." And again she made a note in her book.

"So you fell from a roof," she said.

"No, I jumped."

"You jumped? What kinda behavior is *that,* Mistah Smith?" Ms. Kenner opened her eyes wide and stared at me with deadpan humor. "I bet your wife loved that," she said, finding the weak spot and twisting the knife.

Ms. Stone was assigned as my therapist.

I hated everything about this establishment. I hated its aseptic glitter. I hated its polished-metal, high-tech machinery. I hated the routine of its useless exercises and the mindless optimistic efficiency of its personnel. I hated being trapped.

Ms. Stone was a short perky girl of perhaps twenty-six with short dark hair and dark round eyes and as close to a perfect figure as one encounters. She was an associate of the Mses. Kenner and Stein and aspired to the mythical elevation of co-partner. Attired in her leotard and short shorts and displaying her perfect figure, she nattered along as she addressed my foot; but there was something shy and vulnerable at the center of her dark eyes, and she rarely looked at me directly.

"I've been working here for four years," she explained, "and already I'm an associate. That's good, don't you think? Ms. Kenner and Ms. Stein run a *very* tight ship. Whatever else you might say about them, they run a *very* tight ship—and I admire that. I'm taking extra courses toward my M.A. in physical therapy—there's only one other girl in the office who's doing that. So that's good, don't you think?"

She talked like this as she ministered to my broken foot. I would strip down in one of the cubicles and Ms. Stone would examine me and manipulate my foot and take notes concerning my progress. There was nothing for me to do but to lie on the examination table and contemplate Ms. Stone's figure while I tried to move what was left of my heel and ankle.

After Ms. Stone had concluded her manual work I would be remanded to the exercise room with a further series of exercises to perform.

The exercise room was a spacious, togaed location of bath towels and gym shorts and degrees and varieties of naked flesh all exhibiting some manner of deficiency. Many, like myself, had damaged some portion of their lower extremities, but there were also broken arms and hands on display, not to mention twisted necks, malformed spines, and dysfunctional pelvises. Whatever the orthopedic failure, the Mses. Kenner and Stein and their aspiring staff had some curative manipulation to administer.

All ages were represented, though the establishment might have exhibited a slight predominance of the elderly. There is something affecting about the sight of naked elderly flesh panting under the exertions of high-tech machinery, and I had much opportunity to contemplate this sight from various angles.

The cynosure of the establishment was the array of machinery that glittered throughout the exercise room. Aluminum arms gleamed back and forth, leather headrests shot up and down, leg springs coiled and depressed, electric timers whirred, digital numbers blinked, adjustment screws turned, all in a silent cacophony of ameliorative effort. There were bicycles, pulleys, balances, ski walks, arm pulls, leg extensions—and enough outsize exercise equipment to make a radiologist's office appear antediluvian.

I detested my exercises. I had to stretch my muscles in various ways, balance on either foot, stretch large rubber bands attached to my ankles, balance on boards, work out with various gleaming contraptions, walk and run on treadmills and skiing devices.

I could no longer balance in the simplest manner. Exercises I would once have laughed at now caused me to sweat and stumble. Subtly inspired with the spirit of American competition, the room was earnest with young men and women with muscles aglow who sped away to nowhere on stationary bicycles while I desperately attempted to retain my upright posture on one foot.

When I came home the children clamored to share my new skills. The twins attached the rubber bands to their ankles and knocked themselves over in their enthusiasm. Everyone had a go, including Barbara. Finally they made me take a turn while Barbara looked on in scorn.

"Well, there goes our hiking in the Alps."

"Don't be awful, Mommy!"

"Daddy's going to be okay, aren't you, Daddy?"

"We love you, Daddy," Alexandra said, taking my hand.

"Next time," Barbara said, "do us all a favor and land on your head. You'll do yourself less injury."

"Oh, Mommy," Jenny said. "Why don't you be quiet?"

I was determined to build myself up, but in fact I couldn't walk more than a half-mile without becoming exhausted. At night my ankle would be swollen and black and blue. I hid the ankle from Barbara. It began to dawn on me what I had done.

"How are we today?" Ms. Stone asked as she entered our cubicle. I had changed into my workout shorts and was lying on the examination table; Ms. Stone was dressed in her short shorts and a tank top.

"I'm about the same."

"Oh, don't be defeatist, Mr. Smith. Ms. Kenner says that mental attitude is an important component in physical rehabilitation. We need to *will* health. I just read an article about it in *Physical Therapy Today.* Would you like me to lend it to you?"

"No, I don't think so. I believe you. Thank you very much."

"I think you should read the article. You need to attack your condition from as many angles as possible."

She laid her small cool hand on my swollen foot.

"Now let's see how far you can flex to the left. That's good! Now to the right. You see, that's *much* better. That's really *very* good!"

"How does this work?" I asked. "Do you get Brownie points if I improve quickly?"

"Well, Ms. Kenner and Ms. Stein evaluate every patient at the end of the week, and they set goals for their improvement. If the therapist doesn't achieve those goals, then we need to sit down together and evaluate the situation."

"I see. So we're a kind of team, you and I."

"That's right, Mr. Smith! Teamwork—that's the spirit!"

"Well, we'll have to try to achieve our goal, won't we!"

This seemed to please her and she even looked at me with her large dark eyes. There was a strange lateral movement to her body that reminded me of a small bird flitting and hopping about. She was the only part of the routine that did me any good.

The next session she had brought in the article for me to look at.

I opened the magazine and pretended to read. Inside were pictures of healthy young men and scantily clad young women working out on various devices and in various positions with faces craned round to offer large gleaming smiles.

"This is very interesting," I said. "I had no idea it was so interesting."

"Oh, it's one of the modern sciences," Ms. Stone said, and she looked at me and smiled.

"You're getting in on the ground floor," I said. "You'll have a marvelous career."

"I love it," she said earnestly. "I love what I do."

She put her small competent hand on my foot and tried to persuade its broken articulation while I lay back with my hands behind my head and tried not to wince while I concentrated on the firm roundness of Ms. Stone's physique.

"You could subscribe, if you wanted," she said.

"What?"

"To the magazine. To *Physical Therapy Today.*"

I thought about that for a minute before I replied.

"You know, I think that's a good idea. I think that's a very good idea. I've been thinking about what you said—about attacking this thing from as many angles as possible—and I think that's very sound advice. I hadn't thought of it that way before. I'm afraid I was succumbing to a bit of defeatism. But I've been feeling different since our conversation and our talk about being a team. That meant a lot to me. I think I had been feeling a little isolated before that and maybe a little sorry for myself. But I see now that we're in this together—and that I can help you as well as your helping me. I mean by improving and all, and keeping up with Ms. Kenner's schedule. I see now that that's important for me—and for you, too. And that means a lot to me. So if you think it would be helpful to subscribe to the magazine, well, I'm going to do it."

"That's beautiful, Mr. Smith! What you said is just beautiful!"

"You know, now that we're teammates, maybe you'd like to call me David."

"And why don't you call me Irene!"

I particularly detested the exercise where the large pink rubber band was affixed to my ankle, and balancing on the other foot, I was made to perform a series of kicks and stretches. This exercise, which I should have accomplished with ease, taxed all my resources and invariably ended by almost landing me on my can.

"Allow me to demonstrate how this is performed," an elderly man dressed in a white terrycloth robe said to me as I struggled with the rubber band. He had the hint of a European accent.

"You kick"—he said *keek*—"too hard. Just little kicks, so, so, so," and he demonstrated with dancelike movements, his toe pointed. He was a heavyset man but his legs were thin and his calves well muscled.

"Let's see," I said, and I tried the shorter movement.

"There! It's better, no?"

"Yes—a little."

"Little kicks, like so."

"Thank you."

"Everything is in the movement. Otherwise you knock yourself down. Finesse, yes?"

So I was introduced to Emile Flack. He beamed at me from his benign horselike rubicund face and introduced himself with a slight bow—a sturdy balding man in his late sixties, though hale and comporting himself formally like the middle European gentleman he was.

"Emile Flack," he said. "Honored to meet you." His squarish hand was sturdy and powerful.

"When you have been here as long as I, you learn these tricks," he said with a smile.

He explained his ailment.

"I fell from a truck. Is this stupid? From the back of a truck. I was helping my neighbor in the country to harvest the apples and I fell from the back of his truck." He beamed as if he were sharing a joke.

"I'm sorry to hear that."

"*You* are sorry? And me? But it was my stupidity. So! Now I reside here in this delightful establishment where I study new manifestations of the modern spirit. You smile! Ah, you are sympathetic. You are perhaps a sympathetic soul. I looked at you from across the room and I thought, This individual is perhaps a sympathetic soul. No doubt you have read Stendhal? The happy few!"

"Not always so happy."

"Wonderful! Not always so happy. I knew it, I knew it. A sympathetic soul. So!"

He shook with quiet laughter. When he laughed his eyes screwed up in his face so they were hardly more than slits, like the eyes I had carved on jack-o'-lanterns on Halloween to please my children. Emile managed to be both dignified and ridiculous.

"You must allow me to buy you a drink," he said. "It is not every day that one encounters a sympathetic soul."

I still had to endure a series of exercises on the gleaming high-tech machinery, but afterward I limped to the lobby with my cane.

Emile was waiting in the reception area. It took him a moment to lumber out of his chair. He stood before me with a crooked wistful smile, dressed in a brown three-piece suit and holding himself stiffly erect except for the slant of his head, which jutted forward like a chimney that is about to fall.

"Come, my friend. After such trials some liquid refreshment, no?"

He conducted me to a nearby bar, a brown crepuscular establishment with waitresses dressed in red hunting jackets, and we sat in a back booth equipped with brass ashtrays. Emile ordered a vodka martini.

"So you jumped from a barn," he said. "The jactitations of the modern spirit. You see where it lands you—the Stein-Kenner Pavilion for Somatic Melioration. It is positively Faustian, wouldn't you say? No sooner do you act than you put yourself in the hands of . . . a pretty girl."

"Do you mean Ms. Stone?"

"Who is that? The pert little object with the short dark hair? Well, no matter. Margaret, Helen—they're all the same: the modern incarnation of Laocoönian confusion."

"You are no admirer of the fair sex?"

"Not at all, not at all. You misunderstand me utterly. Besides, who am I to say—an old man in a windy corner, yes? I admire women so much that I would save them from themselves—a paradox, yes?"

"What would you save them from?"

"Well, from the Stein-Kenner Pavilion, for one."

"Is it as bad as that?"

"That depends on how you define your terms. By my definition we all reside within the Stein-Kenner Pavilion. I speak anagogically, you understand."

"Well, Mr. Flack, you certainly speak in riddles."

"Emile, my dear boy. Call me Emile. And let's have another drink. We're just getting to know each other."

The waitress set a new round before us while Emile smacked his lips.

"You quite misunderstand my point," he said, settling down to his second martini. "First God created man, and then he perfected his work by creating woman. But like all human beings, they have no true conception of who they are or what they want. The modern world has propelled them into—what? Their own confusion. They are free, forsooth—free from the responsibilities that have molded them since the dawn of time. But they are free to do what, eh? They have no idea. To wear long pants, to smoke cigarettes, to divorce their husbands, to go to the ballgame, to abandon their children, to swear like sailors, to take lovers, to work in corporations, to chew gum in public. Free to loose upon the world their petty ego. You have come a long distance, baby, yes?"

"Well, I suppose they have as much right as we do to louse up their lives."

"Of course they do! Of course they do! But I have no obligation to *celebrate* it, that's all."

"I perceive you are a conservative."

"A conservative? Pooh, pooh. A reactionary, my boy. The dogs have shat all over that other word."

"As for me, Emile, I hope it won't interfere with this burgeoning friendship, but I've always considered myself a liberal."

"A liberal? But of course you are a liberal! What else would you be? But what does it *mean?* That's all I ask. What does it mean? The Rights of Man? But there are no such rights. There is only the right to be eaten—unless of course you mean in the eyes of God. But what could that mean to you?"

"Very little, I'm afraid."

"Precisely! So! And yet the modern world is not without a religion. That would be impossible, literally impossible. Listen," he said. "I will explain to you the modern religion." And he smiled across the table with genial humor. "The modern religion is not money. It is not even the cult of experience, though it often looks that way. No! A hypothesis stands behind these idols of the tribe. What modern man believes in is history and the self. By history I don't mean the sobering experience of generations of other mortals. No! Insofar as modern man even knows that this exists, it is precisely this that he is in revolt against. By history modern man means something entirely different—he means the secular continuum that allows him to achieve himself. By history he means that empty space whose purpose it is to be filled by—his biography! And the meaning of life is precisely that—to fill up that space. But to fill it with what? With the self, of course!"

Emile looked at me triumphantly, as if he had just demonstrated a difficult point in geometry. Taking another sip of his martini, he smacked his lips and proceeded.

"For modern man, the self is an entirely new entity undreamt of by historical man. For modern man each self is, as it were, an Aristotelian entelechy, a potential, a precious seed that must be nurtured to its own maturity. This is the purpose of life. This belief is entirely different from the traditional one in the immortality of the soul. That belief was based in transcendence and is meaningless without it. But modern man's idea of the self is entirely secular. The purpose of each and every life is to fill up the empty continuum of its own history with the potential of one's own particular self. So! Insofar as one achieves this, one's life is meaningful. It makes no difference if it is a question of making fortunes or painting pictures or seducing scullery maids or finding God. Such details pertain to the various potentials of the individual selves. But woe betide the man—or woman, of course; perhaps especially now the woman—who doesn't realize this potential! Such a life has not achieved Meaning—and as such is hurled into the outer darkness of Failure. And there, my friend, we have the dogmatics of modern religion, the inner principle by which the contraption ticks."

I had attended to this with a mixture of astonishment, admiration, and exasperation; but it was the latter that broke out when I said, "What's wrong with that? What's wrong with people trying to achieve their potential?"

"Aha, I see! You want to know what's wrong with that? You want me to say it in so many words? But of course you know the answer yourself. We all do. It is the worm that eats at the center of modern man. For to fulfill a potential you must *have* one, otherwise the whole thing is a charade. But people don't possess this wonderful potential on which they have staked their all. They have duties, responsibilities, relationships, desires. They have families, friends, neighbors, occupations. They have—though this

they hardly know—they have immortal souls. But as for potential
—all they have is emptiness, foul wind, ravening egos. All they
have is the potential to travel from megalomania to despair."

I was lying on the exercise table in one of the small Stein-Kenner
cubicles and Irene Stone was ministering to my foot; she appeared
to be entirely absorbed in what she was doing.

"You know, I've been thinking about what you said about
mental attitude," I said.

"What?"

"About mental attitude. I think you are on to something."

"It's a scientific fact." She smiled. "The neural connections in
the brain promote healing throughout the body. A low serotonic
function can affect the entire health of the system."

"I think I'd like to try that flexing again," I said. "I don't think
I was giving it my all."

Again she laid her cool hand on my foot and I felt the effect in
my serotonic functions.

"You have to keep your knee immobile," she said impatiently,
and she placed her other hand on my exposed knee.

The cool small impact of her hand was like the essence of
something distinctly modern—Reddi Wip, perhaps. I lay back
and thought I was going to weep.

Ms. Stone's eyes were fixed on the performance of my foot.

"Harder!" she commanded.

I tried, and it was difficult work.

After the flexing I lay breathing on the table. Ms. Stone was
finishing her notations, and as she wrote I could detect the small
movement of her breasts.

She talked to me now as she worked.

"You know, I'm going to a wedding this weekend, it's a friend
of mine from college and she's marrying a guy she met this summer. He's an accountant and has to travel a lot because his firm
has branches all over the country, and Mrs. Hirsch, that's my
friend's mother, she's very snooty and doesn't think that Bill is
appropriate. I think that's just terrible, don't you? I mean, when a

mother says to a daughter that she thinks her fiancé isn't *appropri-*
ate. I mean, that's just medieval, don't you think? But the point
is, they're having this humungous wedding with five hundred
guests or something, and all this time Mrs. Hirsch is saying that
Bill isn't appropriate. Don't you think that's weird?"

"Well, I don't suppose the mother's opinion makes much difference."

"You don't think so?"

"Not if they really love each other."

"No, I guess you're right. I hadn't thought of it that way. Still,
I think it's awful of Mrs. Hirsch. I mean, I don't think it's *nice.*"

"Do you know what was nice?" I said.

"No, what?"

"Telling me to subscribe to that magazine. That was nice."

"Oh, that! That was nothing."

"No, it wasn't nothing. It was nice. It was a good piece of
advice. And I'm thankful."

"Are you? Are you really?"

"Yes, I am."

"Well," she said, "you're nice to say so!" And she beamed with
pleasure.

One day Gordo arrived at the office in a wheelchair. I was prepared because Barbara had helped him order it, but it was a shock
to see him in it nonetheless. He was strapped into the gleaming
metal contraption as if for execution.

He came out of the elevator powered by a large black electric
box affixed to the back of the chair, which made an audible whirring sound like some huge susurrant insect.

At first neither of us said a word. Gordo swung precipitously to
his desk and came about sharp, as if on ice. Marie and I exchanged
looks. He struggled for a while to lift himself into his desk chair.

"Well, aren't you going to help me out of this thing?"

"Of course, Gordo. Just wait a second."

"You don't need to act as if the thing doesn't exist," he said.

"I wasn't trying to act that way. I didn't know what you wanted."

I helped him translate himself from the wheelchair to his desk while Marie hovered at my side. Gordo was still a powerful man and I could feel the ripple of his muscle under his sports coat.

"That's better," he said.

"You'll just have to get used to this goddamned thing," he said. "It makes a goddamned racket."

"Not so bad," I said. "It sounds like an x-ray machine going on and off."

"Ah, an x-ray machine! That's good. Good ol' Smith. What an eye for comparisons. So," he said, swinging toward Marie, "did you ever think you'd see me like this?"

"No, indeed—and I'm very sorry to see it."

"Oh, it's not such a big deal. I'm just fishing for sympathy."

Barbara brought his lunch to the office and I watched while she ministered to him, setting out his food, fixing his napkin, carefully pouring the Heineken she had provided down the side of the glass so it wouldn't form a head.

"He shouldn't have alcohol," I said.

They both looked at me blankly, as if my comment wasn't worth a reply.

Later Gordo said to me, "I should have married your wife."

The next week I again had drinks with Emile Flack. The physical therapy didn't seem to accomplish anything, but I looked forward to my sessions with Ms. Stone and to the intellectual stimulus of Flack's harangues.

Emile and I seated ourselves on a leather banquette and ordered drinks from the costumed young woman. She seemed particularly obliging today though Emile noticed her not at all, an oversight that I attributed to his European hauteur, as if the disposition of a mere waitress could concern him no more than a fly on the wall.

"I have bought you something," Emile said, looking at me slyly as he slipped an object wrapped in brown paper onto the table before us. "Go ahead," he said. "Open it."

It was a small squarish book bound in purple and set in a kind
of heavy utilitarian type similar to that used on an old-fashioned
typewriter. I looked at the book and saw that it was written by
Dr. Emile Flack, Litt. D., and that it was titled *In Praise of Inequality.*

"My goodness, Emile. What do we have here?"

"Oh, it's nothing, it's nothing," he said dismissively and
looked away. "It's just a book I wrote some years ago. It's not the
book that counts—it's what's in it."

"I see."

"Yes. I want you to read it. I don't take credit for it in any
personal sense. I hold no store by originality. Truth is too important for partiality. This whole cult of originality, make it new and
all that—what is it but an admission of the idiosyncratic? There is
nothing *new* about the truth. No, no! It is we who are new, if you
want. The new barbarians! The first Europeans in two millennia
to have forgotten the truth."

"I'm not European."

"European, Western, American—it's all the same. No, no—
you won't escape that easily!"

"Well, tell me what it's all about."

"But it's all in the book," he said, tapping the purple cover
with his squarish finger. "It's what Brooks Adams called the degradation of the democratic dogma. Do you know Brooks Adams?
Much sounder than his brother really. A more radical thinker—
gets more to the *root* of things. All this talk about the dynamo is
really deplorable, a kind of modern paganism, don't you think?
But that's beside the point. What I mean to say is this. The root
of the matter, the etiology of the disease, has to do with that word
equality. We have made a fetish of it and it has led us woefully
astray."

" 'We hold these truths to be self-evident,' " I said. "That kind
of thing?"

"Yes, yes, yes! 'Life, liberty, and the pursuit of happiness'—
another idiot phrase. You Americans are so proud of your famous
declaration, which is really no more than a third-rate piece of
eighteenth-century propaganda, whereas your Constitution, the

most original document ever to come from the New World, is honored in the breach."

"It's the Constitution," I said, "that keeps us from murdering one another every day."

"Precisely! Exactly my point! The Constitution isn't chockablock with that woeful cant about equality. Quite the contrary. The Constitution is built upon a profound sense of man's inherent sinfulness. His *inequality.*"

"We're all equal in evil," I said.

"Exactly! Equal in original sin. A profound point! But we are not equal in our struggle against that sin. There lies the point. There lies the very point I want to make. Democratic egalitarianism, which appears to be rooted in humanism, in fact degrades the human being, for it reduces this most amazing of God's creatures to a vulgar least common denominator. Democratic vulgarity! Democratic resentment! It is the great sludge tide that is overwhelming the world. Look at the language we speak, the food we eat, the buildings we raise to house us and work in. Everywhere the most intimate details of our daily lives proclaim the appalling vulgarity of the common soul, from the profanity of our language to the greasy cheapness of our food. So! Think of it, my dear boy. We live in a civilization where you cannot procure a drinkable cup of coffee!"

"The coffee in America has improved."

"The Devil is a quibbler. I speak as a friend to humanity, not a quibbler. Essence reveals itself as the exception, my dear boy, not as the average. There lies the crux of the matter. Excellence is the exceptional. A civilization that honors humanity is one that cherishes the exceptional, for it is only in the exceptional that the essence of humanity is revealed, and it is only this exception that can lift humanity out of the mud. We need this greatness as we need air to breathe—not the pettiness that we ourselves produce and on which we choke. In the light of this essence we are all illumined, as we are illumined by Shakespeare, though we could not possibly write *Hamlet.* I speak in dead earnest. Shakespeare reveals our common humanity, but we are not Shakespeare. But imagine a civilization that no longer even knows how to *read*

Shakespeare! This is what we call the degradation of the democratic dogma."

"I see," I said. "An edifying discourse."

"Edifying to be sure! The modern soul cries out for edification! Think of the staggering smallness, the littleness of human beings, each of them daily filling his sack and emptying it. Each of them yawning in the same manner, stretching in the same manner. Each getting up, going to sleep, having the same thoughts, the same desires—and each imagining these thoughts intensely his own, intensely significant. Multiply this, not by millions but by billions, and what do you have? Farce! The question is not how to take each of these creatures seriously. The question is how to take *any* of them seriously. Ants scurrying on a fleck of mud in a corner of endless space."

"I've read that book."

"Of course, my dear boy! I do not profess originality. I told you as much. I simply press home the implications of your own point of view."

"*My* point of view?"

"But of course—for our purposes."

"And this is what you say in *In Praise of Inequality?*"

"Oh, I say many things. Read it, read it. But yes! This is what I say. *Inequality* is the law of excellence, which is to say of humanity. This is the Ariadne's thread that will lead us out of the labyrinth. So! I speak as a friend of humanity, a friend of humanity. Shakespeare and we are equals in our sinfulness—no one teaches that better than Shakespeare. But otherwise it is Shakespeare, it is the Shakespearean civilization, that towers above us. This is what I say."

It was early winter and I took the boys to play football in the park. It was a brisk day, the wind was up and the clouds were scudding across the sky, but the sun was warm as it beat from the tops of the buildings that crowned the empty trees. Lofty light bathed the park in majesty and seemed to leave us poor forked creatures far below.

At first I tried to play with the boys but I found I couldn't; I couldn't run to catch the ball. The memory of deep pain was coded in my cells and my brain wouldn't issue the command to come down hard on the heel. After a while I gave up.

"Gee, Dad, this isn't much fun," Mat said.

"No, it isn't. I'm sorry."

"Maybe we should go play with those kids over there."

"That's a good idea."

"I don't want to," Timmy said. "I don't want to play with those kids."

Mat looked at him and didn't say anything.

"Why don't you want to play with those kids?" I asked.

"I just don't want to."

"He's *shy*," Mat said. Timmy looked at his brother and then looked at the ground.

"There's nothing to be shy about," I said.

"I'm not shy. I just don't feel like playing."

"We don't have to play," Mat said. "We can do something else."

"You can play, Mat. Timmy and I will watch."

Mat walked over to the other boys and started talking to them. For a while he just stood on the side and watched. But after a while they called him and he started playing with the other kids.

Timmy sat next to me on the bench and watched his brother. I could hear him breathing in small little-boy breaths, and I wanted to tell him to run and play with the other kids, but I knew he wouldn't and I knew he was now too old for there to be anything I could do to assist, so I just sat there and tried to will him to know that I loved him, though I knew that this too was futile and didn't really help.

I thought then of how I had loved to run and jump and climb as a kid and how it had never occurred to me that a time would come when I couldn't do these things; and it seemed to me that a nail had been driven through my foot and into the ground and that I had driven the nail myself. Only as I thought about it, it seemed that the nail was driven through my heart.

* * *

The next time I saw Ms. Stone she was limping. She limped about
the cubicle preparing for my therapy as I lay on the table watching her.

"What happened?"

"Oh, it's nothing." She shrugged. She was dressed as usual in
short shorts and a tank top, and with her short dark hair and
tanned skin, she looked terrific.

"No, really—don't be like that. I want to know what happened."

"Oh, I pulled my hamstring running. Here." And she turned
and stretched her leg behind her and ran her hand along the top of
her leg to the bottom of her buttock.

"Ouch!" I said. "That must hurt."

"Oh, not that bad. I rub it with Ben-Gay."

"I see. You look in terrific shape," I said.

"I am."

"Well, you look it. I mean, you really look great. In great
shape, I mean. Like you really work out."

"Oh, I do. I work out every day. You need to keep up your
tone."

"Well, your tone looks terrific. Where is it that you pulled your
muscle?"

"Here, right here." Again she turned and demonstrated.

"You'd never know," I said. "I mean, it looks great."

"You can't see," she said. "But you can feel. Here, put your
hand here."

I put my hand on the back of her thigh just under her buttock
and I felt the smoothness of her skin and the firmness of her
muscle.

"It feels okay to me," I said.

"Can't you feel the tautness in the muscle?"

"Well, maybe a little."

"It's like a tautness," she said. "A hardness."

"Here," I said. I massaged her leg. "Does that feel better?"

"That feels great!" she said. She laughed. "Hey!" she said. "Who's the professional here?"

"Well, you should have it massaged," I said. "It will relax the muscle. You'll pull it worse like that."

"You are right," she said. "You are really right."

"Here, let me do it for a minute."

I had been lying with one hand behind my head so I could see her better, but now I sat up and swung my feet off the table. I put my hand on the back of her thigh and massaged it gently. Ms. Stone was completely at ease, as if we were exchanging homework assignments.

"That feels great!" she said brightly.

"Does it?"

"I really should pay *you*."

"The tautness runs up and down the muscle," I said.

I reached down and touched the back of her knee. Then I reached up and touched her left buttock, where I let my hand rest.

"You are tight all over," I said. "You're in very good shape but you are too tight."

"Do you think so?"

"Yes."

I was massaging her at the top of her thigh so that half my hand was massaging her buttock.

"Maybe we'd better stop," she said.

"Doesn't it feel good?"

"No, that's not it. It feels fine."

"Well, just be patient," I said. "It will be over in a minute. If you leave it like this you'll have a charley horse."

"It's just I'm supposed to massage *you*."

"You can massage me," I said. "Go ahead and massage me."

She put her hands on my shoulders. With a little pressure I pulled her closer to me. I could smell the sweetness of her body. A great sadness came over me and a sense of utter futility.

"There," I said. "That's enough, don't you think?" I removed my hand. "You should really have that done every day," I said. "I mean, until the tightness goes away."

For a while she didn't say anything. She stood with her head down, as if catching her breath.

"Yes," she said vacantly. Then, as if finding herself, she lifted her head and smiled. "Thank you."

"I can do it on Wednesday if you are still tight."

"Yes," she said. "Thank you."

I went out into the exercise room and the barren space seemed even more unattractive than usual. The neon lights cast a shadowless glare. While I exercised I was mindful of Irene Stone on the other side of the room. She was trying to ignore me, but when I lifted my head I could see she had been watching but now quickly turned away.

Barbara and I took Gordo to the doctor. It was not the first time Barbara had accompanied him, but he was becoming more and more unwieldy and this time I decided to go too.

"There's no need for you to come," Barbara said coolly. She was dressed smartly, as she always was, with a scarf fixed with a gold pin and her chestnut hair swept up from her forehead, and I thought again how handsome she was and how much I admired her.

"Oh, it's no bother," I said, though I understood perfectly well that that wasn't the message she wished to convey. She regarded me a moment while she adjusted an earring.

"Well, suit yourself," she said. "We've got to be going. I promised Gordon I'd pick him up in the station wagon."

"I'll only be a minute."

"I don't have a minute. Meet me out front if you are going to come."

As I rode down in the elevator I studied the back of Kelly the elevator man's neck. Kelly had been there as long as we, which was now fourteen years, and the back of his neck was pitted like the surface of a Stilton cheese. I never tired of studying this neck, which filled me with thoughtful, fascinated horror.

"Anothah good day it'll be, Mr. Smith."

"Is that what they say, Kelly?"

"Ah, so they do. Sunshine, Mr. Smith, but cold—very cold."

"I'll keep it in mind."

Limping across the lobby, I took pleasure in the shine of the mirror and of the brass lamps and in the sparkle of the cut-glass chandelier. I reveled in everything about our building and I never wanted to live elsewhere.

"Good day, Mr. Smith. Your wife just left before you."

"Yes, I know."

It was the officious new doorman, a strapping lad who was busy ingratiating himself with the maids and au pairs of the neighborhood. Barbara didn't approve of this lad and had her eye on him, and I didn't envy him that.

The station wagon was waiting when I limped to the curb. Barbara was behind the wheel. I got in beside her and the doorman shut the door. Barbara didn't say a word.

"Kelly says there will be sunshine," I said.

"Does he."

We were waiting for a red light to change. From where we sat I could see down Park Avenue, already bumper to bumper with business folk off for a day in corporate land.

"But cold," I added. "Unseasonably cold."

Barbara didn't answer and the car took off with a bound. We swung west toward Madison.

Barbara was a skillful dangerous driver. She liked to maneuver in traffic and she liked to go fast. These qualities represented a personality she had repressed in deference to her adult responsibilities, though one I still recognized, like the foundations of an older house.

"Look out for the bus," I said, and was sorry the minute I had spoken. I invariably second-guessed Barbara's driving and this was a poor idea.

Barbara didn't bother to respond, though she went a little faster.

Gordo owned a brownstone in the nineties between Madison and Park. Barbara swung to a halt and I got out and stood on the sidewalk breathing gratefully of the air, which was clean and brisk with sunlight.

Gordo issued from the front door in his wheelchair and behind him stood a young man. This young man had been acquired to tote Gordo up and down stairs and to facilitate mobility generally, and Gordo treated him with gruff casual impatience, as if it were the young man who was impaired.

The young man lifted Gordo, though not easily, and carried him down the stairs of the brownstone and placed him in the front seat of the station wagon, where I had previously been seated.

Gordo looked at me from inside the car.

"What are you doing here?"

"Why, am I in your way? I thought I'd come for the drive."

"For the drive? What is this, a picnic?"

"Will you need me, Mr. Tate?" the young man asked Gordo brightly.

"Are you going to push me around?" Gordo asked me.

"Why not? You've pushed me around for long enough."

"Then I don't need you," he said to the young man. "Mr. Smith here can be my gofer. You meet me at the office at—what time should we say? One o'clock?"

"That sounds good to me," the young man said.

Then the young man went to the top of the stairs and carried down the wheelchair.

"Do you know how to close it?" he asked me.

"Is it that hard?"

"Easy as pie." He showed me the latch on the side and how the chair closed and opened and how it locked in place. Then we went to the back of the car and I opened the back door and the young man placed the wheelchair inside.

"Thanks!"

I climbed into the back seat and stared at the back of the heads of Gordo and Barbara. It seemed to me entirely plausible that I wasn't actually there.

Barbara pulled away. Her driving seemed even more terrifying from the back seat but less real, and somehow I managed not to say anything.

"How have you been?" Gordo asked my wife.

"I'm fine, Gordon. I'm a little nervous about today, that's all."

"About the doctor? What's to be nervous about? He can't tell us anything we don't already know."

I was continually impressed by Gordo's stoicism. He was a large brave unhappy man, and I remembered how much I liked him.

"What is it he is going to say?" I asked.

Gordo craned himself around and looked at me over his shoulder. He was wearing a brown tweed sports coat with little hairlike threads that protruded here and there like the bristles in a mustache, and as he looked at me his eyebrows bristled in the same fashion.

"He's going to tell me I should take a vacation in Tahiti. He's going to tell me I should buy cheap and sell dear."

Gordo turned around and stared out the front window and after that there was silence while Barbara drove skillfully and too fast through the accumulated traffic.

When we got to the doctor's office I got out of the car and went to the back door and got out the wheelchair. I was afraid I wouldn't be able to open the contraption and that Barbara would lose her patience with me, but the chair opened easily and locked into place. Feeling pleased with my accomplishment, I wheeled the chair to Gordo's door.

It wasn't easy getting Gordo out.

"We should have kept the young man," I said.

Barbara looked at me impatiently.

"Just hold still," Gordo said. "Just let me get a purchase on your shoulder."

I crouched down and Gordo used my shoulder to leverage himself into the wheelchair. He was a strong heavy man and I could feel his weight bear down on my shoulder so I had to brace myself to support him.

Gordo let himself fall into the wheelchair. He looked at me with gloating amusement.

"Not in such good shape, eh, Davey boy?"

"Well, Gordo, I didn't know you weighed fifty stone."

"The young man lifts me up and down as if I were a bride."

"That young man," I said. "You really ought to marry him."

"Make an honest young man of him, eh?"

"It's the only decent thing to do."

"Come on, David," Barbara said. "Since you are here you might as well park the car."

"Yeah, and watch out you don't scratch it," Gordo said.

Barbara wheeled Gordo into the lobby.

I drove the car around the block, looking for a place to park. Because of my foot I drove with my left foot, with my right foot protruding over the dividing section into the passenger's space. Cars were double-parked up and down the side streets and in various places delivery vans made the streets impassable. I waited behind a garbage truck while a taxi vented its horn behind me.

Finally I parked in a parking garage three blocks away and limped back under the empty trees. Clouds had gathered and a chill bothered the air, but I was thankful to be outside.

I rang to be admitted into the doctor's office and told the receptionist I was accompanying Mr. Tate. Apparently the doctor had already taken Gordo, for neither he nor Barbara was in the waiting room.

"Where is Mr. Tate?" I inquired.

"He and Mrs. Smith are with the doctor."

"I see. Well, I'm Mr. Smith."

"Oh," she said, and I thought she looked at me curiously. "Well, your wife and Mr. Tate will be out in a little while. Why don't you take a seat in the waiting room?"

The same interior decorator must furnish all doctors' offices in Manhattan, with their plush floral chairs and low-lying coffee tables with magazines laid out like fish in an ice bin. I leafed through a New Yorker, but there was nothing to read but a thirty-page second installment on the subject of asbestos and a lengthy profile of a geneticist living in Tennessee. I contented myself with the cartoons.

After a while I stood up, but there was nowhere to go and I sat back down again.

"Will they be long?" I asked the receptionist.

"I couldn't really say. Not much longer, I shouldn't think."

There were only three other persons in the waiting room, a corpulent middle-aged man who blinked repeatedly while he read a magazine and picked absently at his lips, and a woman in her middle thirties with a long pointy nose accompanied by her whining seven-year-old son. The boy kept touching his mother while she batted him away with a nervous surreptitious swat as if he were a persistent unwanted lover.

"Mama, can we go to FAO Schwarz after the doctor? You promised me you'd take me to FAO Schwarz." And he fumbled at her skinny thigh with a persistent hand.

Her thigh leapt convulsively to the side a quarter of an inch. *"Please,* Michael!"

"But Mommy—*please,* Mommy! You promised."

"We'll see. I told you, we'll see!" And she parried the hand that fumbled for her breast.

I had an urge to take the child and shake him, and I buried myself in *The New Yorker* so as not to embarrass the skinny uncomfortable woman with my observations.

"This way, Mrs. Dole. Dr. Krooks can see Michael now."

The nurse led the woman and her clinging whining child through the left door, and in the momentary confusion I went through the right.

I walked down a corridor, peering into the cubicles to either side. At the end of the corridor I came to a closed door where I paused. For a while I couldn't hear anything. Then I heard a murmur from the other side of the door, and then I thought I heard Barbara. I knocked slightly and opened the door.

The doctor looked up sharply. He was sitting behind a large brown desk that made him look comically small, as if his feet couldn't reach the ground, and he appeared elderly and stern and minatory, as if he were the dispenser of some ultimate truth inhospitable to the illusions of mankind.

At the same time that he looked up Barbara craned round in her chair, and instantly, like some word suddenly remembered, I could feel with my eye through the softness of her clothes the womanliness of her body.

"Yes?" the doctor said, and it wasn't friendly.

"Excuse me," I said. "I'm Mr. Smith."

"It's all right," Gordo drawled. He was sunk in his wheelchair with his chin resting on his hands in a removed, saturnine pose. "It's just Smith, my partner."

"I see. Well, why don't you come in, Mr. Smith?"

"Thank you."

I sat down next to Barbara, who again looked at the doctor.

"Let's see. What was I saying?"

Dr. Dickerson was a small gaunt austere man, a WASP of the old school with bow tie and stern impartial countenance.

"You were saying, doc," Gordo said, "that the picture is pretty grim."

"Yes. I wish I could contradict you, but I try never to mislead my patients, I don't see the point, and certainly not with a man of your education. Your disease is fatal. It has now entered its tertiary stage. We have medicines that can retard the symptoms but not cure the disease. You could live for another year, another two years—I'm not a soothsayer. What is certain is that your condition will continue to deteriorate, you will continue to lose motor control—possibly you will lose it entirely. I cannot say. I'm sorry, Mr. Tate, Mrs. Smith"—with a nod toward Barbara—"but those are the facts."

Barbara and Gordo waited in the reception room while I walked back and got the car. It seemed to me a very long time since anything good had happened and it seemed to me that perhaps this was now the ongoing unstated nature of things.

I drove back slowly around the block and we got Gordo back into the car.

"What a cheery guy," I said.

Barbara looked at me coldly. I looked at her and it appeared to me that she had been crying.

"It's nothing I didn't know," Gordo said.

"It's the shits," I said.

"Yeah," he said. "Isn't it? It's the shits."

* * *

Emile and I were sitting in our favorite haunt drinking dry martinis when he said to me, "My dear boy, I perceive you are not happy."

"Happy?" I said. "Is happiness one of the virtues?"

"Not precisely a virtue," he said. "It is more like a propaedeutic to all the virtues—like courage. It's a kind of hygiene, if you will. You know it's much easier to be unhappy than happy. You have to work at happiness. You have to count your blessings, and all that."

"I see. And what do you count as my blessings?"

"Well, my dear boy—I don't mean to pry, I don't mean to intrude, but there is of course the delightful Mrs. Smith. Not that I've had the honor of making her acquaintance—not yet—but I've had the pleasure, the great pleasure of *sighting* her, if I may use such an expression, when on occasion she drops you off outside the estimable Stein-Kenner Pavilion, and, if I am allowed to say so— and this is a subject on which I pride myself for the accuracy of my insight—she is an outstanding woman, an outstanding woman!"

"You're right about that," I said.

"So there you have it. There is one blessing right off the bat— and a rather significant one it is. You know, I suspect you are rather like me—a closet monogamist. Am I right? Do I hit the nail on the head? A closet monogamist!"

"Let's have another drink."

Emile stirred his martini thoughtfully and looked at me with genuine concern.

"You know, my dear boy, I've grown very fond of you, very fond of you."

"And I of you, Emile."

"Yes, yes. But that's not the point. You seem to me such an interesting specimen of the modern spirit."

"Ah, I see. Rather like a frog."

"You joke. Always the jokester. But actually, if I may say so— and in its own way this is a sort of compliment—I perceive you are living in despair."

"In despair?"

"Quite so. I don't mean just unhappiness. No! I mean the state of despair—an ontological category, though replete with psychological manifestations!"

"That's most flattering," I said.

"I don't mean it to be flattering. I mean it objectively, the way your physician might say that you were living with cancer."

"Is it that bad?"

"Oh, worse! Considerably worse. Cancer, after all, is just a dirty trick of the cells, nothing for which a man need take personal responsibility. It's not unmanly."

"But despair is? The state of despair is?"

"No offense, my boy. I wouldn't say it if I didn't think you could take it. But yes—despair is not becoming to a man. It's a misunderstanding, a piece of stupidity."

"So now I'm stupid. A fellow could get hurty feelings, Emile."

"There is stupid and stupid, David. An error for one mind is a piece of stupidity for another."

"Well, I don't know what you are talking about. I'm not living in the state of despair. My daughters would say I was living in the state of New York."

"You are like a drunken man who says he is not drunk. Have you ever been drunk but not *known* you were drunk?"

"Well, yes, I suppose I have."

"So! That's how it is with despair. You are in a state of despair but you don't know you are."

"I see." I thought about that while Emile watched me from across the table out of unmovable green eyes.

"Tell me," I said after a while. "What is it that you call despair?"

"Aha! Now we are getting somewhere."

He hitched himself nearer to the table and leaned forward as if in conspiratorial confabulation.

"Despair is not to live in accordance with your nature. It so happens that human nature must center itself on the eternal or it will die. A sickness of dizziness overcomes the human soul living in mortal time. All is passingness, no footing is afforded for the soul, our nature hungers for a point of permanence but no such point can be found. In this whirlpool the soul is sucked down and dies. This fact is no big secret, it is nothing new. It is only modern man who has discovered that he can live without the eternal. And what is the result? Look around you—an age of *merde*. We live in the Age of Merde. And yet we think it is the highest pinnacle of human achievement. So! It is a joke. Literally, a bloody joke."

"So that's despair?" I said. "That's the state of despair?"

"Yes. The state of despair is the objective state of the soul when it tries to live separated from the eternal. I call it the divine, but it makes no difference, you can call it the eternal if you please."

"They are interchangeable?"

"For our purpose."

"Well, I don't mean to hurt your feelings, Emile, but I disagree."

"Aha! So!"

He drew back as if I had uttered a vulgarity. His green eyes flickered and fell.

"I'm sorry to disappoint you," I said, "but isn't it the old story of the turtle?"

"The turtle?"

"Yes. A little boy asks a wise man what does the sky rest on, and the wise man tells him the earth. Well, what does the earth rest on? The sea. And the sea? A turtle. But what, O wise man, does the turtle rest on? The wise man looks at the little boy and nods his head. It's turtles, my son, all the way down the line."

Emile Flack looked at me and then he gave a forced, hearty laugh. "I see!" he said. "You are being flippant. That too is a symptom of despair—flippancy, the modern man's armor. No, I'm sorry, David. You can't palm me off that easily. I know you. I know who you are. How do you say? I have your number."

"Cucumber," I said. It was something the children used to say, but either Emile did not hear or he was so nonplussed by my response that it didn't register. He came forward with the ponderous impressive movement of the water buffalo.

"The soul must continue to grow throughout life," he said. "It is rooted in the darkness of its origins. Its shoots reach into light.

At first it is intoxicated with the passion of becoming. This is natural. But think of that word *intoxicated.* Its root is *toxic,* as in poison. The soul flowers with such strength that it shoots beyond itself into new life, and this too is natural. Thus the cycle of nature is completed. But what of the soul? Its petals drop into the soil from which it sprang. Only its essence, its aroma, can escape upward into the heavens. But if the soul does not mount above the cycle of becoming, it must be cast back into the fire like grass."

"And that is despair?"

"Despair is the turning away from our being. It is to think we *are* grass. That is despair. To misunderstand the soul for grass."

"And that is what I am doing?"

"That is what we all do. All of us moderns. I do not exempt myself. Perhaps it is unavoidable. Perhaps we live in the age of grass. But some of us *must not make the mistake of thinking we are right!* That is where you come in. It is like living in an age when all the physicists have a problem wrong. It is up to a few physicists to say, We still do not have the solution!"

"Well, I do not claim to possess any solution."

"Yes, but the solution lies there before you."

"Does it? Well, I cannot make the leap. When I leap I only . . . break my foot."

"Yes, you bruise your heel. But behold, it brings you to me!"

Behold, it brought me to Irene Stone.

"Is your muscle still tight?" I asked her that Wednesday as soon as we were alone in our cubicle. I made my voice sound casual.

She was not entirely at ease. She did not look at me directly and her cheek colored slightly when I spoke.

"Oh, it's much better," she said, and her voice was normal.

"That's good. No more tightness?"

"Just a little."

"Let me see."

She turned from across the room and showed me the back of her thigh.

"I can't see anything from here," I said.

"Do you want to massage it?"

She came forward and stood in front of me while I sat on the exercise table. I put my hand on the back of her leg directly under her left buttock.

Her leg was warm and firm and again I was overcome by sadness.

"Maybe you shouldn't massage me," she said.

"Why not? Doesn't it help?"

"Yes. But just . . . maybe you'd better not."

"Don't be afraid," I said. "I'm not going to hurt you."

"But maybe, you know, it's not a good idea."

I tried to decide how old she was and decided she couldn't be older than twenty-six.

"I won't hurt you," I repeated. My hand was caressing the back of her thigh.

She put her head down and rested her forehead on my shoulder.

After a while I lifted her chin and kissed her gently on the lips. I had moved my hand so it was on her buttocks and had pulled her to me. I did not kiss her long, though it seemed to me I had not kissed anyone in a very long time.

"Aren't you married?" she asked.

"My wife is leaving me."

"Oh. I'm sorry."

"It's not your fault. Can you come out and have a cup of coffee with me?"

"Not till after work."

"What time is that?"

"Not till five o'clock."

"I'll be waiting for you downstairs."

I took Irene to a coffee shop across the street. I had thought of taking her to the bar with the costumed waitresses where I went with Emile, but reasons of decorum prevented me. Besides I did not wish to make Irene tipsy.

The coffee shop was run by a family of foreign extraction—I could not determine whether Greek or Israeli or Yugoslav, all cultures that doubtless profess to despise one another. The place was really less a coffee shop than the simulacrum of a European café, with cappuccino and espresso and butter cookies that tasted like papier-mâché and were topped with glazed half-cherries as red as Christmas balls and tasting like dollops of plastic. Irene and I took a table in the rear.

We were served by one of the buxom daughters. Unlike her father, a professionally pleasant man with red cheeks and blue watchful eyes, the daughter was dark and scowling and had recently brazenly overcharged me for espresso, though I purchased the bitter brew from her almost every day. I had been impressed with her self-righteous insistence that the extra twenty-five cents represented the regular price, and had concluded by backing away from her truculence. The incident provided me with some insight into the stubborn nature of human cupidity and resentment, and I now regarded her *faux* good humor with amazement and begrudging respect.

"I'll have a decaffeinated cappuccino with fat-free milk," Irene said.

"Do you want a piece of cake or something?" I asked.

"Oh, I can't have a piece of cake at this time of day! I'd have a sugar high. One piece of cake is like eating two candy bars! It destroys the metabolic dynamic of the entire system. I might as well have caffeinated coffee!" And she uttered a bark of laughter at such absurdity.

The waitress regarded us with stolid boredom. I ordered a double espresso and a piece of chocolate cake.

"Irene," I said, "are you ever unhappy?"

"Unhappy? Well, of course I'm unhappy *sometimes.* Everyone is unhappy sometimes, don't you think? I mean, it wouldn't be normal if you weren't unhappy sometimes."

"Yes, but I mean *really* unhappy."

"Really unhappy? Let me see. Well, I guess I was *really* unhappy when my dog died."

"When your dog died?"

"Yes. He was run over by a car when I was twelve. Even now I don't like to talk about it. It was *horrible.* It happened right in front of my parents' house. I can remember it now as if it was only

yesterday. Poor Benji! I heard this terrible yelp and then this
screeching of brakes, and I just *knew* what had happened. I mean,
it was just as if I had been gifted with second sight or something.
I just *knew* Benji had been killed."

"You poor kid."

I took her hand across the table. It was a warm, small-boned
hand, and it rested inside my grasp like a limp sparrow.

"I hate to think of you as unhappy," I said. "You seem to me to
have been born for happiness."

"Do I?" She turned this observation over as if it were a new
brand of nylon she hadn't encountered before.

"Well, I *am* happy," she announced with conviction after a
moment's thought. "I mean, I like my job and my skin seems
much better and I get along beautifully with my roommate
Karen. At first I wasn't sure, but now we get along beautifully
. . . But what about you, ah, Mr. Smith? Are you happy?"

"Don't call me Mr. Smith," I said.

"Well, then—David. Are you happy?"

"I'm not very happy, Irene. That's the point of this. That's
what I'm trying to get at."

"I thought as much," she said. "I mean, it's not all of my
patients who *jump* off of *roofs*."

We both sat thinking about that for a while.

The buxom larcenous daughter brought the coffee and set it
down in front of us on square little napkins on which was printed
the name of the coffee shop.

"I mean, jumping off roofs is *crazy*," Irene said once the waitress had withdrawn. "No offense intended."

"That's all right, Irene. But listen, do you think you could tell
me what it is that makes you so happy?"

"What makes me happy? Well . . . I work out a lot. I can
truthfully recommend that. And then . . . I like to keep busy. I
don't like to *brood* about things. I mean, even after the death of
Benji I didn't become morbid or something like that. I think that
must be the secret of it. And then I like people."

"That's wonderful," I said. "That's really wonderful! Listen!"
And I reached across the table and tried to reclaim her hand,

which I had relinquished when the unfortunate daughter had appeared. "I want you to try to help me, Irene."

"Oh, I'd like to help you, Mr. Sm— David. How could I help you?"

"I'll tell you what I've been thinking. I've been thinking, Irene, maybe you could . . . marry me."

Her face changed utterly. Her jaw literally fell.

"Marry you! But Mr. Smith!"

"For chrissakes call me David!"

"Yes, yes—David. Oh, my God, David! Marry you?"

"It was just a thought."

"But aren't you, you know, *married?*"

"Yes, I suppose I am. Of course I am. But that's not the point."

"Well, I think it very much *is* the point! And I think Mrs. Smith would think so too."

"The point is happiness, Irene. Mrs. Smith can't make me happy."

"That's terrible," she said.

"Yes, I suppose it is. It's not Mrs. Smith's fault. I don't want you to think it's my wife's fault. In fact my wife is a wonderful woman. A wonderful woman. It's my fault, you see. It's entirely my fault. But that changes nothing. It doesn't change my unhappiness. Do you see what I mean? Do you see what I'm getting at?"

"I don't really think I do. You say Mrs. Smith is wonderful, and I'm sure she is. She is the mother of your children, for goodness' sake! I mean, I think that's just so wonderful right there. And then you say she doesn't make you happy. You say it's your fault. But then you say maybe *I* can make you happy. But why, Mr. Smith? Why should I make you happy if the mother of your children doesn't? Can you tell me that?"

This profound observation brought me to a halt.

"It's just a feeling I have," I said after a while. "Just an instinct I have."

"Do you think it's because of what happened this afternoon?" Irene asked. "I mean what happened in the cubicle."

"No," I said. "That just confirmed my feeling."

"You think I could make you happy, and that's why you kissed me?"

"Yes—something like that."

"That's sweet," she said.

"Sweet? Is that what it is?"

"Yes. I think you are sweet." And she reached over and patted my hand; I had never succeeded in regaining hers after the advent of the coffee.

"Thank you," I said, and I bent over and kissed her hand. At the same moment something passed over me that might have been the wings of madness. It seemed I had ceased to have any connection with my actions.

"This is what I want you to do," I said, and my voice sounded foreign in my own ears, as if I were overhearing the conspiratorial babble on some undisclosed Watergate tape. "I want you to think over what I have said. I don't want you to try to answer me now. I want you to call me at my office sometime later in the week so we can find a time to examine where we go from here. Okay? Okay? Please don't say no. Here, just take the number. I don't want you to try to say anything right now. Just remember—and try to have a little pity for me, for my state of nerves. Okay? That's all I ask. Okay?"

That was my conversation with Ms. Stone. When I was alone in the street I started to laugh. I was overcome by a kind of giddy hilarity, as sometimes overtakes one in a vulgar comedy, and after a time I was laughing so hard that people looked at me as they passed, giving me a wide berth.

I didn't have the slightest idea what I was laughing about.

Irene didn't call me at the office—she called me at home. And Barbara answered the telephone. I don't know exactly what Irene said—something sweet and insipid and well-meaning, no doubt; something to the effect that she, Irene, didn't intend to steal her, Barbara's, husband. But the effect was spectacular.

"Listen, young lady, whoever you are," I heard Barbara say, and her voice could easily have pierced steel. "Don't you ever call my house again. Do you understand? *Never call this number again!*"

She slammed down the phone.

Then she came into the study.

"I don't want that dingbat calling us at home, do you understand?"

"Darling, I had nothing—"

"I don't want her calling me and I don't want her calling the children. If you need to have little girls—"

"Darling—"

"—little girls, keep them out of the house. If that dingbat ever calls one of my children, I'll shoot her. Do you understand? Don't make the mistake of thinking I'm fooling. I'll shoot her dead!"

I didn't think she was fooling for an instant.

Later that evening she came back into the study. "What breaks my heart, David, is that you should turn out to be a shit—that you should have allowed it. Because you are intelligent you think you are measured with a different measure, but you aren't. You imagine you are innocent because you never meant anyone any harm. Well, it's a kind of stupidity—you, who pride yourself on your lucidity. Let me tell you something—I'm not going to leave you right now. Why should I? Why should I start over? It bores me. But you had better get down on your knees and thank God— you, the great male adventurer out discovering new continents! What did you think you'd find out there, anyway? The promised land? Milk and honey in the desert? In fact I'm the boat you sailed on, and you've known that all along. If I were as stupid as you, you'd drown in a minute. You'd sink to the bottom of the sea."

It must have been three months later that Annette called one evening at ten o'clock to inform us that Mrs. Grotton was missing. She had not been seen since early that morning when she had driven away in her Corvette. Frank Grotton had alerted the police.

I stood by the telephone while Barbara spoke to her father in a low, concerned voice.

Had she been acting peculiar? Had she gone to the club? Could she have driven to the city? Had he called her friends?

"Dad," Barbara said into the phone, "had Mom been drinking?" Her forehead wrinkled as she listened to the answer and she bit her lower lip.

"What did he say?" I asked after she had hung up.

"About what?"

"About her drinking."

"You know Dad," Barbara said. "He doesn't admit there is such a thing as a drinking problem—certainly not in this family. Mom should have gotten help years ago."

"Do you think that's what it is? Do you think she's out somewhere drinking?"

"How should I know? How in hell should I know?"

She went into the bedroom and started packing an overnight bag.

"What are you doing?"

"I'm going out to Dad. He won't say it but he needs me. He'll just drink himself into a stupor."

"I'll go with you. I don't want you going alone."

"Suit yourself."

"What is it?" Jenny asked.

"It's your grandmother. She's disappeared."

"Disappeared? Well, good for her. It's about time."

"Don't be stupid, Jenny. She could be really hurt. Now you're responsible, young lady, while we're away. Do you know that word *responsible?*"

"Yeah, yeah, Dad—it's what bankers are."

"Don't be a wise guy, Jenny. I want you to make sure Alexandra and your brothers get to school on time—and I expect *you* to go to school as well."

"I'm sorry," Alexandra said to her mother, "I'm so sorry. Will Grandma be all right?"

"Yes, darling," Barbara said, and she hugged her second daughter. "Grandma will be fine, I'm sure."

"Do you want me to come with you?"

"No, I want you to look after the twins and yourself. I'll call you in the morning."

I drove the Mercedes and Barbara sat next to me and fidgeted with her nails.

"Don't do that," I said. "Don't pick."

She looked at me distractedly but continued picking her cuticle.

"Do you think she got in a car accident?" I asked.

"I don't think so. The police would have that information. I'm just afraid she's done something really loopy. I'm afraid she's gone around the bend."

I reached over and took her hand, and she let it rest limply for a while in mine, like a small animal that is warm though it is already dead; then she pulled it away.

"Do you realize I have no vices?" she said to me in desperation and disgust, apparently out of the blue. "None at all. I don't even smoke."

Then we were silent and I drove swiftly into Long Island.

Annette and Charles had arrived before us. They greeted us at the door. Frank was pacing back and forth in the study, dressed in slippers and an ascot beneath his smoking jacket, and his face was dull purple.

"No word," he said. "No word at all. These damn police! They can't even do their job."

"Don't be like that, Daddy," Annette said. "They have been very cooperative. You know they have been cooperative—you said it yourself."

"Yes, of course—but why can't they find her? I mean, my God, how hard can it be to find one seventy-year-old woman?"

Annette took us aside to consult.

"She went to the club at eleven," Annette told us, "and had drinks at the bar and spoke with Mrs. Wick and with the new bartender. No one noticed exactly when she left, but she didn't stay for lunch. That's the last we've heard for sure. However, a bartender in Port Jefferson reports seeing a woman who meets her description drinking in his bar at three P.M."

"In Port Jefferson?" Barbara said, aghast. "What in the world would she be doing in Port Jefferson?"

"That's precisely what we don't know," Charles said gravely. "No one can account for her behavior."

Charles was dressed as usual in a dark blue suit and expensive silk tie, and he spoke with the measured decorum appropriate for a funeral parlor.

"Have people checked the bars?" I asked.

"The police have done the best they could," Charles said. "Obviously we'd like to keep this as quiet as possible."

"Why don't we fan out and check the bars?"

"The bars, the bars," Annette said. "Precisely what I think. Oh, David and I always see eye to eye!"

"At this hour?" Charles said. "I hardly think that's appropriate for the women."

"They can stay with Frank then. The point is, she's probably at one of the bars."

"I think David is right," Barbara said. "You men should check the bars." Then, "My God!" she burst out. "If she was seen in Port Jefferson at three o'clock, she could be *anywhere.*"

"I *do* think we should keep this quiet, though—don't you?" Annette asked me, taking my hand. I put my arm around her shoulders.

"The first thing is to find your mother."

"Yes, yes, exactly! Exactly what I think! But will you find her? Promise me you'll find her, David."

"I'll do my best." And I kissed her on the cheek.

"I think I'll come with you," Charles said. "No need to split up."

"Whatever you want."

I got into the Mercedes and Charles got in next to me. Barbara was already tending to her father and had hardly bothered to say goodbye.

I decided to drive to Port Jefferson, where Marilyn Grotton had last been sighted, and to work out from there. There was small chance of our finding her, but I wanted to be useful to Barbara while remaining out of her way.

For a long time we drove in silence, but as we approached Port Jefferson, Charles shifted his bulk uncomfortably and cleared his throat.

"You don't think there is any danger in our going to these bars at this hour, do you?"

"Danger?"

"Well, you know. It's rather a rough area, wouldn't you say?"

"No, I don't think there is any danger. Anyway, if Marilyn is there she can protect us."

"Very funny. Of course her behavior is appalling. I can't imagine what's gotten into her. A thing like this could be plastered all over the papers. It could be harmful for all of us."

"Don't be silly," I said. "What do the papers care about us?"

"We have positions to maintain," he said with dignity.

"Let's just find Marilyn."

I regretted Charles's presence and didn't want to talk to him, but there was something else I had to say.

"I'm worried about Annette. She seems to be taking this rather hard."

"Oh, no need to worry about Annette," he said sententiously. "She's a brick, my wife, a brick!"

I found the bar with difficulty. It was a sleazy rundown saloon in a crummy part of town and the sight of the place offered little consolation.

"My God!" Charles said.

"Come on, cowboy."

We went into the bar and almost no one else was in it, only two beefy rednecks drinking beer at one end of the counter and some punky kids playing pool toward the entrance. I went over to the bartender.

"Hello," I said. "I'm looking for a lady who was in here earlier today. She is about seventy years old and she was dressed in green and her name is Mrs. Grotton—Marilyn Grotton. She would have been here at about three."

"Oh yeah?" the bartender said. "Well, I wasn't here at three."

"Oh. Well, is there anyone who was?"

"Is this the lady the cops was looking for?"

"Yes, that's the one."

"Still haven't found her, eh?"

"No."

"What she do, run away?"

"Not exactly. If you could help us it would be greatly appreciated. We're worried about her. She might hurt herself."

The bartender, a thin unhealthy-looking man with deep parallel lines that indented either cheek, looked like he smelled perpetually of stale cigarettes. He had thin lifeless hair the color of cigarette smoke that hung down around his head. Now he scowled and turned away.

"I'll get the owner," he said, and as he walked away he muttered something under his breath. The men at the end of the bar watched us with amused, hostile indifference.

"Nice place," I said, turning to Charles, who watched me reproachfully, as if from a great distance.

The owner was a stout large man wearing an apron. His face was fat and solemn and splotched with red broken blood vessels, but his intelligent blue eyes looked amused.

"What can I do for yous?"

"It's about the woman who was here earlier—the one the police asked you about."

"Oh, her. Well, what is it? Still haven't found her?"

"No, we haven't. I'm her son-in-law, and as you can imagine, the family is quite concerned."

"She was a pleasant lady," the owner said. "A very pleasant-mannered lady."

"I see."

"She had some martinis. I'd say she'd had some before."

"You mean before she arrived."

"Yes—previous."

"Was she drunk?"

"Drunk? Oh, I dunno. What's drunk? Like I say, she was a pleasant-mannered person, not at all disagreeable. We chatted for a while—about the weather and that sort of thing. You know. Nothing outa the ordinary."

"I don't suppose you see customers like her every day," Charles said.

The owner looked at Charles but didn't bother to answer.

"Like I said," he said. "A very well-mannered lady." Then he made as if to turn away.

"Listen," I said, detaining him. "Don't mind him. We're overwrought, that's all. We've been looking all day. We have reason to believe that Mrs. Grotton isn't well. If there is anything else you can tell us—anything at all, anything you didn't tell the police—we would be deeply obliged. And it would be doing Mrs. Grotton a favor."

"I wouldn't worry about Mrs. Grotton," the owner said.

"Oh? Why not?"

"Because that bird can look after herself."

"Why do you say that? What leads you to say that?"

"Listen," the owner said, and he led me aside. "Haven't you ever gone on a bender? We all need a bender from time to time, right? Judging by the looks of your friend here, your mother-in-law was long overdue for a bender."

"Listen, Mr.—what's your name? I'm sorry, I missed your name."

"O'Connor."

"O'Connor. Listen, Mr. O'Connor, I'm glad you liked my mother-in-law and I don't disagree with what you say about a bender, but the truth of the matter is that my wife is worried sick about her seventy-year-old mother, who isn't in the best of health. Now if there is anything you can tell us, anything at all, I would be deeply grateful. Why did you say that we shouldn't worry about Mrs. Grotton?"

"Listen, buddy," Mr. O'Connor said, leaning toward me and speaking in a lowered voice. "I didn't tell this to the cops because . . . because why should I? I mean, it's none of their business, right? If a nice-mannered lady wants to go on a little bender, well, that's her business. It's a free country, right? But I'll tell you why I don't think you need to worry about your mother-in-law. You don't need to worry about her because she left with a nice-mannered *man*. Okay? They was two nice-mannered people having some drinks in a civilized fashion. So what I suggest is that you just leave her alone and by and by she'll come home wagging her tail behind her."

"With a man?"

"That's what I said. With a nice-mannered man. He was sitting at the other end of the bar. They had some drinks and then they went out together."

"My God!" I said. "But Mrs. Grotton is seventy years old."

"What does that got to do with it?" he said. "You think there's some statute of limitations on having some drinks with the opposite party? You think people seventy don't need some human companionship?"

I was stunned by what I had just heard and I didn't care to debate the issue further with Mr. O'Connor. I thanked him as best I could; he wouldn't accept any money.

"Don't worry about your mother-in-law," he assured me. "She's a game old bird."

"What was *that* all about?" Charles asked as we drove home.

"Nothing, Charles. The man had nothing to say that would interest you in the slightest."

It was two A.M. by the time we reached the Grottons'. Barbara and Annette were still awake though Frank had fallen asleep in his wingback chair.

"Did you find anything?"

"No—nothing."

"We were entertained," Charles said, "by some vile personage in a working-class dive who claimed to have seen your mother this afternoon. Frankly, I consider it highly unlikely that Marilyn Grotton would have frequented such an establishment. The man was probably just fishing for a reward. I can't help observing that I was never in favor of this junket. We learned absolutely nothing."

When Barbara and I were alone in our bedroom I told her what O'Connor had told me.

"My God!" she said. "You mean she picked up a stranger in Port Jefferson?"

"Who knows what she did? O'Connor says they left together. They may have parted at the corner for all we know."

"But she's—mad!"

"There is nothing we can do. She could be anyplace on Long Island. She could be anyplace in the country."

"You don't think she's . . . dead?"

"Why should she be dead? She's probably asleep in some motel. Or maybe she's still out drinking."

Barbara sat staring for a while. I tried to stroke her hair but she flinched unconsciously, like a thoroughbred mare.

"What will we tell Daddy?"

"Maybe we won't have to tell him anything. Maybe she'll show up in the morning as O'Connor predicted."

"Fuck Mr. O'Connor," Barbara said. Then she lay down on the bed without removing her clothes and very soon she was asleep.

When I knew she was deeply asleep I went downstairs and poured myself a whiskey, and then I came back upstairs and sat by the window watching Barbara sleep. I could detect under the middle-aged woman the lines of the girl I had loved, but truly she could almost have been a different person, so much had she changed.

The next morning they found Marilyn in a bar in Riverhead. She seemed happy although hazy about who she was and what was wanted of her. The police brought her home and led her up to the front door, much to Charles's chagrin.

She recognized Frank and the girls but had no idea who I was.

"Now let me see," she said. "Where is my purse? What have I done with my purse?"

She sat in a large chair in the study and suddenly she looked thoroughly confused.

"Here it is, Mama," Annette said. Annette had been crying.

"Oh, yes, here it is all the time. How foolish of me. *J'ai mal à la tête, j'ai mal à la tête.* But who are all these nice people? Shouldn't we offer them a drink?"

"Where have you *been?*" Frank said. "Where in the name of God have you *been?*"

"Been? Been? Now let me see. *J'ai mal à la tête, j'ai mal à la tête.*"

"Don't excite her," Dr. Thayer said to Frank Grotton. "I'm sure she'll tell us everything later on."

"Do you remember anything about where you've been for the last day?" Barbara asked, stooping down next to her mother.

"Why, I've been right here. Haven't I been here? Let's see, what *have* I done with my purse? How silly of me. *J'ai mal à la tête,* girls. I really should lie down."

Later, when we were on the Long Island Thruway driving home, Barbara said, "We'll never know what happened to her."

"I don't imagine we ever will."

"She's going to have to be institutionalized for a while. We should find out about the Betty Ford Clinic."

"Will your father ever agree to that?"

"He'll have to. He'll just have to."

"And what about the repulsive Charles?"

"What does he have to do with it? How does he count?"

"I'm just saying you might run into opposition."

"What do I care about that? She is my mother and I will take care of her."

"I know you will," I said.

As I put the car away in the garage I reflected on my mother-in-law and on all the years I had known her, and the more I thought about her the more upset I became. Marilyn and I had had our ups and downs but she had mellowed with the years and it came to me with surprise that I loved her. I had no desire for anything hurtful or harmful to visit her, and as I thought of her perched merrily at three in the afternoon drinking martinis in the Three Bells Tavern in Port Jefferson and subsequently departing with a well-mannered stranger, my heart smote me with rumor of impending disaster.

I let myself into the apartment. It was still afternoon and the children were at school. I went into the bedroom and I saw Barbara sitting at the edge of the bed.

"How are you?" I asked.

She looked up but didn't say anything.

"What do you think is really wrong with her?" I said.

"Alcohol."

"Alcohol? Do you think it's only alcohol?"

She looked at me and I saw then that she didn't look right.

"*Only* alcohol? Well, what else would you like it to be? Manic depression, schizophrenia, a lifetime of living with my father, a lifetime of feeling unloved, a lifetime of being her parents' child, a lifetime of feeling inadequate? What else do you want it to be?"

She was shaking. Her lips were shaking, her hands were shaking, I thought she was going to cry. I went to her and I put my arm around her but she pulled away impatiently. And I felt come over me the weight of my errors, none of which I could truly unthink, and the weight of my responsibility toward her; and I felt how much I loved her and how much I always had loved her and always would love her; and I felt overpowered by a sadness for the irremediable inadequacy that we call love, which is ultimately all we have to offer one another.

She began to laugh.

"*J'ai mal à la tête,*" she said, and she laughed. "*J'ai mal à la gorge, j'ai mal au cou, j'ai mal aux genoux, j'ai mal aux seins, j'ai mal à l'oreille, j'ai mal à la main, j'ai mal aux doigts, j'ai mal au nez, j'ai mal—*"

"Barbara—"

"*—aux cheveux, j'ai mal au nombril, j'ai mal aux fesses, j'ai mal à l'estomac, j'ai mal au coude, j'ai mal à l'esprit, j'ai mal à—*"

"Barbara, Barbara."

All this time she was laughing—laughing hysterically. I held her and tried to laugh with her but her laughter frightened me and I could not fathom its meaning nor its provenance nor its likely end; and suddenly and for the first time I saw open between us a distance that was not just the distance of estrangement but was I thought the very space of madness. And I was afraid.

"Barbara," I said. "Barbara."

Slowly she calmed down; but she lay on the bed smiling to herself enigmatically, as if savoring a joke that amused her hugely.

"I'll end like my mother," she said.

"What do you mean?"

"Just like my mother."

It turned my blood cold. "Don't be preposterous," I said. "You are nothing like your mother."

Suddenly she swung and hit me, hard, with the flat of her hand. It caught me on the side of the head next to my eye.

"Barbara—Jesus!"

Now she was laughing again—not hysterically but sardonically, from her throat, like a disillusioned middle-aged woman.

She reached up and I thought she was going to hit me again and instinctively I shied away.

She gave a sob, half in amusement, half in despair, and gripping me by the front of the shirt, she pulled me down on top of her. Biting and kissing, she pressed her face to mine. Then she pushed me back.

But not far. She kept me locked with her arm, and though her face was averted, I could see that she was crying.

"Hold me, damn you," she said through gritted teeth. "Why can't you *hold* me!"

Gordo's health had stabilized under the influence of an experimental drug, and though the prognosis remained the same, his mobility had improved. For his birthday that November he came to dinner at the house, and Barbara cooked a roast beef and Gordo sat in his wheelchair at her side and presided over the table like a magnanimous Roman emperor visiting a provincial court.

Gordo was jolly and avuncular and relaxed that evening and the children, who loved him, acted solicitous and contained—including Jenny, a sure indication of esteem.

The high point of the evening arrived when Mat told Gordo a joke that Gordo had told the twins many years before. The joke had to do with an idiot king and a royal secret that was passed from generation to generation at the moment of the king's death. The secret concerned the reason for the family prohibition against drinking out of the farther lip of any cup or glass. And why was the family prohibited in this manner? The answer is demonstrated when the contents of the cup spills into the experimenter's lap.

Now, this story had become a no-no in our family, since it entailed the tipping of the contents of a cup into the lap of the unwary; when Gordo had first introduced the joke a glass of wine had spilled all over the dining-room table, to uproarious laughter on the part of Gordo and the children and looks of consternation on the part of my wife. Since then Barbara had allowed the joke to be told but never demonstrated. Now, however, with perfectly straight faces, Mat related the story and Gordo played the stooge, while Barbara with a wry and not entirely convincing smile allowed the joke to proceed.

Gordo ended by spilling a glass of water into his lap.

After the party had concluded, when Gordo had dried himself and bid everyone adieu and the children were in their rooms preparing for bed, I went and sat by myself in the study and allowed the images of the day to reel slowly through my mind until they finally approached something resembling a meaning.

"Daddy?"

I looked up and saw that it was Alexandra.

"What is it, darling?"

She came toward me. At fifteen Alexandra was dark and slightly pudgy, a quiet thoughtful child who had perhaps received less attention than her siblings by reason of her steady disposition and precocious good sense; but the sight of her now, with a concerned frown on her usually smooth and placid features, stabbed me, as the sight of my children invariably did, with a paroxysm of love.

"Daddy," she repeated, and she came and stood next to me. "Is Uncle Gordo going to die?"

I hesitated for a moment before answering. "Well, honey, we're *all* going to die."

"I don't mean that. I mean is Uncle Gordo going to die *soon?* You know, because of his disease."

"Yes," I said. "I think he is going to die soon. The disease he has is fatal."

"Does he know it?"

"Yes, of course he knows it."

"He's very brave," she said.

I took her and pulled her closer to me so I could hold her against me.

"Yes," I said, "he's very brave. He's a brave good funny man who has been our dear friend. Are you frightened, darling? Are you very upset?"

"I don't think so—not very. But, Daddy, where will Uncle Gordo *go*? Where will he be after he is dead?"

That stopped me. I realized I had no good answer for my daughter.

"I don't know," I said after a while. "I don't know where Gordo will be. But I do know this, he will live on in our minds. He will live on in our minds and in our love."

"Can we do anything to help him?"

"We can tell him we love him."

"I *do* love him, Daddy. I love him *terribly*. And I will *never* forget him."

"Well, then, that's one place where Uncle Gordo will be."

"But, Daddy, do you think there is a God?"

Again I paused. "I don't know. I think there probably is . . . and also there probably isn't. I suspect there is a sense in which both statements are true."

Alexandra thought about my words, but they didn't seem to satisfy her.

"For me," she said, "God is as certain as breathing. He is *more* certain. It's we who are uncertain. If *we* were more certain, then we'd know God more certainly."

"That makes sense to me," I said. Then I added, "Does that help you with Uncle Gordo?"

"I don't know. I don't understand death. It frightens me for Uncle Gordo. It doesn't seem fair."

"No, it doesn't."

"But"—she surprised me—"if God exists, then not a single thing about Uncle Gordo can pass away. And I am certain about God."

I was moved by Alexandra's thoughts; she was heir to that religious strain that I could trace for generations in my family. She was ahead of me on this, as I hoped she would be on many other matters. But I had thoughts of my own. Alexandra had not lived long enough to know how terrifying it can be to reflect that not one jot of your life can pass away. Trapped with your mistakes for eternity—what is that but a Nessian shirt of despair? Better to pass out of oneself forever, to flow away as spent water flows into pure.

What I had wanted to say about God was this: that He exists, but that His existence makes exactly no difference—except for the fact that without Him there would be no existence at all.

The world *is*. It towers above us like cliffs out of the sea. It is the desirable, we reach out for it—yet when we reach, it is no longer there. It disappears, we are terrified, we are moving in the dark. Yet the world remains—terrifyingly. It is that into which we fall. We search for words to express this, but we cannot find them—and that too is the world, the lostness of the world. And so we turn to each other, we embrace, we cry out in the surpassingness of coming together. But when we are spent, we lie alone in the closeness of the world listening to its small sounds, its breathings. We reach out, and our hands touch and then fall apart. We stir, we rise up on an elbow, and all about us stretches the world. It is a vast plain peopled with cities and towns and valleys, with sunlight and the dappled sides of hills. It is that which we love.

And all of this will be taken away.

Sometimes I dream of Hélène. She is trying to tell me something but I cannot tell what. I stretch out my hand but I cannot reach her. Her lips move, she says something, but her words are blown away. I cannot make out where we are nor whether she is alive or dead. I reach out, and then I awake—and it seems my heart is broken.

If we could live our lives again, would we? I don't mean if we could change them, if we could get them right. I mean the same life, *your* life, with all its little dirts, its lies and cheating and compromises, the long afternoons—the sudden splendor of the afternoons—the entire thing in its occasional grandeur and its daily tawdry detail. Would you?

For myself, nothing could make me relive those days after

Hélène was dead. I would turn away, I would disappear, I would consign myself to darkness.

If anything remains after death, if, clarified and refined, the mind bothers with the fever of mortality, I pray that it views it under the cool light of eternity and not in the distorting glare that we knew.

I remember one summer in Maine with Barbara and the children long ago before I knew Hélène, before I had ever dreamed of Anne Stokowski. It was when the children were very young and we were very happy.

The twins turned one that summer and were just beginning to walk, and Barbara was having the devil of a time with them. I had taken three weeks from the office and we were spending it on Harpswell, on the bay across from Bailey Island.

The weather was beautiful that summer but unseasonably cold during the nights, so cold that the children had to be dressed in little hoods when we put them to bed. Barbara and I slept on the sleeping porch and we held each other all night against the cold. In the morning at five I would hear the gulls and then I would hear the lobster boats go by, and then the sun would come up and the air would begin to warm and for an hour I could fall deeply asleep.

My two girls slept together in the west room, where the swallows had built under the eaves. When I put them to bed we would lie together and hear the shrill swift calls as the swallows darted in and out just beyond us. I told the girls how lucky they were to be living with swallows, and they believed me. They both drew pictures of the swallows wheeling in to nest under the eaves, and I kept the pictures with me for many years.

The house had a high porch with no railings that faced the bay, and this proved a nightmare for Barbara with two small boys just learning to walk. We did not want to discourage their efforts, but neither did we want them toppling four feet off the porch onto the lawn.

I commenced taking the two girls for walks up the dirt road to relieve their mother of their pestering, for they were both jealous of the boys. I bought a flower book in Brunswick and we took it with us on our outings and picked the wildflowers we observed and identified them. We kept a lined book with specimens and names and characteristics, and the girls became adept at identifying the local varieties of flowers.

But mostly what we liked was to pick berries. My girls were berry gourmands; they liked nothing better than to settle down in a large field of blueberries or before a large bush of raspberries and to eat themselves sick. I never knew either girl to throw in the towel before my patience gave out and I announced it was time to return home.

We could not leave, however, until we had filled a container with berries for their mother and their baby brothers. They were conscientious about this and often held me to the mark when I would have proved delinquent.

The house we had rented was spacious and occupied a headland overlooking the bay. The water glistened at full tide, and we could see out to the ocean where on the Fourth of July the local regatta dotted the horizon with its sails; but when the tide was low the water pulled back like a sheet to reveal the smudge beneath. Instead of the great granite boulders I was accustomed to, the littoral was mud-slicked, flecked with barnacled stones, and the water, frigid at best, was too shallow for swimming. Nonetheless it was Maine, and when you are tired of Maine you are tired of life. We were thirty and not at all tired.

To attain the shingle you had to snake down a sheer precipice which the children couldn't negotiate unaided, so it required both adults to reach the beach. I would help Barbara maneuver the descent in the morning and then would return at noon for the ascent. But the kids needed constant surveillance, and it was after this summer that Barbara bought our lacustrine cottage in Connecticut.

"I'll be damned if I'm going to spend another summer playing nursemaid to the children," she said. "I want someplace where I can just sit on the beach and let them *play*."

In her boredom she elaborated a game with Jenny called fish,

fish. They had been reading "The Fisherman and His Wife," about the man who could summon a magical fish out of the sea, and one afternoon Jenny determined to try this exploit herself.

"Fish, fish, come out of the sea," she chanted, standing in the salty mire and pointing at the shallows with her small finger.

Barbara was standing behind her, and as luck would have it, she had a small pebble in her hand; and when Jenny said, "Fish, fish, come out of the sea," Barbara tossed the pebble into the water, where it landed with a plop.

Jenny stood transfixed. We had a policy of strict probity with the children, and it never occurred to Jenny that her mother might be ribbing her. She was convinced she had summoned a fish out of the water.

"Mommy!" she said. "I think I called a fish out of the sea!"

"Try it again!" Barbara said.

"Fish, fish, come out of the sea," Jenny called in her high-pitched treble. Sure enough, there was another little plop, as if a fish had stuck its nose out of the water.

When I came down to gather my family at noon, Jenny ran to me wide-eyed.

"Daddy, Daddy—there *is* magic!"

"What are you talking about, darling?"

"I can call the *fish* out of the ocean!" She was entirely credulous, an instant apostate from my lessons of enlightenment.

I looked at Barbara and I saw the mischief in her eye, and then quietly, behind Jenny's back, she started to laugh.

We stayed for only three weeks that summer, but every day was an adventure. Mat contracted roseola infantum and we were up with him every night in the shivering night for an entire week. Some adventure! Yet it seems like an adventure now.

One night there was a blackout on the entire peninsula. A heavy storm was up, and the lines that lighted Harpswell must have gone, for there were no lights for the entire island.

"We have no candles," Barbara said. "We have a flashlight but no candles. You'd better drive down to Bailey's and get some."

"Why do we need candles?"

"This could last all night, David. Mat is sick. We need to be able to see."

I went outside and the wind was up. There wasn't a light anywhere. Rain was falling and the wind was thrashing in the trees.

I got into the car and I sat for a moment and felt the wind shake the entire automobile. Then I turned on the headlights and began to drive. As soon as I began to drive everything was fine.

The peninsula was a hole of darkness. The rain whipped about me and the trees roared. I drove slowly, my headlights hardly piercing the dark. I was the only car on the road.

When I reached Bailey's I bought the candles, and I bought some bread and milk, and I bought a Reese's peanut-butter cup for Barbara because Barbara loved Reese's peanut-butter cups.

"Some storm," Mr. Bailey said.

"Is it going to last long?"

"I couldn't say."

"What about the lights?"

"Welp, I couldn't say. Sometimes it goes for a couple of days like this."

I got back into the car. The sense of adventure had dissipated but I wanted to get back to my family. I drove slowly up the peninsula, mindful of falling trees.

Our house lay below me to the right, but when I looked there was nothing but impenetrable darkness. Again I was seized by fear. Everything I loved most in the world was concentrated somewhere below me in darkness. It seemed to me they could be swallowed in darkness. All that stood between them and darkness was a handful of candles that I was bringing home.

One day in bright sunlight we took the children to visit the Chartwell House. The house stood on a large hill and was still an operating farm worked in the manner of the previous century. It was a weekday and no one else was there and to my surprise the children loved it.

We visited the mansion and wandered through its rooms and afterward we went down through the fields to the barn. The farmers had been mowing and the hay lay in rows in the meadow. It was very hot and the snakes were out in the grass and I caught a garter snake for Barbara.

We went into the barn and it was cool inside and smelled of hay. A man was harnessing two large horses to a wagon.

"Howdy."

"Say hello, children. Say hello to the nice man."

Barbara took the girls over to see the horses and began talking to the man. I put the twins down on a gunnysack on the hay. They were sweating profusely and I wiped the perspiration from their small matted foreheads. Their little faces were red and tired.

Barbara came over to me.

"That man says he'll give the girls a hayride."

"Is that okay?"

"Of course. He does it every day."

"Whatever you say," I said.

"Look, Daddy, look!"

The girls waved as they rode out of the barn.

Barbara came and sat next to me. The twins had fallen asleep.

"Alone!" she said. "Can you believe it?"

We moved away from the sleeping children. Barbara lay down in the hay.

"Come," she said. I lay down next to her.

"How long has it been since we've been alone like this?" she asked.

"Two weeks. Three weeks."

"Two years," she said.

I undid the buttons on her blouse.

"You naughty boy."

I undid her bra. "Adam lost Paradise for this," I said.

She lay back in the hay and smiled. There was hay in her hair. Sunlight fell over her blond breasts and onto her large strawberry nipples.

"Do you think it was worth it?" she asked.

"Oh, yes," I said. "It was worth it."

John Herman grew up in New York City and received a Ph.D. in English from Berkeley. After living in Paris where he taught at the Sorbonne, he returned to New York and entered publishing. He has been an editor at Simon and Schuster, the editor-in-chief of Weidenfeld and Nicolson, and the editorial director of Ticknor & Fields. Married, with two daughters, he lives in New York City. *The Weight of Love* is his first novel.

JAMES WYATT

EBERRON

STORM
DRAGON

DRACONIC
PROPHECIES

BOOK ONE

STORM DRAGON
The Draconic Prophecies · Book 1

©2007 Wizards of the Coast, Inc.

Cover art by Raymond Swanland
First Printing: August 2007
Library of Congress Catalog Card Number: 2006937508

9 8 7 6 5 4 3 2 1

ISBN: 978-0-7869-4710-2
620-95948720-001-EN

U.S., CANADA,	EUROPEAN HEADQUARTERS
ASIA, PACIFIC, & LATIN AMERICA	Hasbro UK Ltd
Wizards of the Coast, Inc.	Caswell Way
P.O. Box 707	Newport, Gwent NP9 0YH
Renton, WA 98057-0707	GREAT BRITAIN
+1-800-324-6496	Save this address for your records.

Visit our web site at www.wizards.com

THE DRACONIC PROPHECIES
BY JAMES WYATT

Storm Dragon
Dragon Forge
Dragon War

THE DREAMING DARK
BY KEITH BAKER

The City of Towers
That Shattered Land
The Gates of Night

THE DRAGON BELOW
BY DON BASSINGTHWAITE

The Binding Stone
The Grieving Tree
The Killing Song

Dedicated to the memory of my father, David K. Wyatt
and to my son, Carter Wyatt.

PART
I

When the Eternal Day draws near,
when its moon shines full in the night,
and the day is at its brightest,
the Time of the Dragon Above begins.

Showers of light fall
upon the City of the Dead,
and the Storm Dragon emerges
after twice thirteen years.

Tumult and tribulation swirl in his wake:
The Blasphemer rises, the Pretender falls,
and armies march once more across the land.

CHAPTER
1

A distant rumble of thunder.

Thunder is his harbinger and lightning his spear.

Gaven stared up into the darkness of his cell, trying to clear his mind. Trying not to sleep.

He remembered perching on a cliff face, watching a storm blowing over the sea, brooding on those words. No. That had not been him. That was the other.

Wind is his steed and rain his cloak.

The words whispered in his mind in a voice that was not his. They filled him with foreboding. Echoes of a coming doom. His skin prickled. Another peal of thunder, more distant. Sleep closed in around him.

"No no no—no sleep," he murmured. He forced his eyes open.

The Storm Dragon rises.

"Make it stop make it stop make it stop." The prayer that had been his constant companion for twenty-seven years.

He remembered standing in the stone courtyard, head thrown back, arms spread to the sky, and singing to the storm. Exultation. Lightning danced along the high tower walls, and thunder beat a cadence for his song. Until the dwarf guards tackled him, wrestled him to the ground, and beat him into unconsciousness.

. . . the endless dark . . .

The darkness swallowed him, drawing him into nightmare.

He lay entombed in the depths of Khyber. Creeping things crawled and slithered over his body. The legs of a centipede undulated across his face, his lips. He tried to lift his head, to raise a hand, to scream. He couldn't move, couldn't draw breath.

A spear of blinding light shot up from the ground, impaling him before it broke through the ageless stone above him, soaring up and up until it reached the sky, stabbing through a storm cloud to touch the heights of Siberys.

Khyber and Siberys. The Dragon Below and the Dragon Above. A bridge of light joined heaven and earth.

. . . a ray of Khyber's sun erupts to form a bridge to the sky . . .

On every side, creatures began to move—writhing, snaking, quivering. Eyes stared at him from the darkness, dimly reflecting the light. Eyes that formed no intelligible faces, leering from quivering masses of amorphous flesh or glowering alone in bestial skulls. Mouths gaped at him, toothy maws biting, serrated sucking parts trying to bore into his flesh. Tentacles grabbed at him, coiling around his limbs and probing his head.

The Storm Dragon descends into the endless dark . . .

A tentacle worked its way into his mouth, smothering his scream.

* * * * *

The waves of the Lhazaar Sea crashed against the rocks at the base of the walls of the fortress. The walls rose hundreds of feet, unbroken by windows or balconies. Four towers stood at the corners of the fortress, and a watchtower at the center pierced the night sky. This was Dreadhold: the greatest prison of the Five Nations, kept by the dwarves of House Kundarak to hold the world's most dangerous criminals—the most bloodthirsty, sadistic, and evil villains to plague civilization. Its impregnable walls also contained those who posed a significant threat to the fragile peace—or to the interests of the dragonmarked houses—but who could not be executed.

Gaven slept fitfully in his cell, the roar of the breaking waves far below nothing more than a faint whisper through the stone. His eyes shot open, and he sat up with a gasp, staring around at the utter blackness of the tiny room. He threw off his threadbare wool blanket, oblivious to the chill, and groaned. Though he couldn't see them, he felt the walls closing him in, and the moist air stifled him. He staggered off his bunk and fell into the cell's iron door, fumbling around with his hands until he found a shutter at the level of his chest. He slid it open, and a few beams of light, gray and cold, spilled into the room, shining on the sheen of sweat that covered his face. With the light came the merest breath of fresher air, and he gulped it like a drowning man.

Gaven slumped backward against the door and sank to the floor. His thin shirt did little to shield him from the cold, but the iron felt good against his back. Amid the silence of the prison night, the door at his back and the stone floor beneath him reminded him where he was, which actually reassured him. His eyes darted around as if he were still in the throes of the nightmare that had awakened him. Everywhere his gaze fell, writing covered the walls and floor.

"Gaven!" A hoarse whisper came across the hall. "What did you see?"

"The hordes of the Soul Reaver," Gaven rambled, making no effort to lower his voice. "Wild. Gibbering. Swarming out of the earth." He pressed his palms to his eyes. "Brilliant light, spilling up from the depths—a ray of Khyber's sun, a bridge to the sky."

"What else, Gaven? Tell me what else you saw!"

The lingering memories of his nightmare started to fade, replaced by a memory of the old man's mouth pressed against the shutter in his own cell across the hall. Gaven had seen him—out in the yard, in the library, always under the watchful eyes of the dwarf guards—but the image of his mouth was fixed in Gaven's mind. Pale, cracked lips surrounded by white hair, a tongue occasionally darting out to moisten them. That image merged in Gaven's mind with the vision of the Soul Reaver's hordes—tentacles, eyes, gaping mouths—and sent a wave of nausea through him.

"Tell me what else," the old man rasped.

But the vision had faded. In its place came words, something he had read once—or had he? Gaven could no longer tell which memories were his.

"When the Eternal Day draws near," he recited, "when its moon shines full in the night, and the day is at its brightest, the Time of the Dragon Above begins. Showers of light fall upon the City of the Dead, and the Storm Dragon emerges after twice thirteen years."

"The Storm Dragon will come for us, Gaven."

Gaven's laugh was utterly without humor. He stumbled to his feet, bracing himself against the doorframe. Black hair fell over his face, but he didn't bother pushing it back. He reached into a pocket in his thin breeches and found the tiny steel stylus the guards had allowed him, then stood shakily on his bunk. He stretched as high as he could toward the ceiling, and scratched what words he could remember into the stone, describing the gibbering hordes, the brilliant bridge from earth to sky. The Time of the Dragon Above and the Time of the Dragon Below. Showers of light falling to earth, and brilliant beams of light rising from the earth.

He was still writing when the room shook, throwing him from his bunk and sending him sprawling to the floor. In the dim light spilling through the shutter in his door, he saw a crack form in the ceiling and begin to spread. The shaking resolved into a rhythmic pounding—something large smashing against the tower.

"Gaven!" the old man across the hall yelled, in a hoarse voice Gaven had never heard before. "They're coming! They're here for us!"

Gaven curled up on the floor of his cell and shielded his head with his arms as shards of masonry fell from the ceiling. After one more thundering crash, the tower shuddered, and the ceiling collapsed. Gaven rolled to his right, and a great stone slab just missed him. He looked up in terror and awe, and for the first time in twenty-six years, he saw the Ring of Siberys stretching across the sky.

* * * * *

Darraun stood and surveyed his handiwork. It had taken every ounce of power he had in him, but he'd managed to weaken the magic reinforcing the walls of the tower enough for Vaskar to break a great hole in the tower's ceiling. One great crack stretched down the wall of Gaven's cell and into the cell across the hallway. Haldren's. The way into Haldren's cell was probably too small for Cart, the warforged, but Senya was already making her way down into it. The lithe elf avoided heavy armor for exactly this reason—she liked being able to slip into tight spaces. She preferred tight-fitting clothes beneath her leather coat for a different reason. She and Haldren had been lovers before he ended up in Dreadhold, so it was fitting that her short, black curls and painted face should be his first glimpse of freedom.

Cart jumped into Gaven's cell and shifted the rubble around the cowering prisoner. The warforged moved the heavy stones with ease, metal cords and leather sinews shifting and pulsing beneath his armor plates as he worked.

Above Darraun, Vaskar circled through the sky, making short work of the manticore guardians as they swooped and dived around the dragon. Some fell victim to great blasts of lightning from his mouth, others he tore with his teeth and claws. One he slammed with his tail so hard that the beast crashed into the side of the watchtower. The three wyverns perched on the roof around Vaskar's hole watched the aerial battle with interest, as if they longed to join in, but they were well trained and wouldn't abandon their riders. They shifted their weight restlessly on their two clawed feet, flexed their leathery wings, and slowly pulsed the stingers on their tails, arched up over their backs like scorpions.

Everything seemed to be going according to plan.

Darraun jumped down into Gaven's cell. Huddled on the floor, Gaven looked up at the warforged, his eyes wide. Darraun remembered that the first warforged had been created only thirty-four years ago, and Gaven had been in Dreadhold for the last twenty-six. Had Gaven seen warforged during his imprisonment? Darraun somehow doubted that many warforged ended up in Dreadhold. So many people considered them less than human. It was hard to imagine that anyone would think a warforged criminal of any kind was too important to execute.

Darraun moved to the door and rested a hand on the cold iron. He closed his eyes in concentration, sensing and visualizing the magic that flowed through it, keeping it securely locked. He slid his hand slowly up, then down, looking for just the right place.

"Don't you want to be rescued?" Cart rumbled behind him, extending a three-fingered hand down to Gaven. "We're friends. We want to take you out of here."

Darraun smiled at the way the warforged mimicked the voice of a child coaxing a nervous or reluctant pet. Cart had made a serious study of human behavior, considering that he had spent most of his short existence as a soldier.

Darraun found what he was looking for—a knot of magic that would respond to the properly enchanted key. It was a simple matter to tangle that knot further, break some connections, cross some lines. It would take time to sort that out and get the door open, and by that time Gaven would be long gone.

Haldren's head appeared in the crack above him—Senya had evidently succeeded in getting him out. He was an old man, Darraun saw, his hair almost completely white, only a few streaks of coppery red suggesting what he'd looked like in his younger days. His skin had the pallor of prison, his hair was wild and his beard unruly, and his lips were cracked and dry. He still had his presence, though. As soon as he extracted himself from his cell he took command of the operation.

"Darraun," he barked, "help the warforged get our prophet out of there. We don't have much time."

We have time, Darraun thought, but he followed his orders.

Gaven had taken Cart's hand, but he still stared warily at the warforged. He seemed vaguely pathetic. He was a half-elf, so he didn't look old despite his sixty-odd years. His long hair was wild but still black as night, and he had no beard. He was still well muscled, his chest and arms displaying the strength that had been nearly legendary in his time. His dragonmark stretched across the skin of his neck and upper chest before disappearing beneath his threadbare shirt.

"Gaven," Darraun said, moving to stand beside him, "the guards will be here any moment. We have wyverns on the roof, ready to carry you away. You'll be safe with us."

Mumbling incoherently, Gaven tore his gaze from the warforged and shuffled forward. Too slow—Darraun could hear the guards shouting in the hall beyond the heavy iron door. He met Cart's eyes and nodded. The warforged stooped over, put one arm around Gaven's legs, and lifted the prisoner to his shoulder. Gaven went limp, without a sound of protest or a struggle. Perching on the fallen stone slab, Cart clambered out of the cell and onto the roof.

Above him, Darraun heard Haldren's voice. "You see, Gaven," he said, "I told you he would come for us. Behold the Storm Dragon!"

If Gaven made any response, Darraun couldn't hear it. He looked around the shambles of the cell. Writing was scratched into almost every possible surface. He picked up a shard of stone at random from the wreckage strewn across the floor and turned it over in his hands, straining to read the faint, tiny scratches on what had been part of Gaven's cell wall.

. . . recapitulates the serpents' sacrifice, binding the servant anew so the master cannot break free.

Darraun raised one thin eyebrow and shoved the masonry shard into a pocket of his leather coat.

"Darraun!" Haldren roared above him. "We fly!"

As he scrambled back up onto the roof, Darraun heard shouts through the door. The guards had come and found their own door locked to them. He smiled, but he also slid a wand from his coat pocket as he vaulted into the saddle of his wyvern, eyeing the crack leading into Haldren's cell. Vaskar had already taken to the air with Haldren on his back, and Senya's wyvern lifted off behind it. Cart had put Gaven on his own mount, and the man's arms were wrapped around the thick chest of the warforged.

As Cart's wyvern lifted into the air, Darraun heard Gaven mutter, ". . . its moon shines full in the night." Then Darraun followed.

*   *   *   *   *

Gaven looked down in front of the wyvern's strong wings, and a thrill went down his spine. Below them, the Lhazaar Sea churned violently as dark clouds and gusting winds rolled in across the eastern ocean. Gaven clung tighter to the adamantine-plated body of the warforged, who had introduced himself as Cart, back in the cell. He forced his attention off the ocean below and onto Cart. He had seen warforged before, but only from a distance. The plates looked like heavy armor. Subtle engraving decorated the edges, but Gaven could tell from the way the plates moved along with the slightest shift in Cart's body that they were attached, somehow, to the body underneath, which seemed to be made of wood, fibrous bundles, perhaps some stone, and other kinds of metal. The strangest thing, to Gaven's mind, was that Cart was undeniably alive, not like some automaton made for the battlefield. He saw cords and bundles pulsing between the plates, and the warforged moved constantly just like a living person—the smallest shifts of posture, turns of his head, fidgets. Gaven had the clear sense that a sword cut would make Cart bleed, and a blow to just the right place could stop that ceaseless motion forever.

He turned his head to get a better look at the dragon. The Storm Dragon, Haldren had said. "The Storm Dragon emerges after twice thirteen years," Gaven whispered. "Where did you come from, Storm Dragon? You plan to walk in the paths? It's a long road ahead of you."

The warforged turned his head, trying to see Gaven over his shoulder or perhaps hear his mutterings better. Gaven closed his eyes, pretending to sleep. He felt the warforged shift, turning back to watch where he was flying.

Falling—

Gaven started awake, still safe in the saddle though his arms had slipped from the warforged's chest. He blinked, trying to clear his mind from his nightmare—a strange light spilling up out of the earth, gleaming on bronze scales.

CHAPTER
2

The Lord Warden scowled, his rage written plain across his face. Of course, Bordan thought—so brazen an attack on Dreadhold was unheard of, even during the chaos of the Last War. The fact that the dragon had been able to penetrate the tower walls was astonishing. Two prisoners escaping before the guards could respond . . . well, that was simply embarrassing.

Bordan settled back in his chair and stroked his neat beard, watching the other two people in the briefing. One was a Sentinel Marshal, who had introduced himself as Evlan d'Deneith. He was frowning, which Bordan could tell had become a habitual expression for him. Evlan wore his age and his station well. The gray at his temples made him look distinguished, and he had the body of a much younger man beneath his mithral mail and black surcoat. Above the collar of his mail on his neck, the Mark of Sentinel was just visible, an abstract tracing of color on his skin that resembled the head of a dragon with long spines trailing behind the neck. Like Bordan's own dragonmark, Evlan's was an intricate weaving of blue—more a part of his skin than a tattoo, and far more elaborate than any birthmark. The skin that bore the mark was slightly raised, and Bordan knew that the 'mark gave Evlan powers similar to those of a wizard. The bodyguards of House Deneith used the powers of the Mark of Sentinel to protect their charges from harm, and the Sentinel Marshals used the same powers to protect themselves as they pursued dangerous criminals across Khorvaire.

Seated beside Evlan was another dwarf of House Kundarak, much calmer than the blustering warden. The warden had introduced her as Ossa d'Kundarak. She had not yet spoken a word. A scarlet shirt of fine silk stood out against her black skin. She sat with her hands folded on her lap, studying Bordan as carefully as Bordan examined her. Bordan had heard that House Kundarak maintained a small force of soldier-assassins called the Manticore's Tail—or *Ghorad'din* in the Dwarven language—and he suspected Ossa represented that organization. Ossa's dragonmark wasn't visible, but her surname indicated that she carried the Mark of Warding, which the heirs of House Kundarak used to protect banks and vaults in every city of Khorvaire, as well as the prison of Dreadhold.

The Lord Warden, Zaxon d'Kundarak, wore his red-brown beard long, with braids hanging down on either side of his mouth. He was clearly struggling to keep his emotions under control, and that spoke volumes. For a dwarf nicknamed "the Old Rock," any trace of emotion that leaked onto his face demonstrated the true extent of his fury. The clearest sign of his emotional state was an angry flush of red on his bald pate, and he compulsively ran his hands across the top of his head as if trying to hide it. Each time he did, Evlan could see the tracery of the Mark of Warding across the back of his left hand, resembling rays of light emanating from a shape that some thought resembled an eye and others identified as a coiled dragon.

"Where's the damned elf?" the Lord Warden said, starting to pace again. "I have no intention of giving this briefing twice."

"That won't be necessary, Lord Warden." The elf slipped through the door, his movements making no sound, his black garb seeming to meld with the shadows. "I am sorry to have kept you waiting," he said. "I am Phaine d'Thuranni." He sat in the empty chair and did not move again, except to let his gaze rest on each of the others in the room. His dragonmark, the angular Mark of Shadow, started on his cheek and ran down his neck. Deception and illusion were the powers of the Mark of Shadow, as well as espionage.

"Glad you could join us, Thuranni," the Lord Warden said. He swept his gaze across the four dragonmark heirs. "I am grateful to your houses for offering your services to help us handle this . . . situation."

The Lord Warden's eyes lingered on Ossa as he said this; the honor of House Kundarak would recover more quickly from this blow if a Kundarak managed to retrieve the fugitives. Dreadhold was operated by House Kundarak, whose Mark of Warding and expertise with security made it well suited to keeping prisoners confined and the prison secure. But all the dragonmarked houses had an interest in the great prison, since it held many of their most dangerous secrets.

"The first prisoner is Haldren ir'Brassek, a noble of Aundair." Speaking seemed to help the Lord Warden bring his emotions back under control, and his face slowly set into a stony mask. "He was a general during the war—a hero in some circles and a villain in others. He recaptured the city of Cragwar twice, but he was also responsible for the massacres of civilians at Twilight Creek and Telthun. He led troop movements in violation of the Treaty of Thronehold before he was finally captured and brought to trial for his war crimes. He was sentenced to Dreadhold rather than face execution because many officers in Aundair's military remain loyal to him, and Aundair feared what would happen if Haldren were martyred almost as much as they feared his escape. I have already received communication from Queen Aurala to the effect that Aundair will be most distressed if ir'Brassek returns to his homeland." A thick hand ran over his bald head again, and the Lord Warden took a deep breath, staring at the floor.

"I am not familiar with the ir'Brassek family," Evlan said.

"It was once a prominent line in Aundair," the Lord Warden said, "but it has diminished. The fugitive has a few cousins, I believe, who maintain the appearance of luxury despite the loss of their ancestral holdings. The general sense in Aundair's military was that ir'Brassek wanted to restore his family name to prominence. He had some success in that regard, but obviously took it too far. I think it unlikely that he will make contact with the cousins."

"And the other prisoner?" Bordan asked.

"Gaven, formerly of House Lyrandar. A strange case. He worked for his house during the war, prospecting for Khyber dragonshards for use in their galleons. All that time crawling around the depths of Khyber must've driven him mad." The Lord Warden glanced at Phaine. "House Phiarlan claims he was involved in the Paelion affair."

Bordan nodded. The Paelion family had been a part of House Phiarlan, an elf house that bore the Mark of Shadow. Phaine's house, Thuranni, had also been one of the Phiarlan families. Some thirty years ago, the leader of the Thurannis had led his family in a brutal slaughter of the Paelions, claiming to have evidence that the Paelions plotted against the rest of the dragonmarked houses. If Gaven had been involved, then he was part of the reason that House Thuranni was no longer a part of House Phiarlan.

"During his trial," the Lord Warden continued, "Gaven swung between incoherent muttering and murderous rage. He's a strong man, and it was difficult to keep him restrained long enough to pass judgment. There was a suggestion that he was possessed, but an exorcist examined him and found no evidence of that. He was convicted, and House Lyrandar declared him excoriate."

That explains the "formerly," Bordan thought. Gaven wouldn't be recognized as a Lyrandar any more, and other members of the family would be forbidden to give him aid. That would make him easier to find.

"Why Dreadhold?" Bordan asked. "Why not execute him?"

"Two reasons," Zaxon said. "His betrothed made a rather impassioned plea for his life, asking that he be imprisoned in case some day he recovered his senses. Also, his house expressed an interest in the content of his lunatic ravings and requested that he be kept alive. When they learned that he was writing in his cell, they requested a report of what he wrote. I don't know whether they considered it useful or not."

"What did he rave about?"

"They say he always had an interest in the Prophecy of the dragons, and it's all he's talked about for the last twenty-six years. Half his speech is prophetic mutterings—perhaps it makes sense to him, but to everyone else it's nonsense. Just about every inch of wall and floor in his cell was covered with bits and pieces of the Prophecy." Bordan saw Phaine shift slightly—the first disruption of his unnatural stillness.

"How did he write them?" Evlan asked.

"We gave him a small metal stylus so he could scratch his writings on the walls." The Lord Warden's eyebrows bristled as he glared at Evlan. "Before that, he demonstrated that he would resort to writing in blood given no other means. In twenty-six years, he never used the stylus for anything but scrawling on his walls, and we're quite confident that it had nothing to do with his escape."

"I assume that you kept a copy of all information sent to House Lyrandar," Bordan said. "I would like to see it."

The Lord Warden nodded. "I think you're wasting your time. It's nonsense, and there's a great deal of it. But I'll let you sort it out."

"Is he marked?" Evlan asked.

"Ah," Zaxon said, and the hand went over the bald head again. Bordan's eyes narrowed. "He failed the Test of Siberys in his youth, and he did not carry a dragonmark before his imprisonment. However, he manifested a Siberys mark five years ago."

Bordan saw the surprise register on the other three faces in the small room. The Siberys Mark of Storm meant that Gaven had significant power—power that House Lyrandar would much rather have under its control than loose in the world. Bordan smiled behind his folded hands. That might make the chase more interesting.

Ossa changed the subject, speaking for the first time. "He was to be married." Her voice was gruff, and she tugged at one of her thick braids as she spoke.

"Yes," the Lord Warden said. "Rienne ir'Alastra was his betrothed. She was actually the first to suggest that he was possessed, and she helped the Sentinel Marshals find him and bring him into custody." He nodded at Evlan, acknowledging his order's role in Gaven's arrest.

"Did she marry someone else?" Bordan asked.

Zaxon was starting to look exasperated. "I have no further information about her, as she is not and never has been a prisoner of House Kundarak.

Now, our guards have reported communication between ir'Brassek and Gaven—their cells were across the hall from each other. As far as we know, these conversations were typical for Gaven: he'd report his dreams or recite bits of the Prophecy, but ir'Brassek seemed eager to hear all that."

"Is it possible they used a code to plan the escape?" Evlan said.

"Anything is possible," the Lord Warden said, "but I believe it highly unlikely. The conversations always occurred in the middle of the night and seemed to be precipitated by Gaven starting from sleep, awakened by a dream. After telling ir'Brassek about the dream, Gaven would write it down. It's all recorded on the walls of his cell."

"They weren't confined to their cells at all times, were they?" Bordan asked.

"Of course not. Gaven occasionally had to be confined for long stretches, when he'd go into a violent phase. But ir'Brassek wasn't considered particularly dangerous or an escape risk. They both worked in the mines. They walked the courtyard when Gaven was able. And they had access to the library."

Evlan leaned forward in his chair. "Did they speak together at those times?"

"Gaven rarely spoke at all outside his cell, except to rant. Ir'Brassek approached him a few times, but Gaven either ignored him or flew into a rage, and he gave up after a while. Gaven never read, barely walked, and worked only because we forced him to."

"He was here a long time," Bordan said.

"Twenty-six years, yes."

"Was he any different before his mark appeared?"

"Not at all."

"Was there any change in him after Haldren arrived?"

The Lord Warden shook his head. "None. He gives the sense that he's not quite present, like his mind's off in the Realm of Madness while his body's trapped here."

"What are we up against, Lord Warden?" Evlan asked. "Besides the Siberys mark, what can we expect of these two?"

"Haldren ir'Brassek is a sorcerer, hence his lodging in the Spellward Tower. He likes fire, burning things down. He could, of course, be anywhere by now." A trace of Zaxon's seething rage returned to his face.

"And the Lyrandar?" Phaine said.

"Gaven no longer has the privilege of carrying the name of his house. He is . . . accomplished. He had a reputation for great physical strength, perhaps a result of clambering around in the caves of Khyber for years. He favors a greatsword in combat, taking advantage of that strength. And he also has some facility with magic beyond what his dragonmark grants him. Although the full extent of the power of his dragonmark has never been seen."

"Was there any manifestation when the mark first appeared?" Bordan asked.

"Yes," Zaxon admitted. "We had to move all prisoners and guards underground for an hour to wait out the storm."

Bordan enjoyed watching the others' eyebrows rise. He got to his feet.

"Lord Warden, House Tharashk thanks you for your confidence in us and the detailed information you have provided. On the honor of my house, I swear that I will not rest until these two prisoners are safely returned to your custody."

The others scrambled to their feet as well. "Lord Warden," Evlan d'Deneith blurted, "House Deneith promises a tireless effort to recover these fugitives. I will personally select a team of the finest Sentinel Marshals to assist me in bringing them to justice." He gave a small bow.

Phaine d'Thuranni was the next to speak, in his whispery voice. "The finest of House Thuranni are also at your service, Lord Warden."

"For the honor of House Kundarak," Ossa d'Kundarak said, "the Ghorad'din will hunt them to the depths of Khyber."

The Lord Warden stared at them. Bordan hid a smirk behind his hand as the Old Rock searched for a response to all these oaths and boasts. Finally, his eyebrows bristling again, he blurted, "Well, what are you waiting for? They're probably in the Demon Wastes by now!"

Bordan was the first out the door.

* * * * *

Bordan paced the courtyard of Dreadhold, ignoring the drizzle of rain that heralded a larger storm. Stark stone walls loomed over him, windowless and forbidding. Stout dwarf guards watched him from ledges on all sides, crossbows in their hands and axes at their belts. One archway led back into the prison interior, blocked by a heavy portcullis backed by iron-banded doors. When he was ready to leave, he could signal to the guards, and the gate would open. He tried to imagine being a prisoner—to spend all his days surrounded by those walls, those watchful guards, iron and stone on every side. Even the sky was granite.

Shaking his head to dispel those thoughts, he replayed the Lord Warden's briefing in his mind, sifting his memory for details that might be important in his coming search. He had a pretty good idea of what the others would do. Evlan would assemble a troop of Sentinel Marshals that would march across Khorvaire like overblown city guards. They'd probably question

Gaven's family, find the Aundairian officers loyal to Haldren, follow up on people mentioned in the briefing. Phaine would pull together a small team of Thuranni elves more suited to assassination than investigation. They would probably pick up the trail first, and it might just be a question of whether the fugitives stayed alive until their hunters could return them to Dreadhold. Bordan wasn't sure about the other dwarf, Ossa. He didn't know much about the Ghorad'din, but he thought it was more of a covert military force than a group of trained inquisitives. It was possible that they were brought in just to make sure House Kundarak had a hand in retrieving the prisoners that had been in its care, but Bordan had no real reason to doubt their effectiveness. He just wished he had a better idea how they would go about the task.

For his part, he would start with the documents Zaxon had promised—copies of the reports sent to House Lyrandar describing Gaven's ravings.

CHAPTER
3

G aven stared at the emerald orbs of the dragon's eyes, overwhelmed at the size and majesty of the great bronze beast. Behind those eyes, bony ridges swept back to form a crest around the back of his head, crowned with a pair of curving horns. Smaller horns jutted out along the edge of the crest, at the lower joint of his jaw, and on the chin of his beaked snout. Thick scales overlapped to form an armored plating over the front of his neck and his belly, while smaller interlaced scales covered the rest of his body. Above the muscles of his shoulders, a pair of membranous wings stretched upward and fanned the sea air. Spiked frills adorned the back of his neck down to his wings, stretched between his forelimbs and his flanks, and extended up from his long, heavy tail. Vaskar was larger than any creature Gaven had ever seen. Gaven focused on the emerald eyes and tried to listen to the words coming from the dragon's mouth.

"Listen to me, Gaven." The dragon's voice was surprisingly soft, coming from such a large creature, and it was as clear and low as the ringing of a huge bronze gong. "The Prophecy is finding its fulfillment. The Storm Dragon is ready to claim what has been set aside for him. But you have a part to play. You must—"

Haldren cut the dragon off. "We need your help, Gaven."

Vaskar drew his head back on his long neck, lifting it high. Clearly, the dragon would not lower himself to asking for help, but Haldren had no such qualms.

"You know the Prophecy better than any dragon or mortal alive." Haldren leaned forward, letting the light of the campfire dance on his face. "I've been listening to you for three years, and it's clear I haven't heard a tenth of what you know about the Prophecy. Vaskar has been studying it in Argonnessen for six human lifetimes, and there are gaps in his understanding—gaps only you can fill. Please, Gaven—please help us."

Vaskar snorted, and a bright yellow spark flared at his nostrils. Gaven started, staring up at the dragon. The Storm Dragon, he thought. He wants the Prophecy, so he can be the Storm Dragon.

Gaven looked around their little camp. They had flown through the night, and the first glow of dawn was beginning to spread across the edge of the sea to the east. The rocky cliffs of Cape Far loomed dark in the west, blocking his view of the Ring of Siberys. Cart had built a small campfire on the rocky beach between the cliffs and the sea, and Darraun was cooking some fish that he and the warforged had caught. Gaven had not been starving in Dreadhold, but the fish smelled better than anything he'd tasted in over twenty years.

He was free! The thought struck him for the first time. The dawn sky, the dancing flames, the cooking fish—he had not seen and smelled and felt these things in years. He could walk where he pleased, and no one would herd him back to his cell when the sun set. He could—he looked up at the slowly brightening sky—he could bask in a storm, and no one would wrestle him to the ground and shove him back into confinement. A gust of wind brought a salt smell off the sea, and Gaven had a sudden longing to sail again.

"Gaven?"

He turned his gaze back to Haldren. The elf woman had washed and cut the old man's hair and beard, and he'd put on a new set of clothes—tall boots, warm breeches, a shirt with just a hint of a frill at the collar, a short jacket, and a heavy traveling cloak. He looked twenty years younger. His pale blue eyes were striking, almost hypnotic. Compelling. Gaven found himself nodding.

"What . . . what do you need to know?"

Haldren sat up and flashed a triumphant smile at Vaskar.

The dragon lowered his head to speak to Gaven again. "The Time of the Dragon Above, Gaven," he said. "It is beginning. The sun is approaching the center, spring is dawning, and I saw the moon of the Eternal Day waxing in the sky. Irian draws near, and the Storm Dragon is rising. Tell me what you know about the Time of the Dragon Above."

Gaven recited the words he had spoken to Haldren earlier that night, back in Dreadhold. "When the Eternal Day draws near, when its moon shines full in the night, and the day is at its brightest, the Time of the Dragon Above begins. Showers of light fall upon the City of the Dead, and the Storm Dragon emerges after twice thirteen years."

"Yes," Vaskar hissed, "for two cycles of thirteen years I have been withdrawn from the world, and now I have emerged."

The blond man, Darraun, approached with a wooden plate loaded with fish and some dry bread. He handed it to Gaven. Gaven took a piece of fish in his fingers and put it in his mouth. It tasted even better than it smelled, and he ate with relish.

"What else, Gaven?" Haldren asked. "What is to happen during the Time of the Dragon Above?"

Gaven closed his eyes again and lost himself in a sea of memories—words mingled with images that had haunted his dreams. What is to happen? he thought. So very much. Vaskar wanted to be the Storm Dragon.

One memory surfaced in his mind: his hand traced twisting Draconic letters carved into stone. Was it his hand? Had he been there, or was it the other? Or was this a dream, a figment, and not a memory at all? He opened his eyes and stared at the crackling fire. This is what's real, he thought. This is what's now.

Still staring into the flames, he read the words from the carving in his memory, if the memory was his: "In the Time of the Dragon Above, Siberys turns night into day. Showers of light fall from the sky. The Eye of Siberys falls near the City of the Dead."

Vaskar glanced up at the Ring of Siberys, shining brightly in the night sky. "The City of the Dead," he murmured. "In Aerenal."

Haldren looked at Vaskar, then back at Gaven. "The Eye of Siberys, Gaven," Haldren said, leaning toward him again. "What else can you tell us of the Eye of Siberys?"

New words sprang to his mind almost unbidden. These he had read by firelight—torchlight—and he thought he remembered Rienne at his side as he read them. He couldn't see her, but he could feel her beside him, and it made his heart ache even as rage surged in it. He spat the words out of his mouth—they tasted bitter. "The Eye of Siberys lifts the Sky Caves of Thieren Kor from the land of desolation under the dark of the great moon, and the Storm Dragon walks the paths of the first of sixteen."

"The Sky Caves of Thieren Kor!" Haldren said, the excitement in his voice undisguised. "They are in the 'land of desolation,' Gaven? The Mournland, do you think?"

A nightmare. Gaven remembered waking up in Dreadhold, stumbling to the door, and whispering to Haldren how he had staggered across a land where nothing lived. And then he'd found words to anchor the vision, words with their cold solidity, only hinting at the terror of his dream. He repeated the words, savoring them as a shield from the nightmare. "Desolation spreads over that land like a wildfire, like a plague, and Eberron bears the scar of it for thirteen cycles of the Battleground."

Haldren furrowed his brow and looked to Vaskar.

"Shavarath, the Battleground, draws near to us every thirty-six years—that is its cycle," the dragon explained. "So thirteen cycles of the Battleground would be four hundred and sixty-eight years." He did not pause to perform the calculation.

"Four hundred and sixty-eight years?" Haldren repeated, ignoring the food that Darraun had set before him. "That is how long the Mournland will persist?"

The dragon snorted softly. *If* those words refer to the Mournland."

"It seems the most likely candidate," Haldren said.

"One can never be certain," Vaskar responded. "Your century of war is not the only desolation this world has known. You humans are too quick to assume everything in the Prophecy applies to your works. Some dragons would argue that the Prophecy doesn't even acknowledge your existence, though of course I think they are mistaken. Nevertheless, we will seek the Sky Caves in the Mournland."

Gaven watched as Haldren and Vaskar dissected the Prophecy, ignoring him now. He was glad for the respite from questions. He stared at the dawn as it reddened the sky.

"But first we need the Eye of Siberys," Vaskar rumbled. He looked at Gaven again. "The City of the Dead in Aerenal, when Siberys turns night into day." He turned his beaked snout toward the sky.

Another image flashed in Gaven's memory, another dream—yellow crystal pulsing with veins of golden light, carved to a point and bound to a blackened branch, plunging into a body that was shadow given twisting form. He shuddered.

"What is it, Gaven?" Haldren had seen the shudder. "What did you see?"

"The Eye of Siberys," Gaven said. "A dragonshard, a huge one, the size of my hand. Formed into a weapon, a spearhead." He shook his head, trying to dispel the image from his mind.

Haldren looked up at Vaskar, who lowered his head close to Gaven again.

"A weapon?" the dragon said. "To be used against what foe?"

The endless dark, Gaven thought, where *he* waits. "The Soul Reaver."

A look of triumph flashed onto Haldren's face, and Gaven suddenly understood what was happening. The dragon knew a great deal about the Prophecy already, and he wasn't sure Gaven was worth the trouble. Haldren had probably used Gaven as a bargaining chip in negotiating his own rescue. And Gaven had just proven his worth, providing their first glimpse of a real hope of victory. Probably they knew the Storm Dragon would have to face the Soul Reaver, but this was the first they had heard of a way to win that fight.

The part of his mind that had kept him alive in Dreadhold reminded him to dole out such valuable insights slowly, to keep himself useful as long as possible.

"So the Eye of Siberys will raise the Sky Caves of Thieren Kor under the dark of the great moon," Vaskar said. "And it will serve as a weapon against the Soul Reaver." His eyes narrowed. "Is there anything else?"

Gaven didn't want to remember any more. He wanted to taste the smoke in the air, savor the fish Darraun had cooked, smell the sea and its freedom, watch the sunrise. Those things were real and present, not vague memories that might not even belong to him. He shook his head.

"That's enough for now, Gaven," Haldren said. "You've already helped us a great deal."

Gaven stared at the line of blood spreading across the horizon, trying to see nothing more than a beautiful sunrise.

* * * * *

"What is he?" Senya asked, staring at Gaven. She picked at her fish with her fingers, gingerly placing a small piece in her mouth and sucking the oils off her fingertips.

Darraun watched her with amusement, not sure how to answer her question. "Just a man," he said.

"How does he know so much about the Prophecy?"

I wish I knew, Darraun thought. But Senya didn't need to know the extent of his curiosity. "Vaskar thinks he learned it from another dragon."

"But why would a dragon teach him?" She tried to take a bite of the hard bread, but couldn't find a way to do it delicately. She balanced the plate on her knees and used both hands to break the bread into smaller pieces.

Why, indeed? Darraun shrugged, wanting to drop the conversation. To his relief, the warforged lumbered over to stand beside them. "Hello, Cart."

"Darraun, Senya," Cart said. "How's the fish?"

"Delicious," Senya said, looking back at Darraun as she said it. "Best I've ever had on the road."

"Thank you," Darraun said with a small bow of his head. "I take pride in my cooking."

"I hope your wands and scrolls will be as useful when we start fighting," she said, her face clearly indicating that she doubted they would be.

Cart rubbed his chin, a mannerism he'd certainly learned from a human sergeant during the war. "Are we spending the night here, do you know?" he said. "The general didn't tell me to set up the tents, but if we're camping I want to do it before it gets any darker."

Darraun looked back over at Gaven, Haldren, and the dragon. "I suspect we'll be moving on tonight," he said. "Forty miles is still too close to Dreadhold for anyone's taste, I expect."

Senya grimaced, looking over her shoulder at the wyverns. "I don't think I can begin to say how much I dislike those things. I feel like the stinger could stick down into my back at any second."

"It certainly could," Darraun said. "I hate the way they bounce with every flap of their wings. But I have a feeling we won't be flying anymore tonight."

"What?" Senya said. "You just said—"

"I said we'd be moving on. Not flying."

*   *   *   *   *

Gaven enjoyed a respite from questions as Haldren ate and conferred quietly with Vaskar. He took that opportunity to look around this strange group, his new companions. He'd had plenty of time to examine Cart as they rode their wyvern to this shore, and he knew Haldren's appearance well from Dreadhold, though the cleaned-up, well-dressed version beside the dragon bore little resemblance to the disheveled character he remembered from their neighboring cells.

Darraun was the blond man who had helped Cart get him out of his cell. Gaven had seen the man work some magic with his cell door, which probably meant he was an artificer, skilled with the magic of items and constructs. Scrolls and wands protruded from the pouch at the man's belt, confirming that impression. His fair hair was short and fine, and he had a day's growth of beard. His skin was tan from travel, and his cloak carried the dust of many roads. He wore a hardened leather cuirass and carried a large metal mace with a flanged head. Still, something about the way Darraun carried himself made Gaven suspect that he would not be in the forefront of any battles.

The elf woman—he'd heard Haldren call her Senya—was about as different from Rienne as Gaven could imagine a woman being. Her black hair was curly and cut short, in contrast to the way Rienne's flowed like silk. Senya's skin was pale despite all her travels outdoors, where Rienne's was a rich mahogany. The lids of Senya's eyes were heavy and tinted with a bluish black powder, and her full lips were painted red. She wore a leather coat that hugged her chest before flaring out around her legs. It was cut to reveal more of her throat and breastbone than was probably safe. He noted an amulet at her throat, shaped like a shield and studded with adamantine, that probably more than made up in magic for what her coat lacked in protective value. She wore soft leather leggings and boots that rose to her knees. The heels of her boots made them better suited to a social function in Fairhaven than walking on the rocky shore of the Lhazaar Sea.

Finished with his meal, Haldren got to his feet and lifted a hand to the others. They rose at his summons and walked quickly over to where Gaven sat studying them.

"My dear friends," Haldren said, taking Senya's slender hand and including the warforged with a smile, "and more recent acquaintances," he added with a gracious nod to Darraun and then Gaven, "this day you have done a great service to Aundair and, indeed, to the world. And, of course, you have done a great favor to me, in liberating me from Dreadhold, the prison they said was impregnable."

Haldren laughed, and Senya laughed with him. Gaven glanced at the others, but kept his attention on Haldren.

Vaskar wants to be the Storm Dragon, Gaven thought. Vaskar thinks that's a service to the world. He noticed that Darraun was staring at him. The artificer had barely smiled at Haldren's humor. Gaven decided to ignore the stare and continue watching Haldren.

"Vaskar and I have discussed the Prophecy with Gaven," Haldren continued. "We have learned much that is useful, and confirmed much that we already knew. We believe that Vaskar was correct, that the Time of the Dragon Above has begun, and the Eye of Siberys will soon fall from the sky."

He paused for dramatic effect, clearly enjoying the attention of his companions. This was a man used to addressing crowds, Gaven realized, and used to having his pronouncements greeted with cheers.

"And so we are going to Aerenal," Haldren announced.

"Aerenal?" the elf blurted. "That'll take weeks!"

"We will not be riding, Senya," Haldren said. "My magic will transport us now. We'll rest this morning at an inn in Whitecliff, in Q'barra, do some business in the city, and tomorrow head on to Aerenal."

"How soon do we depart, Lord General?" Cart asked.

"Immediately," Haldren said. "Grab your pack and we will be on our way."

"Should I clean up the campsite, remove our trail?" the warforged said.

"No. Let them find it. They'll assume we're still on the wing and look for us tomorrow within fifty miles of this site." Haldren grinned. "And we will be over a thousand miles away."

Senya left the cluster and retrieved her pack. Cart followed her example, while Darraun quickly rinsed an iron cooking pan in the surf. In a moment's time, they returned and stood around Haldren, ready for him to work his magic.

Before he did, he addressed the group again. "I neglected to mention, my friends, that Vaskar will not be accompanying us to Aerenal. The elves hold an ancient grudge against dragonkind, and Vaskar would draw too much attention to our mission there. He will rejoin us later. Vaskar," he said to the dragon, "thank you for your part in freeing me—and Gaven. Without you we would still be in Dreadhold."

The dragon nodded almost imperceptibly, then glided over to the wyverns, which shifted nervously at his approach.

"Please join hands," Haldren said, seizing Gaven's left hand in his right and pulling him to his feet. Darraun took Gaven's right hand and Cart's left, and Senya connected Cart back to Haldren. With a smile around the little circle, Haldren began a brief incantation.

The last thing Gaven saw was Vaskar closing his jaws on the neck of a wyvern and tearing out its throat.

CHAPTER
4

An instant of blackness laced with silver, then green, then they stood in a lush forest alive with the droning of insects, the songs of birds, and the screeches of monkeys greeting the dawn. In sharp contrast to the windswept coast they'd just left, the air was warm and heavy with humidity. The ground rose sharply in one direction, and peering through the broad leaves of the forest, Gaven caught a glimpse of white-capped mountains in the distance.

Haldren looked quickly around the little circle, then dropped Gaven's hand.

"Welcome to Q'barra," he said with a broad smile. "Whitecliff should be a short walk." He glanced around to get his bearings, then waved his hand at a thinner patch of forest. "Downhill."

"What are the chances someone will be looking for us there?" Senya asked. "Looking for you, I mean."

"It's almost inconceivable," Haldren said. "They'll be expecting us much closer to Dreadhold."

"They know you're a sorcerer," Darraun said.

"True, but they can't search a thousand-mile radius."

"How many major settlements are there within a thousand miles of Dreadhold?" Senya said. "It seems likely they could narrow that search quite a bit."

"Most of eastern Karrnath would have been in my reach. They don't know our destination, so they have little reason to look in Q'barra."

"Except that it's been a haven for refugees and fugitives for seventy years," Darraun said, frowning.

"True enough," Haldren said. Gaven could see that he didn't like having his pronouncements questioned, but he remained gracious. "We will exercise caution as we approach the town. They know what Gaven and I look like, of course, but they don't know any of you. They'll be looking for a dragon and people on wyverns. We have no dragon and no wyverns, so I do not anticipate any difficulty."

The memory of Vaskar killing one of the wyverns flashed in Gaven's mind.

Haldren started walking, ending the discussion by turning his back on Darraun—rather pointedly, Gaven thought. Senya followed without a moment's hesitation, and Darraun trailed after. Cart lingered by Gaven.

"So you're my faithful hound," Gaven said to the warforged.

"Hound?"

"It's your job to keep an eye on me, make sure I stay with the group?"

"It's my job to keep an eye on everyone," Cart said with a shrug. Gaven was struck at how human the warforged managed to seem, despite a face that was essentially a featureless plate of metal with a hinged jaw. Gaven nodded, and they walked shoulder to shoulder behind Darraun.

* * * * *

For all the concerns Senya and Darraun had expressed, the group walked out of the jungle and into Whitecliff with little difficulty. Apparently this frontier town was accustomed to people appearing out of the forest and strolling into town. Had they been lizardfolk of the sort that infested the jungle, Gaven was sure they would have been given a very different reception. A wall of white stone surrounded the town, presumably quarried from the cliffs of the Endworld Mountains just to the north and west that gave the town its name. The guards at the gate wore coats of metal scales and bristled with weapons. Each one carried a halberd and wore a sword, a dagger, and a crossbow. The sentries asked a few questions about their business and the length of their stay, but Haldren handled them with ease.

After a quarter-century in Dreadhold, Gaven felt overwhelmed by this first taste of civilization. The morning streets, lined with buildings made of the same chalky stone as the town's walls, were crowded with people—thronging the marketplace, visiting the temples, opening shops for the day's business. Considering the town's location near the eastern edge of nowhere, it seemed awfully crowded to Gaven. Any one of these hundreds of faces could have been someone looking for them—a Sentinel Marshal or a Tharashk inquisitive. The dwarves made Gaven most nervous, reminding him of his jailers and making him wonder how many had ties to House Kundarak. The freedom he had tasted and savored at the campfire began to sour in his mouth. Looking constantly over his shoulder hardly seemed like freedom at all.

Haldren led them through the streets, leading Gaven to wonder how the Aundairian knew the place so well. That thought made Gaven realize he had no idea of the crime that had brought Haldren to Dreadhold. Had he spent time as a fugitive, hiding in the frontier of Q'barra before he was captured and imprisoned? What had he done that made them hunt him to the farthest reaches of Khorvaire? And to what lengths would they go to recapture him?

Probably the same lengths they'll go for me, he thought, quickly surveying the faces in the crowd around him.

They reached a section of town where the stone buildings were dingy gray, and Haldren stepped through the doorway of a small hostel. A faded sign above the door showed only a unicorn that might once have been gold, but now looked dull brown. The door had been painted green a long time ago, but knives, fists, and armored shoulders had chipped away much of the color. The wooden floor inside was adorned with a frayed rug that displayed another yellow-brown unicorn marred with stains that made up a rainbow of unpleasant colors.

This was the sort of place that catered to people who would rather not present themselves at a hostel run by House Ghallanda, where they'd be required to show identification papers. A glimmer of recognition flitted across the face of the desk clerk when the man saw Haldren, but he bowed his head to hide it, taking the money Senya held out and handing over two room keys without a word. Haldren took one key and handed the other to Darraun, and they climbed a narrow flight of stairs.

"Senya and I will be here," he said as they reached the room whose number matched his key. "Darraun, you and Gaven have the one across the hall. This is not the safest hostel in Whitecliff. We've had a long night, so get some rest. Cart, stay nearby. We'll eat in a few hours, gather some supplies we'll need for the trip, and get a good night's sleep tonight."

He opened the door to his room and pulled Senya inside. Darraun rolled his eyes and turned to the door across the hall, unlocking it with the key Haldren had given him. He pushed it open and stood back for Gaven.

The room was tiny, and the furniture worn, but it was mostly clean. Gaven walked in and sat gingerly on one of the two narrow beds. It felt a bit like his cell in Dreadhold, but he wasn't sure that was a bad thing.

Darraun was still standing outside the open door, urging Cart to join them inside. "I know you don't need rest," he said, "but doesn't it feel good to get off your feet once in a while?"

"No," said Cart, and shuffled into the room. With the great bulk of the warforged, the room seemed much smaller. Darraun came in, pulled the door closed behind him, and threw himself down on the bed with a contented sigh.

"That was a long night," he said. "Are you tired, Gaven?"

Gaven shrugged. Fatigue pulled at his limbs, but he didn't want to sleep. Not really. Sleep for him was torment as often as rest. He lay back on the bed and stared at the ceiling.

"Well, get some rest," Darraun said, closing his eyes. "We've got a grand adventure ahead of us."

Despite his best efforts, Gaven's eyes would not stay open. Listening to Darraun's steady breathing, Gaven was soon asleep, and the dreams came.

* * * * *

The rope bit into his waist, under his arms and between his legs. Uncomfortable, but not agonizing. He swung in blackness, the light of his glowstone too feeble to reach any surface on any side of him. He had no idea if his rope was long enough to reach any kind of floor beneath him, or how far it might be to another wall he could use to aid his descent. He lowered himself as slowly as he could, straining his eyes to see anything—anything at all.

Rienne's voice called to him from above, where his rope slowly coiled out through a series of pulleys. Her words were swallowed in the open expanse around him.

Then the light of his glowstone fell on a roiling cloud of darkness, and the cloud engulfed him—a cloud of silent black wings. He lost his hold on his rope, and he fell. He called out to Rienne, but the rope kept spinning out, never slowing his fall.

He was flying, broad wings outstretched in a darkness that was somehow not so dark. A churning river flowed beneath him, and he followed its course farther and farther into Khyber's depths. He came to a cascade and swooped over the edge, then alighted on the bank of a pool at the bottom. He watched a series of images dance across the swirling water of the pool, and he saw a face—a great reptilian snout topped with a massive horn. A dragon's face. His face. Then he turned, his snaky tail splashing in the water, and he saw the nightshard. Almost perfectly clear, the enormous crystal held a vein of pure purple-black color, pulsing with dim light in its heart.

He groaned, every inch of his body aching, the hard stone beneath him pressing against his wounds. He had a vague sense that he had been unconscious for a long time, and he wondered vaguely why he wasn't dead. The nightshard, though, was pulsing with violet light. He stretched out a hand, bruised and bloody, and touched it.

His mind exploded with thoughts and memories—his own and the other's. He fell back to the rock floor, his eyes glued to the nightshard, and could no longer determine who he was or how he'd arrived there. A distant voice echoed in the vast cavern above him, but it no longer sounded like anyone he knew.

* * * * *

"Gaven?"

For a moment the hand that was gently shaking him belonged to Rienne. Her head was on his shoulder, her silky black hair spilling across the bed, and they were twenty-five again. Then he woke, and there was Cart, leaning over him like a mother. When the warforged saw Gaven's eyes open, he straightened up.

"Time to eat."

Gaven shook his head to clear the dream from his memory, and sat up on the bed. The door stood open, and Darraun was not in the room. Gaven thought he heard voices from across the hall.

"Were you here the whole time I slept?" he asked.

"I was. Your faithful hound," the warforged said. There was a smile in his voice, though his face wouldn't allow it.

"Did I say anything while I was sleeping?" Gaven tried to make the question sound casual.

"Who's Mara?"

"What?"

"I'm joking," Cart said. "During the war, I knew a man who talked in his sleep. Usually about whatever woman had most recently claimed his heart. We used to give him a hard time."

Gaven tried hard to imagine the warforged as just one of the men and women in a squad of soldiers. For a moment he saw Cart in battle, an axe raised over his head, strange, cold light glinting on his adamantine plating.

"No, you didn't say anything," Cart said, gently hitting Gaven's shoulder with the back of his hand. "You snore when you sleep on your back, though."

"Sorry," Gaven said. Dreadhold had taught him to avoid confrontation, back down, apologize.

"Doesn't bother me. And Darraun snores louder. Come with me. Haldren's waiting." Cart stepped aside and waited for Gaven to get to his feet, then followed him out the door.

Darraun stood in the doorway to Haldren's room, speaking quietly to the old sorcerer. Gaven could see Senya behind Haldren, buckling her sword belt at her hip. Haldren saw Gaven emerge from the room, and cut Darraun off.

"Ah, Gaven!" he said. "I hope you are well rested. Shall we eat?"

Without waiting for an answer, Haldren swept out of the room and down the stairs. Cart followed Gaven at the rear of their little procession.

Haldren was willing to settle for substandard accommodations for the sake of privacy, but he had extravagant taste in food. He led the way to Whitecliff's finest restaurant and ordered for everyone.

"It has been almost two years since I have enjoyed a fine meal," he said, "with all due respect for our friend Darraun's expertise at the campfire. Gaven, I can barely imagine how starved you must be for such a repast."

Starved was the wrong word—Gaven couldn't remember what a fine meal tasted or smelled like. He remembered the smell of the fish on the campfire, though, and his mouth began to water.

When the food came, it was overwhelming. Half a dozen aromatic smells blended together to form something exquisite. He attacked his plate.

"I am pleased to see you enjoying your meal so much, Gaven," Haldren said. "It is far better than the offerings at our last lodgings, is it not?"

Gaven nodded and took another bite of pheasant.

"Pheasant can be both dry and dull in the wrong hands," Haldren said, addressing the table at large. "But when prepared by my good friend Marras, it is never either." He gestured toward the kitchen. "So, Gaven, how was your sleep?"

Haldren clearly hoped that the good food would help to draw him out. Gaven chewed slowly, considering how to respond, then swallowed and said, "Not so different than Dreadhold."

"Ah, yes," the sorcerer said, his voice hushed. "Probably best not to mention our last lodgings by name, don't you think? Wouldn't want to attract any undue attention."

Gaven looked around. His eyes met those of a dwarf who quickly looked away. The pheasant suddenly did not taste so exquisite.

"Did you have pleasant dreams?" Haldren leaned forward as he asked it.

"No." For an instant, Gaven remembered his dream about Rienne, but then darker images flashed into his mind.

"What did you see, Gaven?"

Gaven's eyes fixed on the old man's mouth, just as he had seen it through the shutters in their doors in Dreadhold. A dribble of pear-cider sauce stained Haldren's white beard.

"I don't really remember."

Haldren exploded. "Damn you, Gaven, don't get coy now!" His voice was a rasping whisper, barely able to contain his fury. "I brought you out of that place because of the information locked away in that twisted little brain of yours. If you suddenly get clever and decide to start withholding information, I'll send you back there—or off to Dolurrh. Don't think for a second that I won't kill you if you stop being useful."

Gaven glanced around the table. Senya studied her plate while Cart peered around them to see if Haldren's outburst had attracted the attention of nearby patrons. Darraun watched the two of them with unconcealed fascination.

Gaven took a bite of his squash.

Clearly convinced that he was dealing with an idiot or a madman, Haldren brought his anger under control—to Senya's visible relief—and tried a different approach. He made his voice light, conversational, and he lowered his eyes to his plate as he spoke.

"Did you see the hordes of the Soul Reaver again, Gaven?"

Writhing tentacles in the darkness, a blinding beam of light stretching up to the sky. Gaven tried to remember his dream about Rienne and found that he couldn't. Her hair became a mass of writhing snakes, reaching for him.

"No," he said.

Haldren saw his unease and pounced. "What is it, Gaven? You remember something else?"

"The Soul Reaver itself," Gaven said, as if in a trance. Haldren leaned forward in his chair. "Falling or flying down from a great height, sinking into a chasm as deep as the bones of Khyber. Endless dark beneath the bridge of light. There the Soul Reaver waits."

Besides Haldren, who wore a look of smug satisfaction, the other three stared at Gaven with varying degrees of surprise. Senya might have been awed—her mouth was partly open, and her eyes wide. Darraun smiled, but there was something else in his expression that Gaven couldn't read. And Cart's face, of course, was a mask, but he rubbed his chin in a way that looked thoughtful.

Well enough, Gaven thought, let Haldren think he won this one.

Better that than to reveal what he had really dreamed.

Chapter
5

The meal finished, Darraun took charge of Gaven and Cart.

"The three of us need to stock up on supplies for our little jaunt to Aerenal and wherever else Haldren's magic takes us," he explained to Gaven as they left the restaurant. "Haldren and Senya are going to try to make contact with some people in Aundair who will be helping us later."

"Helping us do what?" Gaven said.

Darraun arched an eyebrow at Gaven. That was the first time he'd heard the half-elf ask a question, and he was eager to see more of the workings of the mind behind Gaven's recitations of the draconic Prophecy.

"Ah, I'm sure Haldren will explain it all to you later," he said.

"I'm sure he won't," Gaven said. "He won't let me in on his plans any more than is absolutely necessary to get information out of me."

"What do you think Haldren wants from you?"

"He knows some of the Prophecy, and Vaskar knows more. But two years in a cell across the hall from mine made him think I know more than the two of them combined."

"Wild nightmares and vague visions?" Darraun said. "He could get that from a raving madman on any street corner in Fairhaven. There has to be more to you than that."

Gaven stopped walking and waited until Darraun turned to face him. "That makes two of us, then. I'm not the only one here concealing his true face."

"Three of us, actually," Cart interjected. "I'm really quite complex." He turned his head to look at both of them. "Many-layered."

Darraun gaped at the warforged then burst into laughter. Gaven's eyes were still fixed on him, though, so he resumed a casual stroll in the general direction of the city's mercantile district.

"Very well, Gaven," he said. "Clearly you are more alert and perceptive than Haldren gives you credit for. Haldren is one of those people who believes he is more intelligent than he actually is. But what he lacks in reasoning, he more than makes up for in cunning and charisma. You will find that his most dangerous quality is his ability to inspire fierce loyalty in others." He glanced at Cart and hoped that Gaven was perceptive enough to catch his meaning.

Gaven watched him for a long moment as they walked, then evidently decided against prying any deeper into his secrets, just as Darraun had hoped he would. He figured Gaven would renew the subject if he ever managed to catch him alone, so Darraun resolved to avoid being alone with Gaven. He decided to try what he hoped was a more innocuous approach.

"I understand you were quite an explorer, years ago," he said.

"Of sorts," Gaven said. "More of a prospector. I lowered myself into caves and fought monsters, looking for Khyber dragonshards for my house. The elemental galleons of House Lyrandar . . ." He trailed off, a scowl falling over his face. "My former house," he muttered.

Darraun tried to shift Gaven's thoughts away from the family that had disowned him. "Lyrandar galleons and airships require nightshards to bind the elementals that power them, correct?"

"Airships?" Gaven's eyebrows shot up at the mention of them. "They were made to work? They were a dream of my house for a long time, but I never knew . . ."

This approach wasn't working either. Darraun cursed himself. He was dredging up too many painful memories.

"House Lyrandar put airships into service about nine or ten years ago," Cart said. "Just about every nation used them in the last years of the war, and now House Lyrandar operates passenger lines."

Darraun saw Gaven's eyes light up and decided that if Gaven ever ran off, the airship lines would be the first place to check. This, he thought, is a man that wants to fly.

"So the Khyber dragonshards bind the elementals to the vessels?" Darraun asked again, trying to bring the subject back around to nightshards.

"That's right," Gaven said. "They have a peculiar property of binding. With the right magic, they can hold just about anything—even a human soul."

"Almost like some sort of possession?" Darraun asked.

"Sort of, yes." Gaven's face darkened again, and he didn't elaborate further.

"So all your expeditions into the depths of Khyber—is that how you learned so much about the Prophecy?"

Gaven stared blankly ahead, showing no indication that he'd heard the question. A cloud passed over the hot noonday sun, and Darraun glanced at the sky. "We'd better get our supplies and get ready to go," he said. "I understand it can rain pretty hard here in the jungle, though it usually comes in short spurts."

He quickened their pace, and they found shelter in a provisioner's shop. Heavy drops of rain started falling a moment later.

The shopkeeper was attentive to their every need, which meant Darraun was unable to keep up his line of questions. He stayed busy ordering the things they'd need for their journey, but at one point when the merchant had vanished into a back storeroom for a moment he found himself staring at Gaven's dragonmark. The intricate pattern almost seemed painted on Gaven's skin, fine tracings of blue beginning just at the ridge of his jaw, on his left side, covering the whole front of his neck, and extending down under his shirt. It probably covered his whole chest, and Darraun could see part of it extending out his short sleeve to reach his left elbow. The skin beneath the mark was redder than the rest of Gaven's pale flesh, giving the whole 'mark a purplish tinge. There was something vaguely draconic about the part that covered his neck, which must have been how the dragonmarks had earned their names.

The Mark of Storm. Darraun glanced at a window spattered with rain and wondered if Gaven's mark had anything to do with the weather outside. The rain was coming down hard now, so hard that Darraun could hear the drops splattering on the cobblestones outside and driving against the shutters of the shop. He sighed, glancing down at the fine clothes that would soon be pasted to his skin. Natural storms were one thing, but a storm caused by magic was a more unpleasant prospect. Would Gaven make it rain for the length of their time together?

All the more reason to get this over with quickly, Darraun told himself.

* * * * *

"Cart, what do you think of this?" Gaven held up a leather belt studded with wooden beads and decorative stones, supposedly made by one of the nearby lizardfolk tribes. He was aware of Darraun's gaze lingering on him, but he chose to ignore it. Darraun had been asking a lot of questions, and Gaven wanted to get him away from Cart and ask some of his own before he submitted to any more interrogation.

"Interesting," Cart said, taking the belt in his three-fingered hands. He looked down at the battered belt that held his battle-axe at his waist. "I could certainly use a new one, but I don't know about this."

"It would be a different look for you," Gaven said. The shopkeeper had returned and engaged Darraun in further discussion. Darraun deftly avoided any question of their destination, planned activities, anything that might help pursuers track them down. "What's your connection to this group, Cart?" Gaven asked. "How do you know Haldren?"

"He was my commanding officer," Cart said.

"He was a sergeant?" Gaven was stunned. "I got the sense he ranked higher than that."

"And you assume I was just a private," Cart said. "Lord General Haldren ir'Brassek commanded the Third Brigade of Aundair, Gaven. I might have made colonel and commanded a regiment myself, but Aundair's armed forces value a skill in magic that I completely lack. I was part of the general's staff."

"I'm sorry, Cart," Gaven said. "I . . ."

"I know. You were thrown in Dreadhold before the warforged proved their worth on the battlefield, almost a decade before Chase received his commission, I believe."

Cart's voice was a little too loud, and Gaven thought he saw the shopkeeper's eyes dart in the warforged's direction at the mention of Dreadhold. Damn, Gaven thought. All of Darraun's careful work undone by one slip.

"Chase?" he said, keeping an eye on the shopkeeper.

"The first warforged to hold a command over human soldiers. He served in Aundair and proved himself far more competent than the Lord Major in command of the company. In 981 his general promoted him and relieved the Lord Major of his command, but the Lord Major complained to the Queen."

Gaven watched the shopkeeper excuse himself and head into the back of the shop again.

"Sorry to interrupt you, Cart, but we need to get out of here."

"What?"

"Fast. Darraun!"

The man whirled around. "What is it?"

Gaven nodded in the direction the shopkeeper had gone. "He's going to get the authorities. We need to go." Grabbing Cart's arm, he hustled to the door. Darraun stared for a moment at the provisions spread over the countertop, then ran after them.

They hurried up the street away from the provisioner's, the rain drenching them. Only when they were about to turn a corner did Gaven risk a look back at the shop—just in time to see a trio of soldiers arrive and peer through the shop door.

"What in the Ten Seas happened back there?" Darraun said as they turned the corner.

"My fault," Gaven said. "I got Cart a little riled up, and he let a mention of Dreadhold slip out. The shopkeeper heard it and took the first opportunity to get out and summon help."

"The fault was mine, then," Cart said. "I'm sorry, Darraun. I don't even remember mentioning it."

Darraun sighed. "We were about to finish the deal, too," he said. "Now what do we do? We should find Haldren and get out of town, but we don't have supplies."

"We find Haldren first," Gaven said. "Tell him what happened, and figure something out from there."

"The general is not a forgiving man," Cart said. Gaven could hear the trepidation in his voice.

"Put the blame on me. Tell him I blurted something about Dreadhold. He can get as angry at me as he wants to, but he has to answer to Vaskar about my fate, and something tells me he wouldn't want to have to tell the dragon he killed me."

The warforged strode along in silence, making Gaven wish for the hundredth time that he could read Cart's unmoving face.

"Back to the hostel, then," Darraun said, turning a corner and leading them back to break the news to Haldren.

*   *   *   *   *

"I wonder what he's telling them," Cart said. He stood by the door of their little room, occasionally pacing as much as the tiny space allowed.

Gaven sat on the bed, staring out the window to the street below, watching for any sign that guards were coming after them. Darraun had insisted on breaking the bad news to Haldren himself, and neither he nor Cart was clear on which version of the story Darraun would tell. So far Gaven had not heard any shouting, but Haldren did not strike him as the yelling kind. For that matter, he couldn't be sure Darraun was still alive.

"Do you hear anything in there?" he asked the warforged.

"I can hear them speaking," Cart said. "I can't make out what they're saying. You can tell when the general is really angry, because he whispers. It's frightening."

The general, Gaven thought. He began to understand what Darraun meant about Haldren's ability to inspire loyalty. Haldren hadn't been a general in at least three years, but he would always be "the general" in Cart's mind.

The door flew open, banging hard against Cart's shoulder. The warforged stepped out of the way, and Haldren came barreling into the room. "We are leaving now," he said, very quietly.

Gaven looked around as if he had a pack to load, then got to his feet.

Darraun slipped into the room behind Haldren, eyes lowered.

"Circle up," Haldren commanded. Senya entered, fumbling with the last buckle on her pack, and quickly joined the others in a circle, taking Haldren's right hand. Darraun stooped to lift his own pack to his shoulders, then took Gaven's hand, still avoiding his eyes. Haldren glared at each of them in turn, not even sparing Senya his withering stare, then began another incantation.

Gaven blinked, and he was in another forest, sweltering hot and buzzing with insects. Haldren freed his hands and stormed away from the circle.

CHAPTER
6

re you Arnoth d'Lyrandar?"

Evlan watched the old man carefully. Every reaction was important. Any twitch or shift of the eyes could reveal whether Gaven's father was aware of his son's escape or had any idea of his whereabouts.

"I am," the man said. He was hoarse and short of breath, but he stood as tall as Evlan despite his age. The hair was gone from the top of his head, but what remained still bore traces of black amid the gray and white. His dark eyebrows bristled. "What is this about, Sentinel Marshal?"

"My name is Evlan d'Deneith. I'm here to talk to you about your son."

Arnoth turned to the stairs behind him. "Thordren?" he said, and the young man who had kept a respectful distance on the stairway came to stand beside him. Thordren strongly resembled what his father must have looked like in his youth—fine, black hair cut above his shoulders and combed away from his face, high cheekbones, and proud brown eyes.

"I'm sorry," said Evlan, "I meant your other son."

"My other . . . Gaven?" The old man's skin went ashen, and he slowly sank down onto a bench. Then he seemed to recollect himself, and he looked away. "I have no other son, Sentinel Marshal. He was excoriated a long time ago."

"All the same, it's Gaven I need to talk to you about." He shot a pointed glance at the other man, but Thordren sat down on the bench next to his father, his eyes glued to Evlan.

"Is he dead?" Arnoth's eyes told Evlan almost everything he needed to know. Excoriate or not, Arnoth loved his son, and as far as he knew, Gaven was still locked away in Dreadhold.

"No. At least, not as far as I know. He has escaped."

"Escaped? From Dreadhold?" Arnoth got to his feet again, Thordren fluttering after him, trying to get him back to the bench.

"Yes," said Evlan. "According to House Kundarak, there was a dragon involved."

The old man's eyes went wide. "Where is he?"

"That's why I'm here," Evlan said. "I take it you have not received any communication from him?"

"Not in twenty-six years, no."

"Were you aware that he manifested a Siberys mark during his imprisonment?"

"Yes. House Kundarak has kept me informed of developments."

"You have seen the reports of his ravings?"

"Ravings?" Arnoth said. "You think he is mad?"

"His mind hardly seems stable, if you'll pardon my saying so."

"You underestimate his mind, Sentinel Marshal. He is not all brawn."

Evlan shrugged and tried another tack. "Does the name Haldren ir'Brassek mean anything to you?"

"Ir'Brassek?" Arnoth scratched the side of his face. "Wasn't he an Aundairian general? Tried for war crimes?"

"Yes. Are you aware of any connection between your son and ir'Brassek?"

"Gaven and Haldren?" Arnoth seemed genuinely confused. "No. I can't imagine that Gaven would associate with such a person."

"They occupied adjacent cells in Dreadhold," Evlan said, a reminder that Gaven was no less a criminal than Haldren.

Arnoth shook his head and looked back at Thordren. "No, I've never heard their names connected." He looked back at Evlan. "Did Haldren escape with Gaven?"

"Yes, they fled Dreadhold together. Mounted on wyverns."

Arnoth raised his eyebrows and sank back down to the bench, to Thordren's obvious relief. "Gaven is free," he muttered, running a hand through his short gray hair.

Thordren spoke for the first time. "Sentinel Marshal, my father is in poor health. I must ask—"

Evlan cut him off. "He has escaped, but he is hardly free. He is a fugitive from justice, and the combined efforts of Houses Deneith, Tharashk, Kundarak, and Thuranni will locate him eventually."

"House Thuranni?" Arnoth said. "They'll kill him!"

"Probably. Certainly you can appreciate that it would be better for Gaven if I find him before Thuranni's assassins do. If you have any information that might help me locate him . . ."

"If I knew anything, I would certainly tell you, Sentinel Marshal," Arnoth said, and Evlan believed him. "And if I hear from him . . ."

He trailed off. He couldn't quite bring himself to promise that he'd turn in his son. Evlan would have marshals watch the house.

"Thank you. I have just one more question for you. Do you know where I might find Rienne ir'Alastra?"

*   *   *   *   *

The shadows pooled and thickened in a corner of the little room. A sword blade took shape out of the darkness, glinting dully in the dim light that filtered through the shutters of the room. Then the hand that held it appeared, covered in a black glove. Phaine d'Thuranni stepped out of the shadows, lowering his sword as his eyes swept the empty room. Another form took shape in the dark corner, and Phaine made a hand signal: Stand down.

Either they had received bad information, or they had arrived too late. Phaine shifted his sword to his left hand and used his teeth to pull the glove off his right hand. He bent over the bed beside the window, placing his palm on the mattress. A trace of a circle rumpling the blankets showed that someone had been sitting there not long before. Very recently, in fact—Phaine could still feel the heat.

Phaine shot Leina another hand signal, and she stepped to the door, pressed an ear to it, and shook her head. Then something on the door caught her eye, and she examined it. She knelt and looked at the floor, then stepped away from the door, signaling to Phaine: Look here. She pointed at the door and the floor.

Phaine crossed the room in two steps and looked where Leina had pointed. There was a mark on the door as if something had struck it. Perhaps the metal head of a mace, but not a hard blow. The floor was scuffed.

"A warforged," he whispered. "Pacing here beside the door, and the door hit him when it opened." The other elf nodded. Search it, Phaine told her.

Phaine pressed his own ear to the door then opened it silently. There was no one in the hall, and the opposite door stood open. Taking his sword in his right hand again, he stepped quickly across to the other room. Empty. The two beds were pushed together, their blankets piled on the floor. He found white hairs on the bed—presumably ir'Brassek's—and curly black hairs that must have belonged to the woman the innkeeper had described, the beautiful elf. Phaine snorted. He didn't like to imagine an elf dallying with an old human like ir'Brassek.

He stepped back across the hall, no longer making an effort at silence. "What did you find?" he asked Leina, who knelt on the floor beside the window.

"Come have a look," she said.

Phaine crossed the room and looked over her shoulder. The window sill was thick with grime—except where a fingertip had traced patterns in the dirt.

Without thinking about it, Phaine reverted to hand signals: *Over there.* Leina got out of the way, and Phaine knelt on the floor to study the patterns. At first, they were incomprehensible, but he knew there was something—the shapes hinted at letters, in the ornate Draconic script. But they'd been written on top of each other, and he found it almost impossible to distinguish them. He breathed the words of a simple spell, and the letters slowly resolved themselves in his mind.

He read them aloud, translating them from Draconic to Elven. "The Bronze Serpent seeks the face of the first of sixteen."

"What?" Leina said.

"The Prophecy. Come. Let's get out of here."

The shadows in the corner darkened again, and Phaine stepped into them. When he vanished, Leina took one last look around the room, then followed.

* * * * *

Rienne ir'Alastra whirled on Evlan, a picture of righteous fury. "I assure you, Sentinel Marshal," she said, "if I had any idea where Gaven was, I'd tell you, just as I did all those years ago."

She set her jaw, trying to make herself believe the words she spoke. Back then, she had honestly believed that she was helping Gaven by leading the Sentinels to him—she thought they would help him, restore him to his right mind. Instead, they had locked him in Dreadhold, and she had spent two and a half decades blaming herself for all the tortures she imagined him enduring there. Now he had escaped, and this Evlan d'Deneith seemed a little too skilled at reading the ambivalence she felt.

"I am sure you will do what's right," Evlan said. He smiled slightly, but his eyes fixed on her like a hawk.

She turned her back on him again. "I appreciate your confidence," she said.

"I spoke to his father this morning," Evlan said. The sound of his voice drew a little closer. "Master d'Lyrandar does not believe that Gaven is mad."

"Love blinds him."

"Perhaps. Although he was careful to remind me that, technically, he has only one son."

"The censure of House Lyrandar means little to Arnoth."

"And what about you, Lady?" he whispered, uncomfortably close now. She could feel him behind her.

Rienne stepped forward and whirled on him again, resting a hand on the hilt of a dagger in her belt as she did so. "What about me, Sentinel Marshal?"

"You were engaged to be married. Gaven has been in Dreadhold for twenty-six years, and you have not married anyone else. Might love be blinding you as well?"

"My marriage to Gaven would have been advantageous both to my family and to House Lyrandar. It was a political allegiance. After Gaven's arrest, my value in such a bargain diminished significantly. House Lyrandar has made other alliances with other noble families, and the ir'Alastras have waned in influence. Surely you, a scion of House Deneith, can appreciate what is involved in such an alliance."

Evlan raised his palms as if to deflect the force of her anger. "I married a woman I loved."

"Well, aren't you lucky?"

Evlan met her glare and held it for a long moment. "Very well," he said at last. "If you hear from Gaven, please contact me immediately. I don't imagine that I need to remind you of the consequences if you do not."

"I would hate to imagine that a Sentinel Marshal is leveling petty threats at a member of Aundair's nobility, however much my family's influence has fallen."

"Farewell, Lady." Evlan turned and strode out of the hall.

Rienne watched his back until the servants had ushered him out the front door and closed it behind him. Only when she heard the satisfying slam of the door did she turn and run to her chambers.

* * * * *

Bordan looked up through the shattered ceiling of Dreadhold's tower to the dazzling arc of the Ring of Siberys overhead. He tried to imagine the force it must have taken to break through the thick stone, the size and sheer strength of the dragon that had done it. Blinking several times to clear the dust and drowsiness from his eyes, he set a thick sheaf of papers down on the bed beside him and stood up to stretch his back.

He walked around Gaven's tiny cell, reading whatever words his eyes fell on, hoping that something would leap out at him that would help him understand. He could certainly see why so many people thought Gaven was at least halfway across the Sea of Rage, practically lost to madness. Disjointed fragments full of strange imagery and obscure descriptions covered the walls. Bordan had been wrestling for hours with numbers: twice thirteen years, the first of sixteen, shards of three dragons, thirteen cycles of the Battleground, nineteen turns of the thirteenth moon.

The thirteenth moon? Bordan thought. To the best of his knowledge, there were only twelve. And he could only guess at references for most of the rest of these numbers.

His eyes fell on a scrap of writing at his eye level, and he read the words aloud. "The cauldron of the thirteen dragons boils until one of the five beasts fighting over a single bone becomes a thing of desolation." Bordan stroked his beard. "Very well, Gaven, let's play this game. Five beasts fighting over a single bone—is that your code for the Five Nations? Are we talking about the Last War here? And Cyre, bless it, has become a thing of desolation. So Galifar is the boiling cauldron of the thirteen dragons? It's a boiling cauldron because of the war. Thirteen dragons—thirteen dragonmarked houses!"

He looked up at the Ring of Siberys again. "But there were only twelve dragons before House Phiarlan split, Gaven. Is that why you conspired against them? Did you orchestrate the schism so there would be thirteen dragons and your precious Prophecy would make sense?"

He looked around the room again, at all the writing on the walls, the rubble on the floor, the crack in the ceiling through which Gaven, formerly of House Lyrandar, had escaped.

"So your Prophecy would come true?"

CHAPTER

7

The Aerenal jungle teemed with life. Even discounting the insects that swarmed around them, the sounds of movement were everywhere—gibbons leaping through the canopy overhead and whooping at each other, the hiss of an emerald-scaled snake coiled around a nearby branch, the harsh cries and elaborate songs of a dozen different birds. More alarming, something large rustled in the undergrowth not far enough away, off to Gaven's right.

"Welcome to Aerenal," Haldren announced. He swept his arm grandly around him, taking in the jungle, then pointed behind Gaven. "The City of the Dead lies in the valley in that direction."

"The City of the Dead?" Darraun paled, but Haldren ignored him, shouldering past Gaven to walk in the direction he'd indicated.

Gaven followed, falling into step beside Cart. Senya slipped between them as she hurried to catch up to Haldren, and Darraun brought up the rear, grumbling to himself. Gaven saw a clump of ferns shake slightly, opposite where he'd heard the rustling a moment before. Without thinking, he reached over his shoulder to where his sword should have been, and cursed softly when his hand met only empty air.

"What is it, Gaven?" Cart said, slowing his pace. "Did you see something?"

Senya darted forward, shouting, "Haldren, look—"

Another rustle in the undergrowth, then a creature collided with Haldren, knocking him to the ground. It was covered in sable fur like a panther and resembled a cat in its general form—a cat the size of a horse. Two long tentacles arced up from its shoulders, trying to rake at Haldren's flesh even as it clawed him with six feet and bared long fangs. Gaven found that looking at it was like peering through a curved glass—it seemed to shift position without moving.

Haldren did not cry out or make any exclamation. Calm and sure, he chanted a few words of power that grew in volume until they became a thunderous shout that blasted the beast off him, sending it sprawling on its back. As Haldren got to his feet—a little unsteadily, Gaven noticed—the beast flailed its six legs in the air for a moment before managing to right itself. Senya had already reached it and swung her sword toward its head in what should have been a deadly blow, but her weapon failed to connect. To all appearances, it passed right through the creature's head.

Cart took up a position between Haldren and the beast, waiting in case it threatened his commander again. Darraun produced a slender wand from his belt and reached toward Haldren, working magic to stanch the bleeding. For a moment, Gaven thought about running—getting as far away from Haldren and his team as he possibly could, and making his way on his own. Then he saw the rest of the beast's pack emerge from the ferns, forming a wide circle around them. He cast his eyes around for a branch or even a stone he could use as a weapon, but then the beasts closed the circle. One pounced at him, rearing up to plant its front paws on his shoulders, trying to knock him down. Gaven planted his feet and stayed upright, raising his hands to grab the thing's head just as it tried to bite at his neck. Its middle pair of legs tried to tear at his chest and sides, but it couldn't quite reach him.

His dragonmark was burning. The shadows around him deepened, and the sky grew dark. Gaven growled with the effort of wrestling the beast, and a rumble of thunder rolled overhead. He felt disconnected from the struggle—he was in the storm brewing in the sky, looking down at his tiny form far below—and the storm brewed in his blood. Lightning flashed in the clouds above, and Gaven felt it jolt across the Mark of Storm on his chest.

The beast's tentacles bludgeoned his back, but he barely noticed. His hands held its jaws open and twisted its neck around. With another rumble of thunder overhead, he snapped its neck and roared as he threw its corpse away.

Gaven had become the storm. He was killing with his bare hands, a primal force of nature, and the sky met his savagery with equal fury. Unbound, no longer locked within the walls of Dreadhold, not restrained by convention or decorum, not confined by the limits of his flesh, Gaven's fury flashed across the sky, making shadows dance across the forest.

Two beasts lunged for him, but he held them off, one with each hand. His muscles screamed in pain, but he exulted in the raw physicality of it. For the first time in years, he was completely in the moment, ancient memories and prophetic nightmares exorcised from his mind. An ear-splitting crash of thunder made one of the beasts flinch slightly, and he pressed the advantage, pushing it off him. Finally able to bring two hands to bear on the other beast, he grabbed it and swung it around him, crashing its hips into the snarling maw of the first creature. Darraun appeared at the edge of Gaven's awareness, bringing his heavy mace down hard into the ribs of the beast he'd thrown.

A monstrous roar answered the thunderclap, and another beast crashed through the jungle to enter the fray. If the beasts they'd been fighting were the size of horses, this one was a small elephant, though it was as wiry and compact as the others. Trying to follow its movements made Gaven's eyes ache.

Gaven's eyes rolled skyward, and he lost himself in the storm. The dragonmark that covered his chest was a mirror of the thundercloud overhead, surging with power and flashing with lightning. The wind howled around him, and he let it hold him upright as he gave himself over to the tempest. The rain began to fall.

He was aware of shouts and bestial howls of pain, but if the downpour fell on him, he did not feel it. He opened his eyes, but he felt so far away, so high above the battle that he could barely make sense of it. Darraun stood in front of him, hefting his mace in both hands as if to protect Gaven from the great beast. Haldren was at the artificer's shoulder, his magic searing flesh from the beast's skull, and Cart drove his axe again and again into the creature. The beast's tentacles thrashed through the air, but its roars of pain and rage were drowned out by the howling wind.

The wind lifted Gaven off the ground, and light exploded around him. Gaven felt rather than saw the location of each remaining beast, and bolts of lightning impaled each one, tying them briefly to each other, to the churning clouds above, to the burning dragonmark on his chest.

The world fell silent, and the wind set Gaven back on his feet. Small hailstones pelted him, but the storm's power was spent. He shook his head, trying to make sense of the ground beneath his feet, the fire in his muscles, the frenetic movement around him. Haldren's mouth was open wide as though he were shouting in Darraun's ear, but there was no sound. Darraun nodded to Haldren and ran somewhere behind Gaven, just as Cart's axe felled the great beast.

Then Haldren's red face was inches away, apparently yelling at Gaven. The half-elf shrugged and tried to turn away, but Haldren grabbed his shoulders and continued his tirade. Gaven watched little flecks of saliva form around Haldren's mouth, and he remembered all the times he'd seen that mouth through the shutters in their cell doors. Nausea gripped his stomach, and he curled around it. Haldren released his shoulders and let Gaven drop to the ground.

The silence was strange. With his eyes open, Gaven could perceive the chaos left in the wake of their battle, but when he closed his eyes it was gone. The jungle was silent, and he might have been alone. The earth was warm beneath him, and the ferns made him a soft bed. He felt himself start to drift, so he opened his eyes, and found himself embroiled in chaos again.

Darraun and Haldren stood over him, apparently bickering. Haldren no longer looked like he was yelling, which probably meant that he was getting angry. Darraun rummaged through a large pouch at his belt. Gaven had seen scrolls in there before, so he supposed that Darraun was looking for a spell that would restore his hearing. He closed his eyes again, relishing what might be his last taste of peace and quiet.

His ears started ringing, and Gaven looked up. Darraun was still rummaging, so he wasn't responsible. Gaven rolled onto his hands and knees, letting his head hang between his arms for a moment, then he pushed himself shakily to his feet. Darraun said something.

"Just ringing," Gaven said, pointing to one ear. He heard the sound of his voice, but it was muffled and strange.

Darraun frowned, and Haldren crossed his arms impatiently. Haldren said something—Gaven could hear his voice now—and stomped away. Gaven watched him help Senya to her feet while Darraun talked, a rapid stream of syllables that didn't quite resolve themselves into language in Gaven's ears.

Senya moved slowly, and Gaven noticed a lot of blood staining her clothes and armor. But something about her suggested that something besides her physical injuries slowed her down—she looked distant, almost vacant, as she got to her feet and looked around. Her eyes didn't seem to linger on Haldren at all, almost as if she didn't see him there. She turned slowly where she stood, as if she could see through the thick growth of trees to scan the horizon.

Gaven's ears cleared enough that he could hear Haldren's voice, coaxing her, almost pleading in its tone. Senya lifted an arm to point into the distance, and Gaven could clearly hear her words: "The City of the Dead awaits us."

CHAPTER

8

Gaven took an involuntary step backward as the weight of Senya's words—the weight of what they were doing here—finally registered in his mind. He was no longer in his cell, dreaming of the Prophecy and remembering all the research he had done into its mysteries. No, he was in the jungle of Aerenal, outside the City of the Dead, waiting for the Eye of Siberys to fall in fulfillment of the Prophecy. He was helping to bring it about.

That was what had landed him in Dreadhold in the first place.

Haldren's eyes narrowed and rested on him. "What is it, Gaven? Did you see something?"

"With respect, Haldren," Darraun said, "I'm particularly interested in what Senya is seeing right now." Senya took a few steps in the direction she had indicated, her eyes still fixed on some distant point.

"Senya will guide us to the City of the Dead," Haldren said. "But the Prophecy—Gaven, what did you see?"

Gaven didn't answer. Instead, he lifted his eyes skyward. The clouds of his unnatural storm had cleared, but the sky was beginning to darken. Even in the deepening blue, the Ring of Siberys was visible, glowing faintly. By the time the sun's light faded, the ring would be as bright as the sun—turning the night into day.

Haldren followed Gaven's gaze, and remembered the words Gaven had uttered before. "When Siberys turns night into day," he muttered. "Yes, Gaven. The Time of the Dragon Above is here. All is coming to pass as the Prophecy declares."

Gaven shuddered. Some part of him wished he were back in his cell with his nightmares. That seemed preferable to living them out.

* * * * *

Senya led them through the jungle as though following a distant call, and as they crested a hill, the forest cleared before them. The City of the

Dead lay exposed to their wondering gazes. Wide streets ran straight and long between hulking buildings—sloping pyramids crowned with pillared temples, squat ziggurats decorated with elaborate skull motifs, graceful domes with chiseled arches, winged pillars, and flying buttresses. Great eldritch fires leaped skyward atop towering columns and danced inside the galleries of ancient temple-tombs.

Gaven saw no sign that the jungle encroached into the city—no trees adorned the streets, no vines clung to the ancient stones. No wall surrounded it, either, but the line between the vibrant life of the jungle and the calm stillness of the City of the Dead could not have been more clear. Where ferns and grasses ended, stone began. People walked the streets, though not in any great numbers—and Gaven couldn't be certain whether those people were themselves alive. In the elven homeland, the spirits of long-dead ancestors still inhabited their desiccated corpses, speaking to the living within their ancient tombs. The City of the Dead was the center of the elves' ancestor worship, where the Undying Court continued to guide the spiritual and political affairs of the elves, unhindered by the death of their mortal bodies. Even the guards at the gate might be undying soldiers conscripted to guard the elders' rest.

Senya insisted on leading them to a towering arch set up as an entrance. Two guards wearing helms decorated to resemble skulls crossed their spears in the archway as Senya approached, and easily a dozen more stood beyond. One spoke in Elven. Gaven couldn't make out any words, but the hostility in his voice was unmistakable. Senya stepped forward proudly and replied in the same language. She spoke more slowly, and her voice wasn't muffled by a helmet with a skull mask, so Gaven caught a few words: "the right of counsel," "revered elder."

The guards looked at each other and moved their spears out of the way slowly, as if it caused them pain. Gaven watched them stare at Cart as the warforged lumbered past, and he thought he heard one of them make a spitting sound as he followed Cart through the arch.

Then he was surrounded by the monumental buildings of Shae Mordai, the City of the Dead. He felt as though he had stepped into a tomb.

"Haldren?" Darraun said.

Darraun had been lingering behind as they entered the strange city of monuments, but now he hurried to catch up to the front of the group, where Haldren walked beside Senya. Gaven noticed that he still seemed pale, and wondered if the necromancy of the elves unsettled him. Haldren barely glanced over his shoulder to acknowledge Darraun.

"Why are we entering the city? Didn't Gaven say that we'd find what we need near the City of the Dead, not in it?"

Haldren stopped and turned around. "Indeed he did, though I was not aware you had overheard that part of our conversation." His pale blue eyes burned into Darraun. "However, Senya has access to an unusual store of knowledge here within the city, and I would not miss the opportunity to tap it while we're here."

The Right of Counsel, Gaven thought—the privilege to confer with her ancestors within their tombs. The tradition of the elves attached so much weight to that right that the elders would be compelled to answer her questions. He wondered what they might have to say about the Prophecy and Haldren's plans to fulfill it. The elves were the ancient foes of the dragons, sporadically warring with them since their first arrival on the island continent of Aerenal. The elves studied the Prophecy as a matter of survival.

For that matter, what would they say about him? He had not missed the hostility of the guards at the gate, and he felt certain that elves more ancient would share that distaste for a half-elf violating the sanctity of their tombs. And what of a half-elf who carried so much knowledge of the Prophecy?

The sound of his name drew Gaven out of his reverie. Darraun had stepped closer to Haldren and lowered his voice, but he was gesturing in Gaven's direction.

"Yes, we do have Gaven," Haldren said, turning his icy gaze on him. Gaven looked away. "But Senya's additional information could corroborate what Gaven has told us—or contradict it. Or it could expand our understanding further. Besides, we have time. The Ring of Siberys is at its brightest, and the Eye should fall tonight. It might turn out that our hasty departure this afternoon was actually advantageous. Now come! Senya's family is waiting."

"Family?" Darraun said. He looked slightly relieved and turned to Senya. "You have family living here?"

"The living members of my family left Aerenal many decades ago," Senya said, her voice little more than a whisper. "But the dead remain."

She started walking again, and Haldren took her arm. Darraun stared after her. Cart clapped him on the shoulder as he and Gaven walked past, and Darraun trailed behind them.

Senya led them down a wide, quiet street into the city's heart. The city seemed almost normal as they passed through—merchants beginning to pack up their wares for the evening, loading their carts and rolling up the tents they'd erected in front of the gigantic stone buildings. Most of the people on the street were alive, Gaven could see now, though a few had painted their faces to resemble skulls or corpses. All were elves, and they clustered together as Senya passed with her non-elf allies in tow. The hostility on their faces was clear.

They turned a corner, and the trappings of life fell away. Twin rows of towering monuments stretched before them, many-tiered pyramids topped with thick columns, each column supporting a blazing beacon in honor of the dead who resided within. The air was thick with incense, wafting out the open doorways of the temple-tombs. This was the heart of the City of the Dead, where the Aereni priests performed the Ritual of Undying, which bound the spirits of revered elders to their bodies so they could continue sharing their wisdom with their descendants through the ages. Gaven stopped in his tracks.

He had been here before.

The power of the memory overwhelmed him. He had stood on this spot—seen the same line of ancient temples, heard the roar of the blazing beacons, breathed the thick, scented air. He had been here with a friend, an elf, who sought the counsel of his ancestors just as Senya did now.

No, he told himself, that was not me. That was the . . . other.

"What is it, Gaven?" Darraun tried to follow Gaven's gaze. Cart had stopped a few paces ahead and turned to see what held them up, while Senya and Haldren walked further ahead.

"Nothing," Gaven said, shaking his head quickly. "Sorry." He started walking again, and Darraun stayed close beside him.

Senya started up the stairs of one of the great pyramids. Haldren lingered just long enough to look back at the others and hurry them with an imperious gesture. Cart hustled forward, and Gaven quickened his pace, pushing the memories aside.

He climbed the stairs slowly, with Cart on one side and Darraun on the other. Two more elves wearing skull helmets flanked the open doorway, holding their spears apart so the three could pass. Their stares told Gaven that he was not welcome here. He also remembered that from before. He had been nervous that these guards—or their ancestors, more likely—would see through his disguise and try to prevent him from entering, bring the wrath of the city on his head. His heart started pounding, but this time, as before, he passed through the entrance without incident. The guards crossed their spears across the entrance behind them, and the ancient stone swallowed them.

They climbed a narrow staircase inside the temple-tomb, so long that Gaven began to feel the walls close in around him, until they finally emerged onto a high balcony overlooking the street they had just left. Haldren stood in a narrow doorway, his back to the room behind.

"We'll wait here," Haldren said. "There are certain rites Senya needs to perform. We'll all go in when she's finished." He looked at Gaven for that last

sentence, and Gaven thought he heard an emphasis on the word all. He also
heard Darraun swallow hard at Haldren's words.

Gaven turned around and stepped to the edge of the balcony. The air was
clearer up here, above the clouds of incense that settled at street level. The
western horizon was blood red—"Evening red, clear skies ahead," he whispered, remembering the old sailor's proverb. The Ring of Siberys shone across
the sky like a million tiny suns, lighting the night sky in a pale imitation of
day. As he looked, a shooting star darted down from the Ring and disappeared
above the distant forest.

More memories surfaced in his mind. He had climbed the dark and
narrow stairs beside his friend, Mendaros, and waited on this balcony as the
elf made his petitions to his ancestor. Then Gaven had knelt in the small room
behind him, and learned much that was still locked in his mind. Mendaros
Alvena Tuorren had been his friend, probably Senya's great-uncle or cousin far
removed. And now Senya and her lover had brought Gaven here because of
the knowledge he possessed.

"Gaven, we're ready," Haldren said behind him.

Gaven turned to see Cart and Darraun shuffling into the chamber. Haldren extended a hand, inviting Gaven to join them, a broad smile on his face.
Gaven's pulse quickened. What did Haldren hope to learn here?

Gaven followed Darraun into the small stone chamber. It smelled of
death, clouds of incense unable to mask the acrid scent of the embalmed
corpse that stood and watched them enter. Pale flames flickered in empty
eye sockets, and Gaven felt them burning into him as he approached. Senya's
ancestor was draped in ancient finery, rich velvet and brocaded silk cloak-
ing her withered flesh. Long black hair fell around her desiccated face, pale
paper-thin skin stretched tight over her bones, and her clawlike hands held a
slender gold rod. Senya knelt on the floor before her ancestor, and Cart took
a similar position behind her.

Gaven cast a sidelong glance at Darraun as they sank to their knees,
noticing his wide eyes and the sweat beading on his brow. He'd seen this
reaction on the battlefield during the war. Soldiers faced with the undead
soldiers of Karrnath, animated from the corpses of earlier battles, often
suffered more from their own fear than from the blades and arrows of their
enemies. He wondered if Darraun had fought in the war, perhaps suffered
at the skeletal hands of Karrnathi forces. He gave the man credit for facing
his fear at Haldren's command. Haldren knelt in front of Gaven, just behind
Senya's elbow.

"Senya Alvena Arrathinen," the deathless thing said. Her shriveled lips
barely moved, as though the cold, clear voice emerged magically from

somewhere inside her head. Gaven was surprised at the purity of the voice, a far cry from the rasping whisper Gaven had expected. "What are you doing here? You are not a credit to your family." She spoke in Elven, and Gaven wondered who else in the room understood her words.

Senya held her head high. "I am a warrior, and my skill at the blade brings honor to my ancestors."

"Martial skill is not honorable when it is used for the pursuit of profit."

"The Valaes Taern would not agree," Senya said.

Gaven held back a smile. The warriors of the Valaes Taern had been mercenaries in the Last War until they annexed part of southern Cyre to form the nation of Valenar.

"Your family is not of the Valaes Taern."

"Nevertheless, I fight with honor in a worthy cause."

Her ancestor made a sound like a long sigh and stepped closer to where Senya knelt. "You have invoked the Right of Counsel, and tradition requires that I answer your questions, as much as I might wish to deny you. What counsel do you seek, Senya?"

Senya glanced over her shoulder at Haldren, and Gaven caught his first glimpse of fear in her eyes. Haldren put a reassuring hand on her shoulder, and she turned back to her ancestor. "I seek knowledge of the Prophecy of the Dragons," she said. Her voice sounded high, strained.

"The knowledge of the dragons should be used only as a weapon against the dragons."

"I have invoked the Right of Counsel, as you said. Grant me the knowledge I seek."

"There is more to wisdom than knowledge. You would do well to heed my counsel."

Gaven watched Haldren take his hand from Senya's shoulder and bring it to his mouth. The old man had to restrain himself from jumping into the argument. Gaven rather enjoyed seeing Haldren faced with someone he could not charm, bully, or dominate. He hoped to see many more examples of Haldren caught powerless.

"Give me knowledge, and trust my wisdom and that of my allies," Senya said. Haldren nodded approvingly behind her.

"You have given me no cause to trust either." The ancestor cast her burning eyes over Senya's companions. Gaven was sure she dwelled longest on him. Was she studying his dragonmark, perhaps? Or did she somehow recognize him? "On the contrary," she continued, "to all appearances you are rushing headlong into folly and destruction. I would not assist you in this."

"You must," Senya said.

Gaven was impressed at how Senya handled herself. For a moment he wondered if Haldren had established a magical connection between his mind and Senya's so that he could speak through her. But Gaven decided it was more likely that Haldren had fallen in love with a woman who shared some of his talent for debate.

The undying ancestor drew herself up, bristling with anger. "I am bound to give counsel to deaf ears and show the path to blind eyes."

Triumph rang in Senya's voice. "Tell me, revered elder, how the Storm Dragon shall claim the place of the first of sixteen and become a god."

CHAPTER
9

T he Storm Dragon?" The elder's voice was quiet, and the fire in her eye
sockets dimmed. She fixed her gaze on Senya, then on Haldren for
a long moment. Gaven watched the old man hold her gaze without
flinching. Then the deathless elder turned her burning eyes on Gaven, and he
forced himself to meet those eyes.

"Who is this, Senya?" the ancestor said, her eyes still locked on Gaven's.
"Who is this hybrid you have brought into the city of your ancestors?"

Senya rose to her feet and stood between her ancestor and Gaven. Gaven
looked at the floor and took a deep breath.

"Answer my question," Senya said.

"Kneel!" The ancestor's shout rang with supernatural power, and Senya
dropped back to the floor. Gaven saw that Haldren had been about to rise as
well, but he planted both knees back on the floor at the elder's command.

"You came to ask my counsel," the ancestor said, "but you have proven
yourself unwilling to heed it. I will give you the knowledge you seek because
I must, but I will not tolerate insolence from the likes of you, Senya Alvena
Arrathinen."

She turned her back on them, and Haldren shot a glance over his shoulder
at Gaven. Gaven looked away.

"It can be no accident that you have come here on this night," the ancestor
continued. "You seek the Eye of Siberys, and your question suggests that you
would help the Storm Dragon rather than hinder him. So be it." She turned
to face them, and again her eyes burned into Gaven's. "The Eye of Siberys lifts
the Sky Caves of Thieren Kor from the land of desolation under the dark of
the great moon, and . . ."

Gaven found himself speaking the rest of the sentence in unison with the
ancestor. ". . . the Storm Dragon walks in the paths of the first of sixteen."
The Draconic syllables of the Prophecy coiled and snaked through his mind
as he spoke them in Elven. Those words had become a part of him.

The ancestor stepped closer to Gaven. "I have told you this before."

Gaven shook his head slowly, trying to wrench his eyes away from the ancestor's piercing stare. "I am just a man," he gasped.

I am not the other, he thought—I am not the one who was here before.

"In the first age of the world," said Gaven, "sixteen dragons transcended their mortal forms to become like the Dragon Above who had made them. These are the first ascendant. In the second age of the world, the first elders of Aerenal transcended their mortal forms to become the second ascendant. In the last age of the world, the Storm Dragon takes the place of the first of sixteen, the Gold Serpent whom the world has long since forgotten. The third ascendant." Words spilled from Gaven's mouth without thought, the narrative of his nightmares: "A clash of dragons signals the sundering of the Soul Reaver's gates. The hordes of the Soul Reaver spill from the earth, and a ray of Khyber's sun erupts to form a bridge to the sky."

Images filled his mind as if summoned by the words he had spoken: the gibbering hordes of tentacled monsters, the brilliant column of light bursting up from the ground.

"The Storm Dragon descends into the endless dark beneath the bridge of light, where the Soul Reaver waits. There among the bones of Khyber, the Storm Dragon drives the spear formed from Siberys's Eye into the Soul Reaver's heart. And the Storm Dragon walks through the gates of Khyber and crosses the bridge to the sky."

The deathless elf stared at Gaven in silence for a long time, and Gaven could not turn his eyes away. He was dimly aware of the others—Haldren glaring at him, Senya gaping in amazement, Cart watching with curious interest. Darraun's eyes were elsewhere, probably avoiding contact with the undying thing he seemed to fear.

Finally the ancestor turned her gaze away from Gaven and wheeled on Senya. "Your question is answered, my counsel given. Depart from here, and may you bring honor and not shame to your family."

Senya pressed her forehead to the ground then stood and busied herself around the brazier that burned in the corner of the room—Gaven had not noticed it before—but the ancestor interrupted her.

"I do not care for your prayers and offerings. Be gone!"

Startled, Senya hurried from the chamber, Darraun right on her heels. Haldren and Cart followed. Gaven tried to avoid the ancestor's gaze as he moved to the door, but she placed herself in his path.

"Who are you?" she demanded.

"I am just a man," he said again. "Gaven, once of House Lyrandar."

"Go then, Gaven. Twice you have come to me now. The third time, you will finally find what you seek."

Gaven hurried after Cart. He did not think he breathed until he was back on the street.

When he reached the street, Haldren snarled at him. "What in the Realm of Madness was all that about?" The sorcerer's face twisted in rage.

Gaven shrugged, his eyes darting everywhere but in Haldren's direction. He wasn't sure what had happened, but he certainly didn't want to tell Haldren what he suspected.

"How did she know you?" Senya asked. "Why did she say you'd been here before?" Her voice held none of the fury of Haldren's outburst, and Gaven allowed his eyes to meet hers. But he quickly looked away, and shrugged again.

"Who did she think you were?" Haldren demanded.

Gaven sat on his haunches and stared at the ground.

Darraun put a hand on Haldren's arm. "Why are you so angry, Haldren?" he said. "What did you expect to happen in there?"

Haldren straightened and seemed to calm down a bit, but his eyes were still narrowed in suspicion, and he didn't answer Darraun. "Have you been here before? Is that how you learned about the Prophecy?"

I have not been here before, Gaven thought. I just remember being here. He ran a finger along a groove between the cobblestones. But what had the ancestor meant with those words? The third time, you will finally find what you seek?

Senya fell to her knees in front of Gaven, trying to make him meet her eyes. "Gaven, that was my ancestor in there, and she said you had been there before," she said. "Why did she say that? What's your connection to my family?"

Gaven kept his eyes on the ground. Senya Alvena Arrathinen, he thought. What is your relation to my old friend Mendaros? No—I never knew him, he reminded himself, shaking his head. That was the other.

"Damn you!" Senya drew her hand back as if to slap him, but Cart's words stopped her.

"It seems those showers of light have begun," the warforged said.

Gaven looked up at the night sky. The Ring of Siberys made it look like an overcast day; the sky was dark blue gray and studded with points of golden light. Streaks of fire crossed the sky as dragonshards fell from the ring and rained to earth.

A few dragonshards clattered on the stone streets nearby, and Gaven heard others striking the buildings above them. He had been a prospector—that's what he'd told Darraun. To a prospector's mind, there was a small fortune to be made here. Siberys shards were the most precious dragonshards, useful primarily to the dragonmarked houses, who sent prospectors to Xen'drik to find the products of showers like this one. Properly attuned, a Siberys shard could enhance the power of a dragonmark in a variety of ways. House Lyrandar built them into the helms of their galleons—probably their airships as well—so that a dragonmarked heir of the house could control the elemental spirit bound into the ship. Clearly many of the living residents of the City of the Dead shared that point of view. They were scrambling after the shards that landed in the street like chickens after a handful of seed.

But Gaven was not here to make a fortune, and the shard they sought was no ordinary dragonshard. As he looked, one shard flared brighter than all the others and streaked across the sky. It grew brighter as it fell, stinging his eyes. When it landed, he heard its impact, like a great spear striking the earth. It was close, no more than a mile outside the city.

"The Eye of Siberys," Haldren said. "Move!"

Gaven did not need Haldren's command—he was already on his feet and three strides ahead of Haldren. Darraun kept pace with him at first—spurred, no doubt, by his eagerness to leave the City of the Dead—but Gaven soon left him behind.

The guards at the gate started to close ranks as he approached, probably assuming that he was fleeing the scene of a crime or trying to escape an angry watch patrol. Gaven prepared himself to barrel right through the guards if necessary. It proved not to be necessary—either the guards noticed the lack of any pursuit or they figured the city was best rid of the foreigners anyway.

It felt good to run. For so many years he had been confined to a small cell or given his exercise in a tiny yard where he just walked, slowly, counting his paces like the passing of years. Now the wind whipped his hair behind him, cooling the sweat from his face. His arms and legs pumped hard, his muscles protesting the exertion but also exulting in his speed. He remembered riding on the wyvern's back behind Cart, feeling the dragon's muscles as it flapped its wings hard to propel them through the air, and for a moment he felt as if he were flying.

A hundred yards outside the city, he realized he didn't know where he was running. Three more steps, and he realized he didn't care. He would run until he reached the sea, and then he would take flight and run across the waves. The wind blew at his back, and he could almost feel it lifting him off the ground.

In the jungle ahead of him, he saw a flicker of golden fire lighting a wisp of smoke, and he remembered why he ran. He turned toward the glow. The wind blew his hair into his face, and he lifted a hand to brush it aside. Then he was upon the source of the golden fire, and he stopped running.

The wind billowed around him, lashing the ferns and the leaves of the overhanging trees like a tiny cyclone, then it blew itself out. Gaven looked down at the Eye of Siberys where it lay, nestled in the tiny crater of its impact, where the earth had formed a sheltering hand to hold it. Blackened ferns lined its bed, burned from its heat, still blowing out wisps of smoke that twisted and danced in the dying wind. He fell to his knees and stretched out a trembling hand to touch it.

It was warm, not hot as he'd feared. Its yellow surface shone with light reflected from the Ring of Siberys high above, and veins of gold in its heart pulsed with a light of their own. He scooped it up with both hands, holding it in front of him like a chalice full of holy water. As he stood, he heard thunderous footsteps behind him, and he pulled it close to his chest as he turned to face his companions.

Darraun reached him first, wild amazement in his eyes. He was breathing too hard to speak, and he bent over double to catch his breath before Haldren and the others reached them.

Gaven cradled the Eye of Siberys close. Its warmth spread through him and set his dragonmark tingling.

CHAPTER 10

"T" hat was quite a run," Darraun said, trying to smile as he panted.
Gaven ignored him, his gaze fixed on the pulsing veins of gold in
the heart of the dragonshard.

"Gaven?" No answer.

Darraun shot a nervous glance over his shoulder at Haldren, who ran as
fast as his old legs could carry him. He was still a bowshot away, though Senya
and Cart were closer.

Stepping closer to Gaven, Darraun tried to get a good look at the crystal, good
enough to analyze the magic in it. "Gaven, if you'll let me look at that . . ."

Gaven turned away, shielding the dragonshard against his chest, his eyes
still glued to it.

Darraun put a hand on Gaven's shoulder. "Gaven, look at me." He shook
him gently, then harder. Gaven pulled away but didn't raise his eyes.

"This is not good," Darraun muttered. "I'm sorry about this, Gaven." He
swung his fist at Gaven's chin as hard as he could, hoping to snap Gaven out
of this trance.

A deafening clap of thunder shattered the air, and Darraun found himself
on his back two strides away from Gaven, gasping for breath. His ears rang,
but he could still hear the footsteps approaching.

Senya and Cart stopped dead near where Darraun lay. Cart fell to one knee
beside him.

"Are you injured?" the warforged asked, his voice heavy with concern.
Darraun shook his head. "What did he do to you?"

Darraun sat up. Gaven still held up the hand he had used to block Darraun's punch, but his eyes remained focused on the dragonshard in his other
hand. Senya stood behind Cart, staring at Gaven as if she were entranced. A
clap of thunder rumbled somewhere in the distance.

"I'm not sure," he said. "I think the dragonshard is enchanting him somehow, so I tried to wrench his attention away from it. Evidently he's got some
attention to spare—enough to defend himself anyway."

"Evidently," Cart said. He lifted Darraun to his feet and shifted his shield on his arm, his right hand coming to rest on the head of his axe.

"Do we need to take him down?" Senya whispered.

Darraun turned around just as Haldren caught up with them, breathing heavily from the exertion. "I don't think—" he started to say, but Haldren cut him off.

"Gaven!" Haldren stepped forward, extending a hand to Gaven. "Give me the Eye of Siberys now!"

To Darraun's surprise, Gaven looked up at the sorcerer, holding the dragonshard in his left hand, as far from Haldren as possible.

"Not until you tell me exactly what is going on," Gaven said.

*   *   *   *   *

Seeing the Eye of Siberys and touching it, Gaven's mind flooded with memories. There could be no doubt that it was the dragonshard of his visions—he had seen that crystal shard carved to a point and bound to an ash-black staff to form a spear. He'd seen it plunge into the twisting shadow body of the Soul Reaver, in fulfillment of the Prophecy—

There among the bones of Khyber the Storm Dragon drives the spear formed from Siberys's Eye into the Soul Reaver's heart.

As he continued gazing into the dragonshard's liquid depths, Gaven found himself very aware of the present. The Eye had earned its name. Staring into it was like opening a great eye onto the world. He saw Darraun approach, with the others straggling behind. He saw Darraun pulling his hand back for a punch, and it took little more than a thought for him to react, blocking the punch and knocking Darraun away, without ever looking up from the dragonshard. He saw as he had never seen before—he saw every living thing nearby, from the gibbons in the trees to the ants crawling along the ground. He saw each tree, the orchids nestled in their branches, the lianas coiled around their trunks, and the ferns shielding the earth.

And then he saw himself, far more clearly than ever before. He remembered who he was, the man he'd been before Dreadhold, before the memories of the other came and coiled in his mind. And he saw the man he'd become, stumbling along behind Haldren's lead in a fog of confusion or madness. He realized that he did not want to be that man any longer. It was time to confront Haldren, who had reached him and demanded the dragonshard.

"Not until you tell me exactly what is going on." Gaven stared into Haldren's pale blue eyes, which were open wide in surprise.

"Very well, Gaven," the sorcerer said. Gaven enjoyed seeing Haldren caught off guard. "Very well. We have no secrets here. What do you want to know?"

"You think Vaskar is the Storm Dragon of the Prophecy," Gaven said. "You're helping him raise the Sky Caves of Thieren Kor so that he can walk in the paths of the first ascendant and become a god. What's in it for you?"

"A noble enough goal in itself, don't you think?" Haldren had recovered his wits, and his voice was smooth.

"I don't know about Vaskar, but most people don't aspire to seize godhood out of a benevolent desire to make the world better," Gaven said.

"On the contrary, Gaven, most of us believe that the world would be a better place if we had the power to shape it according to our will."

"I'm sure you'd like the same power. How do you plan to get it?"

"In exchange for my aid in acquiring divine power, Vaskar has agreed to help me acquire power that is more temporal in nature."

"Which throne do you plan to seize?"

Haldren smiled. "The only throne worth holding."

Something gnawed at the edge of Gaven's mind—a fragment of the Prophecy, a flash of a vision or a nightmare, but he banished it. He would not be the madman any longer. "Thronehold?" he said. "A new Galifar?" Before the Last War, all Khorvaire had been united in a single empire ruled from Thronehold. The scions of old Galifar had warred for a century over the right to sit in that throne.

"Something like that, yes. You know that I appreciate your assistance, Gaven. I can assure you of a position of power in the new world."

"Why were you in Dreadhold?"

"For no worse crime than yours," Haldren whispered. Gaven could tell that he had struck a nerve. "I disagreed with our Queen Aurala over the way the war should be prosecuted."

"Sounds like you should have been stripped of your command, maybe thrown in an Aundairian jail. Why Dreadhold?"

Haldren's voice dropped to an urgent whisper, and he stepped closer to Gaven, speaking right into his face. "You were already imprisoned at the time, Gaven, but at the end of the war the nations decided they could put the horrors of the war behind them if they locked some people up. I was a scapegoat—they locked me up so they could believe that all the death and destruction was the work of criminals. I was fighting a war, damn it!"

"And now you're going to start the war all over again."

"It will be different this time. With Vaskar's help—"

Haldren reached out suddenly and tried to snatch the Eye of Siberys from Gaven's hand, but Gaven yanked the Eye back away from Haldren, simultaneously thrusting his other hand forward. There was another thunderclap, but this time Haldren only stumbled back a few steps, while Gaven flew backward, landing hard a few paces away.

Haldren smirked and strode to stand over Gaven. "I won't underestimate you again, Gaven." He crouched and took the Eye of Siberys from Gaven's limp hand. Gaven stared wildly up at the sorcerer, every nerve in his body tingling. "I expect the same consideration in return." He turned away, stowing the dragonshard in one of the many pouches he wore.

Gaven sat up and glared at the sorcerer's back, embarrassed that Haldren had gotten the shard from him so easily. Then he slowly got to his feet and looked around at the others. Senya had Haldren's arm, apparently congratulating Haldren, though she kept glancing back at Gaven, too. Cart stood near Haldren as well, demonstrating his loyalty to his commanding officer, awaiting orders. Darraun had turned his back on the group and was looking at the surrounding jungle.

Gaven reviewed his situation. He was stuck on an unfriendly island with a war criminal who wanted to rule the world. And who, Gaven reminded himself, was his only means of getting back to the mainland. His most likely ally was Darraun, who was clearly hiding something, maybe a great deal. The warforged was completely loyal to Haldren—Darraun had said as much, and Cart's behavior reinforced it.

His eyes lingered on Senya. She was still something of a mystery to him, but the prospect of unraveling that mystery was starting to grow more interesting. She glanced back at him, caught his stare, and flashed him a coy smile before looking back at Haldren.

* * * * *

Haldren conferred briefly with Senya, then announced his plans.

"Tonight we'll make camp in the jungle," he said, "but not here. We need to get far enough from the city that the elves will leave us alone."

"And far enough that we won't be bothered by treasure-seekers scouring the jungle for dragonshards," Senya added.

"We need supplies," Haldren said with a glare at Darraun, "so Senya will return to the city and secure them. The rest of us can relax for a short time. As soon as Senya returns, we march."

With that, he settled himself onto the ground. He was still breathing heavily from his exertion, Gaven saw, which gave him a slight feeling of satisfaction. Cart stood guard by his general, and Darraun busied himself with his pack, preparing for another march. Gaven sat as far away from Haldren as he thought the sorcerer would allow—still in sight and earshot.

He closed his eyes and imagined that he still held the Eye of Siberys, trying to remember the thoughts and feelings it had stirred in him. He'd seen the man he was before, and he clung to that memory—a sense of self that kept him in the present. But over and over he found his thoughts straying to what he had not seen: the man he could become.

In his youth, before he'd taken and failed the Test of Siberys, he'd had a clear idea of his future, even if it was not one that he would choose. His father expected him to manifest the Mark of Storm and work for House Lyrandar. Arnoth had groomed his eldest son to take over his dynasty, ignoring every indication that Gaven would have preferred a different life.

Failing the Test of Siberys had given Gaven an excuse to pursue something different, and Rienne had given him the opportunity. Together they explored the depths of Khyber—still working for House Lyrandar, but in a way of his own choosing. With Rienne at his side, he had never worried much about his future, as long as she was in it.

He saw Rienne at his side in Khyber's depths, holding a flickering torch up so he could read the words scratched into the cavern wall.

The Eye of Siberys lifts the Sky Caves of Thieren Kor from the land of desolation under the dark of the great moon, and the Storm Dragon walks in the paths of the first of sixteen.

He saw a great mass of stone suspended in the air, floating above a blasted wasteland. A storm churned the sky above him, and he thought he saw a dragon wheeling in the air. A flash of lightning showed him bronze scales.

"We march, Gaven. Come!" Haldren's barked command jerked him out of his vision, and for a moment he was in his cell in Dreadhold. Then the walls dissolved into jungle, and he scrambled to his feet.

* * * * *

They walked through the jungle in the cold light of the Ring of Siberys, Cart and Senya leading the way. Gaven counted his footsteps as he'd done in the exercise yard in Dreadhold, trying to keep his mind from straying. His count approached three thousand before Haldren finally called a halt and ordered Cart to pitch their tents.

Gaven helped Cart set up the camp, partly to keep his mind off other things, and partly because he simply enjoyed the quiet company of the warforged. They built a fire, which Darraun used to cook another fine meal. Gaven realized that he hadn't eaten since their luncheon in Whitecliff that afternoon, and just the smell of Darraun's cooking was a delight.

"In the morning we return to Khorvaire," Haldren announced as they ate.

"Where are we going next?" Gaven asked.

"Senya and I discussed that question earlier, and I am of the opinion that Darguun is the best possible destination for tomorrow's journey."

"Darguun?" Gaven asked. "The goblin lands?"

"Indeed," Haldren said. "Are you aware of the rebellion that carved the lands of Darguun as an independent entity?"

"I knew of the rebellion, yes. But I assumed that those lands were destroyed along with the rest of Cyre."

"They were not. And the goblin leader, Haruuc, was recognized as ruler of a sovereign nation in the treaties that ended the war. It remains something of a frontier land, though, which is why it suits our purposes. We should be able to do business there without interference from the dragonmarked houses and their agents, who are presumably still searching for us across the length and breadth of Khorvaire."

"Darguun it is, then," Gaven said.

Haldren scowled at him. "I am glad you approve. And now we are going to bed." He got to his feet and extended a hand to Senya. "I suggest you all do the same—it has been a very long day."

Senya took his hand and kissed it. "I'll be there in a moment," she said, indicating the remainder of her meal. Haldren's scowl deepened, and he disappeared into his tent. Darraun took his pots over to a nearby stream to clean them, and Cart started patrolling a wide circle around the campsite. Gaven supposed he'd do that all night.

With a glance at the tent where Haldren waited for her, Senya set down her platter of food and reached for a large bundle beside her. Gaven watched as she pulled out a greatsword in a fine leather
sheath and brought it over to him.

"I picked this up in the city," she said with a smile. "I thought you'd like to be armed before we get into another fight."

"Thank you, Senya," Gaven said. "That was very thoughtful." He pulled the blade a little way out of the sheath and admired the fine edge and elegant scrollwork. The pommel bore a skull decoration, which seemed fitting—given both the elves' preoccupation with death and the purpose of any weapon.

Senya stared into the dying fire. "I'm still a little confused about what happened back there," she said, pointing over her shoulder toward Shae Mordai. "Have you really been here before?"

"I think your ancestor mistook me for someone else."

"That hardly seems likely, does it? We go to them for their wisdom."

Gaven shrugged.

"Do you think Vaskar is really the Storm Dragon, Gaven?"

Gaven looked at her, and she turned from the fire to meet his eyes.

"I don't know," he said. "I think I've seen him in my dreams, the color of his scales." The color of his scales—that thought sparked something in his mind. The Bronze Serpent . . .

He shook his head. Here and now, he told himself. Stop living in dreams and memories.

"I thought he was at first," Senya said, "but I don't think so any more." She looked back into the fire.

"You think this is all a fool's errand?" Gaven said. "Then why go along with it?"

"Well, even if Vaskar fails, Haldren still has a chance at getting what he needs. And besides," she said, "I didn't say it was a fool's errand." She looked at him sidelong. "Want to know what I think?"

"What do you think, Senya?"

Haldren bellowed from inside the tent. "Senya!"

She leaped to her feet but stopped to look down at Gaven again. "I think the Storm Dragon is you."

CHAPTER
11

When Darraun returned from the stream, he found Gaven staring into the embers of the fire. He saw Cart walking his tireless circle outside the camp, and waved to him as he came near. He sank down on the fallen log beside Gaven.

"Quite a day," he said.

Gaven made a sound a little like a laugh and nodded.

"This time last night I was landing a wyvern on top of Dreadhold."

"How did you end up a part of all this, Darraun?"

"Haldren figured the group needed someone with my skill set, to work on Dreadhold's defenses. And help keep everyone alive, I suppose. He planned the whole thing from his cell, you know."

"How did he do that? We were kept in the Spellward Tower—he couldn't use any magic there."

"Not in his cell, no. Except the magic of his tongue. You've probably noticed by now that he could talk a sphinx into answering its own riddle for him. So partly he persuaded the guards to help him out. And he also used some magic to talk to Vaskar, when he was out of his cell for exercise and such. Again, he talked his way out of the usual restraints and the constant supervision."

Gaven shook his head. "So he told Cart and Senya to find an artificer, and they got you?"

"Senya talked to people in Aundair who were loyal to Haldren, and my name came up."

Gaven turned to look at him—a little too closely, Darraun thought. "You made sure your name would come up," Gaven said.

Darraun let a trace of a smile show on his face. "What do you mean?" he said.

Gaven shrugged. "So are you a true believer in Haldren's cause? Anxious to see him sitting on the throne of a new Galifar? Or are you just along for the ride?"

"Something like that."

"Something like which one?"

"What were we talking about?"

Gaven arched an eyebrow at him and stopped asking questions.

"So," Darraun said, "now that you know all about Haldren's plans, what are you going to do?"

"Do?" Gaven scratched his chin. "At this point, it seems I'm along for the ride whether I like it or not."

"I take it you don't like it."

"It's better than Dreadhold, but I don't look forward to spending the rest of my life on the run from Sentinel Marshals. If I'm going to be free, I'd like to be really free."

"And you think helping Haldren will get you there?"

Gaven scoffed. "No. I think helping Haldren will get me dead."

"So you're along for the ride for now. Not long-term."

"Why am I telling you all this?"

"Because I could talk a sphinx into answering its own riddle for me."

"I thought that was Cart."

Darraun laughed. "Don't underestimate Cart's powers of persuasion."

"Believe me, I don't. I saw the way he jumped at that . . . thing." Gaven gestured out toward the surrounding jungle.

"The displacer beast? Yeah, Cart can handle himself in a fight."

Gaven stared into the dying embers.

Darraun shifted so he could see Gaven more easily. "What would you do if you were really free?"

Gaven raised his eyebrows, but he didn't look away from the fire. "I have no idea," he said.

"You didn't spend the last twenty-six years making plans?"

Gaven shook his head. "It never occurred to me that I might get out of there. I spent that whole time . . . I don't know. I wasn't thinking about the future." His brow furrowed. "Well, I wasn't thinking about my future."

"Just the Prophecy."

"Right."

"The future of the world, the future of countless people whose names you don't know. Great events and terrible cataclysms. And no idea where you fit in to it all."

"I never would have thought it had anything to do with me," Gaven said, looking up. "The Prophecy was just a hobby for me, until—" He broke off and looked back to the fire.

"Until what?"

"I don't know. Until I was in Dreadhold and had nothing else to think about."

Darraun cursed to himself. He'd been so close, but he'd pushed too hard and Gaven had shut him out again. Until . . . what? he wondered. What had made the Prophecy take such a hold over Gaven's mind?

And how could he not know his own part in it?

*   *   *   *   *

Haldren roused them early and set Cart to work packing up the camp. Gaven found it increasingly difficult to sit around the campfire and eat with these people. He'd fought with Haldren when he found the Eye of Siberys, and he was chafing under the sorcerer's barked commands and patronizing explanations. He'd shown a little too much of his thoughts to Darraun last night. And Senya kept looking at him in a way that made him distinctly uncomfortable. After eating as quickly as he could, he got up to help Cart roll up the tents.

All too soon they stood in a close circle again. Senya held Gaven's right hand and Darraun his left, and both seemed as though they believed Gaven could understand a secret language of squeezing his hands. He almost pulled both hands free in frustration just as Haldren completed the spell and brought them, in the blink of an eye, to Darguun.

The hobgoblin lands presented a stark contrast to the steaming jungles of Aerenal. The air was no less sweltering, even so early in the morning. But the towering trees and lush ferns were replaced by dry grasses, stunted shrubs, and barren outcroppings of red and gold rock.

"The Torlaac Moor," Haldren announced.

Gaven surmised that Haldren was the only one of the group who had been here before. The rest looked around at the alien landscape with curiosity and perhaps fear.

Haldren gestured to the rising sun. "To the east is the Khraal rain forest, which is not too different from the jungle we just left on Aerenal." Gaven could see a green haze on the horizon he supposed might be the canopy of a distant jungle.

"Jaelarthal Orioth," Senya said. "The Moonsword Jungle."

"I'm not sure what Khraal means in the Goblin tongue," Haldren said. "It probably describes a peculiar form of disembowelment, knowing their language. And knowing the jungle, for that matter." He turned and pointed in the opposite direction. "To the west, the Seawall Mountains divide this land from Zilargo. Just north of here, the Torlaac River marks the end of the moor, and wide plains make up the rest of the goblin lands. Far to the north, goblins dwell in ruined cities built by the good people of Cyre. Beyond that region, to the east, is the Mournland."

"I see no settlements nearby," Gaven said. "Where are we supposed to get supplies?"

"Have faith, Gaven," Haldren said with a patronizing smile. "As I did when we journeyed to Whitecliff and Aerenal, I chose a destination outside of a settlement and out of sight, lest our sudden appearance startle the natives. And far better to startle an elf in Aerenal than some bugbear going about his business in Darguun."

He laughed at his own joke, and Senya smiled at him. Darraun and Cart were busy scanning the horizon.

"In any case," Haldren continued, "there's a small town on the river just down in the valley there, to the north. It carries the rather quaint name of Grellreach."

"Grellreach?" Gaven said. "I don't understand."

Haldren started walking to the north, with Senya and Cart falling into place beside him. Clearly, Cart was not going to allow Haldren to fall victim to another surprise attack.

"Grells are hideous aberrations said to dwell in the Seawalls near here," Haldren explained as he walked. "They've been described as flying brains with beaklike mouths and long, barbed tentacles. Can you imagine living in a town named after such a thing?"

"I take it that it was not originally a Cyran settlement," Darraun said with a wry smile.

Haldren laughed. "No, it was not."

* * * * *

The spell had set them down a considerable distance from Grellreach, despite Haldren's easy confidence. They walked through the morning, with the sun growing hotter as it neared its zenith, before they even came into sight of the town. They walked through fields of grain nestled between the wreckage of ancient settlements and monuments. Wheat stalks brushed up against weather-beaten blocks of reddish stone, the vague outlines of long-fallen buildings. Here and there a farmhouse stood at the feet of an ancient colossus, clearly built from stone salvaged from the toppled statue. Gaven had to remind himself that, as easy as it might be to think of the goblins of these lands as brutal savages, they had once ruled a mighty empire that stretched across the length and breadth of Khorvaire.

Farmhouses appeared more often, and at last the party came within sight of the town's wooden palisade. Haldren called a halt. "We need to be careful how we approach," he said. "I'm certain I can get us all inside, if we're careful and play it right. People of Darguun are not generally fond of elves—and I have no idea how they'll react to Cart. So Darraun and I will draw near the gate first. And I will do the talking," he added, with a commanding glare in Darraun's direction.

Darraun nodded, and the two of them closed the remaining distance to the town. Cart took a few long paces after Haldren, then dropped to one knee to wait and watch. Gaven found himself more or less alone with Senya. She gazed after Haldren too, and Gaven shifted uncomfortably.

"It's funny," she said, without turning toward him. "Haldren was in Dreadhold for three years, and he's basically had only one thing on his mind since he got out. You were there, what? Twenty-six?" She turned to face him now. "And you're afraid to look at me. I'm starting to wonder if you found a way to become deathless while you were locked up."

Gaven felt his face flush, and he turned away from her.

"Or is it your destiny that keeps you focused on higher things?" she said. He heard her step closer behind him, and he swallowed hard. "The Storm Dragon must have more important concerns—the realm of the spirit, not the flesh." Another step, and he could feel her presence close to him, electrifying, like a storm brewing overhead.

Gaven found it strangely hard to speak. "I'm not the Storm Dragon, Senya," he said. "I'm just a book in which the Prophecy is written."

He heard the creak of her leather coat behind him and felt her light touch on his shoulder, tracing his dragonmark where it disappeared beneath the collar of his shirt. "And written on," she said. Her finger tugged on his collar as she traced the dragonmark downward. "But who wrote it, I wonder?"

Gaven closed his eyes, and Rienne was there with him, touching him, letting him lose himself in her skin. He felt Senya's hands on his chest, and she pressed herself against his back. He pulled away, whirling to face her again.

"You don't want me," he said, shaking his head violently and looking down at the ground. "You want the power you think I represent. You're wrong about me, Senya."

She stepped close again and breathed into his ear. "So what if I am? What do you want, Gaven?" She put a hand on his chest and started to slide it downward.

He took her shoulders in his hands and gently pushed her away, looking straight into her bright blue eyes. "I don't want you," he said.

He couldn't quite read the expression that twisted her face. It was clear that she wasn't used to being refused, and her hurt pride made her angry and defensive. But her eyes held something else, something that her anger couldn't quench.

"Senya!" Cart's voice surprised them both, and Gaven saw Senya's pale skin flush red. "Gaven!" the warforged called. "Haldren is signaling! Time to move!"

Gaven wondered how much Cart had seen or heard, and what he'd tell the Lord General. His mind filled with a string of curses directed at Senya and himself, even as his feet carried him quickly to the gate of Grellreach.

CHAPTER
12

Darraun took in the scene while he waited with Haldren for Gaven and the others to catch up. His travels had taken him over most of Khorvaire, to Xen'drik a couple of times, and now to Aerenal, but Darguun was a new experience. It wasn't uncommon to see the three races of goblinkind—the burly bugbears, proud hobgoblins, and sniveling goblins—in the rougher parts of many cities, and they were more common the closer you came to the fringes of civilization. Here, though, they were everywhere, from the guards at the gate to the merchants hawking their wares in ramshackle stalls that lined the main street.

Four hobgoblins stood proudly at the gate, wearing piecemeal armor—mismatched plates and bits of chain over a basic suit of leather—that was at least clean and well maintained. They leaned on polearms that were as motley as their armor, watching impassively as Haldren led the group through the gate. The guards were all almost a head taller than Darraun and looked considerably stronger, so he was glad that Haldren had so easily talked his way past them. Just past the gate stood a bugbear who looked like he was normally kept chained and as if he might begin a savage rampage at any moment—head and shoulders taller than the hobgoblins, covered in matted fur, and armed with a wickedly serrated sword. Despite his appearance, he too let them pass without incident.

If one could forget that all the citizens of this town were goblinkind, Darraun reflected, it would not seem very different from Whitecliff. The buildings were constructed from stone blocks salvaged from the surrounding ruins, but they were well made. Street vendors hawked food, clothing, and tools from push-carts and wagons pulled by donkeys or oxen. Many of the buyers were women, and children ran and played on the rutted dirt streets.

One thing made this place different from Whitecliff in a way that Darraun didn't like. People stared at them wherever they walked—particularly at Cart, he noticed—and Darraun squirmed under their curious gaze. He had made a living out of blending in, and to be attracting so much attention made him nervous.

"Senya and I will get the supplies," Haldren said as they made their way down the town's main street. "We won't spend the night here, so there's no point in getting a room—even assuming we could find one that would take us." He called a halt in front of an open-air building—some sort of restaurant or tavern by the looks of it—crowded with rowdy hobgoblins, probably drunk even in the early afternoon. "Why don't you three find a table here and pass the time until we're finished?"

Some of the nearby hobgoblins stared at Cart and pushed out their chests in a way that Darraun recognized as a sign of aggression, so he wasn't sure Haldren's idea was a good one. But the sorcerer was already walking away, his arm locked around Senya's waist. "And watch your tongues," Haldren said over his shoulder, shooting a glare at Gaven.

With a sigh, Darraun led the way to a table in the quietest corner of the place, making a wide circle around the aggressive hobgoblins near the street. "Do either of you speak Goblin?" he mumbled as they took their seats.

Gaven shook his head, and Cart said, "A few words—the kind soldiers throw around."

"Let me order, then," Darraun said, as a rail-thin goblin woman approached the table.

"Azhra dam?" Her voice was a high growl.

"Two ales," Darraun answered in Goblin, and the goblin woman vanished in the crowd.

"I hope Haldren comes back quickly," Gaven muttered.

"I agree," Darraun said. "Cart, some of these men were looking at you in a way I didn't like."

"I noticed that," the warforged said, "but I'm used to it."

"Kak-darzhul!" Three of the hobgoblins Darraun had seen before stomped to their table, and the one in front addressed Cart. The warforged turned to face the one who had spoken. He was almost as big as Cart, and his arms were as thick as Darraun's legs.

"He doesn't speak Goblin," Darraun said, pronouncing his words carefully to avoid any insult.

"Tell him I think his ancestors' swords couldn't cut the tail from a lizard," the hobgoblin said.

Darraun started to explain the hobgoblin's insult to Cart, but the warforged interrupted, rising to his feet. "Your ancestors couldn't sharpen sticks to use as spears," Cart said in perfect Goblin.

Darraun bit back a laugh. Naturally, the language of insults would be what Cart had learned from goblin soldiers.

The hobgoblin pounded his chest with one fist, raising the other hand toward Cart. Cart mimicked the gesture, and the onlooking goblins backed up, making a wide circle with Cart and their leader at the center. Cart and the hobgoblin clasped hands and started to push.

Darraun had never seen this form of contest before, but it was easy enough to see what was going on. Right palms together, each man pushed to his left, trying to force his opponent off balance. Their feet were firmly planted on the dirt floor, so Darraun surmised that a single step would mean defeat.

He also quickly saw what he hoped none of the goblins could discern: Cart was holding back. He would win eventually, but he was letting the goblin feel that the contest was a close one. Darraun smiled. Cart continued to impress him, demonstrating an amazing sympathy for the emotions of flesh-and-blood people.

A dozen goblins circled the contestants, shouting, laughing, and making wagers on the outcome. Cart showed no sign of exertion, of course, but his opponent grunted as his biceps bulged, veins pulsing. He leaned in closer, baring sharp fangs in Cart's face and snarling to intimidate him. Unfazed, Cart bent his legs to lower his center of gravity, and with one last push he sent the hobgoblin sprawling on the ground. Cart gave his chest one more resounding thump and returned to his seat, among the yells and jeers of the onlookers.

A quick glance around confirmed Darraun's suspicion that a lot of money had just changed hands. He figured that meant that their chances of nursing their drinks in peace were almost zero, and his fears were confirmed when a big bugbear stepped into the circle, drawing a chorus of loud cheers.

The bugbear pointed at the defeated hobgoblin, who tried to slink away. "Prax is so stupid he doesn't know that the kak-darzhul have no ancestors," the bugbear growled.

Many in the crowd laughed, but several looked with wide eyes toward Cart, wondering how he would respond to what they considered a grievous insult.

Cart leaned close to Darraun and whispered, "What did he say?"

Darraun translated, and Cart stood up. "Well, I wasn't drinking anyway," he said with a sigh. In Goblin, he addressed his challenger. "I'd rather have no ancestors than have ancestors too weak to throw stones."

The crowd murmured a mixture of approval and offense, and the bugbear roared as he pounded his chest. Cart seized his outstretched hand, and the contest began. Darraun could see that the warforged had found a closer match, but he predicted another victory. From what he could hear of the wagering, it seemed the bettors favored the bugbear, and Darraun briefly considered placing a bet.

Again, Cart gave the appearance of a good fight before forcing the bugbear off balance. The big man took two steps and didn't fall, but it was no less humiliating a defeat. More money changed hands, sending the music of clinking coins all around the circle. Challengers began to line up. Darraun looked around for the ale he'd ordered—if he was going to watch fights all afternoon, he wanted to do it with a drink in his hand.

He didn't see the goblin who had taken his order, but Gaven caught his eye. The half-elf watched intently as the next contest began, and Darraun watched the muscles in his arm flexing. Did he want to get in on the action? he wondered.

Cart defeated four more challengers, and the crowd grew boisterous. The next one in line showed some hesitation, to the derision of the onlookers, and Gaven got to his feet before Darraun could stop him.

"All right, Cart," Gaven said, "I don't know the formalities of the challenge here, but I know how to do the wrestling." He beat his chest as he'd seen the goblins do and raised a hand to Cart.

"Well, I should think of some way to insult your ancestors," Cart said, "but I'm afraid I'm running out of ideas. And I have nothing but respect for House Lyrandar, in general."

"Chaos take House Lyrandar," Gaven said, "and your makers in House Cannith, for that matter. Let's do this."

Cart beat his chest, seized Gaven's hand, and started to push. Gaven pushed back, hard, and Cart had to stop holding back. Darraun's mind flashed back to the jungle, the previous night, when he'd tried to punch Gaven and ended up flat on his back. He imagined for a moment that he heard a rumble of thunder in the clear blue sky.

The bets favored the warforged now. "I could have made a fortune here today," he muttered to himself, shaking his head. "I've never seen people so eager to make losing wagers."

It was over quickly. Cart's left foot shifted slightly, then he stepped back with his right. A silence fell over the crowd, then the few spectators who had won money started to cheer, and then the circle closed. Hobgoblins and bugbears swarmed around Cart and Gaven, jabbering at them in Goblin, throwing out a few words of congratulations—and curses—in Common. Darraun smiled. They'd won their acceptance.

They had also attracted a great deal of attention, which had been exactly what Darraun had hoped to avoid. Still, there was no sign of Sentinel Marshals appearing on the scene, no city watch coming to investigate the disturbance, no brawl breaking out. He was starting to like Darguun.

* * * * *

Gaven spotted Senya first, peering around the edges of the bar, looking for them. Haldren hung back, wearing new clothes. Both of them carried new backpacks loaded with goods. Gaven looked down at his own worn shirt and breeches, the same clothes he'd been wearing in Dreadhold before his release. At least he had a sword.

Haldren and Senya were having a hard time finding him, surrounded as he was by rowdy goblins waiting their turn to buy him a drink. Gaven stood, prompting some shouts from people nearby.

"Haldren!" he called. "Over here!"

Haldren looked around, spotted Gaven, and scowled. He hit Senya's shoulder and pointed at Gaven, started toward the unruly crowd, then thought better of it, waving impatiently in Gaven's direction.

"Cart, Darraun," Gaven said, "our escort has returned."

Cart leaped to his feet, breaking the hold of a trio of inebriated hobgoblins who had been draping themselves over his shoulders, trying to get the warforged to drink. Darraun was not thronged by as many admirers—his command of Goblin and his ready wit had won him some friends, but those qualities were not as impressive to the goblins as the sheer strength Gaven and Cart had demonstrated—so he was able to extricate himself from the crowd and get over to Haldren quickly.

Gaven waded through the crush. With every step, goblins grabbed at his hands and jabbered at him, making him wish he could understand a word of Goblin. He hoped it was compliments or well-wishes they threw his way, rather than insults and challenges, but he figured he would never know. The crowd closed behind him as he passed, and he realized with a smile that their departure wasn't going to quiet the party.

"Would you care to explain that spectacle?" Haldren said to Darraun as Gaven drew near. His voice was a threatening whisper.

"Well," Darraun said, "a hobgoblin challenged Cart to a kind of wrestling match, which Cart won. Then he beat a bugbear, then people were lining up to challenge him. Then Gaven—"

"Relax, Haldren," Gaven interrupted. "We kept our mouths shut, and no one here cares a damn who we are or who wants to find us. Looks like you two got what we need. We stayed out of trouble and had a little fun. No harm done. Let's get on our way."

"I will be the judge of what incidents are important or otherwise," Haldren said. "And I will remind you, Gaven, that I am in command of this expedition."

Gaven took a step toward Haldren and looked into his weathered face. "I don't like taking orders, Haldren. I'm not a good little soldier. I never obeyed my father. And the fact that you orchestrated my escape from Dreadhold doesn't mean that you own me."

Haldren's face went purple with fury as he returned Gaven's stare. "Perhaps it would be best if you continued to think of yourself as a prisoner, then. I wouldn't want you getting ideas that you are free to travel about as you please. You are part of this expedition whether you like it or not."

His eyes rested on the pommel of the sword slung on Gaven's back, as if he were noticing it for the first time.

"Where did you get that sword?" he whispered.

Gaven reached over his shoulder and drew the blade out of its sheath, without moving away from Haldren. "You like it?" he said. "Senya got it for me in Shae Mordai."

"Senya?" Haldren whirled on her. "You armed this madman?"

Senya stood her ground to Gaven's surprise—and, evidently, to Haldren's as well. "I thought it would help our cause if he didn't get torn to shreds by another pack of displacer beasts," she said.

Haldren's fury was palpable as he turned back to Gaven. "Clearly, I underestimated you. I took you for an idiot with nothing in your mind but the Prophecy, and now even Senya is doing you favors. But listen to me, Gaven—all of you, listen well. This isn't about the Prophecy or Vaskar's dreams of godhood. It's about my destiny, and I will not be denied what is due me. If you think for a moment of standing in my way, I will crush you. Any of you," he added, with a glance toward Senya. "Don't question whether I can really will." He thrust a finger into Gaven's chest. "I will snuff your life like a candle."

In his mind, Gaven saw himself bringing his sword around, cutting right into Haldren's belly so he would die slowly and in great pain. The hand holding the sword tightened, the muscles flexed, his other hand itched for a grip on the smooth leather of the hilt. Something held him back, though. Perhaps it was just his better judgment, or the stares of the goblins who were circling them, watching the argument even if they couldn't understand the language. But some part of Gaven's mind whispered words of the Prophecy.

Gaven growled as he slid the sword back into its sheath. He took some pleasure, at least, in seeing the briefest flinch cross Haldren's face as the huge blade swung past. Several people in the crowd groaned with disappointment.

Gaven pushed his way through the encircling goblins and strode toward the gate of Grellreach. "Lead on, then, Haldren," he said.

CHAPTER
13

Haldren led them a short way outside of town, then gathered them into a circle. Gaven brooded as he walked, and the others seemed happy to share his silence.

"What's our next destination, Lord General?" Cart asked. The warforged was the only one who didn't seem subdued after the confrontation, and Gaven wondered what he had thought of Haldren's threats.

Haldren didn't answer. He seized Senya's hand in his left and Darraun's in his right and began the now-familiar chant of his spell without waiting for the others. Cart and Gaven quickly closed the circle. Senya clung fiercely to Gaven's hand before Haldren completed the spell that yanked them through space once again.

They stood in a mountain valley, barren rock stretching up on two sides. The bands of red and gold in the cliff faces suggested that they had not traveled far from the Torlaac Moor with its outcroppings of similar stone. Haldren gazed upward at something behind Gaven, so Gaven spun around, pulling his hand from Senya's grasp.

A towering ruin loomed before them, what had once been a grand city nestled among the mountains. A broken wall formed a ring at the head of the valley, each end blending seamlessly into a cliff wall. A gate was built into the wall on a massive bridge straddling a dry river bed. Colossal statues flanked the gate, mostly crumbled away but still showing traces of what looked like gnome features. The carvings were odd, and Gaven stared at them for a long moment trying to puzzle them out.

"Paluur Draal," Haldren announced. "We are high in the Seawall Mountains now, in land claimed by Zilargo. This city is one of the most important ruins of the ancient goblin Empire of Dhakaan in Khorvaire. Scholars from the Library of Korranberg have explored and catalogued it extensively, but they say there are many secrets yet to uncover."

"And what are we doing here?" Gaven said.

"We are looking for a map," Haldren said. "Specifically, one that will point us to the Sky Caves of Thieren Kor."

"So if this is a Dhakaani ruin," Senya said, "why are there gnomes guarding the gates?" She was staring at the same carvings that had puzzled Gaven.

"Those carvings were originally hobgoblins, or perhaps bugbears. However, several races inhabited Paluur Draal over the centuries—kobolds, humans, and gnomes most recently. By the time the gnomes settled here, the original statues were worn to mostly smooth pillars, so the gnomes carved them again in their own image."

"And where are we going to find this map?" Gaven said.

"We're going to look for it, as I said."

"Out here?"

Haldren didn't answer, but started walking toward the gate. Cart followed on his heels, with the others trailing more slowly after.

Heavy drops of rain began to fall as they entered the ruins, forming tiny craters in the dry earth. Gaven glowered up at the slate gray sky with a sense of satisfaction. Anger brewed like a storm in his mind, furrowing his brow and hunching his shoulders, and the rain seemed like a proper complement to his mood. He flexed his hands and arms as he walked, itching for a fight—for anything that would let him give vent to his frustration. He was tempted to attack Haldren outright, but he doubted he could take the sorcerer, Senya, and Cart by himself. He wondered which side Darraun would take.

So intent was his glare at Haldren's back that he barely saw the ruined city as they walked through it. He had an indistinct impression of stone buildings in varying states of ruin, none too different than what they'd passed in the fields outside Grellreach. They wandered along streets paved with shattered cobblestones and clambered over piles of rubble that blocked their way, and slowly made their way toward the cliff face at the back edge of the ancient city.

But Gaven noticed no details, took in none of the grandeur. His attention was solely on Haldren's back, imagining his new blade striking the sorcerer down. Despite his rage, Gaven couldn't swallow striking anyone in the back. He'd draw the sword, call for Haldren's attention, give the man a moment—no more—to ready himself, then bring the blade across and down. No. A quick death would be too good for Haldren. Gaven imagined summoning the fury of the storm itself, lightning falling to blast the sorcerer's smug grin from his face.

Thunder rumbled in the distance, and Gaven could feel the burning tingle of the storm coursing through him. He smiled and opened his mouth to call for Haldren—

A mountain troll emerged from a fissure in the cliff face. The troll's gray hide was covered with warty bumps like gravel. It was three times Gaven's height when it reared up, bellowing a rumbling roar, then it shambled forward using one rubbery hand to help it over the slippery ground, a splintered log held in the other hand.

At last! Here was the chance Gaven had been craving. The attack of the displacer beasts had caught him unprepared, the argument with Haldren had filled him with rage; but now he had a sword in his hand and a reason to fight. Gaven looked up at the enormous creature. A grim smile lit his face, and lightning flickered above them.

Then the creature's smell—a mix of carrion and excrement—hit him and nearly knocked him off his feet. Gaven was glad for the sword in his hand but nervous about his lack of armor. He circled to one side and let Cart take the brunt of the troll's initial charge.

With a word, Gaven made crackling lightning erupt along his elven blade. He ran forward, put all of his rage and frustration into his swing, and brought the sword around in a wide arc. The blade bit deep, and the lightning coursed up the creature's body. It howled in pain. Gaven glanced behind it—and noticed two smaller trolls emerging from the cave entrance. Perhaps that first roar hadn't been anger but a command, summoning the creature's followers to its aid.

"More on the way!" Gaven shouted.

The mountain troll's club came at him, and Gaven ducked, feeling the wind from the massive limb sweep over him. His attack had drawn the troll's attention. Either that, or the creature was smart enough to recognize an unarmored foe as a soft target. Following the big troll's lead, the other two moved in.

Gaven looked up at the trolls surrounding him. The big one was twice the size of the other two, but even the smaller ones were head and shoulders taller than him. Their claws reached for him even as the mountain troll raised its club.

Gaven kept his sword up, batting aside the smaller trolls' tentative slashes and grabs. The trolls stepped back, and Gaven dodged as the massive club came crashing down. He knew he couldn't outlast them in a hand-to-hand fight. They were too big, too fast, and too damned strong.

He focused his mind and chanted the syllables of another spell. Gaven's body erupted in violet flames, and the rain hissed into steam as it touched him. All three trolls recoiled.

The mountain troll turned from Gaven with a grunt and swung its club hard into Cart. The warforged took a couple of steps back, then shook off the blow and renewed his assault. Senya darted around the mountain troll's feet, finding its most vulnerable spots, the weaker parts of its thick, stony hide, and slashing at them with her light blade.

The two smaller trolls overcame their initial shock at the appearance of flames around Gaven, and one took a swipe at his back. The claws raked his skin, but the troll roared in pain as the violet flames engulfed its claws, searing its rubbery flesh. Both trolls backed away. Gaven brandished his sword with a roar of his own, and they scurried further back, unwilling to be seared by Gaven's fire.

"Gaven!" shouted Haldren.

Gaven tumbled and rolled back the merest instant before an eruption of flame struck the trolls, Even so, it seared him badly—the flames around his body burned the trolls that attacked him, but did nothing to protect him from other fires. He got back to his feet in a fury. Haldren had cast the spell, he was sure, and didn't seem to mind that Gaven had been caught in the blast. Despite his rage, Gaven had to admit that the spell had been effective. Both smaller trolls lay on the ground, their unmoving bodies charred black from the flames, and the mountain troll showed signs of serious injury. It could have been much worse.

Thunder rolled overhead, and Gaven leaped at the giant troll, channeling all his anger into each swing of his blade. It dropped to one knee, nearly overwhelmed, and Senya ran up its back to drive her sword into the base of its skull. The troll fell hard, throwing Senya to sprawl on the ground, but it did not move again. The fight was over. As Gaven tried to catch his breath, silence fell back over the ruins of Paluur Draal.

Gaven whirled on Haldren. "So what is it, Haldren? Are you dragging me along to help you on your fool's quest, or do you want to get rid of me?" He stood nose to nose with the old man again, and grabbed a fistful of Haldren's shirt. "Because if you want to get rid of me, I'll go. There's no need to kill me."

"Don't be absurd, Gaven."

"Absurd? You nearly blasted me into the fires of Fernia!"

"Hardly," Haldren said.

Gaven suddenly felt like a small child getting a scolding, and his anger boiled. He pulled Haldren up so his toes just dragged on the ground. "I'm not an idiot, Haldren."

"Of course, Gaven." No trace of fear came through in Haldren's voice. "I wasn't trying to hurt you, certainly not kill you. I simply realized too late that you had moved into the area of my spell. I did try to warn you."

Gaven realized that his threatening steps toward the retreating trolls had taken him closer to the center of the fiery blast, so Haldren's excuse might have been true. That possibility did little to diminish Gaven's rage, though. He pushed Haldren away and stalked over to Darraun, who crouched on the ground beside Cart.

It seemed the troll had gotten one good blow in before it fell. Cart's left arm looked badly hurt—or did it hurt? Gaven realized he had no idea if the warforged felt pain. In any event, Darraun ran his hands over the damaged arm, and his touch straightened bent plates and knotted broken cords back together. It was amazing and strangely fascinating—although, he realized, it wasn't too different in principle from the way a healer's magic knit flesh and bone back together. That was just a magic he was more used to seeing.

While Darraun tended to his injuries, Gaven traced a finger in a groove that ran through the stone on which he sat. He didn't like to watch a healer's magic when it was his flesh being knit together. A flash of light drew his eyes up to Haldren, who had just cast a spell to brighten the darkness inside the cave from which the trolls had emerged.

"Finished," Darraun said, and he rose to join the others, who were gathered around the cave entrance, staring upward.

Gaven started to get to his feet, but the groove he'd traced caught his attention. He had run his finger along a straight part of the groove, but it was not straight for long—it traced the outline of Kraken Bay.

"Behold!" Haldren announced, sweeping his arm across the cave entrance. "The sixteen gods of Dhakaan!"

Gaven brushed a thin coat of mud away from the stone, his heart racing. He glanced up at Haldren, but the sorcerer was completely absorbed in the spectacle within the cave. He looked back at his work, smiled, and tried to sweep mud back over the map he had uncovered.

* * * * *

Darraun looked over Haldren's shoulder at the cavern beyond. The cave might have been natural in origin, but the ancient builders of the place had carefully enlarged it, hollowing the ceiling and smoothing the walls. The debris of a thousand years and the more recent remnants of the trolls' habitation littered the floor, but as Darraun's eyes followed the arches up he realized that the grandeur of the ancient city was far better preserved here than anywhere else they had been so far.

Sixteen enormous figures stood around the far wall, their stone heads near the ceiling and their feet a troll's height above the floor. Most of the figures were proud hobgoblins, dressed in archaic armor and carrying ornate weapons. Two loomed taller than the others, bugbears with their hairy hides and fang-filled mouths, and one goblin crouched near the center of the frieze, half the size of the burly bugbears. As Darraun looked, Haldren started naming them.

"On the left end is Norrakath the Hunter, who slew the great serpent and roped in the sea with its corpse. When humans first came to Khorvaire, they identified him with Balinor."

Norrakath was a fearsome bugbear, leaning on a bow that seemed to be made of the bones of some beast—perhaps the ribs of the great serpent. He was a far cry from any representation of Balinor Darraun had ever seen, though the god of the hunt was sometimes depicted as a half-orc. Balinor smiled in every depiction Darraun had seen. Norrakath, on the other hand, snarled like a beast.

Haldren continued. "Beside him is Uthrek the Keeper. He was so fearsome a god of death that the early humans adopted him completely into their beliefs, though his Goblin name disappeared. He remains the evil god of death, the Keeper."

Uthrek was so gaunt as to be almost skeletal, perhaps intended to be an undead hobgoblin. Darraun had seen the Keeper depicted in similar fashion, but he was more commonly shown as a grossly fat human, hungry for the souls of the dead and a god of greed as well as death.

"Kin to Uthrek, beside him is Korthrek the Devourer, likewise adopted into human myth as one of the Dark Six." The god of the stormy sea was a hobgoblin with the many-toothed jaws of a shark.

"Next is Tauroc the Hammer, god of the forge. Obviously identified with Onatar." Darraun was used to seeing Onatar depicted as a dwarf, but he could easily see the similarities between this hobgoblin smith and the burly Onatar. The god's hammer, in particular, appeared the same as in many modern depictions of the god.

"Then we have Kol Korran, or I should say Rantash Mul, the Thief." Darraun started in surprise—this hobgoblin bore no resemblance whatsoever to any depiction of Kol Korran. Perhaps modern humans valued trade more highly than the ancient hobgoblins did, because Rantash Mul was sickly, sinister, and unpleasant. Kol Korran, by contrast, was usually shown as fat and cheerful.

"Next is Dukash the Lawbringer, sort of a culture hero of the Dhakaani. I'm afraid we humans neutered him when we identified him with Aureon. His exploits as a hobgoblin are something to read about."

Darraun could see the contrast. Aureon was the god of knowledge as well as law, and he was usually depicted as a somewhat frail, elderly wizard—sometimes even as a gnome. Dukash, in contrast, was the most vibrant figure before them now. He looked ready to leap out of the frieze, and his craftiness shone in his eyes.

"And now we come to the great mystery of the Dhakaan Empire," Haldren said, pointing at the figure in the middle. Its body had the erect posture of a hobgoblin, though it was taller even than the hulking bugbears at either end. Its face, however, had been completely obliterated. "This god was the greatest of the goblin pantheon. When the humans conquered Khorvaire, they identified some goblin gods with their own gods—Aureon and Kol Korran, Onatar and the other Sovereigns. Six goblin gods worked their way into human myth as the Dark Six. This one alone was suppressed, forgotten, struck from written legend, and wiped from memory."

A voice at Darraun's shoulder startled him. "The first of sixteen." Darraun had not heard Gaven come up behind him.

"Yes, Gaven, the first of sixteen," Haldren said. "The Gold Serpent whom the world has long since forgotten."

It took Darraun a moment to remember where he had heard the words before, but then he could hear the cold, clear voice of Senya's deathless ancestor in his mind. Snippets of that strange conversation between Gaven and the undying elder flashed through his mind.

In the first age of the world, sixteen dragons transcended their mortal forms to become like the Dragon Above who had made them.

"Wait," Darraun blurted, causing Haldren to turn and face him. "Senya's ancestor said that sixteen dragons became gods in the first age of the world. So you're suggesting that these sixteen dragons were the gods of the goblins, and fifteen of those gods are also the gods of the Host and the Dark Six?"

"Indeed," Haldren said. "That is exactly what I am saying."

"But why was that sixteenth god forgotten?"

"That is the great mystery of Dhakaan. It might be that the god was so closely identified with the Dhakaani that the humans obliterated any record of him in order to quell any resistance from the goblins they conquered." Haldren paced as he spoke, and he sounded as though he were thinking out loud. "Perhaps they believed that wiping out all memory of the god would also extirpate all memory of the goblin empire. On the other hand, the words of Senya's ancestor suggest that the god himself abandoned the world. Perhaps he stopped granting spells to his clerics. Or perhaps the goblins grew convinced that their god had abandoned them in allowing their defeat at human hands, and they themselves obliterated his memory. It could be that he abandoned the world because the world forgot him."

"I'm still not clear on what happened with the other fifteen," Senya said. "You said the humans identified some gods with gods of the Host, and adopted others like the Keeper? Those are the Dark Six?"

"Exactly," Haldren said, putting a hand on Senya's back. "As far as we know, the first humans to come across the sea worshiped nine gods—the Sovereign Host. They encountered the goblin pantheon of sixteen gods, and apparently they were willing to believe that they had lived in ignorance of six more. But those six were the most destructive and evil of the fifteen, the Dark Six, and they were made inferior to the Sovereigns."

Darraun shook his head. "And all sixteen of these gods—the nine Sovereigns, the Dark Six, and the missing one—all of them were actually dragons who became gods during the first age of the world?"

"Correct. And according to the Prophecy, there's a vacancy in that roster of sixteen gods. Khorvaire will have a new god—Vaskar, the Storm Dragon. Right, Gaven?"

Darraun looked at Gaven. He was staring up at the statue with its marred face, apparently lost in a trance. Then his lips moved, but no sound came out.

"What was that, Gaven?" said Darraun. "What did you say?"

Gaven's voice was a whisper. "The Bronze Serpent seeks the face of the first of sixteen," he said. His voice trailed off, though his lips kept moving.

Haldren stepped forward, his face purple with rage, and slapped Gaven hard across the face. "Speak," he said, "so I can hear you."

Strong and clear now, Gaven repeated his earlier words. "The Bronze Serpent seeks the face of the first of sixteen." A wind stirred the stale air in the cave. "But the Storm Dragon walks in his paths. The Bronze Serpent faces the Soul Reaver and fails. But the Storm Dragon seizes the shard of heaven from the fallen pretender." The wind swirled around Gaven, kicking up a whirlwind of dust and pebbles around his feet and whipping his hair around his face.

The color drained from Haldren's face, and he took two steps backward, away from Gaven. "No," he murmured. "The Bronze Serpent . . . Vaskar is the Storm Dragon! He must be!"

Senya grabbed Haldren's arm. "But what if he's not, Haldren?"

"No!" Haldren's eyes were wild, and he stumbled backward. Cart took up a position between Gaven and Haldren, as if to ward his commander from an attack. Darraun stayed out of the way, watching and waiting to see how the situation played out.

"What if it's Gaven?" Senya clung to his arm, her voice an entreaty. "Look at him—the Mark of Storm he wears. The wind blows at his command, the rain outside—"

With another crash of thunder outside the cave, the wind swirling around Gaven died. Gaven slumped to his hands and knees and stared at the ground, shaking his head.

"You old fool," Gaven said, then lifted his eyes to Haldren. "Vaskar's not the Storm Dragon. You've hitched your chariot to the wrong horse."

Haldren found his feet and pulled his arm away from Senya's grasp. "And you think you're the one?"

Darraun couldn't read his voice—it might have been an accusation, but there was a hint of genuine wonder.

Gaven scoffed. "The Storm Dragon? No. No matter what Senya says."

The mention of her name made Haldren wheel on Senya. "You have betrayed me," he whispered.

"I'm trying to help you," Senya said. Darraun had expected her to cower in the face of his wrath, but she stood her ground and met his gaze. "Abandon Vaskar, Haldren. He's doomed to fail. It's not too late! If we work with Gaven—"

Senya broke off as Haldren turned his gaze back to Gaven, fury burning in his eyes. Gaven had dropped his head again and was staring at the ground. Haldren shook his head.

"No," he said. He grabbed Senya's hand and yanked her toward him, then reached out for Cart's hand. "Take hands. We're leaving."

Cart took Darraun's hand, and Darraun bent over Gaven, helping him to his feet and holding on to one hand. Senya gently took Gaven's other hand in hers.

Haldren began the words to his spell, and Darraun found himself lost in the rhythm of them. He looked around the troubled little circle. Haldren's eyes were closed as he focused on his spell; he was suppressing his anger in order to keep his mind clear. Cart stared impassively ahead. Senya's eyes were on Gaven, her brow furrowed, and she clung to his hand. Gaven's head hung down, and Darraun couldn't see his eyes.

The spell built to its conclusion, and Darraun felt the first tugs that would carry them across hundreds of miles. In that instant, Gaven's hand wrenched free of his. Haldren shouted the last syllable of the spell as if he couldn't choke it back, and they were gone.

PART
II

In the Time of the Dragon Above,
when Siberys turns night into day,
and showers of light fall from the sky,
the Eye of Siberys falls near the City of the Dead.

A fragment of celestial light,
the Eye sees, and in it all is seen.

The Eye of Siberys lifts the Sky Caves of Thieren Kor
from the land of desolation
under the dark of the great moon,
and the Storm Dragon walks in the paths
of the first of sixteen.

The shard of heaven falls to earth a second time,
and its light brightens Khyber's darkness.

CHAPTER
14

Rienne stood at the railing of the small airship and gazed at the churning waters of Scions Sound far below. An unnatural storm blew out of the Mournland, churning the dead-gray mist that marked the borders of that desolate wasteland into a roiling frenzy, and sending long tendrils of smoky gray reaching for them. So far, the skill of the ship's windwright captain had kept the air around them calm—and free from the grasping reach of the mist. Rienne shuddered. The mist stood in her mind as a symbol of the mystery that cloaked the destruction of Cyre near the end of the Last War. It was impenetrable, inscrutable, and deadly. Within its embrace, nothing could survive for long. Wounds did not heal, plants did not grow, and horrible creatures born of flesh and metal warped by magic stalked the deserted ruins of the nation that had once been the jewel in Galifar's crown.

Securing the use of the Morning Zephyr had been a little tricky, but she'd managed it. It was primarily a matter of convincing her friends in House Lyrandar that Arnoth had authorized it, without letting Arnoth know that she'd borrowed the vessel. If Gaven's father knew that she was looking for Gaven, he'd want to be involved. And if he was involved, that Sentinel Marshal who had barged into her house would be involved soon after.

She told herself she would probably get the Sentinel Marshals involved soon enough anyway. After all, Gaven was a fugitive from Dreadhold. Whatever reservations she had about her role in getting him captured and convicted, the fact remained that he was a criminal. For all she knew, he might prove dangerous—even to her. Perhaps especially to her—the one responsible for turning him in to House Deneith in the first place. She might have to call in another favor once she reached Vathirond, to ensure her safety in case she actually found him.

"Lady Alastra?" The first mate's voice stirred her from her thoughts. She turned to see that the young man's face, normally smiling broadly, was creased with worry. "The storm is growing worse, and the captain isn't sure she can fend it off much longer. We might need to alter our course slightly, which could delay our arrival in Vathirond."

Rienne sighed. "A slight delay will probably not matter," she said.

"Yes, lady. In the meantime, the captain suggests you take shelter below." The young man smiled briefly, nodded a small bow, and disappeared back into the wheelhouse.

Rienne looked around the deserted deck. She had not even realized that the crew had left her alone, either in deference to her or in fear of the brewing storm. She turned around again and stared into the gray mist. Something stared back, she thought—something powerful and malevolent. She shuddered and made her way below.

Back in her cabin, the bundle of silk propped against her bed caught her eye immediately. She lifted it and sat on the bed, tenderly resting the bundle on her lap and carefully pulling at the wrappings. Beneath the silk was a fine leather scabbard tooled in gold, and she drew out the gleaming blade of her sword, the weapon she called Maelstrom. She removed a scrap of silk that caught on the blade as she drew it, and ran her finger carefully along the razor-sharp edge.

Rienne had not wielded Maelstrom in battle since the Sentinel Marshals had taken Gaven into custody. She had adopted the dress of a noblewoman and settled down in Stormhome. She had made herself useful to her family and lived a quiet and profitable life, making the most of her connections to House Lyrandar despite what she had done to Gaven.

But at least once a week, sometimes every night, she had closed the door to her chambers and brought out Maelstrom, polishing the blade and oiling the leather that wrapped its hilt. She kept it carefully wrapped and secure, in case she ever needed it. She hoped this journey wouldn't be such an occasion, but she was glad to have Maelstrom with her. Some part of her soul sang as she touched it again.

* * * * *

The storm threatening from the Mournland diminished as they made their way farther south, though their route took them alongside the dead-gray mist all the way to Vathirond. Rienne watched the city as it came into view—stone buildings forming tiers and bridges at the bases of its many tall towers, a gray metropolis set in stark contrast to the surrounding green hills—but her mind was consumed with thoughts of how she might find Gaven.

She started her search in the docking tower. A larger airship had docked at roughly the same time as her vessel, and she scanned the disembarking passengers carefully, on the off chance that Gaven was among them.

She tried to anticipate the effects of twenty-six years in Dreadhold on his appearance, as well as any magic he might use to hide his face. More than a few passengers responded with nervous stares or angry rebukes as she tried to peer into cowls and under the wide brims of hats meant to conceal.

After one passenger drew steel, Rienne abandoned that approach, making her way through the crowds to the city streets. She ran down her mental list of contacts in Vathirond—distant relatives, people who owed favors to her family, and a few very old friends—and chose the most likely suspect. Looking around the streets, she quickly got her bearings and made her way to Subsidence, the neighborhood perched along the stream that flowed alongside the city, carrying its filth into the Brey River.

Krathas was a half-orc she believed had some connection to House Tharashk, though he didn't carry the Mark of Finding. His residence in Subsidence suggested that he didn't benefit much from this connection, and Rienne wondered if he were an excoriate like Gaven. She had never met Krathas, but Gaven had spoken of him a few times, and she had the impression that Gaven trusted him.

Setting foot in Subsidence reminded her of descending into Khyber. Danger was near—she could feel it—and she loosened Maelstrom's silk wrappings.

"Look, Marsh," an oily voice purred from an alley to her right, "we found ourselves a noble mouse. A half-elf mouse. Half elf, half mouse." The man laughed, loud and grating.

Rienne sank into a combat stance, and she could feel the hesitation already taking root in her opponents' minds. A quick glance showed her two assailants, emerging from the alleys on either side of her, and she heard a third trying to sneak up behind her. Keeping her attention on the position of the three attackers, she pulled again at Maelstrom's wrappings, trying to free the hilt so she could pull the blade loose.

"Ooh, the mouse has been to fencing school." It was the same one that had spoken before, foolishly drawing attention to himself before he was close enough to attack. He was a lanky human with a weirdly asymmetrical look to him, like one side of his body had grown just a bit faster than the other. He sort of half limped, half shuffled toward her, a leering smile spread across his angular face.

"I'm not sure about this, Jad." The one coming in from her left was an orc, clearly brought in on the operation for his size and strength, though he displayed more sense than his leader at that moment.

Jad responded to Marsh's hesitation the best way he could imagine: he shouted, "Get her!" and sprang forward, his gangly arms flailing wildly.

He held a wavy-bladed dagger in each hand.

Rienne managed a firm grip on the hilt of Maelstrom but didn't have time to draw the blade. She didn't need to. She ducked slightly, batted Jad's left arm aside with her sword—silk, scabbard, and all—and pushed his right arm so the dagger slashed across Marsh's chest. Marsh yelped in pain and surprise, and Jad staggered backward. She could see the doubt gnawing at his mind, and she used their hesitation to quiet her mind.

While her eyes kept careful watch on the two assailants before her and her ears listened for the approach of the man behind, her innermost mind quieted, opened—like a flower opening to the new sun—then focused, channeling her inner energy into a fine point, a sharp edge of energy that flowed into her limbs. She focused the energy and held it, waiting.

The one behind her hung back for that first instant, but then he came charging in. Without turning, Rienne crouched, gathered her soul energy, then released it, springing straight upward. She slammed down on the back of the third attacker, cracking his skull with Maelstrom in its sheath, then landed on her feet behind him. The third assailant fell like a stone, and his head bounced once off the stone walkway.

Jad and Marsh stood flanking the prone body of their companion and gaped at her. Marsh started backing away first, keeping a wary eye on her in case she decided to charge after him. Rienne took the opportunity to draw Maelstrom from its sheath.

That was enough. Marsh and Jad turned tail and ran, leaving their unconscious ally to Rienne's mercy. She touched her lips to Maelstrom's blade and slid it back into the sheath. She started to return the blade to its silk wrapping, then thought better of it. She unrolled the silk and wound it around her waist, then carefully placed the scabbard into its folds so she could draw the blade more easily if she were attacked again.

Only then did she check on the third attacker, the one whose face she'd never seen. She rolled him over onto his back—he was a handsome young man—and checked the pulse in his throat. Aside from a large bump on his head, he'd be fine when he woke up.

He was lucky she'd never freed her blade.

* * * * *

Krathas stared at her across a filthy desk covered with scraps of parchment, and Rienne stared back. The sign on his office door had identified him as an inquisitive affiliated with House Tharashk's Finders' Guild. Rienne wondered what kind of business he attracted in Subsidence—certainly not jobs that paid very well, if his office was any indication. He was clearly past his prime, his

hair thinning and white and his face deeply lined, though he was still muscular and tall—very tall. He had made a show of welcoming her in and clearing
a chair for her to sit on, though he fell silent as soon as she mentioned Gaven's
name. That was when the staring began.

At last he broke the silence, though he didn't look away. "Last I heard,
Gaven was in Dreadhold," he said, watching her carefully. "In fact, I heard
you were the one who put him there."

She held his gaze. "I thought he was possessed and needed help."

"You thought his actions might disgrace your family and get in the way of
your social climbing."

Rienne felt a surge of anger but held it down, making sure no trace of it
showed on her face. "Is that what he told you?"

"Something like that."

"When did you talk to him last?"

"Sixteenth of Zarantyr."

"Zarantyr? Three months ago?"

"Sorry, was I not clear? Three months and twenty-six years ago. Just before
they locked him up."

Rienne sighed and looked away. She remembered that month, all those
years ago. It had been a cold winter, and she'd spent many hours staring out
windows at snow-draped fields and blank white skies. She looked sharply at
Krathas again.

"Just before? The sixteenth?"

"That's right."

"That was after his trial. Was he here? In Vathirond?"

Krathas stared at her for another long moment. "Not then, no. I spoke to
him at a Sivis message station. They let him put his affairs in order before they
locked him up."

"What did he ask you to do?"

"I'm afraid that's between him and me, Lady Alastra. I'm sure if he had
wanted you involved, he would've contacted you."

"Krathas, if you're not inclined to help me, I shall be forced to consult with
another member of your esteemed House Tharashk. It would be unfortunate
if I accidentally mentioned to them how a certain half-orc inquisitive used
to give Gaven leads on finding dragonshard deposits for House Lyrandar. I
understand that's a business House Tharashk would rather keep a tight hold
on."

She had hoped to avoid playing that card. She wasn't positive that Gaven's
information had come from Krathas—Gaven had always been very cagey
about revealing his source. And she wasn't sure that House Tharashk hadn't

known about it, perhaps collected large fees from Gaven for that information. She had leaped from a couple of hunches, and she dearly hoped they proved accurate.

Krathas's face registered nothing, but he was silent again for a long moment, studying her. When he spoke again, his voice was much quieter. "He told you that?"

"Something like that."

"There's no way you can prove that."

So her hunches had been on the mark. "Do I need to?"

Krathas took a deep breath and let it slowly out through his nostrils. "Very well, Lady. What is it you want from me?"

"Gaven has escaped," Rienne said, watching Krathas carefully. His eyebrows raised, but she couldn't judge whether he was genuinely surprised. "I have a hard time believing you hadn't heard that already."

"My sources aren't what they once were."

"I hope that won't diminish your usefulness to me. I want to find him before the forces of the four dragonmarked houses who are scouring Khorvaire at this moment do, and that's where I need your help."

"If I didn't know he escaped, how can I possibly know where to find him?"

"I know he was arrested here in Vathirond, and you just told me he contacted you after his conviction and had you do something for him. I assume there's something here he cares about, maybe even something he'll come back here for. What is it?"

"It's been almost thirty years, Lady."

"I assume he planned for the possibility that it would be even longer before he was able to return. That's why he contacted you."

For the first time, Krathas smiled, revealing uneven rows of broken teeth. "I begin to see what Gaven admired in you, Lady Alastra."

Rienne returned his smile. "Wait until you see me in a fight."

CHAPTER
15

Gaven found himself staring up into the face of the Traveler.
At least, he assumed it was the Traveler. A goblin was carved in the great frieze, crouching at the feet of the mysterious sixteenth god, stepping out of the line formed by the other fifteen gods. She wore a quirky smile that seemed out of place in the ancient sculpture of Dhakaan—an expression that made this one goddess seem more real than the others in their majestic stillness. Gaven shot a grim smile back at the trickster-god and sat up.

His smile fell from his face when he saw that he was not alone. "Senya!"

"Come," she said, "we need to get out of here." She stepped over to him and extended a hand to help him up. He stood without her help.

"What do you think you're doing?"

"I think I'm helping you achieve your destiny. Now move!" She started out the cave entrance, and he followed, reluctantly.

"Senya, wait a moment—"

"No! Haldren could be back any second. We need to be out of sight and as far away as we can get."

That got Gaven moving. He followed Senya as she retraced their steps out of the ancient city. Gaven cursed to himself all the way. He had hoped to make a clean break with Haldren and all his business. He wanted to be rid of them all, certainly including Senya.

They made their way down the rocky valley, following the dry riverbed as it wound between the cliffs. The ground sloped steadily downward along the ancient river's course to the sea. Soon the wall of Paluur Draal with its enormous carved guardians was out of sight behind them.

Feeling they'd put enough distance between them and the city, Gaven lunged forward and grabbed Senya's arm, pulling her to a stop. "How many times do I have to tell you that I am not the Storm Dragon?"

"You can say it all you want," she said. She stepped closer and looked up into his eyes. "Sooner or later you'll realize you're wrong."

"I also made it clear that I'm not interested in you."

She put a hand on his face and pressed herself closer to his chest. "You'll come to recognize that mistake as well."

He stepped back and pushed her away. "Listen, Senya, you are the one making a terrible mistake here. Go find Haldren. Maybe Vaskar's not the Storm Dragon, but you can still go with Haldren. Maybe you'll end up the queen of something."

Senya scoffed. "A queen at Haldren's side? I'd rather spend the rest of my life in the Realm of Madness."

"I thought you loved him."

She threw her head back and laughed. "Love him? That old man?"

"You only stayed with him because of the power you thought he could give you."

"He was much more exciting when he was younger."

"I have nothing to offer you, Senya. I can't even pretend to love you, and I have no plans to seize any throne, mortal or divine."

"What are your plans, then? Maybe I have something to offer you."

Gaven threw up his hands and continued down the valley. "I don't have any plans. I didn't think past getting away from all of you, and I even failed at that. You want to come with me? Fine. We'll end up dead or back in Dread-hold together."

Gaven walked for a while in silence before looking back over his shoulder. Senya trailed behind him, her eyes fixed on the ground as she picked out a path on the rocky trail. She was smiling.

*   *   *   *   *

"Damn you to the outer darkness, Gaven." Haldren quivered with fury. Darraun was nervous that he might end up taking the brunt of the sorcerer's anger again. After all, he was the one who had let go of Gaven's hand.

They had appeared on the shores of a lake, large enough that the opposite shore was nearly invisible. Darraun's hunch was Lake Brey, somewhere near the uneasy border between Breland and Thrane. The wind blowing off the water was cold, and Darraun pulled his cloak around him.

"We're going back," Haldren announced. "Join hands."

Darraun cast his eyes around, looking for a distraction, anything to buy Gaven more time. Nothing caught his attention. "Wait a moment, Haldren," he said.

"Join hands now." Haldren was not going to wait. Cart had already seized one of Haldren's hands and held the other out to Darraun.

"I'm just thinking—"

"Stop thinking and join hands. If he harms her because you're too busy thinking, I will reduce you to dust and scatter your remains across the Ten Seas."

Darraun took Cart's hand, and Haldren intoned his spell. Darraun considered yanking his hand away at the last second as Gaven had done. A world of possibilities began to form in his mind, then Haldren finished the spell and they were back in Paluur Draal, staring up at the sixteen goblin gods.

No sign of Gaven or Senya.

"Senya!" Haldren yelled. His voice echoed around the cave, but that was the only reply.

Cart moved immediately to the cave entrance and looked outside, while Darraun made a show of examining the floor.

"I was just thinking, Haldren," he said, scanning the ground as if looking for tracks, "what if they were still caught in the magic of your spell and got shunted through space, just not to the same place we were?"

Haldren snorted. "I thought I told you to stop thinking. And you know the spell doesn't work like that."

"On the contrary, I've seen teleportation spells go horribly awry."

Haldren moved to stand beside Cart, turning his back on Darraun and looking out at the ruins nearby. "It would have been one thing for the spell to carry us to the wrong location, but quite another for it to transport us correctly while taking them elsewhere."

Darraun stood behind the others. He couldn't see much past the corpse of the mountain troll they had slain earlier.

"Senya!" Haldren shouted again.

Darraun grabbed his shoulder. "Don't! You'll draw every troll and wyvern in the city down on our heads."

"I don't care!" Haldren whirled around as he shouted, and emphasized his last word by shoving Darraun backward, simultaneously blasting a gout of fire from his hand.

Darraun fell to the ground and clutched his arms to his body. His shirt and cloak smoldered but didn't ignite, and his leather cuirass protected his chest, but his face and eyes stung with the heat. Haldren turned away and started out into the city. Darraun sat up and glared after him.

"Are you hurt?" Cart extended a hand to help him stand, and his voice was full of concern.

Darraun took his hand and pulled himself to his feet. "Not badly, no." He scowled. But I'll make him pay for that, he thought. When this is all over.

"Let's go, then." Cart hastened after Haldren, his sense of duty to the Lord General replacing his concern for Darraun.

Darraun lagged behind, watching his feet as he walked. He didn't want to be the one to spot Gaven or Senya, and if Haldren did find them, Darraun wanted to be as far away as possible.

Something on the ground caught his eye, and he stopped. There was a groove, either cut into the stone or marking the space between two ancient cobblestones. Drying mud covered the ground around it—mud that had been smeared across the stone. He crouched and traced his finger along the groove. It was the shape of Kraken Bay—he'd found the map they were looking for.

"Haldren!" he called. "You need to see this!"

Haldren wheeled around and walked back to within a few yards of Darraun. "Did you find their tracks? Are we on their trail?"

Darraun brushed mud away from the region northwest of Kraken Bay. "Not them," he said. Haldren threw up his hands and started to turn away. Darraun pointed to a strange symbol carved into the stone, where he had cleared the dust away. "But I think I've found the Sky Caves of Thieren Kor."

*　*　*　*　*

As the western sky grew red, the valley opened up, and a stream poured out from under the mountains. Gazing down the valley, Gaven saw other mountain streams joining its flow, and it widened into a river far ahead.

Senya spotted a grassy patch near the stream bank and threw herself down. "This river should lead us all the way to Korranberg," she said, starting to remove her boots.

"Is that where you're heading?" Gaven asked.

"There's a lightning rail station there. We could get from there to pretty much anywhere west of the Mournland." Senya got both her boots off and started massaging her feet.

"The Mournland," Gaven echoed.

Words from the Prophecy echoed in his mind: Desolation spreads over that land like a wildfire. Haldren and Vaskar had taken those words to refer to the Mournland. He saw it, briefly, in his mind—a barren plain, unbroken by any sign of life or civilization, the earth itself reduced to ash. Then he saw his hands half buried in the scorched soil, tasted the acrid air. He shook his head, trying to dispel that image. Senya was watching him curiously, and he forced himself to look at her. She is here now, he reminded himself. The rest . . .

"So that's what they call Cyre now?" he said. His mouth was dry, and the words scratched his throat.

"It was a beautiful land, before," Senya said. "Did you ever go there?"

"Many times." Faces sprang to Gaven's mind, people he hadn't seen in many years. How many of them were dead?

"Cart and I went there once after the Mourning. Just a short way in." She shuddered. "Far enough. I don't ever want to go back."

"Haldren's going there—or Vaskar, perhaps. Or both of them."

"Looking for the Sky Caves. Haldren told me."

"Thunder!" Gaven sighed. "I'm glad to be done with Haldren and his schemes." Even as he said it, though, it rang false. Looking for the Sky Caves of Thieren Kor in the Mournland sounded like quite an adventure—and to explore them would be the chance of a lifetime. The knowledge they must hold . . .

He sat down on the stream bank, a few paces downstream from where Senya had started dipping her feet into the water. The stream showed him the Ring of Siberys overhead.

"Shall we stop here for the night?" Senya asked.

Gaven looked up at the sky. The red in the west had faded to a narrow band above the mountains, while the Ring of Siberys shimmered gold above him. It wasn't as bright as it had been the night before in Shae Mordai, but it still shed enough light that they could make their way farther down the valley if they wanted to. Realizing that the previous night they'd been in Aerenal made him feel exhausted.

"Yes, it seems quiet enough," he said. "And open. Less chance for anything to sneak up under cover."

Senya rummaged through her pack and tossed Gaven some dried meat. "I have to say, I'll miss Darraun's cooking."

Gaven scowled, thinking of the fragments of conversation he'd had with Darraun. "Haldren said he was a more recent acquaintance. How long have you known him?"

"Darraun? Only a few weeks. Cart and I recruited him to help us break into Dreadhold."

"How did you find him?"

Senya shrugged. "We asked around. Haldren still has a lot of friends in Aundair. In the army mostly. I think Darraun has friends in intelligence."

"Intelligence? The Royal Eyes?"

"Mm-hm. It was almost like he'd planted his name at the end of every trail we followed. He knows what he's doing."

"Does Haldren know that?"

"I don't know. Why?"

"I'm not sure I'd trust someone who went to such lengths to make sure you chose him for the task."

"Oh, Haldren doesn't trust him."

Gaven laughed. "Of course not."

*   *   *   *   *

The sky grew dark over the ruins of Paluur Draal. Cart paced slowly back and forth, watching for more trolls or any other trouble. Darraun finished copying the map he'd found. Haldren knelt beside him, pointing out details and criticizing his work. Darraun entertained himself with thoughts of strangling the sorcerer as he put the finishing touches on the paper.

Haldren stood, brushed dried mud from his knees, and looked up at the darkening sky. "Damn," he muttered. "We're not going to find them now."

Darraun double-checked his map and rolled it up. "At least we found what we came here for."

"Indeed, and the information in the Sky Caves could very well make Gaven irrelevant to us. As for Senya . . . well, I shall have to trust that she can free herself from his clutches eventually."

"Free herself? You think he's captured her?"

"Of course. What else?"

Darraun opened his mouth but closed it again, remembering Haldren's temper. He would not be the one to shatter Haldren's delusions.

"Cart," Haldren said, "find a secure location and set up camp. Darraun, I'd be grateful for some of your cooking, if you can make something palatable from the supplies we have left. I need to contact Vaskar and inform him of our progress." He glanced around, then pointed to a small stone house near the trolls' cave that was mostly intact. "I'll be in there."

Haldren went into the little house without a backward glance, and Cart busied himself inspecting other structures nearby. Few of the ruined buildings offered much shelter, and Darraun suspected that the trolls had kept the area around their lair clear of competing predators. All the same, something emitted a horrible dying shriek from the house Haldren had entered.

Darraun started to throw a meal together while Cart checked on Haldren. Darraun shook his head as Haldren rebuked the warforged for disturbing his privacy. Darraun waited until Cart had returned and busied himself setting up their camp in another little house. Then he rummaged in a pouch at his belt until he found the right scroll. He spared a quick glance at the warforged, who was rummaging through their supplies, then began to whisper the words inked upon the scroll. A final glance at the warforged, then Darraun uttered the final syllable. With a slight tingle across his skin, Darraun became invisible.

The spell didn't quiet his footfalls, so he moved as quietly as he could up to the house Haldren had claimed. He crouched in the doorway and peered in to where Haldren stood before a shimmering image of the bronze dragon's head. The image was speaking.

". . . than the Lyrandar whelp could anyway. Meet me as we planned, give me the Eye, and everything will be fine. You will receive your reward."

"What about Senya?" Haldren's voice was agonized, and Darraun almost felt sorry for him.

"She is irrelevant."

Vaskar's head vanished in a shower of sparks, and Haldren sank to his knees, his chin on his chest. Darraun watched him for a moment, but the sorcerer didn't move. Darraun slunk away, glanced around to make sure he wasn't in Cart's sight, and dismissed the spell of invisibility.

Waste of a good scroll, he thought.

He finished preparing the meal and ate some. The rest was cold before Haldren emerged.

CHAPTER
16

A splashing in the stream jolted Gaven from his sleep, and he scrambled to his feet. The sky was growing bright in the east, shedding enough light into the valley that he could see Senya kneeling on the bank. She had removed her leather coat, baring her shoulders, and she washed her face and hair in the stream.

Gaven sighed and lowered himself back to the ground. "You startled me."

Senya spun around, surprised by Gaven's voice. Her startled look dissolved into a laugh. "I didn't hear you move. Sorry I disturbed your sleep."

"That's all right. We should get a start on the day."

Senya sat on the ground, stretching her legs out in front of her and leaning back on her hands. Her wet hair clung to her cheeks and neck. She had washed the pigment off her eyelids and lips, which to Gaven's eyes enhanced her beauty. Gaven was painfully aware of the smooth, bare skin of her shoulders, the gentle curve of her collarbones, the graceful arc of her throat. She teased one corner of her mouth with her tongue and smiled. "It's still early."

Gaven turned away. "You never give up, do you?" He pulled his boots on.

"Not when I know what I want."

He stood and shouldered his pack and his sword. "Get dressed. It's going to take days to get to Korranberg." Without waiting for a response, he started walking downstream.

Subdued by his rebuff, Senya trailed behind him in silence, and he lost himself in the monotonous rhythm of walking. Step after step, mile after mile—the scenery changed little, and nothing distracted him from the thoughts that surfaced and subsided in his mind. It was a bit like sleep, especially when the nightmares began—

Enormous wings beat the air, and the morning sun gleamed on scales of every color—red and black and blue; silver, gold, and copper. Dragons wheeled and dived, grappled each other, furies of claws and teeth. Raw elemental power spewed from their mouths—fire and lightning, searing acid, virulent poison, and bitter cold.

He felt the earth tremble beneath his feet and saw a column of blinding light spill up from the ground, casting sickly shadows on the dragons fighting overhead. And he knew what was coming: the hordes of the Soul Reaver.

"Gaven!" Senya's voice jolted him back to the present, and he caught himself just before he slipped over the edge of a low cliff. Off balance, he fell backward and sat on the rocky ground. Beside him, the stream tumbled over the cliff and began to broaden, forming a wide, slow river as it left the valley and wound among the foothills of the Seawalls.

"Are you all right?" Senya clutched his shoulder.

He didn't feel all right. His skin was clammy, and his stomach churned. He dropped his chin to his chest, trying to keep his head from swimming. He cursed under his breath. The Eye of Siberys had given him clarity, but it was slipping away.

"What is it?" Worry creased Senya's face.

"It's nothing," he croaked, but Senya was clearly not convinced.

"Here, why don't you lie down for a moment?" She wrapped an arm around his shoulder, trying to guide him into a more comfortable position.

"It's nothing!" he repeated, pushing her away. "Don't mother me." Rienne had mothered him from time to time, and he'd accepted it from her. Not from Senya.

"I'm sorry," she said. She looked hurt, so much that Gaven almost regretted his words.

He stood, slowly, with Senya hovering nearby. He was a little unsteady on his feet, and Senya put a hand on his arm as if to steady him. He decided against brushing her hand away, and let her help him down the little cliff. Then they continued, side by side, along the river.

*   *   *   *   *

Darraun gazed at the brightening sky as Haldren finished his spell. He blinked, and the ruined city disappeared around him, replaced by the churning waters of Lake Brey. The sun, no longer hidden behind the surrounding mountains, shone in his eyes and glared off the lake so that he had to look away.

Darraun shivered as he surveyed the near shore. They stood on a rocky bluff overlooking the lake. To the north, the land sloped down to the water, and in the distance he could see a small fishing village. Shielding his eyes against the sun, he looked to the south, where the shore curved off to the east. Darraun figured that the city of Starilaskur, one of the larger cities in the north of Breland, stood in that direction, not too far beyond the lake. That meant they were probably not far from Hatheril, a tiny hamlet that was only important because of its position at the intersection of a caravan route stretching west from Starilaskur and a lightning rail line heading north to Aundair.

A gateway to anywhere I want to go, he thought. He shook his head. Maybe when this is over.

Haldren shielded his eyes and looked out over the lake as Cart stood watching, impassive.

"What are we looking for?" Darraun said.

"Vaskar, you fool."

Darraun looked back over the lake, squinting into the glare. The sky was light blue and clear of clouds. A flock of gulls swarmed near the village to the north, stealing from the fishers' morning catch, and what might have been pelicans soared over the waters to the southeast. Nothing in the sky was large enough to be a dragon. Then something in the water caught Darraun's eye.

A moment later, the shape rose up from the water, leaping into the air and beating its wings fiercely to stay aloft. The sun gleamed on Vaskar's bronze scales and shimmered in the drops of water cascading off his body and spraying from his wings. He caught the air under his wings and glided over to the bluff where they stood, alighting gently near Haldren.

Haldren smiled, though it seemed to require an unusual effort. "Hail, Storm Dragon!"

"Show me the Eye of Siberys," Vaskar said.

The smile fell from Haldren's face, and he reached into a pouch. He produced the Eye of Siberys but held it close to his chest as he displayed it to the dragon.

"Here is the Eye," he said. "We found it outside the City of the Dead, as Gaven predicted."

"Excellent." Vaskar hissed. "And Paluur Draal? Did you find what you sought there?"

Haldren winced at the mention of the city, as if its name was enough to remind him of what he had left behind there. "I did."

Sure you did, Darraun thought, I was just along for the ride.

"The map, Darraun." Haldren held a hand out to him without taking his eyes off Vaskar, still clutching the dragonshard to his chest.

Darraun slid the map he had copied from the ruins out of its case and handed it to Haldren. The sorcerer fumbled to unroll it while keeping a grip on the Eye of Siberys. He pointed to the map as Vaskar lowered his enormous head to see it.

"We found a map carved in the pavement of a plaza in the city," Haldren explained. "The outline of Kraken Bay was very clear. Naturally, the locations on the map were marked with their ancient Dhakaani names, when they were labeled at all. But certain geographical features are unmistakable." He shifted his grip on the map and traced his finger over it. Darraun noticed that the Eye of Siberys disappeared at some point in that process, and he wondered if Vaskar noticed it too. "The Seawall Mountains run parallel to the western edge of Kraken Bay. They turn to the east here, at Marguul Pass, then there's the gap where Kennrun stands now—a Brelish fort on the border of Darguun. Then more mountains rise up from the plain—and that's where the Mournland begins now. If you continue following the line of the mountains, you hit Lake Cyre, here. But the map indicates the Sky Caves here, to the southeast of the mountains." With a flourish, he indicated the strange symbol Darraun had transcribed on the map.

"You seem reluctant to deliver the Eye as we agreed, Haldren," Vaskar said. "Why is that?"

"What? Reluctant?" Haldren stammered. "Not at all!"

"Where is it, then?"

"Well, I returned it to its pouch so I could more easily hold the map."

"Give it to me."

Haldren drew it out but cradled it to his chest again. "I will deliver it as I promised, Vaskar. I'm a man of my word. But—"

"Give it to me now."

Darraun could see Haldren struggling against the command, which must have carried a magical weight. In the end, his resistance failed, and he extended the Eye to Vaskar. The dragon plucked it from Haldren's outstretched hand with a gigantic claw. Darraun couldn't see what Vaskar did with it.

"What about your end of the bargain?" Haldren said. "The aid you promised me?"

"Don't worry, Haldren," the dragon said. "My promises are as good as yours. A flight of dragons is on its way to Aundair as we speak, ready to do battle at your command."

Haldren's face lit up. "A flight? How many dragons?"

"More than enough for your purposes. No army in Khorvaire will stand against you."

* * * * *

"Tell me about the Prophecy."

The Ring of Siberys was bright enough to shine through a thin layer of clouds. Gaven and Senya had laid out their bedrolls in a bend of the river, so their camp was surrounded by water on three sides. Gaven was exhausted from the day's march, but so far he'd been unable to sleep. Apparently Senya had the same problem.

"What about it?"

He heard Senya's bedroll rustling, and glanced over to see her propping herself up on her elbows. "Well, how does it work? I mean, does it describe events that are sure to happen? Is the path of my life spelled out in advance? Am I just following a story that's already been written, like . . . like a stage actor or something? Is that what life is?"

Gaven laughed. "An actor trying to follow a script you've never read, fumbling your way through lines you're making up as you go? That feels about right."

"But you can read the script."

"No. I see bits and pieces of the script, as if it's been transcribed by a madman. Unconnected scenes. Lines here and there, with no idea who's supposed to be speaking."

Senya put her head back down and was silent for a long time. Just as he began to think she'd fallen asleep, she said, "I don't believe it."

"What?"

"I don't believe there is a script."

"But you believe in destiny. You seem set on making sure I fulfill mine."

"That's different. Destiny is . . . it's like the highest hopes the universe has for you. Like—like my mother wanted the best for me. And you can either fulfill your destiny, or you—" Her voice became strangled, and she stopped trying to speak.

A wave of thicker clouds drifted across the sky, and the night grew darker. Gaven brought his hand up to his neck and traced the lines of his dragonmark. Suddenly he was an adolescent again, adrift at sea at the mouth of Eldeen Bay. This was his Test of Siberys, a rite of passage of the dragonmarked houses, a trial meant to force his dragonmark to manifest, if he was to bear one. Heirs of the houses usually developed their marks in times of great stress in their adolescent years, so the Test of Siberys had been developed to create just the right stress.

Most children spent the Test straining in the desperate hope of forcing a mark to manifest on their skin. Gaven saw himself on his knees, pouring out desperate prayers to each god of the Sovereign Host that no mark would appear on him. The sea was calm, under the command of a Lyrandar windwright, and he drifted for days, pouring out his prayers. Some dragonmark heirs would call up a wind to move their little boats, while others would develop a protective mark that would inure their bodies to the burning sun. Still others would call up great billowing banks of fog to shield themselves from the heat. Gaven did not. Day after day he knelt in prayer under the sun's unblinking gaze, and his prayers were answered.

At the end of the test, an elemental galleon came to his rescue. Some strong cousin lifted his body, weak and weathered from the scorching sun, and carried him aboard. He was feverish, and most of the faces surrounding him were blurred together, indistinct. But one face was clear in his memory— his father's, trying to smile at him but unable to hide the disappointment etched into every line.

At least there could be no doubt that this memory was his and not the other's.

CHAPTER
17

Noon sunlight glittered on the domes and spires of Korranberg, the oldest and one of the most important cities in the gnome nation of Zilargo, nestled among the foothills of the Seawall Mountains. From his perch at the edge of a cliff, Gaven could see the whole city spread out before him, and miles of fields stretching out to the sea. The city was a fascinating mix of old and new; the ancient buildings of the city's great library pressed between the more recent construction of shops and markets. He was struck by how green the city looked from his vantage point—ivy clung to gracefully arched walls, gardens sprawled over spacious courtyards, and flowers burst in a rainbow of colors to celebrate spring's height.

Behind him, Senya snorted. "Gnomes," she said. "How do they defend this place? It's right next to Darguun, and these mountains are full of kobolds."

"I suspect the city isn't as defenseless as it looks," Gaven answered. He pointed at the city wall nearest their position. "Look at the holes along the top edge of the wall. I'd be willing to bet there's some kind of mechanism that will pump boiling oil or acidic fire out of those holes in case of an attack. In fact, I'll bet the jets shoot out far enough that the ivy is unharmed."

Senya snorted again, adjusted her pack on her shoulders, and started along the winding path that would take them down the cliff and into the city. Gaven took a last look at the city and the sea then followed her down.

* * * * *

Gaven was glad he had taken the time to admire the city from a distance. From inside, the elegant spires and sprawling gardens were lost in the bustle—much of which occurred at waist level. He was not the tallest of men, but in Korranberg, making his way along streets crowded with gnomes, he felt like a giant—and he attracted about as much attention as a real giant would have. Senya only reached Gaven's breastbone, but the majority of the people on the streets only reached her chest. Gaven noticed that she kept her arms in front of her chest as they moved through the city, and he couldn't blame her. He kept his hands at waist level, making sure to maintain a space between himself and any nearby gnomes.

They were not the only "tallfolk," as the gnomes referred to them, walking the streets of the city, but there were few enough that Gaven felt acutely self-conscious. As he had in Whitecliff, he found himself constantly wondering who might be watching him, ready to turn him in. Considering the Zil reputation for trafficking in secrets, he felt sure that word of his escape had reached even distant Korranberg. It was probably just a matter of time until someone identified him and summoned the authorities, so he decided to give them as little time as possible.

Trying not to attract any more attention than absolutely necessary, he seized Senya's hand and pulled her through the streets toward the lightning rail station he'd spotted from his vantage point above the city. He would get them on a carriage and out of Korranberg before any wheels could be put in motion to stop him.

Unfortunately, their great height relative to the natives didn't help them part the crowds on the streets. It was midday, and many people seemed to be taking a respite from the day's work to eat, socialize, and shop. Gaven and Senya's progress was painfully slow, but no one tried to arrest them or actively hinder their progress. The lightning rail station came into view as they rounded a corner, and Gaven let out a long sigh.

The sight of armored guards at the station sent a jolt of panic through him. He pulled Senya to a sheltered spot on the side of the street and stopped his headlong rush.

Senya fell into a ready stance, dropped a hand to her sword hilt, and stared around looking for enemies. "What is it?" she whispered.

"Relax. You're drawing stares."

She straightened and leaned close to him, transforming their appearance from nervous fugitives to amorous lovers. She brought her lips close and murmured, "What's going on?"

Gaven felt his face flush, but passersby were averting their gaze, so he went along. He lowered his head to speak right in her ear. "It just occurred to me—what if Haldren gave up on finding us in Paluur Draal and came here instead? What if he had Cart or Darraun alert the authorities here? There could be Sentinel Marshals waiting for us in there. I don't want to just stroll in."

Senya reached behind his neck and started twirling her fingers in his hair, which seemed to him to be taking the ruse too far. "It's not Haldren's style," she whispered. Her lips touched his ear, and her warm breath sent a tingle down his neck. "He'll want to find us himself. I can't see him relying on the Marshals or anyone else to do it for him. Besides, we know too much. If we're captured, we could tell them about his plans and make his life very difficult. He doesn't want us caught."

"That makes sense. Let's go, then." He started to pull away.

She held him, keeping him close. "Not before you kiss me."

"Senya." He put his hands on her waist and pushed her back, a little less gently than before.

Her mouth was half pout, half smile as she followed him into the station.

* * * * *

"I'm sorry, master, but I can't sell you a ticket without seeing your papers. If you've lost your papers, House Sivis has an outpost in the upper story where they will gladly help you replace them."

The agent at the ticket counter was a human woman attached to the Transportation Guild, a branch of House Orien. The scions of House Orien carried the Mark of Passage, which enabled some to transport themselves instantaneously across great distances, making them ideally suited for courier work. The Transportation Guild operated caravan lines as well as the lightning rail, competing fiercely with House Lyrandar's overseas shipping lines.

The woman was cheerful enough, but Gaven could tell that she was already calculating how to deal with him if the situation got ugly. It wasn't until Senya produced her papers to buy her passage that Gaven had even considered this possibility, which irked him most of all. Securing new papers would be impossible. The gnomes of House Sivis, whose Notaries' Guild issued important documents like identification papers, would send him back to Dreadhold in a heartbeat.

"Look," Senya said beside him, tugging the neck of his shirt open, "he's a dragonmarked member of House Lyrandar. Don't you think you could make an exception?"

The Orien agent stared at Gaven's huge, elaborate mark. "An heir of Siberys," she breathed, not really speaking to them.

"Yes, I'm an heir of Siberys. I'm just trying to get to Vathirond to see my family. Can't you help me?"

Her eyes narrowed. "House Lyrandar has an outpost here. Why not appeal to them?"

Gaven sighed, leaned on the low counter, and spoke in a low voice. "I came here to work for my cousin in the Lyrandar outpost," he said. "But . . . well, it didn't work out." He looked meaningfully at Senya, hoping to convey some sense of scandalous behavior. "So now I'm not in any position to ask a favor from my house here—so I've come to House Orien." He could see the young woman starting to soften. "And it's not any great favor I'm asking. I'm paying for passage, after all."

The agent's eyes shifted between Senya and Gaven, then she gave a resolute nod. "Very well."

Gaven smiled warmly. "Thank you so much. I'll remember your kindness."

Senya put down the money, and they walked toward the lightning rail. A row of decorated wooden carriages, strung together like pearls on a string, hung suspended in the air above a line of glowing blue stones set in the ground. Lightning danced between the stones and similar stones embedded in the bottoms of the carriages, giving the lightning rail its name. Even the empty air shimmered with magic.

The carriages in the rear were meant for passengers—passengers of means, who would ride in luxurious comfort. At the front of the long line, the crew cart held the bound elemental that would propel the coach in the same manner as bound elementals propelled the galleons of House Lyrandar. The conductor stones kept the carriages suspended in the air, but the elemental moved it forward, unhindered by wheels grinding against the earth.

Senya clung to his arm as they walked, evidently enjoying the ruse they had adopted, but Gaven noticed that she kept glancing behind them. After a moment, she stretched up and planted a kiss on his cheek, then whispered in his ear, "There might be a problem."

Gaven kept walking without looking back. "What is it?"

"The agent has summoned a pair of men, half-elves I think, which might mean your house."

"Or House Medani, which could be worse."

"And they're coming after us now. Pretty quickly. Yes, they're Medani. I see the basilisk emblem now."

Gaven quickened his pace, seizing Senya's hand as he hustled to the waiting coach. Senya showed their tickets to the coachman as Gaven looked back. They were close—two half-elf men, as Senya had said, with the basilisk emblem of House Medani on the lapels of their long coats. The coats billowed behind them as they walked, showing the long, slender blades both men wore at their belts. Medani's Warning Guild provided a wide range of services, from tasters employed to detect poison to inquisitives trained to root out lies. Assuming these two were the latter, Gaven hoped to avoid any contact with them.

Making sure the Medanis were watching, Gaven boarded the lightning rail coach. He saw them start to run toward the coach, then he hurried in after Senya. "Quick. Get to the front of the coach."

Senya obliged, pushing her way past a handful of other passengers who were waiting politely to get into their private compartments. Gaven followed her, peering into the compartments they passed. Each was like a small but elegant sitting room, with three lushly upholstered chairs, a small table, and walls paneled with matching mahogany.

At the far end, a door led into the next coach forward. Gaven checked over his shoulder again. One of the Medani agents caught his eye and held up a hand. Gaven nudged Senya forward, and they went through the door.

"Master Lyrandar!" Gaven heard the agent call.

"Off the coach," Gaven told Senya. "Now."

She pushed her way through more boarding passengers then paused at the bottom of the stairs, looking back at Gaven for more instructions.

"Stop them!" one of the agents shouted.

Gaven took off at a run. He moved toward the crew cart at the front of the lightning rail. Senya's boots clomped on the marble tile behind him, and shouts arose farther behind them. Seeing Gaven's size and bulk, the passengers and House Orien workers in his path stepped out of his way, rather than obeying the Medani agents' orders to stop him. One man looked like he might try to stop Senya, but Gaven heard Senya's sword slide from its sheath, and her footfalls didn't falter behind him.

They reached the cart immediately behind the crew cart, and Gaven threw himself beneath it, hoping Senya would follow. He scurried forward on his hands and knees, crawling between two columns of sparking lightning that danced between the conductor stones, then Senya crashed into him. Lightning erupted around him, connecting the two conductor stones and arcing up around the cart. The force of Senya's body sent him hurtling forward along the underside of the cart, propelling him between two more pairs of orbs, sending up three more bolts of lightning before he managed to roll free to the other side of the cart.

The lightning had knocked the wind out of him, and he lay on the hard floor for a moment trying to catch his breath. Senya ran and fell to her knees beside him.

"Ten Seas! Are you hurt?"

He still couldn't speak, but he sat up in answer. She scrambled to her feet and grabbed his arm to help him stand.

"Now what?" Senya's voice was frantic, and there was a commotion coming from the other side of the cart.

Gaven pointed weakly at the cart they'd come under. Senya seized his hand and dragged him to the door of the cart.

His nerves started to reawaken, and they screamed in protest.

They had climbed aboard the steerage cart, where dozens of people—

gnomes, goblins, orcs, humans, and a very subdued-looking minotaur whose horns had been sawed off—squeezed onto narrow benches. These were people who couldn't or didn't want to pay standard fares, which would have entitled them to comfortable seats, sleeper bunks, and meals in the galley cart. Here they could get where they needed to at a fraction of the cost, but they had to endure close quarters—increasingly close as the lightning rail made its way through Zilargo and into Breland, picking up more passengers on the way—and sleep in their seats.

Gaven led Senya to the empty seats near the minotaur, and he felt the cart lurch forward as the lightning rail started its journey. He collapsed on a bench, while Senya crouched beside him.

"Well, they didn't keep us in the station," she whispered. "So did we leave them behind? Or did they come back aboard to search for us on the carts?"

"I guess we'll find out," Gaven said. Pain started to cloud his vision. He closed his eyes, feeling consciousness swirling and slipping away.

* * * * *

"Gaven?" Senya's voice was close and urgent. Gaven fought to open his eyes. The pain had diminished, though one shard of it seemed to have traveled to between his eyes and taken up residence there. His dreams had been echoes of what his body had endured—lightning coursing through his body—though in the dream there had been a taste of exhilaration in the midst of the pain.

Senya had disguised herself as best she could—her leather coat was stowed somewhere, replaced by a more or less formless linen shift. She had pulled her hair back into a short ponytail that made her look almost like a young human girl—except for the shape of her ears and eyes. Her sword was nowhere to be seen, though Gaven couldn't imagine that it was far from her reach.

"How are you feeling?" she said.

"Well enough. Head's pounding a little." He winced as he spoke. "A lot."

She held a waterskin to his mouth and poured some water in. It was warm but clean, and it helped the pounding in his head.

"I've walked every cart," she said. "I didn't see the men who were chasing us. Vond says that a couple of Orien men came in here while I was gone, but he made sure they never laid eyes on you."

"Vond?"

Senya pointed behind him, and Gaven turned slowly around. The minotaur was planted on the bench behind him, staring fixedly at the door that led to the next cart back.

"This is Vond," Senya said. "Vond, this is Gaven."

"Know that," the minotaur growled, not shifting his eyes from the doorway.

"Nice to meet you," Gaven said, feeling awkward. Vond didn't respond in any way, so Gaven turned back to Senya, arching an eyebrow at her.

"Vond has been very helpful, keeping an eye on you while you slept," Senya said. "Not to mention scaring the Oriens away."

"I can imagine," Gaven muttered.

"Anyway, I think we're safe."

"Safe? Maybe until we get to Zolanberg. Then they'll send a team of inquisitives or Sentinel Marshals or gnome soldiers or something to search every cart until they find us. Seems to me we're trapped. But at least we're safe here in this cozy little cage."

"How far to Zolanberg?" Senya asked.

CHAPTER
18

The only reason the village of Bluevine appeared on maps of Aundair was its wine: a fine vintage with a distinctive indigo color. That claim to fame made it perfect for Haldren's purpose, Darraun reflected, which seemed to be getting all his old friends drunk enough to pledge their support to his cause.

Ten people gathered around a table in the back room of a Bluevine winery might not seem like much to a casual observer, Darraun thought. The guests Haldren had gathered, however, represented a significant concentration of power in Aundair. If he wanted to start another war, he could do worse.

Darraun sat at the foot of the table, trying to avoid drawing notice. That was easy enough, as Haldren commanded attention—preaching his vision of a new Galifar reunited under his rule as if it were a message of salvation. Many of the assembled notables received the message as if their salvation did depend on it, nodding or grunting or sometimes shouting their approval of the Lord General's words. Darraun was almost certain Haldren had woven some magic into his words, though subtly. Sometimes even he felt swayed by the rhetoric.

Looking around the table, Darraun made sure he had fixed every participant in his mind. Most were officers who had served under Haldren in the war. None of these were a surprise. Colonel Kadra Ware, Lord Major Parron ir'Fann, Major Rennic Arak, and Lord Colonel Deina ir'Cashan. Ir'Fann and ir'Cashan were not old noble families—the officers or their parents had earned titles during the war. All four of them had lost any importance they might have had when Haldren was stripped of his rank and imprisoned, so they all had good reasons to support Haldren's return to power. Ware and ir'Fann were the most vocal in their approval of Haldren at this gathering, but all four nodded at times and seemed very receptive to his message.

General Jad Yeven was also not a surprise, though he had been Haldren's equal rather than his subordinate. The two had collaborated a great deal during the war—sometimes in actions that, while showing initiative and ability, landed them in trouble with the crown. Unlike Haldren, though,

Yeven had reined in his insubordinate streak at the end of the war, which had probably saved him from Dreadhold. Yeven sat with his arms crossed and a thoughtful scowl on his face—clearly, he would need more convincing, but he was willing to listen.

The other two were the interesting ones, and Darraun watched their reactions carefully. Darraun knew of Arcanist Wheldren only by rumor. He was supposed to hold great influence among the researchers of the Arcane Congress. Any involvement of those wizards was interesting, not least because Queen Aurala's brother, Lord Adal, maintained close ties with the Congress in his role as minister of magic. Adal was also the chief warlord of Aundair, however, and was well known to want the throne of Aundair—and, indeed, of all Galifar—for himself. Wheldren's involvement in Haldren's schemes could mean that Adal was also involved, or there could be a personal connection between the two that Darraun wasn't aware of, perhaps dating back to Haldren's magical education. The wizard was completely inscrutable. His face didn't move as Haldren spoke, and he never uttered a word.

And then there was Ashara d'Cannith. By law and longstanding tradition, the dragonmarked houses generally stayed out of political affairs. Their neutrality allowed them to pursue their activities across national boundaries—and to avoid too much government interference in their business. House Cannith was in a fragile state, though, with three branches of the house working almost independently. There was some speculation that the house would split the way House Phiarlan had during the war, with Merrix d'Cannith of Sharn going his own way. Jorlanna d'Cannith led the northern branch of the house from an enclave in Fairhaven, and Darraun had heard rumors that Jorlanna was interested in seeking closer ties with the throne of Aundair. Darraun had no idea what Ashara's relationship to Jorlanna was, but she had warmed quickly to Haldren's speech.

"Dragons."

Darraun realized he'd been so caught up in gauging the reaction of Haldren's audience that he had barely heard a word Haldren had been saying. Someone had asked Haldren a question, and that had been his answer—and it had left the rest of the table speechless.

"That's right, friends," Haldren went on. "At this moment, a flight of dragons is making its way from Argonnessen to a rendezvous point in the Starpeaks. The dragons are coming to Khorvaire to fight at my command. And no army will stand in their way."

Arcanist Wheldren spoke for the first time. "The dragons of Argonnessen do not fight for human causes."

"Do you doubt my words, Arcanist Wheldren?" Haldren said, smiling.

He gestured around the table. "Those who know me will attest that I do not make idle boasts."

"I have no doubt that the dragons are coming as you claim. I question only their reasons for doing so."

"You prove yourself as astute as your reputation suggests," Haldren said. "You are correct, Wheldren. The dragons have their own reasons for fighting in our cause. Will that make their breath less deadly, their teeth and claws less sharp, their presence less fearsome to our foes? No." He slapped the table for emphasis. "They will drive our enemies before us in terror."

Colonel Ware shouted her approval, and Darraun noticed a smile behind General Yeven's hand as he stroked his chin thoughtfully.

Haldren leaned forward, planting his palms on the table, and a conspiratorial tone entered his voice. "But in the dragons' view, greater events are afoot than the reunification of Galifar. The dragons act in accordance with their understanding of a great prophecy, which they see revealed in the movements of the stars and moons, in the bones of the earth, and even in the flesh of the races of Khorvaire, in dragonmarks. They would not be coming to fight on our behalf were it not for their belief in the Prophecy."

"Our victory is foreordained!" Lord Major ir'Fann laughed, pounding his fist on the table.

Darraun noted how carefully Haldren responded. He smiled and laughed slightly. He did not confirm the Lord Major's interpretation of his words, but neither did he correct it.

And his audience was won. The four loyal officers clinked their wine glasses together, already celebrating their victory. General Yeven was smiling openly now, his eyes not quite focused in the room, as if he were seeing the dragons flying in front of his armies, breathing terror and devastation before them. Ashara d'Cannith leaned in to share a joke with Major Arak, clearly caught up in the excitement. Only Arcanist Wheldren seemed to have noticed Haldren's careful choice of words. He was not, perhaps, fully won over to the cause, but neither was he going to run back to Arcanix and tell Lord Adal all about this treasonous gathering.

Darraun stared into his glass, swirling the wine. Greater events afoot, indeed, he thought. Haldren had no idea.

* * * * *

Bordan hated Zilargo. It wasn't the gnomes themselves, but the constant feeling of being watched, almost overseen. There was a reason he worked alone—he'd worked hard in his house to earn the privilege of working without supervision. Among the gnomes, he felt as though every step he took was being watched and evaluated, and at any moment he could be judged a threat to the social order and dealt with. He knew only too well that the agents of the Trust, responsible for maintaining peace and stability, didn't look kindly on people like him.

On the other hand, that constant watchfulness proved helpful sometimes. After Gaven and his elf companion ran through the lightning rail station in Korranberg, evading the idiotic Medani agents, dozens of gnomes could describe everything the fugitives had done from the time they entered the city to their hasty departure. They came in from the north, but walked around to the west gate to enter by the main road. Gaven's eyes had lingered on a well-crafted suit of plate armor, but he hadn't bought it. The pair had shared an intimate moment just outside the rail station—or had they? The elf had looked wary a moment before, as if expecting an attack, so the intimacy might have been a cover. Bordan couldn't argue—the eyewitness reports were thorough and useful.

There was much they couldn't tell him, though. Who was Gaven's elf companion? He'd only been out of Dreadhold a few days, which didn't seem long enough to persuade some new romantic interest to risk her life running from the authorities in a lightning rail station. She didn't match descriptions of Gaven's betrothed. It might be possible to mistake a half-elf for a full elf, Bordan supposed, but he had been told Rienne had brown skin, not the pale ivory of Gaven's current companion. He figured she must be part of the group that had broken him out of Dreadhold, but that left plenty of questions unanswered. Starting with where Haldren ir'Brassek was.

In contrast to the detailed reports of Gaven's activities, there was no indication that Haldren had been in Korranberg at all. Even though Gaven had evidently made no effort to alter his appearance, Bordan tried to imagine every possible way that Haldren might look different than he did in Dreadhold, but the basics—a male human about sixty years old—drew a blank from the gnomes of the city council. It seemed clear that he had not been here at all. He and Gaven must have split up—and perhaps split up the rescue party as well. Certainly there had been no dragon sightings in the region.

Bordan left the city council hall and made his way through the crowded streets to the lightning rail station. He didn't expect as much detail from the Orien and Medani witnesses to the event, but there were certainly some things they could tell him that the gnomes couldn't. Starting with the agent who sold them passage.

"Of course I remember them," the young woman said. "He was an heir of Siberys with the Mark of Storm. Hard to forget."

"You checked their papers?"

The woman flushed crimson. "I checked hers. You'll see her in my log, there." She pointed to the sheaf of parchment Bordan was idly flipping through while he listened. "Both her identification papers and her traveling papers were issued in Fairhaven. I remember thinking she'd come a long way."

"And the man?"

Her color deepened, and she spoke as if to get the painful truth out as quickly as possible. "He had no papers."

"He had no papers," Bordan repeated, his voice flat.

"He was an heir of Siberys! He hardly had to prove his identity. I could see the dragonmark right there!"

"Calm down. I'm not here to challenge your decision. I'll leave that to your house. What was their destination?"

"They bought passage to Vathirond."

"Did they say why?"

"He said he was going there to see his family. He came here to work for his cousin, he said, but something happened between his cousin and the woman, I think, so they were going home. Or that's what he said."

Bordan found what he sought on the parchment pages. "Is this her? Senya Arrathinen?"

The woman leaned forward to see where Bordan pointed. "Yes, that's the one."

Bordan picked up his pen, jabbed it into the ink, and scrawled what little information the log held into his notebook. Senya Arrathinen, citizen of Aundair, residence in Fairhaven.

"This shows her destination as Vulyar," he said.

"Does it? Hm. Well, that makes sense."

"It does?"

"Certainly. When traveling papers show a destination on the other side of the Mournland, I don't pay much attention. We're obviously not carrying you across on the lightning rail, so I assume whatever your destination may be is just your next stop on the way to where you're going. And Vathirond makes sense, being just this side of the Mournland."

"But he told you Vathirond was their final destination."

"He did, but that was after she bought her passage. Didn't register in my mind."

"I see. So they're on the lightning rail, bound for Vathirond. Where does that cart stop?"

"Zolanberg first, then Sterngate, where Breland will check the passengers pretty carefully. Then up to Starilaskur, then Vathirond."

"Four stops. That should be more than enough. They can't run like that every time."

CHAPTER

19

T he steerage cart grew dark as the sun sank over the forests of Zilargo. No lights would come on, Gaven knew—everbright lanterns might shine in the other carts, but steerage passengers went to sleep when the sun went down and rose at dawn. Or else they sat awake in the dark.

Gaven sat up through the first watch of the night, thinking they were probably the longest three bells of his life.

The lightning rail came in to Zolanberg at the start of the second watch. Gaven sat on a bench, cradling a gnome woman on his lap as if she were his young child. He tried to remember her name as he stared at the cart door, waiting for it to open. Lightning flashed along the length of the car as it came to a slow stop, and Gaven allowed himself a quick glance at Senya. She was mostly hidden behind Vond's huge, hairy body, but he could see her legs draped along the bench on one side. This was the best plan Senya could come up with. Her idea was that a man traveling with a small child would not be suspect, and a woman traveling with the minotaur would be carefully avoided. For his part, Gaven had been too sore and tired to think of anything better. He shook his head, trying to prepare himself for what would probably turn into a terrible fight—or at least another headlong flight.

It seemed to take forever for the door to open. Gaven supposed that made sense. If they were searching for him, they wouldn't want a rush of passengers disembarking all at once. There were many travelers, mostly gnomes, standing by the door, waiting to get off, and if Gaven hadn't been twice the height of most of them he might have tried getting lost in that crowd. It would have been a mistake. When the door finally opened, the people standing nearby agitated toward the door, but a loud voice commanded them to form a single line to get off and have identification papers ready.

Gaven's heart beat a rhythm of panic. He still had no identification papers. What would he do if someone asked to see them? It would have been smarter, he reflected, to bluff the staff at the Sivis enclave into giving him papers instead of bullying the Orien agent. Probably harder, but safer.

The disembarking passengers filed off slowly. As their numbers thinned, Gaven could see past them to the gnome guards who scanned the faces of each passenger. Gaven let out a cautious sigh. Zil soldiers were one thing—one he suspected he could deal with. Medani inquisitives or Sentinel Marshals would have been another matter. The guards mostly waved the passengers through with no more than a cursory glance at them and their papers, though Gaven did see one gnome who looked like she might be scanning for magical auras. They paid more attention to the few orcs and humans who got off the cart, staring closely into their faces and checking their identification.

When all the departing passengers were off the cart, a gnome with a lantern climbed in and walked around. He made a wide circle around Vond, though Gaven saw his eyes linger on Senya's legs for a while. He peered more closely at the remaining tallfolk on the cart, pausing to harass a half-orc with completely irrelevant questions. Then he stood in front of Gaven, shining the light into his face.

"That your child?" the soldier demanded.

"Yes." The gnome in his arms gave a small cough, sounding very much like a sick child. "She's not feeling well."

"Poor thing, crowded into the steerage cart. What's her name?"

Gaven swallowed hard, then blurted out the first name that popped into his head. "Rienne."

"Pretty name." He leaned in close, trying in vain for a better look. "You have your papers?"

Gaven jerked his head toward the bench he sat on. "In my pocket."

The soldier chewed his tongue, trying to decide whether to insist on seeing the papers. Then he laid a gentle hand on the gnome woman's shoulder. "Feel better, sweetheart," he said. Then he was gone.

Passengers were finally allowed to board, and the steerage cart grew crowded. Only when the new passengers were getting settled, the door was closed, and the lightning rail finally started moving did Gaven release his hold on the gnome in his arms, setting her down on her feet beside him.

"Rienne?" she said. "That is a pretty name."

Gaven shrugged. "Thank you so much for your help. You probably saved my life."

"Yeah, me and the fact that the guy they sent in to look for you was a family man." She no longer sounded like a child, but like a streetwise woman of middle age. "Whew! It was getting hot in there." She fanned herself with one hand to emphasize the point. "Not that I'm complaining, mind you. It's been a good long time since I had a pair of strong arms around me." She noted

Gaven's discomfort, and put a hand on his arm. "Oh, don't worry, sweetheart, you're not my type." Her eyes widened. "Way too big."

* * * * *

He stood overlooking a blasted canyon, desolate of life, like a wound that refused to heal ripped into the earth. Wolves that were not wolves howled, too close at hand, but he did not move. The only sign of life was a churning cloud of smoke and steam that billowed up from a rift in the floor of the canyon.

He fell until he was in the canyon, peering through hot smoke to a great furnace below. He felt a steadying hand on his shoulder. He clasped it in his own hand without tearing his eyes from the eldritch machine, the source of all the smoke. Dragonfire fed the furnace, and fiendish figures tended it.

Beside the great machine, whose great canisters and ichor-filled tubes were too bizarre for his mind to comprehend, a mass of crystal jutted up from the cavern floor. A silver serpent writhed and coiled in the heart of the crystal, as if it were the largest dragonshard ever seen. Caught within its coils was a smear of darkness. Gaven could feel the serpent's rage, a palpable fury radiating like heat from the crystal far below him.

A quiet voice came over his shoulder, words lost in the noise of the furnace like the haziness of dream. Words sprang to his lips in answer—

"Two spirits share one prison beneath the wastes, secrets kept and revelation granted. They bind and are bound, but their unbound whispers rise to the Dragon Between, calling to those who would hear."

A great blast of flame erupted from the furnace, jetting upward to engulf him.

* * * * *

"Gaven!" He struggled to wake up, images and emotions from his dream slow to clear from his mind. Senya was on her knees next to him, shaking him awake. She seemed deeply concerned. "Gaven, are you all right?"

"I . . . I think so." Gaven sat up, rubbing his forehead. "I was asleep."

"You were?" Senya looked perplexed. "But your eyes were open, and you were saying . . . something."

"What did I say?"

"I don't know. Half the time, I think you were speaking another language. You sounded confused, and then you screamed, and that's when I shook you."

Gaven looked around. The other passengers tried not to stare, but everyone glanced his way from time to time. He wondered how many of them understood Draconic, assuming that was the language he had been babbling.

He turned back to Senya. "Thank you for waking me," he said. "It wasn't a pleasant dream."

"You're welcome." The worry melted from Senya's face, and she smiled, then looked up at the window. "Sun's almost up anyway. I think we're due at Sterngate around noon."

Gaven groaned. He felt like he had barely slept, and he didn't feel up to another confrontation of any kind, let alone a border crossing. His body was still recovering from its brush with the rail, and sitting upright proved to be a greater effort than he could manage. He slumped back down on the bench. He didn't think he'd be able to sleep again, but he could at least rest his body.

Despite the sun beginning to peek in the windows, darkness swallowed him again.

*   *   *   *   *

Gaven opened his eyes to see Senya leaning over him again, anxiety on her face. He woke quickly, feeling clearheaded and almost well rested.

"Was I shouting again?"

"No, but we'll be at Sterngate soon. I didn't want to wake you any sooner than I had to."

"Thank you. I needed sleep."

"I talked to Vond and Juni, and they're both willing to help us like they did at the last stop, assuming the guards board the cart again. Might be best to be consistent, especially if they're comparing what they see to a passenger list compiled in Zolanberg."

Gaven shook his head. "It'll never work. They're never going to let me across the border without papers."

Senya looked like she was about to argue, then thought better of it. "So what do we do?"

"How far to Sterngate?"

"Not far. We've already turned east toward Marguul Pass, I think."

"So the thing to do is to make sure I'm not on the lightning rail when they come looking for me." He got to his feet and strode to the door leading to the next cart back.

"What are you doing?" Senya asked.

Gaven opened the door and looked around. A small platform jutted out the end of the steerage cart, separated by a short gap from a similar platform at the front of the next cart. "I'm not sure yet." He pulled his head back in and looked at Senya. "Your papers are in order, right? They'll stand up to border scrutiny?"

"Yes."

"Good. Stay here. Stick with Vond if you want. They'll be so busy going through his fur with a comb that they'll barely look at your papers, if I know border guards. I'll see you once we're across."

"What are you doing?" she asked again.

"Still not sure. But I'll figure it out."

* * * * *

Evlan d'Deneith watched the lightning rail approach Sterngate. He stood tall, his arms folded, two good marshals at his back, confident that he was about to make the arrest that would put the final flourish on a long and distinguished career. He'd capture Gaven, who would lead him to Haldren ir'Brassek, and the two would lead him into a comfortable retirement.

Silent lightning arced around the crew cart and along the trailing coaches, flaring blue as they slowed. He watched carefully, in case his quarry tried to jump from the cart before it reached the station, and he had two marshals on the other side doing the same. Two more marshals walked the length of the station. He had spread a net that Gaven could not possibly escape. Evlan drummed his fingers on his arm, impatient.

The carts came to a stop. A platoon of Brelish soldiers stepped forward to open the doors on each cart, barking orders to the passengers inside. All passengers would disembark and file through a checkpoint where their papers would be examined before they would be allowed to leave the station or reboard the lightning rail.

Evlan signaled to one of the marshals behind him, and she followed him aboard the crew cart. They would make their way backward, searching every cart until they found him. The other five marshals would stay in place, watching for any escape attempt.

The crew cart was a maze of arcane devices, cramped quarters, and storage areas. There were hundreds of places a man could hide, but Evlan searched every one. Satisfied that Gaven could not be aboard, they moved to the next cart back, the steerage cart. The passengers had already cleared out, but Evlan could guess from the smell that it had been crowded on the journey from Zolanberg. He wrinkled his nose as he moved through the cart, peering under every bench.

When he reached the rear of the cart, Evlan stuck his head out the door. The marshal he'd left outside gave him an all-clear signal, and he scowled. If Gaven hadn't been seen leaving the lightning rail, then he must still be aboard. He returned to his search.

He opened the door leading to the next cart back, and was struck by the pungent smell of ozone, presumably from the lightning discharges that occurred as the lightning rail moved along its line of conductor stones. He thought it was strange that he hadn't noticed it when leaving the crew cart, but he attributed it to the stench of the steerage cart—the ozone smell was a striking contrast. All the same, he lingered in the space between the carts, peering to the sides and down. He glanced up, and noticed dark clouds blowing in from the west. A storm on the way.

"What is it?" the marshal behind him asked.

"Nothing." He slid open the door to the next cart and went through, ready to search every compartment until he found the fugitive.

* * * * *

Gaven shifted just slightly, looking up from under the small platform at the end of the steerage cart. He saw the door sliding shut behind the Sentinel Marshals, and he let out a long, slow breath.

That was close, he thought. Something made that marshal suspicious.

"Lord Marshal!" a voice cried from the station, very close. Afraid he'd been spotted, Gaven pulled his head back down, clinging to the underside of the platform. His heart pounded, and his muscles started to shake from the exertion of holding himself in place.

The marshal's next words hit him like a punch in the stomach. "We've got the woman!"

CHAPTER
20

Lightning flashed along the crew cart as it started moving again, and a long rumble of thunder answered it in the sky. Gaven took advantage of the sound to jump to the roof of the next cart, where he'd seen them take Senya. His feet slipped on the damp surface, and he started to fall before his hands caught the beam that ran the length of the cart. He hung there for a moment, breathing slowly, before pulling himself back up to a crouch, straddling the beam.

He still hadn't decided what he wanted to do. A loud voice in his mind told him to forget Senya. It seemed clear that the Sentinel Marshals were trying to lure him out of hiding by holding her, and he wasn't eager to fall into their trap. She had chosen to follow him around. He had made no request of her, and he told himself he owed her nothing.

On the other hand, the ruse that had kept him safe at Zolanberg had been her idea. And more importantly, she was at the moment the only person in Khorvaire who was actively trying to keep him out of Dreadhold. That thought had brought him as far as the roof of the cart she was in.

But he stopped there. The lightning rail was just out of Sterngate and wouldn't reach its next stop, Starilaskur, until the middle of the night. If he was going to attempt some kind of rescue, it made more sense to do it under cover of darkness and closer, at least, to his destination. He tried to find a position that would let him relax without slipping off the cart's roof and shield him from the brunt of the wind. He ended up lying facedown on the beam with his arms and legs spread wide to keep him balanced. It wasn't very comfortable, and the rain was coming down harder. At least it was warm. He sighed. It would be a long ride to Starilaskur.

He closed his eyes, suddenly exhausted again. But every time he started to drift into sleep, he felt as though he were slipping off the beam and he woke up with a start. The third time that happened, he opened his eyes and saw a pair of booted feet planted on the roof beside him. Then something hit his head, and everything went black.

* * * * *

A sharp crack of thunder startled Evlan, and he glanced out the window. The storm raged. Trees bent over in the wind, and from time to time a particularly strong gust set the lightning rail to rocking. He'd never heard of high winds blowing the lightning rail off its conductor stones before, but that didn't mean it couldn't happen.

He looked back at his prisoners and was pleased to see Gaven stirring. The marshal had hit him too hard. Still, Gaven was lucky Phaine d'Thuranni hadn't found him first. At the hands of House Thuranni, he'd be dead instead of nursing a headache.

Gaven groaned and looked around. His eyes fell on the elf woman first—he looked at her face, which was set in a grim expression, then to the ropes binding her to her chair. He tested the strength of the ropes binding his own wrists, without putting much effort into breaking them. Only then did he seem to take in the rest of the compartment—the wood paneling, the upholstered chair, the ceiling ornamented with filigree. And then he saw Evlan.

Evlan took that opportunity to introduce himself. "Ah, Gaven," he said. He watched Gaven's eyes drop to the dragonmark on Evlan's neck, then flick over his armor and the heavy bastard sword at his belt. "I am Evlan d'Deneith, Sentinel Marshal of House Deneith, and you are under arrest."

Evlan wasn't sure what to expect from his prisoner—resigned defeat or spirited defiance. He'd seen fugitives go both ways, and a range of emotions in between, upon finding themselves captured and bound. Sometimes they pleaded for their lives or for the lives of their companions. He certainly did not expect the reaction he received.

"A clash of dragons signals the sundering of the Soul Reaver's gates," Gaven said, his eyes wide but fixed on Evlan's neck. On his dragonmark. Evlan found himself looking at Gaven's own mark—a huge, sprawling Siberys mark that extended from his jaw down beneath his shirt.

"Ah, yes," Evlan said. "They did tell me that your mind was off in the Realm of Madness." He sighed and sat down in the seat next to Gaven. He glanced at the woman, whose face had not changed. "Listen, Gaven. Your friend here has been singularly uncooperative. She didn't tell us where to find you, and she says she doesn't know where Haldren ir'Brassek is. So I need you to think very hard in that warped little mind of yours and see if you can tell me where he is."

Gaven stared at the woman.

"Gaven?" Evlan said. "Look at me, Gaven."

Gaven turned his head.

"Where's Haldren ir'Brassek?"

"A clash of dragons signals the sundering of the Soul Reaver's gates." Gaven didn't look at Evlan's dragonmark this time, and Evlan thought he detected the faintest hint of a smile.

"Yes, you said that already. Are we the dragons, Gaven, you and I? Two heirs of dragonmarked houses? Is our confrontation cosmically significant?" Evlan got to his feet and spat on the floor. "I'll tell you what's significant, Gaven. You're going back to Dreadhold, and you're going to rot there. I haven't decided yet what to do with your friend Senya, but I'm fairly certain it will involve rotting in a cell somewhere too. This is no clash of dragons. I'm a Sentinel Marshal, and you're a criminal and a fugitive from justice. You're mine now. Can you understand that? You're mine."

"The hordes of the Soul Reaver spill from the earth, and a ray of Khyber's sun erupts to form a bridge to the sky."

Evlan spun on his heel and left the compartment. He barked an order for another marshal to relieve him, and he started toward the galley cart to get something to eat. He would need to keep his strength up to deal with this one.

As he reached the door at the front of the cart, a gust set the cart rocking again, and Evlan nearly lost his footing. He gripped the handle mounted beside the door, cursing the storm under his breath, and yanked the door open.

A brilliant flash of light exploded in his face with a crash of thunder, sending him sprawling backward into the cart, blind and deaf. The cart shivered from front to back. Evlan lay on his back, gasping for breath. Someone grabbed his hand and tried to pull him up, but he couldn't seem to plant his feet on the floor. He heard shouts—quiet, as though they were far away, though he could feel breath on his face. His sight started to clear at the same time, though blue-green lights danced across his vision. He found his feet at last, mumbling his thanks to whichever of his marshals had helped him stand.

And then he saw Gaven. The prisoner had broken his bonds and forced his way out of the compartment. Two Sentinel Marshals lay on the ground by his feet, unmoving. The storm wind howled through the cart, entering by the door that Evlan had opened. It swirled around Gaven where he stood before blowing out a broken window beside him. Hail drummed the roof, and constant flashes of lightning engulfed the cart like a slow, steady heartbeat of the storm.

Evlan drew his sword and charged. The cart lurched to starboard, sending him careening. His shoulder slammed into the wall of the corridor, but he kept his feet. A few more steps and he was there—at the heart of a churning maelstrom of wind and thunder. The air itself buffeted him backward, thunderclaps ringing in his ears.

"Merciful Sovereigns," he shouted. "What are you?"

"Don't you remember?" Gaven's voice was a peal of thunder. "I'm a criminal and a fugitive. And I'm yours. Your doom."

He stretched out his hand, and lightning coursed outward, swallowing Evlan in another burst of blinding light.

* * * * *

Gaven looked up at a purple-gray sky. Wind lashed the tall grass across his field of vision and blew rainwater onto his face. He sat up with effort and watched the last cart of the lightning rail disappear behind a curtain of rain in the distance. A few yards away, a conductor stone sparked with the memory of the carts' passing, as if imitating the angry sky. He looked around, saw another depression in the grass nearby, and crawled over to where Senya lay flat on her back, staring blankly up at the sky.

He tried to speak, but his voice came out a croak. He coughed, sending a jolt of pain through his throat.

Senya's eyes flicked to his face, then back to the sky. "What does the Prophecy say about me, Gaven?"

He watched her face for a long time, watched her eyes follow the clouds as the sky slowly began to clear. Finally he stood up, bent down to take her hand, and lifted her to her feet.

"I think that's up to you," he said, his voice still gravelly.

"How do you know so much of the Prophecy?"

Gaven found his sword, liberated from the Sentinel Marshals' custody, a few paces away, and Senya's pack nearby. They shouldered their gear and walked to the conductor stone, then to the next one on the line, leading them slowly toward Starilaskur. Gaven thought about his answer for a long time before speaking.

"Years ago, I made it my life's work to learn all I could about it."

"My ancestor said she'd talked to you before."

"That's what she said."

"Well, did she? Had you been there before?"

Memories flooded Gaven's mind, recent past and ancient history blurring together. "I don't know," he said.

"You don't know? Why not?"

"Maybe you can help me," he said. "Does the name Mendaros mean anything to you? Mendaros Alvena Tuorren?"

Saying the name conjured his old friend's face in Gaven's memory—even as he realized that those memories were not his. Mendaros had never known Gaven, though Gaven remembered him clearly.

"The name's a blot on my family's honor," said Senya. "He's reviled as a traitor to Aerenal."

"Why?"

"He conspired with dragons. He opened a door for one of the most devastating attacks against Aerenal in a thousand years."

"Did he? That's a story I'd like to hear sometime."

"Why are you asking about Mendaros? He's been dead for centuries."

Centuries, Gaven thought. That helped put the memories in context. "How many centuries?"

"I'm not sure. Four, maybe five?"

"And he was a relative of yours?"

"Fairly distant, but yes. Naturally, my family would like to emphasize the distance, not the relation."

"How long has your family lived in Khorvaire?"

"About as long as Mendaros has been dead. Coincidentally." Senya stopped, grabbed Gaven's arm, and whirled him to face her. "But it's your turn to answer questions now. What does Mendaros have to do with you and the Prophecy?"

Gaven sighed. "During the war, I worked for House Lyrandar, hunting for the dragonshards they needed to build galleons—or, rather, to bind elementals to power the galleons. Khyber shards are found underground, so I spent a lot of time crawling around tunnels. And the Prophecy was sort of a hobby of mine, something to think about as I traveled. It turns out that Khyber holds a lot of secrets about the Prophecy, maybe even some things the dragons don't know."

"And Mendaros?"

"Well, at one point I found . . . something—a record left by another scholar of the Prophecy. Evidently it was an ancient record, at least four centuries old, because it mentioned Mendaros. As a contemporary."

"What did it say about him?"

Gaven remembered his laugh—a loud, easy laugh. "Not much. It indicated him as a source for some information about the Prophecy. Much the same information that your ancestor gave us in Shae Mordai."

"You knew what he was going to say, you recited the words along with him, because you'd read this ancient record. And that's why my ancestor thought you'd been there before?"

"Something like that."

"I see."

They walked in silence, conductor stone to conductor stone, following the magical line that stretched off past the horizon. The sun broke through the clouds, and Gaven pointed out the hint of a rainbow over the mountains to the east.

"How far to Starilaskur, do you think?" Senya asked.

"Got a map?"

"No."

"Well," Gaven said, "I figure we must have been about half the way from Sterngate when we jumped off. At least six days on foot."

"Six days! I'm exhausted just thinking about it."

"I agree. I suppose we could just wait for the next lightning rail and try to jump aboard."

"People die doing that."

"I know. I was joking."

"Wait—we're near the end of the Seawalls, right? We can't be far from New Cyre."

"New Cyre?"

"A refugee town, more or less. After the Mourning, Breland gave a little patch of land to surviving Cyrans. It can't be more than a few days east, nestled up against the mountains."

"New Cyre it is, then." Gaven turned his steps away from the next conductor stone, setting his course to run along the line of the mountains instead. "From there, we'll try to find a carriage or something to carry us to Vathirond."

"And what's in Vathirond, anyway?"

Gaven shrugged. "After twenty-six years? Who knows? Maybe nothing but memories."

CHAPTER
21

V ery well, Gaven," Senya said, "if you're going to be a fugitive, we're
going to do this right."
Senya's hunch had proved accurate, and they had reached New
Cyre after dark on their third day of travel. Now she was dragging Gaven
through the tiny village.

"What are you talking about?"

Gaven was exhausted. They had pressed hard to reach New Cyre before
resting for the night, and he wanted nothing more than to find a comfortable
bed. Despite their stops in Shae Mordai and Grellreach, the last time he'd
slept in an inn had been Whitecliff, and he was almost ready to go back to
Dreadhold just for the beds.

"We're going to get you some papers."

"How are we going to do that in a town this size? I think it might have a
pickpocket or two, but a forger?"

"Would you mind keeping your voice down?"

"Sorry." Gaven glanced around at the darkened windows.

"And trust me."

Gaven watched in bemused wonder as Senya—heir to a noble warrior line of
Aerenal—found the few people in New Cyre who were still awake, asked just the
right questions, and led him to what must have been the only house anywhere
between Starilaskur and Darguun that could get him forged papers. He stayed
up through the night watching the forger—a gnome with a thick accent who
must have been a renegade offshoot of House Sivis—carefully tracing the lines
of a magical sigil that would convince any inspector that his papers were authentic. The sun brightened the sky behind the Seawalls by the time they finally left
the forger's house, Gaven admiring his new identification and traveling papers.

"Keven d'Lyrandar," he said, trying to get used to the name. "This makes
me really uncomfortable, pretending to be a legitimate heir of my house."

"It's either that or wrap yourself like a mummy to hide that dragonmark,"
Senya whispered.

Shutters were starting to open in the village, and Gaven was suddenly aware of the stares they drew as strangers who had arrived in the night.

"Well, it might work, as long as I don't show these papers to any other Lyrandar."

They stood at the door of one of the village inns—New Cyre, though small, had enough transient residents to support a handful of inns—and found it locked. Undaunted, Senya pounded on the door until a sleepy-looking woman opened the door.

"Respectable folk aren't about at this hour," she said, scowling at Senya.

"Please," Gaven said, cutting off Senya's retort, "we've been traveling for days and just need beds."

"Time for sleeping's done."

"We understand, but—"

"If you understand, then why are you asking for a place to sleep? Why don't you go to the Jorasco place? The halflings'll take anyone who shows enough silver."

They'll also look over my papers with too close an eye, Gaven thought.

Senya interjected, "Silver? We'll pay gold." She produced two galifars to emphasize her point, and smiled as the woman's eyes fixed on the gleaming coins.

"And will you be needing one room or two?"

"Two," Gaven said.

"Please, come in."

* * * * *

New Cyre by daylight was a strange experience. To Gaven's mind, it was easy to imagine that he was in Cyre. The fashions and architecture he'd seen on his previous visits to that nation were on proud display, and the people spoke with the lilting accents of Cyrans. In his cell in Dreadhold, Gaven had heard only vague and conflicting reports of what had happened to Cyre, the nature of the magical cataclysm that had engulfed the nation. Most of Cyre's residents had been killed in an instant, he had heard, but here was a village full of refugees who had been lucky enough to escape the Mourning, presumably because they had been traveling or fighting abroad when it occurred.

As they walked to House Orien's enclave, Gaven found himself thinking of his own home, House Lyrandar's island refuge of Stormhome. When he was convicted and sent to Dreadhold, his family had declared him excoriate, cut out of the house, and he was no longer welcome in Stormhome. He felt an odd sort of kinship with these displaced Cyrans, who spoke so lovingly and passionately about the home they had lost.

Gaven hardly dared to breathe as another agent of House Orien examined his papers. She stared at them a long time, reading each word carefully, and Gaven felt sure she would recognize the forgery. When she handed the papers back to him with a smile, saying, "Enjoy your trip, Master Lyrandar," he could scarcely believe it. He shot several glances back over his shoulder as he walked to the coach, certain that she was summoning a Sentinel Marshal to arrest him. But apparently the forgery was a success. He and Senya boarded the coach, settled into a pair of comfortable seats, and began to relax as they started to move.

Only when they were up to full speed did Gaven stop looking out the windows and actually look around the coach. It was similar to the lightning rail coach—the well-appointed ones, not the steerage cart—but on a smaller and slightly less lavish scale. Instead of a private compartment, they had a cushioned bench with a high back, affording them some privacy. The ceiling was elegantly carved with the unicorn seal of House Orien. There were no passengers in the only other seats Gaven could see, the ones across the aisle to his left.

He drew a deep breath, savoring the woody smell of the coach, and let it out slowly. He turned his gaze back out the window, trying to ignore the warmth of Senya's body beside him, and watched the mountains drift slowly past. The effect was hypnotic, and his eyes started to droop.

"Who's Rienne?" Senya's question jolted him fully awake. He didn't remember ever having mentioned Rienne to Senya.

"You tell me," he said. He wasn't going to give more information than he had to.

Senya laughed at his guarded answer. "That's what you called Juni, remember? The gnome on the lightning rail? The guard asked your daughter's name, and you said Rienne." She watched his face, and he concentrated on keeping it impassive. Her smile faded. "Do you have a daughter?"

"No," Gaven said. "I just gave him the first name that popped into my head."

"But whose name is it?"

Gaven turned to look out the window again. "Before . . . all this happened, I was to be married." He glanced at Senya and saw her eyebrows rise. "Rienne came from a minor noble family, and our marriage would have been advantageous to both our families. House Lyrandar is always looking for political alliances while officially maintaining the neutrality demanded by the Edicts of Korth, and the families it makes connections with stand to gain a great deal of wealth and prestige." He paused. "So that's who Rienne is."

"A nice arranged marriage, then?" she said, leaning closer. "Loveless? Passionless?"

Gaven turned to look past Senya out the windows across the aisle.

"Was she human? Is she an old woman now?"

"She's a Khoravar, elf-blooded like me."

"And she's in Vathirond? All this time I've been helping you reunite with your long-lost love?"

"No, she lives in Stormhome, as far as I know." He scowled. "Seeing Rienne again is not a priority."

"Oh, I see." A mischievous smile crept onto Senya's face. "The romance ended badly?"

Gaven scowled, and Senya's smile disappeared. "My life ended badly," he said. He waved his new papers in her face. "I'm living someone else's now."

He turned back to the window and smiled grimly at the clouds darkening the afternoon sky.

* * * * *

As soon as she stepped into Krathas's office Rienne knew that there was news of Gaven—and that it wasn't good news. The old half-orc's face spoke volumes.

"There's been an incident," he said.

Rienne put a hand on a chair back, then stumbled around it to sit down. "What happened? Is he dead?"

"I don't think he's dead, and I'm not even sure what did happen. There are people working hard to keep this quiet."

"Tell me."

Krathas took a deep breath, then plunged in. "What I hear is that a team of Sentinel Marshals captured Gaven on the lightning rail near Sterngate."

"Captured him? But he escaped."

"Apparently. There was some kind of storm between Sterngate and Starilaskur, and one carriage was blown open."

"Blown open?"

"Sort of funny, isn't it? They call it the lightning rail, but then a lightning storm does this." Krathas smiled weakly.

"One carriage—the one where Gaven was?"

"It appears so."

"So he called in the storm and used it to escape. That means he's in Breland somewhere."

"Probably. Quite possibly trying to get here—that lightning rail line runs through Starilaskur and on to Vathirond."

"There's something else," Rienne said. Krathas's eyes were fixed on his desk.

"One of the Sentinel Marshals was killed," he said.

CHAPTER
22

The coach stopped too often, but never for long. At some point in the night, they had a longer stop to bring a new driver aboard and change the magebred horses that pulled the cart, but even so, Gaven figured they were moving most of the day. And within two days of leaving New Cyre, the coach pulled into Starilaskur, eastern Breland's largest city. They stayed in a hostel that night, which was a vast improvement over trying to sleep sitting up on the coach's bench. The next day, they boarded a new coach bound for Vathirond.

Another two days of endless rolling and bouncing, punctuated with fitful attempts at sleep or conversation, brought them almost to Vathirond's gate. Gaven awoke from another nightmare to a child's loud voice in a bench near the front of the cart.

"What is it?" the boy said.

"I'm not sure, sweetie." The child's mother kept her voice low, trying to calm him. "Probably a dragonhawk."

"But dragonhawks live in Aundair. We're still in Breland." He sounded as though he couldn't believe his mother's ignorance.

"But we're in northeast Breland now, actually not far from Aundair."

That seemed to satisfy the child, and Gaven closed his eyes, settling back into his bench with a smile. Then Senya, sitting by the window, hit his chest. She was staring intently out the window.

"What is it?"

"Look." She pointed out the window and up, skyward.

He leaned over her and peered out, trying to follow the direction of her finger. At first he saw nothing but the gray clouds that had been hanging in the sky for days, glowering but never quite getting around to storming. Then he saw a shape flying in the clouds. Presumably, the same shape the child had seen.

"That's no dragonhawk," he whispered.

"Vaskar?"

"Probably. It's big enough."

"Where's he going?"

Gaven glanced at the sun, still low in the sky. "More or less eastward. To the Mournland. To raise the Sky Caves of Thieren Kor."

They watched the dragon soar in and out of the clouds for a long moment.

"What do you think it will be like, if the Storm Dragon succeeds?"

A vision from his nightmare flashed into Gaven's mind: numberless legions of soldiers marching beneath bone-white banners bearing a blasphemous rune, leaving carnage and devastation in their wake. Senya and the coach around him suddenly fell away, and he stood on the desolate plain in the army's wake. Vultures flapped their heavy wings and peered at him sidelong before returning to their grisly feast. In the distance, above the marching legions, dragons soared among the clouds.

"Gaven?"

He was back in the coach, though he still felt the clammy air of the battlefield on his skin. Senya stared at him, eyes wide, her back pressed against the window. He curled around his stomach, resting his forehead against the smooth wood of the bench in front of him.

"Are you all right?" Senya whispered.

"Do I look all right?"

"What is it? What did you see?"

He turned his head back and forth, feeling the wood against his skin. Senya put a tender hand on his back, and he tried to concentrate on the sensation of her touch.

"I don't want to see any more," he said. "I just want to be here, now. Blind like everybody else."

* * * * *

"Lady Alastra?"

Rienne looked up from the cup of warm wine she cradled in her hands. The messenger was a young half-orc cursed with a face that could break mirrors, with wide-set black eyes and a nose and mouth that were both like ragged holes in his gray skin. He wore a sleeveless shirt that showed off his muscles, and his black hair was cropped close to his head.

"Yes?" she said, trying to smile.

He looked awkward, uncomfortable around women perhaps. She noticed a flush in his cheeks, and he didn't meet her gaze. "Krathas sent me," he stammered.

"Of course he did. You have news?"

"I'm to tell you that he has arrived by Orien coach. Er—not Krathas. He's the one who told me. But I don't know who he is. Uh, I mean, I know who Krathas is. I don't know who has arrived by Orien coach."

A brain to match his face, Rienne thought. "I do. Thank you."

The messenger's smile revealed jagged rows of crooked and broken teeth, and did nothing to improve his looks. Rienne returned the smile as best she could, then ignored the boy as he murmured some pleasantry, bowed, and made his exit. She sipped her wine, trying to calm her nerves and her pounding heart.

Gaven is here, she thought. Now what?

*   *   *   *   *

Gaven was dimly aware of Senya saying something beside him, just as he had vaguely noticed the busy plaza they stood in. But the thing that had captivated his attention since they emerged from the Orien station was a ship, ringed with a circle of dancing flame, floating in the air across the plaza. She was moored to a tower that proudly flew the kraken banner of House Lyrandar. A Lyrandar airship.

He had to fly one.

His mind spun, trying to remember all he had learned about the research his house had been doing, trying to make these ships work. The ring of fire must be a manifestation of a fire elemental bound to the ship, probably granting her propulsion rather than levitation. Piloting the ship, then, was almost certainly just a matter of imposing one's will on the elemental bound into her, not too different from piloting an oceangoing Lyrandar galleon. He wondered if his dragonmark would help him do that—his lack of a mark had hindered him in his previous attempts to pilot galleons.

"Gaven!" Senya pulled on his arm. He tore his eyes away from the ship—the most beautiful thing he'd ever seen—and looked at her.

"What do we do now?" she said.

Her question jolted him back to the present, and to something that he had been turning over in his mind for days. "I'm not sure we do anything."

"What?" She arched an eyebrow at him.

"Listen, Senya. I meant to have this conversation with you back in Korranberg, but we got so caught up in . . . things, and I never got around to it. But now that we're here, you could go anywhere you want, do anything you want. It doesn't make any sense for you to shackle yourself to me, especially since there's a strong possibility of real shackles in my future. I have no idea what I'm going to do, and I don't want to tangle you up in whatever mess I end up making. I think we should go our separate ways."

"Without me you'll be bound for the cold northeast in a week's time."

"I can handle myself. And besides, I know people here."

"After all these years? People move, you know. Or die."

"That's not the point."

"The point is you want to get rid of me."

"Yes," Gaven said. He watched her eyes narrow and her nostrils flare in anger.

"Too bad. I'm not leaving."

Gaven sighed. "Senya, I appreciate all you've done for me already. I have enjoyed your company these last couple of weeks. But I couldn't—I don't want you to suffer because of your association with me."

"It's too late for that. Ever since the lightning rail, they know me."

"Those people won't be bothering us again."

"No, but I'm sure they checked the passage records in Korranberg. They know who you're traveling with—they know my name. And that's all they need."

Gaven put his hands to his temples. "I'm sorry, Senya. I wish—"

"You seem to have forgotten that I chose this. Not just in Darguun, either. I was in this up to my neck when I got on that wyvern's back in Q'barra. I've made my choicees. So what do we do next?"

He shook his head. "Let's see if Krathas is still alive."

*   *   *   *   *

"Lady Alastra, there's one more thing you should know." Krathas spoke cautiously, and Rienne moved her hand to Maelstrom's hilt instinctively.

"What?"

"Gaven has not been traveling alone. He has a companion." Rienne raised her eyebrows, and Krathas flushed. "A woman."

"That's his business," Rienne said, trying to ignore the icy claw touching her heart.

Krathas was visibly relieved. "Just thought you should know."

"I appreciate your concern, wasted though it may be."

Krathas inclined his head in a small bow.

"So where is he now?" she asked.

"On his way here."

"Krathas, would you do me the favor of allowing me to greet Gaven alone?"

"Of course, Lady." Krathas got to his feet and worked his way around his desk. He laid a hand on her shoulder and smiled. "Olladra's fortune."

Rienne returned his smile warmly. "Thank you."

As Krathas shuffled out the door, she sank into his desk chair, her heart racing. She'd been in Vathirond nearly two weeks, working with Krathas, waiting for this day. She had rehearsed her eventual meeting with Gaven in her mind so many times, but it was different each time—she had no idea how he would respond to her, what he might say to explain his behavior, whether he would forgive her for hers. And in her mind, it had always been the two of them, trying to pick up where they left off all those years ago. She'd been so naïve.

"Here it is, right where I left it."

It was his voice, just outside the door. Her mouth went dry.

"Looks like it hasn't been painted in thirty years." A woman's voice.

Rienne drew a deep breath through her nostrils and let it out slowly through pursed lips. Then the door swung open.

In her mind, this encounter had always started the same. She was cool, a little distant, aloof. Her voice low, she said, "Hello, Gaven," and he was thunderstruck, surprised. She began with the upper hand. The reality was drastically different.

He stood framed in the doorway, so beautiful to her eyes. She was overwhelmed with a rush of the love she'd felt so strongly, so long ago, and had worked so hard to suppress these last decades. Then came a wave of remorse—this was what she had done to him. The weight of twenty-six years in Dreadhold was clearly visible on his face and in his posture. His hair was long and unkempt, and his face looked haggard. Then she saw his dragon-mark, and she gasped.

"Rienne." His voice was flat, betraying no surprise or emotion.

The woman stepped into view behind him, peering over his shoulder into the office. She was an elf, pretty in a fey sort of way, with eyes too big for her face and stained with blue makeup. Her lips were full and also painted, the bright red of a streetwalker, and she wore heeled boots and a chest-hugging coat to match. Rienne scowled.

"Rienne?" the woman said. "So she is in Vathirond after all. What a nice surprise!" The red lips twisted into a sardonic smile as she looked at Gaven.

This was nothing like Rienne had imagined.

"Where's Krathas?" Gaven said.

Rienne stood. " 'Where's Krathas?' Hm. It's good to see you, too."

Gaven stepped into the room. "I'm s—no, I'm not sorry. What do you expect me to say?" His voice and his face came alive with anger. "The usual pleasantries don't seem to fit. The last time I saw you, a pack of Sentinel Marshals were dragging me out of the room. You put on quite a show of grief, as I recall. No, Rienne, it's not good to see you. I didn't come here to see you, I came to find Krathas. Where is he?" Without waiting for an answer, he stepped into the room and started peering into the shelves that lined the walls.

"Well said, Gaven," the streetwalker chimed in.

Rienne put her hand on Maelstrom's hilt and stepped around the desk to face the woman. "Would you leave us? We have a lot to talk about."

The red lips pouted, but the mocking smirk lingered at their corners. "And miss all the fun?"

Rienne noticed the woman's hand settling on the hilt of her own sword, which she hadn't seen before. Perhaps she wasn't a streetwalker after all.

"We haven't been introduced," Rienne said. "I am Rienne ir'Alastra."

"Yes, I know. The one Gaven was to marry. I gather it ended badly."

"And your name?"

"Senya Alvena Arrathinen." Rienne heard the first hint of an elvish lilt in her voice.

Gaven began looking around the desk.

"Pleased to meet you, Senya," Rienne said.

"Remember what Gaven said about the usual pleasantries?" Senya smiled and blinked her too-long eyelashes at Rienne before dropping the smile and stepping past her into the room. "What are we looking for, Gaven?"

"An adamantine box, about the size of a small book, but thicker. Maybe two small books."

Rienne felt a surge of fury replace the love and guilt she had felt on first seeing him. "You will not ignore me, Gaven."

He glanced at her, then bent to open a desk drawer. "I'm not ignoring you, Rienne. I just have nothing to say to you."

"Well, I have some things to say to you."

"Go ahead." He slammed the first drawer shut and slid another one open.

"Don't you think I deserve an explanation?" she said.

He glanced up at her again, then back down. "No."

"I think I do. I loved you once, Gaven, and you made me believe you loved me."

He straightened and folded his arms. His mouth was a thin line as his eyes bored into her. "Funny way of showing your love," he said, "turning me over to House Deneith."

"I had to! You were out of control!"

Rienne heard the window behind her shake in its pane as Gaven bent to the desk again. "You had to," he said with a snort.

"Gaven, please talk to me." Rienne had lost any shred of control she might have had over the situation, and she resigned herself to pleading with him. "I need to understand what happened—and what's happening now. What is going on?"

Gaven stood again and looked at her. She saw something in his eyes—pity, maybe, or compassion—and thought for the first time that all might not be lost.

"A great deal has happened, Rienne. I . . . I do regret your part in it."

Rienne felt her face flush as tears sprang to her eyes. "I do as well."

He held her gaze for a moment, then pushed past her to search the drawers on the other side of the desk. "So I think it would be best if you don't have any part in what's happening now," he said. Rienne felt the breath squeezed out of her chest. "You should go."

He was so close, she could just reach out and rest a hand on his back. For a moment she thought that if she did, her touch would bring everything back to normal, would bring him back to her. Just as she began reaching for him, the elf woman interrupted.

"Didn't you hear him?" Senya said. "You should go." Her hand was back on the hilt of her sword.

Rienne walked around the desk and stopped in the doorway. She turned back to Gaven and produced a thick box from beneath her outer cloak. "Is this what you're looking for?"

Gaven leaped around the desk and snatched the heavy metal box from her. "Krathas gave it to you? Or did you steal it from him?"

"Steal it?" Blood pulsed at her temples as fury surged in her heart again. "I have done things I regret, Gaven—a great many things. But I have not stooped to theft. Or murder."

"Murder?" Gaven barely glanced up from the box, which seemed to consume his attention. She wondered again what was inside. What was so important to him that he asked Krathas to keep it safe?

Her throat was tight, and she blinked back a fresh wave of tears. It was too much to bear. "Goodbye, Gaven." She kept her pace tightly under control as she strode out of the room and down the hall, without a backward glance. Only then did she break into a run. She ran down the stairs, out of the building, and into the street, and a shadow detached itself from an alley to follow her. She pulled Maelstrom from its sheath and turned to face this new attacker. The poor fool would bear the brunt of her fury.

"Lady Alastra!" His voice brought her up short, and she lowered Maelstrom's point. A dwarf hurried up to her, dressed for the neighborhood except for a signet ring that gleamed in the starlight. "Are you hurt?"

"I'm fine," Rienne answered. "Who are you?"

"A friend," the man said, but his tone was not convincing. "Gaven in there?"

Rienne's eyes darted back to the building that held Krathas's office, and that was apparently the only answer the dwarf needed. He turned and ran back the way he'd come.

S he's going to turn us in, you know," Senya said. "We need to get out
of here."

"In a moment." Gaven had set the adamantine box on the desk
and was on his knees in front of it, carefully manipulating a set of dials set
in the front. For twenty-six years he had clung to these numbers, the key
to unlocking the one thing he still owned in the world outside Dreadhold.
They were the numbers of the Prophecy, and as he set the dials to open
the box the Draconic verses danced through his mind: the land of thirteen
dragons, three ages of the world, sixteen gods. Then five beasts at war, three
shards of three dragons for nine, and another thirteen—thirteen moons.
He stared at the numbers before opening the box. "And the Storm Dragon
emerges after twice thirteen years," he whispered. Then he shook his head
and opened the box.

Senya gasped, and Gaven felt a chill wash over him. It had been haunting
his dreams, but he had not seen it in so many years. Cradled in black velvet,
the clear crystal glowed with a purple-black light from a writhing vein of color
at its heart. It mesmerized him as it had when he had first found it, and he
stretched out a hand to it without consciously willing it. His hand brushed
against Senya's as they both touched its surface, which seemed to jolt them
both out of a trance.

"A nightshard?" Senya said, drawing a hand across her eyes. "What's this
all about?"

"It's called the Heart of Khyber," Gaven said quietly, "sort of a dark twin
to the Eye of Siberys. It—" He stopped, listening. Yes, there were footsteps in
the hall, slow and heavy. "They're here. Come on."

Gaven shut the adamantine box and spun the dials. Senya moved to the
door, still open from Rienne's departure, and quickly jumped back, taking
cover behind the jamb.

"Stay where you are!" a gruff voice shouted from the hallway. "Gaven the
excoriate, surrender yourself to the Ghorad'din!"

"Dwarves," Senya whispered as Gaven leaped to cover on the other side of the open door and slammed it shut. "House Kundarak."

"Elite dwarf soldiers, no less," Gaven muttered. "How many?"

"I saw two, but they were just coming around the corner. Might be more."

The footsteps were right outside. "Open this door!" the same voice yelled.

"Surrender? Open the door?" Gaven's tone was mocking. "Just like dwarves to expect someone else to do all your work for you." He slid his sword out of its sheath, holding it in one hand and the box in the other.

The words were barely out of his mouth when a body slammed hard into the door on the other side. The door was strong, but not strong enough to withstand an angry dwarf. It slammed open toward Senya, who knocked it back into the dwarf charging through. The dwarf stumbled, and Gaven brought the hilt of his sword down to ring on the man's helmet, sending him staggering backward into his companions.

That moment of confusion provided Gaven a chance to size up his foes. Three of them, all dwarves, two women. They all wore the manticore sigil of House Kundarak, the Mark of Warding, but Gaven didn't see a dragonmark on any of them. The man and one of the women were dressed to fit in to the slum where Krathas's office was located, which suggested that they had been here for a while, ready for him. Gaven silently cursed both Rienne and Krathas for this new betrayal. The third dwarf, evidently the leader, was a handsome noblewoman wearing a silk shirt of a rich red that complemented her marble-black skin. House Kundarak didn't send inexperienced warriors far from their mountainous home in the east—these would be elite warriors, a real challenge.

I'm going to need both hands, Gaven thought. He tossed the adamantine box behind him, where it landed with a heavy thud on Krathas's desk.

Senya stepped out from behind the door to face the dwarves, the tip of her sword pointing at the face of the nearest foe. The dwarf glowered at her, evidently incensed at having had the door pushed in his face. He hefted his spiked mace and charged. Senya smiled, shifting her sword ever so slightly.

The dwarf threw his weight sideways and crashed into Gaven, knocking him to the floor and sending his sword clattering to the floor. Gaven barely had time to roll to the side before the mace crashed down where his chest had been. He rolled with his momentum and came up on his feet, but his sword was on the other side of the angry dwarf.

He glanced at Senya as she parried the other soldier's short sword. "Come to think of it," he said, "I like your plan. Let's get out of here."

The leader of the dwarves planted herself in the doorway in response, her grim smile seeming to indicate that she looked forward to Gaven's attempt to get past her. Gaven spat a few arcane words, sheathed his body in crackling blue flame, then lunged toward the dwarf who had knocked him down.

"That's right, knock into me now," he said with a grin.

As he had hoped, the dwarf avoided his lunge, which provided Gaven the opening he needed to reach his sword. He lifted the blade and swept it in a wide arc that forced the dwarf back another couple of steps. That gave Gaven room to reach the desk and pick up the box with the Heart of Khyber in it.

He glanced at Senya, who was still on the defensive, warding off a flurry of cuts and jabs. "Come on," he said. He jumped onto the desk and threw himself at the window.

Heavy shutters splintered around him, and he fell. Another syllable of a spell brought his fall under control, and he floated gently from the second-story window to the street below. He looked up just in time to see Senya hurtle out the window, somersaulting in the air and landing hard on her feet nearby.

A crossbow bolt bit into Gaven's shoulder, and he glanced around. He hadn't seen a crossbow on any of the dwarves upstairs, which meant there was at least one more waiting here on the street. He heard one of the dwarves follow Senya out the window, and he knew the others wouldn't be far behind. Shaking his head, he broke into a run.

Rain hissed into steam as it made contact with the flames wrapping his body, and he laughed as he ran. He felt the wind at his back, and he willed it to carry Senya along with him, and it obeyed his will. His feet barely touched the ground—he felt the cobblestones brushing the soles of his boots as he ran. Then the cobblestones ended, and it was rocks and grass that kissed his feet as he ran along the river out of the city. He let the fire wash off his body and felt the rain splatter on his face and drench his clothes. No more thought of pursuit entered his mind. He was the wind, carrying Senya as he blew—he was the rain, dancing in the wind and pattering on the ground. He was the storm.

When he finally stopped running, he stood with his face to the rain, his arms outstretched, and laughed. Senya collapsed on the ground at his feet, and still he laughed.

* * * * *

Rienne watched the dwarf approach through the rain, and she knew that Gaven had escaped. The dwarf's scarlet shirt stuck to her skin, revealing the outline of her dragonmark beneath it. Her shoulders were hunched, and she walked slowly despite the downpour.

She came close to the doorway where Rienne stood out of the rain and gave a small bow. "I am Ossa d'Kundarak," she said. "You should have come to us first."

"I know." It was an effort to speak. "You followed me?"

"You were followed from Stormhome, yes. We had a suspicion that you might try to contact him."

"What happened?"

Ossa shook her head, as if she weren't at all sure what had happened. "We found him, of course, in Krathas's office, with the elf woman. They refused to surrender, drew arms against us, and then jumped out the window. They got away," she added, quite unnecessarily.

"You had someone on the street, surely."

"Kerra hit both of them with her crossbow. She thinks the woman must be pretty badly wounded. But it didn't slow them." She shook her head again, bewildered. "They ran fast. Impossibly fast. And when we ran after, it was like—" She looked away, into the sky where lightning danced among the dark clouds. "Clearly, he used magic to impede us. The wind blew in our faces, slowed us down. Thadar was struck by lightning."

"Is he badly hurt?"

"He's at the House of Healing now, but he'll be fine. Thank you."

"It's quite a storm," Rienne said, turning her eyes to the sky as well.

"Unnatural, surely. Must be related to his dragonmark."

"I suppose. I've never seen anything like it, and I've worked with House Lyrandar most of my life."

"Let me say again, Lady Alastra, you should have come to us. He's clearly dangerous."

Rienne nodded.

"Did you talk to him at all?"

"A little, yes."

"Did he say anything important? Anything that might suggest where he is going, what he's up to?"

"He said precious little. I was hoping for some kind of explanation, anything that would help me understand what happened to him. I got nothing."

"What was he doing here?"

Rienne was not ready to betray him again. She answered as vaguely as she could. "Looking for Krathas."

"Do you know why?"

She shrugged. "Krathas was his only friend left after his trial. I think he was looking for someone he could trust."

"What about the woman? What's she doing with him?"

"Isn't it obvious?" Her stomach tightened, and she felt a bit light-headed.

"I suppose it is. You look pale. Are you unwell?"

"It's been a trying evening. I think I'd better get inside, warm up, get some rest."

"I understand." Ossa bowed again and started to turn away. She stopped and looked back over her shoulder at Rienne. "You will contact us if you should run into him again?"

"I will." As she said it, some part of her thought she actually might. The idea saddened her more than her encounter with Gaven had.

"Good night, Lady Alastra."

"Good night."

CHAPTER
24

The wind blew itself out in cyclonic eddies once Gaven stopped running. Lightning blasted the ground near where he stood, and his laughter died with the winds. He looked around at the river, the fields of grain on either side, and the city in the distance. Only then did he notice the small pool of blood spreading from Senya's body, and he fell to his knees beside her.

Several crossbow bolts had hit her as they ran from the dwarves. Some had fallen out, but three penetrated deeply enough that they remained firmly lodged—one in her lower back, one in her shoulder, one in her thigh. The one in her leg had gone deepest, and Gaven couldn't imagine how she had continued running so far. Her breathing was shallow, her skin bone-white, and her eyes wide and staring. Murmuring a prayer to Olladra, the goddess of good fortune who watched over healers, he set to work extracting the bolts.

It was grim work. Senya had lost a good deal of blood, and she barely had strength to groan as he pulled the first one out. Fortunately, the bolts were little more than sharpened sticks with fletching, so they didn't take more flesh with them as he pulled them out. By the time he got the second one out, her eyes were closed.

"You shouldn't have left Haldren," he whispered as he set to work on the third. "Darraun would have had you closed up and back on your feet in no time."

To his surprise, Senya managed a weak smile, and her eyes fluttered open. Her lips moved a bit, but no sound came out.

"I know," Gaven said. "If you were still with Haldren, you probably wouldn't have been hurt. I told you it was dangerous to come with me. I'm surprised you made it this long."

He suddenly felt very alone. He missed Darraun's conversation, even his prying questions. He worried that Senya might not recover from these wounds. And he had driven Rienne away.

He took off his shirt and tore it up to make bandages, binding Senya's wounds to the best of his ability. He pulled a blanket from her pack, spread it over her, and sat beside her, watching the sun's last glow fade from the western clouds. When it was dark, he opened his adamantine box and turned the Heart of Khyber over and over in his hands, watching the vibrant coil of purple-black twist and pulse in the crystal's depths.

* * * * *

The night was well into the fourth watch, and part of Gaven's mind reasoned that he was hallucinating. Even so, the inky coil of color in the heart of the nightshard seemed to have taken on a draconic face, and he had the distinct sense that it listened to him and might answer. So he asked the question that had haunted his mind for most of thirty years.

"Why have you done this to me?"

"You were the one who found me," the dragon said, though Gaven's lips moved as it spoke.

Gaven remembered stretching his broken hand out, despite the pain, to touch the perfect nightshard. The Heart of Khyber.

"You've ruined my life."

"I've given your life purpose." Its voice was Gaven's, but lower.

"I don't want that purpose," he spat. Chasing the Prophecy, manipulating history so that he—Gaven!—could become a god.

"Then choose a new one. But you can't carry on without one."

"Who are you?" Another memory—a draconic face reflected back at him in the swirling waters of a dark pool.

"Who do you think I am?"

Senya stirred in her sleep. Gaven thought she looked better.

"You're me," he muttered. "And you're a dragon who's been dead for five hundred years. With your dying will, you stored your memories in this damned nightshard—you gave them to me. Without having any idea what you were doing to me."

Choose a new one, he thought. He turned the Heart of Khyber over in his hands, thinking of its bright twin.

* * * * *

Senya emerged from unconsciousness to the sensation of warmth spreading through her shoulder—a warmth that brought chills in its wake, like the kisses of a lover. Her eyes fluttered open, and she saw a halfling man crouched beside her on the ground, smiling at her. His hand was the source of the warmth, and the dragonmark visible on his bare upper arm confirmed her first guess: he was a healer of House Jorasco. She returned the smile briefly, then looked around in a panic.

"Where's Gaven?"

The healer's smile flickered but didn't die. "Good afternoon, Senya," he said. "You're safe now. Don't worry."

A couple of other halflings busied themselves around a wagon nearby, but there was no sign of Gaven.

"What happened?" she said. "How did you find me?"

"You were attacked by bandits," the halfling said, a look of concern on his face. He put a hand on her forehead, checking for fever, but seemed satisfied. "You suffered some serious wounds, but you're going to be fine now. Your traveling companion, Keven d'Lyrandar, summoned us and paid for our services. I expect he'll be waiting for you at the House of Healing in town." He watched her reaction carefully.

"I understand," she said. "Thank you."

He shifted his attention to the wound in her leg, effectively hiding his face from her view. "You mentioned someone named Gaven?"

"It wasn't bandits that attacked us," Senya said. "It was Keven's cousin, an excoriate of his house named Gaven."

"I see," the healer said. Senya could only see the back of his head. "And he loosed the crossbow that wounded you?"

Senya's pulse quickened, and she was suddenly sure the halfling saw through her lie. "No, he wasn't alone. There was an old man, a sorcerer I think, and a warforged, and another human with a crossbow. He's the one that wounded me."

"I see," the halfling repeated. Senya felt the warmth spreading through her leg, unknotting the muscles and washing away the ache.

The healer smiled and pulled his hands away. "I think you're ready to be moved." He looked up and signaled to the other halflings, still avoiding Senya's eyes. The others brought a stretcher over and gently rolled Senya onto it, then carried her over to the wagon. When they had loaded her in and carefully strapped her down, they clambered aboard, and the wagon started rolling.

Senya watched the clouds drift across the sky and wondered where Gaven was. She knew that the chance he lingered in Vathirond's House of Healing was next to none.

* * * * *

Gaven crouched on the horse's back, thrilling to the feel of its muscles as it galloped along the road. He hadn't ridden in more years than he could remember, and it had taken a while to get his body into the rhythm of the horse's stride. Once he did that, though, he felt like he was running, his muscles moving in perfect synchronization with his mount's. The wind blew his hair back from his face and cooled the sweat from his skin. Best of all, his mind was completely submerged in the pounding hooves and flexing muscles, the rush of speed and wind. Any time his thoughts began to stray toward Rienne or Senya, he forced them back to the horse and the run.

Hours and miles sped by under the mare's stride. Vathirond—along with Rienne and Senya—fell farther and farther behind him, and he thought as little as he could about what lay ahead. He lost himself so completely in his flight that he nearly fell from the saddle when his mount abruptly slowed.

They had reached the Mournland. A wall of gray mist hung in the air like a funeral shroud, swallowing the road ahead, and the horse would not get any closer.

"It's all right, lady," he murmured as he dismounted. "You've done well. You see if you can find your way back to the barn I stole you from, huh?"

He lifted a bag from the mare's saddle and slung it over his shoulder. It held the scant supplies that would sustain him in the Mournland—journeybread that would keep him nourished and full, and a magic waterskin that would never run dry. He regretted the theft, but there would be enough threats to his life in the Mournland without adding the worries of starvation or thirst.

He patted the mare's flank and let her go. She loped away from the wall of mist without a backward glance. He watched her until she was out of sight, then turned back to face the mist. He had the fleeting sense of a presence in there, something watching him. Waiting for him—impatient, hungry.

A chill ran down his back, and he drew his sword. He was suddenly struck by a feeling of awesome solitude. No one was here to cover his back, no one to share his anxiety—or to make him feel brave, like Rienne used to. No one at all, except perhaps the creatures lurking in the mist.

He checked the sky for the hundredth time, looking in vain for any sign of Vaskar. He took a step closer to the wall of mist, then extended his sword until the point sank into it. The blade met no resistance—in fact, for just a moment, Gaven felt as though something were gently pulling the sword into the mist. He stepped forward, sinking the sword all the way into the fog, bringing his face to within a hand's breadth of the vaporous pall. His movement didn't stir it; even his breath made no eddies in the mist.

He looked around as if taking a final survey of the living world before crossing into the land of the dead, then stepped in. The mist was cold on his skin. He stepped forward again before he dared to take a breath, letting the clammy mist into his lungs. There was an odor to it, not putrid exactly, but definitely a smell of death. The mist closed in around him, and he hurried forward, eager to push through to the other side.

Tendrils of mist coiled around his limbs as he moved, tugging at him.

With every step, he felt a weight of exhaustion settling on him. He stopped, shook his head to clear it, and pressed ahead, but he began to wonder why he bothered. He could see no end to the mist ahead, and when he looked over his shoulder it seemed to stretch forever behind him. He dropped to his knees, his heart heavy, his muscles too tired to move.

An old dream filled his senses. Staggering across a blasted landscape where nothing lived. Falling to the ground, seeing his hands sink into earth that was half dirt, half ash. The taste of the air, bitter like bile.

"Have I been here before?" he asked the mist. "Or did I dream of this moment?"

He lifted one knee out of the dust and planted a foot on the shifting ground.

"It doesn't matter," he said. "Either way, I'm here now." He shifted his weight forward and pulled himself up until he stood with his chin on his chest. "And I have work to do."

The mist began to swirl around him. He smiled as he felt the air stir—the breath of wind restored his strength. Great gusts cleared the air around him, showing him the ground at his feet and a path ahead. He walked between receding walls of billowing fog, and soon the dead-gray mist was gone.

The land around him was a desolation. He had crossed into another world—the verdant landscape of Breland was lost in the mist, far away, unreal. Beneath his feet, the ground was a layer of fine sand or ash on top of smooth rock. He saw nothing alive on this side of the mist. No trees, no birds overhead, not even weeds. The sun hung low in the east, its feeble light drowning in a distant fog. Above him, the sky was the gray of a corpse. Even the wind around him died.

Gaven stepped forward, visions from his dreams crowding his mind. Another step, and the sand around him stirred, jolting him back to his senses. Something formed itself from the ground beside him, taking on a vaguely human form, gaunt arms and a gaping mouth and eyes of sickly green fire. The sight of it sent a wave of unreasoning terror through his body, and he stepped back—right into the grasping claws of a second ghoulish creature.

"Thunder!" He wrenched himself free of the creature's grasp and hefted his sword in his trembling hands.

A third monster surged up from the sand, and Gaven swallowed his fear. He swung his sword in a full circle around himself, biting into each one, sending three sprays of ash into the still air. The creatures didn't flinch—they were upon him, their claws tearing his skin and pulling him in three different directions.

With a single arcane word, Gaven pulled a cloak of fire around his body, its warmth dispelling the lingering chill of the awful mists. The creatures drew back in obvious pain, giving him an opening to slip through, to put all three in front of him. As they tried to circle him, he sent a crackle of arcane lightning into his sword, then lunged to his right to intercept the creature moving around that side. The blade bit deep, and the thing's form lost some definition, but it didn't slow its advance. It slammed into Gaven's shoulder, one claw cutting a gash down his chest. The wound flared with green fire, and Gaven shouted in pain. The creature clung to him, even as Gaven's fiery armor engulfed it. It brought its face right up against his, its eyes staring into his. In an instant, Gaven thought he saw a distillation of all the pain and misery that filled the Mournland.

Desolation spreads over that land like a wildfire, he thought—like a plague. In the creature's eyes, he saw a roiling gray mist spreading across the verdant land, leaving nothing alive in its wake. More, he felt the despair of every living thing that was swallowed in that mist, every spirit that lingered in this graveyard, every person who had lost a relative or friend to the Mourning. He fell to his knees, the creature still staring into his eyes.

Then he brought his sword around, cutting right through the thing's waist, making it dissolve back into the sand.

The other two creatures came at him from opposite sides, stalking in cautiously. Gaven stood and stepped backward, a little unsteady on his feet. A soft breath of wind blew up his back, chilling his sweat, and he filled his lungs as though to draw strength from the moving air.

The creatures pounced, and Gaven exhaled. The breeze at his back swelled, and he became the wind. He stretched out his hands, and the wind blasted forth to tear at the creatures' sandy forms. They staggered backward as the wind continued to drive at them, ash streaming out behind them. He was the fury of nature, all wrath and destruction. He smiled grimly as the power of the storm coursed through him.

A crack of thunder rent the air, and Gaven became the lightning, joining blasted earth to gray sky. His feet lifted off the ground, and the lightning shot out of his hands with the wind. The instant of the lightning strike stretched into an eternity in his mind—he was storm, and he was everywhere at once. This was power like he had never tasted before, and he exulted in the destruction he wreaked.

The instant ended. He came down hard on his back, a few paces from where he'd been standing, staring up at the clear, dead sky. He lifted his head with a tremendous effort, just long enough to make sure that the creatures were gone. Two patches of sand were blackened and smoking, but there was no other sign of the monsters. He let his head fall back on the ground.

The magical flames around his body had gone out, but his body still burned with pain where the creature had raked his chest. His dragonmark also stung, as though lightning still coursed along its intricate tracings. He groaned, tried to lift his head again, and failed.

"Welcome to the Mournland," he said.

*   *   *   *   *

Gaven rested for only a moment—long enough for the sting to fade from his dragonmark, though the wound on his chest still burned. He struggled to sit up, every muscle in his body protesting, then slowly got his feet under him and stood up.

He looked at the sun as it disappeared below the horizon, scanned the sky again for any sign of Vaskar, then turned to look for Nymm, the largest moon. It was just rising out of a gray haze to the east, orange and round.

"The Eye of Siberys will lift the Sky Caves of Thieren Kor from the land of desolation under the dark of the great moon," he said to himself. "The great moon's full now. I've got two weeks."

He put his hands on his knees and let his head hang.

"Two weeks to reach the Sky Caves. If I can stay alive that long."

He found his sword where it had fallen on the ground, heaved it onto his shoulder, and started walking.

CHAPTER

25

Vaskar perched on an eruption of stone, overlooking a plain of jumbled rock and sand. He had been watching the great moon's ascent through the sky, and his patience was rewarded as it neared its apex. A hint of shadow appeared at the edge of its disk. He clutched the Eye of Siberys tighter in his great claw and rumbled deep in his throat.

"The eclipse is beginning," he murmured, "the dark of the great moon." He stretched his neck and his wings to the sky and roared. "The time is at hand!"

He watched, waiting for the perfect moment, as Nymm slowly disappeared in the world's shadow.

When its light was completely quenched, he raised the Eye of Siberys high, holding it gingerly between his two front claws. "Do your work," he whispered. He gazed into the golden crystal, and he saw.

He saw the desolation of the Mournland and the life-leaching energies that still permeated the land. He saw the twelve moons arrayed in the sky above him, Nymm shrouded in its eclipse, and he perceived the forces aligned to make this moment possible. He saw the Sky Caves slumbering beneath the ground, and he called to them. He felt them begin to stir, responding to his call.

For a moment, he saw himself—small and insignificant among the events of the moment. But he did not like to see himself, and he certainly didn't like feeling small.

"The Storm Dragon has emerged!" he cried. "I will walk in the paths of the first of sixteen!"

He closed his eyes, and the earth began to shake. The ground trembled so violently that Vaskar took to the sky, pounding his wings in the still air to rise above the tumult. The plain below him looked like a troubled sea, sand erupting in geysers and boulders rolling wildly in every direction. He flew in widening circles, watching the earth churn in an area the size of a large island.

Soon there was direction in the movement below him—a general tendency toward the outside of an enormous circle. The ground swelled, sand sliding and boulders rolling downhill from the center of the bulge. Vaskar flew to the edge of the swell, not wanting to be directly above whatever emerged.

As he continued his flight, the sand at the crest of the swell fell away, revealing a jagged dome of reddish stone. Slowly it rose higher and higher above the surrounding earth, and Vaskar caught sight of a cave entrance in the face of the rock, sand pouring out of it as it lifted into the air.

"The Sky Caves of Thieren Kor!" he roared.

The more rock emerged from the earth, the faster it rose, and in another moment it had broken free entirely. The rumbling thunder of the earth below came to an abrupt stop. In the sudden silence, an enormous island floated a hundred feet up in the air, rounded at the top, a jagged point at the bottom like an inverted mountain. Sand and rubble poured from dozens of holes, spilling down the sides and trickling into a great crater in the ground below it.

Vaskar tightened the circle of his flight, surveying the Sky Caves from every side, trying to decide where to enter. The cave mouths seemed to form patterns, characters of the Draconic script, but every time he tried to read them he thought they shifted, aligning themselves in different patterns. Finally, impatient, he chose a cave near the top and landed on its lower lip, scrabbling at the edge until he could get all four claws on solid ground.

"The Storm Dragon walks in the paths of the first of sixteen," he said. "I am here. Reveal your secrets to me!"

He advanced into the winding tunnel.

* * * * *

Gaven felt the earth rumbling and hefted his sword, expecting an attack—something springing from the ground, perhaps, or some enormous monster that shook the earth with its steps. The rumbling grew until it threatened to knock him off his feet, and in that moment he glimpsed the eclipsed moon above his head.

"No," he breathed.

Exhausted as he was, he ran. The wind cradled him and sped him on. The sky darkened as clouds rolled in—the first real clouds he'd seen since entering the Mournland—and covered the Ring of Siberys, the stars, the eclipsed moon. His steps and the wind around him kicked up a storm of sand and ash in his wake.

He occasionally glimpsed creatures moving in the night around him, from scavenging vermin the size of dogs to an enormous war construct he spotted in the distance, lumbering across the landscape. One spiny crab-spider thing snapped at him with fangs and pincers as he ran, but he didn't slow at all, and it quickly grew tired of the chase. Nothing else came close enough to threaten him.

Rain began to fall. It cooled him as he ran and soothed the burning wound across his chest. He saw it form craters in the sandy ground and drain away.

The land around him was flat and featureless. The map he'd found in Paluur Draal and committed to memory was his only guide, and he had no better way to navigate than trying to keep his path straight in the direction he'd first chosen. The bank of gray mist hung off to his right, sometimes nearer than others, but otherwise he could see nothing to indicate where he was, where he'd been, or where he was headed. He slipped in and out of an illusion that only the ground moved at all, that he hung in the air, running in place. He lost all sense of time and distance—he could have been running for hours, days, weeks.

But then a darkness appeared before him in the distance. At first it looked like a dark cloud, a heart of a storm in the midst of an overcast sky. As he drew closer, though, it began to take shape. The first feeble daylight illuminated the clouds overhead, casting it in silhouette. It was huge, like a mountain hanging upside-down in the air above the blasted landscape. It floated over an enormous crater, the remains of the cyst from which it had burst forth.

A part of Gaven's mind that was not quite his knew all about the Sky Caves of Thieren Kor. In a different life he had learned all he could about them, poring over fragments of the Prophecy collected in great draconic libraries. He had waited a dragon's long lifetime for the opportunity to explore them and plumb their secrets, and when that lifetime had ended, he—that other he, the dragon of the nightshard—had made sure that what he had learned would someday be remembered.

So Gaven remembered, and the knowledge flooded back to him. The Sky Caves were ancient—they had floated above the untouched wilderness of Khorvaire when dragons first ventured forth from Argonnessen to challenge the fiends that ruled the world. Thieren Kor was a placename in the language used by the fiends, meaning "mountain of secrets." Countless battles had raged beneath that floating mountain, in the skies around it, and within its twisting tunnels—dragons and demons tearing at each other, spilling oceans of blood to gain control of its secrets. When the dragons emerged victorious from the eons-long war, the first dragon to explore the Sky Caves in their entirety became a god, the first of sixteen.

Now Vaskar hoped to follow where that ancient dragon had led. And Gaven felt, for the first time, a surge of envy—he wanted that knowledge, and that power, for himself.

He roared, giving vent to the frustration that had simmered in him since he felt the earth rumble and saw the darkened moon that had propelled him across the Mournland. The brooding clouds thundered in answer to his roar, and lightning danced around the floating mountain. And the wind that had blown at his back swirled in a whirlwind around his feet, lifting him into the air. Higher and higher it carried him, until he stepped forward and alighted in one of the many mouths of the Sky Caves of Thieren Kor.

"Vaskar!" he shouted, sending echoes dancing through the twisting network of caverns. He tensed, gripping his sword in both hands, expecting an attack at any instant. All that emerged from the darkness before him was his own voice in a hundred fragments.

Gaven limned his blade with a pale blue glow, lighting the cave ahead, showing him three tunnels converging on the same mouth—one leading up and to the left, one up and to the right, and one more or less straight ahead. The tunnels were like the boring of some enormous worm—round, smooth, and wide. Stretching his arms wide, he could not touch the walls on either side, and the walls curved together far above his head. He started along the right-hand passage, following it as it wound in an upward spiral. At each branch, he bore right, ensuring that he could find his way back to where he started if the need arose.

After the fourth branch, he found himself teetering at the edge of another cave mouth, his momentum almost carrying him over the brink. He threw himself backward, sending his sword clattering to the floor and sliding toward the cave mouth. He stopped it with his foot then scooted forward to grab it. He got back on his feet and turned around, continuing to follow the right wall.

The next cave opening didn't catch him by surprise, but it did make him stop and think. He'd been blindly following the right wall, as if it would lead him to some destination. But what was his destination? He didn't recall any mention of a specific location within the Sky Caves that might be important—a vault of knowledge or library of some sort. Finding Vaskar seemed like a hopeless endeavor, especially if the dragon were trying to avoid him—he could never hear or see the dragon before Vaskar noticed his approach. So what was he trying to do?

He moved back into the passage he'd just left. The walls were striated in broad patterns of dark and light stone, which he had noted only casually before. As he examined it more carefully, he realized that there was a definite shape to it. He couldn't see it all at once, but as he moved farther in to the tunnel, the parts formed a whole in his mind, a Draconic character representing either a hard th sound or the sixth of some sequence. He continued slowly along, reading more characters—short a or a moon, a sh sound or a beast, or horns. *Thash,* meaning storm—or the horns of the sixth moon, the crescent phase of Eyre.

He stopped, retracing the tunnel he'd been following in his mind. He turned and followed it again, his eyes closed, trying to visualize the path he was walking. It, too, took shape in his mind—another Draconic character, a long e sound or the number nine. Was that part of another sequence, or an attachment to the word and phrase he'd already pieced together? The number nine could be part of a calendrical expression connected to Eyre's crescent phase. Or *thashe* would turn "storm" into an adjective—he had a feeling there might be a "dragon" attached to that somewhere. Or this character could be connected to other symbols formed by the other passages of the Sky Caves.

His mind reeled, and he put a hand out to rest on the solidity of the cavern wall. He had suddenly gained a new depth of respect for the Prophecy. He had learned endless passages of it in Draconic lifetimes ago, and he'd translated them so often in his mind that they spilled out of his mouth in his own language quite naturally. But he began to appreciate what a poor vehicle language was to convey the meaning of it all, how feeble these words and phrases seemed in comparison to the layers of meaning he was experiencing.

Trailing his hand along the cavern wall, he turned and walked farther into the tunnels. He no longer cared about finding his way back. He opened his mind and explored the Prophecy.

CHAPTER 26

When Gaven was a young man, a casual hobby of collecting snippets of the Draconic Prophecy had given him the merest glimpse into its intricacies and complexities. It had made him think that perhaps there was more to life than working and sleeping, eating and getting drunk, getting married and having children—some greater purpose beyond the mundane activities of life, something unfolding behind the scenes. Many people he knew who shared his interest in the Prophecy found that it gave their lives a sense of immediacy, of urgency—life lived against the context of impending catastrophe. Some of the best-known fragments of the Prophecy did seem to concern the most earth-shattering events—the death of empires and the decline of races, natural disasters on an enormous scale, battlefields where thousands upon thousands fell. And he had understood it then as most people did: as sort of a script for the unfolding events of history, preordained and unalterable, revealed through the gods of the Sovereign Host or perhaps binding even them to its dictates.

Discovering the nightshard, the Heart of Khyber, had given him a better sense of the scope of the Prophecy and of the age of the world. He had learned pieces of the Prophecy that had been fulfilled before humans or elves ever walked the earth, and phrases that could not be fulfilled for another thousand thousand years. His earlier sense of immediacy had largely washed away in a dragon's perspective on the Prophecy: the world would not end that year, or the next, or during Gaven's lifetime, but individual events on a smaller scale still carried enormous weight. The appearance of the Storm Dragon seemed to be a central point in the Prophecy from this perspective—possibly the most important event that any human, elf, or dragon alive would ever experience.

Walking the Sky Caves of Thieren Kor showed Gaven the Prophecy in its proper context. In some sense, Senya had been right. If the Prophecy had anything to do with destiny—the destiny of individuals or of the world—it was destiny as Senya had described it. The Prophecy was not a foreordained sequence of events but an infinity of possibilities. Most people used their limited understanding of the Prophecy to justify their action or their inaction, but Gaven came to understand it as a context for action. The Prophecy was reason to act, to watch for opportunities and seize them when they came.

But after days spent tracing the winding tunnels of the Sky Caves, a greater wisdom seemed to dance at the edges of his understanding, like the layers upon layers of meaning in the words of the Prophecy. Exactly like that—to one way of understanding, the words of the Prophecy weren't even Draconic anymore, they were their own language. The Prophecy seemed, in his mind, like the language of creation, the words that called the world into being and spoke it through its course, the tongue in which all things were named. Then, somehow, it was no longer about fulfilling what had been predicted, but about continuing the course of creation that had been established in the beginning, acting in such a way as to become a creator in one's own right. A co-creator alongside all the beings, mortal and divine, who had heard and understood and spoken that mystic language in the past, and all who would do so in ages yet to come.

With that greater wisdom came power, enormous power—the power of the Storm Dragon, whether he chose to accept that title or not. What he decided to do with that power, though, was up to him.

* * * * *

Gaven closed his eyes and walked a stretch of tunnel for the sixth time, trying to get a sense of its convoluted path, the meaning it tried to convey to him. He stopped. Something had changed. He felt the hair on the back of his neck standing up, his skin tingling, and his mouth had gone suddenly dry. The dragon approached.

He stood still, waiting for it. I am the lightning, he thought.

Then lightning engulfed him, flowing through his body and out through his limbs. It sank away into the tunnel floor and sputtered harmlessly out his hands.

He opened his eyes and turned to face Vaskar. The dragon filled the tunnel, wings pressed against his body, legs pulled in close. He crawled forward, more snake than dragon, his emerald eyes fixed on Gaven.

"You shouldn't have come here, Gaven," the dragon said. "The secrets of the Sky Caves belong to me, the Storm Dragon. I don't need you anymore. The Prophecy is laid bare to me now."

Gaven hefted his sword. If that were true, if Vaskar had learned as much from the Sky Caves as he had, the dragon would be a deadly foe.

"Did you hope to thwart me?" Vaskar said. "Would you prevent me from unlocking the secrets of this place? You pathetic creature."

"You arrived before I did. You've been here for days. What have you learned?"

Vaskar roared. "Insolent hatchling. I shall tear you open and feast on your bones!"

Gaven remembered seeing those gaping jaws closing on a wyvern's neck. Suddenly the dragon seemed like nothing more than a ravening beast. Vaskar had learned nothing. "Will you usurp the Devourer?" Gaven said. "Does the world need two gods who eat without thinking?"

"You dare mock me? Are you too dim-witted to fear me?"

"I know better than to fear you, Vaskar."

Another roar, and another blast of lightning from the dragon's mouth coursed across Gaven's skin, through his bones, and harmlessly out his hands and feet. All his hair stood on end, and his dragonmark tingled, but he felt no pain. I am the storm, he thought.

"It appears I underestimated your magic," Vaskar growled. "But will your spells ward you from my teeth?" He lunged, faster than Gaven would have thought possible in such a tight passage.

Gaven stumbled backward, surprised. The dragon's snout knocked him to the floor, the teeth slashing his shoulder. Vaskar pressed his advantage, pinning him to the ground with one massive claw. The dragon brought his mouth close to Gaven's face.

"Now the Storm Dragon will feed." Vaskar hissed.

Gaven grimaced. The dragon's claw was tearing at the wound in his chest, and fear seized his gut. He saw death in the dragon's jaws, and pictured his own neck severed like the wyvern's had been. Then his eyes fell on the ceiling behind Vaskar, its bands of light and dark, and he perceived what he had missed before—a new word in the language of creation.

"No," he said, and a clap of thunder exploded in Vaskar's face, knocking his head back and shaking the tunnel around him. The dragon growled and pulled back, but he found himself stuck in the tunnel.

Gaven scrambled to his feet and drove his sword into the dragon's mouth, cutting a deep gash.

Vaskar pulled his head back as much as he was able, spitting blood that sizzled and hissed where it splattered on the rock. He narrowed his eyes at Gaven. "What has happened? These are not your spells or even your dragonmark at work. What power do you wield against me?"

"If the Prophecy had opened itself to you, you wouldn't need to ask."

Vaskar lunged again, his head lowered this time. Gaven's sword glanced off the armored plates on top of the dragon's head, which hit him full on. He managed to dodge out of the way of the two curving horns, but the force of Vaskar's charge carried him off his feet and backward. With no ground under his feet, nothing solid in his reach, there was nothing he could do but ride it out.

The tunnel fell away behind them. Vaskar emerged into the open air and spread his wings. Only then did he let Gaven fall.

Days had dawned and passed since Gaven had entered the Sky Caves, and the sun was somewhere high overhead, hiding behind a towering mass of thunderclouds. Storm winds swirled around them, and Gaven couldn't see the ground through a cloud of dust. It was enough to note that the dust was a long way down.

Gaven's stomach lurched as he fell, but he closed his eyes and calmed his mind, calling upon the power of his dragonmark. The wind tugged at him, slowing his descent, and he spread his arms and legs wide to catch it. Power surged through him, and he harnessed it, summoning wind and storm and bending them to his will. He stopped, cradled in the palm of the wind, and he exulted as it lifted him. He looked up to where Vaskar wheeled in triumph, and he gripped his sword tightly in both hands as he soared toward the dragon.

Seeing him, Vaskar recoiled in surprise. Then Gaven was on him, swinging his sword back and forth. The heavy blade clanged against Vaskar's bronze scales, catching flesh behind and between them. The dragon's claws batted at him, almost as though Vaskar hoped to knock him from the air. Gaven rewarded his efforts by cutting another bleeding gash between two of the dragon's claws.

The clouds rumbled with thunder, and the wind howled as though it echoed Vaskar's pain. The dragon gave a mighty flap of his wings and pulled away from Gaven's assault, but the wind snatched him and dashed him against the side of the Sky Caves. For a moment his claws scrabbled at the sheer rock face, then he pushed off and into the air again, swooping directly at Gaven, his enormous teeth bared, his wings folded to cut through the gusting wind.

Again, power surged through Gaven's dragonmark, and he funneled it outward. A cyclone lifted Gaven up and out of Vaskar's path. When the dragon hit the whirlwind, he veered hard to the left, rolling over on his back as he swerved, stretching his wings out wide to bring his flight back under control. As he rolled, he spat a bolt of lightning at Gaven, but it flowed through Gaven's body to dance in the clouds, touching off a cascade of light and thunder.

I am the storm, Gaven thought. He stretched his arms out then brought his palms together in a great clap. Winds buffeted Vaskar from either side, crumpling his wings, and another blast sent him reeling backward. The dragon was clearly working hard to stay aloft, and one of his wings looked oddly bent, perhaps broken. He beat his way through the wind to perch in one of the cave openings. Snaking his neck around, he let out a roar that drowned out the dying thunder.

"Thief! Betrayer!" he cried. "I freed you from your prison, and this is the gratitude you show? You stole my prize! Usurper!"

"The prize is not yet won," Gaven said, his voice echoing in the thunder. He stretched out a hand, pointing at the characters formed by the gaping cave mouths. "The Crystal Spire has not yet risen, bridging the realm of mortals and that of the gods."

"What?" The dragon drew his head back, evidently surprised at Gaven's words. "But the Sky Caves—'The Storm Dragon walks in the paths of the first of sixteen!' What have I not fulfilled?"

"Have you learned nothing? Are you blind? The Prophecy is written plain before you, and you have no eyes to see it. On a field of battle where dragons clash in the skies, the earth opens and the Crystal Spire emerges."

As he spoke, the characters of the Prophecy danced in his mind, the layers of meaning that language couldn't capture weaving themselves behind his words.

"A ray of Khyber's burning sun forms a bridge to Siberys's heights."

Images flashed in Gaven's mind from the tortured dreams of his last night in Dreadhold. Gibbering hordes rising up, following the brilliant light up from the depths of the earth. The hordes of the Soul Reaver.

"I will cross that bridge, Gaven! Not you!" Vaskar's rage was all the more unsettling because the dragon's face lacked any human expression. "I am the Storm Dragon!"

The bronze wyrm leaped into the air, lurching toward Gaven on his bent and broken wing.

The wind swelled into a hurricane with Gaven at its eye. Lightning flashed all around him, engulfing Vaskar and limning his scales in brilliant light. The winds battered the dragon and swept him off his path, carrying him around Gaven in a wide arc. Vaskar flailed his wings helplessly. The wind grew, howling through the cave tunnels, sending tremors through the whole mountain. Vaskar whipped around in the wind until he crashed into the side of the Sky Caves, sending a shower of rock in a whirling cascade to the ground.

Vaskar clung weakly to the rock face for a moment, then he let himself fall. He folded his wings and plummeted through the whirlwind, disappearing into the blooming dust cloud below. Gaven lifted his arms to the lightning-scarred sky.

"The Bronze Serpent has fallen," he said, his words disappearing into the wind. "Must I then be the Storm Dragon?"

The wind carried him higher and higher, until he looked down on the top of the Sky Caves. At the same time, the wind lifted the dust and ash from the ground below into a whirling sandstorm that grew to engulf the floating rock.

Gaven lowered his hands, and the wind began to die. The whirling column of air that held Gaven aloft carried him down. As he sank, the sandstorm lost its fury—but even as it settled, it pulled the Sky Caves of Thieren Kor back down to earth with it.

Gaven came to rest on a level, featureless plain of dust. Somewhere beneath his feet, the Sky Caves slumbered again.

PART
III

*The cauldron of the thirteen dragons boils
until one of the five beasts fighting over a single bone becomes a
thing of desolation.*

*Desolation spreads over that land like wildfire, like plague,
and Eberron bears the scar of it for thirteen cycles of the
Battleground.*

*Life ceases within its bounds,
and ash covers the earth.*

CHAPTER
27

Darraun stayed in camp, staring into the fire. It was easier that way. Earlier, he had made the mistake of wandering out to look at the dragons.

On every ledge jutting out from the cliff they perched or wheeled through the air like seagulls. More huddled in circles on the ground outside the camp. Great four-legged lizards—some squat and strong, others long and sinuous—with wings folded alongside their scaled sides or fanning out above and behind them. Long tails lashed along the ground, and teeth like swords tore the flesh of the game and fish they caught. And these monsters, these dragons . . . they spoke.

It was the speech that really unnerved him. It was one thing to see a score of dragons as something like a flock of birds, riding the wind and roosting on the cliffs as if they jockeyed for the best roosting places and squabbled over fish. It was something very different to recognize them as a collection of intelligent creatures, gathered in this place for a purpose—a purpose they took very seriously. It made them less like a flock of animals and more like an army.

Of course, the closer Darraun got to any dragons, the larger he realized they were. Again, as they circled in the sky above, it was easy to imagine they were no larger than eagles. But when he rounded a corner and found himself face-to-flank with a red dragon, it struck him that many of these creatures were the size of a horse, and a few were larger than Vaskar. He stumbled away from a blast of flame that he was pretty sure had been meant merely as a warning, and retreated to the camp.

He caught enough snippets of dragon conversation on his brief stroll outside the camp to confirm that the dragons gathered here shared Vaskar's philosophy, more or less.

"We're not mercenaries," a large black dragon had protested within his earshot. They spoke Draconic, of course, which made Darraun a little unsure of his understanding.

"Of course not," a smaller silver had answered. "This isn't about serving a human army. It's about the Prophecy."

Darraun stared into the fire. What part of the Prophecy did the dragons think they were accomplishing by fighting for Haldren? He thought he remembered Gaven saying something in the City of the Dead about a "clash of dragons," but that seemed to imply dragons fighting other dragons. Or dragons fighting people with dragonmarks. Or dragons fighting the Storm Dragon. Or the Storm Dragon fighting Vaskar, for that matter.

"Thinking about the Prophecy makes my head spin," he muttered.

"That's why I don't think about it," Cart said. His voice startled Darraun, who had been so wrapped up in his thoughts he'd forgotten the warforged was there.

Darraun arched an eyebrow. "Just do as Haldren says, and trust everything to work itself out?"

"Trust Haldren to make everything work out. That's why he's a general."

"What's that all about, Cart? You're anything but stupid. You could think for yourself, but you choose not to."

Cart stood a little straighter, still staring away from the fire as if he were on watch. "I think for myself where it's appropriate, and I obey orders where that's called for. That's why I was part of the general's trusted staff."

"But you're not in the army anymore. And Haldren isn't a general any more. By obeying Haldren, you're disobeying his superiors. You're disobeying the queen."

"My loyalty is to Haldren, not to Aundair or Queen Aurala."

"I see." Darraun picked up a stick and stirred the embers of the fire.

"It's what I was made to do," Cart added.

Darraun watched the sparks rise from the coals and climb into the sky, glowing with all the brightness they could muster before winking out.

* * * * *

The first light of dawn gleamed in the sky when Haldren's grand pavilion opened, vomiting a stream of drunken generals, majors, and captains, staggering and weaving their way to bed. Their tents were safely away from the dragons' roosts, so there were no ugly encounters between belligerent commanders and short-tempered dragons. Darraun watched them emerge and disperse, making sure to keep his disgust from showing on his face.

"Well, I suppose that's my cue to go to bed," he said to Cart.

The warforged nodded, still staring into the distance. Darraun stood and shuffled out of Cart's sight. With a tent between himself and the warforged, Darraun rubbed the fatigue from his eyes and circled back as quietly as he could manage. As he approached the pavilion, he heard Haldren's voice, and he hurried closer.

". . . interested in celebrating," the sorcerer was saying. "Now that they've seen the dragons, they have no doubt of our victory."

There was another voice, this one quieter—but Darraun couldn't make it out from behind the tent. He made his way to a flap, dropped to the ground, and crawled inside, disturbing the fabric of the pavilion as little as he could. He stayed on the ground, behind the great table Haldren had set up for the feast.

"I am exceedingly grateful," Haldren said. It was a protest. "You have certainly fulfilled your end of our arrangement, and I believe my plans are assured of success as a result. And in turn, I have performed my obligations to you. If your plans are not turning out as well—"

A harsh growl cut him off. "You let him get away from you." The voice was Vaskar's. Darraun risked raising his head above the table to scan the inside of the tent. He was relieved to see an image of Vaskar's face floating in a large silver mirror, not the dragon himself.

"You hardly seemed concerned about that at the time," Haldren said. "You told me the Sky Caves would render him obsolete."

"I admit that I did not consider the possibility that he would appear at the Sky Caves and wrest their secrets from me."

Darraun's mouth fell open. No, he thought, I didn't consider that possibility either. Well done, Gaven.

"And you did not destroy him?"

"Do not mock me, Haldren. He acquired tremendous power in the Sky Caves, power that should have been mine. He could not have done that if he had remained in your custody."

Haldren's voice dropped to barely a whisper. "In case you have forgotten, he kidnapped Senya when he made his escape. I would have pursued him across the Ten Seas, but you dismissed them both as irrelevant. I owe you nothing."

"Idiot," Vaskar snorted. "I have seen two mates and half a dozen hatchlings die. They are irrelevant. We seek greater things. Would you abandon the throne of Khorvaire for her? Should I put aside a chance at godhood for the sake of your lust or love or whatever you call it?"

Darraun heard the rustle of cloth. Haldren did not answer for a breath— two breaths, five. Darraun began to panic. Had Haldren heard him somehow? His heart beat so hard he was sure Haldren could hear it in the silence.

Ten breaths, and still neither Haldren nor Vaskar had spoken. Keeping his head sideways, Darraun raised one eye above the table to see what was going on.

Vaskar's head still hovered in the mirror, but Haldren had turned away from it, his hands clenched over his temples. Unfortunately, that meant he stared right at the table where Darraun hid. Darraun ducked his head back down, but it was too late.

"A spy? Darraun?"

Haldren's confusion lasted only an instant, and in the next, a blast of fire exploded around Darraun, engulfing him as well as the table and the wall of the tent behind him. Searing pain shot through his body as he rolled away, under the flaming edge of the tent, and up to his feet outside. Clenching his teeth to quell the pain, he scrambled to the nearest tent.

"Darraun!" Haldren cried behind him. "Traitor! Coward!"

Darraun ducked into the nearest tent, hoping Haldren's cries hadn't woken the occupant.

"Who's there?" A man's voice came from the ground at his feet—very close. The inside of the tent was pitch dark, and the man's voice was thick with sleep and drink.

Darraun took a deep breath, focused his mind, and changed.

Quickly. Hair long, height the same in case the tent's occupant could make out his outline. Breasts, waist, hips—the face could wait a moment. The new form made certain parts of his clothing too tight, but in this case that was an advantage. Voice—soft, husky, seductive. "Haldren sent me to see if you need anything." Pose—chest out, one hand on a cocked hip.

"Sovereigns, is he trying to kill me?"

Darraun heard the man lie back on his furs. He changed his face—round and soft, with full lips and heavy-lidded eyes. It was a face he'd used many times, and it had proven its effectiveness. He started peeling off his clothes, glad he hadn't been wearing his leather cuirass.

"No, no. Go away, girl."

Darraun stepped out of his breeches. Haldren hadn't shouted again, but Darraun knew that didn't mean he'd abandoned the chase. Haldren was too smart and too angry to continue yelling. There was some commotion outside, a susurrus of voices trying to stay quiet.

"What's going on out there?" the man on the ground murmured. "Is something burning?"

"Give me a blanket," Darraun said. "I'll go see."

The man grunted. Darraun bent down and felt around for a blanket. He pulled one off the pile and wrapped it around himself, making a few adjustments to his body as he did so. His new identity complete, he stepped out of the tent.

*　*　*　*　*

"How much did he hear?" Vaskar asked.

"I have no idea," Haldren said. "He certainly wasn't there during the feast, and I made sure I was alone in the pavilion before I contacted you. But he could have come in at any point after that."

"We spoke mostly of Gaven. Why should he care?"

"I don't know."

"Perhaps your success is not as certain as you believed," Vaskar said.

"Nonsense. Everything is set in motion. Nothing can rob me of victory now."

"Nothing? You've had a spy in your midst since you escaped from Dreadhold. How many other conversations has he heard? You told me yourself he had intelligence contacts. It's possible the queen knows every detail of your plans."

"Indeed."

"Perhaps now you will reconsider my request."

Haldren sighed. "Very well, Vaskar. We will choose a different field of battle. We'll conform to your damned Prophecy."

*　*　*　*　*

Getting away from Haldren had been easy enough. Finding a new suit of armor to fit a new body shape and blending in among the hundreds of camping soldiers was not too difficult. The real challenge would be getting out of a military camp located miles from civilization and surrounded by dragons.

The changeling who had been Darraun was getting comfortable in her new body, new identity, and new name—Private Caura Fannam, an enlisted soldier under the command of Major Rennic Arak. She wore her tawny hair pulled awkwardly into a tail down her back, a fashion popular with many female soldiers. A long shirt of leather studded with heavy steel rivets was standard issue for Aundair's light infantry. She carried a short spear—not her favorite weapon, but easy enough to use: "Put the sharp end into the enemy," she'd heard a training sergeant say once. In practice, she knew the hard part was pulling it back out in time to put it in the next enemy, which was why she preferred shorter weapons. But if all went well, she'd have no reason to use her spear as anything but a part of her disguise.

Even with dragons surrounding the camp, soldiers couldn't abandon military protocols—sentries were posted at various spots around the edge of the camp and patrolling the perimeter, probably at least as much to make sure no one left as to intercept anyone coming in. Caura knew they'd be on heightened alert since Haldren had discovered Darraun spying on him. She smiled—how easy it was to think of Darraun as another person entirely.

"Where are you supposed to be, soldier?" A sentry's voice rang out nearby, and Caura started. She'd thought she was well hidden in the shadow of a supply cache. She couldn't see the sentry.

"Uh—I . . . I . . ." The voice was a young man's, just on the other side of the supplies. The pieces of a plan started to come together in her mind. Jumping to a decision, she stepped out of her hiding place.

"I'm ready," she announced. She looked expectantly at the other young soldier, hoping he would follow her lead. She spotted the sentry at the edge of her vision, but tried to act as if she hadn't noticed him.

"What's this?" the sentry demanded. "What are you two up to?"

Feigning surprise, Caura turned to face the sentry. She stood at attention and gave a salute. "Private Caura Fannam, sir."

"Answer the question, Private, since your lover here seems to have lost his tongue."

"Lover?" An instant of concentration brought a flush of color to her cheeks. "Oh, no, sir. We're on our way to report for sentry duty, and I had to stop to, ah, use the latrine, sir. He was just waiting for me." She saw a second sentry hanging back from the scene, ready to get help if a situation developed.

"What's your name, soldier?" The sentry addressed the man beside her, who had fumbled his way to attention as well.

"P-p-p—"

"Do you have a problem with your tongue, Private?"

"Yes, sir, he does," Caura interjected. "A terrible stutter. That's why he's not in Communications."

That drew a harsh laugh from both sentries, and a blush she suspected was genuine from the other soldier. But it covered her new friend's initial hesitation in responding to the sentry—one more step toward getting out of the camp alive.

"Private Jenns Solven, s-s-sir." Jenns saluted. He seemed to be warming up.

"All right," the sentry said, "get where you're supposed to be. Don't let me see you sneaking around like that again, Solven. And keep your eyes open tonight, the both of you. Word is a spy's been discovered—pretty high up, too. So don't go fooling around when you're supposed to be on watch! The Lord General's depending on you."

"Yes, sir!" Caura and Jenns said in unison, saluting again. The sentry returned the salute and turned to rejoin his partner. She and Jenns stayed at attention until the two sentries were well on their way. She heard more laughter, then the sentries were gone. Jenns let out his breath and visibly sagged.

"Thank you," he said. "I don't know who you are or why you helped me, but I think you just saved my life."

"Well, now it's time for you to return the favor," Caura said with a smile.

CHAPTER
28

luevine was exactly the kind of place that Phaine despised. A village small enough that everyone knew each other meant that strangers like him drew attention. The people loved to talk, they were never satisfied with terse answers, and they took umbrage at his habitual silence. On top of that, the weather stayed warm and bright. He vastly preferred the shadowy alleys, darkened skies, and comfortable anonymity of Khorvaire's large cities.

The flip side, though, was that even a secret meeting like the one Haldren had held in Bluevine could hardly be kept secret in such a small town. The fugitive had admitted only a few people inside the room during the feast and had sworn them to silence, which of course meant that everyone in the village knew some version of what had happened inside. Getting information wasn't difficult; just sorting out the truth from the wild speculation and rumors was problematic.

Almost everyone he interviewed claimed to know someone who knew someone who had been in the room, but few could name the source of their information, and those that were named denied that they'd been present. Several times, between interviews, he told Leina he wished he could just find a throat to slit and be done with Bluevine for good.

Through all the gossip and exaggeration, some hints of a consistent picture eventually began to emerge. Haldren had clearly stayed in Bluevine for several days. He had been accompanied by another human man, younger, and a warforged. There was no indication that the elf woman or the Lyrandar excoriate had been there. After the first day, other strangers had arrived: seven men and women, some of them clearly of noble birth, though all of them acted like they were entitled to royal treatment.

Beyond those bare facts, Phaine found little agreement, which made sense to him. Many people in the town would have had occasion to interact with these ten outsiders in various ways, so it was natural that a consistent picture of them would emerge. He had yet to find anyone who claimed they had actually been present at their gatherings, though, which would explain why there were so many different stories about what had actually taken place.

Given that all the stories were probably the inventions of various villagers, it amused him that every one attributed some sinister purpose to the gathering. He figured that adequately summarized the village's attitude toward outsiders. If a group of strangers came to town and met in secret, it was almost certainly for a cultic ritual, a political conspiracy, a depraved orgy, or an arcane summoning. At least, those made for better stories, more likely to get repeated. Phaine supposed that if it had been a casual gathering of old military friends sharing war stories over glasses of Bluevine's famous vintage, that story would hardly have captured much interest.

Finally, Leina pointed him to a promising lead—a dour old farmer who acknowledged, after some badgering, that his grandson had been pressed into service pouring wine for the strangers. He refused to come into the village center, so Phaine followed Leina out to his farmstead. He knocked at the door and waited, knocked louder and waited more, and finally saw the farmer for himself as the door swung open. The man's face was leathery and deeply lined, and one big hand was clutched around the handle of a scythe.

"What do you want?" the farmer demanded.

"Good afternoon," Phaine said, forcing a smile. "My associate tells me that your family has some information about the strangers who visited your charming village a few weeks ago."

The man's hand clenched his scythe harder. "I told her we don't want to talk about it."

"Perhaps Leina neglected to mention that some of these people are fugitives. One of them escaped from Dreadhold."

"She told me. I'm not surprised."

"It is very important that I learn everything I can about these people and what they were doing here. If your grandson has information that might help find them, it's imperative that I speak to him."

The farmer's knuckles whitened on this handle of his scythe. "Listen. My boy was there, and maybe he heard things that would help you. But we'll never know, see? The bastards cut out his tongue."

* * * * *

Under normal circumstances, Senya did not sleep. She was an elf, and four hours spent in quiet meditation rested her body and mind like a full night's sleep. During this trance, her mind would run through a series of mental exercises of memory and reflection that she had practiced tens of thousands of times. Humans would call them dreams.

But circumstances were not normal. She had been badly injured, and her body needed a great deal of rest. She entered her trance in the late morning, and her mind wandered strange paths of fevered dreams. She surfaced from her trance in a panic and stared wildly around the room, trying to remember where she was. Darkness surrounded her, and something held her down where she lay. "Gaven?" she whispered, but then she remembered seeing him, spread-eagled on a great stone slab, covered in blood. Was that memory, or fevered imagining?

Panic welled in her chest, and she started thrashing to escape whatever held her. To her surprise, the bonds came away easily, and she realized that she was lying in a soft bed, swathed in linen sheets and warm blankets. Other memories returned to her—their flight from the dwarves in Vathirond, the wind that carried her when she couldn't run any more, the healers who tended her and loaded her into their wagon. And the knowledge that Gaven had abandoned her.

At least he's not dead, she thought—but the thought gave her little comfort.

She fumbled her way out of the sheets and sat up in the bed. She wore something soft and loose, a nightgown or something very different than the leather she'd been wearing last. She swung her feet down to the bare wooden floor and slid along the bed until her outstretched hand touched the wall. Then she got to her feet and slowly shuffled along the edge of the room, keeping her right hand on the wall and her left stretched out low in front of her. She felt ridiculous, but the darkness was so complete that she still couldn't make out the room's dimensions or features.

Her left hand brushed something she quickly decided was a nightstand, and she worked her way around it. She'd no sooner reached the other side of it than she found another wall, then heavy curtains. She fumbled at the windows, and her eyes finally came alive as dim starlight filtered through thick glass into the room. She was about to turn back to survey the room, but something in the sky caught her attention.

It was Nymm, the largest of the twelve moons. It hung high in the sky, right near the top of her view out the window. At first she thought it was just in a crescent phase, nearly new or just beginning to wax again. But its shape was strange—its color, too—and she realized that a shadow blocked its light, an eclipse. Words danced at the edge of her memory, something about the great moon, something her ancestor had said in Shae Mordai. But it eluded her, and she returned her attention to her immediate surroundings.

The room was small and simply appointed, but cozy in its way. She'd already discovered the bed and the nightstand. One chair stood near the other side of the bed. There was one door, opposite the window. Her coat and her sword hung from a hook on the back of the door.

A good start, she thought. Now where are the rest of my clothes?

Her eyes fell on the nightstand again, and she noticed the two drawers it held. She stepped to it and opened the top drawer. Sure enough, her clothes were there. She pulled them out and set them on the bed.

My boots, my pack—where are they?

A few steps took her to the other side of the bed, and there they were. Her pack was neatly arranged beside the bed, with the elegant, impractical boots standing perfectly next to it. She breathed a sigh of relief and sat down on the bed.

"Well now, Senya," she whispered to herself, "what are you doing?" She ran her fingers through her hair. It felt clean, silky. "They're taking care of you here. Are you going to bolt out in the middle of the night?"

Her thoughts ran back over her conversation with the halfling who had tended her, the way he avoided her gaze as he asked about Gaven. She thought about their ride on House Orien's lightning rail, the House Medani inquisitives they'd avoided at the station in Korranberg, and the Sentinel Marshals of House Deneith who had captured her when the rail stopped in Starilaskur. Was it unreasonable to fear that House Jorasco's healers might turn her over to the Sentinel Marshals or some other house?

The more she considered the possibility, the more she convinced herself that the halflings would almost certainly hand her over as soon as they saw that she was recovered. She took off the nightshirt the healers had put on her, stuffed it into her pack, and put on her own clothes. She was lacing her boots when she heard a creak outside her door. She froze and listened, but the sound did not recur. Was there a guard posted outside her room? Had he heard her moving around?

Taking care that her boots made no sound on the wooden floor, she crept to the door and lifted her sword belt and coat off the hook. She pressed her ear to the door, cringing as it jiggled in its frame. She heard nothing but the pounding of her blood in her ears.

She started to inch away from the door again, but another creak from outside stopped her. She tried to bring her breath and her racing pulse under control and listen. She heard voices whispering outside. With agonizing slowness, she stepped back from the door and tugged at the hilt of her sword. It didn't come free of its sheath, and she almost swore out loud. A glance confirmed her suspicion—the halflings had peace-bonded it, attached it to its scabbard with leather straps designed to make it impossible to draw in anger. It would take too damned long to undo the knots holding it in place.

She reversed her grip on it and readied herself to swing the weighted hilt as a club, if the need arose.

The metal latch clanked softly as it moved, and a sliver of light spilled into the room from the hallway. The hinges squeaked softly as the shaft of light grew wider. When the light fell on the empty bed, there was a pause, and Senya coiled, ready to strike.

The door flew open, and a man rushed in, holding a longsword in his left hand. Senya stepped up to meet him, swinging the pommel of her sword as hard as she could. The attack had caught him by surprise and might have been deadly if she'd managed to pull the blade free, but instead it glanced off his mailed shoulder. He whirled to face her, but his eyes were clearly still adjusting to the darkness. Pressing that advantage, Senya batted at his sword with the basket hilt of her blade, trying to knock it from his hand for her own use.

He kept his grip on his sword and used that moment of connection to swing Senya around until the light from the hall fell full on her face, reversing her initial advantage. Only then did he wrench his sword free, sending Senya's sword skittering across the floor.

Blinking into the light, Senya put her hands up in a gesture of surrender as she tried to size up her opponent. He was not a tall man, but his body was strong. He looked to be about Gaven's age, but he was human, which probably meant he was considerably younger than Gaven's sixty-odd years—certainly younger than Haldren, though his hair was lightly dusted with gray. His armor was gleaming mail, and he wore the black surcoat of the Sentinel Marshals.

Behind this man, an armored halfling in the gold and green of House Jorasco held an everbright lantern—the source of the light shining into her eyes. His other hand was on the hilt of his sword, still in its sheath.

"Senya," the Sentinel Marshal said, "I am Sentinel Marshal Arrakas d'Deneith. You are under arrest. Stop trying to fight."

"Why?" Senya demanded. "So you can give me a quick and painless death?"

"The murder of a Sentinel Marshal is serious business, Senya. But frankly, I'm more interested in finding Gaven and Haldren than in punishing you for your part in it. If you cooperate, I can make sure your sentence is light."

"Hm. A very considerate offer." She shifted almost imperceptibly closer to where her sword lay on the floor, but Arrakas raised his sword as he stepped between Senya and the blade.

He jerked his head toward the halfling in the doorway, without taking his eyes off Senya. "Pick up the lady's sword, will you?"

The halfling scurried into the room and snatched Senya's sword off the floor, clutching it to his chest as if he were afraid she might leap at him and try to wrest it from his grip.

Senya smiled and started toying with the top of her bodice. She might not have her sword, but she'd found in the past that her body was often a more powerful weapon. "Well, Arrakas," she said, her voice low and breathy, "it seems you've bested me. Now I'm yours."

She saw the blood rise to his face, and noticed that even the halfling seemed to be having some trouble swallowing. She stepped closer to Arrakas, letting her coat fall to the ground and trail behind her. His eyes locked onto hers, which was not where she wanted them. She reached up to brush her hair back from her face, and slowly trailed her hand down the side of her face to her neck, her bare shoulder, her collarbone. To her satisfaction, his eyes followed her hand downward, and she stepped closer again, close enough to feel the warmth of his body.

She cupped his face in her hand, felt the flush in his cheek. Men were so easy to manipulate. She let her fingers slip softly down his chin, tracing the thin line of his beard, then down his neck, and she smiled slightly as his eyes closed. She ran her fingers along his shoulder, which he probably couldn't feel through his armor, and squeezed his upper arm to make sure his attention stayed on her hand.

The halfling watched her with undisguised excitement in his eyes, which made her slightly sick, but suited her purposes. She dropped her hand to stroke the back of his, and saw him shiver slightly from the light touch.

This is it, she thought. Last chance.

She stepped forward again, pressing the softness of her body against his armored chest and letting her breath brush his neck. At the same moment, she deftly slipped the sword out of his hand and started bringing it up to strike.

Arrakas's other hand was behind her, though. Before she could bring the sword to bear, something hard came down on her head, and she crumpled to the floor.

CHAPTER
29

What do we do now?" Jenns looked at Caura with wide eyes and bit his lip as he waited for her answer. He might be nervous, but so far he'd proven more than willing to follow Caura's lead.

"Act like sentries," Caura said. "We'll walk the perimeter, insert ourselves between two real patrols."

"Then what?"

"Did you have a plan at all before I found you? Or were you just going to make a break for it?"

"I hadn't really thought it through," Jenns admitted with a smile.

"Good thing I found you, then." Caura returned the smile. He might have been young and naïve, but he was endearing. "At the right spot, we'll alter our course and slip out. I think I know a place where we'll be out of sight and mostly avoid the dragons."

"Can I ask you something, Caura?"

"You can ask, but I won't promise you an answer."

"How do you know so much about the camp and things?"

"I pay attention."

"Sure, but they keep us on a pretty tight leash. Like they want to make sure we don't figure out too much."

"I'd say that's a pretty accurate assessment." Caura had heard Haldren give instructions to the commanders who followed him, a long list of rules to make sure that the rank and file didn't learn too much.

"You're not really just a private, are you?"

Caura smiled at him again, chastising herself. She shouldn't have answered the innocent questions—her answers clearly led right up to a question she didn't want to answer.

They walked in silence for a moment, then Caura guided Jenns into an excellent imitation of a sentry patrol around the perimeter.

"Want to hear my crazy thought?" Jenns said.

"Can I stop you?"

"I think you're the spy that sentry was talking about."

"What on earth makes you say that?" Caura carefully modulated the tone of her voice, making sure that her face did not flush. A perfect lie.

He shrugged. "I told you it was a crazy thought."

"How do I know you're not the spy? Why are you running out of here?"

"Me?" Jenns chuckled. "You saw me back there. I'd be a pretty pathetic spy."

True, Caura thought. But you'll do for now.

"So why the daring escape?" she said.

"Do I have to answer that?"

"I guess not. Fair is fair."

Caura entertained herself trying to imagine the reason this innocent young soldier would desert his post and flee the camp. A romantic entanglement struck her as the most likely reason, although abject terror seemed like another strong possibility. She wouldn't ask again, mostly because she didn't want to put herself in a position of feeling obligated to reveal anything more to him.

The western side of the camp was bounded by cliffs overlooking the stormy Eldeen Bay. Their path took them alongside the cliffs briefly, and Jenns gasped when he saw the dragons wheeling in the air over the water and perching on the cliffs. He walked in silence, wide-eyed, until they turned their backs on the bay and the dragons, heading along the northern perimeter.

The sun appeared over the horizon, shining in their eyes as they walked, and the camp was coming alive. Bugle calls roused soldiers from their tents, and the shouts of sergeants assembled them into formations for inspection.

"You'll be missed soon," Caura observed.

Jenns raised an eyebrow. "What about you?"

"Me too," she said. "We'd better get moving." She pointed to the line of trees in front of them, blocking part of the rising sun. "That's the Whisper Woods up ahead. Our best chance of getting out of here." Alive, she added silently.

Caura kept their pace slow and steady until they got within bowshot of the trees. At that point, instead of continuing southward around the perimeter, they veered toward the woods and picked up the pace. They had only covered half the distance when a shout arose behind them.

"What did he say?" Jenns said, a panicked look in his eyes.

Caura turned to run. "Not sure, but it sounded a lot like 'Halt!' " she yelled. "Come on!"

"We're going to die," Jenns groaned as he hurried behind her.

A few arrows flew lazily overhead, then a few more thunked into the ground near their feet as the archers found their range. More shouts erupted from the camp, and Caura thought she heard the tromp of pursuing feet far behind, but she didn't dare slow down to look backward. Jenns had caught up his initial lag and kept pace with her. A quick glance confirmed the terror she expected to see on his face.

"We'll make it," she gasped.

But the trees didn't seem to be getting any closer, and they weren't dense enough to guarantee cover from their pursuers. She started to feel guilty for leading Jenns to his death, then she reminded herself that she'd already saved his life once. So she hadn't caused his death, merely delayed it.

The arrows started falling short, the shouts faded in the distance, and no one seemed to be gaining on them. Caura saw a look of hope begin to dawn on Jenns's face as they came closer to the sheltering trees. She shot him what she hoped was a reassuring smile, but he wasn't looking at her. As she watched, the color and the hope drained from his face, and his steps faltered.

"Sweet Sovereigns, protect us," he breathed, stopping his headlong run and falling backward onto the ground.

Caura slowed her pace but didn't stop, searching the forest ahead for a sign of what had terrified him. The forest's edge was thinly scattered with trees, but a covering of ferns and bushes promised more cover, and just a few yards in the trees grew more closely together. Everything was lush with spring growth, and a gentle breeze stirred the branches in a soft susurrus.

Then she saw it: a dragon snaked among the trees. Its green scales helped it blend in among the leaves and ferns, but its eyes were fixed on her. It was one of the smaller dragons she had seen around the camp, but that still meant it was roughly horse sized. And it looked hungry.

Caura stopped dead. She cast a glance over her shoulder. Jenns was still on the ground, looking desperately back and forth between her and the dragon. Far behind him, a clump of soldiers from the camp had stopped to watch—they had evidently spotted the dragon before Jenns and didn't want to approach it any more than he did.

"Caught between the Kraken and the Hydra," she muttered. The expression made her think of the two rocky islands that marked the entrance to the dangerous straits of Shargon's Teeth, poised like twin monsters waiting to devour ships passing between them. "Well, that's nothing new."

"What do we do?" Jenns shouted.

"Follow me!"

Caura ran, turning her course just to the right, aiming for a spot a little south of where the dragon waited. She saw the dragon whip around, keeping even with her, but after a moment it disappeared into the heavier trees. She glanced back and saw the soldiers move again, ready to catch them if they circled back toward the camp.

Caura and Jenns reached the woods, charging into the undergrowth with a clamor of rustling leaves and branches. When they were out of sight of the camp and the pursuing soldiers, Caura put up a hand to stop Jenns. The forest settled around them. She listened. Birds fluttered, a few squirrels or chipmunks scurried at their feet, and something large stalked nearby. Too near. It stopped when it couldn't hear them moving anymore.

Caura was painfully aware of how loud she and Jenns were breathing after running so hard. She held a finger to her lips and tried to catch her breath. After a moment, though, she heard the dragon resume its stealthy movement toward them.

She realized the flaw in her thinking. She'd been treating this dragon as a strange reptilian leopard or something, a big predatory animal stalking them through the woods. This was not an animal—not any more than Vaskar was.

"All right, dragon, you've got us," she said.

Jenns goggled at her, but she held out a reassuring hand. If dragons could argue with each other over the Prophecy, then certainly they could talk to her before eating her. Maybe this one could be talked out of eating her.

The rustle of its approach grew louder. It wasn't trying as hard to sneak up on them. Getting closer. Caura saw branches bending and swishing back into place as it passed—thirty paces, then twenty, fifteen. It must have been crawling along the ground to remain so well hidden, and it used the trees for cover as much as possible. But at ten paces it couldn't possibly keep out of sight any longer, and it reared up on its hind legs like a bucking horse, revealing itself in its terrible majesty.

Jenns let out a tiny whimper and took two steps away from it. It was much smaller than Vaskar, more like a sleek, agile tiger than the lumbering behemoth she was more familiar with. Its scales were mottled green and gray, resembling the patterns of light and shadow on the forest growth. Its head bore a crest that stretched high as it reared up, and it spread its wings to look larger, breaking branches and pushing saplings aside. For a moment, Caura wondered if she had misjudged—its behavior was not too different from that of a threatened predator ready to strike. But then she noticed its eyes. They watched her with evident curiosity, flicking occasionally to the terrified Jenns behind her.

The dragon's snout was long and narrow, tipped with a wicked point that made it look almost like a bird of prey. As it looked at them, the flesh at the corners of its mouth stretched back to reveal its sharp teeth. Caura's heart leaped, but then she recognized the expression—the dragon was smiling.

"And now that I've got you," it said, "what am I to do with you? A pair of deserters, are you?" Its voice was low and smooth, almost seductive.

"That's right," Caura said. Jenns whimpered again. "We don't have the stomach for the coming battle."

"I think my course is clear, then," the dragon said, its grin growing wider. "You'll be my main course. I do have the stomach for you."

Caura resisted the temptation to groan at the dragon's awkward wordplay. At least it hinted at a strategy for keeping the dragon busy, and she leaped at the opening. "But if we're deserters, shouldn't we be your dessert?"

The dragon opened and closed its mouth in a gesture Caura discerned as a laugh. "Well spoken, meat. But who ever heard of eating meat for dessert?"

"Don't you think it's sweet to meet us?" Caura glanced over her shoulder. Jenns stared at her with his mouth hanging open, incredulous. But the dragon was still enjoying the game.

"Perhaps I'll eat your sweetbread for dessert."

"Oh no, we're not well bred."

"Are you suggesting I was born in a well?" The dragon fanned its wings, breaking more branches. Caura thought she detected an impatient tone in its voice. At the thought, her mind went blank.

Jenns stepped forward to stand beside her, then bowed before the dragon. "We hope your offense doesn't run deep."

The dragon laughed again, and furled its wings. "The male joins in the game!"

Caura shot Jenns a smile and picked up the thread. "There must be tastier game in the forest."

Jenns added, "I fear you'll find us too gamey for your taste."

"I think perhaps you're too tasty to let this game continue." The dragon's tongue flicked out and brushed its lips.

"No, not at all," Caura shot back. "Haven't we amply demonstrated our bad taste?"

Again the dragon flapped its lower jaw. "You have indeed. I suggest you flee before I change my mind."

Caura almost retorted, but Jenns grabbed her arm and pulled her away from the dragon as fast as their legs could run.

CHAPTER
30

I s there news?" Rienne sat in Krathas's office, her elbows on her knees, looking at the floor to avoid the half-orc's gaze.

The half-orc shifted some rolled papers on his desk. "There is. The woman who was with him—she's been captured."

"Really?" Rienne hated the tone of her voice, but she couldn't keep the spite from her voice.

"Indeed. As I understand it, she was badly injured while she and Gaven fled from the dwarves." A twinge of guilt pricked Rienne's heart—she had unwittingly led the dwarves to Gaven. "Somehow, Gaven sent healers from House Jorasco to find her and bring her back to the city for care. A Sentinel Marshal apprehended her at the House of Healing."

"Where's Gaven?"

"I don't know." He paused, but something on his face indicated that there was more. Rienne waited.

"At about the same time as the Jorasco healers set out to find Senya, a horse was stolen at the eastern edge of town. It's possible that was Gaven."

"The eastern edge? Is that near the House of Healing?"

"Not particularly, no. Gaven might have ridden east."

"East—toward the Mournland."

"Right." He rubbed the side of his face. "There's one more thing. The horse—it found its way home."

Rienne sat back in her chair, trying to absorb that information. Krathas found something interesting on his desk and kept his eyes low.

"Well, that might not mean anything," she said after a moment. "I can't imagine a horse would willingly ride into the Mournland. Perhaps he just let it go and made his way in on foot."

"Maybe so." He didn't say any more, but Rienne could read his thoughts on his face: he didn't like Gaven's odds of surviving in the Mournland on foot.

"Why would he go in there?" She remembered her view of the roiling gray mist from the airship deck, the sense of a malevolent presence in the Mournland. The thought of walking into the Mournland made her shudder.

"I hoped you might have some idea."

Rienne shook her head, replaying her conversation with Gaven and Senya in her mind. "He didn't say anything." She shrugged, feeling helpless. "It was so hard to see him. Not at all what I expected—or hoped for. He seemed so strange."

"Strange how?"

Rienne considered her words, trying to express the thoughts that had been nagging at her since her encounter with Gaven. "He was . . . absent. He had no interest in talking with me. He didn't ask me for an explanation or offer me one. I thought he would be angry. I didn't expect him to just not care."

"He's had years to get over his anger."

"So have I. But all he cared about was that damned box. What was in it, anyway?"

Krathas shrugged. "I don't know."

"He never told you?"

Another shrug. "I never asked."

"He accused me of stealing it from you." The memory stirred her anger.

"I promised him I'd keep it safe. He came to my office and found you holding it. I think I can see why he might have been upset."

"And as soon as I left, those dwarves ran in. He probably thinks I summoned them."

A look of profound sadness settled on Krathas's face as he stared at his desk.

Rienne's anger melted away. She reached out and clasped the half-orc's folded hands. "I can't see him go back to Dreadhold, Krathas. It's my fault he went there in the first place. I want to help him, but I don't know how."

Krathas looked into her eyes. "Don't you?" His voice was gentle.

Rienne sat in silence for a long time. Krathas held her gaze for a while, then looked back down at his desk. Finally, Rienne sighed.

"I suppose that means I'm heading to the Mournland."

* * * * *

"Desolation spreads over that land like a wildfire," Gaven muttered. He lurched forward and fell into the dust. "Like a plague." He spat dirt out of his mouth. "A plaguefire, a virulent plague, a wasting sickness, a spreading cloud that burns and wastes and destroys."

He scooped up a handful of the sandy ground and let it spill out between his fingers. A shadow of a dream flitted through his mind.

So many thoughts were in his mind, he couldn't cling to one. He slowly got to his feet.

"Two spirits bound in one prison beneath the wastes," he whispered, his eyes unfocused. Twisting caverns forming letters, letters bound together in infinite combinations of words, words that danced unfettered in his mind. "Secrets kept and revelation granted, the Secret Keeper and the Messenger." He started to walk forward, stumbled, stopped and stared at the sky. "They bind and are bound, but their whispers are unbound."

"Destroyer!" he shouted. "Tearer and reaver and flayer of souls, the Soul Reaver." He staggered in a different direction beneath the featureless sky. "The Soul Reaver waits in the endless dark, where it is forever night, the un-day. Beneath the bridge of light, there will descend the Storm Dragon, the Dragon of thunder and lightning and wind and rain and hail."

Something dark jutted up from the barren ground, tracing jagged lines against the gray horizon. Gaven turned and reeled toward it. It meant something, he knew.

"There among the bones of Khyber the Storm Dragon will drive a spear— the Eye of Siberys bound to a branch of ash, an ash tree's branch charred with ash, a victim of the storm."

The object began to take shape as he drew nearer—blackened branches stretching up from the earth to the sky, a memory of life where nothing else grew.

"Drive the spear into the Soul Reaver's heart!"

A distant rumble of thunder testified to the storm that had passed and left the tree scorched by lightning.

"Where is the Eye of Siberys now, Gaven?" Gaven's voice was suddenly clear and coherent, though lower than usual. As if startled by the sound of it, he fell to the ground again. He tore at the pouch at his belt until he got it open, then pulled out the heavy adamantine box and opened it.

The nightshard captivated him, pulsing with its purple-black light, and he mumbled at it as if answering its question. "The Storm Dragon seizes the shard of heaven, a tiny fragment of Siberys's glory, from the fallen pretender, the bronze serpent."

"Where is it now?" he said, clear and low again.

"Vaskar. The Bronze Serpent used it, it lifted the Sky Caves of Thieren Kor from the earth, he had it."

He scrambled to his feet once more and lurched to the burned tree. He started to fall when he reached it, but he caught himself on its blackened trunk, smearing his hands with ash.

"Drive the spear into the Soul Reaver's heart," he murmured again.

He walked his hands up the trunk, stretching as high as he could, just barely managing to get his hands around the lowest branch. In one smooth movement he pulled himself up onto the branch, then climbed until he was near the top of the tree. He planted himself on a high branch and reached up to another one that seemed the right size. It broke off easily in his hand, almost throwing him off balance. He steadied himself and hefted the branch in his hand.

Perfect.

"There among the bones of Khyber the Storm Dragon drives the spear formed from Siberys's Eye into the Soul Reaver's heart." Shadow given twisting form writhed in his thoughts, a distant echo of a long-ago dream. "It was my hand on the spear," he whispered.

He climbed slowly back down to the ground, his mind suddenly clear. Studying the sky to find his bearings, he set his face to the west and started walking.

*   *   *   *   *

Rienne patted her new horse's nose as the stable hand cinched the saddle. The mare hadn't come cheaply, but she had a House Vadalis pedigree—she was magebred for speed, and the previous owner had boasted that she ran as fast as a Valenar horse. Rienne doubted that claim, but felt sure the mare would be fast enough for her needs.

Rienne checked the saddlebags, loaded with the journeybread and water she'd need for her journey. She had also secured a sizable amount of cash from the bank operated by House Kundarak, knowing that the dwarven house might soon block her access to her accounts. She smiled wistfully. It was like the old days, setting off on another dangerous adventure, and a far cry from the settled life of a sheltered aristocrat that she'd adopted without Gaven.

"She's ready, Lady," the stable hand said with a small bow. "Safe travels."

"Thank you," she said, dropping a few copper coins into the girl's hand. She led the mare out of the stable and mounted on the street. Reaching over her shoulder to make sure Maelstrom was securely strapped to her back, she gave the horse a gentle nudge with her heels and started riding out of town to the east.

She was happy to put Vathirond behind her. She couldn't help but identify the city with her disastrous encounter with Gaven, a meeting she preferred to forget. As soon as she cleared the gates, she urged the mare to a gallop, exulting in her speed.

"I'm sorry I doubted you," she whispered in the mare's ear. "You put the steeds of Valenar to shame."

* * * * *

"She must know something." Ossa d'Kundarak glared across the table. "People don't ride off this close to the Mournland for fun."

Bordan shook his head, staring down into his wine glass. "It doesn't make sense. Senya told the Sentinel Marshals that Aundair is where the action is, and the last I heard from Phaine he was there, close on Haldren's tail. Anyway, if she knows where he is, why not just contact you or the Sentinel Marshals? Why chase after him herself?"

"She doesn't want to see him go back to Dreadhold."

Bordan looked up and met Ossa's gaze. "She turned him in twenty-six years ago."

Ossa shook her head. "She only turned him in because she thought he was possessed and hoped to get him cured."

"And what happened the other day?"

"I think she hoped for a happy reunion, picking up where they left off before he went mad. Then he appeared in town with his new elf ladyfriend, and there went her hopes for getting married at last."

"Oh, come now." Bordan swirled the wine in his glass.

"I'm serious. Twenty-six years, she never gets married? I tell you, she's been pining for him. So she ran out into the street, angry. You should've seen her—Natan said she was ready to cut him in half. But she didn't want him to get caught. She knew he'd escape, somehow. Ten Seas, maybe she helped him escape."

"Damn," Bordan breathed. "You're a suspicious one."

"I'm still alive."

"So what do you suggest?"

"I suggest we follow her, and I'll bet you fifty crowns she leads us right to Gaven."

Bordan drained his glass. "I'm not a betting man. And following her will be no easy task—she rode out of here on a magebred horse, remember, and not the draft kind."

Ossa tugged at one of her long braids. "Then what's your suggestion, d'Velderan? Following people is supposed to be your specialty."

"Well, if I told you my suggestion was that we forget about Rienne and join Phaine in Aundair, you'd accuse me of not listening to you. And I have been listening. I'm just not sure I believe your reasoning."

"Sovereigns! What's it take, man?"

"Hold on," Bordan said quickly. "I didn't say I don't believe you. I'm just not convinced yet. But if I were convinced, I think I'd suggest that we secure the use of a small airship from House Lyrandar. An airship can at least keep pace with a magebred horse, though she's a little obvious. But if I'm going into the Mournland, I'd rather do it in the air than on the ground."

"I happen to know," Ossa said with a grin, "that House Lyrandar has a small airship in town at this moment that would be ideal for that purpose."

"And if this turns out to be a chase after the dragon's tail, it'll be easy enough to turn the ship around and take her to Aundair."

"Have I convinced you, then?"

Bordan smiled. "Close enough."

CHAPTER
31

The moment Gaven pushed through the gray mist, leaving the Mourn-land behind him, his chest erupted in stinging pain. One of the ghoulish creatures had slashed his flesh when he first entered the Mournland, and Vaskar's claw had torn him further. But the wounds had gone numb in the dead air of that desolate land, neither healing nor festering as long as he remained there. At first he was afraid that some contagion in the mist had contaminated the wounds, entered his blood, and started an assault on his body from the inside. He washed the wounds carefully in the first clear stream he could find, and the bright red blood he rinsed from them reassured him that they were still, somehow, fresh and relatively clean.

The wounds taken care of, though their sting remained, he climbed up a hill near the streambank to get the lay of the land. Putting the wall of dead-gray mist behind him, he surveyed the surrounding landscape. To his right and ahead, gentle hills, some covered with tilled fields, others painted with wildflowers and prairie shrubs, rolled on as far as he could see. To his left, the horizon was shaped by mountains—a small range fairly close—then a level gap, then more mountains. As best as he could figure, that put him somewhere southeast of Vathirond, looking at the northernmost extent of the Seawall Mountains. A careful study of the northwestern sky showed him what might be the smoky haze of the city, far in the distance.

The thought of returning to Vathirond gave him pause, and he sat down on the hill to eat some dry journeybread and consider it further. Since cutting the wood from the ash tree, his mind had been fixed on his destination, and he'd given little thought to how he would get there. Going through Vathirond presented numerous dangers: the Kundarak dwarves who had nearly arrested him on his last visit, Senya, whom he'd abandoned in the House of Healing there, and of course Rienne. He groaned. No, that was a city he would prefer not to see again.

He scanned the horizon, trying to think of another city he could use to launch his journey. But this time, something in the sky caught his attention.

"Vaskar!" he spat. But looking again, the dark shape in the clear blue sky did not resemble a dragon at all. Far too large to be a bird, though he supposed a dragonhawk was a distant possibility. But the air shimmered around it—

No, a ring of fire. An airship!

Gaven rested his hands on the ground behind him, damp with dew, and watched the airship soar closer, all his plans pushed aside. How high she flew! And there were people aboard! People who could stand at the rail and peer down, see the whole country spread below them like a grand banquet. His eyes drifted down to the hills and fields, trying to imagine what they would look like from so high in the air, but his gaze always returned to the majestic ship, the pinnacle of House Lyrandar's achievements.

As she flew closer, he could make out more details of her shape and construction. She was about the same size as the one he'd seen moored in Vathirond—he wondered if she might be the same one. She came from the right direction, from the north along the wall of mist. Then he wondered what different sizes existed—how large was the largest airship? How majestic a vessel something like a flying galleon would be!

A sudden thought put an end to his speculation, and he stared blankly into the sky as he ran through its implications. An airship coming from Vathirond, coming closer to where he was, southeast of the city—where was she bound? Would she continue along the mist, heading somewhere in Darguun? Or soar over the Mournland to reach Valenar, perhaps? One of those possibilities, certainly, because otherwise . . .

Otherwise she was coming for him.

He scrambled to his feet and raced down the hill, no other thought in his mind than finding cover to get out of sight. What a splendid view the airship's decks must offer, indeed! The whole landscape spread out below—one might even be able to make out a person on the ground! Especially if the crew had sighted him while he was still in the Mournland, where he would stand out from the barren ground like an ogre at a society gala.

Unfortunately, the land offered little in the way of cover. Crawling or crouching his way through tall grasses or crops might have helped him elude a pursuer on the ground, but it would do little to conceal him from the view of watchers on the airship. What shrubs there were held little more promise: they were scattered widely, so while he might be able to hide under one, he couldn't move from there. So if they had already spotted him, hiding would just give them more time to reach him.

He jumped back down to the streambank and stopped, surveying the land again. The stream tumbled through a narrow, rocky ravine on its way down from the mountains. It probably passed very near Vathirond by the time it joined up with the Brey River and poured into Scions Sound. The ravine didn't offer much in the way of cover, but it might be better than nothing. Gaven looked up to the sky.

The airship was much closer, and she flew considerably lower. That probably meant her crew had spotted him. He crouched back against the side of the ravine, trying to get out of sight. But he couldn't find a position that blocked his own view of the airship. He cursed and clambered back up to the grassy bank.

"What am I doing?" he wondered aloud. "I have walked the Sky Caves of Thieren Kor. I sent Vaskar flying away with his tail between his legs. I will not hide any longer."

He stood and waited as the airship drew closer.

*   *   *   *   *

"Fifty crowns!" Ossa slapped her hand on the bulwarks. "I told you we'd find him here!"

"And I told you I'm not a betting man," Bordan retorted, peering through a spyglass. "But I have to admit that you were correct. It certainly seems that we've found our man." He watched as Gaven tore down the hillside and crouched in a ravine. "He's seen us. And he thinks to hide."

"Where can he hide out here? Nothing but open field as far as the eye can see."

"He appears to have reached the same conclusion." Gaven had climbed out of the ravine and stood on the streambank, head high, watching the airship approach.

"Ha! We've got him!"

Ossa was a little too pleased with her victory, in Bordan's opinion. Certainly it was reasonable to be concerned about the honor of House Kundarak after the dwarves allowed Gaven's escape from Dreadhold. But part of the reason for Ossa's crowing seemed to involve the fact that she had been right and Bordan—an heir of House Tharashk who bore the Mark of Finding—had been wrong. With every exclamation of triumph, Bordan heard an undertone of condemnation, as if the dwarf said, "If we'd taken the course you suggested, we'd still be chasing the dragon's tail." He had very quickly grown tired of Ossa's voice.

"We don't have him yet," Bordan said, a little too sharply. "Remember what happened to the Sentinel Marshals."

"What did happen to the Sentinel Marshals? I heard some sketchy reports, but I'm not clear on the details."

"No one is. I think House Orien and House Deneith are trying to keep it quiet. I can hardly hold it against them. If they blame the storm, House Orien loses business—people won't want to ride the lightning rail in a lightning storm. If they blame Gaven, House Deneith looks bad for letting such a dangerous fugitive escape again, and we all come under tremendous pressure to recapture him. The whole reason we're in on this chase is that House Kundarak"—*your House,* he added in his mind—"wanted to keep the facts of his escape quiet as long as possible."

"So it's true," Ossa breathed. "Just like when I chased him in Vathirond. Gaven caused the storm? Or he brought it down to the lightning rail?"

"So it appears. Evlan was definitely killed by lightning, and there was significant evidence of wind blowing through the cart. But just the one cart. It seems that Gaven was the center of the storm—and I don't mean the calm eye of the hurricane."

"These storm clouds, then . . ." Ossa gestured at the sky.

"Churning chaos!" Bordan swore. "The sky was clear when we spotted him!" He and Ossa gaped at each other for a moment, then Bordan whirled around and shouted to the pilot, "Take us down! Now!"

A roar of thunder overhead drowned out his last word but made his point just as effectively. Lightning danced around the prow of the airship as a gust of wind set her rocking wildly in the air. Bordan had to clutch the bulwarks to keep his feet as the pilot steered her in a sharp descent. The ground rushed up beneath them, and as they turned in their descent, Bordan lost sight of Gaven.

Instead of looking overboard, which made his stomach lurch, Bordan found comfort in watching the pilot. All around him, the crew retied broken ropes and retrieved spilled cargo, a whirlwind of activity. But the pilot was a still point in the chaos. His hands were white as they gripped the wheel, but no trace of panic was visible in his eyes. He exuded confidence and competence, which helped Bordan keep the terror from welling up in his own chest.

Thunder rolled and lightning crackled, and the pilot seemed locked in a war with the wind over control of the ship. Her timbers creaked, the ring of fire leaped wildly around her, something in the prow snapped loudly, but the pilot managed to keep her under control and bring her to the ground. A bump rocked the ship as some part of her keel touched the earth, then an ear-splitting crack as that something broke. The fiery ring disappeared as though the ship had sucked it in, and Bordan had to pull his hand off the bulwarks as it flared hot. The ship groaned loudly as she settled, then everything fell silent. Bordan watched a smile start to form at the corners of the pilot's mouth.

A great shout went up from the crew, celebrating a safe landing. Their roar was answered by a rumble of thunder, then a series of deafening cracks as lightning struck the earth around them. Bordan's eyes went wide as gouts of flame reached out from the ship toward each lightning strike, as if trying to join the heat of the lightning, before disappearing back into the wood. Bordan put a hesitant hand back on the bulwarks, found it perfectly cool and wet with rain, then jumped up to stand on it and look for Gaven.

A blast of wind dashed him from the bulwarks and clear of the grounded airship, landing him flat on his back in a field of rain-drenched grass. For a moment he could only lie there, staring up at the angry sky, straining to breathe and then to sit up. He raised his head, finally, just in time to see two bolts of lightning strike the airship. Flames leaped up on the deck in the lightning's wake, and an instant later the entire ship erupted in an inferno. Bordan threw his arm across his face to shield it from the fire's heat, and he rolled farther away from the ship.

Sailors jumped off the ship, some of them trailing flames or smoke as they came. Ignoring them, Bordan leaped to his feet and ran to the prow of the ship. As he neared it, the source of the attack finally came into view: Gaven hovered in the air, riding a column of swirling wind that blew dirt, leaves, and smoke in a cyclone around and beneath him. The fugitive's long hair whipped around his face, and the dragonmark on his bare chest and neck crackled with lightning.

CHAPTER
32

Gaven was the storm—raw, destructive fury. Some part of him regretted wrecking the airship, damaging a thing of such beauty. Somewhere in his mind a voice cried out for the safety of the people on board. But that voice was drowned in thunder and roaring wind.

Lightning struck the downed airship, sparking new fires on the deck, splintering timbers and sending sailors hurtling overboard. He felt a knot of anger in his gut, rage that lashed out in great gusts and rumbling thunder to smash and burn and destroy. Fury that silenced every voice of reason and compassion in his heart.

Something caught his eye, movement at the edge of his vision, and he turned his head to see a man on the ground, running toward him. He held a sword in each hand, as though he thought he could cut through the cyclone that held Gaven aloft. Lightning followed Gaven's glance, splitting the ground just behind the man, who tumbled into a forward roll across the grass, found his feet at the end of the roll, and kept running. Gaven scowled, and another bolt struck right in the man's path. That made him falter. The man leaped to the side and came down hard, one of his swords skittering away across the grass. Gaven looked back at the airship and frowned.

Destruction was so easy. He had acquired the power of the Storm Dragon, and it would be so simple to take up that mantle and become a god of devastation, a rival to the Devourer. Simple and so tempting. He looked back at the man. He was still advancing—so determined to meet his doom.

"Curse you," Gaven muttered. "Don't make me kill you."

With a breath, Gaven sent a gale to blow the pest away. The man faltered in the face of the wind, turning his head to draw breath, but he strained, still pushing his way forward. Gaven waved his hand, and the wind whipped into a cyclone. Gaven sent it for the man, hoping to lift him off his feet and carry him away.

But the idiot dropped to his knees, sank his fingers into the earth, and held on tight to wait out the wind. Gaven roared his frustration, and the wind howled in answer before blowing itself out.

Gaven tried to swallow his rage, and he forced the wind around him to set him down. He was tired, and he clutched the ash-black staff in both hands, leaning on it as his feet settled to the ground. The man looked up, grabbed both swords, and got to his feet.

"What's your name?" Gaven called.

The man gave a small salute with his twin swords. He stood a head shorter than Gaven. He was not strongly built, but his movements were quick and precise. His hair and his neatly trimmed beard were dark brown, but his temples were gray. His armor was well-worn leather, and the shoulders of his cloak had been bleached almost white by the sun.

"Bordan d'Velderan, heir of House Tharashk," he said. "I assume the formalities of declaring your arrest and demanding your surrender are pointless."

Gaven sighed. Surrender—the idea held some appeal. To stop running, stop fighting for his freedom and whatever feeble hold on sanity he still had. Surrender and let fate run its course.

No. He shifted the staff to his left hand and drew his greatsword.

"You're all alike, you know," Bordan said, stepping a few paces closer. "You criminals and fugitives. You all think you're better than the law, more important. You think you've done nothing wrong, you're just misunderstood, you've been treated unjustly. You think the law should make an exception for you. Every petty thief and small-time thug thinks the same way you do."

"Don't be so sure you can see into my mind," Gaven said. At the same time, he wondered—should he not return to Dreadhold and pay for his crimes?

Bordan stepped closer. "See? That's exactly what I mean. You all think you're different than the others. Sure, Gaven, you're unique—just as every dragonshard that falls from the sky is unique. But they're all the shattered parts of the same dragon."

Gaven saw the sky above the City of the Dead, the Ring of Siberys shining bright as dragonshards rained down, clattering on rooftops and cobblestones. Then the bright streak that was the Eye of Siberys. A shattered part of the same dragon? Perhaps, but one with a part to play.

Bordan leaped for him, his swords moving in a deadly, whirling dance. Gaven swung his greatsword reflexively, cutting a low arc toward the other man's legs. Bordan adjusted the pattern of his blades to deflect the blow, their clashing blades sparking, and the momentum of his charge carried him past Gaven.

No, Gaven decided. He would not surrender. He had a part to play. He jammed the staff into the sheath on his back, then stepped forward, his greatsword whirling toward Bordan's head. Bordan crossed his blades to stop

Gaven's sword and hold it, trembling against the bigger man's tremendous strength.

"You think you're better than all the others," he said, "but you're not."

Gaven wrenched his sword free and swung it in another low arc. Bordan stumbled back out of his reach, unable to parry in time. Gaven pressed his advantage, trying to keep him off balance by driving him farther backward. Unable to recover his footing, Bordan threw himself backward into a roll. As he came up, he batted Gaven's greatsword aside and found a balanced stance again.

"I don't want to kill you," Gaven said.

"Why not?" Bordan's swords blurred as they parried Gaven's swings and exploited every opening, putting Gaven on the defensive. "Would that violate your criminal's code? You've murdered before, Gaven. Why not kill me too?"

"I didn't say I won't. Just that I don't want to." Gaven stomped one foot on the ground, unleashing a thunderous blast of air that knocked Bordan backward, battering him off his feet. He raised his greatsword and advanced. Destruction was so easy.

Bordan lolled on the ground, still reeling from Gaven's concussive blast. Thunder rolled overhead, and Gaven growled his fury.

An axe clanged against his sword as he swung it down, then the dwarf holding it barreled into him and knocked him to the side. He recognized the scarlet-shirted, long-braided leader of the dwarves from Vathirond. He staggered under her weight, and wrestled to free his body and his sword from the tangle.

Bordan had found his feet and his swords, and was circling around him for a clear swing. With a heave, Gaven swung the dwarf around, planting her between Bordan and himself.

"Bastard," Bordan growled. He lunged and cut a long line in Gaven's arm, the only exposed skin he could reach.

With a growl of pain, Gaven pushed the dwarf to the ground and sent her axe flying, bringing his sword up to block Bordan's flurry of steel.

He was floating, disconnected from the blur of steel, the sweat, the straining muscles. He saw it all—saw it so clearly. The flurry of Bordan's swords resolved itself into weaving patterns, just as the tunnels of the Sky Caves had revealed their patterns to him. Seeing the paths of the whirling blades, he had no trouble blocking the strikes, cutting through the defenses. The dwarf found her feet and joined Bordan's assault, but his sword was fast enough to block them both.

"Velderan," he mused. "Part of House Tharashk. Do you carry its mark, the Mark of Finding? Is that how you found me?"

Bordan's eyes narrowed, and he paused before answering.

"Rienne led us right to you," he said.

Rienne. A fresh surge of rage welled up in Gaven's chest. A blast of lightning exploded around Bordan, lifting him off his feet and hurling him away. The dwarf staggered back as well, though she kept her feet this time.

Rienne led them to him. Rienne summoned the dwarves to Krathas's office in Vathirond. Rienne sent for the Sentinel Marshals who arrested him twenty-six years ago. Why?

"Rienne is here?" Gaven said. He pushed past the dwarf—she and Bordan no longer mattered—and strode toward the fallen airship.

Apparently Bordan didn't realize that he'd become irrelevant. Gaven heard him charge up behind him, and swept his sword behind him in a half-hearted, one-handed swing. He half turned around, thrust a palm toward Bordan, and drove him back in a blast of wind. Then he broke into a run, carried by the wind.

* * * * *

Rienne hunched down in the saddle and urged the magebred mare to greater speed. The cloudy sky ahead of her grew blacker by the minute, and lightning flashed among the clouds. That probably meant that her pursuers had found Gaven.

She had first spotted the airship shortly after leaving Vathirond, and she kept telling herself that it was unreasonable to assume the ship was following her. Even so, she had tried to choose paths that blocked her from the sky. She didn't suppose it mattered—if they were trying to follow her to Gaven, they would have a better chance of finding him than she did.

And she suspected that was exactly what had happened. When she reached the edge of the Mournland, she turned to the south mostly on a hunch, and she saw the airship do the same. Not long after, though, she lost sight of the ship. When storm clouds had started to form over the sky ahead of her, fear clenched her heart.

What am I afraid of? she thought. That they'll catch Gaven? Or that he'll kill more innocent people?

She reached the crest of a hill and almost fell out of the saddle in surprise. The land sloped gently down the other side of the hill to a wide, bowl-shaped valley, then rose up into steeper hills, the foothills of the Seawalls. On the far side of the valley, she saw the airship lying askew on the ground, an inferno of leaping flames and splintering wood. Lightning danced in a ring around the ship, occasionally striking a high point on her shell. An enormous thunderhead towered in the sky above the conflagration, as though the smoke billowing up from the ship were somehow feeding the storm.

As the mare charged down into the valley, Rienne's stomach sank—the airship was the Morning Zephyr, the same ship she'd taken from Storm-home to Vathirond. The smiling face of the first mate appeared in her mind, and she strained to remember his name. This disaster was her fault. The ship wouldn't have been in Vathirond if she hadn't borrowed her for this journey.

But who had commandeered her for this voyage?

Rienne settled back into the saddle and urged the mare to even greater speed. She assumed Gaven was responsible for this disaster, which meant he was probably down there. She didn't know what she'd do if she found him, but she knew she had to be there.

As she drew closer, she could make out people around the wreck of the airship—and even people still on her deck, trying to get the fire under control. With each pounding hoofbeat, she called on the Sovereign Host to protect the innocent people who were caught up in this maelstrom. A new burst of fire erupted on the deck, sending a group of people scattering, jumping over the bulwarks, shouting.

While still a bowshot from the wreck, Rienne saw two people running toward her. One was a dwarf—possibly Ossa d'Kundarak, if the scarlet shirt were any indication. That would explain the Morning Zephyr being here: a dragonmark heir on such important business could probably call in favors to secure the use of a Lyrandar ship. And if the human beside Ossa were also an heir of a dragonmarked house—well, that would be twice as many favors.

"Lady Alastra!" Ossa stopped running and shouted at her, waving his arms wildly over his head. "Stop! You're in great danger!"

Danger? From Gaven? But how did he know she was there?

She reined in the mare right in front of Ossa and her companion. She noticed the human eyeing her carefully, but she ignored him and spoke to Ossa. "What did you tell him?"

"Tell him?" It seemed Ossa had been unprepared for her leap ahead in the conversation.

"Gaven. If he knows I'm here and wants to hurt me, I can only assume you told him that I led you to him, which might be technically true but could give the wrong impression." She saw Ossa and the human exchange a surprised look. "But he thinks I came here with you on the Zephyr, so he's probably looking for me there." She nudged her mare forward. "Thank you for the warning."

"Wait!" Ossa called, but Rienne ignored her. She urged her mount to an easy gallop and didn't look back.

She rode up beside the airship. Another gout of flame burst from the hull—reaching for her, it seemed. Her horse screamed, reared, and backed away from the ship. She guided her mount in an arc around the ship, keeping their distance from the flames.

"Gaven!" she shouted into the roar of the inferno. She could barely hear herself.

No one moved on the deck any longer. She saw a clump of people moving away from the ship's bow, but she didn't see anyone who looked like Gaven—or any sign of a fight going on among those people. She looked behind her and saw Ossa and the human man running toward her again. She didn't have much time.

She guided her mare as close to the airship as she dared, then brought her to a stop. With a word and a calming hand, she steadied the horse then nimbly jumped up to stand on the saddle. The mare shifted slightly, and Rienne teetered, but she found her balance, tensed, and sprang into the air. She somersaulted through the air and landed on the airship's bulwarks.

"Gaven!" she cried. Where was he?

As if in answer to her unspoken question, the deck before her exploded outward in a shower of sparks and splinters. A gust of wind carried tongues of flame and clouds of smoke up from the cabin below, and she threw her arms up to shield her face from the sudden heat. As soon as she dared, she lowered her arms and peered through the billowing smoke.

He stood on the deck before her, silhouetted by the raging flames. He took a hesitant step toward her, accompanied by a crash of thunder and a bright flash of lightning from above. She couldn't see his face, and she wasn't immediately sure whether he intended to use the sword in his hand.

"Gaven, please hear me out," she said, holding her palms out to him.

He took another step then slumped to the deck.

CHAPTER
33

S o where do we go now?" Jenns said. He licked his fingers, savoring the last taste of the meal Caura had cooked.

"Where do you want to go?" Caura avoided his expectant gaze, staring into their little campfire.

"I hadn't really thought about it."

"Churning Chaos, man! Did you have any thought in your head besides getting out of that camp?"

"Not really."

"Well then, Jenns," Caura said, leaning back on her hands. "We seem to be safe for the moment. Tell me about yourself. Why were you in such a hurry to get away from the camp?"

"Do I have to?"

"I think you'd better."

Jenns sighed and leaned forward, gazing into the fire. "I'm Jenns Solven, from Passage. You ever been to Passage?"

Caura nodded, remembering the bustling city, and the person she'd been there.

"So you know it's a pretty big city, sort of a hub for the lightning rail and caravan routes. And of course House Orien has their big enclave there."

"Are you attached to House Orien?"

"I'm the youngest of three brothers. My father works for House Orien. Both of my brothers work for House Orien. I fled. I joined the army a week before the signing of the Treaty of Thronehold."

Caura arched an eyebrow. "How old are you?"

"Twenty. You don't look any older. How long have you been in the army?"

Caura suddenly remembered that the face she wore was a great deal younger than Darraun's, and quickly covered her mistake. "No, I'm twenty-one. I joined up when I was just sixteen, though, so I thought maybe you were younger than you are."

"Just sixteen? What drew you in?"

Caura tilted her head and glared at him. "We're talking about you, remember?"

"I can't help it," Jenns said with a sheepish grin. He avoided her eyes. "I find you fascinating."

Oh, here we go again, Caura thought. "I think you're just dodging the question."

He looked up and smiled. "Fair enough. I joined the army when I was eighteen. I was still in training when the war ended, and I never saw combat. Truth is, that suited me just fine. I wanted to get out of my parents' house, and the army was all I could think of. Well," he added with a mischievous grin, "it was the best way I could think of to make my father crazy."

"Did it work?"

"Oh yeah. He wrote letters, he got various Cannith heirs to write letters, he pulled all the strings he could to bring me home. So one day my sergeant comes to my barracks, sends everyone else away, and asks me if I want to go home. I said, 'No, sir,' and that was that. Sergeant Kessel was a good man." The smile slowly faded from Jenns's face as he stared into the fire. "So I joined the army to get away from my father. I never wanted to fight. And then the treaty was signed, and I thought I got lucky—I never had to fight."

His smile reappeared for a fleeting moment. "Except that for some people, the war wasn't over. Lord General ir'Brassek ordered my unit into the Reaches, in violation of the treaty. I saw combat after all, which mostly meant that I pissed myself and hid when those damn huge Eldeen bears started tearing into our ranks. Sergeant Kessel was killed."

"I'm sorry," Caura murmured.

Jenns tried to smile.

"So the Queen called us back—I still don't know how she got the Lord General to listen. They put the Lord General up before the Tribunal and sent him to Dreadhold, gave all the units below him drudge duty as far from the borders as possible, and that was that. Two years I've been in the army now, and that one assault into the Reaches is my only combat engagement. And that doesn't bother me a bit."

"And then, out of nowhere, you're mobilized and sent to the middle of nowhere on the coast, no idea why, and you learn that the Lord General's back and about to violate the treaty again, and you want no part of it."

"Pretty much. Though I'm less concerned about the treaty than I am about the bears."

"Not to mention the dragons," Caura added.

"Please don't mention them again." He smiled.

"So you fled in panic, without taking the time to put a plan together?"

"Well, yeah. I figured I had to get out before we started to march."

"What?" Caura sat up. "I thought we weren't marching for another week yet."

"You didn't hear? No, the orders came down just before you found me in the camp. I guess it wasn't widely known yet, since most people were still asleep. Change of plans, straight from the Lord General."

Change of plans, Caura thought. So everything I learned is useless.

"What's wrong?" Jenns asked, his voice full of concern.

I am really slipping tonight, Caura thought. He must have seen me scowl. Control, Caura—it's all about control.

She smiled, erasing the tension from her face. "I must just be tired," she said. "It's been a long day, and I didn't sleep much last night."

"You sleep, then. I'll keep watch."

"Don't bother. I'm a very light sleeper. I'll hear anything coming through the woods toward us. And if you're walking around on watch, I won't get any sleep."

"All right, then. It won't be the first time today I've put my life in your hands."

Caura returned his smile, then pulled her cloak around her and lay down facing the fire. She closed her eyes and felt the exhaustion grip her, pulling at her consciousness and stilling every movement of her body.

"Caura?"

Her eyes shot open.

"I'm sorry," Jenns said. "I just wanted to thank you."

"I'm glad for your company, Jenns. We'll make plans in the morning."

"Good night."

"Night."

* * * * *

Poor boy, Caura thought.

She stood by the fire, looking down at Jenns as he slept. She thought he looked like a child, though he was only ten years her junior—his body curled tightly around the warmth of the dying fire, his face unlined, untroubled.

How long will you search for Caura Fannam? she wondered. Will you think I've been kidnapped or killed, like a fool? Or are you smart enough to discern the truth?

"Safe travels, Jenns," she whispered. His brow twitched, and Caura hurried away, afraid he might awaken.

As she walked, she made herself a new person, ensuring that neither Jenns nor anyone from Haldren's camp would ever find a Caura Fannam in all Khorvaire. Of course, Haldren might suspect he was searching for a changeling, but that wouldn't make it any easier to find the spy who had been in his midst so long.

Constrained by armor made to fit Caura's slender body, the changeling decided on a male elf—fewer hearts got bruised when he took male forms, it seemed. Elf eyes were hard to do right, especially without a mirror, but he enjoyed the challenge. He decided on long hair, raven and straight, figuring he'd braid it back when he got a chance. A slim but muscular body, pushing at the limits of the armor. He found a strap he could loosen to give him more room in the chest—room in the right places, anyway. He sketched the face—bright blue eyes in an almond shape, chin a little angular, smooth, fair skin, high cheekbones. He'd fix details when he found some still water or a mirror. He hated traveling without a mirror, but he had left Haldren's camp rather abruptly.

That would do for the time, he decided. Except for a name. He passed the time as he hurried through the night turning name ideas over in his mind. By the time the sun came up, he'd settled on Vauren as a given name, and fell back on a family name he'd used as an elf before—Hennalan. Vauren Hennalan. It was funny, he reflected, how the name he chose shaped the persona he adopted. Vauren shared its consonants with the name of a paladin he'd known, lifetimes ago it seemed, and that made him want to act nobly. The last time he'd been a Hennalan, he had been a little mischievous, though, so those two streams flowed together and began to shape a personality for him.

Crafting a personality took a lot longer than shaping a face and body. He hadn't really had time to figure Caura out. That seemed to be the time when he was most vulnerable: while he was still deciding what kind of person to be, he was faced with temptation to be the kind of person who opened up, who shared secrets, who cared about people. That probably explained his slips at the campfire the night before.

Perhaps Vauren wasn't the best name. How could he be as noble as the name demanded and still be a spy?

CHAPTER
34

Gaven!" Rienne rushed forward and gathered him in her arms, trying to get him back to his feet. He seemed unconscious, and he was probably twice her weight even after his stay in Dreadhold. She glanced around, frantic for anyone who could help, but the Morning Zephyr seemed deserted. Worse, flames began to engulf the upper deck, spreading out from the hole Gaven had blasted through it. "Gaven, you've got to help me get you out of here."

He didn't stir, and Ossa and the human were too far away to help. Rienne took a deep breath, steadied herself on one knee, and slid her weight beneath Gaven, shifting his limp body onto her shoulder. She groaned. "I must be out of practice, because I know you haven't gotten any heavier."

The heat stung her eyes and face, and she heard the deck creaking beneath her. "Here we go." She tried to imagine she was deflecting a charging enemy, using his momentum to throw him, but the only momentum Gaven had was what she gave him. So she leaned forward as much as she dared, then quickly rocked back, using the movement of his body to roll her up onto her feet. She staggered backward under the weight, but managed to find her balance.

Something gave way, and the airship rolled hard to starboard, nearly throwing Rienne back into the flame-ringed hole in the deck. Just trying to keep her feet beneath her got her moving, and she managed to run around the shattered planks to reach the starboard bulwark and struggle over it. Her feet kicked open air. With Gaven on her shoulder, she couldn't see how far she was above the ground, so she tried to brace herself for a hard landing and protect Gaven as much as she could.

To her surprise, the ground wasn't far at all. Her feet hit first, and she toppled forward, sending Gaven sprawling. The impact knocked the breath out of her. She rolled onto her back to look at the inferno behind her. The airship's hull started collapsing under its own weight, devoured by flames, but she had landed clear of the snapping timbers and leaping flames. She fought to fill her lungs again, panted to catch her breath, then scrambled over to where

Gaven lay. The position of his limbs looked awkward, and his head seemed twisted around too far—panic rose in her throat.

"Sovereigns, no, he can't be dead," she said.

He coughed weakly, and she breathed again. Eyes still closed, he turned his head to a more natural position and shifted one leg.

She clutched his face, leaning in close. "Gaven? Wake up, Gaven."

To her amazement and relief, his eyes fluttered open. It was a moment before recognition registered on his face, then when he tried to speak no sound came from his throat.

"Come. We need to get away from this ship."

"Are you—?" Gaven began, then he broke into a fit of coughing.

"Take it easy," she murmured, stroking his cheek.

"Are you going to turn me in again?"

"What?" she said. "I just saved your life. Can you get up?"

Gaven lifted an arm and tried to lift his body after it, without much luck. Rienne got to her feet and took his hand, and managed to get him sitting up. He held up a finger and took a deep breath, trying to steady himself.

"Why are you doing this?" he said.

Rienne put her hands on her hips and looked down at him. "Because I love you, damn it. I'm not going to turn you in again. But I need you to tell me what's going on. If you can do that, I'll get you out of here, I'll join you on the run, I'll make myself a criminal for you. Just let me in."

Gaven lifted his eyes to meet hers. "I'll explain everything," he said.

"Wonderful. Now let's get out of here."

He held his hand up. She took it and heaved him to his feet, then wrapped his arm around her shoulder. "Lean on me," she said, and they hobbled as quickly as he could manage away from the burning wreckage of the Morning Zephyr.

Rienne spotted her mare—as well as Ossa and the human, trying to grab the mare's reins as she bucked and neighed. "That's a good girl," Rienne whispered. "Don't let the bad people catch you." She whistled, high and long and loud, and the mare's ears pricked. The horse reared up again, backing away from the others, then ran past them to reach Rienne.

As the mare ran by, the human saw his opportunity. He grabbed the horn of the saddle and leaped onto the mare's back. The horse tossed her head and screamed, but the man held on. His feet found the stirrups and he clutched the reins, but he let her keep running to Rienne.

"No!" Rienne shouted, waving her arms over her head. "Go back or throw him or something!"

"Bordan d'Velderan," Gaven muttered. "And his Kundarak friend." His hand went over his shoulder to his scabbard, but he found the ash staff instead of his greatsword's hilt. He looked at Rienne with wide eyes.

"I'm sorry," she said. "It must still be on the Zephyr." As she spoke, she drew Maelstrom from its scabbard.

She saw the man, Bordan, draw back at the sight of her steel, but then he hunched over the mare's back again, guiding the horse directly toward her.

"He's going to try to use you to get at me," Gaven said. "Clearly, he doesn't know you very well."

Rienne shot him a grim smile and focused her thoughts as she settled into a ready stance, Maelstrom poised over her head. She waited, utterly motionless, as Bordan drove the mare forward, faster and faster. As he drew near, he leaned out, reaching down as if to grab her waist and hoist her up.

Rienne only wished she could see his face as she grabbed his arm and used the mare's speed to throw herself into the air. Her feet went up in a wide arc, and her body followed. Suspended above her would-be captor, she slammed both feet into the side of his head, sending him tumbling from the saddle. She landed astride the mare and pulled on the reins. The mare wheeled around and trotted back to where Gaven stood over Bordan.

"Leave him, Gaven," she said, reining in the mare beside him.

Rienne clutched Gaven's arm and helped him swing up behind her. He put his arms around her waist—a little hesitantly, she thought—and she had to stifle a gasp. It had been so long since she'd felt those arms around her, she had all but forgotten how it made her feel.

She urged the mare back to a gallop, no destination in mind but away. This time, though the hoofbeats filled her ears, all she felt was Gaven pressed against her, holding her. After almost thirty years, she had finally come home.

CHAPTER
35

I think it's time to honor your promise," Rienne said.

She sat on the edge of a hard, lumpy bed in a squalid inn, somewhere in northern Breland. She didn't know the name of the town, and she didn't care. Gaven stretched in the bed, and for the first time in two days, he didn't wince in pain. That confirmed her assessment that he was well enough to start talking.

"Rienne," he said, "I promised to marry you a long time ago and under very different circumstances. I think—"

"Not that promise, you ogre." She slapped his shoulder. "Don't pretend you don't remember. You promised to explain everything."

"Can I eat breakfast first?"

"No. Get started."

"It'll be time for luncheon before I'm done explaining, and you won't be able to hear me over the rumbling of my stomach."

She quirked her mouth at him, then broke into a full smile. "Very well, we'll get some food, and you can tell me everything while we eat. And if I'm pleased with the story, we'll buy you a new sword before we head out of town."

Gaven grinned. "Thanks, Mama."

She cupped his cheek in her hand and smiled at him. How long since he had called her that? It was an old joke between them—he complained that she mothered him, but she knew he appreciated it. And no matter how many times she reminded herself that she had many reasons to be angry at him, she couldn't help but thrill at every such recollection of their old life together. And to savor the feeling of his skin under her fingers.

He insisted that she turn away while he stood and dressed, which made her smile even more, thinking of the evening she had bathed him, tended his wounds, and dressed him when he was too weak to do it himself. But she resisted the temptation to nettle him further by peeking over her shoulder.

* * * * *

They were quiet as they left the inn and went in search of a fruitseller. Rienne couldn't think of anything to talk about besides the coming explanation, and Gaven seemed deep in thought, as if composing the words he would say. Her mind raced through all the things she thought he might say to her, and her mood grew darker. Her thoughts kept circling back to the elf woman in Vathirond, the one who had been arrested.

She watched Gaven pick out fruit. He checked each piece over for bruises or rot, used his thumb to test its firmness, and finally brought it to his nose before deciding whether to buy it. They bought a small bag of plums, a block of sharp cheese, and a fresh loaf of bread, then started back to the inn. By the time they reached the corner of the building, Rienne scowled down at the dirt road beneath her feet, tormenting herself with thoughts of Gaven testing the fruit of that elf strumpet.

"Hey," Gaven said, coming to a sudden stop just outside the door to the inn.

Rienne's sword flew into her hand as she whirled around to face him; it whistled softly as it bit through the air—and neatly cut through the plum that Gaven had tossed at her. She caught one half in her left hand, and the other landed in Gaven's outstretched palm. He laughed, and she couldn't help but smile again.

"I see Maelstrom hasn't lost its edge," Gaven said, pulling the pit out of his half of the plum and holding it up to her. Rienne's cut had divided the pit in half. His eyes found hers. "And you haven't lost yours, either."

She brought the point of her sword right under his chin. "And don't you forget it," she said, trying to scowl again.

He winked, and her face dissolved into a smile. She returned Maelstrom to its sheath, took a bite of her plum, and started up the inn stairs.

Back in the room, she sat cross-legged on her bed while he sprawled across his, devouring a plum.

"Where to start?" he wondered aloud, wiping juice from his chin and tossing the pit aside.

Rienne cut a piece of cheese from the block. "Perhaps at the point where you started acting like a madman?"

"Hm, no. I think I need to go further back." He pressed his palms to his eyes and drew a deep breath. "All right," he sighed. "Our last descent together, those caves in the Starpeaks. Remember?"

"How could I forget? I was so worried when you fell. I tried so hard to catch the rope! I was about to grab it, and then a swarm of bats came up from the shaft, thousands of them. I couldn't see my hand, let alone the rope, and by the time they'd flown by, the rope was gone."

Gaven let his hands fall to the bed and stared at the ceiling. Rienne waited, but he didn't continue. She stood and leaned over him. His eyes didn't register her presence.

"Gaven?"

His voice was distant, dreamy. "I fell. Down and down through endless dark. The pain . . ."

She sat beside him on the bed and put a hand on his chest. "You were so badly hurt."

His head jerked up, and she saw his eyes come back to focus on her face. "You found me. But not until after—" He sat up, taking her hand in his.

"After what?"

"Did you look in that box that Krathas gave you?"

"No. What was in it?"

Gaven reached into the pouch at his belt and produced the adamantine box she'd given him in Vathirond, the one he'd left in Krathas's care so long ago. As she watched, he opened it, his eyes gleaming as he peered inside. He stared so intently that she grew worried and started to push the lid closed. Only then did he turn the box so she could see its contents.

Her breath caught in her throat. A long time ago, a very different Rienne had made a career out of exploring the depths of Khyber, far below the sunlit world, searching for the dragonshards that formed there. Legends held that Khyber shards were formed from the blood of the Dragon Below, one of the three primordial; dragons who had shaped the world at the dawn of time, the progenitor of fiends and the father of all evil. Those legends gave nightshards their other common name: demonshards.

Legends aside, nightshards were valuable—especially during the Last War. The dark crystals were suffused with magic, making them extremely useful in the creation of certain magical items. They carried a particular affinity for magic of binding, which made them essential for the artificers and magewrights who crafted elemental vessels for House Lyrandar: seafaring galleons early in the war, airships in more recent years. She and Gaven had made a small fortune procuring nightshards, because they had been good at finding them and good at selling them to the right people at the right price.

But she had never seen a nightshard like the one in Gaven's adamantine box. It was larger than her fist, and the swirls of midnight blue in its heart pulsed with barely contained energy. She reached out and touched its hard surface, and it seemed for an instant as though her fingers might sink into the crystal to touch the writhing serpents of color inside.

"The Heart of Khyber," Gaven said, and his hushed tone gave voice to the awe in Rienne's heart.

She moved her fingers slowly over the smooth facets, then suddenly jerked her hand back, wrenching her eyes away from the crystal to Gaven's face. The largest nightshard she'd ever seen—the largest demonshard. Her original suspicions about Gaven's behavior resurfaced—could the exorcists have been wrong? A shard this large—perhaps it held a spirit powerful enough to hide its presence from their examination.

Gaven must have read the fear on her face, because he snapped the box shut and took her hand. "I'm not possessed," he said, his eyes searching hers. "But in a way, you were right. Something was in the shard, something that entered me when I touched it." Rienne tried to pull her hand away, but he held it tight. "Not a spirit, though—it didn't dominate me, control me. Just knowledge. Memories. A whole lifetime of memories, incredibly ancient and wise."

The mystery that had haunted Rienne for nearly three decades was starting to unravel. She felt dizzy. "But whose memories, Gaven?" she said.

"A dragon's."

A dragon's memories. She tried to imagine the thoughts and experiences of a dragon's long lifetime, and found that her mind wasn't up to the task.

"So many memories, Ree. I still can't keep them straight." His eyes were staring, out of focus again.

"Which ones are really yours, you mean?" Sometimes, before all this happened, she would remember doing something as a child, or thought she remembered—it turned out Gaven had done it in his childhood. They had been that close, once. They had shared so many stories and memories that they had forgotten whose were whose.

He nodded. "At first, it seemed like the dragon's memories were mine, and the memories of my life as Gaven were the figments. I knew you, but it felt like I knew you from a long time ago, like you were someone I cared about when I was young."

Tears sprang to Rienne's eyes. "You weren't yourself. I thought I'd lost you."

"You had. I became the dragon, in a way, and tried to live his life, pick up where he'd left off. It took me a while to figure out that time had passed, and I've only just got a sense of how long it had been."

"How long was it?"

"I think somewhere between four and five hundred years."

Rienne whistled softly, casting her mind to what she knew about Khorvaire's history. Four or five centuries past—the Five Nations united into one empire of Galifar, Cyre alive and flourishing. A world that could barely imagine the horror and violence of a century of war.

"Twenty-nine turns of Eternal Day and Endless Night," Gaven murmured. His brow was furrowed, and his eyes closed.

"What's that?"

He held up a finger, and she sat back to wait. He rocked slightly, as if he were lost in the rhythm of some unheard song.

His eyes opened. "The Storm Dragon slumbers for twenty-nine turns of Eternal Day and Endless Night, and then withdraws from the world, to emerge in the Time of the Dragon Above."

"What are you talking about?"

"Turns of Eternal Day and Endless Night—Irian and Mabar, the planes of light and darkness. Irian draws near every three years, Mabar every five. Every fifteen years they draw near in the same year. Twenty-nine cycles of fifteen years is four hundred and thirty-five years. I think that's how long I was—"

He broke off and lay back on the bed.

"Not me," he whispered. "The other."

Rienne lay beside him, propped up on one elbow. She ran her fingers through his long hair and watched his eyes, staring wide at the ceiling, darting around as if there were something to see. Her heart ached, and tears stung her eyes. What must he have endured? So many years of this—not certain who he was. And still he was haunted, she saw it in his eyes.

"What do you see?"

Gaven looked at her, and a smile danced on his lips. She smiled down at him and buried her fingers in his hair.

"So many horrible things, Ree," he said. "Such horrible things."

"Hush," she whispered, stroking his cheek.

He sat up, pushing her aside. "No, thunder, no," he muttered, his gaze darting around the room.

Rienne pulled gently on his shoulder, trying to get him to lie down again. "Shh, Gaven, relax." His sudden unease sent a jolt of panic through her. This was too much like before—she didn't understand what he was saying, and she didn't know how to keep him under control.

"Help me, Ree. I don't want this."

"I know. I know. Relax, love."

"No!" He pulled free of her touch and stood. "I can't relax. That's when the dreams come."

Rienne took a deep, steadying breath, calming her racing heart. "Can you tell me about the dreams?"

He stalked to the door and turned to face her. "It's all the time now, even when I'm awake. Sometimes I know I'm dreaming about things that have already happened—some things I did, some things the other, the dragon did. Sometimes they blur together—I'll dream about my fall, say, and then I dream that I'm the dragon, putting my memories in the nightshard. Other times I think they're past events, but not anything I experienced." He pressed his palms to his eyes again. "But the future ones are the worst."

"You dream about the future?"

He slammed his fists into the door behind him. "All the time. Why can't I just live my life, here and now? Why do I have to see so much?"

She held her hands out to him, and he came and took them. There was so much she still didn't understand, but at that moment it didn't seem to matter. She kissed his hands, then brought them to her cheek, savoring the touch of his skin. "I'm here, Gaven," she murmured. "Here and now."

CHAPTER
36

Gaven did his best to recount his travels from the cold Lhazaar coast to Q'barra, to the City of the Dead in Aerenal, to Darguun, and then north from Korranberg on the lightning rail. Some parts were hard to tell, particularly the parts where Senya played an important role in the story. Other parts were hard to remember—his confrontation with the Sentinel Marshals on the lightning rail, for example, was confused in his memory with the dreams that had haunted him.

Whenever he started to lose focus, though, Rienne was there. At the beginning of his tale, in particular, it was hard to mention his dreams and visions without starting to slip into them, but her touch always brought him back. She asked gentle questions that clarified her understanding and sometimes helped him refine his own. Finally, she asked the question that struck to the heart of the situation he was in.

"So Vaskar is trying to become a god, and Haldren wants to be king of a reunited Galifar. What do you want?"

He frowned. Why should that be such a difficult question to answer?

"I'm still trying to figure that out," he said. "When I left Vathirond, I thought I knew what I was doing. I decided I wouldn't accept a destiny that somebody else had placed on me, that I would forge my own destiny."

His thoughts went back to the night outside of Vathirond, alone with the Heart of Khyber. The dragon's words had stirred something in him—a sense of purpose, the idea of choosing a purpose. But the purpose he'd chosen, pursuing Vaskar into the Mournland, had led him down paths he didn't want to take. He had felt as though he were still pursuing the dragon's purpose, not his own.

Rienne drew him out of his reverie. "Can you say more about that?" she asked. "Who was trying to place a destiny on you?"

"Everyone. The lords of the dragonmarked houses and the Sentinel Marshals had decided that my destiny was to rot in Dreadhold. Haldren and Vaskar had the idea that I would be the accessory to their greatness, like some kind of seer that validates their dreams by declaring them the fulfillment of the Prophecy. And then even when I thought I was choosing my own course, the dragon in the shard still seemed to be foisting his destiny on me, trying to make me finish what he couldn't. I didn't want any of those things."

"To forge your own destiny," Rienne mused. "That's heady stuff, Gaven—the sort of thing that legends are made of."

"I know. That's what bothers me. Before all this happened, I never really thought of myself as a person of destiny. I failed the Test of Siberys, and figured I'd live my life as a minor player on the stage of the drama of the dragonmarked houses." He had wanted to fail the Test of Siberys—precisely because his father expected the opposite. Arnoth had dearly hoped Gaven would manifest a dragonmark and carry on his work in House Lyrandar.

"It seems Siberys herself chose you for a greater destiny than that," Rienne said, reaching up to trace her finger along his dragonmark.

"Perhaps," Gaven said. "Although I feel more like I stumbled onto a different stage when I found that nightshard, and I'm trying to fumble my way through a play I don't know."

"So to forge your own destiny means taking control of the play. Becoming both player and playwright."

"Mm." Gaven nodded. "Heady stuff, as you said."

"So what did you think you were doing when you left Vathirond?"

"I thought I would be Vaskar's nemesis—and Haldren's, too. I thought I would be the agent of the Sovereign Host, punishing their pride and bringing their plans to ruin. So I went to the Sky Caves of Thieren Kor thinking that I had to stop Vaskar from gaining the knowledge there."

Vaskar hadn't gained the knowledge of the Sky Caves. But was that Gaven's doing, or Vaskar's own failure? He hadn't even seen Vaskar until he'd been in the Sky Caves for days, walking the paths and exploring the Prophecy. Why hadn't Vaskar gained the same understanding—and the same power—that he had?

Again Rienne prompted him out of his silence. "That seems like a worthwhile goal."

"Yes. The thing that worries me . . ." He trailed off again.

What worries me, he thought, is that I might become a god.

"The thing that worries me," he said, "is that the only way I could stop Vaskar was by claiming the knowledge of the Sky Caves for myself. I set out to become his nemesis, but ended up playing the part of the Storm Dragon in his place."

Rienne's brow furrowed. "The Storm Dragon . . . Gaven, what about these storms? The lightning rail near Starilaskur, the Morning Zephyr—I've never seen a Lyrandar heir throw that kind of power around. Even the tales of other heirs of Siberys don't say anything about storms like those."

All these storms, he thought. And not just the disastrous ones—rainy weather had followed him across the Five Nations. Wind swept around him in his anger. Lightning blasted his foes. He had the power of the Storm Dragon, whether he wanted it or not.

Did he have a choice about how to use it? Or was the script already written, just waiting for him to play his part through to the final act?

"It seems I've been cast in a role I wouldn't have chosen," he said.

"So turn it into the role you do want."

"How do I do that?"

Rienne got to her feet and held out a hand to him. "Why don't you begin by deciding where we're going next?"

He took her hand and walked behind her out of their room and out to the inn's stables, pondering her question. They were in Breland, somewhere near the border with Thrane. He had very little idea where Haldren or Vaskar were, though he guessed that Haldren would be in Aundair. The lord general had kept his plans to himself, for the most part—Gaven knew Haldren's ultimate goal, but nothing of how he hoped to achieve it. As for Vaskar, Gaven had told him what he had to do to reach his goal. "On a field of battle where dragons clash in the skies, the earth opens and the Crystal Spire emerges." Vaskar would seek to bring that about.

The thought of chasing Haldren and Vaskar all around creation made him feel tired, especially when he thought about the people who were chasing him at the same time.

Rienne pressed a coin into the stable boy's hand and led the magebred mare onto the street. Gaven stopped in his tracks. "Darkness take my destiny," he said. "I've been away for twenty-six years. I want to go home."

Rienne turned to him, eyes wide. "Do you think that's wise?"

He waited while she swung into the saddle, then climbed up behind her. "Wise? No, probably not. I'm an excoriate and a fugitive, so going back to the primary enclave of House Lyrandar in all Khorvaire is not wise."

"But at least it's a city of Khoravar, like us," she said. "Our race won't make us stand out the way it would in, say, Korranberg."

"And we know the ways of the house," Gaven added. "We can lie low there pretty easily." He swallowed hard. "Rienne, do you think my father would see me?"

"Of course he would. Oh, Gaven, he never believed the charges against you. Why, if I had told him I was going to look for you, he would have insisted on coming along."

Gaven gave a laugh that was half sob. "You've seen him recently?"

"It's been a few months, but we've been in fairly regular contact. I need to tell you, though, he's not in the best health."

"What's wrong?"

"Mostly he's getting old. He was still walking around when I saw him last, but he moved pretty slowly."

Gaven drew a deep breath. "I remember him the way he was before our last descent," he said. "Healthy, maybe seventy, still vibrant and strong. Not much older than I am now, I suppose." He'd been taller than Gaven, and more slender, but they had the same hair. The same large hands, and the same laugh. Once, when laughter came more easily to Gaven.

"Your brother has been running the household," Rienne said.

"Good for Thordren," Gaven muttered. "And I suppose his mark's a greater mark now?" Thordren had only just taken his Test of Siberys the last time Gaven saw him.

"I believe so, yes," Rienne said. "He's grown into a fine young man, Gaven. You shouldn't begrudge him his success."

"You're right, of course. He and I just chose different paths in life. He chose to follow our father and run the family business, and I rotted in thrice-damned Dreadhold for twenty-six years. And look how successful we've both been at our chosen careers!"

"Gaven—"

"No, I'm sorry. I was being stupid."

"To Stormhome, then?" Rienne craned her neck to look back at him, a smile on her face.

"To Stormhome."

She gave the horse a gentle kick, and they rode like the wind.

CHAPTER
37

When Gaven and Rienne reached the Thrane river, they knew they had left Breland. The Treaty of Thronehold had defined borders between the once-warring nations, but those borders were fluid and inexact things, and they mattered most when they were crossed by roads. Riding overland as they were, it was nearly impossible to tell that they had left one nation and entered another.

They avoided a large city, Sigilstar, situated along the river, and passed quietly through several small villages spaced about a day's travel apart—a day of riding on a cart pulled by oxen, that is, not a day on the back of a horse magebred for speed. On the third day, the river widened gradually, slowing from its headlong rush to a much more leisurely pace and finally coming to rest in one of the branches of Scions Sound, once the heart of the Five Nations. The warm breeze carried the smell of the sea, and the abundance of songbirds signaled that spring had well and truly come to this part of Khorvaire.

They spent the afternoon visiting shops. Rienne kept a careful eye on her stores of coin, knowing that House Kundarak had probably blocked her credit by that time. She bought Gaven a sword, new clothes, and a coat with a high collar that concealed his dragonmark. She replenished their supplies of journeybread, preparing for more long days of travel. That night, they enjoyed a comfortable inn in the small town of Sharavacion, the largest settlement they had dared enter since leaving Vathirond.

"Did you see the docks on the sound as we rode into town?" Rienne asked as they settled into their room.

"What about them?"

"Their size, mostly. This place might not be a bustling metropolis or a center of high culture, but it sees some shipping trade."

"Hm." Gaven leaned back in a chair and rested his hands on his belly, feeling comfortably full and quite tired after a pleasant meal down the street.

"I'm thinking there's some chance we can hire a ship here to take us to

Stormhome. Maybe even a Lyrandar galleon—I might still have a favor I can call in."

"That would be good." Gaven closed his eyes and put his hands behind his head. He liked the thought of riding on a ship, especially a fast ship, rather than spending any more time on horseback.

He heard Rienne sit down on her bed and sigh. "Gaven?" she said.

"Hm?"

"What do you think Haldren and Vaskar are doing now?"

Gaven opened a sleepy eye and cocked an eyebrow at Rienne.

"Because you were talking the other night about becoming their nemesis, bringing their plans to ruin. I know that might not be the destiny you want to pursue, but I was just thinking about . . . well, what happens if they succeed?"

"I don't know what they're doing," Gaven said, looking up at the ceiling. "They didn't exactly inform me of all the details of their plans while I was with them. And when I saw Vaskar in the Sky Caves—well, we were too busy trying to kill each other to make conversation."

"I understand that," Rienne said.

Gaven thought she sounded a little testy, and he wasn't sure why.

She sighed, and when she spoke again her voice was quieter. "I'm just scared, I guess. Scared that Haldren will plunge us back into another century of war. Scared that Vaskar really will become a god, or gain the power of one."

"I don't think Vaskar will succeed. There's too much he doesn't understand, and he didn't learn anything from—"

Gaven stopped abruptly as words and images rose unbidden in his mind.

The words of the Sky Caves, woven thick with meaning . . .

The words he had studied in his draconic existence . . .

All flowing together with images from his nightmares.

The earth splitting. A colossal eruption of blinding light—a ray of Khyber's sun, a shard of the Dragon Below's might.

The hordes of the Soul Reaver emerging from the depths where they have long hidden in the darkness, unafraid of Khyber's cold light. Pouring forth from the cracks in the earth, swarming over the plain that lies in the sunset shadow of the mountains of stars.

Tearing into the soldiers massed there, shrieking and howling.

Soldiers cursing and hacking and dying. Fires in the sky and raging across the plain.

A clash of dragons signals the sundering of the Soul Reaver's gates . . .

Dragons fighting dragons . . .

. . . dragons wheeling in the sky . . .
. . . a clash of dragons . . .
. . . the armies gathered on the plain.
Dragons . . .
. . . Storm Dragon . . .
"Gaven?"
The images faded.

He lay on the floor of the room, where his chair had deposited him when he leaned too far back. Rienne was on her knees leaning over him, a look of concern mingled with fear on her face. Her hand stroked his cheek, brushing the hair back from his forehead, presumably checking him for fever.

"I'm all right, Mama," he said, trying to smile.

She clearly believed neither his words nor his smile. "Here, let me help you to your bed. Oh, Gaven, I let you do too much before you were fully recovered. You need to rest."

"I'm all right," he repeated, but he accepted her help in lifting himself onto the bed, and lay down again as she commanded. He chased the last fragments of dreams and visions as they scurried away from the rigidity of consciousness.

"What happened?" Rienne asked. "Did you faint or just slip? I didn't think you were leaning that far backward."

"Shh, shh." Gaven whispered. "I need to dream some more."

"Sleep is a good idea." Rienne's anxious fluttering transformed in an instant into soothing ministrations. She lay a blanket over him, stroked his hair softly, hummed an old tune that echoed the grief of wars long past. Eventually, she seemed to convince herself that he was asleep, despite his wide eyes staring toward the ceiling—but seeing only nightmares.

* * * * *

Rienne awoke with the first rays of sunlight creeping into the room. She stretched, rolled over to check on Gaven—and then leaped to her feet. Gaven was gone. The blanket she had draped over him the night before lay smoothed on his bed, and the pillow was fluffed. That, at least, told her that Gaven had gotten up and left the room in a more or less sound state of mind. She started for the door, stopped, and went back to lift Maelstrom from its place beside her bed. Then she went out to look for Gaven.

She was down the stairs and starting out the inn's door when a voice stopped her. "Good, you're up." She whirled and saw Gaven sitting by a fireplace in the front room. She laughed.

"Sorry to be such a slugabed. Sleeping 'til dawn—I ought to be ashamed of myself."

"Are you ready to go?" Gaven said, standing up and walking over to join her. He didn't smile.

"Well, almost. I left my things upstairs and—"

"Grab them and let's go."

Rienne started to say more, but decided against it. Gaven waited by the door as she ran back up the stairs to collect her pack. She hurried back down, and Gaven held the door open for her. He led her at a brisk pace toward the docks.

After a moment she hurried to catch up and walk beside him. "Gaven, are you all right?"

"Of course. Why?"

"Did you sleep at all?"

"No. But I dreamed a great deal."

She waited a moment for more explanation, but quickly realized he wasn't going to volunteer it. "Why the dawn rush this morning?"

"I'm anxious to get home."

Rienne pulled Maelstrom, still in its scabbard, from the sash at her waist and swung it at his stomach. "Stop."

He obliged her, scowling.

She stepped in front of him and looked up into his face. He didn't meet her eyes. "Listen to me. You promised to explain everything. I didn't take that to mean everything up to that point. You haven't fulfilled that obligation—you can't start the curt and cryptic act again. Because I can unsave your life, you know." She pointed the tip of her scabbard into his throat, gently, to emphasize her point.

He met her eyes, still scowling. She saw the muscles in his neck and shoulders tensing, and for an instant she feared he might actually attack her. Then, slowly, his frown dissolved, and he almost smiled. "I'll explain everything on the ship."

"What ship?"

He smiled broadly at that. "You'll see. If you start walking, that is. Come on!" He circled around her, laughing as he hustled toward the docks again.

Rienne made herself draw a calming breath. She could smell the sea air off Scions Sound, and she managed to catch some of Gaven's enthusiasm for the journey ahead. She hurried to catch him, slapped her scabbard against his rear, and laughed at the expression of outraged surprise on his face. He joined her laughter, even as he drew the greatsword from his back.

"Careful with your little sword, there, Lady Alastra," he said. "Don't make me use this."

"I'll put Maelstrom up against your great big hunk of scrap metal for any wager," Rienne shot back. "That's an orc's weapon—just swing it wildly back and forth and hope you hit something." She noticed as she spoke that Gaven still carried the black wooden staff he'd had when she found him outside the Mournland. He had attached it to his scabbard with some care. She started to ask him about it, but he cut her off.

"There she is," Gaven said, pointing with his sword.

He was pointing to a ship—and not just any ship. She was a great galleon, with two masts and an elegant aftcabin. Circling her, behind the mainmast, was a circle of elemental water, arcing high above the aftcabin and disappearing into the water on either side, reminiscent of the fiery ring around an airship. The water was in constant motion, churning in great rippling waves. She flew the kraken banner of House Lyrandar.

"Holy Host," Rienne breathed.

Gaven laughed. "Now do you understand?"

"Who's her captain?"

"Ah, that's the rest of the surprise." He sheathed his greatsword beside the ash staff, took her hand, and dragged her to the gangplank.

"Gaven! And the lovely Lady Alastra!" The man perched at the top of the gangplank was lean and weathered, his skin almost as dark as Rienne's from exposure to the sun. His blue eyes gleamed behind an aquiline nose, and deep wrinkles etched his face, accentuating his warm smile. His hair was a close-cropped sprinkling of black and gray, revealing the tracings of a dragonmark that started at one temple and extended behind his ear, making one more appearance on the side of his neck before disappearing. Half a dozen gold rings glittered along the edge of one gently pointed ear. He threw his arms wide as Gaven started up to meet him.

"Jordhan!" Rienne cried. She dashed up the gangplank behind Gaven, gripped Gaven's arm and swung past him, nearly sending him toppling off the side. She leaped into the grinning captain's arms, making him stumble backward onto the deck as he returned her enthusiastic embrace.

"Now do you see why I was so anxious to get here?" Gaven asked, laughing.

"I can't believe you didn't tell me!" Rienne didn't relinquish her hold on Jordhan, but spun him around so she could see Gaven over his shoulder. "How long have you known he was here?"

"I came out for a walk very early this morning and spotted the Sea Tiger here. I had barely settled in my seat at the inn when you came downstairs."

Finally Rienne released her tight hold on the captain, though she kept her hands on his shoulders as she looked at his face. "Look at you! You haven't changed a bit."

Jordhan winked. "And you're as lovely as ever, Rienne."

"Are you sure about this, Jordhan?" Gaven asked, clapping the captain's shoulder. "It's an enormous risk you're taking."

Jordhan kept his eyes on Rienne as he spoke. "I've been playing it safe for far too long."

"What have you been doing?" Rienne asked, finally relinquishing her grip on him. "I haven't seen you in—"

"Twenty-six years?" Gaven interjected.

Jordhan looked down at the deck. "Give or take." He brightened. "Come on, I've got your old cabin ready for you."

"It's just like old times, isn't it?" Gaven said. "Coming back from someplace desolate and dangerous, a load of Khyber shards in the hold—you did load the dragonshards, didn't you, Jordhan?"

They all laughed. Rienne's thoughts went to the Heart of Khyber, the one dragonshard they did carry on this journey—the cause of all their trouble. She squeezed Jordhan's arm. "It's wonderful to see you," she said. "And we're so grateful."

"It's nothing. I owe you two my life many times over."

"We wouldn't have had to save your life if we hadn't dragged you into such trouble," Gaven said. "Thank you, old friend."

Rienne looked back over her shoulder as she and Gaven started down the stairs to the little aft cabin they had shared on so many journeys, so long ago. Jordhan watched them go, a little smile on his lips and sadness in his eyes.

CHAPTER
38

I always figured Jordhan would be at your door courting you as soon as I was off the scene," Gaven said. He couldn't look at her; he busied himself with his hammock while she rummaged in her pack. Even as he said it, he wasn't sure what he wanted her to say in response.

"Jealous?" she asked.

"Me? I suppose I was at times. And furious at what seemed like a betrayal compounded. And once in a while, late at night, maybe glad at the thought of my two best friends happy together, even if I couldn't share that joy."

He felt Rienne lay her hand gently on his back. "Oh, Gaven," she whispered. He turned a little, and met her eyes gazing up at him. She shook her head slowly. "He came by a few times in the first months. He was the only friend we shared who understood what I'd done, and his friendship meant the world to me in those months. But he never courted me."

"What would you have done if he had?"

"Now why would you ask a question like that?" She turned to her pack again, jingling the buckles for a moment. "He stopped coming within a year's time. It was just too painful for both of us—you were always so conspicuous in your absence. But when he stopped coming, it was even worse."

Something clenched in Gaven's chest, and he stepped behind her, resting his hands on her shoulders. "You were alone."

She took a deep, sobbing breath, and Gaven enfolded her in his arms. She turned around and buried her face in his chest.

"I always imagined you at home," Gaven said, "carrying on with your life—the life of a beautiful noblewoman with the world at her feet. I still can't quite believe you never married. And when I escaped, you came looking for me."

"Of course I did." She lifted her tear-streaked face to him. "Oh, Gaven. I know Dreadhold must have been terrible for you, and I'm so sorry, but—"

"But you were as much a prisoner as I was." She started to bury her face again, but he put a gentle hand under her chin and lifted it. "I'm sorry, Rienne."

She straightened her back and shoulders, stretching up toward him. Kissing her, he knew beyond doubt that all was forgiven.

* * * * *

House Lyrandar's airships were certainly their crowning achievement, but Gaven simply exulted in the speed, power, and grace of the Sea Tiger, seabound as she was. A water elemental was bound into the hull, channeled through arcane traceries carved into the fine Aerenal wood, and manifest in the enormous ring of churning water that surrounded the ship. The elemental lifted her from the water, carried her over rough waves, and propelled her along, even as the wind filled the sails at Jordhan's command. They saw the lights of Flamekeep after sunset on the first day—a journey that would have taken at least two days on horseback. There was no faster vessel on the sea.

The sea—Gaven had forgotten how much he loved it. Though still enclosed within Scions Sound, he could almost taste the open water, blue spread forever above and below him, the water lifting him up, and the wind surrounding him. It was much like flying on an airship, he imagined—with the land stripped away, nothing stood between him and the sky. It made him feel like he could soar with the gulls overhead, as easily as the black-and-white porpoises in the water rode the Sea Tiger's bow wave.

Even in the course of a day's travel, Gaven could see and feel the weather changing. Summer arrived later in Aundair than it did in Korranberg, certainly, and it brought more rain, especially thunderstorms. During the second night, they came upon a terrible storm. At the first resounding crack of thunder, Gaven sprang out of his hammock and went up on deck, where the rain drenched him. All around him, the crew of the Sea Tiger struggled to secure loose objects as the ship tossed on the churning sea, and he heard the night pilot order a mate to wake the captain. The command made sense—only an heir of the Mark of Storm could reliably command the ship's bound elemental, and the night pilot did not carry that dragonmark.

Before the mate could rouse Jordhan, though, Gaven lifted a hand to the sky. A flash of lightning silhouetted him, then another bolt struck him. He laughed as its power coursed through him, splintering off from his other hand into five harmless showers of sparks.

The rain stopped, and in a moment the wind died down—enough still to carry the Sea Tiger on her way, but no more. Sailors stood around Gaven in awe, staring skyward at the Ring of Siberys shining through a hole in the towering thunderheads above them—a hole that moved slowly across the sky as they continued their northward journey.

Gaven stayed on deck until morning, delighting in the storm's distant dance, the flashes of lightning all around them. When the sun rose in a crystal blue sky, the sailors around him cheered, clapping him on the back in congratulations. But he mourned the storm's passing.

* * * * *

The morning of the third day brought a glimpse of Stormhome, its towers and bridges gleaming pink in the dawn's first light. Beyond it, the sea stretched on seemingly forever, fading into white at the horizon. Avoiding the site of his ancestral home for the time being, Gaven found a place to stand on the deck where he could not see any land—just rolling ocean. He knew that the Frostfell lay beyond, holding the far north in a perpetual winter, but from where he stood it was a fantasy, all land was fantasy, there was only him, the Sea Tiger, and the endless, boundless sea.

"You don't seem pleased to be home." Rienne's voice startled him—he had so completely fallen into the illusion of solitude. He turned to see her crossing the deck toward him. Stormhome rose up behind her shoulder.

He shot her a weak smile then turned back to the sea. "Stormhome hasn't been my home for a very long time."

"Despite its name," Rienne said as she stood beside him, leaning her shoulder against his.

"Despite its name," Gaven echoed sadly. "They cut me out, Ree, like a healer cuts out gangrene. What am I doing going back there?"

"What are you doing?" Rienne said. "What destiny will you forge?"

"I don't know." Fleeting thoughts of a life on the sea passed through his mind—to spend his days and nights on the open water, under the open sky.

"If you don't know what you want, you're sure to do what someone else wants."

Gaven turned again, saw the warmth in her eyes and smiled. Then his eyes drifted over her shoulder to Stormhome, drawing closer as the Sea Tiger surged forward. His smile turned into an eager grin.

House Lyrandar's ancestral home—his home, for the first half of his life— occupied an island off the coast of Aundair. Its towers rose gracefully from the hills of the island, accentuating the natural contours of the land. Arching bridges and ornamented domes made the city into a work of art, glittering under a sky kept perpetually blue by the weather magic of House Lyrandar. Despite the city's position at the mouth of Scions Sound, at the northern edge of Khorvaire, the power of the Mark of Storm kept the weather warm and fair. There were buildings Gaven didn't recognize—the city had changed some in twenty-six years—but the closer he came, the more he felt glad to be there, even if he couldn't quite say it was home.

Rienne pointed to a prominent tower on the north side of the city, and Gaven's mouth hung open in delight. The tower was tall and slender, decorated with krakens whose outstretched tentacles formed spurs radiating out near the tower's top. Moored at one of these spurs was the largest airship Gaven had yet seen, considerably larger than Jordhan's impressive galleon. She boasted two elemental rings, one of white-hot fire and another of roiling cloud, occasionally flashing with lightning.

"Do you think," he asked Rienne, "that while we're here, I might get a chance to ride an airship?"

Rienne looked puzzled for a moment, then realized: "Ten seas! Of course, you've never been on one!"

"I'd never even seen one until I went to Korranberg."

Rienne took his hands in hers and clutched them to her chest. "You'll ride one, I promise," she said.

She turned to face the city, and he wrapped his arms around her. She leaned back into him, and he savored her warmth, her smell, the way her hair tickled his nose. It was almost enough to make him forget Stormhome as they sailed to the docks.

*   *   *   *   *

"I can't thank you enough, old friend," Gaven said, clasping Jordhan's hand in his own. "I hope this doesn't land you in any trouble."

"I never saw you," Jordhan answered. "Either of you."

"That's right. And neither did your crew."

"They won't say anything unless I tell them to. Don't worry."

"I'm not worried," Gaven said. "How long will you stay in port here?"

Jordhan's blue eyes scanned the towers that rose above the harbor, and he scratched his chin. "Not long, I think. This is the one place it's hard for a freelancer like me to find work. Why? You think you'll need a way out of here?"

"I hope not, but I don't really know what's next. I just thought it would be good to know my options in case I do need to leave in a hurry."

Jordhan shook his head. "Think you can stay out of trouble?"

"No way," Gaven said with a laugh.

Jordhan embraced Gaven, then turned to Rienne. Without a word, Rienne threw her arms around him and held him tight for a long moment.

"Stick to him, Ree," he said with a nod to Gaven. "You two should be together."

"I plan to," Rienne said. She took Gaven's hand and stood back.

"Thank you again, Jordhan," Gaven said.

"I still owe you my life," Jordhan replied. "At least once or twice."

"But who's counting?"

"Sovereigns keep you," Jordhan said.

"Winds' favor," Gaven replied. Holding Rienne's hand, he strode off the Sea Tiger and into the city.

* * * * *

Rienne had been right: in a city full of half-elves, Gaven felt far less conspicuous, almost as though he belonged there. It helped that he knew the streets and buildings of Stormhome far better than any other city in Khorvaire. He found himself confused a few times by newer buildings that had altered the course of streetways, but overall the city had changed little while he was in Dreadhold. From time to time he was almost able to convince himself that it was still 970, that he'd never found the Heart of Khyber, never done the things that earned him his imprisonment, never been to Dreadhold. He even felt younger.

Rienne corrected him at each wrong turn, and soon they stood looking up at the three-spired tower where Gaven had spent his childhood, his father's house.

"Do you want me to wait?" Rienne asked. He gave her a puzzled frown. "I thought you might want a chance to talk to your father alone."

"Is there any reason he wouldn't be delighted to see you?"

"No, not that I know of."

"Well then, you're coming in." He took her hand and squeezed it, then he knocked on the door. It swung open immediately. Gaven didn't recognize the young man who stood in the door, but Rienne did.

"Good afternoon, Jettik, we're here to see the elder Master Lyrandar."

From the look on young Jettik's face, Gaven assumed that the boy guessed who he was. He gritted his teeth, planning how to keep the boy quiet—or, if all else failed, how to escape to a safe hiding place. Then he realized that Jettik's eyes were fixed on Rienne, his white lips quivered, and his eyes were red as though he had been crying.

What is going on? he thought.

"I—I'm sorry, Lady Alastra," Jettik stammered. The act of speaking seemed to break a floodgate, and fresh tears sprang to his eyes. "The master . . ." He wiped his nose on his sleeve and tried to draw a steady breath. A dread gripped Gaven's stomach, and he put a hand on the door frame. He already knew what the boy was trying to say.

Jettik started again. "The master passed away this morning."

"Oh no," Rienne breathed, squeezing Gaven's hand. Gaven heard the words and felt the squeeze, but both seemed distant, as though he looked down on the whole scene from a mile in the air.

"Th-th-the younger Master Lyrandar is upstairs, Lady, if you want to . . ." Jettik trailed off.

Gaven only vaguely realized that Rienne was looking to him for direction. Did he want to see his brother? Some part of his mind thought that Jettik's words should have stung—he should have been the younger Master Lyrandar, not his younger brother—but he was too numb to feel the sting. It was impossible: he had been cut off from his family for so many years, and he had come hours too late to see his father one last time. Hours. Did he want to see Thordren?

Rienne led him forward into the entry, clutching his arm and looking up at him with eyes full of concern. She had evidently made the decision for him, or made her own. They were going to see Thordren.

His brother had been a headstrong adolescent when Gaven saw him last, barely more than a child. The two brothers had never been close, had never really been anything more than casual acquaintances who happened to live under the same roof. Now Thordren ran the household in their father's illness—no, he had just inherited the household. He could throw Gaven out of the house if he wanted to, he—

Holy Host, Gaven thought, he could have me arrested in no time. What are we doing here?

"Rienne." A rich tenor voice came from the staircase that curved upward along the opposite wall. Rienne wrenched her eyes from Gaven's face and looked up at Thordren.

"Thordren, I'm so sorry," she said. "I didn't know—"

"Of course," Thordren said. "It's good to see you anyway, though of course I wish the circumstances could be other than they are. But do I know your companion?"

Gaven had his back to the stairs, but now he turned to face his brother.

"Gaven," Thordren said, his raised eyebrows the only indication of his surprise. "This is unexpected."

"Hello, Thordren."

Gaven watched a series of emotions work themselves out on his brother's face, surprise and rage and grief and regret prominent among them. The silence stretched until it was awkward, with Rienne looking back and forth between them as if waiting for one of them to spring at the other.

"I'm sorry," Rienne sobbed at last, when the silence had become unbearable. "We shouldn't have come."

"No," Thordren said. He started down the stairs again. "It's good that you're here. I apologize for being ungracious."

Thordren had reached the bottom of the stairs and crossed the room to stand by them. He threw his arms around Gaven, clinging to him with desperate fierceness. Gaven stood awkwardly for a moment, then returned his brother's embrace. When Thordren finally pulled away, his face was wet with tears, and he gave an embarrassed laugh.

"You will always be my brother," Thordren said.

Gaven pulled him close again.

CHAPTER
39

The Aundairian ambassador looked as though he had been dragged from bed and brought before the Cardinals—which, Vauren supposed, was not far from the truth.

Silver Flame, he thought, *I feel much the same way.*

Vauren's path away from the Whisper Woods had led him to the border of Thrane, Aundair's neighbor to the east and south. He'd been far enough ahead of Haldren's marching armies that he had little trouble slipping across the border without papers. Within three weeks of leaving Haldren's camp, he'd found his way to the city of Thaliost, where he managed to secure identification and traveling papers for his new identity. He had also used a contact in Thaliost to get a message back to Fairhaven, though he didn't expect any kind of response.

Armed with a letter of introduction provided by the same contact, he had made his way to Flamekeep and found his way into the livery of a Knight of the Flame, which made him distinctly uncomfortable. On the one hand, he knew he was by no means the first foreign spy to infiltrate this chamber and this supposedly holy order. On the other hand, it shaped Vauren's personality in unfamiliar ways. He wasn't accustomed to piety, but he was becoming pious. He had even started cursing like a Thrane. He feared it would interfere with his work.

He stood, stony-faced, at the great chamber's edge, as the ambassador hurried forward and bowed before the Diet of Cardinals. Vauren could see the man trying to compose himself as he held the bow a little longer than strictly necessary.

"Revered Lords," the ambassador said, absently straightening the folds of his robe, "to what do I owe this honor?"

One of the cardinals seated near an end of the crescent-shaped table got to his feet. "Ambassador," he said, "we have received some very disturbing reports from the north, and we hoped you could shed light on their significance for us."

"Reports from the north?" the ambassador repeated. Vauren pitied him. He was an aging diplomat, his hair thinning and his waist spreading, and he clearly had no idea what he was in for at this meeting.

"I will not waste your time weaving shadows, ambassador. Aundairian troops are marching north of Thaliost. What is their purpose?"

The ambassador was obviously stunned, and he stammered a reply. "I—I have not been informed of any troop movements."

"Are you quite certain, ambassador?"

"Yes, of course! I am sure it's nothing, just training exercises or war games."

"War games," the cardinal said gravely. "Tell me, ambassador, what kind of war game involves large numbers of dragons?"

"Dragons?" For the first time, the ambassador smiled, if nervously. "Revered Lords, someone is playing a terrible joke—"

"This is no joke, ambassador. We have not heard anything from you to suggest an explanation other than the one that seems obvious: Aundair is planning an imminent violation of the Treaty of Thronehold, in an attempt to reclaim the lands of Thaliost."

"That's ridiculous!"

"I might be inclined to agree with you, ambassador, were it not for the dragons. I wouldn't presume to guess what damning bargain your queen has made to secure the assistance of dragons, but I assure you that Thrane takes this threat very seriously. We have already notified our ambassadors in Breland, Karrnath, and the Eldeen Reaches in order to secure the assistance of those nations in protecting ourselves from this violation of the Thronehold accords. Aundair's arrogance will not be ignored. We hope you will urge your queen to reconsider this brash move before all Khorvaire is once again engulfed in war."

"I assure you, Revered Lords, Aundair is not planning an invasion. They would have notified me, recalled me. Unless . . ."

The ambassador fell silent. No one needed to finish his sentence for him—Vauren knew that everyone in the room could think of one very good reason for Aundair not to recall its ambassadors. A sudden departure of diplomatic personnel would alert Thrane to the imminent invasion. If a handful of aging diplomats had to be sacrificed—well, that was the smallest price Aundair would pay in a renewed war.

Vauren stared blankly at the ambassador, careful not to let any of his thoughts register on his face with even the slightest twitch of muscle. Some part of him—the Knight of Thrane part, he supposed—wished he could help the poor man, leap to his defense and Aundair's, explain the whole situation.

He wished he could put a stop to Haldren's madness before it cost any more lives. But he knew that was not an option.

I'm as much a slave to my orders as Cart is, he thought.

He was surprised to realize that the thought of the warforged brought a twinge of sadness. Would Cart's be one of the lives lost in Haldren's scheme? What about Jenns? Had he survived alone in the wilderness, or starved to death, or perhaps been rounded up again by Haldren's marching armies? And Gaven? Had the Sentinel Marshals tracked him down yet and dragged him back to Dreadhold? Or killed him?

Vauren suddenly felt light headed. In his mind, the grand chamber became the center of a swirling vortex of history—events unfolding inexorably around him, dragging him and everyone whose life he had touched into annihilation. Haldren and his armies marched in the north, dragons winging overhead. He'd last seen Gaven far to the south, but he imagined Gaven and Senya making their way northward, drawn by some unalterable destiny to reunite with Haldren on the same terrible battlefield. The fate of Khorvaire seemed bound up in the strands of these people's lives—caught in the maelstrom.

A pair of knights led the ambassador out of the room. Vauren assumed they were not escorting him back to the embassy. He'd be a hostage in the upcoming conflict, another life dragged under by the storm.

* * * * *

Vauren tried to relax. He was no longer dressed in the uniform of a Knight of Thrane, but he still felt the role constricting him. He leaned on the counter at a busy Flamekeep tavern, keeping an eye on the people coming and going without appearing to do anything but study his drink. He let the laughter and curses of the other patrons wash over him, hoping to absorb some of their freedom and coarseness. He felt altogether too clean and pure after his time in the Cathedral of the Silver Flame, and in danger of becoming a prig. Self-righteous morality didn't sit well alongside a career built on duplicity.

He had considered simply discarding Vauren and starting afresh on a new identity, but something held him back. Perhaps it was just the fact that he'd been three different people in such a short span of time. He had barely had time to get to know Caura, and he didn't want to discard Vauren so quickly. It was still early, he told himself—there was still time to shape Vauren's personality and keep him from priggery.

There was little else he could do in Thrane. He'd stayed in the Cathedral just long enough to learn where Thrane's generals expected to engage Haldren's forces—an old battlefield called the Starcrag Plain—and the size of the force they expected to marshal. Of course, if Breland or Karrnath decided to get involved, the number of troops could increase significantly, but by the time Vauren had left the service of the Knights of Thrane, those nations had made no commitment to Thrane's cause. If they did, that would be important information, but there were other spies who would probably hear the news first.

Finding Gaven, though, was something that no other agent was likely to accomplish.

A combination of a careful reading of the Korranberg Chronicle—the most widely read source of news in Khorvaire—and a thorough roundup of gossip had given him a sketchy idea of Gaven's movements. There was the chase through the lightning rail station in Korranberg. The Chronicle hadn't reported the identity of the fugitive, but it was easy enough to guess that it was Gaven. From Paluur Draal, Korranberg was the closest major city and lightning rail station. Then the lightning rail disaster in Breland. The Chronicle painted it as a freak storm, but the rumormongers spoke of Sentinel Marshals killed in the incident. Vauren had spoken to a pair of travelers who had been aboard when the carts stopped in Sterngate, who had told him about the Sentinel Marshals searching every cart, looking for someone. Clearly, Gaven had been traveling north from Korranberg.

The disaster had occurred near Starilaskur, he knew, which lay in north-eastern Breland. The lightning rail line ran from there to Vathirond, then north into Thrane. But Vathirond also stood at the edge of the Mournland—not far at all from the Sky Caves of Thieren Kor, according to the map they'd found in Paluur Draal. And Vaskar had spoken, in Haldren's tent, of meeting Gaven at the Sky Caves.

And there was the lost airship. A man attached to House Lyrandar had gotten too far into his cups and told Vauren that an airship had failed to return after leaving Vathirond under unusual circumstances. Someone had bribed or persuaded the captain to take the ship on an unscheduled voyage, and she had flown out of town to the east, toward the Mournland.

Could Gaven have persuaded members of his family to let him borrow a ship, or to carry him into the Mournland? It seemed unlikely. He was an excoriate as well as a fugitive. By aiding Gaven, the captain would have been risking excoriation himself, as well as criminal charges. Someone very close to Gaven might have taken that risk, Vauren supposed. Perhaps Gaven had seized control of the airship? Again, unlikely—but not impossible.

He pondered the mystery of the lost airship as he ordered another cup of wine—or the vaguely wine-flavored water this place served. On a positive note, though, he could drink it all night without worrying about clouding his wits. While he waited, he leaned back against the bar and surveyed the crowded tavern.

A group of dwarves tramped in, and Vauren studied them. They were travel-worn, their cloaks dusty and their boots caked with dried mud. That wasn't unusual—at least half the patrons of this tavern looked much the same. Vauren had chosen a tavern near the southern gate of the city for just that reason: it was popular among travelers newly arrived in Flamekeep. He turned back around as the barkeep set his wine down with a grunt.

Something caught Vauren's eye as he turned, and he considered the implications as he sipped his wine. One of the dwarves, sporting a fine silk shirt of brilliant red, had revealed a signet ring as she pulled off her gloves. If Vauren's brief glimpse had been accurate, it was the snarling manticore seal of House Kundarak.

That could mean many things. House Kundarak maintained banking operations across Khorvaire, so some of its members traveled constantly from enclave to enclave. These dwarves did not look like bankers, though—they were battle hardened and armed to the teeth. Well, Vauren supposed that traveling bankers would have to be well armed and ready for combat, to protect against the threat of bandits. Still, House Kundarak also operated Dreadhold. Who would House Kundarak employ to track a fugitive from Dreadhold?

Vauren closed his eyes and listened to the sounds of the tavern, trying to locate dwarf voices amid the din. No luck, but that didn't surprise him—they hadn't struck him as a boisterous group. Holding his cup, he turned around on his stool, leaning against the bar again, to all appearances a handsome elf searching the crowd for companionship. He saw them arranging themselves around a table across the room. There were five of them, and they grumbled as they tried to fit their broad bodies comfortably at a hexagonal table. Vauren spotted burn marks on the clothes of at least three of the five.

There was no way Vauren could hear their quiet words at six paces, not with four other tables full of much rowdier drinkers between him and the dwarves. He concentrated on watching their lips. That meant he had to stare more intently than he would have liked, but the dwarves weren't looking around much. It was a risk he was willing to take.

The table's attention seemed fixed on the one in the red shirt, so Vauren pegged her as the leader. Unfortunately, Vauren stared at her back, watching the heads of the others bob in agreement but getting no idea of what she had said. Finally one of the other dwarves said something Vauren could read, and he knew he'd found a trail to follow.

"Couldn't we seize her family land in Stormhome?" the dwarf said.

That question told Vauren a great deal. Although House Lyrandar owned the island of Stormhome, the dwarves were clearly discussing a noble, not an heir of the house. Even House Kundarak couldn't seize an estate that belonged to another dragonmarked house. The question probably related to someone who had aided a criminal or a fugitive—seizing land would be a way of putting pressure on such a person. It was by no means a certainty, but it seemed probable that they were talking about Rienne ir'Alastra, Gaven's former betrothed.

He watched for a while longer without attracting the dwarves' attention, but he couldn't make out any more words to confirm his hunch. He needed closer access to these dwarves. When one of them got to his feet and made his way outside, Vauren saw his chance.

He left his drink on the bar with a silver coin, and slipped through the crowd to the door. Stepping outside, he looked up and down the street. Dark and quiet—perfect. Light spilled out the tavern windows, forming little bright pools on the cobbled street, but the other buildings were dark, and no one else walked the street. A splashing sound from the alley next to the tavern alerted him to his quarry's location. He wrinkled his nose in disgust—he expected better manners from House Kundarak.

He untied the length of silk rope he wore as a belt and tied a knot in it as he hurried to the alley. The dwarf leaned his forehead against the wall of the tavern as he relieved himself. In one smooth movement, Vauren stepped behind the dwarf and slid the rope around his neck, pulling it tight.

He cursed the hardiness of dwarves as he waited for the air to give out and the body to fall limp. The dwarf struggled hard, trying to work the fingers of one hand under the silk as he reached behind him with the other to gouge at Vauren's eyes. Vauren kept the pressure constant while keeping his own vulnerable spots out of reach, and finally his patience was rewarded—the dwarf fell first to his knees, then face down in his own puddle of urine. Vauren released the rope, and a wracking breath reassured him that he hadn't killed the dwarf.

That's strange, Vauren thought. Why didn't I kill him?

"My descent into priggery is complete," he muttered aloud. He pulled a dagger from his belt and bent to slit the unconscious dwarf's throat, but again he found something staying his hand.

"Oh, Vauren, you weak-willed Thrane." He dropped the dagger on the ground. "Only one thing to be done." He rolled the dwarf over, looking closely at his face. He glanced toward the street, making sure he was well cloaked in shadow. Then he changed.

He pulled off his clothes as he worked on his face, transforming it into a perfect copy of the dwarf at his feet—chiseled features, neat beard, shaven pate. Then he pulled off the dwarf's armor as he compressed his body to dwarven stature. He liked dwarf bodies—solid, strong. The skin firm, almost like marble.

He put on the unconscious dwarf's armor and checked himself over. He found identification papers and traveling papers in a coat pocket and studied them carefully. He repeated the name softly to himself several times: "Natan Durbannek, Natan Durbannek." He always preferred choosing his own names, but it was useful in this case: taking someone else's name helped him become someone more unlike himself. He didn't know Natan Durbannek, but he knew what House Kundarak's elite agents were like. So as he shaped his body, he also sculpted his heart—hard, sharp.

Ruthless.

He picked up the battle-axe that lay at the dwarf's side. Without a moment's hesitation, he brought it down hard on Natan Durbannek's neck.

* * * * *

The young Sentinel Marshal ran through the streets of Stormhome as fast as her feet could carry her. Watching Arnoth d'Lyrandar's house had seemed like the most boring assignment imaginable, and before the lightning rail disaster she had spent countless hours in her hiding place, wishing that she was with Evlan d'Deneith instead of sitting on her ass. After the lightning rail disaster, she had spent hours wishing she'd never entered the Sentinel Marshals, wishing she could be anywhere in Khorvaire other than that street in Stormhome.

But the assignment suddenly seemed anything but boring. She had to get word to someone before it was too late. She only hoped that someone could act on the information in time. She burst into the little message station operated by House Sivis, out of breath, her legs and lungs burning.

"Quickly!" she panted. "Send a message to Karrlakton! The Lyrandar excoriate, the fugitive from Dreadhold—he's here!"

CHAPTER
40

H e grew steadily weaker for a long time," Thordren said, "but the end went quickly. The healers said they couldn't do anything for him—his body just didn't have the strength to go on. Then it was just a few weeks ago he took a turn for the worse. He could barely draw breath enough to speak. So we started making sure all his affairs were in order, making sure everything was legally transferred over to me. He slept most of the last two days, and this morning—he didn't wake up."

Gaven sat with his hands over his face, his elbows on his knees. His mind was filled with memories of a much younger man, still healthy and vibrant and—gruff, often angry, always busy.

"It sounds like it was a peaceful end," Rienne said.

"Yes, very. I was actually asleep in the chair in his room when he died. We had a healer from House Jorasco here for about a week, I guess. She came in and woke me about dawn, and she observed how slowly he was breathing, and the next time I woke up he wasn't breathing at all. Very peaceful."

"Not very like him, is it?" Gaven said. "I would have figured he'd go out fighting, the cantankerous old—"

Rienne squeezed his knee, and he broke off.

Thordren laughed. "I can see what you mean." He stared at Gaven for a moment. "Anyway, I've been handling most of the business, as he grew weaker. Though Aureon knows I couldn't have done it without father's guidance, at least not at first."

"How is business?" Rienne asked. "Are you going to be all right?"

Thordren scoffed. "I'll be fine. Father was a genius, and I've learned a lot from him. I have plenty of money, and shipping contracts enough to keep it that way for the rest of my life. That is, assuming we don't end up back at war."

"What?"

"You haven't heard?"

"We've been at sea," Rienne reminded him.

"Of course. Well, the rumor is that Aundair's massing troops in Thaliost, or that's what Thrane says. Aundair denies it, of course, but there's a great deal of saber-rattling going on."

"Haldren," Gaven said, lifting his head from his hands.

Thordren gave him a quizzical look.

"Haldren ir'Brassek. He was in Dreadhold, escaped with me. Damn, he moves fast."

"Are any other nations getting involved?" Rienne asked, gripping Gaven's knee tightly again.

"Karrnath and Breland are making lofty proclamations about the importance of the Treaty of Thronehold and preserving the peace after so much tragedy, but otherwise keeping out of it. So far."

"What about the Eldeen Reaches?" Rienne asked. "They've got to be nervous that they're next on Aundair's list."

"As a matter of fact, just today I heard news of a skirmish on the Eldeen border. Some Reacher scouts had crossed into Aundair, presumably looking for signs of a troop buildup, and they tangled with an Aundairian patrol."

Rienne shook her head. "More bloodshed."

Gaven stood and walked to the window. Stormhome spread out below him, and the sea sparkled in the afternoon sun. In the distance, looming shadows were all he could see of Aundair.

. . . vultures wheel where dragons flew, picking the bones of the numberless dead . . .

Gaven started as though he'd touched fire, and stepped back from the window. He blinked, trying to get the image out of his mind, the sight of a battlefield strewn with corpses, a sky blotted out by the black wings of carrion birds, the earth torn open and violated.

Rienne was beside him, her strong hand between his shoulder blades. "What is it?"

Gaven sat back down, pinching the bridge of his nose and squeezing his eyes shut. "It seems that I no longer have to sleep to start dreaming."

"You're having visions?" Thordren asked.

Gaven looked up, studying his brother. That question was the first hint he'd given of concern about Gaven's mental state.

Does he think I'm mad, or possessed? Gaven thought. *Has he simply been trying to placate me until help can arrive?*

He stood and stalked to the window again, this time searching the streets for a marching force of Sentinel Marshals or some other authority on their way to arrest him.

"Gaven?" Rienne was beside him again, her face full of concern.

"Tell me something, Thordren." Gaven turned around, leaning back against the windowsill and crossing his arms. "Twenty-six years ago, House Lyrandar excoriated me and the tribunal threw me in Dreadhold. You've obviously gotten on with your life, and you're doing well."

"I don't un—" Thordren began, but Gaven cut him off.

"Why did you welcome me back with open arms?"

Thordren looked as though he didn't understand the question. "Because you're my brother," he answered.

"I'm an excoriate. Technically, that means I'm not your brother any more. You have no obligation to me. In fact, you're prohibited from giving me aid or shelter. You could be arrested just for having me here. Why did you let me into your house?"

Thordren's bewildered look changed as he gradually made sense of Gaven's questions. "You don't trust me," he said. "You think I've already summoned the Sentinel Marshals and I'm just keeping you busy until they get here? Is that it?"

"I'm really hoping to rule out that possibility right now. Tell me why you took me in."

Rienne held his arm. "Gaven, why—"

"No, Rienne," Thordren said. "I understand why you're suspicious, Gaven. If I were in your position, I would be too. Well, I hope I would have the presence of mind to be suspicious. I'm not sure I would."

"You're risking everything for me."

"And you can't understand why I would do that. But Rienne's risking everything, too. Do you understand that?"

"Not really," Gaven admitted, "but it's harder for me to imagine what she might be hiding."

Thordren's eyes were bright with tears again. "Did Dreadhold make you forget what love is?"

Gaven turned back to the window. "My betrothed delivered me to the Sentinel Marshals. My family disowned me, cut me out. Nobody spoke in my defense at my trial. It wasn't Dreadhold that made me forget."

Rienne moved behind him and clasped his arm, but she was evidently at a loss for words. He stared blindly out the window, savoring the bitter taste of anger in his mouth. He heard Thordren step away and then settle in a chair. He started to turn back around, but something in the street below caught his eye.

Dwarves. If they hadn't been in Stormhome, he probably wouldn't have noticed, but in the home of the half-elf House Lyrandar—a single dwarf might not draw the attention, but half a dozen of them, trying to look inconspicuous, certainly did. When he spotted a scarlet shirt on a dark-skinned dwarf, he was certain.

"You bastard." Gaven whirled to face his brother. "You almost had me convinced with your little speech about brotherly love."

"What are you talking about?" Thordren looked genuinely confused.

"Those thrice-damned Kundarak dwarves are on their way," Gaven said.

Rienne gasped, and stepped to the window. "How many?" she asked.

"I saw five."

"Gaven, I had nothing to do with this," Thordren said. "Please, you have to believe me."

"They've probably been watching the house since you escaped," Rienne said.

"It doesn't matter any more how they found me. I need to figure out how I'm getting out of here." Gaven started out of the room, but Rienne grabbed his arm.

"How we're getting out of here," she said. "We're still in this together, Gaven."

"The airship," Thordren said.

"You have an airship?" Rienne asked. "Here?"

"Not here. But close. Rienne, you know where the bakery is?" He gestured to the west, and Rienne nodded. "If you turn right at that corner, there's a mooring tower halfway up the next block. It's not hard to miss. She's called the Eye of the Storm. Take her with my blessing."

Gaven stepped close to his brother and clasped his shoulder. "Thank you, Thordren. I'm sorry I mistrusted you."

Thordren smiled and nodded. "Hurry," he said.

"And I'm sorry for this," Gaven added, punching him hard in the jaw. Thordren spun halfway around before hitting the floor, unconscious. "But things will go much better for you this way," Gaven added.

Rienne took his hand and pulled him out of the room and down the stairs.

Just as they reached the bottom of the stairs, a pounding erupted from the door. Jettik hurried toward it, but Rienne stopped him with a gesture. The boy looked confused, glancing between Rienne, the door, and the stairs, as if waiting for an explanation from Thordren. Ignoring him, Rienne led Gaven through the house to the kitchen and yanked a back door open.

A dwarf stumbled through the door and collided with Rienne. Rienne let herself fall backward under the rushing dwarf's weight. Keeping her hands and knees between the dwarf's body and her own, she lifted him up and hurled him into the iron cookware hanging on the opposite wall. He collapsed in a

JAMES WYATT · 2 6 1

heap of pots and armor, jerked slightly, and fell still.

"Natan!" a voice shouted outside, then, "Around back!"

Gaven grabbed Rienne's hand and pulled her to her feet as he charged out the door. As he ran west down an alley, he turned his face to Rienne. "You have to lead the way—I don't know any bakery around here."

"It's only been there about ten years," Rienne said with a smile, but then she pointed to their right and up. "I think that's where we're heading."

Gaven followed the direction of her finger with his eyes, and saw the distinctive shape of a small mooring tower jutting above the surrounding buildings. "Got it," he said. "The Eye of the Storm."

"Let's hope she's ready to fly."

"Do you know how to fly an airship?" Gaven asked.

"Sovereigns, no. That's your job, heir of Siberys."

Gaven growled and made a sharp right turn into another alley, trying to steer more or less toward the mooring tower. Just as Rienne made the turn, a crossbow bolt clattered against the wall of the alley.

"Fortunately, these alleys haven't changed much in thirty years," Gaven said. He pointed ahead. "We're going right at that T, though it leads away from the tower."

"If you say so."

They ran at top speed, and once again Gaven felt the wind pick up around them, carrying them so their feet barely touched the ground. When they reached the branching alley, the wind carried them smoothly around the corner without slowing. At the same time, though, a man came hurtling from the opposite branch, falling into stride right behind them, evidently carried by the same wind. Gaven barely caught a glimpse of him as he rounded the corner, but that was enough to identify him without wasting time on a backward glance.

"Bordan," he growled.

"That's right, Gaven." Bordan had to shout to be heard over the wind. "We found you again. The rest of your life will be like this, you know, as long as you keep running."

"Still better than Dreadhold," Gaven replied.

"And Dreadhold's far better than you deserve!" As he shouted, Bordan leaped forward and threw his arms around Gaven's legs, bringing them both to the ground.

Gaven landed on his side and kicked hard at Bordan's head. As his foot connected, a blast like thunder threw Bordan backward. Rienne helped Gaven stand, and they kept running down the alley. They made a sharp left turn, then stopped short, faced with a blank stone wall.

Lightning flashed in the darkening sky. Gaven shouted a curse, but a peal of thunder overhead drowned him out.

"I guess the alleys have changed a bit," Rienne said. She drew Maelstrom and stepped back to look the way they had come. "The dwarves are almost here, and Bordan's right behind them."

"If they want a fight, I'll give it to them." Gaven wreathed his body in flames as he drew his sword and stepped beside Rienne to face the onrushing dwarves.

Rienne looked at him sadly. "Gaven, I don't want their deaths on my conscience."

"You're a criminal now, Ree. You can't afford a conscience."

The dwarves slowed their approach, demonstrating more caution than they had last time. There were five, and Gaven thought three of them looked familiar from Vathirond. There was the scarlet-shirted leader Rienne had identified as Ossa. The one who had crashed into the kitchen had been in Vathirond as well—he'd knocked Gaven to the floor and almost cracked his ribs with his mace. The woman who had fenced with Senya was there too. The fourth wore the heaviest armor, a steel breastplate with a few other plates of metal protecting sensitive spots, and hefted a greataxe as long as Gaven's sword. The fifth kept to the back, her empty hands poised in front of her body, preparing to cast a spell. Bordan walked more slowly, trailing the dwarves by a dozen yards or so.

Ossa stepped ahead of the others and addressed Rienne, pointedly turning away from Gaven. "I know from experience it's pointless to ask for Gaven's surrender," he said, "but there is still a chance for you, Lady Alastra."

"Surrender?" Rienne said. "You don't know me very well, Ossa."

"There are few witnesses to the events near the Mournland, and it's not too hard to believe that he enchanted you and forced you to aid him. I certainly can't think of a more logical explanation for your behavior."

Gaven sneered. "You're wasting your time, Kundarak."

"Am I?" Ossa finally acknowledged Gaven's presence with a glance. "She delivered you to justice once, she can do so again. And certainly escape with nothing more than a slap on the wrist. You needn't spend the rest of your life a fugitive, Lady Alastra."

"No," Gaven interjected, "You're wasting your time chasing me at all. Two of us escaped from Dreadhold. Haldren's the one fomenting war and planning his conquest of Khorvaire. Why are you spending all your energy chasing me?"

Bordan stepped forward at that. "When you're just a harmless, misunderstood victim? Is that it, Gaven? We're chasing you because you're a dangerous fugitive. You expect us to just let you run around Khorvaire crashing the lightning rail and airships as the mood strikes you?"

"If you hadn't been chasing me, neither of those accidents would have happened," Gaven said.

"What makes you think you're so damned important, Gaven?" Bordan pushed his way through the rank of dwarves and thrust his face into Gaven's, heedless of the shield of flames around Gaven's body. "You think you're more important than the people you've killed? Is your life worth more than theirs?"

"Haldren's about to plunge the world into war again. Do you understand that?"

"You're the one who doesn't understand, Gaven. Yes, Haldren's a mass murderer. But you still have Evlan d'Deneith to answer for. You might be less evil than he is, but that doesn't mean you're good. You've earned your place in Dreadhold—or worse. So we're going to take you in, whether it's now or later. And then we'll find Haldren and take him in, and put an end to this nonsense. And the world will be a better place when you're in a cell again."

Gaven snarled, and lightning answered him, dancing around the spires of the mooring tower above them. "Take me in? You?"

"We will prevail, Gaven." Bordan's smile was calm and confident, which only infuriated Gaven more.

"How? You can't handle me."

It was not Bordan who answered, but Ossa. Her voice, too, was calm. "We don't have to handle you, Gaven," she said. "We just have to handle her."

Gaven realized his mistake at once. While he'd been yelling at Bordan, the dwarf in the back had cast a spell on Rienne, freezing her in place. Gaven sent a hurricane blast of wind down the alley, sending Bordan sprawling on his back and forcing the dwarves into half crouches. But two of the dwarves held Rienne's arms, and they started pulling her stiffened body away, letting the wind lighten their load. Ossa pressed the tip of a dagger to Rienne's neck.

"Careful, Gaven," the dwarf shouted over the gale. "The wind seems to have caught my blade."

Gaven saw a prick of crimson well up on Rienne's neck. The wind caught it and drew it in a line across her throat, as though demonstrating what Ossa threatened to do. With another rumble of thunder overhead, Gaven made the wind stop. His shoulders slumped.

Rain began to patter on the cobblestones around them, to hiss and vanish in the flames that still licked across Gaven's body, to spatter Ossa's scarlet shirt with darker spots like blood. The dwarf spellcaster spoke another spell and snuffed the magic of Gaven's fiery shield. Gaven stared at the tip of Ossa's blade and the dimple it made in Rienne's throat.

"If you harm her," he growled, "I swear that I will hunt down every person that so much as knows your name."

Two of the dwarves moved to seize Gaven's arms and pull them behind his back. As they clamped manacles around his wrists, he saw Bordan get to his feet and look up at the sky.

"I must admit my surprise, Gaven," Bordan said. "I knew you were powerful. But when did rain last fall in the streets of Stormhome?"

PART
IV

The greatest of the daelkyr's brood,
the Soul Reaver feasts
on the minds and flesh of a thousand lives
before his prison breaks.

The Bronze Serpent calls him forth,
but the Storm Dragon is his doom.

A clash of dragons signals the sundering of the Soul Reaver's gates.
The hordes of the Soul Reaver spill from the earth,
and a ray of Khyber's sun erupts to form a bridge to the sky.

The Storm Dragon descends into the endless dark
beneath the bridge of light, where the Soul Reaver waits.
There among the bones of Khyber
the Storm Dragon drives the spear formed from Siberys's Eye
into the Soul Reaver's heart.

And the Storm Dragon walks through the gates of Khyber
and crosses the bridge to the sky.

CHAPTER

41

The Starpeaks jutted up above Thaliost as if a fiend imprisoned in the earth had pushed them upward in its struggles to escape. Senya stood on a rocky overlook at the edge of the mountains, with Arrakas d'Deneith at her elbow, never letting her stray too far. The dramatic landscape spread out below left her speechless. To the southeast, hills spread out from the mountains like ripples frozen into earth. Boulders littered the rocky ground, gathered in places into enormous cairns commemorating fallen soldiers from untold centuries of warfare. On the eastern edge of the plain, a dark forest stood out against the background of the jagged field. A chill wind blew out of the mountains at her back, moaning as it blew through gulleys and chasms in the bare rock.

It was easy to see why Aundair considered this land Aundairian soil: the only natural feature that divided the land was the Aundair River, which flowed into Scions Sound just south of the plain. But at the end of the Last War, the Thronehold Accords had established the new border between Thrane and Aundair somewhere in the middle of this plain below them, and extending on an indeterminate path through the Silver Woods beyond. By demanding that Thrane's borders include Thaliost, the Thrane delegation to Thronehold had almost undercut the peace process. Had the memory of Cyre's desolation not been so fresh in everyone's memory, this plain might have seen another decade of war.

"The Starcrag Plain," Arrakas said, gazing down with Senya onto the rocky field below them. "So just to the north—" He pointed an armored finger to the left, to the mouth of a wide valley that opened into the plain. "Bramblescar Gorge. Not too deep into that charming valley, just across the border in Aundair, we'll find your Haldren camped and ready to launch a new war over Thaliost. We'll reach his camp by nightfall."

"You're making a mistake," Senya said. She knew her protests were futile— she had run through the same arguments at least a dozen times since Arrakas had captured her in Vathirond. "He won't jeopardize his plans for my sake."

"Don't worry," the Sentinel Marshal said, still staring at the valley. A grin touched the corner of his mouth. "You're not the only dragon in my flight."

Senya suppressed a shudder at the mention of dragons, though she knew the phrase simply referred to a tavern game. She wondered how much Arrakas knew about Haldren's plans. Was he prepared to venture into that valley and come face-to-face with a real flight of dragons?

Senya found herself much less nervous about a score of dragons than she was about her inevitable encounter with Haldren.

Arrakas signaled to the half a dozen Sentinel Marshals at his command, and they started down the craggy overlook toward Bramblescar Gorge.

*   *   *   *   *

Senya's sharp elf ears heard the pounding hoofbeats a second before any of the human Sentinel Marshals who surrounded her. She wheeled her own horse around to find their source, but two Sentinel Marshals spurred their horses toward her, anticipating an escape attempt. They wrested the reins from her hands and seized her arms before Arrakas's sharp command cut through the din.

"Release her!" The marshals obeyed, though one kept hold of her reins. Both looked daggers at her, and Senya returned the glare. Between them, she could just make out a party of perhaps a dozen knights charging across the plain.

Arrakas had clearly seen the knights as well. "Harkas! Lucan! Give Senya her reins and turn your horses around."

The anger on the marshals' faces turned to surprise, and they did as their officer commanded. Senya saw the approaching knights more clearly—they wore plate armor and full helms, and carried shields and lances with the tips held high, gleaming in the sun. Their shields bore the silver arrowhead of the Silver Flame, marking them as Thranes. A regular border patrol? Or scouts from an advancing army, massing on the Thrane side of the border to face Haldren's forces?

"Senya," Arrakas said, "you will be silent while I talk with these knights. You will not speak without my leave. Do you understand?"

Senya nodded, even as she wondered what kind of trouble Arrakas feared from her—and how she could cause worse.

Arrakas nudged his horse forward to await the Thranes' arrival. Senya saw him straighten his cloak, ensuring that the large brooch at his throat was clearly visible, since its chimera symbol marked him as an heir of House Deneith and a Sentinel Marshal.

The knights rode hard to meet them. The leader of the charge circled a raised hand in the air as he came to a halt, and the others spread out to encircle the intruders. When all the knights were in position, they lowered their lances in unison—all except the leader, who sat unmoving on his steed, his face covered by a full helm. Glancing around the circle at fourteen shining lances leveled in her direction, each carried by a heavily armored rider on a barded warhorse, Senya started to reconsider the idea of causing trouble.

After a few heartbeats, Arrakas gave an exasperated snort and addressed the knights' leader. "Knights of Thrane," he called, "I am Sentinel Marshal Arrakas d'Deneith, traveling your lands in pursuit of a fugitive. Under the provisions of the Treaty of Thronehold pertaining to the order of Sentinel Marshals, I claim safe passage."

"With all due respect, Sentinel Marshal, as far as I am aware the Treaty of Thronehold is about to be torn to shreds. I need to ask where you are going." The knight's voice was muffled by his helm. Senya thought it odd that he had not removed it to speak.

"The fugitive I seek is in Aundair," Arrakas said, "and if I find him quickly then Aundairian forces will not enter this plain."

"So you seek General ir'Brassek," the knight replied.

Senya raised an eyebrow. Could she be imagining that his voice sounded familiar? And why would a Thrane even know who led the Aundairian army, let alone call him General?

"Your scouts and spies are to be commended," Arrakas said.

Senya could see that the Sentinel Marshal was as surprised as she was. She glanced at the knights on either side—their lances were still lowered, and one horse pawed the ground impatiently. This meeting would not end well.

"Six Sentinel Marshals," the knight observed, "and one elf. Who is that, a captured fugitive?"

Arrakas shot Senya a quick glance over his shoulder. "Yes," he answered. "She is an associate of ir'Brassek, an accomplice to his escape."

"Did you capture her in Thrane?"

Arrakas took a deep breath before answering. "No."

"Where, then? In Breland?"

"Yes. Vathirond." Arrakas's voice betrayed his frustration.

"So you have already transported her across one national border and are about to bring her across another? Has she yet stood trial?"

Arrakas drew himself to his full height, still a head shorter than the towering Thrane leader, and his horse pranced in place. His face was crimson, and Senya tried unsuccessfully to suppress a grin. The knight had caught Arrakas in an act that was questionable at best, possibly illegal even under the broad authority granted by the Treaty of Thronehold. That explained Arrakas's nervousness at the knights' approach, as well as his command for Senya to remain silent.

"Sir, you have detained us long enough. There is a great deal at stake here—as you yourself observed, the Treaty of Thronehold and the peace it established may soon lie in ruins. I must demand that you allow us to continue on our way."

"I'm afraid I can't allow that, Sentinel Marshal."

Arrakas drew his sword, and the swords of his six marshals sprang to their hands at once. "Thrane will hear of this."

Something about the knight's voice as he responded jolted Senya. "I certainly hope so," he said, and she suddenly knew where she'd heard his voice before. She threw her head back and laughed, spurring the knights flanking her to wheel on her again, and she kicked herself for not realizing sooner. What appeared to be plate armor under the tabard of the knight leader was actually the armored plating of a warforged soldier. And not just any warforged.

It was Cart.

As the surrounding knights charged, Senya leaned over and grabbed the reins of the rider on her left, pulling his horse closer. Too close for him to swing his sword. He turned in his saddle to face her, trying to free his sword arm. She brought her left hand, clenched around his reins, up into his throat. His horse reared, and Senya leaned over to grab his sword hand. She yanked the sword from his hand as the rider toppled backward out of his saddle.

Senya yanked the reins farther back, keeping the horse off balance, and it finished her work—one of its hoofs crushed the fallen man's chest. Releasing the reins, she brought the dead man's sword around in a wide arc to her right, just in time to block the other marshal's sword as it sliced down toward her leg. As she found her balance in her saddle, she kicked the other horse's flank, sending it prancing forward, carrying the rider out of reach. She sat up, wrapped her reins firmly around her hand and wrist, and took stock of the battlefield.

The Sentinel Marshals were terribly outnumbered—there had been at least two foes for each Sentinel Marshal before Senya made herself part of the equation. Still, they were hardened warriors, and they had so far acquitted themselves well against Cart's soldiers. Four soldiers in Thrane colors lay dead or dying, one of them crushed beneath his bloodied horse. Cart was locked horse-to-horse with Arrakas: she saw him raise his axe high over his head as he pushed Arrakas away with his shield. The man Senya had unhorsed lay motionless on the ground, but he was the only Sentinel Marshal who had fallen.

The other Sentinel Marshal brought his mount under control and wheeled it around to charge her. Senya braced herself in her stirrups and kicked her horse forward to meet the charge head-on. Both horses shied at the last moment, rebelling against their riders' evident desire to bring them into collision. Senya was thrown from her saddle and hit the ground rolling. She somersaulted away from the stamping hooves and stood again, relieved to have solid earth beneath her feet again. She was no more used to mounted combat than her horse was, bred as it was for speed and not war.

The Sentinel Marshal kept his seat and held his sword low as he charged. Senya settled into a relaxed, balanced stance and watched him come, looking for the perfect place to strike. The marshal drew his sword back as he came nearer. She waited as long as possible, then dropped to the ground, slicing her slender blade along the horse's flank. The sword's point traced a line of blood along the charging horse's skin, then caught the saddle strap and cut through it. The horse screamed and bucked, sending rider and saddle flying through the air.

"What would the Valaes Tairn think of me?" Senya muttered. The warrior elves of Valenar revered their horses almost as much as they did their ancestors, and they frowned on attacking an opponent's horse. Senya's mind leaped back to Shae Mordai, and she was off guard when the marshal charged her again, this time on foot.

"Die," the marshal snarled. His sword arced toward her neck, and she lifted her left arm just in time to prevent the blade from cutting deep where her neck and shoulder met. As it was, the sword cut through the leather and flesh of her arm, struck and broke bone, and lodged between the two bones of her forearm before the marshal wrenched it free. Senya felt blood spatter her face and blinked hard to clear her eyes.

"Not yet," Senya gasped.

Her opponent reeled backward with the momentum of pulling his sword back, and she drove her own blade into his belly. He collapsed on the ground, staring blankly up at her, his face contorted in pain. She stabbed him again, in the throat, then rolled him over to stare at the ground. Dropping into a crouch beside him, she took stock of the battlefield again.

Cart and two of his men, still on horseback, ran down a Sentinel Marshal who was trying to flee on foot. Two other men in Thrane colors fought on foot against a second marshal. Otherwise, the battle was over. Senya ripped the midnight-blue cloak off the marshal she'd killed and, using her teeth and one hand, tried to rip it into bandages she could use to bind her arm. The wound was excruciating, and her right hand shook violently as she worked.

Her trembling hand slipped as she tried knotting the first bandage around her arm, sending a fresh jolt of pain from the wound. Her head grew light, and she put her right hand on the ground and lowered her head to steady herself. Just as her vision cleared, a weight settled on the back of her neck, accompanied by the gentle bite of a blade resting against her skin.

"I lost four good soldiers for you." Cart's voice was heavy, and his axe blade on Senya's neck shifted as he spoke.

"You call those good soldiers?" Senya said. "They had the Sentinel Marshals outnumbered two to one, and I took out two marshals by myself. "

"I said they were good soldiers." Cart lifted his blade off Senya's neck, and she pushed herself to her feet and faced him. "Not champions. It's good to see you again, Senya."

Senya smiled, but she had stood too quickly, and she slumped to the ground in a dead faint.

CHAPTER
42

The streets of Stormhome were choked with people, most of them staring into the sky. Bordan had been right: it had not rained within the city walls in the memory of any living resident, though the rolling hills of the island enjoyed mild showers from time to time. The people of the city acted as though the world were about to end.

Let them, Gaven thought. Let it rain. Let the world stop. Arnoth d'Lyrandar is dead.

In front of Gaven walked two dwarves, trying to remain calm and gentle while they nudged people aside to clear a path. Another walked behind him, a hand on his manacles and an axe at the ready. Ossa and the dwarf spellcaster guided Rienne. The last time Gaven had stolen a look backward, the tip of Ossa's dagger was still pressed into the skin of Rienne's neck. Bordan brought up the rear of the strange procession, seeming nearly as disconcerted by the rain as the residents of the city were.

Rienne was manacled and walking under her own power, so the paralyzing spell had ended. He briefly toyed with plans for an escape. He tested the strength of the manacles, trying not to alert the dwarf holding them. He didn't think they would give—they were probably reinforced with magic—and he thought they might even be dampening his own magic. With his hands free and alert to the threat of the spellcaster, Gaven was sure that he could handle the five dwarves and Bordan by himself. With Rienne, he might be able to handle them with his hands still bound. But as long as Ossa's dagger was pressed into Rienne's neck, he couldn't take the chance.

Gaven didn't know where the dwarves were taking them. He had assumed at first that they'd bring him to Stormhome's jail, to hold him until they could arrange transport back to Dreadhold. But the jail was near the center of the city—unless it had relocated during Gaven's imprisonment—and they were headed toward the northern neighborhoods. A few dragonmarked houses had enclaves in the northern district of Six Corners, but neither the dwarves' House Kundarak nor Bordan's House Tharashk were among them. House Deneith's

Sentinel Marshals also occupied a large tower in the city center, not far from the jail. The docks were situated to the southeast, but Gaven realized that he didn't know where in the city airship mooring towers might be concentrated. That became his working assumption: The dwarves and Bordan would load him on an airship for immediate transport back to Dreadhold.

The rain fell harder as they walked, and the mood of the people in the streets grew worse. When lightning flashed in the sky, Gaven heard a woman scream, and he suddenly realized the flaw in his theory. Bordan and Ossa were not stupid enough to put him on an airship—they had both been aboard the *Morning Zephyr* when storms forced her to the ground.

The dwarf behind Gaven yanked on his manacles, and he stopped walking. The leaders of their cavalcade were embroiled in an argument with a group of men who had apparently objected to being pushed aside. The dwarves kept their voices calm, but the men yelled and waved their arms.

"Gaven, listen to me." The dwarf behind him still had a hand on his manacles, and he whispered up to Gaven. Gaven moved his head in the slightest nod.

"It's Darraun," the dwarf said. Gaven almost whirled around to face him. "Don't move. Listen. If we ever get out of these crowds, I'll release your manacles. As soon as you feel them loosened, you need to run, and fast—the way you did in Aerenal. I'll take care of Rienne—just get out of here."

Gaven nodded again, almost imperceptibly. The dwarves in front managed to force an opening into the crowd, and the dwarf who claimed to be Darraun nudged him to start walking again. As they made their way through the crowd, a hundred questions arose in Gaven's mind. In the forefront was what possible reason there could be for him to trust the dwarf of House Kundarak who said he was a human artificer named Darraun.

So Darraun was a changeling—rather, a disguise adopted by a changeling. Gaven had known there was more to the artificer than he let on, and Senya had suggested that Darraun might have connections in the Royal Eyes of Aundair. It fit. But it left open some much larger questions. Why had Darraun been working with Haldren? And why had he infiltrated Ossa's group of dwarves? Was he helping Gaven now in order to return him to Haldren or for some other purpose? Did Gaven want his help, or would it come with a cost he would be unwilling to pay?

The crowds grew thinner but more serious as they entered the Six Corners neighborhood, named for the junction of three roads in an elegant plaza outside the House Orien enclave. The people glowering at the sky there were heirs and functionaries of the dragonmarked houses, speculating at what failure House Lyrandar, their colleague and competitor, might be experiencing.

Gaven kept his arms tense, straining against the manacles to be sure he'd know as soon as—

The manacles clattered to the ground.

Gaven roared, and lightning flashed in the sky. He whirled and thrust his arms out in front of him, and a gust of wind followed his arms in a mighty blast. Bordan, Rienne, Ossa, and the dwarf spellcaster were knocked to the ground, and Ossa's dagger clattered to the cobblestones. Darraun was already running to Rienne, and the blast of air knocked him forward, into a somersault, and back up into his run.

Gaven ran, the wind howling at his back.

He hadn't even thought about where he would run—he'd been too busy thinking and worrying about Darraun. He knew Six Corners well from his childhood, but he wouldn't rely again on a mental map of streets and alleys that was years old. He looked over his shoulder. The Darraun-changeling was locked in battle with Ossa and one other dwarf, and Rienne fought beside him, using mostly her feet since the manacles still bound her hands. Bordan and the other two dwarves ran behind him. As he slowed to look behind, they gained several paces on him.

He had no choice. He had to trust Darraun to get Rienne safely out of there—if the changeling could free her hands, they'd be fine. So without any other plan in mind, he did as Darraun had told him: he ran like he had in Aerenal.

The wind blew like ragged wings at his back, speeding him through Six Corners and beyond, outside the city to the rain-spattered beach. He swept along the sand, leaving only the faintest of footprints. Waves rose up to drench him in their spray, and lightning flashed across the water. Rage and fear and grief overwhelmed him—they took shape around him like forces of nature as powerful as the storm, and he howled with the voice of the wind.

Sandy beach gave way to sharp rocks that cut his feet as he ran across them, but he felt no pain. His pursuers were lost in the distance, Stormhome had been swallowed in the mist and rain behind him, and even Rienne and Darraun were all but forgotten. Storm clouds blotted out the sunset and swallowed the stars. Soon he climbed above the tumultuous waves as the rocky beach rose toward the jagged cliffs at the far end of the island.

He ran, buoyed and buffeted by the wind, until he reached the highest bluff. Part of him imagined running off the point and either plunging down onto the rocks or somehow running onward, upward, becoming one with the storm. He stood at the precipice for a moment, suspended in the air, his eyes fixed on the waves crashing against the jagged rocks below, and then he sank to his knees, lifting his gaze to the storm clouds that brooded over the cliffs.

"Father!" he howled to the sky, and the wind howled along the cliffs and blew itself out.

Gaven slumped to the ground.

The rain pounded his back, stinging his skin, and the waves thundered as they crashed against the cliffs. His body clenched like a fist around a knot of grief in his belly, and he pounded his hands against the rock. The storm began to wane and the knot in his gut loosened, and his breathing went from shallow gasps to a slower, deeper flow of air.

He drew one last, long, shuddering breath and uncurled his body, lifting his head to a sky that began to show patches of blue. He saw ships navigating the bay and imagined their crews' relief at the passing of the freak storm. The waves started to quiet, and gulls took to the air again, calling to each other with keening cries.

Arnoth d'Lyrandar is dead, he thought, but life will go on. It must.

He stood, taking another deep breath, and looked behind him for any sign of his pursuers. The beach was still deserted, but a ring of fire flickered in the sky, growing quickly larger as the airship it propelled drew nearer. He watched it warily, feeling power welling up within him while hoping he would not have to use it again—he was so tired. Finally he saw a figure in the prow, arms waving in the air—Rienne. The airship was the *Eye of the Storm,* his brother's vessel.

Gaven turned back to the sea and thought of Thordren, and his father, until Rienne called down from the airship above him. "Gaven! Are you all right?"

He looked over his shoulder and saw a rope ladder hanging over the ship's bulwarks, dangling just outside of his reach. Rienne leaned out over the top of the ladder, a look of worry on her face.

"I'm fine," he called. He walked slowly to stand just below the end of the ladder, and carelessly jumped up to grab the lowest rung. "Don't worry about me," he said as he started to climb.

The airship jerked in the air, nearly throwing Gaven off the ladder. He saw Rienne clutching the bulwarks, her eyes wide. "I'm not worried about you," she hollered back. "I'm worried about how long Darraun can fly this thing. Hurry!"

Gaven clambered up the ladder as fast as he could, even as it writhed and jerked in his hands. Rienne helped him over the edge, and shoved him aft, where Darraun clutched the wheel—and wore Darraun's face again. That face was chalk white, and his eyes were wide. He didn't give any sign of recognition as Gaven approached him.

"He's been trying to convince the elemental that he has the Mark of Storm," Rienne explained, "but it's a losing battle."

Gaven saw a pattern on the changeling's skin that suggested a Lyrandar dragonmark, but it wouldn't fool even a casual observer, let alone grant Darraun the magical ability to control the airship.

Gaven moved to stand behind Darraun and reached his arms around the smaller man to clutch the wheel.

Be still, he told the elemental, channeling his will into the helm and into the conduits that bound the elemental to the ship. *A true heir of Storm commands you now.*

The ship stopped bucking, and Darraun slumped to the deck in front of Gaven. Rienne took his hand and led him out of Gaven's way. Pulling Darraun's arm around her shoulder, she led him below decks. Gaven stepped closer to the wheel and settled into a comfortable stance. A smile blossomed on his face as the ship responded to his every thought, soaring smoothly away from the island and into the clearing sky.

Since Darraun had first mentioned airships to him in Whitecliff, Gaven had been waiting for this moment. Since he had first laid eyes on one in Korranberg, he had dreamed of standing at an airship's helm. His smile broadened into a boyish grin, as a single thought ran over and over through his mind:

I was born for this!

*　*　*　*　*

Bordan fell to his knees on the sandy beach. The dwarves hadn't been able to match his speed, though he wouldn't be surprised if they ran all the way to Storm Point before they flagged. He glared up at the airship receding into the rain, the sign of his defeat. Gaven had escaped him again.

The storm lashed him, though it had diminished as Gaven got farther and farther away. Gaven had been the cause and the center of the storm. Bordan was sure of it. A harder rain had begun almost at the moment that he'd knocked on Arnoth's door. The thunder that accompanied Gaven's kick—he rubbed his sore head thinking of it—and the wind that had literally carried him out of the city made it clear. The storm obeyed Gaven's command—or at least echoed his emotions, overriding the will of Esravash d'Lyrandar, the house matriarch, and all the Lyrandar heirs who worked together to maintain the paradisal climate of Stormhome.

Despite his boasts to Gaven's face, Bordan found himself grappling with serious doubt for the first time in his career. Perhaps he could continue finding Gaven—but he'd found Gaven twice already and been unable to apprehend him. What if he never caught him? And even if he caught Gaven, could he hold him? Or would he meet the same fate as Evlan d'Deneith?

Could even Dreadhold contain a man with the power of the storm at his command?

The beach grew darker, as though a new storm cloud covered the sun. Bordan felt rather than heard a presence behind him, and he leaped to his feet.

A pool of shadow had formed on the white sand, roiling like smoke at the feet of Phaine d'Thuranni. An elf woman garbed in black stood just behind Phaine. Both elves had weapons drawn.

"Damn it, Thuranni, I didn't hear you approach."

"Few ever do," the elf replied, taking a step forward. The darkness moved with him, clinging to him as he walked.

"What's this about? Did you follow Gaven here?"

"Yes. He escaped." Another step closer. "Again."

"Now, wait a moment, Thuranni. If you had any inkling of his power—"

"I believe I do."

"Did you see that storm?" Bordan said. "Do you know what he's done?"

"Far better than you do."

"Do you know what he's been ranting about all these years? What he's been dreaming?"

Phaine wrinkled his nose in disgust. "My blood is from an undiluted line of Aerenal, *human*." He drew out the last word with a vicious sneer. "I know."

Bordan's gaze flicked between the two elves. "What are you doing?" he said. "Gaven is the enemy here."

"Of course," Phaine said.

The elf woman spoke for the first time. "We can't let you fail again. He grows stronger each time."

"Why don't you get him, then?"

"We will," Phaine answered.

"And this is what we'll do to him," Leina added.

Both elves' swords spun in a burst of motion, and Bordan fell to the blood-spattered sand.

CHAPTER
43

The sun was dipping below the horizon, setting the last shreds of storm clouds ablaze with yellow and red, when Rienne returned to the main deck. Gaven watched as she looked up at the sky, and he smiled at the way the sunset glowed in her hair and eyes. She leaned against a railing near the wheel and smiled at him.

"How's Darraun?" he said.

"Exhausted, but he'll be fine." She glanced at the hatch leading below. "I suppose we owe him our lives, or at least our freedom."

"Again," Gaven said. He remembered his first glimpse of freedom from his cell in Dreadhold: the Ring of Siberys framed within a ragged hole in the stone ceiling, the warforged jumping down and trying to coax him out, and then Darraun, finally, standing at his side and bringing him back to his senses. It seemed so long ago, and Dreadhold just a memory of a dream.

"Did you know he was a changeling?" Rienne asked.

"No idea. I remember that almost from the beginning I knew he was hiding something. He didn't quite fit in with the others—he was the only one who would even think of challenging Haldren, for one thing. And Senya thought he had some connection to the Royal Eyes. But a changeling?" Gaven shook his head, remembering the dwarf who had released his manacles—the same one who had barged through Thordren's back door and landed in a pile of cooking pots—and struggling to find any similarity to the familiar human artificer. "No, I can still hardly believe it."

"It sort of makes you think, doesn't it? Anyone you talk to could be a changeling, really—even someone you think you know. How can you ever be sure?"

Gaven had no answer for that.

Rienne watched him for a while, her eyes following the slight movements of his arms as he steered the airship over the sea. "So you're flying an airship," she said at last, a smile spreading across her face, gleaming white in her dark skin.

Gaven returned the smile. "I am," he said. "It's wonderful."

"Is it hard?"

"Not in the least. She's really not very different from a ship on the water. And the elemental does most of the work."

"It seemed to be plenty of work for Darraun."

"Oh, it was. These wheels are made to channel the power of a dragonmark —they're the same ones they use on the seagoing galleons. They won't work for just anyone."

"It's fortunate he was able to do it at all."

"Yes, but not altogether surprising. Artificers are good at making magic work the way they want."

Rienne ambled a few steps toward the prow. Gaven watched her as she stared ahead for a moment, then to the right, then to the left. She searched the horizon for a long moment, then turned back to him and asked the obvious question. "So where are we going?"

He gave her a sad smile. "If you don't know what you want, you're sure to do what someone else wants."

"That's my line," she said with a grin, but then her face grew serious, and she stepped closer. "So what do you mean by that? Are we still talking about you and your destiny, or are you making some kind of comment about me?"

"I mean it's time for me to decide. I've spent my whole life squirming under the pressure of other people's expectations, without ever deciding who I want to be and what I want to do. It's time for me to grow up, to stop defining my life by whining, 'No, I don't want to do *that*.'"

Rienne laughed at his exaggerated voice.

"Do you know," Gaven continued, "before my Test of Siberys I must have prayed to each of the Nine Sovereigns a hundred times, asking that I wouldn't show a dragonmark?"

Rienne frowned. "You never told me that."

"It's true. And I always felt like my father knew it, or at least blamed me for failing the test. I think he always figured that once my mark manifested, I'd come around—I'd be the dutiful son he wanted me to be, and follow in his footsteps. I guess I must have figured that if I did get a mark, I would pretty much have to. And that's why I wanted so badly not to get one."

"I don't want to do *that*." Rienne mimicked Gaven's whining voice.

"Exactly. I never wanted to do what I was supposed to do."

"And yet you served your house well, all those years with me."

"By working around House Tharashk to get better deals on dragonshards. By working outside the system."

Rienne stepped closer. "Very well, you rebel. So now you're fighting against expectations again. Some ancient dragon inside your head wants to become a god, but you're not going to do that. Haldren wanted you working for him, but you weren't about to do that. You're supposed to go back to Dreadhold and rot like a dutiful prisoner, but I note we're not sailing east to Dreadhold. We're sailing west. So what are you going to do?"

Gaven's brow furrowed, and he looked away. "I think I'm going to be a hero."

"Really?" Rienne almost laughed, but she reined it in when she saw the seriousness of his eyes.

Gaven blinked back tears. "The elder son of Arnoth d'Lyrandar could be nothing less."

She closed the distance between them and placed a hand on his chest. "He was proud of you, you know."

Gaven nodded, but he stared down at the wheel. "The memories of him that come most readily to my mind are the stern father, judging and distant and gruff. I don't know why those are so much easier to remember than the kinder moments, the times he made it clear how much I meant to him. The way his eyes would shine when he talked about me, positively beaming with pride." He looked up and found Rienne's eyes. "That's an expectation I suddenly find that I want to live up to."

She held his gaze, then reached an arm behind his neck to pull his mouth down to hers.

*   *   *   *   *

The changeling was dreaming—he knew that much, but the knowledge did nothing to help him navigate the chaos. A jumble of identities, names and faces and personas, stumbling through one unlikely crisis after another. At last he stood in his true form in the awesome presence of a goddess.

"The Traveler," he said. "Bless your ten thousand names."

But the Traveler wore the face of his paladin acquaintance of recent months—a tall half-elf with short red hair and blue-gray eyes—and she glowed with an argent radiance like the Silver Flame of the Thranes.

"Who are you?" she asked him.

"Auftane Khunnam," he said, and he was a dwarf, all black and brown and sturdy, strong.

"Who are you?" she asked again.

"Haunderk Lannath." Human, sandy hair, scheming.

"Who are you?"

"Darraun Mennar." Prying, planning, blond.

"Who are you?"

"Caura Fannam." Poor Jenns. Compassion, care.

"Who are you?"

"Baunder Fronn." Simple, stout, stupid.

"Who are you?"

"Vauren Hennalan." Brave, honorable, prig.

"Who are you?"

"Natan Durbannek." Another dwarf. A killer.

"Who are you?"

"Aurra Hennalan." Mischievous elf.

"Who are you?"

There were so many, and the Traveler seemed unwilling to accept any answer he gave.

"Who are you?"

He awoke, sweating and shaking, panic racing through his veins. He was in a swaying bunk in a pitch-dark cabin, and he couldn't remember where he was or—most importantly—who he was supposed to be. He put his hands to his face and felt his features: male, human, thirties. Aboard an airship. Who was with him? Kelas? No. Janik and Dania? No. Haldren? Closer, but no. Gaven, of course.

Real memories started taking shape in his mind, crowding out the confused memory of his dream. His most recent dwarf persona, Natan Durbannek. Helping to capture Gaven in Stormhome, and then helping him escape. Piloting the airship from one end of the island to the other, which made him tired just to remember it.

What in the world had he done? He had revealed himself to Gaven and Rienne, tripling the number of people in the world who knew that he was a changeling. And why? Had it been essential for his mission?

He tried to roll out of his bunk and ended up in a heap on the floor. He curled inward, clutching his head. What was his mission? What in the Traveler's ten thousand names was he doing here?

"Make it solid," he whispered. This was not like him at all—he had never in his thirty years questioned a mission or lost his grip on an identity. He struck his head against the floor and reverted to the training disciplines of his youth. "Who are you?" he said. "I am Au—Au . . . What the blazes is my name?"

"Darraun," a woman's voice said. He scrambled on the floor, turning himself to see the woman standing in the open hatch of the cabin, silhouetted in front of a night sky dimly lit by the Ring of Siberys. "Or that's what Gaven calls you, anyway."

"Rienne," he said. He felt like a child just learning the names for everything in the world.

"That's right. I'm Rienne." Her voice sounded bemused, but her face was still in darkness. "Are you all right?"

"Am I . . . ? No." He started to get to his feet. "That is, I think so." He reached out and grabbed another swaying bunk, trying in vain to steady himself.

"Do you need more sleep?" Rienne took a step farther into the room, and her features began to resolve in the darkness. "Do you want me to help you back into bed?"

"No! Not more sleep. No, thank you." He managed to stand, and put a hand on her shoulder.

"Good, because Gaven wants to talk to you before we get much closer to Haldren's camp."

"Haldren's camp? What in the Ten Seas does he think he's doing?"

"You'll have to ask him that."

"All right," the changeling said. Darraun, he thought. Darraun Mennar. "You go ahead. I'll be there in a moment."

"Are you sure?"

"Quite sure." Darraun Mennar. Darraun was polite, friendly. "Thank you."

Rienne turned, halfway out of the cabin, and smiled back at him. "You're welcome." Then she was gone.

He buried his fingers in his hair, ran them down his face, wrapped himself in his arms, ran his hands down his legs. He knew this body—he'd worn it for months. He knew Darraun. He was ready. He started out the cabin door.

But Gaven and Rienne knew he was a changeling. He stopped dead. What would that mean? How would they treat him now? Did it matter if he acted like Darraun or not?

Best to appear familiar, reassure them that he was the same Darraun that Gaven knew. He took a deep breath, and wished that Darraun were a little braver. Vauren Hennalan could face dangerous and uncertain situations like this with ease. Darraun had been worried about finding himself lost in the Aerenal woods.

Shuddering at the memory of a city filled with the undying, Darraun climbed the stairs to the main deck.

* * * * *

"Have you seen Haldren's camp?" Gaven demanded as soon as Darraun's head came above the level of the deck.

To his credit, Darraun answered without hesitation. "Not the camp where he is now. His forces marched after I left." As he spoke, he climbed the rest of the stairs and came to stand near the helm.

"Why did you leave?"

"Haldren discovered me spying on him."

Gaven arched an eyebrow. "I'm surprised you got out."

"That's because you know more about Haldren's capabilities than about mine. Haldren makes a show of his power. I do not."

"Fair enough. I've always known there was more to you than you let on."

Gaven remembered Cart interrupting their conversation in Whitecliff, insisting that he, too, was "quite complex." He chuckled, and noticed Darraun doing the same. Their eyes met, and at the same time, they said, "Many-layered." Then both men burst into laughter.

"Clearly, I missed something," Rienne said, folding her arms and smiling.

"I'll explain later," Gaven said. "What can you tell me about Haldren's movements since he left Paluur Draal?"

"He was quite distressed at your disappearance—or at Senya's, really. He was convinced you had pulled her out of the circle to use as a hostage. From that point on, your knowledge of the Prophecy meant nothing to him. He would have tracked you down and killed you, or tried to, to get Senya back."

"How touching," Gaven said. "If only Senya shared his devotion."

Darraun raised both eyebrows. "If only. So we met with Vaskar on the shore of Lake Brey, and Haldren gave him the Eye of Siberys."

"Vaskar has it?"

"As far as I know he still does, yes." Darraun paused. "From there we went to Lathleer, in Aundair, and laid low for a few days. When we were in Whitecliff, Haldren sent word of his escape to a few of his closest friends in the army, and that blossomed into a meeting with seven of them in Bluevine. He swayed them to his cause, promised them a flight of dragons to assure their victory, and sent them off to gather troops."

"A flight of dragons?"

A clash of dragons . . .

A sense of doom gripped Gaven's heart.

"That was Vaskar's end of the bargain, in exchange for Haldren's help in getting the Eye of Siberys and extracting whatever other information he could get out of you. Vaskar persuaded a fairly large number of dragons to come and form the vanguard of Haldren's army."

"And by the rumors of war I heard today, I assume that Haldren has amassed his army, gathered his dragons, and begun his march toward Thrane."

"That's right."

Gaven thought over what the changeling had told him. Darraun's manner had seemed perfectly straightforward—he could read no trace of deception. The story all made sense, and fit with what little he already knew about Haldren's movements. He couldn't help himself—he liked Darraun, he always had, and knowing that he was a changeling and a spy did nothing to diminish that.

I've got no choice but to trust him, he thought.

He glanced at Darraun and broke his silence. "Do you know where they're camped?"

"No. The original plan was to strike down the coast into Thaliost, but Haldren changed the plan after he discovered me."

"How do you know?" Gaven asked.

"Before I escaped the camp, he gave orders to march, a week ahead of schedule. After I got away, I spent some time in Flamekeep, where I learned that Thrane is concentrating its defense on an old battlefield called the Starcrag Plain."

"The plain that lies in the sunset shadow of the mountains of stars," Gaven said. Again the dread gripped him, and he took a deep breath.

"What?" Darraun said, but then he nodded. "Yes, it's to the east of the Starpeaks."

"They're attacking there in order to fulfil the Prophecy. Sovereigns," Gaven said, "it's going to be a bloodbath."

CHAPTER
44

While Darraun and Rienne slept, Gaven was left alone on the deck. The Ring of Siberys shone bright overhead, and the approaching dawn stained clouds in the eastern sky red. To his mind, they whispered warnings of doom: the shining ring of dragonshards that lit the night foretold the consummation of a prophetic cycle, the emergence of the Soul Reaver and the revelation of the Storm Dragon, while the bloody signs of dawn spoke plainly of the cost that would be paid in human lives.

He turned the airship inland, and absently guided her between the darkness of the Whisper Wood on his right and the shadows of the Gray Wood on his left, following a narrow strip of grassy land between the two forests. He was grateful that the navigation didn't require more attention—his vision seemed to keep slipping between the reality that presented itself to his senses and something deeper, the language of creation.

The Prophecy was written everywhere. Everything he saw spoke of its past and its potential. As he piloted the *Eye of the Storm* between Aundair's primeval forest and its younger offspring, making his way to the jutting Starpeaks, he saw the words that had made them and heard distant echoes of the language they strained to speak. And images of his nightmares flashed through his mind, tastes of the horrors those lands would see.

Vultures wheeling over fields strewn with corpses. The howling hordes of the Soul Reaver boiling up from Khyber and spreading out across the land. Legions of soldiers beneath the banner of the Blasphemer. Dragons in the sky.

The visions blended and blurred together, weaving themselves into a tapestry of horror in which he could no longer discern individual threads. Haldren's march to war would not be the end of the nightmare.

* * * * *

Rienne emerged from below decks at dawn, and Gaven watched with a tired half smile as she stretched and practiced with Maelstrom at the keel. Darraun came up a little later, rubbing his stomach.

"Do you think Thordren had any supplies stashed away?" he asked no one in particular.

"You're welcome to look below," Rienne said, "but don't get your hopes up."

Darraun disappeared back down the forward hatch, and Rienne hopped up onto the bulwarks' railings, keeping perfect balance as she practiced complex sequences of lunges, parries, and ripostes. Gaven watched carefully, and chose a moment when her balance seemed most tenuous to jerk hard on the wheel, making the ship lurch to port.

Rienne didn't miss a step in her exercise, but Darraun let out a cry of pain from the cargo hold. A moment later his head appeared in the hatch.

"Everything all right?" he called to Gaven.

"Fine, sorry," Gaven said. "Did you hurt yourself?"

"Just cracked my head on a beam." He rubbed his scalp, then checked his fingers for blood.

"Maybe you should go back to being a dwarf," Rienne suggested.

Darraun scowled and dropped below again.

"Do you think I hurt his feelings?" Rienne asked.

"I don't know."

"Aha!" Darraun yelled from below. "We've got breakfast!"

Rienne stepped lightly from the railing to peer down the hatch. "What did you find?"

Darraun emerged with an armload of small boxes and a strip of dried beef dangling from his mouth. "Lady Alastra," he mumbled around the meat. He left his sentence unfinished as he began setting out the foodstuffs he had gathered—pickled vegetables, dried fruits, nuts, and salted beef. When he had swallowed, he addressed Rienne again. "Lady Alastra, I hope that we have the pleasure of traveling in each other's company under better circumstances so that I can cook you a proper meal. But for the present, please enjoy these . . . erm, trail rations, with my compliments."

Rienne and Gaven laughed. "He really is quite a cook," Gaven added. "I'll vouch for him."

"There are many men to whom I would entrust my dinner," Rienne said, bowing slightly to Darraun. "There are precious few to whom I would entrust my life. I don't know if I can bring myself to entrust both to the same man, but it would be an illustrious honor indeed."

Darraun smiled awkwardly, then busied himself with the food.

* * * * *

With the help of a box of spices he unearthed from his pack, Darraun managed to make even the preserved food palatable, which earned him a new measure of respect in Rienne's eyes. As the day wore on, Gaven found himself dozing at the wheel, while Rienne and Darraun took turns pacing along the prow. They left the Gray Wood behind and followed the curve of the Whisper Wood's edge along to the south, then left it as well, making straight for the eastern edge of the Starpeaks. Any movement on the rocky plain below brought a moment of intense scrutiny and heightened tension, then a return to the interminable waiting once the lookout realized it was just an animal or a farmer or a gust of wind below.

Rienne and Darraun were so focused on searching the ground below that it was actually Gaven who spotted the first real threat. "Check the sky," he called, "four points to port!"

The sun was high in the sky, but beginning its descent behind the Starpeaks on the airship's port side. Darraun had to cup his hands around his eyes, but Rienne spotted it immediately.

"A dragon," she said.

"Are you sure?" Gaven shouted. "It's not very big."

Rienne wheeled and gave him an incredulous stare. "Not very big?" she said.

"No, he's right," Darraun said. "Compared to Vaskar, this one's small, immature. No bigger than a bear."

"If you mean one of those Eldeen bears that the druids send before them in war to tear up enemy infantry, I'll grant you that." Rienne gripped Maelstrom in a trembling hand.

"Yes, that's exactly the kind of bear I mean," Darraun said.

The dragon closed on them quickly—it had clearly seen them before Gaven spotted it. The sun gleamed dull red on its scales, and Gaven's mind filled with the image of the *Morning Zephyr* in flames outside the Mournland. He had a sudden, unsettling realization.

"How do I land this thing?" he called.

"*Land* her?" Darraun said. "I don't think you do. That's why they have mooring towers."

"Well, start looking for a mooring tower. I don't want to be in the air when that thing breathes fire on this ship."

"No," Rienne said, "you should be able to do a ground landing in a ship this size. Smaller airships like this are designed to moor just about anywhere."

"Then take a look beneath us, and tell me where to set her down." He glanced at the onrushing dragon, now close enough that he could distinguish its horns and the predatory curve to its mouth. Rienne rushed to the starboard side and peered over the edge.

"Rocky, very steep—and trees to the east. I don't see—"

"Oh, damn it to the Darkness!" Gaven swore. He stretched one hand to the clear blue sky, and the sun went dark, blotted out by a black thunderhead that appeared from nowhere. He jerked his hand downward, and a bolt of lightning thundered out of the sky and struck the onrushing dragon. For an instant, it hung suspended in the air, engulfed in burning light, then it plummeted downward.

Spreading its wings, the dragon pulled out of its fall and swooped back up toward the airship, sending a blistering gout of fire from its gaping maw ahead of its flight. The flames parted around the keel and licked up around the bulwarks, but it seemed that much of their energy was pulled into the ring of fire surrounding the ship, making it flare brightly for a moment, then fade back to normal.

Gaven smiled. "Looks like I was more worried about the fire than I should have been," he said.

"Don't get too confident," Rienne shot back.

As if reinforcing Rienne's warning, the airship lurched suddenly to starboard. The wheel jerked free of Gaven's hand and started spinning wildly.

"Concentrate on the helm,"' Rienne said. "Let me and Darraun handle the dragon."

When Gaven touched the wheel again, flames leaped out from its wooden spokes and seared his hands. Gaven cried out, more in surprise than pain, and eyed the wheel warily.

"The dragon's breath gave the elemental a taste of freedom," Rienne explained. "You need to remind it who's in charge."

"Maybe riding horseback isn't so bad after all," Gaven grumbled as he approached the wheel again.

"You ever let a stallion think he's in charge?"

"Good point." Gaven seized the helm again, ignoring a new flare from the wheel. *Be still!* he commanded the elemental, and he felt it rebel against his control—very much like a spirited horse pulling against its reins. For an instant, the fire that formed a ring around the airship flickered and died away, letting the airship fall freely, but Gaven stretched out his will like a whip and brought both elemental and ship back under control.

Which meant that he could do nothing but watch as the dragon's fiery breath engulfed both Rienne and Darraun where they stood on the deck. Rienne tumbled away and stood up again barely singed, but Darraun could do nothing but huddle on the deck and weather the blast's greatest force. In the wake of its breath, the dragon swooped in and alit on the deck, stretching its wings into the air to keep its balance.

As the flames died around Darraun, wisps of smoke trailed off him, but to Gaven's surprise he leaped toward the dragon as though he'd just been immersed in water rather than fire. As he hefted his mace, Gaven noticed a ring on Darraun's hand that glowed red as if it had been newly forged in the inferno, and he suspected that the artificer had turned the ring into a magic ward against fire before the dragon's onslaught.

The dragon's enormous wings made it seem considerably larger than a bear—even an Eldeen bear. Its head whipped away from Darraun's mace, then arched back around to bite at his shoulder even as it lifted its front claws to tear at him. It was caught off guard and off balance, though, as Rienne tumbled into it, slamming both feet into its chest. She knocked it backward, and Maelstrom was ready to cut at its neck as it yanked back. The magic blade only nicked its scaled neck, and it retreated a couple of steps to regain its balance, all four feet firmly on the deck. Its neck swept back and forth as it sized up its opponents.

At almost the last moment, Gaven remembered.

An arcane word sheathed him in cool fire that would protect him from the dragon's breath. Then fire spewed from the creature's mouth in a great blast that engulfed all three of them and started several small fires on the deck. Gaven took cover behind the wheel, and his fiery shield protected him from the rest of the blast. Darraun laughed it off, and again Rienne bounced clear of the worst of it—her constant movement in battle was both her strongest offense and her best defense. She proved it by leaping onto the dragon's back and bringing Maelstrom down hard into its neck, spraying a gout of steaming blood onto the deck. The dragon thrashed and reared, throwing Rienne backward off the deck.

Darraun lunged to the prow, his panicked look telling Gaven everything he needed to know. The dragon leaped into the air, pushing away from the airship so hard that the prow bobbed downward, then spun itself in the air to plummet downward, following Rienne to the ground—out of sheer malice or perhaps blind fury. Gaven released the helm, and a gust of wind lifted him off the deck. A quick glance around showed him that Rienne was still falling, and an equally quick gesture brought a whirlwind out of the brewing storm to lift her safely out of her fall. With the merest thought, he impaled the dragon on another bolt of lightning. After Rienne's deadly blow, the dragon had no more strength to evade or resist the blast, and its charred corpse spiraled away like an autumn leaf, dry and drained of life.

But as the airship swept past Gaven, caught in a terrible maelstrom of air dragging her to earth, he realized it would take considerably more effort to stop her fall.

CHAPTER
45

The *Eye of the Storm* did not simply drop out of the sky. Snared in the whirling currents of air born of Gaven's storm, she spun in a great wheel through the air, her magical buoyancy still fighting against the downward pull. At the same time, the elemental bound within her flared to rebellion in the absence of Gaven's control, coursing visibly through the arcane channels carved into the hull. Gaven didn't see Darraun immediately, but after a moment spotted him clutching the wheel, struggling to control the ship as he had in Stormhome. A valiant effort, but one doomed to failure.

Gaven's first impulse was to crush the airship between irresistible blasts of air, to shoot her through with lightning and scatter her flinders to the wind. Destruction was the easy path, the purest manifestation of his power. So simple, so tempting. The impulse startled him—his friend was aboard that ship. Why would he destroy her?

Gaven snarled his frustration, and lightning coursed around him. Destruction was easy. It was far more challenging to create, to build, to save. His anger was a tight knot in his gut—he felt it as he roared, like nausea. He wanted to curl his body around it, cradle it in his arms and vomit it out.

The wind tore at him in a manifestation of his rage, and the airship bucked against Darraun's control.

No, Gaven thought. I need to let it go.

Layers upon layers of rage and resentment fueled the storm. The dragon's attack mattered little, just the fury of a misguided minion, now undone. A thin layer of anger, easily sloughed away.

Haldren's brewing rebellion angered him, the way Haldren had used him, manipulated him, coerced him. Was that truly significant? Haldren had also engineered his release from Dreadhold, and his attempt at conquest would soon be quashed. The world would return to its uneasy peace. Another layer gone.

The howling of the wind diminished, and Darraun managed to tame the blazing elemental fire in the airship, leaving only the bright ring.

Twenty-six years in Dreadhold . . .

Haunted by visions, plagued by nightmares, abused by guards and fellow prisoners alike . . .

So utterly alone in the wilderness of his mind.

Waking from sleep, night after night, to stumble to the door and speak his dreams through the shutter in the door—he'd done it long before Haldren had come to occupy the cell across the hall, as though giving his dreams voice would help exorcise them from his mind.

Carving the words into the floor and walls of his cell—writing them in his blood before they finally relented and gave him a stylus to scratch the stone. Trying to make them solid, to ground them, to fix them into the present.

It had nearly driven him mad—perhaps he had gone mad.

He wished for true freedom—freedom from the ceaseless pursuit of Bordan and the Kundarak dwarves, freedom from the visions that still besieged him day and night. That anger seethed and bubbled, fierce and hot. He squeezed his eyes shut and roared again. The wind snatched away his cry and carried his boiling anger with it. His knowledge of the Prophecy might have seemed like a curse in the past, but he was using it to his advantage. It had given him power and insight. It was a gift.

The Heart of Khyber with its stored memories. The dragon who had altered the course of his life. A hard shell of resentment.

"I've given your life a purpose," the dragon said. Its voice was Gaven's.

"I didn't want that purpose."

"But you chose a new one. You can't carry on without one. And you will never again be content to live an ordinary life."

Another gift. The hard shell broke and fell away, leaving a blazing core of molten fury.

Lightning seared through Gaven's body, and he hung in the sky. Lightning flowed through each hand and foot and poured from his mouth as he screamed.

Rienne shook him gently awake. He sat bolt upright—he heard the jangle of chainmail.

Tears streamed down Rienne's face. He was too stung by her betrayal to resist the Sentinel Marshals.

The person he loved most in the world sent him to Dreadhold. This anger was thick and hot, and would not fall away so easily.

At night in Dreadhold, waiting for the nightmares to come, he lay in his bunk and nursed that anger.

Rienne testified to the Tribunal. She wanted to convince them he needed help, but instead she convinced them of his guilt.

He glanced down to where she hung in the air, held aloft by the winds at his command. Again the urge to destroy welled up in him. It would be so easy to let her fall.

Four Sentinel Marshals struggled to restrain him. He wanted to get to Rienne, to break her neck, to tear her small, lithe body apart with his bare hands.

"Let him live, I implore you." Rienne was pleading for him, even as he tried to reach her. "By all that is holy, have mercy! If he is mad, who knows but that he might one day recover his senses?"

For twenty-six years he'd nurtured a lie—a lie that let him focus his anger outward at her, instead of inward. Rienne had not betrayed him, she had tried to protect him. She had acted out of her love for him. He had kept her out while the Heart of Khyber had wormed its way into his heart—he had betrayed her.

"Don't you think I deserve an explanation?" she said.

"No."

"I think I do. I loved you once, Gaven, and you made me believe you loved me."

Sobs wracked his body. "I'm sorry, Ree," he whispered, and he imagined that the wind carried his voice down to her.

The knot of his anger was stripped down to its core.

"Let me see you, Gaven." Arnoth stood over the parched, feverish body of his son.

Gaven huddled under a blanket that chafed against his sunburned skin.

"Let me see him," Arnoth said.

Someone pulled the blanket off him, and Gaven felt his father's eyes searching him, looking for any sign of a dragonmark. In vain—Gaven had failed his test.

A blur of faces surrounded him, but one face stood out clearly—his father's, trying to smile.

"I am not you!" Gaven cried into the storm.

A young Gaven held an orb of magical light in his palm, full of excitement at his first successful spell. "Look, father!" he cried.

Arnoth stood in the doorway, leaning against the jamb, smiling with pride. "Well done, Gaven," he said. "Keep practicing." He turned away, returning to his work.

Gaven dismissed the spell and refused to try it again for a week's time.

All his life Gaven had resented the firm hand of a domineering father, and had blamed Arnoth for every act of rebellion he had committed. He had imagined a father who was determined to mold his son into a replica of himself, and he'd been blind to the pride Arnoth took in the son he had—not the son Gaven thought he wanted.

"Why don't you apply yourself, Gaven?" An older Arnoth frowned in the doorway as Gaven packed supplies for an expedition into Khyber, hunting for dragonshards.

"I am applying myself," Gaven said, not looking up. "And doing good for the house."

"But you could do so much more! You have greatness in you, Gaven."

Greatness? Gaven thought. You mean I have you in me. I am not you!

Gaven had avoided any achievement of consequence, and used his father's high expectations as an excuse for his own failure. He had clung to the image of a stern and distant father because that was an image it was easy to blame—and for years he had channeled his anger at that image instead of at himself.

A fresh wave of grief surged through him.

I love you, father.

Lightning blasted the rock around Gaven's feet, and only then did he realize that he had come down to the ground. He blinked and looked around, and saw Rienne standing ten paces away, staring into the air with wide eyes. He followed her gaze to where the *Eye of the Storm* floated calmly under a slate-gray sky.

* * * * *

Darraun managed to get the ship down close to the ground, and Gaven and Rienne climbed back aboard. Darraun was glad to relinquish the helm, but worry creased his face.

"I spotted Haldren's forces," he said, gesturing vaguely to the south. "They're on the march already."

"We should have no trouble catching up to them," Gaven said as he settled himself in at the helm. Darraun had done well piloting the ship this time; the elemental seemed much more docile already.

"Not to the ground troops, no," Darraun said. "But I also saw the dragons taking wing."

"The dragons," Gaven grimly. "A clash of dragons . . ." He rubbed his chin.

"Gaven?" Rienne said.

Gaven put both hands to the wheel again and lifted the airship higher. "Thordren named this vessel well—we're flying into the eye of the storm, now, friends, and I think we've just seen our last bit of calm weather."

"What do you mean?" Rienne demanded, coming to face him across the wheel.

"Vaskar knows the Prophecy, or at least this part of it: 'A clash of dragons signals the sundering of the Soul Reaver's gates.' Vaskar's whole purpose here is to open those gates, so he can fight the Soul Reaver and be the Storm Dragon, claiming that divine power. But it has to be a clash of dragons. What are the dragons on the Thrane side?"

Darraun came closer, leaning back against a nearby railing. "Other dragons, or people with dragonmarks?"

"There have to be dragons, and they have to be part of Vaskar's plan. I'm sure he hasn't just left it to chance, hoping some dragonmarked heir is fighting on Thrane's side for some reason and will fight a dragon for the sake of the Prophecy."

"You think he's double-crossed Haldren," Rienne said.

"Exactly. He promised Haldren he'd bring dragons to fight alongside his armies—military might unknown in the Last War and unsurpassed among the armies of Khorvaire. And then he turned around and brought another group of dragons to fight on the other side."

"Will it work?" Darraun said. "How can he make the dragons fight each other?"

"From what I understand, it often doesn't take much. Dragons often don't get along with each other. They're territorial. The whole continent of Argonnessen is carved up into dragon territories, and many areas are hotly contested. And when they're not fighting over territory, they fight over the Prophecy. It only takes a spark to ignite a conflagration."

Darraun looked puzzled as Gaven spoke, but when he'd finished he burst into laughter.

"What?" Rienne said.

"What a web of lies Vaskar must be weaving. It's funny: I always thought Haldren was a conniving manipulator who could bend almost anyone to his will given a moment of conversation. I never stopped to think what kind of dragon joins forces with a man like that."

"Exactly the same kind of dragon," Gaven said.

"Right. When I was camped with Haldren's forces, after the dragons joined up, I remember wondering what part these dragons thought they played in the Prophecy. I assumed they wanted to help Vaskar fulfill it. But now I think those dragons are over in Thrane, just waiting for Haldren's dragons to come into sight so they can initiate the 'clash of dragons' long foretold."

"So then what do Haldren's dragons think they're doing?" Rienne asked.

"He's brought them here with some other piece of the Prophecy," Gaven said. "I'm sure of it. There's something at the edge of my mind—'where dragons flew.' "

Gaven closed his eyes. He remembered seeing his reflection, touching glass, starting as though he'd touched a fire. The reflection in the mirror—an image of desolation.

The vision that had sprung to his mind in his father's house, in the shadow of death. He whispered the words that had come to him: "Vultures wheel where dragons flew, picking the bones of the numberless dead."

"Gaven?" Rienne had come around the wheel and laid a gently hand on his back.

He opened his eyes, but he could not see the world around him any more— only his vision. Words and meaning from the Sky Caves of Thieren Kor took shape in his mind, expanding that fragmentary premonition of doom:

> *Dragons fly before the Blasphemer's legions,*
> *scouring the earth of his righteous foes.*
> *Carnage rises in the wake of his passing,*
> *purging all life from those who oppose him.*
> *Vultures wheel where dragons flew,*
> *picking the bones of the numberless dead.*

Gaven shuddered and shook his head, and saw Rienne's face staring up at him in deep concern.

"He brought them here with a lie," he said finally. "They think they're fulfilling a part of the Prophecy whose time has not yet come. But they believe it guarantees their victory."

CHAPTER
46

Senya had trouble keeping up with Cart and his patrol. Her thoughts kept dwelling on her imminent reunion with Haldren, and she did not press her steed as hard as the others did. She would have to flirt with him, flatter him—ultimately seduce him in order to assuage his anger. It was a ridiculous game, but one which she had enjoyed and excelled at for years. She no longer had the heart for it, and thinking about it repulsed her.

Cart and the knights who rode with him gave up any pretense of being Thranes. They stripped the Silver Flame from their shields, and Cart doffed his helmet. They rode north through Bramblescar Gorge, a narrow valley choked with the dry, thorny plants that gave the place its name. Layer upon layer of dark slate formed the rough walls of the gorge, cut away by an ancient river that had since run dry. On their left, the lowest hills of the Starpeaks rose up toward the towering heights beyond, sheltering the valley from rain and blocking the evening sun. On their right, the first green shrubs and trees of the Silver Woods crowned the rocky walls. Except for the steady drumming of hoofbeats, the air was still and silent. Nature seemed quieted by the impending battle.

Senya barely noticed when they passed a clump of sentries posted at the southern end of Haldren's camp. Cart's pace slowed to an easy walk as they made their way among the clusters of soldiers preparing for their last night encamped. Senya's horse no longer needed urging to keep up with the others, and Senya came to the command post far more quickly than she wanted to.

"Lord General!" Cart dismounted in front of the grand pavilion Haldren had erected for himself—a tribute to his greatness, Senya was sure.

Smile, Senya told herself. You're glad to see him again.

She forced a smile onto her face then tried to make it look genuine.

"Enter." Haldren's voice was gruff.

Wonderful, Senya thought dryly. A foul mood will make this so much more pleasant.

Cart waited while Senya dismounted, then held the flap of the pavilion open for her to enter before him. Steeling herself and refreshing her smile, she stepped once more into Haldren's presence.

"What is it, Cart?" Haldren stood over a small table, and he didn't look up from the large map spread out before him.

"Reporting from patrol, sir," Cart said behind her. "See what I found."

Haldren glanced up, his face taut with irritation. His face softened and he straightened when he saw Senya.

"Hello, Haldren." She made her voice husky, alluring, and she forced her face to keep smiling. Tears welled in her eyes.

Haldren strode around the table to stand in front of her. He clasped her shoulders and let his eyes wander over her face. A soft rustle told her that Cart had stepped out of the pavilion.

"Did he harm you?" Haldren said.

It took a moment for Senya to realize that he meant Gaven, not Cart. She shook her head.

He threw his arms around her and pressed her to his chest. She reached around him to caress his back before she realized that his intention wasn't amorous. His body shook with sobs.

"I'm sorry," he moaned, burying his face in her hair. "I came back as quickly as I could, but he'd already taken you away."

Taken me? Senya thought. Ten Seas, the old fool thinks Gaven kidnapped me!

She clenched him tightly.

"I would have searched the world for you," Haldren said.

The tears broke free of her eyes and streamed down her face.

The old fool loves me, she thought. The idea seemed totally foreign to her.

* * * * *

Haldren's heart soared alongside the dragons as he watched them take to the sky, bright under the morning sun. Riding at his right hand, Cart nodded approvingly, appraising the number of dragons and their strength and size. They numbered nearly a score. Had so many dragons been assembled in a single cause in the entire course of human history? Only Senya, on his left, cast a pall over the moment.

"These dragons and their Prophecy," she muttered. "What do they think of our march here below, I wonder? Are they serving our needs, or are we cards in their hands? Are we playing the dragons, or are they playing us?"

"This is not some tavern game of chance, Senya," Haldren scoffed. "This is war."

He raised his voice so the other commanders around him would hear, and lifted a fist into the air. "The dragons lead us to victory, swift and certain!"

A chorus of cheers from behind him washed away the shadow cast by Senya's doubts, and Cart signaled the other commanders to begin the march. Haldren smiled, satisfied that his plan was unfolding perfectly. An army larger than he had ever commanded during the war marched before him, and its vanguard was an invincible flight of dragons. Before the sun reached its zenith, this great legion would spill out of Bramblescar Gorge onto the Starcrag Plain, and according to Cart's reports, they would meet Thrane forces at the border before nightfall. His conquest of Khorvaire was about to begin!

And fate had given him a token of his coming victory by returning his Senya to his side. Though she was clearly troubled by her ordeal, he was confident that she would return to him fully before long. Everything he desired was within his reach.

They rode in silence at a slow walk behind the marching legions. As the narrow gorge widened he was able to survey the full strength of his forces. His banners fluttered in the wind of a brewing storm, the formations of his soldiers bristled with spears, and the earth thundered in concert with the sky under the boots of tens of thousands of marching feet. Haldren's thoughts were full of glory—victory on the battlefield, the conquest of all Khorvaire, his coronation as emperor of a new Galifar, Senya at his side. What could stop him?

Bursting with pride, he watched the columns of troops begin their advance across the Starcrag Plain as he had ordered, each rank perfectly aligned behind the one before, exactly in place. These were the best troops that Aundair had to offer, and they served only him, not a soft and foolish queen in far-off Fairhaven. The other commanders—Lord Major ir'Fann, Lord Colonel ir'Cashan, Rennic Arak, Kadra, even General Yeven—had all acknowledged the brilliance of his strategy. They had all agreed that victory was sure, and praised him as the greatest general Aundair—no, Khorvaire—had ever known. The Thranes would be the first to fall, but only the first in his long campaign of conquest. After this initial victory, he knew he could count on the support of Arcanix and even House Cannith. The wheel was in motion, and nothing now would stop its inexorable turning.

"Lord General?" Cart's voice was quiet, but something in his tone told him that there was a problem. How could there be a problem?

"What is it, Cart?"

"Look to the sky, Lord General." Cart pointed up into the distance, in the direction the dragons had flown.

Haldren squinted in the direction Cart had pointed, then cursed his aging eyes and called for a spyglass. Peering through the lenses, he could clearly see the tight clumps of dragons—his dragons—advancing toward the Thrane forces arrayed against them, far across the plain. "What? I don't see—"

But then he did. More dragons lifted into the air, and they were behind the advancing Thrane lines. They closed with his dragons with murderous speed, and the sky erupted with fire and lightning as the two groups of dragons met. They swooped and dove at each other, tearing with fang and claw, great bursts of deadly energy erupting from their mouths. Some fought on the ground, wings and tails buffeting each other.

Haldren's hands trembled as they clutched the spyglass tighter, pressing it to his eye as if looking harder would reveal a different interpretation of what he saw. But there was no other explanation: the Thranes had dragons fighting for them as well. At least a score of them.

Senya's soft voice behind him hit him like a pronouncement of doom. "A clash of dragons signals the sundering of the Soul Reaver's gates."

As if responding to her words, the earth began to shudder, answered by a rolling crash of thunder across the sky.

CHAPTER
47

A t the beginning of time, one legend said, the great dragon Siberys danced through the void, setting the stars in their places. Khyber prowled behind, consuming stars as fast as Siberys could scatter them. Eberron sang, apart from the others, and life began to blossom in the void.

Finally Siberys turned to confront Khyber, to stop the dark dragon from consuming the stars. The two dragons fought, tearing at each other in their hatred. At last Khyber arose victorious: Siberys was torn asunder, her body broken into numberless fragments. Then, thirsty for blood, Khyber wheeled upon Eberron.

Where Khyber lunged, Eberron snaked aside, around. The bloodless battle, the fierce dance continued for eons, neither dragon gaining ascendancy over the other. At last, Khyber grew tired, and Eberron enfolded and imprisoned Khyber in her own body. The struggles of the primordial dragons had come to an end.

Both dragons slumbered after their long warring, and hardened into earth. And so the world was born, Eberron forming its surface and Khyber its dark depths. The fragments of Siberys's broken body encircled Eberron in a great ring that shone in the night. The Dragon Above, the Dragon Below, and the Dragon Between. Always Eberron stood between the Dragon Above and the Dragon Below.

Some parts of the Prophecy suggested that one day the divisions between them might be healed, but an event of such grand proportion was little more than a distant dream. Once in a very great while, though, the gulf could be bridged.

* * * *

Gaven raced the *Eye of the Storm* toward the Starcrag Plain, following the path of a dry gorge between the Starpeaks and the forest to the east. Rienne and Darraun rested below, recovering from the dragon's attack. Gaven wasn't sure what he had to do, but a burning urgency spurred him on. Could he stop Haldren's advance, prevent the clash of dragons and save Khorvaire from another terrible war? Failing that, could he prevent Vaskar's ascension?

He didn't know. And yet, somehow, he was satisfied. He was acting—he had made the decision to intervene in these events, to try, at least, to make events work out for the better. He vastly preferred that to a life spent floating on the currents that carried him. He would set his own course, choose his own destiny.

Destiny is . . .

The highest hopes the universe has for you. Like . . . like my mother wanted the best for me.

The memory of Senya's words made him think again of his father. Arnoth had wanted only the best for him, even if his idea of what was the best didn't often match Gaven's. Why had Gaven not realized that until his father was gone?

The valley he'd been following opened out into the wide expanse of the Starcrag Plain, and Gaven saw the battlefield for the first time—with his eyes. It was hauntingly familiar as the landscape of his nightmares. The northern lands had whispered to him of their past and their destiny, hinting at the Prophecy and the words of creation hidden in the hills and trees. The Starcrag Plain screamed centuries of anguish. This was not the first time the plain had been a battlefield—ancient cairns, piles of weathered stones, littered its edges, and the ground itself spoke to him of horrors past and horrors yet to come.

In the present moment, he saw the regimented lines of Haldren's forces marching across the plain toward the waiting Thranes massed along a line he presumed was the border set by the Treaty of Thronehold. He saw dragons wheeling above the plain, clawing and biting at each other, blasting fire and icy frost from their gaping jaws. The battle had already begun—the clash of dragons. He was too late to prevent it.

He gripped the helm and blinked hard, struggling to keep his vision focused on the scene before his eyes, to clear away the memories of his nightmares. Haldren's forces marched onward, heedless of the dragons battling furiously in the air and on the ground between them and the Thranes. They shouted as the *Eye of the Storm* soared over them, then shook their spears and shields when it was past.

Then Gaven saw his nightmares come to life. Thunder rolled overhead, and the earth groaned in answer. Rienne raced to the deck, and Darraun trailed after. The airship drew near the center of the plain, dangerously close to a pair of blue dragons swooping and tearing at each other, and the earth below began to crack. Eberron was opening a path—small and brief, but a bridge nonetheless—for Khyber and Siberys to touch once again.

At first the crack was a midnight scar across the face of the plain, its blackness drawing in and swallowing what little sunlight filtered through the storm clouds above. Then an awesome, unholy light began to grow in its deepest core, and the earth trembled again as the light swelled in the depths and began to erupt toward the surface, to reach for the sky. For a moment it seemed like an enormous, many-tentacled beast formed of the most brilliant light, oozing out of the fissure in the earth and sending exploratory tendrils in every direction.

Then the light burst forth and roared heavenward with a sound like a titan's sword being drawn from its sheath, sharp metal cutting through the air. It stood tall and straight, stretching from the fractured plain up to the clouds, and the clouds melted away from it, churning and swirling in a storm of protest as the light broke through.

"On a field of battle where dragons clash in the skies, the earth opens and the Crystal Spire emerges," Gaven said. "A ray of Khyber's burning sun forms a bridge to Siberys's heights."

"What does it mean?" Rienne asked, her face twisted in horror. Her body was half turned away from the Spire though her eyes were glued to it, as though she wanted to look away but couldn't quite force herself to.

"It means the Soul Reaver's gates are sundered," Gaven said. "His monstrous hordes are about to spill out of that rift and tear into the armies on both sides. Nobody win this battle."

"You called it a bridge," Rienne said. "Does that mean it has something to do with the Storm Dragon's ascension?"

"You said it in the City of the Dead," Darraun said. "You said, 'the Storm Dragon walks through the gates of Khyber and crosses the bridge to the sky.' "

Gaven nodded, only half listening to Darraun. His nightmare continued to unfold before his eyes. Darraun muttered a curse, and Rienne gripped Gaven's arm, convincing him that the scene was not merely another waking dream.

The creatures that began to exude from the rift could not have existed in a sane world. Some resembled earthly beasts, but they had been so twisted by the corruption of Khyber that they were barely recognizable. Tentacles sprouted from their sides or backs or protruded where their mouths should have been. Joints bent in obscene ways. Faces erupted from wounds in their skin and then retreated back into horrible bodies. Others could not be compared to anything natural—they were mounds of flesh or agglomerations of bone covered with parchment skin, or slimy things that slithered on pale bellies or skittered on innumerable legs. Blank eyes stared out from pale gray faces, and hundreds of humanlike eyes covered an oozing mass of half-congealed blood.

Worse, somehow, than the sight of the creatures vomiting from the gulf was their sound—part keening, part lunatic babble, part predatory growl. It began quietly as the first monstrosities emerged, but it grew louder with each successive wave, building until it drowned out the other sounds of the battlefield and battered at the walls of Gaven's sanity. He couldn't form words with that babble assaulting his mind, and he couldn't hope to be heard above the cacophony if he did.

A blast of lightning engulfed the ship, followed by a deafening crash as an enormous copper-scaled dragon smashed into her hull. The impact knocked Gaven off his feet and slammed him against the bulwarks. The ring of elemental fire surged out to engulf the dragon's body, charring its flesh and making the airship buck and roll. The dead dragon plummeted down, pulling the *Eye of the Storm* down with it.

Gaven leaped up to grab at the helm, desperately hoping to regain control of the airship before she crashed to the ground. He sensed the elemental's acquiescence to his will, but then he felt the impact rumble through the hull. He had slowed their fall, but he was too late to stop it. Timbers groaned and then cracked, the ring of fire sputtered and went out. The airship lurched backward, jerked to port, and was still.

Rienne had kept her feet through it all, and Maelstrom was already in her hand. She swung it through slow repetitions of the whirling patterns of strikes and blocks she favored in battle. The sword seemed to sing in her hand, adding a voice of storm and steel to the mounting clamor around them. Darraun pulled himself to his feet and slid his mace out of the loop in his belt. Gaven looked up at the darkening sky, calling out to the brewing storm. If he was to be a force of destruction, best to use that power in a cause like this—to help protect the soldiers of both armies from the slaughter that surged toward them. If Vaskar was determined to be the Storm Dragon, let *him* face the Soul Reaver.

In the blink of an eye, the hordes of the Soul Reaver swarmed over the bulwarks of the grounded airship, and Gaven forgot himself and his friends in the storm of battle. Eyes wide open, he plunged headlong into the nightmares that had plagued him for twenty-six years.

Roaring with horror and fury, he swung his greatsword back and forth, cutting through alien flesh, shattering bone, spilling blood and ichor onto the deck. Shouting arcane syllables, he created fire and lightning to sear his foes, summoned invisible and irresistible forces to push them back, cast spells to guide his blade to the vital parts of tentacled things that refused to die. Bile rose in his throat as unspeakable horrors stared him in the face and spat oozing slime onto him in their death throes. He lashed out in reflexive fear to sever tentacles that grasped at him. The wailing ululation of the horde battered at his ears and at the ramparts of his will, threatening to break his concentration and reduce his resolve to quivering terror. And all the time the storm's fury built around him, torrents of rain and hail, blasts of wind, and eruptions of lightning that tore great holes in the teeming carpet of aberrations that covered the Starcrag Plain.

Without warning, the battlefield fell silent, and the raving legions paused. Gaven's ears rang in the sudden quiet, and he seized the opportunity to check that Rienne and Darraun were still alive. But the respite was brief. A moment later, every monstrosity raised its voice in a shriek, lifting arms and tentacles and limbs into the air, and the onslaught resumed. Gaven roared and spun his blade in a wide circle. A whirlwind followed his sword through the air and forced the nearest creatures back, giving him room to assess the battlefield.

He glanced up at the Crystal Spire, towering above them a bowshot away, a radiant beacon through the driving rain. He saw what had made the creatures pause: a figure hung suspended in the shaft of light, roughly human in size and shape. It was smaller than many of the creatures he had already slain, but even at that distance, it projected an aura like a low grumbling roar, tearing at the very roots of his sense and will. Long tentacles thrashed the air around its face, and clawed hands stretched up to the sky.

"Tearer and reaver and flayer of souls," Gaven whispered.

The hordes renewed their assault, and Gaven lost himself in the battle again.

* * * * *

Haldren surveyed a battlefield over which he no longer had any control, clutching his reins until they bit into his palms. The full extent of Vaskar's duplicity had made itself clear: in addition to bringing dragons to fight on both sides of the battle, Vaskar had convinced him to launch his assault against Thrane on this field—here, above the prison of the Soul Reaver. Haldren had known Vaskar would have to face that foe in the end—Gaven had seen the Eye of Siberys used as a spear to defeat the creature. But he had not expected to provide the stage for that battle. Not only had Vaskar undone the advantage he had given Haldren, but he had actually consigned both armies to slaughter at the hands of the Soul Reaver's aberrant legions. Now Haldren would be forced to watch Vaskar's moment of triumph, his ascension to godhood, in the air above the spectacle of his own crushing defeat. And rather than having an ally among the gods of the world, Haldren would have a bitter enemy. It was too much to bear.

His eyes wandered over the field, straining to see the magnitude of the carnage through the driving rain. To his right, ir'Fann's infantry was falling under a renewed press, which meant that his pikemen had been overwhelmed. Near the middle of the field, a clump of Kadra's knights stood in a tight circle as the aberrations advanced over the corpses of their steeds. He lifted his spyglass and saw Kadra Ware herself lying at the center of that circle, bloody and unmoving. To the left, ir'Cashan's troops fled toward the sheltering hills. A group of knight phantoms, well-armored infantry riding conjured steeds of smoke and shadow, ranged back and forth along the rear, looking in vain for a place where their aid might turn the tide of battle. There could be no doubt: the field was lost. Lord General Haldren ir'Brassek had never known such a crushing defeat.

He lifted his eyes to the radiant column at the hub of the spreading devastation, and saw for the first time the tiny figure suspended in its light. He pressed the spyglass to his eye again. The Soul Reaver. Hatred welled up in his gut like bile, and he cursed under his breath. "Kill Vaskar for me, damn him." The creature stretched its shriveled arms upward as tentacles writhed out around its face, and Haldren imagined it urging its subterranean hordes to greater fury as they swept over their foes or calling down the storm to add its wrath to theirs.

"And damn the rain," he said aloud. "Can I not at least see my defeat through clear eyes?"

"It's Gaven," Senya said, pointing at the excoriate's grounded airship. "The storm battles for him."

"You still believe his lies? You still think he's the Storm Dragon?"

Senya turned her gaze to meet his angry glare. "That's our only hope."

"Then hope is lost," Haldren said, biting back his rage.

Cart rumbled on Haldren's right. "We'll see soon enough," he said. Haldren turned to look at him, then followed his gaze back to the towering shaft of light.

A blast of lightning engulfed the Soul Reaver. For an instant, Haldren thought that the storm had lashed out at the monstrosity, but then he saw the lightning's source: Vaskar had begun his attack.

"The Bronze Serpent," Senya said. "He's doomed to fail."

"Good," Haldren spat.

CHAPTER
48

The dragon's roar cut through the wails of the Soul Reaver's hosts. Gaven drove his sword down through the double head of a waist-high monstrosity and glanced up at the Crystal Spire. Vaskar had come to face the Soul Reaver, hoping to bring about the fulfillment of the Prophecy. The sounds of the battle fell away, even the howls of the monsters around him, leaving a strange stillness, and the words of the Prophecy rang in his mind:

The Bronze Serpent faces the Soul Reaver and fails.
But the Storm Dragon seizes the shard of heaven from the fallen pretender.

Had Vaskar accounted for those words? Did he even know about them? Gaven had spoken them to Haldren, but not in Vaskar's presence. Would Haldren have repeated them to the dragon, when they upset him so much?

It didn't matter, he realized. Vaskar was doomed to fail, which meant that the Soul Reaver's hordes would continue to pour forth from Khyber's darkness. Every soldier in the Starcrag Plain would fall beneath them. The monsters would pour into Aundair and Thrane—they might raze Thaliost, or Daskaran across the river. They might reach Stormhome. The idea of Haldren conquering Khorvaire was terrible to contemplate, but the thought of the Soul Reaver spreading his tentacles across the north was much, much worse.

Vaskar was doomed to fail, and that meant the Storm Dragon would have to do what the Prophecy demanded of him: seize the shard of heaven and drive it through the Soul Reaver's heart.

No one could do that but him.

The aberrations crowded closer. Growling, Gaven impaled one of the larger, shambling monsters, left his sword hanging in the wound, and swung his hands together to create a clap of thunder that drove the smaller creatures back. Then he grabbed the sword from the teetering bug-thing and leaped aft, toward the helm.

"Clear the deck!" he shouted. He seized the wheel and willed the elemental out of its quiescence.

"Can she fly?" Rienne called back. "That was a rough landing."

"I'll make her fly." The wind howled, and the airship lurched, then she slowly lifted off the ground.

The elemental resisted Gaven's control at first, protesting as though the damage to the hull had wounded or weakened it. *Fly, damn you.*

Rienne and Darraun fought hard to carry out Gaven's command. Rienne nearly stopped using her sword, instead relying on a constantly shifting stance to overbalance the creatures that came charging toward her and throw them overboard. Maelstrom came to bear only in the one instance where a tentacle wrapped around her leg as its owner hurtled overboard, threatening to drag Rienne off the ship as well. A swift, sure blow from Maelstrom freed her from its grasp and sent the creature plummeting to its doom. Darraun swung his mace, magically enhanced to slay the aberrations of Khyber, beating them back under a constant hail of blows until they had nowhere to go but off the ship.

The *Eye of the Storm* teetered higher, rising above the din of the battle and the gibbering hordes below. Gaven let the winds carry her in a wide circle around the Crystal Spire as the ship swirled faster and faster around the bridge of light. That circular path provided Gaven with a clear view of the continuing battle between the Soul Reaver and Vaskar—be he Storm Dragon or doomed Bronze Serpent—as it raged in the midst of the great column of light.

It would be more accurate to say that Vaskar raged, Gaven thought. The battle was not too different from watching Rienne fight a drunken Eldeen wild man. The Soul Reaver remained calm, moving very little in response to Vaskar's charges, his circling flights and desperate lunges. Each time Vaskar closed in, an invisible force pushed him aside, preventing him from making contact. Gaven couldn't see the Soul Reaver make any counterattack, but it was clear that Vaskar grew more tired with each passing moment. His frustration also built with every failed lunge. He roared and spat lightning at the Soul Reaver, but though the lightning at least touched the creature, it didn't seem to cause it any pain or distress. To his surprise, Gaven felt a twinge of pity for the dragon—he was so misguided, and ultimately so ineffectual, just as he tried to seize tremendous power.

Vaskar pulled back and floated motionless on the building gale for a moment. Carried by the wind, the airship swirled closer to him, and for a moment Gaven thought the dragon would attack the *Eye of the Storm* to vent his frustration. Then Gaven saw a flash of gold: from somewhere on his body, Vaskar had produced the Eye of Siberys. He fumbled with the dragonshard in claws too large to serve as hands, and Gaven saw that Vaskar had clumsily bound the shard to a straight, polished staff, making a spear to slay the Soul Reaver. He was desperate, Gaven realized, and was pulling out his weapon of last resort. The dragon didn't expect it to work—and he was right. Vaskar was already defeated.

Gaven jerked the wheel hard to port and took the *Eye of the Storm* out of the cyclone.

"What are you doing?" Rienne said.

"I need to get off this ship," Gaven said, "and I'm not going to make Darraun try to fly her in that storm."

"No," Rienne said, "I mean, what are you *doing*?"

The airship had cleared the worst of the storm and flew smoothly again, despite the staved-in timbers of her hull. "Darraun, can you take her from here?" Gaven said.

"I can try," Darraun answered. His hands clenched the wheel, and Gaven released it. The ship bucked slightly, then leveled. Darraun nodded, but didn't try to speak again.

"Gaven," Rienne said, "what are you doing?"

Gaven pulled off his scabbard and untied the ash staff he'd bound to it. Touching the staff sparked a torrent of memories— stumbling, half crazed through the Mournland, climbing the storm-blasted tree to pull off the branch, a dream: a yellow crystal pulsing with veins of golden light, carved to a point and bound to a blackened branch, plunging into a body that was shadow given twisting form.

"It was my hand on the spear," he said, more to himself than her. "It seems I will play the part of the Storm Dragon after all." He stood with the staff in his hands and slung his sword and scabbard back over his shoulder.

Rienne lay a hand on his back. "Play the part," she said, "but write it as you go. You are player and playwright."

He looked into her eyes and cupped her cheek in his hand, running a thumb along the curve of her lips.

"I don't know how I could ever have doubted your love," he said. "I never will again."

"Come back to me."

"I will." He kissed her, savoring the taste of her breath, and then jumped over the bulwarks.

A fresh gust of wind caught him up and carried him away from the airship, back to the storm that whirled around the Crystal Spire. Lightning flared and roared around him, and the rain became hail, as though the storm had been holding its full fury back until that moment. Gaven willed himself forward, toward the Soul Reaver, and the wings of the storm carried him there.

Vaskar roared when he saw Gaven approaching. "Do you still think to steal my prize?" he howled over the wind. "Get away, interloper!"

Vaskar's outrage had a very different effect than he had intended. The Soul Reaver followed Vaskar's gaze, turning its monstrous head toward Gaven as he approached. Then, as if the battle to that point had consisted purely of the Soul Reaver playing with Vaskar, the tentacled thing dismissed him. Barely sparing the dragon another glance, it blasted him with waves of energy that made the air shimmer, and the echoes of it made Gaven's head throb with sudden pain. Unconscious or dead, Vaskar fell.

As the Soul Reaver turned its full attention to Gaven, lightning streaked into the Crystal Spire and coursed through the Soul Reaver's withered flesh, though it left the creature unharmed. Wind buffeted it from every side, and the robes it wore flapped furiously around it. In return, Gaven felt his mind engulfed in a similar storm. Thoughts and feelings welled up in no sensible order, like a nightmare galloping through his mind at a breakneck pace. Slights and shames from his childhood sprang to his thoughts alongside the fresh grief of his father's death, while the memories he'd acquired from the Heart of Khyber added their own share of fear and frustration. For a moment Gaven could not even distinguish the torrent of memories from his sensation of the present: the Soul Reaver and the storm seemed like distant thoughts amid the deluge.

Among the torrent, though, Gaven found words that connected the ancient dragon's memories to his own past, walking the Sky Caves of Thieren Kor, and the present moment, tying them all together—

The greatest of the daelkyr's brood, the Soul Reaver feasts on the minds and flesh of a thousand lives before his prison breaks.
The Bronze Serpent calls him forth, but the Storm Dragon is his doom.

The words focused his mind like a bolt of lightning. I wield the power of the Storm Dragon, he thought. If I don't kill the Soul Reaver, who will?

He whipped the storm into a greater fury. Hail battered the Soul Reaver, rain like searing fire burned its flesh, and lightning crackled in a ball around it. Then the Soul Reaver, too, fell from the sky, sliding down the shaft of unearthly light. Gaven watched it descend and disappear again below the earth, and he wished he could believe it dead.

The Storm Dragon descends into the endless dark beneath the bridge of light, he thought, where the Soul Reaver waits. There among the bones of Khyber the Storm Dragon drives the spear formed from Siberys's Eye into the Soul Reaver's heart.

Siberys's Eye—where was it? With a start, he searched the ground below. Vaskar lay crumpled on the rocky plain near the base of the Crystal Spire, one wing outstretched at a strange angle, his neck curved around beneath the bulk of his body, his head hidden from view. The Soul Reaver's hordes had dispersed from there already, moved outward to tear into the armies gathered at either end of the plain. Gaven willed himself downward, and the wind set him on solid ground once again. Drenched with rain, chilled to the bone, he scrambled over and around the rocks to the place where Vaskar's body lay.

The dragon looked pathetic, broken like a child's toy dashed to the ground, and Gaven again felt the welling of pity. "The Bronze Serpent faces the Soul Reaver and fails," he said. "But the Storm Dragon seizes the shard of heaven from the fallen pretender. Where is it, Vaskar?"

Gaven circled the fallen dragon's body, scanning the ground for any gleam of yellow. The ground around Vaskar's body revealed no clues, so Gaven used the ash staff to prod under the dragon's claws. He lifted a claw, and almost jumped in surprise as the Eye of Siberys flashed gold beneath the dragon's massive hand. He scooped up the dragonshard and yanked it free from Vaskar's staff.

He was back in the Aerenal jungle, cradling the warm Eye of Siberys close to his chest, gazing into its vibrant core where veins of gold danced like Siberys at the dawn of creation. It was so easy to lose himself in that writhing dance, to forget his surroundings, to forget himself. Even the sound of thunderous footsteps could barely stir him from his reverie, but he made himself turn and look at Darraun.

Except that he wasn't in Aerenal, and the footsteps had been hoofbeats. Gaven tried to shake his head clear, without much success, and sized up the rider charging him from the north. A knight of some sort, he supposed, clad in heavy armor—no, a warforged. Cart.

Gaven stowed the Eye of Siberys in a pocket and held his ash-black staff as though it were his greatsword. "What are you doing here?" he called to the advancing warforged.

"I'm not here to fight you, Gaven," Cart said. His tone reminded Gaven of the first time he'd encountered the warforged: Cart bending down to him in his cell and trying to coax him out as if he were a frightened child. "I thought you might want some help."

"Help? Why would you help me?"

Cart dismounted and walked closer to Gaven. "Because we are alike, you and I."

"Alike? How so?"

"Each of us was made for a single purpose, Gaven. It's foolish to deny that purpose. I was made for war, and I will continue to war until I finally meet a foe who can defeat me. And I'll die knowing that I lived according to my purpose. What more can anyone hope to do?"

"And for what purpose was I made, Cart?"

"You were made to be here at this moment, to fight that monstrosity down there and do what Vaskar could not. To be a god."

"Of all people, shouldn't gods be free to choose their destinies?"

"What greater destiny could you ask for?" Cart sounded as though he couldn't possibly imagine a satisfactory answer to his question.

Gaven looked up into the storm, feeling the rain striking his skin. The wind lashed his hair against his face. He was the storm: he felt himself raging in the whirling clouds and booming thunder. But he was also a rain-drenched man, feet planted firmly on the ground. "You're wrong about me, Cart," he said. He pulled the Eye of Siberys out of his pocket and started binding it to the ash staff.

"Am I? Then why are you readying your weapon?"

"Oh, I'll play the Storm Dragon's part, for now. You're right—someone has to stop the Soul Reaver, and no one here is going to do it but me." The branch he had pulled from the ash tree seemed made to fit the Eye of Siberys. He jabbed the ground a few times to make sure the dragonshard was securely affixed.

Satisfied, he pulled his adamantine box out of another pouch and sprang it open. The nightshard inside seemed to spring to life at the proximity of the Eye of Siberys. "The Time of the Dragon Above draws to a close," he said, not really addressing Cart. "The Time of the Dragon Below approaches. The Eye of Siberys and the Heart of Khyber are united, just as the Crystal Spire links the Dragon Above and the Dragon Below."

"I agree with Darraun," Cart said. "The Prophecy makes my head spin."

"You don't know the half of it." Gaven lifted the nightshard and tossed it gently away from him. It seemed to float along that path for a moment, then it circled back, drawing a ring of lightning behind it. Like the whirlwind that had borne him aloft, it swirled around him, tracing its path in crackling light.

"Are you coming with me?" he asked the warforged.

Cart nodded.

"Let's go, then." Gaven strode over to the base of the Crystal Spire, to a ledge overlooking the chasm that rent the plain. He tried to peer down into it, but the light blinded him. "The Soul Reaver awaits." Without a backward glance, he stepped off the ledge and fell.

CHAPTER
49

I 've got to get her back on the ground." Darraun's face was deathly pale, and his hands gripped the spokes of the wheel. Speaking seemed like an enormous effort.

"Keep going south," Rienne said. "Behind the Thrane forces. We'll be off the plain in no time." She tried to sound more optimistic than she felt. But she had just watched Gaven fall down into the depths of Khyber, and dread had a chill grip on her heart.

Darraun fixed his eyes just to the port side of the prow as he steered the airship in that direction. His every movement was stiff and clipped, as if moving too fast would break his mind's hold on the elemental bound in the ship. His apparently fragile state did nothing to ease Rienne's apprehension. She leaned on the port bulwark, watching as the chasm grew smaller in the distance behind them, until it was swallowed up in the rain and hail, and she could barely even make out the Crystal Spire.

"See anything?" Darraun grunted.

Rienne shifted her gaze to examine the plain below them. The Soul Reaver's hosts rampaged across the battlefield. She saw Thrane banners cast down in the mud and trampled, though clusters of knights still held their ground against the tide of horrors. I see the world sinking into chaos, she thought.

"The Thranes are still fighting the creatures from the chasm," she said. "Do you suppose Thrane will blame Aundair for that?"

Darraun nodded, and Rienne had to agree in her heart. The situation was grim in any event: If the Thrane army were completely destroyed, the Cardinals would assume that Aundair's attack had been successful. If there were survivors—there had to be survivors!—they would describe how Aundair's forces opened a crack in the earth and brought the monsters forth, and trafficking with the Dragon Below would be added to Aundair's list of real and imagined crimes. It seemed the storm of war had broken again and nothing could stop it.

She leaned against the railing and stared down at the carnage below. Something had to stop it—something or someone. Gaven's talk of being a hero, of choosing his own destiny and writing his own part in the play, stirred in her memory. "Darraun," she said, whirling to face the changeling at the helm, "turn us around, take us north!"

His eyes were wide. "Back into the storm?"

Yes, but not that storm, she thought. "Circle it. We need to get to Haldren."

Darraun nodded and turned the wheel.

"Why should I be content to be a minor player in this drama?" Rienne mused aloud.

A smile quirked at the corner of Darraun's mouth.

* * * * *

Haldren stared through the spyglass at the dragon's crumpled body. Vaskar did not stir. He had watched Vaskar's defeat with satisfaction diluted by growing rage. Vaskar had brought his plans to ruin, so it pleased him to see the dragon's ambitions quashed as well. At the same time, Vaskar's defeat left room for Gaven to seize what Vaskar had sought. Gaven—the pathetic madman that had started all this, without having the slightest idea what he was doing. Gaven was supposed to be a tool, a pawn Haldren could use to manipulate Vaskar and to facilitate his own rise to power. Instead, the bastard had stolen Senya, thwarted Vaskar, and appeared out of nowhere to take part in the ruin of Haldren's plans.

"If I achieve nothing else in this lifetime," he whispered, "I will destroy him."

"You aim to destroy a god?" Senya said.

"He's not a god."

"Not yet. But his power is already greater than yours."

"What did he do to you, Senya? How did he bend you so completely to him?"

"He didn't bend me to his will. That's how you work with your magic and your oratory. You taught me to work that way as well, using my body. And oh, you taught me well—well enough that the disciple became the master. I had you wrapped around my finger. But Gaven—he didn't bend me. He straightened me out."

Senya's words stabbed Haldren's heart and poured ice into his gut. "You . . . used me?" he whispered, quivering with rage.

"Of course." Her voice was not cruel or bitter, just . . . dismissive. Utterly calm and cold. How could he have been such a fool?

He turned away from her and urged his horse forward a few steps. "Do you see the warforged?" he asked, trying to keep his voice as calm as hers.

"I saw him last on the east side of the field, riding hard."

"Has he gone mad? What is he doing?"

"Cart was never good at standing by and watching a battle unfold. He was made for war, as he said, built by Cannith to be a soldier."

"No," Haldren breathed. He had put the spyglass back to his eye, and finally found Cart near the middle of the field. "He was evidently made for treachery. He's talking to Gaven."

"Don't be absurd, Haldren. No one is more loyal to you than Cart."

"If he treats with my enemy, he is my enemy."

"I wonder if you have any friends left."

Haldren surveyed the battlefield again. Ir'Fann's infantry was gone, wiped from the field, leaving a strange calm on the eastern side. No wonder Cart had ridden that way. Kadra's knights had fallen as well, which meant that if she hadn't been dead when he saw her before, she certainly was now. The knight phantoms he'd seen earlier had actually rallied ir'Cashan's troops on the west side, but there was no sign of ir'Cashan herself. Her death had probably caused her soldiers' initial rout. He hadn't seen Rennic Arak or his troops since the crevice opened—they had been at the vanguard, and were probably the first to fall. General Yeven, at least, was still alive: he had taken his command staff and retreated back up Bramblescar Gorge at about the same time as Cart had ridden off.

Haldren returned his gaze to Senya. "No," he said, "none are left."

As he spoke, something in the air caught his eye. A bright flash—lightning, perhaps? He almost dismissed it as yet another effect of the storm, but then he saw it again. An airship, a small one, and she was soaring closer to them through the storm.

"That's Gaven's ship," Senya said.

"He's not aboard, though."

"You just saw him talking to Cart."

"Well, if I can't destroy him, perhaps I can at least destroy someone he loves."

* * * * *

Rienne kept her eyes on the battlefield as Darraun piloted them around the storm. The skirmishes thinned on the south side, the Thrane side, and gave way to random clumps of monsters spreading over the plain to the east and shambling toward the Silver Woods. As the airship rounded the Crystal Spire and the raging storm, she saw more signs of battle—Haldren's remaining troops struggling to hold the monsters off.

"I give better odds to the Thranes," she said.

Darraun nodded. "Without the dragons, Haldren wouldn't have had a chance."

"So he had lost the battle even before the Crystal Spire appeared. His fate was sealed when the other dragons appeared to fight for Thrane."

"Exactly."

"What will he do?"

"Lick his wounds," Darraun said. "He doesn't take well to defeat."

"Do you think he'll try again someday?"

"If he gets out of this alive and manages to stay out of Dreadhold, yes."

"Then I need to make sure he doesn't."

"Yes, we do," Darraun said with a smile. The airship lurched, and his smile disappeared. Shaking his head, he renewed his concentration.

"I'm sorry. I'm distracting you." Rienne turned back to the railing.

The Aundairian side of the field had boiled down to a single pitched battle on the western side. Haldren's troops fought bravely, but they were completely encircled by the gibbering hordes. She watched sadly as the nightmarish host whittled away at the Aundairian formation, every fallen monster quickly replaced by another drawn to the battle from elsewhere on the field.

She pointed to the mouth of the small valley at the north end of the plain, the opening between the rocky wall of the Starpeaks and the Silver Woods where they had emerged into the Starcrag Plain. "There," she said over her shoulder. "That's the way we came, and I expect that's where we'll find Haldren."

Darraun adjusted his course slightly, and they soared past the Aundairians' last stand.

Rienne's first indication that they had indeed found Haldren was a blast of fire exploding around the airship's prow. Rienne tumbled away from the edge of the flames, unhurt, but she heard Darraun let loose a string of vehement and evocative curses. Flames danced along the arcane tracery in the hull, fire answering fire, and she knew that the ship's bound elemental would rebel against Darraun's control as it had when they fought the young red dragon.

"Bring us down!" she shouted, but there was no need. Darraun was already urging the airship downward, though Rienne couldn't tell whether he exerted such enormous effort to force the airship down or to keep her from falling too fast. Beads of sweat trickled down his face, and he squeezed one eye shut to clear sweat or smoke from it—he didn't dare release even one hand from the wheel.

Rienne leaned over a railing on the port side and looked below them to help guide Darraun to a relatively safe landing spot. She was so intent on getting the airship safely down that she almost forgot about Haldren's imminent threat, until another burst of fire engulfed her. She cried out in pain and fell back away from the bulwarks. Darraun must have lost concentration, either because he was injured as well or out of concern for her, because the airship suddenly jerked to starboard and then plunged downward. Rienne scrambled for a grip on something, and finally managed to clutch at a web of rope netting that secured a few small crates to the deck. As soon as she was sure of her hold, she looked at Darraun.

His eyes were squeezed shut, and his knuckles were white on the wheel. The muscles in his neck stood out like cords pulled tight beneath his skin, and sweat glued short tendrils of blond hair to his forehead. She didn't see any sign of serious injury, but if he didn't regain control of the airship quickly they would both be dead. She felt powerless, and she didn't like that feeling.

Keeping a hand on the ropes, she half climbed, half crawled to the helm. She had tried to help Darraun fly the *Eye of the Storm* when they first left Stormhome in search of Gaven, but he had said that if two minds tried to control the elemental at once it was less likely to respond, not more. Darraun had been the obvious one of them to try steering the vessel, both because of his expertise with magic and because his changeling nature might allow him to trick the elemental into believing that he was an heir of House Lyrandar. But at that moment, Darraun was failing, and it was about to cost them both their lives.

She seized the wheel, grabbing two spokes between the two that Darraun gripped. She felt the elemental's presence immediately. It pulled away from the touch of her mind like an unbroken horse shying or bucking from a trainer's hand. She pulled her hands away from the wheel as she imagined a bucking stallion's hooves lashing out at her—the elemental's resistance was so violent it felt physical. The ground was dangerously close, though, so she tried again.

This time she did not pull away when the elemental reacted. She felt Darraun's mental presence there as well, and she understood what he had meant in Stormhome. It would have been easy for the two of them to pull in two different directions, to give the elemental two competing voices to listen to. Too many warriors did exactly that—they let their minds give one command to their swords and their bodies another. Rienne's training had taught her the alternative. Rather than throwing another rope around the wild elemental's neck, she focused her attention on strengthening Darraun's grip, just as the mind could heighten and enhance the body's reflexes. One hand at a time, she shifted her grip on the wheel so that she held the same spokes Darraun did, and their hands touched even as they both grasped smooth wood.

The airship pulled out of her fall so suddenly that the lurch almost threw them overboard, but they held the wheel and managed to keep their feet. Rienne opened her eyes and saw Darraun smiling at her across the wheel, still tense but seeming far less panicked. She returned his smile just as another of Haldren's fireballs burst between them.

It stung her eyes with heat and brilliant light, scorched her face, and even seared her lungs as she gasped in surprise. Pain overwhelmed her, and she slumped to the deck.

CHAPTER
50

Gaven fell.

The cold radiance of the Crystal Spire failed to light the sides of the chasm, so he fell blind, just as he had fallen when he found the nightshard. Time vanished, and his sense of motion failed as well, so he felt as though he hung suspended in the column of light. He might have fallen for a matter of seconds, but it seemed like hours.

Strangely calm, he kept his feet below him and stretched his arms to the side, one hand clenching the spear he had made from the Eye of Siberys. The Heart of Khyber continued its orbit around his body, but the lightning trailing behind it had vanished in the overwhelming light that bathed him. Air rushing past his ears was the only sound, and it faded into a dull roar.

Slowly a shape took form below him—the only feature he could make out in the light. A mouth gaped wide to receive him, like the jaws of Khyber waiting to engulf him when he reached the end of his fall. The Crystal Spire seemed to pour out of that mouth like lightning from Vaskar's maw. The shape grew larger, though he couldn't tell whether he fell toward it or it surged up to meet him.

Then it was upon him: the face of a great dragon carved into ancient stone. Though the storm raged far above him now, he called a gust of wind to stop his fall and planted his feet gently to one side of the dragon's mouth. He barely remembered in time to make sure that Cart landed safely on the other side. To his credit, the warforged made no sound that indicated he'd been worried about the fall. His face, of course, was unreadable.

The First of Sixteen descended to this gate. The Soul Reaver spoke to his mind, bypassing both ears and language, but carrying the same grumbling roar he had sensed when he first saw the Soul Reaver high above the battlefield. *Any who would follow in his paths must be prepared for what lies beyond.*

Gaven peered into the darkness for a sign of the Soul Reaver, cursing the brilliance of the Crystal Spire that blinded his eyes without illuminating the shadows around it. Only the Heart of Khyber in its steady rotation cast a faint strobe of light around the chamber. Gaven had a vague sense of a dome arching overhead and smooth, round tunnels leading off into darkness. "And what if I don't want to follow his paths?" he called into the nothingness.

Cart looked at him strangely—the Soul Reaver evidently hadn't spoken in his mind.

Then I will kill you.

A wail filled Gaven's mind, different from the torrent of thoughts with which the Soul Reaver had assaulted him in the air. That attack had called his own mind up against him, but this was an intrusion, a blast of psychic force so great that his vision began to cloud over. He clamped his hands to his ears but couldn't block the sound, and squeezed his eyes shut to no avail. He dropped to one knee, searching for the still point he had found in his mind before, the focus that would enable him to shrug off the psychic attack again.

"The Bronze Dragon. . . no, the Bronze Serpent . . ."

His mind reeled, and though he rose once more to his feet and opened his eyes to search for the source of the assault, he could do nothing more than stumble half blind along the nearest tunnel, careening off the smooth stone walls.

* * * * *

Rienne opened her eyes and cried out—she was falling. Then she realized that an arm was firmly wrapped around her waist, holding her over a shoulder—Gaven? Her fall stopped abruptly, and Darraun crumpled to the ground beneath her. She rolled free and scrambled back to him, trying to get her bearings at the same time.

The *Eye of the Storm* loomed over them, grounded again, and Darraun had evidently just jumped off the deck, carrying her over his shoulder. It was not a great fall, and he was back on his feet in a moment. "Come on!" he said, "We have to get to Haldren before he hits us with another fireball."

His words reminded her what had happened, and she felt her face as she ran after him. The pain was gone—Darraun must have used some healing magic on her. "Thank you," she called to him, hustling to catch up. He shot a smile over his shoulder at her.

"Thank you for landing the airship," he said. "I was sure we were doomed."

"We may yet be," she said, looking ahead. A white-haired man she could only assume was Haldren was perched on a warhorse not ten paces in front of Darraun. The horse was barded with metal plates engraved with protective runes, and the old man's hands were raised in the gestures of another spell. In front of the horse, holding a slim elven longsword in a ready stance, was Senya. She met Rienne's eyes and her lips curled into a cruel smile.

* * * * *

"Gaven." Cart's voice was calm and gentle, nuanced with his years of studying human tone and cadence. "Shake it off. You can do this."

Smooth stone walls. A thought like lightning flashed through his mind, and he saw—not with his eyes, but clearer—the paths of the winding tunnels, the shapes they formed. The words of the Prophecy.

"The Storm Dragon walks through the gates of Khyber and crosses the bridge to the sky." He muttered the words to himself, sensing the layers of meaning contained in the tunnels around him. Words formed in his mind and bubbled from his mouth, slowly driving back the psychic scream of the Soul Reaver. "The Dragon of thunder and lightning and wind and rain and hail, the Storm Dragon—enters, walks, passes through, bursts through, shatters the Khyber gates, the dragon-gates below the chasm-gate." A vision started to form in his mind, and he laughed.

"Gaven?" Cart had a hand firmly clamped on his shoulder.

"Crosses the bridge, traverses it, spans it, thwarts it." Gaven spoke louder now.

And the Soul Reaver's mental assault broke on this new barrier of words—*I will destroy you!*

The Soul Reaver appeared, looming out of the dark. Shriveled limbs on a slender body, wrapped in a wind-tattered robe and with stoles and sashes bearing twisting runes. Hands like great claws, curling in anticipation of rending either body or soul. And a head like a nightmare from the deep sea—blank white orbs for eyes, surrounded by bony ridges, and four long, twitching tentacles where its mouth should have been. Its skin was living shadow, dusky gray, and its coating of slime glistened in the pulsing light of the Heart of Khyber as it circled Gaven.

Cart charged the monster, but it flicked two tentacles in his direction, revealing a hint of a suckerlike maw beneath them. The warforged staggered sideways into the tunnel wall and slumped to the ground.

"Thunder and lightning," Gaven said, reading the characters inscribed in the wall where Cart had collided, and he sent a bolt of roaring lightning to engulf the Soul Reaver. Gaven felt a psychic echo of its pain in his mind, but it did not flinch or back away. Instead, its four tentacles extended toward Gaven, reaching for his head even as the Soul Reaver's mind reached out. . . .

* * * * *

Haldren shouted the last syllable of his spell, but at that instant Darraun held up a wand and yelled a word of his own. A brief flare of light and smoke was the only manifestation of Haldren's spell.

"Traitor!" Haldren hissed, glaring at Darraun beneath bristling eyebrows. "Spy! I never trusted you!"

"You didn't have to," Darraun said, running forward with his mace over his shoulder and his wand in his other hand. "I still learned everything I needed to know."

Senya grinned at Rienne. "What do you say we let these two sort out their differences?" she said, jerking her head toward Haldren and Darraun. "And we can sort out ours." The elf charged, the point of her sword low to the ground.

Rienne stood still, her sword loose in her hand. "Please tell me you're not going to fight me in a jealous rage over Gaven."

"A jealous rage?" Senya said. "No." She closed with Rienne, bringing her sword up in a thrust at Rienne's heart. Rienne lazily swung Maelstrom up to knock Senya's sword aside, and the elf's momentum took her around to Rienne's right. Rienne turned to follow her.

"What differences, then?" Rienne said, settling into a good defensive stance and awaiting Senya's next move.

"Remember the dwarves in Vathirond? The ones you brought to apprehend us? They nearly killed me, you know."

Rienne felt a pang of guilt. That had been her fault, though not the way Senya thought. "I didn't bring them. They followed me."

"I don't care." Senya lunged, more carefully this time, but she was not at all prepared for the way Rienne fought. Maelstrom beat her sword point to the ground, and Rienne stepped on the blade, yanking it from Senya's hand. Rienne's next step landed on Senya's shoulder, and Maelstrom traced a shallow cut in the elf's neck as Rienne went overhead and landed behind her.

Rienne's new position gave her a clear view of Darraun and Haldren. The sorcerer had still not dismounted, and his horse pranced sideways in a circle around the changeling, keeping Haldren effectively out of Darraun's reach. Another spell shot from Haldren's hand only to fizzle in the air, met by something from the artificer's wand. But Rienne could see that Darraun was tiring.

Senya circled, then stooped to retrieve her blade from the ground. Rienne saw her opening—Senya's defenses were down. But at the same moment, Haldren spurred his horse forward to run the changeling down. Instead of attacking Senya, she ran toward the others, placing herself carefully between Senya and Darraun.

Senya charged again. Rienne stepped to the side and spun as she went past, deflecting the force of Senya's charge upward. The elf's own momentum carried her through the air to land at Darraun's feet, right in Haldren's path. The horse neighed and reared, and Haldren had to fight to keep his seat. Darraun charged forward and swung his mace into Haldren's knee. The sorcerer screamed and fell to the ground.

* * * * *

The pull on Gaven's mind was tangible, as though the tentacles had touched him, wrapped around him, and drawn him in. He staggered forward, unwilling, but unable to resist. He felt he could not balance on his feet unless he kept stepping forward. He tried to lean back, against the pull, but sensed immediately that he would fall backward unless he lurched forward again. He stumbled and felt something bang against his arm, sending a tingle of warm energy through his skin.

The Heart of Khyber. He stretched out a hand and grabbed it, then lost his balance and fell to the ground. The Soul Reaver stepped closer on its spindly legs, and Gaven raised a hand to ward it off—the hand that held the Heart of Khyber.

The Soul Reaver recoiled, and Gaven felt the pressure on his mind ease. He scrambled to his feet, keeping the nightshard between himself and the monstrous abomination, and hefted the spear in his other hand. A sick, burbling hiss came from the Soul Reaver's mouth as it crouched, wary of Gaven's next move.

"Does this frighten you?" Gaven said, thrusting the nightshard forward. "Or is it the spear, foreordained for your doom?"

I am your doom. Pain assaulted every nerve in Gaven's body, an unbearable agony worse than any trauma of body or soul he had ever experienced. His body urged him to flee, to get as far as he could from the source of the pain, to never draw near it again. He turned to run, but the Heart of Khyber held him like an anchor. He would have dropped it in order to flee, but his hand seemed unwilling to release it. It was cool in his palm, an oasis from the pain, and he tried to draw on that coolness to assuage the agony. A soothing chill like water spread out from his hand, and in a moment the pain was gone.

I will destroy you, the Soul Reaver said, *and my hordes will spread over the surface world like a plague. Nothing will stop them!*

A vision accompanied its words, startlingly real, much like the visions that had haunted Gaven's dreams in Dreadhold and even his waking since his escape. He saw an unending stream of horrible monstrosities pouring out of the chasm far above him, unleashing devastation far worse than anything the world had experienced in the Last War. It was a vision of the world overcome with madness and horror.

Doubt began to gnaw at the roots of Gaven's mind. How could one man hold back such a tide of devastation? To do so would require greater power than even he wielded—would it not require the power of a god?

Gaven roared, and thunder shook the earth around him. Sheets of lightning shot out from the tunnel walls to engulf the Soul Reaver, lifting it off the ground and holding it in the air as wave after wave of storming fury poured into its sickly flesh. Still howling, Gaven charged forward, leveling his spear at the Soul Reaver's chest.

The Eye of Siberys bound to a branch of ash . . .

. . . among the bones of Khyber . . .

The Storm Dragon drives a spear into the Soul Reaver's heart.

My hand on the spear, Gaven thought as he plunged it into a body that was shadow given twisting form.

CHAPTER
51

One sharp kick from Rienne's foot sent Senya sprawling facedown on the ground. The elf groaned, but she did not move again. Darraun had overheard only snippets of the banter between the two women as they fought, but it was enough to make him curious what had happened in Vathirond. He wished he'd been there to see it.

Haldren stirred, so Darraun slammed his mace into the sorcerer's skull rather harder than was probably necessary, sending a trail of blood arcing from the sorcerer's mouth. Darraun had been itching to do that almost since he first laid eyes on Haldren in Dreadhold, and he took great pleasure in watching the old man slump into unconsciousness. The artificer put his hands on his knees and paused to catch his breath—and to think hard about what he had to do next.

At that moment, the earth shook violently, nearly knocking him off his feet. Rienne kept her balance easily enough, but fear clouded her face. "Gaven!" she breathed, and she turned to stare back at the Crystal Spire, still piercing the sky with its unearthly light.

"Go!" Darraun said, reading her thoughts on her face. So transparent. "I'll take care of these two."

Rienne hesitated only a moment before bolting to Haldren's horse and throwing herself onto its back. It didn't seem to mind at all, and eagerly ran out of the valley, heading back into the heart of the storm.

"So what am I going to do with you two?" Darraun said to the bodies at his feet. He put his hands on his hips and stared down at them, then began looking around the nearby field of battle. "Let's see what we have to work with."

* * * * *

Writhing shadows gripped the Eye of Siberys and sucked it into darkness, yanking the spear from Gaven's hand. The Soul Reaver's blank white eyes opened wide. Gaven stumbled backward and stared up in disbelief at the creature transforming before him.

Dusky gray flesh became translucent, hard as crystal, with smoky veins of darkness twisting beneath the skin. A core of molten shadow churned around the Eye of Siberys in its chest, where the spear had torn cloth away and penetrated the skin, as if it were dissolving the dragonshard or absorbing its power. Finally the eyes—pale white orbs that bulged in their bony sockets—began to glow with rich golden light, as if the Eye of Siberys had traveled through the Soul Reaver's body and lodged itself in its eye sockets.

As it changed, the Soul Reaver stretched out its clawed hands as if beckoning some distant ally, and in response the earth shook. Great cracks appeared in the walls of the tunnel, and rocks cascaded along the floor. Gaven threw his arms over his head, and for a moment he was back in Dreadhold, cowering in delirious fear as Vaskar smashed the roof over his cell. A great rumbling roar echoed throughout the caverns, answered by a gibbering cry issuing from a thousand inhuman throats. The legions of the Soul Reaver were ready, Gaven knew—no vision had ever been clearer in his mind.

The Soul Reaver's next attack was clearly meant to dismiss Gaven just as it had dismissed Vaskar—a psychic blast that overwhelmed his senses and his thoughts and every nerve that could register pain in his body. Gaven howled in fury and pain, joining his voice to the weird ululation of the monstrous hordes, but he did not break as Vaskar had. He struggled to his feet, standing in the Soul Reaver's path, interposing himself between that monstrous thing of living shadow and the Crystal Spire behind him. He yanked his greatsword free of its sheath and held it before him with both shaking hands.

Idiot mammal. The Soul Reaver's thoughts scraped across Gaven's mind. *You have fulfilled your purpose. Now die.*

Another psychic blast ripped through Gaven's mind, sending his sword clattering to the ground as he brought his fists to his temples and howled. But it passed, and Gaven still stood. He stooped to retrieve his sword as the Soul Reaver stepped closer.

Do you know why I am called the Soul Reaver, mammal?

"The greatest of the daelkyr's brood," Gaven whispered, "the Soul Reaver feasts on the minds and flesh of a thousand lives before his prison breaks."

And you shall be a thousand and one. Another blast tore at Gaven's mind, and the Soul Reaver drew closer still, extending all four tentacles toward Gaven's pain-wracked skull.

"The Bronze Serpent calls him forth," Gaven screamed, pouring his agony into his voice, "but the Storm Dragon is his doom!" He slashed his sword at the tentacles, but the blade clanged against them as if they were solid stone rather than writhing flesh.

So you thought. And you thought to drive your spear into my heart. But your

Prophecy didn't help you, did it? Perhaps you are not the Storm Dragon after all.

One tentacle made contact with Gaven's scalp and attached itself like a leech, and he felt his will begin to ebb. Of course he was not the Storm Dragon, he realized. How could he stand against this monster? In trying to destroy the Soul Reaver, he had only made the abomination more powerful. He tried to bat the tentacle away with one hand, but it held fast. The Soul Reaver was close, so close that its constant psychic grumbling had grown to a roar in Gaven's mind. He could see the ash haft of the spear he'd made dangling from the creature's chest. It smelled faintly of ozone and charred flesh, which made him smile weakly.

A second tentacle touched his head. The pain was fading, along with Gaven's desire to resist. Why should he not feed the Soul Reaver? He should be glad to nourish his master in the last moments before his ascension—

The thought filled Gaven with alarm. Where had that idea come from? The Soul Reaver planned to seize godhood from the Crystal Spire? Gaven tried to make sense of that notion, and he felt the creature's tentacles recoil slightly at that surge of mental activity.

A third tentacle touched, but Gaven swept a hand up to knock it away before it could affix itself. He tried to throw his body backward, away from the creature that fed on his thoughts, but two clawlike hands embraced him and pulled him back. He tried to lift his sword, but he could no longer bring it between the Soul Reaver's body and his own. Gaven could see the palest glimmer of golden light within the churning darkness in the Soul Reaver's chest.

The Eye of Siberys pulsed there like the Soul Reaver's heart, throbbing in a steady rhythm that beat in Gaven's head as well. Shadows twisted around it, like veins carrying its power throughout the creature's body. "The Soul Reaver's heart . . ." he murmured, and then he knew.

His spear had not touched the Soul Reaver's heart. The monster had goaded him into using his spear against its fleshly body, rather than striking its real heart—the Heart of Khyber. Gaven let his sword fall to the ground, and with his last ounce of will, he wrapped both hands around the haft of the ash spear. He gave it one mighty tug, but it would not come free.

Where had the nightshard fallen? Gaven wrenched his head around to scan the ground, even as the Soul Reaver's third tentacle attached itself to his scalp. His thoughts were a jumble of memories and nightmares brought up at the Soul Reaver's call, but he clung to an image of the Heart of Khyber. At last he saw it on the ground behind the creature, where he had staggered backward before.

He had no will left. He feebly tried to pull his head away from the grasping tentacles while keeping his grip on the spear, but he could not move his head beyond their reach. He tried to speak, but the words came out slurred beyond recognition. Still, they formed themselves in his mind. "There the Storm Dragon drives a spear through the bones of Khyber through the Soul Reaver's heart."

Layers of meaning. He stood, barely, among the bones of Khyber, deep beneath the earth. But if the Heart of Khyber was the Soul Reaver's heart, then the Soul Reaver's bones were Khyber's bones. He could drive the spear through the Soul Reaver's bones and into the Soul Reaver's heart, if he could just—

"I am player and playwright!" he cried, and he heaved himself forward into the Soul Reaver's chest. The spear sank deeper into the creature's flesh, and waves of pain rippled through Gaven's mind. He forced his foe backward one step, two, then with one great push knocked it to the ground. Two tentacles tore free of his head, trailing blood from their sickly white tips. Gaven clutched the spear, pulling it downward with all his strength, praying to the Sovereign Host that its tip would find the nightshard.

He felt the spear break bone, and then heard it grate against stone below. He had missed the shard. The Soul Reaver heaved him away, its third tentacle tearing free from Gaven's head, and rolled away from him onto its hands and knees. The Eye of Siberys protruded from its back, shedding pale golden light around the dark cavern. Gaven spotted the nightshard on the ground between him and the bloodied Soul Reaver. As the creature stood and turned to face him again, Gaven could tell that it saw the shard as well. They froze.

The idiot mammal is more clever than I imagined. It made a sound like a gurgling cough, and Gaven saw black blood spill down from its mouth. A fresh wave of pain washed through his head—he began to feel where the tentacles had been boring through his skin and scraping at his skull.

"I am the Storm Dragon," Gaven said. He stretched his hands forward, and a blast of air like thunder shot through the Soul Reaver, sending it staggering backward a few steps. "And I will still be your doom!" He dove forward and clutched the Heart of Khyber in both hands, landing hard on his belly. He tried to roll back onto his feet as he caught his breath, but the Soul Reaver landed on top of him, two tentacles grasping at the nightshard while the other two slashed at his eyes.

Gaven swung his legs to one side and used their leverage to roll the Soul Reaver onto its back. Still clutching the Heart of Khyber in both hands, he put as much weight as he could above it, forcing it down toward the Soul Reaver's chest. It put up both hands to push back, using all four tentacles to attack

Gaven's face. One forced its way into his mouth, tasting of blood and slime, working its way back toward his throat.

Grimacing with disgust, Gaven bit down on the tentacle in his mouth, adding a new taste of bilious ichor. He didn't bite clean through, but it was enough: the Soul Reaver's grip on the Heart of Khyber weakened, and Gaven managed to force the nightshard down to the stone floor. Spitting slime and bile, Gaven drove a knee as hard as he could into the creature's midsection. Holding the nightshard against the floor with one hand, he grabbed again at the spear with the other, raising it and the Soul Reaver's struggling body with it. Guiding the spear toward the hand that clutched the Heart of Khyber, he brought the spear's point, still protruding from the creature's back, down hard.

The spear pierced his hand, and he cried out in pain. But the Soul Reaver stopped struggling as the Eye of Siberys went on to pierce the nightshard, the Soul Reaver's heart. Its withered body, a moment ago writhing with preternatural strength, dissolved into wisps of smoke, snakes of oily darkness slithering away and seeping into the ground. A foul-smelling cloud of gray-black mist arose from the body and then dissipated, leaving Gaven alone, holding the spear he had made from the Eye of Siberys, impaling his own hand against the ground.

A tremendous sob wracked his body, and he dropped his head to the floor. He started to scream even before he pulled the spear free, but then it was done, and the pain was not as bad. He thrust his injured hand under his other arm and squeezed it there as he tried to find his feet. Reeling, he leaned against the wall for support while he waited for his head to clear.

His mind swam with echoes of the Soul Reaver's psychic assaults. The torrents of memory and feelings slowed, leaving him drained and trembling. It was done, or the worst of it was. Perhaps he had saved the world, or at least a corner of it. He wanted to take pride in that—he supposed he would when he was less exhausted.

As the storm of his thoughts stilled, he realized a strange emptiness in his mind. He cast his mind over his memories of the past months. The dragon of the nightshard, a presence in his thoughts for so long, was gone. He still remembered the dragon's memories—but he remembered his memory of them, he remembered experiencing them as Gaven. They were still vivid in his mind, some of them all too vivid, but a little more distant, farther removed from his own experience.

The dragon had vanished, taking its memories with it, when the Heart of Khyber was destroyed.

His only light had also gone out, so he spoke a quick spell and cradled an orb of light in his palm.

"Look, father!" he cried.

Arnoth stood in the doorway, leaning against the jamb, smiling with pride. "Well done, Gaven," he said.

Gaven flexed his hand, and the one orb split into three that danced into the air around him, lighting the tunnel walls.

"Thunder and lightning," he muttered, reading the Draconic character inscribed on the wall beside him. He started, and looked around. "Cart?" he called weakly. "Where did you get off to?"

CHAPTER
52

Trailing one hand along the wall, Gaven retraced his path, back to the base of the Crystal Spire. As he walked, his mind filled with the words traced on and by the twisting tunnel, words that spoke of the Storm Dragon, the gates of Khyber, and the bridge to the sky. The verbs, though—those most flexible of words, allowing so many nuances of action and meaning. The nouns were facts, the bare facts of the situation as it stood. The verbs were possibility.

The ululation of the Soul Reaver's hordes had diminished slightly, and the voices no longer rose in unison. The cries all seemed to be coming from somewhere far above, as though new waves of monsters were pouring out through the chasm from the upper reaches of Khyber and swarming anew over the battlefield.

He rounded one last bend and threw a hand up to shield his eyes from the brightness of the Crystal Spire, which had grown more intense since he left it. Light leaked out to cast deep shadows on the tracings of the cavern wall, and shone on Cart's impassive face. The warforged stood on the dragon's lower jaw, poised at the very edge of the Crystal Spire.

"Planning your ascension, Cart?" Gaven could barely find his voice—his throat was raw from yelling, and the lingering taste of the Soul Reaver's slime made his tongue feel thick.

"Have you come to stop me, Storm Dragon?"

"I don't care, one way or another. I don't plan on passing through that gate."

"What about the Prophecy?"

"There are many ways to bring the Prophecy to pass."

"I try not to think about it."

"Uncommonly wise."

"What god watches over my people, Gaven?" Cart's voice was strangely melancholy, and he rocked ever so slightly on his heels as he stared down into the dragon's gaping maw. "Which Sovereign has our interests at heart?"

"Are there gods for each race and people?" Gaven asked. "Doesn't the whole Host keep watch over us all?"

"Perhaps. But the gods made all the other races. We were made by artificers and magewrights. Does Onatar then care for us, the god of the forge? Or perhaps the warlord Dol Dorn, since we were made for war? Or do they see us as many mortals do—simply as tools for war? There is no god of swords or siege engines. Perhaps there is no god for us."

"You want to be one, then? God of the warforged?"

Cart shrugged. "I am torn. I am not accustomed to feeling so divided."

"I've never heard you speak of warforged as your people before."

"I have always felt that the best way to serve warforged everywhere was to fulfill my own duty, to live out the purpose for which I was made."

"And you were made for war."

"I was. That's why I followed Haldren. He was my commanding officer, and I honored and respected him for that. But he also promised a return to war. I wanted that—I wanted to see the world plunged into violence again, just so I could find purpose again. What is a warforged to do in a world no longer at war?"

"What would you do, then, as god of the warforged? Would you urge them into war?"

Cart stroked his chin. "Power is quite a temptation, isn't it? It's one thing to think of all the good one might do. But I can so easily imagine abusing that power. To become a dark god of war, the destructive mirror of Dol Dorn, calling for war for its own sake. I think the Dark Six would become the Dark Seven."

Gaven nodded. "Exactly."

Cart stepped back from the Crystal Spire, and shadows fell over his face. "Well, Storm Dragon? How will the Prophecy come to pass?"

"The Storm Dragon bursts through the gates of Khyber and blocks the bridge to the sky."

He came and stood across from Cart, on the face of the snarling dragon, and looked up. The Crystal Spire rose forever above him, its light showing hints of movement along the edges of the chasm far above but blocking any detail from his view.

"That's not what you said in the City of the Dead," Cart said.

"No, it's not. But there are many ways to translate Draconic verbs, many layers of meaning that are expressed better in context than in isolation. And if I am to be the Storm Dragon, then I am the context for those words. They can't be interpreted apart from me."

"So you will choose your own destiny after all."

Gaven smiled. With one more glance skyward, he stepped forward into the Crystal Spire.

He dropped down into the dragon's maw, but then wind whipped up from nowhere, whirling furiously around him and holding him aloft. The earth rumbled as lightning probed the chasm, and a shower of rocks tumbled down from above, catching in the whirlwind and circling him. He lifted his hands to the sky high above, where the Crystal Spire broke through the swirling storm clouds, and a great bolt of lightning flashed down through the chasm, striking the stone dragon's mouth and adding to the swirling hail of stone around him. Then he surged up on the wind, sloughing the rock behind him.

He burst up through Khyber's gate in an explosive shower of rock splinters. The cavern went dark as the dragon's mouth collapsed in on itself, great slabs of stone falling in on the gate and dousing the light of the Crystal Spire. Reaching a hand toward Cart, Gaven lifted the warforged into the whirlwind behind him and hurtled up through the chasm.

Flashes of lightning illuminated the darkness around them as they rose, revealing tunnel mouths crawling with gibbering monsters clambering toward the surface. Gaven shot past them, rising faster than he had fallen, emerging into open air in the space of a few gasping breaths. Lightning crackled in the air around him, and great thundering bolts struck the ground below. The whirlwind below him hurled monsters off the brink and into the yawning depth of the chasm, and more lightning blasts sent enormous slabs of earth plummeting down after them. The Storm Dragon stretched out his arms, and sheets of lightning struck along the length of the chasm, shattering rock to fill it in. Thunder rolled continuously like the rumbling of a mighty earthquake, and when it was done, the chasm had become just another scar on the face of the Starcrag Plain.

* * * * *

Haldren's stallion galloped across the plain. Rienne stroked his neck as she rode, encouraging him to greater speed. He was no magebred horse or Valenar steed, but he was amazingly sure-footed on the rocky ground, which more than made up for a lack of raw speed. The earth thundered with the pounding of his hooves—no, she realized, the earth shook from tremors far below the battlefield, which seemed to bode ill for Gaven's well-being.

The battle was over, as far as Rienne could see. Haldren's soldiers had fallen or been routed from the field entirely, and until she drew near the chasm she saw only a few clumps of monsters scattering away from the field—heading for new haunts in the Starpeaks or the Silver Woods. She could see no dragons still aloft, whether they were all dead or driven away or just brought to ground. She spurred the stallion toward the towering shaft of light, a beacon in the midst of the furious storm.

She was halfway across the plain when the beacon flickered and went out. Her mind raced through a handful of possibilities as she spurred the stallion on: Had Gaven crossed the bridge to the sky, collapsing it behind him? Had he failed, proving that he was not the Storm Dragon after all? Had Gaven perhaps been wrong about the whole Prophecy and the Crystal Spire? Perhaps it was not any kind of bridge to the sky, but some kind of beacon or signal, and Gaven had destroyed it.

She drew a slow breath, calming her pounding heart, and tried to lose herself in the rhythm of the stallion's gait.

She lost track of the distance to the chasm where the Crystal Spire had been, and the storm grew even fiercer ahead. Wind whipped her hair and small hailstones stung her skin, and she soon rode into a wall of rain. She guided the horse toward the heart of the storm, where lightning danced around a swirling whirlwind. The heart of the storm must be Gaven,she thought.

A new tide of monsters poured out of the storm toward her, a tumultuous mass of pallid flesh and flailing appendages, sharp claws and writhing tentacles, screaming mouths and staring eyes. They seemed to surge forward, clawing over each other in their haste to reach fresh prey. Each time she fixed her gaze on one creature, it disappeared under or behind the next wave of horrors. Terror and revulsion wrenched her gut, but she quelled them with another slow breath. If these monsters stood between her and Gaven, then she would have to fight her way through the monsters. She pulled the stallion to a halt and slid Maelstrom from its sheath.

There was no discipline to their advance. When they drew close, a monster with a single staring eye and a much smaller fanged mouth leaped ahead of the others and bounded up at her. The gaze of its lidless eye raked across her, blistering her skin as its claws reached for her throat. She drove her blade into its eye and deflected its momentum, sending its lifeless body spilling to the ground behind her. Her arms trembled—that would not do. Combat required discipline, focus, concentration, a perfect unity of thought and action.

Before she could steady herself, the waves broke around her. Action first—thought would follow. Maelstrom went into a dance of constant motion, spinning like a deadly shield surrounding her, blocking the creatures' attacks and biting into their flesh. Many of the monsters reached up to grab her—and a few reached down from a greater height—and those were the first to die. Haldren's horse proved himself one last time, rearing up to strike with its hooves and felling many of the smaller creatures. But before long the horse was pulled screaming under the surging tide, throwing Rienne through the air as he fell.

With a mighty shout, Rienne brought her energy back into focus. Like Darraun piloting the airship alone, action alone would not suffice against these hordes. Rienne came down on the chitinous back of a hulking monstrosity, then bounded off it to a relatively clear patch of ground. As she landed, she kicked a skittering buglike thing out of the way and slashed two other nameless things back, carving herself a place to stand. She banished her fear and lost herself in whirling motion, feeling Maelstrom surge to life in her grip. This was the style of fighting that had given the sword its name: a constant spinning, cutting everything within reach, wheeling the blade through an unending, intricate series of swirling arcs punctuated by sharp thrusts—what she thought of as lightning strikes within the whirlwind.

As she danced, the storm answered her strikes with lightning that shook the earth, and she had the sudden thought of fighting alongside Gaven on one of their subterranean expeditions. She smiled as gore flew from the tip of her blade. No claw could touch her, no tentacle stayed coiled around her wrist or leg for more than an instant before she sliced it through. Wide eyes tried to catch her gaze and assault her mind, sharp teeth tried to close around her but met the constant motion of her blade. Her feet moved with her blade, an intricate dance of steps and lunges that guided her away from dangerous blows and brought her near the weakest foes. She was utterly lost in the dance—no memory or anxiety about Gaven remained in the diamond stillness of her mind, perfectly focused on the battle at hand. A perfect unity of will and action.

The sea parted around her, and Rienne stumbled. A greenish ray of light shot through where she would have been if she had stepped where she planned. She stopped her whirling in order to keep her full attention on the monster before her. Its body was a gigantic orb hovering a few feet off the ground, a magical buoyancy holding it aloft. One great eye stared at her from above a mouth filled with needle-like teeth, and ten more eyes writhed at the ends of long stalks on its upper surface. Years of exploring the subterranean reaches had taught her to fear the beholder above almost all other threats of Khyber. One of those smaller eyes had projected the green light, and Rienne knew the touch of that light could mean her death.

Something lunged at her from the right and lost its head to a reflexive slash of her blade. The monsters seemed hesitant to attack prey the eye tyrant had chosen for itself, but they were also driven by some madness or rage or instinct that wouldn't let them leave her alone.

Slowly Rienne started into a new dance, ready to slash at anything that came at her from the sides or behind, but focused on dodging the beams of light that came from the many eyes of the beholder.

Displaying more coordination than she had yet seen among the Soul Reaver's hordes, two creatures came at her from both sides. The easy response to such an attack broke her rhythm: she ducked toward one and threw it at the other. Before she could return to her rhythmic pattern, though, two rays of light made contact with her body. One seared her flesh, opening a horrible wound in her arm, black around the edges, sending horrible pain jolting through her body. At the same moment, she felt an absurd urge to flee, to turn and run from the horrifying apparition before her, even though it meant plunging headlong into a sea of smaller horrors.

She swallowed her fear, telling herself that it came from the beholder's magic and not herself, and found her stride again in time to dodge two more beams of light. The monster might have been laughing at her, opening and closing its mouth so that its teeth rubbed together. A ridiculous image of the beholder as a butcher sharpening a knife appeared in her mind, and the smile returned to her face. It was time to charge.

With three quick steps she built up enough speed for a great leap at the beholder. She landed just close enough, swinging Maelstrom down with the full force of her jump and cutting a shallow gash in its plated hide. As she brought her blade around for another strike, a bolt of lightning struck the creature, knocking Rienne backward a few steps with the thundering force of its blast.

The beholder swung its large eye around to look for its new attacker, even as it unleashed two more rays at Rienne. She vaulted backward to avoid them, then rolled forward beneath the floating orb. Realizing its danger, it started rolling in the air to bring its eyes to bear on her again, but before it did she drove Maelstrom up through its jaw and into its core. She didn't know what organs the thing might have in its strange body, and she didn't much want to, but her sword must have hit something vital. Had she not rolled quickly to the side, it would have crushed her beneath its bulk as it crashed to the ground.

"Rienne!"

It was Gaven's voice, and it was all she needed to hear.

CHAPTER
53

G aven ran to Rienne, though his feet didn't touch the ground. The wind carried Cart behind him, and his greatsword cleared a path through the howling monsters before them. The fall of the beholder, combined with Gaven's stormy advance, seemed to break the horde's resolve—what had been a tight mob clamoring to get at Rienne quickly dispersed into smaller groups fleeing the field. He stopped beside Rienne just as she got to her feet.

"Are you all right?" he asked.

In answer, she threw her arms around him, clutching him as tightly as she could. He returned her embrace with equal ardor, burying his face in her soft black hair. It still smelled of the sea, and for just an instant he lost himself in the memory of holding her on the *Sea Tiger*.

"What happened?" she said at last, not releasing her hold but turning her head to speak into his ear.

"I'll tell you later." He drew back to look into her eyes. "Where's Darraun? And the *Eye of the Storm?*"

"You came here with Darraun?" Cart said from behind him, his surprise plain in his voice.

"And who's this?" Rienne asked, keeping one hand on Gaven's shoulder as she drew back to a respectable distance.

"Cart, Rienne." The two nodded at each other. "And yes, Darraun rejoined us in Stormhome. I guess I've got a lot to tell you as well, Cart."

"I left Darraun at the airship," Rienne said, "at the north end of the plain. With Haldren and Senya."

It was Gaven's turn to be surprised. "With them?"

"Well, we knocked them out first. He said he'd get them bound."

Cart grumbled, sort of an animalistic growl, but he didn't say anything.

"Will the *Eye* still fly?" Gaven asked.

"I'm not sure."

"Let's get there and see." He stepped forward, and her hand trailed down his arm until it came to rest in his hand. Together, they started to run, and the wind picked up behind them. Cart shambled into a run as well, and soon the wind moved him far faster than he was evidently used to moving.

"The plain seems almost entirely clear," Gaven noted as they ran. "Where did the hordes of the Soul Reaver go?"

"Dispersed into the woods to the east or the mountains to the west, I suppose," Rienne said. "There were so many!"

The *Eye of the Storm* came into view, and Gaven slowed their pace.

"And they were just the vanguard of the host," Gaven said as they came to a stop. "If I had not closed the chasm, they would still be pouring out."

"There she is," Rienne said, pointing at the airship. "But I don't see Darraun."

Cart walked heavily among the bodies that littered the edge of the Starcrag Plain. He stooped at one and rolled it over to see the face, but he stood quickly and continued looking.

"On the ship, maybe?" Gaven said.

Rienne hurried to the airship and scrambled up to the deck. "Darraun?" she called.

Gaven climbed the ropes behind her, and made his way to the ship's highest point at the stern. There he turned in a slow circle, surveying what he could see of the battlefield and Bramblescar Gorge. The battlefield was all but deserted, and the gorge twisted away from him too quickly—he couldn't see more than a bowshot away.

Rienne moved below decks, calling the changeling's name. Rather, the name he had used with them. Gaven scowled. Had he been wrong to put his trust in Darraun?

He returned to the deck just as Rienne emerged from below. "I don't know where he could be," she said.

"It doesn't make any sense," Gaven said.

"What part of it?"

"We trusted him, and he really proved that he deserved that trust. He didn't interfere with me doing what I had to do—quite the contrary, in fact. He put himself at considerable risk to help me. We put our lives in each other's hands."

"You think he helped Haldren escape?"

"I don't know why he would. But—"

"Gaven!" Cart called, thirty paces across the mouth of the gorge.

"Cart's found something," Rienne said. She tumbled off the deck to the ground and started sprinting toward Cart before Gaven had started climbing down. Gaven ran behind her, but he was in no real hurry to reach the warforged.

Cart had been examining corpses. If he'd found something, Gaven wasn't sure he wanted to know what.

His fears were confirmed when Rienne got to Cart's side and fell on her knees. He found himself strangely touched by the depth of Rienne's grief, written plain on her face. She had known Darraun such a short time, just a day, but clearly that act of putting their lives in each other's hands had forged a bond that hurt in the breaking.

It wasn't until he reached her side and saw the body that his own grief welled up in him, clenching his heart and stinging his eyes. His years in Dreadhold had left him with precious few people he could call a friend, and virtually no one he could trust. But he had warmed to Darraun almost instantly, enjoyed the parry and thrust of conversation with him, the dancing around secrets while revealing far more than was said. And in this last day—the day since he had learned of his father's death—he too had come to count Darraun as a true friend, a friend he had trusted with his life.

And now that friend lay among the numberless dead on the Starcrag Plain, his chest foul with blood, his eyes staring blindly at the brooding sky.

Gaven dropped to his knees beside Rienne and wrapped his arm around her shoulders. She melted into his chest with a sob. Her tears seemed to unlock his own, opening the door to a fresh welling of grief for his father mixed with the loss of this new friend. The terror of the battle just ended, the weight of what he'd just done—he was overwhelmed. His body shook with sobs. And as his tears flowed, he realized with a sharp pang of regret that he didn't know Darraun's real name.

* * * * *

The only sound was the croaking of ravens squabbling over the bodies of the fallen. The battlefield was nearly deserted—only a few clumps of soldiers picked their way among the dead, beginning the long, slow task of building pyres or cairns for their comrades in arms. In time, more of the soldiers who had been routed would find their way back to the field. Another skirmish might even erupt, but without Haldren and his dragons there would be no full-scale invasion.

One group of Aundairian soldiers approached the fallen airship, perhaps looking for plunder or just for survivors of the crash. Gaven and Rienne stayed out of sight—the soldiers recognized Cart as part of Haldren's command staff, and hastened to obey his order to search the battlefield for survivors. Aside from that sole interruption, Darraun's funeral preparations proceeded in a solemn peace.

Cart did the bulk of the heavy work in building a little cairn for Darraun near the airship, at the edge of the battlefield where so many soldiers had fallen over so many centuries. The warforged showed no emotion on his face, of course, but every step he took revealed the weight of his sadness. Gaven wondered whether Cart knew that Darraun had been a changeling. It didn't seem right to reveal that deepest of Darraun's secrets if Cart didn't already know, so Gaven didn't mention it.

That thought led his mind down paths that seemed inappropriate, so he didn't give voice to his thoughts out of respect for the grief of the others. But he realized that just as he didn't know Darraun's real name, he had never seen the changeling's true face. Some part of him then began to wonder why the changeling hadn't reverted to his natural state when he died. Shouldn't Darraun's corpse have worn his true face? It seemed to Gaven that death should be the end of all disguises.

None of them could think of anything to say once the cairn was built and Darraun was laid to rest, so they stood in silence for a long time. It was Rienne who finally broke the silence.

"He never made me dinner," she said, laughing even as fresh tears sprang to her eyes.

"I was blind to entire facets of his personality," Cart said.

Gaven laughed. "Well, I think we should have a meal in his honor. Cart, you can watch us eat, in his honor."

"That does seem appropriate," the warforged said.

They walked back to the airship and rummaged through the stores again. Gaven pulled together a terrible meal, with Rienne's help, and they choked it down with laughter as Gaven and Cart shared memories of Darraun's cooking. Cart's tales involved what he considered strange ingredients—clams, potatoes, and mushrooms foremost among them—while Gaven had only a few excellent meals to remember him by.

When Gaven and Rienne couldn't bring themselves to eat any more, Gaven sat back and put his hands behind his head. "What's our next step?" he said.

Cart answered without hesitation. "My place is with the general. Darraun's death means that he is probably free again, and I need to find him."

Gaven's eyebrows shot up in surprise. "Still the soul of loyalty," he said. "Why did you help me, then?"

"I told you. Because we are alike, both of us made for a purpose. I helped you fulfill your purpose—I think. The Prophecy still makes my head spin."

"Did Haldren know you were helping me?"

"I imagine the general saw me go to you, and I expect that he was not pleased. But that doesn't change my duty to him."

"Didn't you once tell me that he's not a forgiving man? Will he even accept you back?"

"If he does not, then I will have to examine my options. Assuming I'm still alive."

"Gaven," Rienne interjected, "if Haldren is free, we have to stop him."

"No. First, because that would put us directly at odds with Cart, and I choose not to oppose him. Second, I don't believe that Haldren is a significant threat to the world any longer. At least not for now."

"Darraun said Haldren would try again someday."

"Perhaps he will, and perhaps we'll be there to stop him. On the other hand, perhaps Bordan and the dwarves will catch up with him first. I have other concerns."

Cart stood. "I will say farewell, then," he said. "I would prefer to tell Haldren honestly that I know nothing of your plans, in case he has vengeance in mind."

Gaven got to his feet and extended a hand to the warforged. "Thank you, Cart." They shook hands. "For everything."

"Thank you," Cart said. "You have taught me much."

Gaven arched an eyebrow, but Cart turned and bowed to Rienne. "Farewell to you."

"Goodbye," Rienne said, returning his bow.

Cart turned back to Gaven and bowed again. "Farewell, Storm Dragon."

Gaven bowed, but he couldn't find his voice until after the warforged had gone.

* * * * *

To Gaven's great relief, the *Eye of the Storm* rose readily off the ground at his command. He tasted again the thrill of flying, bringing the airship up almost to the overhanging clouds while starting toward the north and east.

"What other concerns?" Rienne asked at last, leaning back in her accustomed place against the rail near the helm.

"First of all . . . you," Gaven said, smiling at her. "Whatever I do next, I want you with me."

"Whatever it is, I'll be with you."

"Thank you. That means more to me than you can imagine. But I won't hold you to it—you're always free to change your mind."

"Gaven, you sound so serious!" she said with a small laugh. "What are you planning to do, cross the Dragonreach?"

"Well, Bordan would have a hard time finding me in Argonnessen." He smiled. "Actually, that is what I've been thinking."

Rienne fell silent in the middle of a laugh. "What? Getting away from Bordan?"

"No, visiting Argonnessen."

"Are you mad? Do you want to be dragon food?"

"I pity the dragon who thinks me an easy meal."

"You want to study the Prophecy at the source."

"Yes. I've already learned much that concerns a great deal more than Haldren's little coup and Vaskar's grab for divine power. The Time of the Dragon Above is drawing to a close, but it's just the first chapter of a larger story."

"And what part do you play in the larger story?"

"I am both player and playwright, Rienne."

"What part will you write for me, then? The supportive wife?"

"Sovereigns, no! No, Rienne, you set a greater destiny than that in motion the day you first laid a hand on Maelstrom. I don't know what it is yet, but I'm looking forward to seeing how you write it."

"To Argonnessen, then."

Gaven smiled at her and nodded, trying to banish the visions of carnage from his mind.

Geneeral Yeven pushed the door open and held it for Haldren to pass through. He took some satisfaction from the bruised skin on the side of the old man's face, the eye that was still swollen shut. Haldren walked into the dark room a little hesitantly, all the swagger gone from his step. Perfect.

Yeven followed Haldren in, closed the door, and leaned against it. "General ir'Brassek, I believe you are already acquainted with Kelas ir'Darran." Right on cue, a dim light flickered to life on a desk across the room, and Kelas's face appeared in the dark.

"You?" Haldren sputtered. "Was Yeven working for you all along? You dare bring me here?"

Yeven grimaced. Haldren's spirit was not quite as broken as he had hoped.

"Shut up, Haldren," Kelas said with a small smile. "You know I couldn't answer your invitation to Bluevine. I can do much more from my current position than I could if my inclinations became known. I'm a spymaster, not a general."

"A spymaster, indeed. I suppose Darraun worked for you, then?"

Good guess, Yeven thought.

"No," Kelas said. "We believe he was a Thrane agent, which might account for the disaster on the Starcrag Plain."

That was the story they'd agreed on. Reinforce his sense of failure, keep beating him down. Make him pliable. It was working: Haldren didn't have a ready response. He looked down at his hands.

"Listen, Haldren. It was a disaster, but it's not the end." Haldren looked up, a hint of spirit returning. "We can't afford to try a direct military approach again—neither you nor General Yeven has enough support left in the army to launch another attack. But we still have allies, and we have other means at our disposal."

"The Arcane Congress?" Haldren said hopefully. Arcanist Wheldren had withheld any support from Haldren's initial strike, but he had promised future support if the attack went well.

"I have spoken to both Arcanist Wheldren and Ashara d'Cannith, and we have begun forging new plans. Your assistance could help bring those plans to fruition."

"My assistance." Haldren looked back down at his hands.

Yeven nodded slightly. Haldren understood the full weight of the words: he would no longer be in charge of this affair. He would be helping Kelas. Would he accept? Was his spirit sufficiently broken?

"Very well, Kelas," Haldren said at last. Yeven broke into a smile. "I will give whatever assistance I can."

"I'm very glad to hear it, General ir'Brassek." Kelas stood behind his desk and extended a hand to Haldren, who took it and shook it. He seemed almost grateful.

General Yaven's smile was genuine. The changeling wearing the general's face was pleased.